Book

of

the

Beginnings

CONTAINING AN ATTEMPT TO RECOVER AND
RECONSTITUTE THE LOST ORIGINS OF THE
MYTHS AND MYSTERIES, TYPES AND SYMBOLS,
RELIGION AND LANGUAGE, WITH EGYPT FOR THE
MOUTHPIECE AND AFRICA AS THE BIRTHPLACE.

Gerald Massey

Volume 2

ISBN 1-56459-149-2

3/03

Kessinger Publishing Company
Montana, U.S.A.

A Deep, unfathomed, dark and dumb,
Is left in Africa to plumb.

MOTHER SHIPTON'S PROPHECY OF THE "END OF THE WORLD" IN THE YEAR 1881.

Some relics of the ancient Circle-Craft are still extant in Britain, and we have our misinterpreted Prophecies in common with the Hebrews (see pp. 388—398). According to one of these the World is to end in the year 1881.

The "end of the world" is the end of an Æon, Age, or Cycle of Time, and we have seen the Prophecy fulfilled in the rare Lunar and Planetary Conjunction which occurred on the 3rd of March. It now remains for Scientific Astronomy to determine the length of this particular Cycle of Time and define its relationship to the period of Precession.

The ending of an Old World (or Æon) and commencement of a New is an appropriate date for the birth of A Book of the Beginnings.

March 4th, 1881.

A

BOOK OF THE BEGINNINGS.

SECTION XI.

COMPARATIVE VOCABULARY

OF

HEBREW AND EGYPTIAN WORDS.

HEBREW.	EGYPTIAN.

א

ab (אב), first ancestor, father.	**ap,** first ancestor.
ab, master, teacher, councillor.	**ap,** guide, judge, head, chief.
ab, desire.	**ab,** desire, wish.
abchh (אבחה), destruction (applied to a sword, Ezk. xxi. 20).	**abkh,** to leap, move, penetrate ; **ab,** to brandish ; **kh,** the thing brandished.
abk (אבך), to mix together, to roll itself together (as smoke).	**abkh,** varied or variegated plumes ; **ab,** pied.
abn (אבן), stone.	**ab,** tablet, statue, stone, ivory, horn ; **abn,** stone wall.
abr (אבר), to mount upward.	**apa,** to mount, fly on high.
abir (אביר), the first.	**ap,** first.
abr (אבר), a wing feather.	**apr,** preparer of bows, equip.
abrh, feathers.	**apru,** a fillet of consecration.
abrk (אברך), tender father (margin).	**ab,** holy father ; **rek,** to rule.
abr, poetically of God (Ps. xci. 4).	**abur,** God.
ad (אד), vapour.	**att,** to soar, fly.
add (אדד), to befall, as misfortune.	**att,** retribute ; **at,** destitute.
adon (אדון), a lord, master, ruler, noble ; **adonaim,** a triad (Gen. xviii.).	**atnu,** captain ; **atennu,** titles ; **aten,** rank, quality, highest ; **aten,** solar orb ; **atenu,** penetrator, former, and ruler.
adm (אדם), red, red man.	**atum,** the red deity, red sun.
adm (אדם), applied to the female sex (Num. xxxi. 35 ; menstrual flux (Lev. xii. 7 ; xv. 27).	**atem,** the "Mother-Goddess of time," or periodicity.
adm (אדם), to dam.	**atem,** to shut up.
adr (אדר), twelfth month, amplitude, width.	**atr,** the limit, boundary, space, measure, distance.
agm (אגם), a collection of water, reeds.	**akhem,** a whelming wave ; **akh,** reed.

HEBREW.	EGYPTIAN.
ahb (אהב), to desire, wish for, sigh after, love, be attached.	**hab**, wish ; **hap**, to unite in marriage.
ahd (אהד), joined together.	**aahti**, dual deity, lunar ; **ahti**, legs, womb, bellows.
ain (אין), nothing, negation, not.	**en**, no, not, negative.
aiph (איפה), a measure of grain.	**ap**, a bushel of grain.
ahl, ten, house, habitation, dwelling.	**ah**, house, stable, camp, storehouse.
au (או), desire.	**uha**, desire.
aob (אוב), python.	**app**, Apophis, serpent.
aob, a soothsayer, diviner.	**ap**, to declare, show, manifest, guide.
aob, a bottle.	**ap**, measure of liquids ; **ab**, a water-bottle.
aud (אוד), to gird, encircle.	**at**, circle.
aud, to press down, as with misfortune.	**att**, destitute.
aun (און), negation.	**en** or **na**, negation.
aun (און), iniquity.	**un**, bad.
ophn (אופן), symbolic wheel, or circle.	**api**, the symbolic winged disk.
aur or **avr** (אור), fire, to burn.	**afr**, fire, to burn.
auth (אות), a sign, a type.	**at**, a type.
as (אז), behold, then.	**as**, behold ; **ash**, then.
as (עץ), an idol.	**as**, a statue, a typical image.
atsb (עצב), image, idol, representation of the female.	**asb**, seat, feminine symbol.
asd (אזד), gone.	**as**, to go away ; **aas**, go, haste.
as, formerly, former time.	**asat**, period of time.
asn (אזן), give ear.	**as**, lo !
asq (אזק), a chain or fetters, in the plural.	**uskh**, a collar.
asrch (אזרח), people of a district, natives, native.	**rekh**, people of a district, native.
achch (אחח), to burn, as fire.	**akh**, fire.
ach (אח), a fire-pot.	**akh**, a censer.
akd (אכד), to bind.	**akh**, to suffocate.
achd (אחד), the first one, first day of the month.	**hek**, first in rule ; **hek-t**, queen ; **hek**, title of Amen, as lord of the first region.
achor (אחור), the hinder or bottom part, rear end, the west, the latter time.	**akar**, Hades, amentes, the underworld, the west.
akph (אכף), to push, spur, drive on.	**kefa**, hunt.
achu (אחו), reeds, grass, Nile-grass.	**akhu**, reed.
achs (אחז), to enclose, encompass, seize, lay hold fast, grasper, holder.	**kes** or **keks**, to bind, bend down, subject.
atun (אטון), fine linen.	**at** and **atun**, a kind of linen.
atm (אטם), stop the ears, shut.	**atm**, listen, hear, to shut.
atr (אטר), to enclose with a hedge, bound.	**atr**, limit, boundary.
aib (איב), an adversary, enemy.	**app**, the Apophis, enemy of the sun.
aiphh (איפה), a measure of grain, modius.	**apa**, bushel.
aish (איש), typical male, vir, virile.	**ash**, tree of life, symbolic ; **as**, secreting part of the body ; **ash**, emission.
akl (אכל), corn, grain.	**aka**, grain, corn.
akr (אכר), husbandman, digger, to plough.	**akau**, ploughshare.
amh (אמה), cubit.	**meh**, cubit.
al (אל), ancient name of the supreme deity, interchanges with Baal.	**ar** or **Har**, the son, the Lord.
alph (אלף), to bind, to bind up or together.	**arp**, to bind, a bundle.
alh (אלה), to be round, move in a circle.	**aalu**, orbit or orbits.
alph (אלף), head of a family or tribe.	**kherp**, the first, principal, the majesty, the prow.
am (אם), typical mother.	**hem**, typical female.
am, truth.	**ma**, truth.
amn (אמן), to stay, sustain, support, to found, make firm, sure.	**min**, to place firm, fix, found.
amn, to nurse a child ; **amnth**, a nurse.	**menâ** or **menat**, the nurse, the nursing mother.
amth (אמת), truth.	**mut**, truth.
amm (אמם), to join together.	**am**, together with.
anq (אנק), to be pressed.	**ank**, to squeeze.
anki (אנכי), I.	**ank**, I, the king.
ans (אנס), to urge, compel, force.	**ans·ra** (*Ritual*, ch. xlii.), the opposer.

HEBREW.	EGYPTIAN.

anph (אנף), breathe, emit breath.
anush (אנוש), son of Seth.
ash (אסה), to injure.
asa (אסא) (Aram), to heal, physician.
asir (אסיר), prisoners bound.
aph (אפ), swine's snout (Prov. xi. 22).
aphud (אפוד), image of an idol.

nef, breath.
anush, the wolf, Sut-Anubis.
ush, hurt.
usha, doctor.
sehar, overthrow.
aph, boar.
apt, Goddess Thoueris; **hept**, a shrine, the **hema** image; also the **hept**, sign of peace and plenty.

aphll (אפלל) judgment.
aph, even.
aph, anger, breathing wrath.
aphl (אפל), to set, be hidden, obscured.
aphah (אפעה), viper.
aphn (אפן), to twist.
aphr (אפר), some kind of head-dress or ornament, a mitre in Syriac.
azb (אצב) uncertain root, perhaps to labour, to toil (Gesenius).
azl (אצל), noble.
ar (אר), a hero, strong man, giant.
ara (ארא), lion, strong, Ares.
arg (ארג), to weave.
arkh (ארכה), healing.
arh (ארה), to pluck off, gather grapes.
arch (ארח), to decree, appoint a time, make a covenant.
arch (ארח), a period, a course of time (Gen. xviii. 11).
ark (ארך), length, space, continuance of time.
ash (אש), foundations; **ashb** (אשב, unused root).
ashph (אשף), a magician, enchanter, to evoke spirits or practise magic.
ashh (אשה), a sacrifice.
ash (אש), fire, fever.
ashr (אשר), to become the spouse or husband, attain puberty.
ashr (אשר), happiness.
ashrh (אשרה), a sacred tree.
asartha, Pentecost offerings of first fruits, as loaves of bread and measures of meal (Josephus, 3, 10, 6).
ashthun (אשתון), rest.
avh (אוה), to desire, to wish strongly.
avth (אות), to be, exist.
avth (אות), to be, to exist, being, essence, body.
avth (אות), a sign, mark, sign for marking portions of time.
avph (אוף), to measure.
avr (אור), light, lightning.
avn (און), substance, born.
ath (את), out of.
athi (אתי), for **at**, a feminine thou; **athun**, a she-ass.
athmcha (אתמחא), to be crucified.
athn (אתן), hard substance.
athn (אתן), perennial.
athr (אתר), place of God.

ap, judgment.
ap, equal or even.
auf, chastise.
hap, to hide.
hefa, viper.
pena, to turn, reverse.
apru, fillet, proof of consecration.

aasb, leisure; **asft**, idleness, fault.

as, noble.
ar, the Divine Son and Hero.
ru, lion.
ark, to weave.
ark, thirtieth of the month, end of period.
arr, vine, grapes.
ark, oath, covenant.

ark, a time, end of a period.

rek, time, rule, reckon.

asb, throne, seat.

shefi, terrify, terror, demoniacal.

as, sacrifice.
ashr, inflame.
sherau, pubescent.

sher-sher, joys; **sheri**, rejoice.
asru, tamarisk tree.
ashrta, meaning determined by a slice or portion of bread, corn, and a measure.

as, rest; **tun**, seat.
uha, to desire strongly.
au, to be.
af, born of; **aft**, the flesh; **apt**, the essence.

aft, the four quarters.

ap, measure.
afr, fire.
af, flesh, born of.
ut, out of.
ahti, womb.

makha, balance, level, or crossing.
atn, some hard substance, tin
aten, to make the circle.
athor, place or habitation of Horus.

ב

beth (ב), the letter B, house.
baush (באש), bad, wicked; **bash**, to stink, a stench.

pa, hieroglyphic house; **bu-t**, belly, vagina.
besh, naked, wounded, hostile, revolt, mystical sense.

HEBREW.	EGYPTIAN.

bar (באר), to declare, explain.
brr (ברר), void, purge, be empty.
bara (באר), fountain.
bbh (בבה), aperture, cavity.

par, show, explain.
per-t, void.
ber, to boil up ; **per**, flow out, pour out.
beb, a well, sense of round, circular, cave, cavern.

bbh (בבה), the apple or pupil of the eye.
bib (ביב), hollow, the pit.
bd or **bdd** (בד) (בדד), to separate, be separate, apart.
bda (בדא), to form, to fashion, used of a potter.

bab, anything round.
bab, hole, the pit.
bet, the foreigners, outsiders.

puta, to form, to shape, the former personified as the potter is **Putha**, the Egyptian **Buddha**.

bdd, to devise or feign.
bhmh (בהמה), Behemah.
bht (בהט), some kind of stone for pavement.
bua (בוע), sense of swelling up.
bgd (בגד), raiment, vesture, garments.
bgl (בעל), the lord, ruler, the husband.

put, to figure, type.
bekhama, hippopotamus.
baaiut, syenite granite.
bua, boast.
pkt, some kind of royal linen or tunic.
bak-al (Bak-Har), **bak**, hawk, sign of rule ; **har** (Al), the Lord.

bva (בוע), to bubble up.
bvg (בונ), to cook, to bake.
bnt (בנט), to bind, gird about, related to the priest's dress.
brbr (ברבר), fatted fowls
beka (בכא), lamentation.
bqa (בקע), to cleave open, divide, divisions, half.
bqr (בקר), dawning of light.
bkrh (בכרה), offspring, firstborn, young.
br (בר), corn.
bra (בָרא), to form, fashion, create, produce ; **bra**, to beget.
bsr (בשר), rejoice, be and make joyful.
buq (בוק), to empty, emptying, depopulation.

bab, to exhale.
pefs, to cook, bake.
pini (t), pshent, crown (*Denk.* iv. 71, *a*).

ber-ber, tip-top, enviable.
beka, to pray.
pkhkha, to divide, divisions ; **peka**, gap, divide in half.
peka, extend ; **pekai**, to flower.
bakh, to engender, fecundate, conceive.
per, grain.
per, cause to appear visibly ; **per-t**, proceed, emanate from the creator.
sher, joy ; **sheri**, rejoice (P. article the).
beka, bring forth, naked, squat ; **bekai**, waste, deficiency, void.

bush (בוש), be ashamed ; **besh**, put to shame and silence, shame ; **besr**, nakedness ; **bezluth**, a making naked.
bchn (בחן), watchtower, beacon.
bchr, (בחר), to have pleasure, to love, to mature ; **bechur-mut**, the first-begotten of Death (Job xviii. 13).
bg (בג), food.
aben-bekn, a tried stone.
btn (בטן), womb.
bka (בכא), to drop, weep, shed, flow by drops.
bnh (בנה), to build, metaphorically to beget.
ben, son.
bqbuq (בקבוק), a bottle.
barak, putting to flight, chasing, expelling, spoiling.
brq (ברק), to lighten, send lightning, also applied to the Great Serpent.
barakah, pools, great waters of Gibeon.

besh, wound, bleeding, naked, mystic meaning.

bekhn, tower, fort, magazine.
bekh, to fecundate, conceive, enfanter.

pekh, food.
bekhn, basalt.
but, belly, vagina sign.
beka, to bring forth, naked, void, squat, depress, bleed.
benn, engender.
bennu, sons.
baakabaka, reversal, topsy-turvy.
baruka, spoils and slaves.

buiruka, *fulsit, fulguravit.*

buiruka, a form of the two waters, *l'eau miroité.*

ב

gah (גאה), high, lifted up, proud.
gb (גב), the booth or brothel, οἴχημα πορνιχόν, τὸ πορνεῖον (Ez. xvi. 24, the LXX).
gb (גב), gibbous.
gb, pit, cistern ; **gba**, a reservoir, marsh, pool.
gbb, to dig.

ka, tall, high, lifted up.
kep, concealed place, sanctuary, Typhonian.

kab, to double, double, turn corner.
kheb, low, lower Egypt, place of waters.

kheb, to dig.

HEBREW.

gbh (גבה), to issue from the earth when hatched (as locusts).

gbul (נבול), boundary, limit, border, margin.

gbur (נבור), the mighty God.

gbur, the mighty hunter.

gbl (נבל), to twist, twist together, wreathe as a rope.

gbr (נבר), a man, vir, as generator.

gd-gd (גדגד), to beat, to thunder.

gdd (נדד), to cut, break in upon.

gdh, banks, stone wall or bank.

gdih (גדיה), a female goat.

gu or **guh** (גו), belly, middle, body.

guih (נויה), dead body, corpses.

gua (גוע), to breathe out one's life.

gv (גו), majesty, to be great.

gvr (גור), to ferment, seethe, effervesce, to draw in moisture.

gvrl (חבל or גורל), lots.

gvsh (עוש, or עיש), the Great Bear (Ibn Esra).

gvsh (גוש), to search out.

gvsh (גוש), to curdle, clot, clod, heap together and make firm, to coagulate.

gil (גיל), a circle, revolution, age; **gul** (גול), go in a circle.

glh (גלה), to make naked, reveal, disclose, be revealed, manifestation, the primeval mode of revealing, the visible word.

gma (גמא), an ark of papyrus.

gma (גמא), Nile reed.

gmm (גמם) (an unused root), to join together, heap up, increase.

gmd (נמד), a staff or rod, a cubit.

gmd (נמד), to sit firmly, to establish.

gml (גמל), complete, mature, grown up.

guph (גוף), to shut upon.

gur (גור), to turn aside from the way.

ghr (נהר), hiding-place.

gn (גן), a garden.

gash (געש), to thrust, be concussed.

grz (גרז), to cut off, separate; **grs**, to break in pieces, expel.

gra (גרע), to scratch.

grph (גרף), to press together, to form a ball.

gshm (גשם), corporealness.

EGYPTIAN.

khep, generate, transform, create, shape, assume shape of (as beetles).

khepr, the world, boundary.

khepr, the creator, the beetle-headed god.

kafa, hunt, seize by force.

kab, to turn, twist, double, redouble; **khepera** twists the horns (*Rit*. ch. xciii.).

khepr, to generate.

kket-khet, to attack, reverse, overthrow.

khet, to cut, break in pieces.

ketui, circle, enclosure, surround with anything.

kahta, she-goat.

kha, belly, body.

kha, corpse.

khu, spirit.

khefa, might, puissance, potency.

kep, fermentation, heat, fertilize, fertilization of the Nile.

kheperu, happening.

Kepsh, the Great Bear, North Pole.

sheps, be concealed; **kapu**, hidden.

sheps, to conceive, be figured, shaped for birth.

karr, circle, orbit, course.

kheru, the word, voice, speech, know, make known.

khem, a shrine or ark.

kam, a reed.

kam, to create, form, produce.

khemat, kind of square-headed sistrum.

khemt, an adult, *homme fait*.

kafa, fist, seize by force.

kar, curve.

kar, secret, under.

khen or **khent**, garden.

khus, ram, pound.

khers, to dissipate, disperse, clear away.

kra, to claw.

khereb, to form, figure, model.

khem, matter; **khasu**, flesh, fleshy.

ד

db (דבב), to speak.

db (דב), a bear.

dbb (דבב), to flow gently.

dbiun (דביון), flux.

dvh (דוה), the woman's illness, menstrual.

dvh (דוה), menstruation.

dbr (דבר), to lead, head, guide, rule, direct, lay snares.

dbrh (דברה), words, precepts, manner, mode; **dbr**, word of the Lord, oracle, logos, edict, the Ten Commandments on stone tablets.

dum (דום), dumb.

dhr (דהר), to go in a circle.

dr (דר), a time, a generation.

dur (דור), generations, times; **dur**, roundabout.

tep, tongue.

tabi, a bear; **Teb**, the Great Bear.

tep, to drop.

tef, drop blood.

tefa, to menstruate; **teb**, to purify.

teph-t, abyss, source, hole of a snake

tepr, head, tie, noose.

tep, tongue, type of utterance; **tapiriu**, an engraved stone; **tapi**, stone; **riu**, engrave.

tem, dumb.

ter, circle of time.

ter, time or times.

HEBREW.	EGYPTIAN.

dud (דוד), to be troubled and agitated.
Dauid (דוד), David the Psalmist.
duh or **devh** (דוה), menstruation.
di (די), having the sense of two, as *Bicornis?*
diq (דיק), a watch-tower, place of look-out.

dlh (דלה), a door.
dath (דעת), the intelligence, understanding.

dr (דר), generation.
dth (דת), law, commandment, degree, statute.

tut, to tremble.
Tet, Lord of the Divine Words.
tua, menstruation; **tb**, **tep**, to drip, drop.
ti, two.
teka, see, behold, whilst hidden; **tekhn**, an obelisk.
terâa, door.
tat, the tat, eidolon, the soul, eternal principle.
ter, to engender.
tet, speak, speech, word, discourse, tell.

ה

he (ה), duration.
hgh (הגה), to murmur and mutter, as the soothsayer, magician.
hgh (הגה) a thought.
hgh, to celebrate.
hgil (הגיל), to rejoice, a religious dance.
hda (הדא), God.
hdm (הדם), to cut in pieces.
hdh (הדה), to stretch out, off r (direct the hand to anything).
hdm (הדם), to overturn, destroy, tread down, level with the ground.
huh (הוה), to breathe.
huh, to desire, long for, sigh for.
huh, to be.
huh, wickedness, fall, ruin, calamity, destruction, misfortune.
hui (הוי), ho! woe, alas!
havoth or **avoth**, cabins, huts.
hvn (הון), to rest.
humm (הומם), destruction.
hm (הם), to hum.
hin (הין), a measure of liquids.
hna (הנע), god or city.
hnh-uhnh (הנה-והנה), here and there.

hrh (הרה), to conceive as a woman.

hsh (הסה), to rest.
ha (הא), lo! see.
hah (האה), cry of joy.

hubnim (הובנים), ebony.
hud (הוד), majesty, honour, glory.
huzzab, the established (Nahum ii. 7).

ha, duration.
heka, charm, magic.

heka, thought.
hak, a time of festival.
hakr, applied to a festival.
hut, the great God.
temu, to cut in pieces.
ta, to offer, direct, with hand outstretched.

tema, terrify, swoop down, subdue.

hu, spirit, the breath; **haa**, breath of life.
uha, want, long for, sigh, desire.
hâ, essence, beginning.
hu, evil.

hui, tear the hair in grief.
hepti, ark or cabin.
hept, peace or rest.
ham-ham, to roar.
hum, locusts.
hin or **henu**, a measure.
hanna, name of a god.
hanu-hana, turn back and return, go to and fro.
ar, to make, image the child, likeness; **her**, function.
as or **hes**, rest.
hâ, to hail.
haa, jubilation; **ahai**, rejoice; **ahaiu**, cries of joy.
habni, ebony.
hut, throne, the upper crown, mystic sun.
hesb, **hesbu**, or **hesp**, a pavement, a district, a hieroglyphic of land, and of Egypt.

ו

uzr (וזר), to carry, sustain.

usr, to sustain, prevail, rule; the **usr** is the sceptre of power.

ז

zab (זאב), wolf.
zbb (זבב), an unused root, but expressive of sound.
zbh (זבה), sacrifice of a special kind.

sab, wolf, jackal.
sebhu, sob, groan, roar.

sabu, circumcise by castration; **sab**, eunuch.

HEBREW.	EGYPTIAN.

zkk (זכך), to be transparent, clear, pure.
zhb (זהב), to shine, be golden, metaphor applied to the heavens (Job xxxvii. 22).
zvg (זוג), to enclose, surround, bind.
zub (זוב), flow, to flow, menstrual.

zun (זון), to nourish, feed, give food.
ziz (זיז), a full breast.
zua (זוע), to shake, agitate, motion.

zv (זו), a precept.
zphth (זפת), pitch.
ziza (זיזא), abundance.
zqim (זקים), chains, fetters.
zmn (זמן), to prepare, appoint, establish.

znb (זנב), something vile or contemptible.
znb, tail, extremities.
znu (זנו), to form, put into shape, figure.
zen, kind, species.
znh (זנה), harlot.
zr (זר), a crown.
zra (זרע), seed, seed of men, race.
zrh (זרה), to winnow.
zrh, an arm, arm of God.
zrh, might, power, strength, help, helper.

zra (זרע), to plant.
zra, to conceive seed, speaking of a woman, be made fruitful (Lev. xii. 2).

saakh, to illuminate, glass?
seb, the star.

sefekh, noose, bind.
sef-sef, purge; **sep**, corrupt; **sep**, time, turn, spontaneous manifestation.
sen, food; **sen-kau**, to suckle.
shes-t, full breast.
sua, priestess, sing loud, shake the sistrum or seshish.
sept, a precept.
sif, pitch, bitumen.
susr, maintain, sustain.
skhem, to prevail, shut place, to imprison.
smen, to prepare, establish, appointed, place of establishing.
snab, fault, stain.
snab, legs.
senu, image, statue, found.
shen, brother, sister, brethren.
khennu, concubine.
shâr, a crown.
sheru, barley, children, pubescent youth.
ser-t, fan.
ser, the arm symbol, arm of the Lord.
sru, dispose at pleasure, chief, arrange, distribute, console.
srut, plant, dig, renew.
ser, a liquid like cream or butter, sacred, private, reserved.

ח

chbur (חבור), a type-name of rivers.
chbq (חבק) (Talmudic), girdle.
chg (חג), a festival, in the Talmud the Feast of Tabernacles, the Passover (Is. xxx. 29); **hgg**, to keep a festival, go round in a circle, dance.
chgg (חגג), be drunk, or get drunk.
chdr (חדר), a chamber, woman's innermost apartment, house of the mother (Cant. iii. 4), inward parts of the belly (Prov. xx. 27).
chdr (חדר), to surround, enclose.
chug (חוג), to describe, draw, or go in a circle.
chud (חוד), to put forth.
chvt (חוט), measuring-line.
chvl (חול), the phœnix.
chur (חור), hole.
chuthm (חותם), a seal, seal-ring, signet.
chzh or **hza**, (חזה) to see, as seers, by abnormal vision; **chzh**, a seer, prophet, one of the zah or sa (see the **chasai**, 2 Ch. xxxiii. 19, margin); **chzion**, vision, revelation, valley of vision, mount of vision.
chta (חטא), sin, grief, calamity, fault, penalty, misfortune, outcast, wander, purify, be purified, expiate, cleanse by a sacred ceremony.
chth (חטה), wheat.
chih (חיה), life, vivify, give or preserve life, feed life, anima.
chith (חית, i.e. חות), the beast of the reeds (Ps lxviii. 31), an image of Egypt.

kabh, inundating; **aur**, river.
sevekh, noose, tie, girdle.
hak, festival, a time; **hekau**, some kind of bread (unleavened?); "**skha-hut**" is leavened bread.

heka, beer, drink.
hathor, habitation of Horus, as the mother; **khat**, the womb.

atr, river measure, limit, margin, boundary.
khekh, a collar.

ut, to put forth.
kept, measured out.

khepr, the transformer, to transform.
kar, hole.
khetem, seal, shut, a signet-ring.
kashi, secret; **sa**, an order of priests; **shaunnu**, a diviner, a divine shau or seer. The Egyptian "sa" equates with "**hasai**."

aati, leprous, accursed, outcast, destitute, unclean.

hut, wheat, white corn.
khu or **hu**, spirit, genius, aliment.

khebt, the hippopotamus, type of Egypt in the North.

HEBREW.	EGYPTIAN.

chk (חֵךְ), mouth, palate, internal parts of the mouth.

khekh, throat, gullet.

chkh (חכה), take captive? (see Is. xxx. 18).

hak, captive.

chlb (חלב), what is best and most excellent.

kherp, to excel and surpass.

chm (חם), heat.

âm, heat.

chma (חמא), to curdle, make cheese.

ham, to conceive, make a child; **kam**, to create.

chmnim (חמנים), images, plural of Hamon, and as the **h** changes with **a**, and these are sun-images, the name identifies them with Amen-ra.

images of **Amen-ra**.

chmz (חמץ), that which is leavened (Ex. xii. 15).

mesi, cake; **mes**, some kind of cake.

chmsh (חמש), womb.

mes-t, place of birth; **mes**, bear, bring forth; **kha**, belly; **khepsh**, womb.

chmth (חמת), a bottle.

hemt, feminine emblem; **hem**, fount or well, with bottle sign.

chn (חן), grace, favour, good-will, beauty.

han, nod assent, favour; **ân**, appear beautiful.

chnn (חנן), making supplication.

hannu, to supplicate.

chnh (חנה), to bow down, incline, prayer.

haniu, adore.

chnp (חנף), to be profane, polluted, impious.

nebt, evil of some kind.

chph (חפה), bride-chamber.

khep, sanctuary, secret place, the uterus.

chpsh (חפש), a beetle.

khepr, the beetle-headed god.

chiq (חיק), to surround.

khakh, a collar; **khakri**, a necklace.

chraim (חראים), excrements (Is. xxxvi. 12; **zuah** in margin; cf. **sua**, Eg.).

aari, fæces.

chrd (חרד), to be frightened.

her, fear, terrify.

chrt (חרט), unused root; to cut in, to engrave.

ruti, to engrave, figure; **karb**, sculptor.

chrishi (חרישי), silent, quiet; **charesh**, secretly.

karas, funeral, place of embalmment; **karast**, the mummy.

chrp (חרף), autumn, fruit season, to pluck, gather, reap.

kherp, a crop; **Repit**, goddess of harvest.

chrs (חרם), the sun.

Res was a surname of Osiris, as the watcher, the eye of heaven.

chrphah (חרפה) (Is. xlii. 3), the shame or reproach, the feminine period.

repa, lady, virgo, feminine repeater, wife of Nile.

chshah (חשה), be silent, still.

kashi, secret.

chshb (חשב), reckoned, to reckon, to think upon, consider.

sap, count, reckon; **saph**, examine.

chshb, the girdle of the high-priest, which bound the ephod (Ex. xxix. 5).

seb-seb, encase, gird; **shebu**, a collar or tippet; **shebu**, traditions; **khesba**, blue, lapis-lazuli.

chsn (חסן), to bind together, be strong, possess power, treasure, abundance.

senh, bind; **senn**, to found, establish; **shen**, granary.

chezb, to destroy, slay.

hesb, destroy, destruction.

chq (חק), an appointed time.

hak, a time appointed.

hkh, defined, established, law, ordinance.

heka, rule.

chqr (חקר), secret depths, hidden, to search beneath.

kar, secret; **khr**, under; **kari**, digger.

chthm (חתם), to shut, to seal, seal up, set a seal upon, a seal.

khetem, to shut, lock, seal.

chthth (חתת), to break, to break in pieces.

khet, to break in pieces.

chth (חטה), wheat.

het, wheat.

ט

tbur (טבור), summit, lofty place, the height.

tepr, head; **tep**, heaven, top.

tebh (טבה), a slayer, to kill, executioner.

tetbu, kill, destroy, exterminate.

tba (טבע), to seal.

teba, seal.

tbth (טבת), month of dirt.

tepht, the abyss, a lake of mud or matter.

thur (טהור), physical purity opposed to impurity, to cleanse in the primal sense.

ter, rub out, wipe out, drive away, obliterate, purify.

HEBREW. | **EGYPTIAN.**

tua (מוא), to be miry and foul.

tu, filth, stain.

tutphuth (טוטפות), written scrolls worn fillet-wise, called frontlets.

tut, word, language; **put,** circle.

tur (טור), an enclosure, wall, fence, boundary.

ter, limit, extreme frontier, boundary.

tchr (טחר), to be illuminated.

teka, to illuminate.

ttah (טמאה), pollution, filthiness, unclean.

taut, slime, venom; **táa,** pollute.

tam (טעם), to perceive.

tam, to spy out.

tam (טעם), judgment, royal decree, sentence.

tma, make just, visibly; **tema,** announce; **Ma,** goddess of justice; **Tum,** god of justice.

tan (טען), to cut through.

ten, to cut in two.

tphth (טפת), a drop.

teft, to drip; **tef,** drop.

---

iab (יאב), to desire, to long.

ab, desire, wish.

ibb (יבב), to cry out, joyful exclamation.

heb, shout of triumph, festival.

igh (יגה), sad, afflicted, grieved.

aka, depressed, subdued, quiet.

iaga, wearied out, exhausted.

akha, dead.

id (יד), the hand.

it, to figure forth with the artist's hand.

idun (ידון), a judge, or judged.

aten, title, officer, hear, listen; **atum,** the judge.

ida (ידע), to perceive, see, know, be aware of, understand, ideal, imaging.

it, figure, paint; **at,** form, type, image.

ihuh (יהוה), supreme deity of Hebrews, rendered Jehovah.

heh, deity, the eternal.

iar (יאר), a river.

aru, a river; also **aur.**

ihr (יהר), union, junction, together.

her, with, together with.

ihm (יהם), to conceive, have sexual intercourse.

ham, to conceive; **kam,** to create.

im (ים), the sea.

iuma, the sea.

ium, the west.

am, the west.

isd (יסד) to found, establish, settle, be based, seated, grounded.

sat, floor, base; **set,** seat, race, rock.

ial (יעל), to rise above, ascend on high.

har, to rise above, ascend on high.

ian (יען), a howling animal of the desert; a name of Baal corresponding to Pan.

an, the ape, the type of speech, a form of Taht, earlier Sut-Anubis, or Bar-Sutekh.

ian (יען), to say, utter, speak, sing, howl.

an, speech of, from, to, speech personified as An.

iaz (יעצ), councillor, chief, leader.

as, the great and noble; **asi,** venerable, august.

ichid (יחיד), the ego, self, or soul (Ps. xxii. 20).

akhet, the spirit, manes, the dead.

iatzr (יצר), potter.

attusa, applied to potters.

iaqb (יעקב), Jacob, "taking hold of the heel," who was to be multiplied.

ákab, a tendon, some part of the body (heel ?); **akab,** multiplied.

igb (יגב), to dig or plough.

kheb, to plough.

iqvm (יקום), the existing substance.

kham, matter.

iqtn (יקטן), little (Arab. Kahtan).

kett, little.

iqim (יקים), a setter up.

khem, ithyphallic.

iqshn (יקשן), fowler.

ushnu, fowlers.

ird (ירד), used of a downward flowing, to pour down abundantly, to flow down, to draw down, pull down, cause to flow down.

art, to milk, or milk.

irch (ירח), a month, that which makes a circuit (monthly), as the moon.

ark, thirtieth of the month.

iarkh (ירכה), hinder part, extremity, end.

ark, end, finis.

ish (יש), being, existence, *esse.*

ash, liquid, seminal source, emission.

ism (ישם), to be set, placed.

sam, remain, dwell.

ishh (ישה), to stand, stand out, stand up.

as, secreting part of body; **ash,** emission; **asut,** testes.

ipha (יפע), he shone forth, to shine forth.

ub, to shine, sunrise; **af,** a name of the sun in the lower hemisphere.

iri (ירי), foundation.

ar, fundamental.

ishi (ישעי), salutary.

usha, doctor, health-bringing.

HEBREW.	EGYPTIAN.

ishi (ישי), Jesse, stem of Jesse (Is. xi. 1), and the root.

ash, tree of life; **Aash**, an ancient deity.

isha (ישע), deliverance and help, raise up, saving; **ishi**, salutary.

shaa, to raise; **usha**, doctor, feed and heal.

ithr (יתר), a distinguished, noble one.

taru, the hero alone.

כ

kab (כאב), to have pain, be in pain, sore, in sorrow, to afflict, to be afflicted.

khab, prostrate, some phase of eclipse; **kabu**, to be poor, weak, miserable.

kab (unused root); in Æthiopic, to roll, roll round, globe, ball.

kab, turn, fold, redouble, roll up, as **Khepr** rolled his globe of earth.

kbd (כבד), liver.

abt, liver.

kbud (כבוד), glory.

khu, glory; **but**, in front.

kbrh (כברה), measure of distance.

kepu, measure; **khepr**, the scarab-headed time-measurer.

kphl (כפל), to double, doubling, two folds; **kbr**, to bind together, to make, multiply.

kab, to double and redouble.

kbsh, coition, to beget.

khep, create, generate.

kbm (כבם or יבם), to be bellied, big, pregnant.

khebma, the pregnant hippopotamus, the genitrix Typhon.

kbs (כבס), to tread with the feet.

kheb, to dig; **khebt**, dance; **khepr** rolled his ball with his feet.

kabs, to force a woman.

kheb, to violate.

kbshn (כבשן), a furnace for smithing.

kafnu, an oven.

kbrh (כברה), sieve.

khip, sieve.

kd (כד), a symbolical pitcher (Ecc xii. 6).

kat, the womb.

khl (כהל), to be able.

kar, power, ability.

khn (כהן), priest, to minister.

ken, title; **kan**, service; **khennu**, sanctuary; **khen**, act of offering.

kuba (כובע), helmets.

kheprsh, helmet.

kvkb (כוכב), a star, the star of Chivan.

Kheb, Typhon; **khabs**, star; **khepsh**, Great Bear.

kv or **kvn** (בו or כון), in Hebrew, Phœnician, Arabic, and Æthiopic, to happen.

khep, to happen.

kvs (כוס), a cup, place of reception, pouch, emblem of sex.

khepsh, female emblem, hinder thigh.

kzr (כזר) (unused root); to break with violence, rout an enemy.

khesr, to disperse, dissipate.

kh (כה), virile strength, might, potency.

ka, the male power, masculine sign.

kir (כיר) (unused root); snare, ensnare.

kar, to entrap, to ensnare.

kla (כלא), a prison.

kar-ti, plural of prison.

klh (כלה), a space of time, complete end.

kar, circle, round, zone, complete.

klch (כלח), a full or ripe old age.

kar, the course; **akh**, age.

kms (כמס), to lay up in store.

khem, house or shrine; **khems**, ear of corn; **khamu**, transfer.

kmr (כמר), priest, priest from thirty years of age.

khemt, man of thirty years of age (ordained?), *homme fait*.

kmr (כמר), blackness.

kam, black.

knp (כנף), a wing, wings.

khen, fly, wave the wing.

knphith (כנפית), corner.

kanbut, ideograph of a corner.

kun (כון), the cake-offering; the μύλλοι offering to Keres.

kuna, pudendum f.

kiun (כיון), a goddess.

ken or **katesh**, the naked goddess.

kun, to erect, to create, form, found.

kna, embrace; **knau**, condition, doing.

ksa (כסא), the full moon, first day of full moon, point of turning back.

khes, turn back.

ksh (כסה), to conceal.

kashi, secret.

kss (כסס), to divide, distribute.

khesr, disperse, dissipate.

kph (כף), hand, hollow, curved, bent.

kefa or **khep**, fist.

kepher is used for covering with pitch and ashes.

khepr, the scarab that covered its eggs with dung.

kphr (כפר), ransom, redemption, atonement.

khepr, to transform, regenerate the dead.

krub (כרוב), a symbolical figure, a griffin or other chimera.

khereb, form, figure, the first form or model figure.

HEBREW.

chbrth (חברת), the coupling-point or place of junction; chprth (כפרת), the mercy-seat and place of the two cherubs; in Egyptian arks the two scarabs, afterwards feather-winged.

krs (כרם), a vine-dresser.

krs (כרש), the belly or womb, a pregnant body.

krth (ברת), to castrate.

kshph (כשף), sorcerer, witchcraft, enchanter.

kthim (כתים), people of the isles and sea-coasts.

EGYPTIAN.

khepr-at, house of the two beetles; the Crab constellation, as place of summer solstice, the point of junction; sign of the god Khepr.

kari, gardener.

karas, the coffin, or place of embalmment, womb of mother earth.

karut, testes; kart, stone-cutter.

sheft, demonial.

khet, navigate, go, sail, i.e. as the seafarers; khet, a ford, a port.

ל

lam (לאם), a people, a nation.

lg (לג), log, measure.

lhg (להג), study of letters.

lvr (לור), begetter of the heir to the childless widow.

lqh (לקה), arts, doctrine, knowledge.

lqhi (לקהי), the learned, imbued with learning.

lhqh (להקה), an assembly of prophets (1 Sam. xix. 20).

luh (לוה), to be joined closely; leui or levi, adhesion, plural. But see "rehiu," and comp. leuiuh (לויה).

lul (לול), to twist round, wind round, go round.

lta (לטא), to cleave to the ground.

lkt, to collect, gather, collect money (Gen. xlvii. 14).

lshon (לשון), the tongue, to tongue.

rema, people, natives.

rekh, reckon.

rekh, to know, be wise; rekh-rhet, Magus.

repa, the heir-apparent.

rekh, to know.

rekhi, intelligent beings, the wise men.

rekhi, pure, wise knowers, intelligent beings, the Mages.

rehiu or reh-h, twin, the twin Lion gods.

rer, circuit, go round.

ret, plant, germ, retain the form, grow, root.

rekh, to reckon, account.

res, tongue.

מ

mbul (מבול), a flood, the Flood.

mad (מאד), strength, force, exceeding might.

mah (מאה), 100.

maur (מאור), light, a light.

man (מאן), to refuse, be unwilling.

msa (משא), a bearing, carrying.

mas (מאס), melt, flow, abroad, run.

mg (מג), a Mage.

mi (מי or מו), male seed.

migdol, tower (of the Mages?).

minqth (מינקת), wet-nurse.

mgl (מגל), a sickle.

mgn (מגן), shield, protector, covering, means of saving.

mkun (מכון), place, habitation, dwelling of God.

md (מד), a measured portion.

mdh (מדה), to measure, extend, applied to a measuring cord.

meh, the abyss of waters; ber, to well forth, be ebullient.

mat, granite; mata, heart, spine, Phallus.

meh, fill, full, complete.

mau, light, shine.

men, no, not, defect, fault.

mes, to bear, give birth.

mes, product or source of river.

ak, a Mage; mak, to think, regulate, watch, consider.

mai, male seed.

makatura, a Migdol.

menkhat or Menât, the wet-nurse.

ma, hieroglyphic sickle; kar (gal), to curve.

makhennu, the boat or ark of the dead, in which they crossed safely.

ma, place; khen or khefn, interior.

mat, a division of land.

matai, rope, pole, tie, means of measuring.

HEBREW.	EGYPTIAN.

b'mu (במו), water, with, in, into.
musd (מוסד), foundation, basis.

mu, water, with, in.
mest, sole of the foot, to be generated and born.

muza (מוצא), origin, a going out, the place from which one goes out, that which goes out or is produced.
msr (מזר), constellation in the north.

mes, generation, engender, birth, born, child, product ; **mest,** sexual part.

mest, sexual part, birthplace; **ur,** oldest, first ; **misar,** star in Ursa Major.
mum, the dead ; **it,** to figure forth.

mmuth (ממות), a corpse, the dead, state of lying dead.
mnchm (מנחם), the comforter.
mnchth (מנחת), resting-place, the grave.
murh (מורה), a teacher, (Arabic) lord ; **mara,** a lord.
mrkb (מרכב), chariot.
muth (מות), the abode of the dead.
mth (מטה), a rod, staff, rod that blossomed, branch, twig, sceptre, expansion, extension.
mth (מטה), the tribe.
mthg (מתג), a bridle.
mtr (מטר), to rain, pour down rain, be watered.
mo (מו), water ; **moab,** water, seed, or progeny of the father.
mut (מוט), to shake, waver, totter, fail, decay, to die.
musb (מוסב), the circuit.
musd (מוסד), a founding, laying foundations, foundations.
msa (מסע), a dart.
mna (מנע), to restrain, keep back, "I will *restrain* its floods."

menkam, kind or quantity of wine.
mena, repose, death, sleep, rest.
mer, person attached to a temple, monk, a superintendent, a deity.
maru-kabuta, chariot.
mut, tomb.
mata, phallus.

mahaut, clan, family, cognate.
mut, mouth ; **ak,** to rule.
matur, growth, renewal.

mu, water ; **ap,** first, ancestral, essence.

mut, end, die.

seb, to encase, girdle round.
mest, place of birth ; **mesaut,** stone-cutters.

mash, an archer.
men, to fix, place firm, anchor fast, impound.

mnaul (מנעול), the Hebrew word for *lock* or *bolt* or *bar* (Cant. v. 5 ; Neh. iii. 3 ; Deut. xxxiii. 25).
mnh (מנה), pound.
mah (מעה), the womb.
mar-keth (מערכת), a pile of the showbread, the showbread, bread of ordering.
msha (משא), retreat.
mla (מלא), to fill, make full, be filled, be full, to satisfy.
mn (מן), manna arabica.

min is written with the sign of the bolt, the hieroglyphic of locking up, as the symbol of Khem.
mna, pound.
ma, the mother ; **hem,** *pudendum.*
merr, cakes ; **khet,** corpse, the dead body.
meshu, turn back, return.
meh, to fill, fulfil, be full, satisfy.

min, a name of Khem, the bull ; **kami,** gum arabica.

men, origin from the parent, creative matter, author, efficient cause.
mrah (מראה), mirror, looking-glass.
mra (מרע), a friend, companion.
mrq (מרק), to cleanse, by washing or anointing, to scour.
msa (משא), bearing ; the "burden of Jehovah" (Jeremiah).
msgr (מסגר), the enclosing, imprisoning, hence a prison.
mshh (משה), to draw out.
mshh (משה), to do at evening, yesternight.

kam (Min), to create ; **khem,** creator ; **kam,** matter.
mau or **maher,** mirror.
mer, love, attach, kiss, will.
rekh, to full, wash, purify.

mes, to bear and bring to birth.

meskar, the birthplace and purgatorial prison.

shu, to extend, stretch, elongate.
masiu, evening meal on the night of the last day of the year.
masu, to anoint, dip ; **masu,** a lotion.

mshuh (משוה), the anointed, prince or priest, consecrated by anointing.
mshch (משח), to anoint and consecrate for office.
mskith (משבית), imagery, chamber of imagery.
mshchr (משחר) (Ps. cx. 3), the "womb of the dawn."
mshkn (משכן), habitation, abode, temple, tent, the Tabernacle of the Israelites, the Tabernacle of Testimony.

mas, to anoint.

mes, to imagine.

meskar, the womb, north pole, place of re-birth.
mesken, the place of new birth ; **mes-t,** sexual part.

HEBREW.	EGYPTIAN.

mshnh (מִשְׁנֶה), double, twofold, one who takes the second rank or place.

msa (מַשָּׂא), tribute.

msa (מַשָּׂא), singing; **hsr-hm-sa** (הַמְשֹׂרֵר הַשָּׁר), the leader of the singing or carrying of the Ark (1 Chron. xv. 27).

shen, two, twofold circle; **shen**, second, the other, the *alter ego*.

mâsi, bring tribute.

sua, to sing loud.

נ

nad (נֹאד), a bottle.

nah (נָאָה), to sit, to dwell, keep at home.

nam (נְאֻם), speech, oracle, utterance, prophecy, the primeval *Word*, the "thus saith" the Lord.

ngb (נֶגֶב), the south, southern quarter.

ngsh (נָגַשׁ), sexual intercourse.

ndr (נָדַר), to consecrate, to vow or be vowed.

ns (נֵס), a banner-pole, ensign, uplifted flag.

nuh, to sit down, to rest.

nuah, to let down, deposit.

nuh, a place.

nua (נוּא), to move to and fro.

nap (נָאַף), to fornicate, commit adultery.

naz (נָאַץ), to be despised, rejected, derided, contemned.

nba (נָבָא), to bubble up, pour forth, prophesy, publish, tell.

nbh (נָבַה), to be high, prominent.

nbhz (נִבְחַז), a deity of the Avites (2 Kings xvii. 31).

ngid (נָגִיד), a prince, leader, noble, one in power.

nud (נוּד), get away.

ndr, vow, vows, vowing, avowed.

nub (נוּב), fruit.

nanm (נָאֻהַם), comfort, consolation, help.

nka (נָכַע), to touch a woman, lie with her.

ndh (נִדָּה), menstruation, menstrual discharge.

nda, to thrust forth, expel, be expelled, an outcast.

nvd (נוּד), to be bulging and belly-shaped.

nvth (נוּת), dwelling-place.

ndph (נָדַף), to dispel, drive hence.

ngd (נָגַד), issued.

nam (נָעֵם), pleasant, soft, tender, gracious, delightful, producing.

nah (נָעָה), shaking, motion.

Noah, lord of the Deluge.

nar (נָעַר), to roar, to shake out, shake off.

nphh (נָפַה), to breathe, blow, breathe out, blow out.

nphth (נָפַת), to breathe.

nphil (נָפִיל), giant.

nphilim (נְפִילִים), sons of Anak, the giant.

nphsh (נֶפֶשׁ), breath, the soul, *anima*.

ntzh (נָצָה), laid waste, desolated.

naza, something cast out, excremental.

naza, a flower.

ntzr (נָצַר), to watch over, depend, preserve, guard, keep.

nchsh (נָהֵשׁ), the serpent.

nsb (נָצַב), to set, fix, make firm, rigid.

na, the bottle; **t**, terminal; **nnut**, receptacle.

nnau, to sit, abject, miserable, placed down.

num, speech, word, utterance; in an earlier form **netem**, denoting gestation.

nekheb, goddess of the south.

nak, to fornicate.

neter, a priest, holy father.

nhas, to erect.

nnu, rest.

nâ, come, descend.

nâu, place.

nnu, go hither and thither.

nahp, to copulate.

nasa, abused, abandoned; **neshen**, plucked; **nes**, broken down; **nasi**, foul and vile.

nehp, to emit, emission, day, wail, complain; **num** and **nub** are equivalents.

neba, palm tree.

Anubis, the jackal-headed deity.

nakht, power, powerful, a giant.

neti, out of.

neht, vow; **netr**, priest, servant, divine.

nubs, dates.

naham, take away, rescue, joy, make rejoice.

nak, fornicate.

neti, being, existence, negative, froth, the sign of bleeding, female source.

neta, out of, compel, afflict, punish.

neft, breathed, gestating.

Nepht, goddess of the house; **nut**, place, house.

netf, to untie, detach.

nakhekh, sprinkle, fluid, essence, seed.

nemt, (pleasant), sweet, delightful, engendering, or gestating.

nahuh or **nnuh**, shake, toss, motion.

Nu, the god; **Num**, lord of the inundation.

nru, awful, victory.

nef, breath, wind, pass, fill the sail.

neft, a fan; **neft**, breathed.

Nepr, a god.

Nep, the god called the "breath of those who are in the firmament"; **nakta**, giant.

nef, breath; **sha**, born of.

nasa, abandoned.

nasi, foul, vile.

nashu, flower-pots.

nasr, a superintendent, governor.

nas, the fire-breathing serpent of Hades.

naspu, to numb and stupefy.

HEBREW.	EGYPTIAN.

nqbh (נקבה), the female (of woman or beast).

ngh (נגה), Venus of the Kabalists.

nthr (נתר), to divide, loosen, break off, separate.

kheba, the inferior, lesser, lower kind; **khep** denotes the hinder part.

ankh, an Egyptian goddess.

nuter, the axe emblem of divinity; **natrau**, to cut, to make work, create.

ס

sah (סאה), measure, a Rabbinical measure, mystical.

sba (סבא), to drink, carousal.

sbb (סבב), to turn, go round, surround, turn, a turn, cause to turn.

sbk (סבך), to bind.

sbka (סבכא), a harp-like instrument.

sgur (סגור), a shutting up, an enclosure, shut.

sdd (סדד), to shut.

sdm (סדם) (Sodom), burning, conflagration.

shr (סהר), roundness, go round, surround.

sod (סוד), a couch, seat, sit, sitting.

sod (סוד), secret, a secret, mystery, "the *secret* of God was on my tabernacle" (Job xxix. 4).

sus (סוס), to leap for joy.

susha, a mare (Cant. i. 9).

suph (סוף), to destroy, make an end of.

suph (סוף), sea—something, sea of Suph.

schr (סחר), to be red-coloured.

shrth (סהרת), supposed *black* marble, marble pavement tesselated in colours.

skk (סכך), covered, hedged, protected.

skk (סכך), to weave, interweave.

skn (סכן), to dwell, inhabit; **skent**, female friend.

skh (סכה), tabernacles.

skuth (סכות), the Ark or Tabernacle.

"**Succoth-benoth**" (2 Kings xvii. 30), supposed image of the Pleiades.

skth (סבת), to be silent.

slh (סלה), "rest, pause, silence?"

sla (סלע), the rock.

smk (סמך), to lay-on the hand in blessing.

smn (סמן), appointed place, marked off (Is. xxviii. 25).

smr (סמר), horror, as if bound with fear, horripilation (Job iv. 15).

sphich (ספיח), a flood, an inundation.

sha, measure.

sebu, drink.

sep, turn; **beb**, a revolution, a round; **seb**, time and period.

sefkh, to bind, capture.

sefekh, number seven, a seven-stringed instrument played before Sefekh.

skhet, shut up, to hinder.

shet, closed, shut.

set, flames; **am**, belonging to.

ser, oblique, involve, enclose.

set, back of a chair, seat, sit.

shta or **shet**, secret, mystery, close, mystic, sacred, a box, chest, ark, or sarcophagus.

seshsh or **sses**, the *sistrum*.

ses-t, a mare leaping.

seft, put to the sword.

seft, pitch, bitumen.

tsher, red.

srut, sculpture, carve, engrave, *tesselated*.

sak, to bind, a cabin.

skht, weaver.

skhen, hall, place, embrace, give life to.

sekht, an ark or tabernacle.

sekht, ark; **bennu-t**, the Phœnix constellation, emblematic of the resurrection.

sekher, to be silent.

srau, private, reserved, involved, oblique.

seru, the rock.

smakh, to bless.

smen, place, dispense, prepare, appointed, place of the eight gods.

smar, bind, enswathe, for slaughter.

Sefa, goddess of the inundation, to make humid, to liquefy.

ע

ab (עב), steps.

abd, to work.

abur (עבור), passing, transition, pass over to an opposite place (1 Sam. iv. 1, 6).

abr (עבר), used of tears and of myrrh-dropping.

agb (ענב), to love, enjoy, pleasure, delight.

agn (ענן), to be shut up.

ad (עד), or **add** (עדד), root connected with time, monthly courses, periodicity, testimony, bearing witness, what testifies, revelation.

ab, steps; **ap**, mount.

abut, work.

apr, the equinoctial crossing, place of Apheru, or Anup, called **Aper**, the crosser; **aba**, pass through, opposite; **ab**, passage.

abr, ambrosia, ointment; **aft**, exuding, distilling.

kab, refresh, enjoy.

akhn, to shut the eye.

at, type of time, circle, deficient, destitute; **att**, speak, manifest; **at**, emanation.

HEBREW.

ad, prince (Is. lv. 4).
aduth (עדות), revelation, a revealed psalm.

adn (עדן), time, a year.

aud (עוד), to surround, go round, make go round.
auth (עות), to be bent, crooked.
aup (עוף), to fly, fly away.
uz (עז), strength, might, power, potency in man and beast.
azr or **uzr** (עזר), to help, aid, a helper.
atp (עטף), to cover over; **atr** (עטר), to crown, a crown.
aug (עוג), to go in a circle.
aitm (עיטם), a place of ravenous creatures.
am (עם), conjunction, communion, together with.
amd (עמד), to stand, stand firm, endure, stand up, be set, placed to bear, column, pillar.
amm (עמם), to hide, conceal, shut, close, be hidden.
amq (עמק), to be deep, unsearchable, "valley of blessing" (2 Chron. xx. 26).
anh (ענה), sing, call, read, lift up the voice, begin to speak, answer, reply (Chaldee **ana**).
anub (ענוב), bound together.

anm (ענם), two fountains.
anq (ענק), to adorn with collar or necklace.
aphi (עפי), full of foliage, flourishing.
atzb (עצב), image of an idol.
atzh (עצה), backbone.
asha (עשה), to make, beget, in the beginning.

EGYPTIAN.

at, prince; **attet**, Word.
atut, speak, speech; **tet**, the manifester, the Word; **atut**, to praise, glorify.
atn, create, make a circle, reckon, the solar disk.
aft, the four quarters.

aut, crook or hook.
ap, to fly, to fly on high.
us, to create, produce, great, extended; **usr**, the symbol of power, puissance, victory.
usr, prevail, valiant, sustain, the Cæsar.
atf, the divine head-dress or crown.

akh, to turn, horizon.
atem, to enclose, to annihilate.
am, together with.

umt, stand firm, *pylon*, beam; **umti**, wall, rampart; **umt-het**, firm heart.

amam, to hide; **amen**, secret place, Hades.

amakh, mature, devoted, devote, strengthen, blessing, to bless.
anu, speech of, speech from, speech to.

nahp, conjunction; **nub**, twin or two; **anup**, together, the double Anup or Anubis.
nem, two; **nem**, waters.
ank, clasp, the Ankh sign.
afa, filled, satisfied.
aseb, God, typical seat.
user t, the vertebral column.
sha, beginning, all forms of commencement.

פ

HEBREW.

peh (פה), the mouth, opening. The **peth** (פת), for secret parts, is the Egyptian **peht**, the hinder part, the rump.
paga (פנע), reached.
peh, this or that, the place.
puh (פוה), to breathe, to blow, to pant.
pun (פון), to set, as the sun.
punh (פונה), "turning itself"; **penah**, face, turn towards.
psg (פסג), to divide, separate, fix limits.

puq (פוק), to go out or give forth, bring to an end.
pah (פעה), to call, cry out, used of a woman in labour (Is. xlii. 14).
pqch (פקה), to open; **peka**, to be cleft.

priah (פריעה), a term for wrapping the skin round the glands in circumcising.
pra (פרע), to loose, let go, begin, make naked, go before.
prsh (פרש), manifestly, fæces, excrements, to be dispersed, separate, declare, be distinctly said.
persh, to break.
pth (פת), *pudenda muliebria* (Is. iii. 17), interstice; **beth**, feminine abode.

EGYPTIAN.

pa, open mouth; **peth**, open the mouth.

peh, to reach.
pa, the, this, it is, the feminine place.
peh, function of breathing; **pef**, breath.
pen, back, one with **pest**, sunset.
pena, reverse, invert, return, turn towards.

pesh or **pekha**, to divide, separate, the division, also **peska** or **pesak**.
beka, to shed or bring forth.

pa-pa, to bring forth, woman bringing forth.

peka, gap, hole, extend; **pka-kha**, divide, be cloven.
pri, to slip, wrap round.

pra, show, appear, cause to appear; **per**, go forth, emanate, proceed.
per, manifest, pour out, come forth, emanate, bleed, pronounce the words, explain.

pershu, to break.
bu-t or **ba-t**, womb.

HEBREW.	EGYPTIAN.

pthch (פתח), open, to open, opening, opened, be loosed.

pethu, to open, as the mouth or a bow.

pthchiah (פתחיה), Jah is Putak, the opener.

putah, the opener, the god **Ptah**.

pthur (פתור), interpretation, to interpret, interpreter.

ptar, perceive, show, discover, explain, interpret.

צ

tzah (צאה), to go out, cast out, excrements.

sa, pass away, corrupt; **shaa**, substance born of; **sah**, the hinder part.

tzb (צב), a lizard.

seb, reptile.

tzba (צבא), go forth, as a star, or light; **zaba**, the starry host.

seb, star, morning, God.

Tzabaoth, Hebrew Lord of Hosts.

Seb, deity of starry time, signs, and circles.

tzbth (צבת) (in the plural, Ruth ii. 16), a handful.

shep, hand; **shept**, a handful, slice.

tzboim (צבעים), hyænas.

tzd (צד), the adversary.

sab, jackal.

St-Typhon, the adversary.

Tzphrda (צפרדע), frog.

khepr-ta, frog-headed god of the earth.

tzud (צוד), to lie in wait, set snares, catch.

ssat, noose, catch.

tzuh (צוה), to set up, constitute.

suha, to set up, erect.

tzuch (צוח), to cry out, joyful exclamation.

sua, cry aloud, sing.

tzuph (צוף), to overflow, drop slowly, ooze; **zufa**, to thrust out, as excrements.

sefa, to dissolve, make humid; **sef**, to purge, purify.

tzuz (ציץ), to shine, be bright, emit splendour, glance invitingly, to flourish (as a woman).

ses, number six, breathe, put on clothes; **ses-mut**, the going mother, register of compatibility, reach land after the period.

tzuq (צוק), to pour or make liquid, as molten metal.

sekh, liquid.

tzur (צור), rock, the " rock of Israel," divine leader; **Zur**, a leader of the Midianites.

ser, rock; **ser**, arranger, disposer, leader, comforter.

tzvar (צואר), to twist.

sep, turn or turns.

tziun (Zion) (ציון), heap, pillar, cippus, sign erected.

senn, to found, statue; **sen**, to guide; **sen**, a name of Esnè; "**sen-hru**," name of the 14th epiphi, the day of the summer solstice, when the eye was full and the year completed.

tzir (ציר), to go in a circle, also a messenger.

shar, crown; **ser**, a child, a consoler or comforter.

tzpr (צפר), to go in a circle, to turn.

sep to turn, a turn, time.

ק

qa (קא), to vomit.

ka, evacuate.

qb (קב), hollow vessel or cup.

kabh, vase of the libation.

qab, a dry measure.

kaab, measure; **kepu**, measure.

qdd (קדד), to cleave.

khet, cut, cleave.

kthm (כתם), gold.

ketam, gold.

kthnth (כתנת), coat of skin, coat of many colours, a sacred and symbolical garment.

khetenu, an image, a similitude, symbolical.

qdm (קדם), eastward, Eden, image of the eternal and of the beginning.

khetam, shut, a circle, closed, seal-ring, with Ankh image of life.

qu (קו), strength, might, rule, give law.

khu, govern, whip, rule, spirit.

qum (קום), to rise, erect, stand, perform, set up, cause to come forth, to exist, restrain, establish.

khem, the Lingaic image; **khem**, he who has power, potency, is master, the bull of the mother.

qoph (קוף), to surround.

kef or **kep**, to enclose, grasp.

qoph (קוף), an ape.

kaf, ape, monkey, the ape used in the mysteries.

qosh (קשׁ), bow.

kesr, arrow.

qvch (קוה), to bind, enclose, knot, fetter, capture.

sefekh, noose, catch, capture.

qlt or **qlvt** (קלט), dwarfed, maimed, curtailed in a member, short-footed, crippled.

khart, the cripple, maimed child-deity, **Har-pi-khart**.

qmh (קמה), stalk of grain.

khems, ear of corn.

qn (קן), abode, nest.

khen, inside, central place; **khan**, pudendum f.

HEBREW.	EGYPTIAN.

HEBREW.

qna (קנא), to become red.
kena, image of jealousy.
Chiun, the goddess.
qnh (קנה), measure of six cubits; beam of a balance.
qnh (קנה), bone.
qtzh (קצה), end, extremity, furthest reach, margin, verge.
qrn, a horn, symbol of male power.
qsh (קש), straw (collected).
kesh, chaff, dispersed.
qthm (כתם), marked, "thine iniquity is *marked* before me" (Jer. ii. 29).

EGYPTIAN.

ken, illness, become ill.
khennu, member.
Ken, the naked goddess.
kan, number.

ken, bone.
khes, to stop, turn back, the verge being reached.
ka, karu, and karunata, male symbols.
shesh, harvest.
khesr, to disperse.
khut, accuser, painted; am, belonging to; khetam, seal.

ר

rb (רב), chief, captain, leader; rbrbn (רברבן), lords.
rah (ראה), to see, to eye.
rosh (ראש), head, summit, highest, supreme.
ruch (רוח), breath of the mouth, spirit, the creative spirit.
rchm (רחם), to be soft, tender, compassionate.
ruham, womb.
rum (רום), high, lifted, raised up.
rann (רענן), green, green things, to put forth green leaves, be flourishing.

rvth (רות), a female friend.
rz (רז), a secret.

rtzd (רצד), to observe, insidiously watch, lie in wait.

repa, lord, governor.

ar, to see, eye.
ras, raise up, south, place of the summer solstice; res, absolutely, entirely.
ru, mouth; akh, spirit; rekhi, pure spirits.

rem, to weep.
ru, mouth, gate, door; hem, female.
rem, to rise up, surge up, be erect.
rennut, a goddess of growth, renewal, harvest; ren-pu, the young shoot and green plant.
Rept, the lady, a goddess of the Nile.
res, watch, be vigilant; rusha, watch anxiously, guard solicitously.
ras, to watch.

שׁ

seht, highness, dignity, excellency.
sba (שבע), full, plenty, abundance.
sbkai (סבכי), the killer of the giant Saph.
sgb (שגב), set up, set aloft.

sdh (שדה), land, field, ground.
sh (שה), cattle, beast.
shd (שהד), record, testimony.
sug (שוג), a hedge, to fence round.

sr (שר), prince; sorah, principal.
soor, power.
sus or ses (שוש), rejoice, be glad, leap, sing.
sch (שח), a thought, to meditate.

schh (שחה), to swim.

Stn (שטן), the adversary, resister.

sua (שוא), excellency.
sib (שיב), elders, grey-headed

sd-rh (שדרה), ranges.
scht (שחט), pressed (Gen. xl. 11).
sichh (שיחה), prayer or speech.
skih (שכיה), pictures, image, appearance, ensign, standard.
sokhoh, to weave, intertwine.

sut, king, royal.
sebu, basketful, quantity.
sebekau, the subduers.
skeb, figure of the deceased set up in the tomb.
set, land, nome.
sa, beast.
sshet, book, papyrus.
sakh, shrine, gate, enclosure, protect; sekt, horizon or house.
ser, chief, head.
usr, power, the staff of power.
shes, singer, draw bolts, open, pass.

saakh, intelligence, influence, illuminate, writing.
sekht, ark, cabin, boat; skat, tow, conduct a boat.
set, to drag; saat, catch, noose; Sut, Typhon.
su, king, royal.
sab, Magus, counsellor; shept, elders of some kind.
set, extended; ru, to be.
skhet, squeeze.
seka, lift up, cry.
skha, to depict or picture; skher, picture, design.
sekhet, net-weaver.

HEBREW.	EGYPTIAN.

subk (שׁוֹבֶךְ), entangled branches.

sefekh, noose, capture, the capturer.

skl (שׂכל), guiding, teachers.

skher, instruct, counsel, plan, educate.

sekhu, watch-tower.

sekaru, fort.

sma (שׂמאֹ), on the left-hand, the north.

semhi, left hand.

smch (שׂמח), rejoice, rejoiced, be glad, make glad.

smakh, rejoice, bless.

smikh (שׂמיכה), coverlet, carpet.

sma, encircle ; **smat**, wrap.

sair (שׂעיר), hairy.

sherau, pubescent.

sair, goat.

ser, goat-kind of sheep.

sarh (שׂערה), barley.

sheru, barley.

sphh (שׂפה), lips, the bank, margin, edge of.

sept, lips, shore, margin.

sphh (שׂפה), devouring.

seba, the devouring serpent ; **sep**, the corrupter.

sephek, to strike a covenant.

sefekh, a binding, tie, register.

sphch (שׂפח), scab-smitten.

sefekh, corrupt.

sphr, book, writings, scribe, secretary ; **Asaph**, co-scribe with *David* the Psalmist.

Sefkh, mistress of the writings, scribe, or secretary of **Taht**, lord of the divine words.

sq (שׂק), sackcloth.

saka, sack.

sqd (שׂקד), bound.

sekhet, net, take, shut up, trap, bind.

sqr (שׂקר), wanton with the eyes.

sakh, salute, pierce.

sr (שׂר), chief, ruler, head.

ser, chief, head, noble.

srt (שׂרט), cut, cutting.

surut, cut ; **serut**, cut down.

sra (שׂרע), stretch out.

ser, extend, elongate.

srph (שׂרף), fiery, burn, burned.

serf, blast, hot breath, jet of flame.

srr (שׂרר), rule, bear rule.

ser, arrange, dispose, rule.

sthr (שׂתר), secret parts.

sheta, secret, mystic.

sthm (שׂתם), shutteth.

shet, closed, shut, box, chest.

ש

shaul (שׁאול), the shades, or valley of shadow, hollow.

shu, shadow, void, destitute, deficient.

shar (שׁאר), kin, blood-relation ; **shereet**, posterity.

sher, child, son.

sharh (שׁארה), female, blood-relations.

sherau, daughter.

shbth (שׁבת), tribe.

shept, a class of men of some unknown kind.

shbi (שׁבי), captives.

Sevekh, the capturer.

shba(g) (שׁבע), seven.[1]

sefekh, seven.

shbx (שׁבץ), embroidered, figured in gold.

sheps, figured.

shbr (שׁבר), break, hurt, destroy.

shab, injure.

shabr, food, victuals, corn.

sheb or **shebu**, food, support, nourishing, flesh.

shbth (שׁבת), ceasing, be still, to cease.

shabti, a sepulchral figure, the mummy.

shd (שׁד), breast.

shet, suckle, breast.

shed, devils.

Sut-Typhon, Egyptian Devil.

shd (שׁד), destruction.

shât, cut.

shdi (שׁדי), Hebrew divinity.

shat, the sow, the suckler, or *Dea Multi-mamma* ; **Shat**, a name of Hathor.

shdh (שׁדה), the mistress, lady ; **shedeur**, casting forth of fire.

shtar, betrothed wife in a secret, my tical sense.

shu (שׁו), vanity, emptiness.

shui, vain, deficient, empty.

shua (שׁוא), vanity.

shu, vanity.

shvd (שׁוד), a destroyer, a mischievous demon, to lay waste.

sheft, terrible, demonial.

shva (שׁוא), to make a noise, crash, be terrible ; **shvh**, to terrify.

shefi, terror, terrify, terrible, demon-like.

shual (שׁואל), fox.

shu, fox or jackal.

shuh (שׁוה), substance, flesh.

shââ, substance born of ; **shebu**, flesh.

shuph (שׁוף), cover of darkness.

sheb, shade.

shuq (שׁוק), watereth, overflow.

sekh, liquid.

shum (שׁום), garlick.

shm, hot.

[1] The oath, covenant, or binding, is synonymous with number seven in the Egyptian **sefekh**, as it is in the Hebrew (שׁבע) r ad " shevag " by some transliterators (who take the *ayin* to have the sound of " *g* ").

HEBREW.	EGYPTIAN.
shushn (שׁוּשַׁן), the lily, so-called.	**ashnn**, lily-lotus.
shush (שׁשׁ), of a white texture.	**sesh**, paper, papyrus, linen.
shchh (שׁחה), worship.	**saakha**, adore.
shcht (שׁחט), to slay animals in sacrifice.	**sekhet**, to slay, sacrifice, a goddess.
shchr (שׁחר), dawn, dawning.	**sha**, rise from; **shu**, light; **kar**, under.
shchiph (שׁחיף), ceiling.	**skhi**, elevated, roof of heaven, sky.
shchth (שׁחת), destroy, lay waste.	**suakh**, destroy, lay waste.
shth (שׁטה), gum acacia.	**ash-t**, gum acacia.
shtch (שׁטח), to spread out, extend.	**st**, to extend.
shtr (שׁטר), to write, inscribe.	**shetr**, engrave (syllabic **shet-rut**).
shtph (שׁטף), to gush out, flow abundantly, overflow.	**seti**, shed, pour forth.
shir (שׁור or שׁיר), to sing.	**sheri**, to rejoice.
shith (שׁית), to set up, to put, to place.	**set**, seat; **sha**, set up; **suut**, stand.
shith (שׁית), dress, attire.	**set**, put on dress.
shkur (שׁכּור), drunk, drunken, drunkard.	**sheka**, drink or drunken.
shkl (שׁכל), to cause abortion.	**skher**, plan, scheme, strike, wound, throw away.
shkm (שׁכם) to rise up early in the morning for some purpose, devotion?	**skhem**, shrine.
shkm (שׁכם), shoulders, as symbol of bearing or sustaining.	**skhem**, prevail; **sekhen**, prop, sustain; **skhem**, the Shrine of the Bearer.
shkn (שׁכן), habitation, dwelling.	**skhen**, hall, place.
shkn (שׁכן), cause to dwell, to abide	**skhennu**, to make to alight; to alight.
shloshîm (שׁלשׁים), number thirty.	**sha**, thirty.
shm (שׁם), thither, whither, thence.	**shem**, walk, go, retrace, traverse.
smd (שׁמד), destroyed.	**sema**, smite.
shmini (שׁמיני), eighth.	**smen**, eighth (Ashmunein).
shmir (שׁמיר), an adamant stone, diamond.	**smer**, an unknown kind of stone.
shmn (שׁמן), anointing.	**smeh**, anoint; **sma-t**, consecrate; **smen**, prepare, anoint.
shma (שׁמע), hear, hearing.	**smat**, turn a deaf ear.
shma, to call, to summon.	**sma**, invoke.
shmei (שׁמעי), famous.	**sems**, distinguished, chief.
shmr (שׁמר), to fasten, to keep, preserve.	**smeru**, to swathe and bind.
shmsh (שׁמשׁ), to minister.	**sems**, minister.
shmsh, the sun.	**shemm**, heat, flame; **sem**, the double solar plume.
shenee, two; **shnim** (שׁנים), two, of a twofold kind.	**shen**, two, twofold.
shnh (שׁנה), circle of the year.	**shen**, circle, orbit.
shns (שׁנס), to gird up.	**shennu**, to wrap round.
shss (שׁסס), to be despoiled.	**shes**, serve, servant, follow, made to serve.
shah (שׁעה), a measure of time.	**sha**, Clepsydra.
shaph (שׁעף), division.	**sheft**, section.
shuph (שׁוף), cover, hide, conceal.	**shap**, hide, conceal.
shphchh (שׁפחה), typical maid or handmaiden, one of a family, as if a noun of unity, the concubine or whore.	**Sefekh**, a goddess, consort of Taht. Her name is number seven. Sefekh is a survival of Khefekh or Khepsh, of the Seven Stars, who was once the "Living Word," degraded as the Great Harlot.
shphchh (שׁפחה), privy member.	**khepsh**, the privy member, called the hinder thigh, the image of Typhon.
shpht (שׁפט), to judge (primary idea to set up).	**sep**, to judge; **sepi**, throne, pile, heap (of witness).
sheft, a judge, magistrate.	**shepta**, some office; **shept**, men of some kind whose office is divine, probably judges.
shphir (שׁפיר), beautiful, beauty, elegance.	**sefu**, colours, paints.
shphk (שׁפך), to pour out blood, also in (שׁפכה) the feminine urethra; **shephek**, the place of pouring out.	**sefekh**, the place of execution.
shphth (שׁפת), to put.	**sept**, put to the sword.
shqd (שׁקד), to watch, lie in wait, as a leopard.	**sekhet**, the cat- or leopard-headed goddess, a watcher.
shqh (שׁקה), water, drink, libation.	**sekh**, liquid, libation.
shqu (שׁקו), drink.	**sheku**, drink.
shqutz, (שׁקוץ), abomination, filthy.	**sek**, corrupt, evil.

HEBREW.

sharash, the shoot of Jesse, the Messiah.

shrb (שׁרב), the desert, mirage, heat, parching.

shrbit (שׁרביט), the royal sceptre.

shruth (שׁרות), bracelets, chains.
sheruth, beginning.
shesh (שׁשׁ), number six.
shsha (שׁשׁא), uncertain; rendered, "I will turn thee back"; "I will make thee go astray"; "I will deceive thee."
shshr (שׁשׁר), vermilion; **srd** (שׂרד), red.
shth (שׁת), buttocks.
sheth, foundation.
shthh (שׁתה), drink, give drink, banquet.

shthi (שׁתי), the warp.
shthm (שׁחם), shut.

EGYPTIAN.

ser, plant, shoot; **sher**, adult youth; **ash**, tree of life, personified by name as the "Sarosh," the Messiah of the Avesta, and the Egyptian **Ser**.
serf, blast, hot breath, sirocco.

user-pet, sceptre of the gods, sceptre of power.
serut, anklet, chain.
surut, to make, build, dig, plant.
ses, number six.
sha-sha, disgrace.

teshr, red.
set, thigh, seat.
set, floor, ground.
set, pour forth, libation; **shethu**, spirits of wine.
setkh, weave.
shatmu, shut.

ת

tham (תאם), to be twin, double, twined together.
thanh (תאנה), coitus.
thnn (תנן), to extend.
thbh (תבה), an ark or chest, ark of Moses, Noah's ark.
thbun (תבון), intelligence, insight, understanding.
thu, tau (תו), cruciform sign.
thudh (תודה), thanksgiving, praise; **taudah**, testimony.
thuph (תוף), to spit.
thur (תור), used of what goes or turns round in a circle, turn, order, a turtle-dove, the bird of return.
thv (תו), desire.
thm (תם), to come to an end, cease, disappear.
thchsh (תחשׁ), a skin, kind or colour unknown, covering of the Tabernacle.
thchth (תחת), lower, below, beneath, nether.

thima (תימא), a desert.
thkn (תכן), to weigh, to measure, a measure.
theken, to set up, to fix.
thm (תם), whole, complete.
tham, upright.
thmim (תמים), truth (plural).

themah, perfect, integrity, just.
thmh (תמה), something astounding, miraculous.
thmid (תמיד), perpetuity, continuance.
thar (תאר), to be marked out, a border.
tashur (תאשׁור), some kind of cedar.
thmruq (תמרוק), purifications of women.

thnim (תנים), uncertain wild beasts of the desert.
thnh (תנה), to distribute.
thnuah (תנואה), alienation.
thnuphh (תנופה), called the wave, or waving, offering.

tam-t, a total of two halves; **tema**, unite; **am**, together, with article.
tennu, create, generate, increase.
tun, to extend.
teb, chest, box, sarcophagus, close, shut.

tebn, to illumine or be illuminated.

tat, cross.
tet, speak, speech, word, discourse, tell.

tef, to spit.
tepr, noose, tie; **ter**, time, season.

teb, prayer.
atem, to annihilate.

tesh, red.

tet or **tuat**, tomb, depth, eternal abode, lower heaven.
tehma, a waste.
tekh, weight, to weigh; **teka**, corn measure.
tekhn, an obelisk.
tem, total.
tam, sceptre.
tem, perfection; **Ma**, goddess of truth in a dual character, article T.
tma, just, distribute justice.
tema, announce, terrify, hover, swoop on wings.
temt, the total circle, completion.
ter, limit, frontier, border.
teshr, red wood.
tem, avoid, negative, prohibitive; **rekh**, wash, purify, make white.
tenemi, make to recoil.

tna, to divide.
tna, turn away, separate.
ta-nep, typical corn; **tenf**, dead ancestor; **tennu**, tribute, ration, offering.

HEBREW.

thmrurim (תמרורים), bitternesses (plural), bitter, most bitter, weeping, or weeping of bitterness.

thnn (תנן), to extend (tent, extent, &c. having similar meaning).

thab. (תעב), to abhor, abominate, abominable, shameful; **tabu**, to be unclean.

thph (תף), circular timbrel, tabret, beaten by women; **teff**, to tap the timbrel, dancing; **tephuzah**, dispersion (Jer. xxv. 34).

thphuh (תפוה), an apple, the *round* fruit.

thphl (תפל), to spit, spit out.

thphs (תפש), to enclose, to hold.

thphthia (תפתיא), lawyers, learned in law, whose answer is almost the same as law.

thrin (תרין), two, from תרין.

thrph (תרף), (unused root). In Syriac, to inquire.

thrvmh (תרומה), heave-offering, offering of food.

theraphim, images, distinct from idols.

EGYPTIAN.

temu-ru, dumb, silent; **rem**, to weep.

ten, to extend; **tennu**, increase, multiply, grow, millions.

teb, to purify, close, shut; **tebu**, chaff; **teph-t**, source, abyss, valve, hole of a snake; **Typhon, Tepi**, the devourer.

teft, to dance, dismiss, send away; **tupar**, tabor or tambourine.

tef, the pupil of the eye, called the *apple*. In English turnips are said to apple when getting round.

tef, to spit, evacuate.

teb, box, chest, ark, chaplet, ring.

teb, answer, be responsible for, hold; **ta**, magistrate; **ti**, interpret.

teriu, two times.

terp, certain rites of Taht; **tri**, to question and inquire.

terp, food, duck, fowl; **terp**, rites of Taht; **mâ**, to offer, give.

ter, time; **ap**, manifest, declare, expose, guide.

NOTE.—The *Hebrew* in this list is but roughly rendered, the consonants only being transliterated as best suited for the purpose of comparison. Also, a word here and there has been selected for some *nuance* of the meaning found to be corroborated by the Egyptian.

SECTION XII.

HEBREW CRUXES WITH EGYPTIAN ILLUSTRATIONS.

ACCORDING to Josephus, the Egyptian writer Apion most strenuously insisted that the Jews were of Egyptian origin. He affirmed that when they were cast out of Egypt, they *still retained the language of that land.* He brings forward a proof which Josephus irately repudiates. Apion's account of the Jews was intended to satirize the worshippers of Sut-Typhon, the AAT, lepers, outcasts, and religiously unclean. These, he says, were driven out, and as they were afflicted with the BUBOS, they rested on the seventh day and called it the Sabbath, after the disease. Apion was playing upon words. Josephus asserts of him, " He then assigns a certain wonderful and plausible occasion for the name of Sabbath, for he says, 'When the Jews had travelled a six days' journey, they had Buboes in their groins, and on that account they rested on the seventh day, that thus they preserved the language of the Egyptians and called that day the Sabbath, for that malady of Buboes in the groins was named SABBATOSIS by the Egyptians. This grammatical translation of the word Sabbath either contains an instance of his great impudence or gross ignorance, for the words SABBO and SABBATH are widely different from each other. The word Sabbath in the Jewish language denotes rest, but the word SABBO as he affirms denotes among the Egyptians the malady of Bubo in the groin."[1]

Apion was impudent or humorous enough, but not ignorant of his subject. He was right in asserting that the Hebrews retained the Egyptian language. Saba, in Egyptian, means solace or rest. SABBA-TOSIS or Saba-tes denotes some secret or veiled form of opprobrious disease, just as in Latin Bubo is the owl, SABU signifying all that is profane, wicked, insulting, and Typhonian. This permitted a pun on the word Sabbo. He was no doubt speaking of the botch of Egypt, the boil out of which broke the plague of leprosy.[2] Tesh is red, and Sabo-tesh, the red boil, as Bubo is the red boil in the groin. Sabo-tesh might also have signified the Sabbo or boil with

[1] *Against Apion*, book ii. 2.   [2] Lev. xiii. 20.

the red spot indicative of leprosy. The Hebrew name for the botch, Shachen, and the Egyptian name for rest, repose, alight, cause to alight, as SKHENN, offer another play upon a word, with the same result. These outcasts of Egypt were, according to their own writings, fearfully afflicted with the botch and leprosy. Diseases of this kind were attributed to Typhon, who was called Baba, the beast. Ba is the beast; Saba the beastly, and those who had the diseases were worshippers of Sut and Sebek (Sefekh), whose name is for ever associated with the Sabbath, because it signifies number seven, and the seventh day, the Hebrew שבע, which the afflicted fanatics kept so gloomily, and in the secrecy of that gloom held up to heaven with piteous appeal their sufferings and their sores; a sad sight and a sorry subject for jest. There was, moreover, another covert meaning in the word SABBATOSIS. The subject has to be further dealt with, and meanwhile it must suffice to say that Sabu (Eg.), not only means to circumcise but to castrate. This was the earlier form of excision practised in the worship of the genitrix, by the Sabeans, who offered up their manhood to the motherhood. Sabu is the name of the ox or bullock, the castrated animal, and of the Eunuch. Seb (Kronus) was the castrator of his father. Sabu-tes means to excise the genitals; tes is the testicle, and the very self. The disease Sabbatosis, the botch of Egypt, and the leprosy, were evidently attributed to the Sabu in this sense, and the lord god of Sabaoth was thus not only the deity of the seventh day, or seven stars, but of the self-mutilated, the Galli, the Attys priests, who became Eunuchs for the kingdom of heaven's sake.

The Hebrew CHETHEM is identical with the Egyptian Khetem, to shut, lock, and seal; it has the meaning of a seal, to seal up, and set a seal upon. The root is Khet, to shut, to seal, and a signet. This will throw light on the form of the word as Chethen, to give one's daughter in marriage, to circumcise, to be a bridegroom, &c. Each is a form of sealing. Khet is likewise to cut, and cutting is the sealing by circumcision. Khet is cut and sealed. To seal is to cut, and the seal is cut. The circumcised child [1] is called metaphorically a bridegroom of blood, that is, sealed (cut and sealed with red) with blood. Aben Ezra says the Jewish women call a son when circumcised the bridegroom. Further, the seal and signet Khet is a ring, and the excised portion of the male is a circle, a wedding-ring of the peculiar rite with which the covenant of the bridegroom is contracted, and the sacred bond is sealed. The word circumcision implies the excised circle. Also, in Egyptian, the form " Heten " is a ring. The rite was symbolical, and the Khet-ring is hieroglyphical. It is the type of reproduction, and if we read the matter hieroglyphically, the covenant of circumcision was instituted as a rite of reproduction, a swearing-in of the male to reproduce his kind, and a protest against

[1] Ex. iv. 25.

all unnatural practices of the earlier time. The proper period of the
ceremony with the primitive races was that of puberty, when the
lessons were taught as in the Maori "young-man making." The
Hebrew circumcision for the second time [1] probably denotes a second
mode; the one in which the circle was excised for the first time in the
solar cult. Hence the foreskins heaped in the circle of Gilgal or the
ring of reproduction. The Jews identify the second circumcision [2]
with the word Periah, now applied to a secondary part of the rite.
The numeral value of the letters in the word Periah amount, by
Gematria, to 365, and that being the number of the negative precepts
of the law, it is said the circumcised person is to be considered to
have fulfilled all those precepts. [3] The number identifies the rite with
the solar year, as did the twelve stones set up in Gilgal, which came
to supersede the Sabean-lunar reckoning, together with some of the
older ceremonies.

The Hebrew words חוד (CHEVD), to tie knots, and CHEEDAH, an
enigma, a dark saying, riddle, parable, as in the symbolical sayings of
old, [4] the sentences of the Hidden Wisdom called Proverbs, have great
light thrown upon them by the Egyptian KHEBT and KHET. The
goddess Khebt carries the knot or tie, the sign of a circle, so much
time (Kept) measured out, and tied up by QUIPU. Kep also denotes
the hidden things, to lurk darkly and lie in wait; Khab is the phase of
eclipse. Khebt modifies into Khet, to shut and seal; Kheti, to go
round, surround, make the CIRCUIT. Khebt was the goddess, but
from the abraded form of Khet we obtain the name of the God.
Khetu is a god of things, we might say of the hidden things
which belonged to the earliest science, and were the secrets of the
learned, but hard riddles, and dark sayings to the ignorant. All this
and more underlies the word חוד applied to the dark sayings, parables,
riddles, and hidden wisdom, spoken of by the Psalmist.

The Talmud [5] says there was a flute in the Temple which had been
preserved from the days of Moses. It was smooth and thin, and
formed of a reed. At the command of the king it was overlaid with
gold, which ruined its sweetness of tone until the gold was removed.
The flute in Egyptian is SEBT : it was a symbolic seven, and the name
of Sebt (Hept or Khept) identifies it with Sut and the number seven.
On account of the Typhonian origin of the Seven, it and the flute
became the synonyms of all that is vile, wicked, profane, abominable,
in the word Seba or Sebt.

It is a Jewish saying that the sun always shines on Saturday. Such
sayings are a mode of memorizing facts that can only be read
symbolically. Of course there is no direct meaning in such a
statement. But Saturday is the day of Sut, and Sut signifies a

---

[1] Josh. v. 2.
[2] Josh. v. 2.
[3] Buxtorf, *Synag. Jud.* pp. 102, 103.
[4] Psalms, lxxviii. 2.
[5] *Eirochin*, f. x. 2.

sunbeam. Suti, the sunbeam, has the determinative of the sun shining ;
and in the hieroglyphic sense the sun always shines on the day of
Sut or Saturday, because it was, so to say, the earlier Sunday or
Sabbath.

Here is another Typhonian illustration.   In the Mishna[1] it is said,
"If a person has slaughtered the animal with a hand-sickle, it is clean
[Casher] and fit to be eaten."   The crooked hand-sickle is a type of
Typhon.   It is extant in the sickle of time (Kronus), and an early
form may be seen in the Egyptian scimetar, called the KHEPSH, a
sickle-shaped scimetar, which bears the name of the hinder thigh, a
special ideograph of Typhon and of the Great Bear.   The Khepsh is
crooked, and Khab means bent, crooked-like, Cam in English and
other languages.   The origin of the shape as bent, crooked, orbicular,
depended on the turning round of the Great Bear, the ancient genitrix
who carried the loop-shaped emblem as her sign of rule and measure.
In later times a moral or immoral meaning was read into the imagery,
and the crooked or bent was made typical of perverseness, wryness,
deflection from the straight rule and right line of rectitude and the
strict accuracy of law as represented by the stretched-out measure of
truth, personified in Mati, goddess of the twofold right.   The coiling serpent, Nenuti, had been an earlier type of the circular measure,
and this was superseded, together with other crooked things, by the
straight rule, the straight knife (Kat), the straight path.   But the
sickle-knife which was permitted to be still used in common with the
knife of stone and of reed was a survival in shape from the earliest,
the Typhonian cult, and can still be identified by the Khepsh sabre
with the Goddess of the Seven Stars and the seven Kabiri, or
turners-round.   So persistent shall we find the primitive types, many
of which were preserved by the Hebrews.

But first of some verbal cruxes in relation to Egyptian.

The Egyptian origin of Hebrew is well illustrated by the name of
the wilderness as MIDBAR.   No satisfactory account of this word has
ever yet been given.   The root MAT in Egyptian, Hebrew, and
Sanskrit, has the meaning of measure and extent.   Mat (Eg.) is likewise time, to fix, appoint, prove, witness, and the middle, or midway.
Par (bar) is the name for a road, and signifies coming out, to manifest,
show, and explain.   The Midbar was a mark of boundary, and a
synonym of the wilderness and desert; the Desert of Arabia.[2]   The
Midbar, as the extent measured and made manifest by a set boundary,
is identical with the desert or wilderness.   In Egyptian the Nome,
district, frontier, and the desert are identical as the Tesh, and Teshr,
with the T terminal, our word desert.   Egypt of all countries was the
land of the desert-boundary, the narrowest strip of land in the world
running betwixt such a double desert ; hence the wilderness, or
waste, was the nearest, most natural image of visible limits to the

---

[1] *Treatise Cholin*, i. 2.   [2] Gen. xiv. 6.

Egyptian mind, and the wilderness was with them a synonym of boundary. The Hebrew Midbars bear the name of the adjacent town, as the desert of Ziph, Maon, Edom, Gibeon, Paran, Jeruel, which shows the Midbar did not express the modern idea of a wilderness. Ezekiel refers to the Midbar of Egypt. "I pleaded with your fathers in the Midbar of the land of Egypt."[1] Possibly the Desert of EDROU HĔREMOS or the Mhiagh of Edair, the Irish Hill of Howth, is a form of the Midbar-boundary named from the wilderness, in the Egyptian sense.

Bunsen, whose Egyptology is often of the most cursory character, and who was personally obsessed with the idea that the so-called Semitic speech was earlier than the Kamitic, and that the rootage of Egypt was in Asia, has asserted that the word MAKATURA for MIGDOL "has no root in the Egyptian language. It cannot come from Mak."[2] But it does, and MAKATURA is of course the same by permutation with Migdol. He derives Migdol from the Hebrew GADAL, to be great. In Egyptian Tura is the tower. Mak means to watch and rule over. The Migdol was a watch-tower. Makatura signifies the watch-tower. "There stood a watchman on the Migdol,"[3] "the Migdol of the watchman."[4] It was the tower of the Mag or mage, the starry watchman of the night. Mak, the mage and to watch, doubly identifies the Egyptian origin of the Migdol as the watch-tower.

The river of Egypt, the Inundation, the "flood of Egypt,"[5] are called the IAUR (or IOR) in Hebrew. That is the Egyptian Aur. But Nahar (נהר) is the name of Nile, the actual river and flood of Egypt, as well as the river of mythological astronomy, the river of Eden,[6] the river of Egypt,[7] the typical river emphasized as THE, no matter under what name. THE river, as Nile was religiously designated, is Aur, and the Hebrew name of names for the river, the typical waters, the mythical floods, is that of the Nile, and the formation of the name is Egyptian. Nahr (Heb.) is a plural for river. In Egyptian Aru is the river, and NÁI is the plural article The; the river is NAI-ARU, or the dual waters of the Nile, the two waters welling from the pool of the Two Truths, or the Vase of HAPI-MU, the biune Waterer.

The divinity of the Psalms who founds and establishes the earth on the floods[8] does so on the Nile and its inundations, which deposited the earth as Khebta; surely then it must be an Egyptian divinity who is celebrated in the Psalms.

According to Josephus,[9] Kimchi, the Seventy,[10] and Ben-Sira,[11] the river GIHON (or גיחון) of the Genesis, is the Nile which flows through

[1] Ch. xx. 36.   [2] *Egypt's Place*, vol. iii. p. 213.
[3] 2 Kings ix. 17.   [4] 2 Kings xvii. 9.   [5] Am. viii. 8.
[6] Gen. ii. 10.   [7] Gen. xv. 18.   [8] Ps. xxiv. 2.
[9] *Ant.* i. 1, 3.   [10] Jer. ii. 18.   [11] xxiv. 37.

all the lands of Kush, the southern lands. It is not that the narrator thought of the origin of the Nile as being in Asia, as Fuerst suggests, but because the narrative was Egyptian at first, the imagery is Egyptian from the first, and the riddle of the mythical commencement can only be solved in relation to the localities as Egyptian. Theirs is the river that runs from the south through all the lands of Kush. Calmet, on the river GIHON, says the people of Goiam call the Nile by that name. The Hebrew name of the river in full is the GICHON, *i.e.* the GIKH-KHAN, an Assyrian synonym for the river Euphrates. If we refer this back to Egyptian, Khekh denotes the tidal water, and Khen means the interior, the lake, the southern (Khent); thus Khekh-khen is the tidal river of the lands of the south. The Nile of Egypt flows from south to north, but the celestial Nile was figured in Khepsh, the north, and only in the Egyptian imagery, and by aid of the Egyptian naming, can this Kvsh of the southern land be reconciled with the same naming, Khepsh, of the celestial north, and only on the theory previously propounded, that the first namers dwelt where the land of Kush (Æthiopia) was yet to the north of them, and Kush, Kvsh, or Khepsh, was their north, whilst Khentu was then their south, and Kheptu-Khentu was their north and south. The Nile thus identified as the terrestrial Gihon includes the celestial river, and proves the mythos to be Egyptian. According to Fuerst, גיחון is derived from גוח, *i.e.* the equivalent rendering of Khepsh, the thigh, as the mouth of source, the great water of the hinder thigh, located in the place of emanation.[1] No explication of the scenery and naming is possible from the Hebrew alone, whereas the Egyptian will make all perfectly plain, and followable in phenomena. This place of source is the well or pool of the two waters and the hall of the two truths, and as such was re-adapted to other localities wherever a fountain rose and formed a double stream. Hence Gihon is found as the name of a fountain on the western side of Mount Zion, where it made a double pool, the upper Gihon being identical with the upper pool,[2] and the lower with the lower pool,[3] the celestial prototype of these being still represented by the double stream of Aquarius.

The Hebrew word SHAKAM, has the general sense of to rise up early, to perform some act, also to enter some place, to bend oneself, the first thing in the morning, although no noun is found in the Hebrew thesaurus as a basis for the verb Shakam, which would denote morning. This implies an original use of the word Shakam, such as included the morning or the act of the morning, to identify the primal meaning, which may be traced by aid of Sakh (Eg.), the shrine or sanctuary, the act of saluting and adoring, also the illuminator, which might be the opening eye of day. Am denotes that which appertains to. The Skhem (Eg.) is also the shrine, and Sekhem-t means to obtain grace. In Egypt going to the shrine was a typical

[1] *Rit.* ch. xvii.   [2] 2 Kings xviii. 17.   [3] Is. xxii. 9.

act of the morning, and the equivalent for rising early, and "Shakam" remained with the Hebrews as an expression having a sacred because symbolical significance when applied to early rising, even without going to the shrine. The Hebrew Sakh (שׂךְ) is the name of a hut or tent.

The Hebrew SHAKAN (שׁכַן) has the same significations as the Egyptian Skhen, the habitation, the place, the dwelling ; whence Skhent, to institute and establish. But in the hieroglyphics the word also means to alight, and cause to alight. This is missing from all interpretations of the Hebrew, yet it supplies the better sense to several passages, especially those relating to the glory, the pillar of cloud, and to the alighting of winged and wandering things. The habitation of the fowls of heaven thus becomes the far more appropriate place of their alighting.[1] Of the eagle it is said,[2] "She dwelleth and abideth on the rock," which is tautological. The Egyptian Skhen makes it, "She alighteth and abideth on the rock." In other instances the sense of to alight adds indefinitely to the meaning, as, for instance, "I will cast thee forth upon the open field, and will cause all the fowls of heaven to alight (remain) upon thee, and I will fill the beasts of the whole earth with thee."[3] "If I take the wings of the morning and *alight* in the uttermost parts of the earth" is a far finer rendering than the A.V. "dwell."[4] So in the passage, "Oh that I had wings like a dove ! (for then) would I fly away, and be at rest. Lo, (then) would I wander far off, (and) remain in the wilderness."[5] The restored sense would be, "then would I fly away and alight afar off in the wilderness."

The chief value of the variant Skhen, to alight, to cause to alight, is this restoration of the nomadic ideograph, which shows the first perception of dwelling, abiding, and inhabiting the earth to have been imaged as alighting like the winged wanderers of the air.

Hebraists have not been sufficiently acquainted with the exact meaning of the word Nqph (נקף) to correctly translate the original of the passage rendered, "And though after my skin worms destroy this body, yet in my flesh shall I see God."[6] Some kind of destruction is intended, but it cannot be by worms. It is true the Arabic NQIPH has the meaning of worm-eaten. But the missing sense and true form of the destruction will be found in the Egyptian NEKHFI, to calcine or be calcined. The reading then will be, "And though this (thing) my עוּר (cover) be calcined, yet in my בשׂר (Basar) shall I see God." AF (Eg.), the flesh, will account for the Hebrew AVR, the skin or cover, and BES, to transfer or transform, pass from one place or shape to another, with AR, the likeness, will render the Hebrew BASAR. The fundamental sense of the passage then is, "And though my likeness of the flesh be calcined, yet in my type of transference

---

[1] Psalms, civ. 12.   [2] Job xxxix, 28.   [3] Ez. xxxii. 4.
[4] Psalms, cxxxix. 9.   [5] Psalms, lv. 6, 7.   [6] Job xix. 26

or transformation shall I see God," a mode of description according to the Egyptian doctrine of Khepr.

In the passage, "Thou shalt engrave upon it (the plate of gold) like the engravings of a signet, 'Holiness to the Lord,'" the word holiness gives no definiteness to the Hebrew Qodesh. Egyptian offers us the clue to understand the word Qodesh in all its applications. Ka is the type, figure, function of thing or person. Tesh is to separate, hedge about, put a boundary to. Tesh is the frontier of a nome. Tesh is blood ; the separating period, the red line or fullstop in the earliest of all *rubric*. TESH-TESH is a title of Osiris in the feminine phase. רּשׁא, to be young, pure, new, is derived from this origin in feminine pubescence. Tesh, to make or be separate, a frontier and limit of boundary, yields the principle of Qodesh. So Mount Sinai was rendered Qodesh by being hedged round and made inaccessible.[1] The cause, object, or result of the separation may be very various as is the use of this word. The woman set apart for seven days would be Qodesh, equally with the priest who was separated and consecrated to the Lord. Hallowed or accursed are secondary meanings in the Hebrew, but to be separated, divided, set or put apart is primary in Egyptian.

Tekh, the hard form of tesh, means the frontier, boundary, crossing, to fix and attach. It is likewise a name of Taht, who represented the new moon. Hence the new moon and the time of the new moon were Qodesh. The first day on which the new moon was visible was a boundary, a limit, a measure in time, and the new moon was the type (Ka) of the tesh or tekh. The moon, the lunar month, and the feminine period are particularly Qodesh. Tekhi (Eg.) was the goddess of the monthly period.

NAAM, in Hebrew, is a word specially employed to express the voice of revelation, the oracle, the voice of God, by which oracles were revealed to the prophets. It is the voice of Jahveh, the Thus SAITH the Lord ; also used for the utterance of oracles.[2] Nam is Egyptian for the word, speech, tongue, utterance. It is literally the voice of periodicity, or again-coming. Nam is to repeat, see, perceive. This repetition includes the inundation and the period determined by a drop of blood, as well as the time for joining and engendering, these being a form of the Two Times, of the Two Truths. Nam has the meaning of guiding and directing on this ground. Nam-nam means to go again, repeat. The nam (namt) is the retreat, the womb, which will be shown in this work to have been the first oracle and mouthpiece of revelation. With the permutation of the M into B, we have Nabi, the prophet ; Naba (אבנ), to announce, manifest, prophesy. A mere hint only is here given, so much has to follow. Enough to know that Nam with all its imagery is Egyptian, and that means getting foothold on granite, instead of losing it among quick-

[1] Ex. xix. 23.   [2] Jer. xxiii. 31.

sands. For Nam is not the earliest shape of the word. The phonetic N is an ideographic Net, and Nam is Netem, a variant of Snatem, and both relate to the gestator and primordial prophesier.

The word SELAH has caused much perplexity to commentators. It is frequently found in the Psalms, it only occurs three times elsewhere, and then in a hymn or psalm.[1] It is generally accepted as a sign of silence, rest, or a note importing a pause, as if it meant the singer was to rest, whilst the instrumental music went on. There is a fuller phrase in Psalm ix. 16, where, instead of the usual Selah, the note is, הגיון סלה, "HEGIUN SELAH." Gesenius suggests that this should apparently be rendered "INSTRUMENTAL MUSIC—PAUSE." But if, as is here contended, the oldest of these Psalms of David belong to the books of Taht, Egyptian ought to enable us to settle the matter. Selah with the R in place of L will be Ser. Ser means something sacred, involved, reserved, and very privately personal. AH denotes a salute. Ser-ah or Selah is a most private and personal salute. We do not get silence specified as one of the meanings of the word, but this may be gathered from the others. Whilst "Huknu" is to supplicate, Huknu read phonetically will be huken. The Egyptian "Hek" has the same meaning in the Hebrew Chug, to charm or the muttering of enchanters. Chug (חוג) is to draw a circle, the circle of magic being an early figure. Chug is also to celebrate, as in Egyptian it is to praise. Huka (Eg.) is magic or thought, to charm and to utter the words of the magic formulas. To charm is to invoke or supplicate. Taking the word HEGION to be identical with HUKEN, to supplicate, we find the truer meaning of Selah to be a pause for prayer, a space of time reserved sacredly to silence and supplication. Meanwhile the music apparently died out in a cadence, for Huken also signifies a CADENCE.

And still further, SERAH is an Egyptian word meaning to reveal and exhibit. "HUKNU-SERAH" would indicate the supplication for the god to manifest his presence. This was done by means of representative images which made motions to the worshippers. The elevation of the host over the bowed and silent devotees is a relic of the same mummery.

"UN-HER-HEB," in Egyptian, signifies the show-face festivals when there was an appearance or exhibition of the god to whom the offerings were made. So in the margin,[2] where we find little leakings-out of the primary sense, Moses besought the FACE (Panim פנים) of the Lord, and the face of the Lord is the same as the shewbread, or bread of faces (Panim), the bread of the show-face festival, hence the relation of the shewbread and bread of faces to Moses beseeching the face to show.

TUBAL is a Hebrew type-name for the metallurgist. Tubal, the son

---

[1] Hab. iii. 3, 9, 13.　　　　　　　　[2] Ex. xxxii. 11.

of Japheth, is a metal-worker. Still earlier Tubal-Cain is an instructor of every artificer in brass and iron;[1] this, be it noted, in the seventh generation of men. In Egyptian TUB or TEB means to purify and refine by fire. TEBA is to roast. Al (ar) is to make, shape, create the form or likeness, and denotes the maker, doer, or shaper. Thus Tub-al (Tub-ar) is the maker who shapes or makes in purifying and refining with fire; he is the metal-worker.

KAM (Eg.) is black, and to create; in Arabic, to arise, to commence. The beginning, in mythology, was with blackness or darkness, as the background of emanation. Kimrir (כמרר), to be darkened, as the day by the obscuration of the sun, is the Egyptian Kam, black; rer, to circuit, go round, encircle. Kam-rer means to enshroud with blackness, hence to eclipse and conceal. The Kimrir of Job[2] are, therefore, eclipsing or eclipses. This suggests that the Kimarim,[3] the priests of the ancient religion, were really the Chimririm, or those who could foretell and explain the causes of obscurations and eclipses. Beginning with darkness, the recurrence of that phenomenon in heaven was the first to arrest attention and wonder, and to demand explanation. The interpreters were the Kimririm or Kimarim; not because they were gloomy and sorrowful or wore black, but because they were able to interpret the recurring gloom of night and the phase of eclipse, whether in heaven or on earth. For the first eclipse studied by the Kimarim was monthly, hence the monthly prognosticators. The root meaning of כמר to be thickened, to boil, bubble up, with the connected sense in Syriac of mourning, is related to this fundamental fact of periodic obscuration, which has to do with the primeval darkness of creation. The two kinds of eclipse are referred to by Job, the celestial and terrestrial, the one naturally following the other. The raisers of leviathan, or the bringers-on of the feminine period, were the causers of eclipse. In Israel the Kimarim were degraded as the priests of an illegal Jehovah-worship[4] and of the golden calf, the symbol of the Elohim who led them up out of Egypt. The Assyrian kings used to keep astronomers who prognosticated from eclipses.

Light seems to me to be shed on the word NAVEH (נוה), rendered " habitation " in the English version[5]—" I have seen the foolish taking root, but suddenly I cursed his habitation,"—by the Egyptian word NABEH, which signifies to be in flower, some kind of flower, probably golden. This would make it, " I cursed his flowering, or his flourishing appearance; " and it agrees with the Hebrew נוה, to be lovely, celebrated, beautified. It would also be less repugnant than cursing the homestead. Nab or Nub (Eg.) being gold, Nabeh may have the meaning of gilded or glorified.

[1] Gen. iv. 22.   [2] iii. 5.
[3] 2 Kings xxiii. 5, and Zeph. i. 4.
[4] Hos. x. 5.   [5] Job v. 3.

The word Tsamim [1] has been a great perplexity. "Whose harvest the TSAMIM eateth up." The TSAMAM [2] is a sort of gin or noose. This will not do for the earlier passage. But may not TSAMIM be the Hebrew plural corresponding to the SAMI (Eg. plural), the conspirators, the Typhonian company of evil plotters? The snare, noose, or tie, is a type of Typhon, chief of the Sami or Tsamim, who make use of the Tsamam in the work of the conspirators. SAM (Eg.) means, to devour.

"Though the root (of the tree) wax old in the earth and the stock thereof die in the ground, through the SCENT of water it will bud." [3] The word RICH rendered scent, as if it were the exhalation of water, has a more appropriate meaning in Egyptian, where " REKH " signifies the washing or laving and purifying of the water. The Hebrew רי for a watering [4] may be the remnant of this Rekh, to wash and water.

The word קדם, rendered "prevented" in the passage "Who hath PREVENTED me, that I should repay?" [5] may be illustrated by the Egyptian SHARMA, which means to make the salaam, or salute, and SHARUMATA to convoy a peace-offering. This was a mode of propitiation for securing favour beforehand, not to call it bribery. The speaker asks, Who hath made presents to me in this wise that I should repay, when all under the whole heaven is mine?

RAMOTH, rendered coral,[6] is a word more probably derived from REMTI (Eg.), to weep,[7] the RAMOTH denoting substances, that are wept, which supplies a principle of naming. This Ramoth is mentioned amongst the precious things by Ezekiel [8] as a production of Syria. So derived, it would be some kind of gum, and may have been a form of the famous Tzri, or balm of Gilead, which is rendered Rosin in the margin.[9] It would then follow that Ramoth-Gilead was named from its oozing gum, balm, or amber.

The word NASPU (Eg.) means to numb, stupefy, render torpid. It appears in Hebrew as NATZB (or Nazb), to fix, make firm, rigid, erect, set. It is used by Zachariah [10] and applied to a shepherd of souls. The shepherd, הנצבה לא יכלכל, (who) does not victual but devour that which is NATZB. Here the Egyptian NASPU extends the sense of NATZB most appropriately, for Naspu signifies, not only to numb and stupefy, but also to abuse, delude, and devour. Then the sense of the passage is that a shepherd will arise who will not victual but devour the foolish sheep who are to be falsely led, abused, and deluded, by their threatened devourer. The rendering of "standing still" has no actual relevance to the meaning.

Jezebel " STIMMIED " her eyes, says the Septuagint, when the English version renders it Jezebel painted her face, or, in the margin,

---

[1] Job v. 5. [2] Job xviii. 9. [3] Job xiv. 8, 9.
[4] Job xxxvii. 21. [5] Job xli. 11. Cf. next verb שלם. [6] Job xxviii. 18.
[7] So written, *Champ. Dict.* 79. [8] xxvii. 16.
[9] Ezek. xxvii. 17. [10] xii. 16.

"put her eyes in painting." This is an Egyptian relic, of which Hebrew gives no account; only by permutation of mim and peh and using the word Shedph for blasting, and inferring from that "to blacken," can we get any approach to STIMMIED. The Hebrew word, however, has in it the elements of STB in Stibium, and in Egyptian Stem is Stibium; to stem or stemmy the eyes was to blacken them with stibium or kohl. With this STEM the eyebrows were elongated and the underlid dyed black. In this way the maidens who had attained puberty made the symbolic eye the sign of their period. They underlined the eye, the hieroglyphic AN, the periodic, and AR, which has the meaning of *fructus*. SMAT, a variant of STEM, is Stibium, also to daub the eyes, a certain period of time, and to wrap up with linen.

The word SHATHAM (שתם) is a *crux* of Hebrew scholars, never yet mastered. It is used only of Balaam the seer, who is called the man whose eyes were *open* (Shatham), and in the margin, whose eyes were shut. The truth is that neither open nor shut will reproduce the sense. The Egyptian Shetam or Satam also means to shut. But that is by no means the whole of the matter. The picture characters of the hieroglyphics exhibit things in themselves, and Shetam denotes a total of two halves. Tam is the total with the same image; the sha (or sa) may have many applications; in regard to which totality, "sha," as a measure would make "shatam," a total of measure. The Sa is a priest, and "Sa-tam" is an Egyptian high-priest, or an unique one, a host in himself. Satem, again, has the sense of covering round either with dress or other form of protection. Wholeness, oneness, totality, composed of two halves, is the meaning of Shatam, and of tam by itself. Balaam was the seer, the man who saw with his eyes either open or shut. Sa or Sha (Eg.) is to dive into, see, perceive, know, discern.

There was an order of priests in Egypt known as the Sa or Sha. The name is written with the jackal sign, denoting the wise men, the Mages. Sha is the earlier form of the word, and signifies secret, mystic, hidden. "Shaa," the name of the substance born of, appears to connect the name with the monthly diviners, the observers of the feminine first cause, as Sha is named thirty, the end of the monthly period, one form of time. "Shannu" is the name of a diviner, and "nnu" is divine; so that the Shannu is a divine or a divining Sha. SATHAM,[1] a variant of Shatham, signifies a revelation. Reading the Sha as sight, Sha-tam is the double sight, and as tam is second, Shatam is literally second-sight or clairvoyance. The seer is a person credited with dual vision, so that "Shatham" signifies this totality, inclusiveness, and oneness, of the double vision which sees with the eyes open or shut.

This is confirmed by the Hebrew form "Sh'ttaim," which means two, and instead of the man who saw with his eyes open OR shut,

[1] Dan. viii. 26.

it should be who saw double or both ways ; the ancients were quite familiar with this phenomenon. All that is secret, sacred, mystical, the innermost of all mystery, apparently including some relationship to or communion with the dead, is expressed by the Egyptian word "Shet," the Hebrew SŌD. Having explained the duality of vision, the briefest rendering would be Shatham, to be a *clairvoyante*, or to see double.

In Psalm lxxiv. 5, 6, the A. V. renders : "A *man* was famous (*i.e.* in time past) according as he had lifted up *Axes* upon the thick trees, but now they break down the carved work thereof at once with axes and hammers." The first word translated by axes is בשיל. Kassil only appears in this passage and in Jeremiah lxvi. 22 for קרדם. Kassil represents the Egyptian Khesr for the arrow, as that which cuts its way. Khesr modifies into Sesr, Sser, and Ser. Sser or Ser means to cut, inscribe, or carve, whence SSRT or SERT is the name for sculpture, carving, and engraving ; the Hebrew שרם, to cut. In the rendering of Kassil, the cutter or carver, as axe, is put in place of the sculpture, and the true meaning is that they once honoured the carver of the trees, but now they lift up the instrument of cutting to destroy the work of the artist. The two words are used for the sake of the antithesis. Khesr (Sser) for carving supplies our chisel, Armoric Gisell, a chisel, used by the sculptor and carpenter. In Polish the carpenter is a KIESLA, and the block or trestle on which stone is sawed is a KAZLY. In the African Limba the KUSALA is a hoe, as the Kassil appears to have been in Hebrew. In Irish, Ceasla is an oar for cutting the water, and CHISEL is an English name for bran, the *shavings* of wheat. So Kasl in Arabic, is the treading out of wheat, and in Zulu Kaffir Qazula is to grind (cut) wheat coarsely. But the same word has travelled a long way when found in the Irish CAISLI, and Cornish KUZAL, which denote *polished* manners.

There is a passage in Psalm xxii. 16, "Dogs have encompassed me, the wicked have enclosed me, they כארי my hands and my feet." The Hebrew word has been rendered by "they pierced," and taken as such in evidence of prophecy, whilst the piercing of the hands and feet in the Crucifixion, which occurs in accordance with this translation, is the fulfilment. We have the indubitable root of this matter in Egyptian, both etymological and mythological. The sense of to pierce does not exist in the original, and in Hebrew the digging, boring, and thence penetrating, is derived from the beetle Khepr. Kef (Eg.) means to seize, lay hold by force. Kep is the fist, a type of seizing and gripping. Khepr is the seizer with his claws ; his name abrades into Ker, to seize, lay hold, contain. The Kra is the claw ; Ker is to seize with a claw. Kar is to seize by the foot, to entrap and ensnare, like the Hebrew Kir for ensnaring. In Maori Koru is a noose, a loop. GIRO, in the African Dewoi denotes chain fetters ; EKURU, KUPA, fetters ; KARR, Arabic, a fetter ; KARA, Sanskrit, a fetter, a binding. Exact representatives of the Hebrew word באר are found in GYRE (Eng.), a circle ; CWR (Welsh), a circle ; GYRI (Latin) circle ; GOURIS, in Chinese, is a girdle, and others might be adduced.

The Hebrew באר, then, is Egyptian, to be determined by the hieroglyphics. The speaker of the passage is encompassed and enclosed by the wicked, who באר his hands and his feet. In the hieroglyphics, KHERI is the victim, caught and bound for the sacrifice. The victims were bound hand and foot.

They were the Kheri *because* bound, and the true sense of the passage is, they have encompassed, ensnared, and incarcerated me. They have bound my hands and feet. The fettering of the victim is then in perfect keeping. Fettering of the hands and feet is the true sense, not piercing, and this is the sense of the Hebrew באר, only it did not prophesy of the Crucifixion. Further, in the parallel passage in the Book of the Dead, which will be adduced, as the original matter, Horus, the "beloved son of the father," is "pierced to the heart by Sut,"[1] but not in his hands and feet. "I have seen Osiris," says the Osirian ; "I tell him the things about this, his great and beloved soul (Horus), pierced to the heart by Sut."

Isaiah[2] exclaims :—"We wait for light, but behold obscurity ; for brightness, but we walk in darkness. We grope for the wall like the blind, and we grope as if we had no eyes : we stumble at noonday as in the night ; we are in ESHMANNIM. . . . We look for judgment but there is none." Here the word ESHMANNIM, rendered in the A. V. "desolate places," and by Jerome and the Rabbins *darkness*, supplies a precious bit of the Egyptian mythology lurking in the Hebrew writings. ESHMANNIM, ESHMOUN, or SMEN, was a name of Hermopolis in Egypt, and in the map of the heavens, Am-SMEN is the place of the eight first gods who existed before the firmament of Ra was lifted, in the time of Sut-Typhon. In the second time, Taht, the lunar god, was made lord of SMEN, and in the solar mythos it was in SMEN that the son Horus was annually established in the place of the father. Another name of this region of the eight is SESENNU, a place of agitation, torment, distraction, desolation, and darkness. Taht, the lunar deity, was lord of this region, which, in relation to the lunar orb, is the region of change of moon. From the eclipse of this change Taht emerges bearing the crescent on his head. SHMENAI means the eighth in Hebrew, and in Phœnician Eshmun was the eighth son of Sydyk. Sheminith is also a Hebrew form of the eighth ;[3] and Isaiah's imagery belongs to Eshmenein, with the Hebrew plural ending Eshmannim ;[4] the eighth region of agitation and distraction, torment and change,

---

[1] Ch. lxxviii.
[2] Ch. lix. 9-11.
[3] Ps. vi. title, and margin.
[4] Psalm xii., title and margin.

the change from darkness to light, which does not come. "We look for the judgment," says the writer, "and it is far from us." This was the region of the judgment seat, and the place of the fourteen trials in the Book of the Dead, half the number of the lunar mansions, through which passed the moon-god. And here he signed the sentence of the dead in the Hall of the Two Truths, and justified those whose lives were pure. This was in Ashmenein. And we, says Isaiah, are in Eshmannim, waiting for the judgment, and groping darkly for the "manifestation to light," but there is none.

SMEN,[1] signifies the "appointed." SMEN was the place appointed for the purging, purifying, and preparing of souls. Hesmen is the Egyptian name for the menstrual purification, and in this region was the Pool of Hesmen (or Natron). The moon in one of its two phases was the woman in her courses, and Smen the place of her pain and torment, out of which emerged the new moon. In the chapter of "making the transmigration into a god,"[2] we read, "I am the woman, the orb in the darkness; I have brought my orb to darkness, (where) it is changed to light. I have prepared Taht at the gate of the moon." This was in Smen, where the feminine moon changed into the male god Taht, or transmigrated, that was, transformed in sex, and the change was made from darkness to light. The woman half of the orb was impersonated as Sef(kh), the consort of Taht Sef is to purge and sift; Sef, to refine by fire; Sephui, to torment, torture, punish; Sefi is dissolution. On the other side, the name of Taht denotes the establisher for ever as the renewer of light. These represent the two halves of a lunation with the symbols derived from sex.

It was in SMEN that the solar god entered his feminine phase, and suffered the agony and bloody sweat, described in the Ritual as the "flux of Osiris,"[3] and the drama assigned to Geth*semane*[4] was pre-enacted there. When the words, "his feminine phase," are used it does not mean that the sun or moon was supposed to change sex; but the red, sinking, ailing, winter sun was lessening, was suffering, was ill, and the illness was described according to the female phase. Typology consists in various things being set forth by means of one original type. Symbolism was a mode necessitated, not a system designed, because the one primitive type had to serve many purposes of expression, and by aid of the Egyptian doctrine of the "Two

[1] Isaiah xxviii. 25.   [2] Ch. lxxx.
[3] Ch. xciv., the "filth of Osiris;" ch. cl., in the eleventh abode, the "flux emanating from Osiris."
[4] This place was in the vicinity of the Mount of Olives, and the name is supposed to relate to the oil (Shmen) prepared from the olives. The Talmudist writers affirm that shops were kept on Mount Olivet by the Children of Canaan, and that beneath two large cedars there were four shops for the sale of doves and other things necessary for the *Purification of Women*. The meaning of SMEN and HESMEN (Eg.) agrees with that of Gethsemane as the place of purification in the Jewish sense.

Truths" the present writer expects to reach the fountain-head of the ancient typology.

Of course here, as elsewhere, the total myth can only be put together by collecting the whole of the scattered remains, some of the most precious of which are preserved in the Hebrew re-writings, and, when complete, it will verify itself and establish its right to the possession of its own members, no matter where these may be found. The present object is to show how certain Hebrew words imply the mythos, and can only be read by means of the Egyptian symbols. The sculptured stones of the first builders have, so to speak, been calcined to make mortar for the later builders, and they reappear without their ideographs and determinatives.

When we use the words EVER, ETERNAL, and ETERNITY, we require the symbols to give definition to the primitive meaning.

On the authority of a word, αἰώνιος (Aionios), found in Greek, human beings are damned for ever, for all eternity, and there is no other foundation for the doctrine of the eternal punishment with which foolish fanatics threaten all who do not think as they do. And yet AIONIOS has no other basis than the Æon, a cycle of time. This is the Egyptian An (or Han, the cycle), with the meaning of repetition. The Eternal was based on periodic repetition. Millions of times is a formulæ of eternity. And four times, the equivalent of the four cardinal points of the circle, is equally an equivalent of Ever. The symbol of these words meaning ever, for ever, is a circle. Heh (Eg.) is Egyptian for the eternal, and it means an age, an Æon, or An, a cycle of time. The Eternal is Æonian at last, and was based on, was a birth of time, the deity who lived and died alternately for ever, not a conception of something abstract and independent of time and space. The perpetual is the periodic.

It is said of the Hidden God in the inscription of El-Khargah,[1] " He has not come out of a womb, he has come out of cycles," and the circle is the image of the cycle. The mode of continuity was by transformation ; one circle running into another. This transformation was represented as the work of Khepr, the beetle-god, the transformer.

There is no other basis than the cycle continually renewed for the Hebrew everlasting. Ad or Gad (עד) means ever and ever, everlasting, eternal, eternity, perpetually. The same word signifies until or *meantime*, as yet, how long, and so long as, during, duration of time, a limit of space, all that is opposed to eternal, infinite, limitless. It is a period whether monthly or a moment. עד means especially the monthly period of women, and according to the Masora the word also signifies twelve times. It was thirteen in the lunar reckoning. The earlier form in Qedim (קדם), the plural of Khet, for old times, shows the same origin, the letter Ayin being midway between A and Q or K. Qedem for Eden is the Egyptian

---

[1] Line 6.

Khetam or circle, the sign of which rounding, closing, and sealing is a seal-ring, the sign of reproduction. The Khet (Eg.) means a circuit, zone, to surround with anything, make the orbit or circle. Khut softens into Hut, the winged solar disk, and At, the type of time figured as a circle. At (Eg.) is a moment, with the circle and exactly the same as the Hebrew AD for the everlasting, perpetual, eternal. The everlasting is simply the ever-recurring and repeating. Aulam or Gvlam (עולם) we must take in the primitive form with the Vav, when it reads Gvlam, or, in Egyptian, Khepr-am, with which we touch bottom.

Am (Eg.) signifies belonging to, and is the place, the Paradise, Eden, or circle of transformation (Khepr) and renewal in time, where the perpetual goings-forth from of old of the Messiah Son are manifested in the circle without beginning or end, hence eternally; he who is periodically re-born from Avlam, Gvlam, or Khepr-am.[1] If we read the Hebrew as the plural of Khevl (Khepr), nothing is changed. It was the plurality of cycles which constituted the continuity of the eternal, the ever-during. Khep is to transform, generate, create, cause to exist. One symbol of this process of transformation was the sloughing serpent, the Hef, the serpent of life, personified as Heh-t, the feminine Heh, with the serpent's head. Thus the ever, Heh or Aye, the eternal, is derived from one cycle of time being transformed into another by periodic renewal; the circle, Heh, being one symbol; the seal-ring, Khet, another; the serpent, Heh, a third; and the beetle, Khepr, a fourth. The circle of Hefa (Kefa) can be traced to the cycle of the Great Bear. The circle of Khepr as sun-god was that of the twelve signs, where the year was at one time renewed with the sun in Khepr (Cancer), and the circle itself is Khepram, Khevelam, or Aulam. The Phœnician GUBULIM means a Quarter. By the circle was the Eternal established, and another Hebrew name denoting forever is Tzemthath צמתת; it is used for establishing for ever.[2] The Egyptian equivalent is Semi-tat, from Sem, a representative sign, and Tat, to establish. Tat or Thoth is the representative of the lunar cycle. Another form of the Semtat, or symbol of the ever, the established for ever, is the tat sign of Ptah, the fourfold cross or cardinal points whereby the solar circle was formed. Semi means to encircle. Semi-tat is to establish the circle, the sign of ever. The first solar circle was framed in two halves, the upper and lower heavens, and the two halves of the moon. These two halves joined in one to make the whole, and the twin-total is in Egyptian Temat. Temat also furnishes a Hebrew word for ever, continual, evermore, and always, as THAMID תמיד. Tem-at means the complete circle, and is identical with our word timed. So in the cypher survives the name and the symbol of Khepr, the creator, former and transformer, whilst Heh or Hoh, represented by the circle,

[1] Micah v. 2.   [2] Lev. xxv. 30.

becomes our O, in Egyptian UAU, the one, one alone, and only one.
The monotheistic sign is at last a nought or a knot, found in the hands
of the goddess of the Great Bear, who created the first circle of time.
The name of the "Ancient of Days," in the Book of Daniel, will
reveal his nature. He is the ATTIQ עתיק. At or Kat (Eg.) is the circle
of time, and Hek or Ak signifies rule and the ruler of the circle. A
title of Amen-Ra, who was born of cycles, is Hek of the first region.

If we render the Hebrew Attiq by the Egyptian Tekh, we obtain
the measurer and recorder of the cycles of time. Tekh as the moon-
god is the measurer, the calculator, and distributor of time; the
counter of the stars. Tekhu is the name of the instrument corresponding to the needle of the balance for measuring weights, the
ancient Egyptian cubit of Tekh.[1] Tekhi, the goddess of the months,
was a measurer of time-cycles. The Tekh, Attiq, Kat-hek, can be
traced back to the goddess of the north, Kheft, as the first ruler
of time, the original Ancient of days. Kheft-ak, Khet-ak, or Kat-ak,
is the old Kheft. The first chronicles, as the word implies, were
records of time and period, and such was the primary nature of the
Hebrew Chronicles; this fact is admitted in a sort of marginal
remark[2] or murmur, *sotto voce*, that these, the subject-matters of
the records, are "Attiq," rendered ancient things. They were in
their first form the registers of the celestial chronology, and, like
the Book of Enoch, the record of the luminaries of heaven, together
with their generations, classes, periods, powers, and names.

Without the ideography it is impossible to fathom the language of
Psalm cxxxix. 15, "My substance was not hid from thee when I was
made in secret and curiously wrought in the lowest part of the earth."
That is in the Hebrew תחתי (Thchthi), the Egyptian TUAUT, the
lower hemisphere. A TUAUTI is an inhabitant of the lower hemisphere. In the Tuaut was the Meskhen or place of regeneration and
new birth. The language of the Psalm is only directly possible to
the solar-child, who was engendered in the TUAUT, and only
humanly possible, because the solar birthplace was founded on
womb-world, and the nethermost parts of the earth are identified
with the matrix. The Tuaut survives in English as the TWAT, a
name of the feminine organ. It was here that the tomb and womb
were one. Hence the "TUAUT" is also the grave or hell.[3]

In the ancient thought there is not an image engraved on one side
of their door of life when it stands open, but is repeated, and serves
the reverse purpose on the door when it shuts, as what we term the
door of death, and in that way was the eschatology founded.

---

[1] Renouf, *Hibbert Lectures*, pp. 116, 117, who is wrong in supposing there is no
such known Egyptian word as TEHU, if M. Chabas (*R. A.* 1857, 72) be right, who
gives the group TEHU, to tell, synonymous with "TET."

[2] 1 Ch. iv. 22.

[3] Psalm lxxxvi. 13.

There is a passage in Job [1] in which the speaker says, " thou dissolvest my substance," meaning the body of flesh, and it is followed by an allusion to the grave. The substance is SHUVAH. In Egyptian this is SHEBU, the flesh, a slice, a certain quantity of flesh. The Shebu is a collar or tippet with nine points. This is symbolic of the nine months' time for sheb-ing, shep-ing, shaping the child, or figuring in the flesh. The Egyptian Sheb and Shep being the same as shape, the Sheb, flesh, is the clothing typified by the Sheb collar, also worn by prisoners. Thou dissolvest my Shuvah is identical with thou unshapest me, lettest loose the sheb-girdle of my flesh, the vestment hieroglyphically rendered with nine points, and by captivity : or, to change the image, it may be read in English, thou un-sheafest me, the sheaf being a form of the binding-up. Thou dissolvest my substance (Shuvah) alternates—according to Kethib—with thou terrifiest me. Here again the Hebrew Shuvah is identical with Shef or Shefi (Eg.), to terrify, be terrible, demon-like. Both are Egyptian, but the context shows the first to be the right lection.

The collar hieroglyphic with all its significance passed into Israel, as we learn by the denunciations of Isaiah. The collar has various names. Khekh is one. Khakri is some kind of necklace. Art Khekh are neck-chains. The determinative of these is the sign of horns and testes ; this indicates the nature of the restraining collar. The collar with nine points alternates with one of thirteen, the same number as that of the knotted loops round the Assyrian Asherah or grove, signifying the thirteen periods to the year which have but one original in nature. The Khekh collar is likewise called Baba, that is Typhon. Typhon the Red was the adversary, looked upon in later times as the destroyer, and at best as only working for good under restraint. The collar was a symbol of this; hence the Khekh collar and Akhekh, the dragon or Typhon, are synonyms. There is a vulgar expression still in use, " Go home and tell your mother to chain up ugly." Translated into Egyptian that would mean Typhon, Baba, the beast, who was chained up with the collar number nine, or the Menat collar, number ten, according to solar or lunar reckoning.

This is enough to show the symbolic nature of the collar emblem, and account for the indignation of the Jewish Protestants at the tricking out of the daughters of Israel in such ornaments. These collars are called " sweet jewels." [2] The " chains" are [3] " sweet balls," which can be explained by the collar with nine BUBU or balls worn by Isis. The " tinkling ornaments about their feet" [4] are " GEKES," one with the Egyptian Khekh, and the Art-Khekh, or chain for the ankle.

When it is asked, [5] " Canst thou draw out leviathan with a hook ? " the word used is CHACH, that is, with the Khekh or Akhekh collar

[1] xxx. 22.   [2] Margin, Jud. viii. 26.   [3] Margin, Isa. iii. 19.
[4] Is iii. 18.   [5] Job xli. 1.

of the dragon Typhon. The Hebrew Chach is a hook, chain, or bracelet, and the stocks. And although the writer knew that Typhon could not be drawn out with the Khekh, he also knew, as did Isaiah, the significance of the symbol; the tinkling Khekhs were calling aloud for the restraint of Typhon, in other words, they were proclaiming that the wearers were marriageable. With us the wedding-ring is the emblem instead of the collar, and to "GIG" is to engender.

The Hebrew writings are full of language which has no meaning without the types by which alone it can be understood, and hitherto it has been read and rendered without these types. It is enough, one would think, to make the ignorant expounders of symbolical language who have drivelled for half a life-time spend the rest in a savage silence, with the tongue held fast between the teeth, as the only amends they can make.

In a passage unexplicated hitherto, the writer of the Book of Ezekiel exclaims, "Woe to the women that sew *pillows* to all *arm-holes*, or elbows," or hands or arm-holes of the hands, whatsoever these may mean. The word rendered pillows is KASATHOTH (כסתות) and only occurs twice.[1] "Woe to the (women) that sew KASATHOTH to all arms and make MISPACHOTH (מספחות), upon the head, of every height, to hunt souls." "Behold, I am against your KASATHOTH, wherewith ye there hunt souls to make (them) fly, and I will tear them from your Jad, and will let the souls go, the souls that ye hunt to make (them) fly."

Let us see what light Egyptian may shed on this passage. The general sense as it stands is that the allurers of men wear some particular images or charms upon their JAD and on the head to ensnare souls. The KASATHOTH are worn on the Jad; the MISPA-CHOTH upon the head. Jad is the hand or the arm. KES (Eg.) means to envelop with little bands; AT signifies typical; UT means magic, to inscribe, wish, command, give directions; and TI is plural, like the Hebrew terminal. KES-UT-TI or KES-AT-TI would denote some form of bracelet or binding for the arms, worn as a magic amulet or as a means of proclamation. There was but one fact the wearer had to proclaim, and that was her period of pubescence. Kesa, in Hebrew, is the appointed time or new moon, the festival of which was *divinely* ordained and made statutory in Israel,[2] and afterwards denounced as an abomination,[3] this was, as Jewish Rabbis acknowledge (as Isa Bar Ali), the first day of the full moon. It was likewise applied to the whole time of the full moon. The appointed time also applied to the age of puberty, when the maiden in Africa put on clothing for the first time, if only a loin-cloth or Basu, or the Zulu Kaffir DWABA and the top-knot, BONGA, formed of crimson clay (BOMVU), worn by the women.

The relation of the feminine period and the ornaments of dress to

---

[1] Ch. xiii. 18 and 20.   [2] Psalm lxxxi.   [3] Is. i. 13.

the moon is indicated by Isaiah,[1] who denounces the "round tires like the moon" which were worn by the daughters of Israel. We still speak of tying the knot in marriage. The sense of Kes (Eg.), to bind, enters into the Hebrew QSHR, to tie, to bind, and קִשֻּׁרִים [2] for the attire of the bride which is coupled with the עדי of the maid ; עדי being a plural form of עד the feminine period. KAS (Eg.) is the knot, to tie a knot, and an entreaty to tie the knot, to bind up the female, as is symboled by putting on the wedding-ring and snooding the hair. The same writer also includes the snood or the caul, a cap of network, in the list of things anathematized. One ideograph of KAS is the loop or knot sign ; one, a bundle of reeds tied up, the Ret emblem of time and indication ; a third is the type of transformation ; a fourth, the tongue. The KASATHOTH were worn *before* marriage, and announced the season of womanhood or full moon. Their relation to the period is likewise *glossed* by KASA (Eg.), to mourn. The bracelet worn in the shape of a serpent holding the red blood-drop of a ruby in its mouth is a KASATHOTH in the emblematic language. They also made MISPACHOTH on the head of every statue. MES (Eg.) is the sexual part, the EMS or HEM. Mes is to bear, generate, conceive, give birth to the child. In Hebrew MESA is a sign of bearing ; at root that is child-bearing in all languages. The "PAKAT" garment is found on the monuments as some kind of linen or tunic ; linen hung up to dry is the ideograph which in itself reads MES, and in the group[3] we have the Egyptian for "MISPACHOTH," and it signifies the linen worn at the time of full moon, or the Mes-pakati of puberty. The prophet objects to these kerchiefs being displayed on the head as a sign of invitation. The Hebrew Qomah applied to the height of the head-dress appears as KEMHU, an Egyptian mode of dressing up the hair. Qomah signifies attainment, accomplishment ; Khem, to be mistress of, grace, and favour. Komah adds another correlative to the meaning of the MISPACHOTH, or top-knots of feminine puberty, which were worn on the head as a kind of investiture and proclamation of ripe age and social status amongst many races, and in a variety of shapes.

Hunting souls to make them fly is apparently meaningless. In the margin it reads, "into gardens." The sense is that the daughters are desirous of refreshment (Naphish), but not anxious that the flowers should be fructified, or the time of flowers be followed by the season of fruit. The soul was figuratively the breath ; they wanted to take the breath of life in a double sense. "But will ye save the souls alive if they come to you?" No! they only lusted to take the life of souls, or hunted them to destroy or disperse and extinguish them.

A kindred illustration of the hieroglyphic language, only to be read by means of the hieroglyphics, occurs in Jeremiah,[4] "A

---

[1] iii. 18.   [2] Jer. ii. 32.   [3] *Egyp. Sal.* 159.   [4] l. 38.

drought is upon her waters, and they shall be dried up, for it is the land of graven images, and they are mad upon EMIM" (idols). The reference here is subtly symbolical. The hieroglyphic HEMA, sign of the lady, wife, seat, place, is the *Ems pudendum*. It is the type of containing and turning back the waters of the red source, so that in the ancient language fish may be caught, or children propagated. The symbol was then adopted as the picture of a water-frontier, the Pehu, Hannu, or Hema; this, in the names of places, marked the water-nome. Such were the EMIM or Hannu that Israel had been so mad upon, and the imagery is peculiarly appropriate in prophesying a drought upon her waters, because they had made so much of the hieroglyphic image of the feminine water-frontier.

The Hebrew name of the divining cup or גביע, by which Joseph is said to have divined, is rendered by κόνδυ in the version of the Seventy. This, as the name of the cup, is also found in Persian and Arabic, and in the Sanskrit KUNDA, a bowl-shaped vessel, or an aperture for water or fire; the Two Truths. This vessel is used in certain Hindu ceremonies for drinking out of, and it was carried in the Procession described by Apuleius. It represented the self-conspicuous image of fontal nature alluded to in the oracles of Zoroaster, " Invoke not the self-conspicuous image of nature, for you must not behold these things before your body has received the purification necessary to initiation." Wilson, in the *Asiatic Researches*,[1] says, the KUNDA was fashioned in the shape of a lotus, the type doubly feminine, the flower that bore the seed within itself, which was therefore adopted as the emblem of the Virgin Mother of Mythology.

Both Athenæus and Jamblichus mention the κόνδυ as being used in the religious ceremonies of Egypt. According to Norden, in recent times the lotus on the water was represented by the dish, cup, or κόνδυ, placed on the water for divination, just as the dish was employed for the same purpose at Shadar, in the Isle of Lewis.

KUNDA is a particular name of the goddess Durga, relating to the vessel, cup, or κόνδυ, which was very primitive as the type of fontal nature. KUNDA, in Sanskrit, is the name of the number nine. The cup is the Egyptian KNAU, Maori KONA, the mother-emblem. With the feminine terminal T, this is the Khent (Eg.) or Hunt; English Quiente; Greek, κόνδυ, Sankrit, Kunda. Kento, in Basunde and Musentando, is the type-name for the female. In Zulu Kaffir, CUNDA is mystically the " woman's Word." The cup imaged the fountain-head of all kenning or knowing and thence of divining, because the mother was the revealer of the Two Truths of time and period, pubescence and gestation, in relation to reproduction. CYN, Welsh, is first and foremost. Khen (Eg.) is to conceive, image, bear; GIN, Gaelic, to beget. All forms of genesis are in this root, and many types of the birthplace are named from it, as KHEN (Eg.), the interior,

[1] Vol. v. p. 357.

also the ark or canoe; Qenn (Heb.), the nest; Ken, Romany, CONI, French Romance, Persian, KHAN, for the abode; Kwan, Chinese, for the granary; QNAH, the garden in Hebrew, and GONA, a farm in Kandin, Kadzina, and other African languages. The CAN, an English vessel or cup, also the KEN, a churn, are named from the same prototype as the Greek κόνδυ. The Hebrew נביע is figuratively a flower-cup,[1] and is cognate in sense with קבעת, which represents the Egyptian Khapat or Khept, called the hinder thigh, but which, like the Hebrew Qebah, denotes the *Genitalia Muliebria*, as the Khep, Kheb, Qeb, or cup. Such was the nature of Joseph's נביע, or cup of the diviner. There was a time when the monthly prognosticators in Israel divined by the image of fontal nature itself, just as the Jains or Yonias of India do to-day, the Q'deshoth being attached to the temples for the purpose of demonstrating certain natural facts in the primitive school of physiology. The Gabia, Khep, or Cup, finally deposited the phonetic KA as the Cup of the Hieroglyphics.

The ATZEB of the Hebrew is vaguely rendered an image, a representation, an idol, without telling us what the image represents. It is associated with the Asherah,[2] and is connected with the woman in travail, bringing forth.[3] But the wherefore is out of sight. In the hieroglyphics the ASEB or ASEP is the seat or throne, the feminine image, the sign with which the name of Isis is written.

As-bu is the place of rest, and the Asb is a type of this, hence the seat. The seat also shows the relation to the woman in labour. The seat or Aseb had various forms based on the feminine type. The Kavvanim made by the women of Israel[4] represented the goddess with the symbolical seat, the Kûn image. The house of the seat (Azeb) is identified with the house of Ashtaroth,[5] As and Hes (Eg.) being names of the seat, the type of the bearer. The absence of the seat in Hebrew has misled the translators of Isaiah,[6] "Bel boweth down, Nebo stoopeth, their idols (Atzeb) were upon the beasts and upon the cattle; your carriages heavy laden, a burden to the weary beast." All the missing sense is restored by reading "their seats" (Atzeb) instead of "their idols." Isaiah identifies the nature of the Atzeb with the seat of the beast. In Egyptian, Hes, the seat, is also the calf, or heifer. So the Atzeb goes with the heifer and calf in Israel. "Israel slideth back as a backsliding heifer; Ephraim (is) joined to the Atzeb."[7] Again, the Atzeb is coupled with the calf of Samaria.[8] And again,[8] the Atzeb is one with the calves. The craftsmen have made the Atzeb, and they say of them, "Let the men that sacrifice kiss the calves." That is kiss the seat, as in the Witches'

---

[1] Ex. xxv. 32.   [2] 2 Chron. xxiv. 18.   [3] Gen. iii. 16.
[4] Jer. xliv. 19.   [5] 1 Sam. xxxi, 10.   [6] Ch. xlvi. 1.
[7] Hos. iv. 16, 17.   [8] Hos. viii. 4, 5.

Sabbath, the symbol of the motherhood. These ideographs infuse new meaning into words. For example, Jeremiah puns with grim coarseness on the name of KONIAH,[1] and on the Atzeb or Kun, Egyptian KNAU. "(Is) this man Koniah a despised broken Atzeb (or Kun) or vessel wherein (is) no pleasure?" This also identifies the hieroglyphical nature of the seat or throne. Without these original images in mind half the meaning of the Hebrew constantly escapes.

The Molten Image of the Calf is denounced by Nahum,[2] "Out of the house of thy gods will I cut off the graven image and the molten image: I will make thy grave, for thou art vile." In the next chapter we read "and HUZZAB (הצב) shall be led away captive, she shall be brought up and her MAIDS shall lead (her) as with the voice of Doves, tabering upon their breasts." Huzzab is a personification of which the Hebrew gives no account, but the Doves show her relation to the Virgin Mother who was represented by the Dove and the Calf. Hus in Egyptian is the Cow, or rather the Calf, the Sacred Heifer or Calf adored under the name of Hus (Isis) in the time of the old empire. HES is likewise the typical feminine seat, couch, or bed, the ATZEB, here written הצב, elsewhere as צב the seat, sedan, or palanquin for persons of distinction, which corresponds to the Hes or Aseb seat and throne of the hieroglyphics. HUZZAB is the goddess of the hinder part, the north, the lower half of the circle, a form of Hes-taurt or Ashtaroth. ASEBI is an Egyptian name of CYPRUS, the great Paphian seat or shrine.

The MEST (Eg.) the sexual part, the place of birth is the name of the mother in the Cypriote MASDU; and the MESKA, the womb in Egyptian, and the eschatological place of rebirth, called the purgatory, supplied the Calf of the Hebrew cult; the MASAK for the door of the Tabernacle;[3] the Spanish MASA for the Mouth; Irish MÁS (of the hill); the Swahili MAZIKA for the burial-place; the Persian MUSHKO, a temple; the Turkish MOSQUE, the Welsh MYSG, the middle, answering to the MESKA as the mid-region or purgatory of the Ritual.

The MESKAH imaged by the Molten Calf is represented by the Calf and Cow in the following languages. MAS, Egyptian, a Calf; MOSCHOS, Greek, a Calf; MOSCHAS, a Heifer; MEUSI, Japanese, a Cow; MOSA, Pahri, Cow; MOSYA, Chopang, Cow; MAOISEAG, Gaelic, a Heifer; MOSHA, Kachari, a Cow; MUSHO, Bodo, Cow; MESA, A.S, a Cow; MASHU, Garo, Cow; MIS-MUSU, African Bambarra, a Cow.

Divine types are found in a vague generalized condition. The Hebrew Menchah מנחה is a sacrifice, an offering, an oblation to the gods. It was at one time the name of blood-offerings, but under the later legislation the word was applied only to unbloody offerings of meat and drink, in which the drink took the place of blood.

---

[1] Ch. xxii. 28. [2] i. 14. [3] Ex. xxvi. 36.

Menchah, the offering, is the type of the goddess Menka, Menkat, or Menâ, and Menât, the Egyptian wet-nurse. Menka is mentioned in the Ritual, " He has engraved a palm on his knee, says Menka." [1]

According to the present writer's view, this goddess is the earliest form of Maāt, the divinity of law, right rule, and true measure, but she was representative of the time of ten months or moons, whereas Mâ bears the name of No. 9. Men signifies liquid measure; Ment the No. 10. Menkat was the first feminine measurer in relation to the water-period. She is portrayed on the monuments in the act of offering two vases held in her hands, [2] the offerer in person, whereas the Hebrew Menchah only denotes the offering. Menka (Eg). means to create, form, work, fabricate, clothe ; and Menkat was the feminine creator and former who clothed the child as the pre-natal nurse. Corn was designated the DRY-NURSE of Rome and Italy; Menka is the wet-nurse; the Twain were personifications of the two truths assigned to the Great Mother in mythology. The one nursed the child with her blood (water), the other with her breath or spirit, she was the quickener of the seed or corn. Menâ is a reduced form of her name, and the Babylonian goddess MENI associated with Gad, who was worshipped with drink-offerings, is probably the same divinity.

The Greek MAGOS was a form of Maka or Menka, the Irish Macha, as a title of Artemis, who was imaged in the great temple at Ephesus as the many-breasted wet-nurse. The month of May was likewise dedicated to Magos at Ephesus, and the name of May is a form of Maka (Menka-t), the Hindu MAYA and Greek MĀIA. Māia is called the eldest of SEVEN Pleiads, but the seven stars were not the Pleiads ; they belonged to the Great Bear, the earliest form of the Genitrix, the wet-nurse found in Menka or Maka. Menka was the first measurer, whose later form was Mā, the luni-solar measurer in conjunction with Taht and Ptah. Ma can be traced in the Greek Themis and Maka in Ar-temis. In Plutarch's *Moralia*,[3] Meragenes says the Hebrews call the brazen vessels used in their ceremonies the " Nurses of God." The vessel imaged the womb or breast, the type of the wet-nurse Menka.

Another reduced deity might be recovered in the person of the prophet Elijah, who will be referred to hereafter.

The Hebrew " BARUK HABA " (ברוך הבא) " Blessed, is he that cometh," is used by the Jews as a salutation to the child when it is brought into the room to be circumcised. The word " HABA " contains various mystic and occult meanings. The value of its letters in Hebrew is considered to amount, by GEMATRIA, to the number eight. The eighth is the day of circumcision, and the salutation is connected with the child's coming on the eighth day to be circumcised. By NOTARICON, these letters, *H B A*, are held to be initials

---

[1] Rubric of ch. ci.   [2] Wilkinson.   [3] *Symp*. lib. vi. quæst. 5.

of three words, הנה בא אליה, "Behold Elijah cometh."[1] The Jews are said to suppose that Elijah enters the chamber along with the child to take the seat left vacant for him in the DOUBLE CHAIR, and they exclaim, "This is the seat of the prophet Elijah."[2] Elijah is the centre of a large number of Hebrew traditions, and this identification of him with the one who comes and with the number eight, appears likewise to indicate that he is a from of the god Taht, or the earlier Sut-Anubis. Sut was the announcer of the goddess of the seven stars, as the one who came annually. Taht, who superseded him, was the messenger, the voice or Logos of the seven gods, the manifester of the Pleroma and completer of the ogdoad. He was the Lord of the Eight, or Eighth to the Seven. HABA, "he that cometh," is the name of Taht's IBIS. HABA is the Egyptian form of Ibis. The word also signifies the Messenger, and the coming or returning one. Elijah commences as the messenger who announces the prophecy to Ahab.[3] Taht superseded Sut, that is Bar or Baal in Egypt, and Elijah is portrayed as the great opponent of Baal in Israel. Taht was the scribe of the gods, and EIGHT years after his ascension into heaven on a chariot of fire, Elijah sent a letter of reproof to Jehoram, King of Judah.

In the Gospel of Matthew the Christ says of John the Baptist, "This is (he) of whom it is written, Behold, I send my messenger before thy face, which shall prepare thy way before thee."[4] . . . "And if ye will receive (it), this is Elias which was for to come." The coming of this messenger is represented as being fulfilled in the advent of John. This contains matter of great moment for a later volume; it may, however, be remarked in passing, that AAN in Egyptian mythology is also the messenger and announcer; first as Anubis (Sut), and next as a form of Taht the lunar god. In a fresco of the second or third century, Elijah is seen ascending on his fiery chariot, and the figure of Mercury (Taht) is present as a part of the picture.[5]

The Atef crown of Upper Egypt, or of the southern heaven, consists of the white crown and double feathers, set on the solar disc. It is the crown of Osiris and gods of the lower world. In Hebrew the word עטף (Atph) has the meaning of clothing and covering, to clothe as with a garment or with gloom. The hieroglyphic is almost recoverable in Job[6] where he says of God, "He puts on (hides himself) in the south, and I see not," which is equivalent to putting on the Atef crown with the insignia of the nether-world, the wearer of which becomes the hidden sun of Amenti, overshadowed, obscured, darkened.

[1] Buxtorf. Synag. Jud. c. iv. pp. 93-95.
[2] Leo Modena, *Rites and Customs*, c. viii.
[3] I Kings xvii. 1.
[4] Matt. ix. 14, 17, 10—12.
[5] *Bosio. Rom. Sott*, p. 257.
[6] xxiii. 9.

The hieroglyphic KAN is a corner of a building, the corner-symbol held in the hand of the mother of the Messiah-child, in the sign of Pisces,[1] the one of the four quarters at which the child was brought forth. In Egyptian the article sometimes follows the noun, and Kanp would thus be the Kan. The word occurs as Kanb, Kanbet, and Kanteb with the sign of a corner. This is extant in Hebrew as KANPH, the corner or extremities of the earth. KANPHOTH[2] signifies the four quarters or corners of the earth. KANBUT (Eg.) means the corner-place. Kan-put the corner of the circle, that is, one corner of the house of four quarters. Put (Eg.) is the foundation; bu (or but), a stone. Thus Kan-but is the corner-stone of the foundation.

In this sense the chiefs of the people[3] are designated corners (in the margin). Isaiah[4] makes the princes of Zoar to be the stay of the people, the corners or corner-stones. The Egyptian Kanbut (and Kanteb) is one who performs service and is the stay and support, whose emblem is the corner, our image of the corner-stone. Kanput and Kanteb are synonymous, because teb and put both mean the circle. The Hebrew word is applied to the highest summit of the temple, and in Egyptian Teb is the summit, the top; as is the pet. The plural of Kanphoth will be explained further on. The hieroglyphic corner has to be built on hereafter. The reader must not think these disquisitions are objectless wordmongering.

There has been no rendering of the Hebrew Kiyor that makes out the meaning. The name is applied to a small hearth or oven.[5] The KARR is an Egyptian furnace, and oven. Next the KIYOR is a Laver or molten sea. The KARUA (Eg.) is a lake, pond, or laver. Again, we are told that Solomon made a KIYOR of brass, and had it set in the middle of the court, and he kneeled down upon it.[6] This was neither oven nor laver. It has been translated SCAFFOLD. The KIYOR in this instance was five cubits long, five broad, and three cubits high. Egyptian will tell us what this KIYOR was.

The hieroglyphic KHARU is a shrine, a tavern, the place of refreshment. The Hebrew KIYOR was evidently the table or shrine of the Eucharist, what is now termed the communion-table. The Egyptians had a kind of bread named KHARUPUS,[7] that is, bread baked for the shrine or altar. This would be baked in the KARR, or oven. The raised Kar represented the upper of the two Kars, the laver, the lower; both were shrines in Egypt. The upper held the bread-symbol of the highest truth; the other, the waters, emblematical of the lower. Both symbols still meet in the bread and wine of the Eucharist.

The Hebrew KALLAH, a technical term for the highest school, has,

---

[1] Hermean Zodiac.   [2] Ez. vii. 2.
[3] 1 Sam. xiv. 38.   [4] Ch. xix. 13.
[5] Zech. xii. 6.   [6] 2 Chron. vi. 13.   [7] *Select Papyri*, xcv. 2.

according to Deutsch, long been a crux for etymologists, so little do the Jews know of their own origines. It comes from the KHA (Eg.), book-library and altar; RU, discourse, word, mouth. Whence KHER, the sacred shrine, the cell of learning; Kher, speak, speech, the word, and the Karheb, a kind of Egyptian priest. AH (Eg.), would add the house of, to Kher or Khal.

The Hebrew Jad (יד) for the hand, is the Egyptian "It," to paint, figure forth, with the hand of the artist for determinative. It has a variant in At, a type, to work, build, form, image, the hand-worker and handiwork. The female as the shaper is the At. "It" therefore includes the work of the hand as well as the member, whilst the organ of working and figuring forth is not limited to the hand itself, which is but one of various jads or types of working. This alone will make sense of the passage,[1] and Israel saw the great "JAD" which the Lord did upon the Egyptians. Hand does not render it, the hand was hieroglyphic for the work done, not literal: AT or KAT (Eg.) is work. The word jad, hand, is used for ability,[2] just as we say a "handy man," which shows the typical use of the hand. Only in the absence of the symbols the Jad has been chiefly confined to one type as the hand, whereas in the original it may also be the womb, the circle, a boat, the heaven round, a house, a place, and twenty other things according to the determinatives. "Jad" is a place in Hebrew; "every man in his JAD,"[3] but the hand is not the only place. At (Eg.) to build, is applied in the Hebrew name of the "Tenons" "JAD," used in building.[4] The hand is a type of holding, so is the tenon, but as the reader will apprehend there may be any number of Jads, whereas the translators have only known of one chief type. Jad also means to consecrate but not by "filling the hand." Of course the hand was used in consecration, but it was laid on the head typically, a mode of figuring forth and constituting sacred handiwork as in IT (Eg.), to figure with the hand.

It is not a part of my work to revise the Hebrew Testament, the oldest portions of which would have to be rewritten hieroglyphically before it could be rightly restored, but two or three applications of the Egyptian "It" or "At" may be made. We read that "Saul came up to Carmel and behold, he set him up a JAD,"[5] rendered a place. "At" (Eg.) is a shrine, a monument, and in Assyrian "It" is a carved stone. When God came from Teman he had horns or emanations coming out of his Jad.[6] Here the Jad is translated hand or side. Had the determinative been present it would have shown the At (Eg.) as the solar circle or disk, the image of Adonai, God of Israel. "At," the circle of the sun, was the Jad whence issued the fiery-hornedness, there was the hiding and

---

[1] Ex. xiv. 31. [2] Lev. xxvii. 8. [3] Num. ii. 17. [4] Ex. xxvi.
[5] 1 Sam. xv. [6] Hab. iii. 4.

manifesting of his power. "At" signifies doing, and the Jad [1] means deeds. Lastly, the hand is frequently used for the mouth. "At" is to utter, put out, it is also that which is uttered. Hence "At" the word, to speak. But we are told that the Word of the Lord came by the HAND of Malachi,[2] and by the hand of the prophets. This may be supposed to indicate the written word, which has no meaning. The word was oral. Besides we find [3] the Lord had SPOKEN by the HAND of Moses. In these instances the Jad signified is not the hand but "At," the word, mouth, or type that needs interpreting by aid of the hieroglyphics, but which never has been interpreted.

In the work of Tabari [4] it is related that two animals came out of the Ark which did not enter; they were produced within it. These were the hog and cat, created as scavengers and to keep down the rats. The elephant gave birth to the hog, and Noah produced the cat from the sneeze of the lion by passing his hand down its back.

Remote as this is, it can be partially read by the Ritual, where the sun is said to transform into the cat or "It is Shu making the likeness of Seb." The alternative shows Shu making his transformation into a cat. Shu was the lion-god and one of the two lions was the cat which dealt with the "abominable rat of the sun," a type of the enemy Apophis. Now when we know that Shu represented breath (Nef) or spirit, we can see how it may be said the cat was evoked from the nose of the lion. We see further that the root of this strange Rabbinical and Haggadistic matter is Egyptian, which is the object of the present investigation.

In the Egyptian Pantheon the Seven Hathors are the Parcæ or Fates, the prognosticators and foretellers of coming events, and these in the Funeral Ritual are represented in the form of seven cows. Thus the seven kine of Joseph's dream which indicate the seven years of plenty and the seven years of famine correspond to the seven cows or Hathors who fulfil their character as the foretellers of events to come assigned to them by the Egyptians. The seven cows are also the givers of plenty who are invoked for food. "He has known the seven cows and their bull, who give of food and of drink to the living, and who feed the gods of the west. Give ye food and drink to the Osiris; feed him." "Give ye to him daily food and drink, oxen, geese, and all good things."[5]

Of Behemoth, the hippopotamus,[6] we read in the English version "He is the chief of the ways of God; he that made him can make his sword to approach unto him." The word rendered sword is Chereb (חרב). The CHEREB is a sword or some other kind of

[1] Jud. ix. xvi.   [2] Ch. i. 1.   [3] Ex. ix 35.
[4] Translated into French by Zotenberg, Oriental Translation Fund, Paris, 1867, p. 112.
[5] Rit. ch. 149; Birch.   [6] Job xl. 19.

cutting instrument, the Chaldee Cherba, Phœnician HARBA, and Greek ἅρπη, but the reading is more than doubtful. The passage is followed by "Surely the mountains bring him forth food." The context shows the meaning to be that, mighty monster as he is, the power which created can feed and sustain him. Therefore it appears probable the word chereb represents the Egyptian "KHERPU" which denotes supply, sufficiency, or enough. The sense of the passage would then be, He that made him can supply him with provisions. Surely the mountains (can) bring him forth food. In a sense he has all the mountains for grazing-ground, though not because these were the particular pasture of the hippopotamus. The imagery is thought of in relation to the typical hippopotamus, the "Great Bear" of the Egyptians. For this reason the Rabbinical writers consider the "cattle upon a thousand hills"[1] also refers to Behemoth whose celestial type was Ursa Major. It is said of Behemoth in the A. V.[2] "Behold he drinketh up a river and hasteth not." The Seventy have it "if there should be an inundation," and this sense is recoverable by aid of the word "AASEH" (Eg.) which means a flood or a deluge of water, and may be derived from AA great, and Sekha flood-time; AASEKHA being equivalent to שׁעשׁ. Thus the passage would mean, Behold in time of a great flood he hastens not, he does not mind an inundation and as for Jordan he could swallow it.

The particular idea expressed by the word THACHASH has never been determined. It is the name given to the skins used for the exterior covering of the Tabernacle.[3] The same thing is named in the Bull Inscription of Khorsabad. Sargon says: "I constructed palaces of skins of TAKHASH, of sandal-wood, of ebony,"[4] &c. M. Oppert characterizes the word as most obscure.

According to Rashi the Takash may be a badger, a sea-dog or dolphin; the Talmud says a marten, others identify the name with the colour rather than the animal. The Arabian Jews call the red-dyed hide of the ram THACHASH,[5] and this is the sense corroborated by Egyptian when we find the word worn down to TESH. Tesh is blood, red. It is applied to the Red Nile, the Red Crown, and to the planet Mars, Tesht. Tesh-tesh is an epithet of Osiris in his inert feminine form, and red phase, the great mystery. Tesh means to separate, leave, be left destitute, set apart. This in relation to the mystical sense which first made it sacred. Teshru is the red calf, red land, a red bird. Tesh, earlier Takash, means red, blood (hence the dyed ram skins), and may of course be applied to anything of that colour: it does not otherwise represent an animal, and cannot represent the grey badger.

The 39th chapter of Job[6] contains allusions which prove a knowledge of the hieroglyphics. One of these is especially intimate.

---

[1] Ps. i.   [2] Job. xl. xxii.   [3] Ex. xxv. 5.
[4] *Records of the Past*, vol. xi. p. 21.   [5] *Niebuhr*, p. 177.   [6] Ver. 9-11.

"Will the unicorn be willing to serve thee, or abide by thy crib? Canst thou bind the unicorn with his band in the furrow, or will he harrow the valleys after thee? Wilt thou trust him, because his strength is great?"   The allusions like those referring to the peacock and ostrich are made in mockery.   The unicorn was the type of Typhon.   The mythical unicorn is the Ramakh, the hippopotamus that dragged and drew round the starry system all night, till men were once more drawn out of the deluge of the darkness.   Will this puller above pull for you here below, that you worship the image of Typhon?   One name of the animal itself is Apt, and Apt (Eg.) is the name of the crib or manger.   The question in Egyptian is, Will Apt (the unicorn) abide by the Apt (crib)?   "Will he plough for you?" is the gist of one question, and Kheb (Eg.) is both a name of the plough and of the unicorn.   Also this constellation of Typhon is called the Plough.   These queries show great familiarity with the hieroglyphic symbols; a convincing proof of this is afforded by an assault on the character of the ostrich,[1] "which leaveth her eggs in the earth."

The ostrich-feather is one of the hieroglyphics, and reads either Mau or Shu, that is, light or shade.   Hor-Apollo says it was adopted because the wing-feathers of the ostrich are of equal length.   This feather is the especial symbol of Ma, the goddess of truth and justice.   It was the sign of the Two Truths and total wisdom of Egypt.   The writer of the Book of Job is aware of the sacred character of the wing-feathers of the ostrich, and asks in effect, Is she either true, just, or wise, or pious?   Does she sustain the character of her wing-feathers?   Does not she leave her eggs in the sand for the earth to warm them or the passing foot to crush them?   He asserts with the Arabs that the bird is impious.   This is the modern realism opposed to the symbolic character of the bird, and even that can only be read as it is written, hieroglyphically.

The tip of the crocodile's tail is the ideograph of Kam, black, darkness, because the crocodile left the land for the water at night, and the tip of the tail was the vanishing point.[2]   To express sunrise, says Hor-Apollo, they depict the two eyes of a crocodile, because, of the whole body, these are seen glaring conspicuously from the deep.[3]   This is the imagery of Job.   "By his neesings a light doth shine, and his eyes are like the eyelids of the morning."   The writer uses the Egyptian symbol of the morning, hence the sole sense of sorrow being turned into joy before such a thing as the crocodile.

"He—the Lord—stretcheth out the north over the empty place." "Hell is naked before him."[4]   That is the "bend of the great void"

---

[1] Job xxxix. 13-17.
[2] Hor-Apollo gives another reason.   He says the tail denotes darkness because with a blow of it the animal will inflict death.
[3] B. i. 68.   [4] Job xxvi. 6, 7.

found in the north, the open abyss, the place of the waters, the region of the hells, in the Egyptian Book of the Dead. This is the quarter where the "Dead things [ghosts and evil spirits] are born beneath the waters, and are the inhabitants thereof,"[1] as in the Ritual. "Though they be hid from my sight in the bottom of the sea, thence will I command the serpent, and he shall bite them."[2] That is the Apophis serpent of Egypt, the dweller in the deep, the dragon of the waters, who lives off the blood of the condemned, and executes vengeance on the wicked. The Apophis is depicted as a crooked serpent set all along with sword-blades, typical of destruction.

On the sarcophagus of Meneptah in the Soane Museum may be seen, amongst various scenes of the valley and shadow of death, one in which a crooked serpent keeps the door of death. This is Job's crooked serpent and door-keeper. "Have the gates of death been opened unto thee? or hast thou seen the door-keepers of the shadow of death?"[3]

The Hebrew word APAP, to *encompass* round, in the passages, "the waters *compassed* me,"[4] and "the waves of death *compassed* me,"[5] is the name of the dragon of the deep, the Apophis monster, that strangled within its coils.

The great serpent of the later Hebrew mythology, called the BARIAK NACHASH, may be explicated by means of the hieroglyphics. It is called the crooked serpent[6] and the piercing serpent.[7] The Typhonian dragon, to whose influence tempests were attributed, is certainly intended; the Apophis or Akhekh serpent, whose heaving, roiling writhing body is set with sword-blades. Akh (Eg.) means fire; Pra (Eg.; Hebrew, Bra) is to manifest, emane, fulminate. This would make the Bariak-Nachash the fulminator of fire. In Egyptian FULGURAVIT, FULSIT, is expressed by BUIREKA. This corresponds to the Hebrew form "Baraq" (ברק), to "cast forth," lighten, or fulminate. The only difference in the Hebrew is the substitution of the letter Cheth for Koph. Another name of this serpent in the hieroglyphics is the destroying serpent, and the Hebrew Barak was called the "thunderbolt." Another title of the serpent is "brass of earth," which tallies with the Hebrew Nachushta; "Nachush" meaning brass, whilst "TA" is the Egyptian word for earth. This will suffice for identifying the Hebrew serpent of evil with the Typhonian serpent of Egypt.

The plural Bariakim employed by Isaiah[8] is founded on another Egyptian word. He uses it for ships, and Bari (Eg.) is the bark, of which Bariakim is the plural.

The mythological and symbolic character is mixed up with these

---

[1] Job xxvi. 5.   [2] Amos ix. 3.   [3] Job xxxviii. 17.
[4] Jonah ii. 5.   [5] 2 Sam. xxii. 5.   [6] Job xxvi. 13.
[7] Is. xxvii. 1.   [8] xliii. 14.

typical beasts, which cannot be simply understood apart from their hieroglyphical nature. Many names of mystic meaning have been rendered by translators who were in the dark and thoroughly ignorant of the thing signified by the word. No Hebrew scholar ever yet knew what was intended by the words " Tan " and "Tannin," which include the whale that swallowed Jonah, the serpent that tempted Eve, the leviathan of Job, the piercing serpent, the crooked serpent, and the dragon of the deep,[1] the dragon that Job claimed to be his brother ; Pharaoh, king of Egypt,[2] and the rod of Moses in its serpentine transformation.[3] It is applied to creatures of the desert and monsters of the deep, also by comparison to the wild she-ass of the wilderness, snuffing up the wind at her pleasure,[4] and lastly, it is used to indicate the old serpent called the Devil and Satan.[5] Thus philologically the serpent that tempted Eve is one with the serpent into which Moses' rod was changed, and the whale which swallowed Jonah is one with the leviathan whom Job wishes had swallowed him [6] rather than he should have been born, and these are all one with the dragon of the waters, who was the cruel Pharaoh drowned for the time being in the Red Sea, but who emerges once more as the Satan of the Apocalypse.

The primary question for us is not, What is the TAN ? There is no " THE " in the case where there are so many. The question is, What does Tan mean as a principle of naming applied to the various illustrations ? Now, Tan in Egyptian means division, cutting in two, to cut off, to divide, turn away, make, become, or be separate. The serpent covered with sword-blades was the piercing or severing serpent. Worms, or destructive animals of the waters, in Egyptian, are Tan-mu, the Tan of the waters ; they pierce and sever in destroying. The River Tan (Iarutan) of the waterman is the river that divides. The period of mourning desiderated by Job was the dividing period opposed to gestation. The wild beasts cut off in remote deserts and isolated on desolate isles are the Tannin on that account.[7] Islanders are the Tena in Egyptian. Lunar eclipses are Tennu ; they cut off the light, and occur at the dividing-place. Tenu is the joint or break, as is the number ten. Tane is one of the Polynesian great gods, the divider of the heaven from the earth personified. Egypt as the Tan, whether celestial or geographical, was the divided heavens or countries.

"Tenny" is the name of lines that give the waved barry look to the shield of a coat of arms. The heraldic colour and blazon of tenny is yellow ; the jacinth in stones, and the dragon's head in the planisphere.

Having the principle of naming, the hieroglyphics supply the means of applying it by determinatives of the different ideas that

---

[1] Is. xxvii. 1.   [2] Is. li. 9 ; Ez. xxix. 3.   [3] Ex. vii. 10.
[4] Cf. Jer. xiv. 6, and Jer. ii. 24.   [5] Rev. xii. 3, 4, 7, 9.
[6] Job iii. 8.   [7] Is. xiii. 22.

have to be expressed by one word. Once cut adrift from these, we have no philological anchorage anywhere. But the hieroglyphic language is like an old sea-bottom, still intact, and rich with the lost treasures of a myriad wrecks.

LEVIATHAN as one of the mythical monsters, or Tannin, is probably the Egyptian REF, or REFI, a form of the Apophis serpent, from REF, or RU, as the typical REPtile, viper, snake, worm, scorpion, or dragon, and TAN, to cut in two, whence the cutting, destroying Akhekh, serpent of night, armed with piercing blades, which represented the power of the darkness and death to sever the circle of light and life in the "bend of the great void" where it lurked. Job's description of leviathan, simply supposed by commentators to be a veritable dweller in the sea, includes all the clothing of the monster of mythology.

Max Müller[1] has shown how the fleets of Solomon must have been to India to obtain the monkeys, on account of the name, which is QOPH, because in Sanskrit the ape is Kapi. "Qoph," he says, is foreign in Hebrew, and the land in which that word is indigenous must be the Ophir of the Bible; therefore it was India. "Kafi" is the original word, and it is Egyptian; Kepi in Persian; Kapi in Sanskrit; Kepos in Greek; Ape in English. The Kafi, a monkey of a peculiar kind, appears in the tombs of the Fourth Dynasty as early as the time of Kufu, with the name of Kafi written over it, about 3733 B.C. It is the dog-headed ape, or Cynocephalus, made so much of in Egypt that it was a co-personification with Taht, of the Word (Logos) itself. It represented the moon and periodicity in its feminine phase, and was therefore a feminine Logos. Jamblichus tells us this Cynocephalus was honoured in the temples on account of certain changes it underwent in common with the moon, by which time could be reckoned! The truth is, the Kaf is a menstruating monkey, and suffered eclipse (Khab) periodically like the moon, and was adopted in the Mysteries, where it took the place of the Q'deshoth, the human demonstrators of primary facts in nature. This Kaf belongs solely to Africa, which is Kafrica, the Ka, inner land, of the Kaf, or Af (born of) the first (Ap)land, and therefore Ophir was in Africa.

It has likewise been argued that Solomon's peacocks (תכיים)[2] were brought from India, because Toki is the Tamil name for the peacock, and Togei in Malabar. But the original of both is the Egyptian Tekh, or Tekai, a symbolic bird. Tekh is a name for the ibis of Taht; Tekai is the Otis Tetrax. The name applied to the peacock is full of significance. Teka is to see, behold with the symbolic eye. Tekhen is to open and shut the eyes, wink, sparkle, illumine, and the TECHI, as peacock, is the bird with the eyes that open and shut with

---

[1] *Lectures on Language*, first series, p. 202.
[2] *Ib.* p. 203. Rev. J. Mateer, *The Land of Charity*.

their winking splendours. Nothing could be more happy than the name Tekhi, from the Egyptian Tekh. Not only is the name of the peacock Egyptian, it exists, without the article prefixed, as the Akh, or Khu, the splendid, illuminated, coloured bird; a sun-bird, the symbol of spirit, lustre, and light.

The ivory in Hebrew is called SHEN HABBIM, ivory, or elephant's teeth (margin). This habbim, says Max Müller, is without a derivation in Hebrew, but is most likely a corruption of the Sanskrit name for elephant, IBHA, preceded by the Semitic article.[1] Again, there is no need of corruption as in Egyptian "Ab" is the name both for the elephant and the ivory. The Ab had earlier forms in Hab and Kab, so that the names of the peacock, ape, and ivory, may be foreign in Hebrew without being derived from Sanskrit, or Ophir being in India, or a navy of a King Solomon having existed that traded with India. The first India known to the Greeks was in Africa, and the earliest Indians were Æthiopic. When Eustathius states that the Æthiopians came from India he means the African India. When Claudius Claudianus, the last of the Latin classic poets, at the end of the fourth century, speaks of the "India, which is painted on Jewish veils,"[2] the India meant is Æthiopic and not Asiatic. Tacitus says many considered the Jews to be the progeny of the Æthiopians, but they would mean the Indians of Africa. India in other classical writers is a name of Æthiopia or the land of Kush. Virgil describes the Nile as coming from the land of the coloured Indians,[3] and Diodorus calls the black Osiris an Indian by extraction. The conquest of India by Osiris or Bacchus is allegorical, and belongs to the sun in the southern heaven. Horus-Khenti-Khrati[4] is a form of this sun of India or the south, the Harpocrates of Khent, the southern heaven. This leads to the derivation of the name of India as a developed form of KHENTU (Eg.), the inner, interior, southern land; extant as far south as U-GANDA, the Patriarch of which was named KINTU, and who, according to Stanley, came and went and was expected to return. KHENTU modifies into the Zend HENDU, Pahlavi HENDO, and India.

Thus Khebta-Khentu is Egypt south, the earliest Hindu-Kush is Southern Æthiopia, and the final, the original form of the Sanskrit SAPTA-SINDHU and Zend HAPTA-HENDU, is the Egyptian KHABTA-KHENTU, or Egypt north and south.

India may or may not be named as the land of the Seven Streams from Sapta-sindhu, the Seven Rivers. But if it were, the celestial Egypt was also the land of the seven streams,[5] and seven mouths were assigned to the Nile. The Romans reckoned the Branches of the Nile to be seven in number, *Septemplicis ostia Nili*. It can be shown,

---

[1] *Lectures*, first series, p. 202.
[2] *Carmen in Eutropium*, Lib. i. 357.
[3] Georg. l. iv. v. 293.
[4] Mentioned in the *Annals of Rameses*, iii. pl. 59, line 8, Birch.
[5] Is. xi. 15.

however, that the typical seven of naming are the Seven Stars of Khepsh (Kush) not Seven Streams. The Indian Ocean, if named from the African India, or Æthiopia, certainly was not called after the Seven Streams. It would then be the ocean of those who had sailed south by the Red Sea, and Khentu (Eg.), means the south, and going south. The ocean would be named first and the land last, as that of the Southern Sea.

The Rabbins say the world is like an eye, and the pupil of it is Jerusalem. The image seen in it is the sanctuary. This belongs to the Ritual where the god is visible in his Disk, which is also the eye. The eye, or its pupil, is the AR, and the eye is made at the place of reproduction, the eye being the symbol of mirroring, making the likeness, conceiving, and it is full when the circle of the year, the round, is completed. Jerusalem represented this centre of the eye, or the place of juncture in the ring, the gem of it.

One meaning of שׁלם (Shalem) is to complete, form the whole, be full. This does not supersede the high place, the summit. But if we take the eye, Aru, and Shalem, in the sense of to fill, complete the whole, we see that Aru-Shalem is just the place of making or filling the eye. As a constellation the eye, a sign of Horus the child re-born every spring, is figured at the place of the vernal equinox, where the hill of the horizon was fixed, and the birthplace of the child, the sanctuary, is found.

The Egyptian Makha supplies a sense missing in Hebrew, where the word אתמחא (Ithm'cha) signifies to be fixed or affixed to a cross, be crucified. The Machba (מחבא) is a junction, the place of uniting and dovetailing. Machaneh (מחנה) in the plural form of Machanim, denotes a dual dance, the up and down of it. Mak (Eg.) means the dance. Machar (מחר) is the morning time, the time of light on the horizon. Makôn (מכון) means a stand, a dwelling-place, the heavenly seat, the dwelling-place of deity, the foundation or basis of a throne. In the feminine form, Makônah (מכונה) is a stand, support, pedestal, a foundation for the world.

Makha (Eg.) is the balance, the equinoctial level, the place of the horizon. Ma is place, and akh is the horizon. Har-Makha was the sun of both horizons, or the level. The first foundations were laid in the four corners; at the chief of these, the place of the spring equinox, was the solar birthplace. Here is the Tser Hill, or rock of the horizon, on which the gods landed from the waters. This was the place of juncture or conjunction of sun and moon, and the birthplace of their son, and from the crossing was derived the symbol of the cross, and the imagery of the crucifixion.

There is a mystery about the use of the Hebrew Mim. The meaning of this addition to words as modifying the idea, says Fuerst, has not been ascertained as yet. The Egyptian M will illustrate the Hebrew Mim. Ma, as place, explains the Mim prefixed in מרעה for pasture, and the time at which an action takes place as in מוֹשָׁב.[1]   Ma, the place, and akha, the horizon, yield Makha the level, balance, or equinox.

The heroic exploit of Samson is connected etymologically with a place called Maktesh, a name applied to Jerusalem by the Samaritans. Tesh (Eg.) is a nome or division of land ; Mak-tesh is the equinoctial division or level.   As this was the place of the mount we may infer that Jerusalem is the Aru (Eg.), the ascent, steps or mount of peace, representing the hill of the horizon in the solar scheme.   Tabariyya is also called Maktesh in the Midrash.   Tab (Eg.) is the point of commencement in the circle ; Ari (Eg.) again is the mount.   The Hebrew Chag is a festival, a feast which was celebrated with dancing.[2] It means particularly the feast of harvest[3] or the Passover.[4]   The harvest and the Passover were the two equinoctial tides.   Khekh (Eg.) is the horizon and the balance, *ergo*, the equinoctial level. Skhekh (Eg.) means to adjust the balance.   Khekh modifies into hakh, a festival, a time, determined by the twin lions of the horizon, and by the double-seated boat ; two ideographs of the sun upon the horizon, at the time of the equinox.   This Chag or Hak is the same as the English Hock-tide, celebrated twice a year, after Easter and at harvest-home, which properly belongs to the two equinoxes.   In the Hebrew name of Chaggiyah (חגיה) we have the god Jah on the horizon (Khekh) who is the Egyptian Har-Makhu.   The name of Cheg-Baal (חגבעל) in Herodotus[5] is probably derived from Sut-Har, a Sabean form of the deity of the horizon.

Beth-Diblathaim is the proper name of a city in the plain of Moab.[6] The plain is the makha, the level, the place of the equinox. Diblathaim reads the dual circle, or double cake ; Dibl, meaning to cake together ; Diblah being a cake of pressed figs.   Teb (Eg.) means a cake, also a cake or Teb of figs.   There was a city of Diblah which was identified with Riblah or Daphne, in the extreme northern border of Palestine. There was likewise a city of Daphne in the north of Lower Egypt. Daphne is derived from Tef (later Tefnut), the Goddess of the North or hinder thigh, a type of the birthplace.   Now the hieroglyphic of the horizon is a cake, and therefore the double cake answers to the double circle of the horizon ; Beth-Diblathaim is the double house of the equinoctial level, where the copulæ occurred at the time of the vernal equinox.   The cake of the horizon and its double house is still preserved in the hot cross bun, or cake of Easter, as already intimated.   The present writer holds that this double cake is the sign commonly called the "spectacles ornament," found so frequently repeated on the sculptured stones of Scotland.   The double house of the horizon, or house of the dual equinox, appears in the Sabean Myth as the double house of Anup (Sut-Har) in Abtu ; Abtu is

---

[1] Ex. xii. 40.   [2] Jud. xxi. 19.   [3] Ex. xxiii. 16.
[4] Is. xxx. 29.   [5] vi. 98.   [6] Jer. xlvi. 22.

designated the double holy house devoted to Anubis. This, in the Solar Myth, was called the double abode of Tum or Har-Makhu, the god of both horizons in An. So ancient was this birthplace that it bears the name of Apt (Taurt), the old Suckler, the Hippopotamus Goddess, who appears also as Ahti, the Double House, or house of reproduction, whose name connects her with the moon.

TERP (teru) is a name of literature, the rites and writings of Taht, the scribe of the gods. A TERU is a roll of papyrus, the equivalent of the Hebrew TORAH or sacred roll of the law. The Torah תורה is the law of Moses, the law or doctrine in the Egyptian sense of religious ritual, written on the roll in hieroglyphics. If, as will be shown, the ancient Hebrew records were in the hieroglyphic signs, then the Torah was the Teru, and the Targum was the writing in which the secret symbols, in addition to the doctrine therein hermetically sealed, were rendered into the alphabet for common use. The Toharoth, a part of the Mishna, treats of what is clean and unclean. This is a form of the two truths. Teru relates primarily to the two times, which were first of all physiological, hence the clean and unclean. Next they were solstitial, then equinoctial. These two constitute the All, the Ter or entire, whole. From this same "Ter" the All consisting of the Two Truths of Egypt, it is now proposed to derive the name of the Talmud as Tar-mat, the total truth of a twofold nature. The work is still divided, according to the Two Truths, into two parts, as the Mishna and Gemara, the legal and the legendary lore. The Mishna denotes the second truth (Ma-shen) or law. Shen, in both Hebrew and Egyptian, means second, and the Semitic Mi stands for Ma (Eg.) The name of GEMARA is possibly derived from KEM (Eg.), to discover, find, invent; hence hidden, dark; and RA, formula, ARA, ceremonial. The Two Truths of Egypt dominate the Hebrew scriptures. These are represented by the two stone tables of testimony given on Sinai. Sinai itself is the twofold in both languages. The written and unwritten law were another shape of this duality. And when Ezra re-rendered the law it was still in accordance with the Two Truths; one part was to be published, the other kept secret as the hidden wisdom.

It is somewhat like our own written and common law, the origin of which latter is unknown, but it has been handed down by tradition, custom, and usage, from a time before covenants were written, and is frequently found at variance, especially in the popular mind, with the written code. Rabbinical traditions represent the Hebrew deity as studying the Scriptures by day and the Mishna by night,[1] which is a mode of acknowledging them to be of the nature of the Two Truths. In this sense the Mishna is the second of two, that is the oral in relation to the written law of the Pentateuch. Both Mishna and Gemara belong to the unwritten law, the second of the twofold

[1] *Jewish Repository*, vol. i. p. 49.

total of truth. It was the character of the Gemara to make examinations of the Mishna as it accumulated. It has been termed a critical expansion of the Mishna. Hence the likelihood that the name comes from Kem (Eg.), to seek, find out, discover, and Ra (Eg.), formula.

The Chaldee word Targum, of uncertain origin, rendered to translate or interpret from one language into another, yields a more particular meaning when derived from the Egyptian as TAR-KEM. TAR means to interrogate, question, sift, distil, indicate, and KEM is to seek, find, discover. TARUU also denotes the stems and roots. The Egyptian experts were designated KEM-sep, and the Targum derived from TAR-KEM is an interpretation of the concealed sense, the dark sayings, allegories, and symbols, of the hidden wisdom, an intermediate between the secret lore and the outside public, and well does the word thus derived express the nature of the process applied in questioning, sifting, modifying, rationalizing, and generally tampering with the materials of mythology, for the Targumists did not remain faithful to the original meaning.

As no Targum on the Books of Ezra, Nehemiah, and Daniel, has ever been known, and as these books were written in Chaldee, this fact further tends to show the meaning of the Targum as the book of elucidation of the secret language ; those written in Chaldee and in the square letter were not in the same category.

"PETAR REF SU," is a formula in the Egyptian Ritual that occurs more than thirty times over in one chapter, the seventeenth, called the Egyptian Gospel or Faith. "Petar ref su" is translated by Dr. Birch, "Let him explain it." Petar means to show, explain, interpret. The Su, however, is not merely him ; he was the royal scribe, the interpreter, the "sole sage, possessed of science," the keeper of the secret wisdom that was only communicated orally ; the voice of the unwritten word. The Hebrew Meturgeman, or interpreter, fulfilled the same office, and will help to explain this frequent "PETAR REF SU." Deutsch, on the Targums, quotes various instructions relating to the regulations of the Meturgeman. "Neither the reader nor the interpreter are to raise their voices one above another ;" "they have to wait for each other until each has finished his verse." The Meturgeman is "not to use a written Targum, but he is to deliver his translation *viva voce*," lest it might appear that he was reading out of the Torah itself. One interpreter was allowed to one reader of the law, while two interpreters were at times allowed for the prophets.

The status of the Meturgeman in Israel had become the reverse of what it was in ancient Egypt ; he was a mere go-between, a translator out of the sacred language into the vulgar, out of Hebrew into Aramaic, and at times the utterer of a lying gloss ; but the origin was the same. Both at first were expounders of the oral and unwritten wisdom, the living tongue of the most ancient tradition.

The uncleanness of creeping things is most definitely laid down in the law, and yet the Talmud affirms that "no one is appointed a member of the Sanhedrim who does not possess ingenuity enough to prove from the written law that a creeping thing is ceremonially clean.[1] This is denounced as sophistry, whereas it is but the blending of the oral and written, the oral going back to the time when creeping things were not considered unclean. A member of the Sanhedrim was bound to be in possession of the Gnosis or Kabala, by which all such incongruities could be explained. "Whoever translates [as Meturgeman] a verse in its closely exact form is a liar," says the Talmud; that is, whoever literalizes that which is symbolical and requires oral explanation of its hidden meaning. According to this, the literalizers are liars and incompetent exponents. Yet the Christian world has never had any other teachers. A gentile inquired of Shammai, "How many laws have you?"—"Two," said Shammai, "the written and the oral."—"I believe the former, not the latter," said the gentile; "accept me as a proselyte on condition that I learn the written law only." Whereupon Shammai ejected him with execration.[2]

The Phœnicians had a kind of judges as recorded by Livy, and proved by the two tablets of Marseilles and Carthage, designated SUFFETES, whereupon it is inferred and assumed that the Hebrews imported their SHOPHETIM or judges from Phœnicia. Goldziher writes: "The consideration of the word Shophet itself leads to the conviction that the office was an institution suggested by Phœnician custom, for it is found in no other Semitic language in the same signification as in these two dialects of Canaan. The Samaritan, in which Shaphat is also found, scarcely requires separate mention. So the Hebrews, as was often the case, must have borrowed the term Shophet together with the corresponding institution, from their cultivated neighbours," *e.g.* the Phœnicians.[3] But the roots of the Hebrews are not always to be found in Canaan, nor were their institutions borrowed there from their neighbours. The Sep in Egypt was a judge. Sep means to examine, verify, judge. The Sep is the throne as a judgment seat; SAB (Eg.), a wise man, a councillor; SUFI, in Hindustani, means the wise; SOPHOO, Greek, to instruct in wisdom; SEFOU, Mantshu Tartar, a master, a teacher; SUIBHE, Irish, sessions, assizes; GAFATE, African Galla, to examine, inquire, search out; SABIT, Hindustani, to prove; SABIT, Malayan, established on evidence, proved; SUBUT, Arabic, proving on evidence; SIFT, English, applied to scrutinizing evidence for judging. The SOPHI was a Persian king. The Swahili SUFFI, a hermit or religious devotee, and with the African Galla, the SOBA is a king. In Egypt, the SHEFT or SHEPT are a sacred order of some kind. The SHEFT or Suffetes were common; not limited to the Phœnicians.

---

[1] *Sanhedr.* f. xvii. 1.   [2] *Shabbath*, f. xxxi. 1.
[3] *Mythology among the Hebrews*, p. 245.   Martineau.

In Egypt, the ancient order of the judges, the SHEPT, had been superseded by monarchy in the monumental times, but the names and signs lived on. The SEP are an order of persons belonging to religious houses. SEP permutes with AP, and AP, if not a judge, is to judge, and means the first, head. The Sep as judge is imaged by the SHEPS (variant, AS), the most ancient ruler, and as AS means the servant as well as the ruler, including the SHUS of the SHUS-EN-HAR, the servants of Har in pre-monumental times, it seems probable that SHUS is the worn down form of SHEPS, who, as rulers, would be the Hek-SHUS kings, the shepherd kings as the judges. The institution of the judges, the SHOPHETIM, is pre-monarchical, pre-solar; it is Sabean, and has a name as old as time, Seb, or the dog-star, Sebt; it is Sut-Typhonian. In the time of Amenophis III. it is found on the tablet of his triumphs over the negroes that they were not ruled by kings or chiefs in the monarchical sense, but by judges, exactly like the SHOPHETIM in Israel. The institution had been retained in Æthiopia and the birthplace. It was once Egyptian, and as such had been carried into Phœnicia and other lands. The earlier Hekshus had passed over Canaan and Palestine before the exode of the Jews, who followed and found many of the outcast customs of earlier Egypt. There is no need to derive the Judges from Phœnicia.

In the harem conspiracy which aimed at the overthrow of Rameses III., Penhi, one of the chief culprits, applied to the sorcerer, saying, " If I only possessed a writing which would give me power and strength ! " " Then he gave him a writing from the rolls of the books of Rameses III., the great god, his lord. . . . Then there came upon him a divine magic, an enchantment for men. He (also) formed human figures of wax, with the intention of having them carried in (to the women's house) by the hand of the land-surveyor, Adiruma, to alienate the mind of one of the girls and to bewitch the others. Now, however, he was brought to trial. They inflicted on him the great punishment of death, such as the holy writings pronounced against him."[1] These magic practices were the work of the godless, whom the Egyptians called the Kheft, after the ancient Typhonian mother, and were prohibited by the sun-god Ra. So in Israel the old customs of witchcraft, sorcery, calling up the spirits of the dead, were superseded by the teacher called Moses—the phrase is used of set purpose—who announced the new Divinity by the name of Jah, who will be shown to be a solar god entirely distinct from the Jehovah of Genesis.

In the Ritual of the instructions given to the reader of a certain sacred book, amongst other things to be done in the purificatory preparations, the sign of Ma, goddess of truth, is to be placed on the tongue in fresh colour (Rui), used by the scribes to denote that he

[1] Brugsch, v. ii. p. 163.

spoke with the tongue of Truth herself when he read the book to Ra. Incense is also applied behind both ears of the priest or prophet who reads the book.

The colour of Ma was red, of which word RUI is the root; red does not appear by name as ma, but N and M permute, and NA is the paint or RUI for writing. Ma must have signified blood, as DAMU derives from ma (Eg.) with the article T prefixed. The red RUI put on the tongue as typical of the truth suggests the natural inference that the blood of the sacrifice which was to be put on the tip of the right ear of Aaron and his sons, and on the right thumb and right great toe, was meant for the mark of Ma, goddess of the Two Truths, the Hebrew Thummim. The red on the ears had transferred the truth to the hearers, whereas on the tongue it applied to the utterance. The mark of Ma in red paint is the probable meaning of the vermilion, red paint, or blood, with which stones are still bedaubed in various parts of the world. If so, each ruddled stone reads Sut-ma, the pyramid of truth; the pyramid, Sut, is a form of the stone of Sut, the simpler stone being the oldest. Sut-ma (Eg.), as a compound word means to make fast, establish truly, and as the pyramid, Sut, signifies an offering, the red stone is the ideograph of a true offering.

We learn from the inscription found in the tomb of Hap Sefa, son of Ai, and high-priest of Anubis, or Apheru, the lord of Lycopolis, that the inhabitants of Egypt, in the time of the Thirteenth Dynasty, were accustomed, rich and poor, to make an offering of first-fruits to their deity, just as the Hebrews were bound to do in later times. The festivals narrated in the inscription took place at the end and the beginning of the year, from the last day of the year (the fifth intercalary day) to the feast called Uak, which was celebrated on the eighteenth of the month Taht.[2] The Hebrews, however, dated from the equinoxes, of which Apheru was the divinity.

In Lightfoot's account of the Temple, the shewbread is described as being laid cake by cake between canes or REEDS of gold. These reeds or canes were not whole, like the reed itself, but represented it as cloven in two or slit up the middle, so that, when the cakes were placed between the halves of the divided reeds, they were the symbol of food contained in the reed. Fourteen of these halves were used in each pile; twenty-eight for the total of twelve cakes, placed in two piles with three half-reeds placed between two cakes up to the fifth, and only two between the fifth and sixth, the lowest cake being laid on the plain table. The number twenty-eight is lunar in the mystical sense. Every seventh day the old cakes were replaced by a fresh offering. The table heaped with bread was, as the vase in the centre shows,[3] a form of the hieroglyphic Hept (or Hetp), the table of the

[1] *La Destruction des Hommes par les Dieux.*   *Bib. Arch.* vol. iv. pt. i. p. 16.
[2] Brugsch, *History of Eg.* vol. i. 196, Eng. ed.   [3] See Calmet's *Dictionary.*

shrine heaped with food, and signifying a pile of food, plenty, welcome, peace. Hept also means the number Seven, and on the seventh day the stale bread, sacred to the priests, was eaten.

The Egyptians, says Hor-Apollo, to " denote ancient descent, depicted a bundle of papyrus, and by this they intimate the primeval food, for no one can find the beginning of food or generation." [1] The papyrus reed was a type of beginning, named Tufi. Af is born of; Ap, the first; Tef, Tep, or Tufi, denotes this commencement. Also, the Egyptians, in making their offerings to the dead or the manes set out their cakes in the tombs upon SCAFFOLDS OF REED.[2] "And the Lord said unto Moses, Thou shalt observe the feast of weeks of the first-fruits of the wheat-harvest." [3] The offering was to include two loaves and two Assarans of meal. This was the Hebrew Pentecost, our Whitsuntide. The fast is assumed to have been first instituted by the Lord for the Israelites to observe. According to Josephus, its name is ASARTHA,[4] which signifies Pentecost. So far from this originating on Mount Sinai or by any direct revelation to Moses, the "ASHRTA" must have been an Egyptian institution even if it did not bear the same name.

"ASHRTA" means a slice or portion of bread, a measure of corn ; that is, the slice and the measure of corn are determinatives of the word Ashrta.[5] It was probably the Sheteta or Shat-sha festival of cutting harvest, whence the symbolic slice of food. Asha is to mow. The Assaran measure of the Hebrews may be the corn-measure of the hieroglyphics, the Kat ideograph of Asher.

In the Annals of Rameses III.,[6] amongst the bread offerings to the temple, are 441,800 buns called "Buns KALUSTA." [7] The Egyptian Kalusta becomes the KALLISTEUS of the Greeks, a kind of cake or bread which they beautified. Apparently it was made of the finest ears of wheat ($\kappa\alpha\lambda\lambda\iota\sigma\tau\acute{\alpha}\chi\upsilon\varsigma$). Rendered with the letter R, these buns are KARUSTA. Ta is bread, food, offering ; KARAS denotes the dead, the corpse or mummy ; Karas, a funeral. A Cornish word, CLUSTY, will enable us to determine the nature of the bread. Clusty means close, heavy, unfermented, dead ; it is also applied to potatoes when they are not mealy. The Kalusta buns were unleavened, like the shewbread of the Hebrews, eaten by the priests only, and offered to them in piles. The PILE will identify the bread under the name of "Marchet" ; and this in Egyptian is Merr, cakes ; Khet, the corpse ; making it one with the "Karus-ta," the offering to the dead, which was unleavened, as a symbol of the dead. This was offered in a pile or in the shape of a pyramid. BUN, in Amoy, denotes the cakes of the dead.

[1] B. i. 30. [2] Wilkinson, *Anc. Egypt*, vol. ii. p. 362.
[3] Ex. xxxiv. 22. [4] *Ant.* iii. 10, 6.
[5] Lep. *Denk.* ii. 25 ; iii. 48, B ; iii. 260, C. [6] Plate 176.
[7] Birch, *Rec. of Past*, vol. vi. 45.

PPA-NEM, or BEH-NEM, in Egyptian, signifies the cakes or bread repeated for the following festival ; from PPA, cake, NEM, repeat, be second, the second festival. This repetition was made by the Hebrews every seventh day. The priests only ate the old loaves of shewbread on the seventh day or festival following.[1]

The head-dress worn by the priests is described by Josephus as a crownlike cap made of thick swathes of linen folded round and round many times. This he calls the MASNAMPHTHES. The high-priest's mitre was of the same fashion in the inner part, but round it there was a golden crown. It is evident from his account that this double mitre worn by the high-priest was a form of the double crown of Egypt, worn by the Pharaohs and the figures of gods.

NEM denotes the secondary form. The "NAMS" was a double head-dress, cap, or wig, worn by Egyptian priests. MES is a diadem, and signifies the anointed or to anoint. TES is to envelop by coiling round and round, just as Josephus describes the thick swathes being wound round and round many times to form the lower part of the mitre. MAS-NAM-P-TES is Egyptian for the secondary diadem (or head-dress) of an enveloped form ; from MES, a diadem or head-dress ; NEM, second ; P, the article The ; and TES, to coil, swathe, tie round and round. And if the S be only the Greek terminal, then MAS-NAM-PUT is still the secondary form of crown, whilst PUT denotes the divine circle of the gods. With the outer crown of gold bound round the MAS-NAM-PUT, we have the mitre of the high-priest called the Mitznephth (מצנפת). Mes-nabt, in Egyptian, means the diadem encircled with gold. Mes is the diadem ; Neb, gold ; Nabt, gold-type ; Nabt, to tie, plait, noose, swathe round. The Nabtu IS the solar disk of gold. Nabt was a title of Amen-Ra, and Mes-nabt in one form is the diadem of Amen-Ra. But the Hebrew Miznepheth was of another type than the double crown of Egypt, the crown of the south and north. Josephus leaves an opening in the lower crown for the plate of gold to be inserted, and that suggests the peculiar pattern of the double crown worn solely by Atum ; the crown of east and west. Josephus gives an elaborate pourtrayal of a cup of gold which rose up out of the Miznepheth like the flower of a poppy or the navel of the pomegranate in shape, and this formed a crown to the double crown previously described. He seems to have gone a long way round not to depict the lotus-flower itself, for that is obviously the original type of flower intended by the EPHIELIS, and on the head of the deity Atum, alone among the gods, will be found the lotus-flower, which he carried as a natural crown, long before crowns of gold had been made by human hands. This will enable us to get at the root meaning of the Miznepheth, the high-priest's mitre, also known as a diadem.[2] Mes signifies in Egyptian the product of a river, the water-

---

[1] Lightfoot, *Of the Temple.*   [2] Ez. xxi. 26.

born. Nef is breath and to float on the water. At is a type, a symbol. All three roots are extant in Hebrew : Mesa, product of the water ; Neph, breath ; and Ath, a sign, portent, symbol.   The lotus floating on the water, bearing the seed up in the flower, or carried upon the head of Atum, was the type of breathing out of the water.   And this lotus crown gives the name of the Miznepheth to the mitre worn by the high-priest of the Hebrews.

It can be still further identified.

The papyrus pattern is found in the fan or *flabellum* of the monuments ; the leaves spread fan-wise as ornament to the hemispherical shape.   And Josephus describes the semi-spherical form with its leaves sharp as the leaves of mint.

The Fan is of course a sign of breath, and one of its names is the Neft ; Mes-Neft is Egyptian for this fan worn as a crown.   Also the papyrus-plant, like the lotus, was a birth (Mes) of the waters, and image of breathing.

The high-priest, says Josephus,[1] wore a long vestment of a blue colour reaching to his feet ; " in our language it is called a Meer (or Mer), and is tied round the waist with a girdle."   MER (Eg.) is to gird round, a circle, swathe, envelop, tie round.   The Mer was a governor and superintendent, also persons attached to a temple as monks, the universal wearers of the long vestment or Mer.   The garment called by Moses the Abanat is designated by Josephus the AMIA.   " We have learned," he says, " from the Babylonians, to call it Amia, for so it is named by them."   This may enable us to recognize the Egyptian AMIHA.   In a hymn addressed to Amen Ra, the deity is described as being " Lord of the high-placed crown, of the fair turban, the white crown ; the coronet and the diadem are the ornaments of his face ; he is invested with the AMIHA ; the double crown is his head-gear ; benignly he receives the Atef-crown on whose south and whose north is love ; the Lord of life receives the sceptre ; Lord of the BREASTPLATE armed with the whip."[2]   The AMIHA has not been recognized, but if Goodwin is right in his rendering, it would seem to be one with the Jewish Amia, therefore a name of the Shent apron.

A stem, BANAT (בנט), is assumed for Abanat, in the sense of to bind, bind about, gird about (Sansk. BANDH, to bind ; Persian BEND), but the stem is not found in the Semitic dialects.   Kimchi and others regarded the word as Egyptian.   BENT (Eg.) is determined by the skin of the beast which was worn by the priests.   This skin was made into an apron called the Shent.   Shent denotes that which wraps, encircles, girdles round.   The sign read Shent is also read FENT, nor is the latter reading, though rare, to be given up.   FENT is a variant of BENT, and the BENT or BANAT or BENTI, we take to be the Hebrew form of the SHENT worn by the Egyptian priests,

---

[1] B. iii. c. vii. 4.   [2] *Records of the Past*, ii. 130.

which survives as the bishop's apron. A Pshent crown is found as a Pinu or Pinut.[1]

Another name given to this vestment by Josephus is MASSABA-ZANES. Mess (Eg.) is a strap ; Mash, to tie ; Mess, a belt ; Sab, to encase, engird ; SANES, to salute, adore, invoke : hence the girdle put on for ceremonial service. A garment was worn about the privy parts called a MACHANASE. It was made of linen, like a pair of breeches, with the top cut off. MAKU in the hieroglyphics is some unknown linen object.[2] MAKUNAS would denote the lower linen object with the sign of the noose or tie. Now, the lotus worn by Atum is a symbol of the female, when the genitrix was represented as containing the seed within herself. The Hebrew imagery, including the priestly petticoats, is essentially feminine, and NAS (Eg.) means her, she, the female, out of. Hence we infer the MACHA-NASE was a feminine garment, in keeping with the skirt.

Josephus calls the piece that was inserted in the void place of the Ephod the ESSEN or Hessen, and says it signified the oracle. SHEN (Eg.) is the circle ; the Shaunnu is a diviner. The Essen was the circle of divination, hence the oracle. Shna is the sacred serpent that often formed the typical circle. The Essen is a modified form of Keshen, the Choshen spoken of by Philo, the two sides of which, he says, were called truth and revelation.[3]

The Choshen (חשן) was a four-cornered gorget worn on the breast of the high-priest. The four corners denote the Aft (Eg.), the abode, and form the square to the circle as in the quadrangular Kaer. The four-cornered gorget, set with twelve precious stones in gold, is best explained by the Egyptian Khu for the four corners, the four supports of the heaven, or circle of the four quarters, and Shen the circle itself. This is supported by the number of the stones which, according to Josephus and Clemens Alexandrinus typified the zodiacal circle, the circle of the Two Truths, whence the Shen or Pshent, the double crown, or Khu-Shen, the circle of the four corners.

The Machashebeth (מחשבת), rendered cunning work, has in Hebrew the meaning of work wrought with skill and art, it is also applied to the strong work of fortification ;[4] Egyptian will tell us more. KHESBET (Eg.) is the name of wrought iron. But the typical KHESBET is the lapis-lazuli stone, the blue, the symbol of heaven. Ma (Eg.) means true, truth, the goddess of the Two Truths, and Ma-Khesbet (Eg.) reads the true lapis-lazuli, an Egyptian expression which distinguished the real from the artificial. Khesbet is also written Khesba for blue and for lapis-lazuli. This is the form of Kesheb, the name of the curious girdle worn by the high-priest, which Josephus states the Jews had learned from the Babylonians to call Amia ; probably another form of Khesba-Ma, the true blue, the

[1] Lep. *Denk.* iv. 71, A.   [2] *Select Papyri*, xxxiii. 5.
[3] *Vit. Mos.* iii. 2.   [4] 2 Chron. xxvi. 15.

real foundation. Kes softens into Hes; and in the Huzzab of Nahum we have an obvious allusion to this Egyptian basis. Huzzab shall be ungirdled and made naked. Huzzab was a personification of the one established on what had been held to be the foundation of truth, whose signs were the Aseb Seat, the Kesheb-ma of Egypt and the girdle Kesheb in Israel. One form of the Khesbet-Ma was worn by the Egyptian judges, and consisted of a figure of Ma carved in lapis-lazuli. Ma represented the dual of truth, and with the feminine article prefixed to her name we have Tema, to distribute justice, whence the Greek Themis, the goddess of justice. Ma, who made justice visible (Tema), was herself depicted blind, or as seeing with insight. The Egyptian twin-total is TEMT, with the ideograph of the two halves made one whole.

In the time of Philo and Josephus it was a matter of dispute with the Jews what the Urim and Thummim were. According to Philo, they were two small images, one of which was emblematic of revelation, the other of truth. Tema, in Egyptian, is the true. Precious stones also are Tameh, and Temes signifies a plate or written tablet. The two feathers of Ma, the goddess of Truth and Justice, would, in the Hebrew plural, render the word Thummim as the total of Two Truths. This exists as תמים for the whole, entire, a whole year; which, according to Jewish reckoning, consisted of two halves. Thummim is perfect and truth,[1] rendered Aletheia (Truth) by the Seventy. The perfect is the double (Tem) or twin truth. Rabbi Nehemiah said, "Every place where it is said 'cunning-work,' there were two figures; in the needle-work there was one figure only."[2] Rameses III. says to the god Ptah, he who created, with Ma, or truly: "I made thee a good breast-plate (Uta) of the best gold, of Katmer (and) silver made with a setting of MEH and of real lapis-lazuli, to be united to thy limbs on thy great throne of the horizon, and the company of the gods of the house of Ptah, who rest in them."[3] Meh is either a precious stone, or inlaid work; may be inlaid stones, or inlayings of precious stones. The Uta, or breast-plate, also denotes the symbolic eye (one form of which is Ma), and means to speak, give forth a voice, like the Hebrew oracle of Urim and Thummim. The lapis-lazuli typifies the blue heaven as the throne of the god who was the lower sun known as Tum and as Af-Ra. Now the Afrim (or Aurim, Urim) is certain to belong to the Thummim of Ma, and as the one represents the perfection of the twin Truth, the other must be solar, relating to the Tum cult of Egypt. Tum, the great judge of the dead, was the sun in the Hades. The breast-plate was that of משפט (Mishpat), or judgment. Tum, sitting in judgment, is accompanied by Ma, the goddess of Thummim. Atum is one with Adonai. Therefore we

---

[1] Amos, v. 10.   [2] *Mishna*, Treatise 18, ch. iv
[3] *Great Harris Papyrus*, pl. 47, 5.

infer that the Afrim belonged to the Af sun that crossed the waters of the under-world. The two figures then would be the red sun Atum, and Ma, the goddess of the Two Truths.

MATSUI RISHON is an ancient name of the Hebrew divinity, said to signify the primary being. RES (Eg.) means the absolute, and UN is being. SHUI (Eg.) is light and shade; the sign of these is the feather of Ma, the truth, with two aspects. MAÃT denotes the Two Truths. Thus MATSUI RISHON is the absolute being as divinity of the dual truth, signified by the feather of Ma, who in the solar cult is creatoress with Adonai or Atum.

It has been denied that there was any female to the Hebrew deity's nature. No Beltis, it has been said, to the Hebrew Baal! But that was implied in the Shekinah, and in the ark of the tabernacle, which was the same symbol as the ark or tabernacle of Ishtar or Beltis, the Baris of Isis, or any other form of the creatoress. The Hebrew imagery being Egyptian, symbolism will tell us more than the written and often re-written letter of the word.

"The women of Israel," we read, "made Beth for the ASHERAH." [1] The word Beth, rendered "hangings," is house in the margin. The Asherah read by Egyptian is the Aser-ah; Ah is the house, and Aser, the tamarisk, a form of the ever-green tree. In Hebrew the Eshel (אשל), according to Fuerst, is a tamarisk. [2] Thus the Eshel is the Egyptian Asru. Neither of the versions nor interpreters have identified this special tree. The Aser-Ah is the tree-house, the grove of the translators, presented to view in the Assyrian Asherah.

It was in a thicket of tamarisk, as described by Plutarch, that the floating ark of the child Osiris was caught, and the tamarisk grew up into a large and beautiful tree, inclosing the child in the heart of it; and the tree became a post or pillar in the palace of the Phœnician Malkarthos and Astarte or Saosis. [3] Asar-Ah is the house of Osiris, the son (Ar) of As or Isis, the house being typified in this instance by a tree. The tree-house was the compound symbol of the genitrix, who was the abode, the tree being one type of the dwelling. The tree-house corresponded to the duality of the nature of the great mother, whose name in the plural is Asheroth. Asherah was known as a Phœnician goddess, whose image was the tree or pillar. Such, it may be hinted, is the meaning of the Asherah, about which much further information has to be adduced. Here it may be pointed out how Asherah is a Phœnician development of the name of Asar in relation to the goddess Asherah. The name of As-ar already contained the tree and house personated by Isis. Ar is the son of, and As (or Hes) means the house, abode, chamber of birth. The tree of Isis was the Ash, the

---

[1] 2 Kings xxiii. 7.   [2] Gen. xxi. 23
[3] Of Isis and Osiris.

Persea tree of life, and her child as Asar is the son of the ash or the house, long before the mother was designated Asherah.

The Beth, rendered hangings, was the tent of the nomads, the Ahal (אהל), an early form of the habitation or hall. Ah (Eg.) is the house, dwelling-place, stable; the Egyptians were beyond the tent. Al (Ar) is the child. Now, if we render the Ahal the habitation of the child, it will show how the same word can signify people, race, family, as the אהליוסף people of Joseph,[1] the child, plural children, of the AH, as the tent; they who were Nomads.

Ahlah (Aholah), a symbolical name for Samaria, likewise means the tent. Alah is a goddess, the habitation of the child, and in her the tree and abode meet under one name. The Alah tree, whichever species, is the same emblematically as the Ashel. Thus the Hebrew goddess Alah is one with Asherah. The tabernacle[2] is the Beth. So also is the inward of the Ephod.[3] The Beth is elsewhere the palace of the king, the divine house. Bu-t and Peht, in Egyptian, denote the uterus. In Hebrew, Beten (בטן) is the womb or inside. Clement gives a curious rendering of the meaning of Thebotha (the ark), as " one instead of one in all places." This is the Egyptian Teb, to be responsible for. It was a representative symbol, and is assuredly responsible for representing the female nature of the Hebrew deity. The Egyptians built their Baris of the gum acacia tree,[4] the tree of Khem, the tree of life. The name of it is Kamai, and Ka is male, Mai, sperm: whence the word gum. The Hebrew ark was built of the same wood. In the hieroglyphics the acacia is Ash. In Hebrew, Shittah (שטה) answers to Ash-tah (Eg.), the acacia wood of the ark (Tah, a boat). The Shetah, when made, is the Egyptian ark, chest, box, sarcophagus, a symbol of the most mystical, secret and hallowed nature, that imaged in one the womb and the tomb. We are told that the ark of testimony contained a pot of manna and the rod that blossomed. This rod or staff is the Matteh (מטה). It was the Matteh of Moab that was broken with his horn, as derisively described by Jeremiah;[5] the Matteh of Moses and Aaron which swallowed the serpents, and caused the Red Sea to divide in twain for the passage through it. The nature of this Red Sea and serpent will be made apparent in the myths. We have now to do with the Matteh, the potent conqueror of the opposing power as typified by the serpent and the Red Sea, which was sacredly preserved in the itinerating tabernacle of Jah. The Matteh is Egyptian, as the MATA of the hieroglyphics, the Phallus.[6] The Matteh being the

---

[1] Psalm lxxviii. 69.   [2] Ex. xxiii. 19 and xxiv. 26.   [3] Ex. xxxix. 19.
[4] Herod. ii. 96.   [5] xlviii. 17.
[6] This was a type of resurrection in the Egyptian eschatology, the image of Khem-Horus as the sun or the risen soul on the horizon. The sexual symbolry is as ancient as it is primitive; for instance, the same type has been found, in France, incised by the men of the Palæolithic age and Art, on a deer's-horn that was buried beneath ten feet of stalagmite, and in all likelihood this was a figure of resurrection with the cave-men as it was with the Egyptians and Hebrews.

male image, it follows that the pot of manna was a feminine symbol, and the two sexual types of source were the tokens of the divine presence. This ark was the holiest of all, placed in the holy of holies behind the second veil.[1] The Egyptians, as Mariette has discovered, used to keep their type of this dual deity in the *sanctum sanctorum* in the shape of the Ankh emblem of life and of pairing. Ankh is identical with coupling and joining together. The Ankh, like the neck and ankle, denoted the join.

We can identify the particular form of the Two Truths by the aid of the imagery as those belonging to the mother and child. There was no fatherhood in the earliest religion or symbolism. The rod that budded is the Renpu (Eg.), the branch, the sign of the young one, the nursling of the virgin mother. In Egyptian, Rennu means the virgin, and Rennut was the virgin mother personified. Her Renn was the nursling and the budding branch, the Renpu was the symbol. The mother and the male child are signified by the pot of manna, and the rod that budded. The sanctity of the Hebrew symbol was so great as to be divinely vindicated by miracles of murder. Nor need we marvel at the watchful jealousy when we know what the manna was!

The MISHKAN is used by Isaiah [2] in place of the Egyptian Karas for the sepulchre or place of the mummy; the ark being a type of both womb and tomb, birth and re-birth.

The Qeresh of the tabernacle of testimony, rendered "boards," is employed in an external sense. Its use for the deck of a ship and for benches shows that it could not be limited merely to boards. To judge by Egyptian, the Qeresh of the tabernacle or portable sanctuary was in Egypt a form of the ark itself. The Karas is the place of embalmment, the coffin of the mummy, and in Hebrew [3] the Karas is the belly. KHA-RESH (Eg.) would be the temple of the belly, *i.e.* the womb. "Beloved of the Adytum, come to KHA," cries Nephthys to Osiris. "Thou who comest as a child each month, to spread the water of thy soul, to distribute the bread of thy being, that the gods may live and men also," says Isis.[4] The god came in the monthly course of feminine periodicity to Kha, to the Karas, to the Adytum, or holy of holies, also under the type of the young moon. This was why the Mishkan, the Jewish tabernacle, had ten curtains, the number of lunar periods that were veiled or curtained round during the nine solar months of gestation, just as we find the Assyrian Asherah with thirteen signs to the circle of the year. There is in all nature but one possible origin for this reckoning. Ten feminine periods curtained round signify the creative work, in the physiological phase.

The people of Israel are said to have swerved from the straight

---

[1] Heb. ix. and Ex. xvi. 33, 34.   [2] xxii. 16.   [3] Jer. li. 34.
[4] *Records of the Past*, vol. ii. pp. 122, 123.

path, become corrupt, and made a "molten image."[1] The same "molten image" was worshipped in connection with the high places by the people of Canaan.[2] Hosea[3] says of the Israelites, "And now they sin more and more, and have made them molten images," and "say of them, Let the men that sacrifice kiss the calves." These were the calves of gold,[4] the same as the molten calf of the Exodus. The "molten image" thus identified with the calf of Israel's worship is the Meschah, the feminine fount called the "lying teacher."[5] This image has been identified with the Egyptian Meska, called the place of birth. MES is birth, and Ka is the type, the seat, tail; Kha, the vagina type; Mest, the sexual part (feminine). In the earlier times the deity of Israel had given to the people the pattern of a tabernacle of testimony, the symbol of the divine dwelling-place, the "tabernacle of Shiloh," afterwards deserted by the divinity. This was called the MISHKAN. Now, the Egyptian Meskhen is a variant of the Meska, and both designate the same thing, the birthplace, the habitation of the child. In the eschatological phase the Meska, or Meskhen, is the place of purgatory and spiritual re-birth in the Akar of Hades. This, too, appears as the Mishkan, or dwelling-place of the wicked in the under-world.[6] The Mes-khen (Eg.) is the interior birthplace or the womb. It was the habitation personified in Isis by the sacred calf, the heifer, Hes; by the cow-headed goddess Hathor, and by Ahti (the womb), a goddess with the head of a calf and body of a hippopotamus. The calf or cow in Egypt was made of gold or gilded; the "golden Hathor" is a gilded heifer. The cast-out Meschah of the later religion was the same image with the Mishkan of the earlier, and had the same significance. Both represented the feminine creatory, the object of worship when religion was in a very primitive phase, but when the cast image or manufactured ark had superseded naked nature, the calf was kissed, or the hindward face of the divinity of the witches Sabbath, instead of the living likeness of Hathor or Ahti.

The root of both Meskhen and Shekinah may be found in the Khen or Skhen (Eg.), the place, hall, bosom, womb, abode of breath. Skhen means to give breath to, sustain, make to alight, as the bird of the waters. The M (Eg.) adds the mother to Skhen, and AH (Eg.) the feminine abode. The Skhen, Meskhen, or Shekinah imaged the birthplace as a natural prototype of the dwelling-place for the presence of creative power. The prophet Jeremiah[7] prohibits the use of the word MESA (משא) applied to the deity. It is to be ignored utterly. "The Mesa (burthen) of Jahveh shall ye mention no more."[8] When people ask what they mean by the burthen of Jahveh and they say in reply, "What burthen?" they are to be forsaken.[9] "As for the prophet, and the priest, and the people that shall say, The burden of

---

[1] Deut. ix. 12.   [2] Num. xxxiii. 52.   [3] xiii. 2.   [4] 1 Kings xii. 28 ; 2 Kings x. 29.
[5] Hab. ii. 18.   [6] Job xviii. 21 ; xxi. 28.   [7] Chap. xxiii.
[8] Ver. 36.   [9] Ver. 33.

Jahveh I will even punish that man and his house." [1]   If the burden of Jahveh be mentioned, Israel is threatened with being utterly forgotten and God-forsaken and becoming an everlasting reproach, a perpetual shame.[2]   Why is this ?   The word MESA in Hebrew means a burthen and to bear, and has some indefinite relation to revelation and the utterance of oracles.   Egyptian will tell us the rest.   The bearing and the burthen are those of gestation.   MESA (Eg.) signifies to engender, conceive, bear, and bring forth the child.   The divinity who bears the burthen of the child, must include the feminine nature, and it has to be shown that the Jehovah of the Genesis was the Genitrix and not a male deity at all.   Jehovah was the Hebrew great mother who bore the burden of her child, and in the later stage of religion, when Jahveh was worshipped in the image of the male, such words as MESA were a reproach ; they were a reminder of the Meska or Meskhen, the symbol of the birthplace.   The Hebrews had not " perverted the words of the living God," but were simply using the words in their original sense, which jarred on the later consciousness.

Maimonides says the chariot seen in Ezekiel's vision was called the Merkabah.   Merkab (מרכב) is a chariot, the chariot of the sun, an emblem of solar worship[3] and of the cherubim.[4]   In the Song of Solomon, it is a seat belonging to a chair.   The seat and chariot are symbols of the genitrix, Kefa, or Chavah, the goddess of the Great Bear, who was the bearer before chariots were invented.   When invented, the chariot is called by the name of Urt, and Chavah or Khab, yet extant as the cab.   Mer (Eg.) is a circle ; Mer-Chavah is the circle of Khab, the Great Bear.   Mer-Kab (Heb.) means a range of space, and this was the circle of the seven stars.   Mer-Kab (Eg.) is the circle of going round in the figurative chariot or bark of the gods in which they rode, as the seven Kabiri or Rishis.   Kabni (Eg.), English cabin, is a name of the ship as the chariot of the waters.   The first form of the chariot, seat, boat, or bearer, was the hippopotamus, Khab, the Hebrew Chavah.   The doctrine of the Merkabah was a great mystery in the hidden wisdom of the Kabala.   The patriarchs are denominated the chariot-throne of the Lord.   These, like the Oans, Rishis, and Kabari, were only seven in number at first, and will be shown to have been the seven of the chariot (Ursa Major).   Maru-Kabuta is an Egyptian name for the chariot.   Ta is the boat, and to go in a boat.

The pillar set up by Jacob is called a Matzebah ; the word is also rendered images, standing images, a statue or pillar of Baal.   "He put away the Matzebah of Baal."[5]   "They broke down the Matzebah of Baal."[6]   The word is also written with the Egyptian terminal Matzebat.   This is the Masteba or Mastebat.   The same variation is found in Mitzraim and Mestraim.   The Hebrew צ repre-

---

[1] Jer. xxiii. 34.   [2] Ver. 40.   [3] 2 Kings xxiii. 11.
[4] 1 Chron. xxviii. 18.   [5] 2 Kings iii. 2.   [6] 2 King iii. 57

sents the Zet or a Tes, which became both T and S; hence the permutation. Matzebah reads, as Egyptian denotes, an enclosure of the dead. And as Sabat is the pyramid of Sut, the pillar-form answers to the pyramid. The Phœnician מצבה was a funeral monument, and one of these memorial stones was erected by Jacob over a grave.

Now, the Mastebahs of the ancient empire were a kind of pillar or pyramid tombs. The Mastebah is described by Mariette (previously quoted) as a sort of truncated pyramid built of enormous stones, and covering with a massive lid the well at the bottom of which reposed the mummy.[1] But to the Eygptian mind, re-birth was not only synonymous with death, it took the place of it, and in the form of Mes-tabah, birth (Mes) takes the place of death (Mut), and Mastebah is the sarcophagus or coffin considered as the place of re-birth. The Teba or Tabah is not limited to the box or chest. It is also the ark of the waters. This represented in a living form was Teb, the water cow, and goddess of the seven stars; the cow preceding the ark and box as a type. Teb or Tep means primordial, the first, and the Teb-ah, or first abode, the womb, was the model of the tomb as the place of re-birth; hence Mes-tabah. The womb Ah-ti is the dual or reduplicating house, and such in the eschatological sense was the Mastebah, the Tebah of re-birth.

The Mastebah was the image of the genitrix, hence the Beth of Al (Bethel), the house of Al (or Ar, the child), hence also the name of Luz,[2] "at first"; Laz being the goddess, consort of Nergal and the Arabian Venus, Egyptian Resh, as a name of the temple. Al, the child, is Baal,—the prefix representing the Egyptian article, and the pillar of Baal is the Matzebat or Mastebat,—Bar-Sut, whose name is written with the pyramid sign. Thus the Hebrew pillar was one with the pyramid, and it was the symbol of Baal, as the other was the sign of Sut, the Bar or Baal of Egypt. The Sphinx was an emblem of the same twofold nature, and the Mastebah of the Sphinx is thus identified with the truncated pyramid and the Hebrew pillar as the place of re-birth. The conical pillar is a well-known emblem of Venus Genitrix. The present point, however, is to identify the imagery as Egyptian and Typhonian, belonging to the primal worship of the mother and child.

The pyramid of Sakkarah has seven steps; the Great Pyramid seven chambers; the temple of Seti at Abydus, seven sanctuaries. One of the two stones of the Druids was the Seven-stone or Syth-stone, called also the Yoni-stone; the stone of the Hebrew deity has seven eyes.[3] The origin of this number seven will be found in the seven stars of the Great Bear or Typhon. Seven, in Egyptian, is Hepti (interchangeable with Khepti and Sebti, Suti or Sut). The pyramid, the pillar, the stone then were types of Sut-Typhon, in whom

---

[1] *Monuments of Upper Egypt*, p. 73. [2] Gen. xxviii. 19.
[3] Zech. iii. and iv.

are summed up the mother and child. The stone is an ideograph of Sut-Typhon. Stone-head and Stone-face are characteristic epithets of Typhon, and the stone as pillar and Seven-stone is the symbol of the Hebrew divinity Jehovah. Also the stone of Jacob, the stone of Israel,[1] represented the deity of Jacob. In the same passage the stone and shepherd are synonymous, " the shepherd, the stone of Israel," and in Egyptian the stone memorial, Mena, and the shepherd are identical by name, whilst, in the feminine form, Menat is the bier, the couch of the dead, and the birthplace as Menat the nurse. The stone is the ideograph of Jehovah.

A city otherwise unknown is mentioned[2] as the M'tzoba of Jah (מצביה); that is, the birthplace or lying-in chamber in which the Hebrew solar god, Adonai, was born, as son of the great mother.

The Hebrew REPA, to bind about, put on a bandage, bind up, represents the Egyptian arp, a bundle, to bind round, bind up. This word is also used[3] in the sense of making the land to bloom again (ארצידרפא). To this answers ARP (Eg.), the flower, or to flower. A variant of Arp is Rep, to grow, bud, and bloom. Words like this carry with them most ancient divine doctrines and personifications called divinities.

REPA, to bind up, to heal, to comfort, is related to the Egyptian Repa in person. In Egypt the Repa was the royal son, the heir-apparent, the hereditary highness, also the divine son, who came to heal, restore, redeem, and save. He was the mystic branch that brought to bloom again, the young shoot of the old tree who furnished the רפא, who is the binder-up, the healer, the physician, the Æsclepios of mythology, and the Comforter of the Hebrew writings. Seb (Kronus), the youngest of the gods, was also called the veritable Repa of the gods, as the son who manifests the eternal in time, the comforter through continuity, the restorer by reproduction, the healing one and saver by repetition of the cycle. The vine was one symbol of this Repa-ship or sonship. Bacchus carries or impersonates the vine. In Egyptian Arp (Rep) is the name of the vine, and of the wine produced from it.

The feminine Repa (Repit) was the goddess of harvest, the periodic reproducer personified as the great mother. The harvest was a form of the annual healing with which the land was made to bloom again, a type of the seed, the comforter, the fulfiller of promise, like the bud, branch, vine, or offspring, the so-called son. Another personification was Repi, the feminine Nile, also a type of periodicity, on account of the inundation.

In parts of France and Germany the tree is still borne, gaily decorated, on the harvest-home load, to be planted for one year

---

[1] Gen. xlxi. 24. [2] In 1 Chronicles xi. 47 (LXX. Vulgate).
[3] 2 Chron. vii. 14.

on or near the master's house, and to be replaced the following year. That is the sign of Rep and the Repas.

It explains nothing whatever to say that the Messiah or Kristos means the anointed. How, when, where, by whom can a son of God be anointed? The doctrine of the divine sonship has to be explained before such names have any proper significance. Enough for the present to show how the Messiah is Egyptian, and where we must seek for the obscure root of the matter, and get it related once more to the phenomenal fact from which names have been so long and completely divorced. Mes (Eg.) means to anoint and to be engendered. Mes is the child, the begotten child of the father. Horus, the Messiah, is called the only-begotten of the father. The root of this matter lies in a doctrine absolutely unknown to the expounders of Scripture.

The first Divine Son in mythology was not the true Anointed; was not the Begotten of the Father. Sut had no father, hence in the development of the doctrine he had to become his own father and was said to do violence to his own mother. This character is the original type of the solar god. The Elder Horus had no father, but was the child of the mother. The feminine terminal in the name of KHART (Har-pi-Khart) shows him to have been the son of the woman. It was the Second Horus who was the Begotten of the Father, the Karast one or Christ of the anointing, re-begettal, re-generation, and resurrection.

The doctrine descended from the time when the Fatherhood had not been individualized on earth, therefore could not be represented in heaven, and the Virgin mother and child were the sole types of Deity. It is easily understood on its own natural ground. But when reproduced by modern theology these primitive ideas are like the fabled giants of old; they stand up against the dawn and cast across the world the shadows that have darkened all our mental day.

To anoint and to be begotten are synonymous. Both meanings were united in the Messiah of mythology. If we read the יה of משיח as the divine name, the Iah or Iach of the Psalmist, " B-Iah is his name,"[1] then MES, the child, the son, the anointed, engendered, begotten, enables us to identify the Messiach as Iach the anointed, the begotten son of the father, the equivalent of Mesiata, an Egyptian deity whose name indicates the typical or anointed child.

Some of the commentators amongst the Jewish Rabbis, who have expounded the sense of the prediction in Zechariah,[2] " I will bring forth my servant the branch," have argued that this was the Messiah, because the name, Mencham (מנחם), the comforter, a name of the Messiah used by the Talmudists, and the word Tzema (צמה), the branch, contain letters of the same numeral value. It is exceedingly likely that the figurative language was thus read in figures. For instance, the word Messiach (משיח), contains the number 358 in its letters. And,

---

[1] Psalm lxv. 5.   [2] Chap. iii. 8.

in Egyptian, Masiu is the night of the last day of the year, and the evening meal of the first day of the new. These are the Masiu. Mas means the child, birth, anointed, and Iu is two. Two days were thus devoted to the new birth or Mas, and with the number 358 these complete the number of days in the Egyptian year, 360. The Messiach, the child, anointed, born as Iach in Israel, was born every year in Egyptian myth. The branch is the hieroglyphic sign of one year. Mencham, however, has another relation to the branch than this. In Egyptian Menkam is a kind or quantity of wine,[1] with the Bacchic branch of the vine for its determinative; the branch and comforter in one! It is the vine on its props, therefore the sustaining branch, as was the Messiah son, who as Horus, is called the substance and supporter of the father.

The words in Genesis,[2] IBA SHILOH (יבא שילה), rendered Shiloh shall come, are much increased in vigour by the Egyptian Uba, to pass through to the other side in spite of opposition; to work the way through as the PASSER (gimlet). The Shiloh, in Egyptian Serah, is the revealer, the consoler; and Uba is a deity, him who passes through or is bound to come. Khem-Horus is called the PASSER. The Shiloh was the RETURNING one. HEB (Eg.) for the Ibis, the messenger, means to return. Whether stellar, lunar, or solar the Shiloh was periodic.

The Mesuauth is the Talmudic name of a fire-signal made by the Jews at the time of new moon. Mesu is birth. At corresponds to the Hebrew word for sign and signal. At is also the time-circle, the round; the earlier Aft denotes the circle of the four quarters of the moon. Meshu (Eg.) signifies to turn back. Thus the Mesuauth is the sign of new moon, as the turner back, the returner of the four quarters.

In the Mishna the names of God in the Scriptures are termed Azkeruth (אזכרות), and the signification, "name of God," as the highest and holiest has arisen out of sacrifice. הזכיר means to sacrifice.[3] In Egyptian, the victim bound for the sacrifice is the Kheri. The Kher, or Har, was the son, word, Logos. With the feminine terminal T, this is the Khart, the child, as son of the mother. Har-pi-Khart, the child, was one great type of the sacrificial victim in the solar myth, as the sun of autumn equinox and winter solstice, that descended and diminished, suffered and died to rise again as the younger Har, the sun of the resurrection. As is sacrifice; one possible reading of the name of Asar (Osiris) is the sacrificial son, and in one character Osiris was the saviour victim. Kheri (Eg.) denotes this victim bound for the sacrifice both in the human form and as the cow. The cow, Hes, was an early type of the mother, and the calf was offered up as her child. The HESM is the spot of sacrifice. Hes (As) was the sacred calf adored as Isis. The Kheru

---

[1] *Denkmäler*, ii. 129.   [2] Chap. xlix. 10.   [3] Is. lxvi. 3.

(calf-victim) with As, sacrifice, is the As-Kheru, which in a plural Hebrew form becomes אזכרות (Azkeruth).   The origin and doctrine of blood-sacrifice, and its relation to deity, will be explained in the " Typology of Sacrifice."   But it may here be pointed out that the Khar or Har, the child, a type of sacrifice, was also the RENN, the nursling, and RENN signifies the Name.   Thus the name of God is equivalent to the son who was the sacrificial victim, or Kheri personified as Har-pi-Khart, the child of Isis, and Egyptian shows us how the name of God becomes identical with the divine sacrifice When, in the Egyptian Mythos, the setting sun-god *prepared his generation* for next day's or next spring's re-birth, that was the MASS or MES, as much as ever it is in Rome ; the MES of sacrifice, the prototype of the Roman Mass called the sacrifice of the Christ, the dead body, which was typified of old by the raw flesh, bread without leaven, or the bloody wafer.   The setting sun was the victim and the sacrifice ; in the physiological sense, the blood of which the flesh was formed for the new birth.   Hence the bloody sacrifice of the Spanish MISA, for the Mass.   The bloody wafer, raw flesh, and unleavened bread were types of this sacrifice, and in German MAZE is a name of unleavened bread.   The living Mes (Eg.) signifies the generative spirit, still typified by the wine of the Eucharist, the blood of the grape, Bacchus, or the vine, the branch of the new life.   This will be sufficient to prove that Egypt has much to tell us respecting the fundamental nature of the Hebrew scriptures and mythology.

SECTION XIII.

EGYPTIAN ORIGINES IN THE HEBREW SCRIPTURES, RELIGION, LANGUAGE, AND LETTERS.

ORIGEN says that all the neighbouring nations borrowed their religious rites and ceremonies from the Egyptians.[1] Sanchoniathon, according to Eusebius, expressly derives his cosmogony from the Egyptian Taht. He says: "These things are written in the cosmogony of Taautus, and in his memoirs, and from the conjectures and evidences which his mind saw and found out, and wherewith he hath enlightened us."[2] That is, he quotes from the Hermetic Books assigned to Taht, the divine scribe, the god of learning, the Egyptian Word, whilst speaking of Taautus as if he had been human. The Phœnicians derived their divinities, including Taautus, and their mythology, from Egypt, as will be made apparent in the course of the present inquiry. The Jews of Palestine were no exception to the rest of the neighbouring nations.

The Jewish historian, Basnage,[3] thought that the Hebrew Moses was a mythological character identical with the lunar deity Taht. Taht is the lord of the divine words, the scribe of truth, the manifester. Moses was the law-giver and mouthpiece of the Deity. Taht carried the shooting palm-branch of the panegyries; Moses the rod. One rod of Taht or Hermes was the serpent sceptre. The rod of Moses turned into a serpent. Taht wore the head of the ibis. The ibis, says Pliny,[4] was invoked by the Egyptians against the serpent. Moses, according to Josephus,[5] invented a wonderful stratagem whereby the army was saved from serpents by means of the ibis. Nevertheless, though the imagery be Egyptian, we shall find another divine prototype for Moses. Meanwhile it is intended to show that the psalmist David is the Hebrew form of Taht, the lord of divine words, the mouthpiece, logos, and scribe of the seven gods.

The name of David or Dud, (דוד) has the same significations as that of Taht. TUT means to unite, engender, establish; DUD, to

---

[1] In Epist. ad Rom. ii. 495. [2] *Cory*, Ed. 1876, pp. 3 and 4.
[3] *El Sched*, p. 109. [4] B. x. ch. xxviii. [5] Ant. ii. 10, 2.

unite, join together, bind, make fast, or establish.   Taht is the servant of RA, DUD is the servant of JAH.   The genealogy also tends to show their identity.

Taht is lord of the eighth region or region of the eight, Ashmuneim or Smen.   These eight have not been explained in Egypt where Taht had superseded Sut when the monuments begin.   According to the present reading, which will be substantiated bit by bit, the first seven of all mythology are the seven stars in Ursa Major, the primal type of a septenary of divinities.   These in one form are called the seven sons of Ptah, in another, of Sydik, and in the Hebrew form the sons of GAISH (עיש from עוש) who will be traced to the seven in the Great Bear, the Egyptian KHEPSH.[1]   Of these seven, whether considered to be one in the Genitrix, or seven, as the ARI (sons, companions), Taht, formerly Sut, was the manifester.   These seven furnished the seven TAAS, seven gods of the word or speech, and Sut (dogstar) or Taht (lunar god) was their word, speech, logos personified.   The seven are represented by Sefekh the consort of Taht whose name signifies No. 7 by which we know that as Taht was formerly Sut, Sefekh was the earlier Kep or Khepsh, and her name may read Sef, otherwise Kef, the Sieve being a well-known sign of alternation.   The eight then are composed of the septenary and the dogstar (Sut Anubis) or Taht, the later lunar manifester.

The Phœnician Esmun is the eighth to the seven sons of Sydik and Esmun is the same as Taht, lord of Smen, the region of eight.   It is now proposed to identify Dud with Taht, as the eighth, and David as the eighth son of Jesse with the manifester of the seven as the sons of Gaish.   An Egyptian deity appears in the Ritual by the name of AASH, who is the hard and immovable.   The Assyrian Assur, god of the eight rays, he who stands alone, probably derives from this beginning.   For Sydik is also known as the god of the eight rays.[2] Ash-ar is the son, Ar, of Ash, As or Hes, whose oldest form is that of the goddess of the seven stars, the son who was first represented by the dogstar.   The Hebrew form of AASH we take to be Jesse the parent of the seven sons, with David for the eighth.   This would identify David with Taht, Lord of the Eight, and the eighth region, both being mythological.   Jesse has eight sons, and as with the Kabiri, nothing is recorded of their mother, the father having taken her place.   Taht is the manifester and revealer.   So David reveals himself to Samuel who comes to select from the eight sons the one who is to be anointed.   Tut means unction, and Taht is the anointed of the Lord.   The imagery shows Jesse to be feminine. Jesse is identified with the serpent and the tree, both feminine symbols.   Jesse is called NACHASH, the serpent.[3]   The Targum to

[1] Job xxxviii. 32, and ix. 9.
[2] Gesenius, *Mon. Phœnician*, pl. 39 ; Movers, *Phœnicians*, p. 527.
[3] 2 Sam. xvii. 25.   Margin.

Ruth iv. 22 says Obed begat Ishai (Jesse) whose name is NACHASH, because there was not found in him iniquity or corruption.   And he lived many days until was fulfilled before Jahveh the counsel which the serpent gave to Chavvah (Eve) the wife of Adam, to eat of the tree of the fruit of which when they did eat they were able to discern between good and evil.   They make Nachash, the serpent, says Jerome,[1] to be another name of Jesse, because he had no sin except what he contracted from the original serpent, and thus David inherited none.   Strange reasons these for calling Jesse after the serpent !   There is more however in the word Nachash than the serpent.   Every one is familiar with the Greek tree of knowledge with the serpent twined round it, fawning and inviting the beholder to partake of the fruit.   In Egyptian the NEKA is the serpent of evil, Sanskrit Naga, the Nekiru or Devil of the African Yula dialect. Neka (Eg.) also means to provoke, play false, and delude.

The Egyptian tree of life is the Ash.   Thus the word NACHASH contains the Egyptian names of the typical tree and Typhonian serpent, which do not directly appear in the Hebrew.   The serpent and tree or stauros are inseparable according to the types.   Jesse has also descended to us as the tree of life (the ash or Persea fig-tree in Egypt) which was to produce the fruit and leaves of healing as an antidote to the serpent, and the fruit of the other tree.   The Jews had not preserved the legend quite correctly, nor had they the buried wisdom of Egypt to refer to as we have to-day.   Still Jesse as the tree of life from whose root the branch was to spring is preserved and the tree is for ever feminine as birth-giver to the branch.   The tree of Jesse with a genealogy is often to be seen in the reredos and east windows of English churches.   There is one at Dorchester in which Jesse is the recumbent root of the tree, and a list of twenty-five names culminates in that of Jesus the latest branch.   The branch of this tree is David.   So is Taht who carries the branch in his hand as his emblem, the branch being typical of the manifester.

Jamblichus [2] makes the remark that Hermes the god of learning and language was formerly considered as the common property of the priests, and the power who presides over the true science concerning the gods, is one and the same universally.   Hence our ancestors dedicated to him the inventions of their wisdom, inscribing all their own commentaries with the name of Hermes.   In Egypt these were assigned to Taht (Hermes), and David is the Hebrew Hermes or Taht.

There is an Egyptian form of the word Taht as Atet, speech, to speak, and this appears in the Hebrew ADUTH (עֵדוּת) the name of the revealed psalm ; [3] Taht or David being the revealer as scribe of the gods and lord of the divine words.   Indeed the Book of Taht is apparently quoted in Psalm xl. 7.   " Then said I, Lo, I come; in the volume of the book written of me."   Taht wrote the book of the

[1] Qu. Heb. in 2 Sam. xvii. 25.   [2] De Myst, i. 1.   [3] Ps. lx.

coming of the solar lord, Har (Horus), and this is one of the Psalms of David the Hebrew scribe of the Lord.

It is said of the " Lord " celebrated by David in the Psalms that " He shall stand at the right hand of the poor, to save (him) from the judges of his soul." [1] And in the Egyptian judgment Har, the lord, is the defender, intercessor, and saviour of the poor souls that have to pass the forty-two tribunals of their judges and the great judgment-seat of Osiris himself. Horus stands between them and the devourer of souls ; he appeals for them in a praying attitude with clasped hands, he who is called Horus the redeemer, the lord of life, the vicarious justifier of those whose lives were right.

Taht the moon-god is the lord of a place variously named Smen (Ashmuneim) Sesennu and Annu. It was the place of dispensing, purifying and preparing as Smen ; the place of agitation, distraction, torment, and change, as Sesennu, and the place of repetition as Annu. As Smen it was Sabean, as Sesennu it was lunar, as Annu solar. From the first it was the seat of the eight gods, the seven of the Great Bear and Sut ; the eighth being the manifester of the seven. When Taht superseded Sut he became the manifester of the seven, because lunar time had been established as truer than the time of the stars. At last the solar Horus was elevated to the divine supremacy and Taht was made subsidiary to the solar measurer of time and saviour of souls from the abyss. Taht the scribe and registrar kept the sacred records in this region, portions of which are said to have been written by the very finger of the god himself. Taht makes the invocations on behalf of the souls in Sesennu, and pleads their cause at the great tribunal. He is the Psalmist of the Egyptian Book of the Dead. On a coffin of the twenty-sixth dynasty, Horus the redeemer of souls in Sesennu, announces to the deceased that Taht himself has brought the books of the divine words or hermetic writings.[2] These books contained the utterances of the soul in its passage from earth, its transit across the Hades and ascent to the presence of the sun expressed by the Egyptian David.

Sesennu from Ses, No. 6, and Sen No. 2, reads No. 8, and is the region of the eight ; the ogdoad in divinities, and octave in music. In Hebrew six is shesh, and zen or shen represents the Egyptian sen, for two. The equivalent for Sesennu in Hebrew with the plural terminal "im," would be Sesenim or Sheshenim. This name is found in the title of Psalm lxxx. " To the chief musician upon SHESHENIM Aduth." In the heading to Psalm lx. it appears as " SHESHAN Aduth."

The Hebrew עדת, is a third form of ATET (Eg.) to speak, speech (Tet, Taht), and SHETU to recite and shout, or proclaim aloud (Sut being the earlier Taht). The thing uttered may be a law, precept, or a psalm. The Hebrew sheshen has the meaning of joy, which does

---

[1] Ps. cix. 31. [2] Lepsius, Abth. iii. Bl. 276.

not apply to these two psalms, one of which, in the A. V. is headed the "Miseries of the Church," and the other, "David prays for Deliverance." Neither of them contains any expression of joy. But may not this name indicate the Sesen or Sesennu of the region of Taht? These two psalms would then contain the utterances of Taht or David in the place of travail, wrestling, distraction, on behalf of souls that suffered from purgatorial pangs in the process of sloughing the clinging skin of the old life, and undergoing the pains of purification in Smen, awaiting and praying and crying for deliverance. Psalm lx. is ascribed to David "when he strove with Aram-Naharaim," which is the name of the Land of the Two Streams, in Mesopotamia, or in the Planisphere, where it is the region of the Two Waters of the celestial Nahar or Nile. That *was* the region of Sesennu in the astronomical allegory.

Sesennu or Smen (Ashmunein) was the place of preparing and re-establishing. The word SMEN means to constitute, make durable, fixed; to establish the son in place of the father. The Myth is alluded to in Psalm lxxx. verse 17, "Let thy hand be upon the man of thy right hand, upon the son of man (whom) thou madest strong for thyself." The son and the man of the right hand was Horus who was established in the place of the father in SMEN or Sesennu, *i.e.* Sheshenim.

We have seen that the SMEN of the Ritual, the region of the Dead, the Shades, the place of change, torment, preparation, salvation, and re-establishing of the mummy for the second life, is reproduced in the Hebrew אשמנים, plural, Eshmannim, of Isaiah,[1] as the desolate places of the dead in the netherworld; SESENNU is extant in the Hebrew plural form of SHESHENIM. Two Egyptian names for one and the same region are thus found in Hebrew. The sixth and the twelfth Psalms are inscribed "to the chief musician on Neginoth; upon SHEMINITH," in the margin "upon the eighth." The usual Hebrew forms of the word for the eighth are S'MONEH and SHMENI. SHEMINITH only occurs here, and in Chronicles xv. 21, and then in relation to music. The eighth of course suggests the octave, but beyond that meaning, Smen is the region of the eight great gods, and SHEMINITH, for the eighth, adds a third form of the name of the eighth region over which Taht was lord, the scribe, the psalmist, who gave utterance to the spirits there, or, as it is termed, wrote the Books of the Dead, fragments of which are contained in the Ritual.

The eight gods of Sesennu are thus addressed in the Ritual:[2] "*Oh, ye chief gods of Sesennu, greatest on the first of the month, less on the 15th!*" that is, in relation to the two phases of the waxing and waning moon. In the Hebrew *réchauffé*, the original subject-matter has been, to a great extent, divorced from the phenomena by which

[1] Ch. lix. 9, 10.　　　　　　　[2] Ch. cxvi.

alone it can be read, and thus it becomes invested with all the vastness of limitless vagueness, and all the sublimity of uttermost indefiniteness. The first of the two Psalms on the eighth region immediately precedes the one [1] concerning the Dabrai of Kush, or hinder part of the north. The cries from the depths uttered by the suffering soul, and written by the Psalmist David, are in keeping with those inscribed by the hand of Taht for the deceased when passing through the place of trouble, torment, agitation, and distraction (Sesennu). "O Lord! how long? Return, O Lord, deliver my soul; oh, save me for thy mercies' sake. Oh, let the wickedness of the wicked come to an end, but establish the just." The children of wickedness, the Typhonian conspirators, were strangled on the floor of Sesennu.[2] The great adversary of the sun and of souls was finally conquered in this place, which was also the Tattu of the solar myth, the region of establishing for ever. The cry for the Lord to return is the same as that of the Osirian deceased for Har, his lord, who is the sun that passes through the world of the dead to illumine the gloom of the shades, revivify the shadows of the dead and make a way for them, by opening the gates of the prison-house, into the land of eternal birth.

The 100th Psalm is still advertised as a Psalm of Taht, in Hebrew THUDH (תודה) the word rendered PRAISE and THANKSGIVING. To "publish with the Voice of THUDH"[3] is to proclaim with the voice of Taht, whose name signifies the mouth, tongue, speech, discourse, to speak, and tell, and who was the psalmist, glorifier, and thanksgiver personified.

Taht, the word, the male Logos, the Egyptian Psalmist, has for consort a GODDESS called the Mistress of the Writings.[4] Her name is written Sefekh, which signifies the No. 7. The present writer holds that she was a survival of the old goddess of the Seven Stars who was called the "Living Word" at Ombos, brought on in the lunar mythos as consort of Taht. In Hebrew the Sephr is a Master or Mistress of the Writings; a keeper of the rolls as well as the name of the Scribe and of the Writings themselves. The psalms are chiefly ascribed to David and Asaph, and these are equivalent to Taht and Sefekh, the Egyptian Lord of the Divine Words and the Mistress of the Writings. One meaning of Sefekh's name is to capture, register, keep; and in the Hebrew Asaph signifies to collect, gather up, gather together, store up. Asaph is the collector. Sefkh is the keeper of the writings. If David be the Hebrew Taht, it follows that the original of the Psalmist Asaph is Sef or Sefkh. Moreover the Jews have a work specially called Sepher or Sifre, of unknown age. It is often quoted in the Talmud as one of the most ancient sources. It is indefinitely older than the Mishna, although it was redacted later from

[1] Ps. vii.
[3] Ps. xxvi.
[2] Ch. xvii.
[4] Wilkinson, Pl. 54.

the oral tradition.[1] Probably this work preserves the name of Sef, the feminine scribe and secretary of the gods who is depicted as the writer, as well as named Mistress of the Writings.

Certain headings and titles of the Psalms are amongst the words most obscure to the Jews themselves. Some of these compositions are called MICHTAMS of David, rendered in the margin golden, *i.e.* goldenly-precious psalms. This is Egyptian. MAK is a composition, whence the Makar or composer, and TAM is the name of gold. Here a clue to the Egyptian origin is preserved.

Psalm vii. is entitled the SHIGGAION of David, the same word with the Egyptian terminal Shiggionoth is found Habakkuk iii. 1. Hebrew does not explain it.   The psalm begins "O Lord, . . . in thee do I put my trust . . . save me.   Establish the just." (v. 9.)

SEKHEN (Eg.) means to support, sustain, give rest. The Sekhent image is the PROP on which the heavens are established, also the double crown. The Prayer of David is to the SUSTAINER ; that of Habakkuk to the establisher who will make his feet firm in slippery places.

SKHENI is an Egyptian god who impersonates the prop as the two arms of Ra. He is the Egyptian Skambha. Osiris is likewise pourtrayed as the Skhen or Prop, in a personification of the divine Sustainer. The fundamental sense, however, of a psalm called שִׁגָּיוֹן may be found in SEKHENU (Eg.), to plead, to tell, to contest. It will therefore bear the sense of wrestling with in prayer, as the speaker does in the psalm.

Psalm lxi. is to the chief musician upon NEGINAH. According to Fuerst, NEGINAH means a song of derision in Psalms lxix. 12, and Job xxx. 9. Nekhi (Eg.) is derision, but if we read "I am thy derision,"[2] no song is demanded. So in Psalm lxix. 12, if we read I was the derision, (נגינה) of the drunkards there is no "Song," and in Lamentations iii. 14, if we should read "I was their derision ; their derision all the day," there is no "Song" or a song of derision has to be understood, which is only explained by NEKHI. Jeremiah says "I was a שְׂחֹק to all my people ; a נגינתם all the day."   He was a laughing-stock, and *probably* the subject of songs of derision, but the Egyptian clinches it.   The word NAKHNU (Eg.) denotes youthfulness and the young. This shows the word Neginah has more meanings than one. Thus the proper interpretation of Lamentations, v. 14, is possibly the YOUNG men have lost their youthfulness ; and that of Psalm lxxvii. 6, "I call to remembrance my youth," in the night, in antithesis to the previous verse, "I have considered the days of old."   The connection, however, between the musical instrument and youth is illustrated by the Nefer (Eg.), which is a viol, and the word Nefer denotes the youth, music being an expression of youthfulness and the voice of its spirit. NAKHEN (Eg.) also

---

[1] Deutsch, *Remains*, p. 66.   [2] Job xxx. 9.

signifies false, lapse, slaughter, destruction. Psalm lv. breathes slaughter against the Ziphim ; and this is one of the Neginoth. From which it follows that the title expresses various characters of the Psalms, although it became a general name associated with the musical instrument.

MASCHIL is a term found in the titles. Hebrew gives no primary account of the word, and it is usually derived from SAKAL, to give instruction. This is the Egyptian Sekher, to give counsel and instruct. But such is not the meaning of MASCHIL. We find it in a " Psalm of David, Maschil ; " [1] " To the chief musician, Maschil ; " [2] " For the sons of Korah, Maschil ; " [3] " To the chief musician upon Mahalath, Maschil ; " [4] " On Neginoth, Maschil ; " [5] " Maschil of Asaph ; " [6] " Maschil of Heman." [7] In this instance Maschil is synonymous with a Psalm or Prayer, which is a cry from the depths, like many of the Psalms :—

" I am counted with them that go down into the pit."
" Thou hast laid me in the lowest pit, in darkness, in the deeps."
" I am shut up, and I cannot come forth."
" Wilt thou show wonders to the dead ? "
" Shall thy loving-kindness be declared in the grave ? "

The speaker is in the MESKAR of the Egyptian Hades.

The Meska, Meskar, or Mesken (Eg.) are names of the birthplace and the eschatological place of rebirth, from Mes, generation and birth, whence the re-generation and re-birth of the Mes-iah. The type exists in the Hebrew MISHKAN, for the tabernacle, habitation, and dwelling-place, the MISHCHAR, for the womb of the dawn ; [8] and the MISHKAB, the couch, which is at once the bed of the living and the dead ; the womb and the tomb, as shown by the various texts. In the Ritual the place of re-birth for the deceased is also called the Meska, Meskhen, or Meskar. Now it will be shown that certain utterances for deliverance found in the Psalms are the same as those in the *Book of the Dead*, therefore we connect Maschil with the Egyptian Meskar. In this way. The Meskar, or purgatory, was the place in the Hades where the souls in bondage awaited and prayed for re-birth. They were in pain, in prison, undergoing the pangs of punishment. In Hebrew this is מסגר, the enclosing, imprisoning, whence a prison or place of confinement, the Meskar. Mas-kher (Eg.) is a cry of supplication for this re-birth in the Meskar, Meska, or Meskhen,—a Prayer or Psalm of the new birth. It may be noted that from the name of this Meskhen, or purgatory in the lower regions, comes the Hebrew Meschen, to be bowed down, low and poor; the state of being low and wretched ; the Maltese, Aramaic, and Arabic Meschen ; Italian, Meschino ; French, Mesquin ; Portuguese,

---

[1] Psalm xxxii.   [2] Psalm lii.   [3] Psalm xlv.
[4] Psalm liii.   [5] Psalm liv.   [6] Psalm lxxiv.
[7] Psalm lxxxviii. [8] Psalm cx. 3.

Mesquinho, and English Meskins.   The Maschil was the prayer or utterance from the depths, the Kars of the Hades.   The continual prayers for the sons of Qorah uphold the sense here assigned to Maschil.   Qorah was fabled to have been swallowed alive by the earth.   Prayers for the sons of Qorah are similar to those for souls in purgatory offered up by the Roman Church.

The blind and fumbling helplessness of the unskilled, the IDIOTES, in representing the myth as miracle, is at times very pitiful, as in this case of the sons of Qorah.   The name of Qorah in Hebrew signifies an accident, a sudden hap, such as was the fate assigned to the sons when the earth opened and swallowed them.   Qora denotes crying and calling.   KHERU (Eg.) means the evil ones, the fallen enemies. But the full form of the word is QORACH, unused in Hebrew, which means to FREEZE and STIFFEN with cold.   AKH (Eg.) denotes the dead, and QORACH identifies the dead below, in the KAR of the underworld, those who were cut off.   QORAH for baldness, has a derivative sense from cutting off the hair for the dead; the Sons of QORACH.   This group of Psalms utters the cries of those whom the earth has swallowed, just as it swallows the souls in the " Book of the Hades." [1]

In one of these (49) the speaker says, " My mouth shall speak of WISDOM "—that means according to the Gnosis—" I will incline mine ear to a Parable ; I will open my dark saying upon the harp."   This was one of the CHEEDAH or KHETU (Eg.), secret things, things shut and sealed to those who re-wrote the mythos as history.   In this psalm the sons of Qorah are the wicked who are laid like sheep in the grave for death to feed on, the unredeemed for whom there is no resurrection ; hence they are the sons of the house of hell.   " I remember thee from the hill Mitzar." [2]   Mitzar is the star of the Mest in the Great Bear, the type of the birthplace, and the speaker is in the place of re-birth.   " Thou hast sore broken us in the place of dragons, and covered us with the shadow of death." [3]   That is in the deep, the place of Apophis, the Hades to which the sons of Qorah had sunk.

One of these Maschils is a prayer of David when " the Ziphim came and said to Saul, ' Doth not David hide himself with us ? ' " [4] The Ziphim belong to mythology.   The Sefr is a gryphon or Typhonian genie.   Sephui is to torment, torture, punish.   Sef to refine by fire.   Shept denotes terror, terrible, to terrify, be demonial.   The speaker, like the Osirian of the Ritual, is passing through the world of the dead ; the Hebrew Sheol.

Psalm liii. is upon מהלת (Machalath or Mahalath) Maschil.   Mâha (Eg.) is the sepulchre, the enclosure of the dead.   RAT (Eg.) is the steps or staircase.   If we read Mak, a composition, the name would denote a Psalm of the Ascent, and the Makalath-Maschil would

[1] *Records of the Past*, vol. x.   [2] Ps. xlii. 6.
[3] Ps. xliv. 19.   [4] Ps. liv.

signify the prayer for re-birth uttered on the steps, well known to the *Book of the Dead*. Now the name given to fifteen Psalms, cxx. to cxxxiv., is in Hebrew "A Song of Ascents." The Hebrew מעלה means a step, ascent, degree, division, the plural being מעלות in the inscription of these fifteen Psalms, or songs of the steps, degrees, divisions of the ascent. עליה stands for מעלה[1] in the ascent of Solomon.

The translators and interpreters have had no clue to the nature of these fifteen steps or degrees, of which they have given accounts as divergent as they have been unsatisfactory; but they may be studied in the Ritual, where there are (apparently) thirty-six Seba or gateways in the great abode corresponding to the thirty-six Decans of the zodiac. They are divided into the numbers twenty-one and fifteen. Some of these look like repetitions, but all that concerns us at present is the fifteen gates of the ascent, which end at the place of putting on the upper crown on the day of the festival of the Adjustment of the Year,[2] at the time of the vernal equinox. This is the Makha, the level, the balance, place of poise, in the region of Annu, the sign of which is the upright " TEKHU " of the scales or Makhu. מעקה in Hebrew has a similar meaning, as the ledge of a level roof. This place of the equinox is also localized in the Hebrew Macha, the name of a region that bounded the East-Jordan land, and lay between it and the north. The Arru or Arrut (Eg.) are the steps, the staircase of the ascent from the underworld, and the god Osiris is pourtrayed as forming the prop (Skhent) of the balance placed at the head of a staircase, which men are ascending, as " Osiris, the lord of Rusta, the same who is at the top of the staircase."

In the Chaldee these Psalms are called a song that was sung on the steps of the abyss. This explanation is said to be founded on a Hebrew tradition,[3] which relates that when the foundations of the temple were being laid there came out of the earth a great quantity of water, to the *height of fifteen cubits*, which would have drowned the whole world, if Achitophel had not stopped its progress by writing the ineffable name of Jahveh on the fifteen steps of the temple. Psalm cxxx. is referred to the same event. The Hebrew tradition is but another name for Egyptian Myth. Fifteen cubits were the typical measure of an inundation.

The steps of the Abyss belong to the Ritual. The God Shu is depicted in hieroglyphic legends as standing on the steps of the Abyss, where, with uplifted arms, he sustains the sun and afflicts the race of the wicked in SMEN (Sesennu).

We shall draw a brief parallel between the fifteen gates in the Ritual and the fifteen Psalms of the steps. The first gate is that of the " *Mistress of Terrors ; the Mistress destroying those falsifying words.*"

[1] 2 Chron. ix. 4.   [2] Ch. 147.   [3] Calmet's *Dictionary*. Psalms.

The prayer in Psalm cxx., the first Step, is to be delivered from lying lips and a deceitful tongue. "What shall be done unto thee, thou false tongue?" "Woe is me," says the speaker, "that I sojourn in Mesech." Mesech is the equivalent Hebrew for MESKA, the place of purgatorial pain, or the purgatory of the Egyptian Ritual. This is supported by the black abodes of Kedar, or black enclosures of Kedar. CHEDAL is used by Isaiah for this world.[1] The Egyptian Khat is a secret abode, the womb of the tomb, the chamber of life or of death.

The second gate is that of the "*Mistress of Heaven and Regent of Earth, destroyer, mistress of created beings or producer of men, creator of all persons is its name. The name of its doorkeeper is Born of Ptah.*" Tum, who is the Great Lord of the Ritual, Lord of the Heaven and Earth, Lord of the doubled-seated Boat, is born of Ptah. In the Hebrew version it is the Lord of Heaven and Earth who is celebrated. "The Lord is thy Keeper."

The third gate is the "*Mistress of Altars, great one of sacrifices, delighting each god in it the day of passing to Abydus, is its name. Subduer is the name of its doorkeeper.*"

The parallel passage is, "I was glad when they said unto me, Let us go unto the house of the Lord." Jerusalem is here the mistress of altars and sacrifices. The going up of the tribes represents the passing to Abydus or Abti, where the double holy house of Anubis and the Pool of the Two Truths are found in the Ritual.

The eighth is a song of degrees for Solomon; it is in praise of children. "Children are an heritage of the Lord, happy is the man that hath his quiver full of them." And in the eighth gate of one series we find, "*Little One is the name of thy guardian.*"

In the ninth song the children are to be like olive plants. And the speaker in the ninth gate says, "*I hold a stick* (or branch) *of the palm tree,*" the type of renewal in the child, the Renpu.

The tenth gate is that of, "*Loud words, exciter of divisions greatly victorious Lord of fear. The name of its doorkeeper is Great Clasper.*"

On the tenth step the speaker says how they have afflicted him, and flowed over him, and made their furrows (divisions). For Great Clasper we have the metaphor of the Sheaf-binder.

The fourteenth gate is that of the "*Mistress of Exultation.*" The fourteenth of the fifteen Psalms begins exultingly, "Behold how good and how pleasant it is for brethren to dwell together in unity." Many more likenesses might be pointed out, but that the space can be better occupied. The present writer has no doubt that these deliverances of the fifteen steps belong to the fifteen gates of the house of Osiris, the Lord, or Atum, the older Divinity of the Ritual; their more perfect literary form is the sign of lateness; the original matter being Egyptian, written in the *Books of Taht.*

In the *Book of the Dead* the form is dramatic. The speaker

---

[1] Is. xxxviii. 11.

personates this or the other mythological character, and what he says is often the merest glancing allusion to the mass of doctrine and dogma, which was in the minds of all initiated readers. This makes the matter remote and the mode of utterance indefinite. So that we can better read the original at times in the plain personal and narrating form of the Hebrew copy. As an example, the spirit who speaks in Ch. 78 on the "turning into a Hawk the God of Time," that is the transformation of the Osiris, who rises as a Divine Hawk (Horus) at the time of the spring equinox, makes various allusions to things that occur in the process of the metamorphosis, the passage through the lower signs of winter as depicted astronomically, and to the deliverance, after passing through all perils and attaining the final salvation in the *peri-em-hru*, the coming forth with the day, or the "manifestation to light." He speaks of the one Lord, the adored, who is the support of the heavens, the establisher of the passage through the dark, the deluge, or death as the "Lord of Urei," the Lord of the Crown of Life, which had on it the two Asps. In this passage he goes through the sufferings of "*Osiris, the great and beloved soul, pierced to the heart by Sut*," that is Typhon, the betrayer of Osiris. In travelling the appointed course the terrors of death and the snares of hell or the hades encompass him. The mouths of the destroyers who lie in wait are said to "*Water for his annihilation.*" He is beset by the "*raging bulls.*" He has to pass and "*turn back the lions*," who are elsewhere called the "turners back."

He "*prays for means from the universal Lord*" to escape; "*Let me come forth and stand on my feet*" is his prayer. He is "*defended by Seb.*" He is "*set in his place*," delivered and preserved by the universal Lord on his Throne. In this chapter we have the subject-matter of the 22nd Psalm, and many of the causes of the speaker's "roaring," including the "bulls of Bashan." "Many bulls have compassed me, strong, of Bashan, have beset me round, they gaped upon me with their mouths as a ravening and a roaring lion. Dogs have compassed me; the assembly of the wicked have enclosed me; they fettered my hands and my feet. Save me from the lion's mouth, for thou hast heard me from the horns of unicorns." The deliverance is thus described in Psalm xviii. 19, 36: "He brought me forth also unto a large place." "Thou hast enlarged my steps under me that my feet did not slip."

The Unicorn, be it remembered, was the sign, we may say the Totem, of Sut-Typhon, and Sut was the wicked encloser of Osiris, the piercer of his brother, yea, his "own familiar friend," and the dogs in the *Book of the Dead* are the accompaniers of Shu, the Lord of Shual, as the punishers and devourers of the damned, the hounds of hades or hell. In the eighteenth chapter of the *Book of the Dead* the conspirators of Sut, he who betrays Osiris, the Egyptian Messiah, are said to transform themselves into goats, or the plural of the unicorn, or antelope, which was one of the types of Sut.

But there is a still more special application of the Egyptian imagery. In the Ritual we read, "*O Lord of the Great Abode, chief of the gods, save thou the Osiris (or my soul) from the god whose face is the Dog. He lives off the fallen at the angle of the pool of fire. Eater of millions is his name.*"[1] This is the dog-faced Mâtet. The Psalmist cries "Deliver my soul from the sword, my darling from the power of the dog."[2] This recalls to the student of the *Book of the Dead* the terrible block and the place of decapitation where the dog-faced deity, Lord of Gore, presides at the execution of the condemned souls.

The Hebrew Jached (יחיד) answers to the Egyptian Akhet, the spirit or manes. The prayer is for deliverance from the dog-faced deity.

The nets that were spread to ensnare the soul in passing through the hades are said to "*reach to heaven and stretch to earth.*"[3] The Papyrus of Nebseni in the British Museum shows the deceased walking away and escaping from a net which the ensnarer of souls had laid in his path to capture him.[4] The 154th chapter of the Ritual is designated the "Chapter of Escaping from the Net."

The dove was retained in Israel as the bird of breath, the type of the soul. In the Osirian cult the hawk was the symbol of the soul. The sun was depicted with the hawk-head, but in the twelve chapters of the Metamorphoses (Ritual, 76-88) the turtle-dove is one of the types into which Osiris or the deceased makes his transformation, and in the Psalms the bird is the dove or turtle-dove (תור), and the speaker exclaims in the solar character, "O deliver not the soul of thy turtle-dove unto the multitude (of the wicked). The multitude or assemblage are the SAMI, who seek to catch the bird of soul or of the sun in their nets. "*Oh catchers of the birds* (souls) *flying on the waters,*" says the deceased walking away from the net, "*do not catch me in them walking away from the earth. The Osiris comes forth and breaks them and goes free.*"[5]

The Psalmist[6] says, "Thou will not leave my soul in Shual; thou will not suffer thy Holy One to see corruption." The word translated holy one is Chasid (חסיד).

The Assyrian KÀSSUDI are the times of ascendancy or turning back of the moon. The first KASSUD of five days ascension in the lunation was given to Anu, the second to Hea, the third to Bel.

The word Khes (Eg.) means to turn back. The Khesr is the turner back or the returner. Khesat denotes the type of turning back in the circuit. KESA (Heb.) is applied to the new moon as one of the

---

[1] Ch. xvii. Birch.
[2] Ps. xxii. 20.
[3] Ch. cliv.
[4] *Vignette* (Pap. 9900).
[5] Ch. cliv.
[6] Ps. xvi. 10.

turners back or returning ones.[1]   The solar turner back is SHU, with the style of Shu-sa-Khes.   KES-KES is the Coptic name of Orion.   Kesil is a Hebrew name of Orion, who was a type of Sut-Har, and a form of whom was the Phœnician divinity Baal-Kaas, one of the starry turners-back, among the earliest observed in the cycle of the year.   The Kesilim, as the stars,[2] probably denote the returners.   All record of the cycles of time depended on these Kesilim or returners in their courses.

The Egyptian sense of Khes is also found in Hebrew as CHESM, to stop, to bar, to turn back, and in CHESAD to bend, crook, curve the neck, turn back.   One type then of this turning back or returning was the ibis, heron, or stork; and in Hebrew CHASIDAH (חסידה) is the name of the stork.   Now, the stork or ibis was the bird of Taht, the lunar god, the bird of return.   "*I return as the ibis among the spirits of the western place.*"[3]   The ibis, as a curious type of the turner back was reputed to administer the enema to itself.   Tâ is a stork or heron and a type; Khes, to return, makes the stork to be the type of returning, and this is the Hebrew Chasidah, the stork, or, we may parallel the Hebrew word with KHES (Eg.), to return, and TEH (Eg.), to tell, or with another name of the lunar god, TEKH, which has the meaning of FULL.   The bird alternates with the ascending moon on the body of Taht.   The Chasid is the returning one, and as Taht returned from the netherworld, Shu ascended from Shual, the Sun from the deep, the stork from over sea [4]—"the stork in heaven knows its appointed times for its passages to and fro"[5]—so the souls of the just were figured as turning back from below in the eternal round of light and shade, night and day.   That which returned again rose again as the sun ascended from the deep and the moon renewed its crescent shape and re-orbed for ever.   The spirits arose in the forms of human-headed ·birds.   The bird was an emblem of breath or soul.   The breath was the mover to and fro in the body, and in death its types, the bird and the feather, were clung to as emblematic of the spirit.   The Hebrew word Ghesr has the sense of moving to and fro as does the returning breath.   With us the goose is the Khesr, or returning bird, still associated with the festivals of returning time.   An Egyptian rendering of the bird of return is found in the form of the KHASHETU,[6] some kind of goose, which was a type of return in common with the stork or ibis, and as KHA means to return, and the Shetu is a goose as the SHET KAB, the SHETENRU, and the SHETENTEP, the Kha-Shetu may be taken for the bird of passage, as the returning goose.

Our goose is the KHES, and thus derives its name from being a bird of passage and return, and as the bird was the type of soul and

---

[1] Prov. vii. 20.   Margin.   [2] Is. xiii. 10.   [3] *Rit.* ch. lxxxv.
[4] *Lep. Denk.* ii. 25.   [5] Jer. viii. 7.
[6] Birch, *Arch.* (Society of Antiquaries), 35, 4, 85.

breath, so the goose is philologically one with ghost or gast (breath and soul) our bird of breath. The CHASIDAH is also the guest or returning visitor. As a bird, whether the hawk of Ra, the ibis of Taht, or the goose, the soul ascended from the lower world as the returning one. Taht, in his second type of An, is said to be created by Ra as the turner-back or returner, AN-AN. "I shall give thee to turn thyself,"[1] and there arose the Aan, as Taht's image in the north, his other type, that of returner, being the ibis. "Thou wilt not suffer thy CHASID to see corruption," is in the symbolic language, "thou wilt not permit thy bird of breath, the turner back, the returner, to die out in the dark dark land of death." Or still more touchingly, "Thou wilt not suffer thy typical returner not to return!" This goes far to identify the divine scribe DAVID with TAHT, the CHASID and scribe of the gods, as in other places it refers to the solar god. For instance, the CHASID of Israel is spoken of in the blessing of Moses. "And of Levi he said, Let thy Thummim and Urim be with thy CHASID whom thou didst prove at Massah, and whom thou didst strive with at the waters of Meribah."[2] The CHASID was the ever-returning one, the sun-god, the god of Jeshurun who rode upon the heaven in their help and in his excellency on the sky.

The word Chasid, however, is somewhat peculiar to the Psalms, and occurs in them twenty-three times. It is found only seven times in all the other books. The speaker is David, the Hebrew form of Taht.

Here is a perfect picture of Typhon, the wicked one. "He sitteth in the lurking-places of the villages; in the secret places doth he murder the innocent; his eyes are privily set against the poor. He lieth in wait secretly as a lion in his den. He lieth in wait to catch the poor, he doth catch the poor when he draweth him in his net." The ANI (Eg) like the עני (Heb.) are the sad and afflicted, hence the poor.

In the Ritual we recover a more definite sense. David in the psalm complains of the evil treatment of the wicked. In the Ritual the Ani are the afflicted who are waylaid, cajoled, ensnared in the nets and evilly treated by the wicked Typhon. "Break thou the arm of the wicked."[3] In the Ritual Typhon is called "STONE-ARM." The Wicked is a title of the Apophis-serpent, and the opposers, the agents of Satan the Accuser, are designated the wicked.

It throws light on the nature of some of these Psalms of the Hades and the night to know that Taht the Psalmist was a lunar god, who illumined the darkness, and of whom it is said: "*Ra created him a beautiful light to show the name of his evil enemy,*" that is to expose the nature of Typhon, the evil power, darkness itself. Ra says to him: "*Thou art my abode, the god of my abode; behold, thou wilt be called Taht the abode of Ra.*"[4] The Hebrew Solar God says: "I have sworn by my holiness that I will not lie unto David. His seed shall endure for ever,

---

[1] *Records*, vol. vi. p. 111.   [2] Deut. xxxiii. 8.
[3] Ps. x. 15.   [4] *Records of the Past*, vi. 111.

and his throne as the sun before me. It shall be established for ever as the MOON, and a faithful witness in heaven." [1] The fulminations of David against his enemies answer to the words written down by Taht who calls himself the "*Justifier of the words of Horus against his enemies on the day of weighing words in the great abode of An.*" [2]

Psalm vii. is entitled "Shiggaion of David, which he sang to the Lord concerning the Dibrai (דברי) of Kush," here called the Benjamin-ite, probably from some relation of the locality to the right hand or side which can be paralleled if not explained by the first chapter of the Ritual in which Taht says : "*I am with Horus supporting the* RIGHT SHOULDER *of Osiris in Skhem,*" the shut place. For Kush or כוש is the KHEPSH of the Egyptian mythology, the hinder part of the northern quarter where the chief transactions occurred in the passage from west to east, from death to life, from darkness to light. This was the black land of Kush, the celestial Æthiopia, and the Hebrew DABAR also signifies the hinder part as the back side of the temple where the Jewish holy of holies was located for mystical reasons ; the especial seat of holiness being the birthplace, the ORACULUM, which represented the Khepsh of the hinder thigh in heaven. Dabar, to be behind, describes the situation and character of Kush or the Khepsh, the place of the Meska or Meskhen in the Ritual. The goddess of the Great Bear when degraded, became the feminine Typhon of this quarter—the Dabar of Khepsh—in the eschatological phase, the Monster of Amenti who was depicted with the tongue thrust out to lap the blood of the wicked. She also carried the noose or tie, once a type of life, but afterwards called a snare of souls. This tie is named Tepr, another equivalent of Dabar, in which sense the Tepr of Khepsh is the tie or snare of the wicked Typhon. The tongue also is Tep in Egyptian. The tongue of Typhon or the wicked, is frequently referred to by the Psalmist. "Under his tongue is mischief and vanity." [3] "They flatter with their tongue." [4] In the Ritual the adversary Typhon is told, "*Thy tongue which has been made to thee is greater than the envious tongue of a scorpion. It has failed in its power for ever.*" [5] The Hebrew Kush, as before said, answers to the Egyptian Khepsh, the hinder part, the night side, the feminine abode of birth determined by the hinder thigh or Khepsh. To this the Hebrew Dabar corresponds ; this it translates.

The Dabar as place was represented in person and by name as Deborah, the prophetess of Israel. The words or Dibrai of Kush are a Psalm of the hinder part, the west and north of the solar circle, where the sun passed by night and the Akar was in travail for the re-birth of the orb or the divinity of day. The time is one of travail, and the pangs are reversed ; it is the wicked, the adversary, who is to suffer that which he has prepared for the just. "Behold, he

---

[1] Ps. lxxxix. 35-7.   [2] Ch. i.   [3] Ps. x. 7.
[4] Ps. v. 9.   [5] Ch. xxxix.

travaileth with iniquity, and hath conceived mischief, and brought forth falsehood : he hath made a pit and digged it (the Ament or Sheol), and is fallen into the ditch he made." [1] The speaker appeals to the covenant : "Have respect unto the covenant, for the dark places of the earth are full of the habitations of cruelty." [2] These are the hells of the underworld described in the Ritual through which the Osiris and Osirians passed.

The Psalmist says, "The assembly of the wicked inclosed me." [3] This answers to the Sami (assembly) of Typhon, the conspirators. Again, "He shall pluck my feet out of the net." [4] And "Our soul is escaped as a bird out of the snare of the fowlers, the snare is broken and we are escaped." [5] The original matter is mythological, and belongs to the phenomena of the solar allegory. In the secondary stage this is applied to the soul, and becomes eschatological. In the myth, Typhon and the conspirators prepare a feast, at which he betrays Osiris. In perfect keeping with the story as told by Plutarch we have the passage, "Yea, mine own familiar friend, in whom I trusted, which did eat of my bread, hath lifted up, or magnified, the heel against me." [6] The heel denotes that hindward part by which Typhon was typified. This is a supposed prophecy of the betrayal by Judas, and the subject of the Last Supper. There is one origin for both.

"I am a worm and no man," says the speaker in Psalm xxii. 6. "*I am that crawling reptile*," cries the Osirian in the eighth abode.[7] This is said "*in the place of dismissing peace, the great and terrible place of the waters.*" Again we read, "The channels of waters were seen and the foundations of the world were discovered at thy rebuke, O Lord, at the blast of the breath of thy nostrils." [3] "He sent from above, he took me, he drew me out of many waters. He delivered me from my strong enemy, and from them which hated me." [9] "Thou didst divide the sea by thy strength ; thou brakest the heads of the dragons in the waters. Thou brakest the heads of leviathan in pieces, and gavest him to be meat to the people inhabiting the wilderness." [10] The Osirian exclaims : "*Hail ! thou who art over the gods. Hail ! thou who hast cut in pieces the Scorner and strangled the Apophis.*" [11] Horus smites the wicked, the enemies of Osiris. "*Horus smites off their heads to heaven for the fowls ; their thighs to the earth for wild beasts, to the water for the fishes.*" [12]

The subject-matter of the Ritual is obvious in the Second Psalm. It is the parallel to the assembling of the Typhonian Sami, who set themselves against the anointed son, Horus, and against Osiris, the lord and father. The wicked conspirators are represented by the heathen, and the netherworld by the uttermost parts of the earth.

[1] Ps. vii. 14-15. [2] Ps. lxxiv. 20. [3] Ps. xxii. 16.
[4] Ps. xxv. 15. [5] Ps. cxxiv. 7. [6] Ps. xli. 9.
[7] Ch. cx. [8] Ps. xviii. 15. [9] Ps. xviii. 16, 17.
[10] Ps. lxxiv. 13, 14. [11] Ch. xv. [12] Ch. cxxxiv.

The opponents say, " Let us break their bands asunder and cast away their cords from us."   In the Ritual the conqueror of the Apophis and the Sami says : " *Apophis is overthrown, their cords bind the south, north, east, and west.   Their cords are on him.   Akar has overthrown him ; Har-ru-bah has knotted him.   The sun is at peace; he goeth forth in peace.   The Apophis and the accusers of the sun fail.*"[1]   " Kiss the Son, lest he be angry," says the Psalmist.   " *Give ye to him glory, ascribe ye it to him,*" says the Osirian.[2]   In a moment of exultation the Psalmist exclaims, " The heathen are sunk down in the pit they made ; in the net which they hid is their own foot taken."[3]   The word Gevi (גוי), rendered heathen, answers to the Egyptian Khefi, who are the godless, the Typhonians, the liers-in-wait of the Amenti, the conspirators against the solar god.   They are the Khefi because in the abyss of the north, the lower region, and thus the name applies to the people of the isles of the north, or the hinder part (גו).

" The kings of the earth take counsel together against the Lord and against his Anointed," in the Psalm ; and in the Ritual these are the Typhonian Sami, who conspire against Osiris, the Lord, and his anointed Son, Horus, who is called the anointed, the holy child, the redeemer, the justifier, the lord of life and eternal king.   It is said, " *He sees his father Osiris.   He makes a way through the darkness to his father Osiris.   He is his beloved, he has come to see his father Osiris ; he is the son beloved of his father.*"[4]   The Messiah[5] is made to identify himself with the Anointed Son in the Psalms.   " All things must be fulfilled which were written in the Law of Moses, and the Prophets and the Psalms, concerning me."   This acknowledges that the nature of the Messiahship and the terms of its fulfilment must be in accordance with those of the Psalms and the " volume of the book written of" the Messiah therein referred to. We read,[6] " When he bringeth in the first-begotten into the world he saith, And let all the Angels of God worship him."   But in what Scriptures ?   The passage is not found in the Hebrew at all; it was added by the Seventy, the Greek translators, and the writer of this Epistle quotes from their version.   It was interpolated from other scriptures extant in Egypt.   Among the mystical phrases addressed to Horus in the Ritual is, " *The one ordering his name to rule the gods* (or angels) *is Horus, the son of Osiris, who has made himself a ruler in the place of his father Osiris.*"   And when Osiris makes his transformation into Horus, his son, as a hawk of gold, it is said, " *Osiris made the generation of Horus ; Osiris figured him.   How was he more dignified than those who belong to the beings of light, created with him ?*"[7]

[1] Ch. xxxix.
[2] Ch. xxxix.
[3] Ps. ix. 15.
[4] Ch. ix. Birch.
[5] Luke, xxiv. 44.
[6] Heb. i. 6.
[7] Ch. lxxviii.

The prayers put into the mouth of David are uttered by Horus or some other form of the sun-god in the original writings of which Taht is the composer. It is the Son, the Anointed of the Lord, who is properly the speaker, as in Psalm xiii., where he asks, " How long shall mine enemy be exalted over me ? " The enemy triumphed in turn over the sun-god during the passage of the darkness, and the change from the old cycle to the new. The cry of the cross is the same as the cry of the crossing, " My God, my God, why hast thou forsaken me ? " [1] uttered by the Redeemer in the depths, the suffering sun of the underworld, the sun who was represented by the reptile (Ref) writhing through the sloughing condition, whose cries are again and again recognizable in the Psalms. " I am poured out like water." [2] He is despoiled of his strength and stripped of his glory. " They part my garments among them, and cast lots upon my vesture." [3]

One form of the divine sufferer is Har-pi-Khart. Kart means silent as well as child. Har-pi-Khart is the dumb god, who opens not his mouth, but points to it significantly. This is the speaker in Psalm xxxix., who says, " I was dumb with silence. I held my peace from good, and my sorrow was stirred." " I was dumb, I opened not my mouth, because thou didst (it)." This was in presence of the wicked, the enemy.

Psalm lxix. is entitled "To the chief musician upon SHESHENIM," and this is expressly a cry from the troubled region of Sesennu. It is a prayer for salvation from the overwhelming waters ; and here it should be pointed out that Seshenin (Eg.) is the name of the lily-lotus, on which the young solar-god was up-borne from the mire of the region of Sesennu. One of the transformations in the metamorphosis [4] is into the lily-lotus of the sun. The vignette shows the head of the god issuing from the flower. The suffering Horus is likewise borne up out of the waters upon the lotus. At Denderah, Horus issuing from the Lotus-flower is designated the "living Soul of Atum." [5]

In the Psalm the cry is, " Save me, O God ; for the waters are come in unto (my) soul. I sink in deep mire (or the mire of the depth), where (there is) no standing. I am come into deep waters, where the floods overflow me." " Deliver me out of the mire, and let me not sink . . . . let not the waterflood overflow me, neither let the deep swallow me up, and let not the pit shut her mouth upon me." That is the sun of the waters in the TES, the mire, or primordial matter, as represented by Har-pi-Khart on the lily ; the breather out of the waters called the " *Lily of the nostril of the Sun.*" " I am weary of my crying " expresses the same character as Remi the weeper, of whom more hereafter.

[1] Ps. xxii. 1.   [2] Ps. xxii. 14.   [3] Ps. xxii. 18.
[4] Ch. lxxxi.   [5] Mariette, *Denderah*, ii. pl. 48, 49.

The miry clay is one of the Talmudic names of hell, corresponding to the Egyptian lake of primordial matter, which in the ritual becomes the miry pool of the damned.   Says the Osirian in this place, after struggling through, "*I stand and come forth from the mud.*"[1]

Osiris was the good shepherd; he carried the crook in his hand. The Psalmist exclaims, "The Lord is my shepherd, I shall not want; he maketh me to lie down in green pastures; he leadeth me beside the still waters;"[2] the Lord is Tzer, the rock; out of this rock flowed the pure waters. "*A well or flow comes out of thy mouth,*" says the speaker, in the Book of the Dead. "*The raging bulls have not been stopped. I pass by them. I lie down. I go to him who dwells in the fields traversing the darkness. I have seen my quiet Lord.*"

"Thy rod and thy staff they comfort me,"[3] cries the Psalmist. The User was borne in the hands of the Egyptian gods; it was their staff and rod of power. "Thou preparest a table before me in the presence of mine enemies: thou anointest my head with oil; my cup runneth over,"[4] is said by the Psalmist.

"*I have received food off the table, and drunk libations at the eventide. I have come to those who are in the horizon with joy, glory has been given to me by those who are in the gate in this mortal body,*" is said by the spirit who has just passed through the enemies in the valley of the shadow of death, and is rejoicing over his deliverance.[5] "He maketh my feet like hind's (feet), and setteth me upon *my* high places."

It is "God that girdeth me with strength, and maketh my way perfect."[6]

"*My face is in the shape of the divine hawk (the soaring bird of soul). My hind quarters are in the shape of a hawk. I am the prepared by his Lord. I go forth to the gate (his way). I have seen Osiris. I am wrapped up by his hands.*"[7]

"Thy right hand hath holden me up, and thy *gentleness* hath made me great."[8]

"*I have seen my quiet Lord.*"[9]

In correspondence with these words spoken by the Horus or Soul in the depths we find, "*I have seen my father Osiris. I have been made and emaned from his nostril.*" This is Horus of whom it is said, "*his hand is strong against his enemies, supporter of his father, snatched from the waters of his mother, striking his enemies, correcting the aggressors.*"

Some fragments of the books of Taht have descended to us in the *Divine Pymander of Hermes Trismegistus.*[10]   In these Taht is called

---

[1] Ch. xcviii.
[2] Ps. xxiii. 1, 2.
[3] xxiii. 4.
[4] Ps. xxiii. 5.
[5] Ch. lxxix.
[6] Ps. xviii. 32, 33.
[7] Ch. lxxviii.
[8] Ps. xviii. 35.
[9] Ch. lxxviii.
[10] Translated into English by Dr. Everard. Also *Hermès Trismégiste.* Traduction complète, par Louis Ménard, with divers additional fragments.

the son of Saturn,[1] and in the Ritual he is Taht, otherwise Sut, who was the first form of Hermes. Other notes of genuineness might be cited. In introducing the Hymn of Regeneration, Hermes instructs Taht, and says, " O Son, do thou, standing in the open air, worship, *looking to the North Wind about the going down of the Sun, and to the South when the Sun ariseth,*" which is according to the earliest orienting, when the two Heavens were North and South in the pre-solar reckoning. This Hymn, or Holy Speech, is one of the Psalms of Taht.

" Let all the Nature of the world entertain the hearing of this Hymn.

Be opened, O Earth, and let all the Treasure of the Rain be opened.

You Trees tremble not, for I will sing, and praise the Lord of the Creation, and the All, and the One.

Be opened you Heavens, ye Winds stand still, and let the immortal Circle of God receive these words.

For I will sing, and praise him that created all things, that fixed the Earth, and hung up the Heavens, and commanded the sweet Water to come out of the Ocean, into all the World inhabited, and not inhabited, to the use and nourishment of all things, or men.

That commanded the fire to shine for every action, both to Gods and Men.

Let us altogether give him blessing, which rideth upon the Heavens, the Creator of all Nature.

This is he, that is the Eye of the Mind, and Will; accept the praise of my Powers.

O all ye Powers that are in me, praise the One, and the All.

Sing together with my Will, all you Powers that are in me.

O Holy Knowledge, being enlightened by thee, I magnify the intelligible Light, and rejoice in the Joy of the Mind.

All my Powers sing praise with me, and thou my Continence, sing praise my Righteousness by me; praise that which is righteous.

O Communion which is in me, praise the All.

By me the Truth sings praise to the Truth, the Good praiseth the Good.

O Life, O Light, from us unto you comes this praise and thanksgiving.

I give thanks unto thee, O Father, the operation or act of my Powers.

I give thanks unto thee, O God, the Power of my operations.

By me thy Word sings praise unto thee, receive by me this reasonable (or verbal) Sacrifice in words.

The powers that are in me cry these things, they praise the All, they fulfil thy Will; thy Will and Counsel is from thee unto thee.

O All, receive a reasonable Sacrifice from all things.

O Life, save all that is in us; O Light enlighten, O God the Spirit; for the Mind guideth (or feedeth) the Word: O Spirit-bearing Workman.

Thou art God, thy Man crieth these things unto thee, by the Fire, by the Air, by the Earth, by the Water, by the Spirit, by thy Creatures.

From eternity I have found (means to) bless and praise thee, and I have what I seek; for I rest in thy Will."

[1] Book iv. ver. 14.

But, to return to the Hebrew writings. In the Book of Job, the palace of the prince of glory is juxtaposed with the Mishkan of the wicked.[1] "Ye say, 'Where (is) the house of the prince? and where are the dwelling-places of the wicked?'" The house of the prince in the Ritual is called the Palace of the Great House, in the region of the hill. The dwellings of the wicked were in the ten Kars or hells of the damned. The Meskhen was the Purgatory.

The son, as Repa and heir-apparent, the prince of peace, the anointed one, had various impersonations in Egyptian mythology, as Horus, Khunsu, and Iu-em-hept. One of these is represented in the Hebrew mythology by Solomon, the son of David. Khunsu, in relation to Taht or the moon, is the lunar son, who fulfils and completes the double circle of sun and moon. As the solar son he is the child of Amen-Ra. Taht bears on his head the half circle of the moon; Khunsu carries on his the full round. He is the fulfiller. And this is the significance of Solomon's name. Shalom (שלם) means to complete, finish, bring to an end, perfect the whole work begun by some forerunner supposed to be the ante-type. The meaning of peace is subsidiary to and dependent on this sense of perfecting some work, and completing and finishing the whole. This is done by the son Khunsu, in fulfilling the soli-lunar circle at the vernal equinox. One of Khunsu's titles is Nefer-hept. Hept means peace; Nefer may be read the good, perfect, plant, youth. The Nefer-hept is really the Hebrew prince of peace, or, as Solomon is designated in the Song of Songs, "the king to whom peace belongs." He is also called the "king of peace with the crown."[2] And as Nefer is the crown, Nefer-hept is the crowned of peace, i.e. the king of peace, synonymous with Solomon, the king of peace with the crown.

The seventy-second Psalm is called a Psalm for Solomon, and the speaker says, "Give the king thy judgments, and thy righteousness to the king's son."[3] Taht was the signer of the sentences passed on the souls of the dead in the hall of the Two Truths. And in praise of the son it is proclaimed with great appropriateness, "In his days shall the righteous flourish so long as the moon endureth."[4] That is the primary imagery. "I will make the horn of David to bud; I have ordained a lamp for mine anointed."[5] The *horn* of the new moon is borne by Taht; the *lamp* of the full moon by Khunsu. It cannot be shown that Khunsu was considered to be the son of Taht, although he is the lunar child, and carries the full moon on his head; but the son in whom the soli-lunar types were both united was Khunsu, the prince of peace, who in the Hebrew myths is Solomon, the son of David.

Jeremiah (xxiii. 5, 6) exclaims: "Behold, the days come, saith the

[1] Job, xxi. 28.
[2] In the *Sohar.*
[3] v. i.
[4] v. vii.
[5] Ps. cxxxii. 17.

Lord, that I will raise unto David a righteous branch, and a king shall reign and prosper, and shall execute judgment and justice in the earth. In his days Judah shall be saved, and Israel shall dwell safely: and this is his name whereby he shall be called, Jahveh-Tzidkenu," rendered, the Lord our righteousness. It has been hitherto assumed that TZIDKENU was to be derived from צדק, with suffix pronoun נו (enu) for "our." Thus, if we read Jahveh as the lord, Jahveh-Tzidkenu is the lord our Tzidek, as in the name of Melchizedek. But there are two passages [1] referring to Jehovah-Tzidkenu. In the first there is to be a king, who is the branch, the Egyptian Repa, called Jehovah-TZIDKENU, and in the second it is Jerusalem which is to be called TZIDKENU, the passage being literally, "and this he shall call *her*, Jehovah-TZIDKENU." Jerusalem can hardly be designated the Lord our Righteousness as well as the Branch! Therefore we need a form of the word which will include both in its meaning. This may be found in the Egyptian as SUTKENNUI.

St   kn   n   u   i

Sutkennui has the meaning of accompanying, conjoining, going together.[2]

TZIDKENU, on any interpretation, applies to two personages and sexes, and these can be derived from the name, if Egyptian, for Sut expresses the necessary conjunction and going together, and KENNU is the name of both the child and a concubine. Sut, the child, was accompanied by the genitrix long before the fatherhood was established, the self-begotten being the earliest form of the divine son. But now the son and the mother are to be called after the husband and father as Jehovah-Tzidkenu. In one sense Jehovah-Tzidkenu would be Jehovah in conjunction with Jerusalem. In another, the Tzidkenu would be the feminine, accompanied by the male god, the mother of the son, she who goes with him. The genitrix is a necessity here, as this son is to be the begotten one, the anointed, the son of the father, not merely that effeminate child of the mother who was the earlier type.

A son is to be born of David in Jerusalem, which represented the Mount of the Equinox, and there the luni-solar child was to be brought forth at the place of the luni-solar conjunction as SUTKENNUI. The conjunction occurred where the sun, moon and star of Horus met in the sign of the vernal equinox, as the Trinity in unity. This can be read by the mythology, with David as the representative of Taht. Taht was the moon-god, who built the ark

---

[1] Jeremiah xxiii, 6, and xxxiii. 16, margin.
[2] *Papyrus, Barker*, 217, Brit. Mus.

of the lunar zodiac and established the month of the moon. Taht is followed by a moon-god Khunsu, who is the child of both sun and moon, the divinity of soli-lunar time. Khunsu is the Prince of Peace, or Nefer-Hept. The Hebrew Khunsu is Solomon the son of David, the promised luni-solar son. And here the Egyptian SUTKENNUI, to accompany, is in perfect accordance with the typology. The son was always of a twofold nature, whether stellar as Sut, or solar as Horus, but the blending of the soli-lunar types in one, as Khunsu, was a particular form of accompanying and of presenting the twin nature of the TZIDKENU BIFORMIS; it was the latest and most perfect fulfilment of the sonship in which the dual nature was reproduced.

Khunsu was the branch personified, in token whereof he carried the branch of the Thirty Years, the number of the Messiah-Son. The VULGATE renders the branch[1] by ORIENS, that is Horus of Egypt, the solar form of the son. But the branch of David promised to him, in the character of Taht the moon-god, is the soli-lunar son who was Khunsu, the Nefer-hept or Perfect Peace in Egypt, and Solomon in Israel. The allegorical nature of the passage and its celestial relationship is proved by what follows respecting the land of Egypt and the north. The days are to come when they shall no longer say, the Lord led them up out of Egypt, but out of the North.

The north is Khept, the Egypt of the heavens, and the allusion is to the beginning in and with the north, the Great Bear and the superseding of Sut by Taht who was again followed by Khunsu the luni-solar son, as the branch of Amen-Ra and Maut.

When the wonderful child is born to Lamech in the Book of Enoch,[2] Enoch says, " the Lord will effect a new thing upon the earth."

The Wonderful Child in this instance was Noah, who initiated the new order of things after the fall in heaven and the flood on earth. The first of these *wonderfuls* (פלאים) was Sut-Anush, the wolf-hound or dog-star type of the son, the earliest male builder of the celestial temple. Next came Sut-Har, the sun-and-sirius type ; then Taht the lunar type, and lastly Khunsu who united the lunar and solar cycles in one cult, as did Iu-em-hept in another, and Solomon in Israel. Each of the last three was a re-builder of the temple in heaven, the perfecter of the work begun by their predecessors.

So far from this being matter of prophecy applying to Jesus Christ, it had been already fulfilled in Khunsu, the Egyptian TZIDKENU or double god, who, according to Macrobius,[3] was primeval among the Egyptians, but who is stated by Herodotus to belong to the order of the twelve great gods of Egypt. He appears on a tablet of the eighteenth dynasty which was found by General Vyse in the quarries of Tourah, where he is called the eldest son of Amen.

The Hiram King of Tyre, who in the Hebrew myths and masonic mysteries is associated with Solomon as co-builder of the temple, is

[1] Zech. vi. 12.   [2] Ch. cv.   [3] Saturn, i. 20.

doubtless a form of the Har, Horus, Oriens, the solar half of the luni-solar god found in Khunsu; this is corroborated by the conjunction of Solomon and Hiram, in fitting out the fleet for India or the south (Khentu). Another personification of the Har-Sun may be found in Solomon's brother Adoni-Jah, who is Jah-Adonai, the Hebrew solar Adon.

Solomon is reputed to have made gold as common as stones in the streets of Jerusalem. It was the same moonshine and solar gold, however, that the Gaelic Khunsu, Con, stole from the giants in the underworld, the golden light which they brought up after vanquishing the powers of darkness.[1]

David continues the character of Taht in several directions. Taht, who supports the *"right shoulder of Osiris"* in Skhem, or the Khem (shrine), is also the opener of the door of the shrine, called Skhem, or the Khem.[2] This character of Taht, as the opener, is typified by the key of David. "And to the angel of the church in Philadelphia write: These things saith he that is holy, he that is true, he that hath the *key of David*, he that openeth, and no man shutteth; and shutteth and no man openeth."[3] This was the two-faced Janus who carried the key, and was called the opener and the shutter, Patulcius and Clusius. The key of David is spoken of by Isaiah[4] as being committed to Eliakim, the son of Hilkiah. "And the key of the house of David will I lay upon his shoulder; so he shall open, and none shall shut; and he shall shut, and none shall open; and he shall be for a glorious throne to his father's house, and they shall hang upon him all the glory of his father's house."

It may be noted that Eliakim corresponds to Har (Ar or El) of the shrine, the Egyptian Khem; he shuts the shrine which his brother Har, the younger, opens, and these two in unity are the shutter and opener who is personified in Janus. The place of shutting was in Skhem; that of opening in Apt, the birthplace, on the horizon of which the mount of peace, Aru-Salem, and Bethlehem as the house of David, formed the dual image corresponding to the Two Truths, two bringers-forth, two horizons, two Horuses, or the dual luni-solar Khunsu.

In the *Midrash Tillim*[5] there is a Hebrew legend, which relates that David was once keeping his sheep when he was carried up to heaven on the back of a colossal rhinoceros, and delivered from his perilous position through the help of a lion. Whereupon he vowed to build a temple to God that should be of the dimensions of the

---

[1] The present writer is not concerned to deny that there ever was an historical Hebrew David or Solomon. These are common names in Israel. All he has to do with are the earliest personages so named, and these he holds to be entirely mythical. The first twelve tribes that Solomon reigned over were zodiacal, and the RIDDLES (חידה), said to have been extant in the time of Josephus, doubtless belonged to the astronomical allegory. Cf. Psalm lxxviii.

[2] Rit. ch. i.   [3] Rev. iii. 7.   [4] xxii. 20-24.   [5] Fol. 21, col. 2.

animal's horn. It has been imagined that the Rabbinical writers based this on the passage in Psalm xxii. 21 : "Save me from the lion's mouth : for thou hast heard me from the horns of the unicorns."

The present writer sees in it one of those fragments of Egyptian mythology found in the Talmudic writings in the same stage of decadence as our folklore and faeryology. David is the Hebrew Taht, the moon-god, who in the Ritual [1] takes credit for first building the ark of Sekari, *i.e.* of forming a zodiacal circle, which afterwards became solar. An enormous horn was the type of Typhon, the unicorn or hippopotamus, and is often alluded to. Sut-Typhon preceded Taht as the time-keeper and announcer in heaven under the types of Sothis and the Great Bear. Also it can be shown that Typhon, the genitrix, as Ta-urt was continued in Astarte, the horned, as a lunar goddess, who preceded Taht, the male divinity of the moon. David borne on the back of the image of Typhon is the exact replica of Taht, otherwise or formerly Sut ; [2] and when the circle was made, and the first four cardinal points were established, the lion was keeper of the corner where the sun was at the beginning of the year of the inundation ; and this sign was a starting-point for Taht, or David, in building the new temple of the heavens, formed of the twenty-eight lunar signs. But when the luni-solar zodiac, or temple, was built, we find Taht seated in the sign of Cancer, as Hermanubis, at the place of the summer solstice. The final temple of the heavens was finished by Solomon, or Khunsu, the luni-solar son, according to the pattern left him by David, or Taht. He filled in and completed that which had been previously outlined. The same mythical matter may be found in the contention of our " Lion and the Unicorn," who fought each other for the supremacy until they became reconciled at last in their embrace of the British Crown. The Lion is supposed to have beaten the Unicorn, whether the struggles were " up and down " the garden or the town.

A Rabbinical tradition affirms that before the destruction of the Temple the Holy One played with Leviathan, but since that event He plays with it no more. This is supposed to mean a temple built in Jerusalem, but refers to the Temple in the Heavens. The Holy One was the Manifester, the Anush who was first of all Sut, the son of Typhon, of whom Leviathan, the female monster dwelling in the deep, was one type. [3] The earliest temple was that of Sut Typhon.

The Talmudic traditions go back to the first time and circle of the Great Bear, which was represented by the rhinoceros, hippopotamus, or Unicorn. Next the lion identifies the point of commencement in the Egyptian sacred year. David's temple was that of Taht, the lunar measurer, and Solomon's represents that of Khunsu, or luni-solar time. The full moon carried on the head of Khunsu

[1] Ch. i.   [2] Rit. ch. xlii.   [3] *Book of Enoch*, ch. lviii. 7.

still determines the time of Easter, or Astarte, in what may be truly termed the Sabean-luni-solar year of the metonic cycle, and the golden numbers of the English Book of Common Prayer.

The names of Taht and David are similar without being identical, and this also can be explained by their different relationship to the double light, Taht, whose full name of Tahuti, shows he was the bearer (Ta) of the Huti, the type of a dual light, from Hu, light, and ti, two, or to duplicate. The Huti is a winged disk. The first winged disk is lunar. Two ibises are given to Taht in the " Destruction des Hommes par les Dieux,"[1] and these explain the sign of a double-winged disk, which at times accompanies the name of this god. The duality applies to the two halves of the lunation. The luni-solar Hut (Huti) symbols another duality, that of the sun and moon conjoined, as they were in Khunsu. This blending of the two in one was represented by the Teb-Huti or winged disk, the emblem of the lord of heaven and giver of life. Khunsu, with the head of the solar hawk bearing the lunar disk, is equivalent to the sign of the Tebhut or winged disk, only he belongs to another divine dynasty. The Tebhut, is the type of HIU and the later IU of the Atum cult. In Ta-huti the dual light is lunar. In the TEBHUT both lunar and solar lights are conjoined. David represents the two blended together in one, which is the meaning of his name of the JOINER, UNITER, or the United, and so this name of דוד is the equivalent of Tebhut, Tevhut, Tahut, or Taht, with the duality of Taht expressed by the two halves of the lunation, and that of David by the luni-solar unity, as it was in IU of the Atum cult.

This duality was finally represented by the Son, who had both father and mother, as the second Horus of the Osirian cult ; Khunsu, the luni-solar son of Amen-Ra and Maut, and by Iu the son (Su), the Iu-su, son of Atum and Iusāas, at On in Egypt, the Iu-em-hept, who comes with peace, and is the Solomon of that dynasty.

Another Egyptian form of the mythical father and son is found in Ptah and Tum, also in Tum and his son IU-EM-HEPT, he who comes with and brings peace, as Iu means both to come and bring. He is the issue of Neb-hept, the lady of peace. Iu-em-hept, as the Repa, is the prince of peace, identical by title with Solomon, called the son of David.

In some respects Iu-em-hept, who was also a form of the dual son, offers a better original for the mythical Solomon, the Solomon known to the Freemasons, for example, than even Khunsu. He was the preacher who reappears in the Hebrew writings as Ecclesiasticus. " I have heard the words of Iu-em-hept and Hartataf. It is said in their sayings,

" After all, what is prosperity ? Their fenced walls are dilapidated. Their houses are as that which has never existed.

[1] See *Bib. Arch.* vol. iv. pt. i. p. 15, note.

"No man comes from thence, who tells of their sayings, who tells of their affairs, who encourages (?) our hearts. Ye go to the place whence they return not. Strengthen thy heart to forget how thou hast enjoyed thyself. Fulfil thy desire while thou livest. Put oils upon thy head, clothe thyself with fine linen adorned with precious metals, with the gifts (?) of God. Multiply thy good things; yield to thy desire, fulfil thy desire with thy good things (whilst thou art) upon earth, according to the dictation of thy heart. The day will come to thee, when one hears not the voice, when the one who is at rest hears not their voices (*i.e.* of the mourners). Lamentations deliver not him who is in the tomb. . . . . . Feast in tranquillity, seeing that there is no one who carries away his goods with him. Yea, behold, none who goes (thither) comes back again."[1]

These are some of the sayings of the Preacher known to us in Ecclesiastes, ascribed to King Solomon.

"Go thy way, eat thy bread with joy, and drink thy wine with a merry heart, for God now accepteth thy works. Let thy garments be always white, and let thy head lack no ointment . . . . for there is no work, nor device, nor knowledge, nor wisdom in the grave whither thou goest."[2]

The Egyptian theme is that of the words which Herodotus tells us were pronounced at feasts when the mummy image was carried round and presented to each person with the expression, "Look upon this! then drink, and rejoice, for thou shalt be as this is."

The song in the Harris Papyrus (500) is said to be taken from the House of King Antuf, and must therefore be as early as the eleventh dynasty.

How ancient are some of the Egyptian Books of Proverbs and collections of wise sayings may be partially gauged by the most ancient book in the world, the precepts and maxims of Ptah-hept in the Prisse Papyrus, which dates as far back as the time of King Assa-Tat-Ka-Ra[3] of the fifth dynasty. It is betwixt five and six thousand years old, and, at that distance of time, appeals to the authority of *the ancients* just as we may appeal to IT as a venerable work of antiquity. In this same Papyrus (Prisse) is also found the 5th commandment of the Mosaic Law: "Honour thy father and thy mother" with the promise annexed "that thy days may be long in the land."

The Apocryphal Book of Ecclesiasticus called the Wisdom of Jesus, the Son of Sirach OR Ecclesiasticus, is admitted in the Prologue to be an Egyptian work brought out of Egypt. Here the Preacher is identified as Jesus. In the Hebrew collection the Preacher becomes the typical wise man, as Solomon, or Ecclesiasticus. The Solomon, whose name signifies Peace, is one with Iu-em-hept, who approaches with peace, to whom the wise sayings are attributed

---

[1] *Trans. of the Society of Biblical Archæol.* vol. iii. p. 386.
[2] Ecc. ix. 7-10.   [3] *Brugsch*, Pl. iv. scutcheon 40.

in Egypt. In the Wisdom of Solomon it is written, " In *the long garment* was the whole world." [1] The long garment is typical of the learned, the Ecclesiastic. And Iu-em-hept is portrayed on the monuments as the wearer of the long garment ; he is Ecclesiasticus, the Preacher, or Word, personified. The Book of Ecclesiasticus is the *" wisdom of Jesus the son of Sirach."* The account rendered of it in the " Prologue made by an uncertain Author " is that this Jesus was the son of Sirach, who was also a son of Jesus, the grandfather of Jĕsus. On one particular line of descent in the divine dynasties Ptah is called " Atef-Atef," father of the fathers of the gods. His son Tum is the divine father, and Iu-em-hept is HIS son. Thus we have the grandfather, father, and son. But Ptah as a son was the first Jesus on this line of descent, that is the Iu-su, or son who comes. He is the Iu or Au in the form of an embryo. Ptah is the father of Tum the second Iu-su, and thus genealogically Iu-em-hept, the third Jesus, is the grandson of Ptah in Egyptian mythology. This relationship of Iusu to Ptah is manifested in a prayer of Jesus the son of Sirach,[2] " I called upon the Lord the Father of my Lord ; " this was in trouble, when he called from the " depth of the belly of hell," or in passing through the Amenti. The true reading of this is, I, Iu-su, called upon Ptah the father of my father Tum, the Lord of An. He had been in the " depth of the belly of hell," his life was " near to the hell beneath," that was in the solar passage through the Amenti or Hades, where lurked the liers-in-wait, and Sut or Satan the Apophis was the accuser, and utterer of " lying words." The accusations against him are made by the " unclean," the " unrighteous " tongue of Typhon, just as in the Ritual.[3] This is in a prayer of Jesus or Iusu, he who comes from the belly of Hades in the new birth.

Iu-em-hept, he who comes with peace, then, is claimed to be a prototype of the Jewish Solomon, the impersonation of peace. " Solomon reigned in a peaceable time. God made all quiet round about him, that he might build an house in his name, and prepare his sanctuary for ever. How wise wast thou in thy youth. Thy soul covered the whole earth and thou filledst it with dark parables. Thy name went far into the islands, and for thy peace thou wast beloved." [4] Of Iu-em-hept (or Nefer-Tum) the gods say, " Hail to thee coming, approaching in (or with) peace." [5]

In an inscription copied by M. Dümichen [6] it is said that a certain part of the Temple of Edfou was " restored as it is in the book of the model of a temple composed by the Chief Kher-heb, Prince Iu-em-hept, eldest son of Ptah." In this inscription the Kherheb or modeller of the Temple, the original designer, would be Iu-em-hept, to whom various arts and sciences were ascribed, including poetry, healing, and building. And in this we have another prototype of Solomon as the

---

[1] xviii. 24.   [2] Ecc. li.   [3] Ecc. ch. li. 5-10.
[4] Ecc. xlvii.   [5] Rit. ch. 15.   [6] *Tempel Inschriften*, i. Pl. 97.

builder of the Temple in Israel according to a book of the model ascribed to David.

One more quotation will show that the canonical writings in which Wisdom figures as the chief character are of Egyptian origin, and not only those that have been excluded as Apocrypha. In this passage wisdom is personified as Hathor, who is nearly one of the oldest of Egypt's divinities. It is but a fragment, but all essence of the kind of utterances assigned to Solomon and IU-EM-HEPT the Preacher.

"I walked in the way of Hathor, her fear was in me (*lit.* my limbs). My heart bid me to do her pleasure. I was found acceptable to her."

"When I was a child, not knowing how to declare the truth (*i.e.* distinguish good from evil, truth from falsehood) my heart bid me adopt the sistrum (*i.e.* the badge of Hathor). God was pleased with it, the good ruler made me rejoice, he gave me this gift to walk in his way (or according to his rule).

"Lead your wives to her truly to walk in the ways of the queen of the gods ; it is more blessed than any other way ; lead them in her way." [1]

Celsus, as reported by Origen, refused to admit the antiquity of the Hebrew Scriptures, and affirmed that they were borrowed from the Egyptians. Much more might be added to show that they contain reproductions of the most ancient Hermean matter. In the first chapter of the Ritual we read : "*Oh, openers of roads ! oh, guides of paths to the soul made in the abode of the Osiris ! open ye the roads, level ye the paths to yourselves for the Osiris.*" [2] This is the voice of him that crieth in the wilderness referred to and quoted by Isaiah : [3] "The voice of him that crieth in the wilderness, prepare ye the way of the Lord, make straight in the desert a highway for our God. Every valley shall be exalted (levelled upward), and the crooked shall be made straight, and the rough places plain." In Isaiah we only get the symbolical language with no clue to the subject-matter, and so it was held to be prophecy. This is assumed to be applicable to John the Baptist, and when we come to the Gospel of Matthew we find the actual proved by the prophetical, whereas the voice of one crying in the wilderness, and the very words it uttered, belong to the solar allegory, and are written in the first chapter of the Ritual, called the "Manifestation to Light." The scene is in the Hades, the wilderness of the under-world. The messenger is Taht, who accompanies the Horus through the desert of the dead. He is the mouth of the gods whereby the promises to souls were announced and made known, as Isaiah has it, by the "Mouth of the Lord." [4] It is by Taht, who is the Mouth of the Lord, that the deceased addresses the gods in the appeal to make the paths straight and level up to

[1] Goodwin, *Trans. of the Society of Bib. Archæol.* vol. ii. p. 356.
[2] Birch, Rit. ch. i.   [3] xl. 3 and 4.   [4] Is. xl. 5.

the divine abode. One form or name of Taht, the messenger in the lower world, is that of Aan, who is designated the "Preparer of the Way of the other World," and with whom we have, later, to identify the messenger John as the crier in the wilderness. Enough at present, to show that the so-called prophet is quoting the Egyptian Ritual,—quoting the words of Taht, who is there proclaimed to be the Messenger in the day of "calling the world," and who is the Mouth of the gods personified, the announcer of Horus, the son, who is the glory of the lord (Osiris) revealed. The so-called witness to Christ in the Psalms, and the testimony to the Saviour in the "Prophets," do but refer to the anointed son, the Iu-Su of Egyptian mythology, whose nature and significance can only be understood by the matter being once more related to the primary phenomena upon which that mythology was founded.

Here, again, is a group of quotations from the "Hymn to the Nile."[1] The resemblance between this hymn and the Psalms is particularly striking. It was written by Enna the scribe, author of the *Two Brothers,* in the time of Merenptah, a supposed contemporary of Moses :—

"*He maketh his might a buckler.*"[2] "*He is not graven in marble.*"[3] "*He is not beheld.*"[4] "*There is no building that can contain him.*"[5] "*There is no counsellor in thy heart.*"[6] "*Every eye is satisfied with him.*"[1]

The Epistle of Jude, for instance, contains a couple of waifs and strays from ancient writings. Jude quotes a passage from the Book of Enoch, found in Chapter 2: "Behold, he comes with ten thousand of his saints, to execute judgment upon them, and destroy the wicked, and reprove all the fleshly, for every thing which the sinful and ungodly have done and committed against him." Again, he says: "Michael, the archangel, when contending with the devil, he disputed about the body of Moses."[8]

And in the Ritual, we read,—

"*I am washed with the same water in which Un-Nefer (the good being) washes when he disputes with Sut (Satan) that justification should be made to Un-Nefer, the justified (Makheru).*"

One form of Horus the good being, Har-Makhu, the sun of the horizon, is the prototype of Micha-El, the Lord of our autumnal equinox (or horizon) called Michaelmas. His dispute with Satan over the Osirian is identical with that of Michael about the body of Moses. This dispute of Horus and Satan was annual.

We have the best reserved until the last. An inscription has been copied by M. Naville from the so-called Chamber of the Cow, in the tomb of Seti the First; it is unfortunately designated by him "The

---

[1] *Hymn to the Nile, Records of the Past,* vol. iv. p. 107.   [2] Cf. Ps. xviii. 2.
[3] Cf. Acts, xvii. 29.   [4] Cf. John, i. 18.   [5] Cf. 1 Kings, viii. 27.
[6] Cf. Is. xl. 13-14.   [7] Cf. Ps. xvii. 15.   [8] Jude, ix.

Destruction of Mankind," which turns a mythical figure into modern fact. It is one of the most precious of the creation allegories,—a legend of the god Ra, who is said to have existed before the raising of the firmament, or the mapping out of the heavens. The inscription is a portion of the " Books of the Prophet, or Horoscopus," of which there were four necessary to be known. This is shown by a rubric at the end.

When Taht reads this particular book to Ra he purifies himself during nine days; prophets and men must do the same. There is a destruction of some mythical race (Rut); Ra complains that the beings who were born of himself utter words against him. "*Speak to me,*" he says to the assembled hearers, "*what you will do in this case : behold I have waited and have not destroyed them until I shall have heard what you have to say. Behold, they are running away over the whole land, and their hearts are afraid.*"

They answer—"*May thy face allow us to go, and we shall smite those who plot evil things, thy enemies, and let none remain among them.*"

The god says, " Go as Hathor !"

This is repeated in the worship of the golden calf.[1] In that story the " Lord said unto Moses," who was with him up in the mount, " Go get thee down, for thy people which thou broughtest out of the land of Egypt have corrupted themselves and turned aside out of the way which I commanded. It is a stiff-necked people. Now therefore let me alone that my wrath may wax hot against them, that I may consume them." Then follows an exterminating slaughter in the camp of Israel. The " Lord said unto Moses, whoever hath sinned against me, him will I blot out of my book," and " the Lord plagued the people because they had made the calf."

In the Egyptian myth the destruction goes forth in the shape of Hathor the goddess whose type was the heifer with the gilded horns, the Golden Hathor who was the lady of mirth and music and the dance,[2] who held the cords of love, and drew all hearts to " *rise up and play*" whilst beating time on the tambourine. In the Hebrew adaptation Hathor or the golden calf is made the cause of the destruction, the re-writers being desirous of turning a moral by means of the myth.

" *Go as Hathor,*" and " *the goddess started, ordered to destroy men during three days of navigation.*" She smote the men over the " *whole land.*" The god Ra says, " *I shall prevail over them and I shall complete their ruin.*" And " *during several nights there was Sekhet trampling the blood under her feet far as Heracleopolis.*" " *It is well done,*" says Ra. " *I shall now protect men on account of this. I raise my hand to swear that I shall not destroy men.*"

Hathor rejoices and says, " *I have prevailed over men and my heart is pleased.*"

[1] Ex. xxxii.   [2] Birch, Gal. p. 19.

The blood that has been shed is then mixed with the juice of fruit to make a divine drink as in the Hindu churning of the ocean to produce the Amrit drink of immortality. This water of life is poured out over the fields, and the goddess came at morning and finding the fields covered with the water she drank to her satisfaction and was filled. The meaning of the myth must remain in abeyance at present as unnecessary for the purpose of comparison. Suffice it that it is so remote as to belong to the pre-creation of time, the establishing and mapping out of the heavens and the making of the moon.[1] In celebration of this deed of Hathor, the gracious goddess heifer-headed, the Deity commands that libations of memorial are to be made to her at every festival of the new year. "*Hence comes it that libations are made at the festival of Hathor through all men since the days of old.*" In the Hebrew account the calf is calcined and pounded to powder, strewn on the water and the Israelites are made to drink of it.

Thus the festival of the heifer goddess was founded on the meaning of the myth, and whatsoever was signified by the Water in the original version was meant by the "water of separation" in the Hebrew Ritual. Also the festival of the heifer goddess was kept in Israel as it was in Egypt, the difference being that the Hebrews offered the red heifer, type of Typhon, and made a water of separation with the ashes of it. And this which is commanded as a statute for ever[2] has exactly the same symbolical significance as the drinking of the water with the ashes of the golden calf infused in it, and both with the drinking of the blood and juice of fruit. Ra then repents him of the destruction and grows weary to be with men.

The walls of the tomb have been so mutilated as to destroy or shatter some most important parts of the inscription. Enough however remains for us to see in dim outline that a drama of the creation was represented briefly, and this has been expanded with numerous details in the Mosaic record. Ra says he is so weary he cannot walk and must have others to support him.

"*Then was Nut seen carrying Ra on her back. They saw him on the back of the Cow.*"

So Jahveh exults in having ridden on the neck of the fair heifer.[3] So the ark of the Lord of Israel was drawn by the two milch kine.[4] The god Ra, imaged by the solar orb, was borne between the horns of Hathor. The Hebrew AGL-AH for the heifer renders the Egyptian Akr-ah the cow of the lower region who carried the sun across the waters of the abyss. Ra is described as descending to earth. "*His Majesty arrived in the sanctuary. The Cow . . . with them. The earth was in darkness: when he gave light to the earth in the morning. Said by the majesty of the god, Your sins are behind you, destruction of enemies removes destruction. Said by the majesty of the god, I have*

---

[1] Plates B and C.   [2] Num. xix. 9.   [3] Hos. x. 11.   [4] 1 Sam. 6.

resolved to be lifted up. Who is it whom Nut will trust with it? Said by the majesty of the god, Remove me, carry me that I may see; and the majesty of the god saw the inner part (of the sanctuary), *and he said, I assemble and give possession of these multitudes of men. Said by the majesty of the god, Let a field of rest extend itself: and there arose a field of rest. Let the plants grow there: and there arose the field of Aaru.* Aaru or Aalu is usually called the Egyptian elysium. But this is to dissipate and dim the definiteness of Egyptian thought.

The Aahru is the house with gates, thirty-six is the number, in the house of Osiris,[1] founded on the thirty-six decans of the zodiac. The creation of the fields of Aaru is the mapping out of the zodiacal circle. Hence what follows; "*I establish as inhabitants all the beings which are suspended in the sky, the stars! and Nut* (our night) *began to tremble very strongly. Said by the majesty of Ra, I assemble there* (in the fields of the thirty-six gates) *the multitudes that they may celebrate thee: and there arose the multitudes.*"

Then Shu is commanded to take Nut (night) and become the guardian of those who live in the nocturnal sky. He is depicted in the tomb in the position of supporting the heaven of night, which is in the shape of the Cow that carries the stars called living beings.

Next, Time (as Seb) is called into being, with his serpents, the symbols of cycles and periods, and instructions are given to him as father in this newly-created land eternally. Then Taht is called, and his luminary, the moon, is created in the inferior sky of night to become the nocturnal abode of Ra. Fuller particulars of this drama of creation will be given hereafter. For the nonce we gather that after the great destruction the deity determines on being lifted up amongst men and entering a tabernacle or sanctuary, and the majesty of the god saw or entered the inner part of this sanctuary. The sanctuary is set in the heavens, in the thirty-six decans, and is the habitation of sun, moon, and stars, and the range of their measured courses. This is the sanctuary imitated in the emblematic tabernacle of the Exodus after the pattern shown in the mount. The opening of the Egyptian inscription with all its lacunæ is the living original of the Hebrew copy.

"*The god (Ra) being by himself, after he has been established as king of men and the gods together, there was . . . .* (lacuna). *His majesty living and well in his old age. His limbs of silver, his flesh of gold, his articulations of genuine lapis-lazuli. There was mankind. Said by his majesty, living and well, to his followers, I call before my face Shu, Tefnut, Seb, Nut, and the fathers and mothers who were with me when I was still in Nun, and I prescribe to Nun, who brings his companions with him—bring a small number of them, that the men may not see them, and that their heart be not afraid. Thou shalt go with them into the sanctuary, if they agree with it, until I shall go with Nun to the place where I stand. When those gods came, they bowed down before*

[1] *Rit.* ch. 146-7.

his majesty himself, who spake in the presence of his father, of the elder gods, of the creators of men, and of wise beings, and they spake in his presence, saying, Speak to us, that we may hear it." This is the prologue that precedes the drama we have already glanced at.

"And they saw the God of Israel, and there was under his feet as it were a paved work of a sapphire stone, as it were the body of heaven in its clearness."[1] Blue stone, chiefly the lapis-lazuli, was in Egypt a divine image. The articulations of the joints, or mouth, or both,—the hieroglyphics used might warrant the *emissions*,—for the utterances are said to be of Lapis Lazuli, MAĀT, just as we should say true blue. In another inscription the *head* of the God is of Lapis Lazuli. Indeed the real stone was distinguished from the artificial, as Khesbet-ma, or true blue. The blue stone was an image of the azure heaven, a type of the eternal, made solid as it were for an enduring foundation.

The Jewish elders saw God upon his sapphire throne; the elders who accompanied Nun bowed down before the majesty of Ra, and did speak in his presence. The Lord of Israel, now established alone, gave to Moses the tablets of stone, on which the law was written by his own hand. The "articulations" (or utterances) of Ra are of "genuine lapis-lazuli," the image of heaven in hue, and of the texture of the eternal. The Hebrew name of the tables of stone, Luch (חלֻ), is the Egyptian REKH, to speak, announce, declare, acquaint, time, epoch. That which was the merest figure of speech for the articulations of Ra and the true blue or genuine lapis-lazuli, enduring Khesbet-Maāt, the stone of the goddess of the Two Truths, has been reproduced in the Hebrew fiction as two veritable stone tablets, engraven by the hand of God Himself. "And the tables were the work of God, and the writing was the writing of God."[2]

On this blue throne has Jahveh been established, a "God by himself," as "King of men and gods together." He reveals Himself face to face with Moses, as Ra calls Shu before his face, and there are three accompanying Moses into the mount, just as Tefnut, Seb, and Nut are with Shu in the divine presence. And "he said unto Moses Come up unto the Lord thou, and Aaron, Nadab, and Abihu, and seventy of the elders of Israel, and worship ye afar off, and Moses alone shall come near the Lord, but they shall not come nigh, neither shall the people go up with them." In the Egyptian myth a small number of the elders, as fathers and mothers, are to ascend with the four. Nun takes the place of Moses, and goes alone with Shu, Tefnut, Seb, and Nut, the four companions, into the mount. In Egyptian mythology Shu is the son of Nun. In the Hebrew the son of Nun is Joshua. The parentage of Nun identifies the sonship of Shu and Joshua.

In the destruction of mankind their blood is poured out over the

---

[1] Ex xxiv. 10.　　　　　　[2] Ex. xxxii. 16.

land for the length of a three days' navigation.   From this a drink
is to be concocted for the gods by mixing fruit with the blood.

"*Said by the majesty of the god: Let them begin with Elephantine,
and bring to me fruits in quantity.   And when the fruits had been
brought they were given.   The Sekti of Heliopolis was grinding the
fruits whilst the priestesses poured the juice into vases, and the fruits
were put in vessels with the blood of men, and there were made seven
thousand pitchers of drink.   And the majesty of Ra came with the gods
to see the drink, and he said, It is well done all this.   I shall now protect
men on account of this.*"

The myth has really nothing whatever to do with any destruction
of mankind.   The beings destroyed are born of Ra, the god.   It is
at bottom a legend of the primitive creation, and the language
used is founded on physiology.   The mixture of fruit-juice and blood,
which is to be the future protection of the human race, is poured out
of the vessels, and the fields are entirely covered with what is termed
"the water."   The avenging goddess, Hathor, came in the morning
and found the fields covered with water, and she was pleased with it,
and she drank to her satisfaction and went away satisfied, and she
saw no men.   Then Ra said to her: "*Come in peace, thou gracious
goddess, and there arose the young priestess of Amu.   Said by the
majesty of Ra to the goddess* (Hathor): *I order that libations be made
to her* (the young priestess of Amu) *at every festival of the new year,
under the directions of priestesses, at the festival of Hathor, through all
men since the days of old.*"

The geographical Amu was at the extremity of the Delta, near
Lake Mareotis, in the last Western Nome, and in the district of the
Cow.   The cow sign in the Planisphere is in the west, and Hathor,
the cow-headed, is goddess of the western hill.   Amu signifies dates,
the place of the date-palms.   M. Naville supposes the young goddess
of Amu to be Tefnut, in the cow-headed character of Hathor.   But
the young goddess, a very young goddess, who was a form of Hathor,
is Shent.   Shent is a name of the nose sign of breathing (as well as
Fent), and the nose and its actions were represented by the head of
a calf.   Shent, the young cow-goddess, is the calf answering to the
golden calf worshipped by the Israelites.   The mount of the west,
sacred to the cow-goddess, in the cow district, answers to Sinai, from
Shen, the point of turning in the circle, and place of the equinox.
Here is another instance which looks like a rendering of the hieroglyphics by some one who was ignorant of the mythical significance
Sinai is the point at which the Israelites are described as turning in
their course.   They turn away from the Lord ; they turn aside to
worship the calf ; they turn back to Egypt ; they bend the knee in
worship of the calf, and the word Shen, or Shena, has all these
meanings.   Shen, to bend, turn away, deflect, twist and turn, bend
the knee, to blaspheme, be enchanted and bewitched.   This one

word would furnish the Hebrew story of the turning away at the western point of turning in the domain of the cow, or rather of the calf. The date-palms of Amu are also in Elim, where there were *seventy* palm-trees and twelve fountains of water.[1]

The goddess Mer is likewise found as a form of Hathor, bearing the solar disk on "her fair neck," between the cow's horns.

The young goddess of Amu is represented in Israel by Miriam.

The pouring out of the blood to the extent of a three days' voyage is a mythical mode of describing the Red Sea, a localized illustration of which was the inundation of the Nile when it turned red, and was under the protection of Mer-Seker, the Silent Mer, and was the image of the mother source, as the Nile was considered to be when red, and called Tesh-tesh, the inert (that is, feminine) form of Osiris. The rejoicing of Hathor over the blood shed is paralleled by the song and dance of Miriam over the destruction in the Red Sea. The bitter waters of Marah, which were sweetened by the tree cast into them, equates with the juice of the fruit poured into the blood of the Egyptian myth. A covenant and a statute are made on the spot by Ra, who orders that libation is to be made to the young goddess of Amu at every festival of the new year at the time of the overflow of Nile. In like manner the Lord of Israel makes for them a "statute and an ordinance, and there he proved them."[2]

The tree of healing is the tree of life, the male source as applied by Isaiah, lvi. 3 : "Neither let the Eunuch say, I am a dry tree." In the elder version this is represented as the fruit of the tree whose juice was mingled with blood.

This bloody business of pouring out the vast crimson sea over the fields is transacted in the middle of the night, just as in the Hebrew story the blood was sprinkled on the lintels and the great destruction was consummated at midnight. Again, it is the first-born of Egypt who are represented as having been slain ; and in the genuine myth the men who are destroyed are the first-born of all creation, born of Ra himself. The blood shed by Ra and Hathor is the blood of a covenant in making which Ra swears "*I now raise my hand that I shall not destroy men.*" He then commanded the blood to be poured out of the vessels over the fields. That covenant, what-soever its origin and significance, is obviously the prototype of the Jewish blood-covenant. "And Moses took half of the blood and put it in basins ; and half of the blood he sprinkled on the altar. And he took the Book of the Covenant and read." And "Moses took the blood and sprinkled it on the people, and said, Behold the blood of the covenant which the Lord hath made with you concerning all these words."[3] The Egyptian myth concludes with the creation of the heavens, the cycles and circles of Seb (time), the two halves of the sky where the moon appears, crescent and full, the establishing of

[1] Num. xxxiii. 9.   [2] Ex. xv. 23-25.   [3] Ex. xxiv. 6-8.

the Aahru, the houses and gates of the sun, and the habitations of the stars.[1] The Aahru, as previously mentioned, consist of the Divisions of the twelve signs. This, too, is modestly imitated by Moses, who makes his zodiac by building an altar under the hill, and erecting " twelve pillars according to the twelve tribes." [2]

These things were the creations of Egypt, who alone can interpret their true meaning for us. As such they are but myths of the profane heathen mind ; old wives' fables and " silly sooth" of the world's childhood. But when reproduced in the records of God's own chosen people they become the direct revelations of the Most High speaking to a real man by word of mouth (uttering on Sinai what is found in Egyptian tombs), the myth is transformed to miracle, the Word is made flesh, the symbol fact, Ra's utterances of lapis-lazuli are turned into two tablets of stone, the writings are divinely inspired, and their fables become eternal truths on which are founded the first revealed religion and the salvation of the human race. These extracts will show, however, that we are vastly indebted to the Israelites for preserving the Egyptian writings, however tampered with in the redaction. They also show to what a height the thought of Egypt soared, and to what a depth it sounded ages on ages before the Jewish people were an ethnological entity. This inscription gives us hope that other extracts from the sacred books of Taht may be still extant and recoverable hereafter.

TUT is the Egyptian word for speech, utterance, language, mouth, tongue. This does not pass into Hebrew as the common type-word for language or speech, and the word Duth (דת), a law, edict, mandate, has been supposed to belong only to later Hebrew. Yet the Jews' language is twice over expressly called Ihu-duth (יהודית).[3] Not the (לשן) tongue of the Jews, but the Tut or speech of the Jews, designated by the Egyptian name. "In those days also saw I Jews that had married wives of Ashdod, of Ammon, and of Moab. And their children spake half in the speech of Ashdod, and could not speak in the Jews' language (יהודית)."

" Then said Eliakim unto Rab-shakeh, Speak, I pray thee, to thy servants in the Syrian language, for we understand it, and talk not with us in the Jews' language in the ears of the people that are on the wall." [4]

The speech of the Jews then is the Egyptian language described by name in Egyptian. The word TUT is abraded from Tahuti (Thoth), who was the word, the mouth, tongue, and pen of the gods, the divine scribe.

It is stated in the Mar Sutra [5] that the Pentateuch was originally

---

[1] *Records of the Past*, vol. vi. p. 103, with Commentary on the *Trans. of Bib. Arch.* vol. iv. pt. i.
[2] Ex. xxiv. 4.   [3] Neh. xiii. 24.   [4] 2 Kings, xviii. 26.
[5] *Sanhedr.* xxi. B. Deutsch, *Remains*, p. 423.

given to Israel in the holy language and in the IBRI writing. It was afterwards given to them in the Aramaic language and in the ASHURITH writing, in the days of Ezra. Israel then adopted the Ashurith writing and the holy language and left to the Samaritans the Ibri writing and the Aramaic language. Here the holy language means the most ancient, and that was Egyptian. Hebrew tells us nothing of the meaning of Ibri or the nature of the form used. Ibri only appears as the proper name of a son of Merari.[1] But the Egyptian scribe's palette, paint-pot, and reed-pen used for forming the hieroglyphics on papyrus is an instrument called the RUI. Papu is paper in Egyptian, and with RUI, the scribe's implements, we obtain the word Papyri. The Hebrew IBRI or Gabrith (עברית) writing, we may conclude was in the hieroglyphics of Kheb or Egypt.

Asha is a corner, and to meander or wind about. The hieroglyphic ha ⊡ shows that Asha means to wind not *round* but with corners, that is, square. The hieroglyphic AS is quadrangular. The mason's square is a corner. Asha-ret is writing that meanders corner-wise or what we term writing in the square Hebrew letter. Ashurith, the writing in square characters, contains the same meaning in Hebrew, derived from Ashur to be straight, rigid, the opposite of flowing, and Auth (אות), a sign, Ashur-auth, the square character. The Ashurith writing in the hard form of Aga is spoken of as the Agarith (אגרת, pl. אגרות),[2] and Aka (Eg.), to twist with the sign of writing corroborates the sense of Asha, the squared. The idea lurks in the Hebrew Agn (אגן) to be crooked, only it needs the hieroglyphic to show the square form of the crook. The earliest method of registering the circle was by the square of the four cardinal points, the corners. This tells us the truth in the plainest manner that the Pentateuch was written on papyrus by the scribe's pen, in the ancient hieroglyphics.

The sacred language and records were those of the hieroglyphics written first in granite, with the chisel for a pen, by the patient scribes of the monumental land. The hieroglyphics as secret signs gave to the Egyptian writings their sacred character, and conferred the authority of a canon. The Ibri writing and the holy language doubly identify the oldest Hebrew as Egyptian.

"Israel then selected the Ashurith writing and the holy language, and left to the Ἰδιῶται the Ibri writing and the Aramaic language." The Hebrews retained the ancient language with the square letter, and left the earlier hieroglyphics to the Ἰδιῶται or those who were unlearned and uninstructed in the later mode of writing. And who are the IDIOTES? is asked. "The Cuthim" (Samaritans). "What is the IBRI writing?" "The Libonaah" (Samaritan).

The Hebrews have the name of Haphtaroth (הפטרות) for certain writings or readings the nature of which has caused much speculation, and it seems to me to be related to the hieroglyphic rolls. Deutsch

---

[1] 1 Chron. xxiv. 27.   [2] Nehemiah, ii. 7-9: and vi. 5, 17, 19.

says former investigators (Abudraham, Elias Levita, Vitingra, &c.) almost unanimously trace the origin of the Hebrew Haphtaroth to the Syrian persecutions during which all study of the Law was prohibited and all copies of it that could be discovered were ruthlessly destroyed.[1] Deutsch thought the term applied to the kind of selections made to be read during the exile. Frankel explained the word as meaning an exordium. But in the parent language HAP means the hidden, to conceal, hide, spy out secretly. HAPU is likewise a name for the laws. Teruu denotes the roll of papyrus, drawing and colours with the symbol of the hieroglyphic scribe. The Hebrew form of the word, TAROTH, does but add the plural terminal which is Egyptian as well as Hebrew, and we have the Teruu, the hieroglyphic rolls of papyrus, whilst HAPHTAROTH denotes either the hidden papyrus rolls or the papyrus rolls of the law. It thus appears on this showing, that the Hebrews were still in possession of the papyri and possibly of the hieroglyphic writing which were preserved and read by the learned when the better known copies of the law were destroyed. Ezra is credited with founding the Great Synagogue, or men of the Assembly, which succeeded in establishing the regular reading of the Sacred Records, and with rewriting the law after the books had been burnt.[2] " For thy Law is burnt, therefore no man knoweth the things that are done of thee, or the works that shall begin."

This burning of the books is the destruction during the persecution when the HAPHTAROTH come into notice. The Haphtaroth being the secret papyrus rolls written in the sacred, that is hieroglyphical language, we now see that the work of Ezra, described with supernatural accompaniments, was that of re-translating the Law from the hieroglyphical or IBRI writing into the Chaldee of Ashurith, or the square letter.

Ezra dictated the translation during forty days and nights, and the five scribes wrote down what they were told by him, which they knew not,[3] as they did not understand the original characters. Ezra drew on his " memory," which had been divinely strengthened for the work. They wrote 240 books, or rather engraved 240 blocks of boxwood, still the favourite for wood-engraving. In this description we see the translator and his five amanuenses engaged in rendering the hidden rolls or Haphtaroth into the common language, and possibly in the square letter, although its introduction is considered to have been later.

Ezra is described as " a scribe of the law of the God of heaven ; "[4] and a " gemr " (גמר) rendered perfect. But the true meaning is not found in the Hebrew. KEM (Eg.) means to discover, find, in the space of an instant. The KEM-SEP belonged to a class of Egyptian experts, and the GEMR was a kem-sep. KEM-RÂ (Eg.) denotes a discoverer of formulæ.

[1] *Remains*, p. 320.   [2] 2 Esdras, ch. i. 4 ; 2 Ez. xiv.   [3] *Ib.* ver. xlii.
[4] Ch. vii. 12.

No marvel if in this process dislocated myths were remembered as history, and Euhemerized; the fables of symbolism represented as human facts, and divine personages were re-cast in the mortal mould. In this transfer the truth that was in the ancient parables when rightly interpreted has at times been completely de-naturalized, whilst that which has been naturalized in its place is true neither to fable nor fact. It was here the obscuring cloud descended on the Ibri writings, and we shall never see clear sky again in that direction until it has passed away.

Fuerst insists that the Hebrew alphabet is not symbolical or founded on picture writing. Nevertheless the characters represent ideographs and are named in the ideographic, not in the phonetic stage of writing. They are hieroglyphics turned into square letters.

Aleph, which denotes the ox or heifer, is in Phœnician the name of the steer. The hieroglyphics will show us why. The Au (Eg.) is a heifer or calf. Au has earlier forms in Khau, Kau or Kaf, just as Aleph hard, is the English CALF. The Phœnician letter retained the form of the head, with horns, but the hieroglyphic Au is the hornless calf, the first figure of ox and cow. Therefore the Aleph must be an ideographic hieroglyphic. The Beth ב corresponds to the hieroglyphic Par, and phonetic P. Beth is a house, and the P (⊏⊐) is the solar house, one half of the dual heaven. Gimel ג (called Gi) is said to be the camel, but one rather sees in it the Egyptian KHI ⚲ modified. The Khi is a water plant and Gima (נמא) is the papyrus rush, Koptic Kam, Talmudic Gmi, the rush, in Egyptian Kam, a reed, and Kami the papyrus. It did not take great ingenuity to convert the Egyptian T ⊐\ into the Hebrew daleth (ד) or the H's, ⚱ and ⚱ into the Hebrew ח and ה. The H, however, is a modified K. This can be traced through the Greek and Phœnician ⊟ back to the hieroglyphic Khi ⊘ called the sieve. The Phœnician letters were derived from the Egyptian hieratic writing, in which the h is a modified Khi. The principle of the sieve was continued and retained in the cross-stroke of the H, and the Hebrew He with the mappiq sign ה is sounded hard like K, whilst the dot preserves the cross-stroke of the modified sieve. The Vau ו is said to be a peg or nail, an emblem of bearing and carrying, and Fa (Eg.) means to bear, and carry as the genitrix, whose name of Apt signifies a peg. Also Au (Eg.) is a hook or means to hook and fasten. But the vau or F of the hieratic, the demotic, the Phœnician and the Greek alphabets, was taken from the cerastes or horned snake, the hieroglyphic Fu ⟋⟍ and visibly continued in the hieratic or cursive writing as ⟨ the Phœnician Ч and Ϥ and the Greek Ⅎ digamma from which in a reversed position was derived the roman F. The horned snake is the likelier original of the Hebrew vau, especially as vau has the numeral value of 6, and the hieroglyphic Fa is also written with six snakes.[1]

In the hieroglyphics the mummy type and the black doll are ideographs of SENN and SHEN, the statue; SENN, to found and establish, SHEN, the mummy. The SAYIN or ZAIN is possibly a form of the statue Senn. The Jad ˙ means a hand, and "It" in the hieroglyphics is an ideographic hand. The Ta also is a hand. The Kaf ɔ represents the hollow of the hand, the *palma cava*. The hieroglyphic Kefa is a fist, a closed hand ▭. The Hebrew Kaf is the hieroglyphic Kafa hollowed out. But the Jad has the numerical value of ten, or two hands, and the Phœnician form of the letter is evidently the Egyptian hieroglyphic for No. 10 (∩) formed of two hands clasped together, cut off at the wrists, and conventionalized.

The capital letter *ℒ* of the English written alphabet, is apparently derived from the hieroglyphic Peh, the tail of the lion(▱). The lion became the phonetic L of the Ptolemaic inscriptions. R and L are interchangeable. In Chinese the L answers for the R; in Japanese the R for the L; and here we have a remarkable connection between the two; both appear to be derived from the lion. The hieroglyphic Ru is a mouth, and the peh, or rump, is also a mouth of the lioness. But there are two mouths, two pehs, two lions, or a dual one. The Ruru is the horizon as the place of the two lions, or the dual one. The horizon is double, one mouth in front and one behind, represented by the double mouth of the lion. Hence the two mouths are figured by R and L, from which it appears that the R and L meet as one in the lion, and are two as signs of the duality of the lion of the double horizon. The lion was feminine at first, doubly feminine, and later it was the male-female. The lion of the hinder part, the north region is Shu-Anhar. He wears the hinder part of the lion as his symbol. The lion or lioness of the fore part is Tefnut. Consequently the Ru (R), mouth, is feminine, and the L of the hinder part is masculine. This agrees with the change in the name of the Rock of the Water from TSER, in the time of Miriam, to SILA, under Moses, when he struck the rock. The change from Miriam to Moses, from Tser to Sila, from female to male, corresponds to the hieroglyphic nature of R and L when both are derived from the lion. It is probable that the Hebrew Lamed ל is a conventionalized representation of the hinder part of the lion, and not an oxgoad, as supposed. In the hieroglyphics the N and M permute with the running water for the sign of both. In Hebrew the letter Mim means a wave. The Egyptian symbol as an ideograph of water is a visible wave 〰〰〰; the plural of this N forms the M, or Mim. The Hebrew Mim, in pronunciation, has the twofold character of the dull labial and the strong nasal sound

[1] Sharpe, *Egyptian Inscriptions*, 78.

corresponding to the Egyptian duality of the water sign, and the unity of origin for both letters. The Ayin ע denotes an eye, and means a fountain. The eye enclosed in the precinct is an ideographic An, ⊂⊃ a pool with an eye. In An was the fountain of the Two Truths which may be denoted by the double strokes of the Hebrew Ayin. An was at the centre of the circle; this, too, is expressed by the Phœnician Ayin ⊙. At this place (An) the eye was figured in the Egyptian planisphere.

Pa, פ, as a letter of the alphabet, means a mouth; the Greek Πι is interpreted in the same sense. Two different P's in the hieroglyphics are pictographs of the open mouth, that of the lioness and the water-fowl. Another peh is the *mons veneris*, or mystic mouth.

The god Taht was formerly Sut. And in the hieroglyphics the Tet sign was the earlier Tset, the two letters of one origin, answering to the two gods. The Tet or Tset was a snake. The Hebrew Tzade צ has the look of a double-headed snake. Evidently it is the same letter as the Coptic zeta or zida Z and English Z (Zed). The Tzade has the numeral value of 90, being the ninth in the series of tens, and the Coptic Theta or Tida, has the value of No. 9; thus the Tset and Tet are united in the double-headed Tzade. The double-headed serpent was finally expressed by the capital letter Z, and this letter is the representative of the Z-shaped serpent, and interchanges with it for the same sign on the Scottish stones. The Teth ט likewise is said to mean a serpent and to twist and knot into each other, as serpents do. As the hieroglyphic serpent Tset becomes both a Tet and a Zed in later language, it may have done so in the Hebrew alphabet, and the Teth, like the Tzade, probably preserves a shape of the double-headed serpent and a proof of its dual origin. The Qoph ק is reputed to denote the back of the head. In the hieroglyphics the head presented back-foremost is the Api, and as no vowel is a primary sound, this is no doubt an abraded Kapi or Qoph. Api the head means the chief one, the first, and Qoph signifies a hundred, it being the first letter in the series of hundreds. As a hundred the Qoph is one, that is five in scores, and Kep (Eg.) the hand is a figure of five. In Coptic the Kappa has the numeral value of 20, that is the one as a score. The back of the head suffices to show the hinder part. But the hinder part signified is the Kep or Khept, the hinder thigh, the feminine cava, and as Qoph modifies into Qo, so in Egyptian Khaf becomes Kha the hieroglyphic ◇— the sign of the vagina and the womb, the Kha, Khat, or Khept. It probably follows that the Hebrew Qoph represents the hieroglyphic Kha.

The reason why one letter permutes with another is to be sought in the hieroglyphical equivalents and has nothing to do with the primal nature of sounds. The Tes divides into T and S, and so the Hebrew Zephon represents the Egyptian Typhon or Khepsh, the North. In like manner the Qoph occasionally interchanges with the Thau ת

and the Api also reads ta, and is rendered Api (ta), ta or tata being the head.

The Resh ר supposed to be the head from " rash " is visibly derived from the hieroglyphic ⌐ the ideograph of Res, to raise up. Res has also the meaning of head as the upper heaven, the south. The shape of this letter in Samaritan, old Aramean, and Palmyrene, shows this is the origin. The determinative of Res is the stand of a balance, and the stand agrees with the meaning of רישה.

The Hebrew Shin ש, pronounced Shi, is obviously derived like the Æthiopic Saut, Ш, and Coptic ⳝ, from the hieroglyphic Shi or Sha ⎍⎍⎍. The Shin represents the third letter value 3, in the series of hundreds: the Sha denotes number thirty, or three in the series of tens. The letter Thau ת is probably the squared form of the hieroglyphic Theta ⇒ a cord with a double loop; as a letter the Tau means a cross. In Egyptian tat (earlier taft) is the cross sign. Symbolically crossing, tying, knotting, are synonymous, and Tha, to make turn back, is equivalent to Tat, to cross over ; ta, knot, a tie, or cross-loop.

The Hebrew alphabet is certainly ideographic because it is based on things and is a reduced form of picture-writing.

The square letter is symbolical. We shall find the square competing with or supplementing the circle in the halos of the saints.[1] The square is typical of the genitrix who was first represented with four legs. The heaven stood on four legs (as it were) over the earth, resting on the four corners. Aft, the four corners, the abode of birth, is the great mother, and the square letter is as much a type of her as is the quadrangular Caer of the Druids.

In this way, by aid of the hieroglyphics, symbolism, and mythology of Egypt we shall be enabled now to get beyond that "original Hebrew" so often appealed to, which has so long served as the last covert and lurking-place of hunted lies. The cave of refuge is found to have a back-door open with a daylight world welcoming us beyond. Egyptian gives us the primaries of language, the very shapes in which Thoughts were THINGED. Meanings that have been pursued in vain for ages can now be run down to earth at last. The typical and symbolical may be read in the symbols and the types of those who created the myths, unless in the meantime the obscurity of the cave has produced in us such visual weakness that the organ is henceforth limited to seeing in the dark.[2]

---

[1] Didron, figs. 5 and 26.

[2] The present writer had made a collection of matter from countries outside of Egypt which implies one common origin, but will not be able to find space for it, so great is the quantity more directly Egyptian. Here is one example of what is known from the Hebrew Scriptures as the Judgment of Solomon.

A certain woman took her child in her arms and went to the pond of the Pundit to bathe. A she-devil having seen the child, and wishing to eat it, took the disguise of a woman and drew near saying, " My friend, this child is very beautiful, is it a child of yours?" Upon her answering, " It is even so, my friend," she replied, "Shall I give the child milk to drink?" "It is good," said the mother; whereupon taking the child in her arms and giving it a little milk, she hastened away with it. The mother ran after her saying, "Whither are you going with my child?" The she-devil fearlessly replied, "Whence did you get a child? this child is mine," and so they both went quarrelling by the door of the judgment hall.

The great Bodhisat having heard the noise, inquired, "What quarrel is this?" but knowing within himself this one is a she-devil because she does not wink her eyes, and also because they are red like two olinda seeds he asked:

"Will you abide by the decision I shall give?" They answered "Even so." He then caused a line to be drawn on the ground and placing the child in the midst, commanded the two hands to be taken by the devil, and the two feet by the mother, saying, "Pull both of you together; let the child be adjudged to the one which pulls it to herself." Now the child being pulled by both came to sorrow, so the mother being in anguish, like as when the heart is rent, let go the child and stood and wept. Then the Bodhisat asked many persons, saying, "Is the heart soft of those who have brought forth children or of those who have *not* brought forth children?" They said, "Oh Pundit, assuredly the heart of those who have."

He then asked them all saying, "Which think ye is the mother?" to which they answered "She who let it go."—

"A CHAPTER OF BUDDHIST FOLK-LORE."

Fortnightly Review, Aug. 1st, 1878.

The she-Devil shows the more purely mythical nature of the matter, which in the Hebrew version has been Euhemerized.

SECTION XIV.

THE PHENOMENAL ORIGIN OF JEHOVAH-ELOHIM.

THE first words of the Hebrew Book of Genesis, " In the beginning God created the heavens and the earth," have simply no meaning ; no initial point in time, or place in space.; no element of commencement whatever, nor means of laying hold to begin with. Whereas the beginnings in mythology were phenomenal, palpable, and verifiable ; they were the primary facts observed and registered by the earliest thinkers. The Egyptians did not begin with nowhere in particular, to arrive at nothing definite in the end.

The Hebrew " BEGINNING " does not enable us to begin. It is a fragment from a primitive system of thought and expression which cannot be understood directly or according to the modern mode. When the ancient matter has been divested of all that constituted its character as real myth, it only becomes false myth, and is of no value whatever until restored to its proper place in the mythical system. This can only be done by recovering the phenomenal origin and mould that shaped the matter of mythology. The primitive Genesis was no carving of chaos into the shape of worlds, according to the absurd modern notion of a creation. The mapping out of the heavens and measuring of time and period were the registered result of human observation, utterly remote from the ordinary notion of divine revelation ; it was a work of necessity accomplished for the most immediate use. The " CREATION " belongs to the mythological astronomy, and has no relation at all to the supposed manufacture of matter,—about which the early thinkers knew nothing and did not pretend to know,— the formation of worlds, or the origin of man, but simply meant the first formulation of time and period observed in the heavens, the recurring courses of the stars and moon and sun, and the recording of their motions by aid of the fixed stars. It was the earliest means of telling time on the face of the celestial horologe which had been already figured for the use of the primitive observers of its " HANDS."

In a description of this creation or beginning of time and formation, found on one of the monuments restored in the time of Shabaka, it is said of the Maker, "A blessing was pronounced upon all things, in the day when he bid them exist, and before he had yet caused gods to be made for Ptah." [1]   So in the Hebrew version, when the two heavens were finished and the starry circle of night and day was limned, the Elohim saw that everything was created good.   But we require to know who was the maker and what were the Elohim here postulated as the creators.   The three first words of the Hebrew Genesis and professed account of creation by means of the Elohim are " B'RASHITH ELOHIM BARA," translated, "In the beginning God created."   Those who have rendered this ancient language and sent forth their versions in hundreds of other tongues were altogether ignorant of the one original which could have explained and corrected the derivative Hebrew, held to be the primeval speech; God's own personal utterance.   With their one book in hand and that uninterpreted according to the Gnosis, unillustrated by the comparative method, they have assumed the preposterous proportions and pretensions of teachers of the world, and yet the very first words of revelation reveal nothing of phenomenal origin.   For that we must seek elsewhere.

The name of the most famous of the Kabalist writings, the SEPHR JETSIRA, or Book of the Creation, which some Jews have ascribed to Abraham, rendered by Egyptian, will show the astronomical nature of the creation therein recorded.   IT (Eg.) signifies to figure forth with the hand of the artist.   IT is likewise a name of the heaven. AT (Eg.) means to build, form, shape, image, type, figure forth, make the circle.   SER (Eg.) is to extend, arrange, distribute, conduct, carve. The SERAU were the conductors, the watchers, disposers, regulators, carvers of the heaven. ITSER or ATSER (including the earlier KATSER) thus denotes the framing and figuring forth of the heavens by means of the stars, which made the earliest cycles of time.

ITZER in Hebrew is to form, to fashion as a Potter.   The Potter is an ITZER.   In Egyptian ATTUSA is applied to Potters.   One framer of the heavens, the typical male creator of Egyptian mythology, is depicted as the Potter at his wheel in the persons of Ptah and Num ; the shapers of the vase or water-jug as an emblem of that which was to inclose and contain the waters.   Still earlier was the feminine Creator, MENKAT, the Potteress.   Ptah is also represented as forming an egg on the potter's wheel.   The egg is another symbol of the circle, hence it is the egg of the sun and moon, that is the circle of their revolutions.[2]   Another apt illustration of this astronomical origin of ideas supposed to have been revealed in some supernatural way, whereas mythology is founded in the natural, occurs in the Nishmath Adam,[3] where the general inhabitants of paradise are represented as stationary, and are called STANDERS.   These are the standers before

---

[1] Goodwin, in Chaba,' *Mélanges Egyp.*, 3rd Series, vol. I.
[2] Rosellini, *Mon. del Culto*, 21.
[3] *Nishmath Adam*, ch. x. f. 39 ; *Stehelin*, vol. ii. pp. 15-16.

and around the throne of our theology; but a select few are permitted
to perambulate and visit others. "In paradise every one has his particular abode, and is not allowed to go out or ascend to the dwellings
of his higher neighbour; if he should do so he is at once consumed
by his neighbour's great fire. Thus they are called standers, because
they stand and keep to their posts and allotted places. There are
indeed some holy ones (the holy watchers) who are suffered to ascend
and descend, to go into the upper and lower parts, walk in all the
quarters of paradise, and pass through all gates and abodes of the
angels." The former are just the fixed stars, the latter the MOVERS
through the heavens, the Planets. These in the Ritual are termed
"Gods of the Orbit," and as the orbits are named the Alu, these are
in their way a kind of אלוהים. The imagery was astronomical before
it became eschatological and was adopted to convey a later doctrine.

The secret wisdom of the Jewish Kabala relates primarily to the
mythological astronomy and the doctrines of the hidden wisdom
concerning the cycles of time. In its later forms, abstractions and
other mystifications took the place of, obscured, and obfuscated the
primordial facts. Although, even of these, the reveries of the Rabbis
and the Kabala in its decrepitude, it may be said they are less false to
the facts than are the Hebrew Scriptures, which re-state the myths as
history. The endeavours of the Talmudists, Haggadists, Kabalists,
at the worst are the efforts of dotage to remember and re-limn
the fading forms of the ancient meanings. They remind us of blind
men trying to read the hieroglyphics with the tips of their fingers;
whereas the "inspired writers" are reproducing the mythic matter
according to a system of falsification. The whole Kabiric doctrine
exists by name in the various Hebrew words, such as KAB, to roll
round; KAPHEL, to double, doubling, be twofold. The deity of
Israel is called a KABIR. KHAB (Eg.) is to give birth. KAB means
to turn round, move, double, and redouble. The ARI or ARU (Eg.) are
the companions, watchers, keepers, guardians, founded on the sonship,
whoever may be called the parent. AR or AL (Eg.) is the child, the
son, with earlier forms in Har, Khar, and Khart. There is no other
foundation for the Hebrew Al or El (אל) than this name of the child,
which has these antecedents in Egyptian. Hence it will be argued
the Elohim are a form of the sons known in mythology as seven in
number, the companions and watchers called the Kabiri or Kab-ari,
that turned round and made the circle and cycle of time. In the
Ritual there are four Kabari, as the Kebi, the lords of the four cardinal
points, the four representative Geni that guard the four corners of the
sarcophagus. These four belong to the Seven Great Spirits of the
Great Bear,[1] in whom we identify the Seven Kabiri of mythology.
The four lords of the corners appear in the Kabala, and the Seven
Spirits of the Great Bear or hinder thigh (Khepsh) are the Seven

[1] *Rit.* Ch. xvii.

Princes of the Chariot of the Kabala. The Seven עירין and קדישין are the Watchers of Heaven, and the councillors of the Most High in the Book of Daniel.[1] The first watchers are the Ari (Eg.), the watchers and companions who are grouped together as the Seven Kabiri, the revolving Ari. The planetary seven afterwards usurped their place, but never were a group of companions in the ark : never could KAB together, as did the seven in one constellation.

Alah (אלה) has the sense of covenanting, making a covenant, a bond, and this is originally based on time and period, as in Egyptian ARK denotes the completion of a period or cycle, and an oath or covenant. עלה (Galah or Alah) signifies to make the circle, to move in a circle. Circle-craft was the essential wisdom of the Kabala. Kab in the reduplicated form of חבב means to encircle, to inclose, surround, protect all round; in the same way כבב is to be round, circular. The Hebrew סבב (Sebeb) identifies the Source or origin signified by KEBEB (Eg.) with the circle, to go round, to encompass, and in one instance it is applied to going about, or making a journey of SEVEN days.[2] So the first Sebeb was the circle of seven (Sebu) stars.

Kabbing, applied to the stars, is clustering and revolving together. The Seven Kabiri are the revolvers together, and the Kabala is the doctrine of the starry revolutions and repetitions.

The Kabala, say the Jews, was first taught by God to a select company of angels in paradise. This is understandable when we know what were the angels of the ancient thought. They were the personified repeaters of periods of time. The angels as SHENAN (שנאן) are synonymous with repeatings.[3] Shen in Egyptian is an orbit, circuit, circle, or cycle. The Hebrew Shanah are years. The Shennu (Eg.), over which Num was lord, are periods of time. The SHENAU are the repeaters of periods of time varying in length. The same sign that denotes AT, a moment, signifies HEH, for ever, or an Æon. It is the circle. Now in the much-derided doctrine of angels found in the Rabbinical writings we learn that angels differ in size and stature. It is asserted by the Talmud that one angel is taller than another by as many miles as a man could travel in a journey of 500 years. Such statements are likely to excite the scorn and derision of those who are ignorant of the fundamental meaning of them, and yet who have constituted themselves the sole authorized expounders of the Hebrew Scriptures.

In the Rabbinical Angelology there are Seven archangels, who have under them a certain number of angels. Orphaniel has under him seventy-one angels; Thagra has seventy-four; Dandael, thirty-six; Gadalmijah, forty-six; Assimur, fifty-eight; Pascar, thirty-five; Boel, forty. This is in the region called the heavens, the first or lowest of the firmaments. The total number of angels is 360, corresponding to

[1] iv. 17.   [2] 2 Kings, iii. 9.   [3] Ps. lxviii. 17.

the number of degrees in the ecliptic. This number identifies the lower firmament with the solar zodiac, the latest of the celestial formations called heavens.[1] This is the lowermost of the three heavens mentioned by Paul, which consisted of the solar, lunar, and Sabean circles. A second firmament, called the heaven of heavens, was divided into ten departments. The division by seven and by ten led to the mapping out of the whole into seventy degrees and nations, which preceded the seventy-two duodecans of the zodiac.

One Jewish expounder of the Pentateuch explains that when the people were divided at the building of Babel, to each nation was assigned a particular portion of the earth, and also a prince to rule over it, and the Rabbis say the earth consisted of seven climates, and every climate was divided into ten parts. The seven climates together made seventy degrees. " Thus were the seventy nations divided among the seventy princes ; the blessed God taking no part in them, because he is pure. Wherefore they are not children of his image, nor bear they any resemblance of him ; but Jacob is the portion of his inheritance." In the Shepha Tal[2] the seventy princes are called the powers of uncleanness, who distribute liberally to the idolatrous nations that are subject to their influence. That is they were Typhonians who derived from the Mother, not from the Male God.

The children of Israel claim to derive from an origin earlier than the division by seventy; their beginning is with the seven, the seven Kabiri, the seven princes of the chariot, the seven Elohim, the seven spirits who preceded the seventy round the throne.

The earliest beginning in mythology is with the heptarchy, as in the seven caves of the sunken Atlantis, the seven provinces of Dyved and the seven divisions of Alban, which a Pictish legend, preserved by the Irish Nennius, assigned to the seven children of the Cruithne. These seven are found in the celestial chart as the seven halls and seven staircases in the great house of Osiris, the Seven Great Spirits of the Bear ; the Seven Chief Powers at the arm of the balance.

Egypt had been divided and subdivided until the number of nomes was forty-two. But the beginning with seven was still shown by the HEPTANOMIS, the seven provinces of Central Egypt, which are found associated with the number ten, in the ten nomes assigned to the upper and ten to the lower country on either hand of the HEPTANOMIS. These are the seven and ten which in the planisphere were the bases of the subdivision into seventy parts. The division by seven, by ten, and by seventy, was primarily celestial. The seventy Princes which encompass the throne of glory are said to be the watchmen who go about the city in Solomon's Song, by whom the decrees of God are brought down to men. The Rabbins give a list of the

[1] *Sepher Herazim, apud Bartol,* tom. 1, pp. 229, 230.
[2] f. 23, ch. iii.

seventy watchers by name.[1] Gabriel is said in the Talmud to have taught Joseph the seventy languages of the world. Here the languages stand for the number of divisions known to the great Kabir, Gabriel.

The Seventy translate Deut. xxxii. 8, "He appointed the territories of the nations according to the number of the angels of God," and not according to the number of the children of Israel. Origen, Basil, Chrysostom, and others of the fathers adopted this reading, which contains the true doctrine: "When the Most High divided to the nations their inheritance, when he separated the sons of Adam, he set the bounds of the people according to the number of the Angels," the Disposers, who as an astronomical quantity were the mythological Israelites, afterwards made ethnological. This is corroborated by the reference to the heavenly bodies in the same book.[2] We are told there are Angels so ephemeral that myriads of them are created and die daily.

As minutes, sixty die every hour; as moments, sixty pass every minute. These are the midges of the angelhood, who sun themselves in one beam of all the glory, and are gone. The angel of 500 years would personify a Phœnix period. AT (Eg.), the name of a child, the lad, is likewise the word for a moment.

Such is the sole origin of angels; they are the repeaters of time and period, and the messengers of the eternal or continuing. The word Angel, derived from Egyptian in accordance with the doctrine of repetitions, is from AN, o repeat, announce, again. Kher is to know, reckon, be the voice, speech, WORD, or utterer. AN, as God, was the Sabean Anush, Sut-Anup; in the lunar reckoning An was a form of Taht, the Logos. An or Un was the goddess of Periodicity. These were each of them Announcers of time, and all of them AN-KHERU or Angels.

"For this cause ought the woman to have power on her head, because of the ANGELS," says the learned Paul, who knew that Angels were repetitions, and here they represent the feminine period. Hair was an emblem of puberty; and as the type of feminine pubescence it ought to be covered and wear the male power—or its symbol—set over it; such covering was significant at one and the same time of modesty and maternity.

"Judge in yourselves, is it comely that a woman pray unto God uncovered?"[3]

Here is an appeal made to a non-existent consciousness which has to be recreated before the language of Paul can be understood, and yet on account of this lapsed sense of ancient decency the woman is compelled to religiously wear the bonnet in all sacred assemblies, and she must not pray to God uncovered.

The Kabalistic lore containing a knowledge of these things was a

[1] Bartoloc. *Bib. Rab*, tom. i. pp. 228, 9.
[2] Ch. iv. 19.
[3] 1 Cor. xi. 13.

form of the Angels' food of Psalm lxxviii. 25, which men did eat of old. In the margin this is identified with the Kabiri, or modified Abari, and called the Bread of the Mighty. The Kabala was first taught by God himself to a select company of angels, in fact to the seven princes of the chariot, and, after the fall from Eden, the angels communicated to man the celestial doctrine as the means whereby he could regain his lost paradise.

One of the Kabalistic books has been attributed by the Jews to Adam himself, or to an Angel named RASIEL, from whom they say Adam received it.[1] Rasiel is the Watcher in the southern heaven. From Adam it descended to Noah, and to Abraham, who carried it into Egypt, where Moses was first initiated into its mysteries. Moses correctly taught its principles in the first four books of the Pentateuch, but withheld them from Deuteronomy. Moses likewise initiated the SEVENTY Elders into the secret wisdom of all the great Kabalists who formed the unbroken line of descent for the tradition. David and Solomon are recognized by the Jews as the masters of the science. No one, they say, dared to write down this matter of the mysteries till Simon ben Jocai, who lived at the time of the destruction of the second temple,[2] by which time the phenomenal origin was overlaid and almost lost.

What the Essenes called the doctrine of angels, meaning the knowledge of the time-cycles and their periodic recurrence, THAT constituted the Jewish Kabala, and with this knowledge, obscured by later redaction, begins the first chapter of Genesis.

The beginning, in mythology, will be shown to consist of figuring time and space by means of the circle, and thus putting a boundary to that which was heretofore the Boundless, the face of heaven being the first dial-plate, or face of the clock on which the circle was drawn. "*My soul is from the beginning, from the reckoning of years*," says the Osirian in the Ritual,[3] and the reckoning of years was the beginning ; the first of these being reckoned by the Great Bear and Sothis.

The beginning was Sabean, and, as it will now be shown, dependent on the revolution of the Seven Stars about the pole. The Kabalist beginning with Adam-Kadmon, *as a male being*, is later. We shall find that all beginning is founded on the female, the Genitrix, not on the Generator. The first Atum (or Adam) is extant in the Ritual, where she is designated "*the Mother-Goddess of Time.*"

"The Mother-Goddess of Time," she who figured the first celestial circle, before Ptah formed his Egg of the sun and moon, as the father of the fathers of beginnings, and who was the ancient Mother of the gods.[4] This mother of all beginnings in time is figured in the Egyptian planisphere as the Goddess of the Seven Stars of Ursa Major, a hippopotamus wearing a crocodile's tail, the most ancient type of the

[1] Bartoloccii.
[3] Ch. xcii.
[2] *Ginsburg on the Kabalah.*
[4] Ch. clv.

water-horse and bearer of the waters.   She has various names already cited, and is known on the monuments as Ap, Apt, Abt, Tep, Teb, Tef, Teft, Kef, Kefa, Kheb, Kheft, Khepsh and Taurt.   Ap (Eg.) is primordial, the first.   Tepi means the first.   Teb is the Ark.   Taurt is the typical chariot or bearer ; the first, chief, oldest.   She is the old Typhon, the outcast of a later theology.   Khab means to give birth to, and she was the first form of the Genitrix who gave birth to time in heaven.   Kefa means to seize, lay hold, grip, and she was the earliest layer-hold, who tied up a knot of time, hence her symbol of the Tie.   Teb means the ark, and She was the primal ark of the unknown Vast, called the waters, hence the image of the water-cow.   Kef means to look, to watch, and Kefa was the sevenfold watcher, the watcher whose seven eyes went to and fro through the whole earth.   Her name as Khebti or Hepti reads number seven.   In the beginning then, it is claimed, was the circle figured by Kefa [1] of the Seven Stars, the Goddess of the Great Bear, and her first child as Time was Seb.

Here it must be observed that Seb-Saturn is a secondary deposit of Kronus.   The first Time born yearly was personified by Sebti (Sothis), the Dog-Star, a representative of Time (Seb) in a dual aspect, or the repeater of Time.   Seb is the earlier Keb or Kebek, that is as now interpreted the child (Khe, ☽) of Kheb the Genitrix, and Mother-Goddess of Time, who bore Time as her child.

The present writer maintains that the Typhonian religion and the Typhonian types are the oldest extant, whether in Egypt or out of it.   Taurt, the Hippopotamus Goddess, is earlier than the Cow, and this will account for Isis being represented in a Typhonian shape,[2] which shows the conversion of the ancient Genitrix into the more humanized form.

Champollion[3] has copied Nephthys, the divine mother, the Gestator in the hippopotamus shape.   Typhon, the old, first, great one, is the "*nurse of the gods*" on a monument of the Sixth Dynasty, and was then divine, not devilish.

Some of this most ancient Sabean lore is extant in the Book ot

---

[1] "Why," asks Dr. Birch, "*why do you make the Great Bear Kefa?   The hind-quarters of a Lion* ☟ *(peh) are used for Kefa, and are always carefully distinguished from the Khepsh* ∽ *sign used for the Polar Constellation.*"   Answer, if here and there the name *Kefa* is used for Khepsh or Taurt, it is not because of any confusion of two goddesses, but only as a variant of the names *Khebma, Kheb, Khep, Kep,* the original *Kefa* of the North.   The distinction was made on behalf of a Solar Kefa of the Western hind-quarter at Thebes, but, in the fourfold type of the ancient Genitrix compounded of the Kaf Monkey, the hippopotamus, the crocodile, her hinder part is that of the lion or lioness.   All four are included in the Goddess of the North.   And here, in mentioning the name of the eminent founder of Egyptological science in England, I should like to thank Dr. Birch for his help, kindly proffered and freely rendered, in answering my questions during a series of years.

[2] Wilk, *Mat. Hieroglyphica,* xix.   [3] 17 D.

Job. Although the cult had been superseded in the mind of the writer, the Gnosis is still there. " *Behemoth*," he remarks, in a passage full of perplexity to commentators, is the first, or " *the beginning of the ways of God.*"[1] The word used is the RASHITH (ראשית) of Genesis, the exact equivalent of Arke. The RASHITH of the ways of God is " B'RASHITH " of the Mosaic creation and of Proverbs viii. 22. But how this can be so could not be seen without the symbolism and mythology of Behemoth.

Behemoth is the Egyptian BEKHMA, the hippopotamus. Bekh means to bring forth, and Ma (or Mut) is the water and the mother. The Bekhma or Bekhmut was the bringer-forth of (or from) the waters. As such she was personified as the Great Mother of Mythology, and placed in heaven as the type of the constellation better known as the Great Bear. Now it has to be understood that with the motion and the circle made by the Bear or Behemoth was the beginning in the heavens, the " Rashith " of the genesis, and that by its periodic revolution the Elohim created the heavens and the earth, or discreted and distinguished upper and lower, and made an attempt to register the recurrence of time and season. Chalmers, on the astronomy of the Chinese, observes that a very ancient and characteristic method of determining the seasons and months of the year, to which the Chinese are fond of alluding, was by the revolution of Ursa Major. One of its names, of which it has several, is "The Northern Bushel." Under this name it is often confounded with the North Pole, and also with one of the twenty-eight mansions in Sagittarius, which has the same name. Its tail is called the "handle." There is a clear statement of this method of determining the seasons in the writings of Hoh-kwantsze : " When the tail of the Bear points to the EAST (at nightfall), it is SPRING to all the world. When the tail of the Bear points to the SOUTH, it is SUMMER to all the world. When the tail of the Bear points to the WEST, it is AUTUMN to all the world. When the tail of the Bear points to the NORTH, it is WINTER to all the world." It is well to keep in mind that the body of the Great Bear was, in ancient times, considerably nearer to the North Pole than it is now, and the tail appeared to move round the Pole somewhat like the hand of a clock or watch. The historical records say that the seven stars of the " Northern Bushel " are spoken of (in the Shoo),[2] when it is said, " the pivot and the gem-transverse adjust the Seven Directors."[3]

The bushel is a type of measure, and this was the first measurer of time in heaven. Kabu (Eg.) is the name of a measure, and the word means to measure. KABT is measured out. Also HEPT (Eg.) is measure and the measure, and the name of No. 7. This initial point of all beginning then was known, and is announced by

---

[1] Job, xl. 19. [2] Pt. ii. bk. i. p. 5.
[3] Chalmers, in *The Chinese Classics*, James Legge, vol. iii. page 93.

the writer of the Book of Job as the circle made by Behemoth or the Bear, the Egyptian Khebt, of the quarter named Khepsh. When the writer of the Book of Job celebrates the potency of the Deity, the great types of the creative power selected are purely Typhonian. They are the crocodile and the river-horse, both consecrated to Typhon. The latter being the image of the genitrix Kheb, who as an earlier Nupe, consort of Seb, was associated with Khebek (Sevekh), the crocodile divinity.

The Jews call the Book of Genesis, "B'RASHITH," from the two first words of the beginning. In the same way the whole series of the cuneiform creation-tablets is named ENUMA ELISH, from the first words of the first tablet, which commences "ENUMA ELISH LA NABŪ SAMAMU;" when the upper region was not yet called heaven. Elish, the upper or raised-up region of the south, answers to the Hebrew RASHITH, as a place, the sky that was not yet called Heaven. The words B'RASHITH, when literally translated, read "In the beginning of" leaving an ellipsis, without stating in the beginning of what! This at least serves to show that "In the beginning" is not the only possible rendering. RASHITH is considered to be derived from RASH, head, chief, with the added syllable ITH, indicating the first in point of time, and therefore in the beginning.

Rashith denotes the firstborn, the first time or condition, the origin of all. Rash also signifies to be set in motion, to move to and fro; to seize, lay hold of, the highest stars, the upper part. As before said, RASHITH is used [1] for the chief of the ways of God, and the true doctrine is alluded to by Wisdom,[2] who says "the Lord possessed me in the RASHITH (beginning) of his way, before his works of old. I was set up from everlasting." The setting-up of Wisdom and the building of her house, be it observed, is connected with the number seven. "Wisdom hath builded her house, and hath hewn out her Seven Pillars."[3] Her foundations were laid in the seven stars which made the first circle in Heaven. So in the Ritual[4] "SEFKHABU built his house for him," is said of the Osirian or deceased. Sefkhabu reads seven horns. Seven horns is the equivalent of the sevenfold one, or single-horn, the hippopotamus, the constellation of the seven stars. There are reasons for supposing that Sefekh (goddess of the seven), consort of Taht (formerly Sut), was a survival of the Typhonian genitrix who made the earliest circle, built the first house, and framed the primordial heaven.

Rabbi Bechai renders "B'Rashith" in order, before all. The Seventy and Philo translate it IN ARKE (Ἀρχή). ARK (Eg.) means periodicity, encirclings, inclosings, and tyings-up. The Ark-symbol is a noose held in the hand of the goddess of the Great Bear, who

---

[1] Job, xl. 19.   [2] Prov. viii. 22.
[3] Prov. ix. 1.   [4] Ch. lvii.

personates the beginning. The word ORACH (ארח) is applied to the feminine period, as the "orach of women."[1] ARKSHA, in Sanskrit, means, regulated by stars.

ARKE, in the Greek mysteries, was the genitrix of the gods. In a Greek mythos also ARKAS was personified as the offspring of Callisto, the Great Bear. At Engyum the divine mother was worshipped as a dual feminine divinity, the same that was adored at Crete as the Great and the Little Bear. ARKIA the mother of Phoroneus was denominated "the first that reigned;" she was the first by whom time was reckoned. Venus ARCHITIS was also a form of the mother, in Arke. The Laplanders likewise designate the genitrix of the gods VIRCHU ARCHA.

Egyptian will help us to render the Hebrew beginning in a tangible form, and not leave it as indefinite as "once upon a time." RAS (Eg.) is the English raise, and RASIT is equivalent to the raised. IT (Eg.) is a name of heaven, and RAS-IT reads the up-raised or suspended heaven. Hence RAS is a name of the south, as the elevated or upper heaven. The determinative of the word RAS, to raise up, watch, in one instance is the sign of suspending and supporting a weight; in another it is the ideograph of heaven, raised up and sustained on three props or rests. The Egyptian RASIT, the propped-up heaven, is paralleled in meaning by the Hebrew ראשת (RESHETH), a bolster, used only once for the bolster of Saul,[2] that which raises up, from RAS, to be high and lifted up. Whether we read RAS-IT, the elevated and suspended heaven, or RAЗ, to raise, hang up, and IT, to figure forth, this will yield the phenomenal origin of the beginning, designated "B'rashith," in Hebrew. Once we can get on Egyptian ground we can tread securely.

This RASHITH of the beginning is the RUSAT or RUSTA (for the word is read both ways) of the Ritual. In the inscription at Denderah, of the time of Kufu, referring to the Sphinx, Rusta is written RUSUT. Primarily the Rusta denotes the raised-up or humanly-figured heaven, and is likewise used as a type of commencement. It has various applications.

RES (Eg.) is to raise up, suspend, be elevated, bow out. The RES, in Egyptian, may be written RES-T, although not found so written. But it is so in the Norfolk RIST, the rise or a rise. RISH is also to rest, and the RISH becomes the "Rest-and-be-thankful" of our ascents. In this sense the RUSTA becomes the place of rest for the dead. A variant of RES is the URS (Eg.), the pillow, bolster, or support, which, with the TH terminal, is the Hebrew ראשת, the bolster of Saul.

The RASHITH of the celestial beginning was the primal resting-place in heaven. RAS, to raise and prop up, becomes the RAÇI of the Hindu astronomers. Thirty degrees make one RAÇI, rendered a

---

[1] Gen. xviii. 11. [2] 1 Sam. xxvi. 12.

sign ; twelve RAÇI make one revolution or circle of the twelve signs. Again, RAÇI has the meaning of raising up, because the heavens of the mythological astronomy were raised up, piled and propped up in building them, just as in piling up so many stones. The RASI-Chackra is the circle of signs ; RASA, the name of a circular dance. RAS, in Assyrian, denotes two roads crossing each other within the canopy of heaven. "IT" (Eg.) is the heaven. So that the raised-up place of the one language becomes the crossing of the other. It is solstitial in the south (RAS), and equinoctial at the crossing, as at the Rusta of the west, the entrance to the underworld in the Ritual.

It was at ROSETTA, in the temple of Atum, that the stone with the trilingual inscription was found (1799), which served as the point of commencement (B'RASHITH) for the deciphering of the Egyptian hieroglyphics. This RUSTA, in the north of Egypt, is the terrestrial analogue to the one we are in search of in the northern heaven. RESH, in Assyrian, is first, beginning. RAS, as a point of commencement, passes into the title of Mercury, as RIS-Risati, the chief of the beginning. The point of beginning for the Egyptian year was in RAS, the south.

There was a Rusta south, and a Rusta north ; also a Rusta of the equinoctial level. Rusta is the southern gateway of the sun when he goes forth to the eastern horizon of the heaven, and the fields of the Aah-ru, the house of the gates or the zodiac.[1]

Horus, in the fifteenth gate, on the day of the festival of the adjustment of the year, or at the time of the vernal equinox, says, "I have brought, I have prepared, the things in Abtu, for I led the road from Rusta."[2] Abtu is the place of beginning. Also, "The Osiris has seen the pool of the Persea, which is in the midst of the RUSTA."[3] This pool was in An, the place of beginning, and of repetition. Again, we read,[4] "Hail keepers of the seven chief staircases ! made the staircases of Osiris, guarding their halls. The Osiris knows you ; he knows your names—Born-in-RUSTA ; when the gods passed, making adorations, to the lords of the horizon." Here are seven keepers of the seven staircases, which were converted into those of Osiris, whose names are "Born-in-RUSTA." These seven are the Seven Great Spirits of Ursa Major. The Rusta they were born in was the circle of the Great Bear, the Rashith of the celestial north.

"In Rasit," as Egyptian, gives us a point of place, which, when identified with phenomena, is a starting-point in space, in time, and a foothold for thought. The full form of the words rendered, "In the beginning God created the heavens and the earth," is "*B'rashith bara Elohim eth ha shamaim v'eth ha aretz.*" The Hebrew BAR, to declare, make manifest, agrees with the Egyptian PAR, or PARA, to show, cause to appear, make obvious, manifest, come forth, surround, go

[1] Ch. xvii.   [2] Ch. cxlvii.   [3] Ch. cxxv.   [4] Ch. cxlv.

round, glide round. PRA denotes visibility, with the eye for determinative. The word is also determined by the symbol of time, and signifies appearance in time. The mode of this manifestation is shown by PRA, to go round, surround, make the round, the image of the cycle of time, in which consisted the "Creation" of mythology.

The primitive Genesis has no relation whatever to the doctrine of creation out of nothing—*creatio ex nihilo*. The word create (Ker-at, Eg.) retains all that was meant by the first creation. KER signifies to curve, and AT is a type, a circle, a time; and by the circle of time was curved, carved, or created the heaven and the earth of symbolism, as will be adequately set forth. The earliest observed creators of a circle of time were the Seven Stars in Ursa Major. The word Bra has also the sense of engraving or drawing, as might be done in forming a circle. The passage may be rendered, "In Rasit the Elohim showed and explained the upper and nether heavens," or heaven and earth; the Elohim being the appearing, encircling, cycle-making disposers, on whose motion and pathway the earliest celestial chart was founded. Hebraists are not aware of the special force of the "ETH" in this passage. In Hebrew את has the meaning of a sign, a type. AT (Eg.) means to type, form, image, the circle. IT is to figure, paint, or portray. AFT (Eg.) is the abode, and the four corners; a first formation, and a name of the genitrix.

ATH in the hard form of עת means something defined, bounded, established. It is especially used for a time, the time, a course of time, definite times of the year, also for a year.[1] The true sense of the passage is, in Rasit (Rusta) the Elohim manifested the typical heaven and earth, leaving the particular point of commencement undetermined. This we affirm to be the beginning with the Seven Stars of the Great Bear, in the name of which, as URSA, we find a form of the RUS in Rusta, and in Rusta was the place of rest. An illustration of this RASHITH may be derived from another meaning of the word. RASHITH also signifies the noose or a network. The altar of the deity, as described,[2] is to have a grating of RASHITH with four rings at the four corners. Netting is typical of catching and laying hold. The goddess Net (Neith) is the knitter in that sense. The tie carried by Kefa (of the Great Bear) is a yet earlier sign of netting. She crossed the first bit of network in heaven.

It is now suggested that the Elohim of the Hebrew Genesis had their phenomenal origin in the Seven Great Stars of the Bear, no matter which of the two Bears was the first observed as the constellation of the pole, and that the Seven Elohim are the same personages and types as the Seven Rishis of India, the Seven Hohgates of the Californian Indians, the Seven Spirits of the Great Bear found in Egypt, China, and Japan; the Seven Khnemu or Pygmy sons of Ptah, the Seven Kabiri, the Seven Sons of Sydik, the Seven Dwarf

---

[1] Gen. xviii. 10, 14.　　　　　　[2] Ex. xxvii. 4.

Sons of Pinga, in the Mangaian mythology; the Seven Dancing Indians of the North American tribes; the Seven SINTOS of the Japanese, the Seven Amshaspands of the Persians, the Seven Sons of Aish, the Seven Sons of Jesse, the Seven Princes of the Chariot, the Seven Titans with Kronus, the Seven Heliadæ of the Greeks, the Seven Companions in the Ark with the British Arthur, the Seven Associates with St. George, the Seven Spirits before the Throne, the Seven Eyes in the Stone, the Seven Bears, the Seven-headed Dragon, the Seven Hathors, Seven Persian Wise Women, the Seven Sisters, the Seven Korubantes of Korubas, the Seven Whistlers, the Seven Pillars of Wisdom, the Seven Gates of Thebes, the Well of Seven Springs, the Tower of Seven Stories, the Seven Doors in the Cave of Mithras, Seven Steps of the Masonic Ladder, the Seven Inclosures of the Jewish Temple, the Candlestick with Seven Branches, the Seven Tablets and Seven Seals.

The name of the Elohim will be dealt with hereafter, and shown to be derived from ALU (Eg.), the first revolvers in relation to an earlier ALV and Kherv, and the Hebrew ACHIM, or brotherhood, as a name of the seven sons and seven companions of all mythology, who sometimes appear as male fellows, sometimes as seven females. For example, the following form of the mythical beginning with the Seven was presented by the Vice-President, Section B, American Association for the Advancement of Science, at the Saratoga Meeting (August, 1879) :—

" The philosopher of Oraibi tells us that, when the people ascended by means of the magical tree which constituted the ladder from the lower world to this, they found the firmament—the ceiling of this world —low down upon the earth—the floor of this world. Machito, one of their gods, raised the firmament on his shoulders to where it is now seen. Still the world was dark, as there was no sun, no moon, and no stars. So the people murmured because of the darkness and the cold. Machito said, ' Bring me seven maidens,' and they brought him seven maidens ; and he said, ' Bring me seven baskets of cotton bolls,' and they brought him seven baskets of cotton bolls ; and he taught the seven maidens to weave a magical fabric from the cotton, and when they had finished it he held it aloft, and the breeze carried it away toward the firmament, and in the twinkling of an eye it was transformed into a beautiful full-orbed moon, and the same breeze caught the remnants of flocculent cotton which the maidens had scattered during their work, and carried them aloft, and they were transformed into bright stars. But still it was cold, and the people murmured again, and Machito said, ' Bring me seven buffalo robes, and they brought him seven buffalo robes, and from the densely-matted hair of the robes he wove another wonderful fabric, which the storm carried away into the sky, and it was transformed into the full-orbed sun. Then Machito appointed times and seasons and ways for the heavenly bodies, and the gods of the firmament have obeyed the injunctions of Machito from the day of their creation to the present." [1]

This is a legend of the seven stars, the seven Hathors, seven cows, bears, or sisters which are met with in the oldest mythologies. The seven cows and the bull constitute one of the mysteries in the Ritual, in conjunction with the four mystical eyes and the four paddles of the sun, arranged according to the four quarters. A knowledge of these things was necessary to the deceased in death; hence the great incentive for the living to keep them in remembrance in life.

The Christian theology is supposed to derive its doctrine of the seven gifts of the Holy Ghost from the Latin version of the text of Isaiah iv. "The spirit of the Lord shall rest upon him, the spirit of wisdom and understanding, the spirit of counsel and might, the spirit of knowledge and of the fear of the Lord." But these seven spirits were extant in Egyptian theology as the seven souls of the solar god, who is spoken of as "Ra with his seven souls." [2] "Hail to thee, O Ra, four times ; hail to thee and thy soul seven times." [3] These Seven personated seven functions or attributes of the sun. They had a still earlier form in the seven spirits of the Great Bear; [4] the first seven spirits of light having their phenomenal origin in the seven revolving stars. The seven gifts of the Holy Ghost are derived from the lady of the seven stars, who as Taurt, was called the "living Word."

The Hebrew Elohim in Job are the sons, the Beni-Elohim, and identical in origin with the Egyptian seven gods of the elements ; the TAAS, a septenary of gods of the word or speech ; the seven spirits of the wind or breath invoked by the Hurons.

The worship of the Elohim marks what is termed the time of the judges in Israel. The judges are the Elohim identified by the name in the Book of Exodus.[5] In the 28th verse of chapter xxii. the Elohim are gods in the text, and judges in the margin. Another Hebrew name of the judges as שפט yields a form of Kheft (Sheft), whose name of Apt signifies judgment and the judge. Also Sebti and Hepti have the value of number seven. These are the typical princes of the people also supposed to have ruled between the time of Joshua and Samuel, who are seven in number, as the princes of the Kabala. In the margin [6] the Elohim of Egypt, that is of Kheb, are the princes, and the seven princes of the Kabalist chariot are the seven stars of Ursa Major, by which we identify the princes who were the Elohim, or Alu-akim, the brotherhood, the gods of the orbit.

The earliest divinities of the Egyptians are called the NUN, NU-TERU or NUNTERU. NUN (Nunu) means a time appointed, a type, an image or portrait, and TER is time. The Nunteru, Nuteru, or Nnu were pourtrayers of time personified as gods. They were of both sexes,

[1] Prof. J. W. Powell of Washington, *Nature*, Jan. 29th, 1880.
[2] *Tempel-inschr.* i. 29.   [3] *Papyrus of the Prince of Wales*, Brit. Mus.
[4] *Rit.* Ch. xvii.   [5] xxi. 6 ; xxii. 8, 9, 28.   [6] Ex. xii. 12.

but the NNU appear as a group of males who are fellows, associates. And there is an ideographic sign called Nnu, figured thus :[1] —

This calls to mind that in the old Siamese planispheres the figures of the stars are circles,[2] not rayed likenesses.   Here the circle is emblematic of those that moved in observed cycles of time and made the circle, of which a loop was the earliest known sign.   The Nnu are here determined by the number eight.   An eight-rayed star is the ideographic sign of the Assyrian god Assur, who is the Great God. This eight-rayed star was continued in the iconography of the Catacombs as the symbol of the manifester.   The number eight, as in the case of Taht-Esmun, denotes the Manifester of the Seven ; that is the Seven who were first represented by the seven stars of the Great Bear, and afterwards by the seven planetary gods.   Name for name, Assur is the same as Asar (Osiris), Ar the son of As, Hes, Isis.   But whereas Osiris was the solar Ar (son), Assur is a star-god, and therefore the Sabean son who in Egypt is Sut-Har.   The eight-rayed star of Assur is the equivalent of the eight Nnu, who were known as the eight great gods of Egypt, but whose origin is unknown.   In the Phœnician mythology Esmun, the eighth son of Sydik, was the Manifester of the Seven, and he was represented with eight rays round his head ; his temple, in which the sacred books were kept, being placed on the top of the Birsa at Carthage.   The Phœnician Esmun was the Egyptian Taht, Lord of Smen or the Eight.   Taht took the position of the earlier Sut as Manifester of the Seven.

Bunsen maintained that Sut was an Asiatic creation, and his rootage, together with that of the Typhonian cult, was not to be found in Egypt.   Nevertheless he was absolutely wrong.   Sut is so ancient as to seem at times entirely new in Egypt.   Bunsen admits that the seven primary gods are indissolubly connected with an Eighth, Taht, who is called by the name of Eight, and is lord of the region of Eight, Smen or Ses-sen.   But he says these numbers cannot be explained from the groups of the gods themselves.[3]   Nor do the monuments offer any direct information as to the origin and nature of the Seven, or their relation to Taht as the Eighth, who is the manifester, in whom the Pleroma is revealed.   In all the representations of Taht, the God of Sesennu, the City of the Eighth, he is always pourtrayed in conjunction with the seven gods as the one who reveals.   These seven cannot be planetary, as Taht, the lunar god, would be one of seven, whereas he is the god Eight.   Nor are they

[1] Burton, *Excerpta Hieroglyphica*, 34.   [2] Plate in *Asiatic Researches*.
[3] Vol. iv. p. 323.

mere elementaries, although the elements were associated with them as seven in number. These seven were phenomenally founded on the seven Elohim of the Great Bear. They are the seven who were associated with seven TAAS, seven elements, seven elementary forces, or seven properties of nature, into which the Egyptians divided the whole as "matter, cohesion, fluxion, coagulation, accumulation, station and division." The seven were afterwards denounced as the BETSH, the children of revolt who were first established on the height of Am-Smen. These were the first movers, revolvers, time-keepers before the raising of the firmament. They are seven in number, with the eighth for manifester or teller of time. But they did not keep true time, they were lazy, the "children of inertness," and got deposed. The later glosses on this subject, which make Ra the creator of the eight, do but confuse the matter ; these came first out of chaos, and the kingdom of Ra was the latest established of three, stellar, lunar, and solar. It cannot be explained except by remembering th at Taht, the lunar revealer, had taken the place of Sut, the dog-star, the first announcer of the seven, and it is through Sut that we have to explain the seven.

Sut, as the first announcer and manifester of the seven, was the son of Typhon, the goddess of the Great Bear, Khepsh, the oldest form of the Goddess Sefekh, whose name signifies the number seven. Taht, the lunar god, superseded Sut, and Sefekh, the mistress of the writings, became his consort, as representative of the ancient Khepsh, Taurt, or Apt, who was called the "Living WORD." The "TAAS," who are the seven gods of the word or speech, represent the Goddess Seven, who was the "living word."

The Great Bear is called the Seven Bears in the Zend. Hathor, the cow-headed genitrix, is septiform in the seven Hathors or cows ; the Great Serpent or Dragon is seven-headed, and so in various ways the one constellation is also the sevenfold in accordance with the phe-nomena, and in no other form of phenomena do we meet with the seven in one satisfying all the requirements of the various illustrations. This is the only source of the seven, who are at the same time one. The seven appear as the seven spirits of the Great Bear, and were also converted into the seven assistants or attendants of the builder Ptah and the seven sons of the Phœnician Sydik, with Esmun for the eighth. So in Hebrew Shmen is number eight, and as place Smen (Eg.) is a name of Sesennu, which is Egyptian for number eight. The eight Nnu are the eight of Smen, the seven of the Bear and the dog-star, the eight that appear in one form as the seven cows and the bull, the husband of the cows, in the Ritual. The Hebrew SMIN also means a being of either gender, and the image or idol was represented as a man with the head of a bull.

The doctrine of the Seven, with the Eighth for their Messiah, as Sut and Taht had been, was known to Micah, who, in speaking of the coming of the manifester, whose goings forth have been from of old for ever, that is Æonian, and who is to be the MASHAL of Israel,[1] says, " This shall be the Peace when the Assyrian shall come into our land, and tread in our palaces, then shall we raise against him Seven shepherds and Eight principal men," which are equivalent to, if not the same as, the eight great gods, with the eighth as the manifester of the seven.

Ibn Sarûk considers the Hebrew חשמן (plural Chashmannim), of Psalm lxviii. 31, to be the same as the Egyptian name of Hermopolis. He is right as to the words being identical, but it does not mean that the people of Hashman or Chashman shall come out of Egypt. The Princes are the eight great gods of Smen, considered as the Seven Kabiri of Ursa Major and Sut, or later Taht, who was the eighth.

We are able to connect the eight-rayed star of Assur and the eight-looped sign of the NNU with Sut, as the predecessor of Taht, the manifester of the Seven Stars. The loops also occur in the sign of SAH for a constellation, which sign is found in the tomb of Rameses IV. at Biban-el-Muluk, directly after the star Sothis, the star of Sut, with a star and eight points annexed to it.[2] Hitherto the star with eight points has been taken to denote the constellation Sah supposed to be Orion. It is now suggested that the eight-pointed star denotes Sut (Sirius), not as the sign of the dog-star constellation or group, as Eratosthenes thought, but as the representation and manifester of the Seven Stars of the Great Bear. This does not exclude ORION as one of the starry types of Sut-Har.

This beginning with the Seven Elohim of the Great Bear and the dog-star will explain how there could be light before the sun, moon, and planets existed. In the Ritual the gods of the circle and of the Seven Aahlu are called the ancestors of light. According to the Hebrew Genesis it was the Elohim who first said, " Let there be light, and there was light," and the light and darkness were divided into day and night. This was before the creation of sun, moon, and planets, or rather before time could be reckoned by their courses, a distinction lost sight of in the literalization of the myth. The seven stars that turned round nightly with the sphere were the primal light-bringers of the first creation. The periods of other stars followed, and Sut was their annual manifester, then that of the moon was registered, and last of all the solar time was observed and kept. These generators and ancestors of light were so ancient they had been sublimated, divinized, and relegated to a kind of spiritual realm beyond the phenomenal creation described in the book of Genesis.

The account of creation, then, in the Hebrew Genesis resolves into a statement that the first motion of the heavenly bodies, observed and registered for human guidance, was the periodic revolution of the

[1] Ch. v. 5. [2] *Mon. de l'Égypte*, pl. 176.

Seven Stars. These, as a constellation, are one ; as stars they are the Seven, and the divinity in whom we shall find the character of the sevenfold one is the deity of the Genesis.

In Hebrew ZMEN (זמן) means to number, to measure out, apportion, arrange, determine, and is applied to appointed times and limits of time, hence to times of festival. The Aramaic SMEN and Maltese ZMYN have the same signification. Also SHMIN (שמים) is the name of the dual heaven. Now the Smen, the eight great gods, were extant before the firmament was lifted or divided into the upper and lower heavens. These were the first creators of the heavens, which are two, or a double one, divided into north and south ; Sut in the south, and Typhon in the north. The Dog-Star and Great Bear are the determiners of south and north, therefore the makers of the two heavens, and as they are the eight Smen in one aspect, so are they the two in another ; hence the name of Smen can also be applied to the dual heaven.

In the Chaldean Creation at the dividing of the whole into two halves, the firstborn of LAKHMU and LAKHAMU were ASSUR and KISSUR, and "Assur" agrees with the God ASSUR, who is now to be identified with the Dog-Star. If this be right Kissur must denote the Seven Stars of the Bear, which would agree with the meaning of the word KISSURA for those who are united and bound together, as in the Hebrew קשר (Qashar) for a confederacy, the constellated group of the Seven Stars, the companions, the Kabiri, Sons, Rishis, Hohgates or KISSURI. Also in the Assyrian dedication of the months the twelfth is assigned to the Seven Great Gods—the zodiacal sign being Pisces—whilst the Ve-Adar or intercalary month is given to Assur, the eighth God. In the Chaldean Oracles the SMEN are described as a septenary of living beings, and there is no doubt the seven planetary disposers came to be regarded as the SMEN. But the seven planets never could be the eight Smen. They were not the first establishers of the heavens. These were the seven of the Great Bear and the Dog-Star, whence the typical eight in number.

If we take the root Sem (Eg.), that is a name of the double plume of the two heavens, it also means representatives, myths, to pass, traverse, conduct a festival. The SAMI are a group, cluster, combination ; and in Sema, to encircle, go round, the number of revolvers is eight. The first form of these was the seven stars and Sut, and the later the seven planetary deities with the eighth god as completer and manifester of the ogdoad. And only in the genitrix, who is the Egyptian goddess of the Great Bear, can we find the sevenfold one, who is both one and seven. This was Khept or Khebt, with many variants of her name. Khebt or Hept signifies seven, also the ark of the seven. Khepsh may have had a form in Khevekh for Sefekh, Number Seven, to have come from ; the SH having been an earlier KH. This would account for the name found as Chavach, for

the cleft, opening, fissure, and feminine cave. Language corroborates this beginning with the seven stars. Khebti, Hepti, Sebti,
and Suti are variants of a type-word for number seven in Egyptian.
These are also forms of the name of the goddess of the seven stars.
Khebti, Kheb, Hepti, Hat, Uati and Aft show the process of wearing
down, and this can be followed in language generally with the
names of Number Seven variously derived from the name of the
genitrix, who is the goddess of the seven stars.

Koopah, Mandan Indian.	Seyth, Cornish.	Hitu, Saparua.
Chappo, Minetari.	Saith, Welsh.	Hetu, Timur and Manatoto.
Kjeta, Lap.	Sate, Hurur.	Hithu, Rotuma.
Kātul, Logone.	Seta, Yakut.	Hita, Marquesas.
Chet, Siamese.	Shāto, Uriya.	Het, Magyar.
Chit, Ahom.	Shat, Deer.	Yidi, Uigur.
Sebatta, Gafat.	Dzhuti, Yeniseian.	Yedi, Kazan.
Shubarte, Tigré.	Tset, Laos.	Yedi, Bashkir.
Subhat, Amharic.	Tsit, Shan.	Yedi, Osmanli.
Subhu, Arkiko.	Tsit, Khamti.	Yedu, Gadaba.
Sabata, Gonga.	Hapt, Biluch.	Yettu, Irular.
Shebata, Kaffa.	Hapt, Bokhara.	Whitu, Maori.
Sibitti, Assyrian.	Hapta, Zend.	Witu, Polynesian.
Sabaa, Swahili.	Haft, Persian.	Aweth or Owith, Pelew
Sabaat, Arabic.	Haft, Brahui.	Islands.
Saptan, Sanskrit.	Heft, Duman.	Edu, Telugu.
Septem, Latin.	Heft, Khurbat.	Idi, Meshtsheriak.
Sheba, Syriac.	Efta, Tater.	Iti, Tarawan.
Sheba, Hebrew.	Epta, Greek.	Itoe, Pome.
Sappoah, Crow Indian.	Hat, Singhalese.	Itoe, Ansoes.

Other names of the Genitrix and her Number Seven might be
followed on other lines of language.

"Let Mete be exalted, who is our root, the root that is one and
Seven," is a formula of the worshippers of the image called Baphomet.

The Mexican mother-goddess Civacoatl, known as the serpent
woman, was reported to be a form of the goddess Seven, as Chicomecoatl, Seven Serpents. Civacoatl answers to the genitrix Kefa,
and the seven serpents to the seven stars. The seven uræi appear in
the Ritual. The seven-headed serpent, or dragon, was a type of
the old Typhonian genitrix. Hence the probability that the goddess
Seven-Serpents was the sevenfold type of Civacoatl. The virgins who
served Chicomecoatl carried in the sacred processions seven ears
of maize.[1]

This type of the seven ears of corn is also pourtrayed in the
Egyptian planisphere.[2] Virgo, as the goddess, bears seven ears of
corn, five in her hands and two on her head. No origin was lost.
This is one form of the goddess of the seven stars brought on in the
zodiac as Virgo. So Hathor was one and seven under the cow type.
In Pharaoh's second dream, behold the seven Hathors (cows) become
the seven ears of corn, and "*the dream is one.*"[3]

Haya in Sanskrit is a symbolical expression for the number seven.
Haya also means the horse as the goer. The first horse that went was

---

[1] Bancroft, vol. iii. p. 352.   [2] Drummond, Pl. 3.   [3] Genesis, xli. 26.

the water-horse, and this, with the typical number seven, shows that Haya is the earlier Kefa, the goer of the seven stars. Another reduced form of Kefa is extant in the Chinese CH'HOO for the North Pole and centre of motion, called the hinge of heaven, on which all turns, the Tëen CH'HOO. So in Egyptian, KHEPU signifies hinges. One form of the goddess Seven in Israel is Deborah of the hinder part, or north. She was the parent of the Princes who are the seven of the chariot, the seven companions. There were no princes in Israel, she sings, until that I, Deborah arose, that I arose a mother in Israel. She preceded the "new gods," and the wars of the Lord.[1] Deborah was the first, the primordial Word, the oracle of the beginning, identical as such with Tep (Eg.), the tongue, and Teb, a name of Typhon, the living Word; one with Wisdom of the seven pillars, and Arke of the beginning. Her name also identifies Deborah with the north, or hinder part. Before her time, we are told that the highways were unoccupied, and the travellers walked through the byways. There was no celestial chart, no roads mapped out, no inhabitants in heaven. Hers was the time of the SHEPHT, the judges (princes), the seven companions who are the Elohim of Genesis, whose judgment-seat was the mount, and who rode on white asses. Following Deborah, "They chose new gods; there was war in the gates." Hers was the reign of Peace. Hept (Khept) means peace and plenty. Hers was the time when mankind were of one tongue, the golden age associated with the name of Sut or Saturn.

Her consort is Lapidoth (לפידות), the lightner; his name signifies lightnings. Another Hero is Barak, whose name has the same meaning. Barak is Sutekh; Bar the Son, the Ar, is one of Sut's names. Sutekh or Barak was the glorious war-god, fierce as fire, the fulminator against the powers of darkness, one of the first, as the star Sothis and son of the Sabean mother, to pass through the Hades of death, cut through the Akhekh of darkness, or make a way out of the swallowing monster of the mythos; the first, as the present writer thinks, to rise again on the horizon of the resurrection as Orion, or Sut-ORIENS.

But if Deborah be Typhon then the most especial Hebrew form of Sut or Bar-Typhon the war-god, is not Barak, but Samson. Samson lived in the time of the Judges, the Shepht, the Princes, the Seven, the Elohim. He was one of them himself, but whereas the other great warriors fight at the head of large forces, Samson is the hero alone. Hitherto the comparative mythologists have not looked beyond the solar type for a witness to Samson. The first celestial hero was not the sun, but the conqueror of the sun and solar heat. He was represented by the dog-star not only as the fire-god, but a god over fire; and at the season when the sun was in the sign of the lion and the heat in Africa was intolerable, then Sut, as Dog-Star, or as Sut-Har (Orion), arose, and as the sun had then attained its supreme height and

[1] Jud. v.

began to descend, the Dog-Star, or Orion, was hailed as the conqueror of this cause of torment. The lion, as is apparent from its place in the zodiac, was the type of the furious summer fire, hence Samson, like the later Hercules, slays the lion as his first feat of strength, and out of the slain lion comes the honey. The ass being a type of Sut Samson kills the Philistines, the inimical forces, with the jaw-bone of an ass. The fox is another type, and Samson destroys their corn by means of the foxes.

Sirius is designated the " Hairy " in Arabic. The SERAU (Eg.) is also a hairy goat-kind of sheep. The star of Sut and hair thus meet in a word. Samson is the hairy one whose strength is associated with his hair. Sut, who vanquished the lion of the summer heat, brought the inundation. So the Ass figures in traditions respecting the Jews, as the animal that guided them to the place of springs in the desert when they were dying of the drought. This is probably connected with the "spring of the jawbone" in the place of Samson's exploit, founded on the story of Sut, bringer of the waters to the thirsty land. In accordance with this, the name of Samson (שמשׁי־ון) contains the Hebrew SHEVN (שׁון), to make water, pour out, cause to flow, pour out plentifully ;. SEFA (Eg.) being a name for the inundation.

If we take " Shem " as the title of the god or renowned hero, or Shema to be bright, glittering, resplendent, SHEM-SHEVN (Samson) is the exact equivalent of the glorious star of Sut, the herald and hero of the outpouring waters of the Nile.

The Targum on 1 Samuel xvii. 4 makes Samson to be the father of Goliath, and that is corroborative of his being a form of Sut. The giant is a personification of a large cycle of time ; the largest of these was the Sothiac cycle, a period of 1460 years—the Goliath of cycles! If we only take the annual cycle determined by Sut, that was a giant compared with the length of a lunation. This latter was reckoned by Taht, who superseded Sut, and the Hebrew Taht, David, is the slayer of Goliath; so the moon-god, Khunsu, is the giant-killer.

Another shape of the goddess of the Seven Stars in Israel is חוה Chavvah or Eve, the mother of Sut or Seth, who follows a form of the Seven Patriarchs, on the line of Adam and Lamech.

Ashtoreth, the horned goddess, commonly associated with the moon as her type, is the earlier Deess of the seven stars. She was represented by and as the moon, accompanied by the seven stars, erroneously assumed to be the seven planets.[1] The seven stars of Ashtaroth or Ishtar are independent of both moon and sun ; they are the seven stars of the Bear.

The horns are not limited to the lunar type, they belong to the cow Hes or As, and it will be argued that Ashtoreth is the Egyptian Ta-urt in the form of the cow or seat, whence Hes-ta-urt. The cow was seven-

[1] Calmet's *Dictionary*, pl. xvi. fig. 13.

fold in the seven cows or Hathors, the horns sevenfold in Sefekhabu. The typical seven do not originate with the moon, but with the seven stars, the Elohim of Ashtaroth.

On the under surface of a scarabæus in the British Museum [1] we see the lady of the seven stars seated on a chair with the mystical seven figured in a straight line behind her. Before her stands a priest or adorer. Between the two there is a symbolic star. This then is the star of the number seven, the goddess of the seven stars, who in Assyria is Ishtar. The number seven is duplicated. In her left hand the goddess holds another seven similar globes or balls arranged circle-wise. These seven disks are identical with the seven balls or globes depicted within the rings on the Scottish stones, as the number of the stars in the Bear constellation.

The Kabalists, who have preserved some of the most ancient images, have the double triangle or six-cornered figure of the two heavens, called the Shield of David, the same figure that, with the addition of a circle round it, forms the SRI IANTRA of Hindustan, and is an ornament in the Royal Masonic Arch. The inscription on it, seven times repeated, is Agla (אגלא). Agl (עגל) means to circle, be round, turn or wind round in a circle. The Aglah is a rolling thing, a car, a chariot. The Agl, Agla, or Aglah was also the golden or molten calf, a symbol of the divinity worshipped in Israel as the Agl-Meskah,[2] that is the birthplace typified by the calf or heifer, a form of the Virgin mother. The six-pointed star or double triangle called the Shield of David is the image of the four corners united to the height and depth, but the sevenfold Agla preserves the seven cows of Hathor, and belongs to the seven stars or the seven Elohim of the beginning.

תור, the Hebrew name of the heifer, is one with Tepr (Eg.), and the heifer was a type of the genitrix worshipped in Israel. Also the whole law and doctrine, precepts, statutes, regulations, and religion of the Jews are named תורה, and Tepr (Eg.) means the oral commencement, the Word of the Beginning. This was depicted in the planisphere by Tef, the genitrix with her tongue (tep) protruding from her mouth as the utterer of the primeval word of revelation, direction, and of law.

The Dove as the Ionah (יונה), or Thvr (תור), is a symbolical figure of Israel. The dove still bears the name of the Ancient Genitrix Tef. It is the Typhonian bird of breath belonging to the pre-masculine period of mythology before the Hawk was adopted. One name of the Typhonians is the Menat, and this is a name of the dove. The dove was a type of the great mother, as Semiramis, it was also an emblem of Juno ; the spirit that brooded over the waters in creation was the dove-like. It signified the same thing and the identical cult in Israel as elsewhere. Tep (Eg.) means to breathe, inhale, and the Thvr was the feminine bird of breath.

[1] Landseer, *Sabean Researches*, p. 361.   [2] Ex. xxxii. 4, 8 ; Deut. ix. 16.

When the Greeks symbolized the Seven Pleiads as seven doves, they had got hold of the wrong constellation in relation to the number seven. The seven doves, like the seven bears, cows, sisters, Hathors, Hohgates, Kabiri, or others, are the seven great stars in Ursa Major. It appears to me that the same mistake may have been made in rendering the Hebrew KEEMAH by the Pleiades.[1] כימה, according to Fuerst, is derived from כום, KVM, in which we have before found a form of the Egyptian KHEBMA, the name of the hippopotamus-type of the Great Bear. Keemah, from KVM, would render one form of the name in the same reduced way that AISH or GAISH may render KHEPSH, whilst the sons of Gaish would be the seven considered as the Elohim, Kabiri, or male companions. The coupling of the constellation with Orion twice over points to its being Ursa Major. Both Bears are constellations of seven stars, and both are circumpolar. Possibly AISH (Khepsh) and KEEMAH (Khebma) may be the two forms of the Bear, or the Bi-Genitrix.

Pythagoras in his Golden Sayings calls the two Bears the hands of Rhea.[2] In another saying he calls the Sea the tear of Time, and that is Egyptian. The Egyptian Rhea is Nupe, the pourer-out of the water; but the water-horse was earliest, therefore Rhea is Ur, or Ta-urt, of the Bear, or, according to Pythagoras, of both Bears.

The Great Bear is still known in Britain as David's Car.[3] In the name of David we have the earlier Dyvid (of Wales) identifiable as the Egyptian Tepht, a name of the abyss of the North, and the goddess of the car, which imaged her as the bearer. Devab (דוב) or Deb (דב) is a she-bear. In Egyptian Tabi is the bear, and Teb, Tep, or Tef is the goddess of the Great Bear. Debab (דבב) means to speak, and Tep (Eg.) is the tongue. Tzebab (צבב) is a collateral form of Debab (דבב) as Zephon is the Hebrew form of Typhon, or Tef, the Bear. Seb-at in Egyptian would be the circle of Seb or time, but the male form of time personified in Seb is later, and Seb is the earlier Keb, Kep, or Kef. Kef-at then is the circle of Kefa, the Great Bear, the first feminine form of time, and identical with Devab the she-bear. Zebab means to cover, to roof over, to bend,. turn, wind round together, as did the seven stars in the Bear. In Egyptian, Kebeb, represented in Hebrew by Zebab, means the source of all. Devab, Zebab, and Kebab meet in the primordial (Ap or Ab), and ancestral Teb, Zeb, Keb, or Kefa, goddess of the Great Bear, whose son was called Baal-Zebub the precise equivalent of Sut-Typhon.

The pole-star is called the "Star of Joudi" by the Arabs. Joudi is a modified form of Khefti, the north, as hinder part. This tends to connect the polar constellation with Judah as her star, and suggests that the meaning of Judea was from Kheft, the hinder thigh, a name of the Great Bear, and that the naming from the north, as Kush

---

[1] Job, ix. 9, xxxviii. 31.   [2] Stanley, p. 9.
[3] Lardner's *Museum of Science; How to observe the Heavens*, p. 153 (Chambers).

or Khebt, was continued in Judea. If we take the Jad to represent a K-sound, יהור contains all the necessary elements of Kheft. The Elohim of GIVAH[1] are the Gods of the hinder or northern region, and the KHEPT (Eg.) is extant in שית from שוה or Gavah, a hut-village, the lowly dwelling-place.

In the first chapter of Genesis the Creator is called Elohim, in the second chapter the Divinity is denominated Jehovah (יהוה), and countless volumes have been written on the two different deities of the Elohistic and Jehovistic accounts of the creation, whereas it will be made manifest that both have one and the same nature under the two different names. Elohim, as in the title of Ashtaroth, the goddess of the Seven Stars, denotes the sevenfold nature, and Jehovah the one who is of a sevenfold nature. We have not far to seek for the sevenfold types of Jehovah of the seven days, seven trumpets, seven times, seven eyes in the stone, seven pipes, seven lamps, seven lights, and seven stars. Of all gods or goddesses, Jehovah is the divinity of the number seven.

The Hebrew writers identify Ashtaroth as Elohim. Elohim takes the place of Goddess and is its synonym. In 1 Kings xi. 5 we read, "And Solomon went after Ashtoreth the Elohim of the Zidonians," where Ashtoreth is a feminine plural, whereas Elohim is a masculine plural. This is in perfect accordance with the mythos of the Seven Stars. Ashtoreth as feminine singular is the goddess Hes-Taurt or Isis-Taurt, the secondary form in Egypt of the genitrix of the Great Bear. Ashtaroth yields a plural form of her name whether as bi-genitrix or the goddess seven. The cult of Ashtaroth is described as being the worship of the "Host of Heaven." Ashtaroth has the meaning of a flock, which is a form of the host. The word rendered host is TZEBA, and Seba is the Hebrew word for number seven, from Sebag, Egyptian Sefekh, number seven. The first host or flock was that of the seven stars, cows, or other animals, and Jehovah of Tzeba or Tzebaoth was the Divinity of the seven stars, the seven eyes in the stone and the seven ewe lambs. The Assyrian ISTARĀT are goddesses[2] like the Ashtaroth of the Hebrew,[3] and their plural form together with the singular as Ashtoreth is only to be found in the constellat on of the sevenfold one. Elohim as a masculine plural corresponds to the seven stars personified as the seven male companions, the seven Kabiri, Rishis, Hohgates, Khnemu, Princes or other male forms of the seven considered as sons whether of the mother or the father.

Another illustration of the sevenfold one is found in the term Elohim which literally means gods, and yet the verb is at the same time in the singular number. This answers to the unity of ASHTO-RETH and the ELOHIM on the phenomenal basis now claimed for both in the constellation of the seven stars, which furnished the primary

---

[1] 2 Kings, xviii. 34.   [2] Great Inscrpt. of Khorsabad, 48.
[3] Judges, x. 6.

type of another duality identified by name as the Hebrew Jehovah-Elohim, the exact replica of Ashtoreth-Elohim as the genitrix, the mother or representative of the seven. It is intended to show that Jehovah is also the mother-goddess and a form of Kefa or Khebt, the Typhonian genitrix.

According to Hebrew scholars the name יהוה is to be derived from a stem הוה (Havah), and this we take for the modified form of Chavah, the heth with mappiq being an intermediate sound. CHAVAH חוה (in Pih, fut יהוה) means to say, announce, declare, show. Kefa (Taurt) was the LIVING WORD. Khab means to give birth to. Hab is the messenger. The mode of annunciation is manifest in Kavah to move in a circle, to set up, establish in the form of a circle. The circle-maker was Kefa or Khebt of the seven stars, the encircler, surrounder, and binder. Chavah (Phœnician חוה) means to live, breathe, respire, therefore one with Havah (הוה), Aramaic Heba. The breather was the pregnant genitrix Kefa, one of whose names is Tep, to breathe, respire, inspire. The great mother is the *enceinte* one, the breather and inspirer of life. Kefa was pourtrayed as the pregnant Water-cow. יהוה, as understood by Hebrews, is primarily the one who brings to be ; the producer of being. So Kefa (Eg.) denotes to be born, and to be born of ; Khab means to give birth to, Khep signifies to generate, cause to exist, to be.

Manasseh Ben Israel considers it is the universal opinion of the Kabalists that the name of Jehovah designates the world of emanations, called the Aziluthic world. In Egyptian As is the seat, the foundation ; Ash is emanation, and Lut denotes repetition, several. Lut also means to create, and retain the form. The same Rabbi observes that the four letters of this name may be variously arranged to compose twelve different words, as was done by the Kabalists, all having the same signification of " to be." Now when the name of Kefa is worn down to AF, and AF to AU, AU (Eg.) still signifies to be ; the past, present, and future of being, the was, is, and is to be. On account of the feminine origin of Jehovah the name is frequently written She in the Pentateuch, and made to read He by the punctuators, after the image of the divinity had changed sex. In fact the word for " He " in Hebrew הו will not only read She but is Heva, earlier Kefa, and when Isaiah iterates his " ANI-HEVA, ANI-ANI-HEVA," I am He, I, even I, am Heva, meaning, of course, the male, it cannot be done without reproducing the original She. The primal " I AM " was of a feminine form, the " I am " announced by Neith at Sais, " I am all that was, and *is*, and is to be." This was the very self signified by the Hebrew הוא, the self of the mother of the gods, and of the title Neith-Tes ; TES meaning the selfhood, and being a special designation of the genitrix.

All came out of the letter He, say the Rabbins, and this takes us into the domain of hieroglyphy.

In Hebrew, H is the enclosure, the Heth, from חות, and earlier חות (CHEVTH), to surround, encircle, enclose. Chevth is the Egyptian Khept, the genitrix, who in the next stage, answering to Heth, is HAT (Hathor), the habitation of the child. Finally, the Chevth, Hevth, and Heth deposit the phonetic H, the letter out of which all came because it was a type of the motherhood. The ה has the numeral value of 5, and the original Khept (Eg.) denotes the fist, a figure of 5, also the creative hand, the matrix. All came out of the goddess in Mythology, the god included, as she was the genitrix of the gods, hence the ה (Heth letter), which, from an early period, stood for the name of Jehovah,[1] must have denoted the female divinity and not the male Jahveh of the later cult. The following list will show how much the Hebrew derived from Khepsh, Khevekh, Khept, Kep, Kheb, and Aft.

GISH (גיש), from גוש, GVSH, the seven stars of the Great Bear.

GVSH (גוש), to curdle, heap, collect in a lump, clot and clod.

GVCH (גוח), to push forth the fruit of the body, to bear, be pregnant and bring forth, to bubble up as water with air bubbles.

GVH (גוה), body, properly belly.

GV (גו), back.

GVI (גוי), fem., Geviah, belly, within, interior.

GVA (גוע), to breathe out.

GVP (גוף), to be gibbous, bowed out, bellying, swelling, stout (gestating).

KVTH (כות), to keep, conceal, the kept or concealed.

KPTH (כפת), to bind about, tie round, be round, bellying, as the womb or pomegranate.

GVTH (עות), to knot together, interweave curve, round out.

KBD (כבד), to be thick, heavy, dense, large, fleshy, pregnant, port, majesty, glory, gestation.

QPD (קפד), to be drawn, rolled, folded together, made ready, be coagulated, congealed, as cheese, or the child in embryo.

KBIR (כביר), great, the great. The Arabic Venus was called Kabir, the great, because she was the great, i.e. pregnant, which is the origin of greatness ; the title of the genitrix, as Pehti, or Peh-peh (Eg.), is the doubly great, the glory in which the Two Truths of puberty and gestation are combined in the image of the dual lioness.

GVL (גול), to go round, to turn in a definite circle.

GVH (גוה), to hollow out, deepen, make concave.

CHVTH (חות), to surround, enclose, of a hedge.

HVTH (הות), to bind about, surround.

HEVD, to be green, fresh, and hale, as a derivative from Kheft, agrees with Uat, to be green and fresh, literally Wet, the name of Uati, goddess of the North, who was the earlier Kheft.

AVTH (אות), to be, to exist, essential being, support, body, be embodied, impersonated.

AVD (אוד), to turn, wind, surround, move, turn circularly, be puissant and mighty, bend, writhe, heave.

AVTH, a sanctuary, abode of being.

AVTH (אות), body, being, person, essential self.

AVTH (אות), to be, to exist, to make a sign of covenant between God and Man, or between the heavens and earth, a memorial sign of time in the division of day from night (Gen. i. 14).

This Avth (or Uth) represents the Egyptian Aft, a reduced form of Kheft the genitrix, who under her first name as Khebt or Kheft is goddess of the seven stars and of the north. As Aft her name denotes the four corners of her circle, the memorial sign of division of the circle into four quarters, Aft (Eg.) being No. 4, the four corners. The Hebrew אות is the foundation of Eth or Uth of the "ETH-Sikkuth,"[2] and in Egyptian Aft-Sekht would denote the ark of the four quarters, the tabernacle of Aft the goddess, the old genitrix who in the hippopotamus shape was the earliest queen of

---

[1] Movers, *Kritische Untersuchungen*, &c. p. 75.   [2] Amos, v. 26.

heaven, Kefa, Kheft, or Kivan. This Avth (אות), which in Hebrew had become an abstract or indefinite term, thus recovers its original significance in relation to the obscured phenomena of the beginnings.

Inscriptions on the tombs and sarcophagi of the Lycians show that the people invoked the goddess PHATE, the Greek Leto, to avenge them on those who dared to violate the resting-place of the dead. Phate also answers to Aft, the Great Mother, the birthplace of the living and abode of the dead. Another of her names, Urt or Ret (Taurt and Rerit), supplied the name of Leto.

It was on account of the feminine origin of Jehovah that it was considered blasphemy to pronounce the name. The Jews, with the Targums and the Seventy, understand that to blaspheme the name of JEHOVAH was to utter it distinctly, say it aloud. Hence the sacredness of the unutterable name. Therefore the man who blasphemed the name[1] may only have pronounced it. That was enough; to utter it was to identify it and proclaim its nature. The man's father having been an Egyptian would account for his knowing the name, and for uttering it he is commanded to be stoned to death.

The Rabbins call the name of Jehovah the name of four letters, it was their mystical Tetractys or Tetragrammaton, the wonderful number of the ineffable name. Now יהוה is really composed of three letters, not four, and the statement conceals a secret not meant for the profane. The younger Buxtorf observes that the name of Jehovah resolves into only three letters, J. H. V., which denote the Being who revealed himself as he who was, is, and is to come. A numerical four or figure of four is of more importance however to the Tetragrammaton than even four different letters. In the Gnostic account of the beginning attributed by Irenæus to Marcus, it is said the Deity uttered the first word of four letters. This word was Arke ($\dot{a}\rho\chi\acute{\eta}$)—the Greek form of the famous Tetragrammaton, which with the Hebrews was the name of four letters. In the later accounts of creation the Deity is postulated as God the Creator, the cause of phenomena; in the earliest the phenomena when personified, supplied the Divinity. "In Arke" was in the beginning, and synonymous with "in the circle" as a type of time. Ark (Eg.), as before said, means to encircle, encirclings, enclosings, settings, endings, weavings; ARKAI is to appoint a limit, fix a decree, and signifies finis. The first circle or Arc observed in heaven as a measure of time was that of Ἄρκτος (Arktos), the Bear whose revolution made the first (Arctic) circle round the pole of the north. The four letters typify the four corners of all beginning. Apt is the name of the goddess of the Great Bear, and of the four corners. Here the secret of the mystery is that Jhvh was represented by the beast that went on all fours, whose name was written with four letters, and who was a figure of four. Apt the genitrix is the abode of the four corners. The

---

[1] Lev. xxiv. 10, 11.

four corners at first represented by the four legs of Apt, the beast, were afterwards depicted by a goddess bending over the earth and resting upon her hands and feet, or on all-fours. Also the hippopotamus has four toes to each foot.

Everything continued by the Hebrews was typical, and they commonly dried their figs for preserving in the shape of four-sided cakes. This is an image of the old genitrix Teb or Apt. Both Teb and Aft are applied to the four corners or quarters. Also Teb (Eg.) is the name for figs and for the box, the Hebrew square cake of figs.

According to Joshua Ben Jehuda, in his commentary on the Pentateuch, the דבח cake was made and baked in the shape of a four-sided brick of clay or gypsum. Teb (Eg.) is the brick, and the four-square loaf thus named after the goddess Teb is still called a brick.

The Hebrews have a Kabalistic figure held to be most sacred and unfathomably profound. This consists of a circle containing three Jads and a Tau, or Qamets.

Kircher says the three Jads mark the three hypostases in the divine nature. By the single Qamets (tau), placed beneath, they are meant to symbolize the unity of the essence common to each person in the trinity.[1] That is after-thought. The figure belongs to a time when there was no trinity and no fatherhood in heaven, but the mother and child only. This is the present writer's interpretation of the figure. The circle or noose is the hieroglyphic of ark or Arkai, one meaning of which is the 30th of the month, as the type of a completed period, and it meant established, finished. Three Jads in Hebrew have the numeral value of 30, and these give to this circle the significance of the noose (ark), carried by the goddess of beginnings.

The Tau Cross, hieroglyphic Tat, or cross, means established for ever. The figure is thus composed of the circle and cross, and the No. 30 shows this to be a figure of " In Arke " the beginning. The three Jads and the Tau also furnish the numerical four on which the circle was founded, the four of Aft, the abode. If the lower sign be the דמק, it is equivalent to a binding, a bundle, the noose (Ark), for an enclosing, as QAMETS means to close, and would be a perfect determinative for the three Jads, No. 30, " IN ARKE." ARKHU is the Assyrian Month or Moon ; ARAKA, a Jain division of time.

The Jews are charged with preserving to a late time the symbol of the Ass-head. This also is an Egyptian ideograph with the numeral value of 30, and therefore equal to the three Jads. The end of a period and completion of the circle of one year is illustrated by

[1] *Œdipus Ægypt.* vol. ii. cap. ii. pp. 114, 115.

the head of an ass figured in the sign of Leo at the point where the Egyptian year ended and was renewed.[1]

Sha (Eg.) is likewise No. 30, and the word denotes various forms of the beginning, and types of cause and commencement.

Learned Jews assure us that the Kabalists constantly added the Jad to a word for the sake of a mystery. The Rabbi Bechai explains that it showed there was a plurality of persons included in the word. The Jad itself was a sign of plurality. It was a hand, and has the numeral value of 10, or two hands, just as the hieroglyphic I with inherent U, is a plural sign. Thus Jhvh denoted the plurality of Havah, a plurality never yet interpreted by the theologians. In the ancient Hebrew letters the Jad has the shape of a kind of zed or Zeta which is identical with the Coptic and ancient Greek Zeta that passed into Z. This letter is the hieroglyphic of Sut (Sebti), and its numeral value is seven. Thus one mystery of the Jad prefixed to Havah might be resolved by the Jad being a sign of seven, the number of Havah, as goddess of the seven stars.

The Jad prefixed is of the same hieroglyphic value as the typographical sign of a hand, still made use of to point with. The phonetic Jad signifies a hand, and in archaic form it had a rude resemblance to the hand. As a numeral it denotes 10 or double the value of one hand. The origin of the Jad can be traced hieroglyphically by aid of the hand. The name Jâd (יוד) includes the Vav,[2] and this relates it to the Egyptian FA, the hand; Fa is an abraded form of Kefa, Kaf, or Kep, the hand; Kefa and Fa are reduced to â, the hand, and this â is equivalent to the Hebrew Jad for the hand. Fâ, the hand, implies a form in FAF, hence possibly the reason why the Jad appears at times in the place of VAV; it also interchanges with the Aleph. Kep (Eg.) the hand is the Hebrew Kaf, called the hollow of the hand, the *palma cava*. כף the hand, the curved hollow of the hand, is likewise the sole of the foot. The primal cave, however, is the womb, as is shown by the Egyptian Kep and Khepsh, the sanctuary of the hinder thigh.

Kaf the hand and foot denotes the double nature of the Jad which gives it the numeral value of 10. The hand and foot, as explained, were types of the Two Truths, upper and lower, before and behind, breath and water assigned to Kefa as di-genitrix. One mystery of the Jad sign of ten is that it stands for the hand and foot of the creatoress Kefa, the mother of all living, which hand and foot are pourtrayed in the figure of Brahma-Maya,[3] as well as in the members of Khepr, the beetle-headed divinity. One title of Athor, the habitation of the Child, is Divine Hand."[4] The "Working Hand" was an image of deity with the Mayas of Yucatan. This

[1] *Planisphere*, Drummond, Pl. 16.
[2] See list of words on p. 138, vol. i.
[3] Lundy, Mon. Christ. J., fig. 26.
[4] Birch, *Gall.* p. 20.

working hand appears as the hand of the artist, the determinative of IT (Eg.) to paint, figure, pourtray; "It" being synonymous with Jad.

We cannot name the hand as Kef (Eg.) or Kaf (Heb.) without at the same time identifying and designating the genitrix Kefa, and that in a particular manner, for the first Kef (hand) was the womb. The goddess Kefa depicted as the hippopotamus had no other hand. That was the earliest working or creative hand, the Kef, Kep, or cave, named before the external hand or foot. This unity of the hand is also part of the mystery of the Jad; Kep (Eg.) is a name of mystery as well as of the hand.

If we were to render the Jad by Aleph then AHEVAH suggests a form ACHEVAH perfectly consonant with hieroglyphic usage, akh and ka being variants of the same sign. A relic of this appears to remain in אכף for the hand.[1] This interchange is not uncommon in the Hebrew. The Egyptian Kar is the Hebrew Akar, the Hades; Akar אכר, the husbandman is Kar, the gardener. Akel (אכל) food, is Kar food; אכף to drive, spur, push, urge on, is Kaf, should, must, receive, take; אכד fortress, castle, is Khet, to be shut, sealed as a fortress.

The Mexicans call the Holy Spirit of their Trinity (that is, the Trinity as interpreted by Europeans) by the name of ECHEVAH. Yzona is the father, Bacab the son, and ECHEVAH remains for the mother. Echevah we take to be the Egyptian Kefa, as goddess of the Great Bear, and identical with the Hebrew Jehovah.

No vowel is a primary in the earliest formation of words, and in cases like this of the Jad in Jhvh we must identify its earliest value before we can begin to discuss the meaning of the name. The Jad as vowel hardens into the consonant, and goes back as representative of ה, ע, פ, and ח, which shows it to be a final development or deposit of a guttural sound. Thus the Jad interchanges with gimel in ידע and נדע, ידם and נדם; with kaf in ישר and בשר, with qoph in יתר and קטר, with ayin in יבש and עבש, and with cheth in ינה and חנה, יאב, and חב. Therefore if Jhvh be a primary name the Jad in it must stand for a guttural or a K sound. If we take it for K it follows that JHVH is a later form of CHEVAH, Kevah, or Kefa. The hand as Jad or יוד, Greek Ἰῶτα (יותא) is a reduced form of Kheft (Eg.) the hand. By spelling the name of Jad, the hand, as we assume it to have been originally written, Kaft, i. e. (יוד) JAD with the K sound, we recover the plural Egyptian form of Kaf in Kaft or Kepti the dual of Kaf which duplicates the hand. Kepti is the di-genitrix and the double hand (or hand and foot) and when abraded into יוד. or Jâd we find the character preserved by the letter being a figure of ten with the numeral value of two hands. In the word יאב, to desire, long for, we have an instance of the Jad being a softened form of the K sound, as יאב is identical with חב, and by taking the Jad (hieroglyphic hand) to be equivalent to the Kaph (hieroglyphic hand), we see that it is a final

[1] Job, xxxiii. 7.

development of the K sound, hence its connection in ·Hebrew with the K sounds, and we are able to restore the original of Jhvh as Khevah, the Egyptian Kh being the true initial sound in the name of Kefa, Chevah or Kheb.

The woman Ivi of the Polynesian mythology can be shown to be a form of the Typhonian Kefa. Ivi in one application is a name of the Widow, the woman that is mateless, as was the first mother in the mythos, the genitrix of the gods. Ivi, Maori Wheva, signifies bone, and the Egyptian Kefa will enable us to correlate the bone, the widow, the Polynesian Ivi, Maori Wheva, Hebrew Chavvah or Khevah. The Ivi or bone of which Taaroa made the first woman means the substance, the body. This answers to Af (Eg.) flesh, the matter born of. In another form Af is Ab, the name for ivory, and ivory the hard bone returns back to Ivi. Af, Ap, Abt (Eg.) are each represented by the hippopotamus as the type of hard strength and substance, the bone of the beginning, the single horn of this animal being the symbol of hardness. Thus Af is flesh, and Aft is the genitrix. Ab is ivory, horn, bone, and Abt is the genitrix, the hippopotamus goddess otherwise Kefa, Wheva, Jhevah, or Ivi.

According to J. M. Arnold [1] there is a negro Eve, the first woman whose name signifies life. It is rendered IYE, the y representing an earlier f, and the name is also found in IFE, as the place of beginning. But this is not the Hebrew Chavvah gone back again: it is a form of the ancient mother of all flesh (Af) the hippopotamus-goddess of Africa who is the original of all the other Eves, and whose name up in Africa had been worn down from Khebma, Khep, Khef, Kef to HAWA in Swahili, IFE the Yoruba abode of the Gods, and IYE for the negro Eve.

Jehovah-Elohim of the Hebrew Genesis is identical with Ashtoreth-Elohim, with Kefa of the seven stars, and Chavvah the mother of Seth and of all flesh; Jehovah denoting the one personage as the genitrix and Elohim the seven-eight as the seven gods and their Manifester Sut. Thus Seth is eighth to the seven patriarchs of one list in Genesis. In the Hebrew Generations we are presented with two forms of the creation legend fused into one. These are commonly called the Elohistic and Jehovistic records. There are likewise two lists of the patriarchs who preceded the flood of Noah with seven names in the one and ten in the other.

Adam.	Adam.
Cain.	Seth.
Hanoch.	Enos.
Jirad.	Qenan.
Methusael.	Mahalalal.
Lamech.	Jared.
Noah.	Hanoch.
	Methusalah.
	Lamech.
	Noah.

---

[1] *Genesis and Science*, p. 155.

Sut in the original myth is one of the Elohim, the eighth, to the seven Alu or Ari the companions, the Kabiri. Arthur and his seven companions in the Ark are another form of the Elohim. In the book of the generations of Adam [1] we have the Sutite or Sethite line of descent, and with one exception [2] in the chapter, the narrative is Elohistic because, as now interpreted, Sut was the manifester of the seven Elohim of the Great Bear. These seven in the Ritual are the "seven great spirits,"[3]—"Anup made their places,"—which seven spirits are Amset, Hapi, Tuautmutf, Kabhsenuf, Maaentefef, Karbukef, and Harkhent S'khem. "Anup places them for the protection of the coffin of Osiris." These seven are behind the constellation of Khepsh, the northern heaven. The "coffin of Osiris" is the square of Ursa Major formed of four stars, also known as the Bier, bier and birthplace being identical. These four stars probably constituted the first four corners, hence four of the seven spirits are the gods or guardian geni of the four quarters. Anup is a form of Sut, a manifestation, also named the Anush or Wolf-Dog. The name of Sut as Suti or Sebti, reads Seb 5, ti 2, or number seven, and in the Genesis Anosh is the son or manifester of Seth, as if the Anosh were the eighth in the star-myth as Taht is in the lunar.

The Anosh is taken to mean the son of man, or man as the mortal, the decaying one. But this is vague, and all too general. Writers on the subject have known nothing whatever of its typology. The Anosh is, according to most interpreters, the Messiah somehow or other, and he is so in the Book of Enoch. Of him, Enoch says, "Before the sun and the signs were created, before the stars of heaven were *formed*, his name was invoked in the presence of the Lord of Spirits."[4] Elsewhere this son of man is called "the son of the Woman, sitting upon the throne of his glory."[5] This is the Anosh, the periodic manifester. He was the son of the woman, as Sut-Anush, and as Har-ur, the son of Isis, before the fatherhood existed, and both facts are acknowledged in the Book of Enoch. Anush, then, is the Egyptian name of Sut, under his type of the wolf-hound. The first Anush in heaven was the dog-star, as announcer of the cycle.

In a chapter on the typology of number and reckoning, it will be shown how the origin is connected with the numbers of the Great Bear. Sebti, as No. 7, has earlier forms in Hepti and Khepti. The name of Suti or Sebti, as god of the Seven Stars, is but a reduced form of the name of the genitrix as Khebti, and Suti must be secondary to the mother, as the son. In the word Khebti or Khepti we have the numeral value of both seven and ten, for Khep is the hand, and ti is either number two or it duplicates the hand; thus Khep-ti (Seb-ti) may be 5 and 2, or twice 5; 7 or 10. This has

---

[1] Gen. v. [2] Gen. v. 29. [3] Rit. Ch. xvii. Birch.

[4] Ch. xlviii. 3. [5] Ch. lxi. 9.

been said earlier in the present work, but is now being brought to bear on the two records, two lists of patriarchs, two forms of the mythos, the Elohistic and the Jehovistic, which have one starting-point and one meeting-point in Khept or Hebrew Khevah, as goddess of the North Pole and constellation of the Bear. We find the seven in the stars, and the two will appear in the ten divisions of time and space. For example: in the Babylonian astronomy, the five planets were called interpreters. There were also twelve chiefs of the gods, one for each sign and month, who presided over the passage of the sun, moon, and planets. Twenty-four stars, called Judges—the four-and-twenty elders of Revelation—were associated with the zodiac, twelve being north and twelve south. Under the five interpreters were a certain number of stars, one of which descended below the horizon every ten days. To complete the year, that of 360 days, it is obvious these must have been thirty-six in number, one to each of the thirty-six decans in which the sun spent ten days, the thirty-six gates in the House of Osiris.

But this reckoning by the stars was pre-solar. The star of ten days would be the Ser (Eg.), chief, ruler, disposer, arranger, consoler for that time. This brings us to a grouping of the days in weeks of ten each, which we hear of among the Egyptians.

One way or another, everything once established, was preserved in mythological allusions after it had been superseded. There is a reference to the week of ten days in the Mendes *Stele* in relation to the consecrating of the queen and uniting her to the divinity. "*Thereupon another ceremony was performed in honour of the queen in the form granted to all goddesses, who there received life a second time, scattering the fumes of incense over her and on each first day of the ten-day week,*"[1] in memory of Menât, whose collar had ten Bubu instead of the nine worn by Isis, although this was not to be publicly proclaimed.

The division of time by ten belongs to the reckoning of that number on the two hands and as the two hands. The ten digits formed the first figure of ten, as two hands. These were crossed in making the sign of ten, and a cross is still the sign of ten. The hieroglyphic ten is formed of the two hands clasped. Teka (Eg.) means to cross and join together, and the sign of ten was made by crossing the digits.

Tekai means a measure, to fix, attach, a frontier; and the first observed crossers of the horizon at regular periods of ten days became the Decani, in Egyptian the Tehani, who in the heavens were the conductors in the reckoning of the nights by tens.

The Egyptian Ephah measure is the hept, and hept is the number seven. In Hebrew measures there are seventy-two zests to one Ephah. In this combination the seven (the revolving stars) of the

---

[1] *Records of the Past*, vol. viii. p. 98.

beginning are related by measure to the 72 of space—the seventy-two duo-decans, into which the ecliptic was at length divided. In this way did one measure run into others.

It is now to be claimed that the twofold beginnings of the Hebrew Genesis are resolved into one, and explained by the universal beginning in the north, with the Great Bear for the first creator of the cycle of time and discreter of the heaven and earth into upper and lower; that this is the phenomenal origin of the genitrix named Khebt or Khefa in Egypt, and יהוה in the Hebrew Scriptures; also of the Elohim, as the seven companions of all mythology, and that Jehovah-Elohim combines both the Great Mother and the companions, Kabiri, Rishis, Hohgates, seven Princes, or Beni-Elohim.

By a well-known law of language Khefti passes into Shefti, and Shefti into Shedi. It does so in Egyptian, where Khefti deposits Suti. Khep, or Kheb, is modified into Seb, Khebt into Sebt (Sothis), and Sebt abrades into Sut, the meaning of Khebt, the hinder part, being still preserved in Sut, the tail or seat. The Hebrew Sheth (שֵׁת) for the buttocks, or hinder-part, can be traced from Kheft or Khept, the hind quarter, the rump of the hieroglyphics in two forms, as the Khepsh ⌒, or hind quarter north, and the Khept ⌒, or hind quarter west. Thus the Shedim, the later devils, represent the Khefti, evil ones, godless, satans of Egypt, and the children of Sheth,[1] are the sons of Kheft, the goddess of the seven (Khept or Hept) stars.

The Hebrew word SÔD, or SEVD סוד, a secret, a mystery, is derived from the Egyptian Khept, the Kep, a mystery, the mystery of fermentation and fertilization, the mystery of Typhon and the female whose name was Mystery in Babylon and Kefa in Egypt. It is in relation to this mystery of fertilization and pubescence that Kheft, to sit or squat on the ground, agrees with סוד, a sitting for a consultation; that is, of a very primitive oracle, which gave forth utterance when the daughter of BABYLON sat in the dust and demonstrated one of the Two Truths.[2] סוד also means to sit down, to GROUND, the same as Kheft. Kep is the inundation, the flowing period, applied to Egypt and to the feminine nature. This flow it was that produced the ground, red earth, of the human creation, and established the basis of building for the body. It was the flesh-maker. It was also one of the two first revealers, hence the consultation, the SÔD, or mystery. SÔD and SHETH meet in one meaning in Hebrew, and both come from Khept, the revealer of the mystery. The mythology corresponds to the philology. Thus Kheft, as the Hebrew Jehovah, becomes the SHADAI of Genesis;[3] the Shadai without the El prefixed, which denotes a male deity. The Elohim, Jehovah, Jehovah-Elohim, and Shadai, all meet in one divinity and starry constellation;

[1] Num. xxiv. 17.   [2] Cf. Isaiah xlvii. 1, 2, in the Hebrew.
[3] xlix. 25; Numbers xxiv. 4; Ruth i. 20, 21.

one name of the old genitrix. Aft means to suckle the child ; Aft is the exuding, the nourisher, or nurse of the child. She is the suckler, the wet-nurse. One form of the wet-nurse is Menât (or Menkat) who bears one of the opprobrious names of the Typhonians. Her peculiar symbol is the breast, or breasts, or rather dugs, drooping down. Her three breasts are all that remain on the monuments of the most ancient mother, the Dea Multimammiæ, many-teated, who is found out of Egypt as the black Diana of Ephesus. In the Hermean zodiac she appears as the female Waterer with her numerous teats all streaming with nutriment. This is the old, old suckler, one of the earliest types of source and sustenance, figured by the primeval man in the human childhood. This ancient genitrix (Khefa or Ta-Urt) also appears in some zodiacs as Rerit, goddess of the north pole, the suckler in the shape of a sow,[1] a primitive type of the multimammalian mother.

According to Tacitus the ESTYI, a German tribe, worshipped the great mother under the type of Rerit, the sow, although he mentions the boar as the symbol used. The sow would represent the mother of the gods, the boar her son. Hest or Est is a name of the genitrix, typified by the cow in Egypt, which had taken the place of the sow. SHAT (Eg.) is the sow, and the ESTYI were the children of the sow. Both cow and sow meet in the goddess Hathor, one of whose names is SHAAT or SHATI, the exact equivalent of SHADAI the suckler ; also Hathor follows Taurt in the secondary or lunar phase, just as Shadai succeeds Khevah or יהוה (Jehovah).

Never dreaming of the imagery still extant to give visible being once more to the types of divinity, Hebraists have interpreted the name of Shadai as meaning the Almighty. But the first powers, forces, and mighty ones, who were recognized in the heavens, were no personifications of power, as the result of abstract concepts in the modern sense of an almighty one, nor were they personifications of thunder, lightning, or winds, but simply the visible turners round in the planisphere. As it could not be known that the earth was a revolving orb, these revolvers, who were identified as the returners back, appeared to have made their way through the earth. The moon was visibly renewed, and might be a fresh creation every month. The sun also that rose again might not be the same sun that set, but that group of seven stars which always kept the same companionship and relationship would be the earliest to demonstrate their identity. These are the first mighty ones, divine ones of typology, the first sailers across the abyss of the waters, as the seven Kabiri or Hohgates, or Elohim ; the first who swam the waters as the seven bears, cows, and earlier hippopotami, or voyaged in the ark as the seven in human form, the seven potent and puissant ones, represented first of all as the genitrix Septiformis, whose type as the water-horse was the embodi-

[1] Lepsius *Einleit.* p. 108.

ment of power and potency. Khepsh, Kep, or Kefa (her names) mean force, puissance, and all that can be expressed by the Hebrew SHADAI, rendered almighty. The old goddess of the Great Bear was personified as the first almighty, as the turner round at the polar centre of the starry system, the initial point of everlasting movement.

The Egyptian Khepsh, the mighty one in the north, whose image is Behemoth, became the CAOUS of the Arabians, of whom they tell such wonderful tales. CAI CAOUS, the son, is said to have reared a city and a palace of great splendour, which was garrisoned by Genii,[1] and afterwards destroyed by an angel of God. The Persian traditions affirm that Cai Caous, the Builder, endeavoured to take heaven by escalade.

As to Shadai, the almighty, it is more to the present purpose that Shad, (שד) in Hebrew, means the breasts, mammæ, paps, the breast of a woman for giving suck, and שדה (Shadah) to moisten, bedew, to give drink, to suckle. These agree with Kefa as the waterer, the inundation, and mysterious fertilization of the Nile, which was female at first, and with KIFI, an Egyptian name of the breast and nipple. They identify Shadai with Menât, the wet-nurse, and with Rerit, the sow. The Hebrew Shadai was the suckler, and the name indicates that personification of the breasted or teated genitrix, the Dea Multimammæ, whose especial types are the hippopotamus, the cow, and the sow. It is possible that Hathor, in her primordial shape of SHAAT, may have had the sow form. But the monumental Egyptians had put that animal out of sight all they could, else, the sow was probably the original of the many-teated type.

Sha (Eg.) denotes all commencement of forms, births, becomings, and fertility; the period of the inundation, the substance born of, to make go out, to extract, cause to flow. Shat is the sow; and from the persistence of the type in Israel as the sacred or the abominable, there can be little doubt that the original symbol of Shadai, the suckler, was the Shat or Shati, the sow, just as in Britain the sow was a type of the goddess Kêd. No picture of the Dea Multimammæ could more effectively present the feminine nature of Shadai than the feminine biunity of the divinity in the description of this divinity of Israel in Genesis,—" Shadai, who shall bless thee with blessings of the BREASTS and of the WOMB."[2] The blessings of the breasts are the blessings of Shad, identified with Shadai.

The Almighty could be equally derived from Kefa, who is mightiness, force, puissance personified; the Being looked on as the power that pulled round the whole starry scheme, or at least led and headed the revolution, hence the appropriateness of the water-cow, the huge Behemoth type. Here it seems to me that in one of the numerous obscure allusions of the Hebrew writings which have been generalized

---

[1] Cf. the seven spirits or Genii of the Khepsh.　　　　[2] xlix. 25.

past recognition in rendering, Habakkuk[1] has identified Shadai and Behemoth, and coupled them together in one image. He is denouncing the ancient worship with its drink-offerings, its exposures of nakedness, its graven images, and he intimates that the violence of Lebanon shall cover them and they shall be overwhelmed by שׁד־בהמות Shad-Behemoth, the wasting or destroying Behemoth, the typical beast, the gigantic animal of legendary lore that was worshipped as the representative image of the Typhonian genitrix Bekhma. The inner thought of such allusions is of more importance than the external phrasing.

Shad, or Shadai, the divinity, when cast out, becomes the Devil, the Shad (שׁד), as devils of a later cult. "They sacrificed unto Shad,"[2] is rendered "unto devils." It is well to note the part played by the Hebrew "points" in shunting the reader off the line of the primitive thought. The origin of the Devil is the result of beginning with the goddess without the god; so Kheft, the great mother, furnishes the name of the evil one, the enemy, the Devil. The worshippers of the mother were the godless, hence the devilish.

The tie is an especial sign of the Typhonian genitrix, and one name of this tie or noose is Tepr (Eg.). The Hebrew tie worn on the head and the hand is called the Tephillin, the prayers, or appendages of prayer. Teb (Eg.) means to pray. The tie, or Tephillin, has the letter Shin on one side of it, the strap is fastened on the back part of the head in such a way as to form the letter Daleth, and the letter Jad is represented on the end of the strap depending from the hand. These three letters constitute the name of Shadai (שׁדי). The tie, Tephillin, is another link between Tef (Typhon) and the Hebrew Shadai.

Still another secret unfolds. Certain of the Jews were accustomed to write the number 15 not with the numerals ten and five, or יה (Jh), but with a 9 and a 6, as is supposed, to avoid writing the sacred name. It was not so. In writing the number 15 with the Teth No. 9, and Vav No. 6, they were preserving the name of Tef, the First One. We shall find various allusions in the later writings to this goddess of the beginning. For example, Kheft is the hinder part, the tail, rendered by the hinder feminine thigh. It is likewise the north, as the hinder part, where the tail of Typhon, as the seven-headed dragon, drew a third of the stars of heaven.[3] Israel is identified with this tail. "The Lord shall make thee the head and not the TAIL,"[4] as she had been in the Jehovah Cult.

The hinder part (Khept) is alluded to by Jeremiah, who charges Israel with saying to a stock, "Thou (art) my father," and to a stone, "Thou hast brought me forth, for they have turned (their) HINDER PART unto me, and not their face." They were worshippers of the

---

[1] ii. 17.　　　　　　　　　　　　[2] Deut. xxxii. 17, and Psalm cvi. 37.
[3] Rev. xii. 4.　　　　　　　　　　[4] Deut. xxviii. 13.

hinder part, the north and its goddess, whose symbol was the hinder (feminine) thigh.   They turned their faces and their images to the north in their worship, and this is represented reversely as turning their hinder part to the Deity.

Again it is written, "The Lord will cut off from Israel head and tail."   "The prophet that teacheth lies, he is the tail."[1]   "She that hath borne seven languisheth; she hath given up the ghost; her sun is gone down while it was yet day; she hath been ashamed and confounded."[2]   This is the genitrix who brought forth the eight gods.   In the Hebrew mythology she bore the Beni-Elohim, the morning stars that sang together in the dawn of creation when the foundations were fastened, and the four corners were fixed.[3]   As Aditi she bore the seven sons in the Hindu mythology.   As Sefekhabu and Khept (Hepti) she is goddess of the seven.   As Jehovah she has the seven eyes in the stone, the seven eyes that run to and fro through the whole earth.[4]   "Sing, O barren, thou that didst not bear, thou that didst not travail with child."   She who was unwedded to the fatherhood, and is therefore called the widow, "Thou shalt forget the shame of thy youth, and shalt not remember the reproach of thy widowhood any more."   The reason for this change proves the feminine nature of the divinity hitherto adored.   "For thy Maker is thine husband; the Lord of Hosts is his name; and thy Redeemer the Holy One of Israel; the God of the whole earth shall he be called."[5]   Which, rendered literally, is, "For thy Baals are thy Makers, Jahveh of Hosts his name; and thy redeemer (the) Q'dosh of Israel, Elohim of all the earth he shall be called."   It is asserted that the Maker is the male, and the husband of Israel who personifies the Great Mother whose peplum was never raised, and who figures here as the barren Widow.   The barren (עָקָר) also applies to both male and female, and she is the UNBEGETTING.   The same strain is continued by Hosea, who treats the "Mother yet no wife," as an abandoned harlot.   The male Lord denounces her, "Plead with your mother, plead; for she is not my wife, neither am I her husband.   Let her put away her whoredoms, and I will have mercy on her children, the children of whoredoms.   I will make her mirth to cease, her feast days, her new moons, and her SABBATHS, and all her solemn feasts, and I will destroy her vines and her fig trees.   I will allure her and bring her into the wilderness, and speak comfortably unto her, and I will give her vineyards from thence, and the Valley of Achor for a door of hope.   And it shalt be at that day, saith the Lord, thou shalt call me Ishi and thou shalt call me no more Baali."   Ishi is the male, the husband.   Then when this union takes place the Begotten Son of the Father will be born as promised by Isaiah.

This imagery is applied by Hosea in his first chapter.   "Go, take

[1] Is. ix. 14, 15.   [2] Jer. xv. 9.   [3] Job xxxviii. 6, 7.
[4] Zech. iv. 10.   [5] Is. liv. 1, 5.

unto thee a wife of whoredoms and children of whoredoms," belonging to her who is made to personate the great mother, and who as genitrix and feminine divinity without begettal is the great whore, whether of Babylon, Egypt, Israel, or Rome, because she was husbandless and bore her child, her branch, without the fatherhood. The bad language and worse sentiments of the prophets are not to be understood except on this theory of the motherhood—preceding the fatherhood—which was worshipped by the Hebrews under such names as Jhvh, Shadai, and Ashtoreth. The change advocated by the prophets corresponds to the introduction of monogamous marriage in the social system. The Lord now says, " and I will betroth thee unto me for ever. I will betroth thee unto me in faithfulness, and thou shalt know the Lord."[1] The Lord is "him that maketh the Seven Stars and Orion."[2] The seven stars were the image of Typhon as genitrix, now treated as the thing made, and no longer as the maker. These represent the great mother and her son, Sut-Har. There is, says de Rougé, a personage who walks with great steps in front of Sothis (Sut), sceptre in hand, and the whip upon his shoulder; the stars that form his constellation comprehend several decans, and correspond in great part to those of Orion. It will be shown that Orion was an early type of Sut-Har, the son of the Typhonian genitrix, and here the seven stars of the mother are coupled with Orion, the son. These represented the primeval mother, and the son born without the father now first found or founded in Israel.

Isaiah, in grimly making merry over the time when Israel shall turn to the Lord, the male Jahveh, and desert the lady of the seven stars, says, "In that day—the day of the ' BRANCH OF THE LORD '—seven women shall take hold of one man, saying, 'We will eat our own bread and wear our own apparel, only let us be called by thy name to take away our reproach.'"[3] The reproach of Israel being the worship of the woman of the seven stars, the Queen of Heaven, here typified allusively by the seven husbandless women seizing upon one man, just as in the Ritual we have the seven Hathors and the one bull, called the bull of the seven cows. The same writer in his anxiety to have the past blotted out and forgotten, conjures his countrymen thus :—" Do not record beginnings; do not dwell upon the things of old. Behold, I will do a new thing."[4]

The feminine origin of Jehovah-Elohim and the status of the degraded divinity will alone account for such gross language applied to the worshippers as is found in Exodus xxxiv. 15 ; Deuteronomy xxxi. 16, and 1 Chronicles v. 25. Only a female Elohim like Ashtoreth could have played the ZONAH (זנה) with her worshippers as described by the Hebrew writers.

When the great mother was degraded and became the Zonah of

[1] Hosea ii. 19.   [2] Amos v. 8.
[3] Ch. iv. i.   [4] Ch. xliii. 18, 19.

the later writers her name of Kivan or Kûn supplied that of the harlot. Khennu (Eg.) is a name of the harlot, the concubine, the one who is not a legal wife, and the Hebrew Zonah, the harlot, corresponds to the Khennu.

One of the Rabbinical names for the creator was HA-MAKÔM, the place, and it was a Jewish saying, "that the whole universe was not the place of God but that God was the place of the universe." The divinity is here the creator, continued after the feminine pattern, imaged by the Hebrew Meskhen or Shekinah. Makôm, the place (numeral value 186), was identified by the Jewish gematria with Jehovah, because, as it was said, the SQUARES of the letters of the Tetragrammaton ($10^2 + 5^2 + 6^2 + 5^2$) yield the same result.[1]

Herein lay a mystery unknown to Buxtorf. The true square was that of the four corners, the Abode, as Aft (Eg.) the reduced form of Kheft. This fact must have been known to the Rabbis, together with the feminine nature of Jehovah, as the place, for them to have given the same value to the four letters which could be conveyed by the figures and produce the square of the place, symboled by the Tetragrammaton. The place occurs as MAQVM מקום and as Makvōn מכון, a place, dwelling-place, the heaven, heavenly seat, foundation, basis, the dwelling-place of the divinity. The Egyptian Makhen was the great double-seated boat of the solar god Tum. Then the word is modified in מען, a habitation, dwelling-place, heaven. This is identified with Saturn, or Baal-Magvōn (בעל־מען), as his seat in the seventh heaven, and the tower of seven stages, of which his was the topmost in the planetary adjustment of the imagery.

This place (Ma, Eg., place) was the abode of Kivan or Kvm, the ancient Khebm of Æthiopia, the hippopotamus, and the two interchangeable names are identical with the Cwm and Cefn (Chûn) of the Kymry. The supreme deity Saturn obtained the name of כון from Sut-Typhon of the Seven Stars. Kivan, the world-founding and sustaining divinity, was the feminine Kivan or Kûn of the seven stars, whose symbols were the place, seat, pillar, mount, and tower. The world was founded and established in the circle of the seven stars of the lady before the courses of the seven planets were observed.

If we read Ma (Eg.), the place, then Ma-Kôm, Ma-Kivan or Ma-Kûn is primarily the place, seat, abode, the first foundation of Kefa, Kivan or Kûn, all forms of the Typhonian genitrix whose son as Sut, (Sutekh) and Saturn, became the Bar-Typhon of Egypt, Baal-Zephon of the Hebrews, Baal-Kivan of Phœnicia and the Baal-Kûn of the Numidian inscriptions. Kefa, Keva, Kivan was the mother before the name was given to the son as the Planetary Saturn.

Kivan, the goddess, the personification of the place, the seat of

[1] *Buxt. Lex. Chald.* 2001.

origin and birth, is the idol of Israel, alluded to by Amos[1] in the text, "Ye have borne ETH-Sikkuth your Malk, and ETH-Kivan your image (or idol), Kôkab your Elohim, which ye made to yourselves." Leaving the meaning of Moloch to be dealt with hereafter, it is claimed that Kivan is the goddess of the seven stars, the stars of the Elohim and of Ashtaroth, which are seven in number on the monuments. Kivan modifies into Kûn, Egyptian Khen, the inner place, the Khennu or Kenau, primarily the womb. Mes means birth (Eg.), and the Meskhen is the birth-place personated in Kûn or Kivan. This will corroborate what has been said of the Mishkan, the tabernacle of the Hebrew divinity Jah-Adonai, whether of the itinerating tent in the book of Exodus or the habitation in Jerusalem,[2] the divine dwelling-place, the Shekinah and Thkivnah,[3] the seat; both of which are identical with the Kana, Egyptian Khen, or Khennu, the later "image of JEALOUSY," the Hebrew קן or קנא.

There is no more universal name for the genitrix than this which is derived from her image, the Quen (Heb.), the hollow receptacle, the nest, Kona (Mao.) pudendum, Kenau, Khent or Hunt (Eg.) the matrix; Chhen (Chinese), Cant (Welsh), Quiente (Eng.), Gene (Vei), Gons or Cons (Cornish), Kuns (Mandan), CON (French), Knai, (Dayak), Kunam (Bathurst, Aust.), Chaan (Favorlang), Yoni (Sanskrit). The Kûn or Kivan of heaven is the Queen of Heaven, Swedish QVENNA, and HEAVEN itself has the same name as this Queen or Kivan. The image of jealousy, denounced by Ezekiel, is the Qaneh. It was worshipped in a lewd and idolatrous manner, and was placed to the north, the seat of the great mother. This image answers by name to Kivan and Ken, who was human first and celestial afterwards. The Qen (קן) "set among the stars."[4] "Record not beginnings," says the anxious prophet, but these beginnings are of paramount interest to the sociologist; they reflect the most primitive thought.

Yahan KUNA was the name of the famous temple of the Mayas, in which their oldest god, their Priapus, Baklum CHAAM was worshipped, who corresponds by name and nature to the Egyptian Khem, found on the monuments with the goddess KÛN. Also CHIAN was one of the offerings made to their goddess of food, along with beans and maize, answering to the Hebrew KAVVAN or cake. In Phœnician CHANNA was a title of Astarte or Cælestis, the Queen of Heaven. The Hebrew deity Herself is also said to be the Qana.[5] "Jehovah, whose name is Qana." And this is none other than the goddess Kûn, worshipped in the wilderness, the naked goddess also called Katesh, Ken or Kennen, the snake-goddess, who in Egypt was a form of Thermutis, the mother Taur.[6] The very divinity, who, according to Josephus, brought up Moses, and who as Tharuis, became his wife.

---

[1] v. 26. [2] Ezra. vii. 15. [3] Job. xxiii. 3. [4] Obad. 4.
[5] Ex. xxxiv. 14. [6] Bunsen, *Egypt's Place*, v. iii. p. 41.

Kivan the star of Elohim can be related to Ken and Typhon by means of the Dog-star or Ken the star of the waters.[1] The dog or bitch is Khen (Eg.) Chiuan in Chinese, and the soul of the genitrix was said to dwell in the Dog-star. The earliest dog, the Fenekh, is an image of Typhon as Khen, or Khena. The Hebrew כּוּן (Kavvan) is a cake, a sacrificial wafer which was prepared for the Queen of Heaven, who has the same name as the cake. This (בּוּן) signifies the founding and fixing of the world. It is hieroglyphical. The cake sign denotes land, earth, place, locality, orbit. It is the ideograph therefore of founding and establishing in space and time. The cake is carried with the divine drink by the Queen of Heaven (one of whose forms is Kefa) in the tree; the cake that was offered to her on earth. Kefa or Kivan was the preparer, the world-founding, and Khep (Eg.) means to create, to form, transform, cause to take shape, as in converting liquid into solid by caking. Kafnu (Eg.) is the oven of the cake. Kivan is the lady (Llafdig) of heaven whose cake is the sign of preparing, forming, creating or founding the world. In Egyptian both "nu" and "nen" denote the type, and according to Jewish interpreters the word כּוּן,[2] to prepare, to create is כּוּנֵן (Kivnen). Khep-nen (Eg.) means to form, create the likeness.

Another name of the "place" in Hebrew is Athar. "Build this house of God in his Athar."[3] "Let the house of God be builded in his Athar."[4] Athar is the name of the Egyptian goddess whose name is written with the habitation. She is the abode of Ar (or Al) the god as son of the genitrix.

SHETAR (Eg.) is a name of the betrothed wife in the mystical sense. The betrothed was the pubescent. Thus SHETAR, or the goddess Ishtar, in the Babylonian myth, is the Shedder personified, and the Sheta is one with Shaat as Hathor. The SHETAR, Hebrew SETHAR (סתר), is the SECRET PLACE of El-Shadai, the secret place (SETHAR) of his tabernacle.[5] The SETHAR was the secret covert and the covering of El-Shadai.[6] The SETHAR[7] is the feminine creatory identified with the nether (female and hindward) parts of the earth, where the Waterer is imaged with the flowing breasts. This bridal chamber of feminine privacy was the secret place of Shadai.[8] The Deity says:[9] "I answered thee in the SETHAR of thunder; I proved thee at the waters of Meribah." En revanche, Isaiah, as the caster-out, replies, and threatens that the waters shall overflow the Sethar.[10] The Sethar is as much the feminine organ of the Hebrew God as were Shetar, the spouse, and Ishtar, the great mother, the better half of the biune nature of deity. Shet (Eg.) means secret, the hidden mystery, the closed, secret, sacred place of the womb or

---

[1] *Calendar of Astronomical observations, found in tombs of the twentieth dynasty.*
[2] Job xxxi. 15.   [3] Ezr. vi. 7.   [4] Ezr. 5. 15.
[5] Ps. xxvii. 5.   [6] Job xxii. 14 and xxiv. 15.   [7] cxxxviii. 15.
[8] Ps. xci. 1.   [9] Ps. lxxxi. 7.   [10] xxviii. 17.

tomb. Shet denotes the crown-house, the abode of breath. Shet is to suckle. AR means the child, to conceive, make, create the likeness. Whence the secret place, as the Shetar or Sethar, is finally the birthplace. The Sheta of the Deity is mysteriously alluded to in the Ritual. " *I have been secret as the secret, the* SHETA TEKA *of the god, knowing what they have in their* BELLIES."[1] Sheta Teka is the hidden in secret, the seer unseen, hence determined by the tortoise. This is in the chapter of turning into a phœnix, the Ben. The allusion is to the first feminine period of time and its shroud of secrecy.

The oracle as mouthpiece of the Deity figured on the Ephod, was the feminine symbol, the Mut, or mother-mouth. This was the same image as that of the Woman who sat in the midst of the ephah called Wickedness, whose resemblance was through all the earth.[2] On account of this similitude, the mouth being the same symbol in ephah or ephod, the weight of lead was cast upon the mouth thereof to dam it up when the earlier worship had been cast out as whoreship.

The Qabah (קבה) is the *genitalia muliebria*, a pleasure chamber, and the vault of heaven, in Hebrew. This is the primitive type of the Kaaba of the Moslem at Mecca, the feminine abode. The נוה, גף, or נב is the belly, the womb. The קבר is a cave, a hole in the earth, a tomb. This was a place of divination founded on the oracle of the womb. Isaiah[3] speaks of the Kabirs who sit in grave-vaults (קברים) and seek declarations concerning the future in the abodes of demons. This origin gives appropriateness to the קברות התאוה or GRAVES of Lust.[4] The Kep, Kab or cave represented the secret place, the abode of Kefa the Typhonian genitrix. Kep (Eg.) is a concealed place, a religious sanctuary. Khab means to give birth to, and the birthplace, symboled by the hinder thigh, the Khepsh or Khept. This is the Hebrew Gab (גב) for the back or hindward part. It is applied to the typical mount of the north,[5] the high place and eminence of the female Cult. In the margin the Gab is rendered the brothel-house, on account of its primitive simplicity as the image of the Gaberoth, the Mistress, the Lady of kingdoms, and Queen of Heaven.

Kep-ti (Eg.) will read the cave of reproduction. Hebron or Kebron the Keb of the renn, the nursling child, was one of the Hills of Kefa, and in Hebron there is a " double cave," a form of the dual house, or house of reproduction, which as Aahti (Eg.) is the womb. The followers of three religions, Jewish, Mohammedan and Christian, vie with each other in adoration of this double Gab or cave. Yet it is identical with the brothel-house denounced by Ezekiel. The Hebrew Gabiah (גביע) includes the Cup and the Mount, as the womb-shaped hill. This is Targumized as AF-GABI (אוגבי) and Af (Eg.) means born of, the Af (Aft) is the place, abode, couch, four quarters, of the ancient

---

[1] Ch. lxxxiii.
[4] Num. xi. 34.
[2] Zech. v. 6.
[5] Ezek. xvi. 24.
[3] lxv. 4.

genitrix Kheb. The Kheb (Kheft) as the thigh type of the north or hinder part supplies the image in Psalm xlviii. 2. "Beautiful in elevation, joy of all the earth, is Mount Zion in the thighs (ירכה) of the north" (or the thigh-like arched hollow of Zaphon, the type of Typhon). The English version says, sides of the north, but it is thighs, as shown elsewhere.[1] Although a city, it was founded on the cave in the mount, the CEFN of the palæolithic men, the Irish CABHAIN, for a particular shape of hill, and the Hebrew GOPHEN.[2]

The abominations committed by Israel in the feminine cult such as are enumerated in Leviticus, and many other places are summed up as Thevgabah (תועבה) or Typhonian, belonging to the worship of שׁד, Shadai or the Shedim in which the calf (heifer) and the female goat also represented the Great Mother, and the Qaba, Gab, or Kep of Tef.

In the Kep (Eg.) the Qabah (Heb.) the cave or womb, celestialized as the birthplace of the seven stars or Kefa, we have the original of the Rabbinical GUPH, the birthplace of souls, a spiritual Eden, which had taken the place of the primitive heaven of the feminine Kep, Qabah or Cefn. They say there is a treasury in heaven called GUPH, and all the souls that were created in the beginning and are to come into the world hereafter, God placed therein.[3] Out of this treasury children in the womb are supplied with souls. The Talmud[4] affirms that the Messiah the son of David will not come till the number of souls be completed which are contained in GUPH, that is not till all the souls created in the beginning and placed in that treasury shall have been sent into the world. This relates to the complete fulfilment of the Great Year of the mythological astronomy.

Kheft modifies into Kêd and Ked, Kefa into Heva. Thus we find a Phœnician race called the Qedmeni (קדמני) who were formerly a portion of the Hivites.[5] And this Qed plays a prominent part in Hebrew as in קדם the past, old times, former times, ancient days, aforetime; קדמה origin, primeval condition, early time; קדמני old, former, most ancient, antiquities; קדמי going before, former, oldest, earliest, first. These words go back to the old genitrix Kheft, Kat, or Hat (hor) the mother of beginnings who was Kefa in Egypt and Phœnicia, and Hevah in Israel. Khept (Eg.) the hinder part apparently passes into various forms of Qadesh (קדשׁ) in Hebrew, which are related to the hinder part. Qadesh, the name of a place in the Wilderness of Paran is identified with the north-western part of the Paran desert; the north-west being the hinder or back part; there was also a Qadesh in the northern part of Palestine. The word is also rendered by Catamy and Catamites. The Qadesh as the

[1] Dan. ii. 32 and Num. v. 21, 27. [2] Josh. xviii. 24.
[3] Rabbi Solomon Jarchi, *in Chagiga*, fol. 5. c. i.
[4] Cod. Jevamoth, Bartol. Tom. iii., 466. [5] Gen. xv. 19.

seat and sanctuary is the hieroglyphic Khept or hinder thigh, the seat of early worship. This suggests that Qadesh is a modified form of Khep-tesh, or Khept-sha (Eg.) the commencement with the hinder side and back part, that is with the north and the goddess of the Khept or Khepsh. Khept wears down into Khat and Kat for the womb, so that Khept-esh would become Katesh or Qadesh. Katesh an Egyptian name of Kûn (Kivan) is identical with that of the feminine Qadesh, who was consecrated to Astarte and to Jehovah in Israel. The word rendered Sodomites[1] is related to this worship of Khept, the goddess of the hinder part, and has never been explicated. In denouncing the practices of the Qodeshoth, Hosea[2] connects them with Israel, " Sliding back as a backsliding heifer." The root of this matter was a primitive manner of congress alluded to by Lucretius, not necessarily unnatural although unnatural practices came to be called by the same name. The subject demands and will receive farther examination, as it is of importance to the evolutionist and anthropologist.

The great mother as Pash is the bringer of Peace. Pash, Pekh, and Peace are identical. Peace in Hebrew is shalem (שלם). Salama is a name of the goddess Venus, and one of the names of the Hebrew divinity is Jehovah-Shalem. Jerusalem was held to be the yoni of the earth and immediately under the name of Jehovah.[3] Gideon built an altar to the Jehovah of Peace in Ophrah of the Abi-ezrites.[4] This character answers to one of the two periods; it is also represented by the woman in Proverbs who says, " Peace-offerings are upon me." The other of the two characters is represented by Jehovah-Nehs;[5] the name is related to the drink-offering (נסך) and pouring out. The peace-offering and drink-offering belong to the two times of the female nature and the two heavens, upper and lower. The Nusa is an Egyptian pedestal, an altar upon which the Nile (the flowing) was represented. The period of peace (Shalem) signified that of fulfilment or gestation. The Arru (Eg.), is the ascent, steps, staircase, to mount. Aaru (Eg.) is also the heaven, Elysium. Jerusalem is probably the Aaru of peace, the Arru (mount) of the lady of the seven stars and seven steps and seven hills. Going up to Jerusalem was going up to heaven, and the idea of heaven being founded on sexual intercourse, this ascent to the high place, and yoni of the earth, at the time of the phallic festival was a primitive mode of going to heaven in the worship of the motherhood. In Swahili the "KILANGO CHA JAHA," or narrow entrance of good luck, is the gate of paradise, and this gate or CHA is the Egyptian KHA, closely related to the *Mons Veneris*. The Mount of Salem presented the same image. Jerusalem is designated the Mishkan of the Lord,[6] and the Meskhen (Eg.) is the place of

---

[1] 1 Kings xiv. 24 : xv. 12 : xxii. 46.
[2] iv. 14, 16.
[3] Basnage, *History of the Jews*, 193-4.
[4] Judg. vi. 24.
[5] Ex. xvii. 15.
[6] Ezra vii. 15.

new birth or the lying-in chamber. Nothing can be more primitive than the Hebrew imagery of the feminine cult.

The mount was an especial type of the goddess of the Great Bear, the solid figure of her supreme height. Her seat was always on the side to the north, the hinder quarter of the circle. "Great Mountain" was the loftiest title of the national divinity of the Santals, and that implies the lady of the mount. Lady of the mountain is one of the chief titles of the supreme Ishtar. In one inscription Nebuchadnezzar says, "I built a temple to the great goddess my mother, the lady of the mountain, the goddess NIN HARRISSI.[1] Ri, lady of the mountain, is a title of great antiquity given to the Genitrix in an Akkadian inscription,[2] and Rru (Eg.) is a name of the ancient nurse and of the mountain. This typical mount is named by Abraham Jehovah-Jrah, rendered Jehovah sees. But Jrah (יראה) also means the hinder part, and is so used by Isaiah in his description of the chariot. The hinder part is the north, and both are identical by name with the Genitrix Kefa, or Jehovah, whose mount is thus acknowledged as the altar of Abraham. This was the seat of Lucifer, who said, " I will ascend into heaven ; I will exalt my throne above the stars of God ; I will sit also upon the mount of the congregation in the thighs of the north."[3] The "image of jealousy" seen by Ezekiel was placed towards the north. There was the Kep or cave in the mount which represented the birthplace of all beginning.

The Hebrew name of the mount[4] is the מצב Matzeb or Matzebah, a synonym of the pillar set up by Jacob. The mount was the natural pillar ; self-erected. Moriah or Arru-salem were forms of the typical mount, the image of the Genitrix on high, the place of birth burial and rebirth. The old Syriac version of the Bible renders the name of Jhvh by Morio. Morio is synonymous with Muru, the mother-mount, the mount of the seven steps or stars, the mount repeated in Moriah. A connecting link between the mount and Jhvh may be found in מורה which according to the Syriac and the seventy means the lawgiver. In mythology the primeval lawgiver is female as in the person of Keres Legifera. According to the Getæ, Zalmoxis received his laws from the goddess Hestia. He was also said to have been clothed in a bearskin as soon as born. The tradition goes to identify Hestia with the Bear constellation as a type of the first, the feminine lawgiver. This female origin of the lawgiver as Jhvh has got mixed up with Moses in the statement of Suidas, who says Musu, a Hebrew woman, was the authoress of the Hebrew laws. In Greek, Meru is a name of the thigh, and from the thigh of the divinity was Bacchus born, that is from Meru, the mount, the mothermouth. Meru the thigh identifies the Greek divinity with Khept the hinder thigh, and with the mount of the birthplace.

[1] E. I. H. iv. 14.   [2] Smith, *Early History of Babylonia*, p. 19.
[3] Is. xiv. 13.   [4] Is. xxix. 3.

Lastly, Kefa is the original of the famous Queen Saba, declared by Josephus to have been Queen of Æthiopia and Egypt, *i.e* Khebt. The Rabbinical writers assert that she was Queen of the Kushite Æthiopia, and the Æthiopian Church has a tradition to the same effect. This tends to show the name of Æthiopia is an abraded form of Kheftiopia, the primordial Khebt named when it was a land to the north of the namers. The first of the name was in the celestial north, the birthplace in the circle of Kefa. In the Koran[1] Saba is known as Balkis, the throne of Baal, the son. The throne is Kes or Hes, with which the name of Isis is written, and the Koran relates some pleasantry practised by Solomon upon the Queen, in changing the throne of Balkis to see whether she recognized it, and was rightly or divinely directed. The throne of the Genitrix was usurped by the son of whom Solomon is a personification. Solomon had been informed that the legs of the Queen were hairy like those of an ass, and is said to have tried an experiment in order that he might learn whether he had been truly told. He laid a flooring of glass over water in which fish were swimming in front of his throne. Over this the queen was led and thinking it was water, she lifted her robe and discovered the legs, and the king saw they were hairy as Esau. Solomon having converted the queen had thoughts of making her his wife. Some will have it that he did not marry her, but others say he did so after the devil, that is Typhon, had by a depilatory taken the hair off her legs. The hairy-legged Saba is identical with the Typhonian figure of Kefa who has the legs of the Lioness.

It is related in the Hebrew Scriptures that Solomon married the Egyptian woman and went after Ashtoreth, that is the Genitrix Kefa, who may be identified by the high place which symboled the seat, and by the Elohim of the seven stars. Possibly she is acknowledged by name as Tirzah the black but comely bride of the Canticles, "Beautiful as Tirzah." Tirzah as a place is described as being the capital of the kingdom of Israel, which lay on the side of Jordan towards the north. Tirzah as person may be Taur of the hinder part, the Sah or seat. Especially as תור is also a name of the turtle-dove, (the Menat) a type of the ancient genitrix in Israel. Moreover, the Hebrew name of תרצה contains the elements of TAURT-sah, characterized as the goddess of the north, the seat, the equivalent of Hes-Taurt, Ashtoreth, Astarte, and Ishtar. The Hebrew TZAH is sufficiently related to the Egyptian Sah.

The lady of the seat is extant in heaven to-night as Cassiopœia seated in her chair. Cas, the Hebrew Kes, Egyptian Hes, is the seat or throne, and the "opœia" probably represents Kep, or Kefa. Thus Cassiopœia would be the seat of Kefa, and not the lady herself, who was represented by the seven stars. Renouf thinks that the constellation Cassiopœia was the Leg. The Leg and seven stars was

[1] Sale, ch. xxvii.

an English public-house sign. The seven stars were the thigh (or birthplace), and the thigh and leg are equivalent to the lady and seat, or Cassiopœia and her chair.

In the year 1825, a medal was struck, for the Jubilee of Pope Leo XII., with his effigy on one side, and on the other the Church of Rome, personified as a woman sitting on the globe like Britannia on her shield, having her head crowned with seven rays; in one hand a cross, in the other a cup was held forth, with the legend "the whole world is her seat."[1] This was the lady of the seven stars, whose seat was the seven hills, identical with Taurt in her first phase, and Hes-Taurt or Isis-Taurt in her second. " Here is the mind which hath wisdom ! The seven heads (or seven rays) are seven mountains, on which the woman sitteth."[2]

It has been said that the name of "JEHOVAH" was the rending asunder of the veil of Sais, which the goddess Isis boasted " no mortal had withdrawn."[3] And when the veil is rent behold it is the old, despised and outcast Typhonian goddess of the North, personified at first as the horse or cow of the water, the oldest form of the motherhood in the world; the mother of all flesh, and of time; the goddess of the Great Bear, the seven stars and seven hills; the Æthiopic Khebma, Egyptian Khebt, the British Kêd, the Virgin Mother, the Widow, and the Scarlet Lady of the modern Rome, whose colour even, like that of " MOTHER REDCAP," is still the hue of Typhon, who was of a RED COMPLEXION.

[1] Elliot, *Horæ Apoc.* vol. iv. p. 30.   [2] Rev. xvii. 9.
[3] Stanley, *Jewish Church*, p. 110.

THE EXODUS.

[NOTE. The AAH-EN-RU is a place of Plenty, a field of Rest, also the Heaven of the Gates, or Divisions, belonging to the Mythological Astronomy, whether Sabean, Lunar or Solar; the Egyptian Elysium was like the latest Heaven of the Book of Revelation, which has twelve gates. The Sabean Heaven had seven gates; the Lunar, twenty-eight; the Solar, twelve, thirty-six, or seventy-two, according to the divisions of the zodiac.

The Bark of Khepr is the Boat of the Transforming Sun and Souls. The APAP is the monster to be found in Darkness, faced in death, and fought with as Evil in all its forms.

The Cross is the TAT of Ptah, set up in TATTU, the eternal.

The EYE is a type of a reproducing circle, on account of its reflecting the images of things.

The WORD-made-true is my rendering of the title of HAR-MA-KHERU. The sentiments and illustrations are entirely Egyptian; chapter and verse can be given for them in the Magic Texts, Solar Litanies, and Ritual.]

Up from the Land of Bondage, and no longer bend
      or sue,
To the paradise of promise in the AAH-EN-RU.

Who ploughed and sowed as mortals, and their furrows
      straightly drew,
They are gods that reap, says Horus, in the AAH-EN-RU.

The bark of Khepr bears us, with the good fruits that
      we grew;
Let them sweat who have to tow it to the AAH-EN-RU.

The gods at rest are hailing the endeavours of our Crew,
As the Solar Bark goes sailing for the AAH-EN-RU.

Strike the AP-AP monster breathless; break his bones,
      and piecemeal hew
The coils he rings them with who voyage to the AAH-EN-RU.

We can never die again; we shall soar as spirits do;
No more turning into Reptiles in the AAH-EN-RU.

We shall make our Transformations, and in linen pure
    of hue,
We shall work in white for ever in the AAH-EN-RU.

We shall find the old lost faces and the nestling young
    who flew
Like Hawks divine, gold-feathered, to the AAH-EN-RU.

We shall see the good Osiris and his son the Word
    made true,
Who died and rose—the Karast!—in the AAH-EN-RU;

He who daily dies to save us, passing Earth and Hade
    through;
Lays his life down for a pathway to the AAH-EN-RU.

Lo! the cross! uplifted in the region of Tattu!
Outstretched with arms of welcome to the AAH-EN-RU.

We shall follow in the Gateways that our god hath travelled
    through:
He will meet us, he will greet us, in the AAH-EN-RU.

Here we talk of all the glory that each morning doth
    renew,
We shall share it, we shall wear it, in the AAH-EN-RU.

Here we filled the Eye of Horus, here we fed the Eye
    of Shu,
To be luminous for ever in the AAH-EN-RU.

SECTION XV.

EGYPTIAN ORIGIN OF THE EXODUS.

A PROFESSED Egyptologist has written respecting the passage of the Red Sea: "*It would be impious to attempt an explanation of what is manifestly miraculous.*"[1] To such a depth of degradation can Bibliolatry reduce the human mind! Such is the spirit in which the subject has been crawled over.

These impotent attempts to convert mythology into history, dignified with the astounding title of the Book of God, have produced the most unmitigated muddle of matter ever presented to the mind of man. There has been no such fruitful cause of misconception as this supposed source of all wisdom, designated the Book of God, ignorantly believed to have been communicated to man orally by an objective Deity. Eschatological interpretations of ancient thought too, can only be judged when we have bottomed them in mythology, and mythology is not fathomed until we have found its natural meanings directly derived from the phenomena of nature. The Hebrew or Egyptian sacred writings can no more be understood, unless we have the original matter in mind, than the allusiveness of the Chinese literary language can be followed by those who are entirely ignorant of the subjects covertly alluded to by the learned. The vanity of building up history out of myth by a process of rationalizing the primeval fables is indescribable!—the likeliest-looking fragments being selected to erect a boundary wall between us and the vast pre-historic past, with the view of defining some sort of historic partition to bump against as beadles used to beat the parish bounds. History is impossible until the unreality of miracles is understood by their being once more resolved into the realities which are masked in the myths. The Hebrew miracles are Egyptian myths, and as such can be explained in accordance with nature.

The sacred writings of the world are not concerned with geography, chronology, or human history. Such things are secondary

---

[1] *Dictionary of the Bible*, Smith, v. 3, p. 1018.

and additional to the most ancient records held to be divine. The Jewish scriptures are no exception. The historic spirit is not there. This is so in writings late as the Talmud, and the reason is because the beginning was not with the historical spirit. Consequently the characters of mythology can no more be reduced to historical proportion than the monsters of the mountain and the mist. The interpretation of sacred—that is, symbolic writings, gets farther and farther removed from their original signification as they become more definite and historical-looking. In their first phase they are indefinitely divine ; in their final phase they are supposed to be definitely historic.

We have to face the fact, and it is well to do so in a manly fashion. We cannot wriggle out of it by squirming ; we shall not avoid the collision by flinching. The light will not be shut out by blinking. The myths of Egypt supplied the mysteries of the world. The myths of Egypt are the miracles of the Hebrew writings, and a true explanation of the one must inevitably explode the false pretensions of the other. Half my labour has to be spent in reducing the Jewish mythology from the status of divine revelation and establishing its *relative* importance by the comparative method, which will be applied incessantly and remorselessly. The key of these writings was lost, and is found in Egypt.

The original foundational matter of the aptly-named Mosaic writings is not, and was not, historical at all, but entirely mythical. The primordial Exodus, like the Genesis, belongs to the celestial allegory. But after the actual coming out from Egypt into Judea the ancient fragments were re-written by those who welded the mythical and historical matter into one mass, and only by restoring the allegory can we divide and discriminate the one from the other.

The Mosaic account of the Beginning called the Creation is allowed by the most learned of Jewish Rabbins, by Philo, Paul, and certain of the Christian fathers, to be a myth—that is, a symbolical representation ; and yet the whole structure of the Christian theology is founded on the ignorant assumption that it was not mythical but a veritable human occurrence in the domain of fact. All translations of the Hebrew writings have hitherto been made under the belief that these were *bonâ fide* histories enacted upon geographical ground, to the everlasting perplexity and confusion of all who have ever attempted to verify the statements.

But it is not the face of history that we behold in these books. 'Tis but the imagery painted on a veil which conceals the features of the face beneath, and prevents recognition of the facts obscured, so that we have neither history nor allegory. The myths of Egypt will be found to have been copied and reproduced, and declared to have been given directly from the hand and mouth of the Lord, whereas there was no revelation or divine origin in the matter. The

Hebrews took them from the Egyptians, with other stolen goods, and were unable or did not choose to render a true account of them; and out of the fragments of ancient mythology a dead wall has been raised around us, and made the boundary of human knowledge for the protection of a faith, against which wall myriads of seekers after truth and spurners of these false limits have dashed out their lives, and fallen, in the apparently vain endeavour to make a free thoroughfare. As history the Pentateuch has neither head, tail, nor vertebræ; it is an indistinguishable mush of myth and mystery. Had it been a real history, Palestine and Judea ought to have been found overstrewn with implements of warfare and work, both of Hebrew manufacture and of that of the conquered races, whereas outside the book, it is a blank. The land of a people so rich that King David, in his poverty, could collect one thousand millions of pounds sterling towards building a temple, is found without art, sculptures, mosaics, bronzes, pottery, or precious stones to illustrate the truth of the Bible story of the nation of warriors and spoilers of nations who burst away from their captivity in Egypt two millions strong. Nor will the proofs be found, not if Palestine be uprooted in the search. The present object, however, is not to find flaws and falsehoods in the "Sacred Writings" and "Book of God" treated as history supplemented and disfigured by fables. There comes a time with all the preservers of the myths when the historical is joined on to the mythical, as in the Hebrew writings—say about the time of Hezekiah—and the divine descent of the gods is made to run into and blend with a line of historical personages; this process creates the monstrous, which has only been explained by miracle. The sacred writings of the Jews were treasured up and preserved in sanctity on account of their symbolical nature; in them the hidden wisdom wore a veil; the same veil that Isis boasted no mortal had lifted from her person was made to cover these writings together with their interpreters, who stood behind the veil and never lifted it. The writings were held sacred from a knowledge of their emblematical nature. They are sacred to the Christian world from ignorance; absolute, unquestioning, unsuspecting ignorance of the meaning of symbolism, and the purely Pagan origin of the teachings. When the veil is lifted from them, all the sanctity will vanish, the glory will be gone. The sacredness consisted in what they have falsely read into the myths, the pictures painted by them on the outside of the concealing veil; their own fond imaginings of the divine realities believed to be verily behind it in the holy of holies.

The chief Jewish teachers have always insisted on the allegories of the Pentateuch, and the necessity of the oral interpretation of the books by those who were in possession of the key. No confession could be more explicit than that of the Psalmist:[1] "I will

---

[1] Ps. lxxviii.

open my mouth in a parable : I will utter dark sayings of old which we have heard and known, and our fathers have told us. We will not hide them from their children, showing to the generation to come the praises of the Lord, and His strength and His wonderful works that He hath done. For He established a testimony in Jacob and appointed a law in Israel, which He commanded our fathers that they should make them known to their children." Parables and dark sayings of old are the allegories of mythology, and enigmas of the ancient wisdom of Egypt uttered emblematically ; the wisdom with which Moses is accredited by Jewish writers. Foremost amongst these parables and mystical sayings are the Exodus, the dividing of the waters, smiting of the rock for drink, and opening of the heavens to let down manna for food. These things which to the modern ignorance are miracles, are parables expressed in dark sayings of old, that is, they are the myths put forth in the manner of the mysteries. It was the same with the Hebrew teachings brought out of Egypt, as with the Egyptian writings, of which Origen observes " the priests have a secret philosophy concerning their religion contained in their national scriptures, while the common people only hear fables which they do not understand. If these fables were heard from a private man, without the gloss of the priest, or the interpretation of the secret doctrine, they would appear exceedingly absurd." And this is exactly how we have received the Hebrew writings.

The Jews always have insisted that two laws were delivered to Moses on Mount Sinai. One was committed to writing in the text of the Pentateuch, the other was transmitted orally from generation to generation, as is asserted in Psalm lxxviii. This oral law was the primitive tradition that contained the Apocrypha, the secret doctrines of the dark sayings and parables, the clue and key to all their hidden wisdom. That which was written was only intended for the ignorant outsiders ; the interpretation was for the initiated. With the re-written version of the Jewish sacred books in our possession, we have been locked outside and left there without the key.

"Woe to the man who says the doctrine delivers common stories in daily words. Every word of the doctrine contains in it a loftier sense and a deeper mystery. The narratives of the doctrine are its cloak. Woe to him who takes the covering for the doctrine itself. The simple look only at the garment, that is, upon the narratives of the doctrine ; more they know not. The initiated, however, see not merely the cloak, but what the cloak covers."[1] That is a Jewish confession of the secret nature of the Hebrew writings. And the Christian world wonders why it cannot convert the Jews to its view of their Holy Scriptures.

As the Rabbi Moses Kotsensis justly says, "If the oral law had not been added to the written law as a gloss, the whole would have been

[1] The *Sohar*, iii. 152 ; Franck, 119.

left obscure and unintelligible, for there are Scriptures contrary and repugnant to each other, and the written law does not comprehend all that is necessary to be known.[1] The foundation of the Hebrew religion was the oral and not the written law, and this matter is extant in the myths. In the Mosaic writings, says Josephus,[2] "Everything is adapted to the nature of the whole, whilst the lawgiver most adroitly suggests some things as in a riddle, and represents some things with solemnity as in an allegory; those, however, who desire to dive into the cause of each of these things will have to use much and deep philosophical speculation."

The same writer remarks with much simplicity, after giving his version of the smiting of the rock, "Now *that* scripture, which is laid up in the temple, informs us how God foretold to Moses that water should in this manner be derived from the rock."[3] The miracle ascribed to Moses was a myth, already recorded in the secret writings of the temple, to be afterwards converted into history.

It is said in the Gemara, "He that has learned the scripture and not the Mishna is a blockhead." The Bible, they say, is like water, the Mishna like wine, the Gemara like spiced wine. The law is as salt, the Mishna as pepper, the Gemara as balmy spice. To study the Bible can scarcely be considered a virtue; to study the Mishna is a virtue that will be rewarded, but to study the Gemara is a virtue never to be surpassed. Some of the Talmudists affirm that to study the Bible is nothing but a waste of time.[4]

In the ancient Jewish work "Sepher," the typical nature of names assumed to be geographical is shown in this way: "The Lord came from Sinai," that, says the Sepher, means the law was given in Hebrew; "And rose up from Seir unto them," which means it was also given in Greek. "He shined forth from Paran," that signifies in Arabic; "He came with thousands of saints," that means in Aramaic.

When Esdras, in a labour of forty nights' duration, had restored the whole body of the Jewish scriptures which had been entirely lost, he was divinely directed to publish some things and show the rest secretly to the wise.[5] This is not quoted as authentic because it is not canonical. Still it shows the Hebrew deity conniving at the same process of suppression and elimination. Again, when these writings were translated into Greek in the third century B.C. by some Alexandrian Jews the process of elimination is very visible. Dates were altered. The threat in the book of Zechariah, that the Hebrews should have no rain if they did not come up to the feast of Jerusalem was omitted, as the translators being in Egypt knew it did not apply. In rendering the Chronicles, the translator gives to the feast of the

---

[1] Buxtorf, *Synag. Jud.* ch. iii. p. 49, Basil, 1661.
[2] Pref. to Ant.   [3] Bk. iii. ch. i. 7.
[4] Buxtorf, *Synag. Jud.* ch. iii.; Stehelin's *Traditions*.
[5] 2 Es. xiv. 21.

Passover the meaning of leading forth (Pask) instead of Pascha, the passing over. After the allegories had been transformed into histories, the true interpretation, that is the symbolical reading according to the principles of the secret tradition, was forbidden to be taught in schools. The Pharisees were so fearful of the Apocryphal wisdom being unveiled and the secrets made known that they sought to prevent people from writing.

Plutarch had evidently heard of the stories told by the Jews as their histories. He remarks, "As for those who tell us that Typhon was seven days flying from the battle (with Horus) upon the back of an ass, and having narrowly escaped with his life, afterwards begot two sons, called Hierosolymus and Judæus, they are manifestly discovered by the very matter to *wrest into this fable the relations (narratives) of the Jews.* And so much for the allegories and secret meanings."[1] He here connects the tales of the Jews, which obviously relate to the Exodus from Egypt, with the myth of Sut-Typhon fleeing from the battle with Horus, and looks upon the one as a fable that has some secret meaning, the other as a fable without meaning, and unworthy of further notice. Still, for our purpose, he helps to identify the "very matter," which is, that the Egyptian fable and the Jewish relations were one and the same thing, whatsoever the amount of history or mystery these might contain.

The Jewish Haggadah deals with the legendary lore of Israel, the parables, myths, dark sayings, and allegories, and it is foolishly assumed that this work turns real history into fables and fantastic falsehoods, and resolves the persons and histories of the Pentateuch into mere symbols. On the contrary, the historical had meantime been evolved out of the allegorical, and the Haggadah preserves fragments of the primary truth. "These things are an allegory," says the learned Paul, a master of the secret wisdom, speaking of the two wives of Abraham, "for these are the two covenants," represented as two marriages ; Agar and Sarah are the two Mounts of mythology, the Sabean and Solar, and Abraham, as the consort of two allegories, must be a myth likewise, or there is no meaning whatever. Myths and allegories will be found full of meaning, and these alone will recover the sense of various supposed human histories.

It is the strangest thing of all that the dreams of Christian theology should not have been broken or disquieted by the fact that Philo, the most learned and devout of Jews, treats the Pentateuch as allegorical and symbolical, which is the nature of the sacred writings. He was a descendant of the tribe of Levi, the holy caste. His son married Berenice, the daughter of King Agrippa. He is recognized by Josephus and by Eusebius as one of the most illustrious of his race. He appears to have been an initiate in the mysteries as Paul was, and it is vain to explain that he was given to allegorical interpretation

[1] Of Isis and Osiris.

when all early sacred writings are allegorical ; nor do we arrive at
their facts by getting rid of their symbols. "Now I bid ye, initiated men, who are purified as to your ears, to receive these things as
mysteries which are really sacred, in your inmost souls ; and reveal
them not to any one who is of the number of the un-initiated, but
guard them as a sacred treasure, laying them up in your own hearts,
not in a storehouse in which are gold and silver, perishable substances,
but in that treasure-house in which the most excellent of all the possessions in the world does lie, the knowledge, namely, of the great
first cause and of virtue, and in the third place, of the generation of
them both. And if ever you meet with any one who has been properly
initiated, cling to that man affectionately and adhere to him, that if
he has learnt any more recent mystery he may not conceal it from
you before you have learnt to comprehend it thoroughly. For I
myself, having been initiated in the great mysteries by Moses, the
friend of God—nevertheless when subsequently I beheld Jeremiah
the prophet, and learnt that he was not only initiated into the
sacred mysteries, but was also a competent hierophant or expounder
of them, did not hesitate to become his pupil."[1] Philo's testimony to
the fact that the "sacred laws," as he calls them, were allegories, is
unimpeachable on the score of character. He could have had no
motive from race or religion for explaining away the early history of
his people. He treats it as *sacred*, which signified symbolic and
secret, and expounds the meaning in his own way. Not in the present
way, nor altogether according to the teachings of the past. For with
Philo philosophizing had taken the place of the physiologizing
attributed to Moses by Josephus.

Philo reads new ethical meanings into the old myths of the mysteries.
He *platonizes* them. As cloud-forms take the mould of earthly
shapes and go sailing off and dislimning in the heavens, so Philo
abstracts and etherealizes meanings which, in the myths, had solidity
as of the rock. The supposed history is so essentially allegorical as
to permit of his taking the liberty of reading into it and shadowing
forth still other allegories.

Speaking of the myths in the Hebrew books, he says truly, "These
things are not mere fabulous inventions in which the race of poets
and sophists delight, *but are rather types shadowing forth some allegorical truth, according to some mystical explanation.*"[2] He knew
something of the facts on which the fables were founded. In
writing of the woman formed from the rib of the man, he gives
us the gist of the whole matter, and describes the very object of the
present work. "*The literal statement is a fabulous one, and it is in
the mythical we shall find the true.*"[3]

It IS in the mythical *we* shall find the true, and the literal version is

---

[1] Rendered by C. D. Yonge.   [2] *On the Creation of the World*, par. 56.
[3] *Allegories*, Bk. ii. par. 7.

the false. He affirms that the writer, in speaking of the Garden of Eden and the two trees, was conveying instruction by means of allegories. By the tree which conveyed a knowledge of good and evil he was intimating that wisdom and moderation by means of which things contrary in their nature to one another might be distinguished. This is obscurely phrased, but in despite of the vague language Philo appears to have known the true nature of the myth. He remarks, "When the soul has received the impression of vice it has become *the tree of knowledge of good and evil.*" This sounds like a generalization, but it is capable of a particular meaning. Again, in regard to the rivers,—of Phison, which encircled the land of Evilat, where is the land of gold, Philo says the "writer is not speaking geographically." Evilat, he asserts, means bringing forth, and Phison, being interpreted, is the change in the month.[1] "The truth is, the sacred writer is here speaking not of any river, but of the correction of manners."[2]

AF (Eg.) denotes the bringing forth, and means birth. LAT (Rat) is to repeat several times. Pi-shen, in Egyptian, is the periodic; Sen is blood. The change of the month relates to the monthly period. We shall see the link between this and the "correction of manners" when we elicit the meaning of the Fall. CARBUNCLE and EMERALD are Philo's rendering of "Bdellium and Onyx," the stones of our version. And he connects the carbuncle with Judah as the symbol of a man who makes this confession, "In respect of whom Leah ceased from child-bearing."[3] Moses, he remarks, has given especial praise to the animal called a serpent-fighter. "This is a reptile with jointed legs above its feet, by which it is able to leap and raise itself on high, in the same manner as the tribe of locusts. For the serpent-fighter appears to me to be no other than temperance, expressed under a symbolical figure against intemperance."[4]

As Philo was more or less a master of the sacred wisdom and the allegorical mode of interpreting its types, every variant of his is worth scanning. He renders the text of Genesis iii. 15, "He shall *watch* thy head and thou shalt watch his heel."[5] He reads Genesis xxxii. 10, "For in my staff did I pass over Jordan," instead of *with* my staff. The whole tenor of translation by men who were uninstructed in the ancient wisdom has been a constant divergence from the primary meaning. They knew that water would be crossed with a staff, as such, rather than in it. But the Hebrew staff MATTEH is one with the Egyptian MATA, the bark in which the sun-god crossed the zodiacal Jordan every year and every night. The Jordan in Egyptian is Iuru-tana (Eridanus). Aru is river, and tana to divide or dividing, the river that divided for the passage in so many mythologies because

---

[1] *Allegories*, par. 20.
[2] *Ib.* par. 27.
[3] Gen. xxix. 35. Philo, *Alleg.* par. 26.
[4] Par. 58.
[5] *Allegories*, Bk. iii. par. 67.

they each and all related to the passage of the solar divinity across the waters. When we find, as we shall, that Jacob was but an impersonation of the sun-god, and his twelve sons of the twelve signs of the Zodiac, it will become probable that Jacob did cross in the MATA or solar bark of Egypt, and not with a staff. MATA also means going across in the ark as the sun did, the crossing being in the "bend of the great void," the nethermost quarter of the circle, where the abyss was located. This passage of the ark called "going in the Cabin" (Mata), is one with the Hebrew Matteh for beneath, downwards, the foundations of the earth beneath[1] and "hell beneath,"[2] the Kar-neter of the Egyptians. The crossing of the waters in the Mata as the bark of the gods thus glossed will explain the passage of the Red Sea, by aid of the "Matteh" of Moses. It is possible to cross the waters in the Mata as a boat, but not in or by the staff, Matteh, whether the rod be that of Jacob or Moses. Mis-interpretation of the original Egyptian necessitates the Hebrew miracle, which is accepted by those in whom a sense of natural law has never yet asserted itself. In this matter, however, the true way of proving what the Hebrew writings do not mean, will be to show what they do, or originally did, mean.

Origen observes, "If the law of Moses had contained nothing which was to be understood as having a secret meaning, the prophet would not have said 'Open thou mine eyes, and I will behold wondrous things out of thy law,'[3] whereas he knew that there was a veil of ignorance lying upon the heart of those who read but do not understand the figurative meaning.

"Who is there that on reading of the dragon that lives in the Egyptian river and of the fishes which lurk in his scales, or of the excrement of Pharaoh which fills the mountains of Egypt, is not led at once to inquire who he is that fills the Egyptian mountains with his stinking excrements, and what the Egyptian mountains are; and what the rivers in Egypt are, of which the aforesaid Pharaoh boastfully says, 'The rivers are mine, and I have made them;' and who the dragon is, and the fishes in its scales—and this so as to harmonize with the interpretation to be given of the rivers."?[4] What man of sense, he asks, can persuade himself that there was a first, a second, and a third day, and that each of those days had a night, when there was yet neither sun, moon, nor stars? Origen tells Celsus that the Egyptians veiled their knowledge of things in fables and allegories. "The learned," he says, "may penetrate into the significance of all oriental mysteries, but the vulgar can only see the exterior symbol. It is allowed," he continues, "by all who have any knowledge of the scriptures, that everything is conveyed enigmatically."

[1] Jerem. xxxi. 37.   [2] Prov. xv. 24.   [3] Ps. cxix. 18.
[4] Origen, *Contra Celsum*, Bk. iv. ch. i.   Cf. Ezek. xxix. 3.

Clement Alexander states, that all who have treated of divine matters have always hid the principles of things, and delivered the truth enigmatically, by signs and symbols, and allegories and metaphors. Yet this foundation of primitive fable has been converted into our basis of fact. "Accepted literally," remarks the learned Maimonides, "Genesis, ascribed to Moses, gives the most absurd and extravagant ideas of the Deity. But, whoever shall find the true sense of it ought to take care not to divulge it." This was sound Rabbinical doctrine. If any readers guessed the secret, especially of the six days of creation, they were commanded or adjured to speak of it only in enigmas. "*The true meaning of the six days' work ought never to be divulged.*" Surely this is evidence enough, yet it has hitherto been offered in vain. In vain the Talmud declares the voice on Sinai and the God descending on the mount to be mere poetic figures ; the Christian world will not believe that. They know better. All such explanations prove the malice of the anti-christian Jews ! The figures have become literal facts for them. The real pig introduced on the stage, in the Greek play, stood no chance after the long successful sham. The men who once taught these things as mythology were in the first childhood of the human race, but those who continue to teach them now as divine revelations and matters of human history might be in their second childhood.

The misreading of mythology on which theology was founded, has created confusion everywhere ; it has obscured the past, perplexed the present, beclouded the future, converted all scientific truth into religious falsehood, and made chaos in the moral domain look like the one only permanent institution in creation. We shall find the Hebrew records are invested with their supremest value in enabling us to see through them and get beyond them to identify their Egyptian origins, and then the myths will abolish the miracles. The Exodus is no less mythical than the Genesis ; no less verifiably mythical. It is contended that if there were a dozen exodes of the Sut-Typhonians, the Disk-worshippers, the Hekshus, the Jews or what not, from Egypt into Syria, THE Exodus of the Hebrew books belongs primarily and proveably to the astronomical mythology ; and its subject-matter has been, to adapt the words of Plutarch, wrested into the later relations of the Jews in composing the epic of that people.

If the reader will refer to the map of the Exodus and the wanderings, it will be seen that had the journey been a real one the Israelites at Moseroth would have almost described a complete circle and come round to a point opposite to Baalzephon and the place of departure. This circular movement is solar and zodiacal. It may be necessary to repeat that the truth now sought to be established in relation to the Exodus of the secret writings, wherein, according to Josephus, the miracle of Moses smiting the rock was already foretold, is, that the first mapping out of countries and giving them names belonged to the heavens ; the primal geography, so to say, was solar, lunar, and stellar ; the first globe ever figured was celestial. A Kabalist image of this may be seen in the tree with seventy-two branches filling in a complete circle with seventy-two countries, or the seventy-two demi-decans of the zodiacal circle, copied by Kircher.

The Burmese constellations are called Coasts of Countries, the stars being mapped out in COUNTRIES. Amongst other names found in their planisphere[1] are Talain, answering to the Tulan of the Aztecs, Yoodaya (Judea), Kothambe (Kedam), Dagoun (Dagon), Tavay (Cf. Eg. Tefi or Tepi), and others common to the mythological astronomy. One of these is Rewade, rendered "large water." In Egyptian Re-Uat is the mouth, gate, outlet, or division of the water.

The earliest nomes of Egypt were astro-nomes, the divisions of the stars, whence comes the name of astronomy ; not merely a naming, but a noming of the stars into groups, constellations, divisions, nomes. The first chart being celestial, the primitive Egypt was in the two upper and lower heavens where the thirty-six decans, gates or divisions of the Aah-ru, preceded the mapping out and naming of the two Egypts and their nomes. The first division was into the upper and nether world of night and day. This is illustrated in a legend of two dancers doing the mill by each lifting the other alter-nately, a form of Kabbing called Kab.t. Kab.t or Khebt, in this sense, is the doubled ; Khebt, the later name of Lower Egypt, had its prototype in the north, the lower heaven of night and winter, the hinder part (Khept), where Typhon or Kep, the Great Bear constellation, was found by night, as deity of the dark side of the circle. All this has to be gone through piecemeal in an account of the mythological astronomy, the solar, lunar, and starry allegories of the astro-nomes. Enough, at present, to affirm that the earliest chart was celestial, and that its divisions and names were afterwards geographically adopted in many lands from one common Egyptian original.

Amongst the stories told as mythology, the same matters were re-lated by the Egyptians themselves of the Exodus out of Egypt and the contention between Sut-Typhon and Horus thousands of years before we read of these things as events in Hebrew history. We shall see the Exodus out of Egypt is the common property of all mythology. Up to the present time it has been the endeavour, in which lives have been vainly spent, to follow the wanderings and settlements of the Israelites solely on the earth's surface. If the pursuers will but turn their attention now to Israel in the heavens, the chances of discovery will be much increased, and there is reason to hope that we may yet come upon the missing Ten Tribes in the skies, from whence they have never descended.

The difficulty of identifying such important spots as those in which

[1] *Asiatic Res.*

the Lord himself is said to have appeared to men is because these names, when they are localized at all, are but the shadows of the celestial places and positions, and it is hard to identify shadows. These astronomical positions and appearances of the Lord, whose excellency was to be seen in the sky and who rode on the heavens, are real objects, and realizable now as ever they were of old. Such sites will not be found in Palestine even though fifty societies be formed for exploration and all the Christian world should join in the search. When the stories were first related by the Egyptians, the localities were celestial, in the AAHRU of the gods, represented by planispheres on the ceilings of temples ; and now Palestine takes the place of the planisphere in consequence of the modern ignorance of mythological astronomy. This much is certain. *Our* Jews did not make the myths or the astral allegories which set them forth. They neither mapped out the heavens nor named the constellations. On their own showing they found the names already applied to places overhead and underfoot when they took possession (or woke to historic consciousness rather) of Palestine. Astronomically and geographically the names were there ; the myths had been taught, and the stories related by other races in earlier times, which stories were condensed finally into a supposed history of the Hebrews who no more enacted that history on this earth (outside their religious mysteries) than they were the originators of the allegoric representations in the heavens.

The Mount Horeb, for example, called the Mountain of the Elohim, is the Egyptian Har, the heaven, of Har, the god ; and Ap, the Mount. Horeb is the Mount of Heaven, or of Horus, the place where Deity is represented as descending to converse with man. Hor, the typical mount in Hebrew, is the Egyptian heaven ; hence the divine character of the Hor, or Horeb. Mount Seir answers to the Rock of the Horizon called Ser, or, with the article Ta-Ser, the Taser Hill, the mount in the solar myth, where the buried sun-god was re-born, and solid foothold attained once more for the continuity of time after the passage of the waters.

Ser, the Rock of the Horizon, was the Mount of Har in Egyptian myth. It was known as Bakht, the land and the mount of the solar birthplace. In the geographical adaptation of celestial names we find Ser, the rock or mount mixed up with Har, the god, in Arabia Petrea, where Hor is a part of, if not identical with, Seir. Again, the name of Mount Sinai on the monuments is known as Bakht, meaning the birthplace of the sun, the new-born Har.

Sinai, the geographical, is supposed to be Serbal, as is likely ; Ser, the rock of Baal or Har, the place of new birth. "I have adored the place of New Birth of the Tser," says the Osirian, in the 21st gate of the Aahru.[1] Sinai, as Bakht then, is the solar birthplace in

[1] *Rit.* ch. cxlvi.

Egyptian mythology, the horizon of the resurrection without the article, called the Akht and Khut.

In the same language SHENI, the equivalent of the Hebrew (סיני), signifies the region beyond the tomb, and the Mount Sinai was the steps of ascent into that region attained by the god and the souls after their resurrection from the Hades. Sheni was the place where the divinity appeared on the horizon.

The Mount Zion, or Zian, the triumphing heaven of the Ceylon Buddhists, called the place of salvation,[1] is identical, in the celestial allegory, with the Hebrew Zion, both being the same as the Egyptian Shena, the region beyond the tomb, attained after crossing the waters and completing the circuit of the heavens.

The whole story of Sinai might be reconstructed solely from the meaning enshrined so safely in Egyptian words, even if we had not the mythology also. But we have the matter as myth, and the naming as Egyptian, long before these appear in the character of Hebrew history.

The TET is an Egyptian name of the tomb, the Deep, lower heaven, or eternal abode, the place of death, *i.e.*, Tet, or the cutting off. Tet is an abbreviated form of Tahuti, the representative of Ra in the nocturnal heaven, one of whose names is Tekh. The Tet, in Hebrew, remains the Thchthi (תחתי) for the underworld. It denotes the nether parts of the earth.[2] It is the nether land of TACHTIYM-Hodshi,[3] the lowest pit,[4] and the lowest hell.[5] The word became a general term for the nether, lower, undermost, but never in common use, and in Exodus, xix. 17, when the people stood at the nether part of the mount, these two, the height and the deep, or Tet, form the natural antithesis belonging to the mythological astronomy. The Tet (Eg.) is the tomb, the void, the world of the mummies, and SHENI (Eg.) is the name of the region beyond the tomb, the mount of the resurrection.

The original names of the towns and districts of Canaan, such as Ashtaroth-Karnaim, Avilah, Berytus, Bashan, Beth-Tappuah or Tebekhu, Ephron (Hebron), Heshbon, Hamath, Judah (Southern), Kadesh, Kison, Megiddo, (Mageddo, near Ascalon), Tamesku (Damascus), and others are inscribed on a pylon at Thebes, containing 1,200 names of places, conquered or garrisoned by the Egyptians in the time of Tahtmes III., some two and a half centuries earlier than the historical Exodus. The number of Syrian names is 119.[6] In fact as Mariette Bey observes, we have before us, most accurately rendered by the hieroglyphic names, a map of the land of Canaan in "a list of 115 names, which is nothing less than a synoptical table of the promised land made 270 years before the Exodus."[7]

---

[1] Upham's *History of Buddhism*, p. 74. [2] Ezek. xxxi. 14 and 16.
[3] 2 Sam. xxiv. 6. [4] Ps. lxxxviii. 6. [5] Ps. lxxxvi. 13.
[6] Birch, *Rede Lecture*, pp. 26-7. [7] *Monuments*, p. 175, Eng. Tr.

In the statement made by Plutarch respecting the flight of Typhon, the myth passes into history represented figuratively. Typhon, he says, fled for seven days, and having escaped, afterwards begot two sons, Hierosolymus and Judæus. That is, the Typhonian religion passed out into Judea, and made its home in Jerusalem. "They who relate this are manifestly discovered by the very matter to wrest into this fable the relations of the Jews." This flight and exode of Typhon from the battle with Horus was depicted in the Mysteries and read in the Northern Heaven, where the outlet of Sut preceded the Nome or Ru of Sut, whence the Setroite Nome of Egypt. Egypt below was a copy and replica of Egypt above, and every nome and name and narrative related of them was primarily mythological; afterwards the fables containing the facts of the astro-nomes were wrested from their meaning, and converted into the facts of fabulous histories.

In Hebrew night and netherworld are synonymous.[1] The day was the other or upper world. The Sabean beginning was on the night side, that of the underworld; and the mythical migration so often met with is from the night to day, from the Sabean to the solar stage of mythology, from the cult of Sut-Typhon to that of Ra. The beginning with night, the negative, the netherworld, where the goddess of the north was the genitrix, the birthplace personified, the bringer-forth, as the ancient mother of the waters, will account for the netherworld being the domain of Typhon, when the religion had changed and the deity of darkness was transformed into the devil of the dark.

The reader has to lay fast hold of one end of the strands of rope we are plaiting for our anchor in the depths, and never leave go till it is finished. We must get well in mind and keep there the fact that Egypt, Khebt, or Mitzraim, are names of the old Sabean birthplace in the north, belonging to the celestial allegory before they were applied geographically to Egypt. They are so old that, as we have seen, Kheb, Kepsh, or Kush was named when Æthiopia was to the north of the namers. The Egypt of the Hebrew writings is mainly that of the astronomical myth, and if the anathemas of Egypt uttered by the divinely-inspired writers have any application to the real country, Egypt-itself furnished and had already applied the language to a locality of the same name, and a Red Sea that was in the heavens, and a monster that was in its waters; had, in fact, supplied the country for the cursing, the means of cursing, together with the whole imagery for clothing the curses with significance. But the Egypt continually intended is the typical Egypt, the Egypt of the allegory looked upon, after they had left it, as a land of mental bondage; and wherever the idols of the genitrix were set up for worship there was Egypt, there was Khebt, the goddess, as well as Khebt, the place.

[1] Job xxxvi. 20.

When the God of Israel says " Behold, I am against thee, Pharaoh, King of Egypt, the great Dragon that lieth in the midst of his rivers,"[1] the language and its application are the same as in Isaiah : " In that day the Lord with his sore and great and strong sword, shall punish Leviathan, the piercing serpent, even Leviathan, that crooked serpent, and he shall slay the Dragon that is in the sea."[2] Here the serpent is one with the crooked serpent of the heavens.[3] The language is typical, and can only be understood by the typology of the subject. The crooked serpent is the dragon of the north, or of Khebt.

The Egypt wherein Israel played the Zonah in the persons of the two women Aholah and Aholibah, was the land of Khebt, the genitrix, a celestial region belonging to the Sabean religion, hence her paramours, who were Sabeans from the wilderness,[4] and men of רב, rendered " common sort," or a multitude, but which are the huge men who are called elsewhere " Sabeans, men of stature,"[5] the giants of the foreworld and the early time.

Jeremiah rebukes the women of Israel for making the cakes and pouring out the drink-offerings to Kivan, the Queen of Heaven. " Jeremiah said unto all the people, and to all the women, Hear ye the word of the Lord *all Judah that (are) in the land of Egypt.*" Again he says to them, " Hear ye the word of the Lord *all Judah that dwell in the land of Egypt.*"[6] " Then all the men which knew that their wives had burnt incense unto other gods, and all the women that stood by, a great multitude, even *all the people that dwelt in the land of Egypt,* answered." This Egypt was not mundane but celestial, religious, typical ; the abode of the Queen of Heaven, who, as Kefa or Kivan, ruled over the mythological Egypt. " Ephraim also is like a silly dove without heart ; they call to Egypt."[7] " They shall return to Egypt."[8] " Ephraim shall return to Egypt."[9] That was in backsliding to the old worship of the female called the " whoredom of Ephraim,"[10] of which the dove of Israel, of Juno, of Semiramis, and Menât was a type.

It was the literalizing of the myth that misled the Seventy in their correction of a supposed error in Zechariah.[11] The writer threatened the dwellers in Egypt that they should have no rain unless they came up to keep the feast of tabernacles. The Seventy, knowing the dearth of rain in Egypt, altered this. But the Egypt signified was the place of the waters and the Waterer Shadai in the north. The feast of tabernacles was a water festival. The water of life had been given of old by the feminine deity, the suckler, which was now

[1] Ezek. xxix. 3.
[2] Ch. xxvii. 1.
[3] Job xxvi. 13.
[4] Ezek. xxiii. 42.
[5] Is. xlv. 14.
[6] Jer. xliv. 24, 26.
[7] Hos. vii. 11.
[8] Hos. viii. 13.
[9] Hos. ix. 3.
[10] Hos. vi. 10.
[11] xiv. 17.

dispensed by the male god. It is noticeable that the Hebrew names for rain are drawn from the Egyptian names of the inundation. מורה is rain; mur, the inundation; מטר, rain; ma, water,—ter, libation; ירה, rain, aur, or aru, the river; נשם, rain; âkhem, a whelming wave of water, as of the inundation.

Are ye not as children of the Æthiopians unto me, O children of Israel? saith the Lord. Have not I brought Israel out of the land of Egypt?[1] The days come, says Jeremiah, that it shall no more be said that the Lord brought up the children of Israel out of the land of Egypt, but the Lord brought *them from the land of the north.*[2] This Egypt of the Hebrew Scriptures was, primarily, the celestial Khebt which always remained in the north, the birthplace of the beginning and the starting-point for the migration found in all the oldest mythologies, always connected with the number seven, as in the seven provinces of Dyved.

In Ireland we have a representation of the seven caves, or sevenfold cave in the cave of the tribe of Oine, called the purgatory of St. Patrick, an ancient Druidic cell, on a small island in Lough Derg, in the south of Donegal. The island is only 126 yards long by 44 broad; on this is a small cavern, and round it are seven tiny chapels, which perpetuate the sevenfold nature of the cave of OINE, the Irish form of the genitrix,[3] KÛN, GWEN, or KIVAN.

Seven mythical caves, grottoes, or underground abodes are the cradle of the race in many American legends. The Quichés ascended from Tulan or Tulan-zuiva, the place of the seven caves; the Mexicans came from Chicomoztoc, the seven caves. The seven principal islands of the Lesser Antilles were a form of these. So were the seven inhabited islands of the Hervey group, which were a copy of Savaiki, the original home of men and gods.

The Nahuas sailed in seven barks or ships, called by Sahagun seven grottoes. The Hohgates (seven in number) came in one boat, and the seven are now the seven stars in heaven. The seven are represented in the Ritual by the seven staircases and seven halls in the great house of the heavens. In the prefaces to the Puranas we are told that Swayambhava dwelt in the country of Puscara, at the farthest point westward. Seven sons were born to him there, and these divided the whole world, or the Seven Islands, among themselves.[4] So Scotland or Pictland was said to have been divided into seven provinces by seven brothers who ruled over it. The names Zuiva, Savaika, Saba, identify the number seven. In Egyptian, Hept (earlier Khept) means seven, and the origin of all is found in Khebt, the north, lower Egypt, the heaven of the seven stars, and the goddess, who was the birthplace personified.

[1] Amos, ix. 7.   [2] Jer. xvi. 14, 15.
[3] *Pagan Idolatry*, Faber, vol. iii. p. 332.
[4] *As. Res.* vi. 470.

The coming out of Egypt is coupled with the gods that were worshipped aforetime, when their ancestors were on the other side of the flood where lay the land of bondage. Joshua says to the people of Israel, "Your fathers dwelt on the other side of the flood (the typical water נהר), and served other gods."[1] "Choose you this day whom you will serve; whether the gods which your fathers served that were on the other side of the flood, or the gods of the Amorites, in whose land ye dwell; but as for me and my house, we will serve the Lord." The gods were the Elohim, a form of the seven, answering to the number of the stars, with Sut as the manifester for the eighth.

When Hosea writes of Israel, "I will give her the valley of Akar for a door of hope," he is employing the language and imagery of the Ritual. The Akar, as in Hebrew, is the lower sterile barren region; the Amenti, Sheol, or Hades. The wilderness of Hosea is the Anrutf of the Ritual, the region of sterility and barrenness which is to be transformed. "Sharon shall be a fold of flocks, and the valley of Akōr a place for the herds to lie down in."[2] The god Shu-Anhar or Ma-Shu was the leader through this dark desert, and the opener of the door of hope for the rescued people who came up out of Egypt. Rahab is a typical name for the Egypt and Pharaoh of the Hebrew mythos. "I will make mention of Rahab," says the Psalmist, among the other dark sayings.[3] "Thou hast broken Rahab in pieces as one that is slain."[4] "O arm of the Lord," cries Isaiah; "art thou not it that hath cut Rahab and wounded the dragon?"[5] This is connected with the passage of the Red Sea, and the overthrow of Pharaoh's host. Rahab personifies Egypt, or Pharaoh, and is identified with the dragon that lieth in the midst of his rivers.[6] Again in Job, "He divideth the sea with his power, and by his understanding he smiteth through Rahab."[7] In the *Book of the Dead*[8] we read of the "Waters of Rubu," which are in the north. The northern hill of heaven is in the lake of the Rubu.[9] Ru-bu is the place of the reptile, the Apophis, the Ru-Ap, which becomes the Hebrew Rahab. For in Chapter lxxxv. Rabu is also Tebu. "Tepiu" is the devourer, and this Rabu of the waters, or Tepiu, takes finally the name of Typhon, the Apep, the Apophis of the waters, or dragon of the deep. Rahab, the dragon, is etymologically a form of the Egyptian Ruhef, a name of the Apophis synonymous with the Hebrew Leviathan. The waters of Rubu, then, are in the north, and identifiable with the pool of Pant, the Red Sea of the myth, in which dwells the monster of many names, all summed up as the Apophis. "Eater of Millions" is his name, "Hardness" is his name, "Baba" is his name, who "is in the pool of Pant," or Red Sea. "Hidden Reptile," one of the names,

[1] Josh. xxiv. 2.　　[2] Is. lxv. 10.　　[3] Ps. lxxxvii. 4.
[4] Ps. lxxxix. 10.　　[5] Is. li. 9.　　[6] Ezek. xxix. 3.
[7] Job xxvi. 12.　　[8] Ch. cl.　　[9] Ch. cix.

will render in Egyptian as "Ru-hab," the equivalent ot Rahab, the dragon lurking in the waters. Ru is the reptile, and Hab to prowl, beset, infest; Hap is hidden. Also Ru-hef denotes the crawling, the gigantic serpent; the Ru-ap, the reptile Apophis.

With the article Tu prefixed we find the Rabu in the Assyrian mythology as the "Tu-rabu-tu,"[1] and in that language Rabu is the beast. Turabutu is the den of the dragon. In Egyptian Tu is the, Rubu (Eg. Ref) the beast-reptile, and Tu a cave or cavern. The Ruhef appears in Sanskrit with the name of the monster Rabu. The Hindu allegory tells how the parts of Barbara toward the mouths of the Nile were inhabited by the children of Rabu. Rabu is represented on account of his tyranny as an immense river-dragon or crocodile, or some fabulous monster with four talons, called Graha, from a root implying violent seizure.[2] Rabu, the river-dragon of India, is identical with Rahab the river-dragon of Egypt, and the river in both cases is the Nile of the heavens, the "Nar" on which the first Ayana, a moving on the waters, was depicted in the planisphere. Rabu the monster of mythology is in the Hindu astronomy utilized as the cause of eclipses. Hence the name given by Wilford to the talons called Graha. This is the name of "eclipse," and means literally the seizure, or if personified the seizer, the Sanskrit Graha being the Egyptian Krau, English Claw or Cray, as in crayfish. Both crocodile and scorpion were the seizers, one with the claws, the other with the mouth. The monster Rabu was represented as seizing and swallowing the sun during an eclipse. Rabu typifies the ascending and descending nodes, and the two parts, the heavenly and the earthly, correspond to the two halves of the Zodiac, and the two regions of all mythology. Rabu was cut in two as the sun severed the Apophis in his passage through the underworld. So the Hebrew deity cuts Rahab.[3] "O arm of the Lord, art thou not it that cut Rahab?" He cuts through Rahab,[4] and "divideth the sea" at the same time; the crossing of the waters included both, because the monster of the darkness was the dragon of the deep.

The original matter and meaning of the Exodus is found in fragments of the Egyptian Ritual or Gospel. In this the solar allegory of the lower world of darkness and the ascent into the world of light is so ancient that it had become mainly eschatological. Still the allegory of the Exodus is there, although charged with a spiritual or theological significance, and the course of the sun is identified with the journey of the soul through the nether northern region where the place of bondage was located.

Khebt denotes lower Egypt, and was analogous to the lower of the two heavens, the hell of theology. Thus the celestial Kheb below was the Egypt of bondage. The Osirian exults that his "arms have not

[1] Smith, *Chaldean Account of Genesis*, p. 90.
[2] *As. Res.* vol. iii. p. 93.　　　　[3] Is. li. 9.　　　　[4] Job xxvi. 12.

been stopped in the place of bondage."[1]   He does not remain in their toils although encompassed by them ; he does not "sit in the nets of them."[2]   From other exclamations we learn that the soul is kept in this Egypt of bondage of which the god Shu opens the gate of the prison-house called the back-door.[3]

The cruel Pharaoh who hindered the coming out of the Israel-ites has been borrowed from the imagery of the Ritual.   Tum is a form of Ra the solar god, and divine type of the Pharaoh. He ruled in the lower world, and in the twenty-third chapter we read, "Tum hinders his coming out ;" i.e. the Pharaoh hinders the souls coming out of Hades, the lower Egypt of the two heavens. "Let me come.   Tum hinders his coming out."   "Let me come out, open my mouth, says Ptah with his brick (book) made of mud, fashion-ing the mouths of the gods by it."   This is said by the Osirian who is being reconstructed for his exodus into the upper world.   Ptah's brick made of mud is possibly one of those said to be made without straw, as one of the bricks made of sun-dried clay, stamped with the name of Rameses II., and surmised to have been made by the Israelites, has the straw still visible in the clay.[4]   It is possible the cruel Hebrew Pharaoh or פרעה is the Af-Ra or Af-rek, the sun in the underworld. For this reason.   Tum is the Af-Ra, lord of the lower world (Khebt or Egypt of the mythos) and judge of the dead, that is, of the souls in their prison-house, where all the plagues occurred and the trials were imposed.   "Af" means to chastise, wring out drop by drop, as did the cruel Ra or Pharaoh of the Hebrew Exodus.   The realm of the Af-Ra or lower sun, is the domain of darkness, and in it there are ten hells or Karti corresponding to the ten plagues of Egypt.

In Arab legend the name of the cruel Pharaoh is known as Ta-muzi.   This is the Arabic name given by Castell[5] as that of the cruel Pharaoh who persecuted the Israelites.   Tamuz is also used to denote the consuming heat of summer.   TAMUZI appears in the Ritual as Ra-Tams or Ra-Tamesa.   "Oh Ra-Tamesa, he who eats the wicked ; oh taker by stealth ; oh stopper, do not steal me!"[6]   Tams means bad luck, and to hold fast in the grasp of the cruel hindering Ra.   It is suggested that this is the Tamuzi of the Arab tradition who is Tum the great judge, the Af-ra (Pharaoh) of the celestial Egypt.   Afra appears in Hebrew as (פרע) Phara, to make naked, uncover, avenging, refuse, go back, let and hinder.[7] Phara, to hinder, is personified in Phara, Afra, the hinderer of the Exodus, who STRIPPED the children of Israel and REFUSED to let them go.

The "PLACE OF PASSAGE," and the "RETREAT OF THE PAS-SAGE," are type-names of the Hades or celestial Egypt.[8]   In the

---

[1] Ch. xxi.   [2] Ch. xvii.   [3] Ch. lxvii.   [4] Birch, *Anct. Hist.* 127.
[5] *Lex. Hept.*   [6] Ch. xl.   [7] Ex. v. 4 ; xxxii. 25.
[8] *Book of Hades,* 4th Division ; *Ritual,* ch. cxxv.

Book of the Hades we also read, " Horus says to Ra's flocks, *which are in the Hades of Egypt and the Desert ; Protection for you, Flocks of Ra, born of the great one who is in the heavens*." [1]   The *Hades of Egypt* is the *Egypt of the Hades* : the flocks of Ra are identical with the chosen people who came up from Egypt and wandered in the wilderness.

The headings of various chapters of the Egyptian Ritual read like a synopsis of the Hebrew story. Such is the chapter of " escaping out of the folds of the great serpent " ; [2] the chapter of " stopping all snakes " ; [3] the chapter of " stopping all reptiles " with picture of the deceased turning back a serpent, [4] the Ap, at the place where it had been ordered to be cut up, " in the house of regeneration of the sun at his falling, where the accusers of the sun are overthrown," together with the Ap, and the sun goes forth in peace ; the chapter of " not eating filth or drinking mud in Hades " ; [5] the chapter of " prevailing over the water in Hades " ; [6] the chapter of " giving peace to the soul and letting it go in the boat of the sun " ; [7] the chapter of " vivifying the soul for ever, of letting it go to the boat of the sun to pass the crowds at the gate,—done on the *birthday of Osiris* " ; [8] the chapter of " coming out as the day and prevailing against his enemies " ; [9] the chapter of receiving the roads, one of these being through the pool, the Pool of Pant, which is the mythical Red Sea. [10]   " I have brought the things of the land of Tum, the time of overthrowing the ministers," [11] looks exceedingly like a hint to be acted on in literalizing the myth in the story of the borrowing from and spoiling the Egyptians, or Egypt, as we have it in the margin. In the Hebrew Apocrypha, the Wisdom of Solomon, [12] we have an account which might have been drawn from a representation of these things in the Mysteries :—

For when unrighteous men thought to oppress the holy nation ; they being shut up in their houses, the prisoners of darkness, and fettered with the bonds of a long night, lay (there) exiled from the eternal providence.

For while they supposed to lie hid in their secret sins, they were scattered under a dark veil of forgetfulness, being horribly astonished, and troubled with (strange) apparitions.

For neither might the corner that held them keep them from fear ; but noises (as of waters) falling down sounded about them, and sad visions appeared unto them with heavy countenances.

No power of fire might give them light, neither could the bright flames of the stars endure to lighten that horrible night.

Only there appeared unto them a fire kindled of itself, very dreadful : for being much terrified, they thought the things which they saw to be worse than the sight they saw not.

For though no terrible thing did fear them ; yet being scared with beasts that passed by, and hissing of serpents,

They died for fear, denying that they saw the air, which could of no side be avoided :

---

[1] *Records*, vol. x. 109.   [2] Ch. vii.   [3] Ch. xxxiii.
[4] Ch. xxxix.   [5] Ch. liii.   [6] Ch. lvii.
[7] Ch. c.   [8] Ch. cxxx.   [9] Ch. lxv.
[10] Ch. cxvii.   [11] Ch. cl.   [12] Ch. xvii.

But they sleeping the same sleep that night, which was indeed intolerable and which came upon them out of the bottoms of the inevitable hell,

Were partly vexed with monstrous apparitions, and partly fainted, their heart failing them ; for a sudden fear, and not looked for, came upon them.

So then whosoever there fell down, was straitly kept, shut up in a prison without iron bars,

For whether he were husbandman, or shepherd, or a labourer in the field, he was overtaken, and endured that necessity which could not be avoided ; for they were all bound with one chain of darkness.

Whether it were a whistling wind, or a melodious noise of birds among the spreading branches, or a pleasing fall of water running violently,

Or a terrible sound of stones cast down, or a running that could not be seen of skipping beasts, or a roaring voice of most savage wild beasts, or a rebounding echo from the hollow mountains, these things made them to swoon for fear.

For the whole world shined with clear light, and none were hindered in their labour ;

Over them only was spread an heavy night, an image of that darkness which should afterward receive them : but yet were they unto themselves more grievous than the darkness.

This is the scenery of the Hades (or Khebt of the Mythos) answering to that of the plague of darkness in the Pentateuch, but nearer to the Egyptian original. It belongs to the mystical abodes of darkness, where the wicked were shut up and fettered in the bondage of a long night. There is the way of absolute darkness. The sun is there but it gives no light to the outcast Khefti, or Egyptians, neither do they hear the voice of the god as he passes through that vacuum of the darkness. There are fourteen of these abodes, the same number as half the twenty-eight lunar signs corresponding to the six solar signs in one-half of the circle. These in Egyptian are the Aat, the original in name and nature of the Hades. Hence the six or fourteen lower signs ranged from the west to the east. In the north was the nethermost corner (the Kab) that held the spirits in prison, detained in darkness. The eighth abode, the place of dismissing peace, is the great place of the waters. "No one has withstood the water in it, the greatness of its terrors, the magnitude of its fear, or the height of its roaring." "Oh the place of the waters! none of the dead can stand in it. Its water is of fire, its glow is of fire, it glows with smoking fire. The thirst of those who are in it is inextinguishable. Through the greatness of its terror, and the magnitude of its fear, the gods, the damned, and the spirits look at the water from a distance." [1] On the sarcophagus of the monarch Nekhtherhebi, a series of scenes in the infernal regions are described in the passage of the sun and soul through the hemisphere of darkness, the fourteen Aat of the realm of night. Here the hells, halls, or holes called Karrs are ten in number, doubtless the ten worst, the "*bottoms of hell*."

"The screams of the damned burst on the ears of the passer-by in a mingled chorus of agony and confusion. They howl as lions, roar as bulls, squall like tom-cats, tinkle as brass, and buzz with the incessant hum of bees," [2] and realize the description in the

[1] Ch. cl. Birch.   [2] Birch, Introd. to the *Ritual*.

Apocrypha, that is, sacred writings. The Apocrypha identifies the plague of darkness in the Exodus, and the Ritual explains both with the aid of mythological astronomy. There is the serpent that dies not, the worm that utterly devours, and the fire that is never quenched ; the hell of flame, wastes and waves of flame, a ceiling of flame : the lake of fire and bottomless pit with Satan bound in chains ; the total outfit of the infernal paraphernalia of the Calvinistic theology is all there to be studied from the origin in relation to the primitive phenomena.

The Israelites in the wilderness are assailed by fiery serpents. "The Lord sent fiery serpents among the people, and they bit the people, and much people of Israel died." Then Moses was instructed to make the serpent of life and elevate it on a pole, and "it came to pass that if a serpent had bitten any man, when he beheld the serpent of brass he lived."[1] In the Ritual we have the chapters of "stopping all snakes" and "of how a person avoids being bitten in Hades by the eaters of the back of the dead,"—the question is how to avoid being eaten or bitten by snakes,[2]—the chapter of stopping the asps,[3] and the chapter said to turn back the asps.[4] In the passage of the Hades the souls are assailed by all kinds of snakes, vipers, and serpents, chief of which is the Apophis, breathing out fire and poisonous vapour. The vignettes show the deceased turning back a serpent.[5] In the midst of these is the serpent of life, the good demon, one form of it being named HEFI. This is an invocation of the serpent of life :—" Oh chief Uræus, serpent of the sun, with a head of smoke, gleaming and guiding (during) millions of years," as the talismanic means of avoiding being bitten in Hades by fiery serpents and flame-breathing reptiles. The "head of smoke gleaming and guiding " for ever, answers to the Israelitish column of cloud by day and fire by night.

Also an Egyptian hymn, copied by Brugsch from the temple of El-Kargeh, celebrates the one God who is immanent in all things, the soul of Shu (breath) to all other gods, and it says of him, " *He travels in the cloud to separate heaven and earth*, and again to reunite them," as the Hebrew divinity travels in the pillar of cloud which separates the children of Israel from the Egyptians.

In the Book of the Hades there is even an allusion to, but no specification of, " the plagues" in the legend of the monkey. " When this god rises he gives up (the pig) to THE PLAGUES.[6] The pig is an emblem of Typhon, the evil enemy who is represented as the cruel Pharaoh whom the God of Moses gives up to the plagues ; and in one of the legends of the same scene—that of the animals—it is said of the ELECT PEOPLE, " They hide those which are in the state of the elect. They, the country belonging to them, is Ameh in the land.

[1] Num. xxi.   [2] Ch. xxxiii., xxxiv., xxxv.   [3] Ch. xxxvi.
[4] Ch. xxxviii.   [5] Ch. xxxix.   [6] *Records*, vol. x. p. 114.

Behold, these are they whose heads issue. What a mystery is their appearance!"[1] These, in the Egyptian myth are the prototypes of the chosen people, who dwell in light while their enemies are enveloped in darkness.

"Food is given to them *because of the light which envelopes them in Hades*." These are clothed in white in the tomb of Rameses I., to represent the children of light passing through the lower world.

In the Book of the Hades the sun-god passes through twelve gates, having the blessed of his keeping on his right hand and the damned upon his left hand. These appear above and below, according to the Egyptian rule of perspective. They are the Israelites and Egyptians of the Hebrew mythos.

In the same book the entrance to Hades is marked by two mountains, one of these is turned upside down; the two form a kind of gorge towards which the divine boat passes, and the twelve gods of the earth are marching, corresponding in number to the twelve tribes.[2] Twelve personages, designated the blessed, that is, the elect or chosen of Ra, are called the worshippers of Ra.[3] They are those who are "born of Ra, of his substance, which proceed from his eye." "He places for them a hidden dwelling." Ra says to them, "Breath to you, who are in the light, and dwellings for you. My benefits are for you. I have hidden you." This was during the massacre of the enemies of Ra, who says, "I have commanded that they should massacre, and they have massacred all beings." "I have hidden you for those who are in the world of the living," the scenery and action being in the region and belonging to the drama of the dead. This is the replica or the original of the transactions in Egypt when the Israelites are sheltered and protected while the Egyptians suffer from the plagues; who are saved during the slaying of the first-born, and who are dwelling in the light of Goshen while the Egyptians are in a horror of great darkness. Goshen or Khu-shen (Eg.), the upper and luminous half of the circle, is identical with the upper position of the children of light in the Amenti. The Book of the Hades was found at Biban-el-Muluk in the tomb of Seti I., where the "Creation by Ra" was likewise discovered; an important fact in considering the Egyptian origines.

The coming up out of Egypt was an astronomical allegory which had passed into the eschatological phase ages upon ages before it was made historical in the Exodus of the Jews. The mythos was formulated in Egypt or in African lands beyond it long enough ago for the story to be carried out by the various migrations into other countries. The coming up out of Astulan (Tulan, or Turan,) has the same origin as the coming up out of Egypt. The allegory was Sabean and pre-solar, hence the journey from the land of darkness before the creation of the sun, and its appearance after they had

---

[1] *Records*, vol. x. p. 114.   [2] *Ib.* vol. x. p. 88.   [3] *Ib.* vol. x. p. 90.

gone some stages on their way. It is so long ago for Egypt as to be almost effaced by time, and being of Typhonian origin it was not perpetuated on the monuments in its primal form, therefore some of the Sabean imagery has to be recovered from its solar guise, which is a disguise.

Plutarch observes that when the Egyptians offer sacrifice upon the seventh day of the month Tybi, which they call the arrival of Isis out of Phœnicia, they print the river-horse, bound, upon their sacred cakes ; besides this there is a constant custom at the town of Apollo for every one to eat some part of a crocodile, and they hunt and kill as many crocodiles as possible, Typhon having made his escape from Horus (Apollo) in the shape of a crocodile. The Egyptian name of Phœnicia is Kefa, and Kheft is the north, the quarter of Typhon, the Hebrew Zephon. The North is the place of the Great Bear or the water-horse, and in the earlier representation of the myth, before Isis, as the solar genitrix, had taken the seat of Taurt (Khebt), it was She, the Great Bear, the water-horse, who came up out of the north, Kefa, or Phœnicia. When the solar had superseded the old Sabean cult, and Typhon was changed into the type of evil, the water-horse appeared as a victim bound upon the sacred cakes. So that Isis, coming up out of Phœnicia, Kefa, Khebt, comes up out of the Egypt of the astronomical allegory, that is, out of the north, where the void, the abyss, was located, because it was the place of darkness and the quarter of the night ; and before Isis came up out of the celestial Egypt it was the water-horse herself who came up out of the waters and carried the light, whereby the first time was reckoned and the first circle described.

The month Tybi bears the name of Typhon, Teb, Tabi (Bear), the first recognized mover in a circle, to whom it was once consecrated. The water-horse came up out of the waters of the north, because, not being within the circle of perpetual apparition, the constellation on that side dipped below the horizon, and was represented at Aphaka as the star of Astarte, which dipped in the lake. The ancient Hindu astronomers, who are said to have attributed an independent motion to the Great Bear about the pole of the heavens with a complete revolution in 2,700 years, called Ursa Major the Dipper.[1] Again, we cannot have the word dip, without naming Tef or Tep, who dipped below the horizon, and rose up out of the waters, as the hippopotamus and as the duck.

Plutarch relates the transformation of the Typhonian genitrix, the mother of Har, into Isis. In the battle between Typhon and Horus, Thoueris is said to have deserted Typhon. Thoueris is Typhon (feminine), as Taur. Typhon was delivered up to Isis fast bound, but she let Typhon go ; whereupon Horus laid violent hands on his mother, and plucked the royal diadem off her head. This, in Egyptian, is the Urt,

[1] Burgess, *Sûrya-Siddhanta*, p. 220.

and he was discrowning Ta-urt. Hermes placed the cow's head on her instead. This was the transformation of Typhon-Taurt into Isis-Taurt, the cow-headed, and it shows the change occurring under the lunar *régime*—Taht being accredited with it—or, rather, the Sabean genitrix passing into the Sabean-Lunar great mother. The cow is called Hes (Eg.), and the combination of the cow with Taurt forms the goddess Hestaroth from Hes-ta-urt, whence Ashtaroth and Astarte. None of the origines were lost.

The primary matter of the mythology found in the Psalms and identifiable in the Ritual is older by untold ages than the Exodus from Egypt. The coming out of Khebt and crossing the Red Sea or Pool of Pant belong to the solar allegory of the Ritual, the imagery of which is reproduced in the Psalms, where the Lord says, "I will bring again from Bashan; I will bring again from the depths of the sea, that thy foot may be dipped in the blood of (the) enemies, the tongue of thy dogs in the same." In the Ritual we read, "*The sun is that Great God, the greatest of smiters, the most powerful of terrifiers, He washes in your blood, He dips in your gore.*"[1] The scene is the same as in Psalm xxii., where the speaker is in the Hades encompassed and beset by the bulls of Bashan, the dogs of the avenger, and the dog-faced avenger himself. These dogs in the Ritual are the "punishers of Shu," they feed off the fallen, the overthrown enemies of the sun, headed by the dog-faced Mâtet, whose name is Eater of Millions. "He is in the Pool of Pant," that is, the Red Sea of mythology and the celestial geography; he dwells there as the "*Lord of Gore.*" In one chapter of the passage through the depths the Osirian says, "I follow the dogs of Horus."[2] There is a desert or wilderness of Tsher, in which the wanderers stray and are environed with dangers; here they meet with the tempter who tries to delude and mislead them. Here they drop and die of hunger and thirst unless supplied with the bread of heaven and the water of life, which are administered by the hand of the goddess Nu.

In the Hebrew version of the myth, Miriam represents the goddess Nu in relation to the water of life. The Egyptian Meri is the lady of the waters, the Nile. The Targumists have a tradition respecting Miriam's well, that was fabled to follow the Israelites and encircle their whole camp till her death. They relate in their legend of the wandering well of water, that it was first of all granted to Israel for Miriam's sake, on account of her watching over the ark of Moses when exposed on the river, which she did at the peril of her life. For this the water followed her and supplied the people of Israel, every one at his own tent door, and encircled the whole camp till the time of Miriam's death; at which time the water disappeared. Miriam's well was said to have found a place in a gulf of the Sea of Galilee, where at certain seasons it overflowed with waters

[1] Ch. cxxxiv.   [2] Ch. xiii.

of healing. The Targumists have got the true tradition. The Bible version does but follow it, limping and halting with its many false pretences. Miriam first represented the water. Hence the outcry at the time of her death and the water's disappearance.

The Well in Israel takes the place of the old Suckler, of Kefa or Nu, who poured out the water of life from the tree. The goddess of the seven stars was the Deess of the waters, and her typical number is found in the well of Beersheba or the well of the seven, the feminine nature of which is shown by the offering of the seven ewe lambs. This was also the well of the tree to be found in the pool of Persea, the ash-tree, for Abraham is said to have planted the tree or grove Aeshel by the well.[1] Another well of Shebah or the seven was named by Jacob.[2]

The Targum of Onkelos, in Numbers xxi., says, "It is said in the book of the wars, that which the Lord did by the sea of Suph, and the great deeds which he wrought by the torrents of Arnon, and at the flowing of the streams which lead towards Lechayàth and are joined at the confines of Moab, and from thence was given to them the well, which is the well whereof the Lord spake to Moses, "Gather the people together and I will give them water." Thereof sang Israel this song,—"Spring up, O well; sing ye unto it, the well which the princes digged; the chiefs of the people cut it; the scribes with their staves; it was given to them in the wilderness, and from the time that it was given to them it descended with them to the rivers, and from the rivers it went with them to the height, or to Ramatha, and from the height to the vale, which is in the fields of Moab at the head of Ramatha." In this account, which is invaluable, the water that runs and follows the Israelites up-hill is certainly symbolic. The whole of the imagery will be identified as Egyptian and its signification explicated.

According to the geographer of Ravenna, the Ganges rises in the Garden of Eden, many thousand miles east of its apparent spring. This statement blends the mythological and geographical. So at Faran or Paran, Clayton, in his Journal,[3] records the fact that no one in a certain place was allowed to put pen to paper, in consequence of a tradition that formerly there was a river there, but that when an European was about to write a description of it it sank under ground and has not been seen since. This was a relic of the wandering well; its importance is in its connection with Paran as a locality in the mythological astronomy.

The rock supposed to be struck by Moses in the desert was, if there be any historic truth in the statement, a very real rock, out of which there gushed real wet water which saved a multitude of men from a horrible death. That is what we have been taught to believe. And here is all our innocent childish faith upset by Paul, who was learned in

---

[1] Gen. xxi. 33.   [2] Gen. xxvi. 33.   [3] P. 33.

the Jewish legends, and did his best to turn them to account in his own teachings. He says this rock was the Christ. That it was nothing more than a figurative rock or metaphor; the rock of mythology, which alone will give us a true account of it. As myth we shall be able to make out both the rock and the water that sprang from it. It was, says Paul, a "spiritual rock, and that rock was Christ." Paul gives a spiritual or new theological interpretation to an ancient Egyptian symbol. Later on we shall see how the rock in Horeb and the Christ of Paul, in Jerusalem, may be one as he asserts. The myth is the sole repository of the meaning. It is written in the Targum that the Messiah was in the desert the "rock of the Church of Zion." Now this rock of the Messiah is identical with the rock or mount struck by the Hindu prince, on which rock he was to build *his* church.

The scene of smiting the rock for the spring or wandering well to burst forth is found in the Hindu writings, which relate of the triple-peaked mount near the fountain of Brimsu, that in the Treta or "Silver Age" an ascetic called Kâk or Kaga dwelt by this fountain, and the Pandu Arjoon with Heri Krishna, came there to attend a great sacrifice, on which occasion Krishna foretold that, in some distant age a descendant of his should erect a town on the margin of the rivulet Kaga, and raise a castle on the triple-peaked mount. While Krishna thus prophesied it was observed to him by Arjoon that the water was bad, whereupon Krishna smote the rock with his chakra (discus) and caused a spring of sweet water to bubble up, and on its margin the prophecy was inscribed: "Oh Prince of Jidoo-vansa! Come into this land, and on this mountain-top erect a triangular castle![1] Lodorva is destroyed, but only five coss therefrom is Jesanoh a site of twice its strength. Prince, whose name is Jesul, who will be of the Yadu race, abandon Lodorpoora, here erect thy dwelling." This prophecy was taken as fulfilled in the person of Jesul, a Bhatti prince of Jessulmer.[2] In this the Prince of Jidoo-vansa of the name of Jesul and of the race of Yadu is literally the branch of the stem of Judah, figured as the reed (Vansa). Jesul is equivalent to Jesu, the Lord, and the prophecy was taken to be fulfilled in the person of a prince so named. Jesul was to be a descendant of the Hindu Christ, Krishna. This has been assumed to be a Hindu forgery? Not in the least. Both the Hindu and Hebrew versions come directly from one original myth. "Thou shalt bring them in and plant them in the mountain of thine inheritance, in the place, O Lord, which Thou hast made for Thee to dwell in; the sanctuary, O Lord, (which) Thy hands have established,"[3] contains the very same subject-matter. The imagery belongs to the time when the fatherhood and sonship superseded the primal motherhood, and the solar cult the Sabean, as will be further

---

[1] Cf. the Egyptian Horus of the Triangle, vol. i. p. 332.
[2] Tod, *Annals of Rajast'han*, vol. ii. p. 243. [3] Ex. xv. 17.

illustrated.   Now, in one of the representations of Rameses II. there is a scene of calling forth the water from the desert rock.   The king had ordered a well to be made at Redesieh or Contra Pselcis to supply the miners and their asses which crossed the desert to the land of Akaitau.   The king is addressed by a deputation, "If," say they, "thou formest a plan at night it is realized by day, and if thou hast said to the waters, Come out of the mountain, the celestial water comes according to thy word." [1]   This language is metaphorical, in allusion to the myth of Egyptian origin which we find in the sacred books of the Hindus and Hebrews.   How idle is it to point out that this Rameses was a contemporary of Moses, and call the scene on the monuments an illustration of the Biblical narrative! [2]   In both cases the imagery of the same myth has been reproduced; Rameses was assimilated to the god who was fabled to have struck the rock. Similarly the name of MOHRAKHA is found in Palestine.   Instantly the spot is identified as the place in which God answered Elijah with fire from heaven, because the word means the place of the burning. [3] But it signifies the same in Egyptian.   "Ma" is place, and "Rekh" is a "brazier," heat, fire.   There is a further suggestion with regard to the legend of Elijah in the fact that the Egyptian "REKAI" means the profane, the scorners, the rebellious, the guilty culprits.   The oath of "RAKA" referred to in the Gospel is also a Maori curse, meaning, May the sun smite you or consume you with fire.   Ra is the sun, Ka, to set on fire.   The Egyptian Ra is the sun, and Kha signifies carnage and to make corpses.   "MEA-RA-KA-HA" in the Maori language expresses a wish for the sun to blast you with his breath.   The author of "Te Ika a Maui," says it endangered the life of the person who uttered this curse.   The Maori Mea-ra-ka-ha is identical with the Hebrew word Mohrakha, the place of the burning and consuming the wicked, and the Egyptian Ma-rekhai, the place of the furnace, and of the culpable and accursed scorners.   One legend underlies the whole. We have seen in the "Creation by Ra" another version of the same scene and circumstances pourtrayed at Sinai.   The new creation by the sun-god is the installation of the solar son of the mother as the supreme deity, the son who comes being set above the mother who brought him forth.   This is illustrated in Israel by the god Jah-Adonai being introduced by Moses in place of the earlier Jehovah. This can be followed more or less in the Eleusinian mysteries. According to the author of "Nimrod," [4] "Eleusin" signifies "the son shall come."   In Egyptian El (Ar) is the son; IU means to come; San is to heal and save.   Thus AL-IU-SAN reads the son who comes as the healer or saviour.   This would be one of the mysteries of the Eleusinia, which were called pre-eminently *the* mysteries, and were consecrated chiefly to Keres.   The initiation was by night, and the

[1] Birch, *Hist. of Egypt*, 124.   [2] Smith's *Dict. of the Bible*, vol. ii. p. 428.
[3] Macgregor, *Visit to Palestine*.   [4] Vol. i. p. 169.

holy mysteries were read to the initiates out of a book called Petroma, a word commonly derived from Patra, a stone, the book being formed of two stones fitly cemented together.[1] The two stone tables of Moses were identical with the Greek stone book of two leaves called the Petroma, the name of which shows that it represented the dual truth of the goddess Ma, typified in Egypt by the twin-feather and the divinity pourtrayed on lapis lazuli or true blue stone. Petru (Eg.) means to show, explain, interpret, reveal, and Ma is truth. The two stones showed the dual nature of the truth, and thus the two-leaved stone book was the Petroma, the Greek form of the two stone tablets inscribed and given to Moses on Sinai at the great scene of initiation there enacted. When these tablets had been presented, strange and amazing objects were seen ; there were thunders and lightnings, and bellowings and awful sounds, the place shook around them, it was at one time radiant with light, resplendent with fire, and then again covered with thick darkness, sometimes terrible apparitions astonished the spectators ; those who were present at these sights being called the *intuitional*. The garments worn by the initiates were accounted so sacred that they were never changed or cast off, but allowed to drop away in rags, the last remnants being devoted to make swaddling clothes or consecrated to Keres and Persephone. As the two stone tables,[2] the thunders and lightnings, the descent of fire, the cloud, and the supernatural appearances of the one scene are found in the other, it may be that the clothes which never wore out[3] were simply those of the initiates which were not to be cast aside till worn in tatters.[4] In both descriptions the first act of the drama was one of washing and purifying.

The Hebrews and Greeks did not borrow their mysteries and mythology from each other. Nor is there any tendency in human nature to make the historical experience of any one race the common property of all, and if these poems and persons of mythology had been based on actual human experience they would not have become universal. They are universally sacred, precisely because they never were limitedly historical. They are divine because they were not human ; they are based on the facts which were common property, and can be reproduced for all by means of the Gnosis. The learned were in possession of the same natural facts below and their astronomical orrery overhead to teach the myths and illustrate the allegories wherever they went. Their facts were independent of time or place, geography or ethnography ; thus they became universal in their acceptation ; and we find the myth of the Exodus as wide-spread as that of the Genesis.

The Hawaiians had a sacred institution called the Ku, a four-days' commemoration of the rising up and deliverance from their mythical

[1] Potter, *Arch. Græc.* vol. i. p. 391.   [2] Ex. xix. 14.
[3] Deut. xxix. 5.   [4] Potter, *Arch. Græc.* vol. i. p. 389.

Egypt of suffering.[1] Ku denotes the rising up. The Khut (Eg.) is the place of the solar resurrection. The celebration of the KU was on four Kapu days. Four Kapu days answer to the four Keb of Egypt, the name of the four representative Genii that stand at the four corners of the world and of the sarcophagus of the dead. Read by the original imagery this institution was the celebration of a resurrection into some other life. Khu (Ku), the rising, is also the spirit name, the manifestation as a spirit or thing of light. Kapu (Eg.) is a mystery, the mystery of new life considered as fermentation. This ceremony has been supposed to illustrate some actual deliverance and rising of the people themselves in this life, just as in the case of the Hebrews. But such is not the origin of sacred festivals and rites. Their Kapu had the same significance as the mythical Egypt of the Jews, it belonged to the Khab, Khep, Kapu, or Khefa of the Great Bear, and of the four corners, called Keb.

The king of the country, named HONUA-I-LALO oppressed the Menehune people. Their god Kane sent Kane-Apua and Kanaloa the elder brother to bring away the oppressed people and take them to a land which Kane their god had given them. The people were commanded to observe the four KU days in the beginning of the month as KAPU HOANA (sacred or holy days), in remembrance of this event because they thus arose (Ku) to depart from that land. The legend further relates how they came to the KAI-ULA-A-KANE (the Red Sea of Kane) and were pursued by KE ALII WAHANUI; that KANE-APUA and KANALOA thereupon prayed to LONO, and then they safely waded through the sea and traversed desolate deserts, and at last reached the promised land of KANE, "AINA-LAUENA-A-KANE."[2] This, says Fornander, is an ancient legend, which also contains the story of water being caused to flow from the rock.

In a Hottentot fable we find the passage of the Red Sea and destruction of those who followed the fleeing ones. HEITSI KABIP was a great sorcerer. He could tell secret things, and foretell what was to happen. He had died several times and come to life again. When the Hottentots pass one of his graves, for like Osiris he has many, they throw a stone on it for good luck. He could transform himself, and sometimes appeared with hair that grew long, down to his shoulders, and at other times it was again short. Once he was travelling with a great number of his people and they were pursued by an enemy. On arriving at some water he said, " My grandfather's father! open thyself that I may pass through, and close thyself afterwards." So it took place as he had said, and they went safely through. Then the pursuing enemy tried to pass through the opening likewise, but when they were in the midst of the divided water it closed upon them and they perished.[3] "Stone of my ancestors divide

---

[1] Fornander, *An Account of the Polynesian Race.*
[2] Fornander, i. 99.   [3] Bleek, p. 75, fable 7.

for us," say the Nama woman and her brothers who are pursued
by an elephant. It opens and they pass. The elephant says the
same, the rock opens but closes on the elephant and crushes it.[1]
In the account given by the Tuscarora Cusic, who sketched the
ancient history of the six nations and was familiar with their traditions
from childhood, we are told that they sprang from a people who were
concealed in a mountain. When they were set free by Tarenyawagon
the holder of the heavens, who had power to change his shape, they
were commanded to go towards the sun-rise as he guided them, and
they came to a river named Yenonanatche, that is, " going round a
mountain," and went down the bank of the river, and came to where
it discharges into a greater river running *toward the mid-day sun*,
and named Shaw-nay-taw-ty, and went down the side of the river till
they touched the bank of a great water. Here the company encamped
for a few days. The people were yet of one language ; some of them
went on the banks of the great water towards the mid-day sun,
but the main body returned as they came, on the bank of the river,
under the direction of the holder of the heavens. Of this company
there was a particular body which called themselves of one household
(like the chosen people of Israel) ; of these were six families, and
they entered into a covenant of perpetual alliance, the bond of
which was never to be broken. These advanced some way up
the river of Shaw-nay-taw-ty, and the holder of the heavens
directed the first of the six families to make their residence near
the bank of the river. This family was named Te-haw-re-ho-geh,
or the speech-divided, and their language was changed soon after.
The company then turned and went towards the sun-setting, and
came to a creek named Kaw-na-taw-te-ruh, *i.e.* Pineries. The second
family was commanded to dwell near this creek, and this family
was named Ne-haw-re-tah-go, or big tree, and their language was
likewise changed. The company still went onward towards the
sun-setting under the direction of the holder of the heavens. The
third family was directed to make their abode on a mountain named
Onondaga, and the family was named Seuh-now-kah-tah, or carrying
the name, and their language was altered. The fourth family was
told to take up their residence near a long lake named Go-yo-goh, or
mountain rising from the water, and the family was named Sho-nea-na-
we-to-wah, or a great pipe, and their language too was changed. The
company still passed onward towards the sun-setting, and the fifth family
was located near a high mountain named Jenneatowake, and this
family was named Te-how-nea-nyo-hent, that is, possessing a door,
their language likewise being changed. The sixth family went with
the company still journeying towards the sun-setting and touched
the bank of a great lake, named Kau-ha-gwa-rah-ka, *i.e.* a cap, and
then went towards between the mid-day and sun-setting, and travelled

[1] Bleek's *Hottentot Fables*, p. 64.

till they came to a large river named Ouau-we-yo-ka, *i.e.* a principal stream. Here they discovered a grape-vine lying across the river, and they began to pass the waters with the vine for a bridge. A part of the people went over, but whilst doing so the vine broke in two and they were divided one against the other, for those who did not cross became the enemies of those who did. This sixth family is said to have gone towards the sun-rise and touched the bank of the great water.[1]

The narrative here begins with a deliverance of the people by the "Holder of the Heavens." This is a name to remember for recognition of the character. The changing and dispersion of language at the places of dividing repeats the legend of Babel. The number of divisions is the same as one-half the zodiacal signs, which were divided into six upper and six nether signs of north and south.

The Mandan Indians, too, hold that they had a subterraneous origin. They were excluded from the light of heaven, and dwelt by an underground lake. The first intimation they had of the light that shone in the world overhead was through a grape-vine, the roots of which had penetrated to their abode. By means of this one half the tribe climbed up into the surface world of light and plenty, but owing to the size and weight of one old woman the vine broke and the other half remained for ever in their underground abode.[2]

The Waraus of Guiana have a similar myth, in which the position is reversed. They say their primary abode was in a pleasant region above the sky; one day a hunter named Okonorote was looking for a spent arrow which had missed its mark, when he found a hole in the ground through which it had fallen. On peering down he saw the lower world of earth lap-full of abundance. Finding the hole was large enough to let his body through, he made a ladder-rope of cotton and descended. He came back again and told the Waraus of this new world of plenty, and counselled a migration thither. They listened with delight to the assurance of an unlimited supply of animal food, and all together resolved upon descending to these fresh hunting-grounds, in total disregard of the will of the Great Spirit. Accordingly the descent (or fall) began through the discovered aperture. The migration continued until an unfortunate woman too stout for the passage stuck, and the hole was filled up, and the sky closed for ever against the Waraus, who were thus confined to this earth without a glimpse of their brighter abode.[3]

The Quiché "POPUL VUH" depicts the ancestors of the human race as travelling away from the place of sun-rise, and then crossing the water, which divided as they passed. They went through as though

---

[1] Schoolcraft's *Information respecting the History and Condition of the Indian Tribes of the United States*, vol. v. 636, appendix, part iii.
[2] Lewis and Clarke's *Exped.* vol. i. 139.
[3] Brett, *Indian Tribes of Guiana*, 389.

there had been no sea, for they passed over scattered rocks, and these rocks were rolled on the sands. This is why the place was called "RANGED STONES, and torn-up sands," the name which they gave to it on their passage within the sea, where the waters were divided as they passed.[1] This is the story of the mythical migration that always occurs in the beginning. Here is the same crossing of the waters that divide for the passage, as in the Hebrew crossing of the Red Sea or "Ium Suph." This spot of the "RANGED STONES" is a replica of the place of the twelve stones set up in the Jordan to mark the spot where the waters were heapéd up to let the Israelites go through dry-footed. When the people had crossed they collected in a mountain called Chi Pixab, where they fasted in darkness and night. The Israelites collected on a mountain on the WESTWARD side of Jordan when Joshua performed the rite of circumcision at the "Hill of Foreskins."[2] In Egyptian mythological astronomy the Khi is the hill or high earth. There were four of these, called the four supports of heaven, at the four corners of the world. The corner is Kab, and the article P is the. In Egyptian, Khi-p-Kab would denote the hill at the corner, one of the four supports of the heaven and cardinal points of the circle.

The Quichés also have a story of their wanderings in the wilderness which have been mistaken for a migration of the people. "At last they came to a mountain where they had been told they were to see the sun for the first time." They also had their confusion of tongues as at Babel, so that no one could understand the speech of another. In the wilderness when starving they were sustained by illusion and by smelling their staves. They had to cross the sea on their way, and this, as we have seen, parted for their passage as did the Red Sea for the Israelites. In the Song of Moses[3] it is said the Dukes of Edom and mighty men of Moab shall be STILL AS STONE whilst the chosen people pass over. In the Quiché account, when the people have crossed the parted waters, and the sun rises, there is a scene of turning into stone ; the gods connected with the lion, the tiger, the viper, and other dangerous animals are not only still as stone but are changed into stone. "Perhaps," says the Chronicler, "we should not be alive at this moment because of the voracity of these fierce lions, tigers, and vipers ; perhaps to-day our glory would not be in existence had not the sun caused this petrifaction !"[4] In the Hebrew mythos the lion is associated with Moab, and Moab is the land of the enemy in the shape of giants, the mighty men who are stricken still as stone.

After the miraculous deliverance "then sang Moses and the children of Israel this song,"[5] and it was on Mount Hacavitz where the Quichés first rested after their passage through the sea that "they began to sing that song called Kamucu, 'WE SEE.'" This was at

[1] Quoted by Tylor, *Early Hist.* p. 308. [2] Josh. v. 1-3.
[3] Ex. xv. [4] Bancroft, vol. iii. p. 51. [5] Ex. xv. 1.

the first rising of the sun, and the Hebrew deity who had triumphed gloriously was the god of Jeshurun who rode on the heaven in their help.[1] The Quichés sang their song though it made their hearts ache, for this was what they said as they sang—"Alas! we ruined ourselves in Tulan, there we lost many of our kith and kin, they still remain there left behind. We indeed have seen the sun, but they— now that his golden light begins to appear, where are they?"[2] And they worshiped the gods that had become stone. In like manner the Israelites made the golden calf and lusted after the fleshpots, and said, "Would we too had died in the land of Egypt."

It was by the miraculous aid of a horde of hornets that the Quichés utterly defeated and put their enemies to rout.[3] In the same way and by the same means the Hebrew deity drove out the Canaanites. "The Lord thy God will send the hornet among them until they that are left and hide themselves from thee be destroyed."[4] "I sent the hornet before you, which drave them out."[5] The first thought of the general reader is that the Quiché version is of necessity borrowed from the Hebrew. There is one origin for both, only we have not hitherto been able to get beyond the Hebrew as the original.

A kindred account is given of the Mexican wanderings, and of their deliverance and guidance under their leader and god Vitziliputzli [6]— the same story as that so fully told of Israel, which is of supreme value mythologically.

After the deluge or the destruction of the world by a flood, the Burmese writings describe the surface of the regenerated world as forming a crust having the taste and smell of butter, the savour of which reaching the nostrils of the Rupa and Zian excited in these beings a desire to eat the crust. The end of their lives as superior persons having now arrived they assume human bodies. These human beings live for some time on this preternatural food in tranquillity and happiness. But being seized with a desire and love of property, the nectarous crust disappeared as a punishment for their crime, and their bodies, deprived of transparency and splendour, became dark and opaque. From this loss of light dark night commenced, and mankind were in the utmost perturbation, for as yet there was neither sun nor moon.[7] What is this but the story of Israel in the wilderness of Zin or Sin? In the Burmese myth the people are called Zian, in the Hebrew Zin is the place. The Israelites are fed on manna which encrusted the ground like a hoar frost. They also sin from greed in going out on the seventh day in search of the manna,[8] and from love of property hold it over till the morning when forbidden to keep any. Further, when the Burmese butter or manna disappeared it sank into the interior of

---

[1] Deut. xxxiii. 26.
[2] Bancroft, vol. iii. 52.
[3] Bancroft, vol. iii. p. 53.
[4] Deut. vii. 20.
[5] Josh. xxiv. 12.
[6] Acosta, *Hist. Nat. Ind.* pp. 352-363.
[7] *As. Res.* vol. vi. 246.
[8] Ex. xvi. 27.

the earth till it reached the great rock, Sila-pathavy, transformed its nature and there sprang out of it a certain climbing-plant which also had the taste of butter. On this again mankind were fed until avarice prevailed and it likewise disappeared.[1] Now this great rock called Sila-pathavy has the most unique relationship to the rock of Israel, and the water of the wanderings. Sila or Sela is the same word as the Egyptian Ser, which is determined by a liquid that is either cream or butter. Ser is also the rock. The first rock of Israel, the rock of Horeb, whence sprang the earliest waters to give life to the people, is always styled Tzer. That is during the life of Miriam or under the rule of the feminine source, for the feminine source was the first anointer. Sila-pathavy signifies this; AVI in Sanskrit denotes a woman in her courses; "put" is to emit. The butter, the manna, the waters of Horeb, all symbol the feminine creative source, hence the pot of manna carried in the ark along with the rod that budded. On the death of Miriam[2] the water of the primitive fount ceases, and Moses strikes the rock to bring forth the waters of Meribah. Here the name of the rock is changed from Tzer to Sela. At root the words are one, but a great change is implied both as a matter of religion and language. In the Burmese account the change in the food was from butter to butter-plant springing from the great rock Sila-pathavy ; in the Hebrew it is from the water rising from the rock called Tzer to that of the rock called Sela. Sela is related to the Shiloh who was to come feeding on butter and honey. "Butter and honey shall he eat, that he may know to refuse the evil and choose the good."[3] That is, the anointed one fed on that which anointed. The Burmese say that, " In the beginning, when men fed on the crust of butter and the climbing-plant, the whole of this food was changed into flesh and blood, but when they began to eat rice the grosser part of that required after digestion to be evacuated. In consequence, the different canals and organs necessary were generated of their own accord, and the different organs of sex appeared, for before that time mankind were neither male nor female. When the difference of sex appeared then men and women married."[4] Here the myth has been vapourized. This " beginning" belongs to the time of the genitrix ; of Atum the "Mother-goddess of time" ; of Menât the wet-nurse, the first giver of the water of life : the time when the feminine period of ten months or moons preceded the reckoning by the solar nine months, and there were thirteen of those periods to the year, as typified in the thirteen branches of the Asherah tree ; the time when men worshipped the great mother, but had not yet begun to call upon the Lord.

The Mexicans relate that when their divine progenitors departed, each left to the sad and wondering men who were their servants their

---

[1] *As. Res.* vol. vi. 247-8.   [2] Num. xx. 2.   [3] Is. vii. 15.
[4] *As. Res.* vol. vi. 247.

garments as a memorial. The servants made up a bundle of the raiment left to them, this was bound about a stick into which a green stone had been embedded to serve as a heart. These bundles were called TLAQUIMILLOLI, and each bore the name of the god whose memorial it was, and the images were more sacred than ordinary gods of wood and stone.[1]

When Tescatlipoca died, disappeared, or was transformed, he left his raiment as a relic with his servant, and a scene is depicted which is the counterpart of one described in the Hebrew writings as occurring to Elijah and Elisha.[2] After Tescatlipoca had been taken away his servant followed seeking him, bearing the garment on his shoulders and wondering whether he should see the god again. At length, on arriving at the sea, he is *favoured with an apparition of his master in three different shapes.* And Tescatlipoca spake to his servant, saying, " Come hither, thou that lovest me so well, that I may tell thee what thou hast to do. Go now to the house of the sun and fetch thence singers and instruments so that thou mayest make me a festival ; but first call upon the whale, and upon the syren, and upon the tortoise, and they shall make thee a bridge to the sun."[3] This was done, and the servant went over the sea, on this living bridge, to the house of the sun. In the Hebrew myth the three appearances answer to the three appeals made by Elijah to his servant, "Tarry here, I pray thee," because the Lord had sent him to Bethel, Jericho, and Jordan. And when they came to the river, Elijah took his mantle and smote the waters, and they were divided before them. Elijah then leaves his mantle to his servant Elisha, as did Tescatlipoca in the Mexican legend. But the Mexican form of this myth has not been tampered with so much as the Hebrew. It shows us what the crossing of the waters was. The imagery belongs to the astronomical allegory. The whale, tortoise, and syren are the three water-signs through which the sun passed in its winter phase, and this passage of the sun is that of the soul in the Book of the Dead, and the dropping of the garment in passing signifies the body left behind, whence the left-off garment, the bundle, represents the god or spirit that has departed, as did the mummy-type in Egypt.

In the passage of the sun through the lower heaven and the six solar signs from west to east, the earliest mapping out of the circle being lunar, we find the fourteen mystical abodes and the fourteen judgment-seats before which the deceased has to pass, answering to the fourteen lunar houses of the zodiac.[4] The first of these abodes is called the head abode of the west. "Hail the head abode of the west! He who has lived in it (has done so) off cakes of thorns." The thorn is the Anbu tree. One of Tum's transformations is into the

---

[1] Bancroft, vol. iii. 61-2.   [2] 2 Kings ii.
[3] Bancroft, vol. iii. p. 62.   [4] *Rit.* chapters xx. and cl.

Anbu or thorn. This we may take to be figurative for wearing the crown of thorns, the crown of justification, the crown of Tum.[1]

"Cakes of thorns" possibly alludes to the manna-like gathering on the thorny acacia and other shrubs. The "cakes of thorns" on which the spirits lived in the first Abode are the analogue of the manna and quails in the Hebrew myth, on which the Israelites were fed in one of their first abodes after crossing the Red Sea.

The anniversary of the fall of manna and quails is kept in the Coptic Church at the time of the autumn equinox, on September 21st, the equinox being on the 22nd, and still associated with the sun's entrance into Libra. This is four days before the festival of the cross (September 26, 1878) or the crossing. In connection with this subject and the miracle of the quails and manna, it is observable that quail-shooting begins at Alexandria on the 5th of September the first day of the Nasi or black days, the five intercalary days, and that the quails migrate on October 31st.[2]

"Moses, our master, physiologised," says Josephus. The secret clue to mythology is physiological, and this was in the keeping of the mysteries ; the outer ring is astronomical because the imagery in which the physiological ideas, as well as others, were expressed was figured first in the heavens. Philo observes that, "*By men learned in philosophy the flux of the catamenia is said to be the corporeal essence of children.*"[3] This is literal fact, the basement of mythology, the blood of the mother made flesh for the child. Here we enter the world of the earliest human thought to which belongs the manna of mythology. Mena is the Egyptian name for the wet-nurse in the mystical sense, she who supplied the flesh-making fluid for creating the child. In all likelihood many things hereby announced will be at first denounced as untrue, solely because of their being too startlingly true, but after the strangeness passes the truth will remain.

The expositors of the Koran, repeating a tradition of the Jews, make the Red Sea divide into twelve different paths, one for each tribe, or every man of Israel. That was just how the Red Sea did divide for each at birth. This is fact, not fable, and in this tradition the physiological and astronomical Exodus commingle. The Red Sea dividing into twelve different paths is zodiacal, and the Red Sea that separates or dries up for each man's individual passage is physiological. Not until the present writer had attained to a knowledge of this dual origin of the myths was he enabled to read them by distinguishing the one from the other, or interpreting the one by the other, or understanding the metaphor in which both are so often blended.

The passage of the Jordan will furnish us with evidence actually topographical in the planisphere. In crossing the river twelve men

---

[1] *Rit.* chapters xix. lxxviii. and cl.
[2] *Egyptian Calendar* (Alexandria, 1878).
[3] *Creation of the World*, par. xlv.

are commanded to take each a stone from the midst of the river-bed, and erect them as a memorial of the miraculous passage.[1] "And they are there unto this day." This, as a statement of literal fact, was calculated to mislead the explorers of Palestine. But its truth to the astronomical allegory may be verified by any one who cares to turn to the planisphere of the ceiling of Isis's temple brought from Denderah.[2] On the verge of the river of Aquarius and on the side near the sign of Pisces there is a constellation of twelve stars, the Astral memorial of the crossing. The stones were erected as a monument in Gilgal, the circle of revolving or rolling round, the wheel-work of the celestial chariot,[3] the Kar-Kar (Eg.), or Karti, of the dual orbit, whose type is the CART; always a vehicle with *two* wheels. When the waters were crossed, the sun, or soul, or Asar had once more attained solid ground on the other side, where the Egyptians located their region of the eternal, called Tattu. Another name of the place was Smen, the region of the pleroma of eight, of which Taht, the moon-god, was lord. And in the same planisphere, close to the constellation of twelve stars, there is a representation of the full moon with eight figures in it. That is an image of Smen, where a luni-solar circle was completed, and the son established in the seat of the father.

The sun, it is said, "has strangled the children of wickedness on the floor of those in Sesen."[4] Sesen is also named Hermopolis, the lunar region of the eight, here indicated by the moon. The eight figures are kneeling in the attitude of the condemned, with their hands bound behind them and ropes round their necks.

In the Mandan and Warau Exodus, the stout old woman that stuck in the passage is doubtless the pregnant genitrix, whose name of Taurt denotes the great old mother; the passage being from her region in the north to a new point of beginning in the south, from the Sabean to the luni-solar circle of time. The Typhonian genitrix took various forms of the stout old woman. The Laps, Finns, and Greenlanders have a pottle-paunched devil or demon which they invoke to go and suck the cows and consume the herds of their enemies, who is the stout old Typhon. The Japanese Kagura seems to be a form of the same kind, and to judge by its immense mouth it still preserves the hippopotamus-type of the Typhonian Khebt.[5]

In the Japanese mythology there is a fabulous or typical animal that is said to inhabit the waters and to be like a monkey. It is called a KAPPA. This is probably a form of the Typhonian genitrix, who united the KAFI, monkey, to the Kheb, or hippopotamus, the water-horse, with the crocodile and lioness in her compound four-fold image.

An African tribe, the Karens, are reputed to have a devil who is

---

[1] Josh. iv. 9.   [2] See Plate.   [3] Ezek. x. 13.
[4] *Rit.* ch. xvii.   [5] Fig. 3, *Demonology and Devil-lore.* Conway.

represented as floating through the air in the shape of an enormous stomach, and the hippopotamus goddess (the Great Bear), is the type of the Egyptian Typhon, who became the devil of their eschatology. She was pourtrayed as the great mother, the pregnant, with a big belly. This to all appearance is the huge stomach of Typhon.

The grape-vine is likewise a landmark to be utilized in the "Typology of the tree." The Exodus from Egypt is marked by a change in the calendar of the year. "This day came ye out in the month Abib."[1] "Observe the month Abib and keep the passover, for in the month of Abib the Lord thy God brought thee forth out of Egypt by night."[2] "This month (Abib) shall be the beginning of months: it shall be the first month of the year to you."[3] The name Abib is always accompanied by the article *the*, as the Egyptians said the Taht, which was moveable, according to precession. The Aramaic, Assyrian, and Jewish calendars show there was a year that once began with the month Ab; the month Sebat being the seventh from Ab, and dedicated to the seven great gods. In Akkadian this month is called "Ab-ab-gar." It is now suggested that this is the month meant by the Jewish Abib. It corresponds to our July, and its zodiacal sign is Leo, and answers to the commencement of the Egyptian sacred year in July.

Talmudic writers say that Moses ascended the Mount Sinai in the month Elul—"*The Lord said unto Moses in the month Elul, Go up unto me on the mountain; and Moses went up and received the second tablet at the end of forty days.*" Elul answers to the moon of August, and it is said to have been in the third month from the going forth from Egypt that Moses went up into the Mount Sinai.

These reckonings cannot be made to agree with the month Nisan as a starting-point, although the month Abib is usually taken to be identical with Nisan.

The new beginning with Ab or Abib is the oldest commencement of the luni-solar year; it goes back to the Sothic year, the year of the Sun and Sirius. We take the dog-star to be the link of connection and continuity between the earliest Sabean reckoning by the Great Bear, and the latest by the revolution of the sun. This point of commencement is marked by the rising of Sothis with the sun in the Lion, and this Egyptian year, the present writer concludes, was the re-beginning under Moses at the time of the Exodus from the mythical Egypt. No beginnings were lost. The four corners of the first, the Sabean circle, remained fixed in the solar zodiac and imagery, as the Lion, the Bird, the Waterer, and Bull. In the year which opens with Ab, the sun was in the sign of the Bull at the time of the vernal equinox, or on the 14th Nisan. Now the latest date for this celestial position was 2,300 B.C., consequently such time cannot apply to the

[1] Ex. xiii. 4. [2] Deut. xvi. 1. [3] Ex. xii. 2.

actual exodus " from " Egypt.   When in the course of precession the sun had receded into the sign of Cancer, the month of celebration was Tammuz instead of Ab, and this will enable us to lay hold of corroborative matter.

In Israel the festival of the month Abib was to celebrate the deliverance from the monster Tamuzi, who had held them so long in lewd pastimes or cruel toils, from which this was now to be the Feast of the Passover, established for an everlasting statute ; at the beginning of the first day of the month Tammuz each year they lamented and wept for Tammuz.[1]   This is an exact parallel to the command given in Exodus[2] and Deuteronomy[3] for the month Abib to be the beginning of months and the first month of the year in which the feast of the Passover was to be kept, because the Lord had brought them out by night in the month Abib.   Now, in Arabic, according to Castell,[4] Tamuzi is the name given to the Pharaoh who treated the Israelites so cruelly, and would not let them go.

The Jews kept two Passovers.   In the Mishna it is asked, What is the difference between the Passover of Egypt and the Passover of succeeding generations ?   The Passover of Egypt was taken on the tenth day,[5] and required the sprinkling with a bunch of hyssop on the lintel and the two side posts, and was eaten with haste in one night, but the Passover of succeeding generations existed the whole seven days.[6]

The first Passover, that of Khebt, was celebrated during four days —the four KU of the Hawaiians—from the 10th to the 14th of the month.[7]   The numbers 10 and 4 are sacred for ever to the ancient founder, who is identified with them by name as Menat and Aft. The Passover of succeeding generations is solar—simply the Easter festival of the sun's crossing at the vernal equinox.

According to Plutarch's report of the Egyptian myth, Typhon was seven days in fleeing from the battle with Horus.   The relations or narrative of the Jews, he says, were wrested into this fable, or, as may be added, *vice versâ.*   Apion asserts that the Jews fled from Egypt during six days, and rested on the seventh on account of the buboes.   Justin relates that the Israelites fled and fasted for six days, and on arriving at Sinai Moses set apart the seventh day as the day of rest.   In the Hebrew writings two different accounts are given of the origin of the day of rest, the seventh day or Sabbath. According to the fourth commandment the Sabbath was instituted to commemorate the coming out of Egypt.[8]   " Remember that thou wast a servant in the land of Egypt, and the Lord thy God brought thee out thence through a mighty hand, and by a stretched-out arm ; therefore the Lord thy God commanded thee to keep the Sabbath

---

[1] Smith, *Dict. of Bible*, vol. iii. p. 1434.   [2] xii. 2.   [3] xvi. 1.
[4] *Lex. Hept.* Smith, *Dict. of Bible*, vol. iii. p. 1436.   [5] Ex. xii. 3.
[6] *Mishna, Treatise* iv. ch. ix. 5.   [7] Ex. xii. 6.   [8] Deut. v. 15.

day." But in the Book of Exodus[1] the Sabbath is said to be a sign between the deity and the children of Israel for ever, because in "Six days the Lord made heaven and earth, and on the seventh day he rested, and was refreshed." The six days' creation, with the rest on the seventh, and the six days' flight from Egypt, with its rest on the seventh, are identical with thē flight of Typhon in the Egyptian myth, in which these various versions can be verified, but only as myth, not as history. Typhon fled on the back of an ass, and barely escaped with life. Two sons were afterwards born to Typhon, named Hierosolymus and Judæus. Typhon on the ass constitutes Sut-Typhon. The two sons of Typhon correspond to Sut in the dual character implied by the name of Sebti or Suti, which was ultimately figured in the form of the double Anubis. The allegory with the secret meaning spoken of by Plutarch belongs to the mythos and the coming out of the celestial Egypt, in which the sabbath of the six days' creation and of the ascent from Egypt will be shown to be identical.

We are told[2] that the number of Israelites who went up out of Egypt with Moses was about six hundred thousand men on foot, besides children and a mixed multitude. The total number of the people,[3] when it is a question of mouths to be fed, is given as six hundred thousand with no mention of children or a mixed multitude. And in the traditions of the Kabalists, the number of the souls of the Israelites is six hundred thousand. Six hundred thousand souls were contained in the soul of the first man. Six hundred thousand was the number destined from the first and fulfilled at last. "The soul of the first man," says the Nishmath Adam, "consisted of six hundred thousand souls twined together like so many threads; of these six hundred thousand there is never one wanting; which shows them to be the model of the upper chariot (a figure of the heavens) in which are to be found six hundred thousand sciences; as is well known to such as are acquainted with those sciences." Another statement is that the number of souls is six hundred thousand, and the law is the root of the souls of the Israelites; and every verse in the law has six hundred thousand explanations, and every soul is formed specially of one explanation. This was the typical number belonging to the mythological astronomy, a "model of the upper chariot" in which Jah rode upon the heavens; the number that always was, and was to be; the number therefore that came up out of Egypt in the Hebrew legend, who are surely the same Israelites in nature as in number.[4] In the *Chronicon Samaritanum*, or "Samaritan Joshua," the same number is implied where Joshua as king wages war against two kings of Persia with 300,000 mounted men called "*half Israel.*"[5] In other legends the same number occurs as the six hundred

---

[1] xxxi. 17. [2] Ex. xii. 37. [3] Numbers xi. 21.
[4] *Nishmath Adam*, f. 6, c. 1; f. 7, c. 1. [5] Juynboll (Leyden, 1848).

thousand beautiful angels, that sang around and encircled the tree of life in the centre of the celestial garden.

The Rabbinical GUPH, the birthplace of souls, is the Hebrew בג rendered the back. But the back is the Bekh, the place of birth called the hinder thigh, on account of the mode of bringing forth and producing animal-fashion. Hence, as seen in the Aramaic and Arabic, GUV denotes the belly, the middle, the midst, the interior. It is the Kep or Khepsh (Eg.), *i.e.* finally the Womb, the Hebrew QEBAH. One of its images was the GEBIA or KUNDA. The celestial GUPH is the Egyptian Kep or Khepsh of the north; the Egypt of the heavens and the 600,000 souls that came out of Guph are identical with those that came out of Kheb or Egypt. On the other hand we are assured that, "They were a few men in number, yea, very few, and strangers in it," *i.e.* the land of Canaan, not in the land of Egypt.[1] "The Lord did not set his love upon you, nor choose you because ye were more in number than any people, for ye (were) the fewest of all people."[2] This has the look of the historical fact, but is at utter variance with the numbers given in the " Exodus." People who were led or left as wanderers up and down a rugged sterile wilderness or desert place during forty years without wearing out their clothes, or their shoes waxing old, and who were fed all the while on manna rained down from heaven, never were either the denizens, inhabitants, or "gipsies" of this world. "Oh, but," says the Bibliolator, "it was all done by miracle." Miracle is the name substituted by the ignorant for mythical. The myth will explain the inexplicable miracle.

And now for a *final proof.*—The "Book of Enoch," to quote its own words, is " *The book of the revolutions of the luminaries of heaven, according to their respective classes, their respective powers, their respective periods, their respective names, the places where they commence their progress (or the places of their nativity), and their respective months, which Uriel, the holy angel who was with me explained to me ; he who conducts them. The whole account of them, according to every year of the world for ever, until a new work shall be effected, which will be eternal.*"[3] It relates solely to the Sabean, lunar, and solar cycles of time, from the circle of twenty-four hours to that of the great year of 26,000 years. From this the following Chapters lxxxiv to lxxxix are quoted :—

CHAPTER LXXXIV.

After this I saw another dream and explained it all to thee my son. Enoch arose and said to his son Mathusala : To thee my son will I speak, hear my word, and incline thine ear to the visionary dream of thy father. Before I married thy mother Edna, I saw a vision on my bed ;
And behold a cow sprung forth from the earth ;

[1] Ps. cv. 12.　　　　　[2] Deut. vii. 7.
[3] Ch. lxxi. sec. 13, Paris MS.

And this cow was white.[1]

Afterwards a female heifer sprung forth ; and it was with another heifer ; one was black, and one was red.[2]

The black heifer then struck the red one and pursued it over the earth.[3]

From that period I could see nothing more of the red heifer : but the black one increased in bulk, and a female heifer came with him.

After this I saw that many cows proceeded forth, resembling him and following after him.

The first female young one also went out in the presence of the first cow ; and sought the red heifer ; but found him not.

And she lamented with a great lamentation while she was seeking him.

Then I looked until that first cow came to her, from which time she became silent, and ceased to lament.

Afterwards she calved another white cow.

And again calved many cows and black heifers.

In my sleep also I perceived a white bull, which in like manner grew, and became a large white bull.

After him many white cows came forth resembling him.

And they began to calve many other white cows, which resembled them and followed each other.

CHAPTER LXXXV.

Again I looked attentively (with my eyes) while sleeping, and surveyed heaven above.

And behold a single star fell from heaven.

Which being raised up, ate and fed among those cows.

After that I perceived other large and black cows ; and behold all of them changed their stalls and pastures, while their young began to lament one with another. Again I looked in my vision, and surveyed heaven ; when behold I saw many stars which descended, and projected themselves from heaven to where the first star was,

Into the midst of those young ones ; while the cows were with them, feeding in the midst of them.

I looked at and observed them ; when behold they all protruded their parts of shame like horses, and began to ascend the young cows, all of whom became pregnant and brought forth elephants, camels, and asses.

At these all the cows were alarmed and terrified ; when they began biting with their teeth, swallowing and striking with their horns.

They began also to devour the cows ; and behold all the children of the earth trembled, shook with terror at them, and suddenly fled away.

LXXXVI.

Again I perceived them, when they began to strike and to swallow each other ; and the earth cried out. Then I raised my eyes a second time towards heaven, and saw in a vision, that, behold there came forth from heaven as it were the likeness of white men. One came forth from thence, and three with him.

Those three who came forth last seized me by my hand ; and raising me up from the generations of the earth, elevated me to a high station.

Then they showed me a lofty tower on the earth, while every hill became diminished.[4] And they said, remain here until thou perceivest what shall come upon those elephants, camels, and asses, upon the stars and upon all the cows.

---

[1] WHITE COW.—The White Cow in the Tomb of Seti represents the nocturna heaven that gives birth to light, or the beings of light.

[2] RED HEIFER.—The Red Heifer or Arg Roud was so great a mystery, says Rabbinical tradition, that even the wise Solomon never fathomed it. In the chapter of transforming into a Nycticorax or Phœnix, the Osirian says, " the thoughts of him who listens to words do not know when I am the Red Calf in the paintings." That is, words may not express the depths of the mystery of the Red Heifer.

[3] *Cain and Abel.* (According to Laurence.)

[4] TOWER.—The tower of the seven stages called Babel.

CHAPTER LXXXVII.

Then I looked at that one of the four white men [1] who came out first.

He seized the first star which fell down from heaven.

And binding it hand and foot, he cast it into a valley; a valley, narrow, deep, stupendous and gloomy.

Then one of them drew his sword, and gave it to the elephants, camels, and asses, who began to strike each other. And the whole earth shook on account of them.

And when I looked in the vision, behold one of those four angels, who came forth, hurled from heaven, collected together, and took all the great stars, whose parts of shame resembled those of horses; and binding them all hand and foot, cast them into the cavities of the earth. [2]

CHAPTER LXXXVIII.

Then one of those four went to the white cows, and taught them a mystery. While the cow was trembling it was born, and became a man, [3] and fabricated for himself a large ship. In this he dwelt, and three cows [4] dwelt with him in that ship which covered them.

Again I lifted up my eyes towards heaven and saw a lofty roof. Above it were seven cataracts, which poured forth on a certain village much water.

Again I looked, and behold there were fountains open on the earth in that large village.

The water began to boil up, and rose over the earth; so that the village was not seen while its whole soil was covered with water.

Much water was over it, darkness and clouds. Then I surveyed the height of this water; and it was elevated above the village.

It flowed over the village and stood higher than the earth.

Then all the cows which were collected there while I looked on them were drowned, swallowed up, and destroyed in the water.

But the ship floated above it. All the cows, the elephants, the camels and the asses, were drowned on the earth, and all cattle. Nor could I perceive them. Neither were they able to get out, but perished and sunk into the deep.

Again I looked in the vision until those cataracts from that lofty roof were removed, and the fountains of the earth became equalized, while other depths were opened;

Into which the water began to descend, until the dry ground appeared.

The ship remained on the earth; the darkness receded, and it became light.

Then the white cow which became a man, went out of the ship and the three cows with him.

One of the three cows was white, resembling that cow; one of them was red as blood; and one of them was black, and the white cow left them.

Then began wild beasts and birds to bring forth.

Of all these the different kinds assembled together, lions, tigers, wolves, dogs, wild boars, foxes, rabbits, and the hanzar,

The siset, the avest, kites, the phonkas, and ravens.

Then a white cow [5] was born in the midst of them.

And they began to bite each other; when the white cow which was born in the midst of them brought forth a wild ass and a white cow at the same time, and after that many wild asses. Then the white cow [6] which was born, brought forth a black wild sow and a white sheep. [7]

That wild sow also brought forth many swine:

---

[1] Four white men. Probably the four superior gods of the upper place.—*Rit.* ch. 135. The four Genii of the four corners. In Egyptian the name of a spirit, Akhu, also means white.

[2] These are the Seven Stars of the Bear, or Water-horse, which were cast out as untrue time-keepers. Enoch (ch. xxi.) is shown these seven stars bound together in the abyss.

[3] Noah. (Laurence.)

[4] Shem, Ham, and Japhet. (Laurence.)

[5] Abraham. (Laurence.)

[6] Isaac. (Laurence.)

[7] Esau and Jacob. (Laurence.)

And that sheep brought forth twelve sheep.[1]

When those twelve sheep grew up, they delivered one of them [2] to the asses.

Again those asses delivered that sheep to the wolves; [4]

And he grew up in the midst of them.

Then the Lord brought the eleven other sheep that they might dwell and feed with him in the midst of the wolves.

They multiplied and there was abundance of pasture for them.

But the wolves began to frighten and oppress them, while they destroyed their young ones.

And they left their young in torrents of deep water.

Now the sheep began to cry out on account of their young, and fled for refuge to their Lord. One [5] however which was saved, escaped, and went away to the wild asses.

I beheld the sheep moaning, crying, and petitioning their Lord

With all their might, until the Lord of the sheep descended at their voice from his lofty habitation; went to them, and inspected them.

He called to that sheep which had secretly stolen away from the wolves, and told him to make the wolves understand that they were not to touch the sheep.

Then that sheep went to the wolves with the word of the Lord when another [6] met him, and proceeded with him.

Both of them together entered the dwelling of the wolves: and conversing with them made them understand that from thenceforwards they were not to touch the sheep.

Afterwards I perceived the wolves greatly prevailing over the sheep with their whole force. The sheep cried out and their Lord came to them.

He began to strike the wolves, who commenced a grievous lamentation; but the sheep were silent, nor from that time did they cry out.

I then looked at them until they departed from the wolves. The eyes of the wolves were blind who went out and followed them with all their might. But the Lord of the sheep proceeded with them, and conducted them.

All his sheep followed him.

His countenance was terrific and splendid, and glorious was his aspect. Yet the wolves began to follow the sheep, until they overtook them in a certain lake of water.[7]

Then that lake became divided: the water standing up on both sides before their face.

And while their Lord was conducting them, he placed himself between them and the wolves,

The wolves however perceived not the sheep, but went into the midst of the lake, following them, and running after them into the lake of water.

But when they saw the Lord of the sheep they turned to fly from before his face.

Then the water of the lake returned, and that suddenly according to its nature. It became full and was raised up, until it covered the wolves. And I saw that all of them which had followed the sheep perished, and were drowned.

But the sheep passed over this water, proceeding to a wilderness, which was without both water and grass. And they began to open their eyes and to see.

Then I beheld the Lord of the sheep inspecting them, and giving them water and grass.

The sheep already mentioned was proceeding with them, and conducting them.

And when he had ascended the top of a lofty rock, the Lord of the sheep sent him to them.

Afterwards I perceived their Lord standing before them, with an aspect terrific and severe.

And when they all beheld him they were frightened at his countenance.

All of them were alarmed and trembled. They cried out after that sheep; and to the other sheep who had been with him, and who was in the midst of them saying; We are not able to stand before our Lord, or to look upon him.

Then that sheep who conducted them went away, and ascended the top of the rock;

---

[1] The Twelve Patriarchs.
[2] Joseph.
[3] Midianites.
[4] Egyptians.
} (Laurence.)

[5] Moses.
[6] Aaron.
[7] The Red Sea.
} (Laurence.)

When the rest of the sheep began to grow blind, and to wander from the path which he had shewn them ; but he knew it not.

Their Lord however was moved with great indignation against them ; and when that sheep had learned what had happened,

He descended from the top of the rock and coming to them found that there were many,

Which had become blind :

And had wandered from his path. As soon as they beheld him, they feared and trembled at his presence ;

And became desirous of returning to their fold.

Then that sheep, taking with him other sheep, went to those which had wandered,

And afterwards began to kill them. They were terrified at his countenance. Then he caused those who had wandered to return ; who went back to their fold.

I likewise saw there in the vision that this sheep became a man, built an house for the Lord of the sheep, and made them all stand in that house.

I perceived also that the sheep which proceeded to meet this sheep, their conductor, died. I saw too that all the great sheep perished, while smaller ones rose up in their place, entered into a pasture, and approached a river of water.[1]

Then that sheep, their conductor, who became a man, was separated from them and died.

All the sheep sought after him, and cried for him with bitter lamentation.

I likewise saw that they ceased to cry after that sheep, and passed over the river of water,

And that there arose other sheep, all of whom conducted them, instead of those who were dead, and who had previously conducted them.[2]

Then I saw that the sheep entered into a goodly place, and a territory delectable and glorious.

I saw also that they became satiated ; that their house was in the midst of a delectable territory, and that sometimes their eyes were opened, and that sometimes they were blind ; until another sheep arose and conducted them.[3] He brought them all back and their eyes were opened.

Then dogs, foxes, and wild boars began to devour them, until again another sheep[4] arose, the master of the flock, one of themselves, a ram, to conduct them. This ram began to butt on every side those dogs, foxes, and wild boars until they all perished.

But the former sheep opened his eyes, and saw the ram in the midst of them who had laid aside his glory.

And he began to strike the sheep, treading upon them and behaving himself without dignity.

Then their Lord sent the former sheep again to a still different sheep,[5] and raised him up to be a ram, and to conduct them instead of that sheep who had laid aside his glory.

Going therefore to him and conversing with him alone, he raised up that ram and made him a prince and leader of the flock. All the time that the dogs,[6] troubled the sheep.

The first ram paid respect to this latter ram.

Then the latter ram arose, and fled away from before his face. And I saw that those dogs caused the first ram to fall.

But the latter ram arose and conducted the smaller sheep.

That ram likewise begat many sheep and died.

Then there was a smaller sheep,[7] a ram, instead of him, which became a prince and leader, conducting the flock.

And the sheep increased in size and multiplied,

And all the dogs, foxes, and wild boars, feared and fled away from him.

That ram also struck and killed all the wild beasts so that they could not again prevail in the midst of the sheep, nor at any time ever snatch them away.

And that house was made large and wide ; a lofty tower being built upon it by the sheep, for the Lord of the sheep.

The house was low, but the tower was elevated and very high.

---

[1] The River Jordan. (Laurence.)   [2] The Judges of Israel. (Laurence.)
[3] Samuel. (Laurence.)   [4] Saul. (Laurence.)   [5] David. (Laurence.)
[6] Philistines. (Laurence.)   [7] Solomon. (Laurence.)

Then the Lord of the sheep stood upon that tower, and caused a full table to approach before him.

Again I saw that those sheep wandered, and went various ways, forsaking that their house,

And that their Lord called to some among them whom he sent to them.[1]

But these the sheep began to kill. And when one of them was saved from slaughter,[2] he leaped and cried out against those who were desirous of killing him.

But the Lord of the sheep delivered him from their hands, and made him ascend to him and remain with him.

He sent also many others to them to testify, and with lamentations to exclaim against them.

Again I saw, when some of them forsook the house of their Lord and his tower ; wandering on all sides and growing blind.

I saw that the Lord of the sheep made a great slaughter among them in their pasture, until they cried out to him in consequence of that slaughter. Then he departed from the place of his habitation, and left them in the power of lions, tigers, wolves and the zeebt, and in the power of foxes, and of every beast.

And the wild beasts began to tear them.

I saw too that he forsook the house of their fathers and their tower ; giving them all into the power of lions to tear and devour them ; into the power of every beast.

Then I began to cry out with all my might, imploring the Lord of the sheep, and shewing him how the sheep were devoured by all the beasts of prey.

But he looked on in silence, rejoicing that they were devoured, swallowed up, and carried off ; and leaving them in the power of every beast for food. He called also seventy shepherds, and resigned to them the care of the sheep, that they might overlook them ;

Saying to them and to their associates ; Every one of you henceforwards overlook the sheep and whatsoever I command you, do ; and I will deliver them to you numbered.

I will tell you which of them shall be slain ; these destroy ; And he delivered the sheep to them ;

Then he called to another and said : Understand, and watch everything which the shepherds shall do to these sheep ; for many more of them shall perish than I have commanded.

Of every excess and slaughter, which the shepherds shall commit, there shall be an account ; as, how many may have perished by my command, and how many they may have destroyed of their own heads.

Of all the destruction brought about by each of the shepherds, there shall be an account : and according to the number I will cause a recital to be made before me, how many they have destroyed of their own heads, and how many they have delivered up to destruction, that I may have this testimony against them ; that I may know all their proceedings ; and that delivering the sheep to them I may see what they will do ; whether they will act as I have commanded them or not.

Of this however they shall be ignorant ; neither shalt thou make any explanation to them ; but there shall be an account of all the destruction done by them in their respective seasons. Then they began to kill and destroy more than it was commanded them.

And they left the sheep in the power of lions, so that very many of them were devoured and swallowed up by lions and tigers ; and wild boars preyed upon them. That tower they burnt and overthrew that house.

Then I grieved extremely on account of the tower, and because the house of the sheep was overthrown.

Neither was I afterwards able to perceive whether they again entered that house.

The shepherds likewise, and their associates, delivered likewise to all the wild beasts, that they might devour them ; each of them in his season, according to his number, was delivered up ; each of them, one with another, was described in a book, how many of them one with another were destroyed, in a book.

More however than was ordered, every shepherd killed and destroyed.

Then I began to weep and was greatly indignant on account of the sheep.

In like manner also I saw in the vision him who wrote, how he wrote down *one destroyed by the shepherds, every day.* {He ascended, remained, and exhibited

---

[1] The Prophets. (Laurence.)   [2] Elijah. (Laurence.)

each of his books to the Lord of the sheep, containing all which they had done, and all which each of them had made away with ;

And all which they had delivered up to destruction.

And he took the book up in his hands, read it, sealed it, and deposited it.

After this I saw shepherds overlooking for twelve hours.

And behold three of the sheep [1] departed, arrived, went in ; and began building all which was fallen down of that house.

But the wild boars [2] hindered them although they prevailed not.

Again they began to build as before, and raised up that tower which was called a lofty tower.

And again they began to place before the tower a table, with every impure and unclean kind of bread upon it.

Moreover also all the sheep were blind, and could not see ; as were the shepherds likewise.

Thus were they delivered up to the shepherds for a great destruction, who trod them under foot, and devoured them.

Yet was their Lord silent, until all the sheep in the field were destroyed. The shepherds and the sheep were all mixed together ; but they did not save them from the power of the beasts.

Then he who wrote the book ascended, exhibited it, and read it at the residence of the Lord of the sheep. He petitioned him for them, and prayed, pointing out every act of the shepherds, and testifying before him against them all. Then taking the book he deposited it with him : and departed.

CHAPTER LXXXIX.

And I observed during the time, that these thirty-seven shepherds,[3] were overlooking, all of whom finished in their respective periods as the first. Others then received them into their hands, that they might overlook them in their respective periods, every shepherd in his own period.

Afterwards I saw in the vision, that all the birds of heaven arrived ; eagles, the avest, kites and ravens. The eagle instructed them all.

They began to devour the sheep, to peck out their eyes, and to eat up their bodies.

The sheep then cried out ; for their bodies were devoured by the birds.

I also cried out, and groaned in my sleep against that shepherd which overlooked the flock.

And I looked, while the sheep were eaten up by the dogs, by the eagles, and by the kites. They neither left them their body nor their skins, nor their muscles, until their bones alone remained ; until their bones fell upon the ground. And the sheep became diminished.

I observed likewise during the time, that twenty-three shepherds [4] were overlooking ; who completed in their respective periods fifty-eight periods.

Then were small lambs born of those white sheep, who began to open their eyes and to see, crying out to the sheep.

The sheep however cried not out to them, neither did they hear what they uttered to them ; but were deaf, blind, and obdurate in the greatest degree.

I saw in the vision that ravens flew down upon those lambs ;

That they seized one of them ; and that tearing the sheep in pieces, they devoured them.

I saw also, that horns grew upon those lambs ; and that the ravens lighted down upon their horns.

I saw too that a large horn sprouted out on an animal among the sheep, and that their eyes were opened.

He looked at them. Their eyes were wide open ; and he cried out to them.

Then the dabelat saw him ; all of whom ran to him.

And besides this, all the eagles, the avest, the ravens and the kites, were still

---

[1] Zerubbabel, Joshua and Nehemiah. (Laurence.)

[2] The Samaritans. (Laurence.)

[3] A supposed error for 35. See the 7th Verse. The Kings of Judah and Israel. (Laurence.)

[4] The Kings of Babylon, etc. (Laurence.)

carrying off the sheep, flying down upon them, and devouring them. The sheep were silent, but the dabelat lamented and cried out.

Then the ravens contended, and struggled with them.

They wished among them to break his horn; but they prevailed not over him.

I looked on them until the shepherds, the eagles, the avest, and the kites came.

Who cried out to the ravens to break the horn of the dabelat; to contend with him; and to kill him. But he struggled with them, and cried out, that help might come to him.

Then I perceived that the man came who had written down the names of the shepherds, and who ascended up before the Lord of the sheep.

He brought assistance, and caused every one to see him descending to the help of the dabelat.

I perceived likewise that the Lord of the sheep came to them in wrath, while all those who saw him fled away; all fell down in his tabernacle before his face, while all the eagles, the avest, ravens, and kites assembled and brought with them all the sheep of the field.

All came together, and strove to break the horn of the dabelat.

Then I saw that the man who wrote the book at the word of the Lord, opened the book of destruction, of that destruction which the last twelve shepherds [1] wrought: and pointed out before the Lord of the sheep that they destroyed more than those who preceded them.

I saw also that the Lord of the sheep came to them, and taking in his hand the sceptre of his wrath seized the earth, which became rent asunder; while all the beasts and birds of heaven fell from the sheep, and sank into the earth, which closed over them.

I saw too that a large sword was given to the sheep, who went forth against all the beasts of the field to slay them.

But all the beasts and birds of heaven fled away from before their face.

And I saw a throne erected in a delectable land.

Upon this sat the Lord of the sheep, who received all the sealed books;

Which were opened before him.

Then the Lord called the first seven white ones, and commanded them to bring before him the first of the first stars which preceded the stars whose parts of shame resemble those of horses; the first star, which fell down first; and they brought them all before Him.

And He spoke to the man who wrote in his presence, who was one of the seven white ones, saying; Take those seventy shepherds to whom I delivered up the sheep, and who receiving them, killed more of them than I commanded. Behold I saw them all bound and all standing before Him. First came on the trial of the stars, which being judged and found guilty, went to the place of punishment. They thrust them into a place deep and full of flaming fire, and full of pillars of fire. Then the seventy shepherds were judged, and being found guilty were thrust into the flaming abyss.

At that time likewise I perceived that one abyss was thus opened in the midst of the earth, which was full of fire.

And to this were brought the blind sheep; which being judged and found guilty were all thrust into that abyss of fire on the earth and burnt.

The abyss was on the right of that house.

And I saw the sheep burning, and their bones consuming.

And I stood beholding Him immerge that ancient house, while they brought out its pillars every plant in it, and the ivory infolding it. They brought it out and deposited it in a place on the right side of the earth.

I saw also that the Lord of the sheep produced a new house, great and loftier than the former, which he bounded by the former circular spot. All its pillars were new, and its ivory new, as well as more abundant than the former ancient ivory, which he had brought out.

And while all the sheep which were left in the midst of it, all the beasts of the earth, and all the birds of heaven fell down and worshipped them, petitioning them, and obeying them in everything.

Then those three who were clothed in white, and who holding me by my hand had before caused me to ascend, while the hand of him who spoke held me; raised me up, and placed me in the midst of the sheep, before the judgment took place.

---

[1] The native princes of Judah after its delivery from the Syrian yoke. (Laurence.)

The sheep were all white with wool long and pure. Then all who had perished and had been destroyed, every beast of the field and every bird of heaven, assembled in that house; while the Lord of the sheep rejoiced with great joy, because all were good, and came back again to his dwelling.

And I saw that they laid down the sword which had been given to the sheep, and returned it to his house, sealing it up in the presence of the Lord.

All the sheep would have been enclosed in that house, had it been capable of containing them, and the eyes of all were open, gazing on the good One ; nor was there one among them who did not behold Him.

I likewise perceived that the house was large, wide, and extremely full. I saw too that a white cow was born, whose horns were great ; and that all the beasts of the field and all the birds of heaven were alarmed at him, and entreated him at all times.

Then I saw that the nature of all of them was changed, and that they became white cows ;

And that the first who was in the midst of them spoke, (or became a Word) when that Word became a large beast, upon the head of which were great and black horns ;

While the Lord of the sheep rejoiced over them, and over all the cows.

I lay down in the midst of them ; I awoke ; and saw the whole. This is the vision which I saw, lying down and waking. Then I blessed the Lord of righteousness, and gave glory to Him.

Book of Enoch, chaps. lxxxiv—lxxxix. Archbishop Laurence.[1]

This is written in the book of the revolutions of the luminaries of heaven, and belongs solely and absolutely to the astronomical mythology.

There is no sign that the Book of Enoch was ever included among the sacred writings of the Jews. It is referred to and quoted in the SOHAR as a book known to the Kabalists, but no claim is made nor clue afforded concerning its origin. Its existence in the Æthiopic was discovered by the traveller Bruce, who brought three copies of the work from Abyssinia, where it stands immediately before the Book of Job in the canonical scriptures of the Abyssinian church, one of which was deposited in the Bodleian library, Oxford, and from this Archbishop Laurence produced his version.

In whatsoever language the work ascribed to Enoch was first written, or whensoever it was last re-written, the matter is most ancient. The Messiah Son, the Manifester of the Ancient of Days, appears in it as the child of the Woman—the *son of the woman sitting upon the throne of his glory*,[2] he who from the beginning existed in secret, and whose name was invoked before the sun or constellations were. That was as Sut-Typhon, the ANUSH (Eg.), of the dog or wolf-dog type, which identifies the Hebrew ANOSH and ENOCH with the Dog-star.

The earliest of all the manifesters of time in the mythologies were the Genitrix (Great Bear) and her son Sut-Anush, or Anup, the Sabean Bar or Baal, who preceded the lunar and solar reckonings. "Interpreter of Belus" Seneca designates Berosus, and Belus is called the *Inventor of Sidereal Science* by Solinus and Pliny.[3] He

---

[1] A pretended "Book of Enoch" has been put forth anonymously by Dr. Kenealy, but it is of no value, either as a translation or as an original work.

[2] Ch. lxi. 9.

[3] Seneca, *Nat. Quæs.* iii. 29. Solinus, lvi. 3. Pliny, *Nat. Hist.* vi. 26.

was so as Baal of the Dog-star, Bar-Sutekh, the son of the mother. He was so in the same sense that the Hebrew SETH was the erector of the pillars described by Josephus.

Sut-Anush appears in the Genesis as Enos, the son of Seth, at the time when men began to worship the Lord instead of or in addition to the Lady. In the Samaritan version the older patriarchs die in the year of the Flood, all except Enoch who is the typical announcer. That is right according to the true myth, and fatal to the false.

The "Book of Enoch," so far as we have it extant, is the Kabalist version of the same series and sequence of events that we find converted into human history in the Hebrew Scriptures. It is genuine Kabala, not the vaporized and vague reflex known as the theoretical Kabala, which consists mainly of metaphysical speculations and mystical misinterpretations of mythology. This belongs to the practical Kabala, which means that it is astronomical, rather than eschatological, and the subject-matter is still verifiable in phenomena.

The Book of Enoch is, on its own showing, a "Book of Parables" or allegories, secret things solely concerning the heavens, to be read by the "characteristical signs;"[1] a book that has been *dropped* from heaven gradually in the sense of having been distilled.[2] There is no human history in it, none to be got out of it. And yet the supposed history of Israel from the commencement in Genesis is outlined in this quotation, and has been identified as such by learned divines. One of two things is sure. Either the Book of Enoch contains the Hebrew history in allegory, or the celestial allegory IS the Hebrew history. The parallel is perfect. Nor is there any escape by sticking one's head in the earth and foolishly fancying that the writer of the Book of Enoch amused himself by transforming a Hebrew history into the celestial allegory and concealed its significance by leaving out all the personal names. On the contrary, it is the allegory which has been turned into later history. History may and does begin with mythology; but mythology does not commence with history. The Book of Enoch certainly contains the same characters as the sacred or secret history of the Jews, and as these belong to the astronomical allegory in the one book, that is good evidence of their being mythical in the other. There can be no doubt that the Book of Enoch is what it claims to be, the book of the revolutions of the heavenly bodies with no earthly relation to human history.

The White Cow of the beginning takes us beyond the Hebrew records to the Chamber of the White Cow in the Tomb of Seti I., the white cow of heaven, of the goddesses Neith and Hathor, who personated the bringer-forth, and the first uplifting of the firmament by Shu. The myth of the two brothers who were at enmity is world-wide, and of this the story of Cain and Abel is a version. The four white men, the seven stars, Noah, Shem, Ham, and Japhet, Abraham,

---

[1] Ch. lxvii. [2] Ch. lxx.

Isaac, Esau, and Jacob, the twelve patriarchs, Moses, the Red Sea, the Judges, David, Saul, and Solomon, are claimed on sufficient evidence to be mythical, and the same characters appear in this book as persons or personifications belonging to the celestial allegory. The seventy shepherds are the seventy princes or angels of the Kabala who descended to the earth when the Tower of Babel was overthrown, who ruled the seventy divisions which followed the seven, whose seventy names are catalogued in the Rabbinical writings.[1]

It is said,[2] "He called also seventy shepherds and resigned to them the sheep that they might overlook them." These seventy are composed of 35, 23, and 12.[3] But the seventy who are twice mentioned have been changed into seventy-two, by the substitution of the number thirty-seven.[4] Laurence characterizes this as an error, because thirty-five is the precise number of the kings of Judah and Israel, before the captivity. On the astronomical ground we see in these two numbers a rectification of the original total of seventy, and the intended substitution of the seventy-two according to the chart of the duo-decans in the solar zodiac.

The description ends as in the Book of Revelation with the prophesied restoration and with the new temple or temple of the new heavens, promised and expected at the end of the great year of Precession and the going forth of the Messiah, Son of the Ancient of Days, as the Word. It begins with the most ancient matter of the Old Testament and concludes with the fulfilment in the New, and vouches for both being the substance of the celestial allegory, which will be fully unfolded in the course of the present work.

The same misapprehension has occurred with some Egyptologists, in their readings of the myths in Egypt, as in our reading of the Hebrew report of them. Goodwin speaks of the origin of the myths as arising from the contests of two rival races of different extraction, those of Upper and Lower Egypt, whose conflict appears to have been perpetually renewed.[5] The same mistake was made by George Smith in rendering the cuneiform tablets. So has it been with the interpreters of the Hindu writings. So must it be wherever there is a determination to see nothing but materials for history in the *débris* of mythology. So the author of *Juventus Mundi* still pursues one of the phantoms which will never condense into historic personality. They have had their time of apparent solidity in the density of our ignorance and the darkness of the past. But now is the day of their dispersion, for a light is dawning that will shine through and through them till their falsehood grows transparent to the truth.

---

[1] Bartoloc, *Bib. Rab.* tom. i. pp. 228, 229.
[2] Ch. lxxxviii. 94. [3] Ch. lxxxix. 7 and 25. [4] Ch. lxxxix. 1.
[5] *Cambridge Essays*, 1858, p. 275.

SECTION XVI.

MOSES AND JOSHUA, OR THE TWO LION-GODS OF EGYPT.

THERE are two lion-gods in the Ritual, attached to the limits of heaven, the extreme bounds of the sun's journeys. Horus says to his father Osiris, "Thou receivest the headdress of the two lion-gods; thou walkest in the roads of heaven, beheld by those attached to the limits of the horizon of heaven." The lion-gods supply his head-dress. That is, they crown the sun-god.[1] It is also said of Amen-Ra, "Thou art the lion of the double lions." The headdress of feathers is found in various forms. The SEM is a double plume of tall feathers, a symbol of the upper and lower heaven, crowning the solar disk. Another crown, the ATF, a type of the fatherhood, has the two ostrich feathers; these denote the two truths of light and shade. "The lion-gods equip the Osiris among the servants of him who dwells in the west at the end of every day daily."[2] These are the servants of Tum. The headdress of the two feathers was put on when the sun-god made his transformation from one character into another at the limit of his course. The "two lion-gods say to Osiris who dwells in his abode, attired in his gate, Thou goest back; no-where in heaven is thy like, embodied in the transformation of a divine hawk." That is, wearing the feather of light. On the other side he wore the feather of shade. The two feathers were worn in a fillet called the APRU. This fillet APRU, in Egyptian, is identified with the feather in the Hebrew Abru (אבר) the wing-feather of the ostrich.[3] The two lion-gods in the Ritual are especially attached to the god Atum, the one wearer of the ostrich-feathers among the solar gods. They are the chosen, preferred and adopted ministers (Sems) of "Tum in the lower country."[4] Tum is said to light the lion-gods.[5] The twin lions are the two brothers,[6] elsewhere the two brethren who make the festival of the sun, that is of Tum on the horizon where they are the founders of his divine abode. Their place is on the horizon, and they support the sun, as the lion and unicorn sustain the

---

[1] *Rit.* ch. lxxviii. Birch.   [2] Ch. cxlv.   [3] Job xxxix. 13.
[4] Ch. xxxviii.   [5] Ch. xli.   [6] Ch. xxxvii.

British crown. They are also named the RUTI or REHIU whom we may call horizon-keepers, RURU being the horizon as the place of the two lions.

The lions have various forms with but one original meaning, as representatives of the two truths, the two heavens, light and shade, the two eyes, or the two horizons. We shall find the two truths were first of all assigned to the feminine nature, the two goddesses of the upper and lower heaven. Corresponding to these we have the two lionesses, the typical form of which exists in Pekht, the lioness-cat, or Pehti, the dual lion, the peh-peh type of double force and vigilance. These were the most ancient. They were represented by the lion and panther, who drew the car or stood beside the statue of the Great Mother as Kubele, and the goddess Amma-Agdistis of the Phrygians. In the figure of Diana of Ephesus her two arms are extended crosswise, and on these she carries two lions. Then the dual image of Sut-Har (Sabean) is called the two lions. Osiris is designated the double lion, lord of the lion city, master of the double strength and Lord of Hu.[1] Hu is the sphinx; the male sphinx being also a form of Shu, with the hinder part lioness. Shu with his sister Tefnut, and Shu with the Khepsh on his head, are other types of the dual lion. It is Shu in his two characters with which we are now concerned. In Shu we can trace the bringing on from the twin female lions to the male and female, and lastly to the dual-male type, personified in Shu and Anhar, who is the Onouris (Mars) of the Greeks. He is addressed thus in the " Hymn to Shu ":—" Thou art greater and more ancient than the gods, in that name which is thine of Aa-Ur (very great). Thou art higher than the heaven with thy double-feathered crown, in that name which is thine of him who lifts up the double-feathered crown." [2] In this passage the lion-god is traced back to his feminine origin, and to the goddess who preceded all the gods, and who is here called the very great, the first, oldest, greatest mother, who was Ta-Urt in the Typhonian scheme and Pekht or Tefn in another. As Tefn or Tefnut she is called his sister.

As Shu and Anhar we have the lion-gods in two male forms. Champollion found the god SHU at Biban-el-Muluk, sitting with fillet and feather, and coloured red, like the goddess MA.[3] He gives another representation of him standing,[4] with two large feathers, as in the sculptures of the temple of Ibsambul, and of a green colour. Red is the colour of the setting sun and the crown of the lower region, and agrees with the sitting posture; green, with the figure standing or up-rising from the underworld. The red figure sitting is SHU; the green figure stands for ANHAR. SHU's name is written with the feather sign ∫, that of ANHAR ∫⊏ with the

---

[1] Brugsch, *Dict. Geog.*
[2] P. 2, lines 3 and 4.
[3] Pl. 25.
[4] 25 A.

vase sign of bringing, and the heaven. SIIU is said to raise the heaven which ANHAR brings. He was the separator and elevator of the heaven from the earth, "millions of years above the earth," and he established it with his two hands. SHU is pourtrayed kneeling on one knee to support the sun with his uplifted hands. ANHAR, in a marching attitude, is the bringer who forces the sun along with his rope. He is the wearer of the long robe in whom is the "whole of Shu," as "in the long garment was the whole world."[1] So IU-EM-HEPT wears the long robe in the second or renewed form of Tum, the Solomon, the completer of the circle in the solar myth. Raising the heaven is synonymous with beginning the circle; and bringing the heaven, with fulfilling the circle.

ANHAR sometimes wears a headdress of four feathers; these symbolize the four quarters of the circle completed by him. It is another illustration of this character that one of the four rams near the Decan of Num personated the soul of SHU as lord of On, the place of return. SHU is the analogue of Har-ur, and ANHAR of Har-Tema: SHU is a god of the southern heaven, and the horizon of the west; ANHAR of the northern heaven, and the horizon of the east. The sun of the south-west, the sun of the left hand, is the sinking sun; hence SHU, as its supporter, kneels: the sun of the north-east rises, hence ANHAR stands up and marches. In the Egyptian planispheres the lion of the south is represented couching; according to Aratus, the progress of the sun through this sign was typified by a couching lion. The lion of Shu is depicted in this position. Another lion, that of MÂTET, is standing. These typify the descending and ascending sun.

They were solstitial at first. Hence the lion deposited in the zodiac marks the point of commencement of the Egyptian sacred and solstitial year. One lion-god was the conductor of the downward sun; the other of the sun that rose again. SHU, in his dual character, is pourtrayed in what is termed Bruce's or the Harper's tomb at Biban-el-Muluk, in company with the black sun-god IU, or AU, who represented Atum in his youthful form. There is an inscription containing a snatch of the hymn being sung by the musician to the harp accompaniment. It is a discourse of the gods, and runs: "*The gods at rest in the divine circle* (the PUT or *pleroma* of the nine gods) *proclaim* (or tell of) *the chiefs who are in the hall of the Two Truths,* ANHAR (and) SHU-SI-RA; *proclaim Shu the son of the Sun; proclaim the chiefs* (or heads of roads) *who are resident in the empyreal region or gate of the dead.*"[2] The double APHERU of the east and west, the double house of Anubis, is depicted in the representation. It is a fragment of a song of the nine gods in place of muses, who sit on the sacred hill and celebrate the lion-gods, the conductors of the sun on the two roads of his eternal round. Sut was a guide of the

---

[1] Wisdom of Sol. xviii. 24.
[2] See Hieroglyphic Text, *Description de l'Égypte*, vol. ii. pl. 91.

sun on these two roads in the characters of Anubis and Apheru, and SHU was the conductor, also in two characters, as SHU and ANHAR.

A hymn to the god SHU, found in the "Magic Papyrus,"[1] furnishes other features and titles for the reconstruction of his manifold character. He is the conductor of the solar bark or ark of the gods in his name of the god dwelling in the divine ark, HAR-SEKTI. He blows off the divine ark with a favourable wind in that name which is his of the goddess MA. MA means wind, and SHU represents breath, or spirit, one of the two truths, by whomsoever personated. SHU is addressed as the "valiant, who is lord of events, and overthrows the wicked every day. The (solar) barge is sailing joyfully, the (solar) ark in jubilation, as they see SHU, the son of Ra, in (his) triumph, he darts his spear against the serpent." The ark of the sun is crossing the waters, and the crew are jubilant at the victory over the Apophis monster, the Akhekh of darkness, the dragon of the deep.

On the astronomical ceilings of some of the royal tombs the divine bark is represented as drawn along through the Hades by certain personified stars. Ra says to the star-gods : "*Pull forward with your rope of the prow. Oh, ye born gods ! oh, shine forth, gods ! Shine forth, gods, at my birth* (in the retreat in Skhem, the shut shrine), *oh, take your crowns of the north, pull with the rope of the stern of the boat of him who is born of me. It is Horus* (the son), *of the royal countenance.*"[2]

In the tombs of the Ramesids, at Thebes, the course of the sun is depicted from childhood to old age by the hours of the day and night. The solar bark appears on the shape of the outstretched goddess, PAINTED BLUE, with the sun in it as a child. Hour by hour the young sun grows up and the conductors of the boat are changed. Towards night the APAP, monster of darkness, rears itself and tries to swallow RA. Twelve spirits draw the serpent away. During the night-hours the god shut in his shrine on the boat is conveyed by spirits through the AMENTES, and towed across the waters all night towards the east. At EDFU he is represented as a child in the morning, a bearded man at noon, an old man bowed and leaning on a staff at evening ; in this character he is called "*the old man who becomes a child again.*"

A visitor to the tombs at Dayr-el-Medeeneh describes a scene wherein a small boat is ascending a cataract bearing a huge beetle, the sacred scarabæus, having a ram's head ; on each side of it is a bird with the human head. This is found where the elongated figures which represent the overarching and enclosing heavens are extended the length of fifty feet across the ceiling.[3] This was Khepr in his boat ; the human-headed birds were souls ; the beetle with ram's head marked the passage from the place of

[1] *Records of the Past*, v. 10, p. 137.   [2] *Records*, x. 131.
[3] *Mummies and Moslems*, Warner, p. 371.

resurrection where the spring equinox was in the Ram up to the Crab (beetle), the place of the summer solstice and top of the ascent to light. The upward journey is pourtrayed by the ascent of a cataract. The writer calls this a conceit. How his interest would have quickened had he known that this was Khepr " MAKING THE KUTE." Making the kute is now applied to shooting down the cataracts. In Egyptian mythology KHUT means going with the current toward the north, but *the* KHUT is the horizon of the resurrection, the place where the souls emerged for the southward ascent against the current up which only the boat of Khepr could climb. This, then, is a form of the ark conducted by SHU. SHU is likewise called " the King of Upper and Lower Egypt," *i.e.* of the celestial Egypt ;[1] the Egypt often intended by the Hebrew writers.

In the Talmud Egypt is described as being 400 miles wide :— " Egypt is 400 miles in length, *and the same in breadth.* Egypt is equal to a sixth part of Æthiopia; Æthiopia to a sixth part of the world ; the world to a sixth part of the Garden of Eden, and Eden to a sixth part of Hell."[2] But neither the Egypt nor Æthiopia intended is geographical any more than the Garden of Eden. The terrestrial Egypt is some seven miles in breadth. In Lower Egypt lies the Red Sea, or Pool of Pant, where the hindering enemy of the sun lurks with his evil confederates to stop and overthrow the divine bark conducted and defended by Shu, who fights the battle of Christian against Apollyon in this, the Valley of the Shadow of Death. He overthrows the wicked far from his father Ra, and the boat proceeds in peace ; his towmen are jubilant, the gods in exultation, when they hear his name as SHU-SI-RA. " I am SHU, the image of Ra, sitting in the inside of his father's sacred eye. If he who is in the waters opens his mouth (or), if he grasps with his arms, I will let the earth fall into the waters' well (the abyss), being the south made north ; being the earth turned round " (upside down). This statement is accompanied by a figure of the sacred eye, an image of the circle which was full at daybreak—" *thou fillest at daybreak the place of his sacred eye in An,*" or at the conclusion of the year. The promise is, that if the Apophis open its mouth to swallow, or put forth his arms, devil-fish-like, to clutch, they will still pass on in the yearly revolution or circle-making, whereas the enemy was a fixture, fast bound, and this appears to have been rendered according to the later knowledge that the earth turned round.

They will escape through the god who makes the earth revolve, and reverses the relative positions. The crossing of the waters, the passage of the darkness and victory over the demons, is actually figured as the earth's revolution, " being the south made north," and contrariwise.

---

[1] P. I. 11, *Magic Papyrus.*
[2] Cited by Bartol. tom. ii. p. 161 ; *Bibliotheca Magna Rabbinica,* 4 vols., Rome, 1675-93, fol.

The earth that falls "into the waters' well," or the abyss MEH of the north, in its turning re-emerges from the dark depths of the lower heaven where dwells the devouring monster, and comes up out of the celestial Egypt, leading its inhabitants into the land of light and of the sacred eye, pourtrayed at the place of the equinox.

In another passage we read, " *I am the chosen of millions coming out of the lower heaven* (*i.e.* the celestial Khebt or Egypt), *whose name is unknown. When his name is spelt on the bank of the river, then it is dried up. When his name is spelt on the land, it is set on fire;*" or as the passage has also been translated, "*If his name be uttered on the bank of the river, oh, then it quencheth; if it be uttered on land, oh, then it maketh sparks.*" [1] The " chosen of millions coming up out of the lower heaven, whose name is unknown," may be meant for Shu, but according to the Hebrew parallel it represents the sun-god. In the fragment from Artapanus it is related that when the Egyptians came up with the Israelites, the fire flashed on them from above, while the waters overwhelmed their path, so that they perished both by fire and flood.[2] This is not found in the Hebrew version, but is in the Egyptian, where Tefnut sends her fire from on high to reduce the enemies to non-existence.

The chosen of millions coming out of the lower heaven is the god of those who came up out of Egypt when "all the hosts of the Lord went out from the land of Egypt."[3] Upon the bank of the Red Sea his " name is spelt " by Moses when the waters dry up or divide, and leave the ground dry while the " Lord looked upon the host of the Egyptians *through the pillar of fire.*" In the second passage the " bank of the river," where the miracle is wrought, is identified with the brink of Jordan, Iarutana, or Eridanus, the river of the division, and Joshua the son of Nun is the representative and fac-simile of Shu the son of Nun. He who leads up the Israelites is the god of the name unknown until it is announced by Moses as Jah-Adonai; the god who is the "chosen of millions," the elect of Joshua and of the people at a later stage of the Exodus.[4] This reading would make the comparison more perfect, but is not essential.

SHU is accompanied by the goddess Tefnut, the Egyptian Miriam, who "*gives her fire against his enemies to reduce them to non-existence.*" So Miriam "gives her fire," in song against the cruel Pharaoh and his host, when they are overwhelmed and annihilated in the Red Sea. Miriam's song reminds us that this Hymn to the god SHU is contained in the " *Chapter of excellent songs which dispel the immerged.*" The IMMERGED are the evil host of Typhon, the dragon Rahab of the deep, lurking beneath the Red Sea. In the Egyptian writings the enemy is represented as the immerged " Raw-head-and-bloody-bones." In the Hebrew the hosts of the opposing Pharaoh

[1] Renouf, *Eg. Grammar*, p. 44.   [2] Eusebius, *Praep. Evang.*
[3] Ex. xii. 41.   [4] Josh. xxiv.

sink to the bottom of the Red Sea. After the overthrow of the enemy it is said of the dead—"*Those who are immerged do not pass along; those who pass along do not plunge: they remain floating on the waves like the dead bodies on the inundation. And they shut their mouths as the seven great dungeons are closed with an eternal seal.*"[1] The same work of progressive destruction that is assigned to Moses and Joshua is ascribed to SHU.

"*Thou seizest the spear, and overthrowest the wicked, in that name which is thine of Har-Tema.*

"*Thou destroyest the An of Tukhenti, in that name which is thine of Double-Abode-of-Ra. Thou strikest the Menti and the Sati in that name which is thine of Young Elder.*"[2]

One of SHU'S names is ANHAR, the celestial conductor, the Heaven-Bringer, not only the bringer to heaven. He is thus addressed:— "*Thou leadest the upper heaven with thy rod, in that name which is thine of An-Har:*" he is also "Anhar, lord of the scimitar." In another section of the hymn we read : "*Hail to you, O five great gods, issuing from Sesen, who (when) not being in heaven, not being on earth,* SHU (as light of the sun) *not existing, have been the morning light ! come to me ! Try for me the river. Shut up what is in it ! What is immersed, do not let it pass out ! Seal the mouths ! Choke the mouths ! as is sealed up the shrine for centuries !*"[3] The five great gods issuing from Sesen are here appealed to as protectors. Osiris is called the "oldest of the five gods begotten of Seb."[4] All we can say of these five in an Osirian legend is that they were time-gods, and that the solar Osiris has been foisted into one of their places. But the name of Sesun, or Sesennu, also signifies to agitate, distract, torment, and fight. This may account for the five reappearing in the Book of Joshua as the five fighting leaders of the Amorites, the kings of Jerusalem, Hebron, Jarmuth, Lachish, and Eglon, who made war on Gibeon, the story of which was found in the Book of Jasher, and the Hebrew account represents them as being totally overthrown by Joshua the servant of Jah-Adonai. The five great gods of Sesen were pre-solar, earlier than Ra, or Shu as the son of Ra. The river is synonymous with the Red Sea (Pool of Pant). "*Try for me the river ! Shut up what is in it ! What is immersed, do not let it pass out.*" So, in the Hebrew version, the Vaheb-suph is coupled with the Arnon. Moses crosses the Red Sea, Joshua the river Jordan, and both passages belong to the same miracle or myth. SESEN, the place of the eight, is close to the river in the planisphere, and the five great gods who issue thence appear not only in the Book of Jasher, they are also the same five lords of the Philistines who dwelt in Geshuri near Shihor (the Nile river) and the land that remained unconquered by Joshua.[5] The five lords who remained that the children of Israel might teach them war and be

[1] *Magic Pap.* viii. 8 and 9.   [2] *Mag. Pap.* p. 2, 9, 10, 11.
[3] P. 3, lines 5, 6, 7.   [4] *Rit.* ch. lxix.   [5] Ch. xiii. 2, 3.

proved by them :[1] they being the pre-solar gods in Sesen the place of Taht, the lunar divinity. These five can be followed a little farther.

In the Book of Genesis we find the conflict of four kings against the five. The four are Amraphel, Arioch, Chedorlaomer, and Tidal. According to the present reading these are kings of the four quarters who superseded the five gods of Sesun who were before the solar zodiac, and possibly the lunar, was established. The battle was fought in the vale of Siddim, which was the place of slime-pits. So Shihor in Hebrew means the slimy river. In the Ritual it is the morass of primordial matter, whether called the Nile or the Red Sea. Then Abram smote the confederate five kings, and—this is the point— one of those who aided him was ANER. Aner, Eshcol, and Mamre were the three who, with Abram, made up another confederacy of four that warred on the five, and put them to rout. This was at the valley of Shaveh, identical with Suph, the Red Sea. The King of Sodom and Melchizedek belong to the earliest Sabean *régime*. It is now suggested that the Hebrew ANER (ענר) is the Egyptian ANHAR,— ANER means to push, drive, precipitate, force along, which is emphatically the character personified in ANHAR, who is said to force the sun along,—and that the five kings belong to the same myth on a different line of derivation from that of the Book of Joshua.

Such being the legend of the Egyptian lion-gods, we are now prepared to prove that SHU and ANHAR have been reproduced as the Moses and Joshua of the Hebrew mythos. And first of the name. According to Fuerst, the etymology of the name of Moses, as given,[2] implies the form (משוי) MASHUI, or MASHEVI. MA (Eg.) is truth, and Shui reads light and shade, the two feathers, two aspects of truth, the two characters of Shu, corresponding to the two appearances of Moses with and without the veil. The head-attire of the two feathers is given to the Osirian as "the image of the great waters."[3] These are named SHU-MA. Josephus explains that Thermutis called Moses by that name because MO (mu or ma, Eg.) is water, and those who are saved out of it are called by the Egyptians USES. It is quite true that SES means to reach land and breathe after the passage of the waters. But the water MA and the breath SES (or Ssu) are more to the present purpose, for these are the two truths, as in SHU-MA or Mashu. Shu is the God of Breath ; he typifies or impersonates the breath of the mouth of Hathor. Ses or SSU (Eg.) means to breathe, respire, reach land again, as did Shu the breather in person emerging from the waters, who, in his twin character, was Ma-Shu. Clement Alexander also derives the name of Moses from "drawing breath."[4] The feather, or feathers, read Ma-Shu, the dual form of truth. In Sharpe's *Inscriptions*[5] the name of SHU is written MAU, with the cubit

---

[1] Jud. iii. 2, 3. [2] Ex. ii. 10. Ch. cxxvii.
[4] Strom. i. [5] 2nd ser. pl. 41, line 20.

sign of Ma, not with the feather, which might only read Shu. MAU and SHU, the two-one, are not only illustrated by the dual feather, but by the lion and the cat. One group of signs now read MAU for the cat, was formerly read SHAU; and MAU for the lion, and SHAU for the cat, do help to give distinctness to the types. Thus MAU-SHAU would read lion-cat; but the dual lion included both, and the duality was expressed by other single signs than the feather. MAU is both lion and cat, and at one part of the celestial circle Shu transformed from the lion-type of MAU into that of the cat SHAU. Moreover, it is the great cat, and some of the American aborigines call the lion the great and mischievous cat. When this change took place and the two were blended, the proper name of the dual type would be MAU-SHAU, or MA-SHU. Also MA-SHU is the actual name of the Divinity in one shape of the double type. As KHU is an earlier form of Shu (in AB-KHU, variegated plumes), MA-SHU had an earlier phase in MA-KHU, and this is extant, with its variants, in the Manyak (Tibetan) MACHEU for a cat; MEKO, African Penin, a leopard; MAGE, Bagrmi, a cat; MECHOU, Carib, cat; MIGHOI, Mongolian, cat; MUCIA, Italian, she-cat; MOCHA, Bodo, cat; MOCHI, Khari Naga, a cat. If we now render the cat-lion or lion-leoparded in the hard form, then MA-SHU is the MA-KHU, identical with the Carib MECHOU and Manyak MACHEU. This in the form of SHU-MA is the name of the pool of the Two Truths, where the Ma is transformed into the MA-SHU. The name and signification of משה include both MA and SHU, and the Kabalists maintained that Moses transferred his soul to, or transformed into, Joshua. That is the pure and perfect myth. Shu is said to be more ancient than the gods in that name which is his of Goddess AA-UR, "the very great," that is in the feminine form brought on from the origin of the Two Truths. One of his names in this character is MA; he is then MA-SHU. This character is also assigned by tradition to Moses, or MA-SHU. It is reported by Suidas that the Hebrew lawgiver and author of the Jewish laws was Musu, a Hebrew woman. Nothing is omitted.

The epicene nature of MA-SHU is preserved in the character of Moses in a remarkable way. In Hebrew At (את) is the feminine form of Thou, and Attah (אתה) is the masculine form. The feminine form is looked upon as being merely the masculine shortened, although, as Fuerst says of it, "The reason for this *abbreviation* has not *always been discovered, and therefore* the LXX. and Syriac read in Ezek. l. c. את (with)." In Deut. v. 27 (in the original, v. 24), the first "thou" is in the usual masculine form אתה (Attah); the second "thou" is in feminine form את (At); that is, Moses in the same verse is described as both male and female. The listener to the Lord is in the masculine gender, and the utterer of the word to the people is in the feminine gender. The symbolical mouth is feminine, as the Ru and Peh of the hieroglyphics; the primeval utterance was by this mouth, preserved in the Hebrew. When Moses, in the masculine character, says he cannot be the mouth, Aaron is appointed for that purpose. Miriam likewise was a feminine mouth to Moses,[1] as Ma is to Shu. "Thou blowest the divine barge off with a favourable wind in that name which is thine of the goddess Ma,"[2] is said to Shu, and the female nature of Moses is retained by a feminine THOU. The name of Moses, then, being of Egyptian origin, we claim that it is MASHU. It is also true that Ma-shâ (Eg.) may be rendered "raised from the water, or the water-raised." In this sense the water-reeds and the crocodile are named Shui. In the form of מַשְׁוִי (Mashevi) we have the intermediate between SHU and KAFI, one of Shu's names as the Ape—a type of the god who, in one character, is personified as the Kafi Ape; he "has the face of a Kafi Ape; the head of hair of a monkey, Aani."[3] By aid of the ape it may be possible to resolve into its primary signification the Rabbinical tradition that Moses was *born circumcised*.[4] Such statements do not pertain to the human being, but to the mythical; and the Moses meant is mythical. As mythical, the statement can be read. Shu was represented by the ape, which, according to Hor-Apollo,[5] was "born circumcised," and was therefore made a type of the priest, or rather it was a prototype, as the priests are said to have adopted circumcision from the Ape.

Shu supports and sustains the heaven of night, that is the most ancient earth as the netherworld of two. The Rabbins say that it was while Moses was digging the foundations of the earth that he found a stone on which was inscribed the unutterable name—the stone of the seven eyes and the stars of the northern heaven, which was succeeded by the heaven elevated by Shu and brought by Anhar.

The double lions are extant in the Hebrew imagery as the twin lions of Judah, the young lion and the old lion that couched. "Judah is a lion's whelp; from the prey, my son, thou art gone up: he stooped down, he couched as a lion, and as an old lion." These are the two characters of the lion-god in his name of *Young-elder* and of NEB-SAATU, *prince of slaughterers.* In the *Chronicon Samaritanum* there is a letter from SHAUBEC, king of Armenia, in which Joshua is designated "the murdering wolf." This is the Samaritan Book of Joshua, considered to be a compilation of the middle ages.[6] But it contains most ancient matter.

SHU has passed into Hebrew in his proper character of gate-keeper. "The gate of the Tser, it is the gate of the transit of SHU. There is the north gate, it is the gate of the door-way; or they are the doors through which his father Tum goes forth to the eastern horizon of the heaven (saying) to those who belong to his race."[7] Shuar (שׁוֹעֵר) is the typical porter or gate-keeper,[8] who as KORE was SHUAR towards the

---

[1] Num. xii. 2.   [2] *Magic Pap.* p. 3; *Records,* x. 141.
[3] *Magic Pap.* ix. 10.   [4] Calmet on Moses.   [5] Bk. i. 14.
[6] Ewald, *Hist.* ii. 39-40. Martineau.   [7] *Rit.* ch. xvii.   [8] 2 Chron. xxxi. 14.

east, identical in position with SHU-ANHAR, who kept the gate through which the sun went to the eastern horizon. SHU is the personified bringer, the turner, turner-back, and returner, the goer to and fro, all of which meanings are found in the Hebrew שוב. SHUKAL is the lion, the fierce lion. SHUAL, the underworld, grave, pit, hell, the Æthiopic Siōl, is the nocturnal heaven supported on his head by SHU, as the starry light of it, its Light-in-shade. This is also the שפלה or sunken land, the underworld that SHU and Joshua led up from. The *gorge* of Shu is said to be the dwelling of Neith; he is hidden in the way of the gorge.[1] SHU is called the En-pe or Na-pe, rendered by Birch the leader of heaven.[2] As ANHAR is the one who ascends, and NA means to descend, the En-pe is further the leader of heaven who descends, as indicated by the stooping position of Shu, the bearer of the sun, and its conductor in the descent from the solstitial height. Shu is specially pourtrayed in the attitude and act of holding up his hands aloft and bearing the disk of the sun above his head. A hieroglyphic legend describes him on the abime of the heaven, on the steps of the inhabitants of SMEN, where he "afflicts the race of the wicked on the steps of the residents in SMEN." In the same text he is identified with Ra and Atum.[3] This portrait of Shu with hands uplifted was so well known that in the porcelain figures the modellers have frequently figured him with hands elevated and the solar disk omitted. SHU holding his hands aloft and supporting the sun, which is saluted by eight cynocephali, typical of the region of SMEN, as he stands on the steps of the residents in SMEN, the region of preparation, purification, establishing the son in place of the father, Shu-Anhar instead of MA-SHU, is the original of Moses on the top of the hill in Rephidim, holding up his hands until sunset whilst Joshua discomfited Amalek in the war that went on for ever.

One of SHU'S titles is SHU-KEBION, Lord of Tebut, rendering victorious his arms. TEBUT (Tebhut) is the winged solar disk, the sun above the horizon. The Keb is the corner, the turning-point; and KEBION, where SHU rendered his arms victorious, is the Hebrew GIBEON upon which the sun stood still while the arms of Moses were held up, and those of Joshua were victorious. The sun supported by the arms of SHU-KEBION is in the Hebrew version up-borne at poise on Gibeon. The word Chabion (חביון) is used by Habakkuk[4] in the description of the god coming from Teman, the luminous emanations of his hand being the Chabion of his power. This has been translated the HIDING and the tent of his power. The Egyptian KAB shows it should be "the redoubling of his power." In Teman, or the south, the sun was in the very furnace and fiery-hornedness of its strength. Gibeon or Kebion is the place of equinoctial poise and turning, the

---

[1] *Magical Texts, Records of the Past*, vi. 123.
[2] Birch, *Gallery*, p. 22.
[3] Birch, *Gallery*, p. 22.
[4] Ch. iii. 4.

recognized place and time of standing still. "The sun stops himself in the west."[1] He is prayed to *prolong* his transformation. The chiefs, one of whom is SHU, sang "Glory to thee, *arresting thy person*."[2] At this time, the standing still of the moon at the level is a fact verifiable every harvest-moon, when the orb rises about the same time for several nights consecutively and, as it were, stands still instead of gaining on the solar time.

The Hebrew Ajalon is an Egyptian name recognized as AARUNA, a topographical place found in a fragment of the "battle of Megiddo"[3] as the valley of AARUNA. But AARUNA belongs primarily to the celestial AARU or fields of heaven.

In the Iroquois mythological astronomy each of the four cardinal points was presided over by a spirit, and the name of the one who presided over the West was KABAUN.[4] At the equinox began the great battle of the lion-gods of the north and south against the powers of darkness which got the better of the solar god in the west, but were utterly annihilated in the east. These two were fabled to keep the balance or libration of the scales, the level of the equinox being the cross-beam, and were figured as contending on the day of the battle between Horus and Sut, when it was "pull devil, pull baker," between the powers of light and darkness, one at each of the two scales.

It was somewhat like the battle of the lion and the unicorn (Shu and Typhon) fought up and down the garden; theirs being in the fields of the AARU. The same conflict was depicted by the Dacotahs as for ever going on between their two gods of the north and south, WA-ZE-AT-TAH WE-CHAS-TAH (north) and ETO-KAH WE-CHAS-TAH (south), who battle for the supremacy of the world, and for warm and cold weather, and will continue, like Jah and Amalek, to battle from generation to generation for ever.[5] In this yearly "set-to" "SHU *and* TEFNUT *make charms to fascinate the wicked conspirators*" of Typhon. "*Tefnut changes her shape into a club*" in the hands of Shu, and as he smites them she cries, "*The cowards are upset by thy blows. I am Tefnut, thundering against those who are kept on the earth* (as the lower region), *who are annihilated for ever.*" "*She is like fire against the wicked ones.*" "*Back, back, ye damned. Shu resists, he prevails against the wicked ones ;*[6] "*O ye wicked ones, the flames of Amen-Ra are in his members.*" In the Quiché and Hebrew versions the enemies are driven out by the hornet. The hornet is the stinger, and the name might be applied to variants of the stinger. The SERKA in Egyptian answering to the Hebrew צרעה (Tzirgah) is the scorpion. This may help us to understand the hornet, for it was in the sign of Scorpio, according to the Lion Calendar, that the great conflict with

---

[1] Ch. xvii.
[2] Ch. xv.
[3] Lepsius, *Denk.* Abth. iii. Bl. xxxi. 6. 32, B.
[4] *Schoolcraft*, v. 409.
[5] *Schoolcraft*, iv. 496. Pl. 41.
[6] *Magical Texts, Records*, vi. 119.

Typhon or Am-Melek began.   ORION sets soon after the rising of
this constellation.   There is a scorpion goddess, SERK, connected
with the four quarters.[1]   Very little is known of her.   But SOTHIS
was consecrated to her, and she has the style of HERT, the mighty.
She is not an evil goddess, so that when personified in her the
scorpion is on the side of the gods.

SEKHET vomits flames against the wicked to suffocate them.   TEF-
NUT is like fire; she gives her fire against them; and no doubt the
stinging scorpion of SERK helped to drive them out.   The Magical
Texts mention the "*Scorpion, the great one of the sun, called the devouring
throat, which swallows.*"[2]   The scorpion of the sun is of course on the
side of the sun; and this was impersonated by SERK, who stings and
drives out the lurking enemy from their holes.   Now when Miriam becomes TZIRAG (צרע), the likelihood is that she takes the shape of the
scorpion-goddess SERK, instead of becoming leprous.[3]   The consort
of Kepheus is the Queen of Æthiopia or Kush, and Moses is said to
marry the Kushite.   The setting of the constellation of Cassiopeia,
the Queen of Kush, corresponds to the celestial position of the sun in
the Scorpion, and the Kushite Queen goes down then and there to
help fight the battle in the underworld.   This, in one version,[4] is
paralleled by the death of Miriam.   SERK likewise means to end, to
be exhaled, which applies particularly to the Water of Mirian!   The
other occurrence takes place where Joshua and the Dog go to spy out
the land of Amalek and the Anakim.

The Samaritan Book of Joshua contains a good deal more of the
true mythic matter than the Hebrew version.   Amongst other important things, a war is described as having been carried on against
SAUBEK, a son of Haman, called King of Persia.   In the Ritual
Sebek is the capturer, as the crocodile-headed deity.   The crocodile
was in later times so clothed with an evil reputation as the type of
Typhon that SEBEK has also suffered—got mixed up with the devouring demon AM-T, the crocodile-headed.   The monster SHESH-
SHESH is one-third crocodile.   SAUBEK, son of Haman, is SEBEK, as the
crocodile of Am, the AM-T.   In chapter thirty-two the speaker says,
" I have made my soul come."   The soul or shade thus constitutes himself in the character of SHU, the Saviour, who here saves the deceased
from the crocodiles.   "*My father saves me from the eight crocodiles.
Back, crocodile of the west (Am); I am not given to thee! Back, crocodile
of the east; I have crossed! Back, crocodile of the south; do not gore me
with thy claw! Back, crocodile of the north; I am the light of the eyes!*"
He is SHU.   In the next chapter he asks, "Dost thou stop SHU?"
This is the war of Joshua with Sebek in the Typhonian phase.

SHU and TEFNUT are a form of the two lion-gods fighting against
the wicked, the Typhonian monsters, devils, giants, or bogies of the

---

[1] Wilk. *Mat. Hier.* 60, A.   [2] *Records*, vi. 116.
[3] Num. xii.   [4] Num. xx.

human childhood, who dwelt in darkness and waylaid the passengers in death or by night.

Rephidim denotes the region of gloom, terror, the dead, the giants, the Apophis or giant in shape of the dragon. It was at the level called the plain, like the Egyptian RUSTA. Then and there came Amalek, and fought with Israel in Rephidim.[1] The place is otherwise called Massah and Meribah. In the blessing of Moses[2] we read, " And of Levi he said, Thy Thummim and Urim be with thy Chasid (חסיד) whom thou didst prove at Massah, and strive with at the waters of Meribah." The Chasid is the turner-back. Khesf (Eg.) means to turn back and return in spite of all opposition. This was what SHU did as ANHAR, and Moses through Joshua. On the journey there are two particular places of trial and strife, Massah and Meribah. Meribah is Egyptian for the celestial inundation. MERI is heaven ; BAH the inundation. In one reference[3] the two are fused together ; in the other they are apparently distinct.[4] Both are right according to the myth. In the Ritual the two chief places of trial are in the west, and in the crossing of the waters of Meribah one of the formulas to be recited four times by the soul that wishes to awe the monsters, is, " I am BAHU THE GREAT ! "[5] that is, he personates the god of the inundation (Meri). AM is the west, and at this point one of the worst Typhonian monsters and liers-in-wait for souls, is the crocodile, expressly called the crocodile of the west, the Ament. *" Back, crocodile of the west, living off those who are never at rest."*[6] Massah (מסה) is the place of terror and dissolving with fear. The type of this terror in the west was the devouring demon, called the crocodile. In Egyptian the name of the crocodile itself is MASUH,[7] or EMSUH. Where the devourer as MASUH waited in the west, was the first place of trial for the dead, who were weighed in the scales there, by the seven chief powers (seven devils also were there), at the arm of the balance on the day of trial.[8] It is designated the "ANGLE OF THE WEST," where Typhon as Baba the beast was the watcher.[9] Amalek is described [10] as the lier-in-wait ; he is synonymous with AM (Eg.), the ruler and devouring demon of Hades.

The crocodile as Am, or the devouring Emsuh, was stationed here in the Ament, the region of Amalek. This is the Hebrew place of trial, called MASSAH, or, without the point, Masah. When the imagery is found in the Book of the Dead it has been rendered more remote because applied to a sort of spirit-world ; the basis, however, is always astronomical, and the main features may be identified in the various planispheres. The Crocodile of the West, for instance, is a constellation lying across the three decans of Scorpio

---

[1] Ex. xvii. 8.   [2] Deut. xxxiii.   [3] Ex. xvii. 7.
[4] Deut. xxxiii. 8.   [5] *Mag. Pap.* Records, x. 149.   [6] Rit. ch. xxxii.
[7] Birch, *Dictionary*, pp. 424-5.   [8] Ch. lxxi.   [9] Ch. xvii.
[10] I Sam. xv. 2.

facing the south, on the downward road of the sun.[1]   The crocodile which fed on souls as they entered the dark river in the later phase of the myth was the swallower of the setting stars in the earlier. The Hebrew version is more plainly zodiacal than the Ritual, and either it was not written for the dead, or it was rewritten for the living.

Hor-Apollo says the Egyptians "denote a rapacious and inactive man by a crocodile with the wing of an Ibis on its head, for if you touch him with the wing of an Ibis you will find him motionless." [2]   In the magical texts a crocodile, carrying a feather on its head, sits on a particular-shaped wheel, inside of which is an *uræus* serpent : a legend calls it "*the turner-of-destruction-crocodile, that which nurtured by impurity ; the great truth, burning its enemies by the entire revolution of its hole in Karrt*"—the abodes of the damned.   Shu is denominated the Repeller of Crocodiles.   "*Thou repellest the crocodile, coming out of the abyss, in that name which is thine of Repeller of Crocodiles.*" This is a type of Am or Amalek as the devourer, in the form of a crocodile. After the battle, "Moses built an altar, and called the name of it יהוה-נס JEHOVAH-NEHS (or NES)."   The Egyptian NUSA is a pedestal or *stand* on which the Nile was represented ; a kind of throne or seat, as the Nusa is the hinder part or back side.   He erected a NUSA for Jehovah or Jah because, as he said, it figured his throne or seat, he who, as god of the hinder part (which was shown to Moses), the lower region from the west downwards, warred with Amalek from generation to generation, or from time to time continually.   The Egyptian TERU, time, denotes the two times of the circle in which the battle was fought from year to year.   In connection with the Nile-stand or NUSA it may be noted that the JAD (Ex. ii. 5), stands for one side or bank of the Nile. Also one of the titles of Shu is connected with the stand which in one form is the Nusa.   "*Thou comest here upon thy stately stand, in that name which is thine of Being in thy Stately Stand.*" [3] Shu was the stand, altar, Nusa, or hand which uplifted the sun and figuratively supported the solar god, whereas Moses is said to have reared an altar or stand.   There is the same choice of *stand* or *standard* in the Egyptian AM-AAT as in the Hebrew NES.

The wars of the Lord are also found in the fifth chapter of the Book of Judges, as the subject of Deborah's song, which is a very precious page of the Hermean lore, and indeed one of the few fragments in the early books of the Old Testament which possess any intrinsic value.   That these are the wars in heaven is shown by the kings who came and fought.   "They fought from heaven ; they were the stars in their courses that fought against Sisera." [4]   In this version the river that takes the place of Jordan, the Red Sea, the Vaheb of Suph,

---

[1] Drum. Pl. 2   [2] B. ii. 81.
[3] *Magic Pap.* p. ii. 4.   [4] Jud. v. 20.

or Pool of·Pant, is the Kishon. "The river Kishon swept them away, that ancient river, the river Kishon;" Deborah sings the song of triumph instead of Miriam or Tefnut, and Barak the lightener is the hero in place of Shu the Light-in-shade. Sisera may be paralleled with the SHESH crocodile, and with Saubek, or the original of all the Crocodile of Darkness, whose image is figured across the west, the place of execution, where, in the Hebrew myth, Sisera is captured and executed. There is an Egyptian version of the myth, in which the woman is the subduer of the evil one. Isis is depicted in the act of piercing the head of a serpent. In other pictures it is the crocodile, Shesh, whose head is being speared, as in the vignettes to the Ritual, and according to Diodorus it was Isis who subdued Typhon at the battle in An (Ant or Antæus) in the north. The piercing of the Shesh by the woman takes the shape of the nail driven through the head of Sisera by Jael.

Moses was only to see the hinder or backward part belonging to the God, the "AKAR." This, when applied to a personified deity, is repellant and needlessly gross. But that is not the meaning. The Akar, in Egyptian as well as Hebrew, is the Hades, the lower region, left side, hinder part, west and north. The Au-kar is the nether place. Moses, as conductor, was only to see the Akar; except in a glimpse of the promised land on the mountain-top, he was not to behold the glory of the Lord in front, nor see the sun upon the horizon of the east.

The general idea in the "Book of the Hades" is that the earth in the west opens and swallows the sun, the gods, and the souls that accompany the luminary below. The goddess Athor, regent of the western regions, received the dead in the west as the spotted cow. The west is also designated "*the good west (who) holds out her arms to take thee.*" [1]

At sunset the earth is said to stretch her arms in the western horizon to receive the god in the embrace of his mother, and in the Mesak or breeding-place he prepares the fresh generation for his new birth next morning. The same process applies to the annual sun. "Oh, enter (or issue from) the east. Come from the belly of thy mother." [2]

The QORAK of the Psalmist belongs to this AKAR of the underworld, and this is the place said to have been made by Moses, who dug a deep pit in the land of Gad, in which he confined the evil demon KARUN, who was only permitted to issue forth and plague the Israelites when they sinned. [3] KARUN is the Arabic form of the Hebrew QORAK. In Egyptian Kar-un would denote a being of the Kar or hole. There is such a being in the Ritual, called AKAR, the viper of Typhon.

Moses was the typical lawgiver in Israel, and the astronomical

[1] Rit. ch. cxlix. Vignette.   [2] *Book of Hades.*   [3] Pirkê, R. Eliezer, C. xlv.

character of the lawgiver spoken of in the blessing of Moses can be shown by reference to an Egyptian planisphere. "Of Gad he said, Blessed be he that enlargeth Gad; he dwelleth as a lion, and teareth the arm with the crown of the head," and "he provided the first part for himself, because there in a portion of the lawgiver was he exalted, and he came with the heads of the people, he executed the justice of the Lord, and his judgments with Israel."[1] It is the same typical lawgiver[2] in another passage, "The princes digged the well, the nobles of the people by (the direction of) the lawgiver, with their staves." And in another of these most ancient fragments to be found in the Hebrew collection it is said, "The sceptre shall not depart from Judah, nor a lawgiver from between his feet, until Shiloh come."[3] The name of this lawgiver is derived from the Hebrew CHEQ, a decree or thing appointed and established, a limit, bound or boundary, a circle, a law. Cheq is identical with Khekh, the collar, and Khekh, the whip-symbol of rule and the ruler. The Khekh is also the balance or equinox, where the circle was completed. The first law-giving depended on recurring cycles of time, and certain stars and constellations were the celestial lawgivers and angels.

The Khekh of the equinox was ruled by the lion-gods, Shu and Anhar, or Shu in his two characters, who pulled at the ropes of the scales until Horus, the coming Shiloh, had conquered Typhon.[4]

Drummond showed from his point of view that this Lawgiver in Israel was the constellation of Kepheus, king of Æthiopia, or Regulus, who is represented as a man with a crown on his head and a sceptre in his hand. In the description of Gad it is said he dwelleth as a lion, and teareth the arm with the crown of the head. Kepheus, the crowned and sceptred Lawgiver, according to Columella, rises on the 7th of the Ides of July, and in the course of a few days he comes to rise under the sign of the lion, and continues to be the paranatellon of Leo, until the sun enters Scorpio. Drummond was right so far, but had not the Egyptian origines for his court of appeal. The Arabians called this constellation both CHEIC, the ruler or lawgiver, and Keiphus. Now, when the sun was in the sign of the lion, Kepheus was visible very low down in the northern hemisphere, at the same time Leo was hidden in the solar radiance. Thus Kepheus took the place of Leo as guide of the sun, or indicator or lawgiver, the Regulus in person, as the paranatellon of Regulus the star (Cor-Leonis) in the lion, and, being so low down in the northern hemisphere, he may be described as seen under the feet of Judah or the lion. In one Egyptian planisphere reproduced by Kircher, the figure of Shu-Anhar, as Kepheus, fills all three decans of the Waterman. He wears upon his head the two ostrich feathers which read MA-SHU; in his stretched-out right hand he holds the sceptre or rod, and in his

---

[1] Deut. xxxiii. 20.
[2] Num. xxi. 18.
[3] Gen. xlix. 10.
[4] Rit. ch. xvii.

left he grasps the ARROW. He is pourtrayed in his marching martial attitude, and, as a paranatellon of the lion, is literally the Lawgiver between the feet of the Lion of Judah.[1] Kepheus, the lawgiver, be it understood, has two stars. One is Regulus, the heart of the lion, the other, the northern constellation.

The Chaldean astrologers predict that if the star of the great lion (qy. the great star of the lion, *i.e.* Regulus) be gloomy, the *heart* of the people will not rejoice. That was one type of the Lawgiver.

In their astronomy the sun was designated the star doubly great and doubly little. He was the doubly-dependent on Regulus, for Regulus marked the solstices in the Sign of Leo and Aquarius. The sun was the doubly great with Regulus in the lion and the doubly little with Regulus in the Waterman. Thus Regulus was the double support of the sun in its two extreme aspects; he was represented by Kepheus or Shu-Anhar, and the dual form of the lion called the twin lion-gods. Here we have one of those things which tend, at first sight, to make Asia look older than Africa; the oldest forms of words being frequently found outside of Egypt. Nevertheless this is the superficial view. Language had gone on developing and modifying more in that land after the migration, that is all. It is evident to me that Kepheus or Kefu is the lion-god Shu, and his name of Shu is the worn-down form of Kefu. We know that the feather Shu is found with the value Khu, and the U is the earlier FU. Shu can be identified by name with Kepheus in his character of Kafi, the Ape. Also Shu, who appears in the Persian sphere with a crown upon his head, is depicted in the monuments bearing on his head the hinder part of the lioness called the Khepsh, and this symbol may supply the name of Kepheus. The Khepsh denotes the north, the hind-quarter, the Heaven supported by Shu. Mars was the planetary type of Shu, and the Twins of the Zodiac are the sign of Shu in the dual character of Shu and his sister Tefnut, a form of the lion-gods as male and female, but no explanation has yet been offered of the constellation Kepheus being one of the types of Shu. This belongs to his Sabean and pre-solar character as the son of Nun before he became Shu-si-Ra. He had a dual solstitial function earlier than that of ruler of the equinox, and he can be identified astronomically as the God of the North who rises figuratively under the lion and is a ruler of the south, the two characters corresponding to the upper and lower lands and heavens.

When the sun was passing through the sign of Aquarius the constellation Kepheus, or Regulus, arose with his consort, Cassiopeia, Queen of Æthiopia, as the attendant of the sun through the abyss. The sun is said to be "forced along by the conducting of Shu."[2] "Shu is the conqueror of the world in Suten-khen" the celestial

[1] Drummond, Pl. 3.   [2] Ch. xvii

Bubastis, the royal birthplace, and the great chief in An, another name of the solar birthplace.

In the lower heaven was the place of judgment in the northern quarter, which included the sea-goat, waterer, and fishes. And of Gad it is said he provided the *first* part for himself; a portion of the lawgiver, or ruler of the north, that is, Gad occupied the first part of the northern quarter, the first of the water signs. The stars of Gad are still found in Capricorn, the sign called Gadia by the Chaldeans, Gadi by the Syrians, Giedi by the Arabians. Rabbi Solomon and others state that Capricorn was the sign of Gad in Israel, as is shown by his being ceiled or celestialized in the first portion of the lawgiver, Kepheus. The Well celebrated[1] was evidently in the portion of the lawgiver that began with Capricorn and ended with the Fishes. The Well answers to the Pool of Persea and water of life to be found in the Waterer or in An (fish) of the final zodiac. The Lawgiver was to remain until Shiloh came. Shu was the support of heaven until the sun-god was reborn from the abyss. Then the Osirian, in the character of the young god, at this point says, "I tell the great whole of Shu."[2] This being the place where the duality of Shu, and of Osiris respectively, became unified; the place of the after-birth. The Egyptians, says Plutarch, celebrate the festival of her (Isis) afterbirth, following the vernal equinox.[3] The afterbirth was the second Horus, the Egyptian Shiloh, or Sherau, the adult son, with the determinative of thirty years of age. One meaning of the word Shiloh (שִׁלֹה) in Hebrew is "the afterbirth." The Shiloh, or Sherau, the adult son, was the younger Horus or the one who came with peace. In the solar myth of Atum this imagery is equinoctial; the Shiloh was born at the vernal equinox. But the Egyptian sacred year began in July with the sun in the sign of Leo, and it is there in the Egyptian planisphere that the symbolism of Jacob's description is visibly present. The Shiloh was to come, "binding his foal unto the vine, and his ass's colt unto the choice vine; he washed his garments in wine and his clothes in the blood of grapes, his eyes red with wine and his teeth white with milk."

The imagery is extant in the sign of Leo, where there are two lions and a whelp, together with the figures of an ass bridled and a man leading a horse to tether it to the Vine, a constellation found in Virgo with branches reaching over into the sign of Leo.[4] The vine and wine (Arp) are synonymous with the Repa, the heir-apparent, the gracious child Horus, who was conceived of the virgin mother, on this side of the Zodiac, as the branch of the vine, or the grapes, to be reborn of the genitrix in the sign of Pisces on the opposite side. The vine or tree constellation is figured in the three decans of Virgo; the virgin goddess bears seven ears of corn, and it may be noted in

[1] Num. xxi. 17.   [2] Rit. ch. lxxviii.
[3] Of Isis and Osiris.   [4] Drummond, Pl. 3 and 16.

passing that there is or was a fresco in the church Bocca della Verita at Rome, in which the goddess Keres was pourtrayed shelling corn, with Bacchus squeezing grapes to provide the elements of the Eucharist for a table below.[1]

The dual character of the lion-god Shu or Kepheus is represented by the double lion of Judah, and it is now suggested that this dual lion of Judah is identical with Shu and Anhar, and with Kepheus, who is represented as the lawgiver, by the star Regulus (Cor-Leonis), in the lion, and by Regulus the constellation Kepheus in the north, who brought in the solar Shiloh or sun of the resurrection at the time of the summer solstice, as Tammuz, Duzi, Adonai, or the child Horus, and the Horus of the resurrection or of Easter at the vernal equinox. According to the Hebrew law, no man was allowed to enter in at the south gate of the Jewish sanctuary, that being the gate of entrance for the Lord.[2] The gate of the south was at the beginning of the Egyptian sacred year, with the sun in the lion, or, in another calendar, in the crab; not at the place of the spring equinox with the month Nisan. The gate is made eastward by the Prophets on behalf of the Repa, or prince, who was Horus REDIVIVUS. These two points in the south and east are indicated by "the Lord came from Sinai" (and) "shined forth from Mount Paran;"[3] also," God came from Teman (or the south) and the Holy One from Mount Paran."[4]

The birth of Moses is associated with the lion in Hebrew tradition.

Albiruni observes that the birth of Moses, according to the report of the Jews, must have coincided with the rising of the "tooth of Leo" and the moon's entering the "claws of Leo." "Cor-Leonis," he says, "rises when Suhail (i.e. Canopus) ascends in Alhijâz, Suhail being the forty-fourth star of Argo Navis, standing over its oar."[5]

Moses can also be identified with Regulus and Kepheus the lawgiver, by means of a description in the book of Isaiah.[6] "Then he remembered the days of old, Moses (and) his people (saying), Where is he that brought them up out of the sea with the *shepherd of his flock?*" The "Shepherd of the Heavenly flock," the Babylonian "SIB-ZI-ANNA" is, according to M. Oppert, the star Regulus. Other Assyriologists say it is a name of Mars. It may be both, as Mars is also the planetary type of Shu, the Egyptian heaven-bringer.

Again, we shall find the character of Shu represented by Moses, who is the registrar of the different stations in the wilderness,[7] and is

[1] Conway, *Demonology and Devil Lore*, v. 2, p. 245.
[2] *Mishna*, Treatise xiv. ch. iv. 2.
[3] Deut. xxxiii. 2.   [4] Hab. iii. 3.
[5] *Chronology of Ancient Nations*, pp. 345 and 347. Translated by Sachau. London, 1879.
[6] lxiii. 11.   [7] Num. xxxiii. 2.

credited with being the inventor of the divisions of lands,[1] that is primarily in the chart of the heavens. SHU is the Egyptian word for the division of land; the Shut or Sheft being a section. The earliest division is that of Shu, light and shade.

As before said, the feather of Shu reads both Ma and Shu, light and shade; he being a god of light and a light in shade. This dual personification is marked in Moses. Nothing proves his identity with Shu (light-and-shade) more than the description of his changefulness from light to dark, from glow to gloom.

Before Joshua takes the place of leader Moses is the light-and-shade in one, and changeful in appearance as the feather, or the sheen of shot silk. In the A. V. and other Protestant versions [2] Moses is said to have put on a veil, in order that he might hide the splendour reflected in his face from the divine presence. The Seventy and the Vulgate represent him as putting on the veil, not whilst he is speaking with the people, but afterwards, to hide, not the glory, but its vanishing away, and as wearing the veil until he returned to the presence of the deity, and the splendour had once more visibly rekindled. "When Moses went in before the Lord to speak with Him he put off the veil until he came out." "And Moses put the veil upon his face again, until he went in to speak with Him." [3] The character permutes and alternates like that of MA-SHU.

The astronomical chapter [4] of the twelve signs or twelve tribes in which the description of the lawgiver occurs precedes the death or disappearance of Moses. He is said to ascend Mount Nebo, whence he vanishes. In the mapping out [5] Nebo is in the territory assigned to Gad. The passage [6] reads literally, with the English put backwards to parallel the Hebrew,

ספון	מחקק	חלקת	‮שם‬-	כי	לו	ראשית	וירא
the distinguished one	the Law-giver	the acre of [or the field]	(was) there	because	for himself	the first	And he saw part

The Rashith or point of commencement for Gad was identified by means of the Lawgiver, because it was in the first part of his area or field. The "fields of the Aahru" (Eg.) is an expression for the celestial divisions. The sign of Gad is the Goat, and in that was the supposed burial-place of Moses, identifiable by means of Mount Nebo in the land of Gad.[7] The Nebo, where Moses dies or transforms into Joshua, answers well to the Mount of the double earth, the Mount of Nub-Tata an Egyptian god. The place of Nebo can be identified in the Hermean Zodiac, where the Goat is Anubis,

---

[1] Artapanus. Euseb. Præp. Ev. 9. 27.   [2] Ex. xxxiv. 33.
[3] Ex. xxxiv. 35.   [4] Deut. xxxiii.   [5] Num. xxxii. 3.   [6] Deut. xxxiii. 21.
[7] The present writer regrets that he is unable to find room for a section in which the stations and districts of the Israelites are compared with the chart of the heavens, more particularly the Hindu, Chinese, and Arabic chart of the twenty-eight lunar mansions.

one of whose names is Nub (Sut-Nub). Also Capricorn, the sign of Sut-Anubis, was called the domicile of Saturn, the star of Israel. The great dog was a type of Anubis, one star of which constellation was called the star of Isis, and Anubis in the Goat rattles the sistrum of Isis.[1] Now in the lion-calendar, when the sun entered the sign of the Goat, the great dog and the dog Procyon were both setting. Here was the grave of the Lawgiver, whether called Kepheus or Moses. Here Kepheus was no longer visible; it was the time of his transformation, or descent, for the constellation Argo sinks beneath the horizon when the sign of Capricorn arises. The pilot, who was Shu, in the forepart of the boat, and the rudder, are visible in Egypt. Shu-Anhar is the god dwelling in the divine barge or Argo, who stands at the prow to strike the Apophis monster of the darkness and the deep, and who, in his triumph, darts his spear against the serpent, when it rears its head to swallow Ra. Nebo, being in the first water sign, also marks the two truths of land and water as they are indicated in the Persian sphere at the place of the equinox in the Scorpion. Nebo is in the plains of Moab. Mu-ab, as Egyptian, reads, "opposite the water." The place was opposite the water which Moses did not cross. He was buried on the boundary. The picture of the devil disputing with Michael about the body of Moses[2] is curiously like the dispute and settlement of the boundary of An between Sut (Satan) and Horus, in the Inscription of Shabaka. When the Sun arrived at the place of the western equinox it entered the domain of Typhon. It was there that Typhon tore Osiris into fourteen parts —the fourteen lunar houses answering to half of the zodiacal circle. No one knew where Moses was buried, but the devil claimed possession of his body, and contended for it with Michael, as Typhon contended with Har-Makhu, Har of the two horizons or of the equinoctial balance, level or plain. At the autumn equinox, our Michaelmas, the dip of the scales was in favour of Typhon.

In the Mythos the sun is received at evening or in the autumn by the Goddess Hathor at the mountain of the west. She is the habitation of Har, the son. The god re-enters her womb to be buried and reborn. This, too, was the burial-place of Moses, who, the Scripture says, died in the land of Moab, AL PHI-JEHOVAH (עַל־פִּי־יהוה). PHI, of course, denotes a mouth, and the PEH (Eg.) sign of the female hinder-part will explain the rest. He entered the mouth of the Void, the Bahu, or Peh of the north, as the sun entered the Peh or Khepsh, carried on the head of Anhar, the Akar or Pit, said to have been dug by Moses.

"The mouth of the well has swallowed him up" is a Hebrew saying of the underworld. The well is the Tepht (Eg.), the void or abyss, and the mouth of Jehovah as the feminine divinity may apply, the horizon or RU being the mouth, but the mouth of the male god can

---

[1] See Plate. [2] Jude, ver. 9.

by no means supply a figure of the entrance to the underworld. The goddess received the sun, the sun stood still. Moses was buried in the west, opposite to the water, or in the first water sign, and in a famous Hawaiian legend of Hiaka-i-ka-poli-o-Pele we find the goddess as the one of the two divine sisters who receives the sun—"*i ka muli o Hea*"—*over the pool or estuary of Hea!* It is related that when HIAKA went to the island of KAUAI to recover and restore to life the body of LOHIAU, the lover of her sister PELE, she came to the foot of the KALALU mountain shortly before sunset, and on being told there would not be light long enough for her to climb it and get the body out of the cave, she prayed to her gods to keep the sun stationary until she had accomplished her purpose. The prayer was heard, the sun stood still ; she climbed the mountain and received the body.[1]

The Abyss in this myth is the ESTUARY OF HEA, the same as in the Assyrian Cosmogony. The two sisters are likewise the same as in the Egyptian mythos. In the invocations of Isis and Nephthys Isis says to Osiris, "I am thy double sister." Ra joins himself to his double mother.[2] One of the Ptolemies calls himself the beloved of the double (divine) mother, otherwise the two sisters.

The passage of the sun in the Goat was marked by the temporary setting of the river of Aquarius. Hence, perhaps, the fable of crossing the Jordan dryshod. Next month, when the sun entered the sign of Aquarius Kepheus again rose, and the Lawgiver was visible as supporter of the heaven. This is Shu-Anhar with the Khepsh on his head, the type of the hinder part and sign of attainment, of reaching and arriving.

This re-arising of Kepheus corresponds to the *rôle* of Joshua after the death or transformation of Moses. "The permutation or transformation of Israel," says the *Kabala Denudata*,[3] "is Mashu:" the true doctrine. The God of the Asar was represented by the transforming twins, Moses and Joshua, Moses being here recognized as the one through whom the Deity was dually manifested. "I am the great whole of Shu," says Osiris in the Ritual. The Hebrews gave the prominence to Moses. In the Ritual the sun of winter is said to transform into a cat. "I am the great Cat," says the Osirian, "which is in the Pool of Persea, in Annu, the night of the battle made to bind the wicked ; the day of strangling the enemies of the universal lord there, the great cat which is in Tattu, in the Pool of the Persea, placed in Annu, is the sun himself, called a cat. For it is like what he has done ; he has made his transformation into a cat.[4] OR it is Shu making the likeness of Seb," (Time). Shu was the earlier lion-god, and his was the true transformation into the cat-lion or leopard. In heraldry the leopard represents those

[1] Fornander, v. i. p. 100.
[2] Obelisk of Hatasu.
[3] ii. 305.
[4] Ch. xvii. Birch.

warriors who manifested the utmost boldness and suddenness in attack; the promptitude of power is typified by the leopard. Our English lion is drawn leoparded like Anhar: it is the lion of the north. Further a young lion is called a cat-lion, and it was in this region that the sun was catted or brought forth as young. Here Anhar becomes the lion-supporter of the sun, on the opposite side of the shield to that of Shu, and as the sun in Anrutef most needed support, Anhar was made the great hero of the twin lion-gods who conducted the sun up out of the very pit.

The total of all that we are here contending for is confessed in the name of the veil with which Moses concealed his face. It is the מסה, one Hebrew rendering of MA-SHU, the Two Truths, the light and shade of the feather. Nowhere in the Hebrew writings is a veil called MASUH or MASHU, except the one worn by Moses,[1] "and this MASHU as a veil," says Gesenius, "cannot be explained on philological grounds;" as the reader will see, it can on the mythological grounds. The MASHU represents the permutation of Ma changing into Shu, or the passage of the sun into the domain of Shu, the shade and veil; this the Ritual designates "*making his transformation.*"[2] MASHU (Eg.) means to turn, just as the changing of Moses is indicated by the MASHU, called the veil. In the Avesta there is a mountain named USHIDARENA said to possess pure brightness—the glory and kingly majesty wherewith Yima the first man was endowed until his fall. From this mountain the fabulous kings descended, and it is a Parsee doctrine that kings and rulers originally came down endowed with a peculiar brightness from heaven. So when Moses came down from the mount the skin of his face shone with such splendour they were afraid to come near him.[3] In keeping with this symbolism of Shu and Anhar, light and shade, are the instructions for building the arks or tabernacles (סכה) for the Feast of Tents celebrated on the fifteenth of Tizri, the first month of the civil year.[4] We learn from the Mishna[5] that a Succah or ark was not valid unless it conformed to certain rules, or as the words are, "which had more sun than shade." It was to be erected equally in sun and shadow; the part open to the rays of the sun was to exactly balance the shade of the covering, because it was emblematic of the equinox, the balance of light and shade, the level of the two heavens of Shu and Anhar, Moses and Joshua, or Ma-Shu. This ark was likewise the Double Abode of Ra, which was typified by Ma-Shu, the light and shade in one personification. The dual meaning of Shu's name as Light and Shade is reflected in the legends that tell of Moses being the first

---

[1] Ex. xxxiv. 33, 34, 35.   [2] Ch. xvii.   [3] Ex. xxxiv. 30.
[4] The Jews celebrated their New Year's Day in London, in the year 1876, on the 17th of September, and in 1880 on the 6th of September.
[5] Treatise, Succah, ch. i.

teacher who set up gnomons to measure the light by the length of the shadow as a mode of time-keeping. Shu, as the father of Seb, is the progenitor of Time.

We have now arrived at the point of time and place where the scene of transformation occurs—at the time of the winter solstice (in the Ram calendar), the turning-point of the lower heaven. Shu does not die : he makes his transformation into Anhar. Moses passes into or permutes with the character of Joshua. Not until he has obtained a glimpse from Pisgah as did Shu, if we may judge by what the Osirian says in this place : " *The Osiris has seen the sun born in the star, at the thigh of the great water ;* "[1] that is, seen it pass into the keeping of Anhar or Kepheus, who takes up the conductorship noose-in-hand, or with the later sceptre of the lawgiver.

In the Ritual the stars or planets are described as hauling the sun along with ropes, the ropes having a noose to them. When the winter sun was low in the nether world by night, or in the winter signs, men looked up at the starry movers through the heavens that retained all their light in their lustre, and never slackened in their speed, as did the sun ; and their thought was, " Pull him along, you glorious goers through the dark. You swift-winged Mercury and blood-red Mars, haul away at the ropes of the sun." " *O conductors of the bark of millions of years ! led through the gateway, clearing the paths of heaven and earth ; accompany ye the souls to the mummies. Your hands are full, bearing your ropes, your fists holding the coils.*"[2] Again, the Osirian, or soul of the deceased, says, " *I make the haul of thy rope, O sun.*"[3] " *I do not fall at the towing of the sun.*"[4]

One starry image of Shu was Mars marching with his noose in hand and forcing the sun along ; for the Ritual[5] says, " *The sun is forced along by the conducting of Shu, who gives blasts of flame from his mouth.*" Shu, then, with his noose is identifiable with the Sun-Catcher of the Maori, Polynesian, and North American Indian myths. The myth of catching the sun is that of measuring time. Until the revolving orbs were tethered, or time was spaced out, there was no reckoning for men to go upon.

In the Mangaian legend MAUI (the Egyptian *alter ego* of Shu) set about tethering the sun to regulate his movements and time him. He plaited six royal nooses, and placed them at six different aper-tures which the sun passed through on his path, and eventually caught him and held him tight, and fastened the end of his rope to a rock. Ra agreed that in future he would not hurry through heaven so furiously fast. Maui slackened the nooses, but Ra still wears them, and they may be seen hanging from the sun at dawn and evening.[6]

The same story is told in the Samoan Islands. There was a man who set himself to build a house of great stones, to last for ever.

---

[1] Rit. ch. xvii.   [2] Ch. lxxxix.   [3] Ch. xxxix.
[4] Ch. cii.   [5] Ch. xvii.   [6] Gill, *Myths and Songs of the Pacific*, 61-2.

But he could not get it finished, the sun went round so fast. At last the Itu, or Atua, caused the *facehere* creeper to grow. With this the man made a noose and caught the sun. Then he built the house.[1]

The Ojibwas have the same tale of catching the sun in a noose of red metal cord. When it had been caught, the animal world was in a state of consternation. The dormouse at last nibbled the cord in two, which set the sun free.[2] The Dog-rib Indian legend makes the mole the deliverer of the ensnared sun.

In the Ute mythology the passage of the sun across the heavens in its appointed course is described as being the result of a fierce conflict between Ta-Wats, the hare god, and Ta-Vi, the solar god. Once on a time, or rather before time was, the sun was accustomed to roam the earth at will and without bounds. At one period he would come so near to men that they were scorched ; at another he concealed himself in a cave, and they nearly perished during the long night of his absence. Then Ta-Wats took the matter in hand, and determined to subdue and tether the erratic solar god. After a long, long journey, he came to the edge of the earth and waited patiently for the wayward Deity. When the sun arose Ta-Wats aimed an arrow at his flaming face, but it was dissolved by his burning breath before it could reach him. He shot arrow after arrow all in vain, until one only remained in his quiver. This was the magical arrow, never known to fail. This he baptized in a divine tear, and shot it. The arrow struck the sun full in the face, and the wayward god was conquered. He was now compelled to appear before the gods in council to receive sentence. This council condemned him to travel across the firmament until the end of time, in one appointed and determined course, by which decision the days and nights, the seasons, the years, with their lengths and recurring periods, were established for ever according to the solar chart.[3]

In addition to identifying the tetherer of the sun with Maui (Shu), it may be noted that Wat is an English name of the hare ; Skhat in Egyptian. The hare-headed Kukufa sceptre is a most ancient emblem of sovereignty, and it bears on it the feather of Shu.

The Vignette to the Abode, chapter cl. of the Ritual, shows a hare-headed god with bow and arrows. The arrow is still another symbol of Shu ; one of its names is the Kesr, the turner-back, and it keeps its character in the Ute myth. Also the Divine Tear is an Egyptian type of creative power.

The bow of Seb is the circle of time, of starry time. The first drawer of this bow, and maker of the earliest circle of time, was the Great Bear. By aid of these facts we can interpret the tradition of the Laps, who relate in their mythological epic the feats of Pawin

---

[1] Walpole, *Four Years in the Pacific*, ii. 375.
[2] Schoolcraft, *Oneóta*, p. 75.
[3] Prof. J. W. Powell, in *Nature*, Jan. 29, 1880.

Parne, the mighty hunter and bowman, an obvious form of Shu-Anhar, also called like him the "Son of the Sun," as well as the off-spring of Kalla. This Nimrod of the far north is represented as hunting along with his fellow giants, and using the Great Bear for his bow. With this bow he pursues and tames such celestial stags as Jupiter and Venus, the "colour-changing hind," in the constellation Cassiopeia. The bow of the Great Bear was the primordial bow of Seb, or time, the first circle of the year. By means of this the primitive observers could reckon the number of years in the revolutions of Jupiter, Venus, and the other planets, which enabled them to establish planetary time. Thus Pawin Parne drew the bow of Seb in its primal shape; and the bow with which he tamed Jupiter and Venus was a type similar to the noose of Shu, who made the "likeness of Seb," and of the *facehere* loop in the Samoan mythos, with which the sun was tethered, so that the proper reckonings could be kept.

The connection with Cassiopeia shows the relation of PAWIN PARNE to Kepheus, who was her consort. Also, the bow identifies the lion-god Shu. "I am the lion-god coming forth with a bow; what I have shot at is the eye of Horus."[1] That is PAWIN PARNE and Ta-Wats in one. In the Egyptian texts RA, the sun, is called "the Runner which no one is able to catch in the morning of his births." The sun is the runner or racer in the Psalms, when he issues from his chamber like a bridegroom rejoicing as a strong man to run a race; to which image the author of *Primitive Marriage* might have pointed as another illustration of the races run at the capture of the bride for marriage. The first tethered time-keeper was KEF (the hippopotamus), and KEFIU (Eg.) means the tethered.

Tethering the sun and building the house are forms of arranging the twelve signs. Shu presides over six of these signs down which the sun hurries, and is represented as being impeded in his course by the six nooses of Maui. The Egyptian Maui is the god of the six descending signs. Six nooses in the hieroglyphics read six months. We thus recover the primitive meaning. Shu is depicted as holding up and staying the sun in its downward course; Anhar as forcing it along in its ascent by means of the noose in his hand.

It must not be thought that the Israelites or Solarites are absent from the Egyptian myth. ANHAR does not only conduct the sun. In the creation by Ra, Nun, the father of Shu, says: "*My son Shu, thou shalt do. . . . thy father in his creations. My son Shu, take with thee my daughter Nut, and be the guardian of the multitudes which live in the nocturnal sky; put them on thy head and be their fosterer.*"[2] That is a metaphor for bearing them up. "*I establish, as inhabitants, all the beings which are suspended in the sky, the stars.*" "*I assemble and give the possession of these multitudes of men.*"

[1] Rit. ch. cxxxii.   [2] *Records*, vi. 105-112.

In these passages Shu is bidden to support Ra by guarding the multitudes that dwell in night or live in the nocturnal heavens; that is in Hades, or Sheol. These transactions were solar and Sabean at first, and secondarily a spiritual sense was read into them, but they were never supposed by the initiated to be human and historical. That notion was a legacy bequeathed by later error to still later ignorance.

Shu (Anhar) is lord of the sanctuary or tabernacle of the god. The Hebrew Joshua is the son of Nun and minister of the tabernacle. He has the care and custody of the sanctuary in which the God of Israel has, like RA, resolved to be lifted up and carried. The Samaritan name of the Messiah, according to De Sacy, signifies the "Returning One;"[1] and Juynboll[2] supposes that the Messiah was called by this name because he was regarded as the returning Moses. MASHU (Eg.) or MESHU means to turn back, return. The night of the last day of the old year, and the evening meal of the first day of the new, were called the MASIU. MESSU was a name of the typical Prince of Æthiopia corresponding to Kepheus, and therefore to Shu, in his character of the "Returning One." Joshua is the Messiah or Saviour, as the returning Moses.

The first words addressed by Jah-Adonai to Joshua are, "Moses, my servant, is dead; now therefore arise, go over this Jordan."[3] In Egyptian Jordan is Iarutana, *i.e.* the river that divides. Joshua leads the Israelites across the dividing river; they pass over on dry ground, and twelve stones are erected as a memorial in Gilgal, on the other side. Then Jordan returned and overflowed his banks again, just as the river of the zodiac re-arises in the train of Kepheus and his consort the Queen of Æthiopia. In the chapter of opening the back-doors and coming forth at the back of the heaven, it is said: "SHU has opened the gate. I have come forth with a rush. I have gone forth, I have gone into the cabin of the boat of the sun."[4] SHU opening the gate for the passage of the Iarutana is identical with Joshua leading the Israelites over the Jordan. The Osirian enters the boat, or ark of the sun, and crosses; he prevails over the waters, streams, pools. When the ark is brought to the edge of the Jordan, the waters divide for the host to pass through. In other words, they realize their name of IARU-TANA, the dividing river of Egypt. "*The Osiris does not arrive from the other side deceived* (or does not go obfuscated) *when he has gone round the heaven at its southern shoulder* SPYING *that to the Osiris are given the winds of the blest, to eat and drink the food of those belonging to the sun.*"[5] He has spied out the land of promise and plenty beforehand, and is not deceived, having "*Thousands of food and drink off the tables of his father; oxen, bulls, red cattle, geese and ducks.*" These, like the Hebrew milk and honey, were sacred types

[1] *Notices et Extraits.*   [2] *Chron. Samarit.* 52.
[3] Josh. i. 2.   [4] Ch. lxvii.   [5] Ch. lxix.

of abundance and offering. The spying out of this land was from the turn of the southern shoulder of the heaven.

Now when Moses deputed Joshua to spy out the land of Canaan he sent him up into a mountain southward to spy out whether the land was fat or lean. This answers to the southern shoulder of the heaven, from whence the Osirian spies out his land of the table, Hept, of the sun, piled with plenty. Joshua was accompanied on his journey by Caleb, the dog, and eleven others. These are, probably, the "*Dogs of Shu*," who, in the Ritual, follow the person of Shu.[1] The spies bring back a huge cluster of grapes from the south. In the south arose the Dog-star, the watch or spy of the gods, who announced the coming plenty to be poured into Egypt's lap by means of the inundation.

Kalb (כלב), the Hebrew name for the dog, is identical with the Egyptian Kherf, Kherp, or Kherb, the first form, model figure, the princeps, as was the Dog-star in heaven. The character assigned to the Kalb as the raging, the furious, is that of the fiery Dog-star, and the god of fury and fire, Bar-Sutekh; Kalb being the same word in that sense as YELP. Chalab is a Turkish god, or typical image; Kilip an Akkadian divinity; Kolpia, Phœnician; Glipo, African Basa. The KALP was a wooden idol, venerated by the Hebrews. Kalb the Kherp was one of the primordial GLYPHS in heaven. Of all the hosts that came out of Egypt, ranging from 600,000 to 2,000,000 souls who were promised the land of plenty, which they never attained, only Caleb the dog and Joshua reached the end of the journey.[2] The imagery on which this was based is to be seen in the Egyptian planisphere, and there only can the reality be found. The Dog-star and COR-LEONIS (Regulus, the sign of Shu in the south) were the two stars at the point where one circuit ended and another began in the Egyptian solstitial year. In one of the Egyptian planispheres reproduced by Kircher[3] there appears the constellation of the Vine to the south-west, near the lion and virgin, and in its branches stands the Dog, looking eastward, spying out the promised land of spring time, and the golden fields of the ascending Sun. The words, "*Shu has opened the gate*" are preceded by "*Those who belong to Nu have opened the gate, those who belong to the Spirits have besieged it.*" So Joshua opens the gate and forces the passage by the siege of Jericho.

The spies who bring back with them the giant bunch of grapes and other fruit report that the cities of the children of Anak were huge and walled round. "And they brought up an evil report of the land, saying, It is a land which eateth up the inhabitants thereof; and there we saw the sons of Anak which come of the giants, and we were in our own sight as grasshoppers, and so we were in their sight."[4]

This region of things gigantic may be found in the mystical abodes

---

[1] Ch. xxiv.
[3] Drum. *Œd. Jud.* Pl. 3,
[2] Deut. i. 35, 36.
[4] Num. xiii. 32, 33.

through which the soul has to pass on its way to the world of light and blessedness. The second abode is called, "*Greatest of possessions in the fields of the Aahru. Its wall is of earth. The height of its corn is seven cubits, the ears are twin, its stalks are three cubits* (said) *by the spirits seven (cubits) in length.*" The spirits also are said to be seven cubits in stature, the height of the corn.[1] Of the fifth abode it is said, "*Hail, abode of the spirits, through which there is no passage. The spirits belonging to it are seven cubits long in their thighs. They live as wretched shades.*" "*Oh, this abode of the spirits. Oh, ye spirits belonging to them, open your road. I have ordered it is said by Osiris, the living lord, Osiris in his illumination. If any condemned spirit sets his mouth against me, or any male or female devil comes to me on that day, he falls at the block.*" The monsters are here called spirits, but the word AKH, meaning how great, would equally render giants, and these are nearly a cubit longer in their thighs alone than the Hebrew giant.[2] Indeed in chapter cix. the inhabitants are eight cubits in height. The passage through the Hades in the eleventh abode is described as the belly of hell. "*There is neither coming out of nor going into it, on account of the greatness of the terror of passing him who is in it.*" That is the devouring demon, the Am-Moloch. The same fear is reflected in the faces of the spies from the land of giants; they had seen the same sight. The Moabites called the giants who dwelt there in times past AMIMS.[3] The Am-am in Egyptian are the devourers. AM is the male devourer, AM-T the female devourer in the Ritual.

Lot's wife fleeing from Sodom is a picture of the escape from Sut, the Egyptian devil, whose domain contains the hells of smoking, fulminating fires, sent forth destroyingly for ever, in blasts that stifle every breath. The Hebrew Shedim are the devils, and Sodom is the place of the Egyptian hells. In this were the nitre, sulphur, and bitumen which furnished the modern fire and brimstone, the circuit of serpents that die not, and the ceiling of everlasting flame. Now in the chapters of "*Leading the Boat from Hades,*" without which there is no escape from the hells, the Osirian cries, "*I have flown as a hawk out of the net of the great destroyer. I have come from the scalding pools from the flaming fields, I have come forth from the mud,*" (the vale of Siddim was that of the slimepits).[4] He escapes from that "*dreadful coast*" in the passage out of this "*Border of Apophis,*" or devil's land. Amongst the tormentors, conspirators, accusers and other associates of Sut are the NASPU,[5] those who render torpid, from NASP or NASB, to numb, stupefy, and petrify. The NASPU are the petrifiers through the terror they create. This word NASPU appears in Hebrew as NATZEB (נצב) to fix, make firm, rigid; and it is applied to the transformation of Lot's wife in the sense of petrifaction. She was (Naspu)

---

[1] Ch. cl.   [2] I Sam. xvii. 4.   [3] Deut. ii. 11.
[4] Gen. xiv. 10.   [5] Ch. xcix.

numbed, stupefied, petrified, or, as our version has it, turned into a pillar of salt. She was petrified in "Siddim which is the SALT (Melak) sea."[1] Siddim, the salt sea, is the pool of salt in the Ritual. "*I have,*" says the escaping Osirian, "*crossed by the northern fields in the region of the captured.*" They placed "*a flaming lamp*" to him and "*an amulet of felspar.*" "*I have buried myself in the well of the pool of salt at night time.*" The "*Wells of the pool of salt are that sceptre of stone*" which has been made. These are the saltpits of Siddim, and the wells of the pool of salt that was a sceptre of stone have a look of the petrifaction attributed to Lot's wife. Salt is in itself an image of petrifaction and purifying, and this was the region of both.

When Joshua had crossed the river Jordan or Iarutana (Eg.) he invested the city of Jericho. Aur, Ior, Iaru, is the river and Jericho is Cho by the river, in Egyptian KAU, and the Egyptians had a city GAU (Diodorus), or Ko, according to Ptolemy. This was geographical, but had been, like Heliopolis and other chief places, arranged and named from the mythical scenery of the heavens. Diodorus relates that after the death of Osiris, caused by Typhon at the autumn equinox, Typhon was defeated by Horus and his mother Isis, on the Arabian side of the river Nile at a spot near Antæus. This city of Antæopolis, where stood a temple on the bank of the Nile, was called GAU or KO, *i.e.* literally IARU-KO. The original of both was in the heavens, and the celestial river was made mundane in the Egyptain ARU and the Jordan. Also, the region of AI, and BEN-BEN is a place in the celestial circle, referred to in the magical texts, the region where Atum sits in his glory, in the pyramidion, at the apex of his power, after the crossing of the waters.[2] It was the work of SHU, the bringer, to lead up the sun and land him on the eastern horizon, after the great conflict in the valley with the swarming powers of darkness.

On the horizon just across the river was the seat of ATUM in An, the red region. This reappears as the city of ADAM. From Jericho to ADAM[3] the waters dried up, while the ark of the God was borne across. Here the circle was completed, the eye made in the equinoctial year.

According to Hipparchus, the Zodiac, *ab Arietis 8 mediâ parte ad 14,* descends with the Crown and Sceptre of Kepheus. In this sign Shu may be seen seated with the Whip of Rule in his hand, close to the triangle of three stars, the terminus of the conductorship of Anhar, and the range of the lawgiver in the northern quarter.[4]

The sun was reborn as the son, the solar Messiah, he who comes. Atum reappears as Iu-em-hept, he who comes with peace. Iu, the son, written in Egyptian, is IU-SU or IU-SIF, *i.e.* Jesus or Joseph. This fact lies at the origin of a sort of identity between Joseph and Jesus.

[1] Gen. xiv. 3.   [2] *Records*, vi. 116.   [3] Josh. iii. 16.   [4] Drummond, Pl. 3.

IU-SIF is the son who comes at the time of the vernal equinox. This was the son conducted up by ANHAR, whose work then ended. In the Hebrew legend we are told that Moses carried the Atzem (עצם) of Joseph up out of Egypt, and this was placed in Shechem at the time of Joshua's death. Atzem is rendered[1] bones. But the word also means self-same, the same, the likeness. AT-SEM (Eg.) reads the Mummy type, also to make the likeness, also the young sun, the typical heir and branch. Sem is the sun with the two tall plumes, and these were placed on the head of the Deity by the lion-gods called the SEMS, his ministers. SEM-PI-KHART was a solar god, and if Moses and Joshua are the two lion-gods, what they conducted out of Egypt and placed in Shechem was the sun-god himself, as Adonai, the son of the mother, the solar disk considered as Aten. SHAKEM in Hebrew is the name for the shoulder as the symbol of bearing. This type was assigned to the male bearer as Horus in SEKHEM, but the first bearer was the female, the Mother ZIKUM in the AKKADIAN, the SKHEM shrine of the genitrix in the Egyptian Mythos, and the σχηνὴ ιερά which was carried about by the Carthaginians.[2] The Arabic SUKHAMAT, rendered podex, is a form of the SKHEM-shrine.

The Egyptian SEKHEM is a secret shrine, the holy of holies, always found in the hindermost room of the temple, surrounded on three sides by a row of cloisters or secluded chambers. The SEKHEM was particularly connected with the great mother and was prominent in the worship of Atum or Aten, the Hebrew Adonai.

This was the Joseph who went out through the land of Egypt[3] whom we shall meet again in the next chapter.

There is a group of avengers or punishers attached to Shu in the Ritual.[4]

" *The Punishers of Shu, who come behind thee to cut off thy head, to chop off thy hand, do not see thee performing the robbery of their Lord.*"
" *The Punishers of Shu have turned away.*" [5]

These are either the same figures or they are supplemented with the " DOGS OF SHU." The punishers belonging to Shu who chop off the hands of the enemies appear in the followers of Joshua[6] as the pursuers of the Canaanites and Perizzites, and the cutters off of the fingers and toes of their captives.

The Dogs of Shu are represented in the Hebrew version by Caleb, the Dog of Joshua, and the dogger or punisher of the enemy, after Joshua's death. The " *swift dogs following Shade, or the person of Shu,*" are rendered[7] by the avengers who come AFTER Joshua in the Book of the Judges, headed by Caleb the dog. Adoni-Bezek, who was mutilated, has a name signifying in Egyptian the revolted ruler Besh-ak, hostile to Adonai, the sun-god.

---

[1] Josh. xxiv. 32.   [2] Diodorus, xx. 68   [3] Ps. lxxxi. 5.
[4] Ch. xc.   [5] Ib.   [6] Judges. i.   [7] Ch. xxiv.

In the Hebrew narrative the followers of Joshua, the avengers and associates of the dog (Caleb), *ergo*, the dogs of Shu, assail the three sons of Anak called Sheshai, Ahiman, and Talmai.[1] NAKA is a name of the Apophis, a type of the criminal, impious deluder. In the Ritual the serpent Ruhak is triple-headed, and Anak and his three sons are a form of the Monster, triple-headed. The Vedic AHI, the serpent of darkness, is triple-headed. The monster Zohak slain by Feridun had three heads. The Chimera killed by Bellerophon was a threefold monster. The three names are all in keeping. Seshai is one. Sesha is the great serpent of the waters in the Hindu mythology. The SHESH-SHESH in the Ritual is a mystic monster of a triadic form, with the Ap-serpent for its tail. AHIMAN answers to the Vedic AHI, and the Zend AHRIMAN the evil being, and the AZHI-DAHAKA of the Avesta. AHI, as the demon VRITRA, is the power that prevents the clouds from pouring out their water, that is the inimical one opposed to fertility. The Hebrew name TALMAI, from תלה to suspend, and מי, the fertilizing waters, reads the suspender of the waters, the Hebrew Vritra. It was not without significance in this connection that Moses of Khorene should refer to the popular songs relating to the triumph over Aj-dahak the serpent.[2]

Out of these "Wars of the Lord," these battles from generation to generation with Amalek, the endless conflict between the sun and the Apophis, the conducting of souls up out of the valley of the Shadow of Death, and the Crossing of the Waters, came the various myths of an exodus or migration of a people as the first fact of their existence, which belong one and all to the mythological astronomy.

The Mexicans depicted the sun of the eastern horizon as being accompanied by hosts of warrior spirits, the bravest that ever fell in battle, who rose up with him and marched in all the pomp and glory of war, as they escorted him towards the mid-day heaven with shouts of triumph until the conquering sun had attained the noonday height. Then they rested, and the women-warriors, chiefly those who had heroically died in childbed, met the sun, and assumed the duty of carrying him on a litter made of rich FEATHERS and brandishing the weapons of war, as the men of the morning had done in the clashing and clangour of conflict, while they bore him downward to the west.[3]

The men of the ascent and women of the descent correspond to the lions as MA-SHU or Shu and his feminine half, Tefnut. This is pourtrayed in the Ritual in a kind of astronomical eschatology, which shows the skeleton of the theological building without stucco or plaster. The deceased is told to pass on. "DEPART, O OSIRIS, GO ROUND THE HEAVEN WITH THE SUN. SEE THE SPIRITS."[4] Taht, it is said, "HAS PREPARED MILLIONS; HE HAS PASSED BILLIONS. THEY HAVE ALLOWED THE DECEASED TO GO. THE

---

[1] Jud. i. 10.   [2] *Windischman Zoroast. Studien*, p. 138.
[3] Bancroft, iii. 365.   [4] Ch. cxix.

CIRCLE OF THE MINISTERS OF THE SEM (the Sems or Lion-Gods) IS BEFORE HIM." "THE OSIRIS GOES IN COMPANY."[1] For the dead spirits or gods are described as swarming through the horizon in crowds. They gather for the battle of the Sun and the Apophis. "THE SUN, HE COMES FORTH: RECEIVE YOUR WEAPONS; RECEIVE YOUR BATTLE ARMOUR." "The doors of the chief horizon of the Sun open; he comes forth."[2]

"For the night of the battle, their march is from the east of the heaven. The battle is made in the heaven and on the whole earth."[3]

The sun *"strangles the children of wickedness on the floor of those in Sesen."*[4]

"The sun rises from his horizon; his gods are behind him. When he comes forth from the Amenti, the despisers fall down in the eastern heaven at the words of Isis. She has prepared the path of the sun, the great chief."[5]

"I am the sun coming forth from the horizon against my enemies. My enemies have not made me to fall."[6]

"O conductors of the bark of millions of years! Ye bruise the Accusers."[7]

"Hail, ye gods of the orbit (Aalu), strangle ye the enemies of the sun. I put forth blows against the Apophis. Strangle ye the wicked in the west."[8]

"Hail, O thou sun in his ark, shining with his light, gleaming with his gleam. The Creator, in the midst of his boat, who smiteth the Apophis daily; say for the children of Sut, who smiteth the enemies of Osiris, they are crushed by the boat. Horus smites off their heads to the heaven for the fowls, their thighs to the earth for wild beasts, to the waters for the fishes. The Osiris crushes all evil spirits, male or female, whether they go from heaven or earth, come out of the waters or cross from the tips of the stars. Taht cuts them up,—a stone out of the buildings of those who possess the ark of Osiris! The sun is that great god, the greatest of smiters, the most powerful of terrifiers; he washes in your blood, he dips in your gore."[9]

Isis, the great mother, preparing the pathway of the sun, corresponds to the women-warriors of the Mexican myth; and this would be still more in keeping with their fierceness when the great mother was pourtrayed as Tefnut, the lioness-headed goddess. In a general way it may be said, the souls emerged with the sun from the horizon east, and accompanied him in his battle-march along the celestial course until they came round to the mountain of the west; and there, where the dead went down, was the Mount of the final Ascension to the land of the blessed, the Mount Manu and place of spirits

---

[1] Ch. cxxx. [2] Rit. ch. xxxix. [3] Ch. xvii.
[4] Ch. xvii. [5] Ch. cxxxiii. [6] Ch. xlix.
[7] Cb. lxxxix. [8] Ch. cxxvii. [9] Ch. cxxxiv. Birch.

perfected, where dwelt the twelve kings who presided over this region of the west.

As Shu and Anhar, in Egyptian mythology, and Moses and Joshua conducted their people with the solar orb round the circle of signs, overcoming the opposing powers postulated by the early men, so in the Toltec mythology HUEMAC (or Huematzin) and QUETZALCOATL conducted their people through the pilgrimage and wanderings recorded in their picture-writings. Huemac, like Moses, wrote the code of laws for the nation, and conducted the civil government. Quetzalcoatl, in relation to Huemac, plays the part of Joshua. When Quetzalcoatl began to give the laws instead of Huemac, he sent a crier to the top of the "mountain of outcry," whose voice could be heard for three hundred miles round.[1] Joshua follows Moses as the leader of Israel, and instructs the people to go up against Jericho (his mountain of outcry), and assail it with a shout that ought to have been heard at an equal distance, as it was loud enough to make the walls fall flat.[2]

THE OLD RED LAND (Huehuetlapallan) was the name of the original home in the north, from which the Toltecs migrated. Their leader, Quetzalcoatl, wore a long robe marked with crosses. The sign identifies him as the one who crosses. Quetzalcoatl attained the land of promise, and in his golden reign an ear of wheat grew so large that one man could hardly carry it. Joshua led the people into the land flowing with milk and honey, where a single bunch of grapes was a load for two men. Moses is placed in a cleft of the rock whilst the Lord goes by, and tradition asserts the print of his body to have been engraved on the stone, visible to this day. The impression of the hand of Huemac is likewise said to have been stamped in a rock.[3]

The lion-gods not only supplied the Hebrews with their mythical Moses and Joshua; the twin typical and transforming lions, the lion of light and the lion of darkness, reappear amongst the twelve symbolic signs called Totemic of the North American Indians.[4] One of these twelve signs is a dual form of the same figure answering to the Egyptian twin-lion. It is a fabulous panther or lynx: the body in both has a human head with horns. But one of the two is marked all over the body with crosses. These, according to Schoolcraft, denote darkness in the Indian symbolism, and this is in perfect accordance here with the Egyptian, as the name of Kak, the god of the crossing, and therefore of the cross, means darkness and night. The other, without crosses, is the same animal in the light. The name of the chimera is given as MISSHI-BEZHIU, not an impossible rendering of MAU-SHU, the twin lions, or lion of light and shade, who is represented as changing into the cat, or becoming leoparded. Moreover Bes (Eg.) is the beast, a tiger, leopard, or typical beast;

[1] Bancroft, iii. 274.   [2] Josh. vi.   [3] Bancroft, iii. 284.
[4] Schoolcraft, vol. i. p. 467, pl. 58.

IU is dual; BAS-IU, in Egyptian, is the twin-beast here called MISSHI, and in Egypt MAU-SHU. The Indians had no lion, but they made use of such beasts as they found in the country.

The Chronicles of Fuentes, of the kingdom of Guatemala, and the MS. of Don Juan Torres, grandson of the last of the Quiché kings, may now be looked at less askancely. The document, having passed through the hands of Father Francis Vasques, historian of the order of St. Francis, has been more than suspected. For it was said to relate that the Toltecs were descended from the children of Israel, whose deliverer was Moses, and who crossed the Red Sea and fell into idolatry, and afterwards separated from their fellows and set out upon their further wanderings under a chief named TA-NUB, till they came to the place of the Seven Caverns, in Mexico, where they founded the famous town of Tula.[1] The children of Israel, who have been sought all over the earth, belong to the heavens; and the heavens, together with their charts and allegories, belong to various peoples of the earth without derivation from the Hebrews. MA-SHU is as good a Moses for the Quichés as for the Jews. TA (Eg.) means to cross over the water; Nub is the Lord; and the Lord who crossed was Tanub, or ANHAR-MASHU.

In the battle of Rephidim we have a rendering of the same original myth as that from which the Greeks drew their story of Hercules and Atlas. When Hercules, in quest of the golden apples of the Hesperides, had come to the spot where Prometheus lay chained, and had shot the eagle that preyed on his liver, that is, when the sun entered the sign of the Waterman, Prometheus, out of gratitude, warned him not to go himself to fetch the golden apples in the keeping of the polar dragon, but to persuade Atlas, the keeper of the pillars which hold heaven and earth asunder (as Homer calls him), to go instead. Atlas consents, and sallies forth to assail the dragon of darkness; meanwhile Hercules takes his stand in the place of Atlas, and supports the heaven himself. Atlas succeeds; he wins the apples, and on coming back to Hercules refuses to take back the burden of the sky upon himself again. In the Mosaic parallel Moses has come within sight of the promised land, or the Hesperides, in the keeping of the monster Amalek. He does not go himself to win the victory but sends Joshua; and whilst the battle is going on Moses takes his stand on the top of a hill and backs up Joshua, not by holding up the heavens for him, as did Hercules, but by holding up his hands; "and his hands were steady until the going down of the sun," and the perpetual battle between the Lord and Amalek was once more won. Jah had once more "spoken by the hand of Moses," as in Egypt.[2] Of course the holding up of the hands, or the heavens either, is only a figure, but the figure surely sets forth the same thing, which thing as myth was the

---

[1] Stevens's *Travels*.   [2] Ex. ix. 35.

common property of both Jews and Ionians, from the Egyptian original of Anhar holding up his hands as supporter of the heaven.

Atlas takes his place again, and in later legend is transformed into or gives his name to a mountain in Libya. So Moses passes away, leaving no trace save the mountain in Moab, in which he was buried, with the mountain for his grave. The name of Atlas, in Egyptian AT-RAS, means the chief (At) or typical supporter of the heaven. RAS, to raise up, has the propped-up heaven for determinative. The lion-gods are those who " do not let the heavens fall."

Also a perfect parallel may be drawn from the Greek and Roman report and the Hebrew Scriptures between Moses and Bacchus. Bacchus, like Moses, was born in Egypt. He was exposed on the Nile in an ark. Orpheus calls Bacchus Mysos, and the Greek Sos renders the Egyptian Shu ; thus Mysos answers to MASHU, as Shu-Anhar, or as Moses. Bacchus was called BIMATER ; he had two mothers—his own and Thyos, his nurse. Moses had his own mother and the daughter of Pharaoh, his nurse. Bacchus, like Moses and Kepheus, was the lawgiver. Bacchus was represented with horns, as was Moses. Bacchus, like Moses, carried the rod which turned into a dragon, and with which he struck water out of the rock. Bacchus covered the Indians with darkness ; Moses the Egyptians. Moses crossed the Red Sea dry-shod ; Bacchus did the same at the river Orontes. A nymph of Bacchus, like Miriam, crossed the Red Sea. Jupiter commands Bacchus to go and destroy an impious people in the Indies, just as Moses is ordered to abolish the abominations of the idolatrous nations. Pan gave to Bacchus a dog as his faithful companion ; in like manner Moses is accompanied by Caleb, the dog. Bacchus warred with and vanquished the giants ; Moses conquered the Anakim. Bacchus is said to have married Zipporah, a name of Venus, one of the seven planets. The priest of Midian had seven daughters ; Moses married one of these, whose name was Zipporah. According to Boyce *On the Gods*,[1] Bacchus was called Jehovah-Nissi ; Moses erected an altar to Jehovah-Nissi. Bacchus was divinely instructed on Mount Nyssa, whence he was named Dionysus.

Now, as before remarked, the Greeks and Hebrews did not derive their mythology and religion from each other. The cult of both was originally Ionian, Yavonian, or Kephonian. The name of the ancient mother, Kefa, is retained in Koivy, a name of the Hellenistic languages. But they derived from one common original in Egypt. Bacchus and Moses are but two other forms of Shu-Anhar. These two lines are equal to each other, because each is equal to a third—the base of a triangle only to be found in Egypt.

Kapi, a name of Shu, modifies on its way to Shu into Khu. Khu means to rule, to govern, and the ruler is the lawgiver ; hence

[1] P. 136.

Kepheus, Kapi, Khu, or Shu, is the lawgiver. This offers one derivation for the name of Bacchus. Khu also means spirit. In the form of Kep the word denotes the mystery of fermentation and fertilization. Bakh (Eg.) means generating, fecundating. Bakh-Khu, then, is the fecundating spirit, personified in Bacchus as lord of the vine, his great symbol. Bakh (Eg.) also means beverage, and SHUT is effervescing wine. Moreover, the name of one of the lion-gods is found to be written with the sign of the winepress, which reads NEMU, the lion-headed Mâtet, whom the present writer considers to be a form of Shu as the punisher of the wicked. The origin and typology of Shu is somewhat obscure. In the calendar inscription at Esneh, Seb (Time) is called the son of Shu. The Two Truths, however, will help us some way. Bacchus is the youthful god of this dual nature. Shu is designated the " *Youthful double force in the circle of Thebes.* Shu is the Dio or dual god, and in the Ritual[1] the exclamation " *O youthful gods! or, two youths of Shu* " appears to refer to his double character. As we have seen, he is the god of the Stately Stand—" *in that name which is thine of Being in thy stately stand,*" or on the standard. One form of the stand or pedestal is the NUSA, and this word in Hebrew denotes the standard. The altar raised by Moses to Jehovah-Nes is called in the margin " the lord my standard."

This NUSA, the stand or pedestal on which the Nile was represented, is the artificial mount answering to the hill called NYSSA. NYS-SA (Eg.) reads literally " out of, behind," and the mount was that of the birthplace in the north, the hinder-part, the thigh out of which Bacchus was born. SHU was the god (Dio) of this Nyssa, as the supporter of the nocturnal heaven ; was himself the NUSA, stand, pedestal, support of the heaven, also typified by the mount. Therefore SHU was the Egyptian DIONYSUS, the prototype of the Bacchus developed or poetized in Greece. Moses and Bacchus were saved in an ark ; and Shu is thus addressed : " *More powerful is thy name than the gods, in that name which is thine of the god dwelling in the divine Sekt.*" The Sekt, or Sekti, is an ark or cabin, very ancient, as its type is that of a double lotus, with a Naos. Moses and Bacchus wore horns. SHU is said to wield the spear to pierce the head of the serpent Nekau (a name of the mischievous being) " *In that name which is thine of god provided with two horns. Thou smitest him who approaches in that name which is thine of smiting double horns.*"[2]

Moses leads up out of Egypt on the way to the land of promise, the land flowing with milk and honey. He bears the magic rod that works the miracles. So does Bacchus. It is said of Shu, " *Thou leadest (to) the upper heaven with thy rod, in that name which is thine of An-har,*" Heaven-bringer.

On his voyage from Icaria to Naxos Dionysus transformed himself

---

[1] Ch. xlvi. 　　　　　　[2] *Mag. Pap.* ii. 7-8.

into a lion, one of the types of Shu. The frenzy of this god is apparently paralleled by a transformation of Shu, to whom it is said, " *Thou didst take the form of a Kaf (monkey), and afterwards of a crazy man.*" [1]

SHU is an Egyptian name of the ass, a Typhonian type degraded in Egypt, but preserved by the Jews, and enshrined in the planisphere. The ass is depicted at the place of beginning and ending of the Egyptian sacred year. On this the young sun-god was to come riding, and as a type of Shu, the ass in that position stands for Sut or for Shu, called the conductor of the sun. Typhon fled from Egypt on the back of an ass, and the ass was stationed in the zodiacal imagery at the initial point of the earliest solar year, where it may be seen close to the vine and the figure of Kepheus the lawgiver in the sign of Leo.

Now in the account of the origin of the Jews given by Tacitus,[2] he observes, "Some say that, in the reign of Isis, the population of Egypt overflowed, and Egypt was relieved by an emigration into neighbouring countries, under the conduct of Hierosolymus and Judah. Many consider them to be the progeny of the Æthiopians, who were impelled by fear and by the hatred manifested against them to change their settlements in the reign of king Kepheus." Kepheus is the lawgiver Shu, and Shu is the Hebrew Moses. Under Shu the Israelites go out of Egypt, where the great mother reigned, that is, the celestial Egypt. Hierosolymus and Judah are a form of the two leaders, like Moses and Joshua, Tisithen and Petiseph, or Moses and Joseph, Danaus and Kadmus, Shu and Anhar, or Shu in his two characters. According to the Egyptian Chæremon the name of Moses, as companion of Joseph, was TISITHEN, when rendered in the Egyptian language. In keeping with the characters of Anhar and Moses as conductors out of Egypt, this name will yield TES, the deep or depth, and TEN, to conduct and drag up out of the TES, as did Anhar with his noose. They were led up by the Ass, say the traditions. The ass found water for them in the desert. Tacitus says the figure of the animal through whose guidance they were enabled to slake their thirst and end their wanderings is consecrated in the sanctuary of their temple.[3] Plutarch speaks of the ass being worshipped by the Jews as the first discoverer of fountains.[4]

Apion tells us that the ass was placed in the holy of holies, and it is declared that when Antiochus Epiphanes went into the sanctuary, after conquering the Jews, he found there a stone statue of a man with a long beard, holding in his hand a book, and sitting on an ass. He took this to be an image of Moses, who built the city, founded the nation, and ordained for these Jews misanthropic and illegal customs.[5]

---

[1] *Mag. Pap.* pp. 8, 9.
[2] *Hist.* lib. 5.
[3] *Hist.* lib. 5.
[4] *Moralia Symp.* lib. iv. Quaest. v.
[5] Diodorus, fragment of lib. 34, preserved by Photius.

The ass was Shu (Eg.), and the figure on it was Shu, called Moses by the Hebrews.

Shu (Eg.) is also a name for the pig, and in the same report Antiochus is said to have offered to the statue of the founder a huge pig and sprinkled the Jews with its blood; he then cooked the flesh, and commanded that their holy books should be defaced and blotted out with the broth, the ever-burning fire extinguished, and the high priest and other Jews be forced to eat the swine's flesh. In doing this he did but make a travesty of most ancient customs with the object of insulting them, by making them eat once more the swine's flesh and drink the broth of abomination.[1] The object of identifying the ass with Shu by name, whether it was his type or only that of Sut, and with Moses, is to note its connection with Bacchus. The ass was sacred to Dionysus. Silenus, a form of Bacchus, rode on the ass, and was said to have been born at Nyssa, the birthplace of Bacchus. In Kircher's *Œdipus* there is a representation of a Græco-Egyptian lamp, on which Silenus is drawn, and he is there mounted on the head of an ass, which is girt about with grapes and vine leaves. It may seem strange to think of Silenus as a form of the Anointed, yet the Anointed was to come eating butter and honey in one account, and in another his eyes were to be red with the blood of the grape. Silenus-like he was to come riding on an ass, which was to be made fast to the vine, the Bacchic type of the fecundating spirit. The Egyptian lamp of Silenus and the ass remind one of the text, "I have ordained a lamp for mine anointed ; upon himself shall his crown flourish." [2] Shu was a lamp or a light (Shu) to the young solar god when he came as the lawgiver in Leo. The ass itself had a dual character, as one of its names Iu (Eg.) denotes. Iu, to come, also means two, twin, double. This is shown by the two asses of the Greeks, placed in the sign of Cancer, following the retrocession of the equinoctial colure from the sign of Leo, or the readjustment of the imagery. The two characters denote the Two Truths, and one illustration of these is afforded in the god BES and the child (Har). BES is the Egyptian Silenus. Silenus always accompanies Bacchus, whom he brought up and instructed ; as Bes stands behind Horus the child ; Bes who is called the "Beast Bes, he who adores his Lord," the child Horus borne on the Lotus. Bes is allied to Silenus by means of the Grape-Bunches at Talmis, where he is represented as Mars, *i.e.* Shu. Silenus is identified with the ass which carried the spirit or mystery of intoxication. BES, like Kep, denotes the passing and transformation of one thing into another, the old one into the young, the blood of the grape into its spirit, flesh quickening into soul. Har the child sustained by BES, and Bacchus supported by Silenus, or borne upon the ass are pictures of the Shiloh described in Genesis,[3] who is to come " binding his foal unto the vine, and his ass's colt unto the choice vine ;

[1] Is. lxv. 4.   [2] Ps. cxxxii. 17, 18.   [3] Ch. xlix. 10.11.

he washed his garments in wine, and his clothes in the blood of the grapes; his eyes red with wine." Here the Shiloh is the solar god who comes, according to the imagery pourtrayed in the planisphere, before Kepheus the Lawgiver departs.

The ass which bore the child was originally feminine, a type of Typhon; Bes is a Typhonian image; there was also a god with the head of a Hippopotamus, conjectured by Wilkinson to have been a form of Bes (Shu). The ass and its foal are found at the end and beginning of the cycle. At first they represented the bringer in the Sabean cult, and in the solar stage the ass was made to bear the solar son, who was personally conducted by Shu, which signifies that it was by means of the lawgiver, Kepheus or Shu, the star Cor-Leonis, that the observers were able to mark the place of the sun in the sign of the lion, where stands the ass and Shu who was the lamp or light of the Anointed as the solar son. AAI, the ass, is pictured in the *Book of the Hades* as a person stretched on the ground hauling at the rope of the sun and drawing himself up by means of it. He has the solar disk on his head, by the sides of which are two ears of an ass.[1] This is the sun-god borne upon the ass, a very rare representation only to be found in the tomb of a Sutite[2] in whose cult Sut had not been altogether superseded by Taht, as the support of Horus. The ass pulling at the rope is also suggestive of the rope carried by Shu to haul the sun along, especially as the ass is also named Shu!

Perhaps the hieroglyphic ass may interpret for us what was uttered by Balaam's when it perceived the angel in the way. The ass (head) signifies No. 30. It is a type of the end of a period, the month, Ark (rekh), or reckoning. Ark denotes encirclings, enclosings, whence cycles of time, an end, a finis. This type is placed in the planisphere just where the year ended, when the dog-star rose and Kepheus was seen under the Lion. The ass was a symbol of Sut or Sabean Baal. He rode the ass at one time, and afterwards wore its head. The ass and Sothis are found together in the sign of Leo. Now for Balaam's parable. Balak is the god Baal. The seven altars built on the top of Pisgah, in the field of Zophim, or the watchers, identify the starry seven, the type of the genitrix and mother of Baal. Balak is the son of Zippor. Balaam belongs to Balak, and am (Eg.) means belonging to. Balaam, the prophet of Baal, rides upon the she-ass of Bar-Typhon, and is called the son of Beor, the equivalent of Bar.

These are representations of the cult of Bar-Typhon opposing the Solarites. An angel is a personified period of repeating. This stands in the way and stops the ass; puts a period or full-stop to the ass ridden by the son of Baal. This ending is first perceived by the ass, hence the ass can go no farther, and Balaam and his Typhonian type are turned back. The parable of Balaam illustrates the

---

[1] *Book of the Hades. Rec. of the Past*, v. x. 130. [2] Seti. 1st.

conversion from the worship of Sut-Typhon, the Baalim, to that of the solar-god Jah-Adonai. This is marked by the rams and bullocks offered up on the altars in Zophim to the Lord. The prophecy corresponds to the parable, " I shall see him, but not now. There shall come a star out of Jacob, and a sceptre shall rise out of Israel, and shall smite the corners of Moab, and destroy all the children of Sheth. Out of Jacob shall come he that shall have dominion."[1] Jacob, as father of the twelve sons, answers to the sun of the twelve signs, the solar zodiac and circle of the sun-god, Adonai, who is to supersede the Sabean Sut. This change did take place, at least as early as the time when the solar year began solstitially with the sun in the lion, or where the lion whelped, and the ass had once brought forth its foal every new year. It is a parable synonymous with the coming out of Egypt, and the escape from Typhon is to be followed by the destruction of the children of Sut. Thus the ass of Balaam is likewise the hieroglyphic of an ending. The kindred " prophecy " of Zechariah, " Rejoice greatly, O daughter of Zion, shout, O daughter of Jerusalem, behold thy King cometh unto thee; he is just, and having salvation; lowly, and riding upon an ass, and upon a colt, the foal of an ass," [2] relates to the same mythical matter as Balaam's, the superseding of the ancient star-god, the ass-headed Sut, by the young solar-god. The prevalent supposition that these prophecies refer to the future events of a personal human history has been and still is the profound delusion of men entirely ignorant of the mythological astronomy and the nature of ancient symbolism. They relate to things that were written and can be read in the heavens:

> Deluded visionaries ! lift your eyes :
> Behold the Truths from which your fables rise :
> These are realities of heavenly birth,
> And ye pursue their shadows on the earth.

Some startling links of continuity are visibly extant in the Coptic calendar of the ancient Egyptian year brought on up to the present time. In the month Misreh (Mesore) [3] the twelfth month of the Coptic year, we find the seventh day of the month is the birthday of Shith (Seth) who is Semitized from the Egyptian Suti whose name, Su or Seb, No. 5 ; ti, 2, identifies itself with the number seven. The 7th Mesore in the sacred year was our 22nd of June, or the time of the summer solstice. The birthday of Sut is thus kept in its true place; the Arabs, however, think it means the Hebrew Seth, which it does in reality, although in a way unknown to them. MESORE means childbirth, the birth of the river and of the child Har (Ar), who was first of all Sut-Har, before the solar Har-pi-Khart. Nine months from this date the Horus of the resurrection was born at the vernal equinox. The Coptic calendar says, " On this day (Mesore 7th) did God send the angel Gabriel, who brought tidings to Joachim concerning our Lady."

[1] Num. xxiv. 17-19.   [2] Zech. ix. 9.   [3] 1878. Alexandria, A. Mourès.

Joachim in some of the traditions is the father of the Virgin Mary. Joachim is a name of Moses; Moses is Shu, who will be identified with Gabriel.   One way or another everything has been brought on.

In Plutarch's *Moralia* Meragenes asserts the identity of Bacchus with the god or a god worshipped by the Hebrews.   Most of the evidence for this he is compelled to suppress, because it is of a kind that could not be uttered except to an initiate in the Bacchic mysteries.   But he points out that the time and mode of celebrating their chief feast in the very midst of the vintage are the same as with the Greeks, and perfectly Bacchic.   He says they sit beneath tents or booths made of vines and ivy, and call the day which precedes the feast the Day of Tabernacles.   Within a few days afterwards they celebrate another feast, not openly but darkly, and dedicated to Bacchus; they carry palm-branches at the feast called KRATEPHORIA, and enter the temple carrying THYRSI.   They have little trumpets, such as the Argives used in their *Bacchanalia*, with which they called upon their gods.   He conjectures that their Sabbaths have some relation to Bacchus, for the Sabbi and Bacchi are the very same, and they make use of that term at the celebration of the mysteries of the god.   He points to the use of the same symbols, as the bells, the brass vessels called the nurses of God, and to the Hina or spotted skin worn by the High-Priest, together with other things which tend to identify the Jewish religion with the Greek worship of Bacchus.[1]   He further asserts that Bacchus is the same god with Adonis.

But, inasmuch as Bacchus is identical with Shu and Moses, he cannot be the same with Adonis, only in bringing on the sonship the types and imagery may be confused.   Sut was the Sabean child of the mother. So was Moses.   Khunsu is the lunar son.   Adonai is the solar son, and Bacchus, the eternal boy, may have passed through three forms of the sonship; hence he was celebrated as the thrice-born.   Some-times the type of the son was changed and the name continued. Kebek, for example, was an ancient star-god, whose name was modified into that of KAK, in the triad of the solar mythos.   In like manner it has to be suggested that a name of the Lion-god, who, in one form, is identified with Nem for the winepress, passed into that of the solar god Num—the star-god of Breath being continued as the sun-god of Breath.

Jamshîd is described by Persian scholars as ascending the chariot or carriage on the new day of Naurîz to succeed the Sabeans and renovate the ancient religion.   Jamshîd is the solar god of the calen-dar in which the day of the new year was at the time of the spring equinox.   In his epoch, we are told, the people increased so fast the earth could not contain them, therefore God commanded the earth to become thrice as large as it was before.   Some maintain that Jam (like the Chinese Yu) ordered channels to be dug into which the

[1] Lib. iv. Quæs. 5.

waters were drained. Others say this had been done by Zû.[1] Zû is probably a form of SHU, who is extant also as the German god ZIU, a name of TIU, the Teutonic Mars, and deity of Tuesday; Shu (or Bes) being the Egyptian Mars, as well as the divinity of Kepheus and *Cor-Leonis*.

The lunar types succeed the older star-gods, and finally the sun succeeds and generally supersedes both, or assumes the precedence and supremacy.

Kepheus (Shu) is king of Æthiopia, that is Kush or Khepsh (Eg.), and it may be the name of Bacchus signifies the Bak or Bekh, the engendered (therefore son) of Kush, for Nyssa also represents the hinder thigh north from which Bacchus was born. Thus, Dionysus, god of the hinder part north, would be repeated in Bacchus, the son of Kush, who went to India, Egyptian Khentu, the south. Moses, not Jah-Adonai, was the Jewish Bacchus, and he stands behind the solar god as his companion and supporter, in the same way that BES stands behind Horus, the child, in the monuments.

"Prince of Æthiopia" was a title of the Repa or heir-apparent to the throne of Ra. Shu (Kepheus) was king of Æthiopia and lord of Nubia. Seb, who was his son, is characterized in the text as the veritable Repa of the gods. The Repa is the returning one, who comes out of Æthiopia, or in the Hebrew mythos, out of Egypt. MASHU, to return, is the name of MASHU, the returner, whence the Moses who not only plays the part of Repa but is also the deliverer in Æthiopia. According to Josephus the young child Moses was adopted and named Mashu by Thermutis.[2] Thermutis, in Egyptian, is TA-UR-MUT, the old great mother, who, as Taur or Thoueris, is the Typhonian genitrix; Kefa of the Great Bear, the Hebrew Jhevah. The serpent, Hefa, is her symbol. She is a form of Kên, the snake goddess, who is the Hebrew Kivan. This old goddess is also queen of the celestial Æthiopia or Khepsh, and Josephus has recorded some particulars concerning Moses in Æthiopia, which have not hitherto received due attention. Moses, he makes out, was a general of the Egyptians, and as such he led an army against the Æthiopians and conquered them. On the way he was infested with a plague of flying serpents; just what the other romance relates of the serpents in the Wilderness. Here again he met the dire difficulty by successful stratagem. He invented baskets, like unto arks, of sedge, and filled them with ibises. The ibis is a stork; it was the symbol of Taht, who was figured ibis-headed. Pliny says the Egyptians invoked the stork against the serpent.[3] Josephus tells us the ibis is a great enemy of the serpent kind. Moses therefore let loose the ibises, as soon as he came to the land which was the breeder of the serpents, and destroyed them. Now Thoueris or Tharvis was the

[1] *Albiruni*, Eng. Tr. pp. 200, 202. [2] *Ant.* ii. 10. [3] *Hist. Nat.* x. 28.

daughter of the Æthiopian king, and when Moses besieged the royal
city of Saba, into which he had driven the king, this accident happened.
She chanced to see Moses as he led his army near the walls, fell in
love with him, and, on condition that she turned traitor to the king,
and delivered the city into its enemy's hands, he consented to marry
her. This she did, and Tharvis or Tharuis became the wife of Moses.[1]
In the Hebrew scripture Moses marries an Æthiope woman. "Miriam
and Aaron spake against Moses because of the Æthiopian woman
whom he had married."[2]

Josephus's story of Moses destroying the serpents and Tharuis
becoming his wife as a result, is the same that Plutarch had heard of
Thoueris and Horus. Thoueris was said to have been the aider and
abettor of Typhon for a time, but she deserted the deity of darkness, and went over to Horus. She was then pursued by a huge
serpent close at her heels ; this was cut in pieces by Horus's men, and
Thoueris joined the side of Horus.

Thoueris and Thermutis are one and the same goddess in Egypt,
who, under the one name, is the foster-mother of Moses and under
the other becomes his wife.

Taurt was transformed or re-typed as Hes-taurt or Cassiopeia, the
lady of the seat and consort of Kepheus. In the Hebrew myth this
traitoress, who yields up the city to Joshua, takes the shape and name
of Rahab. She is called the Zonah, like the lady of Babylon, and
like Thoueris, the concubine (Khennu) of Typhon. As such she is the
head of that line of descent in which Jesse, David, and the Christ were
reckoned ; the primordial mother of the gods, be they Sabean, lunar,
or solar, who was enthroned in heaven at last, as the lady in her
chair, Queen of Æthiopia or Saba, and consort of Kepheus ; whilst
in her primal types of the hippopotamus and the dragon she descended
into hell, and is pourtrayed in the judgment scenes as the devourer
of the wicked, the Rahab of the waters, the dragon of the deep, the
Apophis who wages war eternally with the sun and the souls of the
deceased. The genealogy of Christ is thus perfectly preserved according
to the astronomical allegory. In the beginning was the Typhonian
genitrix, goddess of the north, Khepsh or Æthiopia, variously called
Kefa, Heva, Kivan, Chavvah, Saba, Taurt, Thermutis or Rahab. She
was the mother goddess of Time, which was impersonated by the
star-gods, Shu, Sut, and Seb ; next came the moon-gods—Hes·
Taurt following Taurt—Taht-An following Sut-Anup ; and last of all
the solar- or luni-solar Messiah as Horus, son of Osiris ; Iu-em-hept,
the son of Atum ; and Khunsu, the son of Amen and Maut ; each
of whom was the anointed, the Christ.

The Gemara of Babylon mentions a report of Rahab having become
the wife of Joshua. This is the true tradition which renders the veritable
version of the myth. The story thus correlates with the other sieges

---

[1] *Ant.* B. ii. 10, 2.　　　　　　　　　　　　　[2] Num. xii. 1.

of the Ark-City, which is betrayed by the woman within, as Thoueris betrayed Typhon and followed the conqueror Horus. It is the same story that Josephus relates of Moses and Taruis of Saba, and both belong to the celestial scenery of the north, where Kepheus (Shu) is the consort of Cassiopeia, the Queen of Æthiopia. Rahab, as a Hebrew type-name for Egypt, identifies the traitoress with Khebt or Kush, the earlier Khepsh of the celestial north. Rahab is likewise the harlot, an especial title of the ancient genitrix. Herein is another means of showing that Moses and Joshua were two phases of the same mythical personality as Shu-Anhar or Ma-shu.

In the Egyptian mythos the consort or sister of Shu is Tefnut. She has two characters, one of these is Pekh or Peh, literally the back, rump, hinderpart of the lioness. Tefnut and Pekht or Pekht and Sekht form the double lioness, the twin sisters who gave birth to the sun, as the two mouthpieces or Eyes of Ra. These take the shape of the two midwives in the Hebrew mythos. Also the goddesses in Israel are to be found in the imagery, when they have been suppressed in person. The two lion-goddesses are called the two eyes of the sun; the left eye is said to light the south, the right eye lights the north.[1] The eye was a type of the genitrix, because it reflected the image; AR, the eye, means the reflector. When, in the cuneiform inscriptions, the goddess is called the REFLECTION of the god, the expression reverses the original significance in favour of the male. This is a probable meaning of Sakh (Eg.), to picture and figure, whence the Sakti as the Reflector of the god. The "eye of Horus" is primally the genitrix that reflects the child; hence it is called the "mother of the gods."[2]

For example: when Ra resolved to have his tabernacle and be lifted up as the supreme god, with Shu-Anhar for his son and chief sustainer, the ark, Box or Teb, was committed to the keeping of Shu and Nut. Nut had previously carried Ra herself when the Teb, Tepa, or Tef was the hippopotamus goddess, or the cow. Now Tef denotes the pupil of the eye, the mirror; also the abode, that is the womb, ark, or box, called the Teb, and tabernacle. Tef, the pupil of the eye, was the Reflector, and Tef-nut is Neith, as the reflector or mirror of the god. She was an earlier form of Neith, who carried the tabernacle of Ra; and the eye was a looking-glass before other mirrors were made. The goddess Tefnut, as the eye of Horus the child, passed into the Hebrew symbolism as the mirror-type, called the תבנית (Theba-nith) or Ark of Neith, designated the pattern, likeness, similitude of the tabernacle in which Jah-Adonai had also "resolved to be lifted up." Thebanith is the Hebrew equivalent for Tefnut. This was the mother-mirror. Nut or Night was the reflector of light in her stars, as the dark of the eye (Tef) reflects, and the tabernacle in its most

[1] Hymn to Amen. Boulak.
[2] Granite Altar, Turin. List of Gods, no. 18.

secret parts was the mirror, the reproducer of the image or likeness, the SEE-WITH or SEE-FACE, as the word MA-HER (Eg.), the mirror, means. This See-with was the reflector borne by the women of the temple at the door of the tabernacle, the mirror being a symbol of that which reflected the likeness. The mirrors are called MARAH; this in Egyptian being MAHER[1] (if not Ma-ar). The hand-mirrors were probably the Ankh, filled in with a brass reflector. Ankh is an Egyptian name for a mirror. The Hebrew mirrors are contributed by the women to make the great laver or molten sea. The first mirrors were the heaven above that reflected light, and the water below; and the two sisters who impersonate the two heavens are the eyes of Ra. When the reflector merges into the laver the type is still continued. The Egyptian Laver is a Mer, the mirror is a Maher, and a goddess whose symbol is an eye is named Mer. Mirror, water, and the eye are types of the mother, the reproducer of the image.

The mirror in Japan is held to be the "spirit of woman." It is a symbol of the soul of the sun-goddess, the equivalent therefore of Tefnut as reflector or eye of the sun. The Japanese precious stone, MAGA-TAMA, is also an emblem of the spirit of woman. The Japanese temple of Isa-Naga, or the source symboled by the serpent, contained no image but one vast mirror or symbolic eye. In the temple of Neptune, says Pausanias, they let down a mirror which is suspended and balanced in such a manner that it may not be merged in the fountain with its anterior part, but so that the water may lightly touch its circumference. That was the mirror above and mirror below. After prayer and fumigation they look into the mirror. Whoever looks into the mirror, he says elsewhere, will but see himself obscurely, but the goddess and the throne he will very clearly behold.[2] He further says that he is afraid to disclose the name of Despoina (the lady) to the uninitiated. She was a form of Tes-Neith, the wearer of the red crown.

In the account given by Mackenzie of his visit to the Pagoda at Perwuttum we find the mirror used as a reflector of light, which was flashed into a dark, secret part of the Pagoda, revealing, by means of its coruscations, a silver case in which was set a small oblong roundish *white* stone with dark rings.[3]

The goddess in the Hebrew version is MIRIAM, the sister of Moses. Miriam is the representative of the goddess Meri, one of the Eye-goddesses, who has a dual form. It is said to Amen-Ra, " In rapture is thy mother, the goddess Meru, as thou emittest the irradiation of light and encirclest the world with thy blaze till thou reachest that mountain which is in Akar,"[4] that is till sunset, when he re-enters the hinder part or mouth of the horizon.

Shu is pourtrayed on a pedestal of the god Harsaphes, sustaining the solar bark itself with his uplifted arms. The bark is that of the

[1] Egyptian Saloon, 6689.
[2] *Arcadics.* c. xxxvii.
[3] *As. Res.* 5, 306.
[4] *Mag. Pap.* p. 5. 3, 4.

two heavens, north and south. He is supported on either hand by the two goddesses, MERI-RAS and MERI-MEHI, the dual form of MERI as goddess of the Nile, south and north; Ras is south; Mehi north. The goddesses salute the sun, as do two Cynocephali, the "bards of the sun." A procession of the two Niles, over which the two Meris preside, forms a second picture.[1] The two are but a dual form of one goddess, and their plural name in Hebrew is Miriam. Meri, the Nile-goddess, is called Seker, the Silent; she carries the reed. Seker has a mystical meaning; Ptah, in relation to the feminine phase of Osiris, is likewise called Seker. In another form she carries the solar disk between the cow's horns, like Hathor, and is then the Bearer, Gestator, GREAT Mother.

Miriam in Hebrew means to be fat and stout, from MRA (מרא), to be filled, full and fruitful, and, in an unused form of the word, bellied. So Mehi (Eg.) in Meri-mehi signifies to be full, filled, fulfilled, and the epithet is applied to the cow-goddess as Mehi-urt, the meek fulfiller. This was Meri in the second character, that of gestator, and either the word Miriam represents Meri-Mu—i.e. Meri as mother—or the M is the terminal, which denotes the nature of Miriam as in the twin Meri. The Hebrew AM, for the first form of the Mother of all, the Great Mother, the Queen Mother, the corporeal one, is sufficient to answer for the terminal in the name of Miriam as the Genitrix Meri.

According to the Koran, Miriam, the sister of Moses, was the mother of Jesus. As history, that has no meaning, but it can be utilized as mythology. Miriam, as a form of the Solar Genitrix, would be Mother of the Child (Su) who is Jesus, or Iusu.

In the Arabic Mahometan legends the name of Miriam is Kolthum.[2] Kultum (Arabic) has the meaning of Miriam, to be fat, full, the original of which is to be with child. But Kolthum is also identical with the name of Kartoom, where the blue and white Niles blend and the first swelling is perceived, which denotes the birth of the inundation, the child watched over by the goddess as Meri-ras, and brought forth by Meri-Mehi. The birth is one with the child. KART (Eg.) is the child; UM means to perceive; AM to discover. Khartoom is the place where the child was born and watched over, and Kolthum or Miriam is the perceiver, finder, and bearer of the child.

Meri, the heifer-goddess, is likewise found in מריא, the name of a certain kind of sacred heifer, which was slaughtered for sacrifices and banquets.[3] Some interpreters understand this to be a fatted calf, or fatling. Mer (Eg.) means the cow, and to die; Ia signifies to purify, to whiten. The Meria was slaughtered in front of the ark.[4] The ark of the AAMU was considered vile by the Ammonians and Osirians. The Meria was a type of Meri, the Hathor of the golden calf, and the ark was that of the Aamu, the impure, on account of their primitiveness.

---

[1] Birch, *Eg. Gal.* p. 6.
[3] Is. i. 11. Amos, v. 22.
[2] Weil. *Legends*, 101.
[4] 2 Sam. vi. 13.

The Hebrews continued what the Egyptians had cast out. Meri is the inundation and the goddess of the Nile. This has a mystical aspect, personified in Meri the Silent, who represents another periodic flood, which is repeated in Miriam's being put apart unclean during the woman's week, the time devoted to the mystical inundation. The word צרע (Tserga), rendered leper, as applied to Miriam, and her absence for seven days, is better represented by Serka (Eg.), to be obliterated, to finish; also SERK, the Scorpion, will explain the Hebrew צרעת for leprosy. There is a Rabbinical story of Joseph's coffin, that tells how it floated on the waters when the time for departure had come, and how it was pointed out by an old woman named Miriam, which shows Miriam in the character of the Nile-goddess, the silent watcher still, as when the ark of Moses was left beside the river.

In the etymology of the name of Miriam, in the Midrash to the Song of Songs,[1] the names of the two midwives are given as SHIPHRAH and PUAH; these in the Talmud[2] are identified with Jochebed and Miriam.[3] In the Hebrew, Shiphrah (שפרה) denotes the bright heaven, the upper of the two, the one arched over; the vault above and void below being the two heavens; PUAH (פוה) to breathe, to blow, to utter. This is the Egyptian PEH, the hinder part of the lioness, the bringer-forth personified as PEH-T, PEKH-T or BUTO of the north, the lower heaven. The double lioness reads PEH-PEH or PEHTI, and signifies glory, the double force. Glory, like greatness, was founded upon bigness, being big, gestating. This is the sense of glory found in the Hebrew KABOD. Jochebed's is the sole name compounded with IU (יו). Kabod, like Peh, signifies glory. Pehti is the glory, the double force of Ra, answering to Iu or Ihu, as a divine name.

Iu (Eg.) is not only the name of the young sun-god but it also means double. So read Iu-Kabed is the double glory and the exact equivalent of Peh, duplicated as Peh-peh or Pehti. This then is Jochebed, who equates with SHIPHRAH of the bright heaven, and PEHTI, the glory, the dual lioness. Thus the two midwives are identified by Jewish Rabbis with Jochebed and Miriam, and these again with the two bringers-forth of Ra or of Pharaoh. In the Talmud it is stated that the daughter of Pharaoh who adopted Moses was named BATHIA.[4] Moses became even as a son to BATHIA, the daughter of Pharaoh, as a child belonging rightly to the palace of the Ra. BATHIA is but another spelling of the name of Buto and Peht, the feminine personification of the Peh, Bau, Bahu, or the Void, the primordial Abode and Beth of birth, in the lower heaven of the north, from whence the sun was reborn. PUTA in Sanskrit is the hollow place, the void, or cavity. PUT or PUD is the hell of the childless; FUT, African Balu, hell; BUTO, Fijian, is darkness, place of night. The BUT (Eg.) is the feminine abode; the BED, English, is the uterus;

---

[1] ii. 12.   [2] Bab. tr. Sota, fol. xi. b.
[3] Goldzhier, p. 337. Martineau.   [4] The Talmud, cited by Polano, p. 126.

the PEHT, Hebrew; PUTA, Maori; PATU, Malayalam; BUTAH, Bagu; BHEDA, Sanskrit; BEHUTH, Phœnician. In the African languages, FAT in Fulup; FAD in Filham; FUDI in Soso, are the belly. FUT or AFT (Eg.) is the abode. AFT and FUD in English are the hinder part. The BAITH in Amharic is the little house; BOATH, Toda, conical temple; BOD, Welsh, house; BUTH, Cornish-English; BOOTH, English; BOTHY, Scotch. As feminine personifications, besides BUTO and PEHT, BAHU is an Assyrian name of Gula as goddess of the abode in the under-world. BEUTH is the spouse of Adonis at Biblus. BUTA is a Bakadara divinity, whose type is a stone, the sign of Typhon. PHATE was the Lycian divine genitrix. BUTA-ranga is the Mangaian goddess of the Abyss, and mother of Maui, the Polynesian Ma-Shu.

One of the dual types of the great mother was Venus, the planet, when above or below the horizon; this star was called Zopporah by the Sabeans, and Moses married Zipporah, one of the seven daughters of Jethro. According to the Mythos, Zipporah and Shiphrah are identical. Zipporah, as Venus above the horizon, is the beauty, the brightness, the glory of heaven; one with Jochebed called the mother of Moses, whilst PUAH or BATHIA corresponds to the other consort. The two sister-goddesses of many names, who are the twy-form of the Great Mother, are Zipporah and Miriam, as consorts of Moses. Thoueris or Thermutis was the Great Mother herself, the Goddess of the Great Bear.

It is evident to me that Joshua, the high priest, who stood before the Angel of the Lord with Satan standing at his right hand to resist him, when one Jehovah said unto Satan, "Jehovah rebuke thee, O Satan, even the Jehovah that hath chosen Jerusalem," belongs to the same imagery as that in Jude, where the contention between the angel and Satan is over the body of Moses. The contention here is over the body or person of Joshua, the "brand plucked out of the fire." This may be noted in passing as an illustration of the identity claimed for Moses and Joshua, on the ground of their being the Mau and Shu of Egypt. The transformation of Joshua in this scene is the parallel of the change when Shu, the son of Nun; Shu, the old star-god of the first time, that is the time of Kefa, the Typhonian goddess of the seven stars, is translated to become the son of Ra, Hebrew Jah, the solar god. He had served Typhon (or Satan) before, hence the filthy garments; and Typhon still *claims* him as a servant, and contends for him with the angel, the representative of the time-cycle. Joshua's iniquity is to pass away, and he is to be clothed anew, and be crowned with the Tzniph (צניף); that is, to judge from the Egyptian TES, tie, coil, envelope, and NEB, gold, to have a crown of gold put on his head and become the image of the crowned Kepheus (Shu) in the planisphere. Previous to this change, made visible in the extant imagery, Shu had worn on his head the Khept or hinder-part of the lion, a type of Typhon, the north, the Great Bear, the motherhood. This was his beastly garment, now to be changed by the Lord. Joshua is henceforth to walk in the new ways and keep the new statutes of the sungod ; he and his fellows, who are said to be symbolical men. The branch, the Repa, the young solar divinity, is to be brought forth and placed in charge of Joshua.

The stone with the seven eyes, the seven eyes of the feminine Jehovah, the stone of Typhon, is to be re-engraved by the male god : " I will (now) engrave the engraving thereof." The woman called "WICKEDNESS" with all her symbols is to be cast out. She who had sat in the midst of the Ephah in a certain emblematic figure. This mouth was to be stopped with a weight of lead. The Ephah in Egyptian is the Hept, and the word also signifies the seven, an ark, a shrine, a measure. The Ephah was the image of the iniquitous through all the earth, because it was the feminine type.

A new temple is to be built on a fresh foundation. The ancient dwelling of divinity in the north is to be superseded ; the great mount is to become the plain. The stone is to be laid at the corner, for this foundation is that of the solar zodiac. The seven stars are to be converted into the seven lamps of the Son, as in the book of Revelation. In the Book of Enoch where the ending of a time and a new beginning are represented by the killing of the sheep, one being destroyed by the shepherds every day, each in his season and according to his number, the books are made up by the accountant, and delivered over to the Lord of the sheep, the Ancient of Days, who reads, seals and deposits them. The end is also figured as the destruction of the house or celestial temple ; and " behold three of the sheep departed, arrived, went in and began building all which was fallen down of that house." These three are identified by Laurence with the Zerubbabel, Joshua, and Nehemiah of the Hebrew story ; but they belong nevertheless to the astronomical allegory as re-builders of the temple of time in the heavens. This new temple is identical with the tabernacle created by Ra, in which he resolves to " be lifted up." The two great supports of Ra are Shu and Taht, his solar and lunar anointed ones, his representatives in the inferior sky by night ; these appear as the two supports of the lamp of light, the two anointed ones who stand by the Lord of the whole earth.

In the hymn to Shu it is said the worship of the mortals reached Ra through the intermediation of Shu, son of Ra, lord of truths, and the precise language used is this, " *People present him with their gifts through his own hands;*" Shu being the hands of the god Ra. So the worship of Jah-Adonai reaches him through the intermediation of Moses, who is the hand of the God who is said to speak by Moses, his hand.[1] In the allegory according to Zechariah, Joshua takes the place of Moses and Shu.

There is also a bringing forth of the son (the branch) in the Egyptian text. The aged sun-god says to Seb (time) " *I cannot preserve*

[1] Ex. ix. 35.

myself because of my old age; *I send* (the charge of the serpents or cycles of time) *to thy son Osiris.*" He establishes the solar sonship in the new tabernacle of time.

Taht was created by Ra in this new adjustment, as his abode and luminary, in the inferior sky ; a beautiful light to show or expose to view the evil enemy. "*Thou art my abode, the god of my abode ; behold thou shalt be called Taht, the abode of Ra, and there arose the ibis.* (The stork, or Chasidah, in Hebrew.) *I shall give thee to raise thy hand in the presence of the gods, and there arose the two wings of the ibis of Taht.*" "*I shall give thee to embrace the two parts of the sky, the south and the north,*" and "*there arose the moon-crescent of Taht,*" and the Cynocephalus. These were the two types of the Returner. "*Thou art under my dominion,*" says Ra to Taht. "*All eyes are upon thee, and all men worship thee as a god.*" This is said at the making of the new covenant, to Taht, who is the guardian and scribe of the inhabitants in the northern region.

And of the Hebrew Taht it is written, "I will make an everlasting covenant with you, even the sure mercies of David. Behold I have given him for a witness to the people, a leader and a commander to the people."[1] The word translated mercies has a form which signifies to bend, curve, turn round, whence the name of the Chasidah or stork, the ibis of Taht and type of the crescent moon, the sure returner.

Chasid has various meanings. The same word rendered "mercies" of David is used for a "very wicked thing,"[2] where it represents the Egyptian KHEST, to be foul and vile ; the bending, turning, deflecting of CHASID, and the CHASIDAH, being applied to an immoral action. But the fundamental sense is to be found in the Kasid, the returning one, with the moon for the type of renewal, from KHES (Eg.) to return, to found a road, to construct ; whence KHESF, to return and ascend in opposition to the opposing force, as did the new moon. The Khest (Eg.) is an established district. The Khesm was the holy of holies ; a variant of Skhem. The same covenant was made with David as with Taht, the sure returner and establisher of light.

Again, "They shall serve the Lord their God, and David their king, whom I will raise up unto them."[3] "In that day . . . . the House of David (shall be) as God, as the angel of the Lord before them."[4] "Afterwards shall the children of Israel return and seek the Lord their God and David their king."[5] "And David my servant shall be king over them, and they all shall have one shepherd."[6] "And I will set up one shepherd over them, and he shall feed them, my servant David."[7] The Son that is born of a virgin, the Prince of Peace, sits on the throne of David.[8] Like Osiris, he is at once the everlasting Father and the Repa or Prince of Peace, who, as Horus, is established in the seat of the father by the lunar god Taht, when

[1] Is. lv. 3, 4.   [2] Lev. xx. 17.   [3] Jer. xxx. 9.   [4] Zech. xii. 8.
[5] Hosea, iii. 5.   [6] Ezek. xxxvii. 24.   [7] Ezek. xxxiv. 23.   [8] Is. ix. 7.

the Tat was set up in Tattu, the region of establishing. Says the Ritual,[1] "*Setting up the Tat in Tattu means the shoulder of Horus who dwells in Skhem*," *i.e. the secret shrine;* the son in the Hebrew version is to bear the government " upon his shoulder." In " CHASID " shall the throne be established, and he shall sit upon it in truth in the tabernacle of David."[2] It is founded on the sure returnings of the lunar light, the abode of Ra by night. This Tabernacle had been placed in Jerusalem, the sacred city, the Mount of Peace, the mother-mount where the son was yearly born, as Solomon, or Iusu, or Khunsu, the good peace, the soli-lunar child of Easter-tide, the child therefore of David, so far as he represented the moon-god. The establishment of the throne of the young solar god is intrusted to the lunar god to this day. Taht or David still keeps the covenant, and the full moon of Easter yet determines the resurrection of the Christ. Shu, the star-god, and Taht, the moon-god, were the two faithful witnesses of Ra, the sun-god, whose creation was the latest in heaven, as Kepheus and the new moon ; his supporters and representatives by night in the conflict with darkness, and all its hidden powers ; and these are the originals of Mashu (Moses) and David in the Hebrew form of the celestial allegory. In the new temple built by Zerubbabel, in which Shu (Joshua) was to serve the solar god, these were the two anointed ones of the two gold pipes which fed the sevenfold lamp of light ; the two anointed ones that stand by the solar son as the Lord of the whole earth, who is identified with the number seven as Sevek-Ra, on the Typhonian line of descent, and on the side of the Mother who was now to be cast out as " WICKEDNESS."

These "two witnesses" appear as the two prophesiers in the Book of Revelation.[3] " These are the two olive-trees, and the two candlesticks standing before the God of the whole earth,"—the two lamps of light carried by Taht, the moon-god, and Shu, the star-god, as the witnesses or prophesiers of Ra. These two are present at the measuring for the new temple of the Iu or Ao the Son, the Egyptian Jesus, which is that of the twelve gates, twelve angels, and twelve tribes ; the matter of which is as ancient as the zodiac of twelve signs, and the casting out of the woman here personified as the great harlot, the Scarlet Typhon, called Mystery (Kep, one of her names, means Mystery), the Mother of Harlots, who rode on the beast with SEVEN HEADS. Lastly, the two witnesses to the true, that is solar light, appear on the Mount of Transfiguration as Moses and Elias, the fellow-figures to Shu and Taht in the Egyptian Mythos.

[1] Ch. xviii.   [2] Is. xvi. 5.   .   [3] Ch. xi. 3, 4.

SECTION XVII.

AN EGYPTIAN DYNASTY OF HEBREW DEITIES IDENTIFIED FROM THE MONUMENTS.

WE have seen that there was an ancient Egyptian Chronicle accredited with containing the records of over 36,000 years. The same record is recognised in another way by the tradition of the 36,500 books assigned to Hermes. Nor is there the slightest reason to doubt that the Egyptians may have kept their reckonings during that vast period of time, the whole of which is fully required to account for other actual phenomena, and no signs of numerical exaggeration have ever been detected on the monuments. The tattered condition of the Turin papyrus cannot quite obscure the fact that it contained a chronological system corresponding to that asserted by the traditions of the STELÆ and the books of Taht.

There is a statement quoted by Bunsen [1] from John Malalas (about 900 A.D.), who is followed by Cedrenus (about 1,050), and by a subsequent continuer of the Chronicon Paschale, to the effect that the " Giant Nabrod " (Nimrod), the son of Kush the Æthiopian, of the race of Ham, built Babylon. Chronus ruled over Syria and Persia, the son of a certain Uranus, who reigned fifty-six years. His wife's name was Semiramis. He was succeeded by Ninus, the father of Zoroaster; after whom came Thuras, then ARES and BAAL, to whom the first STELÆ were dedicated. The ARES and BAAL here connected with the first stelæ are Shu and Sut in Egypt. Ares is Mars, and the earliest Baal, the son, is Bar-Sutekh; and the Baal of the first STELÆ, as Sut, is one with the Hebrew SETH, to whom the astronomical pillars are ascribed by Josephus. Certain stelæ are also referred to as the pillars of AKIKARUS, called the prophet of Babylon (or the Bosphorus), whose wisdom was said to have been stolen by Democritus, and on which a treatise was composed by Theophrastus. In Egyptian KHEKHA signifies the numbers and reckonings, and is a name for the stone of memorial; RU denotes the graver of the stone; Rut is to engrave, which suggests a meaning for the name of an erector of the

[1] *Egypt's Place*, v. i. p. 229.

stelæ, as Akikarus. Sut and Shu (Baal and Mars), to whom the earliest pillars were dedicated, are the two primordial recorders in the Egyptian mythology, and both are earlier than Taht, Sut being the predecessor of Taht.[1] Herodotus calls Kepheus the "Son of Belus,"[2] and as the successor to Bar-Sut, the earliest Baal or Bel, this is the true sequence and order of descent.

By aid of the hymn to the god Shu we learn that Shu was also the divine scribe, whose works were included in the records of Taht, lord of Sesen, and treasured up in the royal palace of On. The bringing on of Shu the Star-God as a scribe or recorder into the Lunar Mythos is shown by the AAN, monkey (which was a type of Shu), becoming the co-scribe with Taht.

The stelæ of Baal (Sut) would be records of Sothis, the Dog-star, the star of Sut, the first announcer of celestial time in relation to the Great Bear and the inundation in Egypt. Shu, in his twofold character, has been sufficiently identified with the Moses and Joshua of the Hebrew writings. Sut is Seth, to whom the pillars and stelæ are attributed.

In the fifth chapter of Genesis the seven who preceded Seth are summed up in Adam, the biune parent. "Male and female created he them, and called their name Adam."[3] Adam is the sole predecessor of Seth in one version of the mythos. We might just as well say Eve or Chavvah, for the first producer in mythology is the Genitrix. But Adam will serve, as in the Egyptian Ritual Atum appears as a female, designated the "mother-goddess of Time."[4]

The mother-goddess of time is the genitrix of all the gods, for these have no other phenomenal origin than the cycles of time. The earliest name of Seb (Time) is Keb or Kheb, who in the feminine or dual form is Khebti, and whose place of manifestation was the celestial Khebt (Egypt), or earlier Khepsh (Kûsh), the Æthiopia of the North, and region of the Bear.

The first Time observed and registered was Sut-Typhonian; its types were the Great Bear and the Dog-star. In this time the year began with the rising of Sothis, and the first four cardinal points of the solstices and equinoxes were in the Lion, the Scorpion, Waterman, and Bull; this year and its imagery remaining fixed in the planisphere for ever. Whatsoever was changed and added, the origines are never lost or entirely superseded; the earliest types were stereotyped, and can still be found in heaven above and on the earth below. The bear and dog (jackal, wolf, fox or coyote), the bull, lion, bird, and human figure of the four genii are among the extant witnesses of that early time which began with the genitrix and Sut, her son, to be followed by Shu and the genii of the four corners. Sut and the goddess of the seven stars were the earliest Smen, the eight, of whom Taht was made the lord, when he had superseded Sut. The records of this first time,

---

[1] *Rit.* ch. xlii.   [2] B. 7, 61.   [3] v. ii.   [4] Ch. clxv.

kept on the stelæ or pillars are those of Sut or Seth, who follows the seven patriarchs, and whose son was the Anosh or manifester, identified with the Anush or wolf-hound type of Sut.

Sut was the announcer of the Great Bear cycle, when the heaven was lower and upper, as north and south before the time of the four corners, (the revolution of the Great Bear being observed from near the equator wholly on the north side of the heavens), the records of which were the stones in the Karuadic land. The star-god Shu was an indicator of the solstices as Kepheus in the Waterman, and Regulus in the Lion, and therefore belongs to the figure of the first four quarters.

A sun-and-sirius year also probably began from this starting point; its representative image being Sut-Horus. Sut, in relation to Har, was assigned the earth, and Har the heaven; Sut represented the first of the two truths, the opening one; Har the second. This position was continued in the typology of the Ritual. In the circle of Smen, the place of preparation, it is said of the soul passing through the purgatorial trials, "divine Horus purifies thee; the god Sut does so in turn."[1] He was the purifier in one sense, corresponding to the feminine period of purification. The first starry type of Har in relation to Sut was probably the Wolf, the Anush, which rose in the evening when the Sun and Moon were reunited in the sign of the vernal equinox. Diodorus describes the Dog as being the type of Sut, and the Wolf as the type of MAKEDO; and MAKAI, in the Magic Papyrus, is called the son of Sut, but under the crocodile type. The Dog and Wolf correspond to a dual form of Sut-Anubis. The passage of the sun's entrance into the sign of the Bull was marked by the rising of the Wolf; and Sut (dog) and Makedo (wolf) are called (by Diodorus) the two sons of Osiris. The present point, however, is the identification of Shu (Ares) and Sut (Baal), with the stelæ of the Karuadic land existing before the flood of Noah. Shu, as a star-god, is so old in Egypt that he is called "greater and more ancient than the gods." He was the son of Nun, the Bringer, before Taht became the reckoner and recorder of time, and in the re-adjustment of the myth, according to the solar reckoning, Shu is the adopted son of Ra. In this sense Shu is said to be selected by Ra as his son, previous to his own birth,[2] which is exactly what occurs in Exodus. The sun-god Jah is not born or manifested in Israel until his appearance to Moses in the bush of flame,[3] when he announces himself by name as Jah and EYAH ASHER Jah, the hitherto unknown god.

Shu made for Ra "hereditary titles which are in the writings of the lord of Sesen," that is in the Hermean books of Taht,[4] and here, apparently, we strike upon the connection of Moses with the Psalms of David or Taht.

[1] Ch. xvii.   [2] *Mag. Pap.* i. 2.   [3] Ex. iii.
[4] *Magic Papyrus*, i. 6 and 7.

In addition to the five books the Jews assign eleven of the Psalms (xc. to c.) to Moses. Also there are traditions of the book of Job having been written by Moses, the Hebrew Ma-Shu. Thus the Hebrews have the writings of Shu (Moses) mixed with those of Taht (David), and Shu invented hereditary titles for Ra. Jah is one of the titles of the Hebrew sun-god, found especially in the Psalms. Now the earliest books of Shu, as we have seen, were the stelæ, the stone tablets of the oldest chronology.

Moses being identified as the Egyptian god Shu of the Two Truths, represented by the two stone tablets on which the ten commandments were written, we have in these a survival of the stone stelæ of Shu. Moses is the typical author of the Pentateuch; he is credited with writing the second edition of the ten commandments,[1] and the register of the stations in the wilderness.[2] Moses is Shu; Shu or Su, in the later modification, means number five, and the five books are those of Shu. Su (Shu) for five is the final development of Kafi, the hand, and Kafi is a name of Shu, who, in his dual character, constituted the two hands of Ra, the sun-god, as his supporter and the uplifter of the nocturnal heaven. Taht superseded Shu as well as Sut, and this is reflected in Tut (or Tu) for the number five and a name of the hand. Moses is emphatically the hand of Jah-Adonai, and the "Hand upon the throne of Jah" in the Margin[3] has an apparent relation to Moses or Shu, the hand of the Lord with which he commanded Israel.[4]

In the Egyptian development of the mythology we see Shu discrowning himself as it were to decorate the later sun-god. Horus says to his father Osiris, "Thou receivest the head-dress of the two lion-gods." "The lion-gods supply his head-dress." "The lion-gods have given to me a head-attire. He has given to me his locks, he has placed his head and his neck with his great power upon me," says the Osirian.[5] Osiris was crowned with the feathers by the lion-gods as the universal lord when the solar cult superseded the Sabean.

The change from Shu, the star-god, to Shu-Si-Ra, which occurs in the creation by Ra, is marked when Moses came down from the mount and wrote all the words of the Lord, and erected an altar and twelve pillars at the foot of the mountain. These represent the solar zodiac, and here the twelve stones take the place of the matzebah, or pillar, of an earlier cult, the hieroglyphic of Sut. In the Hebrew mythology Moses reveals the solar god to Israel by the name of Jah, the El-Shadai of the five books. When the new god is elected for worship under the leadership of Joshua and a covenant is made, then "Joshua wrote these words in the book of the law of God."[6] He plays the same part here as Moses in the other books, of whom it is said, "It came to pass when Moses had made an end of writing the words

---

[1] Ex. xxxiv. 28.   [2] Num. xxxiii. 2.   [3] Ex. xvii. 16.
[4] Num. xv. 23.   [5] *Rit.* ch. lxxviii.   [6] Ch. xxiv. 26.

of this law in a book, until they were finished." [1]   Joshua then is a writer of the book of the law, in a scripture indefinitely older in form and substance than the book of Deuteronomy.   Now as the name of Joshua was altered in order that the name of the male god Jah, made known by Moses, might be compounded with that of Shu or Shva ; and as Jah-Adonai is the sun-god Ra who adopted Shu as his son in the solar *régime*, it follows that Jah-Shua is the Hebrew equivalent of Shu-si-Ra, and the original Oshea becomes the son of Adonai-Jah, just as the pre-solar god Shu in the creation by Ra becomes the son of Ra, whereas previously he was, like Joshua, the son of Nun.   Shu, in the character of Anhar, is the elevator of heaven, the bringer, the one who returns, brings back again, countervails, compels, forces a way, raises, restores, equalizes, and saves.   All that can be expressed by the Hebrew שוא, as uplifting, self-sufficing, enough in oneself ; שוה, to countervail and equalize ; שוב, which denotes returning, bringing back, and restoring, is concentrated in Anhar, the typical returner and bringer ; and as SHVA or SHUA indicates this character of the uplifting and self-sufficing one, who follows Moses as the servant of Jah, it is a fair inference that the full name of יהושע means the supporter, helper, and upholder of the god Jah, proclaimed by Moses. Hitherto it has not been known that Jah needed help, and so the name has been rendered, "Jah is help," but in the original myth Ra adopts Shu as his son because he requires support, and his own father Nun tells Shu to become the lifter-up of the sun-god.

Joshua does not appear in the book of Exodus, in which Moses is identified with Shu in his first character of Mashu, until the period of " permutation " or transformation, when Anhar the bringer takes the place of Shu, the up-lifter of heaven.   Also the change of Oshea's name to Joshua occurs in Numbers,[2] at the point where Joshua takes up the leadership for the land of promise, or is sent forth in search and discovers the intercepting Anakim.

Shu, the god of two names, is called the double deity in his name of "young-elder," in his name of "double-abode" of Ra, in his name of the youthful "double force" in the circle of Thebes.   This duality is shown by the change from the leadership of Moses to that of Joshua, and also by the two names of Oshea and Joshua.   In the passage respecting the hereditary titles of Ra, Taht, the lord of Sesen, is called the scribe of the king Ra-Har-Makhu, and the writings are said to be engraved in script, under the feet of the god, in the royal palace of On, to be transmitted from generation to generation. In the exact words of the hymn, as rendered by M. Chabas and Dr. Birch,[3] the "*substance of Shu is blended with that of Ra,*" which is exactly what takes place in the change of Oshea's name into Joshua, in which Shu is blended, as explained, with Jah. It is then said of Shu, "*He made for him* (the god Ra) *hereditary titles, which are in the writings of the*

[1] Deut. xxxi. 24.   [2] xiii. 16.   [3] *Records of the Past,* x. 137.

lord of Sesen, the scribe of the king Har-Makhu, in the palace of On, consigned, performed, engraved in script, under the feet of Ra-Har-Makhu, and he transmitted it (the scripture) *to the son of his son for centuries and eternity.*" Here then we find the Egyptian sacred scriptures ascribed to Shu (Moses) and Taht (David), deposited in the great temple of On, to be transmitted from generation to generation for ever.

The records of Sut, transferred from the stelæ, are not mentioned, as Sut had suffered his degradation and casting out, but these were brought on by Shu and Taht. When the sacred books were assigned to Taht, hieroglyphic writing had been invented. He is the earliest divine scribe as the penman of the gods, and his consort Sefekh is styled mistress of the writings. Previously the burin and the stelæ of the graver had been the chief means of memorial, and the bringing on of the stone records of the past from the stelæ of Sut and Shu set up in the Karuadic land, and their transcription into the hieroglyphics of Taht can be traced through the fragment from Manetho. These, according to his own account, he copied from the inscriptions which were engraved in the sacred dialect and hieroglyphic characters upon the columns set up in the Siriadic land by the first Hermes (*i.e.* Sut), who was earlier than Shu and Taht, and, after the flood, were translated from the sacred dialect in hieroglyphic characters, and committed to writing in books (papyri) and deposited by Agathodæmon (Num), the son of the second Hermes (Shu), the father of Taht, in the penetralia of the temples of Egypt. The three Tahts are traceable as the Sabean Sut and Shu (Baal and Ares), and the lunar god, who, being the third, and superseding the previous two announcers, was knowingly called Hermes-Trismegistus by the Egyptian gnostics. Agathodæmon, or Num, apparently adds a fourth to the divine scribes or registrars, and there is a tradition that Taht drew up commentaries from Nuh, or Num. This is alluded to in the fragment of the Hermean writings entitled Κόρη χόσμου,[1] in which the virgin mother says to her son, " Listen, my son Horus, for I teach thee a mystery. Our forefather Kamephe possesses it from Hermes, who writes the account of all things, and I received it from the ancient Kamephe when he admitted me to be initiated by BLACK.[2] Receive it from me in thy turn, oh, wonderful and illustrious child." The god here called Kamephe is the god of breath, and therefore the name signified is KHNEPH, the Egyptian Nu, or Num. The Hermes, who preceded Num, is Sut or Hermanubis, not Taht, as Taht is the son of Num. The first god of breath was Shu, and the leopard skin is Num, a sign, like the winepress, of the lion-god; Shu was the earlier Num (or Nef), whereas the later Num-Ra was a sun-god. The three bringers-on of the Records were Sut, Shu (Num),

---

[1] *Hermès Trismégiste*, par L. Ménard, Livre iii. 177.
[2] BLACK, rendered ATRAMENTUM, by Canter, or Initiation by Writing, possibly an allusion to the Veil of Isis.

and Taht, the star and lunar gods, before solar time began. The Kabalist doctrine, which they term the Mystery of IBBUR or transmigration of souls, is a form of the Egyptian KHEPR, to transform, change, be re-typed or transfigured as Khepr the Beetle transmigrated into his own son. Speaking of this transformation, Rabbi Menasseh says some among the Kabalists affirm according to the doctrine of Ibbur, that the soul of Seth, being pure and unspotted, passed into Moses to inspire him for the delivery of the law, and the soul of Moses passed into the soul of Samuel through the Ibbur.[1] This is identical with Sut, the Announcer, being followed and superseded by Shu as the law-giver and the two star-gods by the lunar Logos, the divine scribe, Taht; and the solar child, one of whose names, Sem-p-Khart, is equivalent to Samuel, as Sem, the son. Seth, Moses, Samuel, and David form the Hebrew parallel to Sut, Shu, Horus, and Taht. The gathered result in the Records of Sut, Shu, and Taht was deposited at ON as the Hermean books.

According to the Hebrew story it was at ON that Pharaoh gave Asenath the daughter of Potipherah, priest of On, to Joseph as his wife, when he was "thirty years of age," and "he went out over the land of Egypt."[2] Brugsch-Bey has referred to the fact that in ANNU, the ON of the Bible, there existed from very early times a celebrated temple of the sun-god Atum, or Tum, a particular local form of Ra,[3] and his wife the goddess Hathor-Iusāas, to which the Pharaohs were wont to make pilgrimages according to ancient custom to fulfil the directions for the royal consecration in the great house of the god.[4]

Before considering this local northern cult of Atum-Iusāas and their son Iu-em-hept, the Jesus of the Apocrypha, it will be necessary to speak of the god Atum, or Tum as he is generally called, who has already been identified with the deity of the Hebrew Thummin, and the British Tom Thumb. His familiar name of Tum is repeated as an epithet of the Hebrew deity, who is called חם (Thum), a perfect, pure one, in the tenth Psalm. Tum (Eg.) means to complete and perfect in a total of two halves. This is identical with Kak (Akkadian), Koko (Fin), Kokk (Esthonian), COKE (Lap), to complete, and KAK is the form taken by Tum as the completer and finisher of the cycle. In Kak we shall find the Hebrew Jach.

Genealogically Tum is said to be the son of Ptah and Pasht. Also he is called Ra in his first sovereignty. The Ra sun was later than the Har sun. Ra denotes the Rek, the sun by which time was reckoned in the solar year. Ptah was the establisher of that year, or the four corners on which it was founded. Atum is the first

[1] *Nishmath Chajim.* f. 159, c. ii.   [2] Gen. xli. 45, 46.
[3] He was not merely that. Atum was "Ra in his *first* Sovereignty," on a sarcophagus of the time of Amenemha. See the 17th chapter of the *Ritual* for commentary.
[4] *History of Egypt*, vol. i. p. 128. Eng. Tr.

form of the sun of what may be termed the equinoctial year, hence
he wears the equinoctial crown.

The usual double crown of the gods, and always of the kings
of Egypt, is the white and red crown, placed the one within the
other, to represent the upper and lower of the two heavens, and
the two truths of mystic meaning. Atum is the only deity who
wears a double crown, having the one at the side of the other instead
of the two within each other. This double crown is equinoctial,
the other is solstitial. The two different symbols belong to the
equinoctial and solstitial beginnings of the year.

Atum represents Ra in the reckoning by solar time which followed
the lunar and sidereal time. In this way he may be called the son of
Ptah and Pasht, the Egyptian goddess of Pasche or Easter, whose
seat of the double lioness was at the place of the vernal equinox.
Tum is a visible connecting link between the sonship and fatherhood.
He is a form of Har-Makhu, the sun of the double horizon, which
was solstitial at first and afterwards equinoctial, and, as Har-Makhu,
he brings on the name of the son, Har.

Atum was the earlier Aten, Adon, or Tammuz, the son considered
as the child of the mother.

In the stele of the Excommunication Atum is recognized in his
type of the Hut, the double-winged disk of Hu, who is Atum in the
upper heaven, as the "duplicate of Aten," usually called the deity of
the solar disk. But whereas the Aten was limited to the sonship and
to the Har-sun, Atum was developed in one cult into the divine
father and the representative of Ra, as the generator.

In the "PERI-EN-HRU," or Coming forth with (the) day, Atum is
addressed as the "Father of the gods."[1] He is hailed as the creator,
God, the master of being, or visible existence. "*In thy following is
the reserved soul, the engendered of the gods who provide him (it) with
shapes. Inexplicable is the Genesis. It is the greatest of secrets. Thou
art the good peace of the Osiris, oh Creator! Father of the gods,
incorruptible.*"[2]

In the Egyptian gospel[3] the souls call Atum their father. In the
"Chapter of making the change into the oldest of the chiefs," *i.e.*
Atum, the deceased says, "*I am Tum, maker of the heaven, creator
of beings* (which means rendering visible), *coming forth from the
world, making all the generations of existences, giving birth to the gods,
creating himself, Lord of Life supplying the gods.*"[4]

In short, the Egyptian Atum, as the father and creator, is the
divine Adam who appears on earth as the human progenitor, in the
Hebrew Genesis.[5] In one form then Atum is of the earth, earthy.

---

[1] *Rit*. ch. xv. Birch.   [2] *Ib*.   [3] *Rit*. ch. xvii.   [4] *Rit*. ch. lxxix.
[5] TUM (Eg.) denotes the race of human beings, mankind, as the *created* people;
the word is written like the name of TUM or ATUM the Egyptian Adam. The
race of Atum are the created race. Tum has an earlier form in RUTEM for the

It is in the earth as the lower world that the souls are embodied. Even the creation of the woman from the man is known to the mystery of SEM-SEM. In some versions of the Ritual,[1] Ra says, "*When the circumference of darkness was opened I was as one among you* (the gods). *I know how the woman was made from the man.*"

In Jewish traditions the 91st Psalm is assigned to ADAM, and if for Adam we read Atum, we shall recover the veritable El-Shadai as the solar son of the ancient genitrix Shadai, the suckler; he who, as Jah, is identical with Hak and Kak, the earlier Kebek, the Typhonian form of the sun of night, who was brought on as Atum, the Hebrew Adam, to whom the psalm was ascribed. Also the Rabbins have retained much mythic matter, which was rejected when the Hebrew scriptures were selected from such sacred writings treasured up in the temple as the "Book of Jasher" and the "Book of the Wars of the Lord," and those traditions and dark sayings commanded to be transmitted from father to son.[2] To them we are indebted for a further identification of the Egyptian Atum as the Hebrew Adam, in their statement that Adam was originally green![3] Green is one of the colours in which Atum was pourtrayed. Champollion copied from a mummy-lid a picture of Atum as the green god. Green was emblematic of the invisible world out of which life sprang in the green leaf; the flesh of Ptah was also painted of this hue.

Atum is intimately connected with the lion-gods, here represented by Sut and Horus who establish a particular link between Sut and Atum.

"*Oh, Tum! oh, Tum! coming forth from the great place within the celestial abyss lighted by the lion-gods.*"[4]

"*Tum has built thy house, the twin lion-gods have founded thy abode.*"[5]

One title of Atum is Nefer, a word of many meanings, and as Nef is breath, surely the Nefer must include the meaning of the breather or the breathed. Nefer-Tum is the youthful, the newly-breathed form of the god. Atum is depicted with a lotus on his head, the image of reproduction and of life breathing out of the waters. "I have been emaned from his nostril," says the young Horus of his father, and he

---

men.[1] M. Maspero (Æthiopian Inscrip. of King Nastosenen) looks on the t in this word as an inserted dental, and considers the form REM to be the root. But the ideographs precede the phonetics, and with some signs, if not with all the phonetics, Ru is an earlier Rut. By omitting the t from Rutem the deposit is REMA, for the natives. The Rutem are the original created race, and the tri-literal form is first. The name of this primordial race which is earlier than that of the worn-down TUM or ATUM is extant, in the Polynesian language of the ROTUMA. In the Maori, TAMA signifies the eldest son, and TIMATA means to begin.

[1] Ch. cxv.   [2] Ps. lxxviii.   [3] Bartolocci, *Bib. Rabbinica*, p. 350.
[4] *Rit.* ch. iii.   [5] Ch. xvii.

[1] *Bib. Arch.* vol. iv. pt. 2. p. 218.

is called the " living soul (that is breath) of Atum." Nef-ru will read " breath of the mouth," and the Nefer ideograph, a musical instrument, is corroborative. There was a form of the Nefer earlier than the Viol, as Hor-Apollo[1] calls it—the heart of a man suspended by the *windpipe*, signifying the mouth of a good man. The title of Nefer-hept, rendered " the good peace," may also mean " the breather of peace." There is a description in John's Gospel[2] which is related to this subject. The risen Christ comes into the midst of the disciples, " the doors being shut," and says, " Peace unto you." And when he had said this he BREATHED, and said, " Receive ye the Holy Ghost." That is a picture of the Nefer-hept, whether as Atum or Khunsu. Nefer also signifies to bless, and here the blessing is breathed as " peace." In the chapter of " How a person receives the breath in Hades," the deceased cries. " *Oh, Tum! give me the delicious breath of thy nostril,*"[3] the breath of renewed life. The Festival of Tum is the festival of passing the soul to the body. " *My father Tum did it for me. He placed my house above the earth: there are corn and barley in it. I made in it the festival of passing the soul to my body,*"[4] the soul being the breath.

Atum supplied the breath of those to be, and reproduced the image of breathing life, he himself being that breathing image of visible existence in the renewed form of Nefer-Tum, the IU-SU. The proof that the word Nefer has to do with the breath is furnished by the lily-lotus of Nefer-Atum. This lily is borne on his head, or his head appears emerging from the lily, which is mystically called the " *guardian of the nostrils of the sun and the nose of Athor.*" The lily, the symbol of Tum and Athor breathing out of the waters, is the type of Tum, who, in the " Stele of Excommunication," is designated the " *giver of breath to all nostrils.*"

The doctrine of Atum, the breather of souls, with Nefer-Atum as a form of the breathed, the continuer (nefer) of Atum, furnished the myth of the creation of Adam, in the Hebrew Genesis, of whom it is written in the English version, " The Lord God formed man (of) the dust of the ground, and breathed into his nostrils the breath of life, and man became a living soul."

Atum appears in the Ritual as a male triad in one person. It is said, in the 17th chapter, the gods, Hu and Ka, are " *attached to the generation of the sun, and are followers of their father Tum daily.*" That is Atum, the god of the two heavens, whose station is equinoctial, has two manifestations, the one in the lower, the other in the upper heaven ; the one as the god of light, the other as the deity of darkness. In the type of Har-Makhu he unites both ; in the type of Khepr, the beetle-god, he makes his transformation from the one into the other character. The shrine, or secret dwelling, is said to be in darkness, in order that the transformation of this god may take

---

[1] ii. 4   [2] Ch. xx.   [3] Ch. liv.   [4] Ch. lxxii.

place.[1] The name of Ka permutes with Hak, and the original of both is found in Kak, and yet earlier Kebek. Hu is the spirit of light, the good demon of the double-winged disk, and Kak is the sun of darkness in the nocturnal heaven. Exactly the same representation occurs in the Maori, where the word IHO is a correlative, and has the value of AKE, and yet AKE is also the converse of IHO. Hu and Iho are the modified forms of Hak and Ake, just as Har, the upper, is of Kar, the lower. A form of this triad is shown in the passage of the Hades by a picture of the divine bark carrying the solar disk, enclosing a scarabæus. The god Sau is at the prow, and Hakau is at the poop. The beetle represents Khepr-Ra, the transforming sun. If for these we substitute Tum, Hu, and Kak, we have the triad of the Atum cult.

In the earlier mythos of the Mother and Son, the child Horus had a dual manifestation in the light and dark. In this the Har-Sun, the suffering Adonis or Thammuz, was represented as the blind Horus. He is spoken of in an ancient text as sitting solitary in his darkness and blindness. In the Royal Ritual at Abydus he is introduced, saying, "*I am Horus, and I come to search for mine eyes.*"[2] The eye or his sight was restored to the sun at the dawn of day, or it was re-made in the annual circle at the time and place of the vernal equinox. The blind Horus was another form of Ka or Kak, who is called the god Touch, he who had literally to feel his way through the dark, and is the prototype of our "CHACHE—blind-man." CHAEICH, in Irish, means a purblind fellow; CAOCH (Gaelic), blind, empty, void. Kak (Hak), is identified with the blind and suffering Horus by his being pourtrayed as Harpocrates. Kak is yet extant in the form of our Chache-blind-man and Jack-in-the-box.

For Tum is the "*God who is in his box, chest, ark, or sheta, out of which he comes forth from the great place within the celestial abyss, lighted by the lion-gods,*"[3] or springs up from his box like Jack, who also personifies the green man with a black face, as he dances in green leaves on May Day.

The ancient gods, those of Israel included, are now to be mainly met with at the toy-makers'; the divinities of childhood still. In the chimney corner, by the nursery fire, the deities are dozing away their second childhood, save that once a week the strings are pulled, and the puppets are compelled to keep up a kind of nodding acquaintance with the world from the pulpit, which now represents their box, on Sundays.

As before shown, our "Black Jack,"—whether represented by the Jack in his box, or the Sweep in his framework of Spring foliage, or by the "Black Jack" of our winter greens, or the spirit called "Black Jack,"—is identical with Kak-Atum, who is also represented by the image of a black doll, as a sign of life in the lower domain. Also the

---

[1] *Records*, x. 91.　　　[2] Renouf, *Hibbert Lectures*, p. 114.　　　[3] Ch. iii.

White and Black of the gods Hu and Kak have been faithfully preserved in the white Surplice and black Gown of the clergy; and just
as Atum in his box was the black Kak, so the black gown is still put
on when the pulpit is entered by the preacher in the second character.
The guiding star, or the sun in the Hades, the nocturnal sun, the sun
in the winter signs—these are the origines of the black god, the black
Sut-Nahsi, the black Osiris, the black Kak, the black Krishna, or the
black Christ.

The greater mysteries were held at midnight. In truth night was
the earliest time of light, and the evening and morning were the first
day. The Jewish Sabbath, beginning at night, still records this fact.
Night was the mother of all the manifesters of light. The sun of
night, that passed for ever through the underworld, and returned in
spite of death and darkness, was the victorious one, the helper, saver,
comforter, whose first manifestation was the morning; who came to
evoke the religious fervour of those whom the night and its terrors
had already brought into a kneeling attitude from fear. This was
the particular deity made known to Moses as the sun in the Akar, or
hinder part of the celestial circle, by the name of Jah, the great God
of the Psalmist, who praises him by name as Jah or Jach. This
name of Jah is supposed by Fuerst, Gesenius, and other Hebraists to
be a word abbreviated from Ihvh (יהוה), or derived from a different
form of pronunciation. But the writer of the Book of Exodus is right,
and the Hebraists have never known it—Jehovah was not the
same divinity as Jah. If Jehovah had been a male divinity from
the first, he would have represented Khebekh, the son of Kheb
the genitrix; but the positive changes in the naming preclude that
from being a possibility. When, in the fourth chapter of Genesis,
men began to call upon Ha-Shem-Jehovah, the *name* was identical
with the *Son* of Jehovah-genitrix, who is there represented by Sut-
Anush, and later by El-Shadai. Also the Hebrew carefully retains
the ה terminal to the name of Jhv, for the feminine Jehovah, as in
Aloah, a goddess.

If the deity made known to and by Moses had been Jehovah, he
would of course have been known already by that name, and by
making the name of Jah to be identical with Jehovah, the god is
made to bear false witness against himself. The two names have
been confused by translators; the Hebrew Rabbins knew well
enough that Jehovah was not Jah, but a female divinity whose name
was therefore not to be uttered; and when the name was written it
was supplemented by the title of Adonai, or Adonai was employed
in place of it to distinguish the male god from the goddess. The
name by which the deity had not been previously known is Jah.
This occurs in the fragment of an ancient hymn,[1] called the "Song
of Moses," or Mashu, who "made hereditary titles for Ra," and in

[1] Ex. xv. 2.

Exodus xvii. 16, two of the oldest remains of writings, of which we have only a later *réchauffé* in the present Pentateuch. The name originally given in Exodus is Jah or Jach, the god of the far earlier fragments and of the Psalms and ancient poetry; the same as the Egyptian Kak. In the hard form Jah is Kak, and Jach is the intermediate spelling of the name. Kak, Hak, Jach, with other variants, will be found in many languages, including the Hebrew type-name of AKH; AKH, the Assyrian moon-god, the English JACK; Kodiak, IJAK; Saraveca, CACHE; Laos, XACA; Bushman, CAGU; Loanga, CHIKOKKE (a black idol); Ge, black sun, CHUGH-ra; Erroob, GEGGR; Singhalese, JACA (the devil); Seneca, KACHQUA; Port Philip, KAKER; Susu, KIGE; Angami Naga, ACHUCHE; Cuban, JOCAHUNA; Galla, WAK; Gonga, YEKO; Sereres, AOGUE; Finnic, UKKO; Otomi, OKHA; Sioux, OGHA; Arabic, JAUK; Japanese, JACUSI, God of healing; Koniaga, EYAK, the Evil Spirit, and many more. The name depends on KAK, meaning darkness, and on the Light, whether as star, moon, or sun, being the deity of the dark. Kak was the solar god in the Akar; so is JAH, the divinity of the hinder part shown to Moses. Kak is the god of darkness, and the word means darkness. So יה is annexed to a noun,[1] to denote horrible darkness. Jah is the god of darkness. The god of the Psalmist,[2] who bowed the heavens and came down, was the descending sun, the beneficent deity of the dark; the darkness was his secret place. The god of the dark was pourtrayed as the black god.

In Strabo's account of the Exodus we are told that Moses, the Jewish teacher, was opposed to images of the deities;[3] but neither Moses nor any one else could get rid of the imagery which is still extant in the writings and reproducible for the reader. My conclusion, as easy to defend as to suggest, is that the ASHAR, in EYAH ASHAR JAH, is a part of the proper name, equivalent to the Phœnician אסר, an epithet of Baal, the son, as consort of Asherah, the goddess of the tree and the pillar who was the object of secret adoration in Israel when the cult had been publicly suppressed. Asherah, Astarte, Ashtaroth, are finally one with Jehovah as the primordial genitrix; Asher-Jah was a form of her son, the s n who in mythology grows up to become the husband of the mother and the re begetter of himself as his own father. This was so with the earliest Duad of the mother and son, whether Sabean or solar. The Virgin and Child were before the fatherhood was individualized on earth, and therefore before it could be typified or divinized in heaven. Now, this development of the male god from the son of the mother into her husband and the father of souls is traceable in the change from Aten to Atum in Egypt; also in the evolution of Osiris, the father god, out of As-Ar, the Har-son

---

[1] Jer. ii. 31.   [2] xviii. 11.   [3] *Lib.* xvi. c. 35.

of Isis; she who came from herself. The Ar-son is P-ar, *i.e.* Bar, Baal, and this development can be traced in Israel.

"It shall be at that day, saith the Lord [thou] shalt call me 'my husband,' and shalt call me no more Baali," [1] rendered "my Lord," and not inappropriately, for Baal is expressly the Lord, as son of the mother. The Ar or Har (Eg.) means the Lord. Aten, or Adon, is the lord, and the lord is the prince, son, heir-apparent, the Repa of mythology, who precedes the Pharaoh and represents the Har-son that was earlier than Ra. This was the Shem that men began to call upon at the time when the Anosh was born to Seth, or when Sut-Anush was made the male manifester of the female deity.

The earliest god known to any mythology is the son of the mother, the eternal child, boy, or lad. El or Al was the supreme god of the Babylonians; the prince of gods, the lamp of the gods, the warrior of the gods (the characters of Bar-Sutekh). On Assyrian monuments Baaltis and the "Shining Bar" are found in immediate juxtaposition.

Har-pi-Khart, distinguished from Har-pi-Kherp, is not merely Horus, the child; he is the child of the Motherhood solely, that is the Ar, Har, or Khar, with the feminine terminal to his name.

The Asar, who in Egypt was son of the mother, and later consort, is in the Phœnician אסר (Asir) the husband. In Hebrew Asar means the spouse, the wedded consort, whilst Ashar or Gashar signifies to be united sexually, to be married. Ashar-Jah is thus Jah, the husband, distinguished from Baal, the son.

There is no other origin for the Hebrew El, a name of the supreme deity as male, because it belongs to the sonship of the motherhood. It is useless, likewise, to discuss the meaning of Al (El) apart from the earlier forms in Gal, Kal, and Kar, which alone are primary. El is the worn-down form of Hal, or Har, Khar, and Khart, extant not only in Egypt, but in the Fijian god Kalou, called Kalou-Gata, the god who fulfils what he promises; is as good as his word, the equivalent of the Egyptian Makheru, or true voice; Kalewala, the Finnish divine hero; the Greek Kurios, and others, including the Cornish Golly, or Goles, who is still sworn by in England, and is represented by the uplifted hand; Goll, as hand, being equivalent to the Kher sign, which is the oar-sceptre, or hand of Horus in crossing the water.

Asar (Osiris) is the son of As, Hes, or Isis, so El-Shadai is the son of Shadai, the Dea-Multimammæ. "*I am El-Shadai,*" is the first announcement of his name and presence made in the Hebrew writings.[2] This the Targum of Onkelos renders by "ANAH CHIV-LAH SAPUKAH." ANAH (אנה) has the meaning of being brought on by adaptation. Chivlah (חולה), from חול, denotes the bringer-forth, the gestator, and Sapukah signifies the added and joined

---

[1] Hos. ii. 16.   [2] Gen. xvii. 1.

together, the exact equivalent of Ashar-Jah; El, son of Shadai, being brought on as the god attached and wedded to the genitrix, as in the original mythos.

The earliest Ar was Bar, or Baal, and in the Hebrew writings the name of El interchanges with Baal. Baal[1] alternates with El.[2] Baal, the supreme god of the Kheta and the Syro-Phœnician peoples, was Baal-Sutekh, the ass-headed Sut of the monuments. This was the Baal of the heavenly dwelling or the tower of Saturn in the seventh heaven, when Sut had become a planetary god, as Saturn. Al is the son, then, identified with or as Baal, *i.e.* the Sabean Baal, who was Baal-zebul or Baalzebub and Bar-Sutekh. Bar-Typhon (Eg.), Baal-Zephon (Heb.), Baal-Kivan (בעל־כון) of the Phœnician and Babylonian mythologies, and the Baal-Kivan of the Numidian inscriptions, are each and all the son (Al) of the genitrix, who was first the goddess of the seven stars, next of the moon, and lastly of the sun.

Baal is compounded with Jah in the proper name of Baaliah, *i.e.* Jah, the son, as Baal, Bar, or Al, and Baaliah, a Hebrew proper name[3] as a divine name, distinguishes the deity Jah as Baal, who was the earlier son (Al) of the mother. The most varied abbreviations are found in compound proper names, where the Beth becomes a mere sign of abbreviation. It is so made use of for the name of Baal. Fuerst quotes the Phœnician ב׳מם reduced from בעל־מעם with the name of Baal represented by the Beth. We have the B' Jah of Psalm lxv. 5, Psalm lxviii. 5, Isaiah xxvi. 4, which we can now read as a modest annunciation that Baal-Jah is the name signified, only Baal had then acquired a bad reputation. Moreover the B' is brief for either Baal, Ben, Bar or No. 2. These ancient significates are all essence, and this B' suffices to identify the god Jah as the son who was Baal, the manifester, in a twofold form, the same as Sut-Har, Sut-Nubti, the dual Anubis, or the double Horus.

Philo-Judæus, speaking of the mysteries of Baal-Peor, tells us that the votaries opened their mouths to receive the water that was poured into them by the priests.[4] Baal-Peor is called lord of the opening, which this action symbolizes. The Hebrew פעור, rendered by the Seventy φογώρ, a hiatus or opening, is the Egyptian Pekar, a gap, opening. Ar denotes that which is fundamental. Pekar also has the significant sense of being in flower; one of the Two Truths. At their period of pubescence the Maidens were dedicated to Baal-Peor. This identifies Baal-Peor with Sut, or Bar-Typhon, who is designated the Opener. The year was opened by the star named after him. In the Magic Papyrus the "two great goddesses that conceive and do not breed are opened (Sennt, to open the ground, make a fresh foundation) by Sut and sealed by Har." Interpreted by the Two

---

[1] Judges, viii. 33.   [2] Judges, ix. 46.   [3] 1 Chron. xii. 5.
[4] See also Faber, *Pagan Idolatry*, ii. 250-1.

Truths, this identifies Sut with the water (blood) period, and Horus with gestation or breath; the one represents the opener, the other the closer of the womb; the one flesh, and earth; the other spirit and heaven. In the planisphere Sothis was the star of the opening year and of the inundation with which the year opened; it was Bar-Sut the opener, or Baal-Peor. Sut-Har, in the first year, was represented by the wolf, or Orion. Baal was the opener as the child, son, the Khart, or child of the genitrix.

The Phœnician Baal of the earliest time was known by the title of Baal-Itan, Βελιτάν;[1] this was understood to mean the old Baal, the first form of Baal. ITAN answers to the Egyptian ATEN, the circle-maker, the sun of the disk-worshippers. In Hebrew איתן also identifies the old as an epithet of the highest male deity. The "old" here signifies the first in time. Baal or Bar was the old, first, supreme star-god. The terminal kh in Sutekh has long perplexed Egyptologists, but when we find that Osiris at Thebes is called "KHE," the child, and that the Khu, Sieve, stands for a child, there can be little doubt that Sutekh is expressly the child of the mother, Astarte. Also "At," the root of Aten, is the child or lad in Egyptian. Baal-Itan or Aten is the earliest form of the solar Baal and Aten, the Adon of Syria and Adonai of the Hebrews, identified as the son by the prefixed Baal. Further, by aid of the Phœnician Asar, we are enabled to identify the Hebrew El. Asar or Isar, with the divine name of El suffixed, is the Egyptian Asar, as son of the mother. Asar was an epithet of Baal, the son (Bar) or consort of Asherah (אשרה), who was a Phœnician goddess, sometimes synonymous with the Sidonian Astarte.[2] The Asherah image of 2 Kings xxi. 3, is one with the Asheroth of 2 Chronicles xxxiii. 3, so the goddess Asherah is identified by the Seventy and others with Ashtaroth. Asherah, read by Egyptian, is the abode (Ah) of Asar, the child of As (Isis), the Great Mother being personified as the abode as well as the tree,—Hes, or the divine abode.[3] Asir is an epithet of Adonis, who is called אדני־אסר. El-Shadai, Adonai, Baal, are each a personification of the son of the genitrix belonging originally to the cult of Sut-Typhon, which was precisely that of the Romish Church of to-day, the worship of the Virgin mother and her child.

Many secrets of the early religion are enshrined in Hebrew proper names. Thus Aliah (עליה) or Galiah, identifies the god El, the son Al, as Jah. Adonijah identifies Adon with Jah, and Ramiah[4] identifies Rimmon with Jah.

It has now to be suggested that where Jah is announced to Israel as the new god, EYAH ASHER JAH, the status of the earlier El has been changed from the son to the spouse of the mother, and the divine fatherhood is intended to be introduced. EYAH ASHER JAH reads: "I am Jah, the husband," implying the begetter of souls and

[1] Strabo, xvi. 1.
[2] Judges, ii. 3, and iii. 7.
[3] *Rit.* ch. cxlii.
[4] Ezr. x. 25.

thence the divine fatherhood, as an advance on the doctrine of the earlier mother and son. El-Shadai and Jah then we take to be two of the "hereditary titles" or designations of descent of the sun-god, Atum-Harmakhu, which were "*In the writings of the Lord of Sesen, the scribe of the king Ra-Harmakhu, in the royal palace of* ON, *consigned, performed, engraved in script under the feet of Ra-Harmakhu.*"

These writings of Shu may be supposed to have contained the originals of those which are in various traditions assigned to Moses, and to have been carried forth from ON into Syria, together with a version of certain writings of Taht, the Egyptian David; and from thence we infer the writings of Shu (Moses) and Taht (David) *were* carried into Syria and Palestine, to become the Pentateuch, the books of Joshua and Job, the Psalms, and the missing Book of Jasher. In ON the god Atum was worshipped with his consort Iusãas and their son Iu-em-Hept. These three form the Trinity proper of father, mother, and son, in which mythology landed religion at last as it was in the worship of Osiris, Isis, and Horus, or Amen, Maut, and Khunsu; but the worship was characterized by peculiar tenets and types. In the town of Tum, Pa-Tum, the Pithom of Exodus, Tum was worshipped under the surname of Ankh, one meaning of which is the living, and Brugsch Bey makes much of the god Atum of Heliopolis being called Ankh, the living god; as if the living god could only have been known to the Hebrews at Pa-Tum, in Egypt. "This is the only case," he says, "in the Egyptian texts of the occurrence of such a name for a god as seems to exclude the notion of idolatry."[1] Enough for the present purpose that Tum was expressly called the Living; this with the masculine article prefixed would be Pa-Ankh. Tum was also personified as SUTEM the hearer, or hearkener, the Judge who hears truth. He is called SUTEM or "hearing" in the time of King Pepi,[2] (6th dynasty). The ear is a sign of the descent on the Sut-Typhonian line, from Sut to Aten, from Kebek to Kak, Atum having been the earlier Aten. It may be noted that the proper name of Azniah[3] signifies Jah the hearer, from Azen to hear, and Jah, Jach, or Kak is a form of Atum, the god who hears or perceives in the darkness, hence the god of the dark based on the nocturnal sun. Tum-Ankh of Pithom was served not by priests like the other Egyptian divinities, but by two young girls who were sisters, and who bore the title of honour, URTI, the two queens or twin-queen. A serpent was considered to be the living symbol of the god of Pithom, called in the Egyptian texts the magnificent, the splendid. According to Brugsch it also bore the name of נלה, which he renders the smooth.[4] But as the word also signifies to reveal, disclose, open, and is applied to the open ear,[5] the serpent Geleh may have been another type of Tum-Ankh as the Hearer. The consort of Atum of

---

[1] v. ii. p. 346. (Eng. Tr.)   [2] *Records*, x. 91.   [3] Neh. x. 9.
[4] v. ii. p. 374, Cf. Numbers, xxi. 9.   2 Kings, xviii. 4.   [5] Job, xxxvi. 10.

On is named Iusāas; styled Regent of Heliopolis. She is a form of Isis or Hathor, to judge by her head-dress. "Her divine *rôle*," says M. Pierret, "is most obscure; her name itself is a mystery: *On peut le traduire; venue de sa grandeur.*"[1] But a better rendering may be found in perfect keeping with her character. She is the mother of the son whose name is IU-EM-HEPT. She herself also has the title of Neb-hept, the mistress or lady of peace. The accented SĀ in her name implies the earlier Sif; both Sa and Sif are names of the son who is IU. AS is a name of the genitrix, Isis; the AS, the seat, chamber, house, bed, resting-place, maternal abode, the secreting part of the body. IU-SĀ-AS is thus the As or womb of IU-SĀ, IU-SIF or IU-SU, three modes of naming the son IU. IU means he who comes, and Iu-sa, Iu-su or Iu-sif, is the coming son, the messiah of mythology. The HES was also represented by the sacred heifer as a type of the virgin mother. Iusāas is the cow, the chamber, the womb of the coming son, the child that is to be. There is still another meaning. IU signifies double. The Iu was of a dual nature. In the Hermean zodiac one mother, the Virgin, is in the sign Virgo; the other, the gestator, is in the sign of the Fishes; a kind of mermaid. IU-SĀ-AS will read the double-son-house, double-seat of the son, or seat of the duplicated son. She is the double-seat of Atum in An, in person. Perhaps the most complete rendering of the name of Iusāas, *and one that includes the mythological meaning as well as the philological*, is, She who is great with the coming one, that is, with her son who was Iu. The name of Iu-em-hept is variously spelt with the AI, AAI, IU, and AU. It was abbreviated into I-em-hept, and became the Greek IMOYΘOΣ. Both IU and AAI mean to come and to bring, so that IU-EM-HEPT is the peace-bringer or he who comes with peace, who, as the Nefer-Hept, is the breather of peace. In the solar or luni-solar trinity there was one of the three who was for ever the COMING one, the exact analogue of the expected man of America, looked forward to as the "Coming Man." This was the IU, AU, AO, AF, YAV, YAHU, AHU, IAH, IAO, HAK, KAK, KEBEKH, and other variants of the one name of the youthful god. Osiris has the title of Neb-Iu, the coming lord. IE (Iu) was written over the door of the young sun-god Apollo at Delphi. Tum was called Tomos by the Greeks. Thomas "which is called Didymus" renders this duality of Tum by name, and the epithet serves to identify the Didymean Apollo with the sun of the two horizons impersonated in Tum, or in IU as the dual son. Iu-oliter is the name of a Finnic deity who not only comes but also brings fish into the nets of the fishermen of the Baltic; a form of bringing attributed to other messiahs. Hept, in addition to peace, means plenty, heaps of food. Both natures of the father and mother were blended in the later son, and before the fatherhood was founded both sexes were represented

[1] *Petit Manuel de Mythologie*, p. 119.

by the dual child. The son of the mother as IU or the double Horus personified the future of being, the becoming, and was the type of futurity presented by Youth, the image of coming into being, the mythical Iusu or Iusif the coming child. Hence the doctrine goes back to the child in the womb of the great mother, and has to be thought out there as a beginning; hence AU (Eg.) to be, and AU the embryo, the coming being. It is as old as the god Ptah, who was personified as the embryo, and as Sut the ass-headed, for IU is an ancient name of the ass. Now the worshippers of this manifestation of the eternal in time were the "IUS," or Jews, and the doctrine of the coming one of the heavens led to their false and fatal expectation of the Messiah on earth.

All that is expressed in Revelation [1] by the AO, "which is, and which was, and which is to come," is found in the Egyptian "AU," signifying was, is, and to be. The letter U represents the later O. A and I interchange in Egyptian, A being the English I, and in the name of Iu-em-hept the IU has a variant in Au, the AO or alpha and omega of the Greek alphabet and of the Mexican pictographs. We are told that all who entered the temple of the Epicene divinity Serapis, bore on their brow or breast the letters or signs of Io (Iu).[2]

There were different modes of indicating this double divinity and the dual nature of the Iu. For example, the dual signification of the name of the IU or JEW would appear to have been perpetuated in a practice of the Abyssinian artists who, according to Salt,[3] invariably and of set purpose drew only the profile of a Jew, the reason of this curious custom being unknown to him. It was a mode of suggesting the dual expressed by Iu.[4] The dual nature of the IU-God is correctly depicted in the person of the young man with feminine paps. Bacchus was pourtrayed with female breasts. In the Soane Museum there is a Græco-Roman statue of the child Horus—the first half of the double Horus—made in the image of the female. Saint Sophia,

---

[1] i. 8.   [2] Kircher, _Œdip. Ægypt._ v. i. p. 197.
[3] _Voyage to Abyssinia_, p. 395.
[4] The English mediæval JEW-STONES were double. Another illustration of the Iu or Jew in relation to the Egyptian Deity. In my identification of the god Tum, the lower minified sun, with Tom Thumb and the impostor "Saint" Thomas, the crowning illustration was omitted. The recurrence of the _shortest_ day reminds me that this is the day dedicated to Thomas. Also Drake relates in his _Eboracum_, p. 217 (1736), that there was a custom in the city of York for a friar of St. Peter's Priory to have his face _painted like a Jew_ and to be set on horseback with his face to the horse's tail, to ride through the city, carrying one cake in front of him and one behind. The double cake denoted the two paths of the solar orbit. The friar represented YOUL in person, and was accompanied by the YOUTH of the City shouting YOUL, YOUL. The MS. cited by Drake connects the custom with the betrayal of the city to William the Conqueror who had obviously taken the place of the sun-god. Tum was the sun of the hinder part, and is represented by Youl (Iu-el) riding backwards, and the JEW or Iu, and here on Tum's (Greek, Tomos) day we find the same transformation of Tum into Iu—as shown by the accompanying Youth—taking place, that was pourtrayed in Egypt as occurring at the time of the spring equinox, when Tomos "called Didymus" or dual, made his transformation into Iu-em-hept.

intended for the Christ in the Roman Iconography, was delineated as a bearded female.[1] The long and typically feminine robe is another sign, whether this be worn by Jewish high priest or Roman pope. Anhar, who is male-female, twin in Shu and Tefnut, is likewise a wearer of the long robe. The long garment—in which was " the whole world "[2] in the sense now explained—was worn by IU-EM-HEPT. He is figured at Memphis seated, and holding an unrolled papyrus on his knees, as the wearer of the long robe. We have already identified this deity as the Egyptian Jesus, to whom the " wisdom of Jesus " is ascribed as an Egyptian writing, and of whom it is said, " This Jesus did imitate Solomon, and was no less famous for wisdom and learning."[3] A form of this god is found on the monuments at Biban-el-Muluk, with the name of AU or Iu. As Tum-neb-tata, he is the black wearer of the white crown.[4] His portraits were copied by Wilkinson. In one of these he is of a black complexion, in another[5] he is bull-headed, with the name of AU, or SUTEM, the hearer. To denote hearing, says Hor-Apollo,[6] the Egyptians delineate the ear of the bull, and the reason given is that when the bull hears the cow lowing he hastens to respond. AU, the bullock-headed, is the hearer. He has the style of Sutemi, the hearer, resident in the HOUSE OF SHU, and he is the lord of victory. Shu, be it remembered, is the Egyptian Moses, and AU (Iu), the bull-headed, is the dweller in his house. Also he is a form of the black god, otherwise Kak or Jach. He is identified with Atum as the hearer, the bull's ear having been preceded by the earlier types of the ear of Sut, who was the hearer as the long-eared ass, the prick-eared jackal, the square-eared fenekh, and who at last deposits in the hiero-glyphics the ear-type of At, Sut, and Sutem. The ear, says Hor-Apollo,[7] is the symbol of a future act. He is right. AU means to be; the being who was Atum as the old (AU), and Nefer-Tum, Iu-em-hept, or AU, as the future of being, the coming one. AU denotes both the elder and the younger in one person, or the young-elder of the mythos. In the form of AU, Atum will supply another of the origines.

AU, as the son, is AUSU. IU, as the son, is IUSU. And this god of Biban-el-Muluk, with the black complexion, is the black Jesus of Egypt. The black Jesus is a well-known form of the child-Christ worshipped on the Continent, where the black BAMBINO was the pet image of the Italian Church, as popular as Krishna, the black Christ of India; and unless the divine son was incarnated in black flesh, the type of the black child must have survived from that of the

---

[1] *Miniature of Lyons*, 12th century, Didron, fig. 50.
[2] *Wisdom of Solomon*, xviii. 24.　　　[3] Prologue to *Ecclesiasticus*.
[4] *Descrip. de l'Egypte*, v. 2. Pl. 90.
[5] Fig. 561.　　　[6] B. i. 47.
[7] B. ii. 23.

black AU, the black IU, the black KAK or JACH, the black Sut Nahsi, the negro image of the earliest god.

IU-EM-HEPT may now be followed out of Egypt. According to Jablonski, Æsculapius was called IMOUTHOS, and he thinks he was Serapis. There was an Asklepeion, or small temple of Serapis, in the Serapeum of Memphis. Ammianus Marcellinus[1] says "Memphis boasted of the presence of the god Æsculapius."[2] A bronze figure of Iu-em-hept, the Egyptian Jesus, the Jesus of the Apocrypha, may be seen in the British Museum. He is represented as a youth wearing a skull-cap, and is seated on a stool in the act of unrolling a papyrus; perhaps a treatise on medicine, he being the Healer, or Æsculapius.[3]

Wilkinson was certainly wrong in assuming that IU-EM-HEPT could not be the leader of the heavenly deities who is called EMPH by Jamblichus. The figure designated HEMPHTA at the centre of the Hermean zodiac will help to identify him. IU was the same as HU in the Tum triad; and the winged disk, or ATEN, is a form of the Teb-Hut sign of the god Hu, the manifestation of Tum in the upper heaven. The disk has the wings of the dove, the type of that peace (hept) which was brought by IU, the coming son, who was the second Atum, and the child of the lady of peace, Iusāas Neb-Hept.

The mythos of Atum and Jesus (Iu-su) contains the original matter of Paul's doctrine of the first and second Adam; he actually *quotes* it. "*So it is written.* The first man Adam[4] was made a living soul; the last Adam a quickening spirit. The first man of the earth earthy; the second the Lord from heaven."[5] And "as in Adam all die, even so in Christ shall all be made alive."[6] "And as we have borne the image of the earthy, we shall also bear the image of the heavenly." This was represented in the worship of Atum, the red Atum, who was of the earth as the lower sun, and the lord of heaven, "the great god, lord of heaven and giver of life," as he is called in his second phase, typified by the Hut, or winged sun. In the character of Khepr, the type of immortality by transformation, the first Atum transformed into the second as his own son Iu, *i.e.* Iu-su, the Greek Jesus.

"We shall be changed," is a translation of the mystery of Khepr, to change, to transform. This change, or re-birth, was also effected by the mother Nut in her name of heavenly mystery. Hippolytus[7] says the Chaldeans called the man of earth who became a living soul, Adam.

---

[1] xxii. 14.

[2] KHERP (Eg.) is a name of the prince or repa who comes, and the name of Æsculapius or Æsclepius is probably derived from Kherp-iu with the prefix As for the great, noble; or, as Æsculapius is the divine healer, the prefix may represent the Egyptian Usha, a doctor, physician. Thus Æsculapius is the Prince of Peace who comes for the healing of the nations.

[3] Eg. Gal. 578, b. Shelf 3.

[4] ADAM, the name of man in Lughman and Curali, and ADMA in Adaiel, were not derived from the Hebrew.

[5] 1 Cor. xv. 45-9.   [6] 1 Cor. xv. 22.   [7] *Hæres*, vol. vii. p. 97.

This was the Gnostic Adamas, Adam the Red, as sun, or as personification, was of the earth earthy, considered as the lower of two, and he became a living soul in the mythical transformation that was first based on the physiological, in which At-mu is the child of the mother, the embryo made of the red earth, the flesh formation; and the second Adam is the Iu-su, the child after it is transformed by the quickening spirit. Moreover, the youthful god, IU-EM-HEPT, had become a personal being postulated as existing in spirit-world, communicating with the minds of men in this life, and pre-figuring the future in dreams. On one of the Ptolemaic tablets there is a record of the fulfilment of a promise made in a dream by the god Iu-em-hept to Pasherenptah concerning the birth of a son. This was as real to the Egyptian mind as that sealing spirit of promise referred to by Paul.[1] "Henceforth," says Paul, "there is laid up for me a crown of righteousness, which the Lord, the righteous judge, shall give me at that day; and not to me only, but unto all them also that love His appearing."[2] Paul's crown of righteousness is the crown of justification or triumph given by Atum,[3] the lord, the righteous judge of the souls of the dead, at his appearing; when the deceased becomes the lord of eternity, to be reckoned "even as Khepera" the transformer, and to be the master of the kingly crown.

This crown is given to the soul when it has been justified in fourteen trials before the fourteen judgment-seats, that is, reckoning by the twenty-eight lunar houses, through one half of the circle, or the whole passage of the lower heaven. It is said to the deceased who has fought the good fight, "*Thy father, Atum, has bound thee with this good crown of triumph, with that living frontlet; beloved of the goas, thou livest for ever.*"[3]

The day of festival, on which was celebrated this triumph of Horus or the soul of the deceased and of putting on the crown of triumph, is designated "*Come thou to me.*"[4]

We are now able to utilize the strange-looking assertion found in the fragment from Justin out of *Trogus Pompeius*, to the effect that Moses was the son of Joseph. Such was the divine knowledge of Joseph, says the passage, that it "appeared to proceed not from a mortal, but a god." "*His son was Moses,*" whom, besides the inheritance of his father's knowledge, the comeliness of his person also recommended.[5] Moses the son of Joseph! As history this is meaningless, but, as mythology, the statement is verifiably true. The bullock-god AU is the hearer who is resident in the house of Shu—the house of the lion-gods who light Atum, or AU, in and out of the abyss of darkness—and Shu is Moses; AU is the sun-god;

---

[1] Eph. i. 13. [2] 2 Tim. iv. 8.
[3] Ch. xix. called the "Chapter of the Crown of Justification." Birch.
[4] So rendered by Renouf, *Hibbert Lectures*, p. 185. Cf. "Come ye blessed of my father." Matt. xxv. 32.
[5] Cory, *Ancient Fragments*, p. 80, Ed. 1876.

Shu-si-Ra is the son of the Sun. It only remains to be shown that Joseph is a form of the Iu-sif, or coming son, to prove his kinship to the mythical Moses.

First of the name. Sif in Egyptian, is the son, as well as Su or Sa. Iu-sif is the son who comes, and equally the dual-natured with Iu-sa and Iu-su. There has always been a sort of indefinite identity of Joseph with Jesus in Christology which this may, perhaps, explain. IU-EM-HEPT is supposed to be a form of Serapis, the Epicene type of Apis; and it is noticeable that AU has the heifer horns, not the bull's, or rather the calf's head, as AU is the hieroglyphic calf, which may be of either sex, and so is a type of both. According to some, Serapis was a compound of Sirius and the solar Apis, a type of the Sun-and-Sirius like Sut-Nubti. Now certain of the Rabbins identified Joseph with Serapis, and this offers a combination in the sonship particularly appropriate to the Hebrews. They were Sut-Typhonians at first when Sut or Baal, Bar-Sutekh, was worshipped as the son of the mother, and the dual son who united the Sabean and the solar sonship of the Sun-and-Sirius would be a natural link between the Sabean and solar cult. But the particular duality of the Iu-sif is not here in question; enough that the *Talmud* calls Joseph Serapis in the treatise AVODASARA, and that Serapis was a dual type of deity who has been identified with Iu-em-hept and Æsculapius. Serapis was the bull (or calf) of a dual nature. Au (or Iu), the son (sif) of Atum, is the bullock or calf-headed god in the house of Ma-Shu; and in the "Blessing of Moses" he says of Joseph, "His glory (is like) the *firstling of his bullock.*" [1] Au (Eg.) is the calf, which is here identified as the firstling of the bullock, or castrated bull. The name of the bullock in this place is likewise that of the cow,[2] AU or IU (and therefore Joseph as well) being of a twin-type. The dual nature of Joseph's name is shown by his being called ADONAIM. Still more apparent is the myth where Rachel, in naming the child Joseph, says, "The Lord shall add to me another son." [3] Joseph, in the margin, is rendered adding, and IU (Eg.) means duplicating. The other child is Benjamin, son of the right hand. He was brought forth in the birthplace of the Messiah, in Bethlehem-Ephrath. These are the two Horuses of Egyptian mythology, the two halves of Atum.

The two sons of Joseph, Ephraim and Manasseh, are identical with Joseph, and both together are also called Joseph. Ephraim and Manasseh, the dual form of Joseph, are the exact equivalents of the twin brothers in all the mythologies, one of whom is the first-born, but the other becomes the chosen heir. So when the two are brought to the blind Jacob, he stretched out his right hand and laid it upon Ephraim's head, who was the younger, and his left upon Manasseh's head, guiding his hands wittingly, for Manasseh was the first-born, and he blessed Joseph [4] or the two sons as Iu-sif. The Psalmist says: "Let thy

[1] Deut. xxxiii. 17.   [2] Lev. xxii. 28.   [3] Gen. xxx. 24.   [4] Gen. xlviii. 14.

hand be upon the Man of thy right hand, upon the son of man (whom) thou madest strong for thyself."

In the first bifurcation of the dual son Joseph, Benjamin, the son of the right hand, equates with the second Horus, Har the younger; Har of the right shoulder in Skhem. Hence he is reproduced as the youngest child of the mother Rachel, who dies at the time of his birth. Joseph, as the sun of the left hand, the sun that descends to the north, goes down into Egypt, into the pit, sheol, or Amenti; Benjamin ascends to the right hand of the father, he is the sun born in Ephrath or Bethlehem, whence came the young-sun-god whose goings forth had been from of old and were Æonian.[2]

Joseph was thirty years of age when he went out over all the land of Egypt. If an Egyptian had been asked the age of Horus when he came of age and went forth to renew the cycle and finish his father's work, he would have said thirty years. At thirty years the man or the god became KHEMT, the *homme fait*, called the man of thirty years; as the god he was Khem-Horus, the male manifester, the virile adult. Thirty years is a typical number for manhood.

Another name of the adult son is Sheru, the pubescent, the bearded (cf. Sheru for barley), and this is determined by the number thirty. The best of all evidence can be adduced to show that the Joseph who went out over the whole land at the age of thirty years was the Repa, the Sheru, the Lord of the mythos. This evidence is, the present writer conceives, irresistible and irrefutable.

The title given to Joseph [3] in the Hebrew Bible is צָֽפְנַת־פַּעְנֵחַ, but an entirely different version is offered by the Seventy who render it as ψονθομφανῆχ (Psonthom-phanech). Josephus [4] has ψοθομφάνηχον (Psothomphanechon). This has several variants however, in the different copies; no less than eleven forms having been found. Bernard in his note on Josephus thinks the original Coptic name was PSOTHOMON-PONEI, which he explains by ARCANUM ILLE MIHI RECLUSIT. Jablonski, in his letter to Michaelis, writes the title PSOTEM-PHENEH. Whiston, L'Estrange, Lodge, and other English translators of Josephus render the first part of the name as Psothom or Psonthom, and to these two forms it may be finally reduced for the present purpose. It has been sufficiently set forth that the god Atum of Pithom was particularly entitled THE LIVING, that is, P-ANKH. In his transformation into the youthful god he was AU or IU, the SIF (son), and became the mythical Joseph. AU is Sutem, the hearer; Sutem is also the title of Atum. It was as AU or IU-sif that he became the hearer. Thus the two titles of the god are SUTEM and PA-ANKH, and according to the record made use of by Josephus, when " Joseph was now grown up to thirty years of age he enjoyed great honours from

---

[1] Ps. lxxx. 17.   [2] Micah v. 2.   [3] Gen. xli. 45.
[4] *Ant.* B. 2, 6, 1.

the King, who called him PSOTHOM PHANECH,[1] that is, P (the) SUTEM (hearer), P (the) ANKH (living). "SUTEM" and P-ANKH are the two titles of Atum of Heliopolis, and Joseph as the Repa, the Sheru of thirty years, is known to Josephus by these two titles, assumed in the solar allegory every year by the Iu-sif or Son of Atum and Iu-sā-as. But the Septuagint has Psonthom instead of Psothom, and the word "SENT" or Shent is Egyptian, essentially a mystical and divine title on account of the duality which it embodies. In the PSHENT crown it denotes the two heavens, or two lands. In the Pshent apron it includes both sexes. In SHEN or SEN for the brother and sister it designates both sexes under one name. The SHENTI were a form of the twin lion which was at first female and afterwards epicene. SEN also means the second of two; and the double crown of the gods indicated the second, the added and dual character of the two. To put on the SHENT crown was typical of attaining the upper heaven, or the ZENITH, which is the equivalent word in the European languages; and in the African-Mandingo SANTO is heaven.

When Horus was Khemt, or became the Sheru of thirty years of age, he put on the upper crown which completed the PSHENT. When the virgin mother passed into the second phase as the gestator she was called SENTEM (Sntm); PSONTHOM is the same word with the masculine article prefixed, and SENTEM indicates the dual one, whether applied to the mother with child, the wearer of the two crowns, two serpents, or to the double Horus, the youth of thirty who is composed of two halves. It is in allusion to this adding and twinning of the two in one that the bringer-forth, the "Woman," in the Ritual,[2] says, "I have united Sut in the upper houses." In the "Tale of the Two Brothers,"[3] the elder brother who represents the first Horus, is said to reign over Egypt for thirty years, and thirty years is the age of the second Horus when he begins to rule. It is the typical age of the adult (Sheru) god, the second of the two brothers. Now when Joseph was thirty years old he went out throughout all the land, or was made ruler over the WHOLE of Egypt. He rode in the second (SEN) chariot, a parallel to wearing the PSHENT crown or being entitled PSONTHOM, literally the UNIFIED or duplicated P-Ankh the living, meaning that he represented the two characters paired, blended, pshen-t in one, which took place when the divine Repa became Ra, or the twofold Tum was reproduced as IU, the Sif. The Egyptian explains both Psothom and Psonthom, and the evidence is absolutely conclusive at once and for ever.

The Jews, says Petronius, in characterizing their cult, call unto Heaven's EARS. They did so, whether designated Egyptians in Egypt or Hebrews out of it, as the followers of Sut-Typhon, the long-

---

[1] *Ant.* B. ii. ch. vi. 1.   [2] Ch. lxxx.   [3] *Records*, ii. 151.

eared ass, or Tum-Sutemi, or Iu (Sif) the hearer, typified by the bullock. As Iusāas of On, the divine abode of Iu the Son (Sif), the mother, therefore, of Joseph, was a form of the goddess Neith, whom we shall find in Asenath, he would be SIF-NAT in Egyptian, and this is the exact rendering of the Zaphnath in Hebrew; SIF-NAT-P-ANKH is the living son of Neith, the one of the two in the Mythos who never dies. Thus we recover three Egyptian titles in SIF-NAT, the son of Neith, PSOTHOM the Hearer, and PSONTHOM the duplicated or Added. The Hebrew יסף, for the ADDED, contains the exact equivalent of P-SONTHOM, and it is applied [1] to the mother in conceiving *or* Adding, where it expresses the sense of SNATEM the seeded, the gestating.

Asnath, the consort of Joseph, is recognizable as the Egyptian SNAT or SNATEM, a particular title of the mother, rendered the pleasing, reposing, sweet, agreeable, restful, peaceful. The root meaning is the bearing, the seeded (as shown by the seed-pod), and the name contains the elements of AS, the great, and Neith, meaning the great or *enceinte* Neith. There is a full form of this name of the gestating mother in Mut-Snatem, a queen on a monument called the Statue of Turin. Iusāas, mother of the Iu-sa or Iu-sif is the Neith of On. As the goddess she would be called the daughter of Ra the sun-god, and PAUTI means the god or divine image. But according to the present interpretation the Jews in Egypt were worshippers of the Aten Sun, the visible glory; and the Hebrew פרע, to be prominent, stand atop or at the head, would describe the Har-sun on the horizon; this agrees with the Egyptian PRA, to be visible, manifest to sight, and PEHTI means the glory. PEHTI-PRA is the visible glory of the disk-worship.

According to the Psalmist the Deliverer who led Israel up out of Egypt when he "went out," and the burden was removed from his shoulder, and his hands were set free, and his bondage ceased, was JOSEPH. [2]

One very ancient name of the Hebrew male deity is expressed by יהו Jahu or Jaho, which is also the name of a Phœnician solar god. This form enters into the name of Joseph, [3] so that Joseph is Jahu-sif, which in Egyptian is Jahu, the son. Jahu is represented by Ahu (Eg.), a name of Atum, the modeller and framer, as a variant of Hu, Au, and Iu, who is the son. Iu-em-hept was also Ahu-sif, or Atum as the son.

Joseph as the sun-god supported by Shu, the god of the bow, who is figured also as the uplifting hands of Ra, or by Moses with his hands upraised, is delineated in the astronomical chapter. " The archers have sorely grieved him, and shot (at him) and hated him." That is a picture of the sun in the Archer, where he was diminishing daily and

---

[1] Gen. xxxviii. 5.   [2] Ps. lxxxi. 5 and 6.   [3] Ps. lxxxi. 5.

losing strength. But he was sustained and protected by the lion-god of the bow. Shu with his arrow or Mâtet with his bow. "His bow abode in strength, and the arms of his hands were made strong by the hands of the Abir (אביר) of Jacob. From thence is the SHEPHERD, the stone of Israel."[1] The character of Anhar is here pourtrayed. Shu supports the solar disk, Anhar the nocturnal heaven. "Uplifted is the sky which he maintains with his two arms." His hands sustain Ra in the weakness of his declining age, or in the lowest signs from the Archer round to the Fishes. He is the Shepherd as the star Regulus. He is the crosser over the river Eridanus, and the Abir or Abar as Egyptian means the one who crosses, passes through willy-nilly to the other side, one who bored his way, as it appeared to the primitive men, through the earth to ascend on the side opposite. The stars that did this were the mighty ones. Anhar as Kepheus, Regulus, or Mars, was one of the Abirs or Kabirs.

Before being let down into the pit Joseph is divested of his coat of many colours. So is the sun as Tum on approaching the Pool of Pant (colours, paint). The Osirian says to this setting sun, "*Indescribable is thy colour, we are beholding all the colours of Pant.*" "*Glory to thee, O Tum, setting from the land of life, in the colours of the Gate.*"[2] "*Great one who journeys to the Production of Colours, ye are at the Pool* (of Pant)."[3]

Tum was the sun going down into Egypt or Khebt, the north. He was Atum-Adon, and in his dual character Adonaim, as Joseph is designated. He too left behind his coat of many colours in the pit or Pool of Pant. Elsewhere, Joseph, or his Atzem, is brought up out of Egypt by Moses and Joshua.

In the account of the exodus given by Josephus from Chæremon, the myth is manifestly mixed up with the Egyptian history of an exodus. The leaders are said to be two Scribes, called Moses and Joseph, whose Egyptian names were TSITHEN and PETISEPH.[4]

We have attempted to derive the Egyptian name of TSITHEN, as the leader up, from the Celestial Egypt or the Deep. That of Petiseph appears to resolve naturally enough. Atum was the son of Ptah and Peht, the lioness goddess; Iu-em-hept being a form of Atum, who as the Son of Peht was Pehti-sif or Petiseph, the name of Joseph in Egyptian, as explained by an Egyptian expert. Thus we recover the solar Joseph, who was accompanied by Shu or Tsithen in the exodus of the celestial allegory, which is here mixed up by Josephus with Chæremon's account of the expulsion of the lepers, Aat, or Pests of Egypt. At the same time Tsithen, as Moses, supplies another illustration of his being the lion-god Shu, for Clement Alexander states that Moses had an earlier name known as Joachim.[5] Joachim, in Egyptian Iu-akam, reads, "the shield or buckler

---

[1] Gen. xlix. 23-4.   [2] *Rit.* ch. xv. Birch.   [3] Ch. cliii.
[4] *Against Apion*, B. 1. c. xxxii.   [5] Stromata, i.

(Akhem) of Iu." Shu was the shield and buckler, the bowman, the spearman, the warrior in support of Ra and his multitudes. Iu-akam or Jah-akam is an appropriate title for Moses, the manifester of Jah, and leader of his people. Shu in his dual character (with Tefnut) furnished the TWINS, and in an ancient Hindu zodiac the sign Gemini consists of a human figure holding up both hands in the atti-tude of Shu, or Moses, bearing TWO SHIELDS, one on each side of him.[1] As Iu (Eg.) denotes two and akam is a shield, this is IU-AKAM in Egyptian, and the two shields typify the double-support which Ma-Shu afforded the sun-god who here sits in the centre of the zodiacal signs as the AO or IU.

One name or title of Moses was ABIAO.[2] ABI (Eg.) is the leopard or cat-lion, into which Shu transformed when he made the "like-ness of Seb." AO is Greek for the Egyptian AU, the name of the young God in the "House of Shu." ABI-AU is thus identified both as Shu (or Ma-Shu) and Moses.

The Israelites or Children of Ra are the same as those who are found in the Egypt of the Hades and the Wilderness of the Egyptian mythology. Their leaders are the young sun-god, IU, AU, or JAH, and SHU, the older star-god.

Fuerst says *Iual*, rendered "IU OF GOD," or Aliah translated "GOD OF JAH," would be an absolute blasphemy. But IU is the God AL, that is, the Son-God, named as son of the mother, whilst ALIAH positively identifies Jah as Al, the son, and Iu-al as Iu, the son, is synonymous with Iu-sif, or Joseph. אביאסף is a Hebrew proper name[3] which proclaims that God (Ab) is Joseph.

The proper name of Achiu[4] reads, God is Iu, *i.e.* double or twin in Egyptian, who as Iu-sif is the child who comes, and whose coming was of a dual nature, whence the personification of a biune being.

The name of Eliu-ani (אליועני) reads, "to Iu are mine eyes."[5] IU or Au is the Iu-em-hept or AU form of Atum, who, as the son of the mother Iusāas, the child, Sif, is Iu-sif, the Jewish Joseph, the twin or biune divinity.

ELOAH is the name used by the Ten Tribes of Israel for the Elohim of the Two Tribes. Jehovah-Eloah,[6] in the Ephraimite version, answers to Jehovah-Elohim in the version used by the Ten. Because the Ten, the Isharim, belonged to the cult of the genitrix, the goddess of the seven stars, in the first time, whereas Eloah denotes the God in a twofold form whom we now identify with Joseph.

Osiris (Asar), the Son of Isis, is called Osiris-Eloh in the Car-pentras (Phœnician) inscription ; he is also the Neb-Iu on the monu-ments, and that is the dual or duplicative Lord who, as the son of the

---

[1] *Phil. Trans.* 1772. Drummond, Pl. 9.
[2] *Abiao.* I am sure of my fact, but not of my authority.
[3] Ex. vi. 24 ; 1 Chron. vi. 8.　　　　　[4] 2 Sam. vi. 3.
[5] 1 Chron. iv. 36.　　　　　[6] Gen. iii. 21.

mother, is the Iu-Sif, the coming solar son; the exact equivalent of Joseph in Israel, the son who comes and duplicates, as Joseph reduplicates in Ephraim and Manasseh, the two sons or tribes whose divinity is Jehovah-Eloah.

It is known that the vau in אלוה denotes an ancient plural, and אלול, so interpreted, signifies the dual El, as in Har the Elder, called Har-ur or Aroeris. Alala is a title of the Assyrian Tammuz. Elul also represents Har-ur as the name of this dual child of the southern solstice and the western horizon, the Iu-su or Iu-sif, who is the dual Eloah in Israel. אלה is a plural pronoun; אלה is a name for gods;[1] and these we take to be worn-down forms of אלוה, the plural for the God of Jacob,[2] and the Alvak of Magozim.[3] Melkart of Tyre was a form of the dual child of the mother, and he is designated the עלה (God) of fortresses. This is the same as the Alvak of Magozim in the Book of Daniel. The fortresses or rocks are the two horizons of the sun, and the Alvak Magozim, אלוה־מעוזם, is identical with Har-Makhu of the double horizon, or Atum in his dual seat.

Rameses III. relates that he built a grand temple in the North of On for Tum, his FATHER LORD, and made an abode and a lake for Iusāas, and the total number of residents was 12,963.[4] The remains of this temple existed till quite lately, and were known as the Tel-el-YAHOUDEH, the Mound of the Jew. OUR Jews had left Egypt with their IU as Joseph, or as Adonai-Jah, before this temple of the Jew was built.

The worshippers of IU were the IUS or Jews. It was a religious and not an ethnological name at first. The Jews were those who worshipped the son, more particularly the son of the mother, and might be Egyptians, Syrians, or Hebrews. The worship of the mother and son had extended over Palestine in early times.

"Our Bethleem," says Hieronymus,[5] "now our very most august spot on earth, of which the Psalmist sings; 'Truth has arisen from the Earth,' the grove of Tammuz—that is, of Adonis—was casting its shadow : and in the grotto where formerly cried the infant Christ, the lover of Venus was being mourned." So was it, ages before the era called Christian and the supposed incarnation of the God in mortal flesh and human form.

Rameses especially dedicates to Atum, as God the Father, rather than to Jesus as the son of Iusāas ; and Atum, as previously stated, was the sun-god Ra in his first sovereignty. Precisely the same change can be traced in Israel. The dual Eloah, Iusif, was superseded in turn, as Jehovah, Elohim, Shadai, and El-Shadai had been. Hence it is written, "Moreover he refused the tabernacle of Joseph and chose not the tribe of Ephraim, but chose the tribe of Judah, the

---

[1] Jer. x. 11.   [2] Ps. cxiv. 7.   [3] Dan. xi. 38.
[4] *Annals of Rameses III. Records of the Past*, vi. 57-9.
[5] Ep. xlix. ad Paulin. Tom. iv. part ii. p. 564. ed. Martinay.

Mount Zion which he loved."[1] Judah represents the god of the twin-lions, or Moses and Joshua, the god of the law-giver. "The sceptre shall not depart from Judah, nor a law-giver from between his feet, until Shiloh come, and unto him shall the gathering of the people be." The deity of Moses and Joshua, in the ancient fragments, is Jah, and the name of הודה, implies the worship, acknowledging, or manifesting of the god Jah. Judah denotes a new kingdom distinguished from the ten tribes of Israel and the dual Ephraim, and is therefore the representative of the Twelve. But we have not yet done with the cult of Atum; tedious as this tracing may be, it is necessary to prove the religious origines of the Hebrews, with a labour far beyond the intrinsic worth of the writings, which in themselves contain but little original value or authority.

It was as Khepr, the scarab-headed god, that Atum made his transformation from the god of darkness to the lord of light. And in Psalm lxxx. 1, we read: "Give ear, O shepherd of Israel, thou that leadest JOSEPH like a flock, thou that dwellest between the Cherubim shine forth." The Hebrew Lord, Adonai or Jah, is expressly associated with the Cherubim. He rides upon the Cherubim and is the Lord of Hosts that dwelleth between the Cherubim.[2] His seat is between the Cherubim.[3] Sitting, riding, dwelling, his place is between the Cherubs, and these are represented as the Two Cherubs. It is probable, as asserted by Clement Alexander, that the earliest cherubs imaged the two Bears, a dual form of Jehovah as Di-Genitrix, the plural KHEPTI. The solar cherubs were the two scarabs of the Egyptian zodiac, placed in the sign of the crab. These two beetles of Egypt were figured in an Ark with their wings outspread, as in the description of the Cherubim, whose wings covered the mercy-seat, and whose faces looked one to another, after the Egyptian pattern.[4]

Josephus tells us that Moses said he had seen such things as the cherubs near the Throne of God.[5] The Hebrew word cherub implies the same thing as the Egyptian Khepr, the scarab-headed image of the former and transformer. Khepr and Kherf have the same meaning in Egyptian of forming and figuring. Khepr, the type of transforming by rolling and turning round, figured the circle, our cypher. Two beetles in the oldest zodiacs kept that circle of the sun at the place where the solstitial year began and ended, or in Egyptian language transformed. There was the gate that opened one way for the descent of the sun, and afterwards of the souls to the earth, the lower of the two regions; the other way being the outlet to the land of eternal birth, in the eschatological phase of the celestial imagery. Although two beetles were pictured at times, the beetle itself was a biune image of working both ways, with hands and feet so to say, in rolling his globe, and making the circle. This has

----

[1] Ps. lxxviii. 67-8.   [2] 2 Kings, xix. 15.   [3] 1 Sam. iv. 4.
[4] Copied by Rosellini.   [5] *Ant.* iii. 6. 5.

dominated in the Hebrew for hands and feet, or the soles of the feet, Kaph (כף), both extremities being named in the likeness of Khepr, the dual one. Kaphel, double or doubled, is the equivalent of Khepr the double-ended type of the biune deity.

Where the two beetles were placed was the join of the circle, the dove-tailing or two-oneing. It was the place of at-one-ment where the circle of the two heavens was completed; the sign of this conjunction being the two beetles or cherubs. The Kaphareth, translated the Mercy-seat and place of the meeting-cherubs, the tips of whose wings touched, and whose two faces looked one to another, was the seat, abode, throne of the deity, who, as the transformer at the Kab (corner), was Khepr-Ptah. This goes far to identify the lord of the Hebrews, who rode on the cherubs and dwelt between them, with the beetle-god of those "profane Egyptians."

The nature or rather the number of the plural ending in OTH (וֹת), as in Ashtaroth, has no determinative in the Hebrew, and yet the number in Ashtaroth-Elohim and elsewhere depends on it. Plurality in the hieroglyphics depends on the number of the gods reckoned in the god-head. One form of the plural includes nine gods. PUT (Eg.) is number nine; the divine circle of the nine gods; and PUT is a later form of the word FUT or AFT for the number four, the four quarters. Aft is a reduced form of HEPT (or Khept), number seven; all because of the one beginning with the seven stars and the Typhonian genitrix, who in the full form of the name of Ashtaroth-Elohim would be Hes-Taur-Hept, i.e. Isis-Taur-t of the seven stars and the ark, both of which are named HEPT. Khept and Hept modify into Aft (the same goddess) of the four corners. As representative of the seven, Ashtaroth is really Ashtar-hept, the plural being sevenfold. In the reduced form of Ashtar-aft (fut) the plural in Egyptian is fourfold, based on the four corners. It has now to be suggested that the plural terminal וֹת is the equivalent for Aft, number four, the four quarters of the ancient genitrix, called AFT in this character.[1] In the hieroglyphics the Kân (earlier Kafn) is the corner-

---

[1] If, as is here maintained, the North Pole was the centre of motion first observed, the initial point of all beginning, the Great Bear would certainly be the type of number as well as reckoning, and this it will be shown to have been. The name of KHEB-TI (SEBTI and HEPTI) supplies a type-word for the Nos. 7 and 10. When Khaft has been reduced to AFT (variant FUT), for the four corners still represented by the ancient genitrix, we find this is a chief type-name for four. KHAFT and HEPT have also a deposit in KHAT and HAT for No. 4; this may be followed in the names for No. 4, as—

GĀDE, Logone.	EKETSE, Lifu.	HOIDA, Woratta.
KAREE, Albanian.	KUDE-IN, Timbora.	HATARA, Singhalese.
CHOD, Paropamisan.	WUTU, Ende.	YOTS, Japanese.
CHATA, Siah Posh.	WATSA, Netela.	AUDA, Gonga.
CHATUR, Sanskrit.	WATCHU, Chemuhevi.	AT, Karon.
CEITHIN, Scotch.	HAAT, Timur.	AT, Pome.
CEATHAR, Irish.	EHAAT, Manatoto.	AT, Wandamin.
KETURI, Lithuanic.	HATAMI, Palaik.	EAT, Omar.
QUATUOR, Latin.	HAUDDÁ, Kaffa.	ATCH, Lazic.
KITHNUCOTE, Kicai.		

[On the line

sign of the dwelling-place, the typical four corners named Aft. This Kân is figured in Aft or Apt of the zodiac, where the genitrix brought forth the child. The Aft-Kan or KAN-AFT becomes the Hebrew KANPHOTH of the four corners, and the פו is equivalent to Aft or Fut, the Egyptian for number four. Thus the terminal in this case is a plural which has the value of number four, and the four corners,[1] also the four quarters,[2] are KANPHOTH. The Kan, with the article suffixed, is the Kanp, Hebrew Kanph, to be bent or turned at the side, in relation to surrounding with a border. All is explained by the Corner. The corner interchanges with the wing: we say the wing of a building. The Kanphoth are the four corners, a type of the eternal; four times being an Egyptian synonym of "for ever." The Greek τετράγωνος ἀνήρ, a SQUARE man, for a complete and perfect or virtuous character, has the same primitive origin; a geometrical skeleton being thus clothed as a moral figure. "Woe to the land of the double shadow," says Isaiah,[3] rendered "shadowing with wings," where the plural of Kanph (כנפים) denotes the wings. This does not refer directly to the mountain-chains of Egypt, throwing their shadows to the south and north, which was noticeable and noticed at Meroë.[4] The natural fact had been turned into a celestial figure, employed by Isaiah. The Kanphim or Kanphoth as wings, are the four wings of the two cherubs, the four wings of the two beetles of Khepr, the wings of the four corners of the circle established by Khepr-Ptah. The four quarters and wings are synonymous.[5] Four wings are equivalent to the double shadow, and these four wings, this double shadow, were pourtrayed in the KAPHRETH, called the mercy-seat. Israel had dwelt mentally in this land of the double shadow, and therefore of darkness. "Beyond Æthiopia" does not point to Central Africa. The first land was Æthiopia or Kush in the northern heaven, the land of the north, and Khentu, the south. The next was the heaven of the four corners, first marked by the four great stars and then by the four quarters of Ptah, with the sign of the two beetles (Cancer) as the place of transformation. This is the land of the four corners or wings, and their double shadow, of the Cherubim, now to be superseded by the new heaven of a later solar god whose corner is the east, and "Damascus shall be the rest thereof, when the eyes of Israel shall turn towards the Lord."[6] Damascus is the typical throne of Atum, whose double-seated ark was in the

On the line of AFT or FET, for the four quarters, we have the following names of No. 4 :—

PETTE, Tsherkess.	APAT, Tagala.	FAT, Salawatti.
PUET, Atshin.	IBDI, in Akkadian (for the	FAT, Batta.
OPAT, Batta.	square).	EFFAT, Malagasi.
M-PAT, Sasak.	PEDWAR, Welsh.	FUDDAH, Mandara.
OPAT, Bima.	BOAT, Amberbaki.	FADYG, Bishari.
APAT, Bissayan.	EVATZ, Mallicollo.	FUDU, Bode.

[1] Ezek. vii. 2. [2] Deut. xxii. 12. [3] xviii. 1.
[4] Fuerst, כנף. [5] Cf. Deut. xxii. 12, and margin. [6] Zec. ix. i.

corner eastward, the birth-place of the young god Iu-Su, the sun of the resurrection, and the *rest* answers to Hept (Eg.) the peace.

In the hieroglyphics the closed right hand with thumb extended is a figure of six,[1] as Kefa the fist, a measure of six fingers. Also the Egyptian foot or Khep is a measure of six digits. Thus, a fist and a foot were equal to twelve. Khepr was the personification of this hand and foot, with the numeral value of twelve.

The beetle may be said to be six-fingered, having six TARSI on its feet, the feet have thirty joints, corresponding to the six months of ascent and six of descent, together with the thirty days of the solar month; and it was said to live one six months under-ground and the other six above. Such was the image of Time, as Ter or Khepr, the beetle. Now one name of the mythical giant in Hebrew is Gibor (נבור). This, as the Egyptian has no letter G, is a form of Khepr.

The giant when analyzed will be found to be only a repeating cycle of time, either on a large scale or culminating at the Midsummer height, when the solstice was in the sign of Khepr, or Teman, in the south,[2] in "Thy Gibor, O Teman."

The giant (Repha) of the Hebrew writings is described in the likeness of Khepr as having six fingers on each hand and six toes on each foot; literally, the fingers of his hands and the fingers of his feet, six and six;[3] and again, his fingers were twenty-four, six and six.[4] These six-fingered and six-toed giants, or mighty ones, are nothing more than forms founded on the six-fingered Khepr. The particular instructions given respecting the curtains of the Tabernacle are especially true to the symbolic number six (as Kefa) and the principle of Kabbing. "And thou shalt double (Kab) the sixth curtain in the forefront of the tabernacle."[5] This was the tabernacle of the god of the two Cherubs and of the KAPHARETH.

It was in Gob that one of the giants was slain by Elhanan; another was killed in Gath; the latter name is connected with Khepr as Gath-Chaphr (נת חפר).[6] Khat is to go round, reach the apex or height; shut and seal. In "Khat-Khepr," or the Crab, the circle of the solstitial year was completed and clasped. Gob answers to the Egyptian Kab, the corner, angle, place of turning and doubling. The particular corner of the solstice may be in Kab, the place of the inundation or libation in the sign of Cancer, and in the month Mesore.

This was the place of ending and renewal for a luni-solar year, and in the Hermean Zodiac Taht is seated in this sign. He may help us to understand how the giant was killed in Gob. In mythology an end is often represented as putting an end to, and the solar year in comparison to a moon was a giant. For instance, Khunsu is a youthful hero, like David; he is the luni-solar god, who carries the full moon on his head. He determined the circle of the equinoctial year,

---

[1] *Champ. Dict.* 98. [2] Obad. 9. [3] 2 Sam. xxi. 20.
[4] 1 Chr. xx. 6. [5] Ex. xxvi. 9. [6] Josh. xix. 13.

which was marked as with us by the full moon of Easter; but, as the representative of monthly time he was set forth as slayer of the giant, and thence of the giants the type of a larger period.

David, the Egyptian Taht, also slays the giant in Gath, which we connect with Gath-Khepr, the sign of the beetle, where Taht represents the lunar god, and where the circle of the solstitial year ended, and the giant was slain by the lunar hero. In the astronomical chapter [1] we read: " The Lord came from Sinai and rose up from Seir unto them ; He shined forth from Mount Paran, and He came with tens of thousands of saints." And the lunar deity Taht is the god of Seir in the Egyptian mythology. Seir was the name of his temple in the southern Hermopolis. This answers to the celestial station of Taht in the sign of the Crab in the Hermean Zodiac.

The law-giver, Regulus, *i.e.* Kepheus, Shu and Moses, is the shepherd of the heavenly flock ; the shepherd that led up Joseph like a flock ; the " shepherd,[2] the stone of Israel."[3] The shepherd, represented by the star Regulus, was also assigned a constellation, called the shepherd and his sheep ; these arose when the sun entered the sign of Cancer. The one we may look upon as the Shepherd in the bull calendar, the other in the ram calendar. This is doubly the domain of the celestial shepherd-king, as it was likewise the fiery region ; the lion being a type of fire. Cancer, as a symbol of fire, was the antithesis and *vis-à-vis* of Capricorn, the representative of water. In these two signs occurred the mythical destructions by fire and flood. Enough that we identify the Shepherd and the region of the sun in his fiery strength. One of the titles of Shu makes him the lord of TARURA, *i.e.* the furnace of the solar fire. Now when Moses, as the shepherd, was keeping his flock of sheep in Midian, he " *led the flock to the back side of the desert* and came to the mountain of God, to Horeb."[4] It was here the Angel of the Lord appeared to him in a flame of fire out of the midst of a bush that burned, and was not consumed, and the Lord spoke to him out of the midst of the bush. This, according to the record, was the first manifestation of the god named Jah-Adonai in Israel. The place of manifestation can be observed among the celestial pictures of the planisphere.

We have seen that the initial point of the Mosaic calendar was solstitial. The year was to begin with the month Abib, the Egyptian Ab of the bull-calendar, and Akkadian Ab-ab-gar, "fire that makes fire," and as the solstice receded the initial point was placed in Cancer. The Egyptians made use of both. Thus there were two fixed points of commencement ; one with the sun in Leo and the first zodiac of the four great stars ; the other in Cancer when the zodiac of the twelve signs had been established. Ancient astrologers affirmed that Cancer was the horoscope of the world ; it was, according to their tenets, the sign of commencement, of rotation, and growth. They say

---

[1] Deut. xxxiii. 2.   [2] Ps. lxxx. i.   [3] Gen. xlix. 24.   [4] Ex. iii. 1.

further that by its creation the creation of the four elements became complete, and by their becoming complete all growth was completed. This applies to the four corners, as fixed by Taht and Ptah, following the four corners of Shu the star-god, in Leo, Scorpio, Aquarius, and Taurus. In the sign of Cancer is the ὕψωμα of Jupiter, a star of moderate nature.[1] Ptah, later Tum, is one form of the Egyptian Jupiter, and Cancer was his especial sign, the place of the two beetles. The change from what we may term the calendar and four corners of Shu to those of Ptah shifts the month of commencement from Ab (July) to Tammuz or Mesore (June). Now the Jews keep a fast in this month, *in memory of the tables of the law broken by Moses on Mount Sinai.* The breaking of the two tablets was followed by removing the tabernacle and changing its name to the Tabernacle of the Congregation, and afterwards the two tablets were renewed, which shadows forth the change from Abib to Tammuz, and from the sign of Leo to Cancer as the starting point of the solstitial year. This the imagery will show.

The Hebrew סנה (Senah), the bush or tree, is the SHENU, a thorn-bush. The Shenu (Eg.) is the thorny acacia, also called the ash or tree of life. The Hebrew divinity is described[2] as שֹׁכְנִי סנה (Shakani Senah), the dweller in the bush of thorns. *Our* bush of thorns belongs to the man in the moon. The Negrilos of Malaya place their diviners in an arbour made of thorn-bushes, from which the divine voice is supposed to issue, as it did to Moses.

Bonwick describes a pit of a " suggestive shape," made use of by the Tasmanians in their religious ceremonies, which was surrounded with bushes.[3] This was their thorn-bush, whence issued the divine voice, and it was of a feminine type. But the name of Senah or Shena has other meanings. It denotes the place of turning in the circle where it is completed at the mid-heaven, therefore the place of the solstice and of recommencement in the sign of the lion. The lion, as the turner-back, is the SHENÂ. There is a star on the tip of the lion's tail, designated the claw of the lion[4] (β Leonis), called As-Sarfah, the turn, because the heat *turns* away when it rises and the cold *turns* away when it disappears,[4] and the lion SHENÂ was thus the turner away of both heat and cold.[4]

The Shenti are a form of the twin lion-gods. Shenah (Heb.) and Shena (Eg.) denote the place of repeating and transforming of one into another at the year's end. Shennu is the circle, orbit, circuit, *enceinte*, extent. Num is denominated lord of Shennu in the Ritual ;[5] that is, lord of the repeatings, cycles of time, called " Angels " or Shenan. SHENNU (Eg.) means millions, crowds, attendants. The

---

[1] *Albiruni*, Eng. Tr. p. 55.   [2] Deut. xxxiii. 16.   [3] *Tasmanians*. p. 198.
[4] *Albiruni*, p. 346. Eng. Tr. This claw on the tip of the lion's tail has been represented by the sculptors of the lion upon Assyrian monuments. *Bib. Arch.* v. 5, part ii. p. 325.   [5] Ch. xxxvi.

chariots of God are twenty thousand thousands of SHENAN; the Lord is among them in SINAI, his holy place.[1] The Lord who rode on the heavens by the name of Jah in this Psalm was a form of the sun-god, and like Num-ra, is the lord of Shennu, the region of time-cycles, the Hebrew Sinai; lord of Sheni, the Hebrew Shinan, who were the repeaters and repeatings of time and period, personified as the angels and saints of God, which, as the Assyrian SANATI, are years.

In the Persian Zodiac[2] the bush or tree is visible in the sign of Leo, but it is evidently the same (a vine) which fills the three decans of Virgo in the Egyptian planisphere.[3]

The Rabbins say that Moses was bidden to put off his shoes when in presence of the burning bush because they were made of the hide of the ass. The explanation is symbolical. The ass was Typhonian, and belonged to the earlier cult of Kefa and Sut, the dog-star deity, one of whose types was the ass. The pagan writers were right who contended that the Hebrew Jah, Iao, or Ieo, meant the Ass in Egyptian. IU is a name for the Ass, and the Ass was an image of Sut, the earliest El or Elyon. The ass-head is an ideograph of the number thirty, the emblem of the end of a period, and equivalent to the Typhonian tie. The ass belonged to the Sabean sonship, whereas Moses introduced the solar god in Jah-Adonai. Hence the typical putting off of the shoes in presence of the sun-god. The ass, as symbol of the solstice, is found in the sign of the Lion, and when the solstice receded to the sign of the Crab, or the change was made from a bull calendar to that of the ram, the ass is put off, is no longer the determinative of the year or the bearer of the coming Shiloh. The first tables were broken, the tabernacle was removed to the keeping of the cherubs or beetles, and the new god, who is not Jehovah nor Elohim, nor Jehovah-Elohim, is manifested to Moses in the mount of fire. The beetles identify the beetle-god, who is represented in Egypt by Ptah and his son Atum. The beetle Khepr, for certain reasons, was the type of trans-formation, and Khepr-Ra is the sun that transforms from one character into the other of his two manifestations, according as the year ended with the solstice or the equinox. The first form of the God was manifested by north and south; the later was the God of the double horizon. This is visible in the divine crowns. The crown of the north and south, upper and lower heaven, is worn by Atum crosswise, and is the equinoctial crown, showing him to be the God of both horizons, Har-Makhu, Khepr-Ra of the equinoxes; the first Khepr having been solstitial.

See how the symbols govern the sense of the Hebrew words in this case. KAPHASH (כפש),[4] rendered "He hath *covered* me," is given in the margin "hath *rolled me* in," KHEPR, the beetle, having

[1] Ps. lxviii. 17.　　[2] Drummond, Pl. xvi.　　[3] *Ib.* pl. iii.　　[4] Lam. iii. 16.

been adopted as a symbol on account of its rolling its eggs into a globe of dirt to get them hatched. The beetle chiefly chose dung as the proper (lighter) matter to roll, and this was emblematic of the physiological fact that the seed of soul is enveloped in what would otherwise be excremental substance, the flesh-making source. The sneer of the later Hebrew writers at the dungy gods of Israel is directed against both forms of the excremental.[1] The dungy gods or Gillulim (גלולים), a name of idols derived from rolling round and round about, were amongst the most familiar in Israel, as is shown by the maledictions of an after-time. They are designated the GILLULIM OF EGYPT.[2] These were images which illustrated the periodic nature of revolving time. Time in Egyptian is TER. This is a name of KHEPR, the beetle being a phonetic T sign as well as an ideographic Khep. Ap is likewise the beetle's name. Ter-ap, the beetle-image of Time, yields in the Hebrew plural form the TERAPHIM, consulted in Israel for oracular answers. These might have been timepieces, to judge by the name. Ter is time, and Ap is to reckon, estimate, calculate, declare, manifest, typify, or they might have been scarabæi-images of Ter-Ap, the beetle of time, and symbol of Khepr-Ra or Atum. Unfortunately for their character, however, the Teraphim were related to the feminine form of time and period. The beetle that rolled up its substance as a male type was a still earlier representative of the Creatoress as the beetle of the goddess and the moon.[3] And when Rachel sat on the Teraphim and said the custom of women was upon her[4] she sat upon the Teraph symbolically, whether there was any other image of time or not beneath her. The monthly prognosticators made use of the Teraph in the secrecies of the mysteries with the Q'deshoth as their demonstrators. Hence the connection with divination, sorcery, idolatry, and iniquity,[5] the Teraphim that *spoke* vanity to the diviners of lies.[6] Looking in the liver was also a form of consulting the Teraph,[7] and the liver is the Af (Eg.) or Ab. Af is flesh, determined by a drop of blood; Abt is the liver. The liver was a visible type of the fluid becoming fixed in solid blood, and therefore a symbol of the flesh-forming source, which the female rolled up as the beetle did its ball.

Ambrose, archbishop of Milan, identifies Jesus with Khepr, the beetle-god, when he calls him the "Good Scarabæus who rolled up before him the hitherto unshapen mud of our bodies," as Khepr rolled the ball of mud or manure between his feet. This mud is the flesh-forming source of life, the physical basis derived from the mother. For this reason the two divine sisters, Isis and Nephthys, are also represented as rolling the ball before them.

TERUPHAH (תרופה) in Hebrew is the ailment, sore, bruise, to be

---

[1] Deut. xxix. 17.
[2] Ez. xx. 7, 8.
[3] *Hor-Apollo*, i. 10.
[4] Gen. xxxi. 35.
[5] 1 Sam. xv. 23.
[6] Zech. x. 2.
[7] Ezek. xxi. 21.

healed by the fruit of the tree of life.[1] TERUPHAH, from TERFH, is the feminine for healing, SANATIO. The word TERP (Eg.), as in Hebrew, has the meaning of food and sustenance, food being a synonym of giving life. The first food-giver, nourisher, sustainer, was feminine, and the blood was the life. That which was excremental in one aspect was the fostering food of life in another, as the maker of flesh, and the early physiologists began with the flesh-maker, the motherhood.

At the birth of Joseph Jacob leaves Laban, the father of Rachel, who is represented as taking away by stealth the Teraphim or gods belonging to Laban. Now when we learn that Laban is an Assyrian god, who presided over certain diseases, and was worshipped as a secondary deity in the temple of Anu and Vul (or Bin) in Assur, the old metropolis of Assyria,[2] we find an additional reason for the mythological interpretation of these supposed histories. This will explain the scorn of the later Jahvehists for the dungy gods, Baal-zebul and Baal-zebub, of Israel. The Teraphim, in one shape or other, were certainly Egyptian; for the rites of Taht are designated TERP, and Taht was the lunar deity of utterance, the oracle of the gods; whilst An, the cynocephalus, the menstruating monkey, was one of his types, especially related to the determination of periodic time. They also use this symbol, says Hor-Apollo,[3] because it is the only animal that, at the equinoxes, utters its cries twelve times in the day, once in each hour. According to 1 Samuel xix. 13-16, the Teraph images were of the human shape and made of wood. These would very well agree with the cynocephalus or the scarab atop of the fourfold Tat of Ptah, like that found on the ceiling of the Ramession in the central position, between the first and last months of the year. The Teraph then was a type of time. Time is TER (Eg.), AKH means old, and in the Hebrew THERACH (תרח), the name of Abram's father, rendered by the Seventy, THARRA, THARE by the Vulgate, Thara (Luke iii. 34) means to turn, duration, or time. TER (Eg.) is a time or a turn, and Khepr also signifies to turn, change, figure, form, and transform in relation to time. In the Hebrew[4] TERAH is actually recognized by name as OLD TIME, and the passage has had to be amended to make another sense. Terah appears as the idol-maker to whom the Teraphim are attributed. Ter-ak (Eg.) also reads the Time-ruler, and the Teraphim are images of Time, of Ptah, of Khepr-Ra, or Ter-Ra. The representation of Terah as the idol-maker is only a way of saying that in Israel these images were types of Terah or Ter, Time. The earliest form of Khepr-Ra is Ptah, the opener and circle-maker, therefore the Turner. If we call him Ter as Time-god, then his two types of the beetle (Ap) and the frog (Ap) would be Ter-ap, in the Hebrew plural, Teraphim, as images of time.

[1] Ez. xlvii. 12.   [2] Lenormant, *Bib. Arch.* v. 6, part ii., p. 588.
[3] B. i. 16.   [4] Joshua, xxiv. 2.

These are the types of Ptah, who is pourtrayed as beetle-headed and frog-headed. In one instance [1] he appears with the scarabæus over the frog's head, and this double type of Ptah or Khepr realizes the Hebrew plural Teraph, the Teraphim. It is now proposed to identify Terah with Ptah as Khepr or Ter, the dungy-god, who created with excrements.

The "temple of TARA, which is the temple of the sun at Senkereh," is described in the "Inscription of Nebuchadnezzar" [2] as having mouldered into ruin from extreme age, and its symbolic figures were no longer visible. Tara renders the Egyptian Tera or Ter, the name of time, of which the sun was one type, and Tara was also an ancient god in Babylonia.

Ptah appears on the monuments with Num and Neith. He is the son of Num, and in the Jewish traditions Terah was a prince, and a great one, in the palace of Nimrod.[3] In the Talmud [4] the wife of Terah is called Amtelai or Emtelai, daughter of Carnebo. Amtelai is the female Terah, and Car-Nebo contains the name of Num as Nebo, by permutation. Ptah was the image-maker of the gods ; he formed the circle, shaped the vase, and was typified by the egg, the beetle, the imager, and the frog, the transformer. He was the divine artificer, and is depicted in the act of drawing a figure of Harpocrates, who is a type of the lower sun. Jamblichus calls him the Artizan, and we are told that Terah was in high favour with Nimrod, whose son-in-law he was, because he made his idols for him and was excellent in his art.[5] Ptah is called the father of the fathers of the gods, whose symbol of time, the frog or tadpole, was the sign of swarming millions. Terah was the father of the fathers of Israel, Abram, Isaac, and Jacob, whose children were to swarm in multitudes, numerous as the stars of heaven or the sands of the sea. The river Nile has also the title of "*the father of the fathers of the gods*." Now the Nile in Hebrew is Nahar, and Nahor is the father of Terah, the Hebrew Ptah. The river was the parent of Time or Ter, on account of its periodic flood. They who dwelt on the other side of the river or the flood were those who used the river-reckoning, especially in a mystical sense. They were the IBRI and KABIRI, the sons of Eber, of Sutekh, of Kefa, of Sut-Typhon. Ptah is the founder of the solar circle on the four corners imaged by his Tat; the circle mapped out in seventy-two divisions or duo-decans. Terah or Old Time was seventy years of age when he begat three sons in Ur of the Chaldees. This, according to the present reading of the mythological astronomy, represents the time of the seventy angels, seventy princes, seventy elders or shepherds, who presided over the seventy divisions of the heavens, called the seventy years of Terah, before he begat Abram.

---

[1] *Wilk.* pl. 25.
[3] Jellinek, Beth ham-midrash, p. 27.
[5] Koran, *Sale*, Ch. vi. Notes. D'Herbelot.

[2] *Records*, v. vii. p. 71.
[4] Baba Bathra, fol. xci. a.

Abram, the son of Terah, corresponds to Atum, the son of Ptah, under whom the change from the seventy divisions to the seventy-two was effected. Atum is the "sun in his first sovereignty," who wears the equinoctial crown. He is called the father of souls by the souls or gods in the Ritual. "*Atum has ordained to thee the earth*," is said by the Osirian in the Ritual.[1] The children of Abraham were to possess the earth. Atum was the bestower of the crown of justification of souls. "*Thy father Tum has bound thee with this good crown of justification, with the frontlet* (or crown) *of life. Beloved of the gods, thou livest for ever. Tum has ordered to thee the earth.*" This is said in the chapter of the crown of justification.[2] Abram was the justifier in Israel, to whom the promises were made. The justification through Abram, expounded by Paul to the Romans, is the justification through Atum found in the Ritual, the justifier being an express form of this god as Har-makheru, the son who makes the word truth and is thus the justifier.

One of the representations of Ptah, the Hebrew Terah, is designated "the god under his Tamarisk."[3] This tree in Egyptian is the Asru or Aser. It is identical with the Asherah and the Eshel, both rendered "the grove." "Abram planted an Eshel in the Well of Seven and called there on the name of the Lord, the everlasting God."[4] This is one with the Tamarisk of Ptah, and the tree that stood in the Pool of Persea, the Well of the Two Truths, which had belonged to the genitrix of the gods and the seven stars, but was converted to the use of the solar cult in mapping out the zodiac. The typical tree is also called אֶשֶׁל. Abram came and dwelt under the tree in the plain of Mamra. In Egyptian Mam-Ra is the sun of the dead, the Mummies in the lower region. Atum was this sun of the dead that crossed from west to east, through the Hades where the Mummies awaited their judgment and resurrection, or dissolution. MAM written with the two owls or two cubits is the synonym of HER-AB, the crossing over, and of AMTU for the transit.[5] Thus the Mam-Ra is the Sun that crosses the lower region. Also MAMARI (Eg.) would denote the guarding and keeping of the dead; and in Japanese MAMARI means to guard, watch, protect, and preserve. The MOMBOIR in Dutch is a guardian. By comparing 1 Sam. xxii. 6, 1 Sam. xxxi. 13, and 1 Chron. x. 12, we see that the Terebinth tree of Israel is the same as the Tamarisk of Egypt, the Ashel of the one language and the Asr of the other. The Tamarisk of Ptah which is found to embower Atum in the Ritual is the same that covered Abram. According to Kimchi the name of the Ashel tree or grove should be printed with six points. But the recovery of the

---

[1] Ch. xix.
[2] Ch. xix. Birch.
[3] Birch, Gallery, p. 14.
[4] Gen. xxi. 33.
[5] *Denkmäler*, iii. 13, 18; *Todt*, xv. 30. The MAM-RA exists by name in the Maori MAMARU, a name of the Sun in the shades.

Egyptian original will, in the present as in many other instances, enable readers to dispense with this shut-eyed mode of accenting and underlining, in which the nod is as good as (and no better than) a wink to the blind horse. The Kimchi's six points, however, may denote a relic of the ancient knowledge, as the tree was in the middle of the zodiac, the place of beginning and ending between the six upper and six lower signs. It was here the son was established in the place of the father, and Ptah transformed into Atum-Nefer-Hept, or later, Atum transformed into his son, Iu-em-hept.

The Tamarisk tree is found in the "chapter of turning away all injury,"[1] in which we read : —

"*I am the babe*" (said four times, typical of the four corners, or for Ever). "*Oh, Abaur, thou hast spoken like the sun! who preparest the block by the knowledge of thy name, for thou hast come from it for the great sinner. I am the sun preparing the obedient. I am the great god betwixt the Tamarisks; finished is Ans-Ra or the Pied, at dawn. I am the creator of the obedient, the god embowered between the Tamarisks. I go out. The sun goes out in his turn.*" ANS-RA is the sun clothed in linen ; that is, the mummy-sun, the Mem-Ra. He is the Pied, the Ab-ra, because dual, the transforming sun. The Ab-ra, as crosser of the waters, is Ab-aur.

There are ejaculations here which need not be strained one jot in reading them as belonging to the original of the story told of Abram the father of the obedient and his readiness to sacrifice his child. The speaker personates all the characters after the mode of the Ritual. The sun is embowered between the Tamarisks ; Abram dwelt under the tree. The speaker is the sun preparing the obedient for the block, as was Abram. He is the creator of the obedient ; Abram was his father. The babe escapes and comes out sound. "*He it is who comes out sound: Immortal is his name.*" Life has been given to him by the gods, as it was to the child Isaac. This scene takes place just where the sun-god puts on the white crown and "spiritualises by the name of Akh."

The ram is said to have been caught in a SEBEK (סבּך), a word signifying to interweave and to bind. It is the Egyptian Sefekh, a noose, a mode of capture, a bandage, a tie, and means to capture. Sefekh is the crocodile-headed god, called the capturer, and this deity assumed the ram's head when he became Sebek-Ra ; therefore we infer that in the original text the true ram was Sebek, the ram-god, who was represented by the lamb, Ab. The passage out of Taurus into Aries is possibly illustrated by the story of the ram as the type of sacrifice.

A similar representation is found among the Khonds, but referring apparently to the earlier sign. Once they worshipped the goddess of earth, and offered human sacrifices to her, but when they changed to the religion of light and worshipped the solar god they offered up the

[1] xlii. Birch.

bull. They held a festival to commemorate the ceremonial change from the human to the animal sacrifice. At this festival in honour of the light-god, they killed a buffalo to celebrate the time when the light-deity sent a tribe-deity to crush beneath a mountain the goddess of blood, who had so long induced men to offer human victims to her, and dragged a buffalo out of the jungle, saying, " *Liberate the man, and sacrifice the buffalo.*"[1] This is evidently derived from the same original as the Hebrew legend of the ram caught in a thicket, but refers to the time when the sun had left the Twins, and twin children had been sacrificed. This was common in Africa as in Galam, where a boy and girl used to be buried alive before the great gate of the city to make it impregnable.

Hitherto, when the bibliolator has met with legends like this, they have been set down to the missionaries ; generally a foolish inference necessitated by a false theory. In almost every instance, from the time of the Spaniards in America, the missionaries found the traditions in the various lands. The Hawaiians have their pre-historic Lua-Nnu, who is their second Nnu, reckoned, like Abram, the tenth from the first Nnu. By command of God, he, like Abram, is to introduce the rite of circumcision, to be practised by his descendants; he is also commanded to offer a sacrifice to the Lord. " Then Lua-Nnu inquired of God where he might find a proper place, and God told him, ' Go travel to the eastward, and where you find a sharp-peaked hill projecting into the ocean, that is the hill of sacrifice.' Then Lua-Nnu and his son, Kupulupulu a-Nnu, and his servant started off in a boat to the eastward, and in remembrance of this event was one of the mountains named." This Lua-Nnu through his grandson became the ancestor of the two children of the latter, and the original founder of the Mene-hune people, from whom the Polynesians claim descent. In the parallel account of the children of Toho, the Marquesans not only enumerated the twelve sons, but also included the thirteenth child, who, like Dinah, is the one daughter,[2] which means that they were in possession of the astronomical allegory, in the solar form of the Atum Triad with the twelve signs of the zodiac, and of the legends in which the facts and the teachings were enshrined, and orally communicated in their mysteries. The twelve children in each case represent the twelve signs established in the first sovereignty of Ra as Atum.

Abram, we are told, buried his dead wife in Machpelah, in Hebron, having weighed the price of her grave in the balance. The balance in Egyptian is Makha, which also denotes the level corresponding to the Hebrew plain. The sun-god, Har-Makhu of the double horizon, was the deity of the equinoctial level, or of the scales as its image, Atum being a form of Har-Makhu.

Then Abram took another wife, whose name was Keturah. Ketu,

[1] Macpherson, *India*, pp. 108-187.	[2] Fornander, vol. i. 98.

later Hetu[1] (Eg.), denotes one-half of the circle. In the Hindu astronomy the moon's descending node is personified as Ketu, and Ketu-Râ would be the consort of the sun in one-half the circle. Kat-Mut is an Egyptian goddess, from Khept-Mut, the genitrix of the north or hinder part, answering to Ketu. Keturah bore six sons to Abram, corresponding to the six signs in Ketu, the half circle, or in Kheft, the hinder heaven. KETURAH answers to Kidaria, a name of Demeter, and to KUTHERIA, a name of Venus ; all three may be traced to Khebt or Kat (Mut), who personified the lower heaven, the earth or the hinder part. We now see the meaning of the division of the whole land between Abram and Lot, in which Lot chose the right hand half and went east or journeyed east,[2] leaving the other half for Abram. Of course no two men ever divided the whole land or the earth between them, and the talk about their doing so would be sheer idiocy. But the solar gods did so divide the whole earth and the heaven ; the earth being the lower half and heaven the upper. Atum and Abram were the gods of the lower half; and they gave the earth to their children. As Lot is one of the mythical twins, his nature explains his name as the adherer, the one attached (from לֹ, cf. לֹם and לוֹת), answering to the Egyptian LUTI (Ruti) the twins, as lion-gods or as two gates.

Abram, according to Josephus, was the first to publish the opinion that there was but one God, the Creator of the universe. "This notion," he says, "was the result of observing the irregular phenomena that were visible in the motions of the heavenly bodies."[3] Which agrees with the fact that the solar deity took the place of the lunar and Sabean divinities, and to him was assigned the supreme seat when men had become the masters of solar time, as will be amply shown in the course of this inquiry. Eupolemus, according to Eusebius,[4] reported that Abraham, as the inventor of astrology, taught the science of astronomy to the Phœnicians; he is also accredited with teaching this science to the priests of On (Heliopolis) in Egypt. This is valueless refuse as history, but contains true matter as mythology. Eupolemus connects Abraham with the overthrow of Babel and the catastrophe of the Flood. He says, that in the tenth generation, in the city of Babylonia, called Kamarina (which by some is called the city of Urie, and signifies a city of the Chaldeans), there lived, the thirteenth in descent, Abraham. This too can be correlated when we know the nature of the Tower, and the meaning of the Deluge. The covenant of Abram follows the flood of Noah, and the end of the times of the ten patriarchs. The bow or circle in heaven is one witness of a new covenant, and circumcision is another. This was connected with establishing the circle of the twelve signs, as illustrated by the twelve stones of Gilgal on the hill of foreskins. There was a tradition known to Paul,[5] that

[1] Champ., N. D., 207.   [2] Gen. xiii. 11.   [3] *Ant.* B. i. 7.
[4] Præp. Evang. 9.   [5] Rom. iv. 5, 13.

Abram in being circumcised was to become the heir of the world. Rabbi Jehuda Hakkadosh said : "So great is circumcision that but for it the Holy One, blessed be He! would not have created the world ; for it is said, But for my covenant (of the circumcision) I would not have made day and night, and the ordinances of heaven and earth.[1] Abraham was not called perfect till he was circumcised. It is as great as all the other commandments put together."[2] "Behold the blood of the covenant, which the Lord hath made with you above all these words."[3] The Jewish rite of circumcision by excising the prepuce-cover belongs to the later phase of the solar religion. With the worshippers of the sun or star as the child of the Virgin mother, which preceded the cult of the fatherhood, the circumcision was by castration or by the longitudinal slit of the Maori and Fijian rite, rather than by cutting off the foreskin.

"Worship not the sun whose name is Adonai, whose name is Qodesh ; and who also has names occult and not to be revealed in the world. This Adonai will choose for himself a people and congregate a crowd. Then Jerusalem shall be built up for a refuge, a city of the abortive, who shall circumcise themselves with the sword, dash their own blood against their faces, and adore Adonai."[4]

Time was when Adon (Aten) the earlier form of Atum, as the son of the mother, was represented as the unfertile, mutilated, emasculated Sun which set from the land of life, needing all the help that could be given typically from his worshippers who offered him their own emblems of virility in his *effete* condition. That was before there was any tread in the egg ; before the fatherhood of the gods had been founded.[5]

The Solar fatherhood was established in Atum, who was Ra in his first sovereignty, as father of souls. This is marked by the introduction of the title Atef for the father, found in the style of Atum. The Atef crown denotes the solar god as the father of souls in the lower world, whose substance is self-originated, and who transforms into his own son no longer born of the widow but the wife.[6]

Atum is called the "*Soul of the souls reserved in the west,*" in whose following is the "*reserved soul, the engendered of the gods who provided him with shapes. Inexplicable is the genesis ; it is the greatest of secrets. Thou art the good peace of the deceased. Oh, Creator!*

---

[1] Nedarim, f. 31, 2.   [2] *Ib.*, f. 32, I.   [3] *Ib.* f. 32.
[4] *Codex Nazaraeus*, i. 47.
[5] Under the Sabean and pre-solar *régime*, the ape, dog, jackal or fenekh, were the types of the son, the child of the mother, and these were types having tails. This may be related to the symbolical act recorded in *Primitive Culture* (vol. i. 334) of the father or father-in-law in Brazil, who, after a couple have been married, cuts a wooden stick with the knife of circumcision or a sharp flint, supposing that by this ceremony he is cutting off the tails of his future grand-children, so that they may be born tailless. Sut signifies the tail, and the Typhonian genitrix represents the hinder part.
[6] "I am Isis, the widow." *Déveria*, catalogue des MSS. Ég. du Louvre, p. 171.

father of the gods, incorruptible."[1] This is said when the god, with hands drooping, sets from the land of life. Yet he is accredited with power to beget the soul in the mummies of the dead awaiting their re-genesis. He is the father, the creator, the sun who is still virile, even in passing through the barren region of Anrutf. In Israel the solar fatherhood was established in the person of Abram, and its token is the covenant of the circumcision made in the blood of the male which superseded that founded in the emasculation of the male.

A curious illustration occurs in John's Gospel. "Moses therefore gave you circumcision, not that it is of Moses, but of the FATHERS."[2] It was typical of and sacred to the fatherhood. Atum is the divine Father of the Egyptian Genesis, who becomes the Adam of the Hebrew Genesis, the progenitor of the human beings. "*Thy servant is Being,*" is said to Atum, as he descends to "*create the life of the earth*" for the gods. "*Thy person is typified in Sekari.*"[3] This refers to the re-genesis, in which Ptah fashions the flesh anew, and the deceased becomes a living soul. "*I am Tum, maker of the heaven, creator of beings coming forth from the world, making all the generations of existences, giving birth to the gods, creating himself, lord of life supplying the gods.*"[4]

In the Hebrew Scriptures we find two adaptations of Atum, the great father ; one as Adam, the other as Abram. And it is noticeable that the book of the generations of Adam[5] is immediately preceded by the statement, "*Then began men to call upon Ha Shem Jehovah,*" or to assimilate themselves to the masculine divinity. Abram is apparently a Mesopotamian version of the same divinity as Atum. This was known to the learned among the Jews, and is acknowledged in the *Kabala Denudata*. "Know ye that the scintilla of Abraham, our father, was taken from Michael, and the scintilla of Isaac from Gabriel, and of Jacob from Uriel. These are of the substance of Adam primus, according to the mystery of repetition (revolutionis) of his parts, to wit, of the right side and of the left side, and of the middle."[6] This identifies them as the solar triad, and localizes their triple domain in the heavens.

Atum is a form of Har-Makhu, the god of the double horizon, or the right side, left side, and the middle. Har-Makhu was represented in the Kabala by Michael, who, in Christian art, is the god of the scales ; in these he weighs the souls of the dead. Michael still presides over the equinoctial scales at Michaelmas. The scales in which the dead are weighed carry us back to Sut-Anubis, who was the Sabean Har-Makhu, and who was merged into a Har-Makhu whose type was the Sphinx, and, lastly, we have the solar Har-Makhu of the Atum triad. Michael on the horizon, Gabriel in the height, and Uriel in the depth, equate with Abram in the place of Atum as

---

[1] Ch. xv. Birch   [2] John, vii. 22.   [3] *Rit.* ch. xv.
[4] Ch. lxxix.   [5] Gen. v.   [6] *Kabala Denudata*, ii. 303.

Har-Makhu, god of both horizons, Isaac in the height, and Jacob in the lower world.

Jacob is probably derived from the old god Kak, or Hak. Kak means darkness, and Kak is the deity of darkness, one with the Af-Ra, or Atum as the sun of the lower hemisphere. This agrees with the meanings assigned to עקב ; the dark, deceitful, cunning one, and the one born after. Also, Akab or Kakab (Eg.) is some part of the body, a tendon, possibly the tendon Achilles. The name of Jacob is sometimes derived from עקב, the heel. The heel, however, is but a type of the hinder and lower part. These significations assigned to the name lead us to the Egyptian Kheb, the lower or hinder part or place. Kheb likewise means deceit, hypocrisy, to disguise, violate, change, and hits the character of Jacob, the cunning deceiver. The name with the Ayin hard contains the elements in Jach-kheb, that is, the God Jach of the lower world (Kheb), and as Jach answers to the earlier Kak, the full form is Kak-Kheb, the ancient divinity of the under-world, the sun that shone and struggled with the darkness all night long, just as Jacob is represented as wrestling with the opposing power during the livelong night ; or groping through the gloom as the blind god, our "CHACHE blind-man." Jacob presents a picture of the blind Kak when he lays his hands on the heads of Joseph's children.

Kheb (Eg.) is a title, and Kak-Kheb, or Jach-queb, is thus a title of Jach, the god of the Hebrews, whilst Kheb, as a name for nether-world, identifies the meaning of the title. Then Kheb means to change, to transform (Khep) as did Khepr-Ra, the transforming sun. Jacob is the changer, the transformer, who becomes Israel.

The name rendered Isaac (יצחק) contains the elements of Itz-chaq. י has the meaning of emanation, going forth, self-activity, and tends to identify Isaac with the manifester of the solar triad, the sun on the horizon, the goer forth, the visible god, the shoot, the born one, the laugher and mocker, whose character is pourtrayed in the pastimes of the spring equinox or games of May. The Kak is the old man, who became the Gec or Gouk of the first of April, and the object of the laughter and mockery of those who welcomed and worshipped the youthful god, who was the old sun transformed into the new : Tum into Hu, or Abram into Isaac. The significance of י (or יציא) is found in the Egyptian Ash, for emanation, emission, issue. In the Ottawa Iosco, or Ioskeha, we find another Isaac. Iosco is the white sun-god answering to Hu, god of light, the sun in the height, Atum as the white or light god. The triadic solar nature of Abram, Isaac, and Jacob is corroborated by the Jewish belief that Abram composed their morning prayers, Isaac their noonday prayers, and Jacob their evening prayers. This again agrees with Atum, on the horizon, Hu, above, and Hak, below. The Jews have a legend which relates that when Joseph told his dream of the sun, moon, and stars bowing in salutation to him, the father said to himself, "How did my child come to know that my name is Sun?"[1] The twelve sons also identify Jacob with the sun in the twelve signs.

With Abram as the solar god of a new covenant identical with that of Atum-Ra, in which Anhar becomes his confederate and son, we shall be better able to understand the war of the four kings against the five, ending with the victory of Abram. The four kings we take to be a form of the four genii of the four quarters, found in the Ritual, the four superior gods of the Upper Place, the four angels that stand at the four corners of the earth;[2] the four white men of the Book of Enoch,[3] who "came forth first," one of whom seized and bound the star which fell from heaven and was cast out as a false watcher, and another of whom taught the white cows a mystery. The five kings we also take to represent the five intercalary days of the year of 360 days. Five deities are assigned to these five days, says Plutarch—Osiris, Arueris, Typhon, Isis, and Nephthys. The war with them, as Drummond suggested, relates to the re-adjustment of the calendar, to include the 365 days in the Abramic year. But a new reading of the passage is proposed. Twelve years they served Chedorlaomer, but in the thirteenth year they rebelled, and in the fourteenth year came Chedorlaomer and the kings that were with him and smote the Rephaims in Ashtaroth Karnaim, and the Zuzims in Ham, and the Emims in Shaveh Kiriathaim, and the Horites in their mount Seir; that is, the giants, the monsters, were smitten in all four quarters of the circle. Shaveh, in Chaldaic, means the equator. The five kings, or added days, had served the four genii of the cardinal points for a time; but they rebelled, they were not true timekeepers. It was discovered that solar time consisted of $365\frac{1}{4}$ days to the year; hence the four kings fell upon the five in the Vale of Siddim and put them to rout. Chedorlaomer is particularly said to be the one they served. He, therefore, ought to be king of the quarter in which the year began and ended. He is the King of Elam, and in the Astronomical Tablets[4] we find that on the fourteenth of the month Tisri (September) the time of the autumnal equinox, and the first month of the Jewish civil year, a crown is given to the (celestial) King of Elam. The forces of Elam are in service; there is no return of peace to his men. The war with Typhon and Amalek began at the autumn equinox. The name of Chedorlaomer is explained in the Targum of Jonathan to mean the ligament which binds the sheaves. The sheaves elsewhere stand for the twelve signs. So interpreted, this is the one of the four kings who girded up the sheaves, or made up the reckoning, with the five additional days which were found not to fully complete the solar year.

---

[1] *Bereshith rabbah*, sect. 68.   [2] Rev. vii. 1.   [3] Ch. lxxxviii.
[4] *Records*, i. 161.

Now in Egyptian, in addition to the root of the name Chedr, the warrior, the overthrower, there is a word KHETR,[1] related to the time-circle, meaning *occasionally*, and corresponding to the incidental days, the five days intercalated. In Assyrian "Kitar" is a name for AUXILIARIES or irregulars. Bearing this in mind, it appears likely that Chedor-Lagomer is named as the ruler of the intercalary five, called the five kings, who served him for a time and then rebelled. According to Berosus, cited by Apollodorus,[2] there were five different Oans, or, as he calls them, Annedoti, the fifth and final one being Odacon. All these, says Apollodorus, related particularly and circumstantially whatsoever the typical Oannes had taught them. The name is derived from An (Eg.), the fish, and to repeat, be periodic. In keeping with their nature as announcers of time, the rest of the name may be read by the Egyptian Tet, speech, to speak, or utter ; Tet, the word, the Logos ; and there were five different forms of the announcers of the periods of the five planets, independently of sun and moon. In the Druidic system the planets appear as the five, the five angels, who are attendants on Hu-Gadarn. These five the present writer considers to be the five Annedoti of Berosus, and the five kings of the Book of Genesis, who were also superseded as time-reckoners by the god of solar time, called Atum within Egypt, and Abram out of it. The five great gods issuing from Sesen existed before Shu as Shu-si-Ra and the light of the sun, or before they reckoned the time of the stars by the sun. This agrees with the five kings who existed before the covenant of a new dispensation was made with Abram, which new covenant is now made with the sun of the zodiacal circle, the god of the equinoctial and perfect year, who is Atum in Egyptian, Abram in the Hebrew mythos, and Hu in the British.[3]

In keeping with this rendering of the myth, the solar triad found in Atum, Kak, and Hu appear as the three Adonaim or "my lords" in the Hebrew version. Also, the three make use of the name Jehovah, whereas Abram never does, in addressing the Lord or "my lords." The narrator says, "Abram stood before Jehovah" and "Jehovah spake ;" but Abram only addresses Adonai, and says, "Behold, I have spoken to Adonai !" Under Abram, then, was established the covenant of the solar god, the perfect male divinity, and its token was circumcision.

We shall further find that Hak (Kak or Iak-Kab) is identical with the god Jah-Nes, revealed by Moses. Kak, Hak, Iach, Jah, Ioh, Iu, or Au, are all names of the black sun-god, the sun in the Ament or Sheol.

---

[1] *Select Pap.* xv. 3. Birch, *Dicty.* p. 562.   [2] Euseb. *Chron.* v.
[3] The star, says Hor-Apollo (i. 13), is a figure of 5, because, although there are multitudes of stars in the heavens, five of them only by their motion perfect the natural order of the world.

In the Turin Papyrus, among the supposed Pharaohs of the thirteenth dynasty belonging to the cult of Sebek-Ra, who was the Amen of the Typhonians, there occurs the name of Ra-Nehsi;[1] that is, the black sun, or the black (Neh) son (Si) of Ra. The name is written with the foul black bird, "Neh," the later image of all uncleanness, and with the poop sign, ⟩, for determinative, which also became a type of things foreign to the Ammonians. Ra-Nehsi is literally the nigger-god. It was the Typhonian form of Amen, the concealed, or Sebek-Ra, the sun of darkness, and therefore one with Kak, whose name was modified from Khebekh (Sebek).

The altar of Jah-Nes, erected by Moses, identifies Jah as the black god, the sun in darkness, the deity of the hindward part, the lower heaven. The Hebrew נצה, for excrement, agrees with Nehsi (Eg.) the foul, and the black filthy fowl in one, the bird of night and the hindward part.

When interpreted by the mythos there still appear in the Abramic story a current and a colouring from the land of Aram or Mesopotamia. The genitrix Jehovah is superseded by the Adonaim of Abram, the divinity of a new covenant, the token of which was the rite of circumcision. This change is exactly what occurs with Moses and Joshua after the exodus from Egypt. Then Adonai, as Jah, is made known as a new deity to Moses, and the rite of circumcision is enforced by Joshua with the people who had been the reproach of Egypt. Thus the same thing, the introduction of a new divinity and the rite of circumcision, takes place (for the first time) twice over ; also the different deities are identical. This proves the existence of two currents—one coming from the Mesopotamian source, the other from Egypt. But whether ethnological, and to what extent, or only mythological, is another question. The same myth may here have fresh starting-points, but in the celestial allegory only can these be unified. Two sources for the same mythical matter can be established, but these only serve, so far, to prove the matter to be doubly mythical, and will not help us to make Abram, Isaac, and Jacob into historical personages. Still, we repeat there are two traceable currents, and the matter that meets in the Hebrew writings must have met there by two different channels, which appear to emanate from Egypt and Mesopotamia.

One name of the sun that crosses the Ament is Af. The Af-Ra, literally the sun that squats and crawls like the Hef, a reptile, snake, or caterpillar. This is the sun whose symbol is the serpent which typified means of motion without apparent members. The particular type of Atum as the sun of the deep was the Eel that makes its way through the mud of the MEHT, or Moat, of the north. Af, Ap, and Ab interchange. Ab means to cross and pass to the opposite side, to work a passage through like the gimlet, still called the passer. Aper

---

[1] Brugsch, *Histoire*, Pl. 8, 158. Bunsen, vol. ii. p. 624. Scutcheon.

(Eg.) is the crosser over. The name is applied to Anup, who is called the "*clean crosser over the place of birth.*" [1] The Kabiri of Seven Companions, the seven stars, were the first that ever crossed over the waters, the earliest sailors. These become the חבלי, Abari and Ibri, the Hebrews. Eber, Assyrian Ebiru, is the crosser over, the passenger, as was the Af-ra when boats were built ; previously he had to cross in his type of the frog, eel, worm, or snake, and crawl as best he could. Eber, or Heber, occurs by name in the Ritual as the crosser. "*I have flown as a hawk ; I have cackled as a goose ; I have alighted on the road of the west of the horizon as Heb-ur.*" [2] This is in the chapter of making the transformation into the god Ptah. Heb-ur is the old returner, the opposite to the hawk of the east. The Osirian has crossed from the east and alighted in the west. This passage was made on wings through the air ; it was the upper passage. The Hut or winged disk of Hu, the sun above, was also a symbol of the crosser through the air. The lower passage was by water, or through the mud. The frog-headed Khepr could swim ; he also crosses in his boat ; [3] "*The divine passenger* (Hebrew, Eber) *of the boat of Khepr*" [4] is a title of Atum as the crosser, "speaking words to the gods in Asher-ru."

REM was an ancient epithet of the supreme deity. Among the Phœnicians it was a title of Baal. A Syrian god (Rimmon, רמון) represented Adonis in his mourning phase.[5] Zechariah refers to the great mourning of Hadad-Rimmon.[6] REM is compounded with Baal in Bal-Rem, a title of the Libyan Baal.[7] It was applied to Saturn as Baal by the Phœnicians. The name appears as RAMAS (ραμὰς) in Hesychius. REM (Eg.) is also the fish, one of the water-types. Baal-Rem is Sut, the son of the water-cow, or Remakh. The name of Abram, according to Apollonius Molon, signified "the Father's friend." One name of the god Rimmon is MERMER (Akk.), and in Egyptian MER-MER means the friend.

The Mahometan Arabs held Abram to be identical with Saturn, and represented him in the Kaaba as an old man with SEVEN arrows, or lots of destiny, in his hand.[8] The same figure with the seven arrows was worshipped by the Arabs under the name of HOBAL, who was a form of Saturn. This is important to the genealogy of Abram, because the Hebrew solar god as the father, was once the son of the mother whose earliest form was Sut, Bar-Sutekh, Saturn, Sut-Renn, or the Sabean Baal.

There was a temple dedicated to the god Rimmon in Damascus, and the monarchs of Damascus were assimilated to this god, with Rimmon in their names.

The name identifies the sun as the red (רמה, to be red), and weeping

---

[1] *Rit.* ch. xvii.   [2] Ch. lxxxii.   [3] Ch. xvii.
[4] Ch. xli.   [5] 2 Kings, v. 18.   [6] xii. 11.
[7] Gesenius, *Mon.* p. 453.   [8] Movers, lxxxvi.

(Rem (Eg.), to weep).[1] Adonairem is the weeping Adonai, or Tammuz, whose mourning was celebrated by the women of Israel.

We shall find that Rimmon and Abram, who are both of Damascus, represent a character of the same solar divinity, as the weeping, crawling winter sun, called in the solar litanies Remi, the weeper, the sun who as Af-Ra struggled through the Rem (Eg.), a name for the gorge, throat, or passage. Rem, or Ram, is a name in Hebrew compounded with Adonai in Adonai-ram.[2] The same name is also compounded with Iah in the Hebrew proper name of Ramiah.[3] Thus we have the god Rem, Egyptian Remi, identified with Iah and Adonai, and Adonai is Tammuz, the son of the mother, who became the later Atum in the character of divine father of the son.

In Hebrew Rackam is the womb, and in the change of the name Abram (from אברם to אברהם), the Heth only needs the mappiq sign to show us that Abraham is Abracham, the womb-father, hence the father of multitudes. Abram can also be identified with Atum by means of the legends.

In the Egyptian drawings the Af-Ra is pourtrayed as the father of the multitudes of souls. He appears as the god who navigates the lower heaven, and is represented in the act of begettal, revivifying the mummies of the beings who await their resurrection, the natural imagery being applied in expressing the eschatological ideas. As such he is the Mam-Ra.

Abram is said to have been king of Damascus, where there was a village at one time called the "Habitation of Abram." The Egyptian name of Damascus is Tamsakhu, or Tumsakhu, the shrine or gate of Tum. The name of the city is said to have been taken from King Damascus in honour of whom the Syrians consecrated the sepulchre of his consort Arathis as a temple, and regarded her as a goddess worthy of the most sacred worship.[4] The goddess Arathis is the Egyptian Erta, a cat-headed Deess, and therefore a form of Pasht, who was the consort of Tum, and of whom he was re-born as the son, Nefer-Tum, or Jesus (Iu-su), in the Sakhu of Tum, the Damascus in which Israel was to find the Rest or Peace personified in Iu-em-hept.[5]

We shall likewise find the character of Remi, the Af-Ra, the sun that crossed from the west, and struggled through the Ament, pourtrayed in the sufferings of Job.

This book was one of the last to yield up its secret to the comparative method, the solar allegory has been so naturalized as to hide its face beneath an almost impenetrable mask. The "Open Sesame,"

---

[1] ABRAM. Abraum is an English name for a reddish kind of clay. "ABRAM-COLOURED" is a phrase used by Shakespeare (*Coriolanus*, ii. 3) which was changed to AUBURN in the Folio of 1685. ABRAM and AUBURN permute as two forms of one word (see REMN, Eg.) for a reddish colour.
[2] 1 Kings, iv. 6.
[3] Ezra, x. 25.
[4] Nicolas of Damascus, Eusebius, Josephus and Justin, out of Trogus Pompeius.
[5] Zech. ix. 1.

however, was found at last in the name. There is often more in a single word for the present purpose than can be found in any volume of words. Tradition (Apokryphon of the Alex. version) mentions the earlier name of Job as being יובב (Ιωβάβ) who was an EDOMITE,[1] one of the Kings of Edom who reigned before there were any kings of Israel; the Vulgate and the Seventy also identify him as the hero of the Book of Job. Fuerst gets out of the name, written אז ב, the meaning of the turning, returning, whence converted one. In Egyptian BAB signifies to turn, circle, go round, revolve, also a hole, cavern, the pit; in Talmudic Hebrew, BIB is the hollow, the pit. God is said to answer Job "out of the whirlwind," and "Bab" (Eg.) is the name of a whirlwind as well as the void of the underworld. AU (Eg.) means to be old, sad, and afflicted. The earlier form of Au is Af, answering to the Hebrew יו in יובב, and Af is a name of the sun in the lower hemisphere, or BAB, later BAU, the hole of the tomb. Af-bab, the sun of the lower region, represents the Hebrew Iav-bab (or Iobab) and would denote the sad, old, afflicted winter sun stripped of all his power and property, and shorn of all his glory. "Thou puttest thyself as a boundary, a limit round about the very roots or lowermost reach of my feet," is the sense of Job (xiii. 27), where the A.V. sets him in the stocks; and this language is particularly appropriate to the sun in the netherworld. So read, Iav-bab is the equivalent of the Af-Ra, the sun that crawled (Af) through the infernal region, where Satan the enemy, the accuser and tormenter, as the Apophis, was supposed to treat and torture the poor old helpless sun as badly as he is permitted to do in the Hebrew scripture; only in the Egyptian there is no triad of talking tormentors.

The drama of Satan obtaining the divine permission to torment and try the spirit of Job is suggested in Psalm cix., where we read "Set thou a wicked man over him, and let Satan (the adversary) stand at his right hand" to resist him. So Satan stood at the right hand to resist Joshua. So Satan, as Sut, torments the sun-god in the Hades.

In the Ritual the sun and soul are identical. Here is the suffering, tried, and tormented one.

"*It is the sun himself.*

"*Save thou the Osiris from the god, stealer of souls, annihilator of hearts, living off filth. The darkness is of Sekari; he has terrified by prostrating. It is Sut; it is the slayer.*

"*Oh Creator, dwelling in the bark* (Khepri) *forming his own body* (or forming his body eternally), *save thou the Osiris from those who are the guardians and judges. I do not sit in fear of them. Nothing of a nature hateful to the gods has been done by me, because I am the Lord in the great hall* (that is, the judge himself). *The Osiris goes purified to the place of* (re)*birth; he has been steeped in resin* (Tahn) *in the place of preservation.*

"*Kepri in his boat is the sun himself.*"[2]

[1] Gen. xxxvi. 33. [2] Ch. xvii. Birch.

Job is the same personification as Remi the weeper. His "roarings are poured out like the waters,"[1] his afflictions are reproduced in a drama of horrible physical suffering. The character of the Af-Ra is curiously correct. "My flesh is clothed with worms and clouds of dust." "I have made my bed in the darkness; I have said to corruption, Thou art my father; to the worm, Thou art my mother." "I am a brother to dragons, and a companion to owls. My skin is black upon me, and my bones are burned with heat."[2]

The Af-ra, as before said, is synonymous with the worm of darkness making its way through the earth. Af (Eg.), to squat, also denotes the matter of corruption, the blood-substance, the flesh.

This clue enables us to comprehend the mixture of doctrine concerning the hereafter. Man dies and is ended, but Job lives and will rise again; he is the Af-Ra, the Iav-bab, who completes the circle and emerges from the Nuter-Kar. "Man dieth and wasteth away, yea, man giveth up the ghost, and where is he? If a man die shall he live?" Evidently not. "Man lieth down, and riseth not, till the heavens (are) no more, they shall not wake, nor be raised out of their sleep."[3] But the speaker is not a man. He is the solar personification on whose transformation and renewal so much faith has been founded. He will assuredly rise again. "All the days of my appointed time will I wait till my change come. Thou shalt call and I will answer thee." He asserts the resurrection for himself, whilst denying it for man. This belongs only to the solar allegory. Also the other speakers do not refer to the resurrection of man.

We are literally discovering the skeleton of mythology buried in the body of eschatology, and here and there the bones come more prominently into view.

For example, in the passage rendered "I know that my Redeemer liveth, and that He shall stand at the latter day upon the earth," the Redeemer is the גאל or גאול, and the whole solar doctrine now contended for is to be found in this Gavel, or Redeemer, when rightly interpreted.

The Hebrew Gavel represents the Egyptian Khepr—the beetle-headed divinity who redeemed the dead by re-begetting them in the underworld, corresponding to the grave or burial-place, which, in Hebrew, is the QEBORAH; Arabic, KABR; Malayan, KUBUR; Swahili, KABURI; Hindustani, KABR. Khepr symbolized becoming, he was the sun of morning. In a papyrus in the Louvre it is said:—"The majesty of this great god attains this region (the 12th of the subterranean world, corresponding to the 12th hour of night), where utter darkness ends."[4] He transformed to rise again, and was the god of that metamorphosis and resurrection promised to the just. Khepr with folded wings symbolizes the metamorphosis, the

[1] iii. 24.
[2] Ch. xxx. 28-30.
[3] xiv. 12.
[4] Pierret, *Essai*, pp. 72-3.

transformation. Ptah-Khepr is said to fashion his FLESH anew. The process is exhibited as the fecundation of the mummies of souls awaiting their resurrection from the dead, and their change was the ransom or redemptiom of the later phraseology, as in the Turkish KEFR, an expiation, and Hindustani KAFARA, a penance or expiation for sin.   If we read the words of Job thus:—" I know that Khepr liveth, he who is the eternal being, the re-erector, and that he shall ultimately stand and be established on the earth or the horizon," we recover the Egyptian doctrine of the book.

The identity of Khepr the transformer with Gavel the redeemer is also shown by the cognate Chavel (חול), a name of the Talmudic phœnix,[1] which transformed itself by fire every 500 years, and arose renewed from its ashes. This helps to realize the sense assigned to the word NEKB (Eg. Nekf) in the passage " yea, though calcined (like the phœnix in the fire), yet shall I rise again."   The image is also used by Job,[2] " Then I said, I shall die in my nest, and I shall multiply my days like the PHŒNIX " נאול or נאל, חול.   Gal or Gavl is a frequent epithet of God in Hebrew, as the deliverer or redeemer ; and this identifies the deity at last with Khepr, the god of the solar resurrection.   But the Hebrews have not only the divinity of Khepr as God and as doctrine, they have the beetle likewise by the name of Chargal (חרגל),[3] literally Khepr, the circle-maker.[4] The name answers to the doctrine of Gilgal, or the on-rolling, and Khepr was the roller on of his seed-ball, and thence of the sun and the soul.   For the doctrine of Khepr, the raiser up from the dead, is at the base of the Hebrew Levirate, in which the living brother raised up seed to the dead one, and was called the GAVEL.   Khepr signifies to assume the shape of, as the Gavel did of his brother ; also to generate, and Gavel means to perform the marriage duty, as the redeemer or Khepr.[5]   This doctrine of redemption was likewise applied in the Law of Moses, where the man who had sold himself into slavery was ransomed or redeemed by his kinsman as Gavel, Goel, or Khepr.

The sun that suffered and saved the world was considered to be the true sun as Makheru, the perfect as Tum, the constant in all his trials, the overcomer of the Apophis. Such is the character of Job the righteous, true and perfect man and conqueror at last. Also as the sun that rises again from his lowly state of loss and penury, he has

[1] Talmud, Ezekielos.   [2] Ch. xxix. 18.
[3] It appears to me that the beetle Khepr is referred to by Isaiah (ii. 20) : " In that day a man shall cast his idols of silver and his idols of gold, which they made for him to worship, to the CHAPHR (חפר) and to the עצלף," rendered moles and bats. But the images most probably represented the creatures they are to be thrown to, and one of these is the CHAPHR or Khepr, the digger of diggers. CHEPSH (חפש) is a Hebrew name for the beetle (Hab. ii. 11). The bat, according to Hor-Apollo (ii. 53), is the symbol of a woman suckling and bringing up her children well. Its name, STAAKHMU (Eg.), shows it was a flying chimera, in allusion to its dual nature.
[4] Lev. xi. 22.   [5] Ruth, iii. 13.

restored to him twofold all that had been taken from him. That also occurs only in the realm of myth. This view of the book will suggest some new readings of the text and throw some light on the old.

The use of the word בָּשָׂר for the flesh indicates the image of erection and reproduction. This can be corroborated both in Hebrew and by the Egyptian Shar, puberty and promise.[1] The male emblem of Khem and Mentu was the type of the sun of the resurrection, that is on the horizon, and Khepr is the re-erector. Again, as solar god Job says,[2] "O that thou wouldst hide me in the grave, that thou wouldst keep me secret." The word here used is TZEPHEN (צָפַן), meaning to cover, cover closely, enclose, conceal, to be veiled, hidden, dark, to preserve or keep. But the Hebrew terms derived from the organic root are too abstract to convey the whole meaning.

SEF (Eg.) is bitumen or pitch used in sealing up the mummy, and on the theory that the original was Egyptian, the sense is, "O that thou wouldst hide me in the grave, pitched and sealed as is the mummy." This could not be with the suffering god; but he is here made to envy the human mummy.

The Egyptian and Coptic calendar contains many relics of the past. For example, the 17th of the month Hathor, the day on which Osiris entered the Ark, is still marked in it as the first day of the season for navigation in the Indian Ocean! This calender will help us to establish the mythological and solar nature of Job. We read in it that on the first of the month Taht (Tout) Job took a warm bath and was healed of his sores. This was the first day of the Egyptian New Year, which remains the Coptic Norôz or New Year's day.[3]

Also, the calendar contains "JOB'S WEDNESDAY," the next before the Coptic Easter, and on this day many persons still wash themselves with cold water and rub themselves with a creeping-plant called RAARAA EYOUB or GHABEYRA on account of a tradition that Job did this to obtain "restoration to health."[4] This restoration belongs to the sun of the equinox; the other to the solstice or the beginning of the Egyptian sacred year. These doubly identify Job with the solar god who was first the Har-sun (Aten) of the north and south and afterwards the Ra-sun (Atum) of the equinoctial heaven.

The mythical matter of the book has been recomposed and re-applied for human use. As in the Psalms however, the grandeur of the writing is often the result of its indefiniteness, and the mental mist which our ignorance of the mythology leaves us in is one great cause of the magnificence. The solar theory may perhaps explain why the reputed home of the patriarch Job in the "Holy Land" is a kind of Mecca for negro pilgrimages.

[1] Cf. Gen. xvii. 11, and Ex. xxviii. 42.   [2] Ch. xiv. 13.
[3] *Egyptian Calendar*, 1878, p. 21.
[4] Lane's *Egyptians*, v. 2, p. 222. *Coptic Calendar* (1878), pp. 21, 24, 70.

The Land of Uz or עוץ, if rendered in accordance with the myth, is named from the Egyptian Khepsh, or at least is represented by it. With the Ayin hard, the Hebrew word is Gvz, an equivalent of Khepsh. Khepsh is the hinder thigh, the Great Bear, the place in the north where the sun suffered and died to be re-born, corresponding to the Meskar or Meskhen of the solar house.

The student will perceive how closely allied to the bewailings of Job are the Lamentations of Jeremiah, who seems to be the figure of Jah as Remi, the weeper, or Remiah, with the Jad prefixed. His lamentations are essentially those of Remi the weeper, the suffering sun in Rem-Rem, the place of weeping. "I am the man that hath seen affliction by the rod of his wrath. He hath led me and brought me into darkness. My flesh and my skin hath he made old." "Mine eye runneth down with rivers of water." "Mine eye trickleth down and ceaseth not, without any intermission." "Waters flowed over my head."[1] The third chapter is an exact replica of the bewailings of Job. The words, "All ye that pass by, behold and see if there be any sorrow like unto my sorrow," are an express utterance of the suffering Remi. In the person of Jeremiah, Remi is turned into the utterer of the oracles of Jah.[2] Remi-Jah is found elsewhere as Remi-Baal or Jerombaal.

Sanchoniathon quotes the authority of the Jewish priest Jerombaal, who was the servant of the god Ieuo.[3] If we translate Baal by Jah, Jerombaal is Jeremiah. Jeremiah was considered a kind of protecting genius to the people of Israel who was continually pleading for them before the throne of God. Remi the weeper precedes the Messiah Horus, and Jeremiah was also considered to be, like Elias, a precursor of the Christ who was to come. The Psalms of David likewise give utterance to the wailings of Remi the weeper.

"I am weary with my groaning; all the night I make my bed to swim; I water my couch with tears. Mine eye is consumed because of grief."[4]

"I am a worm and no man,"[5] corresponds to the sun that wound its worm-like way through the earth or the depths.

Abram identifies himself in Genesis[6] with the character of the sun of the netherworld, called the infertile sun of Anrutf, the barren sterile region, in his complaint of being childless. This chapter appears likewise to contain a relic of the genuine mythos in the passages :—

"And when the sun was going down a deep sleep fell upon Abram; and, lo, an horror of great darkness fell upon him. . . . And it came to pass that when the sun went down, and it was dark, behold a smoking furnace and a burning lamp that passed between those גזר."[7]

---

[1] Ch. iii.   [2] Jer. 27. 1 ; Dan. ix. 2.   [3] Movers, 128.
[4] Ps. vi.   [5] Ps. xxii. 6.   [6] Ch. xv.   [7] Gen. xv. 12, 17.

It is a picture of the sun-god going down into Egypt, the Khebt of the celestial north, like Atum, as he sets from the land of life, when Nu, the firmament, seeing in her son the Lord of Terror, greatest of the terrible, setting from the land of life, becomes obscured.[1] The smoking furnace and the lamp of fire are in accordance with the legends of Abram's furnace. Also a smoking furnace may be seen in the Egyptian planisphere, as the altar with its fire.[2]

Abram, in various traditions, is reported to have been cruelly persecuted and cast into a fiery furnace by the Chaldeans, from which he was saved by miracle. UR means fire, and according to the Vulgate rendering of II. Esdras, ix. 7, Abram was delivered from the fire of the Chaldees, not from a city, and this belief or superstition, that is an uninterpreted relic of mythology, is said to be general among the Jews.

The Af-Ra was a god of solar fire, whose furnace was the Ament, out of which flew the starry sparks. But Af is the earlier Kaf or Kep (Eg.), which means heat, light, fermentation or fire. Hence fire, in Maori, is kapura; in Assyrian gibil, a burning, and this agrees with Khepr (Ptah), who was the fire-god. Kep modifies into Hep, and we have the Greek Hephæstus, the fire-god and fashioner by fire. Khepr-Ter and Terah were the fashioners by fire, and just as Kepr modifies into Apr or Afr for fire, so does the Af-Ra follow Khepr-Ra; and Abram is the son of Terah, associated with the furnace of the lower sun, the parallel of Atum as the son of Khepr-Ptah, the Egyptian Vulcan.

The first idea of fire or heat would be derived from the sun; and the sun below the horizon, where the fire burned all night to be reproduced at dawn, was the furnace from which Abram escaped. The land of אור was the domain of Khepr-Ra, the beetle below the earth.

The connection of Abram with Saturn can be traced through the crocodile-headed god, Sebek, or Kevekh, a son of the Typhonian genitrix, whose name modified into KAK. When Amestris, the spouse of Xerxes, sacrificed seven children to the god of darkness and the infernal regions,[3] the number identifies the rite with the worship of this solar Sevekh, whose name signifies No. 7, and with Kak, whose name denotes darkness. He was worshipped as the ram-crocodile god at Ombos. There was a temple of Kak, built by Amenhept-Hui in the time of Amenhept III., and in the district of Kak. It is a very old name, as a King Kakau, of the second dynasty, is assimilated to the ancient Kak, the sun of darkness. Kak becomes Hak in the triad of Atum, Hu and Hak, and the black god of Biban-el-Muluk brings on the name and character, as Iu or Au.

In the Book of Revelation[4] there appears a lamb with seven horns

[1] *Rit.* ch. xv.
[2] Drummond, *Œdipus Judaicus*, Pl. 2.
[3] Herod, B. vii. 114.
[4] Ch. v. 6.

and seven eyes, who is represented in the character of the Lord of Lords and King of Kings, receiving the worship of the four beasts, the types of the four corners, and the four-and-twenty elders, the twenty-four judges in the Babylonian astronomy, and of the host of angels. In Egyptian, Sevekh is No. 7, and Sevekh is a form of Sebek, who became the ram-headed god of the thirteenth dynasty. The young ram is, of course, the lamb—the ram that was depicted as a lamb in the Persian zodiac. It was shown in the first chapter that a mother of the Sebekhepts was named Aaht-Abu, the abode of the lamb. The Sebeks, therefore, adopted the lamb as their type of the ram, which means that they worshipped the male divinity in the form of the son of the mother; their cult in the solar, as in the earlier Sabean stage, being that of the virgin mother and her child. They were Typhonians because they rejected the fatherhood, and continued the pre-monogamous mythological types.

The type of the Ammonians was the ram, as begetter; the lamb represented the unbegotten, or rather the self-begotten of the mother, and not the son who proceeded from the father. Sebek, the ram-headed, was the lamb (Abu or Ab) who became the later lamb of God as the type of sacrifice, just as the bull had previously been. Further, there is a favourite terminal in the names of the Sebekhepts of the thirteenth dynasty. It is that of Ab-Ra. We find in the lists, Antu-abra, Her-abra, Nefer-abra, Netem-abra, Saukh-abra, Uah-abra; Ab-ra being the sun, as the lamb, or Sebek-Ra, whose name is synonymous with the number seven. Sebek or Sevekh was the solar continuity of the earlier Sut of the dog-star in the Typhonian *régime*. The seven (Sevekh) are to be found primarily in the seven stars or spirits of the Great Bear, and the seven horns and seven eyes of the lamb in Revelation are rightly identified with the seven spirits sent forth into all the earth, who, in the Book of Zechariah, are the seven eyes of Jehovah. The lamb, the hornless type, as child of the mother alone, corresponds to the first Horus, Har-pi-Khart, the dumb (Kart, silent) child, and the two are blended in one image by Isaiah, in his portrait of the suffering Messiah. "He is brought as a lamb to the slaughter, and as a sheep before her shearers is dumb, so he openeth not his mouth."[1] In the form of Har-pi-Khart he only points to his mouth. He represents the sun born at the summer solstice, the God who descended and suffered and died; who in one myth is the blind Horus sitting solitary in his darkness and blindness; in another he is Kak (or Hak), who feels his way through the darkness by the sense of touch; in another it is the Af-Ra, the crawling lower sun, the eel, worm, or snake; and in another it is Abram. Ab denotes the young sun-god, whose type was the lamb; and Rem (Eg.) the weeper, completes the title and identifies the first Abram with the other forms of the solar god, who was born

[1] Ch. liii. 7.

of the virgin mother, such as Aten, Sebek, Tammuz, and Duzi. This was before the change of name. That change implies the change from the son to the father: "Thy name shall be called Abraham, for a father of many nations have I made thee."

The corresponding change was made in Egypt, when Aten, the son of the mother, was converted into Atum, the father, which was probably in pre-monumental times. The change is further illustrated by the witness of the seven ewe lambs, as token of the covenant made at the well of the Seven (Shebag or Sevekh), when Abram calls upon the name of the everlasting God.[1]

The Abram of the first covenant represents the sun-god Aten, the Har of both horizons considered to be the dual son of the mother. He and Lot are the two Horuses of the two heavens. In this phase Abram laments that he is not a father, and has only Eliezer of Damascus, who is not his son, to be his heir. His condition corresponds to that of Ra, when the weary god complains that he cannot go further without another to support him, whereupon Shu is given to him by Nun to be his son and supporter. "Said by the Majesty of Ra, I assemble there (in the fields of heaven), the multitudes that they may celebrate thee, and there arose the multitudes."[2]

"And He (the Lord) brought him (Abram) forth abroad, and said, Look now toward Heaven and tell the stars, if thou be able to number them: and he said unto him, So shall thy seed be."[3]

"In that same day the Lord made a covenant with Abram."[4]

The result of this covenant is that a son is given to Abram in the person of Ishmael. In the Egyptian mythos Shu is given to Ra as his first son; in the Hebrew version, Ishmael is given to Abram. Shu, in the dual form, is either Ma-Shu or Shu-Ma; a name of the Pool of the Two Truths, and Shu-ma-el is an equivalent for the name of Abram's first son, called Ishmael, born of Agar. "Which things are an allegory," says Paul, "for these are the two covenants, and this Agar is Mount Sinai."[5] We have identified Shu with Mount Sinai and the first covenant of the two tables which were broken and superseded, and Shu-ma-el is identified by Paul as the son of the first covenant, the star-son who preceded the solar son just as Ishmael precedes Isaac. Under the second covenant Isaac is born. He is the solar son, and second of the triad into which the solar god transforms. Agar has the name of the Akar, the hinder part, the north, where Shu is the supporter of the nocturnal heaven. Thus the first covenant of Abram answers to the first creation of the sun-god, in which Shu is called Shu-si-Ra, and in the second covenant the fatherhood is established in the person of Abraham as it was in the person of Atum.

[1] Gen. xxi. 28-33.
[2] Pl. B. line 41.
[3] Gen. xv. 5.
[4] Ch. xv. 18.
[5] Gal. iv. 24, 25.

By means of Makedo,[1] the wolf-type of Sut, and Makai, the crocodile-type, we are able to establish the Typhonian link between Sut and Sevekh, and as Sevekh septiformis is identifiable with the lamb, and this was a type of the old Sebek, or Kebek, who became the solar Kak, the sun of darkness, and as this is in each case the true Hebrew line of the divine descent from the genitrix to the star-son, the Sabean fire-god, and thence to the solar sonship, and finally to the solar fatherhood, we are now in a position to trace the gods of Israel in a connected series.

In the beginning was the genitrix, Jehovah, who bore the first child in heaven, and was worshipped as the one and seven, Jehovah-Elohim. The son appears as Seth, the son of Chavvah, in one form of the mythos, and as the manifester of the seven, who are the Elohim under one type, and the patriarchs under another.

Sut also appears in the person of Melchizedec. Sut, the first son of the mother, the star-god Bar, or Baal, was the primordial Messiah and Anush of mythology; the first male manifester in heaven under the type of the dog-star, and Melchizedec is acknowledged to be the original type of the Messiah in Israel. He is the establisher of the order of the Messiahship in the Hebrew cult, just as Sut, or Sutekh, is the first announcer in heaven. The Messiah-Son in the Psalms[2] is after the order of Melchizedec. Also the Christ of the Epistle to the Hebrews is a Messiah after the order of Melchizedec. Thus the priesthood of Christ is identified with the Messiahship of Melchizedec, the Hebrew form of Sutekh, the Sut of Egypt, who was phenomenally the first manifester and announcer of time in the heavens as the dog-star, son of Typhon, the goddess of the Great Bear. Sut was cast out of Egypt, together with his worshippers, as the unclean. He retained the good character for a while in Israel, yet it was known in after times that, as Melchizedec, he was of an unclean origin, and by degrees the good Sut, the earliest Prince of Peace, became the Moloch, the Tzud, Adversary, Satan and Devil of the later theology. " Melchizedec," say the Jews, was, " in our third tradition, born of unclean parents." " Melchizedec was born of unclean parentage."[3] According to Epiphanius,[4] the mother of Melchizedec was Asteria or Ashtaroth, the Astarte, who is the Syrian mother of Sutekh. This is sufficient to identify him with the Sutekh of the Khita, the Sydik of Phœnicia, the Sut of Egypt, son of the unclean Typhon. Also both characters meet—the good and the evil Sutekh—in Psalm cix. In the Hebrew traditions this Psalm is assigned to Melchizedec,[5] the ruler of unclean origin, that of Sut, the child of Typhon, who in the later cult of both Jews and Egyptians was turned into Satan. This change in the status of Sutekh, or Melchizedec, will explain why the

[1] Diod. i. 18.   [2] cx. 4.
[3] *Jud. quid. ap. Sixt. Senens.* lib. v., Annot, xc.   [4] *Hæres*, 55—67.
[5] Calmet, " Psalms."

Psalm is associated with the name of the Typhonian Messiah, who was degraded into the Satan and adversary of souls. Sut, or Satan, appears by name in the Psalm assigned to Melchizedec, and it is said of him, "Let Satan stand at his right hand," as the typical adversary, exactly the same as the character assigned to Sut, the accuser and catcher of souls in the Ritual.

There is a proper name in the Book of Ezra[1] IU-TZEDIQ, or (יוצדק), rendered Ἰωσεδεχ by the Seventy. This also contains the duality (Iu, Eg.) of Sutekh, which is pourtrayed, in the double Sut as Sut-Har, Sut-Nubti, or the double Anubis, founded on Sut.

The most ancient worship of the mother and son in the Sabean form is that denounced by Amos as continued in the wilderness, where the Israelites made to themselves and worshipped the god of a certain star—probably the eight-rayed star—of Sikkuth and Kivan. These are undoubtedly the duad of the mother and son, identical with Astarte and Sutekh, Chavvah and Seth, the Carthaginian CÆLESTIS and SICHÆUS, the duad which, in the stellar form, constituted the Sut-Typhon of Egypt.

The god SIKKUTH, Greek Σικύτης, typified the emasculated or castrated divinity, who was the CROOT or כרות of mythology, otherwise the Child. The SEKI (סכי) is the castrated one. In the north of England the castrated bull is still called a SEG. USUKKATH (Ass.) means to cut, to wound sacrificially; SUKHAT (Eg.) to cut, wound as a sacrifice. In English, sacrificing is a name for scarifying; and cutting the flesh was a sacred mode of memorizing, extending to castration in the most fanatical phase of circumcision. The identity of the male organ and the memorial under the name of ZAKAR, which likewise means to cut, imprint, and cause to remember, is derived from early ideas of sacrifice. The Hebrew name for sacrifice, as the meat-offering of remembrance, Azkerah (אזכרה) is derivable from As (Eg.), sacrifice, and KAR, the male power and property; expressed by KARIU for the testes, the seed that was passed through the fire to Moloch. The sinking sun was represented as being in this emasculated condition, and those who made themselves eunuchs were assimilating their condition to his; and to be KART or CUT, literally GELT, was to become like this divine child of the virgin mother. The "reproach of Egypt" consisted of this kind of circumcision. The character of the emasculated, or unvirile sun-god was still continued in Ptah-SEKARI, and the mutilated Osiris, after the eunuch-making had been repudiated by the Egyptians. This circumcision is denoted by the word חרף, which means disgrace and shame; it is applied to being violated and deflowered, stripped of honour, made naked, divested, to cut into, to pull or pluck the fruit, to be made desolate, an object of scorn, all of which meanings fit the eunuch. The word CHERP (in Egyptian Kherp), means the first-

---

[1] Ch. iii. 2.

fruits, to consecrate, pay homage; and the first kind of circumcision was a dedication of the first-fruits of the male at the shrine of the virgin mother and child, which was one way of passing the seed through the fire to Moloch.[1]

The Hebrew אות modifies into את, and the ETH of Sikkuth and Kivan, as before suggested, represents the AFT (Eg.) as the abode, couch, or ark of the four corners which bears the name of the Typhonian genitrix. In that case the ETH (Aft) would denote the portable shrine, and Sikkuth, the child-god, as the Aft or Apt, was the crib or cradle, a form of the Meskhen, Hebrew Mishkan, the tabernacle of the mother and child, the divine duad, also represented by the branch and pot of manna. The meaning of Amos is: "Ye have carried the tabernacle of Sikkuth, your Moloch, and Kivan," the genitrix, whose particular star was Ursa Major, the star of Moloch and Kivan, or of Sut-Typhon. Moloch is commonly identified with Saturn, who is the planetary type of Sut; but the first Moloch was Bar-Sut, the Moloch-Bar, who became the Roman god Mulciber (or Mulkiber), who is identified with the element of fire. Kivan, or Kûn, was a form of Taurt or Taur-Mut, the oldest mother continued under the serpent type. The serpent is an especial symbol of the great mother. The two truths, assigned to her from the first, are written with two serpents. These are the mother's hieroglyphics in her two characters of the virgin and the gestator. The two serpents form the Urt crown of life, or rather of gestation and maternity. The serpent erected on the cross-pole, the stauros, is found in the form of an Egyptian standard crowned with the serpent-goddess Rennut, a type of the Two Truths. She is mounted on a Tau cross, and wears the double crown on her head; the standard is the sign of the two lands.[2] Rennut (as Renen) means the virgin, and she is also the goddess of harvest—that is, of the two periods of pubescence and parturition. Hefa is the name of the great serpent of life, and Hefa (or Kefa) is identical with the Hebrew Jehovah and Kivan, who were worshipped in the typical wilderness, one of whose emblems was the serpent of fire. Fire that vivifies is an Egyptian term for the element represented by the serpent of life, the Hefa; the other of the two primal elements being water. This was the serpent called the Nachash, that is the serpent Nak on the Ash, the tree of life—the same dual figure as that of the serpent twined round the tree which has so many variants. "The Lord said unto Moses, Make thee a seraph;" rendered "a fiery serpent." "Make thee a burning," says the Targum of Onkelos, "and uplift it on an ensign" (or standard). In Egyptian SERF signifies a flame and a burning. Ref is the serpent or reptile.

The element of fire, the fire that vivifies, was represented by the goddess HEH, who is the serpent. She is designated "AR-ENTI-

TEM-UN," or the "making of existences (invisible), creator of being (visible)." [1] She makes invisible existence become the visible being. Heh is a modified form of Hefah, whence the Hefa serpent of life, and this is the Hebrew (היה) to live, exist, breathe, existence. Hih is likewise modified from Hevah (יהוה), the Hebrew Jehovah, whose name denotes the being, existing, the one who calls into existence, the one whose essence is revealed in becoming, the first sign of which, as when the mother quickened, or the living breathed, was the breath of life. The title of Heh, as the maker of existences visible, which had been hitherto invisible, with breathing and heaving for the type of visibility, is the fundamental signification of היה, חוה, יהוה, and Talmudic הבא. The Egyptian goddess, HEH, earlier Kefa, is the Hebrew genitrix, creatoress, serpent-woman, Chavvah, or Eve, and the feminine Jehovah ; and Heh is the serpent goddess, the serpent of life, of breath, of fire, of heaving along. For Hefa (Eg.) means to heave, like the caterpillar and snake, with that amazing self-motion without ordinary members which so fascinated the primitive mind. Thus we can also identify the female Jehovah by the goddesses Heh and Rennut, whose portraits are extant, as the divine genitrix worshipped in the wilderness, and whose type in the serpent form was there looked up to as the image of life itself. This was the Serpent of Tum-Ankh at Pithom, who was served by the two young girls, the sisters Urti.

One of the most perfect mirrors of the past is to be found in words, and their modifications supply us with means of measuring the stages travelled. The mythology of Israel begins with the cult of Kefa, or Kevah (the terminal is not in question), the Typhonian genitrix, who, as the mother of Sut or Seth, is also Chavvah. Kef modifies into Hef, and Hevah into Heh.

The worshippers came out of Egypt, and there is a passage called the wilderness. Here we find the genitrix is exalted under the serpent type. Philology registers the change. Kefa becomes Hefa, the serpent of life, and Heh the serpent-goddess. We now know that on this line of language the Hippopotamus-crocodile type was earlier than the serpent Hefa or Heh, and the change corresponds exactly to the change in Israel from the worship in Khept (Egypt) to that in the wilderness. The divinity was the same ; that is, it was still the genitrix, howsoever the types may be changed. This is shown by the image of Kivan and Moloch, who are identified as Sut-Typhon ; that is, the mother and son ; the Sabean mother and son, who passed into the lunar phase as Hes-Taurt, or Astarte and Sutekh. It is also shown by the manna. They fed on the manna during the whole sojourn in the wilderness. This, read typically, means that the *children* of Israel were suckled by Menât, or Menkat (Eg.), the wet-nurse, who appears in Israel, by name and nature, as Deborah, called the

[1] Wilkinson, Pl. 64. *Denkmäler*, K. no. 2. Lepsius, Gods of the four elements.

MINQATH (מינקת), the wet-nurse of Rebekah, and who was primally[1] the Deborah above, or Shadai, the suckler. The manna was emblematic of the feminine reckoning and rule, and the angels' food supplied by the genitrix from the *Gynæceum* above to the *children* below.

The present writer has yet to discuss the various values of the KH sign (Sieve), as a terminal of Sefekh, the name of the goddess and the number seven.

There must have been a feminine Khevekh who was the original of Sefekh, the consort of Taht. The connecting link may be found in Hathor. The crocodile, Sevekh, is a type of the Typhonian genitrix, and this, in the earliest spelling, is Khevekh. Hathor is called the hippopotamus-goddess, the directress (Cf. the Chinese directors, the seven stars), the feminine Sebek in An,[2] and is thus doubly identified as a form of the goddess of the seven stars, the old Kefa of Khepsh, the celestial Kûsh or Æthiopia. The Crocodile is the secondary form of the hippopotamus-goddess; and Kev-EKH, later Sev-EKH, denotes a secondary form of KEV or SEF. This value of the EKH was deposited in KI for the second, another, one more. The child (Khe) is also second to the mother.

Sefekh is the later type, in relation to the moon, of her who was first in relation to the seven stars. Sefekh thus equates with Hes-Taurt, who is the second, the cow type and lunar form of Taurt or Kefa, of the Great Bear. Both Hathor and Sefekh are associated with Taht, the lord of the eighth region. Hathor-Sebek is Hathor-Sefekh; both are bringers-on of the Typhonian genitrix, and Hathor was continued in Iusāas, as a solar goddess, the consort of Atum, and bringer-forth of the Iu-sif of ON.

Hathor-Iusāas, of the great temple of the IU at On, was the mother of the Jewish Joseph, the Iu-sif in Egyptian. Atum, in the lower world, was Kak in Kheb, or Kak-Kheb, the father of the Iu-sif, called Iu-em-hept, and the original of Jacob. In this temple the writings of Taht were deposited, which contained the origines of the Hebrew mythology and Scriptures, and from thence the deities and the sacred records were carried forth together.

The peculiarity of the cult of Atum at ON was its continuity of the Typhonian tenets and types. First the genitrix, in her Sabean phase, was Taurt, or Typhon, who bore the son as Sut. Next she was continued in the lunar phase as Hathor (and Hes-Taurt), who bore the child as Taht, as may be seen in the Ritual (ch. lxxx.); and lastly, she was personated as Iusāas, the WIFE of Atum, called the FATHER-god of ON, and the genitrix, as mother of the young sun-god Iusif, or Iusu, the Egyptian Joseph and Jesus in one.

All three of these phases were followed by the "mixed multitude" that came out of Egypt; hence the pulling apart and the diversity in after times; the worship of the golden calf, of Kivan and Sikkuth

---

[1] Gen. xxxv. 8.　　　　[2] Rosel. Mon. da. C. 58.

and the backslidings of Ephraim. Hence, also, the prayers of the "prophets" entreating the people to worship GOD THE FATHER, who was Atum in On, or in the Sakhu of Tum—Damascus—and their exaltation of the son in whom all was to be summed, and who was Iu-em-hept, the peace, the rest, the healer, and renewer for ever, the second or spiritual Adam (Atum), known in Egypt as Jesus, just as he is set forth in the preaching of Paul.

Thus the phenomenal origin and descent of the male divinity can be more or less traced from the genitrix Jehovah, goddess of the seven stars, whose son as a star-god is Sut, the Hebrew Elyon, and as a solar god Kebekh, or Sevekh. Sut in Israel is also Seth, the son of Chavvah; but El-Shadai is probably a form of the solar son (Al or El) of the mother who came from herself; and therefore on the Typhonian line of descent he would represent Kebek, whose name modifies into Kak, and finally into Jah.

On the monuments there is a dual-natured god with the head of Sut one way and of Horus the other; this is Sut-Har, with the heads of the ass and the hawk. He is likewise represented as Sut-Nubti, the double announcer, who blends the Sun and Sirius in one dual type (after the manner of the Sabean double Anubis). We have the same combination in the British Arthur. As the companion of the seven in the ark who are saved from the deluge, and enclosed in Caer Sidi, he can be identified with Sut, the companion of the seven stars, which represented Typhon, and with Seth, who follows the seven patriarchs of the first Genealogical List; he too passes into a solar god of the twelve zodiacal signs. Sut-Har unites the star-son and solar-son of the ancient genitrix on the way to becoming the solar Har-Makhu, the double Horus of the two horizons, still as the son of the mother alone.

The same combination is more or less apparent in the Akkadian and Assyrian mythology, and in the character of the ancient god Bar or Bilgi. M. Lenormant has shown that in the Akkadian magic books Idzubar is identified with Bar or Bilgi, the fire-god, whose name is rendered by "the fire of the rushes," which was not the solar fire. He is the fire of the month Ab, named in Akkadian as the fire that makes fire.[1] Now the fire of that month (July) belonged to the dog-star, who was the Egyptian Bar, whence we connect the Assyrian Bar and Akkadian Bil-gi with Bar-Sutekh. Bar (Eg.) has the meaning of fervour, fervency, ebullition. In the Assyrian renderings of the Akkadian hymns Bar is sometimes identified with or likened to Nebo, who, we shall attempt to show, was the Egyptian announcer Nub, or Anubis, the earliest form of Mercury.[1] This combination of Sut-Har, Sut-Nubti, founded phenomenally on the Sun and Sirius as gods of time, or the god of twin-time, expressed by the name of Sebti (Sothis), supplies the origin of a Jah-Nehsi, in Israel, on the

[1] *Chaldean Magic*, p. 188. Eng. Tr.

Typhonian line of descent. By which is meant that the god, whether Sabean merely, as Sut, or solar, is still considered to be the son of the mother only, and born of the hinder quarter in the north. El-Shadai, so the present writer considers, is the same solar son of the mother as Jah; there being in this case two versions of the one myth rather than a development from the god of Abram to the god of Moses.

The African mintage of the earliest current coin of the male divinity is manifest for ever in the image and hue of the black god of the negroes, Sut-Nahsi. The black Sut was continued in Sut of Ombos, named Sut-Nubti, and in Har-Sut, with the black type represented by the black bird. At Ombos we can identify the black Sut with Sebek, the crocodile-headed type. Sebek was the earlier Kebekh, that is, according to the present reading, the KHE (child) of Kheb, and therefore the son of Kheb, the genitrix. The name of Kheb modified into Seb, as Khebti did into Sebti, the dual form, or the duplicator of Seb, *i.e.* of time, represented at first by the dog-star. The black god was continued in the crocodile of darkness, Khebekh, Sevekh, or Sebek, and Khebekh modifies into Kak as the solar god of darkness, in which shape he re-emerges as one of the Tum triad, further abraded in the names of Hak and Ka, Jach, or Jah. To this origin in the negro god, and this line of descent through the black star-god, the black-and-golden Sun-and-Sirius god, and the black god who was the sun of the darkness, the Typhonians remained devoutly attached, no matter whether they worshipped Sut-Nahsi in Nubia, or Sutekh in Syria, or Kak in the temple and district of Kak, or Au, the black god of Biban-el-Muluk, or Jah in Israel. And although the deity changed as the representative of phenomena and type of time, this persistence on one line gives a look of Monotheism to the cult; more especially as the Typhonians start at first, and preserve to the last, the line of direct descent from the motherhood. Their single god is such only as the child of the virgin mother. Sut, Sutekh, Bar, Khebekh, Har, are all names of the child of her who gave birth to the boy. They remained true to the natural beginning in physical phenomena, whilst the Osirians and Ammonians went on reforming on the line of the fatherhood. When the fatherhood was introduced at length in the Tum cult, it is Kak (Hak), the one born of the virgin, the descending, dying sun that heads the triad for the Typhonians; and this is the god Jah of the Hebrews, the god of darkness, the black divinity, who becomes the black Iu, the son of Atum, and finally the black Jesus of the Christian cult, the son of the Virgin Mother in the Romish Church, as in the pre-monogamous worship of the Africans.

Now in the passage [1] where Moses asks for the name of the deity, that he may announce it to the people, he is told to say that Jah or Eyah has sent him to them. The form of the phrasing implies a

[1] Ex. iii. 14, 15.

proper name, and this must determine the sense of the previous announcement, "EYAH ASHAR EYAH." Rabbis Jehuda and Ibn Ezra both interpret the אהיה אשר אהיה as meaning the proper name of the Divinity. The proper name intended, however, cannot be Jehovah, according to the very plain statement of the text.

As before said, the present writer sees in this announcement the elevation of the young god Adon (the Aten of Egypt) into the Ashar, or husband, as the type of a god having the character of the begetter. For this is the god of a new circumcision under Joshua, as a rite of reproduction and a protest against the worship of Sikkuth, the castrator. By this same rite we can identify El-Shadai, the god of Abram, who also alternates with Jah in the Psalms, as the same god in Israel (and as Ashar-El) whom Moses announces and Joshua serves. El-Shadai also changes the name of Abram, which had been the type of the sonship under the motherhood alone, the same as Rem or Rimmon, Tammuz, Sikkuth, and Adon, to Abraham, and promotes him to the fatherhood. So in the Egyptian mythology, Atum, who is designated the duplicate of Aten,[1] was elevated to the fatherhood of the gods and men, whereas Aten or Adon was the son of the genitrix before the fatherhood was founded. The child of the womb, as Abram, becomes the father of the womb, as Abraham. This will give an obvious interpretation to the Haggadistic legend which relates that Abraham possessed a precious stone ; this he sacredly preserved, and wore it all his life, but when he died God took the stone and hung it on the sun.

The later Hebrew writers make most painful endeavours to establish the fatherhood on a physical basis, and irately repudiate the child, the impubescent God, who as the Khart, the croot, the כרות, could neither be the husband of the genitrix nor the begetter of his people. It happens that in Hebrew there is one word for the male sex and a memorial, זכר, and both meanings have to be taken together at times to do justice to the passage.[2] The Lord, his ZACHAR,[3] is thus a proclamation of the masculine fatherhood, in opposition to the worship of Ephraim, who bowed the knee to the virgin, widow or Zonah, and dandled the child-god like any devout Mariolator. The language of Hosea concerning Ephraim cannot be understood apart from this past of Israel and the mythological origines. Ephraim was a typical name used as a periphrasis for the ten tribes, the original Isharim, whose cult was feminine from the first. The name dates from the Typhonian genitrix and the north. Har-Ephraim is called the Northerly Mountain of Palestine, and Khebt was the north. The goddess of the north is specially identified in the Jehovah-Aloah (or Alah) of the Ephraimite version. Eph is a modified Keph, as Eph, to bake, is from Kafn (Eg.) an oven. Thus Ephraim denotes Kephraim, and comes from the mother Keph, who personified the birthplace in

[1] Stele of the Excommunication.   [2] Cf. Is. lvii. 8.   [3] Hos. xii. 5.

the north, the celestial Khebt or Egypt. It was here that Ephraim remained in his worship. His were the idols of Egypt, the Baalim, Sut-Typhon; he served the old Zonah, whose images were the Aseb, the dove, the heifer, and the calf of Samaria. Figuratively he still dwelt in Egypt, and literally did dwell in the Egypt of mythology. He had slidden back as a back-sliding heifer after the Lord had brought them forth as the husband and male God of Israel.

"They shall not dwell in Adon's land," nor sit at Adon's feast. "Egypt shall gather them up; Memphis shall bury them." They were to be interred with Egypt's dead. This is entirely metaphorical and belongs to the celestial allegory, by which alone it can be read.[1]

This Egypt, or Khebt, was in the heaven of the seven stars, the ten tribes and seventy divisions of the earliest formation. The Flood of Noah is the end of a period; in fact, it is the termination of two previous periods and reckonings which are extant for us in the two lists of patriarchs, the seven ending with Seth, and the ten ending with Noah. The first heaven of the Elohim and Jehovah was afterwards mapped out in the ten-seventy divisions of the seventy princes, watchers, elders, or shepherds, for the seventy of many names have only one origin in phenomena.

Apollonius Molon, a native of Caria, who in his time was held in great repute at Rhodes and Rome, and who is attacked by Josephus as one of those who forged lies because he was hostile to the Jews, and gave other versions of their fables,[2] relates that "after the Flood," MAN (Adam or Edom) was driven forth with his sons from the primeval home in Armenia, and they moved on gradually through the sandy wastes to the then uninhabited mountain district of Syria. This migration took place three generations prior to Abraham, the wise, whose name signifies father's friend. He had two sons, one by an Egyptian wife, the patriarch of the twelve Arab princes; the other, named Gelos (or Laughter), by a native woman. Gelos had eleven sons; and a twelfth, Joseph, from whom the third (of the patriarchs), Moses, is descended. This is quoted by Alexander Polyhistor, the learned freedman and friend of Scylla.[3] In this version it is the Laugher, Gelos, i.e. Isaac, who is the father of the twelve. Nor does it matter, as mythology, which of the solar triad is considered lord of the twelve signs, whether it be Jacob as the lower sun, or Isaac as the upper; Atum as Kak, or as Hu. In all likelihood this is a directly Phœnician rendering of the myth, not borrowed from the Hebrews.

In this version there are but three generations between the Deluge and Abram; in the Hebrew there are ten, those of Noah, Shem,

---

[1] In tracing the origines and the mythological allusions, the present writer does not enter into their local or later application; he is only concerned with the Myth. In this instance Memphis is used as a type-name for the dwellings of the dead, and it suggests a possible derivation of the name from *Mem* (Eg.), the dead (*Mena* also denotes death), and *Pa*, the city or habitation.

[2] *Against Apion*, ii. 7.　　　　　[3] Euseb., *Præp. Evang.*, ix. 19.

Arphaxed, Salah, Eber, Peleg, Reu, Serug, Nahor, and Terah, which is the division by ten of the celestial allegory, and exactly the same as the ten patriarchs who were before the Flood. After the Deluge the "families of the sons of Noah" are named and numbered "after their generations, in their nations, and by these were the nations divided in the earth after the Flood." And the number of nations into which the new world is partitioned is seventy-two; the number of duodecans into which the solar zodiac was divided. The solar triad represented by Shem, Ham, and Japhet is repeated in Abram, Isaac, and Jacob, another version of the same myth, in which the ten tribes pass into the twelve, in correspondence with the seventy divisions passing into the seventy-two.

That which followed the Flood of Noah is also described as occurring under Abram, who is directly connected with the world before the Flood and the primeval home in the north, the heaven of the Great Bear. For Abram is called by Isaiah the Righteous, from (מזרח) Mizarach. Now although this became a name of the mount in the East, the solar Tser of the horizon, it belonged primarily to the Mitzar of the north, where we find Mitzraim,[1] and identify it with the birthplace by aid of the star Mizar in the tail, the Mest-ru of the Great Bear. The two forms of the mount are referred to by Paul. The "coming out" of Abram as the solar god, and the establishment of the triad, is nothing more than a representation of that system of the heavens which followed the end of the stellar *régime* of the Great Bear, the instituting of the solar triad, and the luni-solar reckoning, which was established under Atum, the equinoctial sun, and also under Noah and Abram. This triad is repeated in the Hebrew fragments. It follows the Flood in the shape of Shem, Ham, and Japhet, and is equivalent to the three generations mentioned by Apollonius Molon as coming between the Flood and Abraham. The various versions of the same subject meet and mingle as mythology.

Now the persistent traditional number of Jacob's family, his children and grandchildren, including himself, is seventy. "All the souls of the house of Jacob which came into Egypt (were) threescore and ten."[2] All these souls, says the record, came into Egypt with Jacob;[3] and these were exclusive of his sons' wives, who are omitted from the reckoning. It is now claimed that the seventy belong to the celestial allegory, and are no other than the seventy princes of the heavens, here called Mitzraim, because they belong to the chart of the Great Bear, and the mapping out by seven and ten and seventy which preceded the solar zodiac.

They are synonymous with the seventy elders who judged the people of Israel, under Moses in Jeshurun of the ten and the seventy divisions of the heavens. In the mapping out of the heavens, or the separating of the sons of Adam, by Elyon, and the setting of the

---

[1] Job, xxxvii. 9.   [2] Gen. xlvi. 27.   [3] V. 26.

boundaries of the people according to the number of the sons of El,[1] this is the division of the ten (the Isharim) into the seventy, which preceded the final chart made by Moses in which the twelve tribes are established and blessed as his latest act in life.[2] There were ten patriarchs who followed the earlier seven, and these correspond to the ten divisions that followed the seven, which were again followed by the seventy. All these preceded the twelve divisions of the solar zodiac.

There were ten tribes of the Apocrypha who went forth to " keep the statutes, which they never kept in their own land."[3] This identifies them with the time-keepers, the disposers, the interpreters of the heavens, who were deposed in favour of the later and truer watchers, when it was discovered that stellar time differed from soli-lunar time. They went forth into a region called Arsareth, to dwell there until the latter time, when they are to return again, and the waters are to divide once more for their passage through. The ten tribes who were carried away prisoners in the time of Oshea were the ten of the time when Joshua was yet known as Oshea, before his name was changed as the supporter of the sun-god, Jah.

In the extract from the writings of Nicolaus of Damascus, preserved by Trogus Pompeius, and quoted by Justinus, the sons of Jacob are ten in number, not twelve. The Jews, runs the account, derive their origin from Damascus, whence Queen Semiramis sprang. Damascus was the first king; after him Azelus, Adores, Abraham, and Israhel were kings. But a more prosperous family of ten sons made Israhel more famous than any of his ancestors. Having divided his kingdom in consequence into ten governments, he committed them to his ten sons, and called the whole people Jews."[4]

Moses, the lawgiver, was "king in Jeshurun, when the heads of the people (and) the tribes of Israel were gathered together."[5] This applies to the first foundation of the tribes, which were ten in number, and belonged to the seventy divisions of Israel in Egypt. The first children of Israel, or the Isharhim, as they are likewise called, were the ten tribes of the ten divisions in the celestial circle, and that Jeshurun which was the heaven of the reckoning by ten. Jeshurun may be read as the region of Jeshur, or the little Jeshur in relation to the ten tribes of the lesser Israel. In the Norse mythology the Asar are twelve in number, the twelve gods of the twelve signs, and the ten were followed by the twelve in the Hebrew mythos.

Here is another illustration of Jeshurun being the heaven of the seven, ten, and seventy. Gashurun (עִשָׂרוֹן) is the name of a measure consisting of the tenth part of an ephah. The ephah is Egyptian as the Hept, and Hept signifies number seven. Thus Gashurun is the

---

[1] Deut. xxxii. 8.   [2] Deut. xxxiii.   [3] 2 Es. xiii. 42.
[4] Cory's *Anct. Frag.* Ed. 1876. pp. 78—9.   [5] Deut. xxxiii. 5.

seventieth in one form of measure, and Jeshurun, according to the present reading, is the measure of the seventy. It has already been shown how the Ephah is related to the number seventy-two. The change from the ten to the twelve tribes is pourtrayed in what is termed the "Blessing of Moses;"[1] he who had been king of the ten tribes now constitutes and blesses the twelve. "Moses commanded us a law, (even) the inheritance of the congregation of Jacob," he who had been king in Jeshurun. Previous to his death he is here represented as establishing and describing the twelve tribes, which may be easily identified with the twelve signs, the congregation of Jacob, and leaving it as an inheritance to the people of Israel, whose deity is the god of Jeshurun, now as Jah-Adonai; he who rideth on the heavens—traverses the circle of the signs—in their help and by the name of Jah.[2] It seems to follow that the divine name of Israel or Isarel (in Phœnician) is derived from that of the god (El) of the Isar or Asar, as the ten-total. It is true that Ashar for number ten is written with the letter Ayin. But the Egyptian Hes, the seat, throne, is Kes in Hebrew. The full consonant is first. Taht, for example, is called the lord of divine words resident in Heshar.[3] Mut gave birth to Amen-Ra in Asher,[4] the modified form of Heshar. Hes (Eg.) or As means the seat, throne, or birthplace, and Har is the child. But Har also signifies number ten, the equivalent of the Hebrew Gashar for ten, and Heshar would be the seat of the ten. If we apply this to Gesurun or Jeshurun, and treat it as a compound derived from Egyptian, it contains the seat (Hes or Kes) Har, the ten and Un or Nu, the fellow-males, and Jeshurun, as place, is the seat of the ten fellow-tribes.

We are told "The Geshurites and Maachathites dwell among the Israelites to this day."[5] Geshur has the meaning of joining, attaching, bridging. Makha (Eg.) is the scales, level, equinox. Now Taht in Hes-har may be seen in the soli-lunar Hermean zodiac in the sign of the Crab, the place of the solstice in the Ram calendar; and it is probable that the Heshar of Taht is the Geshur of David. נשור is a region which was subject to Talmai, whose daughter became David's wife.[6] The Geshurites were among those who were not driven out by the Israelites, but who remained and mingled with them. Hes-har is the upper seat, as in the expression, "*Shu ma men Heshar; Tefnut ma men Hes-kar;*" Shu in the upper seat; Tefnut in the lower.[7] Alluding to this upper place or crown-house of the double heaven and the four quarters, the Osirian in the Ritual says: "He has followed Shu, he has saluted the crown, he has taken the place of Hu, enveloped in the plait which belongs to the road of the sun in

---

[1] Deut. xxxiii.
[2] Ps. lxviii. 4.
[3] *Rit.* ch. cxxv.
[4] Obelisk of the Lateran.
[5] Josh. xiii. 13.
[6] 2 Sam. iii. 3.
[7] Hieroglyphic text quoted by Prof. Lushington, *Bib. Arch.* v. 6, pt. 2, p. 534.

his splendour." Hu was the sun-god in HESHAR, or upper seat. The Hebrew statement, read allegorically, is this: In forming the circle of the twelve signs the place of the solstices and equinoxes remained as in the old Jeshurun, or in the luni-solar mapping out. Whence we infer that the Geshur of David may be the same as the upper Heshar of Taht and Shu. Preparatory to the coming of the Deluge, Yima is commanded by Ahura-Mazda to make a circle of four corners,[1] as a seemly dwelling-place; corresponding to the quadrangular Caer of the British mythos. But the first circle of four corners was that of Apt or Khept, made by the Great Bear, whereas the solar circle was formed by Ptah.

Jeshurun exists by name in the Khordah-Avesta, where it is related to the four cardinal points, each of which has its Geni. There are four prayers proper, addressed to the four quarters, although a fifth has been added, and the fourth is Gah-Uziren. The Zend King in Uziren is called Uzayeireina. With Uzayeireina are associated three others, designated the Navel of the waters (Apanmnapât), Fradat-Vira, the preserver of mankind, and Daqyuma, the protector of the district.[2] These answer to Moses, Aaron, Hur, and Miriam (as the navel of the waters). This helps to prove that Uziren and Jeshurun were the heaven of the four quarters simply, when it was marked only by the solstices and equinoxes. The chart is that of the bull, lion, bird, and waterer, the well-known compound type of the four quarters. The Tamuli of Tranquebar Khuren, or Maid-Ashuren, was a being of vast stature, who had the horns of a bull and used to intoxicate himself with wine. He was born near the Mount Meru.[3] This looks like a form of Shu (Bes and Bacchus) or Mashu in Jeshurun.

Jeshurun, then, can be identified with the first circle of four quarters, in which the reckoning by ten preceded the twelve solar signs. Moses, Aaron, (or AHARON, Arabic HARAN), Hur, and Miriam are a form of the Genii of the four quarters. Heron is a name of Sut. Sut is translated Heron on the obelisk of the Serapeum, Baal-Zephon (i.e. Sut-Typhon) the later Heroonpolis, was the city of Sut as Heron. Sut was the announcer and Aaron was the mouth personified. Thus we have Shu as Moses, Sut-Heron as Aaron; Har as Hur, whilst Miriam represents the female waterer. This was Amset or Mast in the latest pourtrayal of the four, but the male Amset is found to have had an earlier feminine form, the original of which is the wet-nurse, the waterer in the Hermean zodiac, who is likewise represented by the goddess Uati, in the fourfold ram-type of the four corners.[4] These are the genii of the four quarters, and the four stars in the square of Ursa Major. Sut (Aaron) answering to TUA MUTEF, the jackal-headed; Shu (Moses) to HAPI (the earlier Kapi). Hur (Har) to the Hawk-

---

[1] *Vendidad.* Fargard, ii. 97.   [2] Bleeck, *Avest.* v. iii. pp. 15, 16-18.
[3] Bayer, *History of Bactria*, pp. 2, 3.
[4] Inscrip. of Psametik I., *Bib. Arch.*, vol. vi. part 1, p. 287.

headed KABHSNUF, and Miriam to the Dea Multimammæ of the Hermean zodiac, whose place was taken by Amset.

The first mention of the name of Israel is made when that of Jacob is changed.[1] In this passage Jacob is elevated to the status of El, of the Isar, and the children of Israel are immediately named after him.[2] He was then the El of the ten tribes and the seventy divisions of the celestial Egypt, who became the father of the twelve sons, twelve tribes, in the character of the sun-god of the twelve signs.

In the Kabalistic Book of Daniel the Seventy take the form of seventy weeks, or periods expressed by that number. The great Kabir Gabriel announces that at the end of seventy weeks the vision and prophecy are to be sealed, the end will have come with the bringing in of everlasting righteousness and the anointing of the MOST HOLY. "Know, therefore, and understand (that) from the going forth of the commandment to restore and to build Jerusalem unto the Messiah, the Prince, (shall be) seven weeks, and threescore and ten weeks. The street shall be built again, and the wall." Here we have the seven, as well as the seventy, that preceded the heaven (or temple) of seventy-two divisions, in which the young solar god, the anointed son, was, as in the Book of Enoch, elevated to the supreme seat. This Messiah is to confirm the covenant with many for one week, as it is rendered. But this means the covenant of the number seven, the covenant of Sebek-Ra or of Iu-em-hept. The Hebrew Masiach is the Kak or Hak of the Atum triad, who becomes the Iu-Su. Sebek passed into Kak as the sun of darkness, a form of Atum. Mas-Iach is Mas-Kak or Mas-hak. Mas (Eg.) means to anoint, but it also signifies to bring; and the word contains the dual character of IU, who brings peace; Iu, the Su of Atum, being the Masiach or Egyptian Jesus. Hept, the word for peace, also means the number seven. The Iu-em-hept brings peace with the same name as number seven, the name of the seven stars. The ark and covenant are expressed by the same word HEPT, and, in the Book of Esdras, when the Son Jesus comes, he is to be cut off and the world is to be turned into the old silence seven days, as in the *former* judgments. These seven days are the equivalent of the one week in Daniel, and both are expressed by the word Hept, peace, number seven, in the name of Iu-em-hept, who comes and brings this HEPT, whether called Peace, the Sabbath, or a silence of seven days.

The Jains, who worship Buddha or Menu as the Jain-Eswara, affirm that during the golden age the supremely happy inhabitants of the paradise of earth subsisted on the produce of ten celestial trees.[3] The ten trees are identical with the ten divisions, patriarchs, and tribes under another type; also the ten trees are equivalent to the Tree of Ten, the Asherah.

[1] Gen. xxxii. 28.   [2] v. 32.   [3] *As. Res.* v. ix. pp. 257-8.

Further, it has now to be suggested that the "Book of Jasher" constituted the especial Scriptures of the Isar or Iasharim in Jeshurun, under the lion-gods, Mau and Shu, Moses and Joshua, who were represented by the two lions of Judah, in the astronomical chapter,[1] the old lion and the young one, just as the dual lion-god, Shu-Anhar, is called Young-Elder. David taught them the "Ode of the Bow." This was written in the "Book of Jasher." The bow is an ideograph, and represents the circle and a cycle of time. Drawing the bow is figurative for making the circle and typifying a cycle of time; hence the "bow of Seb." The first bow was drawn by the genitrix; this came full circle in the cycle of Gestation, hence the bow of Neith, and the arrow of the goddess Seti. When the bow of time was drawn by Pawin Parne, it was the bow of the Great Bear, the oldest form of the genitrix and cycle-maker in heaven. In various versions of the solar myth the hero-son is made manifest by his power to bend the bow of his father. This feat can only be performed by the one who is predestined, though obscured and unrecognized. The bending of the bow is the symbol of turning the corner at the place of the winter solstice, where the life of the old sun ebbed low and his hands relaxed, and were unable to bend the bow or make the curve of return. At this point the son or successor takes up the bow and proves his divine descent or royal lineage by drawing it and completing the circle. This bow, which is made the means of the trial-test in so many legends, is found at the entrance to the judgment hall of the Two Truths as the "*floor of the door.*" "*I do not let you cross over me, says the floor of the door, unless you tell me my name.*" "*The Bow of Seb is thy name.*"[2] That is one form of the trial-test; drawing the bow itself was another.

The bow is an especial symbol of the lion-gods; the arrow is a sign of Shu. "I know the name of Mâtet, his bow is in his hand,"[3] is said of one of the lion-gods. "*I am the lion-god coming forth with a bow,*" says the Osiris, "*at the time when the Osiris sought the Well, going in peace.*"[4] In the Hebrew mythos "Joseph is a fruitful bough by a Well," and his bow abode in strength, and the "arms of his hands were made strong" when he was supported by the shepherd of Israel.[5] The bow of Joseph as the solar god was the bow of the "shepherd of the heavenly flock (Sib-zi-anna or Regulus, the law-giver, in the sign of the lion), the "shepherd of Israel, that leadest Joseph like a flock,"[6] who in the original mythos is Mashu, the bow-man of the solar god. In Assyrian the star of stars, the propitious star of heaven, is called the star of the bow. The bow in Hebrew is the Qasheth קשׁת of the book of Jasher. "Also he bade them teach the children of Israel the QASHETH." The bow is but a

---

[1] Gen. xlix. [2] *Rit.* Ch. cxxv. [3] Ch. xvii.
[4] Ch. cxxxii. [5] Gen. xlix. 24. [6] Ps. lxxx. 1.

hieroglyphic figure. The arrow in Egyptian is the Khesr. Khes (Eg.) means to stop, and turn back at a certain point, and return by main force, as the arrow from the bow when drawn full-circle. The Khesrs or Khesarim, as already explained, were the returning circle-makers and benders of the bow of Seb.

The book of the bow was the book of Jasher, and with the K-sound for the Jad this would be the Book of Khesr (Eg.), the arrow. The Qasheth (bow) was a particular type of Israel,[1] of Joseph, and of Ephraim. The great Khesr was Mashu, the bow-man who in Israel was the king or lawgiver in Jeshurun, the heaven of the Isharim, the ten tribes that preceded the twelve. The present conclusion is that the book of Jashur was that of the astronomical allegory, belonging to the ten tribes above, whatsoever relations these may have had on the earth below. The ten books or the books of the ten would be GASHAR or ASHAR (עשר). The Hebrew commandments remained ten in number, whereas those of the orthodox Egyptians attained the number of forty-two. The Egyptians ran their nomes up to the same number, and their sacred books were also forty-two. A relic of the earlier ten, however, is extant in the division of these; the books of the Hierogrammatist (Rekhi-Khet), those of the Stolites and the prophets, were each ten in number, and these were the especially sacerdotal books.

The "Sepher of Jasher" may therefore be a reference to the ten books, and these may have been the originals of the commentaries on the Kabalistic Ten Sephiroth.

The present writer infers that the ancient Book of Jasher is not so much lost as it is distributed and re-written. We know how Josephus appeals to certain secret and enigmatical Scriptures, kept in the temple, to corroborate his account of Joshua's miracles.[2] "That the day was lengthened at this time," he says, "is expressed in the books laid up in the temple." Also there was an ancient book of days or chronicles, not now extant, frequently referred to in the Books of Chronicles and Kings. This was the Book of the Ten Tribes, and a form therefore of the Sepher of Jasher. The present Scriptures have been written from such originals, which are now and again cited by name. In the process of re-writing, the celestial calendars and allegorical chronicles have almost been converted into history. Still the mythology is there, more or less, and the book of Jasher is not altogether lost.

The same may be said of the "wars of the Lord," cited Numbers xxi. 14. "As it is written in the book of the wars of the Lord; at Vaheb in Suphah, and in the brooks of Arnon." Vaheb in Suphah has been rendered the Red Sea, but that tells us nothing about Vaheb. Translators and commentators have been unable to see anything but the literal Red Sea or sea-weed in the Iam-suph—

---

[1] Hos. i. 5.   [2] *Ant.* v. 1, 17.

whereas the Red Sea is green and altogether free from weeds—which had to be crossed by the sun or the souls in coming out of Egypt. It was here in the marshes that Horus was born and Typhon lurked. It was here the deceased saw the sun re-born " at the thigh of the great water," at the place of the going forth.[1] Had Vaheb (והב) been the word we might have derived it in accordance with the mythos from Uah (Eg.) to escape ; and Eb (Ub), to pass through, against, in opposition to, or in spite of. That would tell the whole story of the mythical coming out of Egypt and crossing the Suph. But certain MSS. were known to Kimchi in which this word was written אתיהב or אתוהב, ATHI-HEB, ATHU-HEB or ATH-VAHEB.

This is a find, for the ATHU is Egyptian, and a name of the marshes or reedy lakes, the " Suph," of lower Egypt, ranging round from the Sethroite to the Diospolite Nome as the border of the Mediterranean Sea.[2] The Kat-en-Atha, or Womb of the Marshes, was a place near the lake Menzaleh. This name for marshes is derived from ATHU, the rush, osier, papyrus, and other water plants. Vaheb, read by Uah-eb, to escape and pass, describes the passage of escape in accordance with the meaning of deliverance assigned to אתוהב in the Targumic MSS. known to Kimchi, and by dropping the prefix ATHU we have Vaheb simply. By adding it, ATHU-UAHEB names the well-known locality and imagery of the KAT-EN-ATHA in the Egyptian mythos.

The Athuaheb is localized in the north, the hinder part, and Suph in Hebrew means a hinder part ;[3] it also denotes an end, conclusion, fulfilment, as does another Egyptian name (Mehu) of the north. The Athuaheb-Suph is the marsh, the source of the water-plants, out of which came the child borne on a lotus; the lake of primordial matter found in the Ritual, also called the Red Sea and Pool of Pant. Sufu (Eg.) means paints, colours; this supplies the red or paint of the pool.

It is to be feared that Brugsch Bey will have to discover another route for the Israelites, and this, as marked out by the " ATHU " of his map, may lead them across the marshes and the Mediterranean Sea. Not only do we find the mythical source, the Athuaheb in Suph, but the pool or well follows by name ; the well dug by the princes, by the direction of the lawgiver, with their staves. This is the well, the Tepht, the Pool of the Two Truths, *i.e.* the well of Ma-Shu, in On, or An. As this was the birthplace of Ar (Har) in On, and Ar (Heb.) is the hero, Ar-n-on, as Egyptian, correctly describes the place of Har, the Lord, in An, *i.e.* Arnon, or Arona. As a river, ARUNUN (Eg.) is that of the inundation.

It is not written in the Old Testament what the Lord did for Israel in the vale of Arnon, but the Targum of Jerusalem tells us that when the Beni Israel were passing through the defile, the Moabites were

---

[1] *Rit.* ch. xvii.   [2] *Ægyptus Antiqua, Map*, Brugsch Bey.   [3] Joel, ii. 20.

hidden in the caverns of the valley, intending to rush out and slay them. But the Lord signed to the mountains and they literally laid their heads together to prevent it; they came together with a clap and crushed the chiefs of the mighty ones, so that the valleys were overflowed with the blood of the slain. Meanwhile Israel walked over the tops of the hills, and knew not the miracle and mighty act which the Lord was doing in the valley of the Arnon. Thus the miracle of the Red Sea was reversed.

In the one case the waters stood up in heaps and were turned into hills; in the other the solid hills flowed down and fused together, whilst Israel passed over them as if they were a level plain. How beautifully the one balances the other! In the one miracle the Red Sea was turned into dry ground; in the other the dry ground was turned into a Red Sea of gore. The hills that rushed together to make a level plain are a figure of the equinox, to be found in varied forms of legendary lore.

This book of the wars of the Lord was first opened in Egypt, and the leaves of it were read upon the starry heavens. The Lord was one with the God of Jeshurun, whose excellency was seen on the sky, and the wisdom to interpret the mystic signs was confessedly learned from the Egyptians. Thus the book was brought into Israel ready written, and it is the relating of its various narratives as if they were being then and there enacted upon the ground already named, according to the celestial chart, which has been mistaken for veritable histories of the Hebrew people.

We cannot always recover the original matter direct from Egypt, so scarce is the literature for that purpose; but the roots are all there, and the Hebrew versions are not the only branches of the subject. The wars of the Lord were told and re-told in Greece, till finally made permanent in the twelve labours of Hercules. The Phœnicians preserved the tradition of Hercules as sun-god, and his twelve labours representing the journey of the conquering sun through the twelve signs of the zodiac; the Assyrians in the twelve legends of Izdubar, and the British in the twelve battles of Arthur. The wars of the Lord were described in a work entitled *Semnuthis* or *Semnouté*, written by Apollonides or Horapius.[1]

Sem (Eg.), is a name of the double plume with which the Lion-Gods crowned the sun. Sem-p-Khart is mentioned by Eratosthenes as one of the Heraclidæ. Sem-p-Khart (Gr. Semphucrates) indicates the young sun-god as wearer of the sem or double plume called the head-dress of the two Lion-Gods,[2] whose Hebrew equivalent is Samuel.

Attempts have been made to show that Mazaroth was the zodiacal circle of the twelve signs. But this application is unknown to the Seventy, and the earlier circle of the Great Bear has been overlooked

---

[1] In *Theophil. Antioch ad Autolycum*, lib. ii. c. 6.　　　　[2] *Rit.* ch. lxxviii.

altogether; the circle of Khept and Mitzir or Mitzraim, the celestial Egypt, the first Sabean-circle in the north, apparently composed of ten divisions, which were subdivided into seventy. In Mitzr was the primal house, the birthplace of beginning, and the Mazaroth were its signs; these were limited to the northern heaven. The Ten Tribes, the Isharim, as the Kesharim, date from that quarter; the ten tribes that went out into the region called Arsareth, but which is now tolerably certain to have been Asareth, a modified form of Gazareth. Gazar means to be cut off, divided, parted, parts, and Gazarah (גזרה) is the separate and uninhabited land, the place apart, where the Ten Tribes went. Mazaroth was the circle of the northern stars opposed to the south, or rather a constellation [1] that rose in the north, which it would do, especially in very low latitudes; the region of the earliest observation and naming.

Sir John Mandeville heard, during his travels, that in countries lying east and north of the Caspian Sea, enclosed among mountains, were the lost Ten Tribes, "*the Jews of the ten lynages that were clepen Goth and Magothe.*" [2]

There was also a tradition that those who were thus shut up were pigmies. Gog and Magog are the two giants of Guildhall whose original was Gogmagoth, the giant whose stature was twelve cubits, and who was a ruling power in Britain before the coming of Brute or Prydhain.

These legends find a fit place in the mythological allegory. The giant of twelve cubits is one with the Rapha with six fingers and six toes. The pigmies in Egypt were the seven sons of Ptah, who, like the seven sons of Sydik, may be traced to the seven stars of the Great Bear.

The Ten Tribes belonged to the first time, that of the Great Bear, and the reckoning by ten. This time in one myth is that of the ten patriarchs and the ten Babylonian kings whose reigns ended with the deluge; in another, the ten celestial trees; in another it ends with the destruction of the Giants, or the tower of seven stages built by the giants. This was the time of ten days to the week in the year of thirty-six divisions. With ten days to the week there were thirty-six weeks to the year of 360 days.

According to an account given in a papyrus, says Brugsch Bey, [3] the division of Egypt into thirty-six nomes rests on a particular view which connected the terrestrial division into nomes with the thirty-six ruling houses of the heavens in astrology; that is with the thirty-six Decans of the zodiac. In the celestial Khebt, as in the terrestrial, the first nome—in this case that of the first ruler—was dedicated to the goddess of the star Sothis. The archaic Babylonian ideographic sign of a month represents it as three times ten days, and thus carries on visibly the week of ten days.

---

[1] Job xxxvii. 9. [2] Ch. xxvi. 319-324.
[3] *History of Egypt*, Eng. Ed. p. 15, vol. I.

The Chinese have their thirty-six heavenly spirits called Thien-Kong-Sin in the Amoy dialect, who are used as messengers by the Supreme Being. The residence of such spirits is said to be especially in, or near, the constellation of the Great Bear. In the Egyptian Ritual, the spirits of the Great Bear are seven in number, identical with the seven spirits in the Apocalypse, and the "seven eyes" in the Book of Zechariah.

The "Book of Judges" is that of the primordial seven, the seven princes, the Shepht, a form of Hept (Eg.) for No. 7. This yields to the slightest pressure in applying the hermeneutical principles of the Kabala. The Shepht, or seven, were earlier than the lunar *régime ;* they belong to the mythical time of the JEBUSITES, who dwelt in the Mount, and built the city afterwards called Jerusalem, the city of David, the moon-god (Taht). יבוס from יבם is the equivalent of KHEPSH (Eg.), the hinder part north, the region of the Great Bear, the seven gods, Elohim, Princes, or Shepht, and the Jebusites are the Khepshites, the later Kushites named from the region of the Seven. The Shept of the monuments and the "Judges" of the Negroes date from this beginning. Hence the word Shepht in Hebrew means to divide, separate, split off, just as the one divided into the seven, and the seven is one in the Sept. Shepht also means language, Kheft having been the primordial Word, and Deborah of the Judges, or Shepht, is the Word of the Shepht, the ancient genitrix, the mother in Israel. With the seven we find the seventy sons who rode on "threescore and ten ass-colts,"[1] the Typhonian types of the seventy divisions, ruled and governed by the Seven. The celestial Mitzraim and Mazaroth have left their witnesses aloft. The star Mizar is still to be found in the tail of the Great Bear, and near it is a small star not one of the seven, called ALCOR ; this, according to Humboldt, the Arabs name "SAIDAK," a word taken to signify test or trial, because they used it as a test of the observer's keenness of sight. Saidak is Sutekh, and Sydik the father of the seven Kabiri, and Melchizedec. The star Saidak and the seven constitute the constellation of Sut-Typhon in Mesru, Mitzraim, or Mazaroth. From this Mes-ru came the name of the pigmies, the wee folk, and of the mount, high place, elevation, as Mitzar, a poetical designation of a mountain in the Holy Land ; the hill Mizar.[2] This was the mount of the first oldest birthplace in the northern heaven. The north is identified with M'zar in the מזרים of Job.[3] This Mesru, Mestru, meaning mouth of birth, is definitely marked by the star Mizar in the Great Bear's tail ; and this was the celestial Mitzraim, or Egypt of the astronomical reckonings before the names were applied to Egypt in Africa.

This can be followed in the eschatological phase of the Ritual, where

---

[1] Jud. xii. 14. [2] Ps. xlii. 6. [3] xxxvii. 9.

the seven cows or Hathors are a form of the seven of the Great Bear, in which is found the coffin of Osiris, *i.e.* the place of re-birth; and the first of these seven is named the HAT-KA NEB-TER, or the image-house of the entire lord, *i.e.* of the Horus or soul, in its two halves which were united in the Meskar of new birth. It was here that the earthly Horus was refashioned in his heavenly likeness, and made whole.

In this birthplace of creation in space and initial point of motion in time, we shall find the seven, the ten, and the thirty-six—the number of patriarchs who in one of the lists are seven, in the other ten.

In the genealogy of Genesis,[1] seven sons are derived from Mitzraim which has been identified in heaven and on earth as the outlet from the birthplace, the Egyptian Mest-ru. The genitrix and bringer-forth in this region was the goddess of the Great Bear, of the seven stars, seven Rishis, Kabiri, Hohgates, Princes, Elohim, or Patriarchs, and it is now suggested that the seven called the Ludim, Anamim, Lehabim, Naphtuhim, Pathrusim, Casluhim, and Philistim, were likewise named from the seven of the celestial Mitzraim, Khebt or Khepsh.

The Ten are typified in the ten Tribes, ten Patriarchs, ten days to the week, ten months to the (Roman) year, ten moons of the Marquesan Poni, or year;[2] the thirty-six in the Chinese Thien-kong-sin, and the thirty-six divisions in the celestial and terrestrial Egypt; whilst the Great Red Dragon of Revelation, the beast with seven heads and ten horns, whose tail drew to earth a third of the stars of heaven, is our final figure of the ancient Mother, and the ten signs of the Isharim in Mitzraim, the Meskar or Mazaroth.

Probably, indeed apparently, very few of those who came out of Egypt could have understood the real purport of the writings carried off from the temple of Heliopolis; and, as these died out, the Jews of Palestine became more and more a people without a clue to their own Scriptures, so the true mythos was lost to the Rabbins of the Haggadah on the one hand, and, on the other, it was restored as history under the *renaissance* of Ezra.

In reading this sketch of the phenomenal origin of the Hebrew divinities, it should be borne in mind that only such matter can be introduced as is absolutely necessary for the purpose of comparison.

---

[1] Ch. x.

[2] The "Typology of Time and Number" will be set forth hereafter; but it should be noticed that the Marquesans have a year, revolution, cycle, or period of time, called a Poni, consisting of ten Moons, the ten lunar months of Menat. These, together with an inundation, would, in Egypt, make a solar year. The present writer, however, conjectures that this reckoning was based on the ten moons of the female period, in a land above the inundation of the Nile, and in a latitude where the Great Bear, the Dipper, dipped low down in the north during three months, the fact, as well as the three months' inundation, being registered for us in the three water-signs.

The ground is here but roughly broken, that has to be gone over again and trodden until we can finally find a new, a smooth, a permanent path.

It has now been shown that Egyptian was the Jews' language, and held on that account to be the sacred language, the language of the hieroglyphics, symbolism, the myths and the gods. The symbols go with the vocabulary, the myths with the symbols, the deities with the myths. There is no new creation to be found in the most ancient Hebrew writings, language, imagery, allegories, or divinities. They are wholly of Egyptian origin, to be read by Egyptian, to be interpreted and valued as Egyptian of the Typhonian cult. The Jewish new departure and development were made with the oldest of all material. Only because that which is found within Egypt has been looked on as mythological, whereas the same matter out of it has been held to be historical, was it possible to assert that "neither Hebrews nor Greeks borrowed any of their ideas from Egypt," [1] which includes a double condemnation of the historic interpretation.

By the aid of Egyptian mythology we shall reduce the mist-magnified figures of the Jewish writings to their natural dimensions, and when the cloud has been dispersed by a gust of freer breath and fuller life, Egypt will become visible again, and the natural heavens will once more show clear blue by day and starry azure by night. It is only by removing these allegories back from earth to their native heaven that we shall ever gain the proper distance and detachment for seeing how and why it was that the universal gaze of mankind in many lands has been fixed on them in awe and wonder, instead of our having to suppose that the world-wide veneration was elicited from certain assumed historic facts that happened to an insignificant people afterwards known as the Jews of Judea.

The truth is that the later men overheard the innocent prattle of the early childhood as it babbled of heaven and the angels, the gods and the mighty ones, the Messiahs and Saviours, and, through not knowing the simple nature of the primitive mind, matter, and mode of expression, they have mistaken these utterances for something supernatural, mysterious, awful, divine; the oracles of Revelation, and the personal utterances of the very God himself.

During many centuries these writings have presented a problem so perplexing that it has been unparalleled in causing mental aberration and crowding the lunatic asylum of theological literature, and their expounders have been explaining what they did not understand; trying in vain to found eternal truth upon grounds which science has day by day demonstrated to be for ever false. For these expounders

[1] Renouf, *Hibbert Lectures*, pp. 243-4.

of the ancient fragments, whose beliefs are based on legends which have been made to lie, the day is at hand for what the Egyptians termed the "weighing and valuation of words," and the ignorant upholders of the long misrepresentation of the ancient meanings, these blinded leaders of the blind, await their judgment and award; but, as it is with the uninitiated in the Ritual, there is no resurrection for them.   Theirs was the past of fable and falsehood; they have no part or lot, and their teachings will find no place, in a future or a faith that is solely founded on the facts that are eternal.

SECTION XVIII.

THE EGYPTIAN ORIGIN OF THE JEWS TRACED FROM THE MONUMENTS.

"*Nowhere do the inscriptions contain one syllable about the Israelites.*"[1] That is the point-blank assertion of one of the foremost transcribers from the monuments, who is also a devout Bibliolator. It is perfectly true that they contain nothing *direct* for those who accept the Book of Exodus, and who think to find in Egypt a couple of millions of foreigners called Israelites, Hebrews, or Jews, as an ethnological entity entirely unknown to the Egyptians themselves. It was useless seeking for the Israelites on the monuments until we could get somewhat clear of the astronomical allegory, with its Egyptian myths turned into Hebrew miracles; its gods and leaders of the wars in heaven converted into historic personages.

The Hebrew Books of the Genesis, Exodus, Numbers, Joshua, and Judges are invaluable as a virgin mine of mythology; they are of the utmost importance as an aid in recovering the primeval types of Egyptian thought, which, in turn, will interpret the Hebrew writings and permit of their being understood, as they never have been, and never could be apart from their original purpose and manner of setting forth. For the Hebrews, who collected and preserved so much, have explained nothing. There is evidence enough to prove the types are Egyptian, and the people who brought them out of Egypt must have been more or less Egyptian in race, and of a religion that was Egyptian of the earliest and oldest kind.

Undoubtedly there is some very slight historic nucleus in the Hebrew narrative, but it has been so mixed with the myth that it is far easier to recover the celestial allegory with the aid of its correlatives than it is to restore the human history.

Josephus lets us know how the history was composed in accordance with the mythos. When recounting one of the Mosaic *miracles* he observes, "Now as to these matters, every one of my readers may *think* as he pleases; but I am under a necessity of relating this

[1] Brugsch, *H. of E.*, vol. ii. p. 99. Eng. Tr.

history as it is described in the sacred books," [1] that is in the writings which were considered divine because they did not relate to human events.

If, as Bunsen asserts, History was born in that night when Moses led the people out of Egypt, it must have been still-born, and no Hebraist or Egyptologist has ever been able to determine the date of birth. The monuments tell us but little of all that the Christian world has made such a fanatical fuss about. Egypt has told us nothing as yet, except that the Jews were indiscriminately mixed up with the Hekshus and Typhonians.

English Egyptologists might be named,—not such however as Dr. Birch, the soundest and profoundest of them all,—who have gone into Egypt and perused its monuments with the Bible for an infallible hand-book, asking everybody and everything if they knew of such a person as Abraham (he who taught the Egyptians astronomy), or Jacob and his twelve sons, who went down there and grew into a multitude two millions strong? or a Pharaoh, who was drowned in the Red Sea? or a Solomon, who married the daughter of a Pharaoh? or the universal death, in one night, of the first-born and flower of every family in Egypt? or the ten plagues? Surely they remembered the ten plagues, and the inferiority of the Egyptian gods to those of the Israelites, demonstrated by their inability to produce lice? [2] Yet so positively do the monuments deny all knowledge of these and many other things devoutly believed to be historical, that we may almost expect the imperturbable Sphinx to shake its head in stony negation.

Brugsch Bey has spent much valuable time in attempting to establish the history of the Exodus according to the mythos; but Hebrew history cannot be satisfactorily made out of Egyptian myth, and the monuments in answering for the myth refuse to corroborate the history. Hence the statement, "*Nowhere do the inscriptions contain one syllable about the Israelites.*"

The Hebrews never were in Egypt in the current sense; never were other than a portion of the "mixed multitude" congregated in the Tanite, Sethroite, and Heliopolitan Nomes; a part of the people named and execrated as the FOREIGNERS, HEKSHUS, AAMU, APERU, MENAT, FENEKH, or AATI, whose Egyptian designations will not determine their ethnology.

As the latest results of ceaseless research it appears that the Hekshus times and ethnology are just as indefinite. It is now admitted by Egyptologists to be absolutely impossible to ascertain from the monumental records when the so-called Hekshus period began, how long it lasted, or at what date it ended. Here, however, the LACUNÆ of the monuments are supplemented by the indefiniteness of the Hekshus name.

According to M de Rougé, the Hekshus rule extended to 2,017

[1] *Ant.* v. 5, 2.   [2] Ex. viii. 18.

years; whilst the art-remains of the Hekshus periods discovered by Mariette in his excavations are not Assyrian, not Phœnician, never foreign, nor anything other than Egyptian. As to the Hekshus names, Dr. Birch has remarked, "They unfortunately throw no philological light on their origin. They are neither Semitic nor Aramæan, and would, except for other considerations, pass for good Egyptian Pharaohs. They (the Hekshus) did not disturb the civilization." [1] The final explanation is that the names and their bearers were Egyptian, and that the Hekshus reigns do not necessarily denote the conquests of Egypt by the foreigners, except in the religious sense. The leaders of the religious revolt were within the land and native to it, howsoever mixed the multitude of their followers. Herodotus affirms that the Ionians and Carians, whom he places in the time of Psammitichus, but who may have also belonged to the Tyrian camp at Memphis at an earlier period—were "the first people *of a different language* who settled in Egypt;" and when brought to this test, the "different language" of the invaders does not appear in Egypt as the result of the Hekshus rule. The common notion of the continual conquest of Egypt by the Hekshus kings, considered to be the rulers of foreign races, is almost entirely wrong. It is wholly wrong in the beginning and only partly right in the end. There has been the greatest difficulty in the minds of Egyptologists regarding the statements that the proud and powerful empire of the Pharaohs should be continually overthrown and found prostrate at the feet of wandering nomads and tribes of herdsmen and cattle-keepers; nor was it true in the sense generally accepted.

According to the new reading of the data now offered, the Hekshus are not the ethnological enemies and invaders of Egypt, as they have been considered hitherto. The Hekshus were identical with the Shus-en-Har of pre-monumental times; their cult was indigenous and primeval, and had never ceased in the land, although it had been frequently or partially suppressed. For a period, anterior to Mena, of 13,420 years, a date often mentioned in the inscriptions, they had worshipped the god Har, whether as Har-Sut or the Har Sun; the peculiar iniquity of their cult consisting in the god being the Son of the Mother, the oldest genitrix who was Taurt or Typhon, whereas the Osirians had established the divine fatherhood, and adored Osiris or Amen-Ra as generator. The duad of the mother and child had gone forth over the world as Sutekh and Astarte of Syria, Duzi and Ishtar, the Phœnician Baal and Asherah, Hebrew Moloch and Khivan, British Hu and Kêd, and many more that need not be named here as the subject will recur again; this duad in earliest Egypt was Sut-Typhon.

The beginning of mythology with the mother and boy is universal, and still survives in the Virgin and Child of Rome. The

[1] *Rede Lecture*, pp. 23, 24, 1876.

sonship preceding the fatherhood sheds a light on the remark made by Proclus in his commentary on Plato's "Parmenides," who says that in accordance with the theology of the Greeks "even Jupiter and Dionysus are styled boys and youths." The first boy and his mother were Sut-Typhon. Apt, Khept, or Taurt is designated the "great one who has given birth to the boy, companion of the great one who resides in Thebes, the great mother of Kamutf."[1]

Those who repudiated and degraded the old mother still continued her type, or brought her on under other names. As evidence that she was prior to and was converted into Neith, the great mother, it may be pointed out that the sign read HAT-NAT, the House of Neith, was frequently read HAT-KHEB, House of Kheb, who was the Hippopotamus goddess.

The old genitrix Ta-urt became Hes-Taurt or Isis-Taurt, the cow-headed, whence Ashtaroth; and in the Samaritan Pentateuch[2] ASHTAROTH-KARNAIM is rendered by עפנית קרנים (GAPHNEITH QARNAIM), in which we have both Kheb and Neith, as in the goddess Hes-Taurt and as in the two names of the abode, the birthplace. On the granite altar of Turin[3] we find "ISIS IN PAFET" or PA-AFT. Fet or Aft signifies the four quarters, and Pa is the house, Pafet the abode of the four quarters, which, as the Aft, Apt, or Abtu, was the place of the re-birth. This not only belonged to, it was personified by, the more ancient goddess Aft or Apt, the hippopotamus-type of the abode. With this PAFET may be paralleled the Gaelic PABAIDH.[4]

The old Typhon is designated the "mother of the fields of the Aah-en-Ru," i.e. the first creator and establisher of the heavens, and the "Resident of the Abode of the Bier" (in Ursa Major); and in the astronomical ceilings of the Memnonium of Thebes, and the temples of Esneh and Denderah, she is placed at the northern centre as the mother of the revolutions of the heavens, close to the cow Mehur, who gave birth to the sun. This addition of the cow Hes, as the solar (earlier lunar) genitrix, shows the addition of Hes to Taurt, whence Hes-taroth or Ashtaroth. At Ombos, Taurt and Sut-Nubti were the deities presiding over the months. Taurt is called the resident in the pure waters belonging to the abyssal heights of heaven, and regent of the gods.[5] Taurt is also visibly continued as a goddess with the eye on her head, as prototype of Meru, Tefnut, and others. She is visibly changing from the hippopotamus to the human form, and is pourtrayed as beauty and the beast in one image.[6]

She bore the first Ar, Har, Bar, or Baal, the son. Har, as her son, was the earliest of the Pharaohs and not Ra. There are Pharaohs on the monuments before the introduction of the name of Ra. The name

---

[1] Birch, *Gall.* 41.
[2] Gen. xiv. 5.
[3] Pl. 2, col. 6, line 1, *Bib. Arch.* vol iii. part i.
[4] See vol. i. p. 242.
[5] Birch, *Gall.* p. 41.
[6] Wilk. pl. 32.

of " Pharaoh" is derived from Har, the son of the mother, who, as Neith, earlier Typhon, gave birth to Helios, and not from Ra at all. The Har sun is constantly appealed to in contradistinction to Ra. " I served the Horus (Pharaoh) in his house," says the servant of a Pharaoh.[1] The Har being before Ra,—we know of the introduction of the first name of Ra on the monuments,—and the earlier son being the Har (Horus) sun, the son of the mother and later Ar-Hes (Osiris), it follows that the first Pharaohs, Mena, and others, were founded on the Har. They were assimilated to the sun as Har-Makhu or the still earlier Sut-Har, and the Pharaoh was P-Har-Iu, the double Horus, or Horus of the two houses, who first appears as Sut-Har.[2]

There was an evil fact to face in the name of Sut-Har, as it identified the dog. In Coptic Sū (en) Hōr, the star of the dog, is the name of the dog-star. This is the Egyptian Uhar for the dog. Uhar implies Khuhar, and shows the dog to have been the earliest Khart or Har, the son of the mother. Such origines were annoying after the animal types had been made human in mythology and divine in eschatology ! The Pharaoh may have become the Har, and later Ra of the two solar houses (Iu), or the great house, as rendered by de Rougé, but primarily the Pharaoh, was the Har-Iu, the coming son of a twofold nature, and of the Two (Iu) Houses. This was the Har of the Shus-en-Har and the Bar or Baal of the Hekshus, whether worshipped within Egypt or out of it.

The rulers of the Shus are called Heks. The Hek was an Egyptian regent and governor. The Hek-Taui was prince of two worlds. This Hek, as prince and regent, shows the title was founded on the sonship which preceded the fatherhood. The god Hak, a form of Harpocrates, proves the type and identifies the child of the mother solely, brought on as Har, the elder ; Har, the child. The Hek-Shus were the worshippers of Hak, who survived as one of the Tum Triad, the still earlier Kak, god of darkness, or, the invisible being when eschatologically rendered, the Amen of the Hekshus.

A striking illustration of the Typhonian origin or relationship of the god Atum is cited by Renouf, without mentioning the monument. The four names of Sut, as god of Senu, Sut of Uau, Sut of Un, and Sut of Muru, are all clustered together in one inscription as children of the god Tum.[3] That is, when the solar fatherhood was established in Atum, Sut, the son of the genitrix, was given to him as the son of the father in a fourfold local form. Also the twin lion-gods assume the type of Sut-Horus when they are the supporters of Atum-Ra.

The tombs of the kings at Thebes, those in the valley of Biban-el-

---

[1] Sharpe, *Eg Inscrip*. pl. 106.

[2] It should be explained that certain names of the gods are only epithet-titles ; such is that of Har-Makhu, the first form of whom was the star-god of both horizons, as Sut-Har, and the latest, the solar deity, Aten or Atum. The title of Har-Makhu is even applied to the planet Venus, as star of the double horizon.

[3] *Hibbert Lectures*, p. 84.

Muluk, are filled with imagery that connects the cults of Atum and Sut-Typhon, particularly the tomb of Seti I., the devoted to Sut; the one god of the Two Truths being represented by Tum and the goddess by Ma. The typology in these tombs is so entirely unique, so different from the imagery found elsewhere, as to have arrested and repaid profound attention.

The golden age of mythology was the time of Sut, who, as the Renn, the Child-god of the ancient mother, gave the name to Saturn; the first period of existence in Egypt is the golden age, and to that we owe the world-wide tradition of the age of gold. Sut-Nub is the golden Sut, and in consequence gold became accursed in the Osirian religion, because of its Typhonian relationship. In the representations on the monuments from remote antiquity gold was already tarnished and considered at least a root of evil, on account of its symbolical character. Plutarch tells us how at the feast of the sun the worshippers were prohibited from wearing gold. Sut was the primordial manifester of the Seven in Smen. Sut was the scribe of the antediluvian Stelæ in the Karuadic land. The Papyrus collection of receipts for curing leprosy in the time of King Sapti, the fifth Pharaoh of the first dynasty, was inclosed in a writing-case under the feet of Sut (Anubis), who was thus acknowledged to be the lord of divine words, the divine scribe who preceded Taht.

A very early inscription contains invocations addressed to the Anubis of six different localities, i.e. Sut, in a sixfold form, considered topographically.

In the Egyptian Ritual the god Sut takes his turn with Horus as purifier of the soul.[1] He is "god of the house, belonging to his houses, who informs the Bennu (a type of the resurrection) of the things of the gate."[2] "The great one shining with his body as a god is Sut, for Taht faces those who are among them in that band."[3] This is possibly as the Sahu constellation, Orion. In the magical texts[4] Sut is the creator, god; "Thy father is Sut; thy mother is Nu; they vivify thee."

The chief sign of Nunter (Nuter) is the stone Adze, one name of which is Anup, and this is a name of Sut, god of the dog-star, the opener of the year. Sut was likewise called the opener; the adze being a type of the opener. In this instance the likeness or type (Nun) of time (Ter) is related to the opener of the year in heaven, to the birth of the child (Nun) and to the inundation (Nun), as the Nunter, or Nnuter. Sut gave his name to the south (Suten), and royalty was named after him in the image of the sonship. King Kufu, of the Fourth Dynasty, is a representative of the god Sut as the son, Har-Sut, who was probably the god of the Shus-en-Har for thousands of years before the monuments begin for us.

[1] Ch. xvii.   [2] Ch. lxiv.   [3] Ch. lxxxiii.   [4] Birch, p. 20; *Records*, v. 6, 126.

Sut-Typhon was the divinity of Ka Hebes, the eleventh Nome in Lower Egypt, and the Sethroite Nome bears the name of Sut. Sut is one of the gods worshipped in the time of King Pepi, of the sixth dynasty, and occupies the place of Horus the son, with Osiris, Isis, and Nephthys. He appears twice on the same monument, and in each case the name has been partly erased. Taurt, whose name follows that of Sut, was worshipped as Kar-tek, the Spark-holder in Pa-tek, the place of sparks; another goddess, whose name stands next to hers on the same monument, being that of KAR-TES, of PA-TES, the Flint-holder in the place of Flint-Weapons.[1] TES, the name of the flint, also denotes the soul of self, and was continued as a title of the genitrix. Tuot, formerly Tuphium, repeats topographically the "Taht formerly Sut" of the Ritual. It was here that Wilkinson copied a divinity, from whose head project the two ears of the ass or fenekh, which are Typhonian.[2] These identify the figure with Sut, even though he has no name and his legend has been erased. The Tuphium is the maternal abode of Sut, the son.

There was a god, Sebt or Sapt, the full form of his name being Sebti. He is blended with Har of the East in Pa-Sapt-Har, the temple of Sapt-Har, apparently the pyramid-temple at Memphis.[3] This deity was depicted as a hawk with two upright feathers on his head. These equate with the two feathers of truth on the head of Sapt.[4] A pyramid also is one of his signs, and this reads Sapt or Sapti. Sapt, with the pyramid or triangle determinative, was copied by Wilkinson.[5] He is so little known that he has been called a foreign god. But the pyramid is the sign of Sebt, as Sothis, the dog-star, and the two are connecting links between Sebti and Sut, and Sebti or Sapti is a form of the ancient Sut. The combination of Sut and Horus is well known,[6] and it reappears in this Sapt-Har, of the temple pyramid of Memphis. The Anubis-Jackal, which is also the symbol of Sap, serves to identify that divinity as a continued form of Sut-Anubis. As Sut is the earliest divine son, so Typhon, Teb, or Kep is the primal mother, who gave birth to the boy; TAURT being one of her titles. Aphroditopolis, the capital of the tenth Nome in Upper Egypt, was the earlier TEBU; Aphroditopolis, the capital of the twenty-second Nome, was TEP-AH; Apollinopolis Magna, capital of the second Nome, was TEB. These are all in Upper Egypt, and each is named from the old genitrix.

APET, near Luxor, a principal quarter of Thebes, bears the name of the ancient mother, who personated the earliest Apt or Teb, the Crib or Ark of the divine child. On a Memphian tomb of the

[1] Granite Altar of Turin, pl. 2, col. D, lines 5 and 6. Birch.
[2] Vol. v. pl. 46 A, part vi., or the Head of a Gryphon. See Pierret, *Panthéon Égyptien*, p. 48. Paris 1881.
[3] "*Pa-supti*," De Rougé; Brugsch, *Geogr.* i. p. 32; *Rec. of Past*, ii. 101.
[4] *Rit.* ch. xvii.   [5] Vol. v. p. 65.   [6] See Pleyte.

Fourth Dynasty a lady is named TEBT, the female hippopotamus, and is therefore the namesake of the Typhonian genitrix, the mother of Sut.

APT, the reduced form of Khept, supplied the Egyptian language with its type-word for the angel, the messenger, especially the messenger of divine vengeance in the *Book of the Dead.* AP means to manifest, declare, announce, make known openly, and Apt is the feminine manifester, the angel or messenger who was the "LIVING WORD," as goddess of the Great Bear, and of the four-fold type combining the hippopotamus, crocodile, Kaf monkey, and lioness.

The goddess Khut (a modified form of Khept) and Har-Khent-Khuti, were the deities of Athribis (Ha-ta-hir-ab), capital of the tenth Nome of Lower Egypt. These were the oldest great mother and her son. The goddess TUT or DOOD,[1] who was the mother of the great circle of the gods at Abydus, bears a name worn down from Tept. The same name is found in DIDO, the Phœnician Astarte, who can be traced to Isis-Taurt, or Hestaroth.

Enough to show the origin and continuity of Sut-Typhon in Egypt, where the worship never ceased, however much it was suppressed.

Few more precious relics of the past have been left to us out of Egypt than the account of Isis and Osiris assigned to Plutarch. In this he observes:—"We have also another story told us by the Egyptians: how that once Apophis, brother to the sun, fell at variance with Jupiter, and made war upon him; but Jupiter, entering into an alliance with Osiris, did by his assistance overthrow his enemy in a pitched battle, and afterwards adopted him (Osiris) for his son, and gave him the name of Dionysus."

"It is easy to show," says Plutarch, "that this fabulous relation borders also upon the verity of physical science." It is so without accepting his explanation.

One has to feel again and again that the matter is Manetho's, with added explanations. The present story is that of Sut-Horus, the god of the sun-and-Sirius cycle, who unites the ass or gryphon-headed bird with the solar hawk, in a brotherhood of Sut and the sun. Sut is the later Apophis, the Sut-Apehpeh of the monuments, the Sut-Har of the Shus or Hekshus; the Har-Sut of the inscription of Kufu.

The history of religion in Egypt and of the Egyptian origin of Sut-Typhon is bound up with this story. It rightly relates the quarrel which rent the monuments, as being that of Sut-Horus (Sut as brother of the sun), and the Egyptian Amen-Ra, who was identified by the Greeks as Jupiter Amen, also the alliance of the Ammonians

---

[1] DOOD. This modified form of Tepht appears in the English " Dud's-Well," the Tepht being the Well of Source, identical with Dyved. A festival called the DIUD feast, held in the reign of Mary, is recorded thus : "*On the 19th of October, 1566, Walter Macwalter beand callit and accusit of halding ane Idoll feist, called the Diud feist.*"—Halyrudhous, K.S. R., 19 October, 1566, vol. i.

with the Osirians against the followers of Sut-Har, of Sutekh, of Sebek and the ancient genitrix Typhon.

Again he says: "They tell us that Typhon (Sut) made his escape from Horus in the shape cf a crocodile."[1] This shows the passage of Sut into Sebek, when Sut was separated from Har, and Sebek personated the solar Ra.   In consequence of this quarrel and divorce of the sun and Sut, and the adoption of the crocodile type, he says there was a continual custom in the town of Apollo (Har) for every one on a set day to eat some part of a crocodile.

There has never been so good a history of what occurred in Egypt as this, which is recovered from the mythology.

The Shus-en-Har did not cease with Mena, and the monuments of Egypt are figuratively rent from bottom to top with the convulsions of two theologies contending for the supremacy; whole dynasties being effaced from the records because they were the maintainers of the ancient Typhonian cult, the worship of the starry mother and son.   Shus-en-Hár, disk-worshippers or Hek-Shus, have all one meaning when interpreted according to the theology.

Kufu, the founder of the Great Pyramid, was, according to my reading of the ancient tie sign found on his standard,[2] and in the inscription referring to the Sphinx, "a living Har-Sut," i.e. he was assimilated to the divinity Sut-Har,—Sut, the son of the old genitrix. Khept had been modified into Hat (har) as the current type, but she represented the goddess of the seven stars, Hathor's seven cows, and he, the king, was her living son Sut.   He was the "bull of the cows." It was the religion which caused the bad repute of Kufu in later times among the Osirians, as reported by Herodotus, who says: "One hundred and six years are reckoned (for the reigns of Kufu and Kefren), during which the Egyptians suffered all kinds of calamities, and for this length of time the temples were closed and never opened.   From the hatred they bare them, the Egyptians are un-willing to mention their names, but call the pyramids after Philition, a shepherd, who at that time kept his cattle in those parts."[3]   In this version the Hekshus king has become the later Shasu, identified with the graziers.

Philition probably contains the equivalent of P-har-iu; the plural being written with the alternative "ti." P-hal-ti would be a form of the double Horus, who constituted the earliest Pharaoh founded on the Har sonship. The same root, as Al, enters into the name of Palestine, Philistines, and Pelasgi.

The Shus-en-Har were looked upon as temple-closers and enemies of the gods, because they only worshipped the duad of mother and son, and were the nearest approach to monotheists in the past. That is, they did not develop the early typology of the astronomical allegory or carry it into the eschatological region of thought.   They

[1] Of Isis and Osiris.   [2] *Lepsius Auswahl.*   [3] B. ii. 128.

remained true to the one god as a male and the son of the mother. This particular type will be illustrated in a chapter on the virgin mother and her twin child.

The Shus-en-Har or Hekshus, probably had another return to power after the sixth dynasty, for there is a huge gap as if their works and records had been blown out of existence by the avengers who followed them in the eleventh dynasty. The monumental silence is mournfully eloquent with this interpretation of the facts. The track of the Typhonians is marked with rent and ruin, but not of their own making; they were not the destructives of Egypt. These were the Osirians and Ammonians, who sought to erase every sign of their presence; the men who have made of the seventh, eighth, ninth, and tenth dynasties a blank desert. These were the people who wrecked their monumental history to get rid of the traces of Typhon; these, and not the Hekshus, were the cause of the calamity we have still to deplore.

The Shus-en-Har, the Hekshus, and Sebekhepts were the worshippers of the child and mother as Sut-Typhon, and this was the cult that became dominant once more at the beginning of the thirteenth dynasty, which, if the astronomical chronology holds good, must have been about 2,300 B.C.

As the servants of Sebek, they equate with the Shus as servants of Har-Sut. The passage, "Remember that thou wast a *servant* in the land of Egypt,"[1] will in Egyptian identify the Hebrews with the Hekshus, the Shus-en-Har, the servants. Sebek (Kebek) is designated the youngest of the gods, and yet at Ombos he was the oldest form of Seb, or time. He was also identified as Har, the sustainer of the world. The Har, the youth of the god, was made manifest by the lamb, the young ram; the Sebekhept motherhood being represented as the abode of the lamb. This identifies the child of the virgin mother when the ancient star-god had been brought on as Sebek-Ra, in relation to the reckoning by solar time.

He was still the son of the Typhonian genitrix, the old first mother of the gods. Sut and Typhon were the mother and son worshipped at Ombos, the shrine of Sebek-Ra. The goddess of the Great Bear is there distinguished as the mother of beginnings, the abode of birth and nursing; regent of the divinities of the Meskhen, the gracious dandler. It is she who presides over the months with Sut-Nubti, and is called the "Living Word." The priest or worshipper of Sebek (or Sefekh), holds up in front of him a kind of instrument (possibly musical) containing seven wires, the number of Sefekh's name.[2]

In the course of time the followers of this cult grew fewer and fewer in Egypt, and in the Hekshus revolts against the religion of the Osirians they found their natural allies in the worshippers of the mother and child outside of Egypt, who were continually invited to come over and help them, when they made another rush and rally

---

[1] Deut. v. 15.   [2] *Descript. de L'Égypte*, v. i. pl. 43.

for the old religion. The Sebekhepts of the thirteenth, fourteenth, fifteenth, and sixteenth dynasties were Shus-en-Har, or Hekshus in the religious sense, no matter what compound they represented ethnologically. Their reigns were marked by the customary erasure of their names from the monuments, and the consequent blank in the history. How long they reigned is at present unknown, but the astronomical date of 2,300 B.C. for the beginning of the thirteenth dynasty may possibly lead to a closer computation of the period, and at the same time shed a little light on the subject of the Jews in Egypt.

The notion that Egypt was always invaded on these occasions by a foreign race which conquered the people and suppressed their national existence for hundreds of years together, is doomed to extinction. These conflicts were internal and caused by the rival religions, the Shus within were helped by the nomadic Shasus from without, both being the worshippers of the Egyptian Sut-Typhon, or the Syrian Sutekh and Astarte.

A tradition, extracted by Africanus from the work of Manetho, tells us that the Hekshus kings were Phœnicians; that is, the Fenekh. But the Fenekh is another type-name very difficult to identify ethnologically. In the inscription of Shashankh I. the conquered peoples of Edom and Judah are called "the Fenekh," and the "Aamu of a distant land." "As to the Fenekh," says Brugsch Bey,[1] "I have a presentiment that we shall one day discover the evidence of their most intimate relationship with the Jews." An inscription on the rock tablet of the twenty-second year of King Aahmes says: "These stones were drawn by oxen, which were brought here and given over to the foreign people of the Fenekh." Here the Fenekh are identified by Brugsch Bey as the oldest representatives of the Phœnicians on Egyptian soil. It is easier, however, to identify the Fenekh as Typhonians than as a foreign race. The Fenekh, an Abyssinian wolf-dog, was an ancient type of Sut, and this may have been the determinative of the name in the symbolic sense. The Typhonians were all treated as foreigners, whereas the Fenekh as Typhonians would not be named ethnologically. If the Fenekh are named symbolically they may be Phœnicians, Jews, or anything else in race so far as the mere sign goes. The Aamu, for example, can be shown to include various ethnological types. AAMU became a generic name for the Syro-Aramaic races, and there can be no doubt of its relation to the Cow, hence the cow-herd or shepherd was an Aamu. The young priestess of Aamu in the Creation by Ra,[2] is a new form of the cow-headed Hathor, as especial goddess of the town of the cow, the young Hathor being of the heifer type, the golden calf of the Israelites. But the name is also a variant for the unclean and impure, i.e. the Typhonians, which shows the religious virus, but does not furnish a race-name. The HEMI, as cow, wife,

[1] P. 210, vol. ii.　　　　[2] Pl. B. 24.

female, seat, hinder part, helps to identify theirs with the other Typhonian names. The AAMU were also fishermen who dwelt by the lake Mareotis, and it is noticeable that these are the Aahti, and that the goddess Aahti combines the head of the calf with the body of the hippopotamus, and is a younger dual form of the ancient Typhon. The AAMU in the Metternich tablet are inhabitants of the water, determined by a fish and a crocodile.

The name of the Great Mother, as Ashtaroth in Hebrew, has the meaning of herds or flocks. She was the lady of flocks in the sense of plenty, the Dame Habond. Ashtaroth is Hes-Ta-urt, the Typhonian cow, a form of which is found in Aahti. The Aamu were her herdsmen, cowherds, Shus (servants) or Shasu. They were the children of the old and Great Mother, whose earlier type was the water-cow, and later the land-cow. The water-cow of Typhon is a hidden element in the nickname of the AAMU as the cowherds, the adorers of the Aa-Mu, who was the old first genitrix. Aa-Mu reads "the ancient mother," and as the Aa is the cow, and Mu the water, the Aa-Mu is the water-cow or hippopotamus, the old Typhon, whence the Aamu are Typhonians from the first. By their types shall we know them. The general term of the "shepherds" may be rendered by the Aamu, Shus, or the Menat.

One Egyptian root-meaning of the word MENAT or MENTI is to go round. The collar goes round, and that is a MENAT. The doves, swallows, and pigeons wheel round and round, and they are the MENTI by name; to MEN, as in the English "minnying," being to perambulate, to go round. The first motion observed, imitated, and named was that of circle-making. The dove's name answers to Tef or Teb, which in Egyptian denotes movement in a circle. The planets and sailors, called BIB-BU in Assyrian, are named as the goers-round. This going round shows the MENTI were nomadic in their habits, whatsoever their race may have been; so were the AN, who have been termed the wanderers.

The Menat are the despised Aat, lepers, pests, the abomination of Egypt, but not primarily because they were cattle-keepers. Men is the name of cattle, Men-ment denotes herds of cattle. But, as with the Shasu, the name has an earlier signification. These Menat also bore the name of the Great Mother in her Typhonian form, and were her worshippers. Menât (Menkat) is the old wetnurse, represented by the breasts, the Egyptian form of Shadai. Jablonski says: "There was a personification of Taurt under the name of MENUTHIS, who was worshipped in a town of the same name, the supposed wife of Typho."[1] The "wife of Typho" requires explanation. Plutarch calls Nephthys the wife of Typho. But there is no male Typhon apart from Sut (unless we include Bes) who became the son and consort of Nephthys, in a

[1] Jablonski, vol. iv. p. 153.

later phase of the myth, just as he became the son of Atum. Typhon is Taurt, Khepsh, Rerit, or Teb (or Menât even), the first and oldest genitrix pourtrayed as the suckler. Her children and worshippers were the detested MENAT. The orthodox Egyptians looked on them, as the fanatical Protestant does on the emasculated Mariolator. The name of the AATI was hurled at them. The word signifies the unclean, the leprous, miserables, accursed. AAT is a name of the hinder part, the back, and the eagle sign shows it was worn down from Afti, the name of the old Typhon, who was the hippopotamus as Apt, and the sow as Apht (at least the boar is Aph, and Apht is the feminine form), the earlier Khaft, Khept, and Khebt. The Khaft had become a name for the godless, the evil ones, and this wore down (through Kat, the hinder part) to Aat, the name of the pests or Typhonians. So in the Maori, AUTAIA denotes a pest, or the pest. Khept modifies into GAT, German for the stern of a vessel, into HOUTE, Mantshu Tartar, for the poop of a ship, and the Egyptian UTU or UT sign is the poop. The English CUDDY is a small cabin under the poop at the stern of the ship ; the Welsh CWT is the hinder part ; the Fijian KATA is the hull, the lower part of two, corresponding to the hinder part in other vessels of the name. KHEPT is one of those early words that become excremental, as it were, in language, and typical of all uncleanness. They have no such significance in their earliest form ; but in the process of wearing down we have Khat (Eg.) for the corse ; CHADDHA, Hindustani, bubo ; KHUTI (do.) scab ; KHHUT, defilement and contamination ; KUTU, in Maori, Malayan, and Fijian, the louse. KOTHA, Sanskrit, a sort of leprosy ; GAOID, Gaelic, disease ; COTH and GOUT, English, disease ; KIDA, Fijian, epilepsy ; KATO, Kabunga, itch ; KOTO, Gadsaga, itch ; KET, English, filth ; KITTA, Sanskrit, dirt ; CAID, Irish, filth and foulness ; JAD, Polish, virus, venom ; YATU, Zend (the " sin of Yatu ") ; AADWA, Arabic, contagion, contagious disease ; IADAA, to communicate disease ; WATΛ, pus, matter ; OIDOS, Greek, a tumour ; ODAZO, to itch ; UWATI, Swahili, a skin-disease ; ODIEUX, French, loathsome, odious. The total meaning of all these forms of one word was concentrated by the Osirians and Ammonians into the name of the AATI, the Khefti, the people of the hinder part, the Qodeshoth and Qodeshim in Israel, from KAT (behind, backward) and SH (Eg.) which denotes the place and act of going. The Qodeshim of Israel are denounced by the Hebrew writers in a way that warrants this derivation of the word.

A passage in the Koran [1] is said to have been revealed in reply to the Jews, who asserted that if a man accompanied with his wife after the manner of the Qodeshim he would produce a more witty child. In the same chapter Mahomet appears to have endorsed this " survival " from the animal stage. On the other hand the Egyptians [2]

---

[1] Ch. ii.   [2] Horapollo. ii, 40.

adopted two crows for a type of connubial intercourse because they had advanced beyond the status of the Qodeshim.

The word " Aat " also means the orphan, and this was intended to brand the Sut-Typhonians as the fatherless in the religious sense, because they only worshipped the mother and her child, the harlot and the bastard, as they were held to be by the Osirians. This typical taunt of the " Aat," the orphans, has the same force as " the fatherless," and the " ממזר," cast at the Christ in the " Toledoth Jesu," as the earliest divine child, who was without a father.

The sign of the Foreigners, the wicked, tells the same tale. In the form of the Utu, the poop, or stern of the vessel, it is still an ideograph of the hinder part, and consequently a type of Typhon. The Utu, or stern, is a sign of Uti, the goddess of the north, who was a continuation of the ancient genitrix in that quarter. This sign on the monuments has sometimes been taken for the ethnological Yonias, or Ionians, identical with the Hebrew Javan and Hindi Javanas, Latin Juvenes, and Assyrian Kephenes, whereas it is an ideograph of the hinder part, as the north, and of the Yonias or Typhonians in the religious sense, independently of the Hellenes or Ionians of Greece, and is an especial symbol of the Typhonians, who were Yonias as worshippers of the genitrix, whatsoever their race. The opprobrious determinative was always Typhonian, but not necessarily ethnological. It was the sign of the place of going forth or out at the Khepsh of birth. Then of the way of going out of Egypt towards the north, the ideograph of going abroad, and finally the type of the Foreigners in a topographical or geographical sense. When this sign of the Foreigners, the impure, the hinder part, English AFT, Egyptian KHEFT, is drawn in the scutcheon of Ra-Nahsi,[1] it is not meant to indicate either the Foreigner or the impure in the odious sense, but is simply the determinative of the nocturnal sun in the Akar, the hinder side of the north. One of the Sebek-hepts of the thirteenth dynasty is called Sebek-em-Saf;[2] that is, he who is from the hinder part, the sun in the Ament, the Typhonian solar son, who was Sebek-Ra.

The Aati, Menati, and Aamu were charged by their opponents with beastly practices in their religious physiolatry.

Proclus in Timæus,[3] says : " The Shepherds are analogous to the Powers that are arranged over the heads of animals, which in *arcane narrations* are said to be souls that are frustrated of the human intellect, but have a *propensity towards animals.*" The Menat were special worshippers of the great mother Menât, the wet-nurse, who might be represented by the hippopotamus, the sow, the goat, the ass, or the later heifer. These were considered to be beast-worshippers, and

---

[1] Brugsch, *Histoire*, pl. 8, scutcheon 158 ; Bunsen, vol. ii. p. 624.
[2] Brugsch, *Histoire*, pl. 9, scutcheon 196.   [3] B. i.

undoubtedly the female cult took repulsive forms; the religion was manifested by strange rites.

The subject of Sut-Typhon is the obscurest of the obscure, but the impurity and obscenity associated with the name does not, as commonly supposed, relate to the mere intercourse of the sexes. This did not constitute the mystery of immodesty, so frequently anathematized. The uncleanness, the secrecy, were related to the primitive physiological conceptions of creative source. The naked nature of the beginnings have nothing gross in them either to the savage or scientific mind, but are of absorbing interest to the student of the genesis of ideas, the meanings of the myths and religion of the mysteries.

The charge of performing unclean rites is distinctly brought by the Jewish writers against their own people. "They shall no more offer their sacrifices unto devils, after whom they have gone a-whoring. This shall be a statute for ever unto them throughout their generations." [1] The Lashairim, rendered devils, are a particular kind of hairy goat known on the monuments as the SERAU, a goat-kind of sheep, which offered a type of biune being. The Jews continued the Mendisian worship after they had left Egypt. In the language of Egypt, says Herodotus,[2] both a goat and the god Pan are called Mendes. He was right. Men is a name of the goat, and of Khem, the Egyptian Pan, who had earlier forms in Shu and Sut, the first MEN, or Man, as the fecundator of the mother.

The Menat, the Typhonians, whose types of the genitrix were the female goat and the dove, are described by Diodorus in relation to this subject. He says: "There having arisen, in former days, a pestiferous disease in Egypt, the multitude attributed the cause of the evil to the deity; for a very great concourse of *foreigners* of every nation then dwelt in Egypt, who were addicted to strange rites in their worship, so that in consequence the due honours of the gods fell into disuse."

The word "Foreigners" here, if derived from Egyptian, does not preclude Egyptians from being among them, as Menat had become a type name for the foreigner and for all that was held to be foreign to the Osirian and Ammonian religion. The Menat were Typhonians, all mixed up together as regards races; the origin of the name was religious, and the earliest type of the Menat was Egyptian, or rather Æthiopic. For the roots of these matters we have to go a long way back. The uncleanness had its beginning in the earliest time and most primitive condition of the pre-man. No more effective evidence for the doctrine of development is anywhere to be found than in these dark rites of religion. A link betwixt man and the beast was not merely preserved in them, but it was made sacred. This is a subject which can only be utilized by the evolutionist, and the main interest lies where it has never yet been sought—in the anthro-

[1] Lev. xvii. 7.   [2] Herodotus, ii. 46.

pological and sociological point of view. The Rabbins taught rightly that their typical man Adam, of the same name as the monkey UDUMU (Ass.), had carnal knowledge of every tame or wild beast that he could dominate, and was not satisfied until Eve was made for him.[1] When we know what conditions we have come out from, and are still struggling out of on the upward way, we are for the first time in a position to speak of certain facts of the past, and to enunciate a doctrine of hope for the future, and, until we know what we have been we can form no fair estimate of what we are, or are to be. The first inflammatory or inspiring appeal made by nature to man was through the incitement of his sexual appetite, and this at first was indifferently fed before it was educated. What a portrait, for example, of the early mind and taste is presented by the Hippopotamus being adopted as the primitive type of the genitrix, the Great Mother, the Khep, Khepsh, or uterus of creation. Size of the emblem positively supplies us with a measure of progress. Behemoth is first, in Taurt (Typhon), the primordial; then the cow, as Hes-Taurt, Hathor, Neith; the lioness, as Tefnut, Sekht, and Kefa. The cat as Pasht; the vulture as Mut; the frog as Heka—all types of the mother. These types persisted when the feeling to be expressed belonged to the earliest form of religion, and they were the external images, answering to the internal feeling which was a desire for the Great Mother, to be consummated in sexual unition at times with the aid of her living representatives, which were of necessity earlier than the woman-image of the divinity set up for later worship. Nothing can be more natural, however, than that the sexual feeling, being earliest, should be first directed and the object set forth should be the female. This worship, whether the type was animal or human, was continued by the Typhonians and Yonias of various races who were one in their religion. In the pictures of Khu-en-Aten, the disk-worshipper, the female, his wife, standing by his side, is pourtrayed in a state of nudity.[2] The author of *Nile Gleanings* discovered a portrait of Queen Taiiu, of which he remarks, not without a touch of that modern consciousness which in its expression is at times indefinitely more indelicate than the nudity of nature, "Her dress was quite open all the way down the front . . . . The lady does not appear to have worn any other dress. Prudishness was evidently not the fashion of the day."[3] This nakedness of nature, with its primitive appeal, had also become an abomination to the Osirian and Ammonian, and was cast out as unclean. But instead of abusing the Jews (or Menat) for what their laws reveal concerning the early religious mysteries, the evolutionist is deeply indebted to them for their contribution to this, the obscurest history of humanity.

Another Typhonian type was the dove. The name of this bird in

[1] Bartoloc, *Bibliotheca Rabbinica*, i. 76, 77, 78.   [2] Wilkinson, pl. 23.
[3] *Nile Gleanings*, by Villiers Stuart, p. 252.

THE EGYPTIAN ORIGIN OF THE JEWS.

Egyptian is MENAT, and it must have been an emblem of the primal genitrix as it bears her name, both as Menat and the dove, or Tef (Eg.), the Hebrew תור.   The dove was the bird of breath or soul, the later ghost.   An Egyptian statuette of the nineteenth dynasty shows a dove with a human head and wings extended over the bosom, typifying the breath or soul.   It was a type of the goddess " Hathor," in Egypt, and it brooded over the statue of the Syrian Juno at Hierapolis in the shape of a pigeon made of gold.   To call it a solar bird has no significance.   It was the image of the gestator, the bird of breath, and as such is held in the hand or on the sceptre of Hera in the act of visibly incarnating the soul of breath.   It was the bird of the virgin mother who was the brooder, the generator of the soul when both truths were assigned to the genitrix.   Hence the two turtle-doves of the Jewish offering, and hence also the dove of the Holy Ghost continued in the Christian Iconography.   The Jews charge the Samaritans not only with the worship of the dove, but also with a form of circumcision dedicated to the dove.[1]   This was the dove that was synonymous with the sword, and the rite was the " Reproach of Egypt."

The Egyptian priest appointed to kill all the unclean animals was called a MENUI.   This is significant.

The MENAT appear by name on the monuments as a Sinaitic race.[2] Within Egypt the Menat are identifiable by the Typhonian types, one of which is the dove, another the goat; the Aamu, by the cow (including the water-cow); the AATI, by the hinder part, the seat, the image of Typhon: and it is by these typical names that we have to recover the Hebrews from the Egyptian monuments.

The only satisfactory ethnological designation for a people like the Hebrews must be derived from the religious rootage in mythology. In demonstrating the mythical origines it is not necessary to deny certain tribal arrangements of the Jews out of Egypt.   But the name of the Israelites, as before explained, is derived from Isarel or Asharel, the Lord (El) of the Ten Tribes in Jeshurun; the ten who passed away because they were mythological, and were superseded by the twelve of the solar zodiac.   Whatsoever historical fact may be found as a kind of parallel, the ten tribes are based on the ten who pre-ceded the twelve in the celestial chart.   In this connection the house of David belongs to the luni-solar reckoning of Taht by the number ten, and solar twelve; the two being added to complete the total. The severance under Rehoboam is, even according to O. T. history, only a reversion to some previous order of things.

The " Children of Israel " are the sons of the El of the Isar or Gashar, the ten tribes who became the twelve in the latest arrange-ment founded on the twelve signs and seventy-two divisions of the

[1] Nutt, *On a Fragment of a Samaritan Targum*, p. 44.
[2] Chabas, *Antiquité Hist.* 102.

solar zodiac. The earliest rendering of the name of the Hebrews[1] is as the (עברי) GABARI, identical with that of the Kabiri, who are a family (Kab) of companions, watchers, or brethren; the first of these being the seven of the Great Bear, the children of the Typhonian genitrix, the root of whose name, in Egyptian, is Kef, Kep, or Kheb, as in Kafa, the fist; KEF, force, might, the hinder part; KEP, Typhon, concealed place, cave, sanctuary, womb; KAPU, the mystery of life; Kheb, the hippopotamus. With the terminal TI, or T, Khebt may signify the second, or dual Kheb; Kepti, the two hands; Kheptu, the two thighs; Kabti, the two arms, two dancers, or two Bears. With the terminal SH, KHEPSH denotes the place, pool, uterus, or emaning mouth of Kheb in Khush, and afterwards in Egypt. Khepsh wears down to Ash, and in this we have an equivalent of Eve, or Chavvah. In Jehovah we have Khefa, with the Hebrew terminal ה, the letter out of which all came, the sign of the feminine abode, the Ah (Eg.) for house and womb.[2]

The name of " Jew " may also be traced finally to Jehovah, the Great Mother. The Arab name for the Pole-star, " Joudi," the " Star of Joudi," is a modified form of Khepti, as the goddess of the Great Bear. On another line the original Khepsh, Gevsh, or Chavvach, had modified in Chinese, into the form CH'HOO, for the North Pole. Khep or Khef (Eg.), abrades into Ap, Af, Au, and lastly into Iu, the Egyptian I being a developed form of the A. On this line the name of the mother passes finally into that of the son, and intermediately we have the Hebrew יהו (Jhv) as a name of the God, the mysterious and unmentionable one, whose nature was only communicated to the initiated, whether in Israel or among the Phœnicians and Greeks.[3] This is the divine Son of a dual nature, who became the Iu as Iu-sif, Iu-em-hept, and IE-Apollo. The intermediate form of the spelling is applied to Joseph, as יהוסף in Psalm lxxxi. 5, and there only. With the Vav retained, we have the name of the Jew, as in the French Juif; the W in the word Jew represents a letter F, as in the English If, a name of the Yew-tree. The Jews, then, are the IHVS, IVS, or IUS. The beginning of the name of the Jew in Jehovah or Khevah, the genitrix, and its final development in Iu and IE, the Son, the Iusu (or Jesus) is illustrated by the tradition in the first Toledoth Jesu, which relates that the unutterable and ineffable name of God was engraved on the cornerstone of the Temple. The mount of the four corners was typified by a stone. This is referred to by Enoch, who says: " I surveyed the stone which supports the corners of the earth."[4] This stone was discovered by David when he dug the foundations of the Temple, and was placed by him in the holy of holies. The name was stolen by the

[1] Gen. xiv. 13.
[2] Letter ה. The H or Heta in Coptic has the numeral value of 8, the number of Smen the place of beginnings out of which all came.
[3] *Lydus*, de mens, iv. 38, 74, 98; *Cedrenus*, i. p. 296; *Julian*, orat. 5, in matrem deor. p. 172. [4] Enoch, xviii. 2.

Christ who entered the Temple and inserted the word in the flesh of his thigh ; the name which enabled him to perform his miracles. In this legend we have a representation of the bringing on of the name.[1] The name of Iu (יהוּ) shows the nature of the great mystery, as it means twin, and denotes a dual being that was both male and female in one, as Tammuz, Iu-sif, Duzi, and other hermaphrodite deities. Under cover of this the half-feminine nature of IHV constantly escapes detection. The derivation of Ihv from Ihevah shows the correspondence of the etymology to the mythology. Ihv (seph) *is* the son of Ihevah, and we are now in a position to show how Ihv is an abbreviated form of Ihevah, and the God of the Psalmist, who was the Deliverer from Egypt, as Joseph, is the Son Sif, of Ihevah, hence Ihevah-sif, Ihv-sif, or Joseph.

Sut, as the Iu-sif, has been already identified by his type, the ass, named Iu, in the time of the twelfth dynasty. The mother and son worshipped by the Hebrews or Jews in Egypt were Sut-Typhon, the same dual deity as the Sutekh and Astarte of the Kheta. The god who brought them out of Egypt, had, " as it were the strength of an unicorn." The " Rêm " here named is the Rumakh of the hieroglyphics, the hippopotamus Typhon, the mighty beast pourtrayed in the planisphere, as dragging round the starry system, and literally lugging a third part of the stars of heaven up out of the Egypt (Khebt) of the north. This is the first mention of the unicorn in the Hebrew writings.[2] The passage is repeated in the next chapter : " God brought him forth out of Egypt ; he hath, as it were, the strength of an unicorn." [3]

The unicorn is the type both of Sut, the son, and Typhon, the genitrix. One symbol of this dual divinity is a kind of antelope with a single horn—the unicorn of heraldry.[4] This is the type of Sut, the son, and by it we identify Joseph, whose " horns are as the horns of unicorns." The unicorn of Deut. xxxiii. 17 preceded the bullock of Au, and both are here given as symbols of the Iusif or Joseph. Amongst the most ancient things in Hebrew is the word יבם , which stands for כבם, the Jad representing a k-sound. KABM (יבם or) has the meaning of being big-bellied and pregnant, and in this old unused word survives the name of the Typhonian genitrix, the hippopotamus goddess KHEBMA, the procreant Great Mother. The word is applied to the brother-in-law, *i.e.* the brother of the husband, who was compelled by law to marry the widow of his deceased brother, in fulfilment of what is termed the Levirate.[5] This was a reliquary

[1] This story is in the ספר תולדות ישׁוּ, a work assumed by various writers to be a foul forgery, perpetrated for the purpose of blaspheming the name of Jesus. But this, with other stories in the same work, shows me that the Jesus intended belongs to the Mythos, and has been mixed up with Jesu Ben-Panthera. Here let me say that I am greatly desirous of meeting with some Hebrew who is well-versed in the Talmud, Haggadoth, and oral traditions of his people.
[2] Num. xxiii. 22.   [3] Num. xxiv. 8.   [4] Champ, D. 115.
[5] Gen. xxxviii. 8 ; Deut. xxv. 5–7 ; cf. Ruth, i. 15.

bequest from the sociological stage described by Cæsar in Britain, where ten or a dozen men, fathers, sons, and brothers, had their wives in common, and kabbed together like the Kabiri above, the seven of one family, who were the sons of KHEBMA, and the primeval brothers-in-law, when the fatherhood was individually uncertain, but was acknowledged by the Kabiri, grouped together under one Totem, who were desirous of perpetuating the family (Kâbt, Eg. a family) name.

Sut-Typhon occurs by name[1] as a cousin of Aaron, the Hebrew El-zaphan being the rendering of the son of Typhon. The Hebrew writers are constantly complaining of the tendency of Israel to revert to the grosser, earliest type of deity, in Sut-Typhon, who is recognized by the monuments as the great divinity of the Syrian land. In two different accounts of the same transaction, it is written, —in the one,[2] " the anger of Jehovah was kindled against Israel, and he moved David against them to say, Go, number Israel and Judah : " in the other :[3] " Satan (שטן) stood up against Israel and provoked David to number Israel." But there is no real discrepancy. The first form of Jehovah was the feminine Typhon, the later personification of all evil; and if a male divinity be meant, the earliest masculine deity of the Jews was Sut, the son of Typhon, the Lord as the Sabean Baal or Bar-Sutekh. In Egypt Sut was degraded to the position of the Apophis power of darkness, and the Akhekh of evil, the natural opponent of the sun and the light; and the god, who had been united with Har, as Sut-Har, or Sut-Nubti, in the earlier typology, was afterwards transformed into the devil of theology. The same change occurred in the later Judaism. The ancient divinity, the god Sut, was converted into the apostate Satan, the adversary of souls. Nevertheless, Sut and Satan, deity and demon, were originally one and the same. Also this suggestion of numbering has a look of likeness to what we find in the Egyptian mythology, where Sut was prior to Taht as the numberer, the measurer, and calculator; and David, as is here maintained, is the Hebrew form of Taht. Sut was superseded by Taht, because he was not so true a reckoner as the god of luni-solar time, Sut (שט) meaning the one who has turned aside, deflected, or deviated from the straight path, and become unfaithful ; hence the Apostate. Sut-Typhon, the mother and son, in El-Shadai, became the plural devil, as the Shed or Shedim,[4] to whom the Israelites had sacrificed[5] and offered up their children, the Shad-Behemoth of Habakkuk.[6]

Sut appears, in the Book of Job, among the sons of God. In this book he enacts the part of Sut in the Egyptian Ritual, where he is the adversary and accuser of souls, at the head of a company of accusers, when the deceased pass before the judgment seats. The

---

[1] Ex. vi. 22. [2] 2 Sam. xxiv. 1. [3] 1 Chron. xxi. 1.
[4] Deut. xxxii. 17. [5] Ps. cvi. 37. [6] ii. 17.

Chaldee paraphrast renders a passage in Job thus : "There was (an appointed) day of severe judgment, a day of forgiveness of sins ; and the hosts of angels came and stood before the Lord, and the Satan came also and stood in judgment before the Lord." This is a portrait of Sut in the Egyptian Judgment. It is quoted here to show how faithfully the Hebrew writings follow in the wake of Egypt regarding Sut-Typhon as divinity and devil.

Typhon was especially worshipped in Israel as the suckler who was represented by the sow. The Egyptian Rerit became the Assyrian Lilit, Arabian Halalath, and Hebrew Lilith, a succubus and demon of nocturnal pollutions in the Talmudic and Kabalist legends. Naamah, the sister of Lamech, is likewise a form of the Lilith, who can be identified through the Phœnician goddess Ashthar-No'emâ, later Astronoe, whom the Greeks call Nemanun or Astronome, she who they say dwelt at Tyre in the sacred island of Asteria. The Paschal Chronicle identifies her with Astronome by means of the island and the star of Astarte, who will be shown to derive from Hes-Taurt and her star to be the constellation of Ursa Major, before the planet Venus became the type of the genitrix of the gods. As Naamah she is the gracious, mild, tender, pleasant, melting, voluptuous ; and we can see by the Egyptian "Nem," to be delicious, sweet, delightful, and to debauch and deprave, how the one character passed into the other.[1] She was so beautiful that the angels fell in love, and cohabited with her, the product of this union being certain devils called SEDUII.[2] The Lilith of Rabbinical tradition is called Adam's first wife, who left him, and soared into the upper air. The lady has been badly abused by Jewish ignorance, and turned into one of the demons of divinity dethroned, the night-monster of Isaiah ;[3] for theology, in trying to erase and obliterate the imagery of mythology, has scarified and blasted the face of the whole beautiful creation. But see how the symbols live ! Rerit or Taurt (Typhon), the Great Mother, carries in her hands and rests upon a loop, the noose-sign of reproduction, an emblem of the Bearing Mother, bound up for nine months. And in Hebrew Lilith exists as לילאת, Lilath, the loop. This Typhonian hieroglyphic was to be repeated 200 times in the tabernacle of the Lord.[4] In the hieroglyphics Rer means a child, to dandle, and Rerit (Lilith) is the nurse and dandler of the child. In the Rabbinical legends, Lilith has become the destroyer of little children. The hippopotamus, or rhinoceros, was also a type of Rerit or Lilith. This is the unicorn, and the single horn growing out of its nose is strongly marked in the portraits of Rerit, *i.e.* Lilith. In her demonhood she is supposed to obsess little children. Ben Sira states that "when a child laughs in its sleep on the night of the Sabbath, or new

---

[1] *Chron. Pasch.* t. i. p. 66.
[2] Vossius, *De Orig. et Prog. Idol.* lib. i. c. 17.
[3] xxxiv. 14.   [4] Ex. xxvi.

moon, they say that Lilith toys with it, and tickles it. And three times over the parents cry, ' Begone, cursed Lilith,' and each time they pat the child on the nose ; " [1] the place of the horn, and seat of Lilith's power, hence the appropriate pat on the nose, to drive her out. Also Taruth (Hebrew), for the revolvers, is synonymous with her name, as Taurt, the genitrix of the seven revolving stars.

According to the Rabbins, there is a demon who presides over the malady of blindness and the dizziness of delirium ; his name is SHEBRIRI (שברירי). In the hieroglyphics, SHEFI is the demon, terrible, terrifying. Sheb is blind, and RIRI means to go, whirl, or be whirled round and round. This explains the demon SHEBRIRI, who is only traditional in Hebrew. The name of the demon identifies it doubly with Typhon, who was, with Sheb (Kheb) and Reri (Rerit, later Lilit), the whirler-round.

Sut-Typhon is aimed at by Isaiah [2] as the Hilal (הילל), who had said : " I will exalt my throne above the stars of God ; I will sit also upon the mount of congregation in the thighs of the north." It is a compound image. The divinity of the thighs of the north was the feminine Typhon, and her son was Baal-Zephon. Hilal-ben-Shachar is not one of the morning stars, but, as Sothis at its heliacal rising, had been of far more importance than either of these ; no morning star can be connected with the north, as was Baal-Zephon or Sut-Typhon. This is Lucifer ; and Lucifer, as the devil of theology, identifies the Sut or Satan of mythology. The word שׁחר also tends to identify the Black Sut, as in Sut-har, Sut-Nahsi, or Sut-Nubti.

Rer (lal) is the child of Rerit, and Hi (Eg.) means pollution, impurity. Hi-lal, as Egyptian, would denote the unclean son of the sow (Rerit), Sut, the son of Typhon.

There is no difficulty in identifying the Jews, Hebrews, or Israelites, with the cult and caste of the Sut-Typhonians, the Aat, the Menat, and Aamu, within Egypt ; but this, at the same time, is to disperse them there rather than to recover the ethnological autonomy of a Syrian people, ranging from one individual in Joseph to two millions at the time of their Exode. Such a people is not to be found, simply because it never existed.

Brugsch Bey gives the latest results, and ranges through the whole series of the monuments. He remarks :—

" Some have very recently wished to recognize the Egyptian appellation of the Hebrews in the name of the so-called Aper, Apura, or Aperiu, the Erythræan people in the east of the nome of Heliopolis, in what is known as the ' red country,' or the ' red mountain.' According to the inscriptions the name of this people appears in connection with the breeding of horses and the art of horsemanship. In a historical narrative of the time of Tahtmes III. the Apura are named as horse-men, or knights (Senen), who mount their horses at the king's command. In another document of the time of Rameses III., long after the exodus of the Jews from Egypt, 2,083 Aperiu are introduced as settlers in Heliopolis with the words,

---

[1] Bartoloc, tom. i. pp. 69-71.   [2] xiv. 13.

'Knights, sons of the kings, and noble lords (Marina) of the Aper, settled people, who dwell in this place.' Under Rameses IV. we again meet with Aper 800 in number, as inhabitants of foreign origin in the district of Ani, on the western shore of the Red Sea, in the neighbourhood of the modern Suez. These and similar data completely exclude all thought of the Hebrews, *unless one is disposed to have recourse to suppositions and conjectures against the most explicit statements of the Biblical records.*"—Vol. ii. p. 129.

Which is of course impossible with Brugsch Bey, who is so simple a Bibliolator that he takes the whole mass of mythology, mixed up with the slight human data, for unquestionable God's truth. The Jews had no such origin, no such unity, no such autonomy within, no such exit out of Egypt, as he assumes for them. Like others, he looks only for the ethnological entity and name, whereas the Typhonians of Egypt can only be found under their religious and symbolical names, because they were such a mixed multitude.

There was an order of Egyptian priests named the Aperu, which being preparatory corresponded somewhat to the novices of a convent. Aperu means the consecrated, the Preparers, and it is the name of the fillet worn by the Apru. Also the use of the word in the Harris Papyrus[1] will serve to show that the Apru were likewise preparers or makers of roads. "Aperu" there signifies to lay out with roads, one road to fifty-three and a quarter acres being specified. One form of the Aperu may have been the road-makers or navvies. Clearly then, the Aperu as navvies will not distinguish the Hebrews ethnologically nor religiously, although some of those afterwards known as Hebrews may have rolled stones and prepared roads for Rameses. We shall have to fall back upon the mythological and astronomical Apru-iu in seeking an origin for the name.

The Aperu mentioned in the time of Tahtmes III. as being among the many tribes of the Upper Rutenu who had been captured at the taking of Megiddo (Magda) belong to two different Apru, to judge by the two different determinatives of the greater and lesser bird.[2] These two Apru De Rougé considered to be the two Ophras, situated in the land of Manasseh and Benjamin.[3] This is quoted on account of the dual sign. The name Aperu-iu has a dual ending with the IU added. In the Papyrus of Leyden the name is spelt Apuiru-iu. In this inscription they are engaged in drawing stones for building a fortress of Rameses II. The text says, "Now I have heard the message which my Lord made, saying: Give corn to the men and soldiers and Apuiru-iu who are drawing the stone for the great fortress of the palace of Rameses. I have given them their corn every month, according to the good instructions which my Lord has told me."[4] The Aperu-iu correspond by name to the dual sign of the different birds. Now there was a town or city named Aperu, in the Saitic or

[1] Pl. 34 B. line 4.   [2] De Rougé, *Album Photographique,* pl. 51, 52.
[3] *Étude sur les divers monuments du Règne de Toutmès III.*
[4] Chabas, *Mélanges,* pp. 143, 144.

Sutite Nome, and Apru-Iu is the name of the double-house of Sut Anubis. This is Sut at the crossing, the equinoctial Sut, answering to Atum, the equinoctial sun. Apheru or Apru then is a name of Sut-Anubis, and in the annals of Rameses III.[1] he is called FATHER APHERU by name.

In the seventeenth chapter of the Ritual, Father Aper, as Sut-Anup, is designated the "Clean Crosser of the Place of Birth," i.e. in Apheru the place of the two equal roads. He is also the Ap-heru AP MATENNU in person, the opener and guide of Roads over the Hill at the Crossing.

The Hebrews derive their name from Eber (עבר) rendered the crosser over; Eber being the crosser, after whom the Abrahamites of the line of Isaac and Jacob are designated the עברים, the Heberim, or with the Egyptian plural terminal, the APERIU.

Eber, the crosser, is identical with Aper, the clean crosser, and Eber, the father, with Father Aper, and so we continue the Typhonian origin and line of descent by means of Sut-Anubis, who is depicted in a dual form in the zodiac of Denderah, at the equinoctial crossing facing both ways, and presiding over the Apheru, or equal roads, as god of the crossing. The imagery is equinoctial *versus* the solstitial, and belongs to a reckoning different from that of the two heavens north and south. In relation to this, Sut reappears in the form of Anubis-Sapti or Sapt, lord of the east, with the sparrow-hawk head. Here we can connect Sut with the god Atum and the lion gods in the equinoctial myth. The Hebrew reckoning was equinoctial, whereas the Osirians held on to the solstitial. They kept the year equinoctially and, what was considered still worse, did not begin it with the Spring equinox but with the autumn, with the moon at full in the ascending vernal signs and their sun-god the Red Tum or black Ra-Nahsi, going down in the lower signs. It was in Apheru that Atum and Shu wore the four feathers of the four corners as an equinoctial sign. It was in Apheru, the place of the equal roads, and of Aper, the lord of the crossing and guide of the sun, that the gods at rest proclaimed the chiefs who belonged to the hall of the Two Truths, and told of Shu, son of the sun, and of Anhar, son of the sun in Apheru, the two established heads of roads resident in the empyreal region of Apheru. Thus the Aperu-iu of the double horizon can be identified with Sut and with Har-Makhu as Typhonians; the name equates with that of Sut-Anubis, as Apheru-iu the dual Anubis of the crossing, and guide of the two roads, and it is in this sense they may be one with the Hebrews in Egypt. Aperu-Iu really contains the double name of the Hebrews and the Ius or Jews, both of which are combined in the god Aper-Iu, the double Anubis. But the Aperiu remained in Egypt after the Jews had left. There were 2,083 or 2,093 of them settled in Heliopolis in the time of Rameses III., and 800 are

---

[1] Pl. 58, 117; *Records*, v. viii. p. 26.

mentioned as being in Egypt in the time of Rameses IV. And why not? The mythical exodus is of no authority against the historic Egyptian monuments, and the Aperu or Hebrew was not primarily an ethnological name, any more than that of the Typhonians, the Aati, Menat, Aamu, or the Ius. Proof positive can be offered for the origin of the Jews being the Ius, as the worshippers of the coming son, and not a people named ethnologically. As before mentioned, after our Jews had left Egypt Rameses III. built the temple of the Jews or of Judah in the north of An (On). He says in his address to his father Tum, "I made thee a grand house on the north of An constructed of eternal work, engraved in thy name, the house of millions of years of Rameses, ruler of An."

"I made for thee the great western abode and the lake of thy mother Iusāas the ruler of An."

"I made large boats for thy great daughters Iusāas (and) Nebhept."

This "house of millions of years," in the north of An, was known as the temple that stood on the Tel-el-Jahoudeh, the remains of which were lately in existence. This was the mound of the Jew, and the Jew of this temple was the god Iu, son of Iusāas, the Great Mother of the son whose worshippers were the Ius or Jews, no matter of what race, the same Jews theologically, who worshipped the god Hu, in Cornwall.

Josephus is right when he claims that his people were Hekshus. They were not the Hekshus in his sense of the conquering Syrian kings, the subduers of Egypt, but they were of the Hekshus religion, that of the pre-monumental Shus-en-Har, the worshippers of the mother and son. Hekshus applied to the so-called shepherd kings was a nickname, the point of which lay in the word Shus meaning servants, and service. Josephus reports that Manetho in another book said the nation called Shepherds were also called captives in the sacred books.[1]

This is explained by the name of Shus for servants rather than by the later Shasu, the shepherds as graziers; Hek (Eg.) being a ruler, a king, the Hek-shus are servant-rulers or in a sense captive-kings: hence the nickname. The original service was that of the Shus-en-Har; hence the point of the nickname. The ancient theocracy represented a government assumed to be divine, with no monarchy but that of the Divinity, and the priests or judges were his or her law-givers and representatives to the people. It is the oldest form of government in the world. It was the government of the Druids, of the Aztecs and North American Indians; the earliest everywhere. According to a tablet from Samneh in the time of Amenhept III., the same kind of government was found prevailing among the Kushites as is described in the Hebrew writings. This was a theocracy. It is recorded that they were not ruled by kings but by

[1] *Against Apion*, i. 14.

"judges," or, as is now suggested, they were Hekshus, the priest-rulers and priest-ruled people abominated as Sut-Typhonian by the ortho-dox Pharaohs of the Egyptian monarchy. These always had their adherents within Egypt, and hence the wars of the Hekshus or Shepherd Kings. But the Jews in Egypt can no more be discriminated as Hekshus among Hekshus than the Hebrews among the Aperu-iu or Aamu, the Menat or the Fenekh; they were a part of the mixed multitude generally undistinguishable except as Typhonians and worshippers of Sut. Nor will the Hebrew records help us much; they seldom reflect the monuments. They were primarily mytho-logical, whereas the monuments are historical. They mainly con-tain the Egyptian mythology converted in later times into Hebrew history. If there had been a specially Jewish exodus the Exodus of these writings is still mythological. If there were such persons as father Abram and Jacob, and Joseph and Moses, the characters pour-trayed under these names are none the less mythological, for they were mythological from the first, and could not become historical with the after-touches of Esdras.

To begin with, there is a supposed prophecy made by the Lord to the Abram of the first covenant.[1] "And He said unto Abram, Know of a surety that thy seed shall be a stranger in a land not theirs, and shall serve them, and they shall afflict them four hundred years," and this length of time was identified with the "fourth generation."[2] But the prophecy of 400 years would not be historically fulfilled by the assumed sojourn in Egypt. "Now the sojourning of the children of Israel, who dwelt in Egypt (was) 430 years, and it came to pass at the end of 430 years, *even the self-same day* it came to pass, that all the hosts of the Lord went out from the land of Egypt."[3] It is now too late to discuss the absurdity of the Lord literally talking in person to a man named Abram and making a false prophecy to the extent of thirty years, which is corrected to the day! Nor did the ancient prophecy relate to unforeseen events, but to the fulfilment of the time-cycles. The prophet was the Nabi, the announcer. Sut-Nub or Anup was the typical announcer in Egypt, the first prophet of the year, also of a period extending to the length of a Sothiac cycle, and the learned in circle-craft were those who knew and announced the end of the various cycles of time. Their prophecies were safe, and sure to be fulfilled. But the ordinary notion of prophecy has no meaning in heaven or earth when applied to the sacred books. Here, for example, is an illustra-tion of so-called prophecy, and its false interpretation by those who were entirely ignorant of the symbolical language, and its mode of conveying the hidden wisdom.

Isaiah relates how the Lord spoke to Ahaz, saying, "Ask thee a sign of the Lord thy God; ask it either in the *depth* or in the *height*

---

[1] Gen. xv. 13. [2] v. 16. [3] Ex. xii. 40, 41.

above." Ahaz declined. Therefore the Lord Himself gave Ahaz a sign. Then follows the passage rendered in the English version, "Behold a virgin shall conceive and bear a son, and shall call his name Immanuel. Butter and honey shall he eat, that he may know to refuse the evil and choose the good. For, before the child shall know to refuse the evil and choose the good, the land that thou abhorrest shall be forsaken of both her kings."[1] This in the heading is the promised Christ. Numberless volumes have been written to show that this was a Messianic prophecy, and it was one of the cornerstones of Christology until it was supposed that the building could stand without it. Latterly it has been admitted more and more that the Virgin was conceiving or bearing the child then and there! Now this is a prophecy in the modern sense. The speaker foretells an event which he says will happen shortly. In doing so he uses the language of the elder prophets and the imagery which is still pourtrayed in the heavens. The Virgin Mother is extant as Virgo in the zodiac. Amanuel (עמנואל) is the coming son. Al (Ar) has been sufficiently shown to mean the son. Ameni is an Egyptian proper name. There is a sepulchral inscription of one Ameni, of the eleventh dynasty.[2] Ameni or Amenu (Eg.) signifies to come, or the coming one; the Messiah of mythology, hence Amenu-El is the coming son.

The one who comes also brings, and this AMENI to come supplies the French Amener to bring, Amené, brought. Immanuel came annually and was conceived at the time of the summer solstice, as Har-pi-Khart, the child of the mother only. This was Har the child who transformed and became the only begotten of the father, reborn at the time of the vernal equinox, as Har the younger, the Shiloh, the afterbirth, who was no longer the child but "knew to refuse the evil and choose the good," which the child Horus did not, because he was always infantile. One name of the child the consoler, the arm of the Lord, is Ser; the Zend Sarosh, Hebrew Shiloh. Ser (Eg.) also signifies the anointing, and has the meaning of butter or cream, determined by some yellow substance. This is the typical butter and honey on which the child was nutrified. From summer solstice to spring equinox is nine months, and the two Horuses came forth from these two quarters, south and east, as it is written in Habakkuk.[3] "God came from Teman, and the Holy One from Mount Paran." But in the adjustment of the solar zodiac the Virgin Mother and the gestator (in Pisces) are but six signs apart. These two are in the lower and upper heaven, corresponding to the sign both in the "depth and in the height above."

In the zodiac of Denderah the Messiah prince, Har the child, is stationed in the sign of the Scales. But the Arabians made their Mesaiel the protecting genius in the sign of Virgo, and Mesai-El is the same as Mes-Har, or Mesore, the name of the month in which

[1] Is. vii. 14-16.   [2] *Records of the Past*, vi. 1.   [3] iii. 3.

the child was conceived. This was the month of Tammuz in the Jewish-Aramaic calendar, corresponding roughly to June. In accordance with this allegory of the heavens the Hebrews held that there were two Messiahs, or the Messiah who had two manifestations. One was to be born of the tribe of Judah, and a second of the tribe of Ephraim—that is, on the equinoctial sides of the zodiac as represented in some planispheres, and also in the signs of the Lion and the Bull, which were the signs of Judah and Ephraim. Certain Jewish traditions concerning the Messiah were gathered up in the fourteenth century by Rabbi Machir in his *Avkath Rochel*, and published in Hebrew and Latin by Hulsius,[1] in which the Messiahship is based on the physiological and astronomical number and period of nine months. Three kings are to conspire against the kingdom of God and His law during nine months. Also in the sixth sign a king is to rise in Rome and rule over the whole world, and lay waste and persecute Israel for the space of nine months. And, " at the end of the nine months shall be revealed Messiah Ben Joseph, whose name shall be Nehemiah, the son of Ghuziel, with the tribes of Ephraim, Manasseh, and Benjamin and part of the tribe of Gad."[2]

The year began say in Mesore, our June 15th. Isis had then conceived, with the sun in the sign of Cancer. In three months or so she quickens, and Har the elder appears in the sign of the Scales. Six months after Har the younger is born with the entrance of the sun into Aries. The coming son or Amanuel was born every year of Virgo first, as the child fed on butter and honey, and reborn of the gestator Iu-sā-as, in the opposite sign. Thus according to the celestial pictures yet extant the statement is tantamount to saying, " In less than six or at the utmost nine months the land that thou abhorrest shall be forsaken of both her kings." And that is all there ever was in the " Prophecy." It would have had the same meaning if the writer had said the child was to be born of nine virgins, as Heimdal of the Norse mythology was called the son of nine virgins, the nine who became the muses of Greece, and warmed the cauldron of Keridwen with their inspiring breath. Nine breathers and three water-sirens represented the twelve months of the year.

The two women called the wives of Jacob, " which two did build the house of Israel," are identified with the Virgo and gestator of the zodiac, when it is said allusively to Ruth, " Do thou worthily in Ephratah and proclaim thy name in Bethlehem."[3] The prayer is— May she breed and bring forth; may she conceive like Isis (Virgo), and bring to birth like Nephthys; only the typical two divine sisters cited are Leah and Rachel (the mother of Joseph), and the two places are rendered according to the Hebrew. Bethlehem, the house of bread,

[1] *Theologiæ Judaicæ Pars Frima de Messia*, Bredæ, 1653 ; Bartoloc, *Bib. Rab.* tom. iv. p. 28.
[2] *Avkath Rochel*, Hulsius, p 35.
[3] Ruth iv. 11.

represents the house of Virgo who carries the corn, and Ephratah was
the place where the Messiah son, the seed, was brought forth annually
for ever, he who was to be the "PEACE," *i.e.* the Iu-em-hept.[1]

Egyptian may throw light on the Hebrew עלמה (Galmah), rendered a
virgin, as applied to the pregnant and bearing mother of Isaiah vii.
14. Kar represents Gal as the round, circle, or course; Kar also
means to have, bear, carry; MEH signifies to be full, complete,
fulfilled. The course fulfilled by the Galmah may be completed in
puberty, by the marriageable maiden, or in the period of gestation.
In the present instance the fulfiller of the course as the gestator is the
Galmah, the MEHT-den or Mädchen.[2]

The commentators have been, and still are, entirely ignorant of the
astronomical christology and the fundamental nature of the sacred
writings. The "prophecy" of Abram is just as surely astronomical,
although not so easily explained. For this reason. We find the same
date in the Apocrypha,[3] "Behold the time shall come when these tokens
which I have told thee shall come to pass, and the Bride shall appear,
and she, coming forth, shall be seen that now is withdrawn from the
earth." For "My son Jesus shall be revealed with those that be with
him, and they that remain shall rejoice within 400 years. After these
years shall my son Christ die, and all men shall have life, and the
world shall be turned into the old silence seven days, like as in the
former judgments." This refers to a period of time apparently
repeated every 400 years. "And after seven days the world that yet
awaketh not shall be raised up, and the earth shall restore those that are
asleep in her," and there is to be a judgment as at the end of former
cycles. The seven days had the same meaning as those in the story
told by Lucian,[4] who relates that at the Temple of Hierapolis a
man ascended one of the phalli (pillars) twice a year, and remained
on the top of it watching and sleepless during seven days, as
"some suppose" to keep in remembrance the Deluge of Deuca-
lion, or the ending of a period which was thus symbolized. All
such customs belong to the early mode of memorizing the reckonings of time and period. The time-cycle is shown by the "four
beasts" of Esdras,[5] "whom I made to reign in my world that the
end of their times might come through them." Also, these four
belong to the four corners of the lion, scorpion, waterer, and bull, and
therefore are, according to the present interpretation, the same as the
four kings whom Abram overthrows and supersedes; they also
correspond to the four generations of the 400 years. There is a
period of 400 years assigned to Osiris in the lists, and one of 500
years to Seb. We cannot but suspect that the former period is
related to the Sun-and-Sirius reckoning, and to the Iusu, or Jesus of
the Apocrypha, as a form of Serapis.

[1] Micah, v. 5.   [2] See vol. i. p. 396.   [3] 2 Esdras, vii.
[4] De Dea Syria.   [5] ii. 11, 39.

Can the Bride refer to Sothis-Isis? The star Sothis was called the "Lady of the Beginning." She gave birth to the new year, and was a celestial type of commencement. The Bride is to appear again that now is withdrawn from the earth, and she coming forth shall be seen at the same time that Jesus, the coming Son, is to be revealed. The prophecy of the Apocrypha is certainly based on circle-craft, and contains the parable of a period of 400 years. The prophecy of 400 years belongs to the Apocrypha, *i.e.* the secret writings in which the chronology related to the heavenly bodies in Khebt, and not to the Jews in Egypt.

It is different with the period of 430 years. This we are able to utilize by aid of the "Tablet of 400 years," discovered in the ruins of ancient Tanis, *i.e.* Pa-Rameses, which had been the more ancient Tanis or San, the Hebrew Zoan, and was rebuilt or resuscitated by Rameses II. "Marvellous things did he in the sight of their fathers in the land of Egypt, the field of Zoan."[1] The Zoan here mentioned is no doubt the Egyptian San, the place of the Tablet of 400 years, only the writer has associated the topographical name with the mythical legends of the fathers and the parables of the astronomical allegory, and the "dark sayings of old" which the fathers had told them, that they should make these marvels known from generation to generation. The tablet belongs to the reign of Rameses II., and the king is represented making an offering to the god Sut. The inscription runs thus: "A gift of adoration to thy person, oh Sut, son of Nut, give thou a long time in thy service to the Prince Nomarch, royal scribe of the horses, superintendent of the fortress Taru." The dedicator is a prince, governor of the Nome and the superintendent of the fortress of Rameses, within which the Hebrews are described as labouring when they built treasure cities at Pithom and Rameses. It relates that Rameses ordered a large tablet of stone to be made in the great name of his fathers for the sake of setting up the name of the father of his fathers, Seti I., called Ra-men-ma. Seti is named as the worshipper of Sut, and the monument is erected in the great name of Sut; the scene represents an offering to the god Sut in his human form wearing the hut, or white crown, and holding the Ankh and Uas symbols. Rameses is represented "giving wine to his beloved that he may make him a giver of life."[2]

It may be remarked that this monument contains good evidence that Rameses II. was not that cruel persecutor of the Jews, or Typhonians, which some have declared him to have been. It appears from a tablet at Abusimbel, that he had chosen a wife from the hated worshippers of Sut, a daughter of the king of the Khita, and that she adopted the name of Ra-maa-ur-neferu. He was himself a Sut-worshipper like his father Seti, if not so pronounced; he was a Hekshus

[1] Ps. lxxviii. 12. [2] *Records of the Past*, vol. iv. 35.

in religion, if not a descendant of the Hekshus by blood. He appears to claim descent from the Hekshus king Apehpeh, as the tablet was ordered to be erected in the great name of his fathers for the sake of setting up the name of the father of his fathers, and connecting the Setis with their divine prototype in Sut. Sut-Nub, the doubly powerful, is the style of the god Sut on the monuments, and this Hekshus king is assimilated to that god. The god Sut is the object of the celebration, as he was the deity worshipped by Seti I. The adorer of the god says: " Hail to thee, Sut, son of Nut, Aa-pehpeh (or Apehti), in the boat of millions of years, overthrowing enemies before the boat of the sun." In this passage the Sun and Sirius (Sut) are combined, as in the dual image of Har-Sut, or Nubti. The 400th year of Sut-aa-pehti, the great double force, because of the combination of the Sun and Sirius, must be read as belonging to a Sun-and-Sirius cycle, the object being the divinity to whom the Setis were assimilated.

Herr Karl Riel [1] has undertaken to adduce the proof that the date from the year 400 of King Nub relates to the introduction of the feast of a Sun-and-Sirius year in the year 1766, in which the fifteenth of Pachons of the vague year fell on the 15th of Taht, of the fixed year, or on the real normal day of the rising of Sirius. Be this as it may, the present writer thinks the main object of the journey recorded, and of the tablet ordered by Rameses, was to chronicle the year 400 of Sut-Nub for the sake of setting up the name of the divine father of the Setis, and of keeping the chronology of a Sun-and-Sirius cycle of 400 years; also, he is unable to dissociate from it the 400-year-period alluded to in the Books of Genesis and Esdras, which belongs to prophecy, i.e. to the astronomical allegory.

In the divine reigns [2] there is a period of 400 years assigned to Osiris ; and if we could identify that, it might prove to be a cycle of the " Bennu-Osiris," 400 years in length. The same imagery which was applied to Osiris in the later cult belonged to Sut in the far earlier time ; the name of Sothis is for ever identified with Sut, and here the period of 400 years assigned to Osiris agrees with a four-hundred year cycle of Sut or Sothis. " Hail to thee, Sut-Apehpeh *in the boat of millions* of years, overthrowing enemies *before the boat of the sun*, great are thy roarings," is the salutation to Sut as Sothis, *not* to the Bennu as the Phœnix of Osiris. The Egyptian BENNU or Phœnix was the constellation in which Sothis or Sirius (the dog-star) was the chief star. It is believed to have corresponded wholly or partly to the constellations Cygnus and the Eagle (Aquila); the Egyptian phœnix being the swan of the Greeks, the peacock of the Hindus (the bird of Saraswatî and Kârtikêya, who are the Hindu Bride and Son), and the eagle of the Romans.

[1] Leipzig, 1875.　　　　　　　　[2] See vol. i. p. 41.

The Phœnix was called the BENNU of Osiris as the Nycticorax, a bird with double plume at the back of the head. But it was also represented by other birds. Nor is its name derived from the Bennu but from Ankh the living, as in P'ANKH and PANEACH (פענח) applied to Iu, the son, and to Joseph, both of whom personated a phœnix by name. This Ankh was the oriental ANKA, which was also known as the ROC (Rukh or Rook), and Simurgh, which indentifies the ANKA with the Rekh, another form of the Phœnix found on the monuments; a determinative of the Repas as types of time, as well as a spiritual emblem. Hor-Apollo says,[1] "When the Egyptians would denote the *Great Cyclical Renovation* they pourtray the phœnix bird, for when he is produced a renovation of things takes place, and he is produced in this manner. When the phœnix is about to die, he casts himself vehemently upon the ground, and is wounded by the blow, and from the ichor which flows from the wound another phœnix is produced; which, as soon as it is fledged, goes with its father to the city of the sun in Egypt; who, when he is come thither, dies in that place at the rising of the sun. After the death of his father, *the young one departs again to his own country*, and the priests of Egypt bury the phœnix that is dead." Pliny had learned that the life of the phœnix was related to the great year of the Cyclic Renovation in which the stars and seasons returned once more to their primal places.[2] But he gives its period as one of 660 years. Tacitus informs us that opinions vary as to the number of years, the " most common number being that of 500, though some make it 1461,"[3] the length of the Sothiac cycle. "It appears once in 500 years," says Herodotus,[4] and one phœnix period of 500 is certain. Lepsius has proved[5] that the Egyptians were acquainted with the precession of the equinoxes, which they calculated by a period of 1,500 years, or three phœnix cycles of 500 years each. This had to be combined with the Sothiac cycle of 1461 years, and he has shown how this period of 500 years is the third part of an actual period within which a year of 365 days coincides with the true solar year of the latter years. Now the great cycle of precession, called the great year, when calculated by that motion alone, consists in round (or cyclic) numbers, of fifty-two phœnixes of 500 years. But there is another motion of the orbit which works the contrary way and reduces the time in practice to about 21,000 years. If the Egyptians ascertained the length of their cycles by living through them, or if we credit them with as much mathematical skill and astronomical knowledge as the moderns possess with regard to these motions and cycles, they may have corrected the one motion by the other. The length of the great year, according to the second motion, is given at about 21,000 years; and whereas the 26,000 years contain fifty-two phœnixes of 500 years, the 21,000 contain fifty-two of 400 years each.

[1] B. ii. 57.   [2] x 2.   [3] *Ann.* vi. 28.   [4] ii. 73.   [5] *Einl.* p. 165.

What is wanted, then, is a phœnix of 400 years, as the type of the period assigned to Osiris and Abram, Jesus with the Bride (female Sothis?) and Sut. This may be found by the aid of Hor-Apollo,[1] who also tells us that when the Egyptians symbolized a man who had lived to a proper or good old age, they depicted a dying crow; for " *She lives an hundred years, according to the Egyptians; and one of their years consists of four of ours.*" Here, then, is a phœnix of four hundred years represented by Hor-Apollo's crow, which may stand for a kind of Bennu-Osiris of 400 years, the period assigned to Osiris in the divine dynasties. The crow, in English, is a form of the Egyptian phœnix, or Rekh by name, as the rook. The hundred years, which contain four hundred, can be followed in the hieroglyphics by means of the square, on which the " ter " sign of time was sometimes placed, instead of the circular sign used for the reigns of kings, or ages of individuals. The " proper age " of the phœnix, then, was one hundred TETRA-ETERID, identical with the four generations and four hundred years of Abram.

To represent the current year, says Hor-Apollo,[2] they depict (with the sign of the year) the fourth part of an Arura, a measure of land of an hundred cubits; and when they would express a year, they say a quarter. Four of these quarters SQUARED the fourfold year, just as does the added day of our leap-year. Thus the dying phœnix is identifiable with the dying crow or rook, typical of the proper age of 100 years of four years each, or of 400 years altogether; that is, of four generations of 100 years each.

The fourfold year mentioned by Hor-Apollo belongs to the Sothic period, and the heliacal rising of Sothis being about one day later every four years, completes the cycle, 1,460 years, in 365 of these days. The Egyptians, in consequence, called the year of 365 days one-quarter of the fourfold year.

This phœnix would be in the position of those persons who are born on the 29th of February, and will affirm that they have a birthday only once in four years, and their years are of fourfold length, their reckoning being identical with that of the Egyptians; and if its day of re-birth be analogous to our 29th of February, its age will be the one hundred leap-years, or a hundred years of the squared kind.

The ancient phœnix went down into Egypt to die or be transformed into the young one at the time of the great cyclic renewal. The transformation takes place at On (Heliopolis), where the sun-god, Atum, Ankh, or the Phœnix, is changed into the son as Iu-em-hept, the Jesus of the Apocrypha, who, in Esdras, is associated with the cycle of 400 years. Moreover, it was at ON that Abram was reputed to have taught the Egyptians astronomy ! The data agree exactly with the 400 years and the fourth generation of Abram's vision, seen when the sun went down. The seed of Abram are to serve in a land not theirs

[1] ii. 89.   [2] i. 5.

—Egypt is not named—and to issue forth again ; Abram is to go to his fathers in peace, and be buried in a good old age, just like the aged phœnix of 400 years at the time of the great cyclic renovation. The cyclic renovation is the same in the prophecy of Esdras, where Jesus, the son, is to be revealed with " those that be with him, and they that remain shall rejoice within 400 years." " And the Bride shall appear."

There is a Scholion on the Timæus hitherto considered to be of a doubtful character, which led Biot to think the Epagomenæ or five intercalary days were introduced into the Egyptian calendar by Aseth, one of the shepherd kings. Lepsius considers that if the Scholion contains any fact at all it can only mean that king Aseth converted a lunar year of 354 days into a solar year of 360 days and then added the five intercalary days, as if Aseth were a Semite correcting the Semitic lunar year by the Egyptian solar reckonings. But as Aseth is clearly one with Sut (Apehpeh) of the tablet of 400 years, the change in the calendar mentioned in the Scholion, which cannot refer to the introduction of the five added days, does in all likelihood refer to the phœnix cycle of 400 years, by means of which the apsidal motion was allowed for in its relation to that of precession in the final adjustment of the reckonings resulting from the later observations of the heavens. In Genesis [1] the period of 400 years follows the wars of the four kings and the five kings, who are overthrown in the previous chapter.

There is an Egyptian legend which relates how Osiris in the 365th year of his reign came from Nubia accompanied by Horus to chase Sut-Typhon out of Egypt, by which we may understand that the perfect solar year of $365\frac{1}{4}$ days was made to supersede the Sun-and-Sirius year of 365 days. In the battle for supremacy Horus was aided by Taht, the lord of the luni-solar reckonings.

It is only in this our century of Excavation that men have begun to dig and delve down to any depth of rootage, or to discover the real foundations of their knowledge, and in the theological domain the downward explorations have hardly begun. These time-cycles are the subject of " prophecy" in Genesis, Daniel, or Esdras, and not future human history, or the fate of empires. The burning or transformation of the phœnix is paralleled in Esdras by the *burning of the eagle*. " The whole body of the eagle was burnt, so that the earth was in great fear." This in the interpretation of the " vision " is to be followed by the founding of a kingdom " which shall be feared above all the kingdoms that were before it ; in the same shall twelve kings reign, one after another; *whereof the second shall have more time than any of the twelve ;* and this do the twelve wings signify, which thou sawest." [2] Now if we take this to refer to the founding of a zodiac of twelve signs and the introduction of the year

[1] Ch. xv.   [2] 2 Es. xii. 13-16.

or cycle, in which the quarter of a day was added to be calculated as one day in every four years, and we suppose that the one day was taken into the account in the *second month of the year* as it is in our February, then the second king may be said to have more time than any of the twelve, because the leap-year of fourfold length would be reckoned and dated by the month of his reign.

The whole subject has to be considered in a chapter on the " *Great Year*," but to my mind the present aspect of the cycle of 400 years at least suggests that the Sut-Typhonians—the people, so to say, of the Great Bear and the Dog-star—who were the most learned astronomers of Egypt, and the builders of the great Pyramid, were acquainted with the real length of the cycle of precession, and calculated it, as a period of fifty-two phœnixes of 500 years each, and that they also discovered the motion of the apsides, or longer axis of the earth's orbit,[1] which reduces the actual period of precession to some 21,000 years, or in round numbers, fifty-two phœnix cycles of 400 years each. That is near enough for the present purpose. It may be, however, that the Egyptians found out the length of their periods experimentally, by living through them, whereas the moderns can only calculate the total ; and their practical observations would be more trustworthy than any other reckonings. For instance, not long since the distance of the sun from the earth had to be corrected from 95,000,000 miles to about 92,000,000 ; this may have a bearing on the calculation of the period of 20,984 years, and if the measurement of annual variation should be wrong by two-fifths of a second the number would come out as nearly as possible 20,802 years.

It is noticeable in this connection that Rameses placed on the ceiling of the Ramesseion an astronomical projection of the heavens supposed to represent his horoscope. In the inscription which accompanies it the star Sothis (the Dog-star) is said to appear heliacally, or just before sunrise at the commencement of the year, and thus seems to mark the period of a Sothiac cycle, which may have a bearing on the period of 400 years. Unfortunately the regnal year of Rameses is not given. Here and there we may obtain a date for the Hebrew traditions where we cannot for the history. The Jesus of Esdras was to manifest within 400 years. The seed of Abram were to be afflicted in a strange unnamed land during 400 years. They were led up out of that land by the deliverer Joseph. These belong to mythology, and may be related to a Sun-and-Sirius period of 400 years. The date of 400 years on the tablet of San is none the less historical because of any relation to Sut-Har, the Sun-and-Sirius.

---

[1] "The position of the longer axis of the earth's orbit is a point of great importance . . . in fact, by the operation of causes hereafter to be explained, its position is subject to an extremely slow variation of about 12″ per annum to the eastward, and which in the progress of an immensely long period—of no less than 20,984 years—carries the axis of the orbit completely round the whole circumference of the ecliptic."—*A Treatise on Astronomy*, by Sir John F. W. Herschel, 1833.

Dates on the monuments can be trusted, whether they refer to human history or the celestial chronology ; the Egyptians would as soon have thought of falsifying the time in heaven as of forging an historical chronology, or of recording fictitious dates. There remains the fact that Rameses the Second, the rebuilder of Tanis, has recorded a period of 400 years which had elapsed between the reign of King Sut-Apehpeh and some unspecified year of his own long reign. Sut-Apehpeh is probably the second Apepi, considered to have been the last of the Hekshus kings. According to the prophecy, the seed of Abram were to suffer during 400 years, and, according to the supposed history, they actually were in the land of bondage during 430 years dating from the time of Joseph's being sold to Potiphar, an officer of Pharaoh. And there was a Christian tradition preserved by Syncellus, a tradition "received by the whole world," which affirmed that Joseph ruled the land of Egypt in the reign of King Apophis. Here then is a look of history at first sight. Apophis we know, and the tablet of San shows that he reigned 400 years before the year of the record made by Rameses the Second. In Brugsch Bey's account of Joseph in Egypt, the Hekshus king, Apophis, mentioned by the Manethonian and Christian tradition, is there ; but what is wholly missing from the monuments is Joseph himself. Nor shall we find the Hebrew mythology on the monuments, in the shape of Egyptian history, the impossible converse of what we have found, that is, the Egyptian mythology reproduced in Hebrew as history. The Joseph who went down into Egypt in the time of the king Sut-Apehpeh, and led the Israelites up out of it 430 years afterwards,[1] belongs to mythology, and is apparently related to some period of 400 years belonging to the Bride and the Son, as Joseph or Jesus, the Iusif or Iusu. The tablet of San may enable us to utilize the date of 430 years. It is probable that some 430 years do lie between the reign of Sut-Apehpeh and the exodus of the Typhonians from Egypt after the death of Rameses the Second, in the reign of Seti Nekht. But the only interpretation of the facts at present possible is this. The Hebrew "mixed multitude" in Egypt belonged to the most ancient religion, and were worshippers of the mother and son as Sut-Typhon. After the death or expulsion of Sut-Apehpeh, the last of the Hekshus, the Osirians and Ammonians returned to power, and, with the exception of the reigns of the Amenhepts III. and IV., the Typhonians had a bad time of it in Egypt.

"In their time," says the tradition reported by Syncellus, "Joseph ruled in Egypt," that is in the time of the Hekshus of the fifteenth, sixteenth, and seventeenth dynasties. The tradition is undoubtedly right, only we have been all wrong about the particular Joseph. Enough, however, has now been said concerning the Messiah Son, who, as the one who comes and brings, was the Iu-sif of the mythos.

[1] Ps. lxxxi.

Sut was a form of the Iu-sif, as well as Iu-em-hept and the Delphian Apollo. The ass, in the time of the twelfth dynasty, is named Iu; and this was a type of Sut, who was the Iu-sif of the ancient genitrix Typhon.

Sebek was a form of the Iusif, as well as Har-Makhu and Aten of the Disk, who were each the Iu of the two horizons, as the son of the mother. Har-Sut and Sut Nubti were dual forms of the son Iu-sif. When king Apepi set up Sutekh for his lord, and worshipped no other god in the whole land, that was a form of the Iusif. Thus Joseph must have ruled in Egypt during several hundred years from the commencement of the thirteenth dynasty, at least until the time of Sut-Apehpeh, called the last of the Hekshus, as during this period the mother and her son were the sole divinities of the Sut-Typhonians, and these people considered themselves to be the worshippers of the one God. At Tel-Amarna, Aten is often called the one God; he is styled the one God living in truth. Also Kufu of the fourth dynasty, in personating the living Har-Sut, was the adorer of the one God, as the Iusif or son of the mother. The lacunæ notwithstanding, it is apparent from the negotiation between Seken-en-ra of the seventeenth dynasty and the Hekshus king Apehpeh of Avaris, that a possible treaty between them was made contingent on Apepi's consenting to worship all the gods (elsewhere called the nine gods) of the whole land, with Amen-Ra at their head. But he was a worshipper of the one god, Sut, who took the dual forms of Sut-Anubis and Sut-Har, whose twin starry types were Sothis and Orion, or earlier the dog and the wolf. In the scene on the tablet of San, Sut is the one god of the offering, the one god beloved of Rameses: only this one god was not the generator Amen or the father Osiris, but always the child Sut, son or dog of the mother; Har, son of the mother; Aten, son of the mother; Sebek, son of the mother, or Joseph, son of the mother. It was the same Joseph under the many names of Adon, Tammuz, Duzi, Baal, Sutekh, Khunsu, Iu-em-hept, Greek IE, Jasius, and Jesus; the same Joseph who led the Israelites up out of Egypt; the same mythological character, whether stellar, lunar, or solar, considered as the son of the mother who, as the coming one, was the Iusif by name. This was the only Joseph who ruled as Adon over all the land of Egypt in the time of the Hekshus king Apehpeh or Apophis.

After the reign of Apehpeh the religion again changed hands. Sut and his mother had to make way once more for the gods of the orthodox, and there arose a king " who knew not Joseph," *i.e.* who did not worship the Iu-Sif or coming son. At which time the persecution of those who did so worship broke out afresh, whether they were called after the Iu, Jews; Aati, Menati or Sut-Typhonians; their period of bondage began, and lasted, so far as many of them were concerned, until there came the casting-out, called by the name of the

Exodus.   It was a long period of suffering for those who had been suppressed and enslaved in mines and quarries, and compelled to do all kinds of labour enforced by the whips of the taskmasters.   The Jews belonged to that suffering and enslaved people on account of their religion, independently of race.   They speak in their name because they were of them.   The bondage dates itself from the time of the last of the Hekshus or Shepherd Kings until that of the Exode, in the time of Seti-Nekht, which may have been, for anything known to the contrary, exactly a period of 430 years.

"Now there arose up a new king over Egypt, who knew not Joseph ; and he said unto his people, Behold the children of the people of Israel are more and mightier than we.   Come on, let us deal wisely with them, lest they multiply, and it come to pass that when there falleth out any war they join also unto our enemies and fight against us, and get them up out of the land.   Therefore they did set over them taskmasters to afflict them with their burdens.   And they built for Pharaoh treasure cities, Pithom and Rameses."[1]   This description of the Jews holding the balance of power in Egypt is true to the monuments, only the "Jews" must be understood in the religious acceptation of the name.   The children of Israel were the sons of El, Al, Ar or Har, who is the Son, and Elyon the Highest answers to the first Har or El, who was Sut.

The story of Joseph and the wife of Potiphar is mythological.   It is the same that is found in the endeavour of Ishtar to seduce the solar god Izdubar, who repels her advances when she says "Salute me, for I would marry thee."   Various versions are extant.   One of the most striking may be found in Lucian's account of the Syrian goddess.   In this Combabus (Joseph) is beloved by his master's wife ; and knowing that he is to be left in charge over her during the master's absence, he cuts off a certain part of his body, and delivers it over to the king in a sealed box as a precious treasure to be kept until the monarch returns.   The same solicitation occurs as in the case of Potiphar's wife ; the young man, like Joseph, is proof against the lady's passion.   She turns on him, and denounces him to her husband.   Then the box is opened, and the innocence of Combabus established.   The story relates primarily to the Iu-sif, or child of both sexes.   "I am a woman," says Bata, "even as thou art," speaking as the infertile one, in the Egyptian "*Tale of the Two Brothers.*"   This tale contains a form of the mythos reduced to a romance, in which the younger brother performs the same act as Combabus, and cuts off his genitals and throws them into the water.   It contains the same scene between the temptress and the youth as the Hebrew story ; and the foiled lady also becomes the false informer ; as does Potiphar's wife.   The Egyptian papyrus containing the tale, now in the British Museum, was written by the scribe Anna, master of the rolls, and was

[1] Ex. i. 8-11.

in the possession of Seti Mer-en-Ptah, the successor of Rameses II. This "oldest romance in the world," once proved to belong to mythology, can in nowise be claimed as a precious and important elucidation of the history of Joseph in Egypt in the sense adopted by Brugsch Bey.[1] Nor can anything historical be based on the two dreams of the Pharaoh in which the seven kine come up out of the river Nile; one group fat and the other lean, when the seven lean ones devour the seven fat kine; or the seven full ears of corn that come up and are devoured by the seven thin and blasted ears. The imagery is Egyptian, zodiacal, and mythical. The seven ears of corn are borne by the goddess Isis, in the sign Virgo of an Egyptian planisphere. The great mother holds five ears in her hands and carries two on her head.[2] The seven cows were the seven mythical cows of Hathor, the cow-headed goddess. Both were types of plenty: both related to the Nile and the inundation. These visionary symbols are palpably pourtrayed on the monuments. In the Ritual the seven cows of Hathor are invoked by name. They give food and drink to the living (whom we call the dead), and feed the gods of the west; and the Osirian (deceased) prays these types of plenty to give him of their abundance. "Give ye food and drink to the Osiris, feed him; give ye to him daily food and drink and all good things,"[3]—an early form of "Give us this day our daily bread" is thus addressed to the seven cows of Hathor. The cow type of Hathor is a paranatellon of the Scales, the sign next to the Virgin. The seven in relation to the inundation are as old as the Great Bear. The appearance of the seven cows is made prophetical, just as in Egyptian literature the seven cows, or as they are called the "seven Hathors," are the foretellers of events to come, the prototypes of the Greek Parcæ and the Gahs of the Avesta. These seven prophetic Hathors attend the birth of children, and predict their future fate. They appear in the "Tale of the Two Brothers," where they come to utter a prophecy with "ONE MOUTH." The seven years are likewise mentioned during which the brother remains infertile, and these are followed by the time of prosperity and plenty.[4] The "Hathors from Pithom" are especially alluded to in an inscription in honour of Rameses II. at Ipsambul.

Nor has the "Bahr Iusef" any relation whatever to the supposed patriarch Joseph, whose name has been applied by the Arabs to explain the Egyptian Iusif. All the accounts of this canal show that it was made to retain the waters of the inundation; and the traditions connect it with the name of Mena. When the Nile was in flood a vast quantity of water was received into artificial lakes by means of the canal, and dammed off until required for later use. By these arrangements the inundation was doubled, which is exactly what the name of the Bahr Iusef tells us in Egyptian. SEFA

[1] Vol. i. 269, E. Tr.   [2] Drummond, pl. 3.
[3] Ch. cxlix.   [4] *Records,* ii. 144.

(Eg.) means to make humid; SEFI, to liquefy; SEFA is the inundation. and a name of its goddess. IU means to duplicate, and the IUSEF is literally the doubler of the inundation by name. This name is likewise repeated in another form. In the neighbourhood of the Libyan Basin, which was filled by the Bahr Iusef, it was called the MENHE or MENHI canal.

HI (Eg.) is a canal of water, and the word means to inundate. MEN (Eg.) denotes the fixing and placing, to remain, during. Thus the MENHI canal is the canal of the inundation, or of the water that was fixed to remain there until wanted. A MEN is the container of water, as a cask and a vase or jar. Both names say the same thing, which is altogether remote from the patriarch Joseph. If we take the HI or HIU of Menhi as the first syllable represented by the Arabic Iu in Iusef, it comes to the same conclusion. HIU-SEF signifies the canal of the inundation.

It was the Joseph of mythology who was in Egypt under the rule of Apophis the king, Sut-Apehpeh of the Tablet of San, four hundred years before the tablet was set up by Rameses the second. The historical Joseph, if ever there was one, we shall have to seek elsewhere in another way.

We must now look back to the beginning of the 13th dynasty, when the reign of the Sebekhepts commenced, and the great confusion began, to continue during five dynasties. Here the theory of the foreign invasion and conquest of a thousand or two thousand years fails to bridge over the gulf, or fill it in.

"A considerable number of native kings must have reigned between the last king of the twelfth dynasty and the beginning of the foreign invasion. There are numerous inscriptions which prove that sovereigns powerful in the north of Egypt had extended their dominion to the heart of Nubia. The monuments of Thebes, Southern Egypt, and Nubia might be consistent with the hypothesis of a Hekshus kingdom in the north ; but the presence of equally important monuments of the Sebekhepts at Bubastis and Tanis, kings whose names occupy an important place in the chamber of Karnak, would alone be sufficient to overthrow this hypothesis. There is in the Louvre a magnificent colossal statue in real granite of Sebekhept III., with reference to which M. de Rougé says, 'A single statue of this excellence and of such a material shows clearly that the king who had it executed for the decoration of his temples or palaces had not yet suffered from the invasion of the Shepherds. It is evident that under his reign Egypt was still a great power, peacefully cultivating the Arts.'"[1]

Yet it was the reign of Typhon, as proved by the worship of Sebek, the ancient God of Darkness, who had escaped from the battle with Horus in the shape of a crocodile. My own reading of the facts is that at the beginning of the 13th dynasty only a religious revolution had occurred through Queen Sebek-nefer-Ra, who delighted to assume the character of the Divine Genitrix as mother of the son, *i.e.* the Virgin Mother, who alone produced the son from herself without the initial fatherhood, a *rôle* that was tempting to a woman who reigned alone. She was the continuer of Sebek as Ra. The Sebekhepts were no

[1] Renouf, *Hibbert Lectures*, pp. 44, 45 ; see also Birch, *History of Egypt*, p. 74.

doubt native kings, and some of them were treated as such. But when Seti the first, the devoted to Sut, singles out seven of them for special recognition or reverence, this act tends to show they also were worshippers of Sut-Typhon in the solar form of Sebek-Ra and his mother. Also the Hekshus king Apophis so far claimed a kinship in religion, if not in race, by having his own name engraved in hieroglyphics on the right shoulder of the colossal statue of Semenkhara-Mermesh, the 18th king of the 13th dynasty according to the royal Turin Papyrus.[1] This was more like laying a hand on that monarch's shoulder in token of friendship, than the act of an overthrower and destroyer.

But, with the restoration of Sut-Typhon under native kings, the "invasion" and the strife had more or less begun. For the eternal conflict between Sut-Typhon and Osiris was being fought out continually on earth before it was transferred to the scenery of the heavens in the later rendering of the mythos, and Lower Egypt was the particular battle-field.

Sut had once been in possession of the whole land of Khentu in the south and Kheptu in the north; his star ruled in the one, his mother's in the other, and they were the Biune All, in the beginning with the goddess of the seven stars and her son the Dog. Then other gods were evolved, Shu and Taht, Ptah and Osiris and Amen-Ra, and these began to chase Sut-Typhon from the land of their birth,—the driving out of Sut-Typhon being one of the prime causes of the colonization of the world. By degrees the Typhonians were crowded down to the northern extremities of Egypt, where the mixing of race with their co-religionists of Syria and other lands led them to look at times for help from their fellow-worshippers of the most ancient gods. At length the Hekshus, Aamu, Menat, Aati, are limited to a Nome or two, so far as they are visibly congregated together; and at last the main body of them is confined to Avaris, where we find them under the ruler Apehpeh, called the last of the Hekshus kings.

"It came to pass," says the scribe, Pentaur, " when the land of Egypt was held by the impure (The Aati or Aamu) there was no lord-king (*i.e.* of the whole of Egypt); in the day, namely, when king Ra-skenen (Sekennenra) was ruler of the land of the south, the impure holding the district of Aamu (or of Sut-Ra), their chief (Uhi) King Apepi was in the palace of Uar (Avaris). The whole land paid homage to him with their manufactures in abundance, as well as with all the precious things of the inhabitants of the north. Now king Apepi set up Sutekh for his lord; he worshipped no other god in the whole land . . . built him a temple of durable workmanship. It came to pass that while he rose up (to celebrate) a day of dedicating . . . . a temple to Sutekh, the prince (of the south) prepared to build a temple to the sun over against it (query, in rivalry with it?). Then it came to pass that king Apepi desired to . . . king Ra-skenen . . . the prince of the south. It came to pass a long time after this . . .

Four lines obliterated.

. . . with him in case of his not consenting (to worship) all the gods which are in the whole land, (and to honour) Amen-Ra, king of the gods. It came to pass, many days after these things, that king Apepi sent a message to the prince

---

[1] Pl. 7, scutcheon 116, *Histoire d'Égypte*, Brugsch.

of the south. The messenger (being gone?) he called his wise men together to
inform them. Then the messenger of king Apepi (journeyed) to the chief of the
south; (when he was arrived) he stood in the presence of the chief of the south,
who said to him this saying, viz. to the messenger of king Apepi, 'What message
dost thou bring to the south country? For what cause hast thou set out on this
expedition?' Then the messenger answered him, 'King Apepi sends to thee,
saying he is about to go to the fountain of the castle, which is in the region of the
south, seeing that . . . has commissioned me to search day and night!' . .
The chief of the south replied to him, that he would do nothing hostile to him.
The fact was he did not know how to send back (refuse?) . . . the messenger
of king Apepi. (Then the prince of the south) said to him, 'Behold thy lord,
promised to' . . .

Four lines obliterated.

Then the chief of the south called together the princes and great men, likewise
all the officers and heads of . . . and he told them all the history of the
words of the message sent to him by king Apepi, before them (or according to
order). Then they cried with one voice, in anger, they did not wish to return a
good answer, but a hostile one. King Apepi sent to "[1] . . .

The people shut up in Avaris, who are called Aati or Aamu, are
Typhonians first and foremost, whether invaders or not. The
city of Avaris, says Manetho, was Typho's city, in accordance with
the *ancient* theology. It has been discovered by M. de Rougé that
Avaris, the residence of the last Hekshus king, was depicted as the
house of the leg, written phonetically Hat (house), Uar (the leg).
And the house of the leg is identical with the house of Typhon, when
the imagery is interpreted.

The house of the leg is good Egyptian for the leg or thigh constellation, that is Ursa Major or Typhon. The leg or hinder thigh,
the Khepsh, denoted the north as the emaning uterus of creation.
The city of Avaris in the north of Egypt, as house of the leg, represented the place of birth in the planisphere; and it was in the Nome
of Sut. Typhon was reported to be concealed in the Bog of Serbonis,
at the northernmost limit of the land.[2] Avaris is said to have been
built by Saites or Sut.

In the religious revolt described by Pentaur, Ra-Apepi was king in
Avaris, and ruled over the whole north of Egypt. It was in the
time of Ra-Skenen who was the ruler in the south. We learn from
the "Inscription of Aahmes," a captain-general of marines, that he
was present at the taking of Avaris. He says, "We laid siege to
Avaris," "we fought upon the canal of Patetku of Avaris." "We
took Avaris."[3]

After the reign of Ra-Apepi in Avaris, and the driving out
of the Hekshus for the time being, another rush was made from
the south, and the Pests once more profaned the Ammonian gods
with their hated presence. It is the same complaint as that of
Pentaur, but refers to a later onset. Aahmes the captain served under
Aahmes the first king of the 18th dynasty. In the religious sense
Aahmes the Pharaoh was a king who knew not Joseph, and the

---

[1] *Pap. Sallier*, 1. Slightly altered from Goodwin's version.
[2] Herod. iii. 5. [3] *Records of the Past*, vol. vi. p. vii. lines 7, 8, 12, 13.

eighteenth dynasty arose as the opponent and conqueror of the worshippers of Sutekh, or Sut the child, the Typhonian Iusif. Aahmes married an Æthiope woman, apparently the daughter of some royal house, possibly in relation to the war, in which he drove back the "Pests of the south." Through this queen Aahmes-Nefertari [1] the black race mounted the Egyptian throne.

The black blood appears to have wrought in favour of the Typhonian religion; Sut was the god of the Nahsi, and the Aten sun was especially worshipped by the Æthiopians. It breaks out in the person of Amenhept III., whose mother was a black, and whose features show the Æthiopic type. The monarch introduced afresh the Aten disk of the sun, designated the Aten-Nefer, or youthful solar god. This, when rightly understood, was no new thing in Egypt. Among the servants of Sebek, in the thirteenth dynasty, there is a king AIU, whose throne-name is MER-NEFER-RA,[2] the lover of the young sun-god, who was the lamb of the Sebekhepts and the solar child of the Typhonian mother. He also was assimilated to the god as the son, the "IU," who comes, and is the coming one for ever.

Among the kings, in the Chamber of Karnak, who are later than the thirteenth dynasty, and earlier than the eighteenth, there is one styled "NEB-ATEN-NU-RA."[3]   He too was lord of the Aten likeness of the sun, long before the time of the so-called disk-worshippers. The Aten sun, as mere disk, will tell us nothing without the doctrine of the cult. As the sun of the horizon, it is identical with Har-Makhu, a title given also to the orthodox gods. But the Aten disk was the emblem of the divine son, who was solely the seed of the woman; and the Pharaoh assimilated to this type was a representative of the Har-sun, the sonship of the divine genitrix, and not of the fatherhood; he imaged the unbegotten son of the mother, the son of the woman who is the Messiah in the Book of Enoch.[4]

Amenhept III. is known to have married a woman who was evidently foreign, as she is painted of a fair colour, with pink-tinted flesh—the complexion given on the monuments to what are termed the Japhetic races, as opposed to dusky Ham. It is recorded on the Scarabæi that her father's name was IUAA and her mother's Tuaa. This lady, whose name was TAIU, appears to have had a marked influence on the course of religion and politics in Egypt. Some Scarabæi, says Dr. Birch, dated in the eleventh year of this reign, foreshadow the religious revolution that was impending. On the first of the month Athyr, the king had finished a large lake or basin, about 5,000 feet in length, and 1,000 feet in breadth, English

---

[1] Brugsch, *Histoire*, pl. xi. scutcheons 237, 238.
[2] *Ibid.* pl. 7, scutcheon 135.
[3] *Ibid.* scutcheon 216, pl. 10.   [4] Ch. lxi. 9.

measure, and on the fifteenth of the month he held a festival, and launched on this lake the symbol of his worship, the boat of the solar disk, named Aten-nefru. This was the type of the young (Nefer) sun-god, Aten or Adonis, the Iu-su or Iu-sif.

The mother of Amenhept III. represented the boat, as the bearer or genitrix. Her style in the scutcheons is MUT-EM-UA, the mother as the solar boat. Or, as " EM-UA " also means ALONE, she has the significant title of the Mother alone; she who bore the Only One. In the temple of Ra, built by Amenhept at Luxor, she is proclaimed to be the bark that bears the sun. In this same temple there is a remarkable sculpture representing the incarnation, the annunciation, the conception, birth and adoration of the divine child, here born as Amenhept III., the son of Mut-em-Ua, or the mother alone. The scenes are pourtrayed on an inner wall of the holy of holies. The queen, being the earthly image of the mythical genitrix, gives birth to her child as the messiah-son. In the first scene Taht, the Word, Logos, or messenger, and tongue of the gods, announces the coming birth. In the second, Khneph, the spirit or divine breath, and Hathor, the cow-headed bearer of the sun, each takes the queen by the hand and holds the symbol of life, the Ankh, to her mouth. This is the act of incarnation, which has a visible result in the swelling shape of the queen's figure. In the Arabic traditions, Gabriel, whom the Persians designated the angel of revelations, is said to have breathed into the bosom of the virgin's shift, and caused conception.[1] Nef means breath, and Shu, the earlier God of Breath, will be identified with Gabriel. In the third scene the queen is seated on the midwife's stool, and the child is born. In the fourth scene is depicted the adoration of the child, with three human figures behind the god Khneph. The child here born was representative of the Aten sun, the same as Adonis, Tammuz, or Duzi, considered to be the son of her who came from herself, the virgin mother. In the great Harris Papyrus, Rameses III. complains that the revolters and insurrectionists have made the gods in the human likeness, and Queen Mut-em-Ua and her son assumed the divine likeness, as the Mary and child-Christ of the Aten cult.[2]

Queen TAIIU wears a headdress and crown, from which seven gold wires spring and support seven small golden disks. These show her worship to have been akin to that of Sevekh-Ra, the Sun as the Lord of the Seventh Day and the Number Seven; the Sun that was said to " cross in the Eye of Seven Cubits," and who is adored at Ombos by the worshipper holding the instrument containing the seven wires.

In the British Museum there is a magnificent statue of Amenhept III., with the Libyan lips and Kushite type of face. On the back of

---

[1] Jallalo'ddın, *Al Beidâwi ;* Sale, *Al Koran,* ch. xix. note *g*.
[2] Sharpe, *Egyptian Mythology,* p. 18.

this a divine name has been changed. It was a name conjoined with Ra; for the Ra was left on the polished stone, as it was first written. We now know that the missing name must have been Aten, and with the substitution of *m* for *t* it was turned into Amen.

As it is usual to conclude that a woman was at the "bottom of it all," so in this instance it is surmised that Mut-em-Ua was a cause of the religious revolt under the Amenhepts III. and IV. The Aten disk, the especial symbol of the Æthiopians, is a type of the same divinity as the Syrian and Hebrew Adon. It is a remarkable meeting-point of cross ways this, where stands the King Amenophis III. of the dusky race, with his black mother on the one side and his fair wife on the other, both devout worshippers of Aten-Ra, on the Typhonian line of descent.

Amenhept, like Tahtmes, had, in the language of the inscription, "washed his heart," as the Zulus speak of "washing their spears," and carried his conquests to the land of Naharain. He was a mighty warrior and hunter. The memorial Scarabæi tell us that, on his hunting expedition in the land of Naharain, he had speared 110 lions with his own hand. At the temple of Soleb he is proclaimed conqueror of Naharina or Mesopotamia, Singara, Pattana or Padan-Aram, and Assur or Assyria. Now a king's daughter, preciously adorned, was a portion of the tribute paid by the king of the Rutennu to Tahtmes III., in the year 32 of his reign; and my conjecture is that the fair wife of Amenhept was a portion of his Mesopotamian conquests. The great empire of the Khita lay in the vast plain of Mesopotamia, or Naharain of the double river. The inscriptions often refer to the land of Naharain, in the neighbourhood of the upper Rutennu. This is the Aram-Naharaim, Aram of the two rivers mentioned in the Hebrew writings—the land of the two streams, or double-stream land, that lay between the river Tigris and Euphrates.

Of all the peoples known to the past and named on the monuments, the Egyptians acknowledge the Khita as the noblest, and rank them almost as their peers. They are the "great people," and their land is the "great country." They are the Hittites of the Hebrew Scriptures; their origin is one of the unsolved problems of history. But long ages before the rise of Babylon and Nineveh the ancient Khita ruled in the most northern parts of the Syrian land, and their empire extends to a remote antiquity. The object of citing this is to suggest that the Aramean element in the Hebrew writings connected with the story of Abraham may be the result of the marriage of Amenhept with a daughter of the double-stream land of Naharain or Mesopotamia, who would thus be a "HITTITE." The name of the queen's father, recorded on the Scarabæi, was IUAA, and the name of her mother TIUAA, the feminine form of the same. Iuaa is evidently derived from the god IU, the coming one, and as AA means born of or engendered, these appear to be named as the devotees of Iu, the dual son, who was Iu-em-hept at ON, IE at Delphi, Joseph in Israel, and the Jesus of the Apocrypha. Iuaa, of Lower Egypt, would be IUAA-KHEB. That is the nearest approach to an historical Jacob to be anywhere found on the monuments.[1]

Amenhept III. was followed by Amenhept IV., who has been supposed to have changed his name to Khu-en-Aten, the Adorer of Aten. The latest researches, however, point to these two as being different persons. Khu-en-Aten changed the name of the city called after him, Khu-Aten, into Pa-Aten-Haru, the city of delight for the solar disk, or rather, the youthful sun-god, Adon, the lord. He appeared in public riding on the golden court-chariot, like the disk of the sun.[2] His scutcheon and style read like a hymn to the sun. "In the horizon celebrate (ren) the splendour which is in the orb of Aten."[3]

Khu-en-Aten was suckled by a nurse, who was the namesake of the queen-mother Taiu; she is styled the high nurse and nourishing mother of the god-like one. This would assimilate her to the character of one of the two divine sisters of the child. Her husband's name was AI, or, in full, AIU. AIU was a priest or holy father (Nuter-ta), also the fan-bearer at the king's right hand, and overseer of the stud of brood mares; he was versed in the science of law, and has the title of the royal scribe of justice. Aiu and his wife Taiu were promoted so rapidly that their rise was the subject of gossip with the common people, whose comments are inscribed on the monuments. As Aiu was in the law, and is styled "the royal scribe of justice," he may have been a judge, that is a SEP, and AIU the judge, is AIU-SEP, or Joseph. The name of Iu-em-hept is also spelt with the variant Ai, or Aiu, and the ass is both AAI and Iu.

If there be any historical Joseph to be found on the monuments it is in this AIU as a Sep. He was the *protégé* of Amenhept III.; and again, if there be anything historical in Joseph's asserted connection with the king Apophis, it may be identified, as Amenhept is likewise styled an A-peh-peh. In the title of Sut-Apehpeh on the tablet of San, the double lion is the sign of Peh-Peh; but on his own scutcheon the name is written the same as that of the Apophis monster, the Apap, meaning the elevated. One A-peh-peh is therefore as good as another, for the name or title of Apophis. Aiu is a supposed worshipper of Amen, but this name in a case like the present proves nothing. Amen is but a title, without determining the theology. Amen was a title of Sebek, the Typhonian sun-god. AMEN-AU, the hidden Au, is a god of the Sebek family of gods; Kak was an Amen, the hidden, unknown, or coming god, the AMENU-

---

[1] There is in the British Museum a blue porcelain cylinder for holding the stibium used in blackening the brows and eyelids, on which the names of Queen Taiiu and Amenhept III. appear. (No. 2572 b, shelf 2.)

[2] *Inscript. of Amenhept IV.*   [3] *Königsbuch*, Taf. 28, Fig. D.

EL. Also Baal-Amen of the Phœnician theogony, according to the present reading, indicates the sun as the son (Al) of the mother; whereas the Amen-Ra of later Egypt was the divine father. It is of more importance to know that Aiu is an Ar-mer-Maāt, the beloved son of Truth, and that *his* sun is Khepr-Khepr-Ra, the sun of the double beetle, the two cherubs of the Hebrew mercy-seat, as shown by their appearance in the Egyptian sacred ark or portable temple.[1] This sign connects Aiu with the worship of Tum and Ma, and their Two Truths. Also the lions are used in proclaiming Aiu to be the son of Ma, beloved exceedingly. Here then, we have the Thummim of Ma and Atum, the beetles or cherubim, and the two lion-gods in a cluster.

On a monument of the thirtieth year of the reign of Amenhept A-peh-peh, the patron and promoter of Aiu, is represented as receiving the accounts of an extraordinarily great harvest from the storekeepers of Upper and Lower Egypt. In the tombs of Abydus were buried several "overseers of the accounts of the corn placed in the royal granaries." And again, SAP (Eg.) means to examine and verify.

Brugsch Bey[2] quotes a memorial stone of a contemporary family, which mentions that a certain Ha-Aai (Lord Aai, the equivalent of Adon in Hebrew), who was "an *overseer* of the cutters of hieroglyphics" of his unnamed "lord of the land," had two sons, named Har-em-Hebi and Rameses. This looks as though Har-em-Hebi and Rameses I. may have been the children of Aiu, the divine father and scribe of justice. Brugsch Bey says, "Whether Rameses I. was the son, son-in-law, or brother of Haremhebi is as yet undecided. If I say the brother, I am led to this as a possible supposition by the testimony of the memorial stone of a contemporary family, which mentions the *brothers Haremhebi and Rameses* among the sons of a certain *Ha-Aai*, an 'overseer of the cutters of hieroglyphics' of his unnamed 'lord of the land.'"[3] Aiu, the overseer, examiner, and judge of the cutters of hieroglyphics, would be a Sep, one of the Kem-Sep, and AIU-SEP is the equivalent of the Hebrew *name* of Joseph. If this Aiu, an overseer of the cutters of hieroglyphics, and father of Horus and Rameses, be the priest and Suten of the Scutcheons, who became one of the heretic Pharaohs, it will throw clear light on one of the obscurest parts of Egyptian history, for the reading of the facts would demand that AIU should have become the husband also of the queen Mut-em-Snatem, or Neit-em-Mut, and that she should have been the mother or step-mother, and not the wife, of Horus (Har-em-Hebi). Aiu was the *protégé* of Amenhept III., and the friend and right-hand man of Amenhept IV. or Khu-en-Aten, and if there be a Pharaoh on all the

---

[1] Brugsch, *Histoire*, pl. 12, scutcheon, 257.
[2] Vol. ii. p. 8.
[3] Brugsch, *History of Egypt*, vol. ii. p. 8, Eng. tr.

monuments that agrees with the Hebrew story, this is the king, and Aiu is the man who was elevated to a seat at his side.

. The account in Genesis [1] says Joseph was made an Adon over Egypt; so it is said of Har-em-Hebi. He was "an Adon of the whole land for the duration of many years;" he was called to be "the great lord in the king's house." In the Egyptian collection at Leyden there is a monument on which he appears in the character of first official of the court. Lastly, the Pharaoh being so pleased with him, he rose to the position of "heir of the throne of the whole land," and wore the royal crown of Egypt as the Horus of Manetho. A similar description might be given of the elevation of Aiu by Khu-en-Aten, as he was not of the blood-royal, and the king had no sons.

The Hebrew writer relates that Pharaoh called Joseph, and said, "See, I have set thee over all the land of Egypt. And he made him to ride in the second chariot which he had." This is perfectly consistent with the Repa-ship. "And they cried before him, Abrech, and he made him (ruler) over all the land of Egypt." In this passage the meaning has been missed, and "ruler" has had to be inserted to make the sense. But if the word "Abrech" be Egyptian, that would proclaim the ruler. Rek (Eg.) means to rule; it is the older form of the name of Rā. "Ab" signifies the pure, pure one, the priest, the holy father. Ab-rek denotes the priest-ruler, literally his royal reverence. "And he made him Abrech over all the land of Egypt" is the restored sense of the passage, and thus it would mean he made him the priest-ruler, or the priest as ruler over the land. Aiu is the holy father who was made an Adon, and who is the priest-king, the only Ab-rek or Nuter-ta on all the known monuments who became a Pharaoh in Egypt.

The queen of Khu-en-Aten, Nefer-tai-ta-Aten-Ra,[2] had a sister, who appears on the monuments as Netem-Mut, supposed by Brugsch Bey to have been the wife of Tut-ankh-Amen first, and Har-em-Hebi afterwards.[3] But the fresh fact supplied by the statement respecting Aiu and his two sons, Horus and Rameses, suggests a new reading. On the statue of Turin, Netem-Mut or Mut-netem appears as a queen-mother beside Har-em-Hebi, as if he were her son. She places her left hand on the shoulder of the king. The inscription has been taken to celebrate a marriage between Mut and Horus, as it says, "Then was Amen-Ra moved with joy, and he beheld (the king's daughter) and wished to unite her with himself. And, behold, he brought her to this prince, the crown prince, Har-em-Hebi; and all the divinities of the chamber of fire were full of ecstasy at his coronation." There is no word of a marriage of Netem-Mut with Har-em-Hebi. The joining with Amen in the divine marriage only denotes the change in religion

[1] xlv. 9.   [2] Brugsch, *Histoire*, pl. 12, Scutch. 256.
[3] Brug. v. i. 456.

from the disk-worship, as in the case of Ankh-nes-pa-Aten, who became Ankh-nes-Amen.

First she was considered to be the daughter of Horus, by Champollion and other writers; next his wife, by Lepsius and Brugsch Bey. Dr. Birch, unsatisfied, asks, " Was she the wife of the monarch, the divine father Aiu, and a daughter of one of the heretical kings or usurpers ? " [1] That is what the latest discovery points to: If Aiu be the Ha-Aiu, who was father of Horus and Rameses, then it is almost certain that Netem-Mut was the second wife of Aiu, and the mother or step-mother of Horus and Rameses I.

Here the Hebrew version may contain a fact. The name of Joseph's wife, we are told, was Asenath. As (Eg.) means great, to be at rest, reposing. As-Neit is the great or reposing, *i.e. enceinte*, Neit—Neith as gestator. This is the character of Netem-Mut. Her name, written with the seed-pod, shows she represents the goddess as gestator—the bearing mother. The determinative of As, repose, is the knot borne by the brooding mother, Taurt (Thoueris).

Now in the legend preserved by Plutarch, most likely from Manetho, we are told that Thoueris (Taurt) was formerly attached to Typhon as his own concubine; but it was reported that as great numbers deserted daily and went over to Horus, Thoueris deserted also. This lady, according to other accounts, was called Aso. By that name she appears as aiding and abetting the conspiracy of Typhon against Osiris. Here she is called a certain queen of Æthiopia, whose name was Aso. [2]

In Plutarch's narrative we also find Horus impeached by Typhon for being a bastard, but Hermes became his advocate, and Horus was judged legitimate by all the gods. Either there is historic matter mingled with this report, or else Horus and Netem-Mut of the Turin Inscription are assimilated to the two characters of Aso and Horus in their desertion of Typhon. The inscription derives Horus from the belly of Teb-em-Shef, as if he were of Typhonian origin; but he " made a divine shape in it."

The inscription states that on the day the god *made his peace offerings* he brought them to that chief, the heir-apparent, dwelling in the two lands, Har-em-hebi; he went to the royal palace, he placed him before him, at the home of his " great daughter." [3] That is the daughter of the divinity who it is conjectured was the mother of Har-em-hebi and widow of Aiu, and who had fulfilled the part of Aso, and followed Horus in the change of religion from the worship of Aten to that of Amen-Ra.

Har-em-hebi appears in three different monuments in the British Museum, each belonging to the time when he was Repa, or chosen

[1] *Biblical Archæology*, vol. iii. pl. 2, p. 491.　　[2] Of Isis and Osiris.
[3] The word used is " Sheps," a variant of " As," the Great, in the maternal sense, as in Asenath.

heir-apparent, before he ascended the throne as a Pharaoh.[1] These reveal the fact that he was Repa under a disk-worshipper of the Tum-Typhonian cult, or was one himself. He makes his invocation to the sun as Tum, who is said to grow young and be renewed as ATEN, the "Divine Boy," in the arms of his mother Hathor; the one god who begat and gave birth to himself, especially as the son of the Akar or hinder-part, and who is the one adored in the circle of all the other gods after the manner of Joseph in his dream. This is the language of the so-called Disk-worship. The monument of Turin shows that Har-em-hebi, in becoming the Pharaoh, had made his peace with Amen-Ra, the generator and father, and had changed into a persecutor of those who worshipped the Mother and Child only.

It is not necessary, however, to assume that Har-em-Hebi was the son of Netem-Mut. He may have been the son of Aiu by Taiu the first wife. Har-em-Hebi was not considered to be of royal birth; his tomb at Sakkarah exhibits him without the cartouches of royalty.[2]

It is possible that Aiu as a Sep may have been interfused with the Joseph of the mythos. Anyhow, this is all that the present writer is able to contribute towards the restoration of Joseph and Asenath, and it is more than has hitherto been recovered from the monuments.

Horus became the bitter enemy of the Typhonians and the worshippers of Aten-Ra. There was an exodus after his accession to the throne. The Hekshus, disk-worshippers and followers of Sut, had to flee, whether they were "foreigners" in the ethnic or religious sense. He demolished their monuments, and made use of the stones with the inscriptions reversed and turned inwards for his own buildings.

The ecclesiastical writers make the Exodus to be about this time, at the end of the 18th dynasty, but they place it in the (unknown) reign of Akhenchres, daughter of Horus.

Aiu's tomb in the Typhonian valley of Biban-el-Muluk shows, by his portrait, that he belonged to the race of Kush or Phut. "The catacomb of Aiu is of no great extent; the negro countenance of the king is the most remarkable object in it."[3]

Neither on the present nor any other theory, except the astronomical, can Joseph and Moses be made contemporaries. But, if both were Hekshus kings at different intervals, and their fall was each time followed by an exode of the unclean Typhonians, it would be easy for a transcriber to class them together. Also we have to remember that the reporter for us is Josephus.

It must by this time be obvious that the one Exodus of the Hebrew writings belongs to the mythos, and that when we come to historical facts there were several exodes of the Sut-Typhonians or Ius from Egypt. These facts are reflected on the monuments, where

[1] Egyptian Gallery, Vestibule, Nos 550, 551, 552.
[2] Mariette, *Mont. Divers*, pl. 74, 75.
[3] Osburn, *Monumental History*. ii. 341.

the one grand exodus is resolved into three different expulsions, more or less known to Egyptian historians.

All the charges and objections made by Josephus against the statements of Manetho are falsely founded on the assumption that there was but the one exodus from Egypt, and that that occurred as described in the Book of the Exodus. Whereas Manetho, in the account headed "Of the Shepherd Kings," tells the story of the possession and fortifying of Avaris, and their expulsion therefrom when they were driven out by Aahmes, who has got mixed up with Tahtmes, both being named sons of the moon; and he afterwards relates the story of the second possession of the city of Avaris, which had been "left vacant by the shepherds," and of the conspiracy and revolt of the lepers, under the leader and lawgiver Osarsiph of Heliopolis. These accounts include two exodes at least. Another exode followed the ascent of Horus to the throne, and Joseph-Peteseph can only be the human leader of revolt in this case as Aiu the son of Kush, or the Phutite. Josephus, on account of his theory, was compelled to lump together, or to complain that they were not lumped together, the different exodes distinguished by the Egyptian writers.

In his description of one expulsion under Moses, Manetho gives the number of outcasts at 80,000.

Chæremon, in his version as reported by Josephus, calls Joseph and Moyses (Peteseph and Tisithen) the two leaders of 250,000 outcasts from Egypt. Now, as Manetho puts the number of outcasts at 80,000 the coupling together of Joseph and Moses is as obvious a lumping indiscriminately as is the making of Manetho's 80,000 into Chæremon's 250,000.

According to Manetho, this exodus was caused through the king's desire for a sight of the gods. On the other hand, Chæremon ascribes it to the instigation of Isis, who appeared to the king in a dream; and he says that Phritiphantes was the chief mover, not Amenophis. The quarrel of Josephus is that the Egyptians will not give a true account of the departure of the Hebrews from Egypt: Manetho, speaking of one batch, is charged with forgetting that he had already related their departure 518 years earlier.

Josephus is fusing the different exodes and expulsions in one, and in the name of his own people, all being dominated by the mythical Exodus of the sacred writings. The Egyptian writers more or less distinguished between them. Also these writers never would own that "our forefathers came into Egypt from another country."[1] In both cases they were right. Here again Josephus read his history by means of the mythical descent of Jacob and his twelve sons; and the Egyptians were not so beguiled.

Two exodes will account for the increased number given by the later writer, as the result of two expulsions. Manetho traces one

[1] *Against Apion*, i. 1, 25.

expulsion to Amenophis, whom Josephus designates a "fictitious king."

The "fictitious king" was desirous of seeing the gods, as had been Horus, one of his predecessors in the kingdom. Horus then is the first KING who desired to see the gods, and it was he who restored the gods when the heretics were driven out by him ; this identifies the exodus of Josephus, when Manetho's 80,000 were expelled. Also Horus is the Bocchoris of Lysimachus. The Bak is the hawk of Horus ; with this the name of Har-em-Hebi is written, and in the name Bak-Horus we have both the hawk and its meaning identified with the Pharaoh.

Josephus, quoting from the *Egyptiaca* of Lysimachus of Alexandria, says, " In the days of Bocchoris[1] the Jews, being leprous and scabby, fled to the temples, where they got their living by begging ; and as their numbers were vast, there was scarcity in the land. Hereupon the king consulted an oracle, and was commanded to purge the country by expelling the Jews and drowning the lepers, whose presence was obnoxious to the sun. Those afflicted with leprosy were drowned, and the rest were driven out to perish in the desert. But a certain man named Moses led them into the country now called Judea, and founded the city of Hierosyla, which was in after-time called Hiero-solyma " (Jerusalem). In this account at least three different exodes are massed into one. For these supposed builders of Jerusalem were the exiles who were expelled by Aahmes from the city of Avaris, and they are classed with the emigrants who were driven out by Horus, and both are placed under Moses, who led the revolt in the time of the child of Seti-Mer-en-Ptah.

But if for the present purpose we identify the 80,000 exiles, named by Manetho, with the exode of Joseph (under Horus), the following expulsion, which we may term the Mosaic exodus, would possibly bring up the total number of the two to the 250,000 mentioned by Chæremon.

The Pharaoh called Amenophis, like Horus, had a longing to see the gods. These two being the restorers of the gods, which in each case had been thrown down, broken, or blackened over, their desire to see them is sufficiently explained by their wish to restore them to their former dignity. It is the complaint of Pentaur that Ra-Apepi rejected the gods of the whole land, and in the great Harris Papyrus it is said that the gods had been overthrown and lay on the ground ; also, to judge by a phrase in the Turin Inscription, the statues of the gods, in the time of Khu-en-Aten and Aiu, were blackened over and put in mourning, or, as we say, *blotted* out.[2] The second king who desired to see the gods is told that if he would cast out the Hekshus, Aamu, Aat, Typhonians, worshippers of Sut and Aten, the impure and unclean,—the gods, with Amen-Ra at their head, would return.

---

[1] Meier, *Judaica*, Jena, 1832. [2] *Kammhut*, line 23.

There are at least three different exodes. One after the fall of Avaris, when the conquered Hekshus "departed from Egypt with all their families and effects, in number not less than 240,000, and bent their way through the desert towards Syria." These are said to have built a city, and named it Jerusalem.[1] Another expulsion occurred under Horus or Bocchoris; and a third in the time of Suti-Nekht. *This is the particular Exodus of the Jews associated with the name of Moses.* The Hebrews, says the record, "built for Pharaoh treasure cities (Miskanoth), Pithom and Rameses."[2] Meskhenat is an Egyptian name for a temple, a sacred place, from the Meskhen or cradle of new birth. It is noticeable that in the "Annals of Rameses III." the Pharaoh speaks of all he has done in honour of the gods, especially the god Tum, and enumerates the presents he has conveyed as "tributes given to thy splendid *treasury* in Pa-Tum" or[3] Pithom. Rameses, as before said, was the ancient Tanis, the Hebrew Zoan, Targumic צען, where remains of the Hekshus[4] have been found, including the tablet of 400 years.[5] Its restoration was begun by Rameses. The building of Rameses was continued under Men-Ptah, his thirteenth son, the Pharaoh of the Jewish Exodus, as generally supposed by Egyptologists. This Men-Ptah was followed by his son Seti II., also called Men-Ptah or MER-EN-PTAH, and it was in the time of Men-Ptah, the father of Sethos (Seti-Rameses), that the circumstances occurred which led to the latest of these exodes—the one under Moses.

Manetho, as quoted by Josephus, recognizes two Men-Ptahs or Amenophises, though they are not both described as Pharaohs. He says, "This king (Amenophis) was desirous of beholding the gods, as Horus, one of his predecessors in the kingdom, had desired to do before him; and he communicated his wish to a priest of the same name with himself, Amenophis, the son of Papis, who seemed to partake of the divine nature, both in his wisdom and knowledge of futurity; and Amenophis returned him for answer, that it was in his power to behold the gods if he would clear the whole country of the lepers and other impure people that abounded in it." Here it may be observed that in the Egyptian the LEPERS and IMPURE are the Aati and the Aamu. We know from their own accounts that the Jews were eaten up with leprosy, and may see in that fact good ethnic evidence for their being of the ancient African stock. But these terms of the Aati and the impure are by no means limited to the disease of

---

[1] Manetho, *Apud Josephus.*
[2] Ex. i. 11.   [3] *Great Harris Papyrus*, plates, 26, 27.
[4] Mariette, *Lettre à M. le Vicomte de Rougé, sur les Fouilles de Tanis,* p. 16.
[5] A friend, to whom I am greatly indebted for assistance in proof-reading and other matters, remarks on this—"Not so identified by recent writers. One argument against it—the Exodus would then include crossing one branch of the Nile, and no such passage is mentioned." What Exodus? This is a good typical example of the way in which the mythical Exodus makes everything wrong everywhere.

leprosy.   The Aati were the moral lepers, the accursed as Typhonian heretics, the practisers of dark rites, which the Egyptians associated with the origin of leprosy and other diseases.

"Well pleased with this information, the king gathered together out of Egypt all that laboured under any defect in body, to the number of 80,000, and sent them to the quarries which are on the eastern side of the Nile, that they might work in them, and be separated from the rest of the Egyptians.[1]   There were among them some learned priests, who were affected with leprosy; and Amenophis, the wise man and prophet, fearful lest the vengeance of the gods should fall both on himself and on the king if it should appear that violence had been offered them, added this also, in a prophetic spirit, that certain people would come to the assistance of these unclean persons and subdue Egypt, and hold possession of it for thirteen years.   These tidings, however, he dared not communicate to the king, but left in writing an account of what should come to pass, and then destroyed himself; at which the king was fearfully distressed.

"When those who had been sent to work in the quarries had continued for some time in that miserable state, the king was petitioned to set apart for their habitation and protection the city of Avaris, which had been left vacant by the shepherds, and he granted them their desire.

"Now this city, according to the ancient theology, was Typho's city.   But when they had taken possession of the city, and found it well adapted for a revolt, they appointed for themselves a ruler from among the priests of Heliopolis (On), one whose name was Osarsiph, and they bound themselves by oath that they would be obedient to him in all things.   Osarsiph then in the first place enacted this law— that they should neither worship the gods, nor abstain from any of those sacred animals which the Egyptians held in veneration, but sacrifice and slay them all; and that they should connect themselves with none but such as were of that confederacy.

"When he had made such laws as these, and many others of a tendency directly in opposition to the customs of the Egyptians, he gave orders that they should employ the multitude in rebuilding the walls about the city, and hold themselves in readiness for war with Amenophis the king.   He then took into his counsels some others of the priests and polluted persons, sent ambassadors to the city called Jerusalem, to the shepherds who had been expelled by Tahtmosis; and he informed them of the position of his affairs, and requested them to come up unanimously to his assistance in this war against Egypt.   He also promised, in the first place, to reinstate them in their ancient city and country, Avaris, and provide a plentiful maintenance for their host, and fight for them as occasion might require; and assured them that he would easily reduce the country under their dominion.   The shepherds received the message with the greatest joy, and quickly mustered, to the number of 200,000 men, and came up to Avaris.   Now Amenophis, the king of Egypt, when he was informed of their invasion, was in great consternation, remembering the prophecy of Amenophis, the son of Papis.   And he assembled the armies of the Egyptians; and having consulted with the leaders, he commanded the sacred animals to be brought to him, especially those which were held in more particular veneration in the temples; and he forthwith charged the priests to conceal the images of their gods with the utmost care.   Moreover, he placed his son Sethos, who was also called Rameses from his father Rampses, being then but five years old, under the protection of a faithful adherent, and marched with the rest of the Egyptians, being 300,000 warriors, against the enemy, who advanced to meet him; but he did not attack them, thinking it would be to wage war against the gods, but returned, and came again to Memphis, where he took Apis and other sacred animals he had sent for, and returned immediately into Æthiopia, together with all his army and all the multitude of the Egyptians; for the king of Æthiopia was under obligations to him.   He was therefore kindly received by the king, who took care of all the multitude that was with him, while the country supplied what was necessary for their subsistence.   He also allotted to him cities and villages during his exile, which was to continue from its beginning, during the predestined thirteen years.   Moreover, he pitched a camp for an Æthiopian army upon the borders of Egypt, as a protection to King Amenophis.

"In the meantime, while such was the state of things in Æthiopia, the people of

---

[1] An acknowledgment that they also were Egyptians.

Jerusalem, who had come down with the unclean of the Egyptians, treated the inhabitants with such barbarity, that those who witnessed their horrible wickedness believed that their joint sway was more execrable than that which the shepherds had formerly exercised alone. For they not only set fire to the cities and villages, but committed every kind of sacrilege, and destroyed the images of the gods, and wasted and fed upon those sacred animals that were worshipped, and having compelled the priests and prophets to kill and sacrifice those animals, they cast them naked out of the country. It is said also that the priest who ordained their polity and laws was born at Heliopolis, and his name was Osarsiph, from Osiris, the god of Heliopolis; but when he went over to these people his name was changed, and he was called Moyses."[1]

The time was that of Seti-Men-Ptah, when Seti-Nekht-Mer-Amen was but five years old. Seti was himself the "devoted to Sut," and probably Typhonian at heart, which may account for his cowardly conduct; he would not wage war against his own gods to save his own country, which shows the *virus* of the genuine theological *bite*.

Now it is recorded in the Annals of the Rameses who followed Seti-Nekht, that at this time there was a great disturbance or revolution in Egypt; for many years there was no master-mind or hand, and for a time the country belonged to the governors of cities, one massacring another. To be more particular, the narrative runs:

"Thus saith the king Ra-user-ma-Mer-Amen; long may he live! Listen to what I tell you of my worthy works which I performed as king of mortals.

"The land of Kami had fallen into confusion; every one was doing as he liked; they had no superior for many years who had supremacy over the rest. Other events came afterwards; distressing years!

"AARSU or ARUSU, a Kharu (was hailed) among them as chief.

"He placed the whole country in subjection under him. He assembled his companions. Then were abused the things done to the gods as (if) for men. No offerings were made in the interior of the temples. The gods were overthrown; they lay upon the ground. He did according to his wish and plan."[2]

The writer then describes the overthrow of ARUSU and his confederates by the king Seti-Nekht, who was like the war-god Sut in his wrath. He adjusted the whole land, which had been in insurrection. He slaughtered the abominable who were in the land, and *purified the great throne of Egypt*. He was the living ruler of both countries. He took pains to rectify what had been perverted. Each one again recognized his brother, who had been separated as by a wall. He set up temples, with divine supplies for offerings to the company of gods, the Nine, according to the regulations, and sent the last fragments of the Opposition flying into Palestine. This is the very picture drawn by Manetho, and painted by another hand. The same confederacy and revolt are described, and ARUSU and OSARSIPH are one and the same man. This has been suggested by Dr. Eisenlohr, but he attained

[1] Rendered by Gill, *Notices of the Jews*, pp. 9-12.
[2] *Great Harris Papyrus*, pl. 75; *Biblical Archæology*, vol. i. part ii. p. 355; *Records of the Past*, vol. viii. pp. 45, 46.

no firm conclusion in consequence of the obstruction of the Hebrew mythos.

Time, scene, circumstances and persons are identical and identifiable; and if an historic Moses is anywhere to be found on the Egyptian monuments, it must be in this character of ARUSU-OSARSIPH. The name may be read ARSU, ARISU, ARIUS or ARUAS, ARS being the consonantal root. This name we find connected with Moses, in an account of the Exodus from Egypt to Sinai, cited from Justin out of Trogus Pompeius, who says Moses was the son of Joseph, and "After the death of Moses his son ARUAS was made priest for celebrating the rites which they brought from Egypt, and soon after created king."[1] All we have to do with here is the name of ARUAS given to the son of Moses, which is the same as that of the leader of the revolt in Egypt.

But, says Manetho, "the name (of Moses) was Osarsiph, and he is careful to explain that it is derived from Osiris. Sif (Eg.) is the son, Su being a worn-down form of the word. Osarsif will read the son of Asar (Osiris): but a more important interpretation is possible. It may read Osiris as the son in contradistinction to the father. This was the oldest form of the god; it was the child-Christ of Egyptian theology, and would assimilate Osarsif to the first Horus—Har, the child, the elder, the lotus-borne, the child produced by the mother below, the child of the virgin Neith; the child drawn forth from the waters and the mud of the mother-source itself. AR means the typical, the fundamental (the first and elder Har), or the river, the water-source which preceded the breath. SU is the child. Also the one mythological type dominates, correlates, and explicates all the three names, OSAR-SIF (Osarsu), ARSU, and MESSU.

For it is intended to identify the ARSU of the great Harris Papyrus, not only with the Osarsiph of Manetho, but also with the MESSU who emerges at this time as a heretic Pharaoh on the monuments, and as their sole possible historic Moses. Josephus says Moses was named MOUSES because Mou in Egyptian means water. MU is water, and Su is the child. Thus MUSU, like ARU-SU, is the child of the water, or the river-born, that is the first Horus called Harpocrates. Osarsif, as Osiris the child, *is* the Aru-su.

The Hebrew record asserts that the Egyptian princess called the child Moses because she drew him out of the water. Now the typical child of Egyptian mythology was the water-born; was drawn out of the water. So ancient is the imagery of this subject, that the ideograph of SU, the child, is the water-reed. Mes has the meaning of a product of the river. Thus Messu (Eg.) is not only the water-born, but may be read the child (Su) produced from or by the river; hence Messu, the child born of the water. Brugsch Bey finds the very spot in the Nile at which the little ark landed. "Is it by accident," he asks,[2]

[1] *Cory*, ed. 1876, p. 81.   [2] *History of Egypt*, vol. ii. p. 112.

"*or by divine providence* that, in the reign of Rameses III., about 100 years after the death of his ancestor, the great Sesostris, a place is mentioned in Middle Egypt which bears the name of the great Jewish legislator?" "It is called T-EN-MOSHÊ, the island of Moses, or the river-bank of Moses. It lay on the eastern side of the river, near the city of the heretic king Khu-en-Aten. The place still existed in the time of the Romans; those who describe Egypt at that time *designate it, with a mistaken apprehension of its true meaning, as Musae, or Musôn, as if it had some connection with the Greek Muses.*" So grateful are we for the least look of corroboration of anything in the Hebrew story, and so jealous lest it should prove to be mythical! He does not give the signs, but Ta-en-mes (or mesh) also reads the soil (as island or bank) which was the product of the river, agreeing with the name of the child who was drawn out of the water. Unfortunately this might name any portion of land or soil (Ta) produced by the river as MESI. There is an island of MOSHÉ or MOSHA, belonging to the British, to the south of the straits of Bab-el-Mandeb. Still Messu the typical child, the elder Horus, was Egyptian, and doubtless had his island, localized in the Nile, as the place where the divine sister watched over her brother, the water-born. In the case of the child Horus, "His sister took care of him by dissipating his enemies, repelling (bad) luck, she sends forth her voice by the virtues of her mouth; wise of tongue, no word of hers fails." [1] The child of the waters, found in the little ark, belongs to mythology in general. It is Hebrew and Egyptian, Assyrian and Maori, and mythical wherever it may be found. The ark was represented in Egypt by the boat of papyrus-reed, but its earlier form was the lotus on which the child - Horus is pourtrayed as ascending, and kneeling with the finger pointing to his mouth.

The lotus sprang from the mud, and the child was fabled as born in the mud of the marshes. The mud, as product of the river, is the Mes of Mesr or Mitzr. Messu is the child of this Mes in the same sense as was the land of Mesr; and a child or person named Messu would be the namesake and representative of the child Horus, born of the waters or the mud of the primordial source, and therefore identical by name with Osarsif and Arsu.

Plutarch mentions this child of the waters, who was said to have been dropped into the water and drowned. This was he who had divine honours paid to him at feast and festival as Maneros, the dead Horus, who was represented by the black doll, the Men image of death or second life. Others, however, say the boy was named Palestinus, or Pelusias, and that the city of that name was so called from him, it having been built by the goddess (Isis).

Pelusium, the "City of Mud," was, like the child of the river, the

[1] *Hymn to Osiris*, 14.

product and deposit of the Nile. Musu, Moshé, or Messu would be named after the child of the waters, who was the Mes-ar or Mes-ur of the month Mesore; the first-born, the elder-born, the water-born; the new-birth coinciding with that of the inundation.

It can be shown how Messu is the exact equivalent of Arsu, if we hold fast by the type. Messu is the child produced by the waters; Aur, Aru, or Ar (Eg.) means the river, and Arusu or Aru reads the child of the river—the exact equivalent of Messu, the product of the river, the celestial Nile. In the Hebrew version the child was to be called Mashu (משה or)[1] because he had been drawn out of the water. This is the literalization of the myth. Arsu and Messu are identifiable as one, because of the mythical child, and both with the city and the land of mud as the product of the Nile.

Whether Moses is or is not one with the Messu who was governor of Æthiopia, the Hebrew traditions go far to connect him with that country. Moses as an Egyptian general against the Æthiopians is omitted from the Hebrew Scriptures, which are chiefly occupied with the mythical Moses (Mau-shu), and he is therefore all the likelier to be real on that account. Stephen[2] testifies to his being not only a scribe, learned in all the wisdom of the Egyptians, but as mighty in deeds.

" One of my waking dreams," said Livingstone, " is that the legendary tales about Moses coming up into Lower Æthiopia with Merr, his foster-mother, and founding a city which he called Meroë, may have a substratum of fact. I dream of discovering some monumental relics of Meroë." The monuments answer for a Messu of Æthiopia, who lived at the proper time for an historical Moses, and he may be the very man.

The tradition referred to is mentioned by Artapanus, who, in his account of the Jews, says that after the death of the Pharaoh Mempsathenoth, his son Palmanothes was very severe towards the Jews. This king had a daughter whose name was Merrhis; who was married to a King Chenephres, then reigning in Memphis, for at that time there were several kings in Egypt. Merrhis was barren, and she brought up a child of the Jews, and named it Mouses. When he arrived at manhood he was called among the Greeks Musæus.[3] Mer-res was the Nile-goddess of the south, already identified with Miriam.

Josephus relates that Moses, at the head of an Egyptian army, was seen and beloved by Tharvis, the daughter of the Æthiopian king, and that she became his wife. Tharvis, being one by name with Thoueris or Taurt, identifies the lady, whether she be human or divine, with the Typhonian genitrix. These belong to the mythos; but we also learn from the inscription on the tablet of 400 years,

[1] Ex. ii. 10.   [2] Acts, vii. 22.
[3] Artap. Euseb. *Præp. Ev.* ix. 27.

found at San, that in erecting the statue there was a grand deputation, which included the Repa, or heir-apparent ; the superintendent of the Nome ; the fan-bearer at the king's right hand ; the leader of the foreign legions, and captain of the foreigners ; the constable of Khetam, together with various priests and scribes—the royal scribe of the cavalry, the processional priest of Ba-neb-tat (Mendes), the high priest of the god Sut, the officer of Buto, the ruler of the Two Countries, the superintendent of the priests of all the gods, Seti, justified son of the prince, and among the rest was *the royal scribe and master of the horse who was the child of the lady Taa, the singer of the sun*, or *sun-god*, and his name is " PARA-MESSU," which reads Messu of the temple (Pa) of Ra, or Messu who was a priest of Ra. His mother was a priestess and glorifier of the solar divinity, and Messu is named as belonging to the temple.[1]   Para-Messu is a proper name: the AS image denotes a ruling personage, and he is described as the child of the lady TAA, who is the priestess of the solar god RA. Para-Messu is Messu of the house of Ra, and the name shows the child of the temple, and has the look of the child consecrated or adopted for the divine service ; therefore he may have been adopted by TAA, and so called her child. There is nothing in the inscription to clash with the Hebrew story of the adopted child. Moreover, it is a most remarkable thing to characterize the royal scribe and master of the horse, as the child of TAA, the " singer of the sun." It seems to echo the story of the adoption, or to be used in some sense which could not be open to the suspicion of bastardy.

It is now suggested that this Messu, the royal scribe and master of the horse, may have been the same officer that we find in the Scutcheons at the end of the nineteenth dynasty,[2] who was a prince of Æthiopia and a royal scribe.

" Prince of Æthiopia " was a title of the Repa and heir to the throne of the Pharaoh. This Messu may only have been the governor of Kush, or he may also have been the Repa as heir-apparent to the throne adopted by a childless Pharaoh. The prayer of Si-ptah, for children to inherit the throne, possibly points to his own childlessness. In that case we see one reason why Messu ascended the throne. Also it is possible that the priestess TAA, the singer of the sun, may have become that Tā-seser, the queen of Si-ptah, and co-regent with him, whose name is found inscribed with his own on a number of monuments ; and yet they do not appear in the hieroglyphic genealogies, nor in any other contemporary succession.[3]

In an inscription at Silsilis, a prayer is offered that their children may inherit the throne, which phraseology is remarked upon by Rosellini as strange and altogether un-Pharaonic.

[1] Mariette Bey, *Revue Archéologique*, vol. xi. pl. 4, p. 169 ; Brugsch Bey, *History of Egypt*, vol. ii. p. 95, Eng. Tr. ; Birch, *Records of the Past*, vol. iv. p. 35.
[2] Lepsius, *Königsbuch*, taf. 36.
[3] Osburn, *Monumental Egypt*, vol. ii. p. 554.

The tomb of Si-ptah was taken possession of by Seti-Nekht, who had his scutcheons erased, and treated him as one of the heretic usurpers of the throne, which needed purification after their hated presence.

Osburn states that Tā-seser, whom he confounds with the Thoueris of Manetho, had been devoted to the service of the gods in an especial manner, according to a prevailing custom of the princesses of Egypt, and was one of the Πάλλαχες of the Greek historians. These were the consorts or concubines of the god. Tā-seser was a priestess, and appears by the reliefs on the tombs to have been consecrated to Hathor and Neith.[1]

If the name of the Seser for the ruler was added to that of Taa on assuming the throne-title, that would turn Taa the priestess into the Tāa-seser, whence Tā-seser. Seser is the word for rule, and Tā-seser would be the ruler Tā; the feminine Cæsar.

A secret significance may be suspected in the name of Messu's wife Queen BAKT-UR-NRU.[2] Bakt is the worshipper in the sense of servant; Ur means the chief, principal, and in the case of a queen it may be the royal or anointed. Nru is the name of the vulture. This then was literally the chief or royal servant of the vulture. Typically she was the worshipper and therefore the royal representative of the great mother whose emblem is the vulture of Mut. The Egyptians according to Hor-Apollo[3] symbolized the mother by a vulture, because there is no male in this race of creatures; a statement which has to be interpreted by the typology. The vulture had been a sign of the virgin Neith, when the mother alone was looked upon as the producer of the child before the fatherhood was established. But the older, the Typhonian vulture was a black, foul bird, named the Neh, continued from the time when the genitrix was of a Negroid complexion and type, and her children were the Nahsi. If this bird had been depicted as the vulture signified, it would have doomed the monument. On the other hand, and as an obverse side to the same fact, the adorers of the disk and the Typhonians avoided the orthodox vulture, and used the cubit sign rather than the bird for their phonetic M.

This assimilates BAKT-UR-NRU to Taurt or Thoueris, the old mother, whose name would be written T-ur-Mut; and, according to Josephus, Moses was saved from the waters by Thermuthis, who adopted him as her son, she being childless. This would also assimilate Moses to the mythical child of the Typhonian genitrix, whilst Bakt-ur-nru, the consort of Messu, is the chief servant of the ancient mother who first bore the boy. The servant (Bakt) supplies another note of

---

[1] Osburn, *Monumental Egypt*, vol. ii. p. 559.
[2] Scutcheons, Lep. *Königsbuch*, taf. 36, fig. 479; Brugsch, *Histoire*, pl. 13, 278.
[3] i. 11.

recognition. The Shus-en-Har, the Hekshus and Sebekhepts, all called themselves the servants of their god.[1]

Both Amen-Messu and Si-ptah are said to have come from the same town. The standard name of Si-ptah is Sha-en-Kheb, raised or born at Kheb; whilst an inscription at Gurneh, ascribed to Amen-Messu, states that the king was brought up by the goddess Isis at Ha-Kheb. But as Ha-Kheb permutes with Ha-Neith the mythical abode of birth; and as Horus the divine child was born at Kheb, and re-born in Tattu, it has no great topographical value. Both may have been merely assimilated to Horus in Kheb. Ha-Kheb however, as before shown, belongs to the Mother who was older than Neith Stories told of the child of mythology, the young sun-god, with a secret interpretation, were afterwards transferred to and narrated of the hero as actual occurrences, and the character of the miraculous child of the waters is thus formed and fitted to fulfil the historical character of Arsu, Messu, or Moses. For example, the name of Arsu furnished another meeting-point in mythology for the historical and mythical child. ARSU or ARS is some divine personage in the Ritual.[2] "Thou hast hailed Ars (or Arsu) from the conductors of heaven," is said in the "chapter of Going in the Boat of the Sun," of some mystical personage. Shu as Anhar is the conductor of heaven by name; and the god of two names and dual form answering to the plural "conductors of heaven," Shu-Anhar, is called the Young Elder, the double force and double abode of Ra, and Har-Sekti, the Lord dwelling in the divine barge of the sun.[3] "Thou hast hailed Arsu from the conductors of heaven," points to the water-born, the Aru-su Harpocrates, as he is called the "great god," and yet it is said of him "His faults and defects are the same" as those of the speaker. That is, they were human; Har, the child, being the mortal form of the solar son. This will show how the name of a real person now known from the monuments as Arsu would lend itself to being fused and assimilated with Arsu the typical son; Arsu the river-born. It is possible that the Arsu of the boat may be meant for Ma-shu, as he is the Egyptian Mars, the Greek ARES or Ars, the war-god. Arsu (Ares) is mentioned by Hermapion in an inscription translated from the obelisk of Rameses. There is a deity copied by Wilkinson, who says he "may be a character of Osiris. I have only met with him at Philæ."[4] He is a war-god and the son as lord of the two worlds. He wears the headdress worn by Sebek of Thebes, by Ptah-Sekari, and by

---

[1] The vulture-type of maternity, the NARU or NARAU, denotes the family, and in Maori NGARE is the hard form of the word, meaning family and blood relations. This form has persisted in the Hebrew נער, which represents the Maori NGARE, and signifies the young; and to bear, and it appears also in the Albanian NIERI, Zend NÂIRI, for woman, and NARE, in Sanskrit, which supplies a type-word for the human family in general.

[2] Birch, ch. cii.   [3] *Magic Papyrus*, p. 2.

[4] *Mat. Hierog.* p. 52; *Anct. Eg.* plates 54-56.

Harpocrates. All turns on the sonship here, because the character is really pre-paternal. Kebek, the oldest form of Seb, was the son. This Egyptian war-god is apparently the same as Resp. A Typhonian form of the sonship was continued in RESP, as is shown by the ornament worn on his head in place of the sacred Asp. Resp is considered by Egyptologists to be a Syrian deity; but Syria *originated* nothing; the *types* are always traceable to Egypt or the Africa beyond. He is pourtrayed on a monument in the British Museum standing on one side of the goddess Kên, the Hebrew Kivan, the naked Venus, with Khem-Horus on the other. The goddess herself stands on the back of a lion-leoparded, the type of Mashu or Anhar. Resp has an emblem on his head, like that on the top of an Anubis-staff. This identifies him with Sut, and the group contains the typical four, as in Moses, Hur, Aaron, and Miriam, or Shu, Har, Sut, and Kivan, or Hapi (Kafi), Kabhsnuf, Suttef and Amset, the four Rams, the four genii of the four quarters permanently fixed as the lion, scorpion, waterer, and bull.

There is an extant monument in the Mayer Collection of Antiquities, Liverpool, a large stone of libation, which has on it the name and titles of Amen Messu, his divine style of Ra-men-ma-Setp-en-ra having been written and erased twice over. On this monument he is celebrated as a miracle-worker. It is said that the king established both countries, and that he was GREAT IN MIRACLES AT THEBES; a hint which proved most suggestive to the Hebrew writers, who followed it out fully, by identifying Moses with Arsu the god and with Resp.

There is also a Messu mentioned in the Papyrus, Anatasi I. who was an Egyptian scholar, a Suten or scribe, and a Mohar, who was employed in affairs of state and war by Rameses II. Dr. Lauth is inclined to recognize Moses in this man. The objection raised by M. Pleyte, that the style of this Messu is Ptah-Messu, seems to me to be of little weight. Seti II. is both a Mer-Amen and a Mer-n-Ptah.[1] Also, the assumption of the name of Ptah may have been in relation to Si-ptah, husband of Tā-seser, who was the adopter of the child Moses, if there be any truth whatever in the story of his adoption by a daughter of Ra. Be this as it may, there *was* a Messu, as prince of Æthiopia, a royal scribe; who, if Repa, is visibly on his way to the throne; and a Messu did ascend the throne who was for some time a ruler in Egypt, if not the ruler of Egypt. After his death the tomb of this Messu was treated as that of a usurper.

The Hebrews call Moses the child of the river; Mu-su is the child of the water; Messu the child, the product of the river, and Aru-su is the river-child. All these can be correlated under one mythological type. The river of the child is always the Nile. Surely then this child of the river must be the Egyptian king known to the Greeks by the name of Nilus?

[1] Scutcheon, *Egypt's Place*, vol. ii. p. 628.

Dicæarchus, the historian who wrote the Life of Greece and treated of Egypt in its remoter times, as may be learned from a fragment in the *Scholiast* of Apollonius Rhodius,[1] dates the rule of Nilus as being 2,500 years from Sesonchosis (or Sesortosis), and 436 years prior to the first Olympiad. This gives the date of 1212 B.C. for the time of Nilus, whose rule was obviously chronicled as a remarkable event, so remarkable, indeed, as to date an epoch for the Greek historian. Nilus is identifiable with Arusu and Messu by means of the River, and the only corresponding name on the monuments is that of Messu ; Amen-Messu, the heretic king. The Nile is the Aru, Hebrew Iar. With the plural article prefixed this is Naiaru (Nile) ; with the masculine article it would be Paru, the Phuro of Eratosthenes, who thus wrote the name of the Nile. With the feminine article, or prefix Tu, the river-born is Tu-aru, and this is now claimed to be the meaning of the name of Thuoris given in the list of Manetho as the last ruler of the 19th dynasty. The S may or may not be merely the Greek terminal. If Egyptian, the name contains the elements of Tu-aru-su, the river-child, who was Nilus, Messu, or Arusu. Either way the river-name is there as it is in Nilus.

From religious affinity the Greeks would take great interest in this able leader, who rose from the ranks and occupied the throne of the Pharaohs.

The Lacedæmonians held themselves to be of the same family as the Caphtorim of Palestine ; hence their surmise that they were related to the Jews. "It is found in writing that the Lacedæmonians and Jews are brethren, and that they are of the stock of Abraham."[2] It is noticeable that the Lacedæmonian king who found this in the Records and sent the message to the High-Priest Onias, was called AREUS, the same name as that of Arsu or Aruas. When we substitute religion instead of race as our correlating principle we shall read the past more clearly. The Caphtorim date from Khef or Khepsh, the hinder-part. Abram was the sun of the hinder part. The inhabitants of Sais were very friendly to the Athenians, to whom also they said they were, after a certain manner, allied.[3] This relationship of the Yonias was expressed by Hesychius, who intimates that his countrymen were Hellenes in respect to certain wisdom which they possessed. Hellen, the founder of the Greeks, says Cassiodorus, delivered many excellent things concerning the alphabet, describing its composition and virtues in an exceedingly subtle narration, insomuch that the great importance of letters may be traced to the beginning of things. In this description Hellen takes the place of the British Kêd, the personified Tree of Knowledge, whose branches were letters, and Typhon, who was the " Living Word." Callisthenes and Phanodemus relate that the Athenians were

[1] Appendix of Authorities, Bunsen's *Egypt's Place*, vol. i.
[2] 1 Maccabees, xii. 21.
[3] *Plato in Timæus.*

the fathers of the Saitæ. But Theopompus, on the contrary, affirms that they were a colony of the Saitæ.[1] Eusebius chronicles the tradition of the arrival of Kadmus with a company of the Saitæ, who founded Athens and Bœotian Thebes. They were of Egypt, but he thought they came last from Sidon.[2]

Diodorus relates that the most illustrious and able of the exiles came into Greece under the conduct of celebrated leaders, of whom the most renowned were Danaus and Kadmus. But the greater number went into the country now called Judea, which was in those times entirely desert. The leader of this colony was Moses *as he is called*, a man very remarkable for his wisdom and great valour. In this account the Greek and Hebrew exodes are fused together, whether mythical or historical. It was the exodus of the Ionians as Sut-Typhonians, and the theological classification is before the ethnical. The one exodus which, like the deluge, was universal, is entirely mythical, and belongs to the astronomical allegory. But there were various exodes and expulsions from Egypt, and those of the Ionians are mixed with those of the Ius or Jews, on account of the religious and literary origines. The Saitæ are the Sut-Typhonians, the Yonias, Ionians, the worshippers of the mother and child—the oldest and most universal cult in the world, Sabean at first under Sut and the genitrix, and afterwards Solar under Helios. Ius, Ionians, and Hindi Yavanians had one origin in religion, and that religion, as is here contended, was the oldest cult of Egypt and of Æthiopia.

Arusu, leader of the revolt, is designated a Kharu, and this Brugsch Bey identifies as a Phœnician. It is possible, however, that he was a Carian, and this would constitute another link of connection between the Hebrews and Greeks, the Ius and Ionians. According to Herodotus, it was with the aid of the Carians and Ionians that Psammitichus made himself master of all Egypt.[3] He further says of them, "All the Carians that are settled in Egypt cut their foreheads with knives and thus show themselves to be foreigners."[4] Also "They show an ancient temple of Jupiter-*Carius*, at Mylasa, which the Mysians and Lydians share, as kinsmen to the Carians, for they say that Lydus and Mysus were brothers to *Car*.[5] Jupiter-Carius is the sun in the Akar, like the God exhibited to Moses; the Kar being the lower, northern, hinder part. Herodotus identifies these Carians with the Ionians of the camp at Memphis.

The "Proteus" of Herodotus is a form of Nilus. "There is to this day," he says, "an inclosure sacred to him (Proteus) at Memphis, called the Tyrian camp. In this inclosure of Proteus is a temple which is called after the foreign Venus; and I conjecture that this is the temple of Helen, the daughter of Tyndarus, both because I have heard that

[1] *Proclus in Timæus*, b. i. [2] Chron. p. 14.
[3] B. ii. 152, 153. [4] Herod. ii. 61. [5] B. i. 171.

Helen lived with Proteus, and also because it is named from the foreign Venus, for of all the other temples of Venus none is anywhere called by the name of foreign."[1] The historian then introduces his story of Helen, with which we have no present concern. The "foreign" Venus is known to us as the naked goddess Kên, the Hebrew Kivan. "Foreign" is identical with the impure, the naked goddess. Proteus, the sea-born, the child of the waters, would be an equivalent name for Arsu or Messu of Egypt. Homer calls Proteus Egyptian, and Diodorus calls Proteus Nileus, from whom the Nile took its name; it having previously been Egyptus. It is now suggested that the Osarsiph of Manetho was the Arusu of the Great Harris Papyrus and the Messu of the Scutcheons; and that he was the Nileus of Dicæarchus, the Proteus of Herodotus, possibly a Phœnician (Kharu), and probably a Carian.

But if AIU be the Egyptian original of an historic Joseph, and Arsu-Messu of a real Moses, they could not have personally conducted an exodus, as their place of sepulture was prepared, and they were both buried, and had had their grave-chambers violated in the dreary ravine lying apart in a westward offshoot of the Biban-el-Muluk, Thebes, where we find in the tombs the very imagery carried out of Egypt into the Syrian lands. The black god IU was represented there. The celebration of the Lion-Gods was discovered there. The inscription concerning the creation by Ra, and the adoption of Shu, Sun of Nun, as his chief minister, was found there, in the cow-chamber of the tomb of Seti I.

Which then of these three exodes was the Jewish Exodus? Neither, in one sense; each and all of them in the other. First, the Biblical Exodus is founded on the mythical coming forth from the Egypt of the astronomical allegory. This we have to let go altogether, with the legends belonging to it. Then we are for the first time prepared to face the facts and interpret the monuments which have never yet been proved untrustworthy. No approach to any such series of deliberate falsifications of dates as was made by the early Christian chronologers, to bring the lists of Manetho into harmony with what they considered to be the divinely revealed data of "Holy Writ," can ever be charged against the Egyptians.

Nor is there the least reason to doubt what the Egyptian writers have told us on the subject. Hitherto this has been judged by a Jewish history chiefly drawn from the mythological astronomy. The monuments can know nothing of the Jews in accordance with the biblical story of their Genesis or Exodus. They can tell us something of the religious origines, but little or nothing of the ethnological. Egypt knows the "mixed multitude" of Typhonians, the Shus, the Aamu, the Aati, the Aperiu, and other names of the detested worshippers of Sut. The great Exodus of Egypt is figured as the

[1] B. ii. 112.

fleeing of Sut-Typhon out of it, riding on an ass. That is the symbolical mode of depicting the exit of the worshippers. They are described as going forth under the twin brothers, Judæus and Hierosolymus, personifications answering by name to the land of Judea and the city of Jerusalem.

The two brothers of mythology are a dual manifestation of one deity, as in the double Horus, Har-Makhu, Sut-Har, or the dual Anubis; and this duality is expressed by Iu (Eg.), the name of the Ass, and therefore of Sut. Sut is dual as Dog and Wolf, Sut-Anush, Sut-Har, and as Sut-Anubis; and the twins of Typhon are Judæus and Hierosolymus, or Sut North and South. As the name of the Ass and the Son is Iu, the Sut-worshippers are the Ius, or the Jews, and the exodus of Typhon on the Ass, named Iu, is the Exodus of the Ius or Jews of the earliest, *i.e.* religious, naming. These were the Jews as worshippers of the Son of the Genitrix, who was Iu the Sabean, and afterwards the Solar Son.

From the passage of the Sabean into the Solar sonship traceable in Israel, the duality of Iu-Sut points to Sut-Har, the Sun-and-Sirius God, Sut-Nubti, or Sut-Apeh-peh. And in that case Hierosolymus is the Har of Salem, the Lord of Peace, after whom the city was named.

Jerusalem, the City of Peace, was no doubt the place of the mythical Melchizedek, the king of Salem, whom we can identify with Sutekh, the god of the Khita, Sutekh or Sydik the Ruler, whence Melchizedek. But *that* migration must have occurred when the country of Syria and Palestine was first peopled by the Sut-Typhonians and Hekshus, whom we identify with the pre-monumental Shus-en-Har.

Herodotus had learned that the Syrians of Palestine, whom he couples with the Phœnicians, had dwelt in old times by the Red Sea. They also were Erythreans whom Brugsch Bey considers to be the Aperu-iu. These Phœnicians, as they themselves say, anciently dwelt on the Red Sea, and having crossed over from there they settled on the sea-coast of Syria; this part of Syria, and the whole as far as Egypt, is called Palestine.[1]

This was exactly what had occurred from the earliest times; and it must not be forgotten that the name of Phœnicia itself as Kheft was identical with that of Lower Egypt, named as the country to the north or hinder part north, and the two peoples must have got mixed up in the rendering of the one name by other nations.

In the name of the Khita we find the further continuation of Kheft beyond Phœnicia. Kheft modifies into Khet. Kheft is the Egyptian name of the north, and Khet signifies going northward. The Khita went northward from Egypt, and are found seated in the northern parts of Syria. The name is probably an abraded form of Khefta or Khefti, just as Derketo contains a modified form of Kheft. Their

[1] B. vii. 89.

deities were Sutekh and Astarte.   Sutekh is Sut the child (Khe) in Egyptian, and Astarte is derived from the Isis-Taurt of Egypt, that is the most ancient genitrix Taurt in her lunar and cow-headed secondary type.   These were worshippers of the one God known to mythology as Sut, the Son of Typhon; later Astarte or Nephthys, and the still later Nut—the god known as Sut-Har to the Egyptians of pre-monumental times, called the Shus-en-Har.

So ancient was the movement northward of the Sut-Typhonians from Egypt that *Kittim* is mentioned[1] as a son of Javan, one of five who went forth, and amongst whom "*the isles of the Gentiles were divided in their lands, every one after his tongue.*"

Kittim is the plural of the Khita or Kettai, the emigrants who went farther north in their first name of the Japheti (Khefti); and in the second or modified form of the name, as the Khita, Ketti or Kittim. In this sense, Arkite, one of the sons of Canaan, is called "Chetteus" by Josephus.[2]   The same writer also mentions the Judæans (or Juda-deans), who were a nation of Western Æthiopians from Judadas, who descended from Canaan, the fourth son of Ham.[3] Judadas, one of two sons, is evidently identical with the Judah of the tradition reported by Plutarch and Tacitus, who, with his brother Hierosolymus, headed an exodus from Egypt into Palestine, settled in Judea, and founded the city of Jerusalem.

Cottus is named as one of the three leaders of the Titans, *i.e.* ethnically they who were of the Typhonian religion.   According to Sallust, who quotes the Punic Books of Hiempsal, the aboriginal possessors of Africa were the Gætulians (and Lybians), a rough nomadic race, who fed on flesh and on the pasturage of the ground like cattle.

The Jews of the Bible can be identified according to their religion, but not by their race.   Tacitus shows how the confusion of race with religion entered into what he had heard of the Jews.   "It is said that the Jews escaped from the island of Crete at the time when Saturn (Sut-Typhon) was driven from his throne by the violence of Jupiter (the Egyptian Amen), and that they settled in the extreme parts of Lybia.   A memorial of this fact is supposed to be found in their name."[4]   But he follows the derivation of the Judæan name from that of Ida, the well-known mountain in Crete, which name is itself derivable from Kheft.   He likewise reports an exodus from Egypt in the reign of Isis, when that country was relieved by an emigration of the people into the neighbouring countries under the conduct of Hierosolymus and Judah.[5]   He continues: "Many consider them to be the progeny of the Æthiopians (Æthiopum Prolem), who were impelled by fear, and by the hatred manifested against them, to change their settlements in the reign of king

[1] Gen. x. 4; 1 Chron. i. 7.   [2] B. i. ch. vi.
[3] *Ant.* i. 62.   [4] *Hist.* lib. 5.   [5] Lib. 5.

Kepheus (Ma-Shu); while it is sometimes asserted that they are a heterogeneous band from Assyria, a race without a country, who made themselves masters of a portion of Egypt, and afterwards occupied cities of their own in the Hebrew territories, and the parts bordering on Syria. Others, ascribing to the Jews an illustrious origin, say the Solymi, a nation celebrated in the poetry of Homer, called the city which they built Hierosolyma from their own name."[1]

Tacitus makes the time of the flight from Egypt the same as that given to Typhon on the Ass. He says, "They pursued their journey for six days without intermission, and on the seventh, having expelled the natives, they took possession of the country, where they built their city and dedicated their temple." This agrees with the reason assigned for keeping the seventh day as a sabbath,[2] because of the coming out of Egypt, "therefore the Lord thy God commanded thee to keep the sabbath day."

Polemo, the Platonic philosopher, who died about 273, and who was the writer of historical works now lost, is quoted by Africanus and cited by Eusebius[3] who observes: "Some of the Greeks likewise relate that Moses flourished in those times." Polemo, in the first book of his Egyptian histories, says: "In the reign of Apis, the son of Pharonæus, a portion of the Egyptian army deserted from Egypt and took up their habitation in that part of Syria which is called Palestine, not far from Arabia." And Eusebius asserts, "These were the very men who went out with Moses." Both are claimed to be the exodus of the Jews, as they were in a sense, but not the Jews of the Biblical Exodus. The backward blending of the Jews with the Hekshus by Josephus identifies the relations of the Jews with the two sons of Typhon begotten in Palestine and Judea.

In the Talmud it is written, "A Rabbi once said the daughter of Pharaoh (she who adopted Moses) was an Israelite." "How can that be?" "Because she believed in the unity of God." If for unity we read bi-unity, or the unity of the Two-one, there is a profound sense in the statement. The worshippers of this deity whose name is finally expressed by the letters "Iu" as an Egyptian name for the divine duality and an Assyrian name for the god, as it was in the title of Iu-sif, Iu-em-hept, or "Neb-iu," a title of Osiris; Iu, the twin totality of the son, and afterwards of the Iu-piter, were Ius independently of race or place. In this sense Iuaa, the father of Queen Taiu, was a Jew by name, and a born Jew, or worshipper of Iu.

The account quoted from Lysimachus shows that the Typhonians were named as Jews, or the Jewish people, but not from the land of Judea; and it implies that the land of Judea was named from the outcast Jews of Egypt. In like manner Typhon goes out of Egypt to beget the two sons, one of whom is Judæus.

---

[1] *Hist.* lib. 5.   [2] Deut. v. 15.
[3] *Præp. Evang.* Eusebius, lib. 10.

The city of Tel-el Jahoudeh, which stood near to Memphis, was the city of the mound or mount of the Jew; but the name was not meant to be ethnological. The worshippers of "Iu," whether as the dual Sut, Sut-Horus, the ass-headed Iu, the bull-headed Iu, or Iu-em-hept, were all Jews according to the religious origines, but they were Egyptians also by race, and the roots of the race must have gone the deepest, just as the religion was the oldest in Egypt.

Jahoudeh, in Egypt, was not named from the Jews of Syria, supposed to have entered Egypt as the twelve sons of Jacob. There is a land of Judea, or Oude, in India, and the Burmese planisphere shows a country of Jahudia in the heavens. These were named after the divinity Iu, whether in heaven or earth, whose worshippers were Jews in the primal, that is religious, sense. The beginning was with the Star of Joudi, the Great Mother in the North, and her son Iu, the ass.

According to the data and the view of the present writer, no better description of the entrance of the Biblical Jews into a visible existence could be given than that of Celsus, the well-informed Roman, in the Word of Truth (ἀληθὴς λογος). He says, twice over: "The Jews were a tribe of Egyptians who revolted from the established religion." The Jews were "a colony of revolted Egyptian slaves who settled in a corner of Palestine." It is because they were Egyptians in Lower Egypt, an undistinguishable part of the mixed multitude there congregated, that they have not been known and could not be discreted as a separate race. They were identical in religion with the Shus-en-Har and Sut-Typhonians within Egypt; with the Khita of Syria, the Phœnicians, the Judeans of Æthiopia, the Judeans of Crete, the Jews or Hus of Cornwall, the Ionians, Yavanas, or Kivanas of Greece and India.

The Hindus, who call the people of the Western world Yavanas,[1] are still naming them from the hinder part, as the west, according to the solar reckoning, which followed the north of the earlier Sabean typology. The Yavanas, Ionians, Gevim, or Japhetic people were first named from the north, and later from the west, the hippopotamus being the representative of the genitrix in the north, the lioness in the west, as shown by the two different hind quarters.

Ezekiel[2] tells Israel that her Makvrah (מכורה)—in the margin, her "CUTTING OUT" or habitation (in Egyptian, the equivalent MA-KHEPR would mean the place of transformation or change into some second phase) was in the land of Canaan; and "as for thy nativity, in the day thou wert born thy umbilical cord was not severed." The child was still attached to the parental body. "Thy mother was a Hittite," identifies them with the Khita of Syria, or it goes farther back to the parent of all in Kheft, the ancient genitrix in Egypt; the Amorite father also leads back to Ham

[1] *As. Res.* iii. 358.　　　　[2] Ch. xvi. 3, 4.

the Kamite. They must have been a motley medley from the first. Their dispersion in the present is but the obverse image of their mixture compounded in Egypt, where the marriage of Amenhept III., of the Æthiopic features, with the fair Queen Taiu, daughter of Iuaa, was typical of the intermixture of dark and light, Æthiopian and Syrian, that went on continually between the Sut-Typhonians—a mixture still further continued in the Syrian land with the people of the earlier exodes.

On the ground that IU represents the name of Jew, it might be argued that IUAA was THE Jew named from the divine IU, the son who comes; and that his wife's name of Tuaa, or Tiuaa, denoted the Jewess IUAA, with the feminine article prefixed. The daughter's name written ⑂ (Taiu) and ⑂ (Tiiu) [1] may signify the bearer or the reproducer (Ti) of Iu the Sif, who would be the Hebrew Joseph. This is not to be despised as a possible nucleus for a beginning on a particular line deriving from Mesopotamia and the Hittite race. "Thy mother was a Hittite," and Queen Taiu is the daughter of Iuaa and Tiuaa, the male and female Jews. It would account for the two currents, one from Egypt and one from Aram, which meet in the Abramic and Mosaic renderings of the same original mythos. On the religious line of descent the Jews are as old as Iu (the Ass), the dual son of Typhon, the genitrix whose type was the star Joudi, and on the ethnical line they might rightly claim to be not only affiliated to the exiles of the later revolts, the Hekshus and the emigrants during the reign of Isis; not only to be a branch of the Egyptian vine, for there must be a rootage beyond the branch that struck deep in the Æthiopian and Upper African soil long before it fructified in the alluvial land of the Nile; they might go back and back, and claim kindred at last with the black Jews of India who emigrated with the original complexion of the African progenitors of the Egyptians.

The missionary, Dr. Buchanan, records in his Travels in India, that he himself found sixty-five different settlements of Black Jews in India.[2] These belonged to the earliest אמרי or Kamry. They had gone forth wearing the colour of Kam, the colour of the black ass-headed Sut, and therefore of Iu, and kept it; they must have been indefinitely older than the Pentateuch, and consequently were found to be without the five books of the Jews. The cloud of mystery that overshadows their origin is partly due to the darkness of those progenitors whom the Jews were not proud to acknowledge. With a streak of the lighter Hittite complexion among them they were Canaanites of the black type ages before they entered and were merged with the Syrian Canaanites who had preceded them in the land.

[1] Brugsch, *Histoire*, pl. 12, scutcheons 248 and 258.
[2] *Christian Res.* 226, ed. 1819.

Tacitus, in speaking of the Jews, calls them ÆTHIOPUM PROLEM,[1] and the well-known lines of Chœrilus—a contemporary of Herodotus —describe the Solymi in almost Æthiope colours. It is this immense past as Egyptians and Æthiopians which accounts for their persistency of type, and also for that fearful state of leprosy which was a bequest of the African blood.

As a race-name, the Apru or Hebrew agrees with that of the Danakil, who call themselves the Apru or Afru, a still earlier form of the word. The Danakil are a different people to the Dongolawy, who are Nubians, yet the two names, word for word, are one, and the Nubians are still black. The Apru or Afru point backward to the Kafru or Kaffir, the black people of Africa, the land (Ka) of the Afru or Kaffirs. With which may be compared the ÆTHIOPUM PROLEM of Tacitus, and the JUDADÆUS, or Western Æthiopians, of Josephus.

There can be no doubt that such records and commentaries as we have found assigned to Sut, Shu, and Taht, and deposited in the Temple at On, were amongst the 1,100 books attributed to Taht by Jamblicus; the 20,000 ascribed to him by Seleucus; the 36,500 assigned to this scribe of the gods by Manetho;[2] or we should not have had the tenth chapter of the Hebrew Genesis. In this chapter (x. 5) we find the immediate descendants of Noah, the sons of Shem, Ham, and Japheth, are "divided in their lands every one after his tongue" (v. 5), and the dispersion of language has already taken place, yet the eleventh chapter opens with the statement, "AND the whole earth was of one language and of one speech." So confusedly have the ancient fragments been huddled together. The second statement is made as an introduction to the Babel myth, and the destruction of the Tower of Seven Stages in one myth is equivalent to the ending called a Deluge in the other. The Hebrew writers usually class the sons of Noah as Shem, Ham, and Japheth. But in this tenth chapter (v. 2) the order is Japheth, Ham, and Shem. Japheth, as representative of the north, Khepsh or Kush, should be first according to Egyptian naming, from the celestial beginning in the north. Kam (Ham) belongs to the south, and these two are the Khamit and Khebt, the dual and permutable names of Egypt and the heavens north and south, the celestial being primordial. Japheth represents the north by name, and Kam the south; Khebma, the name of the genitrix, being the original of both Kheb and Kâm, which, with the dual terminal, become both Khebti and Kamit. The Hebrew Japheth has been identified with Kheft as the north, and, in accordance with this naming, Homer places the Greek Iapetos at the uttermost boundary of earth and sea, where the depths of Tartarus lie around them, and they have no refreshment from the rays of the

---

[1] *Hist.* lib. 5, ch. ii.   [2] Jamblicus, *Of the Mysteries*, viii. 1, 2.

supernal sun.[1] That is, in the north, as the abyss. The division by three, following the introduction of the solar triad, is represented by the addition of Shem. In Egyptian the equivalent SEM is the name of the tall double plume of the solar god placed on him by the Sems, the twin lion-gods, as servants of the sun of the east and west, the daily sun, the sun of the Semites. Sem-pi-Khart or Semphucrates (Greek) was a solar god as the Sun of the West.

The three names of Shem, Ham, and Japheth stand for the division of the world into three parts, as represented by Herodotus, who says, " I will show that neither the Greeks nor the Ionians know how to reckon when they assert that the whole earth consists of three divisions, Europe, Asia, and Libya." [2] This was the true division in the planisphere, consisting of south and north, with east and west as the equinoctial centre ; Kam, Sem, and Khept are the true names. Kam is the first, as representative of the black race, with its dwelling-place in the south. Sem is the representative of the Red Man, the Adam or Edom, Egyptian Atum. He is midmost. Japheth represents the north. The division is by north and south, Khept and Kamit (or Khentu) ; the two heavens of the earliest celestial chart made in or beyond Æthiopia, with the equinoctial division added and placed between the solstitial two. Shem is said to be the father of all the children of Eber, and Shem represents the Sun of the Equinox, which was personified by Atum in Egypt, the Wearer of the double crown of the Crossing. Abram is called the Hebrew on the occasion of his war with Chedorlaomer, when the solar zodiac is completely established, as it was under Atum. If for Eber the Crosser we date from the Crossing, that is, the equinoxes, we get to the fundamental meaning of the names of Shem and Eber in the astronomical allegory.

The Aperiu, who dwelt to the east of Heliopolis in the red country and the red mountain, also date from this midmost heaven of the three. The red land of AN represented the boundary of the two lands north and south. This middle division introduces the Red Man, the red Adam, the red sun Atum, in place of the Black Sut-Nahsi, the black Sut-Har, the Black Af and Kak and Khebek of the earlier race. In this wise the facts are reflected in the heavens. The red Atum typifies the red race which followed the black race of Kam and Kush, Khaf and Kheb, the race of the Ruti or the red. This change had already been wrought out in Egypt, in premonumental times.

There is no such thing as a beginning with the mythical Noah, and the mythical triad ; one of which, Ham, was black ; one, Japheth, white ; and one, Shem, a nondescript. This triadic or hundredfold difference of hue is an after-result. Black, bronze, red, yellow, and white races are ethnological facts now at one end of the ages, but so

---

[1] *Il.* viii. 479-481. [2] B. ii. 16.

coloured were never grouped together in one ark, or housed in one tent, or born of one womb. The facts were accomplished, the divergence of complexion was already made, when this mixture of myth and ethnology was written; hence the simplicity of the endeavour to account for the difference by starting with it! Possibly those who have steadfastly refused to accept the ape as an ancestor may fall back gratefully on the black man for a progenitor.

The Hebrew writers place Shem first among the sons of Noah, but Shem as a name is a modified form of Kam. Shem is the Hebrew name for the sun, and in Egyptian Shem denotes heat and flame, and comes from the earlier Kâm or Kvm. Let us see what light the sun will shed on this relationship of Kam and Shem when the name is applied to it. For the name of Kam is found in many groups of languages, especially the African and Carib groups. The sun is KAM in Ghagar; GHAMA, in Pakhya; GAMA, Darahi and Denwar; CAAME, Saraveca; KAMOI, Atoria; KAMU, Mawakwa; KAMUHU, Guinau; KAMU, Woyawai; KAMO, Wapisiana; CAMUI, Uacuambeu; CAMU, Barree; CAMUI, Baniwa; KIUMUK, Chemmesyan; KAMISS, New Ireland; HIKHEM, Pumpokolsk; NKOMBE, Mpongwe; De-KOMBI, Kisama; SKEEMAI, Apatsh; KAMOI, Tarakai; KOMARU, Maori. KAM went round the world before Shem was created. This name begins with Egyptian Gipsy (Ghagar), and crosses to the Gabun, the Carib, the Yeniseian, Baniwa, Nepaulese, Atna, North American, Papuan, and Australian groups of languages.

Shem in the triadic division, which followed "the flood," occupies the centre, and represents the sun of the horizon, the division by east and west, especially of the west, called Sem, the place of beginning in the Jewish solar year to this day; hence the relation to Atum, the red sun, the setting sun of the underworld who transformed into the youthful "Iu" on the horizon of the east. This was a new point of departure, in which Shem and Atum (Adam) came uppermost and appeared as the first, whereas they belonged to the later creation of Ra that followed the lunar creation of Taht and the Sabean creations of Shu and of Sut and his mother.

When Trogus Pompeius says the origin of the Jews was from Damascus, whence Queen Semiramis sprang, that is perfectly identifiable in the typology of the mythos as the seat of Tum in the heavens, the celestial birthplace of the Iu. Damascus is named from this place of rebirth, where Tum transformed into his own son Iu-em-hept. The old Arabic name of the city is Meseq, and Dum Meseq is the Syrian form. Meseq is the Egyptian Meska, the cradle of the son. Tum-Meska is the cradle, and Tum-Sakh the shrine, of Tum or Atum as Iu; hence Damascus as birthplace of the Jews and their coming Messiah. Again, Semi-rami (Eg.) reads the likeness of the fish, and this is found as the mermaid form of the genitrix in the sign of the fishes (An or On), where the Great Mother brought forth as Atergatis, Semiramis or Iusāas, the Meska of Tum personified. This was the sole origin of the Jews in Damascus.

Now this birth and origin in Pisces as the place of the vernal equinox can by no possibility belong to the entrance of the Colure into that sign 255 B.C., and it looks as if we should have to go back at least 21,000 more years (or 26,000 according to one reckoning) for the beginning of the typology and imagery brought on by the mythology.

My own conclusion is that the people known to us as the Jews had a ramification of rootage in Egypt extending to the pre-monumental times, and when they came out into Syria there was among them a fundamental basis of the oldest blood in the men of a race that was at least as ancient as the Typhonian religion, although it is not possible to define the proportions in which the Kamite and so-called Semite were mixed in Lower Egypt.

The Hebrew prophets sometimes speak with a sense of the primordial unity of the Jews, and their dispersion over the earth, which can be followed in the religious but not in the later ethnological sense. The remnants of the people who were the outcasts of the whole world, who were to be gathered from the four corners of the earth, from Assyria, from Egypt, Pathros and Kush, Elam and Shinar, and Hamath and the islands of the sea,[1] were not merely a people dispersed from Palestine. These were the earliest Jews—Jews not in the current acceptation of the name, but as the children of Sut-Typhon, the Biune Being whose name and nature were finally indicated by the IU or HU of Egypt, the IHU (יהו) of the Hebrews, the IAO of the Phœnicians, Egypto-Gnostics, and Greeks; the IE (Delphian Apollo); the Assyrian IU; the Mexican and Maori AO; Toda AU; Coptic HOOU; Lewchew JOH; Apatsh HAH; Dacota IAU; Manx JEE; Cornish Jew, British HU or IAU, the younger; the EEWU of Nicobar Islands; HU of Whydah; HOHO of Dahomy, the divinity of Twins; IAO, the Hawaiian Jupiter; Mangaian IO; the AO of the Book of Revelation; JEYE, a name of Krishna; Etruscan AIUS Locutus; and many more. The IU that began as the most ancient genitrix and ended as the Ju-pater; the IU, as their son, uniting both natures in one; He who was for ever the "*Coming One*," and whose name contains the very expression used in the New Testament where we translate "Art thou he that should come, or do we look for another?"[2]

From the first there is a monotheistic look in the Typhonian religion. It begins with the worship of the genitrix of the gods, the Goddess of the Seven Stars, who is one in the beginning. Her son, Sut, the primordial male, is one god, although he has two manifestations in Sut-Anush, two types personated in Sut-Har, the one god with two heads. Sut-Har passes into Har-Makhu, a god of the disk-worship, who becomes tri-form in Atum. But whether dual

---

[1] Isaiah xi. 11.   [2] Math. xi. 3.

or triadic, Sabean or Solar, Sut or Aten, there is a look of oneness about this divinity, because he was the son of the mother, the Iu-Sif, or Iusu, or Jesus. The Aten-disk was a type of oneness, and the disk-worshippers reverenced it with the fervour of a modern physicist. But this monotheism cannot be understood apart from its rootage in phenomena where we find no relation whatever to a supposed conception or revelation of the one God. Moreover IU signifies the Coming One with a twin manifestation, without determining the phenomenon represented. The Biune Being may be a Star-god, a Moon-god, or a Sun-god; he may image the duality of Sebti (Sothis), or Regulus the lawgiver, of Tahuti the lunar-god, or the solar Iu-em-hept. The Iu may be Sut, with the Ass (Iu) for his type; or Au, with the Calf; or Iao Sabaoth (Bacchus); or Ao, with the paps; or Iu-em-hept, in the long garment; or Shu, the young-elder; or Khunsu, with the twin image of Sun and Moon. He began as Sut of the Dog-Star and Wolf, and ended as the solar Iu, the Ao, the first and the last, of the Book of Revelation.

In this way. The perfect solar time was the latest of the seven cycles discovered, and hence the solar god as the Iao-Sabaoth is the God of the Seven of the solar cult. Sevekh has the name of Seven. Iu-em-hept is also named as the god Seven; HEPT meaning No. 7 as well as Peace. The EBΔOMH festival of the Greeks, held on the seventh day of the lunar month, was celebrated in honour of Apollo, to whom all seventh days were sacred, because he was born of Latona on the seventh day,[1] or was the seventh of the planetary gods. The gnostic Chnuphis is likewise a form of Iao-Sabaoth, and has the typical seven rays in token of his being the seventh god of the planetary group. The Sabean and Solar gods of the No. 7 are still distinguishable. The seventh day of Sut or Saturn is Saturday; the seventh day of the solar god is Sunday. But the worshippers of Sebek-Ra would keep their Sabbath on the day of Sut. In this cult the No. 7 was that of the Typhonian genitrix and her first son Sut, whose planetary type was Saturn, and who was brought on as the Solar God of the No. 7, under the type of the Lamb (Ab-Ra), in the time of the 13th dynasty, who is continued as the Lamb with the seven stars in the Book of Revelation and in the Typology of the Roman Catacombs. From Jehovah-Elohim, goddess of the seven stars, to Iu-em-hept, is the range of time from the year of the Great Bear to the year of the Sun as the seventh of the planetary types. Thus the AO or IU *was* the first and the last, the Alpha and Omega, who became the Jesus as Iu the Son, and Joseph as the expected Messiah of the Jews, also the Ju-piter or biune parent of the Romans.

When the foundations of mythology have been thoroughly

[1] Potter, *Arch. Græca*, vol. i. 385, ninth ed.

examined, and the "heavens" taken to pieces and reconstituted to ascertain the nature of their formation and typology, it will be seen how remote from the primary facts are the conclusions of Egyptologists like M. de Rougé and M. Paul Pierret,[1] who hold that the Egyptian religion was originally monotheistic in the modern sense of a conception and a worship of the one male divinity, and that polytheism resulted from clothing the one god in many symbols. Such a view is but the result of reading backwards; this can be amply demonstrated. Their method of abstracting an idea of the one god in the beginning from the writings of four thousand years—and no one knows how much longer even than that—independently of the origin of ideas in phenomena, or their place in point of time, is tantamount to filching it.

Beginning with a concept of Cause, personated in the ONE GOD, simply has no meaning; there was no such beginning. The Egyptian eternal, TEATA, is founded on the establishment of cycle and circle; the everlasting is based on the four corners imaged by the fourfold Tat of Ptah and Osiris, just as the proverbial four times is the synonym of "for ever." The word of words, Nuter (or Nunter), expressive of divinity personified as god or goddess, has no other fundamental meaning than a type of time. Nu, or Nun, denotes the type, image, likeness; and Ter is the time or season. The ideographs alone place us on firm ground underfoot, with our backs against a wall of granite.

Later abstract meanings got out of or read into such words as Nuter and Teta do not reach the origines. When the Coptic translators of the Bible rendered their idea of God by Nuter, the word had attained to a place of primacy; it expressed the first, and the first is the divine; but the type of time and renewal was first, was divine, and the two earliest types of time and renewal *stelled* in heaven were the Great Bear, Typhon, and the dog-star, Sut. Still, the Typhonians, starting on the single line from the Motherhood and her son, Sut, did appear to be monotheistic compared with their opponents. The process of the Ammonians and Osirians was to evolve the one god in Ra from all the rest that preceded him, as personifications of phenomena, and make his predecessors to appear as his manifestations; his seventy-five names, as they are designated. So the Hebrew writers endeavoured to make their language conform to this look of singleness by reading the plural Elohim in the singular number, by making the dual Aloah a form of the one God, by fusing Shadai and El-Shadai, and by claiming to worship the one alone, whether the name be Jehovah, Elohim, Shadai, Adonai, Jah, or any other of more than thirty names or titles. In either case the origines can only be found in phenomena. The "ONE GOD" was Sut of the Dog-Star; Sut-Anush as the dog and wolf (Seth and Anush in the Hebrew), who became Sut-Har under his Sun-and-

[1] *Essai sur la Mythologie Égyptienne.*

Sirius type; Saturn (Sut, the Renn or child) in his first planetary type; Kebek, or Kak, in the solar phase; and, finally, IU as the sun of both horizons, or the equinox, who was the Iu-su son of Tum and Iusāas. Sut in the south, was the child of the mother, her dog. In the east, or at the place of the equinoctial crossing in Apheru—east and west— he was represented as the parent who became "Father APER" in Egyptian and Father Eber in Hebrew. Shem, "the brother of Japheth the elder," was "the father of all the children of Eber," and these two fathers were the SEM-Sun of the West and Sut of the Crossing, who had been at first combined under the dual type of Sut-Horus. SEM (Eg.) means to join two together and combine them in one, and this combination was expressed in the Hebrew Joseph and the Egyptian Sut-Horus and in Jesus.

The origin and evolution of the idea of an Eternal Being as a male can be traced by its mythologic types. First was the IU, the one who for ever comes and becomes; the divine youth, the son of the mother, the eternal boy, the universal lad.[1] Next is the Being who is, and ever continues to be; and, lastly, the Being who inferentially *was* and has been for ever. Thus was developed the idea of him who was, and is, and is to be. The Jews, as before said, continued the worship of the IU as the ever-coming one. The coming was the becoming, and the mode of becoming was expressed by transformation or transfiguration of the old into the young. A definition of the cause of change in everything that changes is given in the formula, "*Khepr khenti khep khet neb em-khet Khepr-sen.*" This has been rendered, "the becoming which is in the becoming of all things when they become;" but it might be varied, according to the doctrine of becoming by transformation, and made "the becoming which is in the transfiguration of all things when they transmute;" for there is no reason why this philosophy of Khepr should not have included the modern doctrine of the conservation, correlation, and transmutation of force.

This coming or becoming one in person was the IU of the mythos, and to him the believers among the Jews, who were ignorant of the true doctrines, had learned to look for a deliverer from the yoke of the Roman rule; and Josephus informs us that during the siege of Jerusalem by Titus the defenders watched for the huge stones being hurled in by the Roman engines of war, and, when they descried one on its way, they cried aloud in their own language, "*The Son cometh!*"[2] This, in the Hebrew or Chaldee, used by Josephus in his first version for the Jews, would probably be ה־בר־עלה (Ha-Bar-Galah), the same word that is used in the texts: "He that dasheth in pieces is *come up*;"[3] "The breaker is *come up*."[4]

It has been said that many will here look for a mystery, as though the meaning were that the Son of God now came to take vengeance

---

[1] *Hymn to Osiris*, 17; *Records*, iv. 102.
[2] *Wars*, b. v. ch. vi. 3.
[3] Nahum, ii. 1.
[4] Micah, ii. 13.

on the sins of the Jewish nation.[1] For myself, the expression contains a stroke of humour that is Carlylean in its ghastly grimness. There is but one name and form of the Son that is synonymous with the Stone. This is Bar, the earliest son, who was the Iu or coming one of mythology, and his name of Sut means a stone. The stone was his especial type. He is called Stone-head and Stone-arm in the Ritual. As Bar-Sutekh he was the destroyer. Bar was likewise the Babylonian Bel, the breaker and destroyer alluded to by the Hebrew writer[2] as wielder of the " hammer of the whole earth." The stone of Bar-Sut belongs to the stone-age, and is the adze (Nuter) of Sut, the Anup of the hieroglyphics. Bar, the son and stone in one, identifies the Sabean son of the Typhonian genitrix. And when the " *coming one* " takes shape as Bar the destroyer and his weapon of stone, it elicits a ringing yell of derision for those who had perverted the doctrine of the Saviour-Son, and looked forward to His coming as a possible reality. The Son, the coming one, had come at last.

Iu had an earlier feminine form in Io, the white Wanderer of the heavens—the lunar goddess, Io. According to Eustathius, Io, in the language of the Argives, was the moon. Io being feminine and lunar was first. She wandered until her child was born, and Hermes, as the male moon-god, set her free. On the feminine side Io goes back to Af, Aft, Apt, Khef, Khept, or Khepsh, the Typhonian genitrix who was the mother of the Iu, whether Sabean or Solar, and also of the Jews. This Iu of mythology still comes and goes in popular belief as the Wandering Jew of fable and romance, whose figure yet retains something of the personality of the Iu, or Jew, who was cyclic, and born of cycles, and so was for ever the coming one, continuing to come. The popular notion of this Wanderer is that he has an illness which is incurable, and at the end of every hundred years he falls into an ecstasy ; out of this he returns each time in the same state of youth he was in when Jesus bade him wander till he himself should come again.[3] This identifies the Jew with the personification of periodicity and the Eternal Youth. Also, he is still the wise sage, like Iu-em-hept, and wears the purple robe of wisdom ; still the healer, like Æsculapius. The name Iu or Iao supplied a verb, meaning to heal, well known in the mysteries of ancient theosophy, as well as in common medicine. The Jew was said to have been converted and baptized under the name of Joseph, which is yet another link in identification of the undying, unresting Jew with the ever-coming Iu. The age of the Jew at the time of his transformation is also given as about thirty years ; the age of the Messiah as Khem-Horus ; the age of Joseph when he went out over all the land of Egypt ; the age of Jesus[4] when he assumed the Messiahship. The name of

[1] *Wars of the Jews*, b. v. 6, 3. Roland, quoted by Whiston in a note to the passage.
[2] Jer. l. 23.
[3] Brand, *Wandering Jew.*
[4] Luke, iii. 23.

CARTAPHILUS assigned to him [1] seems to include a form of Horus, the Khart (child) who became Horus the Youth.   How the old legends have been made to lie against these wanderers of the world, the Ius or Jews, whose consequent fate it has been to follow on earth the restless track of their prototypes in the heavens as wanderers for ever; goaded on like Io; persecuted like the wandering Jew of the fable, for refusing to let the Christ rest on his doorstep; and seldom sympathized with, except under false pretences, and with sinister intent to convert them to a belief that the lying legends are the latest revelation of eternal truth!

[1] Percy, note to the ballad of the *Wandering Jew.*

SECTION XIX.

COMPARATIVE VOCABULARY

OF

AKKADO-ASSYRIAN AND EGYPTIAN WORDS.

AKKADIAN AND ASSYRIAN.	EGYPTIAN.

A.

a (Akk.), water.	**a**, water.
aa (Akk.), moon.	**a** or **aah**, moon.
aa (Akk.), father.	**aa**, old, elder.
aanu (Ass.), where?	**annu**, to turn and look back.
abubu (Ass.), storm.	**beb**, whirlwind.
abaya (Ass.), a water-bird.	**hab**, a water-bird.
ab (Akk.), **abu** (Ass.), father.	**ap**, ancestor; **ab**, priest, as holy father.
abha (Ass.), unpolluted or unblemished, applied to priests.	**ab**, pure man, pure priest, his reverence.
ablu (Ass.), son, from **ibila** (Akk.).	**ap**, first ancestor; **rru**, child, children, a child to nurse.
ad or **adda** (Akk.), father.	**at** or **atta**, father, priest.
adn (Ass.), great water.	**a**, water; **ten**, extended.
adu (Ass.), portent, sign.	**atu**, type, sign.
aga (Akk.), crown.	**aukhu**, diadem.
aga (Ass.), a sacred day, the sabbath.	**uka**, festival, and a name of the week.
agammu (Ass.), pool.	**akhem**, pool.
agarin (Akk.), mother.	**akh**, sustenance; **renn**, the child, nursling; **renn**, to dandle.
agu (Ass.), a crown.	**aukhu**, a diadem.
ak (Akk.), a ring.	**akh**, horizon round.
ak (Ass.), a lord, a king.	**akhu**, the illustrious, the highness.
aka (Akk.), to raise up.	**akha**, to elevate.
akharru (Ass.), the west, hindward part.	**akar**, Hades, the hindward quarter, west.
akh, a name of Sin, the moon-god.	**Aah** and **T-akh**, names of the moon-god.
akh (Akk.), a worm.	**kak**, a worm.
akhit (Ass.), repair? Inscrip. of *Nebuch.* col. 2.	**akait**, loss and injury.
akhkharu (Ass.), vampire?	**akhekh**, the dragon; **aru**, to rise up.
akku (Akk.), very high.	**akka-t**, the height.
aklu (Ass.), noble?	**akh**, noble.
alal (Akk.), a papyrus?	**ar**, a calendar; **ar-t**, a papyrus roll.
alam (Akk.), image.	**ar**, to make the likeness; **am**, belonging to.

AKKADIAN AND ASSYRIAN.	EGYPTIAN.
allala (Ass.), great, noble.	**arru**, form, ceremony, a divine type.
amar (Akk.), enclosure.	**mer**, enclosure.
amatu (Ass.), command.	**mât**, a whip.
amien (Akk.), crown.	**men**, denotes a ring, collar, bracelet, to twine round.
amir (Ass.), a master (ameer?).	**mer**, superintendent, prefect.
ammat (Ass.), cubit.	**meh**, a cubit.
amut (Akk.), blood.	**mut**, mother, water.
an, sign of a god, heaven.	**nuu**, a divine type; **nu**, heaven.
ana (Akk.), measure, number.	**an**, the boundary.
anaku (Ass.), I am he (the king).	**ank**, I, the king.
anaku (Ass.), I.	**ank**, I.
anki (Akk.), heaven and earth.	**ankh**, pair, to clasp.
annabu (Ass.), hare.	**an**, hare.
ar (Akk.), mountainous district.	**aru**, mountain, steps, ascend.
arali (Akk.), tomb, Hades.	**ar**, lower, fundament; **alu**, orbit.
ardu (Ass.), man, servant.	**ret**, men; **aru**, a page.
aria (Akk.), river.	**arui**, river.
arkhu (Ass.), a month.	**ark**, 30th of the month.
arura (Ass.), land-measure.	**aru**, **arura**, an acre.
asabu (Ass.), to dwell.	**asb**, seat, throne, place, or dwelling.
asaridutu (Ass.), pre-eminence.	**seri**, chief; **tut**, honoured, distinguished.
asha (Ass.), criminally, wickedly?	**asiu**, vileness; **ush**, blot.
astu (Ass.), wife.	**shtar**, betrothed wife; **ast**, Isis.
asi (Ass.), jackal.	**shui**, jackal.
asibut (Ass.), inhabiting, (? enthroned).	**asiput**, throne, seat.
askun (Ass.), I fixed (root **sakanu**).	**skhenn**, to settle, prop, sustain.
assinnu (Ass.), typical figure, a breathing image.	**as**, statue; **senn**, typical figure; **senu**, breathing.
at (Akk.), father, king.	**at**, father, priest.
atalu (Ass.), an eclipse.	**ataru**, fantastic, sham, unreal.
azza (Ass.), healed?	**usha**, doctor.

B.

babar (Akk.), white.	**papu**, papyrus.
bahu (Bab.), name of Gula, Lady of the house of Death.	**bau**, the void, the hollow of the tomb; **bau-t**, **peht**, **buto**.
bakû (Ass.), to weep.	**beka**, to pray; **beka**, squat, depress, set down, naked.
balu (Ass.), power.	**ber**, force, ebullience, to boil up.
bap or **pap**? (Akk.), to be opposed, opponent, adversary.	**baba** or **apap**, the Typhonian adversary.
bar (Akk.), all-powerful.	**Bar**, god, the mighty.
barikiti, the blessed.	**baruka**, blessings, benedictions.
barre (Ass.), fatness.	**abar**, fat.
baru (Ass.), half.	**paru**, one-half of the solar house.
basû (Ass.), (verb) to be.	**ba**, to be, be a soul; **su** or **sif**, the child.
bat? (Akk.), to open.	**peth**, to open, open the mouth.
ber-ber (Ass.), a pyramid.	**ber-ber**, tip, cap, roof, summit.
bibbu (Ass.), the planets, the sailors.	**beb**, to turn, circle, go round.
binu (Ass.), to create, same root as **banu**.	**ben**, to engender.
binu (Ass.), wine?	**bennu**, the palm.
birut (Ass.), pure, refined silver?	**ber**, to boil; **ut**, white; **hut**, silver.
bisu (Ass.), evil.	**besh**, evil, wounded, revolt, hostile.
bitu, house, temple, abode.	**bu-t**, the abode, womb.
bitiq (Ass.), work, form, fashion; **bitruti** (Ass.), carved, cut.	**buter**, kind of workman or mason.
buligu (Ass.), division, divided.	**pu**, to divide; **rekh**, race, or people of a district.
bunnu (Ass.), an image.	**bennu**, image of resurrection.
bur (Akk.), to raise, tumefy, swell.	**ber**, to boil.
bura (Ass.), a lighthouse.	**bu** or **pa**, house; **ra**, sun, day or a blaze.
burbur (Akk.), summits; **bur**, high, head.	**bur-bur**, tip, cap, roof, supreme height.
but (Ass.), an interval or space.	**beh-t**, space.

AKKADIAN AND ASSYRIAN.

D.

Dabu (Ass.), bear, the Great Bear.
dada (Ass.), a vase?
dahuti (Ass.), (plural) gifts.
dalkhu (Akk.), applied to an evil spirit.
dam (Akk.), woman.

dannat (Ass.), dimensions, extent.
dapanu (Ass.), a wheel.

dar (Akk.), race.
dâru (Ass.), eternal

darati (Ass.), long, lasting.
datilla (Ass.), river of death.
dessu (Akk.), heaven.
dhe? (Akk.), to revolve.
dim (Akk.), to judge.
dim (Akk.), a phantom.
dir-se (Akk.), name of the thirteenth month (or Ve-Adar); **dir** means dark. So the intercalary days of the Egyptian year are the black days, the Nahsi.
du (Akk.), to go.
dubba (Akk.), an engraved tablet or brick.
dudu (Ass.), to go rapidly.
duk (Ass.), to have, to possess.

dumku (Akk.), omen of luck, prosperity.

dunku (Ass.), happy, holy, prosperous, (?living).

e (Akk.), a house.
ebir (Ass.), I crossed over.
ebiru (Ass.), to cross and pass.

ega (Akk.), a crown.
egiru (Ass.), to dig.
ekal (Ass.), palace.
ekim (Ass.), a class of spirits; **ekimmu**, a bull-like demon (from Akkadian.)
ekur (Akk.), temple, or God.

el (Akk.), splendour.
eli (Ass.), over.
emgu (Ass.), profound power, applied to the magi, august.

emi? (Akk.), people.
en, incantation.
enu (Ass.), eye.
enu (Akk.), or **enuv**, lord.
epar (Ass.), produce? dust.
eratu (Ass.), pregnant.

erim (Akk.), servant, whence **rim**, the Akkadian **rim-aku**, denoting the servant of the moon-god.
es (Akk.), house.
esara? (Akk.), the firmament as the dwelling of the fixed stars.
esiru (Ass.), a shrine, temple.
eski? (Akk.), I carved.
essa (Akk.), an ear of corn.

etiku (Ass.), to cross.

EGYPTIAN.

D.

Teb, Typhon, the Great Bear; **Tabu**, a bear.
tata, vase, dish, jar.
tahuti, dual deity; **tat**, give, gifts.
ter, drive away; **khu**, spirit, manes.
m, mother; **hem**, woman, wife; **t**, article; **Atum**, mother-goddess of time.
tan, spread, extend; **nat**, limit.
teb, movement in a circle; **pen**, reverse, return, wheel round.
ter, all people, community.
tef, divine father; **tepr**, head; **ter**, all time, ever.
tera, time; **ti** duplicates.
tat, death; **aru**, river.
tes, heaven.
tha, to make turn round, revolve.
tem, to judge, distribute justice.
tema, to terrify, hover, swoop.
ter, frontier, limit, extremity; **si**, it.

tu, to go, go along.
tebh, a seal-ring, a brick.
tata, to gallop.
teka, to lay hold, adhere, cleave to; **tekar**, a hook or finger.
tem-khu, announce benefit; **tem**, to cut, as we "cut" cards; **tams**, bad luck.
ankh (t prefix), life, living, live, sacred.

E.

â, a house or mound.
aba, to pass through, opposite; **ab**, passage.
apheru, the equinoctial crossing; **Aper**, the crosser.
aukhu, a diadem.
karu, gardener; **akau**, a ploughshare.
kher, shrine.
khemu, spirits; **khem**, the Bull.

akar, Hades; **kher**, shrine, the Word, Logos, God.
her, heaven, day; **aaru**, elysium.
ari, ascend, lintel; **her**, over.
mak, think, consider, watch, rule; **am**, to discover, invent, belonging to; **aak**, the mage, the illustrious, august and glorious.
ami, inhabitant; **aamu**, Gentiles.
an, some form of speech or invoking.
an, an eye, to paint the eye.
unhu, bull, male lord; **neb**, lord (khneph).
par, produce; **ap**, dirt, to fly.
art, made, conceived; **rattu**, plant, retain the form, grow, renew.
rem, some kind of people, natives, aborigines.

as, house.
as-aaru, house of heaven, the upper.

ser, a holy place.
sekha, to write, depict, cut, represent.
hes, Isis, zodiacal goddess of corn; **su** or **sa**, corn.
tek, crossing, transit.

AKKADIAN AND ASSYRIAN.	EGYPTIAN.

G.

gabdi? (Ass.), glory.	**kab-ti**, double honour; **pehti**, glory.
gabi? (Ass.), reaper.	**kab**, cut down; **khepi**, harvest.
gabri (Akk.), a duplicate.	**kab**, double.
gabut? (Ass.), an ark.	**hept**, an ark.
gal (Akk.), hollow, cave.	**kar**, cave, hole under ground.
gallu (Ass.), name of a class of evil spirits.	**kheri**, evil, enemy.
gam (Akk.), a dwelling, subduer, a trampling down.	**khem**, shrine, prison, bruise, crush, subdue.
gam (Akk.), to bend, be bent.	**kham**, the bent posture of submission or adulation.
gamir (Ass.), accomplishing.	**khem**, to be master of, be potent, have the power.
gan (Akk.), an enclosure, a garden.	**khen**, an enclosure, hall, sanctuary, inner region, garden.
gap (Akk.), hand.	**khep**, hand.
garru (Ass.), food.	**karu**, food.
gasitti or **kasitti** (Ass.), the " warrioress," a title of Ishtar.	**Seti**, goddess of the arrow.
ge (Akk.), a cleft, valley, abyss.	**ki**, land, inside, cut.
gi (Akk.), a spirit.	**khi**, a spirit.
gi (Akk.), a reed tablet.	**kha**, a book.
gibil (Akk.), a burning.	**kep**, to heat; **afr**, to burn, fire.
gig (Akk), sick, plague, affliction.	**khakha**, venom, sting; **khaku**, man vomiting.
gig (Akk.), night.	**kek**, darkness.
gigi (Bab.), Saturn?	**kehkeh**, the old man.
gigim (Akk.), demon.	**khu**, spirit; **khem**, dead.
gil (Ass.), enclosure, rim round.	**kar**, enclosing circle, a course.
gilda (Ass.), applied to some animal (? gelt).	**karut**, testes; **kart**, cut.
gim-gim (Ass.), a god, son of Bel.	**khem**, a god; **kam**, to create.
gin (Akk.), to stand up, be firm.	**kan**, be able, courageous, valiant.
gir (Akk.), vault of heaven.	**aaru**, heaven.
giri or **garri** (Ass.), course, passage.	**kar**, course, orbit.
gisru (Ass.), mighty.	**kesr**, power personified.
gi-umuna (Akk.), a title of Hades.	**ki-amen**, the hidden, inner land.
gu (Akk.), doubled.	**kiu**, a second, another, one more.
gud (Akk.), go to bed, rest.	**ka**, to rest; **khut**, shut and seal, a bound, the grave; **khat**, a corpse.
guddut (Bab.), he tore or cut?	**khet**, to cut, tear, break.
gude (Akk.), to proclaim.	**kat**, inscription, title, proclamation; **kat**, tree of knowledge.
guga (Akk.), title, name.	**khu**, title; **khekh**, sign of rule.
gum (Akk.), man, male.	**khem**, male type of potency.
gusur (Akk.) wood for bridges, beams.	**khus**, build, found, construct.
gusur (Akk.), light.	**khesr**, arrow or sunbeam.
gusuru (Ass.), a beam.	**seser** or **keser**, to sustain.
gutium (Akk.), people in the north of Mesopotamia.	**khept**, the hinder part, north.
guttav (Bab.), the ecliptic.	**khet**, zone, circuit, circle; **tep**, heaven.
guza (Akk.), throne.	**hes** (**khes**), throne.

H.

hantu? (Ass.), circuitous.	**hanti**, returner to and fro.
hedri? habitation.	**hat** or **hathor**, the habitation.
hidu? (Akk.), moon.	**hiti**, sun and moon, conjoined.
hin or **hinna** (Ass.), a cabin.	**hani**, cabin or bark of Sekari.
hirat (Ass.), wife, woman, mother.	**urt**, the bearer.

I.

i (Ass.), masculine plural.	**i** (as **iu**), plural.
ia (Akk.), glory.	**a** or **aa**, glory, praise, ah! oh! hail!
ia (Akk.), pure.	**ia**, wash, make pure.
ib or **ip** (Akk.), region.	**ap**, equal or mid-region.
ibbu (Ass.), white.	**ab** or **ib**, white.

AKKADIAN AND ASSYRIAN.	EGYPTIAN.

ibbutav (Ass.), written guarantee?

hapu, laws, legally; **teb**, be responsible for, seal.

ibdi (Ass.), the square.

aft, four corners.

id (Ass.), hand; **id** (Akk.), power, action.

it, to figure, pourtray with the hand of the artist.

idu (Ass.), to know or make known.

itu, to figure forth.

idlu or **itlu** (Ass.), noble, warrior.

taru, the hero, the unparalleled.

igigi (Ass.), spirits.

akhu, **khu**, or **khekh**, a spirit.

igira (Ass.), warred, from **garû**.

kar, war.

igiti (Bab.), celestial spirits.

akht, light, lofty, spirits.

ikhimu? (Ass.), he devoured.

ukha, to devour; **akhem**, to annihilate.

ikhiqu (Ass.), gathered, bounded, as waters?

khekh, made to recoil, be repulsed, as waters.

illi (Ass.). infant.

ari, child.

im (Akk.), cardinal point.

am, west, the crossing.

inâ (Ass.), eyes.

an, an eye.

innun or **ennun** (Akk.), a period or watch.

un, **unun**, a period or hour.

ip (Akk.), to create.

apa, divine ancestor; **ap**, prepare.

iru (Ass.), to conceive a child; same root as **eratu**.

ar, to make, child, take the form or impression, create.

ir? (Akk.), a complete vessel.

ur, the chariot.

irka? (Ass.), limits.

arkai, limit, end, finis.

irriti (Ass.), accursed?

retuu, unclean, filthy, sanies.

irsu (Ass.), bed.

urs, pillow or head-rêst.

Ishtar (Ass.), mistress, divine spouse.

shtar, betrothed wife.

isdu (Ass.), foundation.

st, floor.

iskhi (Ass.), houses of some kind?

as, house; **khi**, extended, high, vast, elevated; **skhi**, very lofty.

isme (Ass.), he heard; root **samu**.

sema, hear.

issip? (Akk.), king.

as-sep, enthroned ruler.

iti (Ass.), wall, frontier, border, that which supports or upholds.

iti, a boat; **atb**, a wall.

ittu (Ass.), wheat.

hit, wheat.

itu or **idu?** (Ass.), moon.

utu, Taht, lunar god.

Iu (Ass.), a god.

Iu, a god.

izinu (Ass.), smelled?

sena, to breathe.

izzakaru (Ass.), they recorded; root **zakaru**.

sekha, to write, remember; **sekhar**, to depict, plan, picture, instruct, record.

K.

ka, proclaim.

ka, call, cry, say, proclaim.

ka (Ass.), tooth or tusk.

ka, horned.

ka (Akk.), mouth, as door of the body.

kha, vagina-emblem.

kab (Akk.), before, that which is in front.

kaba, horn; **ab**, horn, oppose, pass through, opposite.

kabat (Ass.), rendered the centre (Talbot).

khept, the hinder thigh of heaven, the hind quarter.

kak, (Akk.), to create.

kâ, to create.

kaka, (Akk.), speak.

ka, call, cry, proclaim, say.

kakkarrit (Ass.), an anniversary.

hak, festival; **kar-t**, periodic.

kalu (Ass.), to burn.

karru, furnace.

kan (Akk.), reed, sign of writing.

kan, the sculptor, scribe's chisel.

kan (Ass.), a fish.

an, the fish.

kanul (Ass.), conduit, water-course, gutter, canal (Norris).

khen, conduct, carry; **ar**, water.

kanuli (Ass.), probably for conveying water.

kanru, to scatter, disperse.

kar (Akk.), food.

kar, food.

kar (Ass.), walled round, a fortress.

kar, to go round or be round; **karti** (plural), prisons

kararu (Ass.), to revolve.

kar, a course; **ruru**, turn round, revolve.

karsu (Ass.), belly.

karas, the womb of earth.

karu (Ass.), to invoke.

kheru, to invoke, say, specch, cry.

kas (Akk.), two, twins.

kes, to bind together.

kasar (Ass.), king (? kaiser).

ka, lofty, highest; **ser**, ruler; **seser**, Cæsar.

kaspu (Ass.), a measure of ground, seven miles.

khesf, stop, turn back; **hesp**, district, square, *in calculo*.

kasu (Ass.), to cover.

kas, a coffin, a funeral, burial.

AKKADIAN AND ASSYRIAN.	EGYPTIAN.
kat (Ass.), hand.	**khept,** hand.
kat (Akk.), to accomplish.	**khet,** to accomplish.
katamu (Ass.), the bolt or bar of a door; **katma,** closed, sealed.	**khetama,** shut and seal, a fortress.
katim (Ass.), concealed.	**khetem,** shut, sealed.
katu? complete, a corpse.	**kati,** complete course; **khat,** a corpse.
kazir (Ass.), restorer.	**khesr,** disperse, clear, disssipate.
keba? (Ass.), mysterious.	**kapu,** mysterious.
kep (Akk.), image.	**khep,** image, shape, form, transform, generate, cause to be.
kha (Akk.), fish.	**kha,** fish.
kha'aru (Ass.), to marry.	**kharu** or **aru,** to beget.
khairu (Akk.), man, husband.	**kariu,** the testes.
khammu (Ass.), heat.	**shemmu,** heat, flame.
khar-ra (Akk.), heaven.	**khar-ra,** circle of Ra or day; **aaru,** the heavens.
kharra (Akk.), master.	**kar,** power, property.
kharru (Akk.), the deep, lower heaven.	**kar, akar,** infernal region; **kar,** Hades.
kharub (Akk.), a sort of grasshopper.	**khereb,** a first form, a model figure.
khi (Akk.), glorious.	**khu,** glory, glorious actions.
khilip (Akk.), a god.	**kherf,** the majesty, divinity or princeps.
khul (Akk.), evil.	**kheri,** evil.
khut (Akk.), die?	**khat,** a corpse.
khut (Akk.), day-spring?	**khu-t,** place of the solar resurrection.
ki (Akk.), with.	**ki,** another, second, one more.
ki (Ass.), thy.	**ki,** thou, thee.
ki (Akk.), suffix for land.	**ki,** a particular land or region, within.
kibaa (Ass.), mysterious.	**kepu,** mystery.
kilib (Akk.), the splendid and magnificent?	**kherp,** his majesty, principal, excel, surpass.
kima (Ass.), like.	**ki,** another; **ma,** like.
kin (Akk.), written letter, message. (See **gi.**)	**kannu,** inscriptions, titles.
kinati (Ass.), women-servants.	**khenti,** work-women (weavers).
kip (Ass.), something for enclosing and capturing animals? No. 196 Sayce's *Syllabary.*	**kep,** to receive; **kaf,** hunt, seize.
kippi, (Ass.), curses?	**kheft,** the godless; **khebs-ta,** some place accursed.
kiprati (Ass.), regions, places. (See comment.)	**khepr-at,** the circle of Khepr, the earth or world; **kab,** corner; **aft,** four.
kir (Akk.), word?	**kher,** word.
kiribu (Ass.), an offering.	**kherp,** an offering of first-fruits.
kiriru (Ass.), the fields of heaven?	**kruru-t,** the orbit or completed circle; **aaru,** the fields of heaven.
kiru (Ass.), plantation or garden.	**kar,** gardener.
kirubi (Ass.), sort of cherubs, symbolical figures.	**khereb,** a model figure, a type.
kisalli, an altar.	**khesm,** holy of holies.
kisip (Akk.), measure, valuation.	**hesb,** *in calculo,* account, reckoning.
kissu (Ass.), some sacred book?	**kas,** embalm, bury; **khes,** a religious rite.
kissuta (Ass.), feast-day? (*Ishtar and Izdubar,* col. 2, line 24.)	**khus,** kill, immolate.
kita (Akk.), below, under.	**ki-ta,** the inner land.
kitar (Ass.), auxiliaries, irregulars.	**khetr,** occasionally.
kiti (Ass.), earth.	**kit,** land.
kitu (Ass.), linen.	**khet,** the loom and woof.
kor? (Akk.), an age, time.	**kar,** a course of time.
krb or **garbu** (Ass.), rendered interior.	**kherp,** principal, first, consecrated; **kher,** a cell, a sanctuary.
kud (Akk.), cut.	**khet,** cut, break in pieces, reverse, overthrow.
kuduru (Akk.), warrior.	
ku-kru? (Ass.), a voice, a cry.	**khu-khru,** a voice of command.
kuku (Ass.), rendered boats.	**ka-ka,** boat.
kul (Akk.), seed of animals.	**karu,** testicles.
kulu (Ass.), voice.	**kheru,** voice.
kum (Akk.), fire.	**shem,** fire, flame.
kum (Akk.), linen.	**hema,** hemp.
kummu (Ass.), palace.	**khemu,** shrine, house, place.
kupru (Ass.), cement.	**khepr,** scarab that rolled up a ball of dung or cement for its eggs.

AKKADIAN AND ASSYRIAN.

EGYPTIAN.

kur (Akk.), to conquer; **gurus**, warrior.
kur (Akk.), country.
kur (Akk.), an enemy.
kussu (Ass.), throne and palanquin.
kussut? (Ass.), empire.
kutmuti? (Ass.), golden.
kuttav (Bab.), ecliptic.
kuzbu (Ass.), beautiful adornment.

kar, battle, war, trample, vanquish.
ker, country.
kheri, an enemy.
hes, throne and palanquin.
khesut, district.
ketem, gold.
kat, to go round; **tep**, the heaven
khesba, blue, lapis lazuli, type of the true, beautiful or heavenly.

L.

lakie? (Ass.), dissolute.
likku (Akk.), dog.
liquat? (Ass.), gatherer (of the people of God).
lisanu (Ass.), tongue, language, speech.
liti (Ass.), statutes, divine ordinances, memorials, records.
lubat (Akk.), a beast.
luga (Akk.), to burn.
lule? (Ass.), twisted or wreathed work.

rekai, culpable, profane, scorners.
rekh, the knower.
rekht, pure spirits, wise, magi.
ras, tongue.
ret, to cut in stone, carved stone, to retain the form.
repat, a beast.
rukai, brazier, fire, heat.
rer, circuit, go round.

M.

ma (Akk.), land.
mada (Akk.), a land or country.
magar (Ass.), to worship and pray.
magaru (Ass.), applied to the incidental month of Ve-Adar, which fulfilled or made true.
magusu (Ass.), mage.

mahru (Ass.), face, presence.
mahar, receiver.
mahaz (Ass.), stronghold, fortress and strong place.
mahiru and mahrit (Ass.), facing opposite.
makannu (Ass.), ship, name of a country supposed to mean the ship-region.
makat? (Ass), pathways.
makh (Akk.), supreme.

makhiru (Ass.), an equal.

makh-khaz (Ass.), to strike; *concussit*.
makru, a name of Marduk.
makut? (Ass.), sovereignty.
malku (Ass.), king, monarch, ruler.

mamit (Ass.), an image, a pledge, token or sign of covenant and salvation?
mana (Akk.), coin, money.
manzaz (Ass.), standing, station.
marat (Ass.), daughter.

marhita (Ass.), wife.

marduk (Ass.), the young warrior-god.
maru (Ass.), son.
mas? (Akk.), soldier, warrior.
masak (Ass.), skin, covering.
masati? (Ass.), painted.
maskanu (Ass.), a dwelling.
maskim (Akk.), demon, incubus.

masi? (Ass.), tribute.
mat? (Ass.), strength.

ma, place; **mat**, division of land.
mat, division of land.
mak, to watch and meditate.
makheru, epithet of Horus as the fulfiller or Word made Truth.

mak, watch, think, regulate, rule; **aak**, the mage; **sa**, the Sage or Mage.
haru, face.
mer, a reservoir.
maha, enclosure; **as**, sepulchre.

ma-her, mirror.
makhennu, boat of the dead, also the bark of Atum.
makha, walk, road.
mak, to rule and regulate; **makh**, to be blessed.
mak, match; **makha**, balance; **Har-mak-heru**, Har of the equinoctial level.
khes, to pound, ram down, beat.
makheru, a name of Horus.
mak, rule, regulate; **ut**, sceptre.
mer, superintendent, overseer; **khu**, to govern; **akh**, ruler.
mem, dead; **it**, figure, the mummy image of the dead, and type of immortality.
mana-tata, money (tata, heads).
ses, to reach land or standing ground.
merut, beloved, person attached or related; mu or ma, the mother; **rut**, repeated.
mer-t, persons attached, bound or married; mar-t, a female relationship or office.
maharu, the young warrior hero.
ma, male seed; **ar**, child.
masha, archer, soldier.
meska, determinative, a skin.
mest, colour for eyes.
skhen, hall, dwelling.
mes, reborn; **khem**, the dead; **meska**, purgatory.
masi, bring, tribute.
mat, granite, established.

AKKADIAN AND ASSYRIAN.	EGYPTIAN.

mat (Ass.), a country.

mazzarti (Ass.), fortresses, bulwarks.

me (Ass.), one hundred.

mele (Ass.), lake.

meruhhi, Libya (Meroē).

men (Akk.), personal pronoun.

men (Akk.), to be.

mer (Akk.), crown?

metu? (Ass.), mazes or windings.

mi (Akk.), night, sunset, black.

mi (Akk.), multitude.

mikit (Ass.), furnace. From a root meaning "to burn."

mimpi (Ass.), Memphis.

mis (Akk.), divine hero?

misah? (Ass.), unction.

misari (Ass.), the goddess Mithra ; **masari**, the abode?

misir (Ass.), bands.

mu, to give.

mu (Akk.), year.

mû (Ass.), water ; **mê**, waters.

mudu (Ass.), skilful, accomplished, one who knows.

muk (Akk.), building ?

mukh (Ass.), brain ?

mukilu (Ass.), word, saying.

mul (Akk.), a star.

mulu (Akk.), man.

mumu (Bab.), the waters.

mun (Ass.), eternal abode ?

munihu (Ass.), rest, firm, fast.

munir (Ass.), subjugator.

muntahzi (Ass.), fighting men.

murani (Ass.), young of animals.

mus (Akk.), serpent.

musakir (Ass.), glorifying, honouring.

musaru (Ass.), writing.

mustesar (Ass.), ruler, support.

musu (Ass.), night.

mut (Akk.), to create ?

mutu (Ass.), husband, the male.

musu (Ass.), source, issue of waters.

muzza (Ass.), gathering, mass.

---

mat, a division of land.

mesaut, stone-cutters; **sart**, sculpture, carve, make.

meh, to fill, full, complete, turns numerals into ordinals.

mer, lake.

meru, Egyptian name of Nubia.

men, the bull, the male I personified.

men, to be fixed.

mer, circle, ring, bind, swathe.

mehat, enclosure, with a fold or winding.

mi or **am**, west, Hades.

ma-t, many.

khet, fire, furnace.

mem, dead ; **pa**, house or city.

mas, the anointed one, the prince.

masu, anoint.

mes, to bear and bring forth ; **ari, ar**, the child, children ; **mes-ur**, the birthplace.

ser, to enclose, involve ; **ser**, anklet.

ma, to give.

mu, year.

mu, water ; **meh**, liquid, the waters of the abyss.

mahauit, courtiers.

makht, a mason. .

mak, think, consider, rule.

makheru, true word.

mer, governor, overseer.

mer, a man attached to a temple, a prefect, superintendent.

mu-mu, duplicate of water.

manu, place of spirits perfected.

mena, to ride or rest at anchor, stop, rest. This also reads **menahu**, *Champ.* D. 231.

nar, victory.

meni, soldiers ; **menh**, officer ; **tasu**, weapon of war.

reni, cattle, young.

messi, a serpent called the *sacred word*, Hor-Apollo, B. i. 59, says the serpent was called **meisi**.

sekar, sacrifice, cut, deprive, cut the flesh, castrate ?

ser, engraving, sculpturing, inscribing.

mes, diadem ; **tser**, ruler ; **tser**, the rock.

mesi, night.

mut, the mother.

mata, phallus, the male, the mate.

mes, source, be born, product of the waters.

mes, engender, mass ; **ush** or **mush**, mud ; **us**, to produce, create.

N.

na (Akk.), setting.

nab (Akk.), divinity ?

nabadis (Ass.), deceitfully.

nabali (Ass.), musical instruments rendered harps ?

nabd (Ass.), music.

nabhar (Ass.), all, the whole.

nabnit (Ass.), produce, offspring, germ, production.

nabniti, the whole of the created races.

---

nai, to descend.

nub and **nef**, names of a deity, the Lord.

nebt, evil of some kind.

nefer, the viol or lute.

neft, breathed.

neb, all, the whole, both sexes.

nap, sow seed, grain, corn.

nab, all ; **neti**, existing or in being.

AKKADIAN AND ASSYRIAN.	EGYPTIAN.

nabu (Chaldean astronomy), a title of Mercury and Venus as prophets.

an or **un**, the period, to repeat ; **ap**, to declare manifest, proclaim ; **Anup**, the prophet as dogstar.

nabu (Ass.), fruit ?

nabs, dates, date-palm, or sycamore-fig.

nadan (Ass.), gift, act of giving, giver.

nat, offering, present tribute.

nagab (Ass.), curses or blasphemies ?

naka, impious, criminal, blasphemous.

nagu (Ass.), a district.

ankh, the people of a district.

naku (Ass.), sacrifice.

nakh, to slay.

nakhiru (Ass.), a narwhal ?, (Norris).

nakh-aru, water-bull.

nakru (Ass.), hostile.

kheri, enemy.

nam? (Ass.), to speak.

nam, speech, utterance, discourse.

namir (Ass.), black or dark figure called **khamir.**

kham, black.

namirtu (Ass.), sight or seeing.

nem, see, perceive ; **ma**, see ; **art**, eye.

nanga (Akk.), district.

ankh, sign of a district.

napah (Ass.), the rising (of sun or star).

nahp, the time, conjunction, emission of light, day.

napistu (Ass.), life.

nef, breath, spirit of life.

naplu (Ass.), surpassing, distinguished, extraordinary, admirable ?

nefer, good, divine, handsome, perfect, regal, youthful.

asplu (Ass.), bless ?

neferi, bless.

naqu (Ass.), libation.

nakhkhu, liquid, sprinkle.

nasû (Ass.), to carry, carrying.

nusa, pedestal, base, support.

nasikk-amma (Ass.), **na-siqu**, kiss me.

na-sek, na-ska, come, salute, adhere, play upon (as on a stringed instrument).

natruti (Ass.), guards, protectors, protecting divinities.

neter-ti, two goddesses ; **neterut**, temples ; **neter**, a god, gods, divine.

naze (Ass.), flight.

as, go, haste, flee.

nazir (Ass.), guardian, protector, preserver.

nasr, governor, superintendent, victory.

nazirti (Ass.), treasure.

nasr-t, kind of frontlet, glowing, probably applied to jewels.

ne? (Akk.), the deep.

nu, lower heaven, water.

nen (Akk.), lord ?

nen, type, portrait, rank, a god.

nene (Akk.), plural.

nnu (or **nene**), plural, fellows.

nesu (Ass.), name of the lion.

nas, fire and flame : the lion was a type o fire.

ni (Ass.), us, our.

nu, we, our.

nibit (Ass.), glory, fame.

peht, glory.

nibut (Ass.), noted.

nab-t, epithet of Ammon-Ra.

nigab (Akk.), porter, keeper.

nakhb, title.

nigin (Akk.), interior.

khen, interior.

nigin (Akk.), to explain ?

khen, news, to tell, inform.

nikatbu (Ass.), writings.

nakhbu, inscribe, engrave, indicate.

nimedu (Ass.), fixed.

nemtt, forced, vanquished, place of execution.

nimr (Ass.), leopard.

nem, the spotted skin, leopard-type.

nin (Akk.), any one.

nen, type, form, portrait.

nin (Ass.), son.

nun, little boy.

nin (Akk.), wife, lady.

nen, as the negative, passive type.

nipihu (Ass.), air ?

nif, breath, pass.

niqqu (Ass.), sacrifices.

naken, slaughter.

nisu (Ass.), uplifting.

nusa, a pedestal for uplifting ; **nas**, out of.

nita (Akk.), male.

nnutu, fellows, males.

nizu (Ass.), standards, signs.

nasu, the standard.

nmsuka (Ass.), crocodile.

msuh, crocodile.

nu (Akk.), no, not.

na, no, not.

nu (Akk.), to rest.

nnu, to rest.

nu (Akk.), image.

nu, image, type, likeness, statue.

nûhu (Ass.), rest.

nnu, rest.

P.

pa (Ass.), mouth, speech.

pa, hieroglyphic of the water-fowl with open mouth ; **peth**, open the mouth.

pa (Akk.), wing.

pa, wing.

pa-gri (Ass.), corpses, victims.

pa-kheri, the victim, fallen.

pal (Akk.), a time.

par, to go round, make the circuit of the sun.

AKKADIAN AND ASSYRIAN.	EGYPTIAN.

palat (Ass.), race, family, lineage (see page 351, vol. ii., Trans. of the Bib. Archæol. Society).
palat (Ass.), duration of life.
palu (Ass.), a year, a time, a lifetime.

parakku (Ass.), altar.
parid (Ass.), opening, expanding.
parra (Akk.), a day, light.

passur (Akk.), dish.
pata (Ass.), the whole?

patu (Ass.), to open.
patesi, a title of the early rulers of Babylonia.
pis (Akk.), to be pregnant.

pisan (Akk.), writing.

pisannu (Ass.), papyrus.

pitû (Ass.), to open.
pulug (Ass.), divisions, regions.

pur (Akk.), to explain.

pa-ret, the race; **per-t**, seed.

ret, to retain the form, endure.
par, a round, go round, surround, make a circle.
khakha, altar.
per-t, emanate, proceed.
par, go round, one turn; **ra**, a sun, a day; **pa-ra**, the day; **peri**, the going forth.
pes, paintbox, inkstand.
pat, completed course; **pata**, company of the nine gods; **pauti**, the Biune-all.
puth, to open.
pat, image of God; **asi**, ruler, august, venerable.
pessh, to stretch, extend; **bekh**, to become pregnant.
shen, to write; **p-shen**, the writing; **pes**, paintbox, inkstand.
shen or **shent**, written papyrus, roll; **p**, article **the**.
peth, open mouth.
pu, to divide; **rekh**, people of a certain district, mankind, race.
pur, to explain.

R.

ra (Akk.), to inundate.
ra (Akk.), to bear towards.
rabu or **rubu** (Ass.), prince.
rabu (Ass.), beast.
radu (Ass.), addition.
rak? (Akk.), vulva.
ramu (Ass.), raise.
res-eni (Ass.), raise the eyes.
ri (Akk.), to shine.
rieti (Ass.), monstrous? (applied to the slain dragon).
rîm (Ass.), buffalo or rhinoceros.

rubatu (Ass.), lady or queen.
rubu (Ass.), lord.
rutu (Akk.), troops.

uri, name of the inundation.
raau, come near; **rau**, go near.
repa, prince.
rep-t, beast; **rebu** (in the Ritual).
ret, repeated, several.
ru, gate; **kha**, belly.
rem, to rise, surge up, to erect.
ras, raise; **an**, eye, see, look.
ra, the sun, day.
retuu, sanies, corrupt, filthy in blood.

ramakh, rhinoceros; also reads **rama**; **rem**, a fish or native of the waters.
repa-t, lady; **rubata**, mystical cow.
repa, lord.
ruten, attack.

S.

sa (Akk.), bond.
sa (Akk.), star?
sa (Akk.), field?
sananu (Ass.), to repeat.
sabadhu (Ass.), a staff.
sabakh (Ass.), lie at rest.

sabaru? (Akk.), an image.
sad? (Ass.), king or ruler.
sadû (Ass.), a mountain.
sadhru (Akk.), written.
sakba (Akk.), the mamit?
sakri? (Ass.), magic; **zikin**, tricks.
sakus (Akk.), leader, chief.
sakutzi (Ass.), unclean food (Heb. שֶׁקֶץ).
salmu (Ass.), some token of a completed transaction.
sam (Akk.), price, amount paid in penalty, sum, ransom.

sa, a tie.
siu, star.
sha, field,
shen, orbit, circuit; **an**, to repeat.
sheptu, a stick or staff.
saba, solace; **sabka**, refresher; **sabak**, prostrate.
sefr, typical image, a gryphon.
sut, king, royal.
set, hill, rock, mount of the horizon.
shetrut, engraving.
skab, the mummy-type.
sakher, plan, design, act, picture, represent.
sekh, rule, conduct, protect.
sakhut-si, cake of corruption.
sharumata, to convoy peace-offering.

shem, measure, tribute; **smau**, total.

AKKADIAN AND ASSYRIAN.

samma? (Ass.), history.
samu? (Ass.), ceasing.
santu (Ass.), the year.
sapat (Ass.), lips.
sapru (Ass.), writer ; **siprati**, writings.

sar (Akk.), to put in a line.
sar (Akk), push forward, grow.
sarru (Ass.), king.
sara-ziggar (Akk.), the " sacrifice of righteousness "—month Nisan, zodiacal sign
Aries. (Meaning doubtful.)
sâru (Ass.), the cardinal points.

sarrutu (Ass.), majesty.
satti (Ass.), years.

se (Akk.), corn.
sedu (Ass.), a spirit (divine bull).
sem (Ass.), wheat.
semu (Ass.), hearing.
semiru (Ass.), diamond.

semu-kki (Ass.), drugs, poison ?
seni (Ass.), support, fulcrum.

ses-lam (Akk.), race or region.
shariri (Ass.), refulgent.
sher (Ass.), barley.
sî (Ass.), she.
sib (Akk.), lord, shepherd.
sibbahti, curb, restraint ?
sibbu (Ass.), threshold.
sibit (Ass.), seven.
sibta (Ass.), song, or mode of musical celebration.
siggarra (Akk.), tower.
siggurat-sadi (Ass.), mountain peak.
siikh? (Ass.), corruption.
sik (Akk.), cloth ; **saku**, woven ?
sikkat? (Ass.), gate.
sikru (Ass.), kindness ?
siku (Akk.), sky, heaven.
sikudi (Ass.), the steersman.
simmu (Ass.), destiny.
sini (Ass.), two ; **sun**, plural, "their."
sinik? (Ass.), enclosed or walled round, as a
garden.
sinipat (Ass.), two-thirds.

sippar (Ass.). There were two Sipparas,
one on each side of the river.
sipru (Ass.), law, explanation.
siptu (Ass.), lip.
siptu (Ass.), record.
sirru (Ass.), used for witness-seals.
sita (Akk.), bond.
siten (Akk.), to rule.
siti (Akk.), genitrix.
soss (Akk.), measure of length.

srasa (Ass.), herself.

su (Akk.), bucket.

EGYPTIAN.

sam-ma, true representation.
sam, stay, stop.
shent, the circle, orbit, cycle, period.
sepat, lips.
sefkh, goddess of the writings ; **sep,** persons
belonging to temples ; **ruit,** engrave, figure,
write.
ser, to arrange, distribute, execute, dispose.
ser-t, germinate, grow.
ser, chief, head.
sera, ram ; **sekhar,** sacrifice ; **skher,** a picture, sign, representation.

seri, arrange, place, distribute, organize,
regulate ; **ser,** the mount of the four
corners.
serut, flabellum, sign of majesty.
set, thirty years' festival ; **asat,** period of
time.
su, corn.
shetau, spirits.
shems, ear of corn.
sem, hear, listen.
semir, some kind of stone (*Brugsch*, g. 13,
c. 2) ; **shamir,** Solomon's stone.
shemm, poison, venom.
sen, to found ; **skhen,** prop, support, fulcrum.
rema, people, natives, inhabitants.
shu, illuminated ; **rer,** all round.
sheru, barley.
su, she.
sep, judge, throne ; **sau,** shepherd.
seb-seb, encase ; **sebti,** wall, rampart.
seb, gateway.
seb-ti, five and two, also the flute.
sebt, flute.

sekaru, a fort ; **sut,** hill.

suakh, decay ; **si,** corrupt.
sikhet, weaver.
sekhet, a gate.
skarhu, to soothe.
skhi, sky, heaven, elevated.
sekti, mariner.
sem, adopted, destined.
sen, two, plural.
senhu, to bind, conscribe, a prison.

shen, duad ; **put,** No. 9, and three-fourths of
a circle.
sper, one side.

sep, judge ; **ru,** discourse, chapter.
sptu, lips.
sapti, register.
sirru, to engrave.
sett, catch, noose.
suten, king, royal.
seti, goddess, genitrix ; **set,** female.
ses, the measure of compatibility ; **ssu,** a
length of time—six hours, six days.
shera, female ; **sa,** the person, Eidolon or
self.
shu, a pool or vessel of water. The English
" **so** " is a tub containing twenty or thirty
gallons.

AKKADIAN AND ASSYRIAN.	EGYPTIAN.

su (Ass.), his.
su, his.

su (Ass.), him.
su, him.

su (Akk.), month of Tammuz.
su, the child, son.

sud (Akk.), to extend.
sut, to extend, elongate.

sugab (Akk.), hand.
kep, fist.

sukalis (Ass.), with intelligence. Root **sakalu**.
sakhu, to understand.

sukh (Akk.), to seize.
ska, to take and lead captive, subdue.

sukin (Ass.), prepare.
sukhai, prepare.

sukti (Ass.), covert, shelter.
sekhet, the ark, shut up, hinder.

suku (Ass.), reed (pen ?).
sukha, write, determinative a reed pen.

sulu (Ass.), a mount.
seru, the mount.

sumilu (Ass.), the left hand.
semhi, the left hand.

suntu or **suttu** (Ass.), a dream.
senta, terror; **snatem**, to be at rest, reposing pleasantly.

sunu (Ass.), pronoun "their."
sen, they, their.

sur (Akk.), mighty.
sser, power personified.

surbu (Ass.), king or chief.
ser, dispose, arrange, govern; **ur**, chief, principal; **bua**, head, archon.

sus (Akk.), No. 60.
ses, No. 6.

surqinu (Ass.), altar, table, Hebrew שׁלחן.
ser, an altar, table, sideboard; **khenu**, act of offering, whence **serkhenu**, an altar or table of offering; **serkh**, a shrine; **serkh**, to supply food.

susib (Ass.), to seat. From **asabu**.
asb, a seat.

susru (Akk.), founder, surname of Anu.
sesr, variant of **usr**, the sign of founding, sustaining, establishing, the backbone, sceptre.

susu (Ass.), elephant. From **su**, the tusk.
susu, hard and enduring, as acacia wood.

T.

t (Ass.), feminine terminal.
t, the feminine terminal.

tab (Akk.), to adjust, to place, to add.
teb, to turn, adjust, place, instead, clothe, clad, equip, recompense.

tabin (Ass.), straw; Hebrew תבן.
tebh, corn; **tehaf** (**teha**), straw.

taddi? (Ass.), say.
tet, speak, discourse, tell, say.

tairat (Ass.), returning; "Bel and the dragon" (plate 45, line 8).
ter-t, a time, a while; **rut**, repeated, several.

tak (Akk.), a stone.
tekht, stones.

taktu? (Ass.), jewelled.
teka, sparks, to sparkle.

tal (Akk.), to put through?
tar, sieve.

tam (Akk.), day.
tam, announce, golden, renew, make over again; **tem**, completed.

tâm (Ass.), sun.
tum, setting sun.

tâm (Akk.), forms part of ordinal numbers.
tem, a total.

tamsil (Akk.), figures of constellations.
am, the crossing and transit; **ser**, to arrange, dispose, conduct, confer, regulate.

tap or **tab** (Akk.), to seize.
teb-tebu, to entangle.

tar (Akk.), separate.
tar, sieve.

tar (Akk.), to cut, pierce.
taru, a pike.

tar (Akk.), young.
tera, young bird.

tarud (Ass.), expel?
teru, drive away, obliterate, rub out, wipe out.

tatta? (Ass.), pot.
tettu, vase, dish.

te (Akk.), foundation.
ta, earth, heap, to bear, carry.

te (Akk.), floor.
tai, threshold.

tibu (Ass.), quiver-case?
teb, a cover, equip (the quiver-case ?).

tik? (Ass.), a jewelled crown.
teka, spark, sparkle, twist, join, bedeck.

tiksi (Bab.), name of the seven planets.
tek, cross, transit; **si**, star.

til (Akk.), to complete, be finished.
ter, entire, complete, all.

til (Akk.), life.
terf, lively.

tim (Akk.), cord, line (applied to enclosing).
tami, a hank, loop, noose, or band.

tin (Akk.), life.
tennu, to create, grow, increase.

tipa? (Ass.), to cook.
teb, purify by fire.

tir (Akk.), a jungle.
ter, a limit, to hinder.

tiskhu (Akk.), planet Venus.
ti, twofold; **sekhu**, illuminator.

tsi or **zi** (Akk.), inherent spirit.
tes, the enveloped self, the soul.

AKKADIAN AND ASSYRIAN.	EGYPTIAN.

tsir (Ass.), serpent.　　　　　　　ser, basilisk serpent.

tsiri (Ass.), long, length.　　　　　　ser, extend, elongate; old form tser.

tu (Ass.), day.　　　　　　　　tuai, day.

tuhami (Ass.), twins.　　　　　　tema, unite, twin.

tul (Akk.), hill.　　　　　　　　ter, tower, height.

tum (Akk.), to bring down; tam, the sun.　tum, the setting sun.

tum (Akk.), to produce.　　　　　　tam, produce, make again.

tur-dan (Akk.), powerful chief.　　　tehan, elevated, promoted.

tur-tanu (Ass.), generalissimo of the armies.　tehani, a name of the Repa, when nominated as the prince, the heir-apparent.

turi (Akk.), to pass, leap over?　　　teru, limits.

tutu (Ass.), Ubara-TUTU.　　　　tutu, a divine image of duration; tat, a god.

tutu, father of the gods.　　　　　tut, father, engenderer.

tsulit (Ass.), authority, protection.　　tser-t, ruler.

U.

u or iau, (Akk.), lord; iu (Ass.), a god.　ua, captain, the one; Iu-em-hept, a god; neb-iu, title of Osiris.

ua (Akk.), sole lord or chief.　　　　ua, the one, one alone.

ub (Akk.), quarter, region.　　　　ub, region of sunrise; ubn, sunrise, light, shrine, splendour.

ubara (Akk.), the glow.　　　　　ub, shine; ara, rising, ascending.

ud (Akk.), day.　　　　　　　　ut, light, issue forth, send out, glow.

ud (Ass.), a weight, also No. 8?　　uta, weight; uti (Taht), Esmen or eighth; uts, kind of steelyard.

udda (Akk.), light.　　　　　　uta, light.

uddium (Ass.), the rising of the sun.　ut, light, issuing, put forth, send out.

uddu (Ass.), to go forth.　　　　uta, to go forth, issue forth, put forth.

uk (Akk.), great, paragon, day?　　akh, how great, paragon, day.

ukkum (Ass.), he arose. From kâmu, to rise.　akhem, rising up, swelling, soaring.

ummu, (Ass.), mother.　　　　　mu, mother; m or hem, a mother.

umde (Median), eye.　　　　　　um, to perceive; ma, see, eye.

Umlu-Bit-Umlu (Ass.), name of an unknown temple (first letter not an ordinary um).　meru, a goddess.

umme-da (Akk.), *femme enceinte.*　hem, female; ta, pregnant.

umtat (Ass.), to stop or hinder?　　uamti, a rampart.

umun (Akk.), Hades.　　　　　amen, or menti, the Hades.

un (Akk.), man.　　　　　　　unhu, the typical male.

un (Akk.), people.　　　　　　un, beings; uni, people.

unassa? (Ass.), blazes.　　　　　nasa, fire; nasr, phlegethon.

ur? (Akk.), the nadir, foundation.　　ar, fundament.

urati (Ass.), old?　　　　　　　urt, old.

urakhga? (Ass.), a bird, constellation.　rekh, phoenix.

urakis (Ass.), I or he bound. From rakasu.　ark, bands, enclosings, encirclings, to envelop.

urhu (Ass.), path, road.　　　　heru, road, path.

urkhi, terminus.　　　　　　arkai, end, finis.

urru (Ass.), day.　　　　　　hru, day.

uru (Akk.), to engender, to beget.　ar, to make, conceive, or create the likeness.

urud (Ass.), sculptured figures?　　ret, carved stone.

urukku (Ass.), white-headed?　　rekhiu, pure, wise, magi; rekh, to make white.

uruku (Akk.), evil genius?　　　rekai, wicked, rebel, profane, culpable.

urume, Urumians (Ass.), a people.　rema, people, natives.

us (Akk.), blood.　　　　　　as or hes, blood.

us (Akk.), male, offspring.　　　us, to produce, create; su, offspring.

us (Akk.), great (ruler)?　　　　as, great (ruler).

us (Akk.), to extend?　　　　　us, to be extended.

usabsi (Ass.), to be.　　　　　sheps, conceive, be figured, and born; shep to be; si, a child.

usbi, she sat. From asabu, to sit.　asb, the seat.

nsikha (Ass.), bow down, or make to bow.　sekha, lead captive, subdue.

usser, protect.　　　　　　　user, defend, sustain and maintain.

ussusu (Ass.), name of Anu as the founder.　sesesu, a name of Sut, or the place of his origin in the south, of which he was lord.

ustatil (Ass.), be established?　　　tat, to establish.

usukkath (Ass.), to stab, wound sacrificially?　sukhat, to wound, sacrifice.

ut (Akk), light, white.　　　　　ut, light; hut, white.

AKKADAIN AND ASSYRIAN.	EGYPTIAN.

utu (Akk.), below, lower part?
utukku (Ass.), an apparition.
utuq (Akk.), magical spirits.
usu (Akk.), chair?
usu (Ass.), flesh or body.
uzzu (Ass.), fire?

uat, Lower Egypt, north.
ut, put or sent forth; **ukhu**, a spirit.
ut, magic; **ukh**, spirits.
hes or **as**, seat, chair.
as, flesh; **sha**, substance born of, flesh.
ushu, to destroy by fire.

Y.

ya (Akk.), pure.
ya (Akk.), glory.

ia, wash, purify,
a or **aa**, glory, praise; **ah**, oh, hail.

Z.

zabu (Ass.), young?
zacaru (Ass.), to record, to remember.

zadu (Ass.), to hunt.
zakir (Ass.), renowned.
zali (Ass.), suppliant, submissive?
zamani (Ass.), evil schemes and designs?
zamu (Ass.), conjuror?
zaru (Ass.), arms?
zasati (Ass.), figures?
zdn? (Ass.), probably sandal- or satin-wood.
zibu (Bab.), wolf.
zibit (Ass.), foundation?
ziggurrat (Ass.), tower. (From Akk.)
zikaru (Ass.), memorial, to remember (see above).
zikti (Ass.), potion, poison?
ziku (Ass.), pure.
zikum, the great mother.
ziku-ra (Akk.), heaven.
zilli (Ass.), to engrave or sculpture?
zimu (Ass.), circle, ring.
zippati (Ass.), trees of some kind, probably cedar.
ziru (Ass.), corn-seed.
zmaku? (Ass.), some house of pleasure or worship.
zu (Ass.), parchment for writing?
zu or **su** (Akk.), body.
zubat (Ass.), a veil (*velum mulieris*).

zum (Akk.), to destroy.
zunnu (Ass.), rain.
zunuti (Ass.), foundation.
zuzu (Ass.), a fixture.

sif, son, child.
sekha, to remember, memory; **sekh**, to paint, depict, or write; **ru**, writing.
ssat, to catch in a noose.
skhakr, embellish, decorate.
sharuma, salute, salaam.
sama, culpable, accused of crime.
sam, mythic representations.
ser, the ideographic arm.
sas, embellish; **ati**, form, type, figures.
set, aromatic.
sab, jackal, wolf.
sebt, to prepare, build, wall, rampart.
sekaru, tower or fort.
sekher, to declare.

skhet, hinder, shut up, wound, deprive.
saakh, a pure influence.
sekhem, the shrine of the child Horus.
sekhi, sky.
ser, to engrave or sculpture.
semau, total of two halves; **sema**, encircle.
sefti, cedar oil.

sheru, barley.
smakh, to bless, rejoice.

shu, papyrus, book.
su, the person, the body.
shap, hide, conceal; **shepat**, shame, fem. purification.
sam, to devour.
shen, secondary; **nu**, water.
sunt, to found.
ses, to attain land, re-establish, curdle, a six-sided block, a cube.

NOTE.—All the words in this Vocabulary, with a hundred and forty more not in it, were taken from the lists printed by Norris, Lenormant, Sayce, and others, or from the various interlinear texts. The total has been severely taxed, queried, and abbreviated by Mr. Theo. G. Pinches, Assyriologist, British Museum. Sometimes the word is questioned; at others, the translation; and in a few instances it may be the Egyptian will suggest the true meaning, and determine the right rendering.

SECTION XX.

EGYPTIAN ORIGINES IN THE AKKADO-ASSYRIAN LANGUAGE AND MYTHOLOGY.

HITHERTO Assyriologists have seldom ventured beyond the Hebrew and the so-called Ugrian languages in search of help. Within the limits of the writer's knowledge they have made no appeal to the Egyptian in those difficulties which have furnished the present opportunity. Either consciously or unconsciously, Assyriologists appear to have been so influenced by the Aryan theory of the source of languages, that they have never looked to Egypt for the origines which, be it understood, are too ancient and primal to include the grammar extant to-day. The vocabulary will now be supplemented with further evidence to show that the matter of language, typology and mythology, was the same in Babylonia and Akkad as in Egypt.

Nothing could better illustrate the depth at which Egyptian underlies the Semitic formation of language than the Assyrian verb BASÛ, to be.[1] This, when bottomed, is found to contain the Egyptian BA and SEF (or Shep) blended in one word. BA (Eg.) means to be, with the special sense of being a soul. As already explained, this later form of BA was a deposit from PÂ and PAF, the soul of breath, named from the ghost as the gust, PAF (Eg.) being both breath and a gust of wind. The earliest being was founded on breathing, whence PAF, PÂ, later BA, signified to be a living, *i.e.* breathing soul; the PÂ were human beings, and the parent as breather of being was the BAT (Eg.) of the AR (child, and to make) the vater, pater, and father.

It is admitted that the Assyrian SÛ is an equivalent of the Hebrew הוא, but we only recover the full force of both words by aid of the Vav. Thus SÛ represents SUF, and SUF the Egyptian SHEP, which has the meaning of TO BE and to be UNPERCEIVED. SHEPS is

---

[1] Vide *Discussions in Trans. of Bib. Arch.* vol. i. part ii. p. 281 ; and vol. iii. part i. p. 104.

to conceive, as the woman conceives the child in the womb; to be figured in concealment in the SHEPSH (modified KHEPSH), and Hebrew חשם, the uterus. BA-SÛ thus contains the elements of BA, to be, to be a soul; and SHEP, which describes the mode and place of becoming so, in the first abode of being, recognized as the mother, the conceiver, and shaper of the soul or image of life, which, in another aspect, is called the SHEP or SHEB. SÛ (Ass.) also implies the SU or SIF in Egyptian; the shape, the person, the child. SIF is the child of either sex. BA-SIF is to be, and a child, and BA-SÛ is an equivalent, generalized with the meaning " to be." This tends to show that USABSI, " he caused to exist," or to be, is not necessarily derived from BASÛ, as SHEPS (Shepsi or Shepsa) has the meaning of to conceive, figure, and bring forth, the mother being the bringer-forth and producer of the child in consonance with the earliest cognition. SHEP-SI (Eg.) would equally signify to be the child, or cause the child to be. It is on the line of SHEP only that we shall find the Hebrew הוה to vivify, breathe, quicken into life. As previously explained,[1] the two primates PAF and KEP (Eg.) express the two truths of breath and blood (the mystical water of life), the fundamental factors of being. Kep is the mystery in relation to the water, the fertilization of the red Nile, and gives the name to red as a colour in the Dravidian KAVI for red ochre. On this line of life we have the Hebrew הוא for life; Russian GIVOY, living; Welsh CHWYF, a motion of life, swelling, as in pregnancy; Old German, QVEH; Sclavonic, SCHIVA; Lithuanic, GWYAS; Maori, HAPU, to be pregnant; Sanskrit, JIVE; Dravidian, JIVA; Vayu, I'VI, to be swelling. On the other line are FOF, Gaelic, to swell; FAOB, Gaelic, swelling; PEPO, Swahili, a spirit; PABA (Eg.) the soul; PEVAH (Heb.), to breathe; PABO, Welsh, the producer of life; BHÁVA, Sanskrit, being, becoming, existing; PEFU (Xosa Kaffir), breath or soul, as in PEFUMLO, the soul of man; BOBON, African Nki, a spirit, or God; BAB (Eg.), to exhale; BUBE, Galla, breath or wind; worn down forms being found in the Tamil AFA, breath: Greek, FUO; Amoy, BOE, to be, not yet; and Zend BÛ, to be. Both HEV and SHEP are modified on two different lines of derivation from KHEF or KEP. Khep (Eg.) means to generate, exist, cause to be, by turning liquid into solid, as Khepr, the creator by transformation, does in the pictures at Biban-el-Muluk, or, as the genitrix did in SHEPS, to conceive; Hebrew גבש, to curdle, clot, lump (like butter in the churn), draw and bind together. KEP (Eg.) is the name of that mystery of heat and fermentation in which the SPIRIT of life is evolved from matter in the matrix of the Mater, who was the Egyptian KEFA and the Hebrew CHAVVAH, or יהוה, as the feminine creator. The Assyrian BASÛ contains both of these Egyptian roots reduced and combined to form one word.

The verb RILU used in the second Akhemenian in the sense of

[1] Vol. i. p. 244.

writing, is, says an Assyrian scholar, purely Ugrian, as the Magyar IRO shows. But vain are all such certifications with Egypt omitted. The RU or RUI (Eg.) is the reed-pen and paint of the scribe ; RU (Eg.) likewise denotes the written word, the chapter, or discourse. RILU contains both elements. The reed RU appears in the Hindustani BARU, the reed from which pens are made, and the Polish PIORO for the pen. This RU also occurs in the Assyrian Zakaru, to record. Sakha (Eg.) is to write, depict, pourtray, and RU is the pen or the record, whence SKHARU for the picture, portrait, or record. Moreover, RIRU (Eg.) means to traverse, go round and round, as in the ogham circle, or the circular writing continued to a late time at Cambridge for diplomas ; and the ogham writing is the RURU or RILU in this sense of being circular, whence the Roll. No matter how late the oghams may have been repeated, nothing is earlier than their foundation in the circle, the first writing or " ret "-ing in stone, with the digital alphabet.[1] The first writer or incisor, however, did not use the reed-pen but the graver, and RUT is to engrave, figure, retain the form in stone. Whence SHETRUT from SHET to work, prepare (the stone), and RUT to engrave. The writer was then the RUT, a mason or stone-cutter and polisher. This Ret is the Cornish Roath, to form and figure ; and RHYTHIA, to rub ; the reed is also named from this root. But the word WRITE implies a form beginning with K, which turns RUT into KART, the earlier name of the mason or stone-cutter, and of the Hebrew Stylus or Graver, the CHART used for inscribing. The Kart (Eg.), KARTUM, or Rekhi-khet (ιερογραμματεύς), was the cutter of hieroglyphics. The name of writing as cutting in stone is synonymous with that of the Karti, Kaldi, and Keltæ, and the KART as mason and as race modifies into the RUT. The Magyar IRO goes back to KIRO, the Egyptian Kheru for speech, utterance, expression, or cutting in stone by the Kart or Kar-natr. IRO in Japanese is ACCENT, which answers to the cutting and carving, to emphasize the form.

In Assyrian the Kan is the reed-sign of writing, and the name of the volume, as in the KAN-MAGARRI, a book of worship or prayers. In the hieroglyphics the Kan (Ken) is the sculptor-scribe's chisel, also the cartouche, in which inscriptions were cut, together with the ivory and bone, the hard and enduring material used for carving ; the Kannu being the simple inscriptions, titles, or names inscribed *on* the Kan, *by* the Kan, *with* the Kan. Then the Kan became the reed (English cane) for writing. This shows the earliest application of the word KAN afterwards applied to the written volume. The Kana as reed passes into the Kan as book, and that this was made of papyrus-reed may be gathered from the fact that in the Egyptian KANANA, for PULP, we catch the KAN midway in its passage between the papyrus-reed and the papyrus made from the reed.

[1] N.B. The word RILU is misprinted Ritu on p. 139, vol. i.

The "RAK-RAK SHA LIBBI KANI" rendered "membranes from the interior of reeds,"[1] and "RAKRAKU" found elsewhere, obviously indicating papyrus, are derived from the Egyptian REKH, to bleach, full, purify, make white, and that gives the process of preparing the paper from the pulp, or KANANA in Egyptian. We still produce paper from bleached RAG, and paper in Arabic keeps the name of URAK. In the African Timne the book is named AREKA. The Hebrew IREK, white, only indicates complexion; Egyptian naming goes to origin. SHA or SHU (Eg.) is papyrus, book, or paper, and one of the "SU" signs is the papyrus root.

The Akkadian ideograph of writing in general is read ALAL. It was pronounced Alal when preceded by the determinative for WOOD. From ALAL came the Assyrian ALALLU. One equivalent for ALAL or alala is BUNNU. Bunnu in Egyptian is palm-wood. The BENI is a palm-branch, and it has the graver's chisel for determinative which shows that it was used for incising signs, letters, and dates. The palm-branch, Beni, was the register of Taht, the divine scribe, who carries it in one hand, with the stylus in the other.

The engraved incriptions, tablets, or printed bricks of Elam and Medea are called in Akkadian DUBBA, Assyrian DUPPU. The earliest form of these is the brick; the brick in Egyptian is TEB, and as the word is also applied to the seal-ring (Teb) for stamping, this indicates the superseded engraving on bricks. The Teb or dip is extant in the Ritual,[2] "Open my mouth, says Ptah, with his book, (or brick) made of mud, fashioning the mouths of the gods by it." The Egyptian Teb, a brick, and afterwards a seal, is the root not only of the Akkadian tablet, but of the English "tab," an affixed mark, table, and tablet, the means of recording. The Akkadian DUB and English TAB are both from Egypt, their relationship has nothing to do with accidental coincidence.[3]

Another Akkadian form of the word or name of the inscribed tablet is DIKH. Tekh (Eg.) denotes stones of memorial, as the obelisk (Tekhn), and therefore engraved stones. Also the TEKAR is the graver; TEK means to cleave, adhere, fix; and Tekh is a name of Taht, the penman and recorder of the gods. Now Taht followed Sut as manifester of the eight great gods, and so far back as we can see the materials for writing are known in Egypt, but TEB, the engraved seal and brick, and Tekh, the stone, the graver, and the god, take us

---

[1] *Tr. Bib. Arch.* vol. iii. p. 444.   [2] Ch. xxiii.
[3] DUBA, in Mandingo, and DUBANA in Soso (African), is ink. DUBH, in Gaelic, DUIBHE, Irish, is ink, as the black. The descending scale of words, which is a result of superseded types, is well illustrated by this word. TEB is the brick and seal-ring in Egypt; DUBBA, the engraved brick, in Akkad; DIPI, Cypriote, a statue. In Mantshu Tartar, TEBOU means reckoning, to keep an account. DUBBI is the African Galla name for a history; TIPPANI, Sanskrit, a gloss, a scholion; DUBY, Polish, an idle tale; Latin, DUBIA; and in Irish, DUBHE is a lie. This is an exact analogy to the descent of TEP (Typhon) from first to last.

still farther into this boundless backward past of the great motherland to Sut, who inscribed the records on the stelæ, and to Typhon, who was the tongue of the still earlier expression, as goddess of the Great Bear. For example, Sefekh, the name of the goddess of writing, abrades into SÊKH, for writing, the writer, the scribe. In Coptic SAGI is the tongue, and as speech preceded writing the tongue was the earlier type of utterance. Sefekh's name is determined by two tongues,[1] and in the Ritual,[2] the woman (Sefekh?) says, "I am the tongue OR the writer." As Taurt she could only put out her tongue for a type of the "living word." To denote speech, says Hor-Apollo they depict a tongue. Sefekh—Sekh deposits the English SAGHE for speech; SAIG, a wise saying, and the words SAW and SAY; our SAYING being equivalent to writing in Egyptian. We shall find Sefekh later in the Akkadian SAKH-Magana.

The Assyrian name of the crocodile is given as NAMSUKHA. In Egyptian it is EMSUH, Em (ma) and Nam are both signs of water. SUH (Eg.) is the egg, and KHA (Eg.) is the fish. Thus NAMSUKHA is named in Egyptian as the fish not only of the waters, but also of the egg, the essential distinction of the crocodile considered as a fish. The syllable "nam" however is susceptible of another rendering; it means to repeat, renew, reproduce. So interpreted, the Namsukha is the fish which is reproduced from the egg; a typical Egyptian expression for the beginning. The Arabic TEMSAH, the crocodile, repeats the form of "tem" reproduced, and Suh the egg. The name of the Namsuh fish (Kha) was worn down in Egyptian to Emsuh.

The god Ninib is called "Nin Kattin barzil," rendered by "the lord of the coat of iron." "KATTIN," says the translator,[3] must be the Hebrew כתן (Katen) a coat: which would only describe the war-god as a deity in armour. But the Egyptian KATEN means an image, similitude, a likeness, and this would make Nin to be the god whose likeness is iron! That stamps the antique, effective figure, more like those nearnesses to nature which they used to coin.

Of the Assyrian ITLU, a warrior, Norris observes,—"The primitive meaning of the word seems to be 'noble,' and if ATTILA be a Hunnish name the connection may be admitted. Even the German EDEL might be allied, as we have some Germanic roots in Akkadian, though the resemblance is probably fortuitous."[4] This was written by a scholar of whom it has been said that his linguistic knowledge was so universal he knew Language rather than Languages. Nothing could better mark the prevailing unsuspiciousness of the African origines which has to account for so much assumed fortuitousness.

In Egyptian ATAI is the noble, the chief; AT is the prince, and TARU is the hero, the unrivalled warrior. The At as prince and

[1] Wilkinson, v. 52.
[2] Ch. lxxx.
[3] H. F. Talbot, *Trans. Soc. Bib. Arch.* vol. iii. 523.
[4] *Assyrian Dictionary*, vol. i. p. 234.

heir-apparent is the Ar (son) royal or divine, whence Adar, the god or the Edel. The Assyrian ITLU has the same significance as the Hebrew ITHR, a noble, a distinguished one, and both are represented by the Egyptian TARU, for the warrior, the unrivalled hero; TA and AT often permute. The ITLU as the strong, hard, unbending, agrees with TARU (Eg.), the name for the pike, as a war-weapon. TARU (Eg.) to bruise, afflict and obliterate, is represented in Arabic by AATL, to treat with great violence; UDLAWIE, Polish, to strangle or choke; ODOL, Basque, blood; ATALE, Egbele, (African) blood; DRA, Fijian, blood; DIRRA, Hindustani, a scourge, and THIR, English, to strike dead; DULA, Galla, destruction; TOLU, French Romance, to be destroyed, annihilated; TAIL, English, slaughter; TALL, Arabic, shedding blood with impunity. The cognates are found in a hundred languages. The ITLU as the noble warrior is at one end and the Attila type of the bloody scourge at the other, and both meet in the Egyptian TARU, the hero alone, and the afflicter and exterminator of men, according to the character and the work of the warrior.

The same writer remarks of the title KASAR, a king, and the Greek Καισαρ : "The resemblance is curious. I hardly venture to suggest any connection, but the word might have been borrowed from the Greeks, the name was recorded historically five centuries B.C., and was no doubt known much earlier."[1]

SAR, in the style of the Assyrian kings, constantly follows the monarch's name as a royal title, and, as in Egyptian, is a worn-down form. USUR, to protect, is identical with USER (Eg.), to support, defend, and maintain; the USER sceptre being the symbol of protecting and sustaining Power. So the Assyrian Nasaru, to protect, represents the work of the Egyptian NASRU, who is the superintendent, overseer, governor or victor, and the Sar answers to the Seri (Eg.), chief, head.

User is an earlier Suser for the regulator and arranger, found also in Susru, a surname of Anu as the founder, with a still earlier form in Khuser, from Khes, to found, build, construct, make a road; the first User being the consonantal Khuser, as the sign of power, valour, to sustain and maintain, to rule. This root yields the Akkadian GISURU, as wood and beam for bridges, and GISRU (Ass.), the strong, the mighty; both meanings being typified by the User (Khusr), sceptre of backbone. Khusr also furnishes the Arabic WAZIR, for the sustaining and supporting; Hindustani, GAZIR, the hero; Greek KAISAR, and Latin CÆSAR. In the time of the third dynasty the original Khesr had become the Seser. The Vizier and Nasr both imply different prefixes to a form found in Tser (Hebrew Tzer, Russian Tsar), as the earlier rock-type of sustaining and protecting power.

In "Bel-Sar-usur," meaning Bel protect the Sar, or king, the word

[1] Norris, *Dictionary*, vol. ii. p. 624.

USUR is a verb, so is Khesr (Eg.), to disperse, dissipate and make clear, answering to the Assyrian KAZIR, the restorer. But USUR is invoked in the fragment of an old Ritual, as the "Striker of Fortresses," "who has opened the hostile land like a whirlwind." He is also addressed by the name of Khammu.[1] In Egyptian, Khemu has the same meaning of victorious, prevailing power.

Us, is a title applied to the king in the cuneiform. "US AGGA" is used in old Akkadian inscriptions in the sense of the powerful male. Us (Eg.) means large, vast, extended. AS is great, august, noble, the type of supreme rule. SU (Eg.) is royal, the style of the king. Rubu, again, is found to signify a lord or prince. Rubu-mi is the full style, but the value of MI is not ascertained. In the hieroglyphics the Repa is a governor, lord, or prince. MA (Eg.), the equivalent of mi, makes it the true Repa. Seb is called the Ma-Repa of the gods. The title is applied to the repeaters of the time-cycles, Seb being chief; Virgo, the lady, another; the Phœnix another; Repit, the goddess of harvest, another.

The Repa is the lord, and Repit the lady of repetition. Repat is the lady of heaven, the constellation Virgo. With the L instead of R the word is Lubat, a title of Jupiter. Saturn also is called Lubat-Sukus. Indeed, all seven of the planets are designated Lubat by the Chaldeans as the repeaters of periods. Rubatu is the Assyrian for a queen, or the lady of the gods, and in the Ritual Rubata appears as the mystical cow, a primordial shape of the Repat, the lady of heaven.[2]

The Egyptian and Babylonian kings were crowned as rulers over the four countries, the four quarters, typical of the whole, as the four posts typify the bedstead, and the four corners, the house, or as Aft (Eg.), the number four and the four quarters, is also the Abode. Now the term "KIPRAT ARBA" of the inscriptions seems to me to be doubly related to this formula of four. Sargon is said to have conquered the "KIPRA ARBA" of Syria. Naramsin is called king of the KIPRAT ARBA."[3] This has been rendered the "Four Races." The name "KIPRAT ARBA," says Smith, was probably given to the Syrians on account of there being four races or principal states in that region, and he supports this by pointing to a similar division in Genesis, where Aram has four sons, Uz, Hul, Gether, and Mash.[4] Kiprati (Ass.), however, does not merely mean races or regions, it relates to the four quarters. In Egyptian, Rut means the race, and the four Kab, where stood the four Kabbirs, are the four corners. The kings of Egypt and Assyria were proclaimed to be lords of the four corners or quarters, as the synonym of the whole earth, and at the coronation of the Pharaoh four birds were let fly towards the four corners. The Kebruti would be the men of the four quarters, without implying four different races. KEB-RUTI would also denote

[1] Sayce, *Bib. Arch.* vol. i. p. 30ᵗ.   [2] Ch. clxiii.
[3] *Rec. of the Past*, vol. v. pp. 60, 63.   [4] x. 23.

the several corners, or the four without the Arba ; these were the four corners of the mount of the four supports of heaven, represented by Khibur (Hebron), and other sacred hills.[1] Arba does but repeat the four.

As we see in the Hebrew the terminal "OTH" corresponds to Aft (Eg.) for number four, the four corners, and thus interpreted the Assyrian Kiprati, and Hebrew Kaphereth, answer to Kab-r-aft or Khepr-aft, the four corners of the Kabbirs, and of Khepr, the circle-clasper, in the place of joining and unifying. This enables us to re-found in phenomena.

The light to be derived from Egypt will save the cuneiform scholar much groping among the Akkadian ideographs. The variants of the character "Id" for the hand, supply a particular case in point.[2] An ideographic ID obviously represents the Egyptian IT, to figure, paint, pourtray, with the hand of the artist for determinative. The hand, ID, it should be premised, was the earliest kind of comb, with the digits for its teeth, and as the *m* and *p* permute Khep (Eg.), the hand is identical with Khem or comb. Kame is an English name for the comb. In Egyptian, Khept is the doubled hand or fist, and the terminal ti (two) makes the Khep dual ; thus Khepti is two hands, as Kabti is two arms or hands. Khemti for number ten, is the equivalent of Khepti, both hands. The genitrix as Khepti, is thus the two hands of creation. The two hands as Khebti are a double Kame or comb ; and the double-toothed comb was an especial ideograph of the motherhood. It is found on the tombs of the LURS as a sign of the female sex ; it is carried by the mermaid, who impersonates the Two Truths of the water and the breath of being.

In Assyrian the hand is KATU, an abraded form of KHEPT (Eg.) which wears down to ID, the Hebrew JAD, and Ashanti IDU, for number ten. This ID in a most ancient form, as shown by a tablet in the British Museum,[3] presents the picture of a double-toothed comb, a sign of maternity. The ID, with the value of number ten, is the representative of Khepti and Khemti, the two hands and ten fingers. The double comb, then, was an image of the two hands, and of the goddess Khept, or Apt, who in the first, the hippopotamus form, had no hands, but had four feet. Now the ID sign has an equivalent in NER, a foot. So the Kaph (Heb.) is both hand and foot. Hand and foot are thus a form of Khepti, the latest form of which is ID, the Hebrew Jad for No. 10 or two hands.

The ID, or hand, will show us in Egyptian how the sign, which is also connected with Kar, may have a real relationship, as Kar (Eg.) is the name of the claw, meaning to seize, lay hold, or claw hold ; and the claw is an earlier form of the hand.

---

[1] Brugsch, *Geog.* ii. 76.
[2] See the Rev. W. Houghton's paper on the "Picture Origin of the Assyrian Syllabary," *Trans. Bib. Arch.* vol. vi. part ii. p. 454.   [3] *Ibid.*

Another curious equivalent of ID, is a figure with four knobs. These correspond to the four feet of the genitrix whose name of Apt also signifies the four corners of the first celestial circle or square, that of Khepsh or the Great Bear. The ID in this shape bears the likeness of the Kam, or comb, of the crocodile's tail with four points, worn by the Typhonian genitrix. The same sign signifies power, and Kefa is power and puissance in person. It likewise expresses the idea of the throne and seat, and the old goddess was the seat, represented by the hinder part, the seat or throne being a type of the bearer. IT is also found as place in the Proto-Medic inscriptions of the Akhemenides. IT (Eg.) is place, and a name of heaven. Finally the character attains unity, and is an ideograph of ONE. That one is the old genitrix who was one as the Great Bear, the bearer, and bringer-forth; one as the seat; one as the place, the uterus; dual as the two bears, or the two hands, when the human figure was applied; fourfold and four-footed as the hippopotamus of the four quarters; ten-fingered, as the two hands, the equivalent of which was the double comb. The comb is a reminder that the NIT still bears the name of the genitrix as Neith.

There is a meeting-point between Egyptian and Assyrian in the name of the moon as IDU or ITU, the same as the name of the hand. Uti, the lunar god, is Taht or Tut, and Tut (Eg.) is a name for the hand; Uti or Tahuti (Tut) was the hand (as well as the speech or Logos of the gods), he being the measurer and weigher, and Uti has the value of number five. IT (Eg.) means to figure forth with the hand. This connection of the hand and moon under one name will enable us to read the typology of Job's saying,[1] that if he beheld the moon walking in brightness and his heart was secretly enticed, he did not kiss his hand, or יד, as the true lunarite would have done. The moon as IDU was equivalent to the hand, because it re-shaped its orb of light.

Considerable evidence of common origin might be adduced by means of the different words derived from the same ideographic type. KAF, for the hand, wears down to SU in Akkadian, and SU in Egyptian is the word for No. 5. REKH or LEKH (Eg.) means to know, reckon, keep account: the knowers were the Rekhi. In Akkadian, LIKKU names the dog and the lion, two types of the Rekh, or Regulus as the Dog-star and Lion-God.

The cuneiform sign for number ten ⟨ is a square or wedge-shaped adaptation of the Egyptian ideograph ∩ for ten, formed from the two hands clasped together and cut off at the wrists.

The ideograph of king used in the Elamite and other texts, was pronounced ISSEP in Akkadian.

In the hieroglyphics the ideograph of the great, noble, ruler is the AS throne, with the ruler seated. A variant of the same image reads SHEPS or SEPS. The SEP likewise is a throne. Another form

[1] xxxi. 26, 27.

of the name of the throne is the ASEP, ASEB, or AS-BUT, the feminine type. The Asep as the throne is the Elamite ISSEP which as As-sep reads the great throne, the fitting ideograph for the king.

In quoting the As-but as the full form of the royal seat, it may be noted that the Mandingo negroes designate the house by the name of "HOUSE-BELLY," the belly-house being the womb, and As (Eg.) is the house, chamber, abode; the BUT is the belly, so that As-but is literally the belly-house or womb, the But or Beth of As, Hes, Isis, the divine abode.

The particular ideogram which expresses the name of Akkad is formed by doubling that of the verb "BUR," to rise, swell, tumefy. This is the Egyptian BUR to well, boil, bubble up. Bur-bur denotes ebullition. Bur-bur (Eg.) means the cap, top, roof, and supreme point of height, the summit. Ber-Ber, the summits, is a name of Akkad, and Akhut (Eg.) is the height above the horizon, the place of sunrise or the resurrection (Khut, the mount of the east).

A cross is the symbol of the old Anu of the Assyrian mythology, and ANNU is the Egyptian place of the crossing and equinox, also of Anit (Neith) who brings forth the child of the crossing.

Certain emblems of the gods Shamas and Marduk are named LIMAZI, rendered Cherubim by Smith. One form of the Hebrew cherub was the Egyptian Khepr, the beetle (or two beetles) stationed at the point of recommencement in the solstitial year. Khereb (Eg.) is the model primeval type, first form and figure of the beginning. The Assyrian and Babylonian beginning was equinoctial from the time when the spring equinox was in the Fishes. This is the meaning of the Fish of Hea and of Oannes. Thus the fish was their Khereb,— this, in case there is authority for translating the Babylonian LIMAZI by the Hebrew cherubim. REM (Eg.) is the fish, and ASI are the statues. The fish-statues are pre-eminently the Assyrian types of beginning instead of the beetles and the bears, or hippopotamus. The fish was sacred to Marduk who personates the fish of Hea. The fish (or fishes) is at the point of commencement, the place of the seven gods in the Assyrian zodiac; Pisces being the sign of the seven great gods, Rem in Akkadian is a point of beginning which is in the fish, Rem, or fishes, Rem-rem (Eg.). Therefore it may be inferred that this beginning in and with the fish is typified by the Limazi, or Rem-asi, as the fish-statues. The fish is a Khereb in the sense of a primary type and model figure of the commencement.

The sign "TAK," says the Rev. W. Houghton, is a very puzzling character. It is rendered by the Assyrian ABNU, a stone, although none of the ancient forms have any likeness to a stone. Now the Egyptian ABN is a wall, with the usual sign of the inclosure, rampart, or fortress. TEKA is a boundary, and to fix. The god Tekh is the measurer and limit-fixer of earth and heaven. The Tekht are the masons and stones for building. May not the Akkadian TAK be explained by the Egyptian Teka and Abn, the sign of a boundary wall, an inclosure, or rampart? Ak, Akkadian, to build, with the Egyptian article Tu as prefix, forms the word "tak," which is obviously related to building. Ak, to build, may not appear in Egyptian as the name for building, which is At, but we find Akh, to work, to perform. Also one of the oldest kinds of building was wattling with branches, twigs, and reeds, and the earlier sign of AK, to build, as described by Rawlinson, contains a picture of reed-matting. Matted reeds are wattled or twisted together, and the idea is conveyed by AK (Eg.), to twist, to make a rope or cable, therefore to wattle or make reed-matting as a primitive kind of building. The Irish TOCHARS were wattle-work.

It may be noted that the Egyptian ideograph of the wall is the determinative of Sapti, to construct, and the wall or rampart by name is Sebti, whilst the Akkadian sign [1] that denotes brick and brick-work also determines the month Sivan, the month of brick-making. In Akkadian the month Sivan is MUNGA, and in Egyptian Munka (or Menka) is the name of pottery, utensils, things made, and the word means to make, form, work, build. MUNGA, for the brick-making corresponds to MENKA, for making pottery or other things of earth.

The Assyrian Rabu, a prince, represents the Repa (Eg.), the prince and heir-apparent of the throne of Ra. The Rabu was represented by a sceptre, a staff, or a beam of wood. Standing by itself, says Professor Sayce, the sign would be the sceptre carried by the prince, and hence the prince himself.[2] So in the hieroglyphics the Kherp is both the prince, his majesty, and the sceptre of his authority, and this Kherp is a form of the Rep or Repa, the prince, or branch.

In an archaic Babylonian form a hand is added to show that the staff-sceptre was carried in the hand. So in the hieroglyphics the SER for chief ruler, denoted by the hand holding the wooden Pet sceptre, is the determinative of SER, the chief one, the Kherp; and Ser is a worn down form of Uscr and Keser, or Khuser.

Kheb, Kefa, or Kufa, is the name of the genitrix as the *enceinte* bearer of the child represented by the water-horse. This type, like those of the cow, fish, and frog, was adopted before boats were used to cross the waters. Ta-urt, a name of the northern Kefa, is the chariot when this was the womb. Khept wears down into Aft, another name of the bearer, as the hippopotamus. Teb is also one of her names.

When boats were built we find the earliest type-names were derived from the ancient genitrix. The Kabni (Eg.) is a vessel, a ship, the Cabin of the English vessel. The UBO in Ibu, and EVU in Adampe, is a canoe; the KPERO, African Kiambo, a canoe; CABARR, Scotch, a lighter; CAYVAR, English, a kind of ship; KEFFER, German, a light boat. From Teb comes the TEBA or Ark, and the Tub, an English name for an old ship; the TAVIO, Fiji, part of a canoe;

---

[1] Sayce, No. 507. [2] *Trans. Society Bib. Arch.* vol. vi. part ii. p. 479.

TAPA, Hindustani, a kind of boat; TABO, Portuguese, a ship. Ship and skiff are forms of the name of Kheb; and one of the most primitive boats, was the womb-shaped skiff still used on the lower Tigris and Euphrates, found depicted on ancient Assyrian sculptures. This round hive-like vessel is called the " KEFA," and still retains the name of the first bearer of the waters.

"Enclosed in a box" is given on the tablets as the equivalent of " NU-U-HU." This, says the translator, will afford us a new meaning for the name of Noah, and perhaps the derivation of the word.[1] Unfortunately for the suggestion, this enclosure of Noah, according to the hieroglyphics, might have been NNUH, a rope-noose, to twist and tie, as this is one of the signs of enclosing, and is really a form of the ark itself, a determinative of ark, to surround, envelop, enclose, to appoint a limit, fix by decree, the end of a period. The noose of Taurt was, so to say, the first form of the ark enclosure. This enclosure of Noah (or NUM) may also be a water-vase, can, or khen, a house, or a box even, with which the god Num's name is written as a phonetic Nu, ideographic Num.[2] The meaning of NU-U-HU does not start from the box interpreted by the ark of Noah. But more of this when we come to the Deluge.

In the deluge mythos one of the birds sent out of the ark, rendered the raven, is named " A-RI-BI." Ribi is identical with RAV in RAVEN. The original of both may be found in the phœnix bird, a determinative of Repa or Repat. The phœnix Repa, Ribi, or raven, is the type of the cycle repeated by one period passing or transforming into another, represented by the consuming phœnix or Repa re-arising from its own ashes. The Bennu-Osiris was a form of the phœnix of the year, the symbolical bird of return and renewal. Such is the nature of the Ribi or Repa wherever found.

The scarabæus that rolled up its seed in excrement, and was taken by the Egyptians for a type of the Creator, may be seen in the drawings from the tombs of Biban-el-Muluk busily employed in seizing the seed as it issues from the source, and transforming it into living souls. Thus Khepr the Creator, as generator, is pictured as the " seizer of seed."

The earliest form of the sign of Cancer in Egyptian zodiacs is the beetle, the emblem of Khepr-Ra, who, at Biban-el-Muluk is pourtrayed as the seizer of seed; Khepr in the abraded form of Kêr means to seize with the claws, as did the scarab.

Now the Akkadian name of the month Tammuz (June) is SU-KUL-NA, "SEIZER OF SEED," and its zodiacal sign is Cancer, the Scarab Khepr of the Egyptians. The seizer of seed then, in the occult sense, who is pourtrayed in the zodiac as the beetle, is reproduced by the Akkadian name of the month, SU-KUL-NA.

The year in the Aramaic-Akkadian calendar began with the

[1] Smith, "Chaldean Account of the Deluge," *Trans. Society Bib. Arch.* vol. iii. p. 591.　　　　　　　　　　　　　[2] Lep. *Denk.* iv. 70, f.

month NISANNU, the month of the equinox, the crossing and coming out of ANNU, when the sun left the fish-sign of An, the place of the Babylonian seven great gods. NAS (Eg.) corresponds to the Assyrian Nisu for up-lifting, up-rising; the NUSA being a pedestal for elevating. Nas also means " out of," and as the year began with the sun's up-rising out of Annu, this seems to be the likeliest origin for the name of the month NISANNU. The names for the month of July (roughly) and January in this calendar are Abu and Sabahu (Aramaic, Ab and Sebat), and the names point to their having been the first and seventh months of a year corresponding to the Egyptian sacred year which began with the month Taht (July 20), a Sothic year preceding the solar with the commencement at the vernal equinox.

In the inscription of Khorsabad, the king relates that he has placed between the doors of the temple four KUBUR on NIRGALLI; " towards the four celestial regions I turned their front." The twin-lions of the horizon, the Rehiu or Ruti are an Egyptian type; they supported the sun at the equinoctial level. The four Kubur are a form of the four Kabari, the four companions of the four quarters. The Keb (Eg.) is a lord of the angle; Kab is the corner; Ari denotes the companions, guards, keepers; the four Kabari were the genii of the four quarters, ape-headed, jackal-headed, bird-headed, and human-headed. M. Oppert describes the passage on the NIRGALLU as very difficult, and says the " Name of Nergal does not interfere with the object."[1] The Gallu, in Assyrian, are a class of evil spirits. Nir (Eg.) means victory and to vanquish. The Nirgallu were probably typical of victory over evil spirits. One of Nirgal's types was the cock, a bird of dawn, at whose warning crow the evil spirits were supposed to vanish. The Egyptian Nir (Nar) is a vulture, as the sign of victory or vanquishing.

It is said of evil spirits, or demons, that they devour men like " KIMI." This word is rendered in Akkadian by Ku. These Ku, or Kimi, have been translated sparrows, but the KHEMI of the hieroglyphics is a quail, and this is probably the KIMI of the tablets. The Khu is another hieroglyphic bird of return, though different from the quail. The hieroglyphic Khu is the symbol of a spirit. It was a bird of passage and periodic return, and, therefore, of prophecy. Nam (Eg.) means to announce and proclaim. The Akkadians had their NAM-KHU, the foretelling or prophet-bird, supposed to be a species of swallow.

In the deluge tablet the word RUKI is an epithet applied to Xisuthrus, as denizen of that other world to which he has gone. Ruki has been rendered "remote." Xisuthrus had emigrated to a country where he dwells in the company of the gods. He is in spirit-world, and in Egyptian Rukh is the pure soul; the RUKHI are the holy spirits, the wise and pure intelligences, whether here or in

[1] *Records of the Past*, ix. 19.

spirit-world. The Rukhi, as pure spirits, are shown to be immortal by the phœnix sign of resurrection, and Xisuthrus as a RUKI, is considered to be one of these.

In the Creation legends two kinds of beings are spoken of, called the ADMI and SARKU. The one are a people of darkness, the other of light. Both are entirely mythical, and neither is ethnological, therefore we need not enter into the discussion of the light and dark races on human grounds. The dark people are also called NISI-ZALMAT-KAKKADI. In one of the Syllabaries, says Mr. Boscawen, we find the ideograph for corpse, "PAGRU," accompanied by the signs for black, and rendered in the Assyrian by ADAMATU, and in the later inscriptions we find ADMU used for men instead of the ordinary word Nisu;[1] again, the same sign occurs accompanied by the ideograph for white, and is rendered by the Assyrian Sarku, a word meaning light. In the Kutha tablet, says the same writer, which contains the earliest of all the Creation legends, there is a curious use of two different words for men who are placed in opposition to one another, as though indicating a similar difference to that in the case of the Admi and Sarku. In one instance they are men with the bodies of birds of the field, and human beings with the faces of ravens. Here, the imagery, being Egyptian, concerns us. For these are imaged according to the typical birds of light and darkness, of life and death, of the upper and the under world. "I went in as a hawk; I came out as a phœnix," expresses the typical transformation in the Ritual. The hawk, the bird of light, belongs to the ascending sun or spirits of light. The phœnix or nycticorax is a bird of darkness; with us it is the owl. This is represented by the black bird of night, the raven. Khu (Eg.) is light, spirit, the bird of light and spirit. Sar, as in Assyrian, denotes the chief or head. The Sar-Khu would be the chief spirits. The raven and the corpse ideograph equate with the black doll-symbol, not of death but of the shades below, or of life in the shades, which is a variant of the tie, the symbol of life in the light.

Atum alone amongst the gods has the black doll image for one of his signs. He is the great god of the dark, and judge of the dead in the nether world. It has now to be suggested that the Admi, the dark beings, and the raven-headed, belong to the realm of Atum, the sun of the Hades; and that the Sarku, the other bird-headed people, are the children of light, as in the Egyptian mythology. The sun-god, Tammuz, is identical with Atum, through Adonis, the sun who descends into the lower world, where he is sought for by Ishtar. Atum was the earlier Aten or Adon, the child of the mother, who became the creative father of a later worship, and as such is the pro-genitor of the Admi, or Adamic race of mythical beings, the men of

---

[1] In Persian, also, ADMI signifies man, HOMO; ADAM, in Lughman; ADAM, Curali (Lesgian); ADMA, Adaiel.

earth (the red earth), as the earth is a form of the lower of two heavens, or the mid-most of three regions.

In the Akkadian cuneiform the ideographic sign which renders the idea of god and heaven is a star. The star in Egypt is a hieroglyphic of heaven as the Tep. Tep is the upper, the southern heaven, and the lower heaven is the Tept or Tepht. This modifies into Tuaut, and is written with the star for Tua or Tep. The night-heaven is the lower of two, the Tepht; hence the sign of the star has the value of Tep, the heaven, determined by the duplicative T for Tepht and Tuaut.

UN, the period, the hour, is written with a star. So the year was signified by a star, the star Sebti or Sothis, the dual of Seb, the duplicator of time.

An early figure of the zodiac was that of the human body, the head being in the sign where the sun rose at the time of the spring equinox; the feet in the sign preceding. The head of Osiris, whose body was represented as divided into various parts, was supposed to be in Abtu, the point of commencement in the circle. This human image of the zodiac will explain the expressions employed in the astronomical and astrological tablets of Babylon, such as "from the first day of Nisan to the thirtieth day of Ve-Adar, *head-and-tail completely*, such a one lives," or "*head-and-tail to head-and-tail completely*, so-and-so goes to destruction;"[1] this, like the human type of the zodiac, being a figure of totality.[2]

In the Babylonian creation Anu is said to select certain stars as measuring stars, and regulators of time and period called "period stars." A list of seven of these is given[3] named the "Measures." The proper name is TAMSIL and the determinative denotes a sheep or flock. These were the shepherding stars of the celestial flock. Sil, or Ser (Eg.), means to regulate, dispose, arrange, be at the head. The Ser is also the name of the builder's measuring-line. The guiding-stars and time-keepers were known by the name of the Disposers. Tam, in Akkadian, is a day, but the word Tamsil is the Amsil formed with the T prefix, and T-am is the equivalent of Am-t (Eg.). Am is written with the cross sign, and is a figure of crossing, like Tek of the Tekani (Decani), or stars that crossed every ten days. AMT means in the middle of, that is, in the mid-heaven, the centre at the moment of culmination, the transit or crossing. In the calendar of astronomical observations found in the royal tombs of the twentieth dynasty, the crossing stars are described in seven different positions pourtrayed by means of the human figure, thus:—1. left shoulder; 2. left ear; 3. left eye; 4. in the middle; 5. right eye;

---

[1] *Bib. Arch.* vol. iii. part i. p. 161.

[2] Possibly this type of head-and-tail was also illustrated in the transfer of authority, when the English father presented his son-in-law with one of his daughter's shoes on the wedding-day, and the husband struck the wife a blow on the head with the shoe, showing that she was his, head-and-foot, or completely?

[3] W. A. I. 57.

6. right ear; 7. right shoulder. This chart of the seven positions, and measure of seven degrees, will probably be found to be connected with the Akkadian Tamsil, and the seven measures of starry time. The first Tamsil, whether as constellation or crossing-stars, were the seven stars of Ursa Major, the seven of the Chinese bushel measure, and the seven in number still dominates in the measure by seven vertical lines being drawn to determine the passage of the stars.[1] As so often iterated, for the sake of saving the reader the trouble of continual cross reference, the Great Bear constellation was depicted as the Typhonian goddess of gestation, the hippopotamus, one of whose names is Teb. The star Dubhe, in the Great Bear, still preserves the name of Teb or Typhon in heaven. Also Tabi is an Egyptian name of the bear. The Assyrian name of the bear is Dabu, and this is applied to the constellation KAKABU DABI, the star of the Bear. But the difficulty of Assyriologists has been to determine the nature of the animal when the name was used. For instance, the word SAKH is the Akkadian equivalent for the Assyrian Dabu, and one translator finds the name to be more appropriate to the hippopotamus than to the bear; another doubtfully suggests the beaver, and each without reference to those Egyptian things which determine the names. The Teb was the hippopotamus of Egypt, and the name was afterwards given to the bear, or rather the bear followed the water-horse as the image of the bearing mother, Teb. The Akkadian name of the bear is Sakh, and in Egyptian Sakh denotes the illuminator and enlightener. Sâhu (Sakhu) also means to perambulate, go round, a revolving group of stars. Orion, for instance, is a SÂHU or SAKHU. But the seven stars constituted the first SAKHU. These, with Sirius added, are the eight signified by the eight-pointed star of Sut as before explained.

In Egyptian the number seven in one form is written SEFEKH, in another Sekhef. My own conclusion is that these resolve into Sef or Kef with the value of number five, or the hand, which with the terminal ti signifies number seven, as Sebti, Hepti or Khepti, and that the name of the goddess Seven (read Sefekh) really denotes the secondary form of Sef or Khef, needing the two horns or tongues, as the TI to make the full sign of number seven.

Skhef will deposit both Sef and Khef as types for number seven; Skhef and Sefkh will modify and meet in Sekhu with the passing of f into u. Here alone, in Egyptian, do we unearth a root or typeword for a particular form of the Seven found in SCHUH, Norway Gipsy; SIK, Arago, (Papuan); TSOOK, Skwali; TSEEK-WAH, Skittegats; HUISCA, Guajiquiro; SHAKOEE, Yankton (Sioux); SHAHKO, Winebago; SHAKOPI, Dacotah; SEIGBE, Khotovzi (Yeniseian); SQWITHI, Mingrelian; S'KIT, Lazic; ISGWIT, Suanic; S'WIDI, Georgian; Targumic, Zgtha (זנתא), synonymous with GAISH for a group of (Seven?) stars; SEACHT, Irish; SEACHD, Scotch; SHIAGHT,

[1] See Calendar and Diagram, Renouf, *Bib. Arch.* vol. ii. part ii.

Manx, which latter modify into SEYTH, Cornish, and SAITH, Welsh. SKHF then is probably the older form of Sakhu and Sâhu, the constellation which is identified by the Akkadian Sakh as the seven stars or the sevenfold-star of the Bear. Nor is this the only form of the seven or seventh to be found under the name, for SAKUS was the Assyrian Kaivanu, the Hebrew כיון Kivan, the star of Israel which has been mixed up with the male Saturn; Lubatu SAKUS being a title of Saturn. SAKUS as the planet Seven agrees with this derivation of Sakh for the seven stars, whilst the seven and seventh of Sakhu and Sakus afford good evidence that the earlier typical Sakhu or Sâhu (Eg.) was the constellation of seven stars, and that all these are forms of the word SKHF for number seven.

The Bear is also named Sakh-Khussu, in Assyrian Russu. In Egyptian KHUS means the turner back or returning one, and RUS signifies to rise up, watch, and be vigilant. The seven stars of the Bear were the earliest revolvers and watchers, the illuminators of the mind's eye of the first observers. The Bear is likewise designated, in Akkadian, SAKH-SIKA. SIKA (Eg.) means to drag and draw with the leg for determinative, and the Bear is the constellation of the hinder thigh. SIKA (Eg.) is also the plough, another name of the same constellation. Further, the Bear is called SAKH-MAGANNA, and Magan or Makan has been identified as Egypt, or the ship-region. The Bear of Egypt is the hippopotamus, the Egyptian type of the goddess of the seven stars. The pregnant hippopotamus, the bearer of the waters, was the primordial ark; she was Teb, the living Teba; before boats were built she was the ship of the north.

MA-KHAN (Eg.) means the bearer of the waters, and when the Egyptians could build a boat they named it the MAKHAN, from Ma, water (or the mother), and Khan, to carry, bear, transport, navigate. The Makhennu is the boat of souls, and the primordial image of this in heaven was the group of seven stars, whose Khenit or sailors were the seven Kabiri, of the Sakh-Maganna, the bearer as the Bear. The proof of this is furnished by the seven spirits of the Great Bear being called the planks in the boat of souls, which is the Makhennu. The mundane type of the boat appears in the MAGANA (Tasmanian), the name of the MONS VENERIS or uterus, the primordial Makhen as the boat of the living. In the Kiwomi and Coehetimi dialects MAICHANA is the name for number seven, which illustrates the interchange of the original type-names. In the same way Maganna as the name of Egypt equates with Khebt which also has the value of number seven, from KHEP the hand, and TI, two, whence Hepti for No. 7.

In the Chaldean creation it is said of the god "He made the year into quarters," and the word for quarters is MIZRATA, sometimes written MIZRITI; the etymology is uncertain. MEST (Eg.) represents the Hebrew MITZ in Mitzraim, and is the birthplace; ret or rat is to repeat, be repeated, several. MEST-RAT yields the divisions of the birthplace, and these were the four quarters. Mazzaroth then is first-named from the birthplace of the beginning, formed of the four quarters of the Great Bear, where we find the star Mizar in the tail or Mest-ru. Moreover the Hebrew terminal in מזרות represents the AFT (Eg.) of the four quarters, and Mitzr-aft is the Mitzr of the four quarters, which belonged either to the constellation or the circle of the Great Bear before Mazzaroth had been extended to the circle of the signs and the four quarters of the solar zodiac. The moon is said to complete its hours (make its dual lunation) in Arbati MIZRITI, or four quarters.[1] The division of the circle of the constellation into quarters is marked in the UMAZZIR for " HE DIVIDED " the year into the twelve months. The Maz-arta, a watch, was then derived from the division of the night or circle of the stars into quarters. A Watch was a piece of time long before it was a timepiece.

In one of the twelve romances of mythology, as the Assyrian version of the ancient legends may be termed, in the sixth tablet of the story of Izdubar, the god Anu is described as creating a Bull at the request of Ishtar, who is desirous of being revenged on the solar hero who resisted her blandishments. Ishtar with her two attendants (a form of the two divine sisters) leads the bull against the city of Erech. With this bull Izdubar and his companion Heabani struggle; Heabani holding it by the head and tail, while Izdubar pierces the animal with his sword. This subject is represented on the cylinders where we see the god or hero fighting with the bull. Sometimes two persons are seen in conflict with two bull-beings, and these two bulls correspond to the double-headed bull of Egypt, whose mythology will help us here as elsewhere.

The bull, like the crocodile of the west, was made into an image of the swallower, the mouth of Hades, the Kr-p-Ru, Kherp-ru, or Kerberus. The earth that swallows up the sun and the souls in the west is described in certain passages of the Book of Hades as a two-headed bull which swallowed them in the west to reproduce them in the east.[2] " Honour to the soul which was swallowed by the double bull," says the same text, " the god (Ra) rests in what he has created." The mummies standing waiting in their porch cry to the sun-god, " Open the earth! Traverse Hades and sky! Dissipate our darkness! O Ra, come to us! The earth is open to Ra." The swallowing earth being typified by the bull will serve to explain the subject of Mithras slaying the bull, which it was impossible to read until we knew what it was the bull represented. The bull being also a well-known symbol of the sun, and Mithras a solar god, it was impossible to see how Mithras, the sun personified, could be slaying the sun. The Egyptian symbolism explains both the Assyrian and the Mithraic. The sun is in Scorpio,[3] but he enters the underworld as the destined

---

[1] *Bib. Arch.* vol. v. part ii. pp. 438-440.   [2] Pl. 2; 3, C.
[3] Mithraic monuments according to Hyde. Drummond, pl. 13.

conqueror of the devouring Earth, or comes into conflict with the bull.
The great mountain of Mul-Gelal, the glory of the mountains, the
mountain of the west where the sun set, is said in an Akkadian
inscription [1] to lie like a buffalo in repose. That will serve for an
image of the bull, the earlier cow of the west, or crocodile, or whale.
In the Akkadian magical texts the gate of Hades is kept by the bull
who is invoked, "Oh bull, very great bull, which opens to the interior.
The entrance to the tomb is thy act; the lady with the magic wand [2]
—Nin-gis-zida, a title of the goddess Nin-ki-gal—fashioned thee for
eternity." The station is at the boundaries, the limits which fix the
division between heaven and earth, where the sun entered the underworld of the souls, the mouth of the swallower, whether considered
as an animal, a fish, or the gaping grave.

A passage is quoted by M. Lenormant from the inscriptions to
this effect, "afterwards they lead the bull into the Bit-Mummutu,"
with the remark, "It seems to me that it is connected with the word
mummu, chaos, Hebrew מהמה, confusion; it would then be the abode
of confusion, the state of chaos, which is a very suitable name for
the gloomy and infernal region." [3] But as the Akkadian name of
Hades, Gi-umuna, is identical with the Egyptian Ki-amen, the hidden
land of the interior, and as the Mamit can be identified as the
mummy-type, the Hebrew ממות, it seems more probable that the Bit-
Mummutu is the house of the dead, who are called the Mum (or
mummies) in Egyptian. Also the Mum or Mam (Eg.), a name for
the crossing or passage, precedes the form of AM for the west or
mouth of the Ament. The Bull is a personification of the swallowing
earth, hence an emblem at the gate of the mummy-house of Hades.

A curious figure is mentioned on the tablets and called the
ASSINNU. In the descent of Ishtar to Hades the god Hea
creates a sort of phantom figure, or he takes the figure "ASSINNU,"
breathes life into it, and sends it on an errand to Hades. Talbot
rendered the Assinnu by the figure of a man of clay, Lenormant
by the "phantom of a black man." [4] But the Assinnu is comparatively common. We have it in the English SCIN of the dead,
a phantom; also SWYN in Welsh, as a charm; ZONA, Cornish,
to charm; the TSEEN, Chinese, a demon; the ASNA, Sanskrit, a
demon; AASAN or USUN, Arabic, a typical image or idol; SONA,
Biafada (African), an idol or sacred image; and ZINEY, Wolof
(African), for the devil. The hieroglyphics will show us the character, shape, and colour of the image. SSENU means a typical
figure. SAN is an image, and the word signifies to charm, preserve,
and save. Ssenu and Sena mean to breathe, and the SSENU is an
image of breath. Possibly the Assyrian As-sinnu includes the As
(Eg.) as statue or type, and Sena for breath or breathing. The

---

[1] W. A. I. iv. 27, 2.
[2] Lenormant, *Chaldean Magic*, p. 171, Eng. Tr:
[3] *Chaldean Magic*, p. 170.
[4] *Records*, vol. i. p. 147; *Chaldean Magic*, p. 43.

Sennu itself is a black statue, and as an image of breath or a breathing image it is a variant of the noose sign of life. The Assinnu was black; it is called Namir and Khamir. Na is coloured or black in Egyptian. The Na people, or Nahsi, are negroid, and Kham is also black.

The black Assinnu then is identical with the black doll of the hieroglyphics, which is an image of life in the underworld, or, as we say, of death, the shadow of life, hence its blackness. The Sennu is pourtrayed by the side of Atum, the god of the lower world, who equates with Hea in the male solar triad.

On the death of a righteous man they " bring a KHISIBTA from the heavenly treasury; they bring a SISBU from their lofty storehouse; into the precious KHISIBTA they pour bright liquor. That righteous man, may he now rise on high! May he be bright as that SISBU; like pure silver may his garment be shining white." [1] The SISBU agrees with the SSHEBA (Eg.), a life-giving image, the mummy-figure which was carried round at the feast when the guests were told to look on it as the type of immortality, and rejoice because they also were immortal. SESH (Eg.) means to pass, and BA is to be or become a soul, hence the SSHEB. KHISIBTA renders the Egyptian KHESBET for blue, the lapis lazuli symbol of heaven and of eternal truth. KHESBET or KHISBA is lapis lazuli, the hard blue stone and image of solid heaven, the throne of Ra in the highest heaven, like the Hebrew " paved work of a sapphire stone, as it were the body of heaven in its clearness." This was the foundation-stone of the other world, the stepping-stone of the southern height at the threshold of the door of heaven.

A variant of KHESBET for lapis lazuli is KHEBST (Eg.). The true lapis lazuli was the KHESBET-MA; the KHEBST was inferior, artificial, made of earth. In the inscription of Khorsabad, the king says he placed the DUNU (offerings, tributes) or tablets, some of which were KHIBSTI, made of earth.[2] On these he wrote the glory of the gods. This was the unreal (KHEB, false) lapis lazuli referred to in the Ritual.

Assyriologists have found a mysterious sacred image, mentioned on the tablets, called the "MAMIT" or "MAMITU," the nature of which has caused much perplexity. It is spoken of as a shape of salvation descending from the midst of the heavenly abyss, the " Mamit, Mamit, treasure which passeth not away." It imaged " the one deity who never fails or passes away." Covenants were apparently sworn and pledges taken on the Mamit. It was placed as is the cross in the hands of the dying to drive away evil spirits,[3] but what the image was is unknown. " It was certainly some great mystery, but of what nature has not yet been explained." An oath taken on the Mamit was equivalent to the English " corporal oath,"

---

[1] *Records of the Past*, iii. 135. Talbot.　　[2] *Records of the Past*, vol. ix. 18.
[3] Talbot, *Bib. Arch.* vol. iii. part ii. p. 433.

which, according to Paley, meant an oath taken on the CORPORALE or linen cloth which surrounded the sacred host, the CORPUS DOMINI or mummy of the Lord; and to become perjured by breaking the oath is, in English, to be MAM-SWORN.

The Egyptian mummy figure was the type of the KARAST, the embalmed corpse of the dead, and in another aspect an image of the resurrection. The Assyrians had their CORPORALE or corpse-cloth, and in one of the magical charms instructions are given to take a white cloth and cover the Mamit with it, and then place the Mamit in the sick man's right hand; a black cloth is to be wrapped round the sick man's left hand—the white and black cloth still preserved in the English pall—and then all the evil spirits and the sins which he has committed will quit their hold of him; it is said to be a mystery that God and man are unable to explain. So in the Ritual we read, "Inexplicable is the Sem-Sem, it is the greatest of secrets,"[1] and this relates to the re-genesis for the next life which was typified by the mummy image. Sem-Sem is the equivalent of Shebti the duplicated image (Sem). The relation of the Mamit to the dead is suggested by the name and office of the Assyrian divinity Mamitu, the goddess of fate, who is the determiner of death.

The hieroglyphics will help us as usual, for the Mamit belongs to Egypt, and the name may be derived in one of two ways. MA (Eg.) denotes the likeness, and MAT is dead: the Ma-mat is thus the image in death, or mummy-type. The Egyptian name of the mummy is Mum, the dead. "IT" means to figure forth, picture, image, typify. This "It" is a reduced form of Kheft, the image itself, and Sheft, to fashion. Mum-it or Mum-ta renders the image or type of the dead; the present image of the life that is past, the symbol of saving, or being preserved on a physical plane and thence an eschatological emblem of salvation for the soul. ITI (Ass.) means a thing which supports and upholds as did the Mamit-type in death. In Egyptian, the word Mamit would also read literally the dead in heaven (It); the Mum being transformed into a spiritual body. In the Ritual the dead or the truly living—for the evil alone are the dead—are called mummies, just as are the dead on earth. Mam, in Hebrew, to be lacking, deficient, agrees with the Egyptian Mum, for the dead; the terminal נו or אות denotes the sign of recognition, and the ממות is the name for the corpse as the image of the dead, and the state of lying dead.[2] This is an equivalent for the Assyrian Mamit.

MAMPUS in Malayan means the dead, and MUM (Eg.) is represented (by permutation) in Swahili by MFU, a dead person; by MBA in Nso, and MPAMBE in Marauri, for an idol or divinity. In this relationship the root MM makes very touching revelations in the Maori tongue where the Egyptian Mum for pitch is found in MIMIHA, bitumen, with which the MUM or dead were mummified. MIMITI means dried up or desiccated. MEMEHA is to be dissolved, to pass away. MOMOE is keeping the eyes closed, and being constantly drowsy; MOEMOEA, means to dream; MAMAO, to be afar off, very distant; and MAMAE denotes *the beginning of feeling in pain.*

The word Mamit came to denote a curse and signify a form of incantation, but this was on account of the Mamit, as *thing* and *type* being an image of the dead and token of the hereafter, to which an appeal was made in consecration or execration, blessing, cursing or in covenanting.

The practice of embalming the dead with such perfection as in Egypt necessitates an immense past. It originated in a desire to retain the likeness of life in death, and is at the origin of what is termed ancestor-worship, the true ancestor being, as before suggested, the body or mummy. The cult, as interpreted by Egyptian thought and imagery, does not imply the worship of father and mother or the ancestors of the race so much as the setting up of the Alter Ego or other self. The Sheb-image is the figure or shape of the embalmed dead, and Shebti means the double or duplicate of self.

The SHEB or SHEBTI, the sepulchral shape or likeness, may be followed universally in language under these names. In Zulu Kaffir, SOBI means the likeness; SHABI, in Hindustani; the Shape in English, a picture or likeness; HAVEL, Cornish; EFEL, Welsh, denote the likeness. It was the likeness in death, and in Irish, SAB, ESBHA, and IOBADH are names of death; SHABIM in Arabic, is death; SEBEN in Æthiopic; SEBIN, Chaldee. The SAV, Hindustani, is the dead body, the corpse or mummy. The Sheb image is represented by the OZIBO, African Igu, an idol; ISIAFA, Abadsa, idol. ISAF, Arabic, an image to which sacrifices were offered in front of the Kaaba; the AZAB, Hebrew, idols; SABARU (Akk.), an image. In Fijian the SAVA is a god's house, and the SAUVATU, a stone set up or marked as a sign of Tapu. In Persian the SIPAD is an angel, and the Arabic SABIHAT are the souls of the faithful. ZEPPEL, Circassian, signifies eternal. The Sheb image was a teacher of the eternal, and in Sanskrit the spiritual teacher is an ISHVA. ABTU (Eg.), the likeness, is a modified form of Shebtu, and the Dahome OFODU is an idol or divinity. ABADI, Swahili, means always; EBEDI, Turkish, eternal, everlasting; ABID, Arabic, perpetual; ABAD, Malayan, eternity. When this type of transformation and continuity was carried round at the Egyptian carousal, they drank healths, as it were, to the image of their other selves in spirit-life, their double, and toasted each other to their immortality.

In Assyrian, SHEBER or SIPAR means to send a heavenly message, and the Mamit is the SHEP or SHEB, an image of life to come, a life-giving image; it is called an embodied messenger of heaven. The Mamit is also called the "SAPAR SA SIMA LA LIKRI SAKBA MAMITA," [1] rendered "the jewel whose price cannot be valued is the SAKBA,

[1] Talbot, *Bib. Arch.* vol. ii. part i. p. 42.

otherwise called the Mamita." Again, it is called the "SAKBA! SAKBA, jewel ne'er departing!" That is the Egyptian SHEB in the earlier form of SKAB, determined by the same mummy-type. Skab means the double, like Shebti, or to double and reflect, from Kab, double, with the causative prefix S.

Another Akkadian name for the Mamit is "NAMBARU," which read by the Egyptian NAM, the second, and PRU, appearance or manifestation, shows the application to another, renewed (nam) life. BARU in Assyrian means half, answering to PAR, one-half of the solar house. So read, Nam-baru would indicate the other half or the second life. The Mamit is also called "Salmitu," Salam being to save; the Itu as in Mamitu remains to express the image or sign of upholding and saving. Still another Akkadian name is the NAM-NIRU. Niru (Eg.) signifies victory, and to vanquish; NAM means to accompany and guide. So Anup (Eg.) was the companion and guide of souls. "A concealed wanderer he passes through the land."[1] The An (Eg.) are the wanderers. In this sense Anup is the guide of the wanderers who threaded the unknown ways of the dark, the underworld, and reappeared in heaven. The next guide was Taht. Here it is the human image of the second life. This agrees with the nature of the figure held in the hands of the sick and dying, as the Cross of Christ has so often been clasped for a visible and tangible object of adoration and faith. The God who could be clutched in the death-grasp was a Saviour indeed, and the Mamit type, the Karast, was the risen Christ of the ancient religion. This type of immortality was the one God with a message for men beyond those of the time-reckoners, the stars, moon, and sun, and in the Akkadian hymns it is called the Only God. In clutching the Mamit the dying were going by touch, and laying hold of the god Touch. Now the image of this god is the oldest form of the type afterwards modified in the mummy set upright, or laid out full length. It is a sitting figure, similar to that of the Palæolithic men in the burial of their dead; whereas the Mummy represents the dead stretched out at full-length.

For the mummy Eidolon is connected with the god Sa, Ka, or Kak, called Touch. Kak is our "Chache blind man," who proceeds by the sense of touch in his dark condition. So Kak went through the underworld like the "Blind Horus." The god Kak was the completer of the circle through the underworld; he cabled or bridged the waters through the "bend of the great void," and the Ka image and type of personal identity was represented by the mummy figure as the god of Touch, the god to touch, the deity of the dark who was clung to in the darkness of death, the human image or Ka being moulded after the type of the sun out of sight.

SA is a modified name of the mummy, as well as the deity called

[1] Hymn of Tahtmes.

Touch ; also the Sa is an amulet or talisman, and signifies protection and aid. SA is an Egyptian name for the soul. This shows the Mamit, as Sa, was used for a charm or amulet in Egypt, an image of the personal identity, palpable, and appealing to the sense of TOUCH or feeling in the physical sense, " true as touch," as we find it to have been in Akkad. SEM-SEM (Eg.), the mystery of the re-genesis, also means Touch.

The god was also eaten. KAKA (Kak, Ka, or Sa) signifies to eat, and names the divinity that could be touched and eaten as a primitive method of taking possession in a double sense. The mummy image represented the *Corpus Domini* of the Egyptians, the KARAST or CHRIST of their creed ; the corpse of flesh and type of spirit in one, as expressed by the Latin *Corpus ;* hence it was the Shebti or double. In presence of this image their feasts became sacramental, eucharistic, and the Greek name for the sacrament is derived from the KARAST. In Icelandic the *Corpus Domini* is the HUSL, and to HOUSEL is to give the *Corpus Domini* or sacrament of the supper. In English the HOUSLE, in Scotch the HOOZLE or OUSEL, is the sacrament of the eucharist, and this is administered in the act of houseling. In Egyptian HUS is to celebrate, and the word is related to a purification which is intimately connected with the doctrine of the bloody sacrifice belonging to the ancient cult. USHA means to feed, and to doctor or heal ; whilst USHT signifies propitiation, absolution, and acquittal, the exact equivalent of being OUSELED or HOUSELED. In Mantshu Tartar HISALAMBI denotes the custom of making the libation and pouring out of wine in presence of the corpse. These things have to be traced beyond their reappearance in Greece and Rome for us to ascertain anything of their origines.

In the Assyrian library or collection of sacred books, a catalogue of which has been found, the Kan-Mamiti followed the Book of the soul's descent into the Hades. This answers to the first chapter of the Ritual. What is commonly called the Book of the Dead is the Book of the Mummy. The name both of the dead and the mummy is Mum. One form of the mummy figure is the Tat image, and amongst the first words spoken by the deceased on entering the underworld on his way to join the companions of Osiris are words of exultation that he preserves his identity. On the day of his funeral he proclaims that he is Tat, or the Tat which when interpreted means that he retains his image, his mummy, still intact, and is a type of the eternal (Tat), and represents in spirit that persistence of type sought to be made permanent above ground by embalmment of the body and binding it up with a linen bandage at times one thousand yards in length and woven without seam ! Tat is not only the flesh and bone, but the eternal substance, and the type of this was the mummy Tat, or Mum-at, then Mamit. Consequently this is the Book of the Mamit, the "KAN MAMITI." The " Kan Mamiti" means the papyrus of the Mamit, *i.e.*

of the Mam-it or divine dead. This was buried in Egyptian tombs along with the mummy; hence the papyri from which has been recovered the Egyptian Ritual or papyrus of the mummy, the "KAN-MAMITI." With the Swiss, the mammi is a doll. We have the Mammet in English as an image, a puppet, a doll, an idol, the doll being the final form of the idol. The mammet is an image dressed up, and belongs to mumming. It has been absurdly supposed to mean Mahomet. But Mahomet did not, neither did Mahometanism, introduce the mumming of our Christmas mummers. The mumming image of transformation was especially illustrated in the English mummery, in which the sexes and every individual player were transformed.[1] And so perfectly is the mum or mamit meaning enshrined in English as the type of TRANSFORMATION, that another Egyptian image, the beetle, is called MUM; the beetle that was the symbol of Khepr, signifying the transformer and transformation. "I have seen the city of New Nineveh and Julius Cæsar acted by mammets."[2] "And where I meet your *mammet* gods, I'll swinge 'em and kick 'em into puddles."[3]

The babe is the name of a child's mammet,[4] a toy in human fashion. The bable or bauble was the fool's mammet, a grotesque human figure—the head of a staff, a puppet. Philologically the puppet and bab, or bauble, are the same. Baby in the north of England is used to signify a child's picture. The bab, baby, or mammet was often made of rags, and called baby-clouts, just as was the *mamit* of the Aztecs and Quichés. The mummy image likewise reads TESAS, that is the enveloped form, or a type, from TES, to tie up, encase, coil, and AS, the statue or image. Tes is the very self in person; so that the mummy image, as Tesas, is the statue of oneself; which the mummy was. Now the "ENVELOPED MAJESTY," or tied-up bundle of the Quichés was obviously the mummy, Sheb or Tesas of Egypt and the Mamit of the Assyrians.

When the four great progenitors of the race passed away, the legend says they left behind them that which was to keep them in everlasting remembrance. They called their wives, sons, and friends around them, took their leave, and said, "Remember us well. Never let us pass out of your memory." The aged fathers, having given their last counsels to those they were leaving behind, now sang once more the old sweet song, KAMUCU, which means "WE SEE." This they had sung of old in the first mythical sunrise of the world, "when the morning stars sang together, and all the sons of God shouted for joy," as they shone rejoicing in the primeval dawn, and now, with sore hearts, they sang the old sad song again, while the light was fading from their dying eyes. The new sun rose with its internal light, and they sang the KAMUCU with its annunciatory "WE SEE." Then came the change,

---

[1] Brand *On Mumming*. [2] *Every Woman in her Humour*, 1609.
[3] Beaumont and Fletcher, *Island Princess*, act iv. [4] Gouldman.

and the old men were not. But in their place there was a great bundle. This was never unfolded, nor on rolling it over and over could ANY SEAM BE FOUND. So it was called the "ENVELOPED MAJESTY," which is identical in meaning with the Egyptian "TESAS;" it was made a memorial of these fathers, and held to be very dear and precious in the sight of all. This story relates the origin of the mummy, and connects that type with the ancestors, as in the so-called ancestor-worship. The robe without a seam was represented in Egypt by the bandage without a join, with which the mummy was coiled round and encased as a type of the eternal, the seamless robe of the primitive Karast.

Brasseur de Bourbourg observes,[1] that the Toltec custom was to preserve the relics of their heroes. The bones were bound up with precious stones in a bundle of stuff called TLAQUIMILOLLI. These bundles were tied up for eternity, to be placed at the end of the sanctuary (the holy of holies), and preserved there as objects of religious reverence. The Quichés used to burn incense before this emblem of the enveloped majesty. "One of these bundles was given up to the Christians by a Tlascaltec some time after the conquest. It was reported to contain the remains of Camaxtli, the chief god of Tlascala. The native historian, Camargo, describes it as follows:—'When the bundle was undone in which were found the ashes of the idol, Camaxtli, a mass of fair hair was also found, together with an EMERALD; and of these ashes a paste had been made by mixing with them the blood of children who had been sacrificed.'"[2]

Here the green stone, the Uat (Eg.), was the same type of renewal as the jade stone placed in the tombs of the men of the Palæolithic age; and the image was a mamit or symbol of the mam (Eg.), the dead which had taken on a divine nature through the preserved mummy being a type of immortality. This tends to show that as the first nature of the Eternal was that of Time, so the earliest idea of Immortality was based on the physical fact of embalming or preserving the bodily image intact, to establish a continuity after death, and puts an altogether new aspect on the making of images in the worship of ancestors, the beginning being with the figure present rather than with the departed spirit. The most rudimentary form of this religious instinct in man would be the desire to keep the dead in memory, and the yearning to live on beyond the visible sphere. But the physical comes first, and so we have the spirit or soul of man called by the name of and pourtrayed as the mummy or mamit. Whether it has any relation or not to the name of CAMAXTLI, Kama (Eg.) is the dead, and Khat, the body, shut up and sealed.

It has been remarked by Geiger that in almost all cases the words for body are taken from the dead body or corpse. $\Sigma\hat{\omega}\mu\alpha$,

[1] *Nouvelles Annales des Voyages*, 1858, tom. iv. p. 268.
[2] Bancroft, vol. iii. p. 54.

as had been observed by Aristarchos, is used by Homer for the dead body only, and he asks, " Whence this eccentricity of language, to start from the notion of the corpse in order to name the human body itself?" But language did not begin with the Greek, and Soma is the Egyptian Sama, the shape, image, and representative sign. It is our "same" or "similar." The determinative of Sama is the mummy. SA means the person, the self, and MA is like, according to; whence SAMA, the likeness. Thus the Greek Sama for the dead body is named as the likeness or representative sign of the living, based on the mummy, and Homer is right according to the hieroglyphics. Body, as before explained, represents Puti (Eg.), the image, figure, shape, form, type; the corp, or Kherp (Eg.), is a model or first figure, embodied, and the mum-type of the dead is the earliest form of the *même* or self; the Latin MEMET for me, Myself.

The old Caribs worshipped an inferior kind of deity that was imaged as a Zemi. The Zemi, in Swahili, is a departed spirit; and at Zanzibar and in Uganda the spirits of the departed are called Mu-Zimmu. Mu (Eg.) denotes the dead. The Egyptian SHEMAU are Typhonian genii, an early kind of spirits. Sem (Eg.) being the representative sign, the likeness, the mummy-type, the Zemi would be the image of the dead, whether as Mamit or as a spirit—the likeness preserved in death. The earlier Khema (Eg.) are the dead; the later Shema, or Sem, denotes the similitude figured as the mummy.

According to Peter Martyr, the Maya images or idols of the supposed lesser gods were called Zemes (plural); "Zemes which are the images of their familiar and domestic spirits." The god Zamna, they say, was the inventor of names and letters. He came from the west and was represented in the form of a hand called Kab-ul, the working hand, and worshipped at Cozumel under the sign of a cross, named Vahomche.[1] SAM (Eg.) is the representative sign, to memorize and remember, emblem or image. Sem denotes the west. Semhi is the left hand; also the west, as Am, was imaged by the cross. The ZEMA here is likewise the representative image in death. Moreover we find the mummy-type by name in the MUMAH of the QUICHÉS, who had small subterranean chapels in which they concealed little images, as the Egyptians hid their Shebti or sepulchral figures in the Serdab or dark passage of the underworld, the tomb. These were identified with the spirits of the departed. The sanctuaries of the god of the road who presided over these idols were called MUMAH.[2]

Mum (Eg.) is the dead, the mummy, and Ah means the house. Such chapels and sanctuaries were manifestly mummy-houses, or Bit-Mummu.

In Egypt the Mamit or mummy figure, called the Shebti, the double of the dead, was not a personal portrait of the living, but a generalized type. Hence the Shebti, a bearded image of the male,

---

[1] Brinton, *Myths of N. E.* p. 188.   [2] Bancroft, v. iii. p. 481.

was likewise the representative of both sexes, used indifferently for the male or the female. The type was of prior importance to the individual likeness, and the type of re-arising or re-erecting was essentially masculine, founded on the star or sun that re-arose from the world of the dead. As the sun this was the pubescent, hairy Sheru, Horus the younger, the adult, the *homme fait*, the Khem-Horus whose emblem of erection was typical of the resurrection. Thus the rising again of both sexes came to be figured in the masculine phase, and by means of the male emblems, including the beard. The second life being founded on the image of the second, or re-arising sun, will explain the bearded Shebti found in the tombs with the mummy of the female.

In one of the Bushman "fables," it is the feather of the male ostrich only that transforms into the young bird of the resurrection. "All other mortal things die outright, except the male ostrich and the moon; these two revive again."[1] In the Egyptian mythology the moon is re-born as Taht in the masculine image.

In an account of Easter Island, Mr. J. L. Palmer[2] says of the symbolical wooden images carved by the natives :—"*Be it noted* that one distinguishing feature is a *small tuft of hair which is represented on the chin for both sexes.*" These images thus repeat the bearded Shebti, with their tuft on the chin for both sexes. The resurrection being typified by the masculine attributes, and the pubescent being the *second of two phases*, led to the later notion attributed to the Turks, amongst others, that women of themselves have no souls.

It is the same with the New Zealand image carried by the natives, called a TIKI. This is worn as a memorial of the dead; but it has a generalized character, and one TIKI will serve a whole congregation of friends who gather round it to weep and wail over it in memory of their own dead friends. Like the Shebti, it is not a personal portrait. In fact some New Zealanders who were in London a while since explained that the Tikis were usually made with three fingers only, so that they should not be the image of any one in particular.[3] The primitive TIKI was a type of the dead ancestors or friends, but not of the single individual.

The "owl-head vases" found in the Greek tombs by Dr. Schliemann may be interpreted by means of the hieroglyphics and in relation to the dead.

The vase with female breasts is a dual type of the genitrix, the suckler, the nurse whose blessings, like those of the Hebrew Shadai, were of the "breast and the womb." The vase HES is an image of Isis with which her name is written. Hes or As denotes the secreting part

---

[1] Bleek, pp. 13-14.
[2] *Proceedings of the Liverpool Literary and Philosophical Society*, 1874-5; pp. 286-7.
[3] Tylor, *Early History*, p. 102, 3rd Ed.

of the body, the breast or womb. The vase with breasts represents the two characters and two truths of the motherhood. HESMEN denotes the menstrual purification, and the HESMENI is a Natron vase or laver.

The tomb of Queen Ta-Seser in the valley of Biban-el-Muluk, contains a chamber, the walls of which are illumined with a large collection of exquisitely designed and coloured vases representing gold, silver, and porphyry. It is a long distance from the owl-headed vase to the delicate imagery of this gorgeous chamber, but the ideograph remains the same.

The vase found in the graves of the American mound-builders, and the pitcher placed on the top of the pile raised over the cairn of the African Bongos, have the same significance as the owl-headed vase in Greece.

Under the name of the HENT, the vase is one with the matrix; and Hent also means rites and consecration. The vase HEN is likewise an ideograph of tribute, and signifies to bring as tribute. In this sense we may read the cups cut in the stones of Britain. FAS, in Egyptian denotes some kind of food determined by the image of the female bearer, with a vase or modius carried on her head as the bringer, and the Egyptian form of the word VASE is BAS.

The owl is a very ancient type; it was extant under the fourth dynasty, but was superseded by other forms of the Nycticorax or Phœnix. As a phonetic MU it still bears the name of the mother, and of the tomb, the chamber, the womb. As an ideograph it had the value of MMU or MUM, the name of the dead, the mummy. Mâ, the name of truth and "to see," is often written Mma. The owl is a bird of night that sees in the dark, hence its adoption as a type of the genitrix who reproduced with the tomb for her womb, the mother earth. Hence, likewise, the goggle-eyes of the owl-vases, which represent the Seer in the dark. The absence of a mouth in these figures also shows the "MUM" (silent) or mummy type. The vase is a form of the funeral urn, and in the name of the URN survives that of the RENN (Eg.), the nurse who was Rennut, the virgin mother, and Renn the nursling. RENN means to dandle, nurse the child with the figure of the RENN (mother) offering her breast to the Renn (nursling). The URN-vase with the breasts continued that image of the mother of life in the underworld.

In the Aztec and Maya myths the Great or original Vase, as Akbal or Huecomitl, is as conspicuous a symbol of the water of life as in the monuments of Egypt or the Greek tombs. In Peru it was an important figure, known by the name of Tiki. Tekh in the hieroglyphics signifies a supply of liquid, of drink, of wine, with the vase for determinative. The same idea of the wet-nurse was conveyed by the woman with breasts, pourtrayed in the burial-caves of Europe. Menâ (Eg.) is both the wet-nurse and the vase or jar; as Menkat she holds two vases in her hands, and was the vase-maker, the earliest POTTERESS and Creator.

The hill of Hissarlik contains the HES in its name; that is the vase, the abode, seat, and Isis in one word. Ser (Eg.) means the sacred hill, the place of burial and re-birth in the "Ser Hill" and rock of the horizon. LIK in many languages relates to the dead and the resting-place, as in LECO or LEGO, Greek, to lay asleep; LECHI or LECHOS, the bed, or couch; LOCHOS or LOCHO, a lair, a place for lying in wait; LLECH, Welsh, a cover and hiding-place; Latin, LOCI, a sepulchre; English LIC, a tomb or burial-place; Chinese LEIGH, the lofty hill, the summit. The hill was the first LIK, or ARK of the living and the dead. Hence the typical burial-place in the Ritual. The mountain-land as the UR-KA, AR-KA or ARU-KA (Eg.), the land of the lofty region, supplied the first form of the ark in the cave or the circle on the mount; the Ark on Ararat safe from the waters and easily defended. This preceded the ark-cities like ERUK and RHAGÆ, which were built on the model of the Ark or Aru-ka, whence the LIK in Hissarlik. An earlier form of the word may be found in KESSERLOCK, the name of one of the bone-caverns of the Cavemen, near Thayingen, in Switzerland; and Kes or Kas (Eg.) is the name of the coffin, to embalm and bury.

The cuneiform determinative of things celestial or divine, as a monogram, reads Ilu, god or goddess, and the phonetic value of the character is N. AN is the Akkadian sign for heaven, and with the pronunciation of DINGIR, for God, it is also used as an invocation or incantation. So is the Egyptian N, which denotes the heaven, firmament, space between. NU signifies "come," "descend." In Akkadian as in Egyptian, NU is no, not, the sign of negation; and the same word denotes the image, or to image. So the NU monogram for Zalam (Ass.) signifies an image or picture. NU (Eg.) is the earlier NUN (from Nnu), the type, likeness, portrait, and NUNU is the little boy, the NINNY, who might be the "tiny boy" of the song with the refrain of "Hey ninny-nonny." The NUNU as child is the elder Horus, who was always the child, the little one, the nursling and ninny of the mother, because in him was typified the sun born at the summer solstice, the negative one of the two Horuses. So Nun, the WATER, is the negative of the Two Truths in relation to Nef, the breath. The Egyptian Nunu furnishes the Assyrian Ninus, the divine child of Semiramis. Moreover the divine style of NUTER is applied to the gods in Assyrian. In the Annals of Assur-Banipal (6, 96) the bulls are called "Ili-NATRUTI." "I tore away the bulls, the Ili-Natruti of the treasures of the temples of Elam." These were some kind of protecting divinities. Nuter is the Egyptian name of the Divinity. The plural in Uti cannot be limited to two. As before shown, the number expressed the nature of the Pleroma. UTI (Eg.) is a form of No. 5 [1] and of

[1] Lep. *Denk.* iii. 79 *b*.

Taht. Now Taht is also the representative of eight, as manifester of the seven, which makes it probable that the typical Iluti are eight in number, the Natruti being the same. Eight talismanic figures in solid bronze were placed by one of the Babylonian kings, Nergal-sar-usur, at the doors of the sacred pyramid in Babylon, to guard and keep them against the wicked ones.

A form of the symbolic figure of eight, a variant of the eight-rayed star of Assur and of Sut-Har, and of the eight-looped sign of the eight Nnu, is found among the ancient Akkadian ideographs as

 This is a compound type

of the abode and deity. According to one interpretation it denotes the divine germ within the womb, and involves the idea of pregnancy. Professor Sayce thinks it points to the high estimation in which the mother was held in the Akkadian family, she being as it were the deity of the house.[1]

It is the emblem of the child, who, as the eighth, was manifester of the seven whether as Assur or Sut, and likewise of the genitrix of the seven stars, who was both one and seven in one as Kep, Sefekh, or Hathor, in Egypt; the goddess of the seven stars and the habitation of the god as the child of the mother. Ishtar in Babylonia was a goddess of the seven stars, and one of her emblems is an eight-rayed star. This figure of eight is its equivalent, and here it is placed within the great mother in token of the promised seed, her child who comes and is her manifester. It has exactly the same value as the eight-rayed star of Buddha or of the Christ in the Roman catacombs.

ANU was a deity identical with the Greek Æon, the Egyptian Heh, the Phœnician and Hebrew Ulom, the Æonian, expressive of ever by repetition, by the age, sæculum, or cycle. This shows the AN (Eg.), to repeat, to be periodic. He was the "Ancient of Days," in this sense of the repeater of time, the "old Anu." The names of the old Anu and the young Ninus of Assyria are both derivable from the Egyptian HANNU, the youth, the bringer or contributor, in relation to the primordial element of life, the water. NEN (Eg.) is the young child, the Ninny, the glow or dawn, and the Inundation, the type of periodic time. The name of Hannu contains both Han and Nen, hence their identity; and when Han was reduced to An, it named the fish, the Oan of the Babylonian mythos. AN (Eg.) signifies repetition, periodicity, corresponding still to Nen. This, however, is a secondary phase: in Egypt the first Nen was of a feminine nature, out of which came the Assyrian Nin for both lord and lady.

In the Akkadian mythology Nin-dara represents the nocturnal sun of a system in which UTU is the diurnal sun, the god in the height. This is the Egyptian Hut, the solar disk on wings, an emblem of Hu; Hak,

---

[1] *Trans. Bib. Arch.* vi. part ii. p. 474.

or Kak, the god in the darkness being the form of Tum in the Hades.

Nin-dara, like Atum, is the judge of the dead in the lower world, and is called "Nin-dara, lord, son of Mul-la, measure, and judge"; who is addressed as "Nin-dara, lord, son of Mul-la, decide the fate." Dara, the eternal, is represented by Teru (Eg.), the total, whole, the dual All.

Marduk, a form of Silik-mulu-khi, is called the mediator; an office attributed to Mithra. The word mediator has the later sense of intercessor, but this was not a primary meaning. The mediator was the intermediate one; therefore the messenger. Hea, the father, hidden in the abyss, sends his son into the world as the newly born star or sun from the deep; and this makes him a divine messenger, a form of the WORD, the intermediate one between the father-god and men. He is the friend who crosses a gulf otherwise fixed and impassable. Silik crosses the waters in the ship of Hea, which carried the sun and the souls of the dead who are brought back to life by him. To him, as the crosser, it is said, "To thee is the steep bank of the pit of the ocean."[1] The Akkadian name of Silik-mulu-khi denotes the distributor of good. Ser (Eg.) means to distribute, to console, be the comforter. As the divine messenger, his insignia of office is a reed. The reed of the messenger implies the pen. So Taht, the speech, tongue, word, revealer and messenger of the gods, carries the reed-pen. This reed is probably found in a variant of Silik-mulu-khi's name. "His name," says Lenormant, "sometimes has variations of which we cannot understand the sense, such as Silik-ri-mulu." The Ru or Rui is the Egyptian reed, a reed-pen of the scribe.

Another name of Marduk is Su, and this also is the reed, as well as the son, in Egyptian. The reed (Rui) identifies the messenger as the penman, and the Akkadian can be read by the Egyptian hieroglyphics. Taht, the lunar deity, messenger and manifester of the gods, is the son of Num (Khneph), the deity of the Ark and the deep; the same relationship as that of Silik to Hea (Assyrian Nuah), but the latter appears to be the solar son. He says, in one hymn, "I am the warrior, the eldest son of Hea, his messenger;"[2] this answers to Har-Makheru, as son of Osiris. But the reed-symbol of this messenger witnesses to an interesting adaptation of Taht's insignia to the solar myth.

The name of Nin-gar, the pilot of heaven, is rendered by M. Lenormant, with a query, "Master of the helm?"[3] The pilot and helm are indissolubly united in the modern mind. But before, the rudder was the paddle, which served to guide and propel the boat. The paddle or oar with which the passage was made is the Kheru (Eg.). In Assyrian the passage or course itself is the GARRU; and in Akkadian

---

[1] Lenormant, *Ib.* p. 193.   [2] W. A. I. 4, 30, 3.
[3] *Chaldean Magic*, Eng. Tr. p. 161.

the KHAR-RU is the deep. The boat-oar is a symbol of Har-Makheru, the pilot of the divine bark of the gods, and the ideograph of his title.

The paddle, KHER, was turned into a sceptre, called the Kherp. Kherp signifies a sceptre and a paddle, to be first, surpassing, conse-crated, and to steer. Kher, the paddle, is the same word as Kher, majesty. Kherp, the paddle sceptre, also reads, His Majesty. In one of the Akkadian magical texts the god Nin-gar is invoked, " Come, Nin-si-gar, great pilot of heaven, thrusting forward thy sub-lime tree, thy lance." He is invoked in favour of the king, and in connection with one of the insignia of royalty, a " weapon which causes terror, which wounds for majesty, the weapon which is raised, which is projectile, by the side of majesty." Now as Nin-gar answers to the lord Har, pilot of the gods, or rather the paddle of their boat, for so he was described (whence the paddle sign of Makheru), it would seem as if Nin-gar was the pilot as lord of the paddle or oar, like Horus, Gar or Khar representing the earlier form of Har in both languages; and that the Akkadians had the paddle-image of dividing and cleaving a way turned into a weapon of war and an emblem of majesty. In addi-tion to the Kher and Kherp, the USER also is both oar and sceptre in the hieroglyphics ; and the paddle sign Kher also reads Tet, speech, the Word. Two names of the Logos, KHAR and TET, are thus written with the oar or paddle.

Har-Makheru is the risen Christ of Egyptian theology, the ful-filler, confirmer, and completer, identical with the fulfiller of pro-phecy in the Christian scheme. He is the true Word, or the word made truth, from Ma, truth, KHERU, the word. In Har-Makheru the Word (logos) became truth. This title of Horus is the name of the Assyrian god of dreams, MAKHER, and the meaning of Makheru is most happily applied to a god of dreaming and foretelling in sleep. In the one instance it is the word made truth, in the other, the causer of good dreams to come true. The dreamer prays, " May the dream I dreamed be confirmed ; the dream I dreamed to happi-ness turn. May Makher, the god of dreams, settle on my head." [1] These are the words of the dreamer, and they accord to Makher the identical character of Har-Makheru, the fulfiller, confirmer, the one who makes the word come true, personified as the Word made Truth. MAKHIR (Ass.), equal or an equal, is a synonym of the name of Har-Makheru, the god of the equinox or level of the double horizon. MAK-RU is a title of the divinity Marduk. Further, an Assyrian standard measure of capacity is named the Makaru. The Ma (Eg.) is a mea-sure, and KHERU means due or just. Also the name of MAGRU or Makhru has been read as a title of the intercalary month Ve-Adar, which was the means of making the reckoning come right and true; the month consecrated to Assur, who is thus a form of the Har-Makheru.

[1] Prayer after a bad dream, *Rec. of the Past*, ix. 151.

In the Egyptian mythology the sun of the lower hemisphere is god of the waters of the abyss. This deity in the Tum triad is Kak, the worn-down form of Kebek, the crocodile-headed god of the waters, when the crocodile was the type of the sun that crossed the deep. One name of this sun is AF—a title given to Num, called the lord of the Inundation. In AF and Kak, modified Hak, we have the two Hebrew names of the same deity rendered Jahveh and JACH—Jahveh who is praised by the name of Jach (יה)—which two names are derived from KHEVEKH as the original form of Sevekh, SUCHOS, Kebek, Kak, Jahveh, Jah, Jav, and Af.

In Psalm xxix. Jahveh is celebrated as the thunderer, the god of the waters, who was AF (Num) in Egypt, and who sat upon the flood. His voice is said to shake the wilderness of Kadesh. Kadesh, read as Egyptian, is the wilderness or desert land. Ka is land, an inner region; Tesh is red. The Tesh or Tshr is the desert, as the red land. Lord of the red land (or Ka tesh) was a title of the Egyptian Pharaoh. The lord of the Psalmist [1] is he who sitteth upon the flood. The flood here is "MABUL" (מבול), the special name of Noah's flood; not used for any other flooding, overflowing, or waters, for which the Hebrew has seven other names. In Egyptian Ma and Meh interchange; and Meh is the abyss of the mythical waters, also a name of the north, where the zodiacal waters are placed. Bul or Ber (Eg.) means to boil up and well forth. "I make the waters, and the MEH-URA comes into being," says the god, in a papyrus at Turin. This was the primordial abyss in the north, the place of the bursting forth of Mabul. Meh-ura is the FLOOD and the great water also called the Cow in the Ritual.[2] So that whatever be the meaning of Noah's flood, we must look to the parent language for an explanation. In the monuments, Af (Num) is the lord of the floods, and he is pictured sitting on the flood.

In the Belmore collection, British Museum, this deity of the deluge may be seen sitting on his throne (the Hes, seat), and this has the flowing waters hieroglyphically pourtrayed as his seat. Num sitteth on the flood as a king for ever. In the Hebrew writings we read "The earth is the Lord's; he hath founded it upon the seas, and established it upon the floods."[3] "The voice of the Lord is upon the waters; the Lord is upon many waters. The Lord sitteth upon the flood."[4] "The waters saw Thee, O God, the waters saw Thee; they were afraid: the depths also were troubled."[5] "Thy way is in the sea, and Thy path is in the great waters."[6] The waters and the flood are the same that Num is seen sitting on; they are his seat. The seat is the Hes. The Hes is likewise a liquid, as in Hesmen, and the name of Isis; in Hes meet the water, the seat, and the mother-source personified. Hes was the seat and throne of Osiris.

---

[1] Ps. xxix.
[2] Chs. xvii. and lxxi.
[3] Ps. xxiv. 1, 2.
[4] Ps. xxix. 3, 10.
[5] Ps. lxxvii. 16.
[6] Ps. lxxvii. 19.

The Hes with the waters is the throne of Num, and these waters constitute the seat and throne of the Lord of Israel. Af (Num) is the image of this god of the waters, as lord of frogs   Also his types include the goat-kind of ram as the Sun that entered the waters in the sign of the Sea-goat, and emerged in the sign of the Ram. Kebek the crocodile-headed, is a yet earlier type of the Af-Ra, or sun of the deep.

Jahveh-Jach, who is identical with Af-Hak, the sun in the three water-signs and crosser of the abyss, is the divinity known in the Assyrian mythology under the various names (so read) of NUAH, YAV, EN-KI, ZI-KIA, HEA, and others.   He is represented by the fish, as was the Egyptian lower sun by the crocodile.   The fish was earlier than the boat, but when the boat is built Hea has his ark of the waters like Af (Num) and Hak, in which the gods and the souls that are saved cross over the otherwise impassable abyss.   This vessel is described with details hitherto inexplicable ; every part of it has a term of magical significance.[1]   With this the ninety-ninth chapter of the Egyptian Ritual should be paralleled and compared, as in that, each part of the boat, the Makhennu of the dead, demands its name of the spirit seeking admission for the voyage ; and it is necessary that the name of every part should be known.   The Assyrian Yav is designated the " Inundator of the lands of enemies."[2]   " To the god Yav, who confers the fertilizing rain upon my land, his house in Borsippa I built."[3]   "The god Yav, establisher of fertility in my land, Bit Num-Kan, as his temple in Babylon I built."[4]   Num, like the Egyptian Neb, is the lord ; Kan is the fish, the earlier form of the Khan (Eg.) for the canoe, and this was a house of the fish-god Hea, or Yav, the GAL-KANA-ABZU, the great fish of the abyss.

In the Yoruba mythology, IFE is a region of the earth or lower heaven, out of which the sun issues forth, and is reborn from his burial-place.   In the Keltic mythology, Ifuren is the Hades.   AFA is the Dahoman god of wisdom, who corresponds to Hea.   One reading of Yav's or Hea's name is YEM,[5] which connects him with the waters. IVM or IUM (יום) is an epithet of the god Jah, synonymous with the name of day.   In Egyptian, IUMA is the name of the sea.   The sea is so called from its tidal motion expressed by IU to come, MA being the water ; and as Ma, or Mau, means light, and to see, IUMA is also the coming of light.   So Ium denotes the god as the one who comes, the same as Iu-em-hept, or the Chaldean Imi, who brings the fertilizing rain.

Now the Samoyedes worship a supreme god whom they call NUM, and whose other name is JUMA ;[6] the god who is known in Finnish mythology as Jumala, god of the Iuma, the waters, the abyss, and

[1] W. A. I. 4, 25, col. 1.
[2] Norris, vol. iii. pp. 722-858.
[3] *Inscrip. of Nebuchadnezzar*, col. 5, lines 57, 58.
[4] *Ib.* col. 4, lines 35, 36.
[5] *Ins. of Tiglath Pileser*, par. 7.
[6] Castrén.

identical with Num and Yav. "Tell me where is Num (Jumala),"
said Castrén to " an old Samoyede sailor when walking with him
beside the sea." He pointed to the dark waters and said, " He is there."
Num had retained his character as deity of the IUMA; hence his
name of Jumala. Juma-la is Juma-Ra, the sun of the waters, as was
Num-Ra in the deep. The Assyrian title of Num-Kan reappears as
the Magar Nam-Khan, a name of the sun; Nam is the sun in the
Limbu language; and in Australia NAMBAJANDI is the lord of heaven,
and NABAGEENA is a name of the sun; NOM, African Yam, God;
NYAMA, African Melon, God; NYAMA, African Nhalmoe, God;
NYAMBE, African Diwala, God; NUM, Khotovsi, God; NEAMH,
Gaelic, Heaven; NYAMA, Melon, Heaven; NAMI, a title of Vishnu;
NUME, Portuguese and Italian, Deity; NUHM, Arabian, Divinity;
NEOMA, Chinese, God; NEMON, Irish Druidical, Deity; NAB,
Akkadian, Divinity; NUEBE, African Mbofia, Divine image; NOBU,
Erromango, God; NAF, Welsh, the Lord; NEP, Scandinavian, God.

Num (Neb or Nef) in Egypt does not appear under the fish-
type; but, in the African languages, NIME, Dsuku; NYAB, Mbofon,
and NYAB in Udan, are names of the alligator. NEBI (Eg.) means to
swim and float, as the lower sun did, under one water-type or the other.

The "NUM" or "Yem" sun of the underworld is also related
by both names to the cannibals of Africa, the NYAM-NYAM of later
travellers—the YEM-YEM or cannibals, described by Hornemann as
being south of the Kano and the Niger, and the JUM-JUMS, a cannibal
race adjoining the Niger, who were accustomed to consign their dead
in rude coffins to the waters.[1] The ÂM-ÂM (Eg.) are the devourers;
devouring demons of Hades. N'AM (Eg.) would indicate the devourers
of the water. NAM (Eg.) is the water; NYAM in Dselana; NYIAM,
Guresa; NYIMA, Gurma. NYAM, Pati, means greedy, gluttonous;
NIAM or NYAMA, in Fulah, to eat or devour. NYAMA, Swahili, is
flesh; NYAMA, Zulu, a piece of raw flesh. The earliest NYAM-NYAM
were the devourers of raw flesh. Among the typical devourers
under this name are the NIME or NIMIYE, Dsuka, an alligator;
NOME, Bidsogo, serpent; NAMU, Gurma, scorpion; NOAMA, Koama,
scorpion; NEM and NIMR, the leopard. One Typhonian type of the
sun of the underworld was the crocodile, a devourer; and one of the
ÂM-ÂM or NYAM-NYAM, as the devourer of the waters, is Sevekh,
the capturer. NAMM (Eg.) also means to destroy.

Sacrifices were offered to this sun of night and the deep, who was
a cannibal god of the cannibals, to be propitiated or appealed to
with offerings of human flesh and blood, which were made to the
crocodile, serpent, leopard, or the water, as the representatives of the
divinity of the world's darkness. Language still retains the typology,
and the typology reflects the mental condition of the early children
of the night, who were putting forth their *feelers* through the gloom

[1] *Mission to Ashanti*, p. 192.

in search of the absent light, impersonated as NUM, KAK, AF or SEVEKH-RA in Egypt, HEA or YAV in Assyria, Kolpia in Phœnicia, and YAV or IACH with the Hebrews.

The solar Af is not an uncommon name. Af, in Persian and Hindustani, is the sun; Afa, in the African Doai and N'godsin, is the sun; AFA in Yagusa, IPHE in PUKA, and Avi in Sanskrit, is the same sun-god as the Egyptian AF, Dahome AFA, the Assyrian YAV, and Hebrew יהו.

The Af-Ra, sun of the lower firmament, the breather amid the waters, has the same relation to Khnef, or Num, as the Gnostic Ab-ra-xas has to the solar Chnuphis; and here, likewise, the divinity is named IAO.   AF-RA will explain ABRAXAS, and prove the continuity of the myth and symbols of expression from the earliest times to those of the supposed heretics, who brought on the typology. Af-ra becomes Ab-ra, and Kas (Eg.) denotes some talismanic kind of stone.

The name is found written "ABRESSES" on a Roman gem— ABRESSES NUMEN (for nomen); DAI (for *dei*).[1] The Egyptian Kas also reads SAS; KASM, or SASM, is an emerald, or other green stone. SAS also means a six-sided block of stone, the cube of Anu, the SES-ru.   The Ab-ra-Sas (or Abraxas) is originally the cube-stone of the Ab-Ra.   For this reason: the number six denotes the establishing of upper and lower, in addition to the four cardinal points when the earth was discovered to be a globe; and the three regions, together with the triad of solar gods, were founded, on the sun below, upon, and over the horizon.   Ses (Eg.) means to breathe, reach land, and respire, as did the god of Nef or Breath, the sun that crossed the abyss.

In the later documents of the Chaldean theology it is affirmed that in the beginning was the existing Being begotten of the abyss and Tiamat.   The name of this supreme and primordial Being, the old original god One, is "AUV KINUV," who was worshipped under that name by Nebuchadnezzar.[2] M. Lenormant renders "AUV KINUV" as the Existing Being.   Some of the more recent developments of the ancient doctrines, as in the works of the Gnostics and Kabalists, contain the most ancient matter in a more diffused form, the myth having been *philosophized*, or the personal divinity made merely doctrinal.   So far from AUV KINUV originating in a development of recent date it is a survival and reproduction from the very earliest undated times.   Philosophical or doctrinal applications do not suffice to give a new origin to the most ancient ideas, characters, or names.   KINUV equates with KHNEF and ENUV (Akk.), for the Lord, and with Neb (Eg.), the Lord, who was Af-Khnef.   Nor does

---

[1] Montfaucon.
[2] *Inscrip. of Borsippa*, col. 1, 1, 2; W. A. I. 31, 4; *Chaldean Magic*, Lenormant, Eng. Tr. p. 113.

the ancient god lose personal identity or place in the system established by being vapourized into the Existing Being of the beginning in Apsu with the mother Tiamat. AUV KINUV is a personification, in character, local position, and birth from the abyss, and, even in name, to be identified with the old original god of the Thebiad, Num or Khnef, the Chnuphis of the Gnostics.

Khnef was the "breath of those who are in the firmament," *i.e.* souls, and he presided over the abyss of the waters. Vishnu lying beneath the waters, and breathing umbilically,[1] is the true representative of Khnef, or Auv-Kinuv, the Existing Being who could breathe under water, and was therefore superhuman, and whose chief image was the sun passing through the lower void of the circle.

Af-Khnef, it is now suggested, is the Egyptian original of the AUV KINUV of the Chaldean Gnostics and the Chnuphis of the gems, and that from him in his dual character sprang the gods Yav (Hea) and Anu; the one being identified with Af, by means of the name, and the serpent Hef, which is the type of Hea, or is Hea as a modified form of Hefa; the other, with Khnef or Nef, which in Egyptian becomes Nu, Na, or Anu. The cross of Anu is equivalent to the Ram sign of the crossing, one of the twin ideographs of Khnef, who was the god One of the Thebiad, as was Auv-Kinuv of the later Chaldean theology. Khnef is old enough in Egypt to be called the father of Taht and Ptah. My own belief is that Num (Khnef), the god of breath in a solar form, was a continuation of the star-god Nem, now identified by the lion-type as Shu, the still earlier god of breath or spirit, the "spirit which moved on the face of the waters" by starlight, before the luni-solar time was registered or the Af-Ra was personified.

The Phœnician god of beginnings, named Kolpia, is the same at root. He is the consort of Baau, the void. Bau is a name of Dav-Kina, goddess of the nether-world, and consort of Hea. Num presides over the void called Bau. Kolpia is called the wind. Nef is breath. The name has been rendered by Bochart KOL-PHI-JAH, voice of the mouth of God as Jah. Röth reads it KOL-PIA'H, the voice of breath. But as it is the god of breath, the beginner of the abyss, identifiable as Nef, and therefore of the Egyptian genesis, the name will be Egyptian too. We accept the terminal IA as equivalent to JAH, AHU, HEA, YAV, and Af, the lower sun or Af-Ra, the deity of the deep, but with a totally different derivation for KOLP. This is the Egyptian KHERP, a name of the first, principal, chief, the paddle or oar (to steer) of the gods, also called the majesty. Kolpia is Kherp-Iu, Kherp-Yah, the Af-Ra.

Aku, the Akkadian name of the moon, reads A-Khu. Â (Eg.) is the moon; Khu is a light, also a title. AKHU was worn down to AAHU (Eg.) for the name of the moon and the moon-god. Both

---

[1] Moor's *Hindu Pantheon*, pl. 7.

forms are extant with the article prefixed in the two names of Taht and Tekh, the lunar god, whose duality is expressed by Tahuti, the bearer and reckoner of the dual light.

The god Aku was considered to be the type of royalty, the first divine monarch that reigned.[1] As is the Akkadian type, such is the signification of the name in Egyptian. Akhu means the illustrious, illuminating, noble, honourable, virtuous, magnificent, their highnesses. Another identification with Taht occurs in an invocation to the spirit of Hur-Ki (an Akkadian name of the moon-god), "who makes his talismanic ship cross the river." Says Taht, "I am the great workman who founded the Ark of Sekari on the stocks;"[2] and he claims the first bark to have been lunar. The allusion is to a myth unknown to Assyriology.[3]

"Tutu" is a name found on the tablets. Tutu is called the generator and restorer of the gods, the progenitor of gods and men. Tut, in Egyptian, is a name for the type of the generator; it is the male member. And Taht (or Tut) is the generator personified; one of his titles being the begetter of Osiris. Taht was the lord of Smen, the place of establishing the gods, as the establisher of the circle and of the son in the place of the father. Tutu is said to "*speak*" before the king. Tut (Eg) means speech, to speak, utter, be the tongue or mouth of utterance, which Taht was as the lunar Word or Logos of the gods. Thus the Assyrian Tutu agrees with the Egyptian in two meanings. A divine personage, Ubara-Tutu, is called the father of Duzi, or Tamzi, the son and husband of Ishtar. Tamzi is the young solar god who opened the year in the month of Tammuz or Mesore, and is identical with the elder, the child Horus. Uba is also the name of an Egyptian deity.

Ubara-Tutu appears as the father of the builder of the Ark, against the coming deluge. Ubara, in Akkadian, is the glow of the descending (setting) Sun, which was personified as Tamzi. If we read Tu-tu as the duplicate root meaning to descend, then Ubara-Tutu would be Tamzi and not his father! Whereas Tutu is the father. Tamzi was born at the summer solstice, as the young child, the dwarf, deformed and maimed in his lower members. In the earliest solar myth he was carried across the waters by the great mother herself, in her various natural types of the womb of the hippopotamus, the belly of the fish, or the sow, or the flower of the lotus. Thus, when boats were built, the lotus was an early model. The ark, Teba, takes the name of one form of the genitrix, and the Sekht another. Ubara-Tutu suggests the building of the ark in which the sun-god made the passage.

Now in the first chapter of the Ritual, Taht shows us how he preceded Ptah as the builder of the ark. There is a personal identification of Taht the god with the Tat image of founding and type of

---

[1] Lenormant, *Ib.* 203.   [2] *Rit.* ch. i.   [3] Lenormant, p. 139, *note.*

duration. One form of the Tat symbol is a kind of fourfold pillar-cross, the figure of the four quarters and corners on which the luni-solar circle was established; this was set up in Tattu, the eternal region, when the sun or the soul had crossed. Taht, the deity, identifies himself in person with the Tat image which is also set up by Ptah. He proclaims, "I am Tat, the son of Tat, conceived in Tat, born in Tat." He is the lunar establisher; Ptah, the solar. Taht further claims to be the Workman of the gods.

He says,[1] "I am the great Workman who made the ark of Sekari on the stocks." He asserts himself to be the builder of the ark of Ptah; that is, he gives priority to the lunar ark, and states that he built it; and there can be no doubt that the lunar zodiac preceded the solar. The Assyrian TUTU and Egyptian TAHT are not one and the same deity; but the application of Tut to establish, to beget, be the father, is the same; and TAHT was the lunar establisher, who built the boat which was afterwards the solar bark of Ptah. Also in the Babylonian cosmogony the moon was first created in a verifiable way, whilst the sun is said to be the child of the moon.

In the "Chapter made on the sixth day of the month, the day of being conducted in the boat of the sun," it is said of the sun being towed along through the lower world, and "*Stopping the dissolution of the leg of the firmament*" where it grows weak; "*Seb and Nu are delighted in their hearts, repeating the name—Growing light, the beauty of the sun in its light, is in its being an image for the great Inundater, the Father of the gods*,"[2] which aptly describes the sun-god as the Glow, and the passage makes this to be the living likeness of the father of the gods, one form of whom is Ubara-Tutu. Now the Egyptian father of the gods is SEB (a modified form of Sebti or Sut), and according to Berosus it was the god Kronus (Seb) who appeared to Xisuthrus in a vision and gave him warning of the great flood that was coming to destroy mankind. It was Kronus (Time) who gave him instructions to build a ship. This tends to identify TUTU as the father of the gods who is SEB in the Egyptian mythos.

The Egyptian Tat-image is a type of the four corners on which the circle was founded. This fourfold ideograph of Tattu, the everlasting, is reproduced in the Tetrapolis of Izdubar, composed of Babilu, Uruk, Surippak, and Nipur, which corresponds to the Biblical Tetrapolis of Nimrod. The Tat of Ptah was a fourfold pillar, and Ptah was designated the Workman of the gods. In the legend of Ishtar and Izdubar the goddess is charged with transforming the Workman into a pillar and setting him in the midst of the desert, *i.e.* at the boundary.

The hero of the Chaldean deluge, according to Berosus and the Greeks, was named XISUTHRUS, and he appears as the SISITHES of Lucian.[3] SISIT is an Egyptian word, meaning flame; and it seems probable that it enters into the name of IZDUBAR. Smith at first

[1] *Rit.* ch. i. [2] Ch. cxxxvi. [3] *De Dea Syria,* 12.

rendered Izdubar by Sisit, without showing its significance in Egyptian. Nor is it found unabraded either in Akkadian or Assyrian. Bar is fire. Sisit-bar or SISTU-BAR would denote the flame of fire, and Bar also means height, the supreme fire, not the setting glow. Now the older Akkadian star-god of fire, Bilgi, is continued in Izdubar as solar god, and Bar not only means fire, but as Bar-Sutekh (Eg.) was the god of the fire of the dog-star. Sisit-bar would thus denote the flame of Bar or Bilgi; the name Sistubar would then modify into Izdubar.

Izdubar is undoubtedly the sun; and his twelve legends, like the twelve labours of Herakles, relate to the solar passage through the twelve signs. Hea-Bani becomes his helpmate in his labours, and assists him in slaying the swallowing bull, a type of the all-devouring earth considered as the grave. Hea-Bani figures on the seals and gems as a satyr having a human body, with the *horns* and legs of a goat-like creature. He is the Assyrian form of the Greek Pan and the Roman Faunus. The square-cut ears of Pan are similar to those of the Fenekh, the square-eared Abyssinian wolf-dog, a type of Bar-Typhon; and the name of PANAX is letter for letter the same as Fenekh; so is the Irish FAINCHE, a name of the Fox, another type of Sut. Also the volume known in Sweden as *Fan's Bibel* (Devil's Bible) has a portrait of Fan for its frontispiece. This is a hideous Ape, green and hairy, probably the ape of the Wagner legends, *Anerhahn.* Baal-Ian (בעל-יען) is the name of a Phœnician god answering to the Greek Pan. Pan is Âan with the masculine article prefixed, and the Äan is Pan; or rather Pan is Âan (Eg.), which word, with the full consonant, is Fan. But the ape Kafi (later Hapi), is finally traceable as one of the types of Shu, two of whose names are Anhar and Âan, an equivalent for ANERHAHN. In the Four Genii, Anup (jackal) represents Sut, and the ape Shu. Therefore Pan, Fan the Âan (monkey), is founded on Shu, called the son of Ra, as Bani is the son of Hea. Shu, in one of his more ancient characters, was the "god provided with two horns," "in that name which is thine of *Smiting Double-Horns*,"[1] and this was likewise a type of Bacchus.

Hea-Bani, the friend and companion of the solar Izdubar, the co-conqueror with him of the swallowing monster, which was the bull form of the Apophis, corresponds to Shu, the great assistant and supporter of Ra in the celestial allegory, who "overthrows the wicked far from his father;" who pierces Apophis and repels the monster as the Crocodile. The Bowman of the Gods is possibly intended in the description of Hea-Bani's descent to the underworld, represented as his death. The mourning Izdubar says, "*Mit pa-na a-na irzituv la-ta-na-sik*"—thou dost not take the bow from the ground; the earth has taken and hidden him: the same earth which is personified by the Bull that is conquered by Izdubar

[1] *Mag. Pap.* ii. 8.

and Hea-Bani, in combination, or Ra and Shu, or Jah and Joshua, in the war that goes on for ever. It is in the ninth of the twelve legends of Izdubar that the sun-god bewails[1] the fate of Hea-Bani, enfolded by the mother Earth and covered with her darkness; the tenth and eleventh tablets answer to the sun in the water-signs Capricorn and Aquarius, and relate to the story and characters of the Chaldean deluge; and in the twelfth legend (and tablet) Hea-Bani is raised again from the dead or the underworld at the place of re-emergence, the An of the Egyptian mythos, or the horizon corresponding to the Temple of Bel.[2]

Cuneiform scholars have not gathered much matter respecting the genitrix and the son in the oldest, that is the star-type of the Great Bear and Dog-star. Still these, the true tests of age, are extant, although greatly obscured or effaced by time and the later re-touching.

" *Primus Assuriorum regnavit Saturnus quem Assurii Deum nominavere Saturnum*"—" First of the Assyrians reigned Saturn whom the Assyrians named God."[3] Saturn in his planetary character is but secondary; the first of the name was Sut, the child, RENN or KHE, *i.e.* Sut-Renn or Sutekh, the god of the Dog-star. This was the primordial god. Now an earlier name of Assur has been given as Ashet, or Sut, who was the first Ar (Har), the son. Ashet is a variant of the name of Set or Sut, as in Aseth. The great gods are seven in number, and Assur stands alone. This is shown in the dedication of the months. The month Adar (twelfth) was dedicated to the Seven Great Gods, and the incidental month, Ve-Adar, to Assur. The seven, with the eighth as manifester, were phenomenally the same as those of Egypt, with Sut for the manifester, the planetary application being later.

The Assyrian god Nebo is in some respects identical with the Egyptian deity Taht, as Hermanubis; Taht, the interpreter of the gods, the divinity of learning and literature. Nebo is the god of wisdom, learning and letters. He is designated the Supreme Intelligence; also he is god of the planet Mercury, which connects him with the Greek Hermes. But the rootage must be sought in Sut-Anubis who is sometimes blended with Taht in the process of bringing on the types. Anubis, Anup, or Nub is a secondary and a duplicated form of Sut, also found in the Hebrew Seth-Anosh, or Anosh as the son of Seth, and in the dog and wolf types; Anush (Eg.) being a name of the wolf. Anup is he who announces, as the voice, word, or messenger of the cycle. Anup is the primordial prophet; and Anup passes

---

[1] K. 3060. In the translation of the fragment by Mr. Boscawen, Hea-Bani is said to be struck to the ground by MIKIE and TAMBUKKU, of whose names nothing is known. In Egyptian, MAKHAU means to strangle and steal, or kidnap. TEM denotes negation, to terrify, swoop, subdue, shut up; and BEKA is to depress, set down, naked. It may be in relation to TAMBUKKU as the Naspu, the stupefiers, the deadly narcotizers, that TAMBAK is the name used in Egypt for a peculiar species of Persian tobacco.
[2] *Bib. Arch.* vol. iv. part ii. p. 267. [3] Servius, *Ad Æneid*, i. 642; Movers, 185.

into the name for the prophet, Nabi or Nebo. Anubis the Announcer prophesied the rise of the Nile by his heliacal rising; and the spring, by his heliacal setting. As Apuat, the double guide of ways, ANUP is also identical with Nebo at the morning and evening gate of souls. Nabach (Heb.) means to bark, to howl as a dog; and Sut-Anup was a type of the Dog-star. The dog's bark was an early form of prophecy. The Armenian Nabog and Arabian Nabuk imply the dog or jackal that howled in the dark and prophesied. When the dog, ape, or jackal type was changed for the human form, it was still continued in the hairy man, the Samson whose strength lay in his hair; this is a readable mode of continuing the type, and the statues of Nebo show him with a robe reaching from the breast downwards, and with very long beard and hair.

Sut-Anubis could hardly be pourtrayed at first as the Scribe of the gods; he belonged to a time prior to the invention of writing. He was the voice of the gods however, as the dog, the ass, jackal, and wolf, each of which was an image of the proclaimer. But when the Anosh was continued in the lunar form, we have the writer, the scribe of the gods. SAK, in Akkadian, is a name or title of Nebo as god of the stylus and letters. In Egyptian, SKHA or Saakh means to write, writing, depict, represent, influence, illumine; and the SKHA is a scribe, the typical man of letters. Immediately after the time of Mena, however, Sut-Anubis is the recognized divinity of the writings in Egypt.

The god who particularly presides over the river Tigris is named ZTAK, and in one of the Akkadian magical hymns he is called "the god Ztak, the great Messenger, the *supreme Ensnarer* amongst the gods, like the God of the Heights,"[1] or, in the Assyrian, "who has begotten him." Whether the same deity or not, Ztak the Ensnarer of the Waters equates with Sevekh the Ensnarer, whose type is the crocodile, and whose name signifies the catcher, capturer, or ensnarer. Sevekh (or Khebek) and Sutekh are children (Khe, the child) of the genitrix Typhon, the one solar, the other stellar. Ztak's consort is the NIN-MUK, lady of building, or the building, that is, the abode. MUK (Akk.) denotes building. The MAEKA (Hindustani) is the maternal mansion, and MAGHA (Sanskrit) the typical abode. A fuller form of the name of MUK is found in MENGA, the month of brick-making, and therefore of MENKHA (Eg.), the brick-maker, which tends to identify her with MÂKHA (Eg.), whose full name is MENKA or MENKHAT, the feminine potter, worker, creator, and builder, who holds forth the two vases in her hands. The two vases, as types of the two truths, image the womb and breast. The breast of MENKAT passed into the long breast-shaped vase of that name, with nipple-like stand. The other became the ORC or womb-shaped vase of Egypt and Greece.

[1] Lenormant, *Chal. Magic,* p. 11.

Also MENKA, in the reduced form of MENSA, for the city of pots, or pottery, occurs on the granite altar of Turin[1] as a place of Hathor. MENKAT, the potter and shaper of earth, whether as bricks or vases, supplies the name for Ware (earthenware) in the Hebrew MAGCHAH and MAGCHOTH.[2] The living representative of the potteress and the shaper, as the womb, is still extant in the female maker of the Craggan in Lewis. The name of Menkat, as previously shown, deposits MENÂT, MAÂT, MAKAT, MAKA, MÂYA, and MÂ, together with the goddesses personified under those names, which include the Irish MACHA, Hindu and Greek MAYA, Phœnician MÔT, and Assyrian Nin-MUK. Here the triliteral word is first, and the monosyllabic is last; MA being the latest form of the original Menkha. Ma, to measure, is the earlier MAKHA (Eg.), to measure, and MENKAT is the yet earlier measurer. This is shown by the Menkat vase, a type of liquid measure; and the vase represents the sign of measure, as the TEKHU, an instrument corresponding to our needle of the balance (Makha), for measuring weights, in which case the vase of MENKAT becomes the vase of MÂ.

Mêt (Coptic) and Ment (Eg.) denote No. 10, and in the Hoopah language MINCH-la, for No. 10, preserves the triliteral form of Men and Mâ.

In Sanskrit, MAKI signifies the twin creators, the originators of all beings, otherwise called heaven and earth. In Chinese the beginning, that which is primordial, is called MENG. In the Maori, the twins are MAHANGA. So MAHANGA, the snare, answers to MENÀ (*i.e.* Menka, Eg.), for the collar; and in Irish the collar, bracelet, or anything worn on the neck or arm, is a MUINCE, a form of MANACLE or MANICÆ; in English, the MUNGER is a horse-collar. The reduced form is again shown in MAKH (Eg.), to be ripe; the prior form in MAONGA, Maori, to be ripe. So the MAKH, or MUK, of many languages, is MINGE, in English Gipsy, for the womb, and MIONACRE in Gaelic for the internal parts, whence came the expression for our common origin in the one mould, "We were all *mung* up in the same trough." MUNGE, English for the mouth (the Maori MANGAI, mouth), deposits both MUN and MUG for the mouth, just as MENKA becomes MENA, and MACHA, the intermediate link being extant in Khaling, as MÂCHHA, for the typical old woman or mother, which shows by the accent the original MANCHHA, who becomes the MAKE, English spouse or mate; MKE, Swahili, a wife; and MAKAU, Maori, a spouse.

The primeval goddess and mother of the gods is named ZIKUM, a variant of which is Zigara. A fragment of an ancient Akkadian poem, containing the primordial imagery of all mythology, tells of the tree in Eridu, the celestial birthplace, which is the same tree that is the type of source in the Egyptian mythos, from which Nupe or Hathor pours the water of life. "In Eridu, a dark pine grew," and "its

---

[1] Col. D, line 7.   [2] Neh. x. 3.

shrine (was) the couch of mother Zikum; like a forest spread its shade; there was not (any) who entered not within it. It was the seat of the mighty, the mother, begetter of Anu. Within it also was Tammuz."[1] ZIKUM, who is here personified as the one great mother, is identical with the Egyptian SEKHEM, a name of the shrine itself. Tammuz, called Duzi, the only one, in Akkadian, is born in this shrine. In the Ritual, one form of Horus, the son, is "Har who dwells in SEKHEM," or "Horus who dwells in the shrine," the secret, shut-place, the feminine creatory. A kind of sistrum-mirror, the symbol of reflecting and reproducing, is also named the SEKHEM, the looking-glass being a well-known emblem of the genitrix, following the "Eye," called the "Mother of the Gods."

Davkina, the consort of Hea, is the goddess of the deep. She represents the Bau, Baut, or void, personified in the Phœnician Great Mother Beuth, who was the goddess of Byblus, and in Buto, the Greek form of Sekht or Pekht. The Egyptian Bau is the void, the hole of the tomb, over which Num is said to preside. Tefnut is a form of Pekht, the lioness-headed goddess. Tef means to drip, spit, evacuate, menstruate; like Davkina, she is a goddess of primeval source, as moisture, which is finally blood; hence Davkina is Damkina, and dam is blood. So Tef (Eg.), to drop, is determined by the flower of blood. KENA, in Assyrian, as in many other languages, denotes the feminine abode. The first Tef, Dav, or Dam was the old Typhon.

At this point we are compelled to make another digression. As already intimated, one object of the present work is to interpret the primitive history and sociology from their reflexions in the mirror of mythology and symbolism. The ancients preserved the past in their own way.

A Chinese sage tells us that "Antiquity was illumined by a clear light, of which scarcely a ray has come down to us. We think the ancients were in darkness, only because we see them through the thick clouds from which we have ourselves emerged. Man is a child born at midnight; when he sees the sun rise, he thinks that yesterday never existed." There is some truth in this; but it is easily mis-construed, because the children, waking from their own darkness, and finding gleams of an earlier light in the world after a while, have said it was direct from heaven; the light of revelation no longer vouchsafed to them, and in their ignorance have held it to be divine and solely the divine. Naturally interpreted, it was the starlight that precedes the day. Nor has the light of the remotest past been lost—not one ray of it—however ignorant we may be of the process of preservation, any more than the rays of sunlight which were gathered up in the coal-deposits millions of years ago for the fuel of to-day. To me it seems that nothing has been lost, and the depths of the human consciousness are mental mines as permanent as those of earth. But the way in

[1] *Records*, vol. ix. 146, 147.

which the stereotyping has been effected independently of *us* gives one an awful insight into the taciturnity of the Eternal.

One method of preserving the past was by giving different names to the same things, to be used by the two sexes. The custom was current among the North American Indians, the Kaffirs, in their custom of HLONIPA, and the Caribs. The latter hold that each one of them has a good spirit-attendant for his divinity, whom he calls ISHEIRI; that is the divine name used by the males. But the name used by the women for their attendant-spirits is SHEMUN, or CHEMUN. This can be interpreted by Egyptian mythology.

The earliest deities on the monuments are the SMEN, the eight (founded on the seven stars or seven spirits of the Great Bear and the Dog-star) great gods in SMEN or AM-CHEMUN. The eight Smen, who were the first *determiners* of time and period, became the eight gods of the primitive cult, and the eight spirits in a later phase; the seven with the manifester or Messiah-son, the Asar or Isheiri of the male nature; otherwise the seven cows and their bull, who says (in the Ritual), "When I am the bull of the cows, I am at the upper parts of the heavens," *i.e.* in the south.[1] They were the most ancient gods of chaos and night. These became the " spirits " of various races and peoples; they belonged to the worship of the genitrix, and being so old were afterwards degraded. Thus in Egyptian the Khemu (Shemau) were a questionable class of spirits, and the SHEMAU are Typhonian genii. The SMEN were Typhonian and first, and their worship is preserved in this curious custom of the Carib women still calling on the " SHEMUN " spirits, whilst the men call upon ISHEIRI, a name which looks like that of the son of the mother, the Sheri, or pubescent youth, known as Hesiri or Asar in Egypt; Assur in Assyria; Arthur, in Britain; and by other names of the son who was his own father, when he became the husband of his mother.

The first creation and reckoning of time belonging to Smen, the Smen as the eight, the two as mother and son, terminates with the Deluge, called in the Hebrew version the Deluge of Noah. The seven are represented by the seven patriarchs of one list, ending with Lamech, who produces the triad of sons, as does Noah in the list of ten patriarchs. The seven have but one origin wherever found, or whatsoever they may be called, whether the seven spirits of the Bear, as in the Ritual; the seven Elohim, sons of God, Kabiri, Khnemu, Hohgates, Rishis, or what not; and in the fourth chapter of Genesis the seven of Eve, or Ursa Major, are followed, and the eight Smen are complete in Seth, who is the father of the Anosh, the manifester, the Anush (Eg.), or Sut-Anup. These in one list are the predecessors of the Deluge; and all the earliest history, sociology, and legendary lore of mythology and typology belong to this period of time and mode of reckoning. For example, all the earliest human transactions

[1] Ch. 105.

in the world, related in myth and tradition, belong to the time of the goddess of the seven stars, whose manifester was the eighth; Sut in the Sabean cult and Taht in the lunar. Thus, it is said by Tacitus, "The Jews escaped from the island of Crete at the time when Saturn (Sut, the child) was driven from his throne by Jupiter;" which, when interpreted, was when the worship of the son of the mother was superseded by that of the father, the Ju-pater, and men had personified the male parent in heaven. The same writer remarks, "Some say that in the reign of Isis there was an emigration from Egypt into the adjacent lands." The first appearance of Isis is as Hes-Taurt, the cow-headed genitrix, who followed the hippopotamus-goddess of the seven stars; she was the lunar genitrix, who continued the old Sabean mother, Typhon. This identifies a time in the astronomical chronicles. Both the star and lunar mythos were pre-solar. Further, Tacitus reports that many considered the Jews to be Æthiopians, who were impelled by fear and by the hatred manifested against them to change their settlements in the reign of king Kepheus.[1] As we have seen, Kepheus was an ancient star-god, represented in a dual character by the constellation of that name, and by the star *Cor Leonis*, and by the two lions of Egypt, or Shu and Anhar, the Moses and Joshua of the Jews.

The primitive Chaldeans and Babylonians were known to the Greeks by the names of Chaldeans and Kephenes. The Kephenes were synonymous with Æthiopians. They were descended from king Kepheus. Dicæarchus says the Chaldeans were first called Kephenes from king Kepheus. "Before (the time of) king Kepheus," says Hellanicus,[2] "there were some Chaldees who extended beyond Babylon, as far as Choche," and Diodorus Siculus calls the Chaldees the most ancient Babylonians. Kepheus is identified with Kûsh, called the begetter of Nimrod.[3] Kush, as before shown, is the Egyptian Khepsh, the north, as the hinder part; and in the planisphere Kepheus is the king of Æthiopia or Kush. Thus Kush is not a person, but a quarter, the Egyptian Khepsh, and Kepheus is its monarch.

In the Greek traditions of Kepheus and the Kephenes, Perseus plays a prominent part; and in the celestial allegory Perseus is the son-in-law of Cassiopœia, queen of Æthiopia, or Khepsh (כוש), the Khepsh and Khebm (Kâm) of the beginning belonging to the oldest genitrix, and to the north as the birthplace. Kepheus must have been a son of the Typhonian genitrix, continued as Hathor, but he introduced a new *régime* as a Male Lawgiver.

In the tenth chapter of Genesis, the black race of Ham and Kush are placed before the Akkadians, Babylonians, and Assyrians. Nimrod, the typical progenitor of these peoples, is the founder of Babel, Erech, Akkad, and Kalneh. Nimrod, as affirmed by Berosus, was the

---

[1] *Histor.* lib. v. [2] Stephen of Byzantium.
[3] Gen. x. 8.

first that ever bore the title of a shepherd king,[1] and Kepheus, as Regulus, is the shepherd-king of the heavenly flock, the star Sib-zi-anna,[2] a name of Regulus and of Mars, who was also the planetary type of Kepheus (Shu) in Egypt.

In speaking of the naming of Northern Æthiopia in the first chapter, it might have been pointed out that the birthplace of Bacchus was Mount Nyssa, which, says Herodotus, is "above Egypt in Æthiopia."[3] Nsa (Eg.) is a name of the north, like Khepsh, and of the birthplace in the beginning, the hinder quarter; and this furnishes another proof of the namers of Northern Æthiopia being further south at the time of the naming.

According to Anacreon, AITHIOPAIS, or the son of Æthiops, was a surname of Bacchus. Æthiops is identical with Kush, the parent of the Æthiopians; and Bacchus is a form of Shu or Kepheus, with whom we are about to identify Nimrod and the Kephenes, who are so named after Kepheus, the star-god. The Kepheus meant is the king of the celestial Æthiopia, Khepsh, the north, not a human progenitor of the people. The name of the north is also an element in the mapping out of the land; the Kephenes and Chaldees having been a dual form of the ancient people of the empire, the earliest Kephenes were probably seated in the north.

The Jerusalem Targum renders the statement of Genesis x. respecting Nimrod, the mighty hunter, by saying, "He was mighty in hunting and in sin before the Lord; for he was a hunter of the sons of men, in their languages."

The dispersion of language will be shown to represent figuratively the naming of places in the planisphere, which entered a second phase under Kepheus or Nimrod. There can be no difficulty in identifying Nimrod as Shu or Kepheus, Egyptian Kafi.

The eight gods ruled in Am-Smen before the lifting of the solar firmament; Shu, who is pourtrayed in the act of supporting the celestial vault, is designated the elevator of heaven. In the Egyptian creation, Shu separated the earth and the waters in two masses, and excited the hostility of the evil powers.[4] This creative act was afterwards attributed to Ptah in his name of "LET-THE-EARTH-BE." Shu was pourtrayed as a hunter, with his dogs; but there is more than the hunter in the Hebrew word ציד, which means properly a catcher,[5] and agrees with the Egyptian Tsat, or Sett, a noose, to catch, to catch in and with the noose. This Sett, noose or tie, is carried in the hand as the special type of Kepheus (Shu), and identifies him with the Hebrew ציד, rendered the hunter, but which should be the capturer, as shown by the hieroglyphical sign.

In the Syriac, Arabic, and Septuagint versions, Nimrod is called the giant; the name of Shu also signifies to extend, to elongate; and

---

[1] Cory's *Fragments.*   [2] M. Oppert.   [3] B. ii. 146.
[4] Maspero, *Hist. Ancienne des Peuples d'Orient*, p. 62.   [5] Jer. xvi. 16.

in the *Magic Papyrus*, Shu (Kafi) appears as a giant, the giant of seven cubits.

Nimrod began to be a "Gibor" in the earth. Kafi is a name of Shu, the Greek Kepheus. Kef (Eg.) means force, might, puissance, and Shu bears the ideograph of this might and force in the rump of the lion on his head. He is the image of the נבר of Genesis, the lord of force. This sign of force is the determinative of the word NEM, meaning force, to force back, turn back by force, as the sun is said to be forced along by the conducting of Shu.[1] Nemrut is a name found on the monuments. There were three princes of the name of Nemrut or Nimrod in the twenty-first dynasty, one of whom was conquered by the Æthiopian ruler Pankhi. A Nimrod, the father of Sheshank I., twenty-second dynasty, is supposed to have been of Libyan race. The name has been derived by Brugsch Bey, from Nimr-at, the son of the leopard; but it has been overlooked that Nimr, for the leopard, is represented in the hieroglyphics by Nem, the spotted skin. Nimr, the Semitic name of the leopard, is written in Assyrian Ni-im-ru. In Egyptian "ru" is the lion; the twin-lions are the ruti, the two ru. One of the two lions is a leopard or leopard-cat—the maneless lion.

Shu, the lion of the sun, transforms into the leopard or cat, and becomes the lion-leoparded of heraldry. That is the Assyrian NIMRU.[2] Nem-Ru (Eg.), determined by the spotted skin, is the leoparded-lion. Also Nem means the second, and Nem-ru is the second lion of the leopard-cat type. The Nim-ru, then, is the leopard named as the second lion; the second of the twin Ruti is Nem-Ruti. In Arabic NIMARAT is the plural or *dual* form of the leopard's name, corresponding to NEMRUTI. Shu, as Anhar, or Kepheus with the Khept sign of Nem carried on his head, is the Nem-ruti, the second, the leopard of the two lions or Mau; whence the name of Nimrod may be derived as Egyptian. When the Osirian in the Ritual[3] exclaims, "I am the two lion (or dawn) gods, the SECOND of the sun, Tum in the lower country," that is equivalent to his saying, in this very sense, "I am Nimrod." Nem is the second (the spotted skin), the twin-lions are the Ruti, and Anhar in this character is the Nemrut or Nimrod.

Another meeting-point between Shu and Nimrod can be found in the statement of the *Paschal Chronicle*,[4] where the Mysians are said to be descended from Nimrod; "Nebrod, the huntsman and giant, from whom came the Mysians." Lydia formed a part of the same kingdom of Pergamos as Mysia. Mysia bears the name of Mashu, and Lydia of the Ludi or Ruti. This will explain why names of the mythical monarchs, Nimrod and Assur, have not been discovered on the bricks of the cities assigned to them. They were characters, personifications, not persons, belonging to the heavens, and therefore

[1] *Rit.* ch. xvii.
[3] Ch. xxxviii.
[2] *Rit.* ch. xvii.
[4] Vol. i. p. 50.

divinities. Hence, while their names remained as human or ethnic titles, the real characters were continued as gods under other names.

Although they work without the present clue to his mythological nature, Assyriologists have asserted that Amarud, Marduk, and Silik-mulu-khi are names or titles of Nimrod. Among other names of the god Marduk, Amarud, or Nimrod collected by Norris, is that of Su,[1] the equivalent of Shu in Egyptian. Shu has the meaning of light, and the god Shu is also called the light of the sun; he was the lamp of Ra that showed the position of the invisible sun. Light, splendour, the brilliant, is a meaning assigned to AM-AR (Akk.); so AM (Eg.) is splendour and light. Mar signifies the youthful, splendid, the Red; a name especially applicable to Mars, and to that planet only, which was assigned to Shu as his planetary type. For it should be explained that when the length of the planetary cycles was made out new names were created. But the new phenomena were also assigned to the more ancient divinities. In this way the genitrix of the seven stars was made the lunar goddess as Hes-taurt (Ishtar), and Venus was assigned to her in the two characters called the two divine sisters, Venus below and Venus above the horizon, by which the two truths and aspects of the motherhood were likewise expressed. Thus the types of the Great Mother were Ursa Major, the Moon and Venus. Mars was given to Shu (Kepheus); Jupiter to the dual parent who had been the earlier son of a dual nature,—in Egypt Ptah; Mercury denotes a Sabean form of Taht, and Saturn is the planet of Sut. Assyriologists who identify Marduk with Jupiter, and Jupiter with Nimrod, are entirely wrong. Mar, the Red, is Mars. The Mar in Marduk, and Amar in Amarud, no doubt represent the Egyptian MAHARU, the youth, the young hero, the warrior who was Mars as the planetary type, and Nimrod (Kepheus-Shu), as the hunter, the shepherd, the lawgiver and king of Kush.

Merodach, at Babylon, is described by Diodorus as represented by a figure that was "standing and walking." This is the portrait of Anhar (Kepheus), who is depicted in a marching attitude, with the noose-sign of capture in his hand. The same character is given to the god called Silik-mulu-khi, who says of himself, "I am he who marches before Hea; I am the warrior, the eldest son of Hea, his messenger."[2] The god Marduk, the marcher, is found to be accompanied by four dogs. It is said, on one of the mythological tablets, "The god Ukkalu, the god Akkumu, the god Iksuda and the god Iltebu, are the four names of the dogs of Marduk."[3] The "dogs of Shu," the "dogs following Shu," the "Punishers of Shu," are to be found in the Ritual, although the number is not given; these are the dogs that hunt with the Capturer. The "dogs following Shu"

---

[1] *Assyrian Dictionary*, p. 853.
[2] W. A. I. 4, pl. 30, 3; *Chaldean Magic*, p. 190, Eng. Tr.
[3] *Bib. Arch.* vol. ii. part ii. p. 245.

apparently implies the legend of Actæon, who was torn in pieces by his own dogs ; and in the story of " Ishtar and Izdubar," [1] the goddess is charged with loving the " king of the land," and with transforming him into a leopard, whereupon his own dogs tore him piecemeal. Kepheus was the king of Kush, and as Shu he was the lion-god who made his transformation into the leopard-cat—a change here attributed to the sorceries of Ishtar.

Silik-mulu-khi is the messenger of Hea, who revealed to man the will and knowledge of the god. He is called the " Great lord of the country, king of the countries, eldest son of Hea, who bringest back (into their periodical movements) heaven and earth. Thou art the favourable Giant : to thee is the sublime bank of the pit of the ocean." [2] Exactly the same change of character takes place with Nimrod, Amarud, or Marduk as with the ancient star-god Shu in Egyptian mythology, where he who was a far earlier god than Ra becomes the son of the sun-god as Shu-si-Ra in a later creation, called by the name of Ra. So Marduk and Silik-mulu-khi, two forms of Nimrod, are each represented as being the son of Hea after the establishment of the solar triad of Hea, Bel, and Anu.

It must have been a curious discovery when men found out and individualized the fatherhood on earth, and this fact is reflected in the setting up of the fatherhood in heaven, which was for the first time established under the solar *régime ;* and the father was Atum in Egypt, Hea in Assyria, or Abraham in Israel. After which, the earlier god, who originated as the child of the mother, is called the son of the father. When Ra, the sun, had become the father of the gods, the fatherhood was extended to the past. He is then said to " Create his name as lord of all the gods ; " the name being identical with the sonship as a type of manifestation. They made much of this discovery or individualization of the male parentage by which they had found the father in heaven, whom they enthroned above the ancient genitrix until the name, the Renn, the child of both, came to supersede the father and mother in the later stage of theology.

In the Assyrian mythology the " supreme name " is a secret with which Hea alone, the divine father, is acquainted. He says to his phantom messenger whom he sends to Hades for the release of Ishtar, " Awe her (Nin-ki-gal) with the NAME." " Silik-mulu-khi, as the son of Hea, is his NAME." Hence the magical incantations represent Hea as teaching the NAME to his son ; but it is unuttered, because he and the name are synonymous. And the reason why this secret of the name rests with Hea is because he impersonates the divine fatherhood. Ra is described as the god who covers his limbs with names. This doctrine is echoed in the *Divine Pymander.* " For this reason he hath all names, because he is the one father ; and therefore he hath

[1] Col. 2, 14-17.
[2] " Akkadian Hymn," Lenormant, *Chaldean Magic,* p. 193.

no name, because he is the father."[1] The name was the manifester,
the Anosh, the son; hence the manifestations were identical with the
names. We see the way toward this doctrine of the fatherhood in
the self-effacement of the father at the birth of his son, and the sinking
of his own personal name in that of the son; the doctrine of Smen
(Eg.), or the setting up of the son in place of the father.

The supreme secret taught by Hea, the god of learning, to his son,
when he makes his appeal to his father, is called "the Number."
Numbers were a mode of invocation and conjuration. Amongst
these, Seven is pre-eminent. But there is a secret in Egyptian,
connected with the origin of numbers and reckoning; with the
two hands and with the ten moons of gestation. No. 10 is likewise
related to the son, possibly on account of the ten moons of gestation.
Har, the name of the son of the mother, has been found to mean
No. 10 in Egyptian; and the type-name of the son of the mother,
as Assur or Ashar, also stands for No. 10, as ASAR in Hebrew;
ASHAR, Arabic; SAR, Syriac; ASSER, Gafat; ASHUR, Tigré;
ASSIR, Hurur; ASSUR, Arkiko; ASHIRI, Kaffa.

Khemt, the Egyptian name for No. 3, has also been found with the
value of No. 10. To be KHEMT is to attain adultship and become the
homme fait, the sherau of thirty years, or thrice ten. Har and Khemt
for No. 10 thus meet in the son, who was called Khem-Horus on
attaining maturity, as the pubescent virile god in the character of the
begetter. The son, therefore, represented the NUMBER as he did
the NAME. He was the repeater, and the number ten is the type of
repetition and renewal.

In his "Secret Sermon on the Mount of Regeneration," Hermes
tells his son Tat that "The Number Ten, O son, is the begotten of
souls; life and light are united where the number of unity is born of
the spirit. Therefore, according to reason, unity hath the number
of ten, and the number of ten hath unity."[2]

In the Chaldean Kabala the gods are each designated by a number,
in a series that ranges from one to sixty. A tablet in the library of
Nineveh gives a list of the chief gods, together with the mystical
number of each. The subject will be discussed in the "Typology
of Number." The same system was extant in Egypt, where Taht
is the lord of the No. 8, and Shu, or Su, bears the name of the
No. 5, and Aft of the No. 4. The later name and number are
founded on the four quarters. Each was established in phenomena
as these were mastered and personified. The Tat emblem, designed
by Taht and given to Ptah, is an image of the four quarters. The four-
legged hippopotamus and the couch were likewise types of Apt and
the four quarters; also the stone hewn four-square. When they added
the upper and lower heaven to the four cardinal points the cube was
adopted as the six-sided type of support for the foundation of things,

---

[1] B. v. 34.   [2] *Divine Pymander*, b. vii. 51, 52, Everard.

as the Tat was the type of the four quarters. The Egyptian Ses for No. 6, supplies the Assyrian Sos, and the six-sided block or cube is a Ses. As an emblem of supporting and maintaining power, this also becomes a Seser, following that of the head and backbone of the same name. Now Anu, when raised to the supreme seat, is called the god One, the god whose number is one; and yet he is at the same time identified with the No. 6, as the sign of the single stroke also stands for the Sos cycle of sixty years. The formula of the Templars in their worship of Mete was, that the root of the divinity was one and seven. That of Anu was one and six. The sole foundation for one and seven is the Great Bear. The foundation of the fourfold one is that of the four quarters; and of the six-one, the cube of the heavens, the Seser. Anu was designated the Sesru, the founder and sustainer, when the heavens were formed according to the cube-block of the stone building, when the upper and lower heavens were added to south, north, east, and west, and a luni-solar month was formed with six divisions of five days each. The ancient mysteries are very simple in their nature, when understood; our ignorance has made them appear profound, whereas they are only profoundly simple.

As with the gods and the phenomena which they typify, so is it with the localities, scenery, and imagery of the other world; the world of the astronomical allegory rendered eschatologically, divided into the upper and the nether halves, which range in one reckoning from solstice to solstice,—these having once been the long and the short of it all,—or from equinox to equinox.

TIAMAT, the personification of primordial source as the water of the abyss, is the same as the TAVTHE of Damascus and the THA-VATH— Omoroka of Berosus, the name being identical through the permutation of M and V. TAVTHE is the same word as the Hebrew TOPHET, the place of the dead and unclean things represented by the valley of Hinnom. But the first TOPHET, or TAVTHE, was the hell of waters, and with this agrees the Hebrew תהום (Tahvm) for the deep,[1] which, at the time of the Deluge, was depicted as bursting forth with its overwhelming waters and reproducing chaos. TAHVM, as a plural form, is the equivalent of Tepht (Eg.), the lower Tep or primal point of commencement. Tepht is identical with the Seven Provinces of Dyved that were submerged by the Deluge, the cause of which is thus addressed :—" Seithenin, stand thou forth and behold the billowy rows. The sea has covered the plain of Gwydneu."[2] The TEPHT is still extant in DEPT-ford on the Thames. TIAMAT, TAVTHE, TOPHET, TAHVM, and DYVED are all one, and the original is the TEPHT (Eg.), the abyss, cave, hole of source, the entrance called a door, a valve, and the hole of a snake. This was the passage of the lower heaven first figured as the earth when it was not yet known that the earth was a globe; hence the hole of the worm and the snake; the mud of

[1] Gen. vii. 11.   [2] *Black Book of Caermarthen*, 38; Skene, ii. 302.

the eel; the baut of the grave; the waters of the Tebt (Topht), the hippopotamus-type of the genitrix before the stars, the moon, and sun could be imaged as passing through a void of clear space below corresponding to the vault above.

The Assyrian Beth-zida, or Tzida, the temple of life, repeats the Egyptian TES, or TSUI-TA, the deep, the abyss of all beginning, the place of the waters. Tes (Eg.), the very self, the concealed, indwelling, *enveloped* soul of self, becomes the Assyrian TZI for the inhering spirit of life, and as locality the TSUITA is equivalent to TZIDA. ZUGE is the name of the "Void of procreative Nature," *i.e.* the uterus of creation. This, in Egyptian SEKHA, a shrine, a gate, was worn down to Sesh, the place of opening and issuing forth; the nest, the lotus, the house of preparation (Sesht), the secret place of mystery, ferment, combustion, and generative power in general. Sesht means Alcohol, a first form of spirit. As Saakh it denotes a spirit of illumination and enlightening or inspiring influence. Egyptian will people the Assyrian void with tangible meanings.

The Zuge or Sekha is personified as Zikum, under the tree-type of the producer. The SAQAMAH (שקמה), in Hebrew, identifies the Tree of ZIKUM with the SYCAMORE or SYCAMINE, in which the type passes by name into English. The SAGUMA, in the African Gura, is a house; the SKEMMA, Icelandic, a store-house. The tree-shrine of Zikum, in Eridu, like the Egyptian tree of life, the ash, in the pool of Persea, also stood in the pool of the Two Waters of the waterer as Hea. Here was the place of new birth for the sun every spring, in Eridu. The birthplace and place of new birth is also called the Meskhen. Para is likewise a name of the abode of birth, the Pa, house of Ra. The whole of this scenery is crowded into a line found on one of the cones—the seed-symbol.

In the inscription of Rim-Agu, he is denominated "lord of Bit-PARRA, MIZKEN of ancient Eridu,"[1] who keeps the religious festivals. He is lord of the solar house in Para, the place of new birth in Eridu, that is of the terrestrial copy of the imagery set in the heavens by the Egyptians, the MIZKEN or MESKHEN being a type equivalent to the producing tree, the shrine or womb of the great mother herself, who brought forth in Eridu as Zikum.

The "PAL-BI-RI," or the temple of the great gods, built in the beginning, was a title of the city of Assur.[2] This Mr. Smith did not understand. It is the primitive Pal or Par. In the hieroglyphics the ideographic house of the sun is the Par, phonetic Pa, the birthplace. Pa-ra was the sacred name of Heliopolis. The Pa was a palace, and the first palace and PARadise was the PAL or Par which, in Akkadian, is the sexual part of woman, the Egyptian PAR; PIR, Gond, sexual part, belly; PER, English Gipsy, belly; POR, Armenian; BAR, Hungarian; PRUT, Malay; BAYAR, Canarese, for the belly

---

[1] *Records of the Past*, vol. v. 65.   [2] Smith, *Chaldean Genesis*, p. 68.

or womb; Irish, BRU, the womb, as the abode of birth. From this Pâ or Pal comes the Palat (Ass.), the family and the race. The temple of the god Assur, and of the great gods, built in the beginning, is also found in the Fijian BURE, the god's house and name of a temple. It is noticeable too that the Assyrian PALU, a life or lifetime, is paralleled by the Fijian BULA, for life and to live.

The Assyrian "Happy Fields" are the same as the Egyptian Elysium of the Aahru. The "Land of the silver sky" is one with the upper heaven typified by the Hut, the white silver crown; the summit of this region was at the place of the summer solstice, where the eye was full at midsummer, and the spirit is at peace in the abode of the blessed. The nether-world not only includes the same scenery as the Egyptian, together with the great hall of justice; it is likewise described in the same terms, in the descent of Ishtar into Hades, or Bit-Edi, which is also designated the "house of no return," "the house men enter but cannot leave, the road men go but cannot return."[1] In the solemn festal hymn of the Egyptians, which is probably alluded to by Herodotus,[2] it is written, "Ye go to the place whence they (the dead) return not; feast in tranquillity, seeing that there is no one who carries away his goods with him. Yea, behold, none who goes thither comes back again."[3]

The land of no-return is spoken of in the Song of the Harper.[4] Bit-Edi answers to the Egyptian Aati, the place of souls in the hinder quarter, the Hades, the name of which is derived from Kheft. The Assyrian Hades is called Edi or BIT-EDI, the house of assembly. The Egyptian AA-T is the original of the Greek Hades and Russian AD, the place of spirits. The AA-T denotes an abode of souls. There is also a region, in the Assyrian underworld, corresponding to the seven provinces of Dyved, the seven caves, the seven islands, and other forms of the seven found in the eschatological Netherlands.

In one of the cuneiform texts the seven gates of Hades are spoken of as the seven doors (*dalti*) of the underworld.[5] So the house of Osiris, in the Hades of the Egyptian Ritual, contains seven halls and seven staircases.[6] Seven walls encircle a central place as the heart of all. The seven, with the centre, correspond to the region of the eight, SMEN or SESENNU, in the Ritual—the seven, with Sut or Taht as the eighth, for their manifester. This is the Terui, circumference, and the Troy of the British and Greek mythos. At the centre is placed the palace of justice, in which the judge of the dead sits on his throne to deliver judgment and execute justice. This is the palace of Nin-ki-gal, the great goddess of Justice, who in this character equates with Ma, the Egyptian goddess of Truth and Justice, to whom the Hall of the dual Truth is assigned. In this place of the Hall of the Two

---

[1] Col. 1.
[2] B. ii. 78.
[3] *Records of the Past*, vol. iv. 117.
[4] *Ibid.* vol. vi. p. 130.
[5] *Trans. Soc. Bib. Arch.* vol. iv. part ii. p. 293.
[6] Ch. cxlvi.

Truths was the Pool of the Two Truths, Shuma, otherwise called the Pool of Persea (the Tree of Life), from which the water of life welled forth. So in the Assyrian locality of the judgment hall at the centre of the seven circles arose the stream of the water of life,[1] which in another phase was accounted the water of death.

"BIT-ANNA" is frequently referred to in the Inscriptions, but whether Anna should be read god or goddess has not been always determined. A "shrine of Anna was built on the mound near Bit-Ziba, and dedicated to the moon-god, Sin, as his temple—BIT-TI-ANNA, his temple."[2] M. Oppert renders this the "Temple of the Assizes of Oannes." A temple of the Assizes would be the judgment hall of the Egyptian Annu. Bit-ti rendered by Egyptian is the double house, that is the hall of the two truths and of the Assizes. Anna, as Annu, is a place here, not a person; neither the gracious goddess nor the Fish-Man, but the region of the Hall of the Two Truths, the judgment hall where the Assizes took place, and the moon-god as An, a form of Taht, registered the dooms of the righteous and the rejected. Bit-ti-anna, the temple dedicated to Sin, is in accordance with the dual house in Annu as the lunar type. There were three types—the solar, lunar and stellar, or Heliopolis, Hermopolis, and the double holy house of Anup the star-god, one of whose images is the wolf, Sab, Assyrian Zibi; and Bit-ti-anna was on the mound near Bit-ziba,[3] just as in the Ritual and in the zodiac the double holy house of Anup, in Abti, is found next to the Hall of Two Truths in Annu. Apparently the two houses are the same below as those that were figured by the Egyptians in the heaven above.

The parent language will show us that the name of Babylon does not merely mean the gate of God. It is true the gate became a sign of enclosing, and thus of an enclosure; but Bab, the gate, is in too late a sense. The Egyptian shows us an earlier meaning in Bab, to turn, circle, go round, revolve in a circle, the names of a whirlpool and a whirlwind; Baba, a collar, a chain, a hole; Bubu, drops and beads, which are round; Baba, the Great Bear, the revolving constellation. Bebr is the Egyptian for Babel. The Babels were round towers; and the city of Babylon, like all the olden places, was round, walled round, as we say. Bab-ili was not only the gate of the gods, it was a circle, a Kar, as its Egyptian name of Kar, Hebrew Kir, implies. According to the customary way of writing the name as Bab-il-Ra,[4] it was at one time the circle of the sun-god, although the solar cult was not primary, and Babili, the circle of the gods, was the earlier appellative. Bab, as the circle, is corroborated by the name of the Bibbu, given to sailors and to the seven Lubat, the planets, the revolvers, or gods of the orbit. Babylon below was a copy of the circle above. The

---

[1] Boscawen, *Bib. Arch.* vol. iv. part ii. p. 291.
[2] E. I. H. iv. 63; Norris, iii. 1051. [3] *Ins. of Nebuch.* col. 4, 60-64.
[4] Norris, *Dict.* vol. iii. p. 946.

same root enters into Byblus, of which we are told, "After these events *Kronus builds a wall round about his habitation, and founds Byblus*, the first city in Phœnicia;"[1] which shows that Byblus was founded on the circle. The Bab was as ancient as the circular mounds. Another syllable KA, as in KA-Dimirra, is rendered Gate of God. But the KA is the mouth, as the door of the body, the Egyptian KHA and KEP, the uterus and emaning mouth. The gate of the goddess or mother is the primary sense, verifiable in nature.

E-KI, an ancient name of Babylon, means the mound-city, or more literally the habitation of the hollow mound, which relates it to the circular type of the mound-builders, who began with the earth and ended with brick and stone; the mount with the CEFN or cave in it being a still earlier form of the E-KI, and the swelling gestator, the first great house, the earliest. The Elamite and Hebrew GAN, signifying an enclosure, is the Egyptian Khan, earlier Cefn, Gophen, Kafn, or Kivan, and Khent (Eg.) with the feminine terminal.

The oldest name of Babylon is the Akkadian TINTIR, which has no known equivalent. In Egyptian Ten is the elevated seat, the throne, and Teru denotes the circumference, the circle, the Troy, a form of Sesun, the region of the eight gods. TEN-TERU reads the Throne of this circle or circumference, the type of Am-Smen. From this we derive the Tentyris or Denderah of Egypt as identical with Tentir or Babylon. Ten-Teru is literally the seat of the Troy-circle, that of the Great Bear and Dog-star, the eight stars, who became the seven great gods with Assur in Assyria. Denderah was the great seat of Hathor, the lunar form of the genitrix, whose number eight associates her with the eight gods. The seat and circle were the same in Tentir as in Tentyris, and both were the circles of time, one type of which was the Babel-tower of seven stages with the seat at the top, corresponding to the seven-circled enclosure of the British Troy pourtrayed on the stones, which was extant before the building of Trinovantum.

Ka-Dingira, an Akkadian name of Bab-ili or Bab-ilâni, is also extant in Africa as TENKUR (in the Æthiopic inscription of Nastosenen), better known as Dongolah. Kir or Kar is equivalent to Teru, for the circle; Kar (Ass.) being a fortress,—to be walled round. Thus Ten Kur or Dingira is also the seat in the circle, the circular seat, synonymous with the Bab of El, the circle of the gods, the Bab-ilu or Babylon, which is the equivalent of Bab-Ilium, Ilium and Troas being interchangeable names of Troy, where the seat of the circle was Mount Ida or Kheft. The first forms of the Great Mother as of the circle or PLEROMA of eight gods was Stellar. The second, with Hathor as genitrix was Lunar; and TINGAL the name of the moon in Tamul, TINGALU, in Tulu and Canarese, represent the Egyptian or Æthiopic TENKUR and Akkadian DINGIRA. In Egyptian TEN is the half-moon, the fortnight, and KAR denotes

---

[1] Sanchoniathon, Euseb. *Præp. Evang.* b. i. ch. vi.

orbit or course. In this, the lunar stage, the circle would be that of the double or divided lunation represented by ISHTAR as "Goddess Fifteen," and the eight gods in Sesennu who followed the eight of Am-Smen.

In the inscription of Sennacherib, the king in speaking of his fourth campaign says, "On my return, Assur-nadin-sumi, my eldest son brought up at my knees, I seated upon the throne of his kingdom; all the land of LESHAN and Akkad I entrusted to him."[1] Leshan and Akkad are also referred to in the inscription on Bellino's cylinder (14). Apparently the old names are coupled together, as Leshan and Akkad for Sumeri and Akkad. In this naming, the Sumerian folk-title is related in some way to the language, and the ideographic group expresses the language of some thing or act. M. Oppert reads it, the "*language of warship*." M. Lenormant renders it the "language of those *sitting*," from a sign having the meaning of to put, to place, intransitively to sit. A better term is still in use for the "squatters;" to be placed, to sit, to squat, opposed to Nomadic. We have now to seek for the meeting-point of the language of the squatters and the name of the Sumeri.

The laws of language tend to show us that the so-called Semitic origines are Kamitic, and we have to take that step backwards which language took forwards when the K of Kam was transformed into the S of Sam, and the Kamite became known as the Semite or Sumerian. The race of Kam had passed out of the Nomadic condition in Egypt if nowhere else in Africa, before the KA sign was modified into the SA. The phonetic S was not extant at the time the Maori migrated from the common centre, but it was when the Akkadians branched off from the parent stock; and, but for the evolution of the SA from KA, there would have been no Semite or Sumeri. The tip of the crocodile's tail is the sign of KAM, black. This is found to read SAM in later language.[2] Also SAM as well as KAM must have continued to signify black, for SMAT is to blacken the eyebrow with stibium, and SAM is total darkness. One meaning of Sam (Eg.) is to remain in a place and dwell, or to settle in one locality; and SAM, to assemble, flock together, herd, and form guilds, as did the Egyptian fishermen, called the SAMI. The SAMAT are the common multitude, the Semites in a primal sense. SAM, to dwell, be located, fixed, has also the form Skam, to remain, dwell, make a full stop. And Skam only adds the S, for the person, any one, signified by Kam: thus in Egyptian SAM or SEM has two earlier forms in KAM and SKAM. Kam has the same meaning of remaining, dwelling, camping, as Sam and Skam. Sam can be traced back to Kam; the Samite is the Kamite in the second stage, and the language of the squatters, the earliest settlers, is that of the

---

[1] Col. 3, lines 64, 65.   [2] Sharpe, *Eg. Inscrip.* 242.

Sumeri, as the people who first stayed, remained, settled, in the Sumerian land.

The Semitic name has its parallel in a title of the Egyptian lion-gods in the solar and second stage, when they had become the servants of the sun—they who had existed before the solar god was born. The SEM or SEMS is a title of the lion-gods relating to their secondary status as ministers of the sun. In this stage they are equinoctial gods of the horizon and of the east and west. SEM is also a name of the double solar plumes belonging to the sun of the east and west. The Khept sign then placed on the head of Anhar is that of the hinder-part west, he who had represented the north and south as the king of Khepsh and as Regulus the lawgiver.

" The sons of Kam were Kush, Mitzraim, Phut, and Kanaan, and Kush begat Nimrod, and the beginning of his kingdom was Babel, Erekh, Akkad, and Kalneh in the land of Shinar."[1] As the letters N and M are continually equivalents, Shinar and Sumir are possibly interchangeable names for the same country. Shinar is the total land of the four cities, and, in Egyptian, Sem and Shen have the same meaning of two or twin. Shen is two or double. Sem is the double plume, the circle, the twin-total of the heaven divided at first as the north and south. In this sense Sumeri would be synonymous with Shen-gar, the twin-circle. Later the twin-land, the land of the two streams, or the double land of north and south, would be added to, as Sumir with Akkad, and finally become Sumir and Akkad ; Sumir remaining the land of the settlers and the people of the original tongue, the land that was again divided into the four quarters, represented by the four typical cities which constituted the Tetrapolis of Nimrod.

The imagery can be best read in heaven first. The sons of Japheth are seven in number ; the sons of Gomer and Javan form a second seven. These belong to the circle of the seven stars. The sons of Ham are four. These correspond to the four quarters in the heaven above, which had their likeness in Æthiopia, Egypt, Lybia, and Canaan, with Kam (Khebma) and Japhet (Khept) beyond all. Then we are told that Nimrod became a Gibor in the earth. In Egyptian, the KEB is a Lord of the corner, and the four Lords or Genii are the Keb-ari or Kab-ari. Nimrod became one of these. The same meaning enters into the Hebrew Gibul, to bound as with a border, coast, or other limit. The plural Gubulim, Phœnician, denotes the quarter or quarters. Nimrod became one of the four KUBUR which king Sargon had imaged in front of the four celestial regions or four quarters. The earliest figure of the four quarters is the fourfold Apt; the later form of Khebt. These four were typified by the hippopotamus, lion, crocodile and monkey, the four corners of Khepsh or the Bear. Next followed the four quarters of Nimrod, probably

[1] Gen. x. 6-10

marked for us by the great stars Regulus, Antares, Fomalhaut, and Aldebaran.

Persian legends relate how Nimrod formed the project of being borne up to heaven by four immense birds, called Ker-Kes, in an ark or coffer. In Egyptian, KER is the claw, and means to seize with the claw, lay hold, embrace: KHES signifies to found, build, and construct. The Ker-Kes would thus denote the bird-shaped type of the circle-founder, a form of whom is personified in the Hindu Garuda.

The ark or coffer is an image of the four corners, the earliest being that of the Great Bear. This was represented as the coffin of Osiris; and the four Genii, human-headed, ape-headed, jackal-headed, and bird-headed, stood at the four corners of it, these being four of the seven spirits in Ursa Major. The primitive Ark was that of the goddess who united in herself the four types which are the originals of all the fours belonging to the four cardinal points.

It is noticeable that the bird is not included in her quaternity. Yet there came a time when the bird was introduced, and this apparently by Anhar (Nimrod) as god of the four corners. Anhar is depicted in the human form, also as the lion and the monkey (Kafi), whilst his name of Shu signifies the feather which stands for the bird. The bird as the winged type would take the lead in lifting up the ark in which Nimrod was to be borne aloft; hence the four immense birds, or Ker-Kes, that carried the ark. Shu carries in his hand the ark-sign in the noose or tie which had previously belonged to the ancient mother.

Nimrod of the four quarters answers to a Semite derivation of his name. Nem of the Ruti, the leopard of the twin-lions, was the Nimrod of the two divisions, north and south, Kepheus and Regulus; but in the later form, and in both Hebrew and Assyrian, the leopard is Nimr, and, as already shown, the terminal נת (uth)—later וד—represents the Egyptian FUT for the four quarters, as in Kanphoth, and Nimr-oth is the leopard of the four quarters, the later d-sound being unknown in the hieroglyphics.

Anhar-Nimrod, the great Gibor, the elevator of the heaven founded on the four corners, became the angel Gabriel. The Mahometan legends call him the chief of four favoured angels and the spirit of truth. The feather of Truth belongs to (Ma) Shu. In the legends of the middle ages Gabriel is the second of the seven great spirits who stand before the throne of God; and in the Ritual the ape-headed Kapi or Kafi is the second of the seven great spirits, and the Kafi is a type of Shu-Anhar. This is the original of Nimrod, chief of the four Kabirs or corner-keepers, whose Tetrapolis above was the model of his Tetrapolis in the Plain of Shinar.

In like manner, tradition asserts that the city of JOPPA was built by Kepheus, king of the Æthiopians, and was his seat before the deluge.

Joppa is the modified [1] form of Keppa; PA (Eg.) is the city, and KAFI (Eg.) is Kepheus or Shu. This marks a stage in naming from the astral mythology, with many applications to places lying north.

In Arabic and Hebrew legends 350 kings are said to sit before Nimrod to serve him, and this number, with the four Genii of his Tetrapolis added, would represent the number of days in a lunar year. In another version the kings that appear as his ministers are said to be 365; the number of days in the solar year without the quarter of a day being added.[2] The traditions of Nimrod also mention a period of 400 years during which he suffered in consequence of his having made war on Abraham, and insolently boasted that he was the lord of all.[3] The death of Nimrod is dated, in a Syrian calendar,[4] the 8th of the month Tammuz, and on the 17th of the same month the Jews kept their fast or festival in memory of the first tablets of the law which were broken by Moses on Sinai, *i.e.* in both cases when the solar year was established with the beginning at the time of the summer solstice, and the spring equinox occurred in the sign of the Ram.

The Hebrew form of the word שִׁנְעָר, with the ayin hard, implies the earlier spelling as Shingar or Shinkar. Kar (Eg.) is a land, district, or country, determined by the dual hill; Shen or Sen being two, Shen-kar would be the double land, corresponding to the twin-total found in Sem. The country of SINKAR, coupled with that of Assur, is mentioned on Egyptian monuments of the eighteenth dynasty, which agrees with the Singara of Ptolemy and other of the Greek writers. Sen-kar or Shen-kar then is named and known in Egyptian, where it means the double land, with the additional application of Kar, the circle; and the naming would be in accordance with the mapping-out of the celestial lands by north and south, as in Mitzraim or Khebti, the dual Kheb. Shin-kar was the dual land that Nimrod subdivided into the four quarters on which his kingdom was founded, and the name lives on in Senkerah.

A title of the kings of the ancient Chaldean empire was UNGAL KIENGI KÎ AKKAD: king of Kiengi with Akkad. The meaning of Kiengi has exercised Assyriologists. M. Lenormant sees in it the country as PLAIN, opposed to Akkad as MOUNTAIN—an expression to be paralleled with that of SUMERI U AKKADI in Assyrian inscriptions. KIENGI or KINGI is an Akkadian word, rendered in Assyrian by Matuv, the country. In Swahili, INCHI means the country; INIKU, in the African Opanda, and ENIKU in Igu, mean a forest district, or the bush. In Murundo, EANGA is a farm; HEANG (Chinese), a village; YUNG (Chinese), a wall for defence, a little city. It is a most ancient, primitive, and widespread title, found in the Assyrian NAGÛ for a district; ONCO (Portuguese), a hill; YANG (Chinese), a

---

[1] Pliny, v. 14. Solin, xxxiv. 1.
[2] Jellinek, *Beth ham-midrash*, V. xl., Vienna, 1873.
[3] D'Herbelot, *Bibl. Orient. Nimrod;* also Hyde.   [4] Genesis, xv. 7.

deep recess in the hills ; CNOC (Irish), a hill ; Chinese, CHUNG, KING, CHANG, or HEANG, a hill ; KUANKU, African Mandingo, a mountain ; KONGKU, Lohorong, a mountain. The first builder of a city in the Hebrew Genesis, CHANOKH (חנוך), has a kindred name. It has already been quoted as a type-name for the circles of the dead : the YINGE (Chinese), a circle. CINGO, in Latin, is to environ, engirdle round ; ANK (Eg.), to clasp round ; ANHU (Eg.), to envelope, surround, girdle, encircle. But there is another ANKH, as in the English Hank, a body of people confederated, and this in Egyptian signifies the natives, aborigines, or those who are indigenous to the district or country. Now KI itself denotes the country, land, locality ; and Ankh (Eg.) means the native of a district. The perfect word is found in the Maori, KAINGA, an encampment, bivouac, place of abode, country, and home.

When Nimrod went forth, and the Kushite migration occurred, it was made into the land of Singar, not primarily into Akkad ; and the first-named beginning of the Kushite kingdom was Babel, which, so far as it goes, identifies Babylon. KIENGI, the country of the natives, the district of the ancestral race, the motherland, is the equivalent of Sumeri or Sameri, the country of the first settlers, squatters, or colonists from the land of Kush. Sameri and Skameri commence, ethnologically as well as philologically, as the Kameri, who were there-fore a branch of the black race from Africa.

The Semite came from the Kamite ; and the Kamite was the created (Kâm, to create) race from Khebma, the most ancient genitrix in mythology.

Assyriologists are accustomed at present to look to Akkad as earlier than Babylonia, whereas the titles of KIENGI KÎ AKKAD, SUMERI U AKKADI, MAT SUMERI U MAT AKKADI, always place Akkad last, and make it subsidiary or additional. It is true the most ancient things yet discovered are Akkadian, but these may have remained as slough and drift from the old race that went on growing, shedding, and renewing its life and language in later forms.

In Kam or Kush, the black race of the Æthiopic centre, was the primeval parentage. The name was continued by Kam in Egypt. Kush, Mizraim, Phut, and Kanaan represent the four branches in four different directions ; and Nimrod is the typical leader into Sumeri— Nimrod the son of Kush, of the black race. The mirror of mythology shows the Kamite or Kushite to answer ethnically to the celestial son of Kush, the typical black under each name. And if the name of Sumeri was borne by the people as well as the land, they would be the Kamari of that country ; identical by name with the Kamari of India, the Kymry of Britain, and the Kumites of Australia, who have yet to be brought in.

In the bas-reliefs of Susiana there is pourtrayed a type of race almost purely negroid.[1] Part of the marshy region round the Persian Gulf

[1] Rawlinson, *The Five Great Monarchies*, vol. ii. p. 500, 2nd ed.

was inhabited by people who were nearly black. A remnant of these are yet extant in the LEMLUNS, whom the French traveller, Texier, has described, and who are allied as an anthropological type to the Bisharis on the border of Upper Egypt. M. Lenormant suggests that they probably spoke that "language of the Fishermen" which is mentioned in Assyrian documents as being a dialect different from those of Akkad and Assur.[1] Which further suggests that the LEMLUNS retain the name of the Fishermen. REM (Eg.) is the fish, people, natives; and REN, is to name, or a name. REM-REN is the Fish-name, or the Fisherman by name.

The poet Dionysius Perigetes, in his description of the southern Σκυθαι of India, mentions that to the west of the source of the Indus dwell the Ωριτας.[2] These ORITÆ may now be claimed by name as a form of the AURITÆ in the old Egyptian Chronicle. Thus we have the Afridi in Afghanistan, the Oritæ in the Caucasus, the Auritæ princes in Egypt; and the earliest form of the name is to be found in the Kafruti of the black race.

Berosus tells us that there were in Babylonia originally many men of a strange or barbarian race (ἀλλοεθνεῖς), who inhabited Chaldea and who lived in a savage state after the manner of animals. This answers to the KAM-RUTI spoken of as the uncivilized race, the savages of the later Egyptians, who belonged themselves to the original Kam-ruti, the race of Kam. These were the men of the Palæolithic age, the sons of Kheb, Kam, and Kush (Khebma and Khepsh), the genitrix of the human race, who as goddess of the Great Bear was the primordial bringer-forth, first figured in heaven by a people who were then to the south of Æthiopia—the feminine Adam or Atum, who appears in the Æthiopic portion of the Ritual as the mother-goddess of Time.[3] They carried out the same names as the people of Japhet or Khept (Kêd), who went out into the isles of the north and into the northern parts of India. The Gutium, a people found in the north of Mesopotamia, also answer to the Japheti—the Catti or Ketti of the north, as in Caithness and other countries named from the birthplace. The Gutium are identical by name with the Kefti or Japheti, with another plural terminal added to the Egyptian. From the one root found in the Khef or Kheb we derive KHEPSH (Eg.), KHEBT (Eg.), JAPHET and GEVIM (Heb.), GÛTIUM (Assyrian), KETTI or CATTI and KÊD (British). Nor is the Sumeri name the only representative of the Kamari and Kymry in Babylonia (speaking generally).

The GIMIRRAI are also found in the north-east of Assyria in the eighth century B.C., and in the time of Essarhaddon, who fought with them. These have been supposed to be the KIMMERIOI of Homer, but the country of the "cloud-capped Kimmerioi" was celestial, with various mundane applications. Wherever found, the name implies the

---

[1] *Chaldean Magic*, p. 347. [2] *Descriptio Orbis Terrarum*, v. 1088–94.
[3] *Supplement*, ch. 165, Birch.

people who went north in relation to the cardinal points themselves, or to the north of the particular country inhabited. For example, enormous underground habitations were extant about CUMÆ and the Auvernian Lake, the name of which place is identical with the CWM or COOMB of Britain, and the mound-like GAMM of the Laps, which have become the dwellings of the elves and dwarfs. These were called ARGILLÆ, and were the reputed homes of the "KIMMERIANS who dwelt in darkness." The Cave and Khem, Gamm, or Cam are synonymous, whether applied to the uterus, to a hole in the earth, or the void of the under-world. The people of the same names must have gone forth while the centre, called Kush or Æthiopia, was far up in the dark land towards the equatorial regions of Africa. They were followed by the later wave of the Kaldi, when the place of emanation was lower down in the Kars of the two Egypts, corresponding in Asia to the Keltæ who followed the Kymry over Europe, the men of the Neolithic age, who were the Karti, as the carvers, stone-polishers, and masons (the Karti and Rekhi), the cultivators of the earth (KAR (Eg.), to dig, farm, garden), the buriers and embalmers of their dead in the Kar and Karas; the circle-makers (KAR, to curve; KARRT, circles and zones), the metal-workers or furnace-men (KARA, the smith, KARR, the furnace); the sailors (KARURU, boats), as well as the people of the twin Kars, or Egypt Upper and Lower, an image of which still exists with us by name in the CART, the typical two-wheeled vehicle—an equivalent type for the names of the KALDI and KELTÆ as the KARTI of dual Egypt, whose name was derived from the earlier KARUTI and earliest KAFRUTI.

The cradle of the Akkadian race was the "Mountain of the World;" that "Mount of the Congregation in the thighs of the north" which can be identified by the hieroglyphic Khepsh, the thigh of Typhon. The first mount of mythology was the Mount of the Seven Stars, Seven Steps, Seven Stages, Seven Caves, which represented the celestial north as the birthplace of the initial motion and the beginning of time. This starting-point in heaven above is the one original for the many copies found on the earth below. Ararat and Urardhu are the same as the mount of mythology in the north, the hinder part of the heavens. The type of both can be identified with the north, the back side of the heavens, and the name of the mount in the Egyptian ARTU for the buttock, and Arrtu the ascent. Artu, the buttock, is equivalent to Khebt or Khepsh for the hinder thigh; and ARURUT, the hieroglyphic staircase, is the Egyptian form of the Hebrew Ararat and Akkadian Urdhu. In the solar adjustment of the starry imagery this mount of the north became the mount of the east; but that was later. The Akkadians date from URDHU, the district of the northern mountain of the world. Mythologically interpreted, that is the mount of the Great Bear, the goddess Urt (Ta-Urt), the mount of the four corners called MERU, or the Mesru, still earlier

Mitzru or Mestru, identified as the celestial Mazar and Mazaroth, the region of the Great Bear, marked by the star Mizar in its tail, to denote the Mest (Eg.) of the birthplace.

Urdhu, the name of the mount, represents Ur-tu (Eg.), and the Tu is the mount, the rock, and the cave. Ur means the great, oldest, chief, principal, first. Thus, Urtu, as mount, bears the name of Urt, or Ta-Urt, who is the genitrix and goddess of the mount in the north, the ENCEINTE (Ta) Urt, whose image typified the very primitive crib and cradle (Apt) of the human race, or the time-births which began in the mountain of the north, URDHU, ARARAT, or URRTU, afterwards called the birthplace of man, in all the oldest mythologies; the full form of whose name (Urt) is RERIT (or Ururat), the Sow, the Hippopotamus, the Great Bear.[1]

[1] After this section had been prepared for press, the following notice appeared in the *Athenæum*, July 24, 1880 :—" In an essay on the peoples and languages of Africa contained in the elaborate introduction to his *Nubian Grammar*, which has just appeared in German, Professor Lepsius maintains that the early Babylonian civilization was imported from Egypt." . . . " The tradition of the Babylonian priests that their country was one colonized and civilized from the South Sea cannot be expressed in plainer language ; and this alone overthrows the hypothesis, untenable in every respect, although still pretty commonly accepted, that the Babylonian mode of writing, together with all the higher civilization of Babylon resting thereon, as well as the higher culture of its priests, is derived from a so-called Turanian people, from regions which at the time of the author of the genealogical tables [in Genesis] were still so unknown and barbarous that he excluded them from the civilized world. In the oldest times within the memory of men we know only of *one* advanced culture, of only *one* mode of writing, and of only *one* literary development, viz., those of Egypt ; and we know of only *one* contemporary people which could have had knowledge of this culture, appropriated its results, and conveyed them to other nations—this was the Kushites, the masters of the Erythræan Sea to its furthest limits. It was by them that Babylonia was colonized and fertilized with Egyptian culture. And it is thus only that the thorough-going correspondence between Babylonian knowledge and institutions and the Egyptian ones becomes intelligible. The pictorial writing forming the basis of the cuneiform characters is unmistakably only a species of the hieroglyphics ; the astronomy of Babylon is only a development of that of Egypt ; its unit of measure, that is, the royal or architectural ell of 0·525 m., is completely identical with that of Egypt, which we find described on the walls up to the fourth millennium B.C.; its architecture, that is to say, its temples as well as its pyramids and obelisks, is an imperfect imitation of Egyptian originals ; and so with the other arts. At every step we meet in Babylonia with the traces of the Egyptian models. . . ."

SECTION XXI.

COMPARATIVE VOCABULARY

OF

MAORI AND EGYPTIAN WORDS.

A.

MAORI.	EGYPTIAN.
aata, altar.	**atui**, or **atua**, an altar, a chapel.
ae, yes.	**ia**, yes, certainly.
ahi, fire.	**akhi**, fire.
aho, radiant light ; **aho-roa**, moon.	**aah**, moon.
ahu, move in a certain direction.	**ahi**, denotes the forward movement.
ahu, form, fashion, create in the likeness of.	**ahu**, name of Tum as the modeller and former.
ai, to procreate, beget.	**aa**, to engender.
aitu, sickness ; **atu**, stand apart.	**aatu**, ill ; **aatu**, unclean, destitute, accursed, leprous.
akarua (Mangaian), the north.	**akar**, the hinder region.
ake, from below, upwards, higher up, climb.	**akh**, elevate, lift up, suspend.
ako, teach, learn.	**akh**, a mage.
amai, or **huamo**, swell of the sea.	**ima**, or **iuma**, the sea.
amaia, halo.	**am**, splendour, halo ; **amma**, orb, shedding light.
amar (West Aust.), pool of water.	**mer**, pool of water.
amene, desire.	**amu**, desire ; **amenu**, come (the desired).
ameto (West Aust.), Hades.	**am.t**, Hades, the devourer of the dead.
amiki, to gather up carefully, make a clean sweep.	**amakhu**, duty, fidelity, faithfulness.
amo, bier.	**am-ur**, cemetery.
ana, there.	**annu**, see, lo !
anake, the only one.	**ank**, I, the king.
anau (Mangaian), to give birth.	**annu**, the solar birthplace.
angi, fragrant smell.	**ankh**, living flowers, a nosegay.
ano, again.	**an**, or **un**, again, repeat.
ao, day, daytime.	**hau**, day.
apa, a company of workmen.	**abuu**, company of workmen.
apiti, curse.	**ap**, consecrate, dedicate.
apiti, two together, side by side.	**ap**, equal ; **ti**, two.
apiti, radius.	**apt**, the four corners.
apuru, inclose.	**apru**, a fillet.
ara, means of conveyance.	**urri**, a chariot.
ara, rise, rise up, ascend.	**ari**, ascend.

MAORI.	EGYPTIAN.
ara, path, way.	**hra**, road, path.
aria, appear, likeness, imaginary presence; **aro**, face.	**her**, appear, image, face, apparition.
ariki, chief, leader, priest.	**arkhu**, title of a king; **rekhi**, the mage.
arita, eager to do.	**ruta**, cause to do.
aru, chase, follow, pursue.	**rua**, chase, rush, go swiftly.
ata, reflected image, shadow, whence a spirit.	**aat**, a soul; **atta**, a type, symbol, a mental image.
ate, heart, liver.	**hat**, heart.
ate-ate, calf of the leg.	**ahti**, two legs or shanks.
atete, oppose, resist.	**atat**, to offer resistance.
ati, a word used only for clans and tribes, as offspring and descendants.	**aati**, children, orphans, descendants on the mother's side.
atua, the moon at fifteen days old.	**ahti**, dual lunar deity; **hetu**, one-half.
atua, first, god.	**ati**, title of Osiris as the sovereign.
au, I.	**a**, I.
auau, lift.	**aau**, raise.
aue, groan, alas!	**a**, oh, ah.
auhaha, to seek.	**huh**, to seek.
autaia (E. C.), pest.	**aati**, the pests.
autaki, roundabout, circuitous.	**aut**, the **hek** or hook.

H.

ha, breath, taste.	**haa**, breath of life; **hu**, taste.
haha, seek for.	**haha**, search, seek for.
ha-ha, shout to warn off.	**ha**, hail, ah! hailer.
hae-ata, dawn.	**hai-ata**, beginning of day.
hae-hae, a wailing accompanying the cutting of the flesh as a rite.	**hai**, ah, hail, oh, heaven! invocation.
haka, dance, sing and dance, merrymaking.	**haka**, a festival, a time.
hakari, a festival.	**haker**, applied to some festival.
hake, crooked.	**hak**, crook.
hakere, stint, grudge.	**hakr**, fast, famish.
hakui, old woman.	**aak** old; Mistress "**Heka**."
hama, be consumed.	**am**, the devourer; **ami**, consuming flame.
hamama, to shout; **hamumu**, to invoke, mutter indistinctly.	**ham-ham**, to invoke with religious clamour.
hamu, to gather and glean.	**ham**, find, discover, pick up, fish for.
hana-hana, to be smeared with red ochre.	**an**, kind of ointment, also colour.
hangai, across.	**ankh**, *Crux Ansa'a*.
hango, an implement used for setting seed, a dibble.	The **ankh**.
hao, to draw round, inclose, encircle, encompass.	**hahu**, a circle, drawn round, time inclosed.
hapa, gone by.	**habi**, panegyry, festival of time past.
hapai, rise, lift up, begin, start.	**apa**, rise, first, prepare, essence, ancestor.
hapati, Sabbath or seventh day.	**hepti**, peace, number seven.
hapu, conceived in the womb.	**kapu**, mystery of fertilization.
hapua, hollow valley, depressed; **hifa** (Tongan), downward.	**kheb**, down, lower; **hefa**, to squat down, crawl, go on the ground.
hara, excess, number over.	**hera**, over.
hara, to violate Tapu.	**herui**, evil-doers.
haramai, come here, welcome.	**mai**, come; **heru**, pleasure (come with pleasure or welcome).
hatea, whitened.	**hut**, white.
hau, food used in the "pure" ceremony first offered to the gods.	**ha**, first food, duck-offering.
hau, illustrious, famous.	**ha**, chief, leader, ruler, lord.
haupu, heap, lie in a heap.	**hept**, heaped.
hawa, ventral.	**hua**, excremental.
hawhe, to go or come round.	**heh**, circle, image of the eternal.
hehe, gone astray.	**heh**, wander.
heipu, coming straight together, meet exactly, just and true.	**hep**, a mason's level.
hemi-hemi, back of the head.	**hem**, back.
hemo, to be dead.	**khema**, dead.
herepu, tie up in bundles.	**arp**, packet, bundle, to bind.

MAORI.	EGYPTIAN.
hi, pshaw.	**hi**, impurity.
hi, draw, raise, catch with a hook.	**hi**, draw, drag, probably yoke or hook together.
hi, affected with diarrhœa.	**hi**, impurity, thrust out; **huu**, excrement.
hi dawn.	**hui**, light, hour.
hia, desire, wish, be in love with.	**uha**, desire, wish, long for.
hika, perform a ceremony with magical incantations; **hiki**, a charm.	**heka**, magic, charm.
hikoko, wasted, starved.	**hekar**, starve, famish.
hina, grey.	**unan**, grey.
hine, young woman, or a young girl only.	**han**, young.
hipi, ship.	**hept**, ark, boat, cabin.
hiri, to seal.	**herui**, roll up a writing; qy. seal.
hirihiri, charm, uttered to impart energy; **horu**, yell in the war-dance.	**heru-heru**, an inspiriting cry.
hoa, throw.	**hai**, throw.
hoa, spouse.	**haa**, spouse.
hoe, travel in a canoe, voyage.	**hau**, voyage, transport boat.
hokaikai, to move backwards and forwards.	**khekh**, balance.
hoki, return.	**khekh**, repulse, return.
hokirara, idling.	**uka**, idle, idleness, festival.
hoko, barter, exchange, merchandise; prefix to numerals denoting ten.	**khekh**, scales, number, reckoning.
hono, add.	**hannu**, bring, tribute.
hono, continual.	**han**, to and fro, continually.
honore, honour.	**hon**, majesty, sanctity.
hopu, a swelling.	**kepu**, to be in a ferment.
hopu, catch, seize.	**kefa**, catch, seize.
hore, not; **hori**, be gone by.	**her**, ended, to have finished.
hori, false, deceiving.	**herui**, deceive.
horo, hurry, quick, speedy.	**her**, go along, fly.
horu, yell, to the war-dance.	**hru-hru**, a war-cry.
horu, grunt, snort, snore.	**heru-heru**, to snore.
hou, feather.	**khu**, feathers.
hu, mud, bubble up, still, silent.	**huua**, filth, dirt, fermentation, menses.
hua, cause, fruit, egg, roe, seed, bear fruit.	**hu**, spirit, seed, corn, adult male.
huamo, the sea raised in waves.	**iuma**, sea.
huare, spittle.	**urh**, ointment, oil.
huhi, discomfiture, weariness, miserable.	**hui**, tear the hair in grief.
huhunu, double canoe.	**khenu**, a canoe; **hani**, barge of the gods.
huka, froth, foam.	**huka**, beer.
huka, hook.	**hek**, hook.
hunga, a company of persons.	**ankh**, the native, or natives of a district.
huri, turn round, turn of tide, turn of the year.	**hru**, a day, a turn round.
hurupa, fresh growth of young trees.	**rep**, to bud, blossom, take leaf, grow.
huti, hoist.	**htai**, ceiling; **huti**, the winged disk of the uplifted sun.

I.

ia, current of water.	**ia**, wash, water.
iho, above with reference to below, correlative of **ake**.	**hiu**, **iu**, or **hu**, the sun on high, brother to **hak**, the sun below.
ika, a warrior, famous fighter.	**akh**, illustrious, honoured, his highness.
ike, high, lofty.	**akha**, elevate.
iku-iku, eaves of a house.	**akhu**, horizon, edge.
ingoa, name.	**ank**, I (the king).
inoi, prayer, entreaty.	**hana**, for mercy's sake! adore, pray.
iri-iri, to baptise or anoint.	**urhu**, anoint.
iwi, the tribe.	**uhi** (first Sallier *Pap.* p. 1), **uhi-t**, tribe (Chabas, *Pap. Hiero. d. Berlin*, fol. 1).

K.

kaabo (West. Aust.), kangaroo battue.	**kahabu**, to excite, butt, toss, tear **kafa**, to hunt, inclose, seize by force.
gabbi (West. Aust.), water.	**kabh**, inundation, libation.

MAORI.	EGYPTIAN.
kadjin (West Aust.), the likeness in death.	katen, similitude ; khat, dead body.
kaha, noose, lashings.	kua, tighten, hold, compress.
kaha, boundary-line of land.	kai, land, region, direction, boundary, division of land.
kahia, image of a human figure carved out of the post of a Pae fence.	kaau, or kahu, a figure, the mummy image.
kahu, hawk.	kahau, claw, seize.
kahua, form, appearance.	kaiu, shape, form, figure.
kahu-kahu, the spirit or ghost of a dead man.	khu, or hu, spirit, manes.
kahui, herd, flock.	kaui, herd, cows.
kai, food.	ka, food.
kai, a prefix denoting the agent.	ka, agent, person, function.
kaihe, ass.	âai, ass.
kaka, intoxicated.	khaku, stupid, obstinate, mad, sick, qy. drunk.
kakahi, part of the " pure " ceremony.	khakha, sacred, repulse, whip ; hi, impurity ; kahkahu, engrave.
kaki, throat.	khekh, throat.
kama, quick, nimble.	kem, a space of time, instantly, discover, find out.
kamo, a wink.	kem, space of an instant.
kamu-kamu, food.	kamhu, a joint of meat.
kani-kani, dance.	ken-ken, a dance, dancing.
kapa, flutter, flap, wing.	ap, fly, wing, mount on the wing.
kapo, blind.	khap, blind.
kapo, catch at, snatch.	kaf, or kep, hunt, seize, catch.
kapu, hollow of the hand.	khep, hand, fist.
kapura, fire.	afr, fire.
karakia, say prayers, perform a religious service, repeat a form of words.	kheru, say, the word ; khu, a ceremony.
karau, trap.	kar, trap.
karaua, old man.	aua, old one ; kar, male.
karawa, dam, mother.	kuraa, widow.
kari, dig for, garden.	kari, gardener.
karu, eye.	aru, eye.
kati, shut, closed, block up, stop, leave off, cease.	khet, shut, closed, sealed.
kato, flowing, flood-tide (only).	khet, navigate, go (from port).
katoa, all, the whole.	khuti, dual form of the God as the All, the Whole.
kau-kau, anoint.	kah, anoint.
kauwhau, recite old legends and genealogies.	ka, say, tell, recall ; hau, records.
kava, strong spirits.	kapu, fermentation.
kawa, open a new building with any ceremony, remove Tapu.	kah, touch, anoint.
kawe, handle.	kahu, handle.
kawe-kawe, tentacles of the cuttle-fish.	kahau, claw, seize.
kehua, spirit, ghost.	khu, spirits, manes.
keke, to quack.	kaka, to cackle.
keke, obstinate, stubborn, mad.	khak, obstinate, stubborn, mad.
keke, contrariwise, in an opposite direction ; kaikaa (Mangaian), Boomerang.	khekh, to be repulsed, to return.
kelap (West. Aust.), first appearance of pubes.	kherp, the first, first-fruits, the Pubescent Horus.
kere-kere, intensely dark.	karh, night.
kero, maimed or dead.	kher, fallen, defeated victim.
keti, gate.	khet, port, water-gate, shut.
keto, extinguished.	khat, corpse.
ki, full.	khi, full-height, enlarged, extended, high.
ki, say, utter.	kai, say, call.
kiki, instigate.	khi-khi, to whip.
kimi, seek, look for.	kem, to find, discover.
kimo, wink.	kemh, to stare.
kimo-kimo, to wink frequently.	khem, favour, grace, desire ; kham, incline.
kini, wink, to convey an intimation.	khenni, convey intelligence.
kino, evil, bad, hateful.	khennu, Typhonian adversary, contention.
kita, fast, held tight.	khet, shut, sealed.
kite, to reveal, disclose, discover.	khet, hidden things.

MAORI.	EGYPTIAN.
gobul (West Aust.), a tadpole.	**khepr**, the transformer, frog-headed.
koeke, the old man.	**kehkeh**, the old man.
kohi, wasting sickness.	**khai**, malady.
koiri, bend the body.	**kheri**, victim bound and bent.
koka, mother.	**kak**, feminine sanctuary.
komeme, to burst inwards, stave in.	**khem**, break, break in pieces.
komo, thrust in, put in, insert.	**kama**, bolt, lock ; **khem**, Lingaic.
kona, lower part of the abdomen.	**kanau**, lap, pudendum f.
kona-kona, smell.	**khena**, snuff.
konga, live coal.	**ankh**, live or living.
konia, canoe.	**kheni**, boat, navigate, transport, convey.
kopa, corner.	**kab**, corner.
kopi, doubled together, shut, closed.	**kab**, double ; **kep**, fist.
kopiko, go alternately in two opposite directions.	**kab.t**, go alternately up and down.
kopiro, a duck, to duck.	**khep**, a duck.
kopiu (West Aust.), secretly.	**kep**, concealed.
kopu, womb.	**kep**, sanctuary, womb.
korero, tell, say.	**kheru**, say, voice, speech, word.
kori, native oven.	**karru**, furnace.
koro, person, man.	**kar**, the male person.
koro, fifth day of the moon's age.	**kar**, a course.
korohu, steam, boil.	**karhu**, a jar with steam issuing.
koromahu, steam.	**karumahu**, some kind of drink (obviously distilled).
koropa, food offered to the Atua in the " pure " ceremony.	**kherp**, consecrate, offer, pay homage.
korote, squeeze, crush (Garotte).	**kherit**, victims bound.
korua, dual, you two.	**kariu**, testes.
koti, cut ; **kota**, anything to cut with.	**khet**, to cut, instrument for cutting.
kotua, with the back towards one.	**khet**, reverse ; **kett**, different, otherwise ; **kat**, seat, hindward way.
kotui, lace up, fasten by lacing.	**kat**, a zone.
kou, good.	**khu**, benefit, good.
koura, crayfish.	**krau**, claw.
kowae, pick out, set apart, openings.	**kaha**, light-holes or windows.
kumi, ten fathoms.	**khemt**, ten.
kumi-kumi, beard under the chin.	**kemhu**, a certain form of hair.
kumu, timid, reluctant.	**khema**, spiritless, humble.
kune, plump and round.	**hun**, young.
kura, school.	**kher**, sacred cell.

M.

ma (Adelaide River), eye, see.	**ma**, to see, eye.
ma, in the power of.	**maaui**, in the power of.
maea, emerge.	**maa**, come, approach, shine.
maehe, month of March, Eg. 9th Month.	**meh**, number nine.
maha, gratified in attaining.	**meh**, satisfy, please, fulfil, complete.
mahanga, twins.	**ankh**, pair, couple ; **meh**, fulfilled.
mahanga, a snare, ensnare.	**menka**, a collar.
mahuta, clan, family.	**mahauta**, clan, family.
mai, come hither.	**mai**, come.
maihe, fence.	**mahu**, girth, water-line.
maka-maka, dancing.	**mak**, to dance.
makau, spouse, wife or husband.	**makh**, devoted to.
makuru, having the fruit set, denoting fulfilment of the flower in much fruit.	**makheru**, justified, the word made ruth.
mana, effectual, enable, give power to.	**men**, place firm, fix.
mano, heart.	**mennu**, sustenance.
manu, float, be launched, afloat, rest on the water.	**mena**, afloat, warp to shore, arrive by water, be at anchor.
maonga, ripe.	**makha**, ripe.
marae, an inclosure, inclosed space in front of a house, the yard.	**mer**, a circle ; **mera**, land, limit, region, space, street.
marena, marry.	**mer**, love, attach, kiss, bind.
maru, power, authority, shield, safeguard.	**mer**, superintendent, prefect.

MAORI.

EGYPTIAN.

MAORI.	EGYPTIAN.
maru, killed.	**merau**, die, be killed.
mata, medium for spirit communication.	**mati**, a title of Taht, the medium of the gods.
matau, know, be sure of, certitude, right.	**mat**, truth, true; **meti**, examined judicially.
mate, dead, death, be extinguished.	**mut**, death, end, die.
matua, main body of an army.	**mati**, a mercenary.
mutua, parent, the father, a company.	**mata**, the male; **mahaut**, family, clan.
mau, to carry in the hand, to bring.	**mâ**, to hold in the hand, offer, give.
mau (Mangaian), spring up, light as vapour.	**ma**, wind, vapour, cloud.
mau, fixed.	**ma**, true, truth.
maui, cat's-cradle.	**mau**, cat.
mauri, twenty-eighth day of the moon's age.	**meh**, to be completed and fulfilled.
me, with.	**ma**, with.
meda (West Aust.), membrum virile.	**mata**, phallus.
mehua, measure; **maoa**, ripen, and be completed.	**mehu**, girth, water-line, a measure, cubit; **meh**, number nine.
meka, "true," "true."	**mâ**, true (earlier **mak**).
mel (West Aust.), eye.	**mer**, eye.
memha, be dissolved, pass away.	**mem**, dead, or the mummy.
mere, war-weapon.	**merhu**, war-weapon.
mero, a whirling current of water.	**mera**, a name of the inundation.
miha, wonder; **mihi**, admire.	**mahui**, wonder.
mimiha, a black, bituminous substance found in the sea.	**mum**, pitch.
mine, be assembled.	**men**, a herd.
mit (West Aust.), active and sustaining principle of anything.	**mat**, heart, substance, growing and renewing power.
mohio, wise, intelligent, understand, perceive, discerning.	**mehi**, a name of Taht, lord of the divine words; **mehi**, illumine.
mokai, captive, slave.	**makhau**, despoil, kidnap.
mote, suck.	**menat**, to give suck; **mut**, the mother.
mote, water.	**meht**, abyss of water.
muna, a ringworm.	**men**, go round in a ring.
mure-mure, go round and round.	**mer**, circle, go round.

N.

MAORI.	EGYPTIAN.
na, by.	**na**, by.
nahea, long in time; **nehe**, ancient times.	**naheh**, an age, for ever.
nakahi, serpent; **neke**, snake.	**neka**, apophis serpent.
namu, a small fly.	**nemma**, a pigmy.
nanu, mixed, confused, indistinct, inarticulate.	**nini**, to be amazed, astonished.
nanu, express disappointment, dissatisfaction, disgust.	**nen**, no, not; **nnau**, m. period.
napi, cling tightly.	
nati, fasten, retain, constrict, contract, as by a ligature.	**nehp**, seize, *futuere*.
	nat, limit, noose; **natr**, pull a rope.
nau, come.	**na**, come.
naumai, welcome, or come here.	**mai**, you may.
nawai, denoting regular procession of time.	**nnu**, time, appointed time, time continually.
nawe, be excited, agitated.	**nnuhu**, be agitated, movement; *masturber* (Pierret).
nawe, be immovable.	**nnu**, rest.
nehu-nehu, dusky.	**neh**, black; **nehs**, negroes.
nga, breathe, live, heart.	**ankh**, life, live.
nga, plural the; **nga-huru**, ten.	**nai**, plural the; **har**, ten.
ngaki, tilling the land, clear from weeds.	**nakht**, hard land, corn land, arable land.
ngaore, a fish.	**nar**, a fish.
ngaotu, to work timber with an adze.	**nater**, to work with an adze, the carpenter.
ngatahi, together.	**ankh**, pair; **taui**, two halves.
ngaueue, quake, shake.	**nahuh**, agitate, shake.
ngou-ngou, a fashion of wearing the hair, with a knot at the forehead.	**ank**, to clasp; **ankh**, tie, knot, image of life.
ngou-ngou, a live coal.	**ankh**, living, image of life.
ngt, landmark; **ngutu**, rim.	**net**, limit.
ngu, peculiar tattoo marks on the upper part of the nose, an organ of **nga** or breath.	**ankh**, make covenant, an oath.
niko, tie.	**neka**, compel, with tie; **ankh**, tie, noose.
niu, sticks used for divination.	**nnu**, divine types.

MAORI.

EGYPTIAN.

MAORI.	EGYPTIAN.
noa, free from Tapu, or other restrictions.	**nnu,** time appointed.
noho, sit, rest.	**nnu,** sit, squat, rest.
nohu-nohu, nauseous, unpalatable; **neu** (Fiji), an interjection used by women only; **nonoi,** disfigured, urgent negation, as no, no.	**nnu,** flowing period; **naha,** foul face; **nini,** flux, flood, catamenial; **nnanu,** defile.
noti, knot.	**nnut,** knot.
nui, great, superior, exalted rank.	**nia,** or **nui,** deity.
nuka, deceive.	**neka,** deceive, false, delude.
nuke, crooked.	**neka,** "crooked serpent."

O.

oha, abundant, generous.	**uah,** increase, flourish very much.
ohia, long for.	**uha,** long for, desire.
ope, troop, number of persons moving together.	**ab,** a company.
opure, pied.	**ab,** pied.
ota, green.	**uat,** green.
ota-ota, herbs in general.	**uat,** plants, green herbs in general.
ourourouro (Mangaian), the ha!-ha! or hurrah of the war-dance.	**herheru,** dilatation with joy, an inspiring cry.

P.

pa, stockade, or fortified place.	**pa,** house, abode, city.
pae, horizon, rest, perch, surround with a border; **pahao,** a threshold, margin.	**pe,** heaven; **peh,** arrive, attain, reach; **peh',** hem or border, a water-frontier, a marsh.
pahake, to bask.	**pekh,** or **pekht,** stretch out, basking.
paheke, have a running issue.	**bek,** squat, naked, waste, void, menstruate.
paho, soaring.	**pa,** or **pai,** fly.
pahure, come in sight, appear.	**par,** appear, show, manifest
pai, good, pronounce good, praise.	**peh,** glory.
paiere, bundle, tie up.	**pari,** wrap.
paihau, wing of a bird.	**pai,** wing of a bird.
pakaru, gap.	**pekar,** gap, hole.
pake, crack.	**peka,** divide, division.
paki, girdle.	**peka,** kind of linen or tunic; **fekh,** girdle, band.
pakohu, cleft, rent, chasm.	**pekah,** gap, hole.
pana, thrust or drive away, cause to go away, block up.	**ban,** no, not, unclean; **pena,** reverse, turn back.
pane, head.	**ben,** cap, top, roof, tip.
pao, hatching of eggs; **papa,** Earth-goddess, hinder part, breech; **papa,** father, male.	**pa-pa,** produce, be delivered of a child; **peh,** the rump, hinder part, feminine sign; **på,** men, males.
para-para, sacred place.	**para,** the sacred name of Heliopolis.
pata, hole.	**puthu,** open.
patu, strike, beat.	**pet,** strike.
pehi, sit as a hen.	**peh,** the seat, rump.
pennu, deities.	**pen,** emphatic *the*; **nnu,** deities.
pepe, close together.	**pep,** to engender.
pitau, fancy figurehead of a war canoe.	**ptah,** or **patakoi,** a figurehead of the Kabiri.
po, night, underworld, place of departed spirits.	**bau,** the void, hole of the tomb, lower world.
poka, hole, pit, well.	**peka,** hole, gap, pit, infernal locality.
poti, cat.	**buto** (**pasht**), the cat-headed goddess.
poti, corner, angle, cardinal point.	**fetu,** corner, the four corners or quarters.
pu, precise, very, exactly.	**pu,** it is.
puka, to swell.	**pekht,** stretched out.
puka, passions, affections in operation, as swelling.	**bekh,** to engender, conceive, fecundate.
puku, the silent word, secretly.	**beka,** to pray.
pupa, eructate; **puhi-puhi,** to blow frequently.	**puf,** breath, to blow, a gust.
pupu, to bubble up.	**beb,** to exhale.
putere, go in a body.	**put,** company or body of nine deities.

R.

MAORI.	EGYPTIAN.

Ra, Sun-god, monarch, day, the West as place of sunset.

Ra, Sun-god, king, day; **ruha,** evening.

rahui, a mark to warn people against trespassing in case of "Tapu," and for protection; **rai-ona,** lion (**ona,** of him, of her).

rehui, twin Lion-gods which kept the boundary, as the *Turners Back;* **rehui,** twin-lions.

raka, to entangle, be entangled.

ark, to weave, a noose, envelope.

rako, an Albino.

rekh, full, whiten.

rangai, herd, flock.

renu, cattle; **kaui,** herd.

rapu-puku, bud, put forth buds (**puku,** swell, put forth).

rep, to bud, flower, grow.

rapu-rapu, be in doubt.

rupu, or, either, one or the other.

rara, twig, small branch; **rere,** be born.

rer, nursling.

ratou, they, them.

ret, several.

raua, the two.

rehui, twin.

remu, posteriors, end of a thing.

remn, the limit, extending so far.

renga, to pull up by the root.

renpu, plant, renew, young.

reo, voice, speech, language.

ru, mouth, chapter, word, discourse.

rere, run, place, fly, sail.

rer, traverse.

rere, to and fro, rise and set.

rer, go round and round, on circuit.

reti, snare, catch.

ret, a loop or noose for fastening cattle.

rewa, melt, become liquid.

ru, drops.

rewa, be elevated, ascend.

rru, steps, sign of ascent.

rima, five; **ringa,** hand, arm.

remnnu, the arm, extent.

rino, twist of two or three strands.

ren, noose, or cartouche.

riwha, cleft.

ruha, quarry.

rohe-rohe, to mark off by a boundary-line.

ru, mark, division; **ru-ru,** horizon, place of two lions.

rone, bind, confine with a cord.

renn, cartouche ring, noose for cattle.

roto, the midst.

rrut, those around; **rra,** in the midst.

Rupe, Maui, as Son of the Divine Father.

repa, the prince, son, heir-apparent.

T.

ta, print, paint.

ta, register, the writer.

ta, tattoo.

ta, type.

ta, mallet, maul.

ta, the head of a mallet.

ta, whip a top.

ta, go along.

tae, go in a boat, arrive, reach the utmost limit, be reached.

ta, go, go in a boat, navigate, cross.

taepa, place where the sky hangs down to the horizon.

tep, heaven, and hill of the horizon.

tahae, thief.

tehai, thieve.

tahati, sea-shore; **tahatu,** horizon.

tattu, the established region, the horizon.

tahe, menses; **tahae,** filth.

tua, sanies; **tua,** filth.

tahei, divided by crossing.

tai, to cross; **tat,** the cross; **hu,** adult.

tahi, together, altogether, unique, one.

taui, twin.

tahoe, swim first with one arm then the other.

taui, halves.

daht (West Aust.), sly, cunning, noiseless.

tat, craft.

tahu, husband.

tai, the male; **hu,** adult.

tahu, light.

tahuti, dual lunar light.

taiki, wickerwork.

teka, plant, stick, join, cross, unite, reunite, twist, weave.

taipu, betroth.

tebu, seal ring, be responsible for.

taita, timber fixed in the bed of a river.

tat, fixed, established in the waters.

taka, fasten, tack.

teka, fix, attach.

taka, heap up, a mound, a post.

tekhn, an obelisk.

taka, round, on all sides, wind round.

teka, boundary, cross over.

takahi, trample underfoot.

tekh, throw down, overthrow.

takapau, end of the "pure" ceremony.

tekhbu, anoint.

take, absent oneself.

teka, hide, escape notice of.

take-take, well-founded, firm, lasting.

teka, stick in, adhere, cleave to; **tekhn,** obelisk.

taki-turi, the death-watch beetle, from **taki,** to proclaim, announce, tell; **turu,** the end, or shortly.

taki, announce; **tur,** the extremity or end; **tur,** a name of the beetle-headed God, Khepr.

tak-urua, the Dog-star Sirius; **uri** (Polyn.), dogs.

taka, see, behold; **uhar,** the dog (the announcer of the inundation).

MAORI.

EGYPTIAN.

tamahu, remove Tapu.

tamau, fasten.

tami, repress, smother.

taone, town.

tapu, religious restriction, with especial relation to cleanliness.

tara, influence by charms.

tara, rays of the sun before sunrise.

tara, phallus, mettle.

tari, platting with eight strands.

taroi, tie up.

tarua, tattoo a second time, repeat.

tata, strike, beat, strike repeatedly.

tatari, sieve, strainer.

tatua, girdle, put on as a girdle; **tau,** loop or thong.

tau, bark.

tau, thy.

taua, wear mourning garments, sign of mourning for the dead.

taua, we two.

taua, hostile expedition, a murderous raid.

tautau (Mangaian), the ages.

tau-tau, tie in bunches.

te, article the.

teitei, high, tall, summit.

tekau, ten.

teke, pudendum muliebria.

teke-teke, nudge.

tepe-tepe, clot of blood.

tete, figurehead of a canoe.

ti, a game of telling.

tiemi, play at see-saw.

tihema, December.

tika, right, just, fair and true.

tiki, post marking a "Tapu" place, a memorial, a token.

tinei, put out, end, extinguish, destroy, kill.

tini, hosts, myriads, innumerable.

ti-ti, Mutton-bird, sacred, only goes inland at night.

titi, stick in, a peg, nail; **tete,** stand fixed in the ground.

tito, invent, compose.

to, pregnant.

tohe, thief.

tohi, ceremony, also ceremony before battle; **tohu,** preserve, save alive, spare.

tohu, mark, sign, proof.

toihi, to be split in two.

toitoi, trot, gallop.

toka, to overflow.

tokari, to cut, notch.

tomo, be filled.

topu, pair, couple.

toro, consult by divining, stretch forth the hands.

toro-ihi, sprout, bud.

tu, to stand.

tu (Mangaian), strong enough to stand.

tu, part of the fishing-net which is first in the water.

temau, restore, renovate.

temaiu, band or fastening.

tem, no, not, avoid; **tem,** dumb.

tun, royal seat.

tebu, a clean beast; **teba.t,** purged and purified.

tari, invoke religiously.

ter, indicate.

ter, male member, to engender.

terui, No. 8.

terui, papyrus roll, limits.

terui, two times, twice.

tata, strike, strike terror.

tar, sieve; **ta,** the.

tat, buckle of a girdle; **taau,** a loop.

tâ, bark.

ta, thou, thine.

taau, probably mourning clothes; **taau** to kill; **tet,** death; **ta,** burial.

taui, halves, pair, couple, double.

taau, foray, slaughter.

teta, eternal (Æonian).

ta, knot, tie.

te, article the.

tata, head, princes, heads; **taui,** hill, summit.

teka, a measure, quantity, weight; **tek,** a cross.

kha, Pud. Mul.; **t,** fem. article.

tekhn, wink.

tef, drop of blood; **tef-tef,** drip.

tat, image, type, figure.

thui, to tell.

tem, two halves.

tem, to complete, the whole. (The Egyptian year ended at Midsummer, the Maori with December.)

tekar, perfect, absolute.

tekhn, obelisk, a memorial sign.

ten, cut off.

tennui, millions.

teti, Ibis religiosa, lunar bird.

tat, image of fixity.

teti, the divine scribe, mouth, word of the gods.

ta, to bear, carry, be *enceinte.*

taui, steal.

tua, consecrate; **tuan,** adore, honour, pray; **tehu,** beseech, offering.

tehu, to tell.

taui, two halves.

tata, gallop.

tekh, to be full.

tekar, graver; **tekh,** the cutter and notcher of the palm-branch.

tem, be fulfilled.

tebu, pair of sandals.

tri, adore, invoke, interrogate, question, with hands outstretched.

ter, a shoot.

tu, the rock or mountain.

mentu, the rigid stander, image of erection.

tuia, to net, catch.

MAORI.

EGYPTIAN.

tua, the further side, as the western sea.

tua-ahu, sacred, consecrated place; **tua,** lay under spell; **ahu,** high place.

tuhi, indicate by pointing, draw, delineate, write, paint.

tuhua, obsidian.

tupare, chaplet.

tupehu, blustering, angry.

tupo, cave for bones, in which incantations for the dead were performed.

ture, law.

turu, time, moon at fifteen days old.

turuapo, midnight.

tutu, a message sent to summon people.

tutu, stand erect.

tuaut, the place of sunset, lower heaven.

pa-tua, the chapel in which the Pharaohs were consecrated.

tuhui, to tell.

tu, rock; **huh,** everlasting.

teb, chaplet; **tepr,** tie.

tef, Typhon.

tebhu, chest, sarcophagus.

teru, papyrus roll; **torah** (Heb.).

ter, time, season, limit.

teriu, two times; **ap,** first.

taht, the divine messenger.

tutu, erect image.

U.

u, reach land, arrive by water.

ua, backbone.

ue, paddle a boat, steer with a paddle.

uho, heart, pith, substance.

uka, be fixed, preserved, last.

uki, ancient times, the old.

uku, or **ukui,** white, white clay.

unene, to plead importunately.

unga, cause to be born.

ungutu, meet together.

upoko, head.

uri, offspring.

uri (Polynes.), dogs.

uru, join, be associated with in act.

uruahu, tabooed place, where certain ceremonies were performed.

uta, land, earth.

utu, ransom.

u, go by boat, depart, arrive.

uas, sceptre, the backbone.

ua, boat being paddled.

uai, substance.

uka, a week, a festival, a peg, a column.

aaki, old.

akhu, white.

unun, to flatter, caress, cajole.

ankh, life, to live, be living.

ankh, couple, pair.

api, head.

ur, or **ar,** child.

uhar, dog.

her, with, function of being with.

urhu, anoint, oil; **ahu,** house.

ta, earth, land.

uta, salvation.

W.

waha, carry on the back.

wahina, virgin.

waia, be filled with tears, melt in tears.

waka, spirit-medium.

waka, canoe.

waka-waka, parallel ridges.

wana, a young shoot.

ware, viscous fluid, spittle.

wene, a noose.

weti, weigh.

weu, a single one.

wha, get abroad, be disclosed.

whana, bowed, bent.

whana, company, people.

whanau, offspring, young.

w'hangai, feed, nourish, bring up.

whata, an elevated storehouse for saving food.

whata, elevate, support, hang.

whatero, put out the tongue.

whati, turn and go away, flee, be broken off, separated.

whatu, eye, pupil of the eye.

whatu, weave, lace.

wha-wha, lay hold of.

wheko, become black, very dark.

wheku, a distorted figure in symbolic carvings.

uââ, lift, carry away.

hannu, youth.

uau, melt, in meditation.

akhu, spirit, manes.

ukha, sacred bark.

akha, horizon.

hannu, young.

urh, anoint, oil, liquid.

un, a noose.

uta, weigh.

ua, one, alone.

uha, escape.

anu, to be afflicted, oppressed, forced down.

unnu, beings, people.

hannu, young.

ankh, food, life, living.

uta, a storehouse or treasury.

uts, hang, support, bear aloft.

hut, tongue.

uta, go forth, pass, proceed, alone, separate, divorced.

uta, symbolic eye.

khet, woof, net.

uha, enfold.

ukha, night; **kek,** darkness.

heka, the frog-headed goddess; **hekau,** charm, magic.

MAORI.	EGYPTIAN.
whenu, warp of cloth.	**anu**, plait ; **ans**, linen.
whetau, small.	**ket**, little.
whete, to make eyes.	**uat**, colour for eyes.
whete, or **whetete**, be forced out.	**utu**, or **utut**, command, order, go out, exact.
whetiko, a shell-fish.	**uti**, a fish.
whetu, star.	**hetu**, star, sign of a period.
wheua, bone.	**hu**, ivory, tooth, bone.
whiri, twist, plait.	**herrui**, roll up.
whiti, hoop.	**khet**, ring, bound.
whitu, number seven.	**hept**, number seven.
wiki, week.	**uak**, week, festival.
witi, wheat.	**uahit**, corn.

NOTE.—Vocabularies compiled by Dieffenbach, Mariner, Moore and others, have been used ; but the chief authority is *A Dictionary of the New Zealand Language* by the Right Reverend William Williams, Bishop of Waiapu, New Zealand. London, 1871 : Williams and Norgate.

" There is a continuity in language which nothing equals ; and there is an historical genuineness in ancient words, if but rightly interpreted, which cannot be rivalled by manuscripts, or coins, or monumental inscriptions. "—MAX MÜLLER.

SECTION XXII.

AFRICAN ORIGINES OF THE MAORI.

THIS Vocabulary appears to reverse the dictum of those philologists who continually assert that phonetic decay, and the consequent obliteration of the origines of language, is especially active amongst the primitive races who are now in the lowest stages of culture or of survival. These words were taken down by Europeans who knew nothing of Egyptian, from the natives, who were in possession of no written characters, and who had no knowledge of their language having been written. For unknown ages past the words have lived in memory alone, or rather they have remained like mummies, so carefully preserved that the likeness to life is as recognizable as ever.

So far from the principle of laziness or least effort having got the better of the Maori in their ethnical decadence, they have sedulously sounded to the last the most difficult phonetics, such as the "NG," and still possess one-third more words beginning with the "K" sound in addition to Ng than with the H. The following list shows how the K sound has been continued in words, found in Egyptian in the modified form.

MAORI.	EGYPTIAN.
KAEWA, wandering.	HUHA, to wander,
KAIHE, an ass.	ÂAI, an ass.
KANOHI, eye.	AN, eye.
KANGA, curse.	ANKH, oath.
KAPA-KAPA, wing.	AP, wing; AP-AP, to mount on the wing.
KARA, secret plan, conspiracy.	HERUI, evil-doers.
KAPURA, fire.	AFR, fire.
KARU, eye.	ARU, eye.
KAREPE, grape.	ARP, grape.
KARURE, twist, spin round.	RER, go round, whirl.
KAURUKI, smoke.	RUKAI, furnace, brazier.
KERI, rush along fast.	HER, go along fast.
KURI or KIREHE, dog.	UHAR, dog.
KOKA, dried up.	AKA, to dry up.
KONA, womb.	HUN(T) matrix.
KONAE, turning in a path; KANI, backwards and forwards.	HANA, turn back, return.
KOPI, shut, closed.	HEP, shut, secret, hide.
KUNE, plump, filled out to roundness.	HUN, youth.
KARU, eye.	AR, eye.

In Egypt language continued to grow, although very slowly, and assumed new forms as the young live shoots sloughed off the old dead leaves. The anchorage of conservatism is in clinging to the ground wherein it does not grow. Growth implies change; the quicker growth the greater change. The mummy will preserve its likeness whilst the living race to which it once belonged outgrows the primitive form and features still retained by the death-arrested type. The savage is the genuine conservative. We are apt to look on the Chinese as a very conservative and stereotyped people, as they are in the continuity of their customs, and yet language has been so worn down by them that words are often like coins with the features effaced. An accented vowel is at times all that remains of two or three consonants, and the explorer is constantly confronted with abysses of *abrading*. Language is tenfold less worn down in Maori.

Duplicating the word was the earliest mode of pluralizing it and extending the sense by adding a second, third, or fourth to the first. The principle is especially illustrated in the interjectional domain of words, and the most primitive languages are those which retain most reduplication. Sir John Lubbock has tabulated the result of a comparative calculation made by him, which shows that whereas in four European languages "we get about two reduplications in 1000 words, in the savage ones the number varies from 38 to 170, being from twenty to eighty times as many in proportion." [1]

LANGUAGES.	Number of Words Examined.	Number of Reduplications.	Proportion per Thousand.	
EUROPE—				
English . . .	1,000	3	3	
French . . .	1,000	2	2	Both foreign.
German . . .	1,000	6	6	All but one foreign.
Greek . . .	1,000	2	2	One being ἀβαρβαρος.
AFRICA—				
Beetjuan . .	188	7	37	Lichtenstein.
Bosjesman . .	129	5	38	Lichtenstein.
Namaqua Hottentot .	1,000	75	75	H. Tindall.
Mpongwe . . .	1,264	70	60	Snowden and Prall.
Fulup . . .	204	28	137	Koelle.
Mbofon . .	267	27	100	Koelle.
AMERICA—				[butions, 1869.
Makah . . .	1,011	80	79	Smithsonian Contri-
Darien Indians . .	184	13	70	*Trans. Eth. Soc.*, vol.
Ojibwa . . .	283	21	74	Schoolcraft. [vi.
Tupy (Brazil) . .	1,000	66	66	Gonsalvez Dias.
NEGROID—				
Brumer Island . .	214	37	170	M'Gillivray.
Redscar Bay . .	125	10	80	M'Gillivray.
Louisiade . .	138	22	160	M'Gillivray.
Erroob . . .	513	23	45	Jukes.
Lewis Murray Island.	506	19	38	Jukes.
AUSTRALIA—				
Kowrarega . .	720	26	36	M'Gillivray.
POLYNESIA—				
Tonga . . .	1,000	166	166	Mariner.
New Zealand . .	1,300	220	169	Dieffenbach.

[1] Lubbock, *Origin of Civilization*, p. 404.

This principle of reduplication can be illustrated from the hieroglyphics in which "Uâ-Uâ" means the one or the other; "U-U-U," stands for No. 3; "Uha-Uha," denotes intense desire; (Uha) "Ua-Ua," to revolve a matter in the mind, as we say "over and over again"; "Khi-Khi," to beat or rule (Khi); "Hab-Hab," to prowl round and round; "Ken-Ken" and "Kes-Kes," to dance; "Ker-Ker," to claw; "Khet-Khet," to attack and overthrow; "Am-Am," devourers; "Ab-Ab," to oppose (ab). "Ap-Ap," to mount, rise up (Ap) or Up-up; "Ben-Ben" and "Ber-Ber," for the roof and summit, the topmost height; "Han-Han," to return; "Her-Her," to snore; "Mas-Mas," to dip, dye, anoint; "Men-Men," to perambulate; "Mer-Mer," a friend; "Nu-Nu," the likeness, the little one; "Pa-Pa," to produce; "Peh-Peh," glory; "Rem-Rem," fish; "Ru-Ru," companions, steps; "Seb-Seb," encase; "Sem-Sem," regenesis; "Teb-Teb," to tread; "Sheb-Sheb," slices of flesh or food; "Shen-Shen, to fraternize, ally, form a brotherhood, or companionship; "Shu-Shu," plumes. These words show that in Egyptian the duplicated word was equal to the terminal Ti, value two, and therefore a plural ending. Thus, Peh-peh is the equivalent of Pehti, the glory or force in a double form. Ruru is equal to Ruti; Seb-Seb to Sebti. Sem-Sem describes a second phase; Nunu, the child, a second or duplicated form, and two plumes will read Shu-Shu, or Shuti, whilst in "U-U-U," for number three, the repetition serves the purpose of reckoning. This method of duplicating preceded any other kind of plural by means of the prefix or terminal, and belongs to the stage of language before ideographic signs had been reduced to phonetic values, when the two hands were expressed by Kep-Kep instead of Kepti; a Lower Egypt in Nubia, by Kep-Kep, instead of Khebt.

Numbering or reckoning is a mode of repeating by reduplication, and this in Egyptian is designated Kha-Kha. The throat, a chief organ of utterance in the guttural stage, is the Khe-Khe. To cackle as the goose or the fool and idiot, is to "Kaka," and the deposit of Kaka is kâ, to cry, call, or say. This seems to follow the duplicative mode of pluralizing into the region of the clickers and cacklers; the Quaqua, as the clicking Hottentots name themselves. The Namaquas are a tribe of these Quaqua, and the Qua in their name is presumably a reduced form of Quaqua, as Nam in their language means to talk, and Nams is a tongue. Nam-Quaqua, whence Namaqua, would thus denote the talkers with clicks, or those of the Kaka language, the Cacklers.

The Table proves that the Negroid language of Brumer Island retains the highest number of duplicated words, and next to it comes the *Maori of New Zealand* with its 169 in the thousand, and the following list of Maori words will show how the duplication of the syllable pluralizes and intensifies :—

APO, gather together, grasp. APOAPO, roll together, entangle.
APU, company of labourers. APUAPU, crammed, stuffed.
ARU, follow, pursue. ARUARU, chase.
AWHIO, go round about, wind. AWHIOWHIO, whirlwind, or whirlpool.
HAE, slit, lacerate. HAEHAE, cut repeatedly.
HARI, song. HARIHARI, song to make people pull together.
HOKI, return. HOKIHOKI, return frequently.
HOPU, catch. HOPUHOPU, catch frequently.
HURI, turn round. HURIHURI, turn over and over in one's mind, ponder.
KAPU, the hollow of the hand. KAPUKAPU, the sole of the foot.
KARE, a ripple. KAREKARE, the surf.
KIMO, wink. KIMOKIMO, wink frequently.
MOTU, severed. MOTUMOTU, divided into isolated portions.
PAKI, slap, pat. PAKIPAKI, slap or pat frequently.
TOHE, persist. TOHETOHE, be very pertinacious.

In this aspect the language of the Maori is next to the Negroid type, and both belong to the oldest formation of spoken language. Egyptian had, to a great extent, passed out of this primitive phase, but the hieroglyphics remain, and these in their ideographic stage show us the pictures of duplication, inasmuch as the phonetic B was an ideographic BUBU (or Bub), F was FAF; H was HUH; I was II or IU; K was KAKA; M was MUMU or Mim; N was NUNU; P was PEP; R was RER; S was SUS, and T was TAT. These are the visible representatives of the duplication in sounds.

In tracing the African origines at the antipodes, the Maori language and Mangaian mythology will furnish the chief evidence, but no contribution from kindred sources will be rejected.

TINA or DINA is a type-word for the foot in the Australian dialects. Tena (Eg.) means to divide in two halves, and become separate, which supplies a principle for naming the legs or feet. At this primitive stage we find a few Australian words not recovered in Maori. In another dialect, the Terrutong, which counts two and reckons number three as two-one, the word for one is ROKA, and two is ORIALEK, the rest are added to these. Also in Raffles' Bay, One is LOCA; Two ORICA, and in Egyptian LEKH (or Rekh) means to count, account, to reckon. Rekh interchanges with Ark, which is determined by the noose or knot for one period. So REKH in Maori is to knot the hair; that is the Egyptian ARK, and RIE-REKE is two knots; this answers to ORIALEK, the Second. Thus REKH, to count, is the sum and substance of all their reckoning.

We are often told of tribes that can only reckon two; which is an error. No tribe who ever reckoned on the hands could avoid counting up to ten. It is the base, the two hands, that has been mistaken for the limits. All digital counting implies the two, five and ten, and the two hands necessarily include the ten. For instance, Kap is the hand in Egyptian and other languages, that is one and five, and it is used for both. Kap in the Jhongworong (Aust.) dialect is No. 1. Kabti or Kepti (Eg.) denotes the two hands, and number two in Kamilaroi is Kâdien. In the same language the emphasis and urgency of imperative command is measured by the prolongation of the affix WĀ. The

Maori UA-UA means to be strenuous and pertinacious. UAH (Eg.) signifies augment, increase, very much. UA (Eg.) means go along, a long, long, long way. KHERP (Eg.) is the first, chief, principal, consecrated, his majesty, the type of the One. The KHERP was the first figure modelled by Ptah. In the Boraiper dialect the name of the number one is KEIARPE.

Horus, the " KHERP," was the pubescent Sheru, the adult and hairy god, and in the West Australian KELAP denotes the first appearance of pubes. KHERP (Eg.) also signifies first fruits,—which were offered in one shape or other, including the hair at the time of puberty,—and the word also reads to *produce linen.* KUNG-GUR (W. A.) is the name for a young woman who has arrived at puberty. This corresponds to a proto-Chaldean title of Ishtar in the character of GINGUR. In Egyptian KHEN-KAR would denote the period of puberty. The KWONNAT (W. A.) is a kind of acacia tree. This tree in Egypt was a form of the tree of life. Here the KWONNAT, as a sacred tree, answers by name to the KUNT (Eg.), a fig-tree.

MUTA-MUTA (Tas.) is the bird. In hieroglyphics the MUT is the bird that symbolizes the mother. MAGRA (Tas.) is a name of day. In Egyptian MAK is rule, and RA is day, or the sun. The MAKHU is the horizon, and the sun on the horizon is Makhu-Ra. GIBOR in Wiradurei is Man (Vir). Khepr (Eg.) is the generator. In the West Australian the tadpole is named a GOBUL. This is a form of Khepr, who was the frog-headed transformer in relation to water, and beetle-headed in relation to the earth.

In the hieroglyphics the moon and moon-god are represented by the Ibis or HABU. In North Tasmania the moon is called WEBBA; in the South it is WEIPA. HAPA (Mao.) means crooked and curved, and the curved bill of the Habu made it an image of the lunation or curving moon. In the same dialects the NURSE is called MEENA-MERU. MENA is the Egyptian wet-nurse; MERU means to love, attach, kiss. TET (Eg.) is the mouth, speech, or tongue, and in Port Philip the tongue is named TATEIN. TATANN was a divine title of the god Ptah as the father of beginnings, and in the West Tasmanian vocabulary the name for father is TA-TANA. TUT (Eg.) denotes the engenderer, the male emblem. Tata in Maori is the stem or stalk, and NA means begotten by. KUMI is the Maori name for No. 10, as a measure of ten fathoms, and Khemt is a form of No. 10 in Egyptian. To be Khemt likewise denotes the man or god of thirty years, who was the pubescent and hairy Horus called Khem-Horus, the virile adult. The hair figured on the Shebti or Double, the image of the re-erected life, and on the statues found in Easter Island has been alluded to as typical of Khem, which means the erectile power and potency that supplied the symbol of resurrection. KEMHU is applied to a certain form of hair, possibly to its being twisted to imitate the tongue HU, as a type of maturity. Be this as it may, the Maori KUMI-KUMI not only denotes the beard under the chin, but the duplicated Kumi is the equivalent of KHEMTI or Khemt, as the plural form of Khem which has the meaning of three—the Egyptian plural—and ten; hence thirty or KHEMT, the *homme fait* of thirty years. KUMI-KUMI for the bearded chin and throat tells exactly the same tale. MEDA (W.A.) is the MATA (Eg.), the phallus. MANDO (W.A.) means pubescence. In Egypt MEN and MENTU were two divinities who personified pubescence.

Regaa, Tasmanian, signifies the white man; Reko (Mao.) white; and in Egyptian Rekh means to bleach, full, make white. The Bibi (West Aust.) is the female breast; English bubby. This is explained by Bub (Eg.) the well of source; to be round and to well forth. BÂT (Eg.) means to inspire. In one sense it is to cause a soul to be; Ba being the soul or spirit. BA also denotes a spiritual illumination, hence Bâ-t to inspire will signifiy inspired, the t being a participle. The Fijian BETE, Abyssinian BOUDA, Amazulu ABATAKATI, Zend BUITI, Toda BUHT, are all forms of the BA-T, the inspired or inspiring, and identical in this sense with the Hindu Buddha, the enlightened, illuminated, or inspired one, who as SAKYA bears the name of the enlightened in the same sense from SAAKH (Eg.), illumination, understanding, an inspiring influence; Saakh to influence, illuminate, inspire; SAKR signifying perfect. The word "SIKA" is also used in Fiji to describe the signs of the god or spirit being in possession of the medium or priest; "SIKA" describes the appearance of the inspiring spirit. So in the Ojibwa language to YEESUKU is to prophesy in an abnormal condition. With the aborigines of India the diviner, exorciser, and witch-finder is denominated a SOKHA.[1]

TORO in Maori, means to consult by divination. This is the Egyptian TERU to invoke, ask, interrogate, question, adore. The TARO is a name of the Fijian diviner or magician identical with the Gaelic Draoi or Druid as the magician. The Fijian word Tara signifies to ASK, and when the TARA invokes, questions, or divines, he sits in a prescribed manner with his knee up and foot resting on his heel.[2] The Egyptian diviner probably sat in the same position, as TERU is also the name of the heel.

MAU, in Mangaian, means to spring up lightly. It is the name of the season in which the roots in the soil spring up into life, and answers to our spring and MAY. The Magellan clouds are named "MAU," as if from the rising-up of vapour, or curling up of smoke in the heavens.[3] It is needless to remark how Egyptian! where all is so. MAU (Eg.) is light, brightness, beams. MA, to grow, live; MAAU, the stalk, shoot; also MA is vapour, cloud, puff, or air,—every form of light and lightness, spring and springing indicated by the Mangaian

[1] Colonel Dalton.   [2] Williams, *Fiji and the Fijians*, vol. i. p. 229.
[3] Gill, p. 317.

Mau; the light and vapoury lightness being both combined in Magellan's clouds.

The Maori, Samoans, and Tahitians call the south TONGA, and speak of going up to the south and down to the north as it was in Egypt. HAGI (Tongan) is upward, and HIFO down or downwards. Tonga the south answers to TEN (Eg.), the elevated; KA, region; AKHA (Eg.) is the high, and HEFA the low, to squat down. Amongst the ancient Hawaiian names of the south is Lisso.[1] In Egyptian both RES and SU are designations of the south. RES-SU, as a compound, is the raised up heaven of the south.

TAKURUA is the Maori name of Sirius, the dogstar, which announced the arrival of the Inundation. TAKA means prepare, make ready. URUA denotes the arrival. In Polynesian URI is a plural of the dog, and Uhar (Eg.) is the dog. Teka (Eg.) is to see, behold unseen. Thus Takurua was the watchful announcer in New Zealand as in Egypt. It is natural that heat and light should have been named earlier than fire, and that fire when discovered should be named in the likeness of heat and light. Egyptian contains the chief type-names for heat, light, and the sun, found in all the groups of languages, and these originated apparently under the Motherhood. For example, KEP, the name of the old goddess of the seven stars, supplies a word for heat, fermentation, and light, but with no certain relation to the element of actual fire. The first types were framed and names were formed under the feminine *régime*, and the earliest heat and ferment of KEP related to the fire that vivifies, or the fire of life in womb-world. Hence the so-called goddess of fire, and the female mould of the type in Kep, who was the secret abode, the womb of life. In a second stage or character Kep, the genitrix in Khepsh, is pluralized as Khefti, Khepti, or Khebti. Khepti modifies into Uati or Uti, a goddess whose name signifies heat as well as water. The root KEF or KEP (Eg.) meaning heat, and to heat or light, furnishes the following names of fire found in the various groups of languages :—

QUAFI, in Chamori; GOIFI, in Guaham; CAUP, Annatom; COUVOU, Tocantins; CHÛ, Pacaguara; KOU, Apatsh; KAPURA, Maori; AFR, (Eg.); AVR, Hebrew; AFOR, Arago; FURU, Biafada; URA, Erroob; FOR, Papuan; AFI, Ticopia, Mallicollo, and Fakaofo; YAF, Tobi; AFU, Malagasi; IAF, Satawal; EAF, Ulea, and the Micronesian Group; FAI, Ahom, Khamti, Laos, and Siamese; FI, Japanese, and Luchu; KABUNGO, Aaiawong; APEH, Aino; HPIHU, West Shan; HIPPU, Telugu; HIEPP, Mallicollo; APUY, Tagala; API, Menadu, Buton, Mandhar, Bugis, Sasak, Bima, Sumbawa, Bali, Ende, and Mairassis; APUI, Bashi, Kayan, Korinchi, and Atshin; APEH, Solor; APIE, Batta dialects; APOI, Silong, and Sumenap; APO, Macusi; AP, Guebe; OPOAY, Rejang; EPEE, Catawba; EBE, Takeli; AVE, Yesso; AWA, Mohave; PHU, Shina.

[1] Fornander, *Polynesian Races*, vol. i. p. 17.

Khepti modifies into Khêt and Kat, and these are names of fire in Egyptian. KHETI or fire is the name of an enormous serpent with seven folds, the support of seven gods in the Hades. The name goes back to KHEPTI which in the modified HEPTI is a name for No. 7, originating in the seven stars. Khêt (from Khept) and Set are Egyptian names for fire itself, and this wears down to Ut for fire and heat; also to jet and emit fire. In these succeeding forms of the name we have KUADE, Bagnon; KHOTT, Kot, and Arini; KUT, Cahuillo; KETAL, Araucanan; KATTI, Maipur; KATHI, Baniwa; KUATI, Sapiboconi; KADING, Kasia; KIDZHAIK, Mille; HEDDOO, Begharmi; HOT, Skwali; HATZ, Hueco; HAT, Assan; GADI, Punjabi, and Hindustani; GADLA, Parnkalla; GAADLA, Menero Downs; UKUT, Ternati; WATA, Waiyamera; WATO, Maiongkong; WETTA, Woyawai; WATU, Carib, and Akkaway; WOT, Yakut, and Tshuvash; UTU, Furian; UT, Kirghiz, Baraba, Kazan, Nogay, Bashkir, and Meshtsheriak; OT, Turcoman, Tobolsk, Tshulim, Teleut, Kuznetsk, Koibal, Karagas, Yeneseian, Kumuk, and Karatshai; UD, Uzbek; OD, Osmanli.

Everywhere the mother-mould is first. Kep, Kaf, or Af, signifies BORN OF; the heat or fire of life. In the first phase the genitrix was designated Kartek, the sparkholder, in allusion to her circumpolar supremacy, and TEK, the name for the star-spark, supplies the type-name for the Star as TOGYT, in Fin; TJECHT, Esthonian; TECHTE, Olonets; TAGTI, Karelian; ETAK, Solor; TAKAR, Miri; TEKAR, Abor; TAKAR, Dofla; TOOKUL, Natchez. TEk, the spark, TEKA, to sparkle, furnished the name for fire, which, when produced, was derived from the spark, as TUEK, Motorian; TIKIAI, Saravecca; TEKERI, Daurai; TEKIEEHT, Riccari; TEGHERRE, Atoria and Wapisiana; TOGO, Savara, Mangasela, Yakutsk, Tshadpodzhir, and Nertshinsk; TOGGO, Yenisei; T'JIH, Bushman. In the second stage Khept, Uati, or Ut, is still feminine, for the genitrix was of a dual form as representative of the Two Truths. Now, as here maintained, the first son of the ancient genitrix Typhon was Bar-Sut of the Dog-Star, and he was the primordial god, or male divinity of fire. Hence the names Bar and Sut signify fire, the star being associated with the furnace-heat of the "Dogdays." The earliest form of the great solar god of fire who can be traced by means of the monuments is Kebekh (later Sebek-Ra), the son of Keb or Kep, the Typhonian great mother. Kebekh was the crocodile type of the sun, whose eyes denoted sunrise, and his tail the sunset,[1] or darkness. Kebekh was the sun of the waters and the underworld; his name modifies into Sebek, Khep, Af and Kak, or Sebek-Ra, Khepr-Ra, Af-Ra, and the ancient god Kak, who was continued in the Tum-Triad when that was formed. KAK signifies darkness, shade, night. The same word as the name of the boat, written KÂKÂ, shows a prior form in KF-KF,

---

[1] Hor-Apollo, i., 68.

a duplicate equivalent to the second Kaf, as in Kafti or Khebti, and so KAK equates with Kebekh, the son of, or the second form of Keb, corresponding to KEP-KEP and KHEB-KHEB, to descend, go down, fall down, or set; KEBEKH, KA-KA, or KAK, being the sun below in the underworld. In this form of the sun below, a male solar god was created as the author of fire, and the fashioner by means of fire. Hence Khepr, the Egyptian Vulcan, and Hephæstus, the Greek god of fire, who was represented as the lame and limping divinity of divers mythologies; the crooked-legged Ptah; the Hottentot " Wounded Knee;" and the Greek Vulcan. KAK means darkness; and, in another spelling, Khekh is light. Thus, as will be shown in explaining the name of the star Kokab, Kôkab, or Kab-kab, the fundamental meaning is the light-in-shade, and in the solar phase, Kak was the god of darkness, who supplied the name for god as CHUGH-Ra, the black sun, in Ge; CAGU, Bushman; XACA, Laos; CHIKOKKE, Loango, a Black Fetish God; KIGE, Susu; KACHQUA, Seneca; CAOGARIK, Abipone; KAKER, Port Philip; QUAKER, Nottoways; KHOGEIN, Lunctas; JACH, Hebrew; JACK, English; JAUK, Arabic; JACUSI, Japanese; IJAK, Kodiak; JAGEACH, Radack; JOCAHUNA, Cuban; JACA, Singhalese, Devil; EYAK, Koniaga, Evil Spirit; WAK, Galla; WAKAN, Sioux; ACHUCHE, Angami-Naga; AOGUE, Sereres; UKKO, Finnic; OKHA, Otomi; JEKO, Gonga; AKH, Hebrew and Assyrian.

The name of KAK, the solar god of the underworld, supplies the following names for the sun :—

CHAKI, Paioconeca; KACHQUA, Seneca (sun and moon); KAKKAAN, Kolush of Sitka; KAKETLKH, Ugalents; KAQUI-KEBIN, Andaqui; KAAGH-KWA, Cayuga; GARACHQUA, Onondago; CHOKONOI, Navaho : KIJIK, Ottawa, Sun, and in Ojibwa, light; KAJA, Begharmi; KUYA, Koibal; GEGGER, Eboorr; SHEKKINAK, Eskimo; IAKAI, Ticunas; SAKH, Kutshin; SIGA, Figi; SACCE, Moxos; AQUICHA, Huasteca; WOKA, Dizzela; YUKO; Yakkumban; AHKA, Masaya; OKO, Pujuni and Sekumne; YAH, Waraw; and lastly, we are indebted to Kak, the Sun-God, for the following names of fire :—

CHEK, Uraon; KAG, Nut; CHAKI, Paioconeca; KHAKAR, Brahui; KICHCHU, Budugur; GAGAVAS, Umiray; KAKO, Kaffa; K'AKK, Maya; K'HOH, Kulanapo; YUGA, Intibuca; YACHTAH, Uchee COCHTO, Timbiras : KOKO, Legba; CHICHI, Antes; CHECHAN, Machakali; WAIK, San Raphael; WIKIH, Tshokoyem; WIKE, Talatui; AQUACAKE, Puelche; AKKHI, Pali; AKA, N'godsin and Dodi; OGIA, Ashanti; ICHE or CHU, Pacaguara; EKA, Koldagi; OKO, Aro, Mbofia, Isiele, and Isoama; IKA, Nubian; UGA, Guajiquiro; AHKU Masaya; OKHO, Khwakhlamayu : AGHI, Kuswar; AGI, Tharu; AGO, Pakhya : UGG, Bhatui; AGE, Darahi; AG, Khurbat, Hindi, Ghagar, and Nawer; AKH, Egyptian.

From these lists it may be seen that the Egyptian word, which only indicates heat, the heat and ferment of life, as in the womb, and the mystery of fertilization, in the name of the genitrix Kep, furnishes the type-name for actual fire in the Micronesian group as QUAFI, Chamori; GOIFI, Guaham; EAF, Ulea, and IAF in Satawal. In the New Hebrides we find CAUP for fire in Annatom; HIEPP and AFI as names of fire in Mallicollo; YAF in Tobi; AFI, Fakaofo; AFI, Ticopia. KAPURA is a name of fire in the Maori, and in this language alone do we recover the full form of the word AFR (Eg.) and אור (Hebrew) as the name of fire and light. Af is worn down from Kaf or Kep, the feminine fire, heat or mystery of life, and preserves the same meaning in Af, to be born of. The Maori has frequently retained the oldest forms.

In Tahiti, and other of the Polynesian Islands, Captain Cook found that it was customary for the natives to preserve the bread-fruit by fermenting it into a sour paste; this paste they called MAHI. Now the Egyptian word MÂI was found difficult to fathom. Mariette argued that it had the meaning of bodily humours, including the seminal essence. But we recover a more inclusive and workable sense in the Polynesian "MAHI" for fermentation or fermented; Maori MAHI, to work; MOI, to ferment. Mahi is the Egyptian MAHI to fulfil, applied to the gestator and bread-maker. MAI (Eg.) is the fermenting source of life as the spirit of the male. This meaning of Mahi, to ferment, or to be fermented and fulfilled, will help us to the sense of an unknown kind of Egyptian drink named KARMAHU.[1] The hieroglyphic Jar, Kar, or Karhu, is determined by a vase from which steam is issuing. In the Maori both KOROHU and KORU-MAHU are names applied to steam. The issuing steam implies some kind of craggan or vessel for the fire. Drink, produced by steam, will no doubt include distilled liquors, and as Karr in Egyptian and Maori denotes a furnace; the Karhu is the steaming jar; the KAR-MAHU the drink; and as MAHU means to ferment and turn into spirit, it follows that the steaming signifies distilling, and KARMAHU is drink as a distilled liquor; drink fermented and fulfilled in the jar or craggan. Mahu (Mao.) also denotes the being raised up by force, as in steaming or fermenting. Tane-Mahuta was the strong spirit that forced up the heaven.

The Mangaians, when expressing their belief that the Deity is the essential support, denote it by the word IVI-MOKOTUA, the back-bone, or vertebral column. That is the same ideograph as the Egyptian Usert-Sceptre which is formed of the back-bone, and is the sign of sustaining and protecting power. This emblem was Typho-nian at first, with the head of Anubis on the top; that is, it repre-sented the genitrix Kep or Kef, whose name denotes puissance, force, and power. She was the primordial Power personified, and

---

[1] Smith, *P. H.*, Birch, *Dictionary*, p. 416.

Sut-Anubis was her son. The continuing of the feminine type as a masculine one is shown in the Ritual,[1] where the "SPINE of the Osiris" is said to be in "the shape of that of Pasht." It has been explained how the name of Kefa, Chavvah, or Ihevah passes into that of Ihu and Iu, the dual-natured son; and precisely the same thing occurs in the Polynesian and Maori. The Eve, or Kefa, of Mangaia and New Zealand is found in Ivi, Iwi, or WHEUA. The Maori has no V, or WHEUA would be WHEVA, the equivalent of Khefa or יהוה, as the name of the genitrix, the back-bone and sustaining power, the essential support which was figured at first as feminine and hinder part. In Samoan and Tahitian the typical word for the divinity is Fatu, the name of the ancient genitrix as Fet or Aft. Fatu has a variant in ATU, and the moon, at fifteen days old, is called Atua in Maori. This relates the Atu or Fatu to the lunar Goddess of the four quarters, and to the Goddess 15, a title of Ishtar. Atu, in Mangaian, is strictly the kernel, core, or heart of a thing; the hard, essential, and sustaining part. Very large kernels are called KATU, which shows an earlier form of the name. Katu is the hard form of Hatu (Eg.), for the heart and essence of all. Akâtu (Eg.) is the foot, the sole; and the SOLE of the foot was reckoned an earlier foundation than the soul.

"My heart is my mother," says the Osirian.[2] "My heart was my mother; my heart was my being on earth." That is the Hatu in Egyptian, and Atu in Mangaian. The earliest form of the Hat or Kat (from Khept) is the womb-type of the producer. Wheva, Ivi Iwi, pass into Io. IHO is the heart of a tree. IOIO (Mao.) means the doubly hard, and in Mangaian IO is a constant equivalent for the Atu or Katu, the core, kernel, pith, or heart, which expresses the same meaning as IVI, or the bone. Bone, kernel, pith, and heart are entirely typical of the essential base and support of life. The Polynesian EVE could not be borrowed from the Missionaries as the Eve formed out of Adam's bone, for she preceded the male. Ivi the widow is Ivi the genitrix, who existed before her son grew up to become her consort and to represent both sexes in one. This duality of the Io, or Iu, is also manifest in the Maori IHU, for the nose, which, in the hieroglyphics as the nose of the calf, is the sign of the Au (Iu). The heart of the tree is IHO, or UHO, and UHO is likewise a twin-type as the umbilical cord. The word IHO, or IO, says Mr. Gill, is a common name for God in Polynesia, and he observes, "Most appropriately and beautifully do the natives of Mangaia transfer the name IO-ORA to Jehovah." He little thought how appropriately! He renders the "IO-ORA" by the living God. "ORA," in Maori, means alive, safe, escaped, recovered, well in health. The first who escaped in the passage of the waters, or the void, was the Ora or Horus, the Saviour. ORE means to bore a way through; the OREA is a kind of eel, the

[1] Ch. xlii. [2] *Ritual,* ch. xxx.

type of Tuna and Tum who passed through the waters and mud of the abyss. The Ora, Horus, Koru, Ar, El, or Elyon had the same origin in phenomena, and the type is as old as Sut, who was both the Har and Iu in one.

In catching these last words of the Mangaian mythology just as it was expiring the Missionary was doing good work, but in preaching his gospel he was also re-imposing on the people their own ancient divinities in another shape; the Hebrew version of these being but a portion of the driftage on many shores of one original system of thought long gone to wreck. Where there is sufficient intelligence extant, as in India or China, the native mind recognizes the old matter, newly presented to it as a special divine revelation, and is able to gauge the limits of those who do not so recognize it, and who are profoundly ignorant of the origines. Consequently those who know are not to be converted to the creed of those who do not know.

A common name of God with the Mangaians is "TATUA MANAVA," rendered by Gill a loin-belt, or girdle. It means more than that. TATUA is the belt, and MANAVA (Maori MANAWA) is the very heart and breath of life, as well as the BELLY or seat of life. It is, therefore, a girdle of the breath of life, or more literally a life-belt. The Mangaian and Maori TATUA is the Egyptian TATU, a buckle-symbol of life, which the Egyptians enclosed with their mummies as a type of immortality. "Osiris having set up the Tat and prepared the Tatu (buckle) proceeds wherever he likes."[1] The Tat was the cross of Ptah; the buckle, a kind of Ankh-loop, signifying life. This TATU therefore was the equivalent of the Mangaian girdle of life. The "Tatu" was an image of the eternal (Teta) in Egypt, and here we find that Tatua is the name for the eternal. "Eternity," says Gill, "is often expressed by the phrase 'e rau te TAUTAU,'" i.e. 200 ages,[2] or "e tautau ua atu," i.e. time on, on, still on. The Tautau for ages, time continual, for ever, is the Egyptian Teta, eternal, or time for ever, figured by the circle, the Tat of the four corners, and the Tat-buckle.

The images of the gods and ancestors, as well as the spirits of the departed, are called TIKI-TIKI in Polynesia. They are looked upon as protectors of boundaries and crossings. The Egyptian Tekh is a frontier, and Teka means to cross. These are commonly called the KII without the T prefix, and the Egyptian Akhu, Khu, or Khi, are spirits, manes, the spirits of the dead. The same word likewise denotes the edge, boundary, or horizon. The New Zealanders make little talismanic images of green jade, called TIKI. Tiki was the creator. The word TEK (Eg.) has the important meanings of to twist, to see unseen, with the eye for determinative; to be hidden and escape notice, and yet to behold. This is possibly expressed by the TIKI, which has the head bent down on one side and twisted as if to realize the meaning of Tek; as

---

[1] *Ritual*, ch. cxxix. Rubric. [2] Gill, 326.

may be seen by images in the British Museum. TEK (Eg.) means to amputate, cut short; English DOCK, to cut off, and Dockey, a little meal. The Tiki is not only a dwarf, but is docked of two fingers of each hand, and thus images those who have been cut off, with whom, in slang English, it is "all dickey." Dr. Krapf learned that the dwarf Africans, only four feet high, were called DOKOS, *i.e.* Tekis, or short people. Under this name we have a type of Sut in the ass, designated a "dickey." Tiki was the god of the dead, and the first to make a passage through the underworld. He was the crosser, and Tek (Eg.) means to cross. The Egyptian Tekh is Taht, the lunar-god of the lower world, but not the earliest who made the passage. There is a god, Tekhem, in the Ritual. Tiki has several images, one is a post marking a Tapu place; another is a figure on the gable of a house; another the lower part of the back, the sacrum; the *os sacrum* being a very early form of amulet or charm. The TOKI in Maori and Mangaian is the axe or adze. Eva-Toki is the axe-dirge. "In this scenic dirge," says Gill, "the axes were used to cleave the earth which had swallowed up the dead. They were only mimic weapons made of iron-wood, as the use of stone axes would infallibly end in bloodshed." The Toke in Maori is an earth-worm, another earth-cleaver, and the word means gone away, out of sight.

The axe ideograph, the sign of Anup the opener—the first opener of the underworld, who was therefore the conductor of the Great Mother, of the sun, and lastly of the souls—is the symbol of divinity in the Mangaian mythology, as in the hieroglyphics. In the dirge of the "Blackened Face" the mourner for his lost son exclaims, "Fairy of the Axe! Cleave open the secret road to spirit-land, and compel Vatea to give up the dead." "Puff, Tiki, a puff such as only ghosts can." That is, to crack and split, and the word used is rendered by the Latin *Pedite*. The appeal is followed by a chorus of pretended explosions. Irreverent as this seems, it goes far to identify TIKI with the Hottentot Utixo, who they say is the concealed god that sits in heaven and thunders. Tiki who thunders will be a god of lightning, and his axe (Toki) becomes a link in connection with the axes of the thunder and lightning in many lands. Sut-Anup was the earliest fire-god and LIGHTNER, and before weapons were shaped, or Celts were polished, the flash from heaven descended with its dart of death, which was imitated in the stone-axe and arrow-head, and the fire-stones, lightning-stones, or thunder-bolts, were afterwards confused with the weapons and amulets of the stone age. The stone axe or adze, named Anup, identifies itself as the type of Sut, the first opener; and in a Damara story this is apparently recognized. A little girl's mother gives her a needle. She finds her father sewing thongs with thorns, and gives him the needle, whereupon he presents her with an axe. Going further she finds the lads trying to cut down trees with stones, and says to them, "Our sons, how is it that you use stones?

Why do you not say, '*Our first-born*, give us the axe'?"[1] Sut-Anup was the first-born of the Great Mother; the axe was his.

The ancient Egyptian Adze preserved in the British Museum is identical with the Toki of New Zealand, not only in shape, but also in the manner of tying on the stone to the handle, and likewise with the cinet with which it is bound. The Maori wicker-work is also called TAIKI, and is identical with the Irish TOCHAR, the wattled causeway, the Akkadian TAK for reed-matting, and the English TUCK for weaving; from TEKA (Eg.), to cross, twist, or interweave. The Tima, or hoe of the Maori, is the same implement of husbandry as it was in Egypt, the curious dibble, or pick, placed in the hands of Khem, the primeval plough. The Maori have also a weapon made of stone, or of whale's bone, used for hand-to-hand fighting, called the Mere, or Patu. It is a club of curious shape, which has been likened to a soda-water bottle with the bulb flattened.[2] Some of these war-weapons, made of green jade, were held to be the most precious heirlooms of the Maori chiefs. The names of Mere and Patu agree with the Egyptian Merhu and Pet.

The Merhu is a club or *boat-hook*. Now an early form of the sceptre, which can be traced into the war-weapon, was the paddle-blade called the Pet-sceptre. This is held in the hand as the sign of the Kherp, the princeps, consecrated one, his majesty. Various paddle-blades, as the Usr and Hepi, also approach the shape of the Mere or Patu, and tend to identify the type with the Pet-sceptre of Egypt.

A secret stone used for purposes of divination by the Tasmanians was called "Heka."[3] Hika (Mao.) is to perform a ceremony with incantation. HEKAU is the Egyptian name for magic, conjuring, and to charm. A master of magic, and charmer or conjuror to the king, is called UR-HEKA, the great charmer. The feminine Peh or Hem was a form of the Heka.

A very sacred relic of antiquity was shown to Sir George Grey on the Island of Mokoia, in the middle of Rotorua Lake, during his visit there in 1866. Two aged priests were still keeping watch over their treasured symbol preserved on the site of an ancient temple. This was an image the size of life, well executed in a species of *porphyry*, represented in a sitting posture with the elbows resting on the knees and the face looking upwards, one of those apparently brought by their ancestors who first entered the island, as the stone could not have been procured on that side of the world.[4]

Rotorua means the Double Lake, which corresponds to the Pool of Two Truths. The priests took the Governor, Sir George Grey, to the place where the Giant of Rotorua, called TUORANGI, was interred in a stone coffer or cist, eight and a half feet long, formed of flag-

[1] Bleek, *Reynard in Africa*, p. 90.
[2] See *Early History*, Tylor, p. 202, 3rd edit.
[3] Bonwick, p. 193. [4] *Te Ika a Maui*, pp. 31, 32.

stones with a sloping top like the roof of a house, the ridge of it being curiously carved.[1] Tuarongo (Maori) is the back or ridge of the house ; Tua-rangi would denote the ridge of Heaven, and as Tu means to stand erect, the giant Tuorangi was no doubt a form of the Heaven-raiser and supporter, the giant, the Maori Nimrod. One of the Egyptian gods is termed, "Sole type in the roofed house."[2]

The allegories and their illustrations found amongst the Maori and Polynesians are often so ancient that they resuscitate an almost effaced type. The lizard is one of these. It is extant as the ideograph of multiplying and becoming numerous, but was comparatively superseded in monumental times. The lizard is to the Maori and Tasmanian women what the serpent became in Egypt, a feminine type of the Two Truths on which the multiplying depended. The Eel is another almost superseded symbol. The Athenian comic writers Anaxandrides and Antiphanes scoffed at the Egyptians for considering the eel a powerful dæmon and an equal of the gods. The Eel was sacred to Hapi-Mu, or the Nile, and was also a type of Tum.[3] Hapi-Mu may be rendered the water-concealed. Tum was the sun which made its way through the fabled waters of the deep, and the eel was an appropriate type for the crosser beneath the waters. The eel as a solar symbol—like the frog—is so ancient that it belongs to a time when there was neither boat nor bridge, and the big fish was the boat ; as in the Mangaian myths, where the whales, sharks, and large fish are called canoes. The frog spawned a bridge, as it were, over the surface of the waters, and the eel made its way at the bottom, through the mud of mythology. So the god Shu and the solar God were said to transform into the cat, because this animal could see to make its way by night. Such modes of representation did not originate in worship, but in necessity and utility.

Tum was the earlier Aten or Atun, the circle-maker, the deity of the disk, the one who crossed the abyss, bridged the void, completed the circle when he was considered as the child of the mother. This form of the God whose type was the eel has been preserved in the Maori and Mangaian mythology, in which Atun is Tuna, the divine solar hero who crosses the waters of the inundation in the shape of an eel. TUNE is the Maori name of the eel, and the word eel is identical with El and Ar, the son, who made the passage of the underworld as the Af-Sun, or Atun.

In the story of "Ina-who-had-a-divine-Lover," daughter of Kui-the-Blind, who dwelt in the shadow of the Cave of Tautua, Tuna the Eel-God appears to her, and tells her of the coming flood, and of an eel that will be landed at her threshold. She is instructed to chop off its head and bury it. This was done and Ina daily visited the grave of the Eel-God, her lover. One day she saw a stout green

[1] *Te Ika a Maui*, pp. 31, 32.　　　　[2] *Rit.* ch. cxlii.
[3] Votive Mummy-case in Bronze. Leemanns.

shoot piercing the soil, and the next day this had divided into two. The twin shoots from one root grew into two cocoa-nut trees which sprang from the two halves of Tuna's brains; one red, the other green, the red being sacred to Tangaroa, the green to Rongo, who are the twin-brothers of another mythos.[1] It is at this depth the origines of mythology have to be read.

Tautua, the ridge of rest, answers to the Egyptian Tattu, the eternal region, the place of the pool of the Two Truths, and the twin tree called the tree of life and knowledge; the twin Persea tree of life in Egypt. Tuna the Eel-God, is one with Atun and Tum, who was duplicated in Iu, and who brings peace just as Tuna does. In Tattu was the place of transformation and re-establishing, in the sign of the fish (An); Tun (Eg.) means to divide, and it was here that the dual son was established in the place of the parent. The kernel of the cocoa-nut was called the brains of Tuna, and it was held to be unlawful for any woman to eat an eel.

According to Gill, the blackbeetle was looked upon in Mangaia as diet for the dead.[2] The type remains the same, although differently applied, as in Egypt and Britain, where the beetle was buried with the dead; not for food exactly, but the Scarabæus represented being, self-originating substance, and self-sustaining power; it was also the emblem of the transformation and resurrection of the dead; this in Mangaia had taken shape as food for the dead, or rather the ghosts of the dead. In Koroa's lament for his lost son, beetles, crabs, red worms, and blackbirds are said to be the food of disembodied spirits.[3] The blackbird is the MOMOO, the type of the god Moô, who delights to secrete men and things in his hiding-place. MU in Egyptian is death, and the MUMU bird of death or the dead is the Owl, a bird of darkness and of death; the name of the dead, the mummy, is written Mumu, with two owls.

The Perue, or bird-shaped winged kite, corresponds to the TAUTORU, or three stars in Orion's belt.[4] Toru (Mao.) is three, and TAU is the string of a garment, a loop, thong, or belt. PERUE, the bird, denotes the throat-feathers of the PERU-PERU; the Koko, or *prosthemadera* bird. PURE (Mao.) also means to arrange in tufts. These tufts appear on the kite. The PURU-PURU, with its throat-feathers, equates with the solar-hawk, which has a frill of feathers figured round its neck. The constellation Orion is named after Horus of the resurrection.

The hawk (Maori, KAHU) imaged the ascending sun of the resurrection, Horus or Hu, the spirit; and KAHU-KAHU denotes the spirit or ghost, the one risen from the dead. So the human-headed hawk was the symbol of the dead mummy which had become a soul. In England the kite is both a hawk and the paper toy. The

[1] Gill, p. 77. [2] P. 205.
[3] *Ib.* p. 202. [4] *Ib.* p. 122.

Mangaian kites are all symbolic. One of these is egg-shaped, and corresponds to the constellation of the *Twins* and their parents. The twin-brothers of mythology are represented as coming out of the egg. The Maori have preserved this solar hawk of mythology in the shape of their kite, which they fly for amusement. It is called KAHU (hawk, *Circus Gouldii*), and has the tail and claws of a hawk. It is still made in the likeness of the hieroglyphic "Hut," the solar disk borne on outspread wings. This was the type of the gods Kâ and Hu, the sun below and the sun above the horizon, and where the Egyptians placed the disk between the outstretched wings, the Maori depict the solar face.[1] It is said that two different gods in Fiji lay claim to the hawk.[2] So is it in Egypt, where the hawk is a type of the Solar God, both as Horus and Ra.

In the Fiji Islands, certain birds, fishes, plants, and other things are said to be the domiciles of deities. On Vanua Levu the god Ravuravu claims the hawk as his abode.[3] That is how the symbolism is reported. Now in Egypt the hawk-headed Horus is the Repa, the heir-apparent, the prince, and in Ravuravu the name of the Repa is duplicated in the name of a deity whose dwelling or type is the hawk. In this shape the symbol survives as an ideograph, the meaning of which has to be read in Egypt.

The primeval types and symbols live on in popular games where the actors have no other mode of figuring them. The Maori have another symbolical representation in which a lofty pole is erected on the brink of a river. *Twelve* ropes are attached to the top, which revolves so that each person has to swing round in turn over the water or precipice. This kind of swing is called the MOARI.[4] MERU (Eg.) denotes a ring, a circle; MERUA, a limit of land and water, and this meaning is identified by the position chosen. The sun in the underworld, crossing the waters and making the MEH-passage, was represented in the mysteries as having a narrow escape from the attendant dangers in the abyss of the North and bend of the Great Void, and this passage of danger was imitated in the MOARI. Hence MOARIARI (Mao.) signifies having a very narrow escape.

In Egyptian MEH for the north, the north quarter, is also the name of the number nine, and it denotes a fulfilment; the completion of a cycle and a circle when the sun had crossed the waters of our three winter and water signs. The Egyptian year began in July, with a starting-point also from the solstice in Mesore (June), and March would be the ninth month, *i.e.* MEH, the month of the Equinox. A relic of this reckoning is extant with the Maori, who call the month of March MAEHE or MAEA, although their year ends in December, and MAEA, to emerge, be gathered in, fulfilled, is equivalent to the Egyptian MEH.

---

[1] *Te Ika a Maui*, p. 346.   [2] Maclennan, *Fortnightly Review*, 1870, p. 216.
[3] Williams, *Fiji and the Fijians*, vol. i. p. 219.   [4] *Te Ika a Maui*, p. 363.

An instrument has been found on the monuments, called the KÂ, used for throwing at birds and supposed to be the boomerang. According to M. Chabas, it is 'the Egyptian boomerang. In the West Australian languages the boomerang is named Ky-li. It is thrown by striking the ground to obtain a rebound into the air, and in Egyptian KHA expresses this throwing to the earth, also to rise up. But the full value of Kâ is Kak, or Khekh.

The Mangaian curved club is shaped like the Australian boomerang, and this is named the KAIKAA. KHEKH (Eg.) means to be repelled, repulsed, and to return ; KIK, Chinese, to kick. KEKE, Maori, signifies contrariwise ; in a different line or direction from the one expected. The Keke or Kaikaa then is the boomerang.

Now the word "Boomerang" appears to be a reduced form of BOOROOMOOROONG, the name given to a scene in the most secret of the Maori mysteries at which a tooth was extracted from the boys who were then made into men. A *throwing-stick* was cut with much ceremony, and this was applied to the tooth and knocked against it by means of a stone.[1] The use of the boomerang, the throwing-stick that described a complete circle, was typical of the cycle of life then completed and the entrance into that of manhood. This fact with the aid of Egyptian will enable us to decipher the sign of the boomerang. BURU means the height of attainment. So Poro in Maori means to complete, attain the end, termination, as in the " Porabung " rite. MER (Eg.) is the circle, and ANKH, life. The Kaika stick which fulfilled the circle was possibly a type of KAK, the completer of the solar circle, which, as will be seen further on, would account for its application to the tooth knocked out. KHAKHT (Eg.) means to recoil, also KHA is a stick and KHAT to recoil. KHA-KHAT therefore denotes the recoiling stick, and this may supply the names of the KATURIA used by the Kulis of Gujerat and the CATEIA mentioned by Bishop Isidore of Seville. The name, as Khat or " Cat," still survives in that of the piece of wood used in the game of tipcat, which rises in the middle so as to rebound when struck at either end.

The survival of the myths in ceremonies, games, usages, is totally independent of the proverbial short memory of savages. The thing that had been they repeated like any other act of nature, without troubling themselves about the origin or end, or pausing midway to remember the meaning. And these customs carry their message more simply and safely than any written record in the world when we have recovered the clue to their primordial character. KHEPR-PTAH was one form of the Crosser. He carries the Tat, the cross of the crossing : Ta (Eg.) means to navigate across, and the Tat is the cross symbol. Ptah is styled Tatanan, the father of Beginnings ; our word *tatting*, for crossing the thread, preserves the primal meaning.

[1] Collins, *New South Wales* (1804), p. 364.

The Maori also have their tatting in the game of cat's-cradle, called MAUI. This, by the bye, is the name of the cat in Egyptian. In their "Maui" they were accustomed to represent such scenes from their mythology as the Great Mother bringing forth her primal progeny ; Maui fishing up the land, and other pictures of the beginnings, in the forms assumed by the crossed or "tatted" lines.[1] They were repeating the work of Ptah-Tatanan, *tatting* the figures of creation over again and enacting the scenes set forth by mythology. The first who "tatted," however, and the earliest to cross the waters, was the great mother herself, in her water-types of the hippopotamus and the crocodile. Her "TAT" sign was simply a tie or knot. In her second character as Hathor she is styled MEH-URT, the great or peaceful fulfiller. MEH denotes the number nine, and means a measure, to wreathe, girdle round, fulfil, complete, be filled. Tat signifies to establish and found, as was done in crossing and fulfilling the circle or in "tatting." "Mau," in Maori, means restrained, confined, to be fixed and established, which was illustrated by the MAUI or cat's-cradle, as a mode of typology.

Shortt, in his account of the tribes on the Neilgherries, describes the Toda women as being tattooed on the chest and arms with semi-circles, having *nine points*, and with rows of dots consisting of thirty-six points ; the terminal point of each row being marked by a ring or circle. This tattooing is called GURTU. KARTU (Eg.) denotes the orbit or course which was fulfilled by the gestator in nine Solar months. Guru, Sanskrit, means the pregnant woman, hence the Great, Cornish GRETE, the graced and favoured.

The semi-circle with nine points is the fellow to the Collar of Isis worn chiefly in front and therefore semi-circular, composed of nine Bubu (beads), the number of months assigned to the genitrix as mother of the Sun-God. Guru, the pregnant woman, is she who is both great and girt. KHIRATU in Assyrian is the type-name for woman, from this root, as the gestator distinguished from the child. The thirty-six points showed the number of ten-day periods in the year, determined by the thirty-six decani (Tehani) or crossing stars ; and this number of crossings in the year was prescribed by the Syrian Liturgy as the sacred number of the cross !

The natives on the Murchison River celebrated a festival at which they made a great gathering of eggs. They danced around an oval or egg-shaped pit, and carried the spear in front of the body as priapus simulacrum : the pit itself being fringed with bushes. According to Oldfield every gesture was an appeal to the virile passion. This festival was called the KARO. Kara in Maori signifies the man, the adult male or the old man. In Egyptian KAR denotes masculine

---

[1] *Te Ika a Maui*, p. 347.

[2] Shortt, *Tribes on the Neilgherries*, quoted by Marshall. *Amongst the Todas*, p. 47.

power; the testes are named KARIU and KARTU. Both names have passed into the far islands.

One illustration is this KARO festival. We also find the KHERTU. The Adelaide blacks practise a rite of initiation on their youths in which they suffer the test of their manhood in the shape of a piece of bamboo reed being thrust into the prepuce, and the membrane is then slit by means of another piece of reed to which a sharp edge has been given by rending it. After this trying ceremony the member is named KERTO, the Egyptian name of the testes, the male power and property. The rite was performed at the time of puberty when the boy passed into manhood.

Davis, who had been admitted to the Maori mysteries during fourteen years, says the ceremony of young-man-making, called WORRIN-GARKA, was for the purpose of passing the lad into the state of manhood, and to teach him how to act with a woman. They bestowed on him a seal of admission. It was affirmed amongst the black natives, that the lizard Yura now dwelling in the Milky Way was *the author of the Worringarka.* The rock-lizard in the hieroglyphics is the ideograph of becoming numerous and *multiplying.* The rite of circumcision (not in the fanatical phase of castration) was that of swearing-in and covenanting for the reproduction of human kind; hence the proper time of the rite was at the period of puberty, and the lizard of the Milky Way is as good an ideograph of multiplying as the rock-lizard on the monuments. Also it affords a curious parallel to the Hebrew "Worringarka," or Covenant of Abram, in the making of which the Deity said, "Look now toward heaven and tell the stars, if thou be able to number them. And he said unto him, So shall thy seed be." This was on the condition of his keeping the Covenant of the circumcision.

As to the name of the ceremony, ARIKI (Maori) is the title of the first-born; ARK (Eg.) denotes a covenant on oath and the end of a period; LECKA, in the Gipps' land dialect, signifies to bring forth young. The charms being repeated and the seal conferred, the youth was passed into the ranks of the producers. In the Tasmanian initiation a seal of admission was given. At other times a white stone was presented to be secretly kept from the sight of woman. A girdle of human hair was sometimes presented, others wore a covering made from the pubes forcibly extracted.[1]

Now when the child Horus transformed into the second or virile character, he became the Sheru, the pubescent, adult and hairy God, Khem-Horus, and it can be shown that in their rites the Australians, Tasmanians, and New Zealanders were enacting the drama of Mythology according to the Egyptian characters. One word in Maori will of itself tell the whole tale. TARA is the name of the male member, the masculine mettle, the papillæ on the skin, the

[1] Bonwick, *Tasmanians,* p. 201.

pubes, things pointed and prickly, the spear-point, thorns, spines in the dorsal fin of a fish and the shoots or rays of the ascending Sun, the pubescent Horus of the horizon who had transformed from the nursling child into the Man-god, the begetter, he who was called TARAHUNGA or the begetter of his people, as the father of Maui. The transformation in Egyptian was named KHEPR, and it was effected under the type of Khepr-Ra. The young-man-making rites, when performed in the Macquarrie district, were described as the celebration of the mysteries of KEBARRAH.[1] As the Mangaians and Maori have the Sun-god Râ, there can be no doubt they had him in the character or under the type of Khepr.

One shape of Khepr was Ptah, the crooked-legged, lame god, and in Maori one name of the lame-footed and the cripple is KOPIRI. Also, Khepr-Ptah was the ·frog-headed, as one image of the transformer; and in the West Australian dialect, GOBUL is the name of the tadpole, the transformer into the frog.

The beetle, another type of Khepr, was represented as having no female kind. That is, it was an image of the male god, who was said to beget himself. Of Khepr-Ptah it is said in the texts, " Thou art fatherless; begotten by thine own becoming; thou art without a mother; thou art born by repetition of thyself." The doctrine is illustrated by the KIPPER-Ground of the Australians. This, as the Khepr-ground, would be a place sacred to the scene of transformation or transfiguration. It was a circle of raised earth corresponding, in its way, to the KYVRI-VOL and other British mounds. This hallowed inclosure was far from the haunts of womankind, and a female approached it under penalty of death. Khepr, in the solar phase, did without the female. Other customs, including that of COUVADE, will yet be traced to Khepr.

With some tribes the foreskin was cut off in circumcision with a sharp flint, and placed on the third finger of the left hand.[2] An early form of marriage-ring, employed as a type of reproduction, answering to the seal-ring (Khet) of the hieroglyphics, and the ring of the Hebrews, worn by the bridegroom of blood.

With others a new and sacred name was conferred by sponsors, as in the baptismal ceremony, never to be divulged except in presence of the Chosen. The Maoris made use of a sacred instrument called a WITTO-WITTO; as rendered by Angas.[3] This they whirled round over the fires to keep off evil spirits at the time of certain rites. It was also used to warn off women and children. The name, as WETOI, implies a voice of prohibition.

At the third and last ceremony of the rites of puberty, the sponsors bestow on the fully initiated youth a new name, by which he is known for the rest of his life. In token of this they hang about his neck

---

[1] Angas, vol. ii. pp. 216–224. [2] Angas, vol. i. p. 98.
[3] *Savage Life and Scenes in Australia and New Zealand*, vol. i. pp. 98, 99.

the "WITURNA;" and the ceremony concludes by the men all clustering round the youths, and enjoining them to speak only in a whisper for some months to come.[1] The whispering shows the relation to the revealing voice and the magical word. In English, to whisper is to ROUN. In Egyptian, to Ren is to name, and the name which is here connected with the "WITTO" is WITARNA or WITARENA. In Maori RENA denotes the fulfilment and completion. The Egyptian UTAU, a magical breastplate, worn as an amulet, is the probable representative of the Witarena, which was the sign of the new name (Ren, Eg.). UTAU signifies to be set apart, in solitude, and denotes a mystical voice in relation to magical rites and directions. After the rites of man-making, the youths were denominated "PART-NAPAS," or those who were permitted to take a wife. The Maori sheds no light on this title, but in Egyptian PERT indicates the masculine manifester; the emanating one, the seed, determined by the male ideograph. NAP is to sow seed in the sexual sense.

Among races like these the ancient mysteries may be (or might have been) studied in their simplest nature, unperverted by the later devotion to the Virgin Mother, who produced without the fatherhood, or by fanatical self-sacrifice to the hermaphrodite divinity. The Mysteries were founded to lead mankind from a bestial to a cleanly way of life; to instruct youth at the proper period in matters which are sadly neglected now, or suppressed altogether, from false notions of the fallen nature of the "flesh." The most attractive women were employed as demonstrators of the reality that was set before the initiates to take the place in their minds of misleading fancies. One object of the painful treatment at puberty, prolonged sometimes for six months, was to prevent what the Egyptians termed NNU-HU; NNU, or NEN, denoting negation, and HU, seed, spirit, aliment of life. They desired to save the race and ensure progeny.

It was the teaching of sexual matters in the Mysteries that led to the establishing of such institutions as those of the Qodeshoth, the Pallakists, Nautch girls, and other forms of the Temple Hetairæi and the investing of the Courtezan with a sacred character. The origines here, as in other things, are traceable at last to the simplicity and not to the depravity of human nature; and it was these uterine origines of the teachings concerning the production and preservation of the race, which alone account for what may be termed the uterine religion, in which the Eucharistic celebration of divine love was enacted, and the conjunction of the soul with its source was consummated in the Agapæ of the early Christians, according to the marriage-model of Cupid and Psyche. Davis's plain statement that the rites were intended to teach boys how to behave with women dissipates much mystery.

The customs of circumcision and tattoo were modes of memorizing

[1] Angas, vol. i. p. 113.

and means of biting and branding in the things that were to be had in everlasting remembrance. Matters relating to the sexes were taught to the children at the period of puberty, with the object of ensuring progeny and avoiding disease through uncleanness ; and, as in the Hebrew, the ZACHAR and the memorial were identical. The lizard, in Maori, is named the MOKE, and Moke also denotes the tattoo marks made on the body. Moke probably represents the Egyptian MAK, to make, to inlay, work in, composition, to think, consider, regulate, and rule. The Maka is also the fighter. The Africans of Abeokuta have a vast variety of tattoo marks, among which the lizard (Moke) is the favourite figure.

The word Tattoo is not Maori as it stands, but TUTU means to raise up, cause to stand erect, make fast, establish. This is one with the Egyptian Tat, to establish for ever, eternize, the Tat-cross being the sign of duration or everlasting ; Tattu, the eternal region of the resurrection. The Tut image is the type of the raised-up and established mummy. TA, in Maori, is a name for Tattoo, and this, in Egyptian, is to type, with the symbol of an eye shedding a tear—an Egyptian ideograph of creation.

Hence TA means seed, corn, and to be pregnant, as does the Maori To, that is to be typing or figuring the child. The symbolic eye typing the tear is called the UTA, and the word means health and salvation, a treasury and a storehouse or granary; the health and saving being applicable to the seed. This hieroglyphic eye (Uta) is reproduced in the Maori Ta, or tattoo, and figured just beneath the eye in the faces of the Maori.[1]

The tattooing in Mangaia was an imitation of the stripes of two fish—the Paoro and Avini—and, in the song of INA, we read, "Here are we, Ina's little fish (Avina and Paoro), from which mortals derive their tattooing."[2] "On her way to TINIRAU, Ina invented tattooing."

TINIRAU signifies, literally, forty millions. TINI, in Maori, denotes innumerable myriads. The Tinirau is called king of all fish, it being of the swarming sprat kind. In this legend the type of multiplying and becoming innumerable is the prolific little fish which equates with the lizard of Africa and New Zealand.

The English moke, as a fish, would be the mackerel. The *poisson d'Avril* of the French, for which the fool is sent, is a mackerel ; the striped, cross-barred, or tattooed fish that crossed the waters periodically, and was adopted as a type of the crossing, the fish of the zodiac, the sign of the equinox. "By his stripes we are healed," is a doctrine of tattoo ; and the striped and *mackled* fish was one of the types. The MOKE or Ass was another. He was fabled to carry the cross, the impression of which was stamped on his shoulders and back, because the ass (Sut) was likewise a type of the crossing.

[1] See "Head of a New Zealander," *Origin of Civilization*, p. 55.
[2] Gill, p. 95.

Tinirau, as God, and the father of forty millions, or a progeny innumerable as sprats, was the *second* son of the genitrix Vari, the very beginning, and he is identical in the mythos with ABRAHAM, the second form of the Sun-god, as the father of swarming multitudes, innumerable as the stars of heaven or the sands of the sea.

Tattoo has two aspects, one relating to production in this life, the other to being reproduced in the next. Among the Kingmill Islanders those alone who were tattooed could expect to reach the Kainakaki heaven. This is the belief of various peoples of the Pacific area and others. Fijian women, who have not been tattooed in this world are threatened with having to be scraped by oystershells in the next, and made into bread for the gods. The Eskimo women believe in the efficacy hereafter of tattooing here. The doctrine of reproduction had passed into the eschatological phase.

The name for tattooing or eternizing is also applied to the desiccating and preserving of the human head. The Maoris made a MOKO-MOKO (or embalmed mummy) of Captain Lloyd's head. This they turned into a Christ or Karast (Eg.), the Pepul Kristo, the risen dead, and consulted it as an oracle, a mouthpiece of the other world. So a wild tribe on the east of the Republic of Ecuador are, or were, in the habit of making the mummy Christ by cutting off the heads of their enemies, and removing the skin and scalp from the skull entire. This is then re-stuffed so as to preserve the human likeness as much as is possible, with the eyes and mouth sewn up ; and the image is then consulted as a god.[1]

The Maoris have a ceremony called the WHANGAI-HAU, rendered "feed-wind" by Shortland.[2] Hau denotes food used in the "pure" rite, which sets free from Tapu. Whangai has various meanings, one being to feed ; so Ankh (Eg.) is some kind of sacred food. WHANGAI is to make an offering of food to the Atua or divinity. ANKH (Eg.) is to make a covenant. The Whangai-hau is performed over those who slay an enemy in battle, and some of the hair and an ear of the first man killed form a part of the offering. The ear is eaten by the female Ariki, or chieftainess. The ear eaten at the Whangai is the ANKH in Egyptian, a symbol of the covenant, also called the Ankh, and an emblem of life. Hieroglyphically the Ear, Ankh, is equivalent to the Ankh, as the CRUX ANSATA, and eating the ear was identical with the covenant made on the cross. The ear was a type of Sut and Aten, as gods of hearing. The divinity, as listener in the dark, preceded the seer in the light. Rongo, the name of the Polynesian deity whose house is in the shades, also means to hear, listen, feel.

So Sut-Anubis went by the ear in the dark ; Kak, by touch, and Tum, the sun in the shades, was called Sutemi, the hearer. The ear would be the token of a covenant made with a divinity, as the hearer ; and he, as the primordial male god, was Sut. Now, when

---

[1] *New Zealand*, Taylor, p. 147, note.   [2] P. 232.

Sut or Sat (earlier Khut) has worn down to AT, the word denotes hearing, and is written with the ear-sign ; and the Maori god or hearer is the ATUA, in accordance with Sut or At being the first divinity, as the hearer in the dark, and an outward image of the mental darkness.   Atua (Mao.) also means the first.

The Hakari feast of the Maori was the Hakr festival of Egypt, and the English hock-tide.   Hock is connected with harvest in the hockey-cart, that which brings home the last load of corn.   Also in the hockey-cake, a seed-cake distributed at the Harvest Home.   The Hawkie was a figure dressed up in a woman's clothes, with a painted face, and the head decorated with ears of corn.   This was borne on the top of the harvest-home load of corn.

The New Zealand " HAKARI " was a feast of peace, to which presents of fish were brought by the visitors, also birds' eggs, the roe of fish, and all kinds of seeds.[1]   The children will tell us what the ancient parent meant by the " HAKR " festival, of which we have no Egyptian record.   It was equinoctial, and it happens that the seedtime of Egypt, at the autumn equinox, is our harvest-time, and the same symbols apply to times six months apart.   The Hakari festival is also related to the hearer, as well as to earing and harvest.   Hakiri (Mao.) signifies hearing, but to hear indistinctly, for this god was deaf at times, and the same words that signify hearing in Egyptian also denote deafness.   We retain the likeness of the listening god, who heard indistinctly in our *deaf ears* of corn.   The sun was considered to be the god who was deaf, or blind, or dumb, when in the region of Anrutf, or NARUTF, a name found in Irish, as Narith, for the last day of the year, and also in the English word North.

Not until we dismiss from our minds the crude notion that the same myths have sprung up independently in various parts of the world shall we cease to be paralysed by marvelling at the startling, strange coincidences which continue to increase the further we make research, until the lifted eyebrows of the wonderer elevate him into a sort of effigy of his own wonderful foolishness.   As for the system of mythology said to have arisen from some disease of language, the present writer thinks that must be a creation of the modern time, as he has been quite unable to find it in the past.

By degrees we shall discover certain test-types of the unity of origin in mythology.   One of these is that of the Eight Gods, the SMEN of Egypt and Assyria, which have been identified with the Hebrew Elohim, and Arthur and his seven companions in Britain. It has been mentioned that Cornish children used to figure the city of Troy by cutting seven circles round a centre, the eighth, in the grassy sod, which are also figured on the Scottish stones.[2]   This Troy, as the Egyptian TERUI, is a form of Sesennu, the place of the eight

---

[1] Dieffenbach, vol. i. p. 361.   [2] Leslie, *Early Races*, pl. 57.

gods, and a name for the number eight. It is the number of the Mother and Child in the eight-rayed type of Ishtar. Hathor, the *habitation* of Horus, has a symbolic wheel-like sign containing eight spokes. The same imagery is continued in the eight-rayed star at the centre of a Scotch "Baking Stone," on which the symbolic number eight is *thrice repeated.*[1] The mother was the prototype of both the bread-maker and oven. The ovoid and womb-shaped figures found on these stones are also emblems of the genitrix. Another illustration of this beginning with the Troy-making and the number eight may be seen in the Maori TARI-TARI, which is the name of *plaiting with eight strands,* and of the noose employed in catching birds. The same name and number as in the Egyptian Terui-circle and the British Troy.

So late as the year 1859, a teacher of the new religion landed on the island of Fortuna and found the whole population employed in rebuilding a spacious temple which was supported by a row of eight pillars. It was the house of their gods, and the eight great pillars symbolized their eight great gods. The pillars were formed of trees with branches left in imitation of human arms.[2] These eight great gods who retained their supremacy amidst the crowd of lesser deities are none other at last than the eight great gods of Egypt.

Captain Cook, in his first voyage, describes a symbolical figure, made and venerated by the Otahetians, resembling the shape of a man. It was made of wicker-work, nearly seven feet in height, covered with black and white feathers. On the head of it were *four protuberances*, which the natives called "TATE-ETE," rendered little men. This corresponds perfectly to the fourfold Tat of Ptah, who as the pigmy was the father of the seven Khnemu, and these with their father, as the eight little men, were synonymous with the eight of the double Tat, a continuation of the typical Eight of Am-Smen.

The eight tree-pillars with arms extended were obvious forms of the tree-pillar or fourfold Tat.

The eight of the beginning supplied a type-sign of establishing not only in the circular figure of eight but in the fourfold cross, duplicated as the symbol of establishing. Thus the fourfold cross or Tat repeated, is equal to the numeral eight, and this Tat is identified with Taht, who represented the eight in the lunar mythos.

"Tat" passed into many languages as the type-word for number eight, which marks the naming as occurring under the lunar, the second of the divine dynasties. Our figure of 8, a twofold circle, is equivalent to the two Tats and sign of the Eternal established as the Pleroma of Eight.

Two fourfold figures read Tattu, to establish; Tattu being the region of establishing, the region of the SMEN; the eight gods represented

---

[1] *Past in the Present*, p. 239 ; Dr. Arthur Mitchell.
[2] Gill, *Life in the Southern Isles*, p. 178.

by Tahuti; and, absurd as it may seem, our Daddy-long-legs bears the name of the double Tat, of the god Taht, and the region of the eight. Daddy is an octopus of the air. So the South Sea Islanders call their octopus of the water the sea-spider.

One form of the eight was the NNU group of the eightfold circle, that is, the NEN, and in Swahili NANI is number eight. NANE in Wanika; NANE, Msambara; EN'YE, Krepee; NANGIRI, Yangaro. In Tahiti the octopus is called FAE; Maori, PAE for *all round*. In the Chinese dialects PEH is number eight, as is API in Egyptian; APU, Mangarei; VAU, Marquesas. PAE, for all round, to surround with a border, circumference, is the equivalent of TERUI (Eg.), the circumference and number eight.

With the article prefixed TEKH is a name of Taht, which as Tahuti would in the earlier form be TAKUTI, and the number eight in the Oneida dialect is TAGHETO; TEKRO, Cayuga; DEKRA, Nottoway; TEKIRO, Onondago; and TIKKEUGH, Seneca. Khekha (Eg.) means number and reckoning; Tekh being the reckoner, at the full height or eight, the octave.

Now the son of the genitrix of the Seven Stars was also named Kar(t), Har, or Ar; he is extant under this name as the Polynesian KORO, and in Egypt his earliest form was Sut-Har, brought on as the Solar Horus. Sut, the son (or Har), preceded Taht as manifester of the seven, and these names of the number eight are identical with that of the god of the eight stars, who was Sut-Har, the son of Typhon, and the child denoted by the cruciform sign of eight.

The first circle and circumference of Terui or Troy was made by the Seven Stars with an eighth as their Anush or announcing word, found in Sut, the Anush. This circle or course is expressed by the word KAR for an orbit, in many languages, and for time, as the Sanskrit KAR, to announce the time, and Kara the word; Egyptian KHAR, the voice or word, as in the name of the solar god Makheru. This Kheru or Karu, with the initial letter modified, furnishes the following names of number eight:—WARU, Maori; WARU, Polynesian; WARU, Saparua; WARO, Porne; WARU, Bima; WAR, Papuan; WAR, Salawati; WAR, Beak and Mefur; OUAR, Arago: ORO, Moor; OROI, Mallicollo; ARRU, Savu; ARA, Suanic; WALU, Fiji; WALU, Timur; WALU, Manatoto; WALU, Ceram; WALO, Cocos Island; WALU, UALU, or UALOK in the Batta dialects; UALO, Bissayan; UALU, Kayagan; UALO, Tagala; UALO, Iloco.

Taht, the Lord of Sesennu, a region of agitation and distraction, has a curious relationship to the octopus at Rarotonga, where the cuttlefish was the special divinity of the reigning Makea family, and the superstition was related to a remarkable circumstance. There was a particular pool of water near the usual landing place at which passing vessels filled their empty casks. The water was commonly crystal-clear, but at a certain phase of the moon it became black. This change was doubtless owing to the presence of cuttlefish that went there to spawn.[1]

The octopus is called the divine cuttlefish by the Hervey Islanders. Its name is EKE, meaning a total, the typical octo, height or eight, as in the Manx HOGHT; OCHT, Irish; OCHT, Scotch; ὀκτώ, Greek; OKTO, Gipsy of Norway; OCHTO, Tater; AKHT, Lughman; AKT, Tirai; AGYS, Yakut; ACHAT, Joboka.

The daddy-long-legs and the octopus are figures of eight, and therefore were named as representatives of that number.

The missionary did not learn the nature of the connection between this troubled turbid water and the octopus-worship; but the Pool was surely a form of the pool of the Two Truths. The ibis type of Taht was white and black, as representative of the double lunation, and here the eight-armed Lord of the Pool who turned the water into ink would supply another type of the lunar divinity. The water turned black would answer to the pool of Hesmen, which is a name of the menstrual purification; one of the two primary truths.

These figures in relation to number are among the earliest and most universal. Seth is the eighth on the line of Lamech. Taht as Esmun was the eighth. The Bull of the Seven Cows, in the Ritual, is the eighth. The eight-rayed star was a numeral symbol of this god as Sut in Egypt, Buddha in India, Assur in Assyria, and the Christ in the Roman catacombs. The Fijians likewise have the deity of Number Eight either as three different gods, or as three local forms of the same god. WALU (Maori WARU) is number eight, and Matawalu is a god called Eight-eyes. Kokolo has eight arms, and the giant Thangawalu, who is sixty feet high, has a forehead of eight spans.

Also the Fijian Tangawalu, or assembly of eight, represents the eight gods who ruled in Am-Smen, the ancient star-gods of chaos, before the firmament of Ra was lifted by Shu, or Maui, or Taht became the manifester of the eight in the later luni-solar phase. In another form the primordial eight were personified as the father and his seven sons, who were the seven sailors as the Kabari, the seven Patakoi of Phœnicia, the seven Hohgates of California, and the seven Khnemu or Pigmy sons of Ptah, who stand by his side as builders. In the Mangaian mythology, "Pinga" has seven clever sons who are all pigmies, their appellative being "the seven dwarf sons of Pinga." The equivalent of this name in Maori is PINAKHU, a war-canoe (English, pinnace), the same vessel that is called a PITAU, a war-canoe with a fancy figure-head corresponding to the Patakoi, and therefore with Ptah, in whose image they were formed.[2] These seven dwarfs were very expert as reed-throwers. One day they measured their skill against the divine Tarauri, and every time he was about to throw the reed the seven dwarf sons of Pinga, in fear of being beaten, rushed round him

[1] Gill, _Life_, etc., p. 289. [2] Herodotus.

in a circle and hemmed him in so that he could not throw the reed.
At length Tarauri observed that the legs of one of the seven were
bowed, or a little apart, and through this loop-hole or gap in the living
enclosure he drove the reed with such force that it remained aloft in
the skies for eight days.[1]   This is one way of pourtraying the seven
dwarf sons of Pinga as bow-legged, like the seven Khnemu and Patakoi.
The seven and the eight are both represented in the Mangaian Saivaiki, or spirit-world below.   The typical eight who are symboled
by the eight-rayed star and eight-looped sign of the Nnu, the eight
gods in Am-Smen, are apparently intended in the *Adventures in Spirit
World*, by the Cocoa-Nut Tree, which bears eight cocoa-nuts only,
and by the eight paths leading to the house where Kura, one of the two
divine sisters, was kept a prisoner when she fell into the underworld.
It is in this story that the Mangaian Orpheus descends into the other
world to rescue his Eurydice.[2]   In the Mangaian stories, eight is the
typical number of times that every event occurs, instead of the later
" three times," which belongs to the solar mythos.   This is derived
from the eight of the beginning; like the " eight friends who sit
spying on all heights, on all watch-towers for Mithra."[3]

The Polynesian origin of all things, the arranger of the various lands
in Saivaiki, is the Great Mother VARI, who is the original of all the
gods, corresponding to Ta-urt in Egypt, the Great Bearer; Urt has
the meaning of VERY in English, which in the sense of extremity
equates with the name and nature of VARI.   VARI means the veriest
beginning ; the word is used for describing a new order of things.
In Maori WERI means to take root, the root, rootage.   In Rarotonga
VARI signifies mud, that is the red mud or earth of the Dam.   VARI-
VARI, Mangaian, is muddy ; WERIWERI (Mao.) is offensive and dis-
gusting, for mystical reasons.   URI (Eg.) is a name of the inundation.
WERI (Mao.), for the root, is also a name of the centipede.   When men
could only crawl mentally, their lowly thoughts were expressed by
crawling things, such as the worm, the lizard, the eel, mantis or centipede.   Those things that had the means of motion through the elements
of earth, water, and air, which man did not possess, were accounted
most wonderful, and at this stage WERI the centipede is named as a
type of VARI.   The hundred legs of the centipede made it an early
figure of the Goer, who was represented by the Weri (centipede), the
URRI, Egyptian Car, and the English WHERRY (a boat).   Vari-ma-
te-takere, her full name, means the beginning and the bottom ; the
TAKERE, in Maori, being the keel of a canoe.   Vari personates the
first of the Two Truths of the creative Motherhood, that of the blood
which forms the flesh.   In accordance with this, Vari is said to make
her children out of her own flesh, plucked in pieces from her body.
Vari and Papa are a form of the Two Sisters into whom the Great

[1] Gill, p. 118.   [2] Gill, *Myths and Songs*, p. 221.
[3] *Khordah-Avesta*, xxvi. 10, 45.

Mother bifurcates. Papa signifies foundation. Papa (Eg.) denotes the female who is delivered of the child, the gestator who personates the second of the Two Truths; that of the breath or soul, the true foundation of Existence, the other being the blood or mystical water of source.

The original tribes of the Hervey group claimed to descend from the Great Mother Vari, that is, from the beginning with the genitrix alone. In the "Dramatic Song of the Creation," they sang, "WE have NO Father whatever; Vari alone made us! That home of Vari is the narrowest of all."[1] The ancient mother is described as sitting in it at the bottom of the hollow cocoa-nut shell, with her knees and chin meeting, in the attitude of burial adopted by the cave men in Britain, Peru, Africa (with the Namaquas and Bongos), and the Australian aborigines. Vari, like Ta-Urt in her hippopotamus form, is incapable of talking, and can only make signs; in such wise does mythology reflect the human beginnings.

An island in the Hawaiian group named KA-PAPALA, the land of Papala, is identified with the genitrix as PAPA, who was the base and foundation of Being personified. KA (Eg.) is the land of an interior region, and Papa (Eg.) denotes the feminine producer. But according to Fornander the island bears the still earlier name of NUSA. Now in Egyptian Nusa is the equivalent of Papala, as the foundation. The Nusa is a typical stand, base, or pedestal. Nusa was the birthplace of Bacchus, Osiris, and (to judge by the altar, or stand, erected by Moses) of the Hebrew Jah-Adonai. Nusa (Eg.) signifies out of, the hinder part. Nu is the abode, receptacle, the feminine bringer; SA means behind, and the firmament, or Nu, was depicted as producing the sun animal-fashion, from the Nusa, or behind. The island of Nusa, or Ka-papala, is one with the Mount Nusa in Æthiopia, or the celestial north; one in its mythological nature as it is in name; also Nusa (Eg.) means the She.

Fornander[2] speaks of BABA, an island south of the Banda group, in the Indian Archipelago. He also observes that "KEPA, a land on Kaui, Hawaiian group, refers itself to TEPA, a village on the above-mentioned island of BABA." The exact wording is quoted, but the meaning is not very clear. Enough for my purpose that BABA, KEPA, and TEPA here grouped together, are all Egyptian names of the Typhonian genitrix.

This first Great Mother has a four-fold type compounded of the hippopotamus, crocodile, Kaf-monkey, and lioness, as the goddess of the four quarters. These four are afterwards personified as gods, spirits, or genii of the four quarters belonging to the Great Bear. In the Mangaian mythology there lived four mighty ones in Awaiki, the nether world. These were Buataranga, the ancient mother; Ru, supporter of the heavens; the sun-god (Ra) and Mauike, or

[1] Gill, *Myths*, p. 8.   [2] Vol. i. pp. 14, 15.

Mafuie, the god of fire.[1] These four correspond to the genii of the four quarters who can be traced to Uati (Buto or Kheft), Shu, Har, and Sut; Miriam, Moses, Hur, and Aaron; or the later Columbine, Pantaloon, Harlequin, and Clown, as gods of the four corners, who were all contained at first in the four-fold type of Apt or Fut whose name signifies the corner, and the four corners. Poti (Mao.) likewise denotes the corner or angle where Buata sat to guard the road to the underworld. Mauike, as god of fire, is identical with Bar-Sut, the oldest star-god of fire, far older than the solar god who is here named Ra. Mauike is represented as keeping the secret of fire in the underworld to which Maui descends in the guise of a pigeon, and wrests the hidden treasure from him. It was formerly supposed that fire could only be procured from the four kinds of wood found by Maui in the fire-god's dwelling.

Uati or Uti is a name of the goddess of the north. She is the divinity of the waters, plants, green things, and also of heat; Uat being both wet and heat. Ut is light, and to put forth, emit, jet. The Egyptian Uat reappears in the Uti of Mangaia. Uti presides in Mano-Mano, or spirit-world, in the very depths of the netherland, and at night she climbs to the upper world with her torch to fish for food in a lake. It was she who first taught women to catch the sleeping fish, by torch-light. Also the fen-fire or *ignis fatuus* is designated Uti's torch.

Mano (Maori) is the inner part, and Mano-mano is the duplicate which makes it an equivalent for the Menti (Eg.), the netherworld entered at the west. Uati as goddess of the north was the earlier genitrix of the seven stars, the spark-holder, first bearer of the torch by night, first guide of the waters. UATI as heat, later fire as Ut, is the fire-goddess of the Mongols. Castrén gives a Mongol wedding-song, in which the Great Mother is addressed as the queen of fire. "Mother Ut, queen of fire, thou who art made from the elm that grows on the mountain tops of Changgai-Chan and Burchatu Chan, thou who didst come forth when heaven and earth divided, didst come forth from the footsteps of mother earth, and wast found by the king of gods! Mother Ut, whose father is the hard steel, whose mother is the flint, whose ancestors are the elm-trees, whose shining reaches to the sky and pervades the earth! Goddess Ut, we bring the yellow oil for offering, and a white wether with yellow head! Thou who hast a manly son, a beautiful daughter-in-law, bright daughters, to thee, Mother Ut, who ever lookest upward, we bring brandy in bowls, and fat in both hands! Give prosperity to the king's son (the bridegroom), to the king's daughter (the bride), and to all the people."[2] The old spark-holder, who is here extant as Ut from Uat, was also named TEP, and Tep is fat. Kep, another of her names, signifies the mystery of fermentation and alcoholic spirit, which is a

---

[1] Gill, p. 51.   [2] Tylor, *Prim. Culture*, vol. ii. p. 254.

reminder of the Kava or Ava, an intoxicating drink.   KAWA in New Zealand is the strong drink; KAVA, Rarotonga and Mangaia; A'AVA in Samoa; AVA in Tahiti and Hawaii.   KAAWY in South America is an intoxicating liquor made from maize, or the mandioc root, by being chewed and fermented.   AVA-AVA is tobacco in Tahiti.   The pepper plant is CAVA in Tonga.   COFFEE is an exciting drink.   Sometimes the plant bears the name, at others the drink.   But the intoxicating liquor made in Polynesia, New Zealand, South America, and other parts, known as "KAVA," is not named either from its pungency, its bitterness, or from "Cava," the pepper plant.   It is KAVA without either of the qualities here implied, and it is KAVA or AVA when not made at all, but drawn fresh from a plant.   All forms of KAVA, however, have one quality in common: they are all intoxicating.   And this meaning is found in Kepu, or Kefa (Eg.), the name for fermentation.   At this rootage we find Kefa, force, to seize, lay hold by force, puissance, ferment, to heat, inspire, and Kâ-Kâ, that is Kef-Kef (Eg.) to CHEW, which is the same word with w instead of the f terminal.   Kauen (Ger.), is to chew.   CAWNA (Tongan) to be intoxicated with Cava.   The intoxication was attained by chewing certain plants, and chewing to produce the Ava was, as in Fiji, a sacred ceremonial custom; the ancient Kefa, the fermenter and chewer being represented by old women.   How ancient the name is may be seen by the Maori KAPU, to drink out of the hand. Kaf (Eg.) is the hand, and the first libation of Kava, as palm wine, was drunk from the tree with the hand, for the KEP or primeval cup. The KABH (Eg.) is the libation.

The earth in Hawaiian is KAPAKAPANA.   Taken in its literal sense KAPA signifies to gather up in the hands and squeeze like the dregs of Awa.   And the creation of the earth by the god Kane is the earth strained or squeezed dry by Kane.[1]   The Kapu was also the womb, Maori Hapu, in which the red earth was strained dry and squeezed into shape by the genitrix Kepa.   This description of creation also presents the image of the Khepr (the creator typified by the beetle) gathering the matter up to cover and conceal the seed, or as the beetle may be seen on the monuments taking the liquid matter with his hands to turn (Khep) it into solid.

The Australians have a demon named KOIN, who carries off people in their sleep.   He appears in the form of a native, painted with pipe-clay, and carries a fire-stick.   The shouts of the victim's friends are supposed to make the demon drop him.   At daylight Koin vanishes, and the sufferer finds his way back to the place from whence he was carried.[2]   In Egyptian, KHEN means to carry, conduct, transport, convey, and Khen denotes the carrier, as the adversary, with the determinative of Sut, the ass, or gryphon-headed opponent.   Sut as

[1] Fornander, vol. i. p. 73.
[2] Backhouse, *Visit to the Australian Colonies*, p. 555.

the dog was a form of CANIS, and therefore, of Khen, which name would modify into An, and the headless Khen, or dog of the hinder-part, would equate with Sut in the underworld, where Sut-Anubis was the conductor and carrier of souls, as the Khenu.   This makes it probable that the Australian KOIN, and the Polynesian god Kane may be forms of Sut-Anubis who was the guide through the darkness of death, the PSYCHOPOMPUS, and so in a degraded phase comes to carry off the spirit of the dreamer in the darkness of night.   Sut in his two characters as a dual divinity of light and dark, was represented by the black bird (Neh) and the bird of light.   These two phases are likewise rendered by the black native painted with pipe-clay.   Koin carried a fire-stick, and Sutkenui, the conductor, and accompanier, was the star-god of fire that lighted the way through the underworld.

It has been shown that the name of Shu is also written Mau, and the earlier Egyptologists read his name as Maui.   This is the name under which he reappears in the Polynesian mythology.   Also the Ruti (twin lions) are there represented as RU, the father, and Maui, his son.   These are likewise the "founders of the heavenly abode," as in the Ritual.   The legend of the "*Sky Raised*" tells how the heavens at one time almost touched the earth, and Maui resolved to raise the sky; for which purpose he obtained the assistance of RU. Maui stood at the north and Ru took up his position in the south. These two lay prostrate on the ground, and succeeded in raising the solid blue with their backs; then they rose to their knees; next they stood upright and lifted it with the palms of their hands and tips of their fingers; then they drew out their own bodies to vast proportions and pushed up the retreating heavens to their present position.   The solid blue, answering to the Egyptian Lapis-lazuli, and the Ba or steel, was then pared and polished until per-fectly smooth and lustrous, as we see it now.[1]   This is the likeness of the lion-gods on the horizon sustaining the heaven and not letting it fall,[2] or the twin-lions who support the sun on their backs at the equinox : Shu, who lifts the heaven or sun and keeps the southward gate, with Anhar at the north.   Ru takes the place of Shu, and in another version his title is that of Sky-supporter ; he is known as the " Sky-supporting Ru."[3]   Ru is the lion in Egyptian, and Shu was the lion ; Anhar the lion-leoparded.   Shu supports the heaven which Anhar brings.   The starry nature of the sky-supporter is shown by the story of Maui hurling the body of his father Ru so high aloft that it was entangled among the stars and left suspended there.   His bones, however, fell, and are to be found all over the island in the shape of pumice-stone ; the peculiar light-ness of which would make it typical of the early god of light, which is the meaning of Shu's name.   He was the light in the shades, and Mr. Gill furnishes a specimen of the primitive typology, which is

---

[1] Gill, p. 71.   [2] *Rit*. ch. lxxviii.   [3] Gill, p. 59.

almost unfollowable for the modern mind. When the natives of Puka-puka, in 1862, gave up their gods, one aged man, formerly a priest, was seen coming in with what looked like a lump of coal. This proved to be a deity of pumice-stone, known as KO TE TOKA MAMA, *i.e.*, the LIGHT-STONE.[1] It was blackened over and thus made to typify the light-in-the-dark, or the shades, which was represented by the star-god Shu, in Egypt, and by Maui, or Ru, in Polynesia.

The missionaries have acquired the images without the ideas which they once embodied. For example, this island bears the Maori name for a book PUKA-PUKA, which they tell us is the duplicate of the English word book. Yet it is a native name that retains a more subtle sense than is conveyed by the word book. PUKA-PUKA has the meaning of communicating secretly and without speaking, which is effected by the book. This goes back to Puka, or Huka (Eg.) for THOUGHT and MAGIC; Puka and Huka being synonymous.

Amongst the Tongans Maui is still a kind of Atlas in the nether-world, the domain of Anhar, where he supports the earth on his prostrate body. When there is an earthquake, they say it is Maui trying to turn over for relief, and the world-bearer, or heaven-supporter, is invoked, and the earth is beaten to make him lie still beneath his burden. Here the character of MAUI is merged in that of Ru, whose name in Maori denotes the earthquake, and to shake. This may serve to connect the bones of Ru (pumice-stone) with volcanic action by which they were ejected from the earth. Moreover, earthquake is caused by force from *below*, and Maui's sign (as Anhar) is the rump of the lioness, which signifies force. The footprint or footprints stamped in the earth by Maui when he raised up the heaven are shown in various of the Polynesian islands. In one of the legends the work of Maui is assigned to Tane, who divides the heaven from the earth, and TAN (Eg.) signifies the dividing, separating in two halves. In another the raising of the sky is assigned to Tii-tii, and in Samoa they show two hollow places in a rock, nearly two yards each in length, as the footprints of Tii-Tii, which mark the spot where he stood when he pushed up the heaven from the earth.[2] These footprints are to be found in the Ritual as the "foot and the sole of the foot of the lion-gods," *i.e.*, of Mau-Shu.[3] "Hail to ye feet" is said to the lion-gods.[4] When the Osirian[5] has crossed by the northern fields of the palm-tree he says he has seen the "Footstep and the sole." These, then, are identified with Mau-Shu in the Ritual, and with Maui in Polynesia.

In the Hindu mythology the sun's entrance, in each quadrant, immediately following the Solstice or Equinox, is styled Vishnu's feet. In the solar reckoning three feet are assigned to Vishnu, the

[1] Gill, *Myths*, p. 60. [2] Turner, *Nineteen Years in Polynesia*, p. 245.
[3] Ch. cliv. wrongly given as ch. cxliv. p. 96, vol. i. [4] Ch. cxxx.
[5] Ch. cxxv.

sun-god, representing his three strides through the three regions, of the two heavens above and below with the third midway. These are represented by three stars in the Asterism ÇRAVANA, the twenty-third lunar mansion ; SÂD BULA' (Arab Manzil) ; NÜ (Chinese Sieu). The Sûrya Siddhânta [1] speaks of two entrances (Sankrânti) as the TWO feet of Vishnu. The two feet or footprints were earliest. The Arab SÂD BULA' and Chinese NÜ are in the Waterman ; Çravana in Aquila, where they would mark the solstice in the Lion calendar. This connects the two footprints, or the footprint and the sole, with the two solstices as the sign of Kepheus (Shu), who first lifted up the heaven, and in doing so made the two prints of his feet, one for the south and one for the north ; one for *Cor Leonis*, the other for the constellation Kepheus, which accounts for the expression "the footstep *and* the sole." The heaven was first uplifted and distinguished as north and south to mark the solstices, and the marks were called the two feet of Shu the Lion-God. TII-TII is probably explained by the Maori THEITIA, from TIHEI, to carry a burden on the head or back, and hold it in place with the hands, which describes Shu bearing the burden of the heaven overhead by upholding it with his hands.

Anhar with his noose has been already identified with Maui, who caught and tethered the sun with his slip-noose, by the help of which the orb is let down gently at a measurable rate into Avaiki, and drawn up every morning out of the shades. The reporter of this, who has not the most remote idea of the meaning of mythology, says, " Of course this extravagant myth refers to what English children call 'the sun drawing up water.'" [2] But it is Maui drawing the sun, who in the Ritual is said to be forced along by the conducting of Maui or Shu.

It was some time before Maui could find a rope strong enough to hold the sun fast. Stronger and stronger ropes were twisted out of cocoa-nut fibre, but in vain. At length he bethought himself of his sister's hair, which was very long and lovely. He cut off some of Inaika's locks, and plaited them into a rope. He placed the noose once more at the aperture of the emerging sun, and when Ra ascended Maui pulled one end of the cord and the sun was secured with the slip-knot.

INAKI in Maori has the meaning of falling back on the rear for reinforcement. This legend shows the sister of the lion-god in Polynesia corresponding to Tefnut, the sister of Shu in Egypt, who was also represented by the rear-part of the lioness. The sun-catcher appears in the Little Monedo of the Ojibwa mythos. He, too, is accompanied by the sister, who cuts him out and is his deliverer when he has been swallowed by the Great Fish. [3]

[1] xiv. 8.   [2] Gill, p. 63 ; Grey, *Polynesian Mythology*, p. 35.
[3] Schoolcraft, vol. iii. p. 318. *Algic Res.* vol. i. pp. 135-144.

We find in the Maori myth that when Maui has secured the sun in his six nooses, which represent six months, or one half the circle of the year, from solstice to solstice, the sun slackens in his course, and, weak with wounds, crawls slowly towards the under-world. In his anguish he cries, "Why should you wish to kill TAMA-NUI-TE-RA?" by which they learned the sun's *second* name.[1] "TAMA-NUI-TE-RA" is the Ra in his character of the great (Nui) first-born (Tama), the equivalent of Tum, who is Ra in his first sovereignty. It was Tum who passed through the six lower signs, and was represented as sinking from the land of life. Ra's second name is Tama, which word in Egyptian means the second, to renew, renovate, make over again. In the Egyptian mythology, TAUI is the wife of Ra, as a goddess of the lower world, and in the Mangaian, the goddess TU-Papa, or TU of the lowest depths, is the consort of Ra, the solar god. It was on account of Ra's visits to her being too frequent and too prolonged that Maui had to tether and check the sun-god.

The savage islanders have subterranean regions called MAUI, for the spirits of the departed; but the place of the blessed or fortunate was in the land of SEENA, the land of light in the upper skies.[2] Maui (Mao.) is the left side, the left hand, the north when the east is reckoned the front; and therefore the lower of the two heavens, the one supported by Anhar Maui. SHENI (Eg.) is the region beyond the tomb, in the upper heaven, the heavenly abode founded by the twin lion-gods.

The sister of Shu is Tefnut, or Peht, who was the old great mother, brought on in her lioness-shape, as Peht or Buto. She appears as Buata-Ranga. Ranga is to raise up, whence Rangi, the sky. The Maori has no B, but PUTA is the hole, the void, the place of the dead, the Egyptian Baut, which was personified in Buto as in Buata. Also Poti is the cat; one form of Buto being the cat-headed. Buatar-anga is the consort of Ru, as Buto (Tefnut) was the sister of Shu.

When Anhar brings the heaven which was raised by Shu, he is said to bring it with his MAFUI(ÂK),[3] which M. Chabas thinks was a dart or lance; according to the Mangaian and Maori imagery, his FIRE-STICK. This fire-stick was brought up from the lower world by Maui, who wrested it from the god of fire named Mauike in Mangaia. But in the Samoan dialect the fire-god's name is MAFUIE, and on the island of Fakaofo the origin of fire is traced to MAFUIKE, which word contains both Mauike and Mafuie. MAFUIKE, in this island, is a blind old lady, and the name of the old Typhon, Khep, signifies blind. Mafuike appears in New Zealand as Mahuika, the great mother of Maui. The word Mafuika agrees with the Egyptian name for copper, Mafuka; of course that which would smelt would supply a name for that which was smelted or fusible.

[1] Grey, p. 38.   [2] Turner, *Nineteen Years in Polynesia*, p. 470.
[3] *Pap. Mag.*, Harris, 2, 5; Pierret, *Essai*, p. 31.

The legend of the tree which opened the eyes of those who ate of its fruit, is preserved in Mangaia in a form indefinitely more ancient and primitive than in the Hebrew mythos. From the so-called " Exploits of Maui," we learn that the great mother, called the grandmother of Maui, dwells in the darkness of the under-world. Here she is known as Ina the blind, who, in her groping blindness, tends a few sparks of fire, with which she is unable to cook her food. Ina the blind is the old spark-holder, whose name of Khep (Eg.) means blind. Khep, the blind spark-holder of night, is the Egyptian great mother. In this region grew four NONO trees, one of which belonged to each of three Mauis, and one to the sister. Maui, pitying the benighted condition of his grandmother, climbed his own tree and plucked an apple. Biting off a piece he threw it into one of Ina's blind eyes, whereupon it was opened and she saw. Maui plucked another apple and threw a piece of it into the other eye, and that was opened likewise.[1] The four trees correspond to the four corners and four genii of the Great Bear. These four were followed by the four of Shu with their four representatives in Sut, Har, Kapi, and Uati, who are here called the three Mauis and Maui's sister. Ina now makes Maui lord of all below and above, and in her instructions says : — " As there were four species of Nono so there are four varieties of cocoa-nuts and four of taro in Avaiki (or Savaiki, the Egyptian name for number seven, this being the region of the seven stars or sparks below the horizon)." The four trees, whether those of the old mother or of Maui (Shu) in the second time, are equivalent to the four-fold tree or Tat of the four quarters.

In various mythologies the Saviour descends into the Hades, is buried underground or in the belly of a fish during three days. By aid of the *Exploits of Maui*, this can be bottomed in phenomena. In one version of the fire-myth, the god who keeps the secret of fire in the underworld is Great Tangaroa of the tattooed face, who is called Maui's grandfather. In wrestling with him Maui causes the death of Tangaroa. He then puts the bones of the ancient god into a cocoa-nut shell and shakes them until the god comes to life again. This resurrection occurs on the third day, when the re-emerging Tangaroa is found to have entirely lost his old proud bearing, and looks scarred and enfeebled.[2] This belongs to the lunar myth, and can be explained by the three days of the moon's disappearance, which were afterwards applied to the buried god in the solar myth. The connection of Tangaroa with the moon is proved in the Maori, where the twenty-third day of the moon's age is called TANGAROAMUA, and the twenty-fourth is TANGAROAROTO.

The name of Shu written with the feather is paralleled in the Maori myth by the pigeon-type of Maui in the form of which he makes his aerial voyages. When Maui made his transformation into

[1] Gill, *Myths*, p. 66. [2] *Ib.* pp. 68–69.

the pigeon he took the name of Rupe. It was in the form of the pigeon that he went down into the underworld and the abode of the god of fire. A rude representation of Shu as the supporter of the sun-god when he resolves to be lifted up, is also perceivable in the Maori myth. Maui ascends to the place of his father, who is here called Rehua. Rehu, in Maori, denotes the setting sun, *i.e.* Tum in Egypt, the primordial Ra. He begins to set the old god's house to rights, as the aged Rehua was too feeble to do this for himself. Amongst other of Rupe's performances is the arranging of a cross-beam, by which we may understand an image of the Balance or Equinox. This is said to have been so indifferently done, that Kaitangata, another son of Rehua, was one day killed through hanging on to the cross-beam, which gave way and he was dashed down; his blood ran over that part of the heavens staining them ruddily, wherefore, when men see the crimson flow of sunset in the sky, they say, " Ah, Kaitangata stained the heavens with his blood." Tangata, the human being, the man, shows the human form of the solar god who was of the earth as Atum; the mortal as Horus the child, who descended at the western crossing in autumn, and fell below the horizon at sunset daily, or set from the land of life, and tinged the heaven with all the colours of Pant, here called blood.[1]

The transformation of Maui is depicted as his death. At the end of his career, or journey, he comes to the dwelling of his ancestress, HINE-NUI-TE-PO. HINE is generally used only in addressing a young unmarried woman, or a girl. This, therefore, is a form of the Virgin-mother; literally, Virgin-Great-the-night; the great mother of the underworld, who is seen in the distance, opening and shutting (Mut-like) where the sky and horizon meet. Maui has to pass through her. So Moses, the Hebrew Maui, entered the mouth of Jehovah. Maui enters the womb of HINE-NUI-TE-PO, and is half-way in, when the bird, the Tiwakawaka, bursts out laughing at the sight. This woke up the great mother, who was sleeping, and so Maui was crushed to death between her thighs.

Maui is called the son of Ra, answering to Shu, as the son of Ra. Ra was the tutelary god of Bora-Bora. The title of Ra was made part of the style of kings, as it was in Egypt. In Mangaia the rule of each temporal sovereign was called a MANGAIA, or reign of peace, the equivalent of the Egyptian Hept for peace, luck, and plenty; or a Koina-Ra, a bright shining of the sun.[2] The Egyptian Pharaoh was the Sun incarnated. The Mangaian Ra was called the "Man who holds the Sun." The Pharaoh was the Har or later Ra, sun of the two houses. BORA-BORA, the shrine of the one Ra, is equivalent to the double Par (house) of the other. The Maori PARU, for the thatch on the roof of the house, renders the Burbur

---

[1] Grey, pp. 88, 89.   [2] Gill, p. 63.

(Eg.), the cap, top, roof; and Bora-Bora is the equivalent of Para, the house of Ra, duplicated to express the twin heavens.

According to Gill, it is a standard expression in hourly use in Mangaia for the wife to call the husband her "Rua-ra." This he renders "sun-hole." But it contains more than that. Rua is not only a "hole" in the Polynesian and Maori tongues, it also means two, twin, double. Her RUA-RA was her double sun; her sun by night and day; and the husband is lovingly invested with the dual character of the Pharaoh as the sun of the two heavens. The husband designates the wife as his ARERAU, translated by his "well-thatched house." The house, in its reduced estate, is still the house of Ra, and husband and wife preserve the royal style and impersonate the sun and double-house of the kings and queens of Egypt.

In the myth of Rata's canoe we have the creation of the double-seated boat of the sun. The Mangaian Rata in the fairy land of KUPOLU resolves to build *a great double canoe* with the view of exploring other lands. KUPOLU answers to KHEPRU who crosses in the solar boat. RA-TA in Egyptian would denote the sun that navigates and crosses the waters in the double-seated boat of KHEPRU. In Maori RATA signifies cutting through, to be sharp, red-hot, which agrees with the red sun of the cutting through and crossing. Upon his way to build the boat Rata beholds a furious fight between a beautiful white heron (Ruru) and a spotted sea-serpent (Aa). The heron is a type of Taht the moon-god, and appears as the fisher, the same as in the hieroglyphics. The Aa represents the Apap serpent of the waters. The fight therefore is between darkness and the lunar light. "They fought hard all through the night." At dawn the weary white heron sees Rata (as sungod) passing, and cries, "Oh, Rata, finish the fight." The serpent asks to be left alone in the struggle, which is but "a trial of strength between a heron and a serpent." Rata does not interfere; he goes on his way—being in a great hurry to build his boat. But the white heron says reproachfully, "*Ah! your canoe will not be finished without my aid.*" The lunar mapping-out preceded the solar. Taht the moon-god built the first ark or boat laid down on the stocks, which became the double-seated boat of KHEPR, Ptah-Sekari or Tum in the solar myth. At last Rata assists the heron and chops off the head of the serpent. Then the birds of Kupolu finish the boat in a single night. In this myth of Rata's canoe occurs the story of the Polynesian Noah (and Jonah), Nganaoa. NGA (Mao.) means to breathe, take breath, and is commonly connected with MANAWA for the belly and breathing. Nawe (Mao.) also signifies to set on fire as NGANAOA sets on fire the fish that swallows him. Nganaoa on board Rata's canoe represents the god of breath who was Shu first of all in Egyptian mythology, and afterwards Nef the sailor and breather in the waters. Nganaoa puts out to sea in a mere calabash, a type that preceded the grand new

double-seated canoe of Rata, the sun of the crossing, and had to
serve before boats were built, or the crosser was depicted as walking
the waters. According to Hor-Apollo[1] the hieroglyphic sign of
a pair of feet walking the waters, denotes an impossibility or a
miracle. The two signs however read Han or Nen, the name of a god
who was the bringer in relation to the water. Shu-Anhar was one of the
bringers. The pair of feet on the water is equivalent to the water
carried by a pair of feet, and the vase or pipkin sign of An (Han) is
paralleled by the calabash, without its top, of the breather NGANAOA.
After various refusals Nganaoa is taken on board the ship of Rata,
his plea being that in case the monsters of the deep rise up against
Rata he, Nganaoa, will destroy them. One day they fell in with a
great Whale which opened its wide jaws, one below the canoe one over
it. Nganaoa jumped inside the enormous mouth, and on looking
down into its stomach, lo! there sat his long-lost father and mother
awaiting their deliverer. The hero and saviour then kindles a fire
within the belly of the fish, when the monster writhing in agony seeks
relief by swimming to the nearest dry land, and the father, mother,
and son walk out of the mouth of the stranded and dying whale.
This was one of the primeval legends of the race. Nganaoa is identical with Anhar, who stands at the prow of the solar barge or double-
seated boat, ready to dart his spear at the Apophis, when it rears its
head to swallow the passengers, and it is said of the monster, "a
fierce flame devours him, consuming from the head down to his soles,
and roasting all his limbs with fire." The foundational phenomena
is that of the star-god, who was Shu-Anhar, being the earlier crosser
of the abyss of darkness or passer through the monster before boats
were built, and when the double-seated canoe was shaped by Taht
and Rata, the crossing sun, Anhar (Shu) was taken on board as the
son and defender of Ra.

Much that is missing in Egypt is recoverable in the Mangaian
and Maori treasury of the mythos. The transformation or KHEPR
also takes place at KUPOLU, where dwelt Maaru, an *old blind
man*, and his boy named Kationga, *bite-and-smell*. English children
are still told to bite their bread and smell their cheese.[2] The old
man when dying tells his son to drag his body, when dead, to Nikao
(the Noke, Maori, is an earthworm), and cover it with leaves and
grass. In four days the son is to go and see if there are any worms
crawling about, if so he must cover it once more. Still further he is
to return again in four days, and *something will follow him*. Peace
will be restored to the island, and the son will become king. Here
the old blind man is one with the blind Kak of Egypt, and "CACHE"
blind man of Britain, both being representative of the sun in the

---

[1] B. i. 58.
[2] At least it was so among the canal boatmen with whom the present writer's
childhood was mainly spent.

dark, the blind black god who transforms into the child of light. Kationga is Har the younger, the divine Repa. He goes to the old man's grave at the end of four days, and finds the place covered with crawling worms. He re-covered the grave, and went to it in another four days, when he found the resurrection occurring in a strange fashion. The grave was heaving with life, and then and there was born the first litter of pigs in Rarotonga. Pigs are still called the "worms of Maaru," and the worms become pigs. Now the Maori native name for the pig is KUHU-KUHU, and in Egyptian KAK or KUKU is the word for worm. Also HEKAU is the pig as one of the beasts—a type-name having to serve for several uses. Thus the name of the god Kak is an Egyptian name of the worm, and the modified Hek for the pig. The pig was a type of sacrifice in Egypt, and in the May festivities of the year 1852, a thousand pigs were killed in Rarotonga.[1]

If the reader will now turn to the zodiac of Denderah, at the end of this volume, there is to be seen an illustration of the original myth. In the sign of the Fishes as the place of the spring equinox we see the full moon and in its round stands Khunsu, the child-prince of peace, holding a pig in his hand in the act of offering. He is the prince of the pig. This sign is related to the yearly festival of sacrificing the pig and eating it at the time of the spring equinox. It was the festival of the full moon of Easter which dominated and determined the resurrection of the sun, and the pig slain, the pig of the planisphere, is that of the full moon.

The old blind man turning into worms or KAKU is the God KAK, or HAK, the sun in the lower world, and the sacrifice of the pig was the same in Polynesia as in Egypt. Herodotus remarks that a tradition is related by the Egyptians respecting this matter, giving an account why they abhor swine at all other festivals and sacrifice them in that (the festival of Bacchus), "but it is more becoming for me, though I know it, not to mention it."[2] It was simply because the sow imaged the Multimammæ, who was an early type of the genitrix, and it was offered up as a symbol of the prolific breeder, hence an ideograph of plenty associated with the prince of plenty.

The Maori MAERO signifies to be listless, weak, and emaciated, which describes the character of MAARU in accordance with that of the dying sun of the underworld. The Mangaian myth presents a pathetic picture of the sun in Anrutf (the region of stinting and starving), the aged man (or god) who is too feeble to procure food, and who is fed by the son as the food-bringer until the son himself has become a mere skeleton through starving to feed the aged one ; a picture that was reproduced as the well-known Christian Janus, than which nothing is commoner in iconography, notably in ancient cathedrals such as Chartres, Strasburg, and Amiens. This is described

[1] Gill, p. 135. [2] B. ii. 47.

by Didron as, " A man with two heads on one body, seated near a table covered with food. One is sad—and has a beard. The other is happy-looking, young, and has no beard. The older head represents the expiring year—the 31st of December. The younger, the new year—the 1st of January. The former sits beside an empty part of the table. He has exhausted all his provisions. The latter, on the contrary, has before him several loaves of bread and several dishes. Moreover a child (a little servant) is bringing him others. This child is a further personification of the new year; he is the complement of the younger head of Janus. Nevertheless a child accompanies the older as well as the younger man—but on the old man's side, the child is as if he were dead, and the door of a little temple is being closed upon him, whilst on the young man's side the child is issuing joyfully from a similar temple. One is dying and leaving the world, the other is full of life and about to enter it." [1]

" I have united Sut in the Upper House, through the old man with him," says the woman, in the Ritual, who reproduces the twin-being as the young one.[2]

In Samoa they say only pigs die, men finish, or in Egyptian thought, they are transformed if worthy. The pig in the judgment scenes is the type of dissolution and eternal death, because the probability is that in the earlier time of the pig, the Typhonian genitrix, men had not evolved the idea of eternal life. We have to read their thought in the status of their types.

It was customary at Rarotonga to bury the hog's head with the dead. This was mythically related to the boar's head, brought home as a decorated trophy at Christmas, but the type was limited to the expression of one of the Two Truths in the later phase, when the winged bird, the phœnix, dove or hawk represented the risen soul. This was not so when Maaru transformed and rose from the dead in the shape of the pig as a type of plenty.

A form of the solar Horus may be traced in the Olo, Oro, or Koro of the Polynesians, one of the most important of their deities. He is the Koro of Mangaia; the war-god of the Society Islands, said by some to have been the brother of KANE, *i.e.*, Sut, as in the compound Sut-Horus. He is also said *not* to be one of the gods who sprang from chaos and primeval darkness, as did the first eight gods of Egypt.[3] Koro (or Oro) like Horus is a form of the son who is established in the place of the father in the region of Tattu.

Koro in Mangaia is the son of Tinirau, whose proper home was in Motu-tapu. MOTU (Mao.) denotes an island, and TAPU means sacred. So Tattu the place of establishing for ever, was represented by a sacred island in the Nile. A story is told of the process whereby Koro the son managed to get established in place of his father.[4]

---

[1] Didron, *Iconographie Chrétienne*, p. 546. [2] Ch. 80.
[3] Fornander, vol i. p. 45. [4] Gill, 100.

Once in every year the father and son met at the same spot and danced with the fishes. Moreover the sacred island like that described by Herodotus was a floating isle. It was in Tattu or An, the fish-sign, that the sun "lodged dancing" at the place of the level, or the vernal equinox. In the Mangaian myth the fishes themselves come to land and join in the TAUTITI dance in which the hands and feet all move at the same time. The name of this dance may be derived from TAU (Mao.) the year, and TITI, to stick in a peg. The name of the period and festival in the Egyptian UAK also means a peg.   The annual TAUTITI registered another year in the eternal round; hence the circular dance. The emblem of the "Tautiti" was a belt or girdle, which passed from the father to the son. That this fish-dance was astronomical may be gathered from another which was known as the crab-dance, in dancing which the performers imitated the side-movements of that fish.   One witness[1] remarks that the "graceful Tautiti dance stands opposed to the "crab," in which the side movements of that fish are most disagreeably imitated." The "crab" in Maori is named REREPARI from RERE, to go to and fro, rise and set as the heavenly bodies, go both ways, and PARI, the high shore, or sea cliff. This is in consonance with the crab's being the high sign of the summer solstice, and the crab-dance would be an illustration of the sun passing through the sign of the fish that lived in two elements and went in two ways or sidewise.

This myth preserves a sign of its solar nature in a way most unique. The sun of the two heavens and two halves of the circle is represented by the father and son who meet on one night of the year, when they join hands to form the circle and dance the TAUTITI.   The father is seen by his son to ascend a cocoa-nut tree, and it is observed that both in climbing and in twisting off the nuts one by one he makes use of only one hand, and to the great astonishment of the watcher he does not allow his body to touch the tree.[2] Each of the two suns had but one hand or side of the circle divided in two halves.

Koro the Son, who learns the father's magic, gets possession of his girdle and becomes king of the fish.   The son supersedes the father in the fishes, as he did in the fixed year of the zodiac. Koro is the Egyptian Har, who in one character is called the avenger of his father, and as conqueror of Typhon, is a war-god. "Tautiti" is given as a name of Koro, the renewer of the circle. And as the branch or shoot (Renpu) of the mythical tree of life he is celebrated as the planter for ever of the fragrant tree, the red-berried pandanus, which "graces the sacred sandstone."

This is why the crab was what is termed an "object of worship" in some of the southern isles.[3]   It was preserved as a symbol the significance of which was known more or less. Certainly less to the

---

[1] Gill, p. 256.   [2] Gill, p. 101.
[3] Gill, *Life in the Southern Isles*, p. 278.

English missionaries than to the initiated natives. The English witnessed their reverence for the symbol, but had absolutely no knowledge of the thing signified, and could not read their hieroglyphics or render their hidden lore.

The fish-god Tinirau has a daughter, the goddess ATURE, who is a fish-goddess. A fish named the ATHURE (Bream) is sacred to her. This fish in shoals makes an annual visit to one particular part of the northern shore of Mangaia in March, the Maori MEH. The fish-goddess is known as Athor or Ater, the fish (Atergatis), in the Hermean zodiac. In the Ritual the land attained after crossing the waters in this region of the fishes is Tattu, the place of establishing for ever. It was here the fish landed Hercules, and the whale Jonah, the place where the fish-goddess brought forth. In the lunar myth it was Hermopolis; in the solar Heliopolis. One name of Athor is MEH, the fulfiller in MEH, the place and the time of fulfilment. Ature the fish-goddess is identical with Atergatis or Derketo, the fish-tailed Deess and Syrian goddess described by Lucian. We do not find ATHOR in Egypt expressly called the fish-goddess; her extremity is out of sight, or rather she begins in the crocodile and hippopotamus goddess. Also she appears with a bream or a perch on her head. Athor, the habitation of Har or KORE, is the Egyptian Venus, and her fish-type shows us how she was the goddess who rose up out of the foam, after being poetized by the Greeks, with her fish-form turned into the tenderest fleshliness.

The Kamilaroi and Wiradueri tribes, who formerly occupied a large territory on the Darling and its tributaries, have a traditional faith in "Baiame" or "BAIMAI," literally "The Maker," from BAIM, to make or build.[1] They say that Baimai made everything. He makes the grass to grow, and provides all creatures with food. Baimai gave them a sacred wand, which they exhibited at their "Bora," the initiatory rite of admission to manhood, and the sight of this wand is essential to make a man. The first male maker was found in the procreative image represented by the sacred wand. In the Wiradueri and other Kamilaroi dialects the man (Vir) is named Gibir, the Egyptian Khepr, or Creator with the seminal source. Conterminous with the Kamilaroi is what is termed the Western Australian dialect. In this BEMA is the semen which shows how BAIME or BAIAMAI was the procreative spirit personified. BAIAMAI, interpreted by the sacred wand, the typical wand that budded, can be recovered by means of the hieroglyphics in which the BAH is the phallus, and MAI is the seed of man. The Bâ is also the branch in leaf. From this Bah or Bâ comes the Bat, the father or procreator. This image of deity belongs to the "Non-revealed religions," and yet the rod of Aaron which budded was the wand of Baiamai.

---

[1] William Ridley, Paddington, Sydney, Australia, remarking upon Sir John Lubbock's *Origin of Civilization*, p. 205. *Nature*, Oct. 29th, 1874, p. 521.

BATU or Bata, in Puto Nias, is a divinity said to have charge of the earth; his full style is BATA-DA-DANAU. BATA appears in the Ritual in the chapter of transforming into the "Soul of the Earth." He was represented by a serpent: "I am Bata, the soul of the earth, whose length is years, laid out and born daily. I am the soul of the earth in the parts of the earth. I am laid out and born, decay, and become young daily."[1] Tan or Tann (Eg.) is also a name of the earth. Ptah was a god of the earth, the lowest of two regions, and one of his titles is Ptah-Tatanan. Patu (Mao.) denotes the lowest, the lowest batten on the roof of a house.

NGARU is a name of the Polynesian victor-god who fights with the powers of evil, the monster of the waters, and the devourer of the Hades, and unites in one the characters of Izdubar and Ulysses, Hercules, Khunsu, and Jack the Giant-killer. He fights with a shark during eight days; he is buried in the earth during eight days—the typical number eight belonging to the time of the eight gods—he is buried as a Black and rises again as a White. He descends into Hell and puts it out by letting in a deluge. He ascends to a region above and slays the Giant. In all his conflicts NGARU comes off the victor, and the equivalent NARU (Eg.) signifies victory. NASRU has the same meaning of victory, also a governor. Naru, and Nasru enter into the names of the gods Nergal and Nisrock.

In Egyptian Tep is the Ap, and Ap means first, ancestral, that which is born of, as in the earlier Kep. Tep denotes the point of beginning. Tep is the sacred mount, the starting-point of the whole. All that is primary, initial, and primordial, is expressed by Tep. Tep is the upper heaven, and the Tepht is the lower. So is it in the Maori and Polynesian language. Tupu denotes the very beginning, and to tupu is to commence. Tupua in Mangaian means from the very beginning which is personified in Vari the great mother, who is Tep or Typhon in Egypt; Teb, the hippopotamus; Tepa, the heifer; Tep, the tongue; Teb, the ark; Tep, the keel of a boat; Teph, the cave, cavern, cefn, or womb. Tupuna (Mao.) as a plural means the ancestors, male or female. The Mangaian TAEVA-rangi, the celestial aperture out of which the divine Papa or Foundation put forth her hand, is the Egyptian Tepht, the hole of source, the aperture of the abyss in the beginning.

The god TEIPE, one of the thirteen Mangaian gods, was "supposed to be incarnate in the centipede,"[2] which means that the centipede was a type of TEIPE. Teipe is the Egyptian Tep of the beginning, a first type, whether applied to Vari or to the male god Teipe. Tef in Egypt was likewise applied to the male, as the first, the divine ancestor, when the fatherhood was acknowledged. Tef, Teipe, or Tipa was claimed by the Maori as their divine ancestor, their deity. In the Maori address to Sir George Grey, in 1861, the chiefs gave up their

---

[1] Ch. lxxxvii., Birch. [2] Gill, *Life in the Southern Isles*, p. 95.

god. "That is Tipa," they said, pointing to a carved image. "We who belong to these five tribes, take our origin from Him; he is our ancestor; the source of our dignity; we give him to you; also his mat and his battle-axe. We cannot give you more."[1] So they presented their deity to the English, who have given the same god back again as our Devil. Tef (Eg.) means divine, and the first El was the Tef-El, son of Tef or Typhon, who has now become Taboo instead of Tapu. TUPI was also a Mangaian, Zaimuc, Dyak, Aztec, Mexican, Chiquito, Tamul, and Guarini god.

As TIPOKA, in New Zealand, Tef had become the divinity of death. Akh (Eg.) signifies the dead, manes, spirits. In Mangaia TEIPE was the god of human sacrifice. The Maori name thus obtained something of the later character of Typhon, as destroyer. TUPHUI signifies a typhoon, and TUPUA is a title of the Taniwha, the Maori monster of the waters, and representative of the Apophis demon of the deep. Not that they ever acquired the downright devil of the Christian theology, who was reserved for missionary revelation. The Mangaians called their evil spirits "bright evil spirits;" they were luminous by night when the sun shone in the underworld.

The Mangaians have a goddess, the cruel Moto, called the "Striker," who is for ever beating with the flail of death in the shadow land. In the hieroglyphics, MUT, or MUTI, to die, has the striker for determinative. Moto, or Momoto, in Maori, is to strike blows with the fist. From this striking of Moto it is said that the art of cloth-beating was derived. This may recover a hieroglyphic, the determinative of Mata to beat, or strike, which may be the sign of hot-pressing. In connection with the cruel Moto the Mangaians have what seems to me a crude form of the Assyrian descent of Ishtar into the Hades.

Moto, in the underworld, takes the place of the Akkadian Nin-ki-gal. Ngaroariki is a queen (Ariki), like Ishtar. Ngaro (Maori) is to be hidden, absent, lost sight of, as is the moon in its descent and passage out of sight, when it has been stripped of all its glory. On one occasion Ngaroariki was cast into a bush of thorns by four MEN who correspond to the Genii of the four quarters, but she came out again beautiful as ever. With this we may connect the four quarters of the moon and the bush of thorns in it. Moto is the hater and envier of her lustrous loveliness; and once, when the queen had stripped herself for a bath in a secluded place, Moto fell upon her. "With a keen shark's tooth she shaved off the whole of her hair, which was so profuse that it made *eight* large handfuls. Her face was next so disfigured that it was impossible for any one to recognize the once beautiful queen. Her pretty yellow ear ornaments of stained fish-bone, and her fine pearl shell, daintily suspended from her neck, were snatched away. Her gay clothes were all taken from her, and she was wrapped round in a single piece

[1] Taylor, *New Zealand*, p. 131.

of old black tapa, so that poor Ngaroariki, utterly forlorn and changed in appearance, hid herself in the forest." [1]

Ishtar, we are told, had set her mind and determined on going to the place of Nin-ki-gal; so Ngaroariki had fixed her mind on going to the fountain near the place of Moto. She went, although her husband warned her not to go, and tried to dissuade her from her purpose, for she loved to have her own way. Like Ishtar, she was despoiled of all her "queenly ornaments." Ishtar is restored to the upper world, and has all her ornaments returned to her through the interposition of the Sun. Ngaroariki has her stolen treasures returned, and is restored to her pristine beauty through the interposition of the king Ngata, her husband. In each case the desolate condition of the queen is announced by a messenger—the one in the assembly of the gods, the other at a "grand reed-throwing match in honour of the king." This mythical representation has not been recovered directly from Egypt; here the stem of the fork is missing.

The Mangaians have another goddess or demon, Miru, who is deformed in figure and terrible of look, and who feasts on the fallen souls of the dead. Miru dwells in the west, and is the devouring demon of the Hades. Her name denotes the west and the pit, the hole or void, to which the west is the entrance. This, in Maori, is MURI, the hinder-part, the rear, the Egyptian Akar. In Miru we have a form of Am, the devourer of the Hades, called the destroyer, the mistress of the west, which was the Ru or mouth. Muru, in Egyptian would denote the mouth of death, or gate of the dead, *i.e.* the grave or Hades, the pit-hole or the west. MI, in Egyptian, is the west, as a variant of Am. MI (Ass.) is the black. The particular Egyptian form of the Mangaian Miru and Maori Muri is to be found in the word Amru or Muru, a name of the cemetery, and a quarter—the west.

In the Ritual the monster Amt, the Devourer of the Dead, is pictured in the scene of the Great Judgment, with the head of a crocodile, the fore-part of a lioness, and the hind-quarters of a hippopotamus. AMT, the Devouring Demon of the Hades, and a name of the western crossing, is repeated in the Maori AMETO for the Hades.[2] The dead, the setting souls and setting stars, were represented as being swallowed down by the crocodile of the west. In Mangaia some of the wise men insisted that the spirits still lived on after passing through the belly of Mura and her followers.[3] This, too, is the doctrine of the *Book of the Dead*, where the spirit [4] says: "No harm was done me; I received no impurity in passing through thy belly." The belly of Hades, howsoever personified.

The ghosts of the dead were described as wandering disconsolate along the margin of the sea. Their great delight was to follow the

[1] Gill, pp. 132, 133.   [2] *Te Ika a Maui*, p. 24.   [3] Gill, p. 161.
[4] Ch. 155.

sun. A place called Ana-Kura was one of the meeting points where the disembodied spirits gradually assembled for their final departure. For this they might have to wait some months. The precise period of passage was fixed by the leader of the band. When the distinguished chief had resolved to depart he issued his commands. Messages were sent to collect the stray ghosts who still lingered near their ancient haunts. With last looks and farewell tears they assembled at Ana-Kura and there watched intently for the rising sun. At the first sign of dawn they moved to meet him, and then the multitude followed in his train; he in the heavens above, they over the ocean beneath, until, late in the afternoon, they all assembled at Vairorongo, facing the setting sun in the west, with their eyes fixed on him as he sank in the ocean, and following him, they flitted over the waters in the path of the sun-god Ra.[1]

Now let us turn to the *Book of the Dead*, and the " Chapter of Going Forth to the Heaven where the Sun is."[2] This describes the Sun as issuing his commands for the gathering together of the Dead who are waiting to be taken on board the solar bark.

" *The sun is shining on that night. Every one of his servants is living. He gives a crown to Horus on that night. The deceased delights while he is one of the same. He has come to thee, his father, oh Sun! He has followed Shu, he has saluted the Crown, he has taken the place of Hu enveloped in the plait which belongs to the road of the Sun when in his splendour. He has chased that chief everywhere in the horizon. The Sun has issued his commands in heaven. On thou great God in the east of heaven! Thou proceedest to the bark of the sun as a divine hawk of time. He has issued his commands, he strikes with his sceptre in his boat. The deceased goes to thy boat. He is towed in peace to the happy West.*" The journey of the dead is from the west to the east through the underworld, and then round again to the west following the track of the sun. "The road is of fire, they whirl in fire behind him." And there in the west was the Mount Manu, the place of spirits perfected, the point of ascent from a completed circle. Ana-Kura is the red cave, and the same red rock is found in the Egyptian Annu or An, the " Boundary of the Land." Tum, the god of An, was also lord of the double-seated vessel; the sign of the festivals, and the Tongans have the " double canoe of Tongans sailing through the skies."[3]

On the monuments the red crown is the symbol of the lower sun, world, or Egypt, the type of the nether one of the Two Truths of mythology, the feminine of source, as place, person, or principle, hence it is red. The divinities wear the red crown as emblem of the lower world, and the spirits in passing through the Hades are invested with the red crown. Not only is the red crown worn, the region is red, the Osiris (as Tesh-tesh) is red, the pool of Pant is red, the mythical Red

[1] Gill, pp. 157, 158.   [2] cxxxi. Birch.   [3] Gill, p. 167.

Sea. Says the Osiris, " I have anointed myself with red wax." ¹   " I
have provided myself with the leg-bone of a red bird."   " Thou
mayest go ; thou art purified." ²   For this red sign was typical of the
menstrual purification in Smen, the region of purgation and preparation.   The imagery is older than any artificial crown, and is extant
in the earliest natural stage with the Polynesians and Maori.   Their
dead in passing through the Hades, following the red sun of the
lower world, are likewise wearers of the red crown.   They " are
arrayed in ghostly network and a fantastic mourning of weeds picked
up by the way, relieved by the fragrant heliotrope which grows freely
on the barren rock.   A *red* creeper, resembling dyed twine, wound
round and round the head like a turban, completed their ghostly
toilet." ³   NET is a name of the red crown, and the goddess Net
(Neith) carries the sign of netting or weaving on her head.

At Rarotonga the spirits of the dead were supposed to meet at
Tuoro, facing the setting sun, waiting for the moment of leaving.
Tuoro was the limit of earth and point of departure for the under-
world.⁴   TERU is Egyptian for the utter extremity and limit of the
land.   The first object seen was the BUA tree, or tree of life to those
who laid hold of it without the branch breaking.   The Bu-Tree is the
palm of Egypt, and in the Ritual the Osirian says of the passage
after death, " I have crossed by the northern fields of the palm-tree." ⁵
That was from the west, the point where sun and spirit entered the
Hades.

" Explain to them what thou hast seen in the *Region of the Captured*,"—the region of the captured, through which the deceased
had passed.   In the Mangaian myth there was a circular hollow
beneath the bua tree, where Muru spread the net to catch every soul
that fell, through laying hold of a dead branch instead of the living
green one.   Here was the region of the captured.   In the Ritual the
pool of the damned and the trap are in a fissure of the rock.⁶   There
are the liers-in-wait, who watch with noose and net to capture souls.
At the angle of the west is the watcher Baba with the net, and he
who " lives off the fallen at the angle of the pool of fire, the Eater of
Millions is his name." ⁷   One name of the Mangaian watcher with the
net that catches fallen souls is AKA-ANGA.   In the Ritual AKA is the
great squatter, who hides as the lier-in-wait for fallen souls.⁸   " ANGA,"
to turn in some other direction, is equivalent to that western corner or
angle where the liers-in-wait are found.   The Mangaians have a proverbial saying in regard to the dying—" Will he be caught in the net
of innumerable meshes ? "   The deceased in the Ritual cries, " Oh
father of the gods, mother of the gods in Hades ! save ye the
deceased from the wicked netting of the dead," or deficient ; the one

---

¹ Ch. cxlvi.   ² *Ib.*   ³ Gill, p. 156.
⁴ Gill, p. 169.   ⁵ Ch. cxxv.   ⁶ Ch. cxxx.
⁷ Ch. xvii.   ⁸ Ch. lxxviii.

who had not power enough to break through the nets.[1] Again he exclaims exultingly, "I do not sit in the nets of them."[2] One chapter of the Ritual before cited is that of "escaping from the net,"[3] with a vignette of the deceased walking away from the net.[4] "Oh, catcher of the birds (souls) flying on the waters, do not catch me in your nets; they reach to heaven, they stretch to earth! The deceased comes forth and breaks them when they are stretched (says the hidden god). I have made men to fly with wings."

In the Egyptian, hell and the net are synonymous. Aat is the region, the Hades, and also a name for the net.

The Mangaians have a well-known proverb that presents a ludicrous picture of the souls caught in the net of Aka-anga, who flap their wings in the vain effort to escape from its meshes, besmeared with filth, and floundering deeper in the mire. This mud and its bemirement are likewise presented in the Ritual.

Off the south-west coast of Vanua Levu there lies a small island, which is imagined by the natives to resemble a canoe. In this canoe the souls of the deceased are said to pass over the waters of death.[5] The canoe of the dead is the Egyptian Makhennu, the first form of which was the Great Bear, as the boat of souls. MA is the dead, Khennu the canoe. This preceded the ark built by Taht, and the double-seated boat of the sun.

PARA was the sacred name of Heliopolis, or An in Egypt, named from the celestial birthplace in An above. This is the Assyrian Parra, and Fijian Bure or god's house. AN is a name of the fish, and in the fish-sign the god was re-born. This fact and its meaning were carried forth by the Maori. "PARA-PARA" is the name of their sacred place; likewise the name of the first-fruits of their fishing, which identifies the symbolical value of the fish offered to the gods. PARA-PARA is also identical with the Mangaian BORU-BORU, dedicated to the sun-god Ra.

The name of the Haitian Elysium in the west, the paradise of the happy dead, is Koaibai. Like the Aaru (Eg.) it is a field of feasting and a place of plenty. In Koaibai grows the Mamey-tree, the fruit of which supplies the dead, who assemble by night to pluck from their tree of life. The living will eat very sparingly of the Mamey-tree, on account of its belonging to the dead, who in Egyptian are the MUM, hence the mummies. KAUI (Eg.) also denotes the dead. BAI is some kind of sacred food, and KOAIBAI is the name of this Haitian heaven and Eden of the Mamey-tree.

"At first sight," says Max Müller, "what can be more startling than to see the interior of the world, the invisible or nether world, the Hades of the Mangaians, called AVAIKI; Aviki being the name of one of the lower regions, both among Brahmans and Buddhists. But we

[1] Ch. cxlix.   [2] Ch. xvii.   [3] 154.
[4] Papyrus, 9,900, British Museum.   [5] Williams, *Fiji*, vol. i. p. 205.

have only to look around, and we find that in Tahitian the name for Hades is Hawaii ; in New Zealand Hawaiki, and more originally, I suppose, Sawaiki; so that the similarity between the Sanskrit and Polynesian words vanishes very quickly." [1]

The original of these names is to be found in the Egyptian SEVEKH, which is the name for the number seven. The Hervey group consists of seven inhabited islands, and one of these is Mangaia. The seven isles are said to be the visible representatives above of another seven in Avaiki, or SAVAIKI, below. At the Penrhyns, when referring to death, they speak of going to SAVAIKI. The seven below have become shadowy and impalpable, and the seven above are described as the embodiment of the seven in the underworld, as if these latter were spirits. [2] The Mangaian Savaiki is another form of the seven belonging to the nether-world of mythology, derived by name from Sevekh, number seven; the seven spirits of the Great Bear; the seven caves or islands of the sunken Atlantis ; the seven submerged provinces of Dyved. In the fragment from Marcellus, on the islands of Atlantis, we read that it is recorded by some of the historians who have treated of " the external sea, that in their time there were seven islands situated in that sea (the Atlantic) which were sacred to Persephone." [3] The seven isles belong to the world and time of the earliest mythos, sunken in the north, the region of Sevekh, the crocodile type of the sun below, and of the goddess of the North Pole.

PO, another name of the netherworld, is equivalent to Avaiki. [4] And Po or Pu is an Egyptian name for the north or Buto, the bau, void, hole of the tomb. Po is the place of departed spirits in Maori and in Egyptian Bau, the deep, also signifies spirits as well as the void. But this mythical and submerged land identified with the number seven, which belonged primarily to the celestial allegory, had a real existence in Khebti (Egypt), the land of the seven outlets to the Nile, the original Khebti-Khentu, a double land, as north and south. Kepti, or Hepti, is number seven equally with Sefekh or Savaiki, because the TI is two, and KEP, the hand, is five. It is evident that the Mangaians had both forms of Savaiki, or Egypt, from one of which people emerged on the horizon north-west, and from the other came up out of the earth, as the original home of gods and men. [5]

Mangaia is the seventh as the southernmost of the Hervey group of seven islands, and its name signifies " PEACE." PEACE in Egyptian is " Hept," which is also the name of number seven. MENA (Eg.), for repose and rest, answers to Mangaia for Peace. But this word Mena, for peace and rest, also signifies the warping to shore, coming to anchor, arriving at the resting-place, or attaining land. So interpreted, Mangaia, like Menapia, would be named as a first landing-place.

[1] Preface to Gill's *Myths and Songs from the South Pacific.* [2] Gill, p. 16.
[3] Marcellus, *Æthiopian History, Proclus in Timæus.* [4] Gill, p. 4.
[5] Gill, *Myths*, p. 125.

The Maori are accustomed to call the natives of the Hervey islands their "ELDER BROTHERS;" and one name of Mangaia is "AUAU." This is a duplicated form of AU, which in Egyptian means the old, the old one, the most ancient, and therefore the first, hence a title of dignity. In Maori AU signifies THOU—the pronoun of dignity still in English—denoting THE AU, or the old one; the old age in Egyptian. In Maori AUAU, to lift or raise up, has an earlier form in Hapai, to lift up, raise, carry, begin. So in Egyptian AU or AAU, the ancient, has earlier forms in Af and Kef, who was primarily the old one born of. As place, Kheb or Kef, abrades into AU or AÂ, the ancient place, the island rising up out of the waters. In the secondary form this is the Aât or Khepht, the AU, Af, or Khep, with the plural terminal. Thus AU-AU is a duplicated AU, equivalent to the Vewa KIBA-KIBA, the Fijian HIFO-HIFO; Kep-Kep, the name of Nubia, and Kheb-Kheb (Eg.), which, as duplicative forms are equivalent to Khebt, Kheft, Aft, or Aut, in Egyptian. An equivalent of KEP-KEP is found in UÂ-UÂ, a name of Nubia in the time of the sixth dynasty. UÂ-UÂ is literally one-one, and therefore denotes the second one, like Kep-Kep. In the form UAUAT, the plural terminal is added. UÂ is the one, the one alone, solitary, isolated. UAT is a name of the North and of Lower Egypt. Thus UA-UAT in Nubia was once the lower Egypt of inner Africa, and UÂ-UÂ is a worn-down form of Kefa-Kefa or Kep-Kep. So Uat is the secondary form of Kefa, the goddess of the north. AUAU, of the seven isles of Savaiki, whose names associate it with peace and the number seven, or "Hepti," the earlier Khepti, is a form of Khebt, the lower of two Egypts, named from the celestial birthplace in the north, where the two Egypts were the region of the Great Bear, as the Kep (Khepsh) above and the Kept or Khebt below; or the Khep north, and Khept west. The seven islands are representative of the seven below, the seven isles, lands, caves in the Akar of the north-west, out of which all issued in the mythological beginning.

In the Hawaiian traditions the ancestors came from "MOKU-HUNA," or "AINA-HUNA-A-KANE," the concealed land of Kane. The god Kane appears in the Hawaiian mythology as the lord of the waters.

The "land of Kane" so frequently referred to in the Hawaiian folk-lore, is the land of the living waters of Kane. This spring of the water of life is described at its source as an overflowing fount attached to a large inclosed pond, which was crystal-clear and had magnificent banks. It had *three outlets;* one for Ku, one for Kane, and one for Lono. Its water had the power of restoring the dead to life; it was the fabled fount of immortality.[1] The three outlets are remarkable because the fabled or mythical waters of the Pool of Two Truths are but two. Hor-Apollo tells us, however, that when the Egyptians denoted the rising of the Nile, which they call NUN, they

Fornander, vol. i. p. 78

depicted three water-pots, neither more nor less, to signify the triple cause of the Inundation, one for the ocean, one for the earth, and one for the southern heaven.[1] The triple cause was more probably the three lakes. But it is possible that there was another triad intended, that of evaporation in the upper heaven, the water that irrigated the earth, and that which went to the sea; three feeders in the three regions of heaven, earth, and the abyss imaged by the triple fount, corresponding to the three outlets for Ku, Kane, and Lono.

In the following chant of the Land of Kane, the words "Pali-uli" signify the *northward-flowing*; the course of the Nile in the hidden land of Khen, the interior of source :—

> " O Pali-uli, hidden land of Kane,
> Land in Kalana i Hau-ola,
> In Kahiki-Ku, in KAPA-KAPA-UA a Kane.
> Land with springs of water fat and moist,
> Land greatly enjoyed by the God." [2]

The name of Kane being taken, as before suggested, for the Egyptian Han or Nen, this is the land of the Inundation; the land of the bringer, who was Nun the father of Shu, and Han or Nun the youth, the child of the mother alone who became An-up the dog-star, and who is identified by name in the earlier form of KHAN as Sut the first bringer of the Inundation. In like manner the name of the typical vase modifies from Khan into Han and An, as the symbol of the bringer.

Atia or Atiu—it is rendered both ways—is a common Polynesian name of the original birthplace. One native account of Atia is that it is an inclosure out of which came the primary gods of the island.[3] That is out of the Hades, the Egyptian Aat, Kat, or Khept for the hinder heaven. In a chant intoned on public occasions by the priests of Rarotonga it is proclaimed that—

> ATIA is the original land from which WE sprang.
> AVAIKI (Savaiki) is the original land from which SOME came.
> KUPORU is the orginal land from which WE sprang.
> VAVAU is the original land from which SOME came.
> MANUKA is the original land from which WE sprang.[4]

This asserts that whereas *some* of the tribes came from Avaiki and Vavau *they* came from the primeval home, called Atia, Kuporu, and Manuka. Manu (Mao.) means to be launched and set afloat. The bird and the boy's kite are Manu. KA denotes the commencement of a new condition of things, besides being the well-known sign of land and country. Ati is a word used by the Maori, who preserve it sacredly, and employ it only in the names of tribes or clans, for the offspring and descendants. So in Egyptian the Aat is the child of the mother alone, and the Aati are the children whose descent is on

---

[1] B. i. 21.
[2] Fornander, vol. i. p. 78.
[3] Gill, *Life in the Southern Isles*, p. 27.
[4] Ib.

the mother's side. At Memphis Osiris is designated Ati, and he was the child of the mother alone as As-Ar, son of Isis. The Aati were the outcasts of Egypt because the children of the mother only. In Maori ATI-ATI is to drive away, expel, and ATIUTIU means to stray and wander. The outcasts of later Egypt were of the same cult as the early emigrants. Ati is a worn-down form of Khepti, a name of those who were looked on as the wicked, godless, enemies of the sun, because they were the children of night, and Typhon, the ancient Kefa and Khept of the hinder-part. Atiu then was the country of the Ati or Khefti, who as the Khêti (Eg.) are the sailors and navigators; Khêti corresponding to the Maori Ati to wander, be nomadic. It has been shown that ÆTHI-opia [1] is an abraded form of KHEFTI-opia as the land of Kefa in the second or plural form of the name, Kheft, Khept, or Khebt; Æthiopia being the Egypt within before the namers had descended the valley of the Nile. For example, an ancient name of Abyssinia is HABESH. That represents the Egyptian Khepsh and Hebrew Kûsh, the name for the north, the region of the Great Bear, when the namers were farther to the south, where the first and singular form of the name is extant, in the province of KAFFA, Lat. 7° 36′ N.; KIFA, about 4° north, and the land of KIVO at the sources of Lake Tanganika. Kaf (Eg.) is one hand, Kafti or Kapti is two hands, and in Kheftiopia, or the modified Æthiopia, we have the doubled or secondary land of the south and north which was finally upper and lower Egypt. And the name of the ancestral land was Ati or Atiu, which is equivalent to the Egyptian Aâti, Afti, and Khept the second, or a dual Khep. Among the Maori names of the north-west wind are Hau-ATIU and Tup-ATIU. Hau means wind, and Tup is to commence or to blow. Thus ATIU in both cases means the north-west. This in Egyptian would indicate a dual form of the hinder part, the Aât, Aft, or Kheft which was at first the hinder part north and afterwards the hinder part west, and the duplicate or plural form may be expressed by Khepti, Kep-Kep, or Uâ-Uâ, as in the names of Nubia. Now another Maori name of the north-west wind is KAPE-KAPE, a duplicative form of Kape which may be illustrated by Kapu applied to the hand and Kapu-Kapu to the foot, an equivalent for the upper and lower, or for the first and second, Kapu-Kapu being a sort of Kapu *da capo;* therefore an equivalent of the dual in Kep-Kep (Nubia) or Khebti (Egypt); only in the Maori the dual is applied to the north-west instead of to south and north, or the upper and lower lands. Khepsh is also the hinder-part north, and Khept the second Khep is the hinder-part west in Egypt.

The Polynesian traditions, says Fornander, all agree in looking

---

[1] The Greek αἴθω, to burn, is identical with the words HEAT, HOT, and UT (Eg.), which are derived from KHET (Eg.), fire, but heat is not a primary meaning; that has to be sought in KHEPT and UATI for the North, and the secondary form of Khep.

westward as the point of emergence from the underworld below the horizon. No matter on which island, or on which of the three groups, Hawaiian, Samoan, or Tongan, the situation of this ancestral land was always indicated by pointing in the direction of NORTH-WEST.[1]

Æthiopia was the UTOPIA, or UTOPU of the Polynesians. As late as the beginning of the nineteenth century the Nukahivans used every now and again to fit out exploring expeditions in their great canoes and start westward in search of their traditional UTUPU; from which they said, the god Tao had brought the cocoa-nut tree.[2] There are reasons for thinking that UTUPU represents Æthiopia or Khepsh. Pu is an Egyptian name of the north, the Po or lower heaven of the Polynesians. Khept and Aat denote the hinder-part which was both north and west. Uta (New Holland) for Hell, corresponds to the Aat (Eg.) or Hades.

As previously shown, the Akar was a region of the hinder-part west in the solar mythos, whereas in the Sabean it was in the north. The Mangaian name of the north is AKARUA. That is a type-word of measurable value. It belongs to a time before the west was considered the Akar in Egyptian, and Akharru in Assyrian. Still another Maori name of the north-west wind is MAURU, and URU is the west. The region and the wind are identical, as in the Egyptian MEH for the north and the north wind. In Egyptian Mâ and Meh are sometimes equivalent, and the Meh, symboled by a nest of water-birds, is the north as the birthplace of the twin source and Two Truths, the water and the breath of life. This water of the Meh (Mehuri) re-appears in Maori as MAORI applied to water fresh from the fount of source. Thus the Maori preserve the water of life under their own name, and the wind of the north, also called Meh (Eg.), which was the breath of life in Africa, is to them the MAURU as the wind of the north-west. It is touching to think that MAURU, the name given to this breath of the motherland, is also the word for being eased and quieted in pain and heartache. Mauri is also the name of the 28th day of the moon's age, and MEHI (Eg.) means to fill, be full, fulfil and be completed; it is also a title of Taht, the lunar god, whose name of Tekh signifies full, and of Hathor the fulfiller.

In Egyptian the Ru is the horizon, as the door, gate, or mouth to the Meh, the abyss in the north. The Ruru denotes the horizon as the place of the two lions, the double horizon of the equinoctial level. The RRU are steps. MEH-RU would thus unite the abyss below and the horizon above. It is possible that the Mount Meru with its seven steps may be the type of this MEHRU, though that is not our object at present. There is an ideograph of the two Egypts, ⌐_⌐ the original of what is known as the Greek "border pattern," which reads MERI or MERUI. It is the visible sign of lower and upper, or MEH (north, the abyss) and RRU (horizon and steps), and it is feasible

[1] Vol. i. p. 25.   [2] L'Univers Pittor., Oceanie, by D. de Rienzi, vol. ii. p. 230.

that the name of Tameri is the land of MEH-RU, whence Meru, and that the ancient Meroë was once the capital of two Egypts under this name. The first lower and upper were north and south, but the Maori Mauru is north and west, and this is in keeping with the Meh, north, and the Ru as the horizon west. Meroë in Æthiopia was due north from the equator, but reckoning from Central Africa or from Habesh (Abyssinia) we shall find the land of the ancient MAURI (Mauritania), howsoever the district was bounded at different times, was always to the north-west of our centre, which travels from the equator down to Lower Egypt. Thus we have a "Mauri," for the country north-west in Africa, answering to the Maori name of the north-west as Mauru. This shifts the duality of Meh-ru or Meru, from north and south to north and west, just as it was shifted when the hinder-part west was called Khept, as the place of going down instead of the north. This name for a land lying north-west of the African centre—always reckoning from the south—would deposit the names of the Mauri land; MARMARICA (a duplicated form) and MAROCCO as the Mauri or Moors went farther north into Spain, or TZEPHON.

From these and other data may be drawn the inference that the Maori people were self-named as the emigrants who came from the north-west, one name of which is MAURU, Egyptian Meru, Meroë or the Meh-ru.

The Mauri name is that of the later Moors, of a land under the Tropic of Cancer and north-west of the equator, as well as of Æthiopia the typical birthplace, and the name of the Moors found on the Egyptian monuments is written MAURI or MAURUI. The original MAURI dwelt in the north-western land lying between the Atlantic and Mediterranean, and their name is identifiable with that of the Maori, whose traditions derive them from the north-west.

They came from the MAURU, and in their language I signifies from, so that the people from Mauru would be the Maurui or Maori. They came from KAPE-KAPE, and Kep-Kep (Nubia) is the primitive plural for Khepti. The Hervey Islanders came from ATIU or Ati, the worn-down form of Khebti. The Nukahivans came from UTOPU or Æthiopia. These names are sufficient to identify the ancestral land from which the migrations went as claimed in their traditions and proclaimed in their songs.

According to Diodorus Siculus, the Egyptians declared they had sent forth many expeditions and established colonies in divers parts of the world, in times of the remotest antiquity. These would issue forth at different stadia of the African development and from divers regions of the country with sufficient initial divergence between the varieties to account for the difference developed in the Australians, for example, and the Maori or Tasmanian wild man ; the black men and the brown men of to-day.

At least three such stages are marked by the Auritæ, Mestræans, and Ruti of the old Egyptian Chronicle. The Auritæ, Afritæ, or Kafritæ name takes the people back to inner Africa, and identifies them with the blacks and the people who named Kûsh and Habesh as their north. The Mestræans are midway towards Egypt, and here the westward course would be taken into the Mauri-land. The Ruti are the people of Egypt known to us. They are, as the name implies, and their complexion shows, a form of the red men.

Thus we have the range from black to red with the variety of intermediate hues which afterwards deposited distinct types, all traceable at home.

A tribe of natives found in Australia still call themselves the KUMITES. KUME in Maori signifies to stretch out, pull out, draw away to a distance. KOMARU is the name of the sail. KHAMU (Eg.) means to let drop, to let fall an arm or branch, to transfer (peacefully). The old rowers and sailors who were dropped from the parent stem, and had to range out vast distances from the ancestral land in transferring themselves, were the Kumi or Kumites.

The identity of the names for boat and body has been referred to. A body of men is, in a Polynesian form, a boatful, the boat itself being a Poti in Maori. The boat-load was the body of emigrants, and as such would offer a type-name for the clan, tribe, or gens. Now, in Maori, the canoe is called a WAKA, and the WAKA is the primary division, which is subdivided into IWIS and HAPUS, or rather the territory claimed by each WAKA is subdivided into districts, each of which is claimed by an Iwi, the Iwis and Hapus being named from ancestors.[1] The waka is the Egyptian KAKA, a canoe.

Mr. Bartlett, the naturalist of the Zoological Society, has identified the oldest dog found on the Egyptian monuments with the wild dog of Australia, known as the Dingo, Maori TINGEI, which word means to be unsettled, roving, wild. The Dingo seen by the present writer in the Gardens, Regent's Park, was a very recognizable likeness of the Egyptian dog. This dog's name is ABUAKAR.[2] ABU is the dog; AKAR signifies the clever, sharp, alert, prepared, excelling, and the Abuakar has a most sharp and active look. It appears, in the tombs of the fourth dynasty, as a house-dog attached to the master's chair, and is also called Tasem, the dweller or domesticated dog.

ABAIKOUR has been found as the Berber name for the greyhound species. This tends to prove the reading here suggested, as the Akar, the clever, sharp, prepared, alert, applies equally to the watch-dog and hound. In Egypt the Abuakar was domesticated. In Australia he appears to have gone wild, i.e. TINGEI, in Maori, whence the Dingo of the colonists.

The powerful people who once occupied the Pacific Islands, and

[1] Shortland, p. 290.
[2] *Trans. Soc. Bib. Arch.* vol. iv. part 1, p. 175 ; vol. v. part 1, pp. 127, 128.

who built the Cyclopean inclosures with walls twelve feet thick, and the canals which were lined with stone, were known to the Lele Islanders by the name of the ANUT. The ANUT, say the Islanders, were sailors who possessed large vessels in which they made long voyages, east and west; many moons being required for one of their voyages.[1]

The ANU is a name of the ancient inhabitants of the Nile Valley With the terminal ti these are the Anuti; ANAU, in relation to the points of the compass, is the Mangaian typical name for "giving birth," and ANNU was the Egyptian name for the typical birth-place.

In Egyptian, Han (or An) means to go to and fro, especially on the water. The Hani is the barge of Sekari. In relation to the water and the barge, the Hanti are the sailors, or literally, the wanderers by water. Hanti or Hant is the equivalent of Anut, and was in Egypt the name of the typical returners or voyagers; being worn down from KHENIT, the sailors. The Maori HUHUNU is a double canoe; this duplicates the HUNU or HANI, which is a bark of the gods in Egypt. The most ancient portion of a race, those who belong to the earliest conditions, sink down as the sediment of later times, and in Tahiti there is a lower order of the common people, a separate and even tabooed kind of folk, including not only the manual labourers, but dwarfs and all sorts of queer and uncanny people. These are termed the MENAHUNE, the name having become an epithet of opprobrium. But may not these preserve the name of the Han, the Anut or Hanti who were the water-nomads that sailed in the Hani, Hunu or Huhunu canoes? MINNA in Tasmanian is the beach. MENA (Eg.) signifies the arriving, anchoring, landing, remaining, and resting, a meaning contained in the name of Mangaia, and so interpreted, the Mena-hune would be the earliest settlers.

This description should be read with globe and atlas at hand. Then it will be seen that the position of the MAURI-land in Africa is north-west of the equator, toward the Atlantic coast. Now, in the second edition (only) of *Te Ika a Maui*,[2] there are some figures, designated "A specimen of a lost language." These were recovered from Pitcairn's Island—a small lonely rock, one mile wide and two and a quarter miles long, at the south-eastern corner of the great Polynesian Archipelago, in lat. 25° 3′ 6″ S. long. 130° 6′ W. It is mountainous, has a poor soil, and no harbour. It is the island upon which the mutineers of the ship *Bounty* landed and lived, amongst whom, we may be sure, there was no Egyptologist. This is a fair copy of the characters, which are here paralleled with some Egyptian hieroglyphics taken from those drawn by Bonomi, and printed for the purpose of comparison:—

[1] Baldwin, *Ancient America*, p. 290.
[2] By Rev Richard Taylor, p. 702, 2nd edition, 1870.

Hieroglyphics found in Pitcairn's Island.

Egyptian Hieroglyphics.

Rudely drawn as they are, the characters are unmistakably Egyptian hieroglyphics. The solar disk, the so-called cake, the ideograph of land, habitation, dwelling-place; the cross, the five-rayed star, the eye, or SPER sign, the bow, the reversed half-moon, the "Kha" (the vagina sign of the birthplace)—these are all Egyptian; all there, howsoever they may be interpreted. It will be observed that the straight line ascending from left to right quaintly crosses a small *globe* which has one *pole* cut off. This is our starting-point.

The only line yet represented as crossing the globe is *the* Line, *i.e.* the line of the equator, and according to the proposed reading we have here a very crude chart in which this line denotes the equator; it cuts the globe across, or in two, the northern side is missing, and the southern half has a point to it apparently meant for the southern pole. The line is too short, and considerably out of drawing, but the science is here in keeping with the art. The hieroglyphic sun is drawn close to the line, and determines the tropical region of the solar path, the line or course travelled by the sun from east to west. At the upper end of the line is the well-known hourglass-like sign of the equinox. Although not known to me as an Egyptian hieroglyphic, it is found on the sculptured stones. It is also the Chinese sign for No. 5, an equivalent of one hand. The first hand reckoned upon was the left, and the west was considered as being on the left hand. The figures on the upper end of the line may possibly stand for two legs, signs of the character **J** from which we derive our written *B*. These with the two short strokes would read BUBI and denote the point of turning round in the circle, the complement of the cross sign of crossing the line. Figures which look like our 5 and 7 are also marked on the line, but our English figures are of Egyptian origin. These, however, may have been added by some Mutineer. Beside the equinoctial cross is the hieroglyphic cross "Am," the sign and name of the western crossing, the Ament entered by the sun when setting. This cross is a determinative of the crossing and transit.

The Egyptian AMTU for the crossing west is repeated in the West Australian AMETO, for the Hades. Next to the AM-cross is the star, a symbol of time and period. Then follows a kind of eye, unless it be the ideographic SPER. The strung bow and a half-moon shedding rays are the last of the upper signs. The human figure to the left below has the KHA sign projecting from the body; this in the hieroglyphics determines the belly, womb, or birthplace. The other two human figures are the signs of KA! KA! KA-KA (Eg.) signifies a rejoicing. Ka is to call, say, cry, proclaim a boundary, to boast, be uplifted. Ka is also the name of the priest, minister, or ruler, and the third figure to the right appears to bear the whip sign of authority. KAHA in Maori has the meaning of a boundary. The word also denotes lineage, the line of ancestry. We now try to read the chart by aid of the hieroglyphics.

The Egyptian North was the *hinder part* of the two heavens, or of the world, and the bird to the right is placed to the north, according to the present reading. It presents a portrait of the hinder-part, not only in the position of its tail, for *its feet are reversed and turned backwards in the drawing*. Feet turned backwards are *antipodes*. The north was the Egyptian antipodes to the south, and Ptah, as representative of the sun in the north below the horizon, was pourtrayed like this bird *with his feet turned backwards to denote the antipodes*.

The name of the north in Maori is NOTA, and as NO means "from," and TA to take breath, this shows the north was, as in Egypt, the place of the breath of life and of birth. NUTA (Eg.) signifies "out of," and the lower world of the north was impersonated by the mother, Neit, out of whom all came.

The sign of locality is also used for the horizon, and this purpose is served by the smaller figure placed between the bird in the north and the cross of the crossing, west. Next to this sign of the horizon comes the crossing followed by the sign of the cross, or to be *in transitu*. These are followed by the five-rayed star.

A star is the sign of time, a period of time. "When the Egyptians represent a year they delineate Isis, *i.e.* a woman (the great type of periodicity), and Isis is with them a star called Sothis." [1] The star is a symbol of Isis in the ceiling of the Ramession. It was

[1] Hor-Apollo, B. i. 3.

a synonym of the Inundation, and thence of the Sothic year. In the present instance it possibly stands for one year. For a whole year or a time they voyaged on in what the Egyptians termed "MAKING THE EYE," a phrase for completing a circle. The circle of the year was completed, and the eye was filled at the time of the summer solstice. The eye was full due south, therefore half way round from the north. In the north the eye was empty; in the south it was full. "I have made the eye of Horus, when it was not coming on the festival of the 15th day." [1] This is said on behalf of the moon making the eye, or lunation. "I have brought my orb to darkness; it is changed to light." The fifteenth was midway, full-moon in the lunar reckoning. In making the eye they would have gone to the southern side of the world, and were at a point due opposite to the north. But there is the possibility that the sign is not meant for an eye; it is unlike any hieroglyphic eye, and but for the stroke beneath would be a fair copy of the determinative of "SPER," a side (given underneath in two forms), which has the meaning of *approaching the side*, or *to approach the side!* In that case the sign would indicate the approach to the other side of the world, or half-way round the heaven. This half of the circle would be indicated by the half-moon and strung bow. The half-moon reads TENA, for a fortnight, as one-half of the total lunation, and tena signifies a measure of one half of a whole. PET (with the variant tep) means the heaven, and is the name of the Bow. "TENA-PET," or "Pet-tena," is equivalent to half-way round the circle (also called Pet) of the heaven, reckoning from the bird stationed to the north. The Bow, "Pet," is still more particularly a sign of the southern as the upper heaven. Thus read as ideographs of ascertained and provable values, the inscription announces the birth-place in the north-west, from which the emigrants set forth by the Atlantic into the Pacific Ocean, and pursued their way for a whole year, or a period of time, until they reached a boundary, or found themselves beneath the southern heaven, and knew that they were something like half-way round the world.

The bird being north, the bow may be taken as south, the cross marks the west, and at the opposite end of the line is the east. The hieroglyphics range through the half circle from north to south. By referring to maps the reader will find that the position of our assumed MAURI-land north-west of the equator corresponds to the position of the larger sign of land and dwelling-place. This emblem of locality is then taken to mean the birthplace and starting-point from the country or city north-west of the equator.

The KHA-sign projecting from the body of the left-hand figure betokens the belly, the body; and the KHAT are the children, the race. These then appear to be the race from the parent KHA or birthplace of the race. The other two figures, read "KA-KA," suggest

[1] Ch. lxxx.

that this inscription may contain a message proudly proclaimed respecting a birthplace and boundary. If this refers to Africa, then the larger of two signs of land (next to the sign of the sun) is perfectly placed north-west of the equator in corroboration. This is apparently the subject of the "KA-KA." Pitcairn's Island may be filled in near the head of the left-hand figure.

Such is my rendering of the characters, which must now take its chance with the other data concerning the African origines.

Every diverse line of development continued in the world-wide radii, every modification of form and feature, every colour and complexion, may be more or less recognized in the African races themselves. All the various divergences were begun in the primeval land, and are visibly continued there to this day. No distinct type in form or colour is found elsewhere, but some incipient or initial likeness of it is extant in Africa. The "promise and the potency" of all that has been evolved in other countries were first manifested there.

The various "blacks," the coffee or the copper-hued men, the red men, the yellow Mongols, and all the colours from black to white, or nearly white, had deposited some portrait of their past and foreshadow of their future selves in the ancestral home before they migrated to modify elsewhere. These types apparently mark the different stages of the migrations and possibly indicate the starting-points from the coasts on the Red Sea, the Indian Ocean, the Atlantic, and the outlet of the Nile. The present quest, however, is mainly limited to the evidence of language, mythology, folk-lore, and ceremonial customs.

That which has haunted us all round the globe like a ghost in Hebrew becomes reality itself in Egyptian. Most precious fragments of mythology have been rejected as too like the Hebrew not to be a modern importation, and some, in this way, have been lost. But the missionaries and navigators did not convey five hundred words and the earliest myths and symbols of Egypt into Mangaia and New Zealand, when these were safely buried underground in the sealed secrecy of the hieroglyphic characters. The error which created that mirage of the lost tribes of Israel lay in the taking of Hebrew to be the primeval tongue, and in mistaking mythology for historic truth. That which was false in the Hebrew delusion is true for the African origines. It is not the lost tribes of Israel that we come up with at last, but the early migrations from the African birthplace, and the last vanishing remnants of those who first went forth. All this and more is to be unravelled and read in language, myth, ceremonies, and customs, the treasury and storehouse of knowledge which, like the geological records, have been carefully kept, for us to come into full possession of when grown up and come of age ourselves.

There is undoubtedly a descending as well as an ascending progression in the course of evolution which has no relation whatever to the mythological creation or fall of man, and furnishes no argument whatever against the doctrine of Evolution, and we who stand on this side of the summit of the early attainment see much more of the descent; but the ascent beyond is no whit the less certain although hitherto hidden like the sources of the Nile. So surely as the Egypt of to-day has degenerated, and in its state of decadence yet furnishes the evidence of a past so lofty in attainments as to present an altitude that seems unscalable to the race who have descended from the ancient heights of the colossal wonders in the lands of the Nile; so have the primitive peoples of the world had their descent, and more or less retain the testimony to the fact in language, mythology, rites, and ceremonies, and often in monumental remains, although these may be less impressive than those of Egypt.

Rites and ceremonies are found permanent, as if graven in granite, amongst races whose character may appear to be shifting as the sand. The race dies out, but the religious customs never. They are constantly continued where the meaning has been lost. The filthiest in some respects are pious in their purification from ceremonial uncleanness, as the Kaffirs, who would not otherwise wash themselves or their food-vessels. There are signs of survival from some higher form of civilization which could not be attained by the Maori, Kaffirs, Hottentots, or Bushmen as they are known to us in the present.

Mr. Ridley, the missionary, was forced to the conclusion that the Kamilaroi and other of the Australian tribes showed the remains of an ancient civilization from which the race had fallen, but of which they retained some memorials. That is, they have suffered the decadence consequent on the arrest of growth indefinitely long ago, Language of itself is the sufficient proof of a pre-historic civilization none the less real because it was on different lines from ours. This alone is a memorial of powers beyond the present reach of the aborigines of many lands; mythology is another.

The West Australians of the lowest type were found by Moore to be in possession of an order of chivalry, to which certain women were chosen as an honour, and one of their privileges consisted in their being empowered to do precisely what is recorded of the British Druidesses, namely to rush between the opposed ranks of fighting-men and prevent their joining in battle.

These poor fellows who meet us at times as they descend the slope of our ascent, and who salute us with the manners of a ceremonial type of greater dignity than ours, are on the downward way from the far-off height at which such manners were first acquired and inculcated. The imperative regulations and perfect *etiquette* often observed amongst people who are considered by the missionaries to be savages or sub-human beings, who were cast out by a Hebrew God at the time of the "Fall," and who are damned for ever unless they accept our proffered Creed of Salvation—accompanied by rum and rifles, pip and piety, and the filthy fraud of Vaccination—their shining traits and nobler qualities, which at times illumine the darkest conditions, are not the rough jewels spontaneously produced by nature in the day of its degradation. They are the reliquary remains of a people who have seen better days. The results attained by the comparative process all tend to establish the unity of origin in language, mythology, religion, and race. There has truly been a " fall " for them, not merely the mythical one. They are the distant dying roots of the grand old tree which struck so deeply by the Nile to ramify the wide world round, so that wherever we may dig we lay bare some proof of its length of reach, strength of grip, and enduring vitality.

The tree was African once. It is English now. In the young green branches is the old life renewed, and may they flourish unfadingly! Already they stretch as widely round the surface of the earth as did the roots of Egypt underground. Egypt was parent of the initial unity in language, arts, laws, religion; and in our English tongue it appears *dreamable* that mankind may ultimately obtain the final unity of the universal race. But is it not possible for this new great green tree to extend a little shelter to the old fast-decaying races that sprang originally from the same rootage? The Kaffirs, the Red Indians, the Maori are withering underneath its shadow, and our tree of life is for them the fabled Upas found at last ; it is the tree of death that takes their life as its darkness steals over the earth, and turns it into one vast graveyard. Is our final message—delivered to them by the typical militant Christian, with a bible in one hand and a sword in the other—to be, " *Believe what we tell you about this book ; be saved at once, and pass off peaceably into another life, as there is no room for you in this, and the white earth-devourers are daily hungering more and more to eat up your ever-lessening lands at last ?* "

SECTION XXIII.

ROOTS IN AFRICA BEYOND EGYPT.

ALFRED RUSSEL WALLACE, co-contributor with Darwin in the discovery and promulgation of the doctrine of evolution, has remarked that "If geologists can point out to us the most extensive land in the warmer regions of the earth, which has not been submerged since the EOCENE or MIOCENE times, it is there that we may expect to find some traces of the very early progenitors of man. It is there that we may trace back the gradually decreasing brain of former races, till we come to a time when the body also begins materially to differ. Then we shall have reached the starting-point of the human family." [1] This has now to be sought for in Africa, the birth-place of the black race, the land of the oldest known human types, and of those which preceded and most nearly approach the human.

Æthiopia and Egypt produced the earliest civilization in the world and it was indigenous. So far as the records of language and mythology can offer us guidance, there is nothing beyond Egypt and Æthiopia but Africa, of this the present writer is satisfied. Although unable to give all the results in these two volumes, he has applied the same comparative process to language and mythology in China, India, Europe, and America, with a like result. All the evidence cries aloud its proclamation that Africa was the birthplace of the non-articulate, and Egypt the mouthpiece of articulate man.

Professor Owen has said that the conditions are unknown and scarce conceivable which could bring about the conversion of the Australian into the Egyptian skull. But that is not, and never was, the question. No evolutionist supposes that the ape of the present could ever be developed into the man of the future, any more than charcoal or graphite can be developed into the diamond. The sole meeting-point was at starting, and from this the one type bifurcates and branches on two routes which are unretraceable.

[1] *Journal Anthrop. Society*, 1864, v. ii. p. 167.

But this impossibility does not preclude the possibility of the Australian and Egyptian skulls having been developed on two different lines from the African skull of (say) 50,000 years ago, and that, again, from the skull of an earlier and more ape-like being.

Certain types which nature evolves for herself become stereotyped for us. There they are, ossified in their permanence, and far apart, as we look back upon them in their isle-like isolation and sharp distinctness, seen amid the ocean of an illimitable past. The Australian can no more *become* the Egyptian than the ape can become human. Nature goes on producing new types, but never copies from the stereotypes.

We are now for the first time approaching a summit in equatorial Africa, from which a descent and development of man are traceable in the valley of the Nile, but where the ascent beyond the summit is out of sight, and the absolute proofs of the origines of inarticulate man are probably buried in the Tertiary deposits.

It is intended in this last section to establish a few links between Egypt and the Africa beyond.

At least the same *namers* who came down into Æthiopia, Nubia, and the two Egypts, to carry the origines of the myths and mysteries, types and symbols, religion and language over the world, may be traced by the names and by the mould of thought and expression throughout central or equatorial Africa.

In the opening section it was suggested that the black race was first, and that equatorial Africa was the birthplace, not only of the human being, but of the original modes and types of expression which have more or less persisted from the beginnings of human utterance to the present time. Inner Africa, the writer maintains, was the land of the earliest namers of things and acts, who were therefore the creators of nouns and verbs which constituted the main stock of language before the descent into Egypt and the dispersion, on the way to developing the thousand dialects of the world from the one mode and form of speech evolved at starting.

Egypt as the mouthpiece of Africa, tells us that Africa was Kafrica, the land of the Kaf, or Kaffir ; and of Af, Kaf, or Khab, which in Egyptian signifies " BORN OF." The types of this birth, OUTRANCE, or utterance, have been continued for us in the images of the KHEB (hippopotamus), the KAF-monkey, and the CAVE of the troglodytes. The genitrix as KHEBMA, is the mother Kheb, and Khebma, Hebrew חם, becomes Kâm, to create ; and finally KAM, as a name of the black people and the burning land of the south. Kheb and Kam are interchangeable names, because they bifurcate from that of Khebma, the mother Kheb. KHEPA (Eg.) is the name of the navel, because KHEB (Kep, Ket), in the equatorial or Af lands, was the womb of the world, and the Cwm, Chvm, Kam, Coff, or Cefn, of the QVŒNS (Fins) and the KVM-ry. In this sense Damaraland is called Dama-QHUP in the

Namaqua language. KHEP (Eg.) means to be, exist, being, generate, create, form, transform, cause to become; CHVI (Heb.), GIV, Sanskrit, Gothic QUIV, to live, on account of this origin. Now we may see how this land of Khebma, whence Kheb and Kam, was named before Æthiopia, Nubia, and Egypt.

KEF (Eg.) means the front, as the face, Akkadian GAB for the front or before, and Khept, the secondary form, is the hinder-part. These two are depicted as the face and hinder-part of the female, who represents the Egyptian heaven. Again, in the first and second hinder-parts of the north and west, Sabean and solar, the Khepsh is first, and the Khept is the second of the two.

The descent from the first KHEB to the second KEP-KEP, or KHEBTI, can be traced. KHEPT, as second, is the hind quarter; KHEBT is Lower Egypt, as the second of two; KHEBT is the underworld, the second of the two. KHEB-KHEB (Eg.) is the primitive plural, as in KEP-KEP (Nubia), and it signifies to DESCEND, come down, go or fall down. In the celestial reckoning and naming, the Great Bear above the pole was in KHEPSH the first KHEB, and below it was in KHEB-KHEB, or KHEBTI.

A form of the singular Khep with the terminal sh, a water-sign, is found in Khepsh, for the hinder thigh, and this furnishes the name of Kvsh, or Küsh, for Æthiopia, or HABESH, the first land of Khept above Egypt, and the name of the birthplace, or outlet in heaven; extant in the Hebrew חסף, to separate and split open, as in parturition, and the Talmudic חסף, for COUCH—which word is also a modified form of the KHEPSH. When another sign of duplicating and naming the second of two was discovered in the terminal T (or ti), the first Khep, or Khepsh, became Khept (Egypt), and Kam became Kamit, another name of Egypt. It has already been shown how the first mode of duplicating the value of a word, or forming a plural, was simply by repeating it. Thus a second application of the name of the Kheb, for dwelling-place, would make it Kheb-Kheb, and this is found in the Egyptian name of Nubia, called KEP-KEP, corresponding to the Hebrew " QEV-QEV," applied to the Æthiopians. As place, KEP-KEP is a second form of the KEP. KHEB-KHEB for the north, as the lower of two lands and two heavens, is extant in Polynesia, where HEFA is the name of the spirit-world to which the dead descend. The land of HIVA is common in the songs and stories. HIFO, with the Fijians, is the Amentes, the place of going down, and a synonym for *below*.

In some places, as at Vewa, the mouth of the underworld named Bulu, the Bahu, or void, is called KIBA-KIBA—a mode of duplicating which makes the word equal to Khebti, the second or dual form of Kheb. Every island and town has its KIBA-KIBA, or cemetery, the lower place of two, that of the second birth named from the womb as the first; such are the KOPU, Maori, womb; KIBO, Malagasi; KEPP, old Bohemian ; COOPOI, Darnley Island ; Te-KAP-ANA, Ombay ; COFF, Cornish, and others. This being the womb, the *hinder* thigh is the Khept, as a secondary type of two. With a different terminal, the thigh in Mutsaya is KEBEL ; in Babuma, KIBELO ; in Utere, KEBELE ; and in Mbamba, KEBELE. The hinder thigh, Khept, denoted the emaning-place to the Khep of the feminine heaven that over-arched the earth and brought forth animal-fashion in the north, at the outlet of the Nile.

Many forms of the first one may be traced under this name, and as KEP (Eg.) is the hand, and Kep-ti two hands, Kabti, two arms, so the earliest Khebt, or Egypt, is the second Kheb, which second form is found higher up in the duplicative KEP-KEP of Nubia. Thus language in its type-words supplies one mode of tracing the descent from the upper and inner country of Africa or Kafrica, into Æthiopia, Nubia, and Khebt, as the lower land of two ; a duality afterwards continued in Egypt, upper and lower.

A rabbinical geographer of the fifteenth century says it is declared by the knowing ones, or the gnostics, that paradise is situated under the middle line of the world where the days are of equal length.[1] If equatorial Africa be the human birthplace, it is there we may expect to find the earliest localization of the paradise and Eden of mythology, in the country from which issues the river that runs through all the land of Kush.[2]

It may be noticed in passing, although the subject will be considered in a chapter on "Eden and the Fall," that CHAVILAH (חוילה) is a form of the name of the genitrix KEFA, or CHAVVAH, and of the words for life itself, the bringing forth, the person and the place of bringing forth, the act of opening to bring forth, in Egyptian and Hebrew. Chavilah is also called the land of gold ; and Nubia means the land of gold, or Nub (Eg.) Moreover there is an African river Euphrates or Eufrates, the chief river in Whydah, which is still revered as the sacred stream, and a procession in honour of it is made annually. The Egyptian name for Elysium, as the place of peace and plenty, the heaven of the primitive man, is the AÂRU, or AALU. This written with the accented sign shows it was the earlier AFRU, and, as no initial vowel is a primitive of speech, still earlier KAFRU. ÂÂ, AF, KAF, and KHAB, all signify "Born of." The Ru is the outlet, gate, place of emanation, the mother-mouth. Afru denotes the place born of, and from ; the type of Elysium being feminine. Ka (Eg.), is an inner land, and Africa, or Kafrica, is the interior land of the human birthplace. "AURKA" is a monumental name for a country in the south of Egypt ; this in the consonantal form is AFRKA. AF and AU have the same value, meaning the old first place,—born of ; RU indicates the outlet, and KA the interior land.

The name of MESRU can also be followed into Africa beyond Egypt.

[1] *Sepher Hamunoth*, f. 65, C. i. Stehelin, v. 2, p. 4.   [2] Gen. ii.

The first form of "physical geography" was founded on the female figure of the woman below (earth), and the woman above (heaven); and whether the representation be of the woman below, with her feet pointing to the Great Bear, or the woman above—the Great Bear itself—Africa, in Egyptian thought, was the womb of the world, and Egypt the outlet to the north, the Mest-ru. In English, for example, the Mus is the mouth answering to the Mest (Eg.), for the uterus. Muslo, in Spanish, is the thigh. In Turkish, Mazhar is the place of manifestation, and Mashaara in Swahili means monthly, which relates to a primary manifestation, as in the Arabic Mizr, for red mud. Mosari, in the Setshuana dialect, is the name of the manifester, as woman. Mizrawam in Arabic is applied to the haunches, and in the African Bute dialect, Muhsir, like the Spanish Muslo, is the thigh, which is the hieroglyphic of the Mesru, the birthplace, whether in the heavens or in Africa. The land which drains into Lake Victoria, for a twenty days' journey, is named the Masai land.[1] Masi (Eg.) is to bring, be tributary; and Mes denotes the source, the birth of a river. Mesru, or Mestru, is the emaning outlet from the Masai land known as Mitzr, or Mitzraim.

Teb (Eg.) means the first movement in a circle; that of Teb, a name of Typhon, or the Bear. One of her types was the Mount Tepr, or Thabor, at the point of commencement, as in Defrobani and Dover. Another type of the oldest genitrix was the water-cow, and the later cow called Tep or Teb. Now on the African Gold Coast there is a rock named the Tabora, which is one of two great objects of adoration: the cow is the other. Both are identifiable by name with the great mother Teb (or Typhon), the first and oldest form of the mythical genitrix. The Yorubas identify a place called Ife, in the district of Kakanda (5° E. long.; 8° N. lat.) as the seat and birthplace of the gods, from which the sun and moon are reborn after their burial in the earth. Ife is also looked upon as the human birthplace and cradle of the race.[2] This renders the Egyptian Af, born of, as place, which as person is Iye, i.e. life, Hauve, Eve, Kepa, or Kheb, who, as the earliest mother, was Khebma, whence Kâm, Khepsh, and Kûsh. Kebeb (Eg.) is the word for source itself; the Hebrew Chabab, to carry in the womb, from Chab (חב) the place of concealment; and in central Africa (8° 8′ S. lat.; 23° 36′ E. long.) we find Kabebe (or Muato Yanvos), also Kupopue (lat. 2° 30′ S.). The root of this name is applied to another form of the birthplace in Kivo, the country at the southern head of Lake Tanganika. According to the native account there are thirteen tributaries to the river Rusizi on its way to the Lake Tanganika, the last and largest of these being the Ruanda river, which discharges its waters into the Rusizi in the gorge of the valley near the entrance into the lake.

[1] Stanley, *Through the Dark Continent*, i. 165.
[2] Tucker, *Abeokuta*, p. 248.

The Rusizi was found by Livingstone and Stanley to be a feeder of the lake, and this river, with its thirteen tributaries, rises in the land of KIVO, south of the southern head of the lake, according to the native report, on the south-western side of one of the mountains, and flows down between two ranges of mountains, the Ramata on the east, and the Chamati on the west, into the lake.[1] The name of the birthplace in the form KEP, means the concealed, the hidden place of the source; KEBEB is the source. KEFI denotes the navel the nipple and the uterus. KEPU signifies the mystery of the hidden source, the flowing source; the mysterious fertilization of the Nile. KEP is a name of the inundation of the Nile, which modifies into HEP, or HAPI-MU, the hidden water of source. KIVO, then, is the Egyptian name for the birthplace, the land of the hidden fountain-head; the mystery of the inundation and its secret source; and so concealed is the *embouchure* of the Rusizi river as it issues stealthily from the land of KIVO that, although Livingstone and Stanley constantly kept their binoculars searching for it, they could not see the main channel until within 200 yards of it, and then only by watching the fishing canoes come out.[2] KIVO is an earlier form of KHEB which is repeated in KEP-KEP for Nubia, and duplicated in KHEBT, as the name of Lower Egypt. Of course it may have been thought that Lake Tanganika was the head of the water-system immediately connected with the Nile, in which case the land of KIVO would be the country of the secret source of the inundation of Egypt.

The name of KHEBMA, the mother, Kheb, Kep, or Khep, who impersonated the womb of the race, is found in abraded forms as that of the womb or belly in various of the inner African languages, as ABUM, in Bagba; IBUM, Orungu; EBOM, Melon; EBUM, Ngoten; EBAM, Bamon; APOM, Pati; IVUMU, Kabenda; AVOM, Papia; VUM, in Dsarawa; VUMU, Kasánds; FUMU, Basunde; FUMU, Mimbosa; PFAM, Balu; BUM, Momenya; BUM, Nso; BAM, Kum; WEMO, Pangela; IWUMU, Mpongwe; and YAFUN, in Fanti. The Y in the latter represents the K found in Kabin (Teor) for the belly or uterus. To these names corresponds the Hebrew IBM, to be bellied, big, great, pregnant, as the KHEBMA was pourtrayed. In WEMO, Pangela, we have the WAME or WOMB. All these names, inclusive of WAME and BUM, together with the Greek Βωμος and Hebrew במה, are derivable from KHEBM, the hippopotamus, who also represented the hinder-part of the heaven; one of her types being the tomb in the mounts and mounds of the Cave-men. These names identify the original type of the KHEBMA, the CWM, QUIM, KHEM (a name of Hathor, the habitation), Xosa, GOMBA; the HEM, HAM, HOME, and AM. The reduced Kâm supplies the name for woman in the African languages, as KOOMARA, in Dor; GAME, Bode; KAMU, in Kanuri, Munio, Nguru,

---

[1] Stanley, *How I Found Livingstone*, p. 505.   [2] Stanley, *Ib.* 504.

and Kanem; UMA, in Dodi, and MA, in Bassa. DEBO for woman in Fula; KYVIQUIS, woman, in Hottentot; T'AIFI, woman in Bushman; WOPUA, woman, in Gurma, Kura, and Dizzela, and DJOF, for the belly in Mahari, are all African, and each word is a form of the name of the oldest African great mother.

The natives of the Soudan have the legend of Eve and her oven. They relate that HAUVE bore so many black babies that Abou the father god said he would have no more darkies. Then she hid them in an oven, from which they emerged black with soot. These were the negroes.[1] Eve, Hauve, Kef, Kafu, Cefn, Kivan, Kabni, Cabin, and Oven, all meet in the name and types of the one original genitrix, KHEBMA. The Cabin, the KABNI (Eg.), the YAFUN woman, the CEFN, the cave, the KABNI, as Eve's OVEN, the Cabin of the primordial ark, the HAVEN, and the HEAVEN, had but one prototype in nature.

Without expecting to find the PLACENTA of the mother earth, to which her latest child was attached, we may do something to further identify the birthplace so far as the articulate has left any record of inarticulate man in that water-region where the human tadpole made its transformation into a being that could go by land as well as water and so make its way out over the world.

In the Dahoman goddess GBWEJEH, to whom are ascribed the attributes of Minerva as goddess of wisdom, it is not difficult to identify the ancient KHEPSH, who was the living word of the Typhonians in Egypt. She also lives in the Egba mythology as IYE or HAUVA, another form of the negro Eve, KEFA, KHEBMA, or KHEPSH. The WEST African kingdom of FUTA also bears the name of Aft, a modified form of Kheft, for the hinder-part west. Aft and fut are interchangeable as in the English aft and fud for the hinder-part. According to Cosmas Indicopleustes, who copied the inscription from the monument of white marble erected at Adule, a port on the Red Sea, in latitude 15°, the King Ptolemy Euergetes, the later conqueror of Æthiopia and Central Africa, penetrated to the Snowy Mountains. He described the great mountain named KHA-KUNI, which was doubtless Mount Kenia, one of the only two snowy mountains known in Africa. The KHA (Eg.) is the high earth, one of the four supports of heaven; KHENI means inland, interior. Ptolemy reported that from this mountain seven chains advanced seaward and one inland towards à province named HANIOT. If this geographical formation be really extant, the seven mountain ranges would be the early African seat of the Lady who sat on the seven hills at Rome, Great Grimsby, or wherever there was a cluster of seven; the eighth would complete the number of the Great Bear and Dog-star, the eight of Am-Smen who were in the beginning, and the cradle of Sut-Typhon and of the oldest mythology would be dis-

[1] Palme, *Travels in Kordofan*, p. 187.

covered in the great mountain of Kha-Kenia. The KHA is also the adytum of the genitrix. HANIOT would indicate the region of the water-source; the HANT or HENT is the fount, the vase, the matrix of the feminine Bringer. Kenia is also called NDUR-KENIA, and NTUR (Eg.) means the Divine, the Goddess or the God. Also one of the rivers that run down from the supposed seven mountain chains into the Indian Ocean is named SABAKI, and this as Sevekh (Eg.), Hebrew שבעה, for number Seven, would denote the river of the Seven, whether as the seven ranges or as the great mount of the Seven Stars. The two provinces of Abyssinia, LASTA and ṢAMEN, answer by name to the Egyptian RUSTA and SMEN, the two regions found in the Ritual.[1] In the provinces of Lasta and Samen rise the sources of the last tributary of the Nile, amid mountains which attain the altitude of 15,000 feet. The name of the RUSIZI river contains a root also found in those of the rivers MeRAZI and MalagaRAZI, which are feeders of the southern sources of the Nile. RAS or RUS (Eg.), to rise up, is the name for the south as the place for rising up and watching, the south being the upper of the two heavens. In the Semitic languages RAS came to mean the head, but RAS Awath, RAS Asuad, and RAS Maruti, in Somali land, facing the Indian Ocean, are not only headlands, they are southern headlands, which corresponds to the meaning of RAS as in the Egyptian triple sense. The RUANDA river flows into the RUSIZI, and both into the Tanganika.[2] RUANTA (Eg.) is the mouth, outlet, or gorge of a river. The RUANDA country is full of gorges or ravines, in which the dark tops of trees are seen. RUANTA (Eg.) is the gorge of a valley as well as the mouth of a river. The KAGERA is "broad, and deep, and SWIFT, and its water, though DARK, is clear." KAK (Eg.) means dark, and RUA, or RAAU, is the rapid river. RWERU, the small lake in Karagwé, eight miles long and two and a half wide,[3] agrees with RURU (Eg.), a pool of water; also a mere drop; this being in the region of the great lakes. The natives of Ihuna Island told Stanley of a lake, a three days' journey round in canoes, named the Akanyaru. "Hamid Ibrahim said the Ni-Nawarongo river rises on the west side of the Ufumbiro mountains, sweeps through Ruanda, and enters AKANYARU, in which lake it meets the Kagera from the south; united, they then empty from the lake."[4] Akhen or Khen (Eg.), is the lake, and ARU, the river; this would thus be named, in Egyptian, as the river-lake.

The Kingani river was said, by the natives, to rise in a gurgling

[1] In discussing the origin of the Hebrew RASHITH, it should have been noted that the "RUSTA," (Eg.), technically means the "Guiding Gates," or the "TOWING-PATHS," as the primitive forms ot the celestial roads and gates of entrance, passage, and egress. To tow is synonymous with leading or conducting, and in Egyptian imagery the sun was towed through the RU'S, which were early forms of the gates, houses, asterisms, sieus, or manzils of the heavens.

[2] Stanley, i. 479.   [3] Stanley.   [4] Stanley, i. 468.

spring on the EASTERN face of the UKAMBAKA mountain. The BAKHU (Eg.) is the birthplace in the east; the birthplace of the sun as old as the solar chart, and the time when the spring equinox occurred in An. Bakh means to engender, bring forth; whence bakhu, the birthplace. Kam (Eg.) is to create.

The Wamrima people appear to be named from the WAMI river, and Rema (Eg.) signifies the people, the natives, aborigines. The Wajiji did not know why the Lake Tanganika was so named, unless it was because *it was so large and long canoe voyages could be made on it.*[1] In accordance with this, Egyptian would offer a more satisfactory derivation for the name of the great lake TANGANIKA than any yet proposed. Stanley found that the natives could not explain the meaning or derivation of the word " NIKA." In Egyptian TAN signifies to extend, spread, stretch, lengthen out, fill up. KHEN is the lake, the water. KHENNU also means to navigate, transport, carry; hence the name of the Canoe. The Khenit are the sailors as conveyers. The KHENT ideograph is composed of three vases with two spouts, answering to the two Niles and the three great lakes. KA means the land or country; also interior. Thus TAN-KHANI-KA (Eg.) reads the vast extended navigable lake in the heart of the country. As before cited, Hor-Apollo claims that one of the three vases of the inundation stood as symbol for the rains which prevailed in the southern parts of Æthiopia, *i.e.* Africa. Again, TAN (Eg.) signifies to rise up, increasingly, become vast, extended, full; and KA is the inner land. NEKA is a type-word for power and puissance. Also, in the African languages, water is NGI, in Nguru; NGI, Kanuri; NGI, Kanem; ENGI, Munio; ANINGO, Mpongwe; ONGOU, Fertit, ENGI, Mumo; INJI, Bangbay: NKI, Ngoala; NKE, Balu; NKE, Bamon. These words agree with ANKHU (Eg.) for the liquid of life. In the Malemba dialect a lake is called EANGA. In the Kaffir languages, however, the Xosa, and others, NIKA is a word expressly used for giving, in the restricted sense of HANDING OVER, or PASSING ON, and TRANSMITTING from one to another.[2] This would especially apply to Lake Tanganika considered as the head of a water-system. In the same language, the Xosa, TANGA is the thigh or place of emanation, like the Egyptian Khep, and the seed of certain fruits, such as the pumpkin and water-melon, which is a type of source WITHIN. So interpreted, TANGA-NIKA is a water-source transmitting from within.

The Urunga people call the lake the IEMBA. IEM or IUM (Eg.) is a sea, and BA (Eg.) is a name of water for drinking. IEM-BA would denote a FRESH-WATER SEA. The name of Tanganika was known to a native of Western Usue as Lake UZIGE. In Egyptian USEKH (with the variant SEKH) means to stretch and range out, vast and broad; the modified USESH signifies the overflow or

---

[1] Stanley, *Dark Continent*, ii. 16.   [2] Davis, *Dictionary*, p. 143.

evacuation, and SEKHA is the name for flood-time and the season of the inundation. Lake USIGE, in Egyptian, is the Lake of the Inundation, and Stanley describes it as "rising and encroaching on its shores so fast that the dwellers on its banks are compelled to move every five years farther inland."[1] The overflow which he predicted has been found to have occurred.[2] Here then, is a lake with a periodic inundation known by the same name as the flood-time in Egypt, which was designated from the inundation of the Nile.

A communication was lately made to the Royal Geographical Society by Mr. E. C. Hore, of Ujiji, who was the first to solve the moot question of the Lukuga outlet of Lake Tanganika, on the long-continued rise of the lake level which has never yet been satisfactorily explained. A succession of extraordinarily rainy seasons, of which we have no evidence, would not, in his opinion, account for it. He says he can bear testimony to an enormous evaporation; but how, he asks, is it that the waters suddenly gained upon the evaporation, as they had never done before? He seems disposed to connect the changes of-water-level with earthquake movements, and at the date of his letter—September 15th—he mentions that his house was shaking with earthquake, as it had been for several days previously. Some years ago, according to one of his Arab inform-ants, there occurred an extraordinary disturbance of the lake-waters, a long line of broken water being seen, bubbling and reeking with steam. The next morning all was quiet, but the shore was strewn with masses of a stuff resembling bitumen.[3]

This opens up a vast vista of possibility; for this region may have been in the past the seat and scene of the largest deluges on the surface of the globe, before the beds and the sheds of the waters had been formed as safely as they are at present. This, of all regions beyond the land of the inundation of the Nile, should be the terrene birthplace of the deluge imagery of mythology.

The origin of TANGANIKA is said on the spot to have been a small deep well that bubbled up from the heart of the earth, and, in consequence of the unfaithfulness of a woman who could not keep a certain secret, the world cracked asunder down to the centre, the fountains overflowed and filled the profound gulf of the earthquake rent, and there was the Tanganika.[4] A similar story is told of the origin of Loch Awe.

Cailleach Bheir is the Gaelic name of a rugged rock overlooking the loch. Cailleach means the "woman of old," who is here personified as Bheir or Beir, the old woman who had charge of the well or fountain on Ben Cruachan. When the sun went down, it was her work to cover up the well by placing a lid on it. One night she fell asleep, and forgot to make the fountain secure. In the morning there

[1] Stanley, ii., 12
[2] Thomson's recent report.
[3] The *Athenæum*, Jan. 8th, 1881.
[4] Stanley, ii. 12-15.

was the deluge: the fountain had overflowed and covered the plain: Loch Awe had taken the place of man and beast. The old woman was turned into stone. Bera is also said to have made Loch Eck in Cowal, above Holy Loch. She is likewise known in Ireland.[1]

The name as Beru (Eg.) signifies the cap, tip, roof, supreme height; the BERU is a well. BERU also means to boil up, ebullition, well up as in the Bore. BU-RU (Eg.) would denote the place of the outlet; hence the fount and flood. Loch ECK corresponds to UKA (Eg.), for the waters of the inundation. AU and AF (Eg.), answering to AWE, mean the old one, the one born of, who as Aft or Kefa was the ancient mother, Cailleach Bheir.

When Stanley asked an African chief what river it was he was voyaging down, "THE River," was the reply.

"Has it no name?" he asked.

"Yes; the GREAT River."

"I understand; but you have a name, and I have a name; your village has a name. Have you no particular name for your river?" ("We spoke in bad Kikusu.")

"It is called Ikutu Ya Kongo,—the River of Congo."

Egyptian will yield more meaning than that. It was in the midst of a long series of cataracts or falls that the river was so named. The traveller counted fifty-seven altogether. Now, in Egyptian, KHUT means going down with the current, or shooting the cataracts, "making the KHUT" is making the shoot. Also, the Khutu are steps, the equivalent of the cataracts. So read, this river of falls is the River of the Steps or Cataracts. KONGO probably represents the type-word for water, extant in Pali as KHONKHA, in Tonquinese as KHUNGU, and in Maori as NGONGI, which duplicates the African NGI. NGAWHA (Mao.) denotes the water that bursts open and overflows its banks; and WHA is to burst forth and get abroad. In Egyptian, KHEN-KHU would denote the interior water or lake that rises up, extends, elongates, and runs with great rapidity.

One group of falls is called the "Falls of UKASSA." "U" denotes place, and KASHA in Egyptian signifies to water, spread, and inundate; represented in English by WASH, GUSH, and GWASH; in Xosa Kaffir by QWESHA; Irish, CAS; Arabic, GHAZIO; Circassian, KHEEZA, applied to swiftness of motion. This reminds us that M'GUSSA is a powerful Water-Spirit who has his dwelling in the lake (Victoria Nyanza) and his priest, who lives on an island in the lake. M'Gussa is said to wreak his vengeance on all who offend him, and his dominion also extends over the rivers that communicate with the lake. The Waganda would not allow Speke to throw a sounding line into the water, lest M'Gussa should rise up in his wrath and punish them.

[1] *Loch Etive*, p. 55.

The Babwendé, whose territory on the Kongo is far away down toward the Atlantic Ocean, have a typical term for a river, or *the* river: it is NJARI. That is the original for the name of the NILE. The word is formed from ARU or ARI, the river, with the definite plural article NAI prefixed. NAIARI is the Nile as the waters, not merely a river. The *j* may represent the *k* in the earlier KARUA, whence the form NACHAR or NACHAL, the Nile, in Æthiopic. In the African Nalu dialect, NUAL is the type-name for water.

The river Niger is also known by the native name of the QUORRA. KARUA (Eg.) means the lake as a source; and Ni, or in the full form NNI, is the flood or inundation. It can be shown that this Ni represents the Egyptian Nun, because in the Bight of Benin the Niger is called the NUN or NIN, as in the word Benin. Thus the name of Niger in full is NUN-QUORRA, and Nun-Karua (Eg.) is the flood from the lake. BENIN in Egyptian would read, the place of the inundation, or the flood of fresh water.

According to Livingstone, the people of RUA, on the west side of Lake Tanganika, live in rock-excavations, and he heard that some of these dwellings were of enormous size.[1] RUHA is the Egyptian name for a stone-quarry, and it will be interesting to learn whether the RUA Mountains have been excavated and chambered, or whether they are remarkable for their natural caves.

In one of the most recent utterances on the subject of the Egyptian origines, M. Renouf says,—"It is in vain that the testimony of philology has been invoked in evidence of the origin of the Egyptians." The language, he asserts, cannot be shown to be allied to any other known language than its descendant, the Coptic. "It is certainly not akin to any of the known dialects either of North or of South Africa, and the attempts which have hitherto been made towards establishing such a kindred must be considered absolute failures."[2]

Possibly we have not set about it in the right way. What is it we are looking for? Sameness in grammatical structure, under the guidance of Grimm's Law? Then such seeking is not likely to find the missing affinity. When we see that in Egyptian the word is in many instances no specialized part of speech, but potentially noun, verb, adverb, adjective, all in one, and that what concerns us as primary data lies far beyond the extant state of speech in Coptic, it becomes evident. that grammar can be no test of original likeness, and the attack on the problem has to be made in flank instead of front. As time was when the word was everything, and distinctions had to be made by other means, words must still count for something in evidence of origin.

The missionary Saker, who translated the Bible into one of the African dialects, was especially impressed with the signs pointing to a common origin for the African languages. He says of the people

---

[1] *Proceedings of Geog. Society*, Nov. 8, 1869.   [2] *Hibbert Lectures*, p. 55.

amongst whom he worked on the West Coast, " They had a language, for they could communicate with one another; but they had no books, their tongue was not a written one. There were no means which we could lay hold of for teaching us the language they were using." So he learned it from them, and was able to re-present it to them in a written shape. In his researches he made the discovery that this was only a dialect form of language, and observes :—

" The language that the people use is a language which prevails with its dialectic differences throughout the whole of that region. I have no trouble there. There are millions and millions of miles that I know nothing about, because the country itself where I live is something like 2,000 miles across it, and there are 2,000 miles more down to the south; yet in the interior districts, so far as I can discover, there is one original tongue broken up into an innumerable multitude of parts. Away in the far east a missionary sat down to learn their tongue, and committed it to paper, and he printed a part of the Scripture. I can read his Scripture. Another man has gone south without any reference to me, or anybody else, and has worked there and learnt their tongue, and written a portion of the Scripture. I can read it. And wherever our brethren have gone, they have worked quite independently one of another, and they have shown us the result, and I can read the whole. And my book goes into their hands. They read it; their people read it. They understand it. Now, what I have done on the coast where I have been living is only one little thing accomplished. Other men have done a little here and a little there, and by and by some good man will be able to take up the work and bring all these languages together ; and who can tell but that he may direct our hearts and thoughts, and our eyes too, to the source whence comes all these broken dialects. It may be that we shall some day discover whence they emanate. I have sought to find it out, but I have failed. I have looked to the Amalic. It is not there. It has nothing in common with it. Of course I could not find it in the Æthiopic. I have looked to the Coptic. It is not there. And whence comes it? I have sought everywhere, but I have not found. They have the tongue. It is beautiful now. In its ruin it is beautiful. They have the tongue, and it is expressive. It is a tongue of power." [1]

The original *language* at the root of these African dialects is no more extant in the modern sense than is the primal type of man. The first matter of speech must have consisted mainly of noun and verb, the earliest articulators of words being mere namers of things and acts ; and even at this stage Egypt is the mouthpiece of the Africa beyond. The following comparative list of words will at least show the identity of *naming* to the extent illustrated in the Kaffir (Xosa and Zulu) and Egyptian :—

KAFFIR.	EGYPTIAN.
ANGA (X.), to kiss ; ANGCO (X.), a sweetheart.	ANKH, to pair, couple, clasp, squeeze.
AWU (X. & Z.), interjection, expressing admiration, *how* great !	UAH, very much, how great !
AYA (X. & Z.) denotes future time.	AU, future time, to be.
AZI (X.), a cow.	AS, or HESI, a cow, the Heifer-goddess.
AZI (X. & Z.), a wise man, man of great intelligence.	ASI, august, venerable, great, noble.
BA (X.), to be.	BA, to be, to be a soul.
BABA (X.), my father.	PÂ, the male ; PÂ-PÂ, to produce ; PEPE, to engender.
BABA (X.), to flutter the wings as a bird.	PEPE, to fly.

[1] *Freeman*, Baptist Newspaper, May 3, 1878.

KAFFIR.

BADA (X.), a plunderer, a robber.
BAKABAKA (X. & Z.), the firmament above.
BALI (X. & Z.), one who reckons ; BALO (X. & Z.), a reckoning, a number.
BAXA (X. & Z.), a fork in the branch of a tree, or a river where two branches meet.
BEBA (X.), to bleat like a he-goat.
BEDU (X.), a ring.
BEFU-BEFU (X.), hard breathing.
BEKA (X. & Z.), to pay respect and to honour.
BEKA (X. & Z.), to set down.
BEQE (Z.), war ornament, a strip of some wild animal's skin.

BI (X. & Z.), badness, vileness, evil, wickedness.
BILA (X. & Z.), to boil as water, effervesce, ferment.
BOBO (X.), a round, corpulent person, a hole.
BUTO (X. & Z.), a company of people, soldiers, or cattle.
BUXA (X.), to sink, as in a bog.
CASA (X.), to break, crush, smash.
CIBI (X. & Z.), a lake, pond, sheet of water.
CIMA (X. & Z.), to extinguish.
COFA (X.), to feel, press, or squeeze with the hand.
COPO (Z.), a corner.
CULA (X.), to sing.
DA (X.), a limit of land or country.
DALA (X. and Z.), old, as old time.
DALI (X.), one who creates or originates.
DALO (X.), an idol.
DEBE (X.), a person who is tattooed in the face.
DEBE (X. and Z.), a drinking cup or bowl.
DIDI (X.), rows, as of stones set up.
DODO (X. & Z.), a man, manhood, vir.
DUKA (X.), lost to view, hidden.
DUMO (X.), fame.
DUNA (X. & Z.), person in authority, a leader, the bull.
EWA (X.), hermaphrodite.
EWE (X.), yes, certainly.
FAKA (X.), the cow is said to "faka" when making udder and filling it with milk.
FANTA (X.), a cleft, fissure, as in a rock.
FEBE (Z.), a fornicator.
FENE (X. & Z.), a baboon.
FEZI (Z.), Cobra species of snake.
FUBA (X. & Z.), the bosom, as organ of breath.
FUNGA (X. & Z.), to take an oath, to swear.
GABU (X.), to part in two.
GADA (X.), cat.
GAGU (X. & Z.), a bold, fearless man.
GALO (Z.), a bracelet.
GAU (Z.), curve, bend, turn.
GEGE (Z.), gluttony.
GEXA (X.), to sway to and fro.
GEXO (Z.), a string of beads.

GIBE (X. & Z.), a snare for game.
GQOTE (X.), speed, go.
GUMBE (X.), a recess, inner chamber.

EGYPTIAN.

BAT, bad, infamous, evil, criminal.
BAAKABAKA, topsy turvy.
PER, to show, explain, a time-reckoning.

PEKA, to divide in two.

BA, the he-goat.
PETU, a circle.
PEF, to puff, breathe hard.
BEKA, to bend and pray.

BEKA, set or sit down, to squat.
BES, skin of beast, amulet for protection ; PEK, magic ; PEKH, the lioness, kind of dress.
BUIA, infamous, wicked, hateful, bad.

BER, to boil, rise up, ebullition.

BEB, to be round, a hole.

PUTU, a company of the gods.

BEKA, to sink down, be depressed.
KHES, to ram, pound, crush.
KABH, water, libation, inundation.

ÂKHEM, to extinguish.
KEFA, the hand, to lay hold, seize with the hand ; KUA, to tighten, to compress.
KEB, a corner.
KHER, to say, speak, cry, utter.
TA, land, soil, country.
TER, time.
TER, to engender, make, fabricate.
TERU, a drawing, a picture.
TEB, to seal, be clean, be responsible for.

TEBU, anything to drink out of, a jug or jar.
TAT, to set up, to establish.
TUT, engenderer, procreator, father.
TEKA, escape notice.
TEMA, to announce.
TEN, to conduct, lead ; TENNUI or TEHANI, the conductor.
IU, dual, twin.
IA, yes, certainly.
FEKA, fulness, abundance, reward.

PANT, the mythical pool.
PEPE, to engender.
BEN and ÂAN, an ape.
PESHU, to sting and bite.
PEF, breath.

ANKHU, an oath, a covenant.
KAB, to double.
KHAI, a cat, T is the fem. terminal.
KAKA, to boast.
KER, circle, zone, go round.
KAHU, corner, angle, turn.
KAKA, to eat, devour.
KHEKH, balance, move to and fro.
KHEKH, a collar ; KHAKRI, a kind of necklace.
KHABU, a cord or noose ; KEF, hunt, seize.
KHET, go.
KHEM, a shrine, a shut place.

KAFFIR.	EGYPTIAN.
HADE (X.), a pit.	AAT, the Hades, the pit.
HANGA (Z.), a strong, brave man.	ANK, I, the king of men.
HLONI (X. & Z.), not to name.	REN, to name; NU, not, no, without.
INYE (X.), one.	UN, one.
KABA (X. & Z.), the navel.	KHEPA, the navel.
KABA (X.), an ear of wheat.	KHEPI, harvest.
KALA (X. & Z.), a crab.	KRA, claw.
KALO (Z.), a loud cry.	KHER, cry.
KAPI (X. & Z.), a guide.	KAPI or AP, the guide.
KAWU (X. & Z.), a species of monkey.	KAF or KAU, a monkey.
KITA (Z.), to take by force, plunder.	KHET-KHET, to attack and overthrow.
KONDE (Z.), a large monkey.	KANT, a large long-tailed monkey.
KONYANA (X. & Z.), the young of animals.	KHENNU, the child, the young one.
KOVA (Z.), to sit on the haunches like a dog.	KEFA, the hinder part; HEFA, to squat.
KUBA (X. & Z.), a hoe, a pick.	KHEB, hoe or plough.
KUBA (X. & Z.), to dig.	HAPI (earlier Kapi), called the digger.
KUBA-BULONGO (X.), a large beetle that burrows in manure.	KHEP, the beetle that covers its eggs with dung.
KUBI (X. & Z.), evil.	KHEFT, evil.
KULUMO (X. & Z.), speech.	KHERU, speech.
KWEPA (Z.), strength.	KEFA, force, puissance, might.
KWETA (X. & Z.), a circumcised lad set apart in a separate abode.	KHET, to seal and shut up; KHATI, cut.
LIFA (X.), an inheritance.	REPA, the heir-apparent.
LISA (Z.), one who gives joy and pleasure.	RESH, joy.
MA (X. & Z.), my mother.	MA, mother.
MAME (Z.), my mother.	MAMA, to bear, as the mother.
MANA (X.), to continue, persistently.	MEN, to be fixed, be firm.
MAWO (X.), exclamation of wonder and surprise.	MAHU, wonder.
MEMEKA (X.), to carry a child.	MAMA, to bear a child.
MENZI (X.), the Creator.	MENKHA, to create.
MINXA (X.), to hold fast by pressure, as a substance between the hands.	MENKHA, pottery, to create, form, fabricate.
MISA (X. & Z.), to cause to stand, set up, establish.	MES, to engender, generation; MEST, the sole of the foot.
MITA (X. & Z.), to become pregnant.	MUT, the pregnant mother.
MONDE (Z.), patience, endurance, long-suffering, steadfast.	MEN, to remain firm and fixed, constantly.
MOYA (X. & Z.), wind, air, breath, spirit.	MÂ, wind, vapour, breath, spirit.
MUNYA or MUNCA (X. & Z.), to suck as a child at the breast.	MENKA, nurse, child-suckling.
NA (X. & Z.), to rain.	NA, water, to descend.
NAKA (X.), to empower a person to do a difficult thing.	NAKA, power, be powerful.
NAMA (X.), to adhere, stick together.	NAM, to join, accompany, go together.
NANYE (X.), none, not one.	NEN, no, not, none.
NCA (X.), to stick to, adhere together.	ANK, pair, clasp, squeeze, covenant.
NOBA (X.), denotes all.	NEB, all.
NTÚ (X. & Z.), human beings, persons, relating to human kind.	NET, being, existing; NET-SEN, they.
NUKA (X. & Z.), to smell.	ANKH, nosegay, living flowers.
NXIBA (X.), to tie, bind, put on, to dress.	UNKH, strap, dress, put on, bind on.
ODWA (X. & Z), alone, only.	UTA, alone, solitary.
OKA (Z.), to search by fire.	AKHA, fire.
PEFU (X.), breath.	PEFU, breath.
PEKI (X. & Z.), a cook.	PES or PEKH, to cook.
PEPO (X.), a gentle breeze, a light gust.	PAIF, wind, gust.
PETA (X.), a bow.	PUT, a bow.
PETA (X. & Z), to bind round, make a hem, rim, or border.	PUT, a circle.
PUPUMA (X. & Z.), to well and bubble up, to overflow.	BEB, to swell up, bubble, and exhale; BABA, to flow.
PUTA (X. & Z.), to fail and die away.	FET, to fail; FETK, to exterminate.
QABANA (X.), to form companionship, fraternize.	KABT, a family.
QADI (X. & Z.), the chief beam of a house or roof.	KAUTI, to build; KAT, built.

KAFFIR.	EGYPTIAN.
QAMBA (Z.), to invent and devise.	KEM, to invent, discover.
QELE (Z.), a circlet.	KER, zone, circle.
QOMA (X.), to serve up meat in the native manner.	KAMH, joint of meat.
QOQOQO (X. & Z.), windpipe.	KHEKH, windpipe, throat, gullet.
QUBU (X. & Z.), swelling, any protuberance of body.	KAB, increase; KHEB, give birth to, be pregnant, the Great Mother.
QULA (X.), a well of water.	KARAA, lake, pond, or welling water.
RAUZA (Z.), to exalt.	RES, to raise up.
RWI (X.), to go rapidly, as a shooting star.	RAAU, swift-going, come near.
SA or SO (X.), to dawn, morning.	SU, day.
SANUSE (X. & Z.), an enchanter, a sorcerer, one who supplies charms.	SAN, to charm; SHANNU, a diviner.
SATYANA (X. & Z.), little children.	SET, the child.
SENGA (X. & Z.), to milk a cow or any other animal.	SENKA, to suck and suckle.
SINDISI (X.), a saviour; SINDISO (X. & Z.), salvation.	SAN, to save.
SITA (X. & Z.), to shade.	SHUT, shade.
SONTA (Z.), to twist a rope, to spin a cord.	SENTA, to found (determinative, a twisted rope).
SU (X. & Z.), belly, womb.	SA, belly.
SUMO (X.), fable, fairy tale, myth.	SEM, myths.
TA (X. & Z.), corn.	TA, corn.
TABA (X. & Z.), mountain.	TEB, the hill, top, height.
TATI (X. & Z.), a very durable wood.	TETA, eternal.
TEBE (Z.), fat of animals.	TEP, fat.
TETA (X.), to speak, utter, speech, be the speaker; TETI (X.), a speaker.	TET, to speak, speech, tongue, utterance, the speaker personified.
TEZA (X.), to gather and bind wood up into faggots to carry on the head.	TES, to tie up, coil round, a tied-up roll, elevate, transport.
THAWE (X.), one of high birth.	TA, throne, chief; TATA, princes, heads, ministers.
TIXO (X.), god.	TEKH, name of a god.
TOVOTI (Z.), temples of the head.	TEB, temples of the head.
TSHA (X. & Z.), new, youth, freshness, applied to the new moon, new year, &c.	SHA denotes all forms of the first, the new, commencement.
TSHABA (X. & Z.), an enemy, desolator, destroyer.	SHEFI, terror, terrifying, demonial, malevolent.
TSOMI (X.), fable, fiction.	SAM, myth, similitude.
TUMU-TUMU (Z.), a large assemblage of huts.	TEMA, a village, city, district.
TUPA (X. & Z.), the thumb.	TEBAU, the fingers.
TUTA (X. & Z.), to carry.	TUT, to carry.
TUTA (X.) an ancestral spirit.	TUT, image of the dead.
UWA, hermaphrodite.	IU, of a dual nature.
VATO (X. & Z.), dress, cover, clothing.	UAT, colouring matter, plants, rags, wraps.
XATULA (X.), to make marks or prints.	KHETU, seal-ring.
XEGA (Z.), be infirm and declining; XEGO (X.), the feebleness of old age, the old man.	KEH-KEH, the old man bent with age.

These words have been quoted without the prefixes that denote the parts of speech to which the words belong in forming the Xosa language. The words are the same in Egyptian where the Kaffir prefixes have been shed, and the language has been constructed on other lines of development. Here we find in the Click stage of language that speech and the personified speaker are the same by name as on the monuments, where Taht has become a mythological divinity, the male moon-god. The magistrate and advocate are there under the same names. The very durable tree, Tata, the sneezewood of the colonists, has the identical title of the Egyptian Eternal. Tuta, the genius, and the ancestral spirit are represented by the mummy image or genius, called the Tutu. Tut (Eg.) signifies to unite, to engender, to establish a covenant; and TATANA (X. K.), to establish a covenant, take one another according to a sacred rite, as in marriage. Lastly, the root of all these variants is expressed by a "T-T," the very sound assigned to the Kaf Cynocephalus as his especial contribution to the language of Clicks. He is the Clicking Kaf, who preceded the Clicking Kaffir, and on the Egyptian monuments he is a type of Taht and An, both of whom represent speech, to speak, and the speaker in person.

This illustrates one of two things; either these words went back from the Egyptian stage to take on the prefixes and include the Clicks, or else the Egyptian has shed both Clicks and prefixes. No evolutionist can doubt that the Clicks denote the earlier stage of language; and the inference is inevitable that the language in which the speaker has risen from the type of the Kaf monkey to the status of a god; the ancestral spirit is typified by the mummy figure, and TAHT has become the divine advocate and saviour, must have advanced from the Kaffir condition. Other instances of this visible development abound. "XOXA" denotes a general and confused conversation, talking together, Kaffir conversation. XOXA is the name of the frog, which, says W. Davis,[1] is onomatopoetic, and refers to the sound of "XO-XO," as that which represents the confused noise of many persons speaking all at once. In the Click condition of language, ONOMATOPOIEIA has a real meaning, and in such sounds as "XO-XO," or "KA-KA," the frog undoubtedly may have named itself. In Egyptian, "Ka-Ka" denotes calling and crying as do the frogs. In Basunde, the frog's "XO-XO" becomes "HUKU," as the name of the frog. In Egypt the frog has attained the status of Mistress HUKU (or Heka), the frog-headed goddess, consort of Num, the lord of the Inundation and king of frogs. HUKU and Huka are modified forms of XO-XO or KA-KA. UKA wears down to KÂ, for the frog's name; and KÂ means to cry, call, say. The frog was the caller and crier, and the self-given name was adopted as a type-word for saying and conversing, especially of manifold and therefore frog-like conversation.

It may be noticed, in passing, that the Sanskrit name of the frog, BHEKA, is the Egyptian HEKA, with a prefix answering to the Egyptian article The. Thus Bheka in the one language is *the* Heka from the other. In a Sanskrit story, Bheki, the frog, became a beautiful girl, and one day she was discovered by the king sitting beside the well. He asked her to marry him. She consented; but warned him against his ever letting her see a drop of water. The king promised that she never should. But one day, when thirsty, she asked the king for some, and he, forgetful of the conditions, gave her water to drink; whereupon Bheki disappeared. Egypt will tell

---

[1] *Dictionary of the Kaffir Language*, p. 246.

us who the king was, for a title of Num is "King of Frogs." His consort was HEKA, or, as *the* frog, P-HEKA. The frog was a type of transformation, as the water-born and breather on the land. Num, king of the frogs, has two characters : in one, as Khnef, he is lord of breath in the firmament above. In the other, as Num, he is lord of the waters. Heka was his mistress in the deep, his water domain. Out of the waters HEKA changed characters with the beautiful Seti, the Sunbeam. In that phase the king found her sitting beside the well. But when Khnef-Ra (the sun) goes down his consort is HEKA, the frog, because of the passage of the waters in the north by night, and the beautiful Seti, wearer of the white crown, disappears as the frog in the deep.[1] This will explain how it is that the story of Bheki, the sun-frog which squats on the·water, has been found in Africa, among the natives of Natal.

The evidence of faeryology tends to show that the frog was a lunar type. In a Russian story the fairy bride of the Prince Ivan is a frog that transforms into a lovely woman. When the prince finds her frog-skin empty he burns it. His wife on coming back from the ball seeks for it in vain. "Prince Ivan," she cries, "thou hast not waited long enough. Farewell! Seek me beyond twenty-seven lands in the thirtieth kingdom." The numbers identify the luni-solar myth. Twenty-seven is the proper number of days during which the moon was reckoned visible, and the three days before it rose again completed the luni-solar month of thirty days, and there is a new conjunction of the sun and moon. In another version the burning of the frog-skin is followed by the flight of the Beauty,·who has to be sought for "beyond *thrice nine lands* in the *thrice tenth kingdom*, in the home of Koshchei the deathless."

In another Russian variant of the story the princess whose fairy skin has been destroyed, has to be sought in the seventh kingdom. That is, the one beyond the six periods of five days each, into which the luni-solar month was divided. The seventh would be the first stage of another new moon. A Turkish story describes the beautiful woman who becomes a frog, and says her "face when she looked *that* way was like the moon, when she looked *this* way it was like the sun," showing the imagery to be luni-solar, or the exact representation of Num's two consorts who are interchangeable as Heka the frog-headed, and Seti, the sunbeam ; the one being his wife by day : the other by night.

In the Zulu tale the frog is represented as swallowing the princess to carry her safely home,[2] which agrees with the transformation into the frog, or Seti passing into Heka as the consort of Num in the waters. But we must identify a few more of the African "roots" which were developed in Egypt, and are scattered throughout the world.

---

[1] *Chips*, Max Müller, v. ii. 251.   [2] Callaway, *Zulu Tales*, p. 241.

The NAM in the African Kiamba is a goat. In Egypt the goat-headed god is NUM. Nome, in Bidsogo, is a serpent, and Num the divinity wears the serpent as one of his types. Num represents the sun of the waters, one of whose types was the crocodile; and in Dsuku, the alligator is Nime. The monkey, which is named KEFU in Krebo, KEBE in Kra, and EFIE in the Anfue language, is KAFI in Egyptian as the cynocephalic type of the god Shu, and the later HAPI a Geni of the four quarters.

NEBO, in Ekamtulufu is heaven. In Egyptian, Nupe is the lady of heaven, or heaven depicted in the female form, the typical heaven that supplied the drink of life as Nupe, and the breath as Neft. The EFAM is a cow in Akurakura, and in Egyptian AFAM is the beast, but the original beast is the Water-cow or hippopotamus, Khebma, who is a goddess in Egypt and a divine type. The Sun in Gafat is named CHEBER, and in Egyptian, KHEPR is the Beetle-headed solar god.

KER (Eg.) is the claw, and KER-KER means to seize, embrace, lay hold, especially to seize with the claw; Ker-Ker is literally to claw with the claw, or claw-claw. This expresses what the scorpion does; and the scorpion is named Kere-Kere in Eki and Owaro; KIRE-KIRE in Yagba; AKAR-KERE, Dsebu, Ife, Egba, and Ota; AKEKERE, Idsesa; IKEKURU, Okuloma; KEKIRE, Hwida and Basa; WAKURE, Padsade; GREASWE, Dewoi; KELE-KELE, Dsumu; KIALEA, Kiamba; KULIS, Timne and Bulom; YARE in the Pulo group, and KAL, KEL, WUR, and EL in other dialect forms. The scorpion goddess, who seizes and holds the Apophis serpent, is named Serka, worn down from Kerka, and the full form is only found in the Ker-Ker of the scorpion which seizes with its fore-claws and stings with the hinder one, and was consequently named KERE-KERE or Claw-Claw.

Here are five divinities, NUM, SHU, KHEBM, KHEPR, and SERK, identified with their types by name in inner Africa.

The bee is KEME in Baga and other African dialects. In Egypt it is made an ideograph of KAM and Kheb. The boy or son is designated TOBO in Udso; DIUBE in Kru, and DEVI in Adampe. HE is named after Tef, Tep, or Typhon, the old first mother before the fatherhood was known. This fact is distinguished in Egyptian where TEFU has become the name for an orphan or the fatherless child. When the father is individualized it is as the Atef, and this name is assigned to the double crown of the fatherhood.

TUT, in Egyptian, is the male member; TUT is the engenderer, procreator, or father; and Tata is a type-name for the father in some thirty or forty other African languages. This Tut was a type of the Eternal as the re-erector and establisher of the mummy. PAPA (Eg.), to produce, supplies forty languages with the name of the father, as Papa or Baba.[1] The producer under this name, as before shown, was originally the mother, the breather and quickener of life.

[1] Chiefly found in the *Polyglotta Africana*, Koelle.

BUKEEM, in Bola, is the palm-tree, the plural being MUNKEEM; BUKIAM in Sarar, with the plural MUNKIAM; BEKIAME in Pepel, with the plural MENKIAM. Now BUK is the Egyptian name for palm-wine; and MENKAM is some kind or *quantity* of wine.[1] Am (Eg.) means the tree, to give, or find; and BUK-AM would denote the tree which yielded the palm-wine, called the toddy-palm. BUK (Eg.) is to fecundate, engender, inspirit, and as such it passed into the name of Bacchus, for the spirit of fermentation and wine.

In the African Gbe language Fire is NASURU; and in Egyptian NASRU is not only Fire and Flame, the word becomes the type-name for the fiery Phlegethon of the Hades, where the consuming Sun of a land which had a soil of fire and a breath of flame, first suggested a hell of heat in that region of the underworld in which the Black Sun (later Red Sun) first impersonated the great Judge of the dead.

The star in Hebrew is KOKAB; Arabic, KAUKAB; Egyptian, KHABSU. But these are abraded forms of a duplicated KAB. Seb is a star; this was the earlier Kheb or Khab. Khab also signifies shade or eclipse, and this is determined by the star. Thus shade and star are both KHAB; these being the two truths of night—the light-and-shade—which are also illustrated by the feather of Shu (light-and-shade). The star then is KABKAB as the light in the dark, and in the African MAHARI, KAB-KOB is the name of the star; this is the duplicated form in full.

In Egyptian MÂ is a type-name for the beast. The accented â (eagle sign) is a worn-down FA, so that the word is really "MFA," and this recovers an African type-name of the beast or animal. The goat is named MFI in Nalu; MVI in Param and Bamom; MBI, Isoama; MPI, Pati; MPIE, Abadsa; MBOM, Orungu. The cow is MFAU in Papiah; MFON, Udomi; MFOU, Eafen, Pati, Kum, Bagba, Bamom, Param, Bayon, Mbofon, and Ekamtulufu; MPON, in Nki, Mfut and Konguan. The MBAME in Wolof is the hog; the MUPUN in Tumu, a ram. "The Beast" was a type-name before the animal was otherwise distinguished, and in many African languages the typical beast is the dog, which is MUMVO in Papiah; MVO, Param; MFO, Dsarawa; MVI, Tuma; MFA, Murundo; MFA, Babuma; MPFA, Ntere; MBUE, Baseki; MPUA, Melon; MPOA, Nhalmoe; MBOA, Muntu and Kisama; OMBUA, Pangela; MBOA, Basunde, Nyombe, Kasands, Ngoten, Kabenda, Mimbosa, Bumbete; and MU in Konguan. The typical beast appears under this name as MMAFT or MAFT, the lynx, with the determinative of Sut-Typhon. Also, with the lion as determinative, and in the worn-down form MAAU or MAU, the name is chiefly applied to the lion, leopard, panther, or cat, the ideographs of Shu and Tefnut or Pasht. The Dog, and Baba, the beast (the hippo-potamus), were to a great extent superseded, these being the images of Sut-Typhon, and of the chaos which preceded the lifting of the

---

[1] *Denk.* ii. 129.

firmament by Shu, and the migration from the celestial Egypt. The older the types, the more do they become inner African. This MF was almost worn out in Egyptian, but survived in the Hebrew מ, and here it is in full force. Not only with one M, for the goat also in N'goala is MOMFU; MAMPI in Pati, and MEMBI in Bagba, where we find the double M expressed by the sound of MIM for M, which is still apparent in the hieroglyphic MM or M for with; M·M having been the ideographic value. Thus we find that MMÂU,[1] the beast, is an earlier form of Mâ, and with the F instead of the accented Â, this is identical with the N'goala MOMFU, and Pati MAMPI. The ideographic MM which preceded the phonetic M is extant in the Welsh MAM for the mother, and in the African Darrunga MIMI for the woman, Malemba and Embomma MAMA, for the mother. In Egyptian the mother is MU, and may be expressed by the phonetic M which was the earlier MIM. The Hebrew names of letters like MIM and NUN are ideographic; this the hieroglyphics prove, and these inner African words are likewise in the ideographic stage.[2] The working of the principle of repetition is not limited to the reduplication of the *same* sounds. KAF, for example, the hand, deposits KÂ, FÂ, and Â; fâ and â also signifying the hand. This accounts for the interchange of GH and F in English; both of which meet in the one word "LAUGHTER," where the GH has the F sound. The ideographs take the student into a domain of derivation never yet penetrated, not only by the current school of philologists, but by any writer on language. The Sisterhood, so to say, of Egyptian, Akkadian, Maori, Hebrew, and English may no longer be seen in syntax or grammar, or be traceable by means of Grimm's Law, and yet the common African Motherhood may be visible in what is here termed the typology.

MANKA is the type-name for woman, in Udom, Mbofon, and Ekamtulufu; MUKA, Wakamba; MOKAS, Babuma; MOKAS, Ntere; MACHA, Gonga; MACHOA, Woratta; MUKETU, Kasange; MANYI, in Makua, and MEYA, Nda. In Egyptian MENKAT, MÂKA, MENKA, and MENA are the equivalent names for the typical nurse, the wet-nurse of the child, the lady of the vases and therefore the vase-maker, the potteress and creatoress of many mythologies. The name of the Irish MACHA—Akkadian Nin-MUK; Sanskrit and Greek MAYA, and Egyptian MENÂ and MÂ—simply denotes the Woman in

---

[1] Birch, *Dict.* p. 424.

[2] Here is another example of the ideographic stage passing into the phonetic. The hieroglyphic sign of the Inundation is both a KHENT and a FENT. The Finns call themselves QVAINS, and this name modifies into QUAINS and FINNS, because the ideographic KF deposits a phonetic K and F. So the APE is KAFI (Eg.), and ÂAN from an original KFN which will answer for KAF, KAN, FAN, PAN, BAN, ÂAN, and AN, including the types of Sut, Shu, Pan, and the lunar An. This primate is found in KÂFTEN (Eg.), for the monkey. The KAFTENS, KAFNS, or QVAINS are those who derive from the female KAF (KAFT), the ape-type of the ancient genitrix, known to the Finns as KIVUTAR, Egyptian KHEPT, and British KÊD.

the Kaffir languages of the Gabun. These are what the present
writer looks upon as the Egyptian roots in Africa beyond, where we
can trace by name the natural origines of the types which became
symbolical in the hieroglyphics.

To denote the mother, says Hor-Apollo, the Egyptians delineate
a Vulture, and they signify the mother by it, because in this race of
creatures there is no male. *Gignuntur autem hunc in modum. Cum
amore concipiendi vultur exarserit, vulvam ad Boream aperiens, ab eo
velut comprimitur per dies quinque,* during which time she partakes
neither of food nor drink, being too intent upon procreation.[1] Which
means that the vulture, the hieroglyphic type of Maternity, royal or
divine, was the symbol of the genitrix as the virgin mother, from
whom men reckoned their descent in the early times as the sole
progenitor. This representation was imitated in the Egyptian tombs
by the small aperture opening towards the north, from whence, according to African ideas, came the breath of life which re-begot the
god or soul in the womb of the tomb for the second life. The name
of the vulture, in addition to its denoting MU, the mother, is NARAU.
This is extant in the English NORIE, to nourish or nurse; Maori
NGARE, for the family and blood relations; Hebrew נער for the
young and to bear; Albanian, NIERI; Zend, NÂIRI, and Sanskrit,
NARI; INOR (Peel River, Australia), INAR (Wiradurei), and INUR
(Wellington), for the woman. This is the type-word for the name of
woman in various groups of African languages, as NYORU in Adampi;
NYIRE in Grebo; NYIRO in Gbe; NYERO in Dewoi; NGEREM, Budu-
mah; UNALI, Biafada. The Yoruba ALO for woman probably shows
an abraded form, as in the Kouri dialects, Kaure and Legba, NYORO
means the head, and woman was not only the first head, but the
NARAU (Eg.), vulture, is also represented by the sign of the vulture's
head. ALO is the woman, and ABALO the man; the plural for a
Kouri population being Nebalo, and Neb (Eg.) means all, composed
of both sexes.

Here we find the hieroglyphic type, the ideograph of the motherhood, both royal and divine in Egypt, which has gone to the other
side of the world, extant by name in Upper Africa as the type-name
for Woman.

In Wolof and Galla, DUG signifies the truth; in Egyptian TEKH is
the moon-god, the measurer, calculator, and reckoner of truth,
and the Tekh is the needle of the balance of truth. One of the
hieroglyphic M's or Em's is the sickle, the sign of cutting. From
this may be traced the Welsh AMAETH, for the husband-man;
English MATH, a mowing; the Latin EMETO, to reap, and Greek
AMETOS, a reaping. This has the earlier form of HAMTU, the
sickle, in the Galla language, and EMATA in Meto; OMATA in
Matatan, for the farm. MA-AUT (Eg.) is the stalk, and the word

[1] B. i. 12.

contains the meaning of that which is cut with the sickle. Still earlier KAMADI (Galla) denotes corn, grain, wheat. AMT (Eg.), the abraded KAMADI, is a name for food, and a peculiar kind of bread, called AMTMU, or food of the dead.

The MAZIKO in the African Swahili is a burial-place. In Egyptian the MESKA, founded on the tomb, was the eschatological place of re-birth for the mummied dead.

Such "types," whether in words, customs, things, or personifications, are the root-matters and objects of the present quest. For example, in a paper recently read on the "different stages in the development of music in prehistoric times," the author, Mr. Rowbotham, showed that although the varieties of musical instruments might be countless, yet they are all reducible under three distinct types: 1. The drum type; 2. The pipe type; 3. The lyre type. And these three types are representative of three distinct stages of development through which prehistoric music passed. Moreover, the stages occur in the order named; that is to say, the first stage in the development of instrumental music was the drum stage, in which drums and drums alone were used by men; the second stage was the pipe stage, in which pipes as well as drums were used; the third stage was the lyre stage, in which stringed instruments were added to the stock. The three stages answer respectively to rhythm, melody, and harmony. And as in the geological history of the globe the chalk is never found below the oolite nor the oolite below the coal, so in the musical history of mankind the lyre stage is never found to precede the pipe stage, nor the pipe stage to precede the drum stage. Now the drum in Egyptian is TEB, and the TUPAR is a tabor or tambourine. TUP means first; AR, to make, and Tupar reads in accordance with facts, the first made; the primary type. The drum then bears the name of the genitrix TEF, Tep, or Typhon, who in her secondary phase carried the tambourine as Hathor. The son of Typhon, Sut, Suti or Sebti (in full) gives the name to the oblique flute, named the SEBT and the MMU. This MMU and SEK to play upon, yields the name for music, thus identified with playing the flute. Sebti or Suti (5+2) has the value of number seven, and the octave really consists of seven notes, the eighth being a repetition of the first. Now the races of Central Africa include all three of these musical types beyond which music has not yet gone. The primitive original of the Egyptian harp to be seen in the Harpers' or Bruce's tomb, is extant as the guitar of Uganda.[1] This process of identifying the African origines with Egypt as their supreme interpreter might be continued until volumes were filled. But we have not yet done with "words."

The following list, which does not contain one-half of my own collection, is taken from various African dialects on the authority of Koelle, Bleek, Norris, Tuckey, Burton, and others.

[1] See fig. 9, vol. i. p. 413, of *Through the Dark Continent.*

GENERAL.   EGYPTIAN.

ABAN (Fanti), a fort. — ABN, a wall, a fortress.

ABOAUN (Asante), doorway; OPUN (Fanti), a door. — UBAN, opening of heaven or of Neith at sunrise.

ACHARA, (Ibu), hay. — KHERSH, truss of hay.

AFA (Doai, N'godsin); IPEHE (Puka), sun; AFA (Yasgua), God. — AF, the sun of the underworld.

AFAHE (Fanti), a feast. — AFA, to be filled, satisfied; AB, a feast.

AGUBA (Biafada), war. — UKP, destruction.

AGWE (Ako), a field. — UAKH, a meadow; AKHA, green, verdure.

AHOM (Ibu), skin. — AM, skin.

AMATE (Galla), embrace. — AMAT, pet.

AME (Bambarra), to understand; HIME (Galla), to interpret; HHAMA (Wolof), to know. — AM or KEM, to find, discover, interpret, be an expert.

APATA (Mbofia), the thigh. — KHEPT, hinder thigh.

ARAHA (Bulanda), EURE (Akui and Egba), ERU (Isoama), ERI (Abadsa), ERE (Aro), OKIRI (Mbofia), goat. — KAARI and AUR, goat.

ARIA (Swahili), a following or faction; HERREA (Galla), an associate. — ARI, companions.

ASHIRI (Fanti), beads. — ASHR, tree of life, with seed-pod.

ASIGE (Anfue), an earring; ASIKA (Puka), chain-fetters; ZAKA (Basunde), bracelet. — USKH, a jewelled collar; SHAKA, earring.

ATA (Adampe), ITA (Yagba and Idsesa), ITAA (Aku), ITO (Yoruba), ETI (Dsumu and Egba), ETA (Anfue), the thighs. — AAT, an abraded form of Khept, the hinder thigh.

ATAH (Boritsu) ATUA (Asante), KETE (Landoro), oats; KETEI (Gbandi), guinea corn. — KHAT, a crop; ATT, grain.

ATATI (Yau), father; TATA or TUTU (Nyamwezi), father. — ATTA, father, priest; TUT, the engenderer.

BAERI (Goburu), oats. — PER, grain

BASA (Z. Kaf.), to kindle as fire. — BESA, warmth, candle, jet, blaze, dilate.

BASO (Z. Kaf.), woman's word for fire.

BES (Dsarawa), fire.

BESI (Toronka, Mandingo, Dsalunka, Kankanka), a charm, talisman, or gree-gree; SE (Mano), a gree-gree or charm; SAIA (N'godsin), earring; ZA (Boko), a bracelet. — BESA, an amulet, protection; SA, collar; SA, an amulet or charm.

BIR (Fanti), pluck. — BER, to boil up, be ebullient.

BUR (Wolof), a king. — BURU, height of supremacy.

DABA (Baga) Dsalunka, Kankanka, Bambarra) DABO (Mandingo, Kabunga), DEBAO (Diwala), a hoe. — TEF, a hoe.

DAGLA (Galla), cross. — TEK, cross.

DAN (Mandingo, Kabunga, Toronka, Dsalunka, Kankanka, Vei, Kono, Bambarra), No. 10; DON (Afudu), No. 10. — TEN, weight of ten Kat; TEN, sign of two hands; TENT, a tithe.

DEBO (Mfut), heaven; DIOBA (Baseke), heaven; DOBA (Diwala), heaven. — TEP, heaven.

DEVI (Adampe), a boy; TOBO (Udso), a boy, a son; DIUBE (Kru), a child. — TEFN, an orphan.

DIN (Banyun), God; UTEN (Anan), the sun. — ATEN, the youthful sun-god of the disk.

DIPE (Mano), a bull; DUFE (Wolof), fat. — TEPA, a fat ox.

DUG (Wolof), DUGA (Galla), truth. — TEKH, a measurer and reckoner of truth; the needle of the balance of truth.

DUGUM (Bode), DEGEM (N'godsin), DEGAM (Doai), the king. — KHEM, to be master, have power, force, authority. TEKHEM, a god.

DUKU (Ashanti), DUKKO (Galla), a veil. — TEKAU, to hide, see unseen.

DUKU (Galla), flour. — TEKAU, flour.

E (Setshuana), yes; EYI (Yoruba), yes; YE-U (Watutu), yes; OUAA (Yalif), yes. — IA, yes.

EBODA (Bini), gree-gree, or charm; EBOTO (Melon), bracelet; IFOD (Anan), gree-gree. — ABTU, the likeness, with mummy-type.

EFA (N'goala), OVIE (Sobo), a king. — KHEF, a title; AP, head, chief, god.

EFAM (Akurakura), a cow. — AFAM, a beast; KHABM, water-cow.

GENERAL. | EGYPTIAN.

EGODE (Adampe), OGODUE (Anfue), OGODU (Isiele), EKUTA (Wun and Bidsogo), WUKATA (Bola), the loincloth.

KHUT, to enfold and conceal.

EHI (Aro, Ibu, and Isoama), a cow.

AH or AHI, cow.

ENAME (Orungu), ENEME (Ekamtulufu and Mbofon), GEMA (N'godsin), NAMERE (Tiwi), the thigh.

HEM, the seat, hind part, the ham ; NEMTT, legs.

ESE (Hwida), OZI (Koro), OWASE (Murundo), ESO (Kaure), EZE (Mahi), God ; OZAI (Ife), OZOI (Ondo), a fetish image ; ESO (N'ki), ESUI (Alege), UOSI (Kouri), sun.

AS, a statue, the great, august, worshipful.

EYA (Ako), ox.

AUA, steer.

EYO (Ako), EWA (Nupe, Goali, and Ebe), OHUA or IWA (Basa), a serpent.

HEFA, snake, viper, serpent.

FATU (Haussa), a cat ; BOUDE (Malemba), BOODE (Embomma) the cat.

PEHT, or BUTO, cat-headed goddess.

FEDU (Karakare), No. 4. FUDU (Bode, Doai, Haussa, Kano, N'godsin), No. 4. FODU (Kadzina), No. 4.

FETU, No. 4, the four corners or quarters.

FIRA (Galla), family, offspring.

PER, seed.

FURU (Biafada), fire.

AFR, fire.

GALB (Beran and Adirar), a bracelet.

KHERP, a first form, or model figure.

GIFTI (Gallo), a mistress.

KHEFT, great mother.

GIREYO (Mano), greedy.

KER, claw, seize hold.

GLIPO (Bassa), GREPO (Dewoi), God.

KHERP, the first, principal, his majesty.

GUDI (Swahili), dock for ships.

KHET, a port.

GUSEBA (Bode), chain-fetters for the neck.

KES, to envelope with bands.

GWETE (Fanti), silver ; KUDEE (Mandingo), silver.

HUTA, silver.

HANGA (Basunde), chain-fetters ; YINGA (Z. Kaff.), necklace of coloured beads ; INGU (Ako), beads ; KUNK (Dselana), bracelet.

ANK, to clasp ; the ANKH, a noose, tie, cross, and circle.

HART (Adirar, Beran), a farm.

HERT, garden, park, paradise.

HATE (Galla), to steal.

ATU, to rob.

HATTE (Galla), to rob.

ATA, or ATAU, to rob.

HESABU (Swahili), an account, reckoning.

HESB, to reckon, calculate.

HIMAMA (Nyassa), mother.

HEM, the female, woman as mother.

HOLEN (Kisi), the eye.

AR (earlier HAR), the eye.

HU (Wydah), HOU (Buduma), God.

HU, God.

HUKU (Basunde), a frog.

HEKA, frog-headed goddess.

IAH (Pessa), IE (Susu), YA (Gbese), YI (Mano), water.

HI, water ; IA, water, to wash.

IGE (Afudu), fire.

AKH, fire.

IGEN (Akurakura), palm oil.

HEKNU, unguent.

IKUM (Fanti), OKUM (Boritsu), a fetish image.

AKHEM, the mummied hawk.

IRI- (Isiele), YUAR (Penin), IRI (Ibu), KUR (Boritsu), HIRU (Kaure), No. 10.

HAR, No. 10.

KABDO (Galla), pincers, tongs.

KABTI, a pair of arms.

KEASFI (Kadzina), small-pox.

ASF, contamination.

KELEA (M'bamba), an idol divinity.

KHER, divine voice or word.

KEME (Baga), KUMU (Vei), KUMI (Kisekise), the bee.

KAM, Egypt with the Bee ideograph.

KINOO (Swahili), a whetstone.

AN, whetstone.

KIRO (Sagara, Gogo, Nyambu, Ganda), night.

KARH, night.

KITU (Swahili), a thing, a tangible thing.

KHETU, things, a god of things.

KOR (Landoma), KURI (Dewoi), GERRA (Galla), EKURO (Bini), IYARE (Tiwi, Kers, and Beran), the belly.

KAR, the belly or womb of Hades ; KARAS, the belly of earth.

KRISTO (Pepel), an idol or fetish.

KARAST, the mummy type, the embalmed or anointed dead ; Egyptian CHRIST.

KUADE (Banyun), fire.

KHET, fire.

KURA (Haussa), a beast ; ARAI (Banyun), a cow ; HORRI (Galla), cattle.

KHERI, a cow.

LEKI (Galla), rule.

LEKU (REK), rule.

GENERAL.	EGYPTIAN.
LUBIA (Wadai), beans; LIBO (Zulu), produce of the soil.	REPI, a Goddess of Harvest.
MAKURA (Kiriman) cocoa-nut oil.	MAKHERU, the anointed, beatified.
MAMA (Kabongo, Kabinda, and Jiji), mother.	MAMA, to bear; MMU, MU, mother.
MANIA (Meto), an armlet or bracelet; MUEN (Ngoten), an armlet or bracelet; MEIAN (Papiah), an armlet or bracelet; MENU N'Goalá), a nose-ring; MINI (Nalu), an earring.	MENA, collar of the nurse.
MANSO (Kabunga), MANSA (Mandingo, Kono, Dsalunka), king.	SU, royal; MENA, shepherd, driver.
MAS (Kanyika), MOSU (Undaza), MUAZI (Marawi, Mahasi, and Songo), blood.	MAS, to anoint, paint, ink, dye.
Masi (Puka, Haussa, &c.), a spear; MASSI (Fulah), a lance; MESE (Z. Kaff.), a sword.	MASHA, an archer.
MASIWE (Tene), a serpent.	MEISI, a serpent.
MAYU (Nyamwezi), mother.	MEHU or MU, mother.
MAZA (Kongo), water; MAZZI (Kabongo and Kabinda), water; MESI (Yau), MAZA (Bwende), NA-MAZI (Jigi), river.	MES, product or source of a river.
MAZIKO (Swahili), a burial-place.	MESKA, the place of re-birth.
MUSO (Afudu), a king.	MES, a diadem.
NAB (Guresa), rich.	NEB, gold.
NABA (Koama), a bull; NYIBU (Hwida), a cow; NAFO (Mose), a cow.	NUHBU, calves.
NABI (Galla), a prophet.	NUB, Anubis the announcer.
NABU (Toma), fire.	NABUI, fire.
NAM (Kiamba), goat.	NUM, goat-headed god.
NEBO (Ekamtulufu), heaven.	NUPE, the lady of heaven.
NIBA (Kru), a river; NABI (Appa), water.	NEBI, to swim and float; NAM, water.
NOM (Ham), God; NYAMA (Nhalemoe), God; NYAMA (Melon), God; NYAMBE (Diwala), God.	NUM, God.
NUEBE (Mbofia) fetish image.	NEBU, cast or model; NAHP, mould, form.
NYABO (Esitako), NABI (Mutsaya), to seize.	NEHP, to seize.
OFIE (Egbele), beans.	KHEP, beans.
OFOMI (Sobo), UPEM (Bulom), war.	UFA, to chastise and whip.
OHA (Orungu), OWI (Fulup), monarch.	UAU, the one alone, the captain.
OKA (Aku, Ife, Idsesa), oats; OKA (Dsebu, Sobo, Bini, Ihewe, Abadsa), maize.	AKA, grain.
OKA (Ibu), fire; OJA, in Ashanti and Fanti, OKE (Abadsa and Isieli), fire.	ARH, fire.
OKE (Ihewe), OKE (Yagba), YEUKE (Wolof), a bull.	KA, a bull.
OKO (Aku and twenty other dialects), a canoe.	UKKA, the solar bark.
OKU (Ako), the dead.	AKHU, the dead.
ONNUKU (Ako), active; OUNYIKE (Ibu), able.	NAKH, power personified.
OSE (Akurakura), a sacrifice.	AS, a sacrifice.
OSI (Ibu), deceit.	USHA, entrap.
OZIBO (Igu), idol.	KHESBA, lapis lazuli.
PEPE (Orungu), night.	BAB, the void below.
PERE (Landoro, Mende, Gbese), a house.	PAR, a house.
PEREI (Gbandi and Mano), house.	
PERI (Kossa), house.	
PERI (Krebo), beans.	PER, grain.
PILA (Nyamban), oats or kuskus.	
POFU (Z. Kaff., BOBO in others), reddish beads.	BUBU, beads of Isis, and the mummies.
RABE (Wolof), cattle.	REPT, a beast.
RAJA (Ako), to cheat; RAKE (Galla), idle, lazy.	REKAI, culpable, criminal, rebels.
SA (Bambarra), dead.	SA, the mummy-image.
SAGA (Mampo), a sacrifice; SAKE (Kano), a sacrifice; SAYAKA (Toronko), a sacrifice.	SKAU, a sacrifice.

GENERAL.	EGYPTIAN.
SAGUMA (Gura), a house.	SKHEM, a shrine or sacred house.
SAHIGO (Landora), sword; ASAKU (Kambali), spear or assegai.	SEKH, for cutting.
SAKUME (Galla), to embrace.	SKHEN, embrace (cf. the Skhem).
SANTO (Mandingo), heaven.	SHENT, crown of the upper heaven; the zenith.
SATHIE (Wolof), to rob and steal; SEHTEH (Haussa), theft.	SET, to steal.
SAU (Fanti), to dance; SEO (Fulah), to dance; SEWO (Mandingo), joy; ZEZE (Swahili), kind of lute.	SHU and SESHU, the sistrum.
SEFA (Z. Kaff.), to clear the mealie-meal from husks; SAFE (Galla), to polish.	SIF, to refine and purify.
SERA (Galla), order.	SER, order.
SET (Fulah), ZAITE (Galla), oil.	SAT, to grease.
SHARI (Swahili), evil.	KHERI, evil.
SIMO (Nalu), hell; ZUME (Dahome), hell; ZUME (Dsarawa), dense forest.	SAMI, total darkness.
SIRE (Okuloma), the leopard.	SER, a camelopard.
SIRU (Fanti), to laugh.	SHERI, to rejoice.
SOGEI (Kisekise), God; SOKO (Nupe), God; SEAKOA (Puka), God.	SAKH, illuminator, inspiring influence.
SOKOA (Esitako), SOKWO (Nufi), SUGE (Susu), TSOKA (Marawi), DSUKU (Mbofia), God; TSHUKU (Ibu), a god who has two eyes.	
SOM (Bulanda), war.	SAM, to destroy.
SOMAN (Ashanti), a fetish figure.	SEMU, amulet figures; SMEN, to establish the son in place of the father.
SONI (Pika), a bee.	SHEN, honey.
SOR (Bulom), an arrow.	SER, an arrow.
SORU (Ashanti), heaven.	SHARU, the lake of sacred principles in Elysium.
SOSU (Ashanti), a measure.	SESH, a measure.
SU (Fanti), to cry.	SUA, to cry aloud, to sing.
SUSUI (N'goala) and ZUZO (Papiah), cotton and thread.	SHES, flax, linen.
TABA (Galla), to play.	TEF, to dance.
TABA (Z. Kaff.), to rejoice, be delighted.	
TAFFÉ (Susi), father.	TEF, father, divine father.
TAKAWE (Galla), to count.	TEKH, the reckoner.
TETE (Nhalemoe), a king.	TATI, thrones.
TEUBA (Wolof), jump, leap, dance.	TEF, to dance.
TIBU (Swahili), scent.	TEF, fragrance.
TOBA (Salum), TUBA (Timbo), trowsers; TOPA (Yala), TAFARO (Landoma), loincloth; DWABA (Z. Kaff.), skin petticoat.	TEBA, kind of dress, linen, wrap, mystical.
TOGEI (Kisekise and Salum), beans.	TEKA, beans.
TOMU (Gbese), king.	TAM, sceptre.
TORE (Tene), war; THURU (Swahili), to harm.	TAAR, murder.
TSHOMA (Galla), fat; SHAHAMU (Swahili), fat.	SMEH, to anoint.
UDEN (Boritsu), a king.	ATN, to rule, a lord.
UTEN (Anan), the sun.	ATEN, the sun.
UZER (Marike), the sun.	ASAR, sun-god.
WAKA (Haussa), to sing; WAKA (Fulah), a song.	UKA, a festival; KAKA, to rejoice.
ZIA (Bambarra), the soul.	SA, the soul.

In a small Dictionary of the Namaqua Hottentot language,[1] another dialect of the CLICKERS, we have the following words, with the same meanings as in the Egyptian :—

[1] *Hottentot Grammar*, Tyndall, Cape Town, 1857.

NAMAQUA HOTTENTOT.	EGYPTIAN.

A, or EIO, yes.

A, cry, weep.

AMA, true.

AM-XUA, blessed.

AN, to beautify, make a show of one's self.

AUP, man, husband, old one.

CABI, to rain.

CAIGHA, fiery, hot.

CAISIN, to be sick, sick.

CAM-CAM, to finish, come to an end.

CAMO, eternal.

CAUP, blood.

CGURI, to pray.

CHAM, to flog, to whip.

CHUBI, altogether.

CKAM, to be hot.

CKEI, to spread, extend.

CKHIP, the black rhinoceros.

CKHUI, to vomit.

CKHU, to cluster.

CKHUMS, grace, mercy.

CKHURI, to creep.

CKOI, to be a lunatic.

CNAM, to love.

COCO, to staunch a wound.

CUM, to grow, breathe.

CUM-CUM, to breathe into, make live.

DAMA, not.

DAMA-QHUP, Damaraland.

DANA, a chief, head over.

DUBU, to dive, submerge, dip.

EIBI, first.

ELOP, God.

GA, wise.

GAGHA, sly, deceitful.

GAKAS, a spirit.

GAU, to rule.

GHUAS, a writing, scripture.

GHUI, a thing.

HAGUP, a pig.

HORA-HOP, the only begotten.

HUKA, long ago.

HURI, to leap.

IP, likeness, image.

IQU, to commit adultery.

KAMA, crooked.

KAMANAS, loins.

KAN-KAN, to praise.

KEI, great.

KHA, to sink.

KHABOP, a slave.

KHAI, to rise, stand up.

KHAP, war.

KHUAP, a cave.

KURIP, a year.

KURU, to create, make.

LAN, to make known.

MA, which; MA, give.

MA, to stand.

MAGU, to trade.

MA-U, to stand holding.

MU, to see.

IA, yes, certainly.

A, ah, oh, alas.

MA, true, truth.

AMAKHU, to bless.

AN, to beautify, paint the eyes, show.

AU, old one; AP, ancestor.

KEP or KABH, the inundation.

AKHA, fire; KHAKHA, venom, sting.

KHAI, malady.

KHEMA, dead; KHAMUI, let fall, drop, render up.

KAM, to create; KHEM, deity.

KHEP, fluid being, with sign of bleeding.

KHUR, speech, word, voice, call.

KHEM, beat, bruise, crush, prevail.

KAB, double, redouble; KABT, a family.

SHEM, heat, summer.

KHI, to extend, spread rapidly.

KHEP, the hippopotamus.

KHAAKA, to vomit; KHAKHA, man vomiting.

KHEKH, number, reckoning.

KHEM, grace, favour.

KHERI, fallen, on the ground.

KHAKU, mad, lunatic.

NAM, to join together, to engender.

KHEKH, to check, to repel.

KAM, or KAMAMU, to create, form, produce.

TEM, no, not.

TAMA, created persons; KHEP, birthplace.

THANI, elevated over, leader, conductor.

TEB, bend low, dip; TEPHT, abyss, deep.

API, first.

REPA, lord; KHERP, the first, the god.

AAK, Magus, old, wise.

AKHEKH, dragon, gryphon, Typhonian, darkness.

KHEKH, a spirit.

KHU, to rule.

KHÂ, book.

KHI, a thing.

HEKÂU, pig.

HAR, the only begotten.

AKHA, old.

HUR, to ascend.

ABUI, likeness, form, image.

KHUU, sin.

KHAM, to crook in bowing.

KAMAMU, produce, create.

KEN-KEN, to dance; AKEN, adore, salute, praise, and glorify.

KHI, large, vast, extended.

KHA, thrown down on the earth.

KHABÂ, less, inferior, lower.

KHI, to rise up, be born.

KAF, seize by force.

KEP, a sanctuary, retreat, concealed place.

KHERP, a first form, model, figure; KHER, a course.

KHAR, beget.

REN, to name.

MA, like, according to; MA, give.

MA, to place.

MAK, to regulate, balance, scales.

MA, hand holding vase.

MA or MU, to see.

NAMAQUA HOTTENTOT.	EGYPTIAN.
NABA, to shine, lighten.	NABUI, fire; NUB, gold; NAHP, emission of light.
NAM, to talk.	NAM, speech, utterance, discourse, converse, accompany.
NAMS, a tongue.	NAMS, vase with a tongue.
NAUIP, a spark.	NAHP, emit light.
NUI, an oath; NU, to take an oath.	NU, a type, appointed.
OA, to beget.	ÂÂ, beget.
OMI, a house.	AM, pavilion, house; KHEM, house.
ORI-AUP, a saviour, deliverer.	HAR or AR, the Saviour-son.
PIRIKU, the Kaffir tribes. Cf. Peleg (Heb.), Pulug (Ass.), Bolg, Irish, the Belgæ, and Bulgars.	P-REKHU, the people of a district, the RACE.
QABAP, an ascent.	AP-AP, to mount.
QAP, a river.	AP, liquid; KEP, inundation.
QAP, one portion.	KEB, one corner.
QKHAI-QKHAI, to darken.	KAK, darkness, black, night; AKHEKH, darkness.
QKHAM, to fight.	KHEM, to fight.
QKHOU-QKHOU, to madden, enrage.	KHI-KHI, to extend, enlarge, elongate, with rapidity, be quick with arms and steps.
QKHUP, a lord or master.	KHEF, chief.
QKUA, to crack a whip.	KHU, whip.
QNAI, to blow.	KHENA, blow, puff away.
QQAM-QQAM, to humble.	KHAMI, lowly, humble.
QUABAS, rhinoceros.	KHEB, hippopotamus.
QUAGU, opposite to.	KHAKU, stupid, obstinate, madly opposed.
SA, to rest.	SA, seat.
SAP, rest.	SEBA, solace.
SAU, to keep, save.	SAU, preserve, save.
SOMI, a shadow, shade.	SEM, likeness.
SORO, to sow.	SART, to sow seed.
SUBU, light, to lighten.	UBU, sunrise; s, causative prefix.
TOROP, war.	TAAR, murder.
TWA, to end, finish.	TUA, slaughter, kill.
VABA, a burst.	PAIF, wind, gust; PAPA, produce, be delivered of a child.
VKA, to go in, enter.	AKA, to enter; FEKH, to burst open.
XAIP, time.	KEB or SEB, time.
XAN, to dwell, inhabit.	KHEN, be within.
XEIGHA, to be angry.	KHAKHA, mad, obstinate.
XHAS, the womb.	As or HAS, the womb.
XHOU-OMI, a prison.	KHEMI, prison.
XKA, to wrap round the neck.	KHAKRI, kind of necklace.
XKKAI, to chew.	KAKA, to eat.
XKHABA, again.	KAB, double, redouble.
XKHOU, to seize, take captive.	KAHAU, to claw, seize.
XKUA, to dawn.	KHU, light, colour.
XNAM, to embrace.	NAM, to join.
XUM, to sleep.	KHEMA, dead.
ZEP, a day.	SEP, a time, a turn, a day.

The following specimen list is taken from the Makua dialect, one of the Eastern group of the Bantu family of languages: —[1]

MAKUA.	EGYPTIAN.
AHANO, concubine.	KHENNU, concubine.
ATATA, ancestors.	ATTA, father.
EYO, yes.	IA, yes.
IHIPA, a hoe.	HEB, earlier KHEB, a hoe.
IKUKU, Python.	AKHEKH, the Apophis serpent.
IKWIPI, fist.	KEP, fist.
ING'OPE, bull and cattle.	NEKA, bull, steer, cattle.

[1] *Handbook of the Makua Language*, by Chauncy Maples.

MAKUA.	EGYPTIAN.
ING'OTO, reptile.	NEKA, the deluding reptile.
INKALA, crab.	KERA, claw.
IPIPI, darkness.	APAP, to rise up vast as the monster (Akhekh) of the dark.
IPITU, hippopotamus.	KHEPT, hippopotamus.
ITELI, a legend.	TERUU, a papyrus roll.
KANA, young.	HANA, youth.
KEKAI, true, perfect.	KHEKH, balance, mason's level.
KIIMO, no.	KHEMA, no, not.
KUMI, No. 10.	KHEMT, No. 10.
MAHIYE, arrogance.	MAAUI, in the power of.
MAKUWARE, a particular dance.	MAK, dance.
MANYI, mother.	MENÂ, the suckler or wet-nurse.
MIRAO, girl.	MAR.T, a female relationship.
MLUKU, god.	REKHI, a pure intelligence, soul or spirit.
MSHAPWE, monkey.	KAFI or KAPI, a monkey.
MTHATHA, hand.	TAT, the hand.
MTU, man.	MT, the race, the mate.
MTUCHI, shade.	TEKA, hide, escape notice.
MUNO, a water-jar.	MUN, a water-jar or vase.
MAM-KWELI, a widow.	KHARUI, a widow.
NAVATA, twin.	NEB, two, twin.
NETHI, freedom.	NNUTI, escaped, out of.
NETHI, a gentleman.	NU, NUT, NUTER, a divine type.
NIPORU, bubble.	NEF, breath ; URU, water.
NRAMA, check.	REMU, the extent, or limit.
OHEVA, bravery.	KEFA, force, puissance, potency.
ONIOKO, hostility.	NEKA, provoke, be false, criminal ; NAKEN, slaughter.
PAKA, cat.	PEKH, the cat-headed goddess.
TARU, No. 8.	TERUU, a form of No. 8 and name of Sesennu, the region of the Eight Great Gods.
UCHACHA, cross.	KHEKH, the equinox.
UHUVA, woe.	HEB, earlier KEB, wail.
UKAKA, urge.	KHEKH, whip.
UKAKA, to push.	KHEKH, to repulse, repel.
UKOMA, to come to an end and cease.	KHEMA, dead, ended.
UKUMI, health, life.	KHEM, to have power, potency, virile force.
UKUNULA, to unclose, let out.	KHANRU, to scatter.
UKWA, death.	AKH, the dead.
UKWIRI, magic.	HUKA, magic.
ULELA, to nurse, to rear.	RER, to nurse, dandle, and rear.
UNELA, to drive.	NAR, victory, to vanquish.
UNETHI, civilization.	ENTI or NUTI, existence, being.
UNUKA, smell.	ANKHU, a nosegay, living flowers.
UPARA, fire.	AFR, fire.
UPUA, to bud.	APU, to open.
UTAI, far, apart.	UTUI, journey afar, be divorced and apart ; UTAI, solitary, divorced, to go forth.
UTHEPIA, to persuade.	TEP, tongue.
UTHONYA, to guide.	TENNU, to conduct.
UTUKA, tie, fasten, imprison.	TEKA, bind, tie, fix, attach.
UVAVA, jump.	AP-AP, up, up.
VATHE, out, forth.	FET, to disperse ; UT, out, go forth.
VATHI, bottom, floor.	UATI, Lower Egypt, Goddess of the North.
WAFA, secret.	KEPA, secret, hidden.
WETA, to walk, go.	KHET or UTA, to go, journey, expedition.
WIPA, swell.	KEP, fermentation, the inundation.
WUPA, to create, to shape.	KHEP, to create, to figure.
YOTELA, whiteness.	HUT, white.

It has been lately asserted by M. Maspero and Professor Sapeto, that in the speech of some of the negro tribes on the Blue Nile, the *clicks*, which were deemed a peculiarity of South African speech, are detected ; and more than this, that an increase or diminution of the prevalence of this linguistic feature could be remarked as the traveller advances towards or from Central Africa. The clicks are not quite extinct in Upper Egypt, as the name of the Copt when pronounced properly is CKIBT or CKOOBT. In Egypt they are no longer extant in uttered speech, but, if the roots of the Egyptian language are to be found in Africa beyond, there ought to be some record of the clicking stage in the hieroglyphic signs. As there is. For instance, the cynocephalic ape of the Upper Senegal is said to utter *clicks* which contain a distinct "d"-sound.[1] If so, he has advanced beyond the ancient Egyptians, who had no sign for D. The hieroglyphic pyramid TA, however, becomes the Greek "Δ" (delta), and if we take the value at T the result is still remarkable, as this ape on the monuments is the representative of language, speech, utterance, as the Word or bard of the gods. He represents Taht or Tet, and Tet means speech, tongue, language, mouth. As Âan, the ape represented Taht in the northern heaven, and the name signifies speech—speech of, speech from, or speech to. Thus the Clicking Cynocephalus personates speech under the two names and forms of TAHT and AAN. The typical voice or speech then, is represented in the "Click" stage by the *Clicking* monkey. The Crane or Ibis was likewise a type of Taht; also T is the ideographic T-T or TET; consonantal phonetics being reduced ideographs; and this double T is given by the Bushmen to the blue Crane in the kind of language especially devoted to it. They insert a "TT" at the end of the first syllable of almost every word of the CRANE'S language,[2] and this TT in Egyptian means speech, tongue, mouth, and language. T represents one of the chief clicks in the Hottentot dialects, and it can be shown that this *Click*-prefix in the one language was brought on and still survives as the T or feminine article "the" in Egyptian. It is extant in the word "Tser;" this sheds the prefix but retains the same value in "Ser," which tends to prove that the T-click still survives in the Hebrew צ (Tzer), and Coptic Djanda.

The Hottentot T-KAU is the buffalo. In Egyptian the bull (or typical male) is the KÂ. T'Kui, Hottentot, is Man (homo); in Egyptian this also is KÂ. T'GOOSE (Hot.) is the cow; HES (Eg.) cow; T'NA (Hot.) man as Vir; T'NAA, the head; NA (Eg.) chief, head; NU, male; T'KOA-RA (Hot.) the sun; KHU-RA (Eg.) light of day. T'AA (Hot.) a hand; Â or AA (Eg.), a hand; T'AIFI (Hot.) the typical woman; AF, KEF,—the Eve,—(Eg.), Genitrix, the one born of; T'SAGUH (Hot.) the eye; SAAK (Eg.) the eye-type of the illuminator. In these and in other instances the Egyptian article Tu (the) completes the Bushman word, and by dropping the prefix, the Bushman word becomes Egyptian. The Tu article of the one is the *Click* of the other. These clicks, for reasons which may be stated hereafter, are amongst the oldest sounds in language, and possibly the

---

[1] Faidherbe. *Revue Linguistique*, 1875.   [2] Bleek. p. 6.

first distinctly conscious imitations of other sounds. The T-click is manifestly the primitive form of the T or The-sound, and according to Bleek, the name of the phonetic sign which distinguishes the palatal click made with the tip of the tongue pressed as flat as possible against the termination of the palate at the gums, and withdrawn with full force, is "Gara,"[1] another name for speech, to speak, utter, voice, word, which in Egyptian is Kheru. "Gara" describes speech or utterance by means of the T-click.

Bleek says, "the Bushman word for 'to sleep' seems to be Phkoinye, beginning with a combination of dental click, aspirated labial and guttural tenuis in which three letters are sounded together."[2] If this complex prefix be omitted we shall have a word answering to the Egyptian Khennu, to alight, lean on, and rest; and sleep is synonymous with rest. The dropping of the click is apparent in other cases, as in Q'Kham, to fight; Khem (Eg.), to fight; Q'Khou-Q'Khou, for Kku-khu; Q'Khup, for Khef; Q'Qam, for Kham; X'Khaba, for Kab; Qkhup (Nam.), a lord and master; Khef (Eg.), chief; Qqam (Nam.), to humble; Khami (Eg.), humble. So in the Makua language the "Um" prefix being dropped Mthatha, the hand, becomes Tat in Egyptian; Mluku, Lukhu; Mtuchi, Tuki; and Mshapwe represents Kafi, the monkey.

Certain words retain their primal value and are world-wide types. The word Kherp (Eg.), for a first formation, a model figure, has been traced to the name of a county in Shrop-shire, and a quarter of the world in Europe. In Coptic it is represented by Sorb, the same as in the Roman Sorbidunum. Another illustration of Kherp is extant in the English Selvage, which is not merely self-edge. Self, the first person, is a form of Kherp, the chief one, but Kherp also means to *produce linen;* and the Selvage is the Kherp-edge, the woven edge or first formation—the Curb-edge. Kerf is an English name for cloth with the wool left on it; another first formation, This name persists in the Soudan and other parts of Africa, and is applied to the most primitive palisade or rudimentary enclosure for cattle, as the Serb or Seriba, which is still a first formation and model figure of the beginning.

One of the Central African type-names is expressed by " U "; the prefix denoting place, just as in Xosa Kaffir it is the prefix denoting person. The U in such names as Uganda, Ugogo, Usakara or Ujiji, signifies the country of. The Egyptian U, is a sign of land, district, canton, line, boundary, edge, direction, and also means Me and Mine. It is a point of departure so primitive that its ideograph is a pullet, signifying "from the egg," an Egyptian phrase for the beginning. Usakara, the land or district of Sakara, bears the name of the oldest Egyptian pyramid known. Uganda, which is far south, is

---

[1] Bleek, *Reynard the Fox in South Africa*, p. 55.
[2] Bleek, *Bushman Folklore.*

the country of Ganda answering to Khenta (Eg.), the name of the south.

In Egyptian Tun means to divide and separate in two halves; Ka is the thing, person, or type. In Xosa Kaffir the wall that divides is called a Donga; the fence or hedge is called a Tango. In Zulu the Donga is a cutting or division in the land. The thigh which is one of two, the divided part of the body, is likewise Tanga in Zulu; Tungi, in Musentando; Dongo, in Fulah; Dango, in Kano; and Tanke, in Wolof. The dividing one is the frog, as Tongo, in Tiwi; Tungua, in Dsuku. Ten, for the division, is also a number 10 in Egyptian as in English, for the two hands, the tithe, and the ten of Ten Kat. This in the form of Tan is the name for number ten in the Vei, Kono, Mandingo, Toronka, Kankanka, Bambarra, Kabunga, Dsalunka, and other dialects. In the Makua language, the division is marked in Thanu for number five, or one of two hands, and by Tani, number five, in Fan; Tanos in Malemba.

The chief type-name in Africa for palm-oil is Mas in the Kanyika, Mas, N'goala and Lubalo; Masi, Basunde; Masi, Kasands; Mazi, Nyombe; Mazi, Congo; Mezeie, Goali; Mosoa, Murundo; and in Egyptian Mas means to anoint; in Hebrew Mashach is to anoint and the name for anointed. Mas in Egyptian applies to anointing, painting, and dyeing. Mest (Eg.) is colour for eyes, the black Mestem, Kohl, or Stibium, made use of for painting the eyes. This was produced from the condensed smoke of incense. So the Maori Kauri, used for tattooing, is made of soot from burnt resin, obtained from the Kauri (*Damanara Australis*) tree, and Kauruki is the name of smoke. In Swahili Masizi is soot, and Moshi smoke; the one being derived from the other. This Mas is an African type-name for smoke, as in the Kanyika, Muis: Matatan, Moes; Basunde, Muisi; Meto, Moisi; Musentando, Muiz; Kabenda, Muizi; and others.

In Egyptian, the Bab is a hole, cavern, or pit; Talmudic Bib for the hollow, the pit; Beabh, Gaelic, for the grave, and in Tiwi, Bebo; in Melon, Babisi is the hell. Baba (Eg.), the beast, is an epithet of the Typhonian devil; the Apap is the Satanic monster and adversary of souls. In Swahili, Pepo is an evil spirit; Bibi, Eregba, is bad; Ebeb, Eafen, bad; Ebibi, Mbofon, bad; Ababa, Bambarra, is to terrify, and Bebon, Ashanti, means guilty.

The ass was a type of Baba, or Sut-Typhon, and in the Fulah language the ass is Babba.

An Âper in the hieroglyphics is a preparer of bows, and Aper, to equip, has the quiver-case for determinative. In the Papiah language Aper signifies war, and the word has earlier forms in Kefir (Haussa), a bow; Kepora (Landoma), a quiver; and Gbaru (Boka), a quiver. The accented â preserves the sign of the original consonant.

Put is likewise an Egyptian name for the bow. In Babuma the bow is the BOTA ; and BUTA in Koro, Utere, Mutsaya, Musentandu, and other dialects.

KHERSHET (Eg.) is a name of war-arrows, and also of the quiver. Shet denotes the arrow. The KURU, in Bornu; KORO, in Kisi; KORI, in Kandin ; EKIRI, in Egbele ; EHERI, in Sobo, is the quiver.

AKAU is an Egyptian name of the axe; this weapon is Aike in Oworo ; AGA, Opanda ; AKE, Yoruba ; IKA, Eregba.

KAR, or KHER (Eg.), is war. This is KARE, Wolof ; KURE, Gadsaga ; GERE, Mano ; GEREI, Kise-Kise ; OKORI, Egbele ; OKORU, Bini ; KELE, Mandingo, Bambarra, Kono, and Kankanka ; KELO, Kabunga ; Kala, Galla ; GALE, Solima ; GULU, Gio ; YORU, Legba and Kaure ; HERA, Buduma ; HARE, Salum. This type-name for war is the same as kill, and Kar (Eg.), means to kill ; the Kheri being the fallen victim, or one bound for the slaughter.

Another type-name for war is found in EKO, Ashanti ; EKU, Nupe ; IKU, Basa ; OGE, Abadsa ; OGEASA, Basa ; OGO, Isoama ; OGU, Aku, and fifteen other dialects ; OKU, Kupa ; OKUE, Ihewe ; YAIKI, Haussa ; YAKI, Kadzina ; AGIASA, Kamuku ; UKIWA, (Swahili), deso- lation. In Egyptian UKA signifies to rob. Thus two type-words deposited in the hieroglyphics as KAR and UKA show that primitive warfare was simple murder and robbery.

Stanley describes the muster for an attack on his party, and says the enemy " came on boasting, Meat ! meat ! we shall have meat to-day ; we shall have plenty of meat ! BO-BO-BO-BO BO-BO-BO-BO-OOH ! " ;[1] BUU is the Egyptian boast, and BU-BU, BA-BA, or BO-BO, signifies boasting.

In another instance the cries of the battle onset were " OOH- HU-HU OOH-HU OOH-HU-HU." In Egyptian " UA-UA " means *hurl yourselves on them !* and " HU-HU-HU-HU " reads strike ! drive ! seize ! pluck !

Again, Stanley writes :—" Tippu Tib, before our departure, had hired to me two young men of Ukusu—cannibals—as interpreters. These were now instructed to cry out the word SENNENNEH, ' Peace,' and to say that we were friends." The " pathetic bleatings " described by the traveller may derive a touch of additional pathos from the mean- ing of " Sen-nen-neh " in Egyptian. According to Stanley, the word made the most earnest proclamation and protestation that the new comers were men of peace. In Egyptian SEN means blood ; NEN is the negative and prohibitive NO ; NEH is to vow, request, pray. " SEN-NEN-NEH " is good Egyptian for " We vow and swear that we are not men of blood," or, more literally " No blood ! we entreat you ! "

" WAKE, WAKE, WAKY, HUH, HUH," ending with clapping of hands, is a greeting accompanying what Stanley calls a " most tedious ceremony " of welcome at Uvinza. If we may read the words by Egyptian, they indicate the hailing, addressing, and invoking, as at a

[1] Vol. ii. p. 201, *Dark Continent.*

festival of rejoicing. UAK, or UAKA (Eg.) is some kind of festival, or rejoicing; "HAIU," means Ah, oh, hail, address, invoke, and HUH is to seek, search, wander (to sunshine), which would particularly apply to the greeting of the travellers.   HU (Eg.) also means white.

Another exclamation of the natives at sight of White-skins was "WA-A-A-A-A-ANTU." WA is a prefix to denote persons, they, the people of a place, answering to UI (Eg.), for they, them. ANTU (Eg.) denotes a bright, light, sun-like colour. In Kaffir, ANDU signifies for the first time. ANDULELA is the name of a particular bright star which appears at the end of autumn.   These travellers were the WA-ANTU in both senses.   HANTU, in the Mintira (Micronesian) language, means a Spirit.

In KIVO, and other places, the intoxicating juice known to Europeans as PALM TODDY is called " ZOGGA."

SEKH (Eg.) is drink, and KHU is spirit; SEKHKHU would be drink with spirit in it, the English Sack. Sekhu (Eg.) is spirit in another sense ; it means the illuminating and inspiring spirit, from SAKHU, to illumine, influence, inspire, excite mentally.   Sakhu likewise denotes fermentation ; Sakhu-hut is fermented bread.

This name for drink and divinity is represented by the goddess SEKHET, who is the Deess of drinking. The inner Africans were also beyond the alcoholic stage of spirit, and had their divine mental illuminator, under the same name.

The divinity, or god, is designated SUGE in the Susu dialect; SOKO in Nupe; SOKOA in Esitako; SOGEI in Kise-Kise; SOKWO in Nufi; TSOKA in Marawi; TSHUKA in Ibu. Sekhet is the feminine form of the same word.

Egyptian may help us to a meaning for the name of the half-human-looking SOKO.

SEKHA (Eg.) is to represent, depict, paint, pourtray, make a picture. The SEKHA, personified, would be the portrait or likeness. Sekab is to reflect and duplicate the image ; and as the SOKO is so like the human type, that the imitation—the ape—sometimes runs close to the later development, there is nothing more likely than that the name is derived from SEKHA, and means the animal of the recognized likeness. The SOKO being a menstruating ape, the likeness to the human creature would increase the similitude. SHOKA, in Swahili, is the woman's word for menstruation. TS'KI, in Japanese, is the monthly period, and SEKHA (Eg.) is the flood.

SECK in Sacramento Indian is blood. This was the first form of SUCK in symbolism.   It was also the earliest ink or paint of the writer. Hence the menstruating ape was made the image of the Word. SEKHA (Eg.) means to paint, write, memorize, and remember. The monkey, Udumu (Ass.), is named in relation to blood as an earlier Adam, the feminine Atum or Dam.

SAMI-SAMI, the name for red beads, corresponds to the Egyptian

SAM, for a representative sign. SEM-SEM means Genesis: "Great is the mystery of Sem-Sem,"[1] and the first form of that mystery we shall find was the red source, represented by the red, the lower crown. SEM is an Egyptian name for myths and symbolical representations, and in the Oji language of West Africa the spider myths are called ANANSE-SEM; ANANSE being the spider, and SEM a fable.[2]

"TARA-TARA" Stanley gives once as paper, and once as a mirror. "Our people saw you yesterday make marks on some TARA-TARA." But the TARA-TARA was written on; *ergo*, it was writing-paper. The note-book, pronounced fetish,[3] was so on account of the marks or writing. TERU (Eg.) signifies drawing and colours, with the reed pen.

The TERUU is a roll of papyrus, and as a plural the word is equivalent to TERU-TERU. Paper, like the mirror, is a reflector of the image! TERU (Eg.) also means to invoke, adore, rub or drive away, in relation to charms, spells, or incantations.

There is a set of figures used in Africa called GOBAR, as the name is rendered by the Arabs whose traditions affirm that "GOBAR," the name of these figures, means dust, from the fact that they were introduced by an Indian who made use of a table covered with fine dust for the purpose of cyphering.[4] But the primitive figurer here meant is KHEPR, whose name signifies the former, or figurer, who made his figure, or shaped his ball, out of the dust of the earth.

The first figure ever made was a circle, which to this day bears the name of Khepr, as a cypher, synonymous with the French CHIFFRES, for figures. The cypher, as primordial figure, still gives the crowning value to all the rest. Khepr and shaper are identical, and Khepr, who shaped the first figure in rolling up his ball with the seed within, was adopted as the figurer. Figures are types, and Khepui (Eg.) denotes types. These had various forms, but the earliest type or figure, the cypher, was shaped in the reckoning by QUIPU, or tying knots in a cord as a mode of cyphering. The Quipu bears the name of Khep (Eg.), to form or figure. The cord in Egyptian is KHABU. Kheb, the goddess of the north, who carries the knotted cord or noose in her hand, as the figure of her period, her QUIPU, is the still earlier cypherer, as the maker of the first circle and cycle of time in heaven. There was also a lunar form of Khepr.

The Mantis, the most prominent figure in Bushman mythology, is charged with putting evil thoughts into the sides of men's throats, where the Bushmen are said to place the mind (qy. as organ of utterance?). The proper name of the Mantis is T'KAGGEN.[5] It may bear on this that KHEKH (Eg.) is a name for the throat, the gullet, the place of utterance, in the guttural stage of language. The Dutch render the T'KAGGEN by the devil, and he is accredited by

---

[1] *Rit.* ch. xvii.   [2] Riis, *Vocabulary of the Oji Language*, Basle, 1854.
[3] Vol. ii. p. 385.   [4] Max Müller, *Chips*, v. 2, p. 292.
[5] Bleek, *Bushman Folk-lore*.

the native mind with the works of darkness. KAK (Eg.) is darkness; the Akhekh was the old dragon of darkness, and KAK is the god of darkness. As a type the Mantis of the Bushmen equates with the Khepr (beetle) of Egypt; and the divinity which it represents, called TOÛQUOA by Kolben, a little crooked-legged, crabbed, inferior captain, answers perfectly to Khepr-Ptah, or Ptah-Sekari.

Peter Kolben has related how the Cape Hottentots regarded the *Mantis fausta.* He says that if one should chance to visit a kraal, it was looked on as the descent of the Divinity among them, and the man or woman on whom it alighted was overshadowed by the divine presence, to be considered sacred for ever after. The fattest ox of the kraal was killed as a thankoffering, and the caul of the animal, powdered with Bukhu, was twisted into a rope, and put on like a collar, to be worn till it rotted off.[1]

Entrails were a primitive kind· of GREE-GREE. The twisting of the hog-pudding and sausage had the same significance. Hence the white pudding of Easter, and the black-(blood)-pudding of Michaelmas; and the symbolic sausages still preserved in the panto-mime of Christmas.

The beetle, in Egypt, represented the maker of the circle, which was imitated by the twisted caul. In the Ritual [2] the beetle Khepr is designated the "twister of the horns"; that is, the curver into a circular shape, the earliest beetle being emblematic of the moon. It also denoted generation, or an *only-begotten;* the scarabæus being typically a creature self-produced, and therefore a symbol of the self-begotten god.[3]

In Whydah, if one of the snakes, which are kept in the temple called the serpent's house, and permitted to leave at will, should, in its wanderings, chance to touch a child, the priests immediately demand the child of its parents, to be brought up as an initiate in the mysteries.[4] This is a type to be read hieroglyphically. The serpent which became a phonetic T was an ideographic Tet. Tet not only denotes the tongue, mouth, language, and to tell; the word also signifies unction, to anoint. Taht personified was the tongue, the teller, the anointer of the gods. But in Whydah the TET, as teller or foreteller, was the snake itself, the living ideograph, which was afterwards drawn as a pictograph to express the same idea.

In the hieroglyphics the ostrich-feather is the sign of truth in its dual aspect; this has many illustrations. One of these was light and shade, the eternal transformation. It was worn by Mā, whose Two Truths applied to day and night, this life and the next. Now the Bushmen have a myth of the revival of a dead ostrich by means of one of its own feathers. A male ostrich is killed and carried home by a Bushman. One of its feathers, stained with blood, floats on a

---

[1] Astley's *Collec. of Voy. and Trav.* iii. 366.   [2] Ch. xciii.
[3] *Hor-Apollo*, Bk. i. 10.   [4] Skertchley, *Dahomey*, p. 56.

gentle wind, and falls into the water, where it gradually becomes a young ostrich. This is compared by the natives to the renewal of the moon. All other mortal things, except the moon and the male ostrich, die outright; these two revive again.[1] These are the Two Truths of Egypt, typified in both instances by the ostrich-feather. Hor-Apollo says the sign was adopted because the wing-feathers of this bird are equal on every side.[2] The feather was probably first of all a symbol of the Two Truths of light and shade in the equatorial land of equal day and dark.

In Dahome the rainbow is the heavenly snake that makes the BOBO beads;[3] and BUBU in Egyptian is the name for beads, especially the symbolical beads of the collar worn by the gestator Neith, who was sometimes represented not by, but as a rainbow. The heavenly snake or rainbow is named DANH (Dahome), and TAHN is the Egyptian name for crystal and material used in making glass or other reflecting substances which typified the eye of Horus, and the mother-mirror.

The African "HONGA" is looked upon by travellers as mere tax or tribute. But if the word be read by Egyptian it is of greater interest. ANKHA means a covenant on oath; Ankh is life, the sign is the cross of life, the covenant of the Ankh is equivalent to swearing "by my life" on the cross.

The Maori HONGI is the salute by touching each other's noses, and smelling and sniffing, a more primitive mode of making the covenant, identical with that of the animals. The Honga is also called Muhonga; and Maa (Eg.) means to come, approach, offer gifts. MHU is to please, satisfy, fulfil.

In Egypt the king was the Ankh (or Ank), the living and ever-living; it being a theory that the king never died, but only transformed. Father Merolla describes the high priest or supreme pontiff of Congo as the GANGA Chilerne, who is reputed to be the god of the earth. He was a form of the ever-living one, who was able in death to confer his character on another chosen for the purpose. He boasted, says the father, that his body was not capable of suffering natural death, and to prove this, when he found his end approaching he called for the one of his disciples who was intended to succeed him, and pretended to communicate to him his great power; and afterwards, in public, where this tragedy was enacted, he commanded his attendants to tie a halter about his neck, and strangle him therewith. The reason for this being done in public was to make known the successor ordained by the last breath of the predecessor. The halter or noose is an ideographic ANKH.

The Basutos hold a kind of parliament, in a court formed by a circle of rushes and boughs, in which public affairs are discussed, and *justice is administered*; it is designated the KHOTTA, and the chief councillors of the king bear the honorary title of men of the

[1] Bleek, pp. 13-14. [2] B. ii. 118. [3] Burton, *Dahome*, vol. ii. 148.

KHOTTA, an appellation signifying the men of the court.[1] The Egyptian KHET was a minister, and TA is the throne. Also KHETF means an accuser, and TA is the magistrate or judge.

At the court of Uganda the warrior chiefs were received by the king with a pot of test-beer. The emperor says, "Drink if thou darest!" The chief turns to the gathered warriors and cries aloud, "TEKEH." "TEKEH" is then shouted in response by the multitude. Being tested or weighed in this manner and found TEKEH, the warrior drinks. Stanley renders TEKEH by "WORTHY"—"Am I WORTHY?" and "Thou art WORTHY!"[2]

In the hieroglyphics TEKHU means weight or weighing, and a supply of liquid; drink or drunk. The word TEKHU also signifies full, and it is the name of Tekh for the god of the moon at full. The TEKHU was a vase which corresponded to the needle of the Egyptian balance, used for measuring weights. This TEKH, for weight or weighing, is the root of the Hebrew בקל,[3] for weighed; the weighing, as testing, being equivalent to the Uganda TEKEH, where the mode of measuring or weighing includes the TEKH of the full cup, which is used as the means of testing and weighing. These warrior chiefs of Uganda were a kind of king's THEGNS, or Thanes.

The name of the Kaffir can be traced a little farther than the root Kaf. For example, Kâfir is a name for the darkness of night in the old Arabian poets. The accent shows the vowel to be a reduced consonant, and the full form is found in KAK (Eg.), for darkness, blackness, shadow, and night. The Kaffir, then, is the Kakfar; in Egyptian, he, him, or it (f) who is created (ar) black (Kak). We do not anywhere reach the origines in the phonetic stage of language. The ideographic signs show that the phonetic K was an ideographic KK; N was NN; M was MM; R was RR; T was TT; P was PP; and Kak, Nun, Mem, Rer, Tet, and Pep deposited the syllabics Kâ, Nû, Mû, Rû, Tû, Pû (in the process of evolving the vowel-sound from the consonant), and finally the phonetics K, N, M, R, T, and P. These origines, however, must be reserved for a section on the "TYPOLOGY OF SOUNDS."

Beyond the root KAF then, there is a KAKF, which in Egyptian would read the black person or thing, and show the Kâfruti were the black race, as the Kâf is the black monkey; and QUAIQUA is a self-given name of the Hottentots. CHIKOKHE is the title of a little black image used as a fetish figure at Loango. KHE (Eg.) denotes a spirit, and KAK is black. Kak was the black god, the sun of the underworld.

QUAIQUA may possibly represent another meaning than Kak, for black, darkness, and the name of the sun of night. KAKA (Eg.) is the tongue of the god Hu, and the tongue is a type of speech.

---

[1] Casalis, 124.   [2] Stanley, *Through the Dark Continent*, v. i. 392.
[3] T'qal, Dan. v. 25.

Kaka (Eg.) is to cackle. Khak, in Amoy, is the clearing of the throat by expectorating. Ka-ka (Eg.) is a duplicative form of Ka, to call, cry, say, and therefore finally to speak. The Quaiqua may have named themselves as the speakers, or, as we might say, and as Egyptian says, the Cacklers. The Kookas of India derive their name from a peculiar sound which they make with their mouths. They likewise are a kind of Kak-urs, or Cacklers, who still preserve this sign of the Clickers. The Caqueux and Cagots of France possibly retain their names from this origin. In Magyar the dumb are called Kuka. Khekh (Eg.), the gullet, Quack and Cough (Eng.), and Quakle (Danish), illustrate the status of the Quaqua, as the mere Quacks and pretenders of speech.

Hor-Apollo tells us that Speech was symboled by a tongue and a hand beneath, the principal sign of language being the tongue the secondary the hand.[1] In such hieroglyphics we have a visible deposit of the remotest past. The tongue and hand have been found as the symbols of Har, the Messiah, Word, or Logos. The ancient genitrix Typhon was the first tongue-type of the Word; the ape (Kafi or Shu) was the hand, the earliest scribe; Kaf being a name of the hand. Tet (Eg.) is the name of both tongue and hand; and tongue and hand, in the Bushman-Hottentot language, are T'inn-T'aa, which, with prefix and terminal, would become Ho-tinn-taa-t. It is not unlikely, therefore, that the Hottentot name was derived by the early settlers from the native names for tongue and hand, the types of language in the early stage of click and gesture speech. "Tt" denotes the especial language of the Blue Crane; "Tet" is speech in Xosa and Zulu Kaffir; Teti is the speaker, who, under the same name in Egyptian, would be the stammerer or clicker with the tongue.

The name Hottentot is thought to be a coinage of the Dutch to express the clicking; and the word Hottentotism has been adopted as a medical term for one of the varieties of stammering. In Egyptian "Tet" is speech, language, and tongue; Teti means to stammer. The earliest language, or "Tet," with the tongue, would be that of the clicks, and the fact seems to be registered by the tet or "tt" of the Blue Crane, and the clicking cynocephalus, the personified Tet of language in the earliest phase.

The present writer heard a clicking Kaffir at Sir James Simpson's, in Edinburgh, who was able, according to his own account, to converse in clicks alone. If the Hottentot be named as the utterer of pre-verbal language, we see how the title of Hottentotism would be derived and applied to some particular form of impediment or non-development of faculty.

Haut-en-Tet, in Egyptian, would denote those who were first of speech. This, on the way from the ape, the still earlier type of the clicker, would become a title of distinction. The "Speakers" is a primordial name. The people of LISANU, tongue, language, speech, was a title in Sumir. The Basques call themselves "those who have speech." The TUNGRI, QUADI, and LELEGES are the Speakers, or those who have a tongue. This is primitive naming, which does not depend on the later differences between one language and another. It implies the languageless or mouthless beings in the background, who bequeathed a type-name for the barbarians and savages as the "speechless" and "tongueless" people of later times. For instance, it is observable that TAMME or TAMMA is "the tongue" in several Hottentot dialects; DEMO, in Tumu (Gabun); DEMI, Kisama; TIMI, Fertit; and that one meaning of Tem (Eg.) is the mouthless and dumb, as the TEM or created people were (figuratively) in the earlier time. TEM (Eg.) is a type-word for the race of created persons,—the same word as Atum or Adam the Red. But the Red was not the created race, because it was developed from the black race. It was urged on a previous page that the Æthiopic RUTEM is the earlier form of REMA for the aborigines; Coptic RŌMI, men. In like manner NETEM abrades into NEM, and SUTEM into SEM; Sutem, the antecedent form of Sem, hearing, being shown by the ear, which is an ideograph of "Sut" and "At"; and this ear is missing from the phonetics of the word Sem, and has to be added by the determinative.

The value of RU-TEM is that it names the TEM, the created people who have found a mouth or language. Ru (Eg.) is mouth, discourse, or utterance. The antithesis of this is shown by TEM, the name of the created persons, also meaning the dumb, the mouthless people, i.e. the tongueless or languageless, as the clickers would be considered by those who had advanced a stage. These, then, are the RUTEM of the Æthiopic inscription; the created people who have found a tongue. ROTUMA is the name of a Polynesian language.

RUTUM is the type-name for tongue in the African languages, where, however, the L represents the R. The Tongue or a Tongue is ARDIM in Runda; LUDIMI, Basunde; LUDIM, Kanyika; LUDIMI, Musentando; LUDIMI, Nyombe; LATHEM, in Bakele.

The wearing-down of Rutem into Rema, previously asserted, can be shown in the African dialects. Ludimi abrades into Limi for tongue; LIMI, Lubalo; LIMI, Kasange; LEMI, Songo; LIMI, Ntere; LAMMI, Wanika; LAMEI, Wolof; LIMELIMA, Bullom; EREM Sobo; OLEMI, Egbele; ULIMI, Swahili; LELIM, Babum; OULEME, Mpongwe; LILIM, Mutsaya; LELIMI, Undaza; LAWEM, Nkele; LELIMI, Mbamba; RAMEZ, Timmani; TELAM, Kanuri; TELAM, Munio; LAMBA, Gurma; ESUROMA, Keamba; DERIM, Mfut; TEKEREMA, Ashanti; PULEMA Padsade. These languages are all African.[1]

[1] This and other names for tongue passed out of Africa as NALEM, tongue, Ostiak; NELMA, Vogul; ELMYE, Tsheremis; LIMTSI, Akush; RAMARE, Arago; RAMARE, Papuan.
Also, RAS is tongue in Egyptian, and LISI, Pika; LUSU, Karekare; MILASO,

The relationship of tongue and nativity is, of course, most intimate, and this type-name for tongue, in the abraded form of Rema, Egyptian, means the natives, the indigenous, the aborigines. In this stage we have the Romany, Rumanyo, Ramusi, Lamut, Lampong, Limbu, and other languages or tongues. The Tem (Eg.) are the created races of mankind, not the descendants; and the name is extant in the Damara tribes. Two of these are known as the Damup. Read as Egyptian, Tem-Ap signifies created first—the race first created. Two tribes of the Damup live on the hills and in a valley, or on the drainage of a lake. The hill-men are called the GHOU-DAMUP. And in Egyptian KHU is the hill, or height, on the horizon.

There is a tribe of Bushmen proper known as the Kubabees; these likewise belong to the Damup (or Damara) land. In Egyptian KABEB means the source. Khab is Born of, and Ap is the first ancestor. The process of wearing down from Kubab to Ab or Ap is apparent in the Hottentot names of KAAB, SAAB, and SAP, which they apply to themselves. In Namaqua XAIP, for time, is earlier than Seb (Eg.), Time. The Sap are the earlier Kab, still earlier Kaf (Kaffir), or Kubabees. Now Seb or Kheb (Eg.) is called KAK-ur, the CACKLER, as the great KAK, under the type of the goose.

The Hottentots identify the baboons with a tribe of the AmaFENE people, or Apemen, also called the Amatusi, who became apes through fastening pick-handles to their bodies, and these turned into tails. Ama denotes the men, in Kaffir. Fene, the baboon, in Xosa and Zulu, represents the Egyptian ÂAN, earlier FEN, whence BEN, the ape. Thus the Ape-men, in Kaffir, are the monkey-men in Egyptian, named in the image of the Ben, Fen, or Aan, the dog-headed ape, or clicking cynocephalus. FANI (Kaffir) means resemblances, things that resemble each other, which shows the Ama-fene are the ape-like. This ape was a type of the Typhonian Kefa, as her portraits prove, and of Shu (Kafi), after whose image the Ama-fene are named. In the second stage the Fen or Ben, as the Âan or Aani, gives its name to the Ainos of Yesso, who are ape-like in their hairiness. The Ainos are mothered and fathered by the Great Bear and Dog or Sut-Typhon. The bear is their chief divinity. They kill it, but, in dissecting, make elaborate obeisances and deprecatory salutations.[1] They place its head outside their habitations, as a protection from misfortunes. Their first human being was a woman who dwelt alone on an island, where she was visited by a dog, who was the

Kaffa : MELASI, Gafat ; LASHON, Hebrew ; LISANU, Assyrian ; LISHAN, Arabic ; LESHONO, Syriac.

Again, TEP and TET are both tongue in Egyptian, which shows the wearing down from Tepht, and the tongue is DUVI, in Brahui ; DUVA, Singhalese ; TOPONO, Yarura ; TOPE, Purus ; TUPE, Coropo ; TAFOD, Welsh ; TAVAT, Cornish ; TEOD, Breton.

[1] W. M. Wood, *Tr. Eth. Soc.* vol. iv. p. 36.

father of the wild hairy Ainos.[1] The dog, or jackal, was a type of Sut; the dog-headed AAN, a type of Shu; but Anup is also a name of Sut, and the dog and bear are Sut-Typhon. It is assumed that the name of the Bosjesmans, or Bushmen, merely denotes the men of the bush. But it is far more likely to be a native name. BESI, or BESISH (Eg.), means nomads or Wanderers, and PES-SH is to range and extend.[2] BACA, or BACISA (in X. Kaffir), is likewise applied to homeless wanderers. If native, it may be the name of the BETSH, or BESHT (Eg.), applied to the Eight Great Gods of the first time, who were born of Chaos; a parallel to the Carib women calling upon the SCHEMUN (SMEN) as the spirits. PITTJO is the Lap name of the bitch; PETZ the Swabian name of the bear, and the Party of the Betsh (Eg.), the children of Inertness, Revolt, and Hostility, were the Eight of the Bear and Sut.

PETSHEI is No. 8 in Pujuni, and PASHT in Deer. The word for eight, in many languages, identifies that number with Taht, as THAT in Thounglhu; Thata, Angami; TETE, Albanian; TITA, Appa and others; Taht having been the eighth as lunar manifester of the seven. Sut was still earlier, and his name supplied the type-word for No. 8 in various languages. Even Sut-ANUSH appears in the ANSH for No. 8 in Kashkari and Arniya; and Bar-Sut in the Ingash and Tshetsh BAR, and the Sasak BALU, for No. 8.

The earliest Put company of the Egyptian gods was not the Nine, but the Eight Great Gods. Api(ta) is found with the meaning of No. 8; and API is the first, the head and chief.[3] To this beginning we can trace the English FAT for eight bushels; PAT, in Cantonese, for eight; PET, in Laos, Ahom, Khamti, and Siamese, for No. 8; and in Xosa Kaffir, Si-boso is eight, BOZO being the type-word for eight or the eighth. The BOZO, or Betsh, would derive from the eight, i.e. from Sut-Typhon, and this origin would supply a root for the BETJA or BISHARI, the BEDJAS described by Burckhardt; the BASHI, the BUSH-men, and others, who may be considered as belonging to the first BATCH of people. The BEETJUAN dialect is akin to the Bosjesman, and retains in its name the Egyptian BETSH or BESHT.

In a letter sent by Bishop Callaway to the *Academy* periodical, the writer says he has been " much interested in examining some drawings made from those in Bushmen caves; among them were some amusing pictures of contests between the pigmy Bushmen and the gigantic Kaffirs, the latter being represented always as disproportioned, stupid giants, and getting the worst of it, like the giants in *Jack the Giant-killer* tales. But what interested me more was the existence of what no doubt are mystical symbols of an old religion—a rayed sun, a crescent, a sun and crescent in conjunction, a cup in a circle, and an EIGHT-RAYED CIRCLE." The eight-rayed circle is that of the NNU

---

[1] Bonwick, *Daily Life of the Tasmanians*, p. 229.
[2] Cf. *Besishti*, Champ. N. D. 429.   [3] Rossellini, Mon. da C. 43.

and the BETSH, the eight gods of Smen who were in the time of Chaos. The sun and crescent may be seen on the head of Khunsu, the soli-lunar child who slew the giants as the piercer of the proud, in what was probably the original of the battle between the pigmy Bushman and the giant Kaffir.

This beginning with the eight or the seven-one of the Great Bear and Dog-Star, the earliest of the origines which survived even in the Seven Sleepers of the cave at Ephesus and their Dog, was extant with the North American Indians in the shape of the eight ancestors assigned to all men by the Pawnees, Ottoes, and others. The Iroquois, when leagued together in the most perfect state of their organization, had eight totems at the head of eight classes of warriors and hunters, and the descent of chiefs was in the female line.[1]

The Californian Indian tribes, near the Trinity River, relate that when their ancestors came down from the north-west they quarrelled with the great divinity worshipped there, who handed them over to the powers of evil or devils.[2] The first of these devils is OMAHA, who possesses the shape of a GRIZZLY BEAR. The second is MAKALAY, a fiend with a horn like a unicorn.

Now the goddess of the Great Bear, in Egypt, was dethroned, and became the evil Typhon or devil, and in the "Magic Papyrus" the crocodile MAKAI is the son of Typhon; the single horn, the unicorn, being a type of Typhon or Sut. Typhon, as Great Bear, was super-seded by the lunar and solar deities, the change being marked by the migration out of the mythical Egypt, or the seven caves of the Sunken Atlantis in the American traditions, and the Mangaian SAVAIKI of the Seven Isles.

The coast-dwellers of Northern California tell of a mysterious people, called the Hohgates, to whom they ascribe an immense mound of mussel-shells and bones still existing on the table-land of Point St. George, near Crescent City. These Hohgates are said to have come to the place seven in number, in one boat; and now they are the seven stars in heaven, that all men know of; their boat having been one day caught up into the vast, to swim the upper sea, and these seven stars are the seven Hohgates that once lived where they built the great shell-bed near Crescent City.[3] In this legend the typical number is Seven, as with the seven great gods of Assyria, to whom ASSUR, the greatest, was the eighth, and the Seven origins or Eundas of the Damaras. The mound-builders are analogous to the builders of the Babels and towers of the seven stages, and the seven Hohgates repeat the seven encirclers of the pole-star in the Great Bear. The name of the Hohgates read by Egyptian means the circle-builders or mound-makers. Heh is the circle, the emblem of the Æon, Age, Eternal. KET means to build circle-wise. The Hohgates or Hehketi were the circle and mound-builders, who, in Britain, "lifted the stone of the Ketti.'

[1] Schoolcraft, v. 73, note. [2] Bancroft, iii. 176. [3] *Ib.* iii. 177.

It has been shown how the north is the region of the great mother, as goddess of the Great Bear; and how that quarter was considered the hinder-part, and the south the front. When these came to be considered as the male and female, Sut, the son (also the phallus), typified the south or the front, and the mother Typhon the north or the hinder part. This imagery is still sacredly preserved in the custom of the Bongos, who bury their dead facing the north and south; the females having their faces turned towards the south, and the males towards the north. These too are children of the Great Bear and Sothis.

Captain Burton describes an African negro as calling on "MAMA, MAMA," his mother, as an expression for a feeling of fear.[1] Mama is the mother in Tongo and Landoma; MMA in Kiriman. This is the Egyptian MAMA, to bear, carry, be pregnant. But it is in the ideographic stage with the double M. The worn-down form of Mu remained as the mother-name; Mut with the feminine terminal. The first Mama above was the goddess of the seven stars, and in the Wakamba dialect MAMA is the name of No. 7.

The last present of many in the long and curious wooing of the Basutos is a fine ox, given by the suitor to the parents of the bride; this is called the "ox of the Nurse,"[2] and is identifiable with its mythological type. In the Ritual we have the "Bull of the Cows," or seven Hathors. Hathor was the nurse, who was the still earlier Taurt, goddess of the seven stars, who is not only styled the nurse, but is the great mother and nurse of KAMUTF, the bull of the mother and nurse.

The Hottentots used to affirm that the name of the first parent was NOH, and that he came into the country through a window or doorway. His wife's name was Hing-Noh. These taught their descendants how to keep cattle.[3] Kolben fancied this fragment of tradition was derived from the Hebrew story of Noah. Both came from one original, which was African, and the Hottentot version can be traced in Egypt, whence it was carried forth afresh in the Hebrew writings.

Noh represents the Egyptian Nu, Num, or Nef, whose name, in the time of the twelfth dynasty, is found in the tomb of Nahrai, at Benihassan, to be written Nuhu.[4] NUHU, or the NUACH of the Hebrew, may be read Nu (Eg.), water; Hu, or Akh, spirit; that spirit of the waters (breath) which is the meaning of Nef. Nu, Nef, Num, Nuh, or Nuach was called the father of the gods, the breath of those who are in the firmament, i.e. the souls. His consort is named ANKH, the ONGA of the Phœnicians and ONKA of the Gephyreans.[5] Her name identifies her as the mother of life. Hing is an earlier form of Ankh, just as King is the still earlier. Noh and Hingnoh are the inner African forms of the Egyptian Nuh and the goddess Ankh, who wears the primitive crown of Hema, or Hemp, on her head, as her sign of the weaver of the web of life.

---

[1] Burton, *Lake Regions of Central Africa*, ii. 333.   [2] Casalis, p. 199.
[3] Rowley, *Religion of the Africans*, p. 51.   [4] Osburn, i. 239.   [5] Pausanias, 9, 12.

According to Skertchley, the supreme divinity of the Dahomans is named MAU. The worshippers deny the corporeal nature of this deity, and assign him a kind of spiritual status;[1] doubtless the primitive type, which was breath as the basis of the Egyptian MAU-SHU, who was a god of spirit as breath, Ma or Mau having that meaning in Egyptian. In relation to this deity we find a primitive form of the Two Truths and the Judgment. Mau is said to have an assistant who keeps a record of the good and evil deeds of every person by means of a tally-stick, the good being notched on one end, the bad on the other. When a man dies, his body is judged by a balance struck between the two ends of the stick. If the good preponderates, the body is permitted to join the spirit in Kutomen, or the land of the dead; but if the evil outweighs the good, the body is annihilated, and a new one is created for the use of the spirit.[2] Here the balance of the tally-stick takes the place of the scales of the Two Truths in the hall of the dual justice or twofold right. Mâ signifies the truth; and the earlier form of the word is Mak or Makha, which is the name of the balance or scales of Mâ. Mau is possibly a form of Shu (Mau-Shu), whose feather is a type of the Two Truths. He is the great chief in An in the Ritual, and was an earlier god than the solar Tum and Osiris. In the judgment hall of Mâ (Truth), Taht is the assistant who keeps the record of the good and evil deeds, and he also employs a form of tally-stick as the recorder and reckoner of the earth—an earlier type than the pen. The dead-land, Kutomen, corresponds to the Egyptian KHUT, the horizon of the resurrection, and MENA, for sleep, rest, and death.

A most ancient and significant name of the moon occurs in the Bushman language as TKAU KARUH. Tekh is an Egyptian name of Taht, or the moon. Akh and Ka are the still earlier forms of Ah, and with the article these become Tka or Tekh. Kheru is the Word, to speak, speech; and Tekh was the Word (*logos*) of the gods. Tekh-Kheru is the Word personified in Tekh, the oldest name of the male lunar deity, and of another measurer, the goddess of the months, TEKAI.[3] Another Hottentot name of the moon is T'ha, in Egyptian the HA, or AH (moon), the softened form of Tekh. So T'GACHUH is the older form of Akhu. T'gachuh is the sky. In Egyptian, Akhu is the elevated heaven, the upper of the two.

Huh is an Egyptian name of the dual deity, also called Hu and Iu; and among the Dahoman gods HOHO is especially the preserver of twins, who are dedicated to this deity.[4]

The Af-sun of Egypt and Assyria is found in Afa, the Dahoman god of wisdom, answering to Hea, whilst OFAN is the name of the

---

[1] Skertchley, *Dahomey as It Is*, pp. 461-5.   [2] *Ib.* p. 461.
[3] The Chinese twelve characters for the double hours of day and night are called TECHI.
[4] Skertchley, *Dahomey as It Is*, p. 468 ; Burton, *Abeokuta, etc.*, p. 221.

Egba divinity of blacksmiths. So Hephæstus (Ptah), the smith of the gods, was a form of the Af-Ra, or the sun in the lower firmament. ATIN-BODUN is a Dahoman deity whose domestic abode is represented by certain curious specimens of Ceramic art.[1] ATEN (Eg.) means to create, as the potter at the wheel. Ptah was represented as the Creator by the potter sitting at the wheel.

There is a cave, says Livingstone, near the village of SECHELE, called Lepelole, which none of the Bakwains dared to enter. It was declared to be the habitation of their deity, and no one who went within had ever come out again.[2] The deity was crook-legged, and the descriptions of him reminded the traveller of the Egyptian god Ptah. In the crook-legged form Ptah is called SEKARI, and by reading the word SECHELE with the *r* instead of *l*, as in Egyptian, we obtain the name of SEKERI, the very title of the crook-legged Ptah. The cave represented the Meskhen of new birth. LEBE, in the Kaffir languages, is the name of the *pudendum feminæ*, the Meskhen, the place of transformation, which would account for the tradition that those who entered never returned. The solar god who appears on the monuments as Ptah-Sekari, the crooked-legged abortion, the embryo, is certainly one with the Hottentot and Kaffir Utixo or "wounded knee."

Amongst the Namaquas in South Africa he is known as Tsuikap (otherwise Kabip and Eibip), which signifies "*wounded knee.*" The "wounded knee," a leg with a knife thrust through the knee, is a hieroglyphic sign which denotes the deprivation of power and being overcome. It is the determinative of SEKAR, to sacrifice, as in the person of Sekari, or Sikkuth, the god deprived of power, the cut, wounded, castrated, or unvirile deity. The original of these representations was the sun below the earth, which was typified as the embryo in the womb, the infertile, feminine, infantile, gelt, or wounded sun, maimed in his lower members, and even as blind, and going on one leg, hopping, and groping his way by the sense of touch. So primitive and near to nature was the imagerial vesture of the early thought.

With the Zulus the deity UTIXO was the hidden god, who was said to have been concealed by Ookoolukooloo, the first ancestor, and in consequence he could not be seen by any one. The character still keeps the meaning of the name in Egyptian, where TEKA is to be concealed, to see unseen. When personified, this is the one who sees unseen, like Utixo.[3]

In his letter to the *Academy* periodical, Bishop Callaway says: "One very interesting discovery was that of the name Ukqamata for the Creator among a tribe of frontier Kaffirs. It is a name almost universally unknown to white men, and entirely so to white missionaries.

[1] Skertchley, *Dahomey as It Is*, p. 468.   [2] Livingstone, *Travels*, p. 124.
[3] Callaway, p. 67.

What the natives said of this Being was more remarkable, more like 'theology' than anything I have met with. And what was especially interesting is that my informants told me it was their tribal name for Utiᵹo before they came into contact with the Hottentots, when they gave it up for the Hottentot word Utiᵹo."

Now when the sun attained the horizon, as the pubescent, virile god, it was in the image of Khem or Khepr, the erector; the god who was Khemt or thirty years of age, or the trinity in unity (KHEMT, the adult; KHEMT, three). Kama (Eg.) also means to create, and UKQAMATA probably represented Khepr or the Khemt Horus, the sun upon the horizon. Another of his names is Eibip, and Abeb is the sacred scarabæus, the type of Khepr's transformation. Another name is Kabip. With the Namaquas, Kabip has a son, named Urisip, the WHITISH one. Khem-Horus was the white one. Uri (Eg.) is the elder, the chief, first, oldest son, as in Har-ur; and Sip means the son. MOKOMA, or "him above," the god of the Mountain Bushmen, and IKQUM'U, the "Father above," another form of the same name, are identical with Khem-Horus, the Begetter, as the sun on the horizon. The Damara god OMAKURU is identical with MAKHERU.

The Yorubas worship the lord of heaven under the name of Olorun.[1] Olo agrees with Ar (Eg.) or Har, the lord who was the child of the mother, the earliest lord of heaven, as Sut, Sut-Har, and afterwards as the solar Har. He was the Renn, a nursling of the mother, who became Saturn as Sut the Renn. Olorun echoes Al, the Renn. Another title of the youthful god is the Repa, or heir-apparent. Seb is designated a veritable Repa of the gods, as a repeater of the time-cycle; and RUPI is the name of the supreme god of the Ediyahs of Fernando Po.

The type-name of the solar god as the son of the mother is Horus, the Egyptian HAR or AR for the child, the Hebrew El. The earlier form is Khar, as in the Khart, the elder Horus, who was always the child of the mother. These names of the sun-god are African names of the sun, as YAKARO, Musu; GUIRO, Kru; GIRO in Kra and Basa; GIRU, Gbe; WURO, Boritsu; HORU, Idsesa; HAR, Wadai; EREI, Udso; ERUA, Okulma; IURO, Bassa; ORE, Sobo; ORU, Egba, Eki, Ife, Ondo, Yoruba, Yagba, Oworo, Dsebu, and Dsuma. KURU is god in Baga; GARA, in Toma; and these also supply the type-name for heaven, the Egyptian AARU or elysium, in various African dialects.

Written with the letter *l* instead of the *r*, we have the divine names of KELEA, M'bamba, a god or idol; HALA, Bulanda, god; YALA, Wolof; ALLA, Mandingo (and twenty-eight other African dialects); ALLO, Kabunga; ALLAH, Haussa and Swahili: ALA, Mano, Munio, and Nguru; ALE, Soso; HALE, Landoro, an idol; ELE, Yoruba, Dsebu, and Aku, an idol or divinity.

[1] Tucker, *Abeokuta*, p. 192.

Horus, the child, the Khart, was maimed in his lower members, which condition was at one time represented by his legs growing together,[1] and having to be divided by Isis the genitrix. This is still the deity of the Barolings, one of the Bechuana tribes, who is described as having only one leg. This representation of the limping one-legged sun of night would be the original of the Zulu Half-men, a tribe of beings with one leg, who found the Zulu maiden in the cave and thought she must be two people. After close inspection, they made the admission, " The thing is pretty; but oh, the two legs!" Here the cave shows the underworld, and these beings were created in the image of the lower sun. The One-half-people were represented by Miru the deformed hag of the Mangaian Hades, who had but one breast, one arm, one leg, and was altogether one-sided.[2] Religious customs of standing, and games of hopping on one leg blindfolded to break eggs, have the same origin as the one-legged creatures. The Zulu Keke is a one-sided, deformed person, who corresponds in name and nature to Kak, the Egyptian god of darkness, the blind and lame one who went by touch.

The Batoka tribes said they knocked the front teeth out of their children's mouths at puberty—a custom which they performed at the same age that circumcision was in other tribes—to make them resemble oxen or bullocks, i.e. the bulls which have been gelt. This can be read in the same way. It was a lesser form of the sacrifice practised in circumcision by castration in the cult of the Aten Sun, the Hebrew Adonai, and of the semi-castration formerly practised by the Hottentots. When Lucian left his hair as an offering to the goddess and her son in the temple at Hierapolis, the meaning of the rite was the same, although the type of adultship had been changed. Hair, tooth, or *testiculus*, was each a type of puberty and of testifying.

In the hieroglyphics, the tooth Hu has the same name as the sun in the upper heaven. Hu also signifies the adult, whether applied to the sun or man. Hu was the white and pubescent form of the solar god (Tum), and Kak the black, impubescent and unvirile form. The tooth knocked out at puberty was a sacrifice to the god of darkness and the underworld, who was the blind god, the lame and limping god, or the Hottentot " wounded knee."

So when the aborigines of the Garrow Hills effect their " transformation into the tiger," or the Khonds of Orissa, who claim to possess the art of Mleepa, become tigers, they are still enacting the representations that belong to the drama of mythology. They transform according to the mould in which the lion-god Shu changed into the cat, leopard, or tiger-type. The Jakuns of the Malay Peninsula hold that the transformation occurs just before the man-tiger makes his spring. This agrees with the change from the

---

[1] Plutarch, *Of Isis and Osiris*.   [2] Gill, *Myths*, p. 173.

lion-god sitting to the leopard up-springing, or Anhar standing up and marching. The Khonds say that one of the man's four souls goes forth to possess the beast; and by the four souls we can identify Shu as the god of the four corners, four feathers, and four genii or souls. As Shu means both soul and feather, the four feathers of Shu are equivalent to the four souls, one of which assumed the tiger or leopard type.

When the French describe the twilight as the time between dog and wolf, that is in continuation of the imagery set in heaven, where the dog imaged the day-star, and the wolf was the herald of the night; and just as Sut (dog) transformed into Anup, and that transformation was enacted in the mysteries, so does the typology underlie the supposed transformation of the Werewolves of France. Exactly in the same manner the type of Ptah with his feet turned backward, to represent the sun of the *antipodes* or lower heaven, was imitated in the description of beings who dwelt in the world of myth and monsters, and who went with their feet turned backwards, and were called *Antipodes*.[1] This sun of darkness, represented as black from the first, and imitated by the blackened faces of our Mummers, has the character of an evil deity in the later phase of various mythologies; but that was not the original significance. The worship was directed to the power which groped its way through the lower half of the circle by night and rose again with the dawn, to become the type of the Saviour in the human darkness; the KRISTO or the KARAST one, the god, whether stellar, lunar, or solar.

The Hottentot god Heitsi Kabip, who transformed and appeared at one time with his hair short and at another with it growing down to his shoulders, and who died and came to life again,[2] is a recognizable form of the double Horus; Horus the child, and Horus the hairy or pubescent, the Sherau, he who died in one character and arose as the sun of the resurrection in the other.

One particular feat ascribed to the miraculous child, the Messiah of mythology, is that of speaking before birth. Apollo was fabled to have spoken from the womb of Latona.[3] In the Mohammedan account of the delivery of the Virgin Mary, the Child-Christ speaks from the womb. And in the Zulu nursery tales, Uhlakanyana, the Zulu Jack or Boots, performs the same feat of speaking before he is born.[4]

The Basutos have the myth of the Saviour, son of the mother, in a very early form. In this we are told that "once all men perished." A prodigious animal, called Kammapa, devoured them all, large and small. It was a horrible beast; it was such a distance from one end of his body to the other, that the sharpest eyes could hardly see it all at once. There remained but one woman on the earth who

---

[1] Pliny, vii. 2.
[2] Bleek, Fable 7, p. 75.
[3] Callimachus, *Hymn in Delum.*
[4] Callaway.

escaped the ferocity of Kammapa, by carefully hiding herself from him. This woman conceived, and brought forth a babe in an old stable. She was very much surprised, on looking closely at it, to find its neck adorned with a little necklace of divining-charms. "As this is the case," said she, "his name shall be Litaolane, or the diviner. Poor child! at what a time is he born! How will he escape from Kammapa? Of what use will his charms be?" As she spoke thus, she picked up a little straw to make a bed for her infant. On entering the stable again, she was struck with surprise and terror; the child had already reached the stature of a full-grown man, and was uttering words full of wisdom. He soon went out, and was astonished at the solitude which reigned around him. "My mother," said he, "where are the men? Is there no one else but you and myself on the earth?" "My child," replied the woman, trembling, "not long ago the valleys and mountains were covered with men; but the beast, whose voice makes the rocks tremble, has devoured them all." "Where is this beast?" "There he is, close to us." Litaolane took a knife, and, deaf to his mother's entreaties, went to attack the devourer of the world. Kammapa opened his frightful jaws, and swallowed him up; but the child of the woman was not dead; he entered, armed with his knife, into the stomach of the monster, and tore his entrails. Kammapa gave a terrible roar and fell. Litaolane immediately set about opening his way out; but the point of his knife made thousands of human beings to cry out, who were buried alive with him. Voices without number were heard crying to him on every side, "Take care, thou art piercing us." He contrived, how- ever, to make an opening, by which the nations of the earth came out with him from the belly of Kammapa. The men delivered from death said, one to another, "Who is this who is born of woman, and who has never known the sports of childhood? Whence does he come? He is a monster, and not a man. He cannot share with us; let us cause him to disappear from the earth." With these words they dug a deep pit, and covered it over at the top with a little turf, and put a seat upon it: then a messenger ran to Litaolane, and said to him, "The elders of thy people are assembled, and desire thee to come and sit in the midst of them." The child of the woman went, but when he was near the seat he cleverly pushed one of his adversaries into it, who instantly disappeared for ever. Then the men said to each other, "Litaolane is accustomed to rest in the sunshine near a heap of rushes. Let us hide an armed warrior in the rushes." This plot succeeded no better than the former. Litaolane knew everything; and his wisdom always confounded the malice of his persecutors. Several of them, while endeavouring to cast him into a great fire, fell into it themselves. One day, when he was hotly pursued, he came to the shores of a deep river, and changed himself into a stone. His enemy, surprised at not finding him, seized the stone, and flung it to the opposite side, saying, " That is how I would break his head, if I saw him on the other side." The stone turned into a man again ; and Litaolane smiled fearlessly upon his adversary, who, not being able to reach him, gave vent to his fury in cries and menacing gestures.[1]

This belongs to the typology of the first period. It is the myth of the mother of time and her child, who was the earliest star that was observed to re-appear periodically. Litaolane is the prototype of the Messiah who in the Book of Enoch is the Son of the Woman, and of all the saviours and messiahs who have conquered the monster of darkness and death by passing through it. The announcer, who was Sut-Anubis in Egypt, is proclaimed by the little charms of divination ; and he is here called the diviner.

A perfect parallel to this may be found in a Neeshenam tradition, which relates that long long ago there lived a terrible old man, the great devourer of the Indians. Around his wigwam on the plains of the Sacramento the blood of the Indians flowed a foot deep. The Indians made war on him in vain. Then the clever old Coyote took pity on them, and rushed to kill the devourer. So the Coyote got into a pit, just outside the *great circular dance-house* into which the enemy used to go to slay the Indian chiefs. When he came next time, the Coyote, armed with a knife, jumped out and slew the slayer.[2] The Coyote answers to Sut-Anubis.

Litaolane is the Renn (Eg.), the nursling of the old first mother. The one woman in the world was the ancient genitrix (Typhon), whose name of Apt also signifies the stable or manger, the crib, the abode, the place of bringing forth. The stone into which Litaolane transformed himself is the sign of Sut.

The imagery can be read in the earliest Egyptian myth, almost effaced from the monuments, because Sut, the Sabean son, who rose as the Daystar, and set and passed through the underworld, or the devouring monster of the dark, and re-arose as the Wolf or Orion, the glorious warrior and conqueror of the Akhekh or Apophis dragon, was superseded by the lunar light borne through the night by Taht and the solar god as Horus the son of Osiris. Kam-appa (Eg.) reads the Apophis of darkness. In matter like this—and there is much of it among the Zulus, Bushmen, and Hottentots,—we reach the roots of Egyptian thought in Africa.

In various parts of Africa it is related that in former times men knew the language of animals, and they could converse together. This is but another way of saying that the animals formed certain ideographic types by aid of which the primitive men could express ideas. Language uttered by means of animals became the language of animals in the later description. In like manner when Pliny relates[3] that the hippopotamus has the cunning to walk backwards

---

[1] Casalis, *The Basutos*, pp. 347-349.   [2] Bancroft, iii. 546.   [3] viii. 25.

and thus deceive and baffle its pursuers, he is doing precisely what is done in the Hottentot fables; the character of the typical animal is conferred on the natural one. The types evolved from the animals are confused with them. The only hippopotamus that ever walked backwards was representative of the Great Bear constellation.

The men who employed the living types were the first hieroglyphists, and these living types were not only the pictures in the book of nature first opened, the early men also represented the types as expressing the human ideas, views, and sentiments. These are the speakers of the African fables, who *had to talk* because the human speakers were not in possession of any other mode of *thinging* their own thoughts and of getting them *reflected* by any other kind of types. The printer's types talk with us, and we have lost the secret of the animal language because we can no longer read the primordial hieroglyphics. Still, the ancient language is not lost: the types have been translated or were continued in pictographs and hieroglyphics. Egypt remains the mouthpiece to Africa, and renders the language of animals intelligible to us. Many of the animal prototypes are still identifiable in the fables with the ideographic types extant in the monuments and mythology of Egypt.

When we see the exaltation of the leopard as the type of Shu-Anhar the lion-leoparded, and the Nimr of Nimrod set among the starry hosts of heaven, it may help to explain why the Africans should consider it a kind of consecration to be killed by a leopard. They are not the only sacrificial victims of typology and mythology.

The fables of animals such as those still extant amongst the Hottentots and Amazulu are not the myths of Egypt in their decadence. These do not denote the senility and decrepitude of a second childhood following a maturity attained in the mythology of Egypt. They still represent the primitive childhood, and in them the child was father to the man. They have now to be studied in the light of evolution, and not to be judged according to the doctrine of degradation; and evolution teaches us that here as elsewhere we have to begin for the first time.

In the South African tales the crab is considered the mother of the tortoise. The giraffe says to the tortoise, " I could swallow you." " Very well," says the tortoise; " I belong to the family who are accustomed to being swallowed." The giraffe swallows the tortoise, who eats its way out again.[1] In an Ojibwa legend the tortoise goes underground and wins the race.[2] In the Bushman version, when the tortoise has thus killed the giraffe, it proceeds to the crab, its mother, and they two live on the giraffe for the rest of the year. This is astronomical imagery. The tortoise on the monuments, called Shet and Apsh, was evidently one of the most ancient Typhonian symbols which were superseded in later Egypt. Two tortoises were

[1] Bleek, *Tales*, No. 15.   [2] Schoolcraft, *Algic Res.* ii. 181.

placed in the zodiac where the Scales now are. The giraffe is an ideograph of Ser, which means, to dispose and arrange. The Ser was the disposer, organizer, and over-lord ; also the name of the measuring line, and a title of Sut or Sirius.

In these fables the Jackal plays the part of the cunning one who always outwits the lion, as in Europe the fox gets the better of the bear. What has been termed the beast-epic of Reynard the Fox is one with the Bushman's celebration of the jackal, and both are identical with the jackal of Egypt. The jackal and wolf were types of Sut-Anup, an earlier form of Seb ; Seb-ti being a dual Seb corresponding to the dog and wolf or the jackal and wolf. The jackal is Seb, the wise beast ; Seb is a name of the councillor.

The jackal in the Hottentot fables is the same wise animal as the fox in the beast-fables of Europe, and the Coyote or prairie dog of the North American Indians. The jackal is the guide of ways to the sun, one of these being on the earth or in the lower heaven ; and in the Hottentot fables the animal is said to have the long black stripe on his back where he was burnt in *carrying the sun*, whom he picked up on the earth as "*such a fine child.*" [1] This wise beast was placed in the zodiac as the guide of the sun's two paths at the place of the spring equinox. The folklore of his travels as the solar guide is not extant in the yet recovered literature of Egypt, but it is to be found all over the world, especially in America. Also, the nursery tales of other nations were outgrown in the older land, or have been lost along with the books of Taht ; but the mythical and astronomical imagery remains for identification.

Here it may be pointed out that the African mythology survives among the American Indians in a far ruder form than is to be found in monumental Egypt. Egypt was the developer and perfecter of the African typology, and remains its interpreter ; but the earliest likeness to the origines is to be found with the Indians, Maori and other of the decaying races who probably migrated before the valley of the Nile was inhabited. In these stories the prairie-dog, the Coyote, is representative of the jackal, the wise animal, Seb, of Egypt, who is personated by the fox in Europe.

The Coyote is credited with doing wonderful things ; amongst others, he procures fire for man. This is usually assumed by the advocates of the fire-myth to mean actual fire, because they have not known that the fire of mythology was that of star and sun.

The notion of Brinton and others, that the early man was so enraptured with the element of fire, when the discovery was made, that he went on his knees at once in front of it and kept it alive ever afterwards with the breath of prayer, is an utterly false interpretation of mythology.

In a legend of the Cahrocs,[2] when the creator, Chareya, first made

---

[1] Bleek, *Fables*, p. 67.   [2] Bancroft, iii. 115-16.

fire, he committed it to the charge of two old hags, and the wise
Coyote arranged a line of animals from the home of the hags to the
edge of the water.   Then he stole the fire, and as the hags pursued, the living line of animals passed it on from one to the other,
like a row of kindling gas-lights, until it came to the water's edge,
and there it was received by the frog, who, just as the hags were
about to snatch the fire, swallowed it, leapt into the water, and
gained the other side with the fire secured.   To go no further
back than the solar allegory, this can be read by the Egyptian
types.   The fire is the sun which crosses the waters of the underworld.   The two ancient hags are the two divine sisters who at-
tended the solar god in his burial and resurrection.   One form in
which the sun crossed the waters was that of the frog-headed god
Ptah, or Num, the king of frogs.   The line of animals takes the place
of the series of transformations extant in the Ritual.   The Coyote
represents Anup, who is the guide of the sun and the souls through
the lower region.

The two foremost and greatest animals in the Coyote's line of fire-
bringers are the Cougar and Bear.   These answer to the Great Bear,
and the lion-leopard, Shu.

Another Cahroc legend corroborates this.   Chareya, the " old man
above" who made the world, as he sat on a certain stool still in
possession of their chief medicine-man, gave to man the power of
assigning to each animal its place and duty, as in the Hebrew
Genesis Adam gave names to all cattle.

The man determined on giving to each of the animals a bow, the
length of which should measure the rank of the receiver.   He called
the animals together, and told them that early next morning the dis-
tribution of bows would take place.   The Coyote was very desirous of
having the longest bow, and he kept awake all night to be the first at
the division.   But, as luck would have it, he fell asleep at the last
moment, and did not appear until all the bows except the shortest had
been given away.   That is why the Coyote had the shortest bow.   The
man, however, took pity on him, and pleaded his case with Chareya,
who decreed that the Coyote should become the most cunning of
animals, as he still is to this day.

The bow of Seb has been already described.

APER, a name of Anup, means a preparer of bows.   Anup, as
guide of the sun in the underworld, is associated with the lessening
light and shortest day, typified by the smallest bow of time.   After
the passage of the waters by Aper (Anup) the crosser, his station is at
the place of the vernal equinox, just when the bow is beginning to be
drawn from the equinoctial level, the fullest, largest bow being
stretched out at the summer solstice.   Shu, the lion-god, had the
great bow.   Moreover, this little bow of Seb and the jackal may be seen
at the centre of the zodiac of Denderah, where the jackal is depicted

as standing on the bow, which is faintly figured in the present copy, but is distinct enough in the original.

This imagery, with the same apportioning and proportionment, is found in another sun-myth of the Pallawonaps, in which it is said, " The sun's rays are arrows, and he gives a bundle to every creature; more to the Lion, fewer to the Coyote." [1] Besides which, in this myth, the coyote is stationed at the spot, or over the hole through which the sun comes up. And here the coyote, who, as the jackal of the monu-ments, is the guide of roads to the sun, quarrels with the sun respect-ing the right of way; the sun insisting that he is travelling on his proper course; the coyote telling him to go round another way, as this was his road. Then after the altercation, the coyote asks the sun to give him a ride round the bow, or upper part of the circle. This the sun does; they ascend a path with steps like a ladder. It gets hotter and hotter for the coyote, but he holds on, winking and blinking, until the sinking sun is level with the western verge of the world; then the coyote steps off and finds firm ground again; he who as Sut-Aper was the equinoctial guide of the sun.

These myths are neither corrupt nor degraded; they mark the earliest stage, and are precious in proportion to their primitiveness. They are the literature of the nursery, which was African, but arrested at a stage outgrown by Egypt itself many thousand years ago. Yet so certainly do they belong to the ancient mother, that she only can tell us what they mean when we point to her symbols and jog her memory.

The Toukaways, a wild predatory tribe in Texas, celebrated the solar resurrection in a most primitive manner. They are said to have made the ceremony typical of their origin. One of them was buried in the earth stark naked; all the rest, being clothed in wolf-skins, howled and sniffed the air round and round the grave wolf fashion. Then they dug up the body with their nails, and a bow and arrow was placed in the hands of the newly risen man by the leading " wolf." [2] That wolf was the living image of Seb, the wolf, and the jackal of Egypt, whose station in the heavens was at the place of the spring equinox, as the guide of the sun on his way. The bow was the " bow of Seb." [3] The buried man represented the sun of the resurrection, ascending from the winter tomb, and emerging just where Seb, the wolf, was waiting to set him on his way. These also were Werewolves.

This was their mode of performing the suffering of Osiris, the descent into hell by Atum, the resurrection of the saviour Messiah as Horus the Christ, at Easter. This was an annual festival, and the burial was followed by a dance. It makes one's heart ache to think how faithfully these poor despised outcasts of earth have cherished their ancient traditions. Even when the surroundings of their exist-ence were the veriest dust and ashes of life, with these they strove to

[1] Bancroft, iii. 549.   [2] Brinton, p. 231.   [3] Rit. ch. cxxiv

keep the dying spark of light alive, and hid their treasures in their rags and dirt.

The dog-star was the announcer of the coming inundation, and the soul of Isis, the Great Mother, was said to be the dog, or to dwell in the Dog-star (Plutarch). The Cherokees have a legend of the deluge, in which a dog prophesies the flood. Isis, the ancient, is she whose son is the sun, and the Mandans, and other Mexican tribes, had their old woman who never died, and whose son was also the sun.[1]

The Acagchemem tribe of Upper California are said to worship the "PANES" bird. They hold an annual festival of the PANES at which they kill a bird, sometimes said to be the eagle, at others a turkey-buzzard.[2]

Tradition represented this bird as having once been a woman, whom the god Chinigchinich had met in the mountain ways, and transformed into a bird. The PANES was killed annually, one part of the ceremony consisting in not losing a drop of blood. The bird was next skinned with great care to preserve the feathers, which were used in making the feathered petticoat and diadem, as part of the TOBET; and the body was either burned or buried within the sacred enclosure, with signs of weeping and wailing from the old women.

It was held that as often as this bird was killed it was made alive again, and also that the birds killed in various places at the same festival were all the same bird. How this could be they knew not, but so it was. Here the PANES was their phœnix, the type of transformation and renewal. The phœnix of the hieroglyphics is the BENNU, or nycticorax, a bird of passage with a remarkable double plume.

The Bennu (says the *Book of the Dead*)[3] is Osiris, who is in Annu. That was the sun in the place of the resurrection or re-birth. But it is properly the bird of the western equinox, the type of transformation where the sun made his change into the feminine half, or entered the female phase. Again, at the time of the spring equinox it was figuratively said that the Osiris had made his change into the divine hawk, the soaring circle in the heaven, or that he had received the head-dress of the lion gods; he was feathered, in short, for the ascending flight. But to return. The part played by the wise or cunning Seb is well illustrated in the story of a man who found a snake lying fast under a great stone. He set the snake free, whereupon the snake wanted to eat him. The man objected, and made appeal to the hare and hyæna (both belonging mystically to the snake side); and they said the snake was right. Then the jackal was inquired of, but he doubted whether the snake could lie under the stone, until he saw the thing for himself. The snake lay down once more; the man rolled the stone on her. "Now," said the jackal, "let her lie there." This is a Hottentot fable,[4] and it reproduces the jackal as the wily

[1] J. Müller, 149. [2] Brinton, p. 105; Bancroft, iii. 168.
[3] Ch. xvii. [4] Bleek, *Reynard the Fox in South Africa*, Lond. 1864.

councillor, Seb in fac-simile. The rôle of the hyæna and hare is true to the original typology in their being on the side of the serpent.

One of the Hottentot stories[1] tells how frightened the leopard is at sight of the ram, and he needs all the encouragement the jackal can give for him to face the ram. This is a readable apologue. The winter sun was represented by the leopard or cat, as the maneless lion, the type of the sun when shorn of his strength. The sun in the Ritual is called the great cat (or leopard) in Annu, the solar birthplace, where the young lion was brought forth, or the sun was renewed. This point was in the Fishes, the place of the spring equinox. Here was the station of the jackal, the guide of the sun in both his phases and on both his roads. The sun of winter was in his feminine phase; hence the cat, leopard, or lioness, the maneless type. This feminine phase is depicted by the fear of the leopard at sight of the ram. It was not from an observation of natural fact that the leopard would be dramatized as in fear of a ram. But the ram signified was celestial, which the sun in his feminine phase or type never entered. The transformation had to take place in the double holy house of Anup, *i.e.* the jackal, in Abtu, and the Hottentot fable may be read as a germ of the Egyptian mythology.

Shu and his sister Tefnut appear as the brother and sister of the Bushman tales. When the cannibals of the cave or underworld pursue the sister, she climbs up into a tall tree, and is described as carrying a vessel of water. The vessel breaks, and the water drips on the cannibals below, who hear the water dripping down with the sounds " KHO-KHO."[2] These relate to the tree and the water of life in the Egyptian mythos. Tef, in the name of Tefnut, has the meaning of DRIP, DRIP ; and Nut denotes the goddess or receptacle of the water; she who carries the vase of water on her head.

In another story the sister has a brother who goes out hunting with his dogs. He sees his sister in the top of the tree, like Nut in the Egyptian drawings, and the cannibals hewing at the foot of it to cut down the tree. He sets his dogs at them, and these kill them all.[3] These answer to Shu and his dogs in the Ritual, who in company with his sister Tefnut are the destroyers of the devouring demons of the underworld, here called the cannibals of the cave. Shu may be likewise traced in these stories under his types of the ape and the lion. In the Bushman fables the types appear in their primitive conditions, which were humanized and divinized in Egypt. Also in these fables there is a lion which transforms into a woman in one story, whilst in another the woman transforms into a lion.[4] This is the exact similitude of the lion-god Shu, who was represented in one half of his rôle by his sister Tefnut, who was the woman or the lioness as a goddess. These two likewise transformed into the character of

[1] Bleek, No. 13.
[2] Callaway, *Nursery Tales*.
[3] Bleek, *Fables*, p. 7.
[4] Bleek, pp. 24, 25.

each other, when the lion Shu became Tefnut in the feminine phase
and Tefnut became the lion in the masculine phase.

Amongst the other fables is one called the "Judgment of the
Baboon." In this we have the same formula as in the English story
or allegory of the "pig that would not go." The cat bites the
mouse, the dog worries the cat, the stick beats the dog, the fire
burns the stick, the water quenches the fire, to elicit the hidden
truth. In the Sephr Haggadah there is a similar allegory in which
the *holy one* slays the angel of death, who slew the butcher, that killed
the ox, that drank the water, that quenched the fire, that burnt the
stick, that beat the dog, that worried the cat, that ate the kid. The
"Holy One" of the Hebrew Haggadoth is the youthful solar god,
who was preceded by the lunar Word and by Shu and Sut. When
the baboon has succeeded in his work he says, "From to-day I
will no longer be called JAN, but Baboon shall be my name." [1]

Now AAN is the name of the dog-headed baboon or Kaf monkey
of the temples and hieroglyphics. The Kaf was originally a
type of Shu the star-god, and a determiner of sidereal time before
lunar and solar or luni-solar time was established. When the phases
and lunations of the moon were reckoned, and the eight gods of
Smen, the "children of inertness," the "sluggish animals of Satan," [2]
were superseded by the new creation, in which Taht the moon-god
built the ark, and became the measurer and recorder of the gods, the
AAN monkey was made the representative of the moon in the
northern heaven. This change is analogous to the change of name
in the Hottentot fable. The AAN baboon was the type of the moon
in the hind-quarter of the heaven, and imaged the hinderward phase
or face of the moon, and in one of these fables it is narrated how the
baboon once worked bamboos, sitting on the edge of a precipice. Up
came the lion to steal upon the baboon. But the baboon had fixed
some plates, *round glistening plates, on the back of his head.* Seeing
these dazzling plates the lion supposed they were the face and eyes of
the animal. So that when the baboon turned round to look, the lion
thought that the real face was the hindward part. This gave the
baboon the advantage; he could watch the lion advance, and when
the lion made his leap, the ape bent forward, and the lion went over
both the baboon and precipice. This was the Hottentot way of depicting the hindward image of the baboon. The curious reader may see
the PLATES which the baboon wore behind painted in brilliant hues
on the back of the Cynocephalus, blue at the head and red at the
tail, in the plates of Champollion's *Panthéon Égyptien.* [3] Blue and red
are the colours of the Two Truths, here applied to the dual lunation.
The plate or disk at the tail of the animal signifies the AAN as
representative of the hindward part, the lunation of the waning half
of the moon. A description in the Ritual [4] of some mystical animal

[1] Bleek, 17.   [2] Taliesin.   [3] Pl. 14 B.   [4] Ch. cxxv.

whose mouth is said to be "twisted when he looks, because his face is behind," agrees with the Hottentot portrait of the baboon with its face behind. The origin of the world-wide allegory of the pig that would not go may be traced to the Great Bear, one type of which was the sow Rerit. This, being the primordial time-keeper, was found too slow when judged by moon and sun; hence the "children of inertness," the "sluggish animals of Satan" (Sut-Typhon), and the "pig that wouldn't go." Thus the roots of the mythos developed in Egypt, with world-wide branches, can be laid bare in Africa beyond. The sow Rerit of the North Pole may also be traced in the world-supporting hog of Celebes.

In the hieroglyphics, Bennu is the name of Osiris *redivivus*, of Horus as Khem, and of the Phœnix type of the resurrection. Also the Ben is the mount, the cap, tip, and supreme height of the god—the pyramidion. This in the pyramid shape, with the seven chambers, was synonymous with the tower of seven stages and the mount of seven steps. The Phœnix is not only an emblem of the manifesting spirit, but as the Rekh it is a determinative of Dreaming. The Manganja people worship a spirit or deity who dwells on the top of a mountain called Choro. He is a beneficent divinity, the dispenser of peace and plenty, like the Egyptian Nefer-hept. Priestesses are dedicated to him as his consorts, as were the Pallakists of the temples in Egypt; the temple in this cult being the mountain-top on which the consort dwells alone with the god. When the people need the spirit's advice, they ascend the mount and lay the necessary offering on the sacred ground in front of the hut, stating their difficulty and desire to the priestess. They then retire, and the priestess goes for the night to the hut of the god, who appears to her in a dream, and inspires her with the message which she is divinely commissioned to deliver.[1] Here the mount takes the place of the temple of Belus in Babylon, to the summit of which the priestess retired for the night, to be visited and inspired by the god in a dream. The name of the Manganja deity is Bona.

The Masonry or mystery of the people of Senegal is known as "Porra." The person to be initiated in this Porra has to dwell in the Porra bush for a certain time, apart from the population. No female must look on him, and he is said to be eaten by the Porra devil. When he re-issues and has had the new name, one form of which is Banna, another Cong, the Porra name conferred on him, he is said to be delivered from the belly of the Porra devil.[2]

With the Kamilaroi of Australia the rite of initiation into the duties and privileges of manhood is called the Pora.[3] Also the Eastern Australians have a mystical dance in a mystic ring, named

[1] Rowley, *Religion of the Africans*, pp. 58, 59.
[2] Harris, *Mem. Anthrop. Society*, ii. 31.
[3] Ridley.

the Porrabung. According to Mr. Threlkeld,. POR means to drop down, to be born.[1] PORO, in Maori, means to finish and come to an end ; *porae* is to anoint. PERU (Eg.) means the coming forth, the manifestation of the adult sun-god as Osiris-Bennu, or Horus-Bennu, *i.e.* Horus as Khem in the image of the begetter. The Bennu is the phœnix type of transformation, and the Manganja BONA, Senegal BANNA and Tasmanian BUNG, are probably forms of the Bennu or phœnix. CONG is the earlier form of Ankh (Eg.), the living one, applied to the sun or soul that issues from the belly of the Hades, and the Meskhen of re-birth.

When the Kaffir youths attain puberty and offer themselves to be made into men, a part of the ceremony consists of making their faces white with pipeclay.[2] So when Horus, or Tum, attained puberty in his second character as the virile sun of the vernal equinox, he was the white god. White, says Plutarch, is the colour of Horus. The white sun-god at this time of attainment assumed the Hut, the white crown. The pipeclay of puberty, with the Kaffirs, is the exact equivalent of putting on the white crown, and must have been an indefinitely earlier act of the same symbolism. Herodotus relates how the Æthiopians, when going into battle, smeared one half of their bodies with chalk and the other half with red ochre.[3] These are the colours of the double crown of the Pharaohs and gods of Egypt ; the red (lower) and white (upper) formed the complete crown. Chalk and red ochre were typical of the TWO Truths, to judge of their survival with the most primitive races of the earth ages before metal crowns were fashioned, or even a fillet of cord could be twisted. In this wise Africa lies behind, and its symbols are anterior to Egypt.

The Namaqua Hottentots allow their young men or boys to eat the flesh of the Hare until the period of young-man making, when they are admitted to the status of manhood, with certain ceremonies of initiation ; after which the hare is forbidden food, because it is a type of things forbidden, relating to ceremonial uncleanness. The type is ostensibly connected with the moon, but has a more secret significance. The root of the matter is, that the initiates are taught to respect the times of feminine periodicity, and not to eat of the forbidden food, the hare having been adopted as the external figure and representative or ideograph of that particular idea. In the hieroglyphics the hare is "UN," the sign of periodicity and of an opening. Hor-Apollo[4] says the hare was chosen to denote an opening, because the animal always keeps its eyes open. It has been suggested by Sharpe that the open period, UN, means the lawful, the unprohibited. In one sense it was so, the period of puberty having arrived. But in the secret sense the "open" was

---

[1] Bonwick, *Daily Life of the Tasmanians*, p. 187.   [2] Dugmore p. 159.
[3] B. vii 69.   [4] B. i. 26.

also the prohibited period, the negative of two, and on that account the hare was a type of uncleanness. The two different messages attributed to the hare by the Hottentots correspond to the two meanings of the type, as the hieroglyphic of "Un," open. The Namaquas relate that the moon once sent the hare to say to men, "Like as I die and rise to life again, so you also shall rise again when you die;" but the hare went to men and said, "Like as I die, and do not rise again, so shall you also die and not rise again." This made the moon so wrathful with the false messenger that the moon struck the hare with a hatchet, and made the cleft, or OPENING, in its lip, which has remained ever since.[1] The hare is a type of periodicity; hence its relation to the moon.

The earliest typical customs relate to puberty and periodicity, and the most primitive and permanent types are also emblematic of periodicity, or, as the Ritual has it, of "time or renewal, coming of itself." One of the chief ideographs of time is a shoot of palm, the determinative of the REN (with the suffix, RENPU), the plant, branch, or shoot of renewal. This root REN is found in EARN, Irish, barley; EORNA, Gaelic, barley, the sprouting grain; ARHAN, Mantshu Tartar, the germs or sprouts of grain; ARHANAMBI (*ib.*), to sprout; ROINE, Irish, hair or fur; ROINEACH, hairy; ROMA, Sanskrit, pubes, hair. Roine and Rom permute in Irish, Sanskrit, and other languages.[2]

Horus, the Renpu, the branch, the shoot, was the hairy or pubescent god in relation to this particular type of renewal. He was the Sheru, and that is a name of barley. The Sheru is the adult, the manly, the man. The true type of virility is found as the Ren, in the Hollen, for the holly; AULANE, French Romance for the hazel; Hebrew, Alon, the oak; and Swedish Ollen for the acorn. At Brough, in Westmoreland, the eve of Epiphany is celebrated as "Holling's" Eve, when there is an annual procession with an ash tree, which is lighted at the tops of its branches; the ash being also a tree of life, or a Hollen, that is, a LEN (or Ren), branch or shoot of the year. This was the day on which "kings were created by beans"; and on the next day the bean was placed in the cake of Twelfth Day, to determine who should be king, the bean being the type of the first Horus, the Renn, who transformed into the Renp, the new shoot, the divine king.

The RENN, nursling, and RENPU, the branch, plant, or shoot, were the two forms of Har, the solar god; and in the

[1] Bleek, *Reynard in Africa*, p. 69.
[2] In like manner, AUBURN and ABRAM are interchangeable names for red in English, and in deriving the name of ABRAM, considered as the red sun of the lower world, it might have been claimed that ABRAM was permutable with Ab or Af, the RENN (Eg.), the Nursling Child of the Great Mother, who preceded the Fatherhood, but the writer desired to take as little advantage as possible of the law of permutation in dealing with the Hebrew mythology.

African Dsekiri the sun itself is ORUNA; in Kambali, URANA; in Hindustani, ARUN; in Sanskrit, ARUNÂ or HARINA, which names are represented by the Gaelic GRIAN and Welsh GREIAN, for the sun: whilst in the Timne dialect the heaven or sky is ARIANNA; in Mandingo, ARYENA; in Soso, ARYANNA; in Doai, SLINA is heaven. Now, the Zulu RANANA is a person with an abundance of beard or large bushy whiskers. He is a form of the Sheru or Renpu personified. And in the African Wun language, the ORONYO is the king, exactly the same as the Breton Roen, a king. In the permuted form, RÔMI, in Coptic, is the male; ROM, in Gaelic, is the *membrum virile*, the *linga*, another type of Horus, the adult. ROM, in English Gipsy, is the husband; and to be ROMMED is to be married. REN and ROM supply type-names for man, as *vir* or *homo*, in RIN, Gyami; RUNA, Quiché; URUN, Murung; ORUNI, Landoma ORANG, Malay, Atshin, Sibnow, Sakarran, Tshamba; REANCI, Sapiboconi; RANUKA, Tanema; RUM, Khong; OLMA, Lap; ERMEU, Coretu, Lan, Thoung-chu; LENNI, Minsi; ILENI, Shawni; AMLUN, Korawi. The Egyptian REN (Welsh, PREN), for the branch, probably furnished the name of the REINDEER, not merely from RENI (Eg), cattle (as in RUNT (Eng.) for an ox), but from the typical branch and shoot. RENA (Mao.) is to stretch, or shoot out. The reindeer is remarkable for its branchy horns, which it shoots periodically. HARINA, in Sanskrit, is a name of deer, antelope, stag; one of five kinds. IREMU (Georgian) is also the stag. HARINA also means green, and both GREEN and HORN are based on REN. These are types of renewal and puberty, named from the same root and for the same reason as LUNA; Maori, RUNA; Keltic, LUAN; the titles of the renewed and horned moon. RANpick is an equivalent, in English, for stag-headed. The head of the stag is depicted (although rarely) on the monuments as an emblem of renovation. The horns appear inverted, that is, shed, in the judgment scene copied by Bonomi from a tomb in Thebes.[1]

Schoolcraft gives the grave-post of Waboojeeq, a famous Indian war-chief, who died about 1793.[2] He belonged to the clan or totem of the reindeer; at least the reindeer is depicted on the tomb-board in the reversed position that denotes death, which agrees with the reversed deer's horns in the Egyptian judgment scenes. In this connection it should be noted that the REINdeer's horns were the chief material used by the artists of the early Stone Age for incising their figures on, the REN being the cartouche in Egypt for the royal names; and to REN was to name; also IRANA in Sanskrit, RENGA in Xosa-Kaffir, mean to proclaim and publish. Thus the reindeer's horn, the branch and shoot, the type of shedding and renewing, was the palæolithic cartouche and means of RENN-ing found in the caves, which were also the graves; so ancient is the type. The stag's horns, according to Hor-Apollo, signify long duration. But the duration

---

[1] See *Hor-Apollo*, B. i. 69; B. ii. 21, and Pl. 2.   [2] i. 357.

was also manifested by transformation and renewal; not merely by the dead bone, but also by the live shoot of the young horn; the type was emblematic of both. The same writer says the "bone of a quail signifies PERMANENCE and SAFETY, because the bone of this bird is difficult to be affected."[1] In a note the editor observes that the quail's bone sign probably signifies "son." Dr. Birch reminds me that the bone here called the "quail's" is more probably the calf's bone. The calf, ÂÂ, denotes the infant, and the word means substance, to beget, issue, and be born. As a determinative the bone, with flesh on it, signifies ÂÂ, ÂU, issue, engendering, birth, born of; ÂUA and ÂUF (or AF), flesh; SHÂÂ, the substance born of; SHEB, flesh. In the form ÂB, flesh and bone, or horn, have one name. Flesh and bone were considered to be the substance born of. This bone is especially the determinative of the SHOULDER, and is therefore a guide to the prevalent use of the shoulder-blade. The Chippewa Indians made their magic drawings on shoulder-blade bones, which they threw into the fire to divine by.[2] The Laps, Mongols, and other races drew upon and divined by the shoulder-blade. The flat smooth surface of this bone adapted it for incising or drawing. It was the LEAF of a very primitive book. LAP in Magyar is the leaf of a book—LAPAS in Lithuanic—and LAPALKA (Ib.) is a shoulder-blade. The calf being the type of an infant, its bone becomes a hieroglyphic guide to the bones of children which have been found within adult skulls. The idea of permanence and safety was connected with the type of renewal and reproduction, which would likewise be represented by the bone of the child, the substance born of, and therefore an ideograph of rejuvenescence and re-birth.

It is with the greatest probability that the Quichés are reported to have slain children on purpose to make a paste of their blood, wherewith to cover the green stone in making up their mummy-type of the resurrection—an early form of the bloody wafer of sacrifice continued by Rome.

Thus the apparent problem presented by the trepanned skulls found in the burial-caves of France can be solved by the typology, which enables us to interpret the primitive ideas by their extant ideographs. These skulls had been trepanned, and flint arrow-heads, together with the *bones of infants*, had been inserted within the cavity of the skulls.[3] Now when the beetle was buried within the skulls found in Egypt, that was as a type of transformation and rising again; Khepr being expressly the re-erector of the dead. The arrow-head, in common with the axe, represents the Nuter of the hieroglyphics—the ideograph of renewal, permanence, protection, summed up as power or divinity; that is, the ability to renew, make permanent, and protect, personified as a god or goddess, was represented by this type of the

[1] B. ii. 10. [2] Tanner's *Narrative*, p. 192.
[3] *L'Archéologie Pré-historique*, by Baron J. de Baye.

Celt arrow-head, the hieroglyphic plane called the Nuter. It was Horus the YOUNGER, the sun of the resurrection, born at the vernal equinox, who rose again; and it was he whose types included the hair or beard, and the palm-shoot of the Renpu. We are told that Horus defended himself against his great enemy, Satan, with a palm-branch, that is with the type of renewal—the RENPU-shoot which he himself impersonated; an image of continuity by reproduction. This type belonged to Taht in the lunar mythos, in relation to the renewal of the moon. In each case the god and the branch are equivalents: both were types of the same fact of renewal, and nothing more. Both were preceded by Sut, whose name is identical with the Shoot, the son of the genitrix, the tree of life. With Sut-Anup, son of the oldest genitrix, we get back to the arrow-head, adze, or axe forms of the Nuter type. Anup is an Egyptian name of the stone adze, plane, or Nuter; and, in passing, it may be noticed that the jackal, wolf, or fox is a type of Sut; the fox in Europe taking the place of the fenekh, wolf, or jackal in Africa. Sut-Anup, in his degradation, was made the representative of Evil, and became our Satan. Now the Japanese still identify the Celts of the Stone Age as weapons of the Evil Spirit, whose type is the fox, and they call them fox-hatchets and fox-planes; and these are identical in name and nature with the Egyptian NUTER, a plane or adze called ANUP, after the divinity whose symbol was the fox, or its African equivalent, the fenekh, or the jackal.[1] The old British broadsword was likewise named a fox. The arrow-heads, then, are emblems of the son of the genitrix, when he was Sut of the Dog-star. He was the first "opener," and the stone was his type. In this image of the child of the mother were the dead buried in the cave of the genitrix and placed in the posture of the fœtus in the womb. The skull was opened, and the type of the opener, Anup, was inserted, to represent another opening out of the underworld, or the re-birth. The typical trepanning was probably founded on the observation of the unclosed skull of the infant; they were reproducing the child in the womb. This conjecture is corroborated by the bones of the infant being placed within the skull of the adult as another type of renewal and re-birth.

In one shape or another, in one place or another, the most primitive types of early expression appear to have persisted and survived. The arrow-head, as a stone monument and emblem of protection, is developed and continued in the grave-stone. The shells and beads of

---

[1] THE AXE. Abram is said to have taken the opportunity, while the Chaldeans were abroad in their fields, of entering the temple in which the idols stood, and breaking them in pieces with an AXE; and in order that he might the more fully convince the worshippers of their folly, he *hung the axe on the neck of the chief idol, which is said by some writers to have been Baal*, as if he had been the author of all the mischief. The same story is told by the Jews, who relate that Abram, the Iconoclast, demolished the images in the workshop of Terah. Baal is Sut-Anup, the opener, whose ideograph is the axe, and the story testifies to the Egyptian origines.—Hyde, *De Rel. vet. Pers.* Ch. ii. *Al. Beidâwi.*

the talismanic Gru-Grus are represented by the Rosary. The "Cross of Christ" reproduces the Egyptian Ankh and Tat, which were buried with the dead. The palm-branch of Taht, the shoot of the Renpu with which Horus defeated Typhon, is still gathered and carried on Palm Sunday by the boys in various parts of England.

The earliest form of ideography was acted before ideas could be otherwise registered, and this still exists in the customs and rites of the primordial drama. These are yet extant where they have never had any other expression. In the absence of literature and pictures the ideography is performed. Thus the "shooting of the Horns" is represented by the African Bongos in a funeral ceremony. These people still bury their dead according to the custom of the Palæo-lithic age. They place the corpse in a crouching posture, with the knees forced up to the chin, like the Peruvian mummies. The body, being bound and compressed to preserve that position, is then sewn up tightly in a SKIN.

The Bechuanas prepare to fix the body in this bent posture by calling in the aid of death. When a person is dying, they throw a net over the body, and hold it in the sitting posture, with the knees brought in contact with the chin until it is rigid in death, which is a very early kind of mummy-making. The body is then carried to the grave in a sitting posture, the head being covered with a skin.[1]

The skin was a type of renewal. In the hieroglyphics the NEM (skin) has the name of repetition, and a second time. In the "chapter of placing warmth beneath the head of the spirit,"[2] the deceased calls the lion (Paru) the "lord of the numerous transformations of skins," which suffices to connect the skin with the shooting and shedding of the hair, as illustrated by Hor-Apollo.[3] The deceased also says his body has been put away; but, addressing the god, he cries,[4] "Thou makest to me a skin"; that is, something to appear in, to cover the nakedness of death. The skin in which the Bongos wrapped their dead always appears in the judgment scenes. He is "sound at the evil altar," and has not been dragged to it; that is, at the judgment-seat, where the spotted skin (Nem) was always present as a symbol of the judge. Hor-Apollo[5] calls it the undress robe of royalty, which the king wore only in presence of the priest who was as the eyes of the gods. The skin of the Bongos was their undress robe, worn by the dead in presence of the gods.

In making their graves, the Bongos sink a perpendicular shaft for about four feet in the earth, and then hollow out a niche in the side of the grave, and insert the corpse into this, so that it may not have to bear any pressure from the earth in filling up the grave. This is a primitive form of the chambered tumuli and tombs. A heap of

---

[1] Rowley, *Religion of Africa*, p. 96. [2] Ch. clxiii.
[3] B. ii. 70. [4] Ch. clxvi. [5] i. 40.

stones, the cairn, is then piled over the spot in a cylindrical shape, and supported by strong stakes driven into the soil all round. On the top of the pile a pitcher is placed, frequently the same that had been the drinking-vessel of the deceased. The site of the grave is then marked by a number of *long forked branches, which are sharpened into horns at the ends,* and carved with numerous notches and incisions. The friends of the deceased are invited to the funeral, and all take part in preparing the grave, in rearing the memorial urn, vase, or pitcher, and in erecting, shaping, and ornamenting the horned sticks. "When the ceremony is finished, they shoot at the stakes with arrows, which they leave sticking in the wood." Schweinfurth says, "The typical meaning of these horn-shaped stakes, and the shooting at them with the arrows, had long since fallen into oblivion; and notwithstanding all my endeavours to become acquainted with the Bongos, and to initiate myself into their manners and customs, I could never get a satisfactory explanation."

Now the fact is, such customs are too simple for the meaning to be lost by those who have not lost their own simplicity in passing on to other planes of thought. The Bongos and others know the meaning of these customs more or less; but the imposing ignorance of the Europeans is too much for them; it shuts them up by making them conscious for the first time of their utter simplicity, and their nearness to naked nature. Remembering the typical palm shoot, the reversed deer's horns in the judgment scenes, the use of the shed horns of the reindeer, and the skin which shoots its hair, we may infer that the Bongos were enacting the "shooting of the horns," which was one of the earliest signs of "renewal, coming of itself," and was therefore applied to the human being in death. Volumes might be filled in tracing these typical customs to their root, and then the explanations be laughed at. But the profound ignorance of the knowing present concerning the past, will fail to impose on the writer of this explanation; he does not mind the laugh; the Bongos and other races do.

On the West Coast of Africa the negroes form figures, apparently made of sand and ashes, which are laid on the rock to dry and indurate, when they look like stone sculptures in low relief. According to Captain Tuckey[1] the fetish-rock on which these rude figures are found is considered to be the peculiar residence of the spirit named SEEMBI. This is analogous to that of the Carib ZEMI; the West Indian CEMI; the ZIMMU of Zanzibar and Uganda; the ZEMES of the Mayas, and the SHEMAU of Egypt. The Ozohim, in Igu, is a spirit, rendered by the missionaries a devil; the USOAHIM being the same in Egbirahima. These are identical with the SAMAN Fanti, a ghost; SCHIM, Dutch, ghost or spirit; SCHEMEN, German, phantom or shadow; English, SHAM; and the SEM (Eg.), an amulet, figure, emblem, image, the mummy-type of the departed. The earlier

[1] *Narrative*, p. 375.

form of these names of spirits is KHEM, the Egyptian name for the dead.

The Mantshu Tartars place a pole or rod at their doors, to make known to the passers-by that they are offering to some spirit. The pole is called a SOMO; and the act of making known, showing and explaining is called SAMBE. So in French Romance a funeral service is called a SEME, the Egyptian SEM, to conduct a ceremony The makers of the rude raised figures on the rock of SEEMBI were also representing and commemorating their dead. One of the figures copied by Captain Tuckey is the hippopotamus—the oldest type of the Great Mother in Egypt. Another is the rock-lizard. This is the ideographic determinative of the words ÂSH, AMMA, MÂT, UMT, and SHENBI, all of which denote many, numerous, multiplied. By permutation of the M and N, SHENBI is equivalent to SEEMBI. The rock-lizard, in Egyptian thought, if applied to the dead, would be the sign of wishing the life renewed a myriad or a million times.

Bastian states that the natives of Bamba say their great Fetish dwells in the bush, where he cannot be seen by any one. When he dies, the priest carefully collects all his bones, so that he may preserve and nourish them, that they may revive again when they acquire new flesh and blood. In the Mangaian myth Tangaroa is a god who dies and rises again in three days. When he dies Maui carefully collects his bones, puts them inside a cocoa-nut, and gives them a "terrible" shaking, and, like the dry bones which were shaken in Ezekiel's vision,[1] and came together again, the bones revive, and on opening the cocoa-nut shell the dead god is found to be alive.[2] This is the doctrine of the mummy, as in Egypt, exactly the same as setting up the Tat image of establishing for ever, and of making the mummy itself. The image was emblematic of the moon, sun, or soul in the underworld, and when the Hebrew priests are said to bring the Atzem, bones, mummy-type, or self-sameness of Joseph up out of Egypt, the original significance was the same as in the act of the priest of the Bamba fetish, who is said to collect and keep the bones of the god until they are clothed again for their resurrection. Also the ATZEM of Joseph, whether the mummy image of Self or some other figure, has its equivalent in the African Akurakura, ESEM, a GRU-GRU or charm.

Captain Tuckey says the word FETISH, meaning a charm, magic, and witchcraft, is in universal use among all the tribes of the western coast of Africa.[3] It is supposed to be derived from the Portuguese FETIÇO, which implies a form in TIKO analogous to the New Zealand and Peruvian TIKI. In the modified form of TES, the fetish can be traced to the Egyptian TES, the very self, the enveloped form, the soul, as we say. TES also means to tie up, coil round, as in making

[1] Ch. xxxvii. 7.   [2] Gill, *Myths and Songs of the Pacific,* p. 63.
[3] *Narrative,* p. 375.

the mummy, based on the embodying of the child by the mother, called Tesas-Neith. TES (Eg.) may be resolved into the (T) SA, that is the mummy image, also the soul which was typified by or as the Sa, earlier Ka. Sa further denotes an Amulet, for protection, help, efficacy.

One form of the SA amulet is the tie or noose emblem of reproduction, but the type of types was the mummy-figure This SA, TSA, or TESA, is represented by the Assyrian TSI, for the life ; Greek ZAO, also SAOO, to preserve and save ; and SOS, safe and sound ; the Ashanti SISA, *one who may be born again ;* Chinese TSOO, to preserve, help, aid, succour, and assist ; Fijian SO, to help ; Kaffir SIZO, help, assistance, succour. The ZE is a fetish in Kiamba ; OZAI, Ife ; OZOI, Ondo ; and ZAZO in Ebe. The mummy image was the Saviour, the KARAST, which represented the primitive Christ, the embalmed or anointed, the original type of the Pepul KRISTO, a fetish image which was not derived from the missionaries. The Egyptian TES for the self, and the SA (T-sa), as the mummy image, is well preserved in the Chinese TSE, the self, himself, or likeness of himself.

With the Egyptian masculine article as prefix the KA or SA becomes the BESA (Eg.), Amulet, for protection ; English BOSH, a figure ; and PAX, an image of the Christ on the Cross; Gaelic BAS for the dead body ; Coptic BASI, the corpse ; the Egyptian god BES ; Polish BOZY or Syn BOZY (Son of God), the Hindu deity PASU ; Mantshu Tartar POUSA, an idol ; Persian PASH, Hindustani BHES for a likeness, and the Chinese P'AK, for the corporeal soul.

The roots of these things are to be found in Africa, where the types are still extant in their most primitive form, as they were before the movement down into the Nile Valley led to the existence, development, and civilization of Egypt itself.

In the African Legba and Barba dialects, the idol or fetish figure is named TORU, the equivalent of the Welsh and Cornish DELW, for an idol or statue. In Xosa-Kaffir the idol is called DALO, and TARAH in Dselana. This was the TARA-TARA, applied to Stanley's *Notebook*, and also to a mirror, the reflector of the image—the book being a reflector of the image of thought. These words were represented in the hieroglyphics by TERU, for the SHOOTS of time and season ; TERU for drawings and colours, TERU and DRAW being synonymous. In Akkadian, TAR means to cut and carve ; TOREIA, in Greek, is carving in relief ; TUREI, Malayan, to cut, carve, engrave ; DOLO (Latin), to cut and carve ; DALA, Xosa-Kaffir, to create. In Gaelic the created, cut, or carven image, figure, or statue is the DREACH. In the monuments the divine artizan Ptah, who is the modeller and potter, appears as the draughtsman in the act of pourtraying the child Horus. TERU (Eg.) also means to invoke, evoke, and adore.

One African name of the fetish, as idol, charm, or talismanic ornament, is the GRU-GRU or GREE-GREE. This Gree-gree, in the

African Kiriman, is the OKUIRI; UKWIRI in Meto; EKURU in Kupa; GIRI in Krebo. GREE-GREE duplicates the type-name, one form of which is AKAR (Eg.) for the charm and silence.

The necklace and bracelet were early Gree-grees. EKURU, Kupa; EWARU, Egba; GIRO, Dewoi, denote chain-fetters for the neck. The EKURU, in Kupa, is also a bracelet or armlet; the AGOR in Ekamtu-lufu, a bracelet; AUKARAT, Arabic, a spherical amulet or charm; CHURI, Hindustani, bracelet; KARA, Persian, bracelet; KEYURA, Sanskrit, bracelet; whilst CORI, in Fijian, means to string beads. The beads with which the Europeans have swindled the Africans out of their own valuable products were all invested with a sacred character on account of this primitive symbolism. The mixed red-and-white bead, so eagerly sought for in Central Africa, as we learn from Livingstone (or Waller), was as much the type of the two truths of mythology as the later red and white crowns of Egypt.

Plutarch tells us that Isis, finding herself *enceinte*, hung a certain charm or amulet around her neck on the sixth day of the month Papophi (Oct. 4th in the Alexandrian year), which amulet or charm when interpreted in Greek, signifies a TRUE VOICE. The voice in Egyptian is KHERU, and the true is MA; MaKheru being a title of the voice, word, or Logos. This was the amulet of the gestator, one form of which is found in the nine bubu or beads of Isis. Still earlier than beads were the berries and the seed-pod of the acacia-tree of life, as a determinative of the seeded or pregnant wearer, the Mut-SNATEM or NETEM. These berries and bubu or beads of Isis were the prototypes of a network of bugles and various coloured beads, made use of in the preparation of the mummy, and worn over all the other wraps and bandages, the network being a symbol of the net (of Neith) with which Horus the child was fished out of the waters of the Nile. The regeneration of the mummy in the tomb, founded on the generation of the child in the womb, was typified by the Scarabæus of Khepr, the transformer, which was woven into this network of beads.

The charm AKAR and the Khart (child) or mystic Word, have the same name as the GREE-GREES, the bracelets, the beads, the berries, and the trees on which they grew, as in GHAR (Persian), laurel; KEER (Eng.), the rowan-tree; GARRUS (French), holly; KAURI (Maori), a pine, the resin-tree; ACHOUROU (Spanish), American bay-tree; HICKORY (American), tree; AAR (Scotch), alder, and English HOLLY, all of them being forms of the tree ot life, first personated by the mother as bearer.

When Isis wore the Akar charm, she was rounding, was *enceinte*, which has the same meaning; and ACHAR (Welsh) is rounded, en-circled; GYROO (Greek), to round or surround; GHERA (Hind.), a circle or circumference; GYRE (Eng.), a circle; and GURU in Sans-krit means the pregnant. Her child was the voice, the Kheru or

Khart that first prophesied and foretold as a type of time, hence CHRAO, CHREO, or CHRESO (Greek) is to deliver an oracle, to chresthen, the divine response; AGOURO (Portuguese), divination, a soothsaying; OGHUR (Turkish), augury; Latin, AUGUR; CARIE, (French Romance), a kind of witchcraft; HOR (Persian), a nativity; HOROSCOPOS (Greek), and many more.

The African GREE or GRU-GRU is just the Egyptian KHRU, the voice (Vach), the word, the utterer, and utterance, the Logos when personified. KHRU is the original of the Kurios, the Khar of the virgin mother, called the Khart or child-Horus. Khar modifies into Har, the Horus of the upper heaven and higher life. One of these represents the fore-shadow and phantom of reality; the other the True Word.

The typical Word, Logos, or messenger, is universal under this name. For instance, Taht, the lunar word, was represented by the crane, which in various languages has the Egyptian name of the voice or word, as in the Gaelic CORRA, a heron or crane; Scottish GRU, a crane; Mantshu Tartar KEROU, a stork; Irish CORR, the crane or stork; Italian GRU or GRUE; Latin GRUIS, a crane; Sanskrit KHARA, a heron.

In India the Khuru became the Guru, a name of the teacher, as utterer of the word of wisdom. Also in Sanskrit KARA is the word, the feminine, or a secret messenger; CELI (Welsh), the mysterious and secret one; GAIR (Welsh), denoting words; KORERO (Maori), to speak, tell, say; GUL (Kanuri), to say; KARU (Ass.), to invoke; KOLLI (Mandingo), to swear; GOLE, (Cornish), to swear; KOL (Lesghic), a mouth; KELO (Goram), the tongue; KLAI (Chinnook), to cry. The poor African's GRU or GREE-GREE was a primitive form of the KHERU, voice or cry.

Another name of the GRU is KLA, the tutelary genius of a person which can be evoked by magical arts. The Ashantis call the KLA the spirit of a man. If the name be used in the masculine gender they say that it stands for the VOICE that tempts a man to evil, and if used in the feminine it denotes the voice that persuades him against the evil;[1] which identifies the KLA with the Egyptian KHARU, the voice or word of two natures or aspects impersonated by the two Hars.

This duality of the Kheru (Har) is denoted by the repetition in GRU-GRU; and "JU-JU" is also a name of the GRU-GRU. Iu (Eg.) is two, twin, dual, duplicative, and therefore the equivalent of Ju-Ju. Written with the Hi, we find Hiu, whence Hu, the tongue-deity of twofold character; the tongue is painted of two colours, and Hu means a spirit of good or evil, the equivalent of the twofold Word. Also Hu is a name of the twy-formed sphinx. HUHU is likewise a

[1] Baseler, *Missions Mag.* 1856, 2, 134, 139.

name of this biune being, and the Dahoman deity Hoho is the double-natured god to whom twins are dedicated.

When the person dies the Ashanti KLA, or tutelary genius corresponding to the Egyptian KA image or genius, the living double of the self in this life, becomes a SISA, and the SISA may be born again ; with which we may compare the Egyptian SES, to breathe, reach land and respire as a living soul after the passage of the waters or in death. SESSAH also means to perambulate and make the circle of the ever-living gods. SES is the opposite to de-CEASE. SUSA in Zulu Kaffir means the cause, ground, and origin of a thing ; SUS (Arabic), root, origin ; ZIZ (Ass.), as before, as you were, restored, and flourishing ; SOIS (Irish), at rest ; SOSO (Zincali), rest.

The KA-LA or personal spirit of the Karens of Birmah is the same as the KLA of the Ashantis, and this is abbreviated into the " LA " of madness or epilepsy, or others of the seven demons so named. The KA is identical with the Egyptian for the personal " la," hence the Kala or Kla. The objection of the primitive races to having their portrait taken is well known ; the portrait, being the image, is, in a sense, the KLA, or Egyptian KA, the living image of the self and personality, an objective form of that which they conceive to be the subjective self and permanent or *reproducible* part. The sun-god Ra has fourteen " Ka's " or images, which are founded on the fourteen days of growing light in the first half of the lunation, his light being reflected fourteen times by the moon, these fourteen reflections are called his Ka's, as fourteen impersonations of his second self.

The Maori KARAKIA is a prayer, incantation, to say prayers, repeat a formula of words at a religious ceremony, perform a religious service. The name of the Papuan " KAR-WAR," in presence of which the native squats to divine the right and the wrong of a thing, is a form of the GREE-GREE of Africa, and bears its dual name, and these are identical by name and in their nature with the Egyptian Kheru, the voice, word, Logos, and the Greek Chrao or Chreo, to deliver an oracle.

The first oraculum was the mother, and the inner voice was the child of two utterances. The fact of this life was then applied to another in the eschatological phase, and to the voice within in the sense of the conscience.

The Hebrew ATZEM or GATZEM, which is applied to the bodily SELF, the bones of the body, the bones of the dead, and likewise to the fœtus within the womb, as the body which is a fruit of the body,[1] explained by the Egyptian KHAT, the body, corpse, or child, and SEM, the representative sign and likeness, is derived from this origin of the Fetish. The joint of the backbone, especially the end one, the bone called LUZ by the Rabbins, was the same type as the hieroglyphic Usert, a sceptre formed of the vertebral column as the sign

---

[1] עצמים, Eccles. xi. 5.

of sustaining power.   A man was held to rise again in the next life from LUZ in the backbone, the nucleus of his resurrection body. Luz represents the Egyptian RUS, to rise or raise up.   The bone, the berry, and other primitive forms of the symbolic Sem or Amulet were worn long ages before the mummy itself could be preserved, and these earlier types have been continued in inner Africa.

The Gru-Gru worn by Isis denoted the other self, as the child in the womb with which she was GURU (Sansk.)   The Gru-Gru of beads or berries worn by the marriageable maiden signified the other second self of womanhood ; the Gru-Gru worn by the Queens of Egypt in the shape of the vulture or the double Uræus serpent was the crown of this second self duplicated in the maternal phase. The Shebti or mummy type placed in the tomb was the Gru-Gru or double, representing the other self hereafter; the child of another life in the womb of death.   This was one aspect of the KLA, the tutelary genius which was finally pourtrayed as the other self, the voice within, the voice of that which lived on through death, ulti- mately called the voice of conscience within ourselves.

Now, when the Bechuana women who are married find them- selves in the condition of Isis, they begin to carry about with them a doll, as the outward and visible sign of the inward grace, and when the child is born, the doll is put aside.   One of these, now in the London Missionary Museum, is simply a calabash wound round with strings of beads.   The Basuto women make use of clay dolls for the same purpose.   These are treated as children, but the names of tutelary genii are likewise given to them.[1]

When the Ashanti woman finds herself *enceinte* she not only puts on her GRU-GRU of beads or berries to show that the flower has set and seeded, she goes at once to the oracle of the priest to have a spirit-consultation, and obtain particulars from the KLA or tutelary genius respecting the *ancestry* and future career of her child.[2]   Accord- ing to the missionary here quoted, the Ashantis hold that the KLA or soul existed before the body, and has had a very long existence indeed, it having been continued and passed on from generation to generation from the remotest time.   But does not this consultation concerning the ancestry point to the indefiniteness of promiscuous intercourse before the fatherhood was known and acknowledged? In mythology the first divine child is the self-begotten ; the paternity not being taken into account.   This inquiry concerning the fatherhood would be an early form of seeking for a Creator.   Bastian saw the Indian women in Peru carrying the doll image on their backs as the Atzem or Sem type of the child that was dead.

What is the origin of the image and idol but the endeavour to pourtray an objective form of an inner and unseen self, the idea of which begins with the child in the womb?   This is illustrated by an

[1] Casalis, *Basutos*, p. 251.   [2] Rowley, *Religion of the Africans*, p. 118.

expression in the Ritual (Chapter of the Scarabæus) "*en-tuk Ka em Khat*," which, according to the primitive thought and hieroglyphic imagery, is literally "thou art the image or soul in my womb." The beetle within the body was the type of transformation and becoming for the future life. It was an image of life in the dead body, as in the womb of the tomb, because the mother-type had been applied to the earth or the void as the place of burial and re-birth of the star, moon, and sun that re-arose from the underworld, and the Meskhen of the new birth. These were both phenomenal and physical, having no relation to a "perception of the Infinite," and on their bases was reared the superstructure of eschatological typology.

The womb was the first εἰδωλεῖον, as the chamber or house of the image mentioned in the texts, which had become the place of the Ka-images set up by the Egyptians with their dead. The symbolry of Sex, and the mother-mould of expression, adopted by the natural desire to produce, were continued when the feeling to be expressed was the desire to be reproduced. Now the Bone-caves have yielded up their buried secret, we find that so far back as the record goes the desire to be reproduced is as manifest as the desire to produce, and in these sentiments only do we reach the root of the Phallic origines. No written language is found in the Caves or the Mounds to tell us what were the ideas of the men of the Palæolithic Age, but these primitive types, the most ancient records of the past, are often more eloquent than words, and their kith and kin are still extant above ground in Africa to-day, awaiting the comparative typologist to become their interpreter, as a means of entering into the minds of those who are still the children of that remote and dumb primeval past. We shall learn more of the tangible roots of these ideas in Africa than from all the classical literature of Greece and Rome, or sacred books of the later religions of the world, and it is exasperating to feel that matter far more precious for the present purpose may be lying unavailable in Dr. Bleek's unpublished collections.

In some languages, to *say* and *do* are synonymous ; but the doing precedes the saying, and the earliest utterance was that of visible speech. The primordial forms of this doing and saying, or express-ing by means of the first intelligible signs, originated with the black races who are so despised and misunderstood by the magni-ficent "Caucasian" conceit of "mean whites," who send missionaries to create in them a sense of their nudity—the absence of which ought to show that they do not belong to the "fallen" race—and a consequent need of being provided with English clothing.

These types, this imagery, the visible expression of a nature other-wise dumb, are to me infinitely more pathetic than the most perfect utterances of poetry. They constitute the root-origines of symbolism ; they were primarily the signs of the simplest, most aboriginal of human needs, those of the outward expression and visible configuration of thought and feeling. The religious is their final phase, and in this they have persisted until the present time; for it will be demonstrated that much of the outfit and wardrobe of our current theology was primarily furnished through Egypt by the naked races of Africa, and that we, in common with them, have been the ignorant victims of misinterpreted typology.

One last illustration of a masculine type. There is a bell in the Edinburgh Museum of Antiquities which was taken from St. Fillan's Chapel. On the top of it the male emblem is figured; the ancient type of KHEM-HORUS, who was the potent and prevailing Har (or Hal) of the resurrection. This was the first part of the mummy that re-arose in death, and the Christian was a simple, at times a very simple continuation of the Egyptian Iconography. The god of this image was the appearing, emanating, and manifesting son, i.e. PER RENN, or the Renp, the masculine, pubescent Horus. It was in the person of Khem-Horus that the son became the father and was considered as both the child and husband of the Mother in One.

Now the name of FILLAN is word for word identical with PER-RENN (the VIR-renn) the manifester in the masculine type represented by the male image, which has the same meaning on St. Fillan's bell as on the deerhorn of the Palæolithic age; the African Fetish Legba, or in the portraits of Khem, Mentu, and Horus the Renn, whose epiphany is celebrated unwittingly on Hollen's (or Holling's) Eve, which still retains the name of Har, the Renn who was the Hairy One. HARREN in English signifies the Hairy, or made of hair, and the Hollen (Holly) is the typical tree and namesake of the Har-Renn. Naming, in the same way and from the same type, is represented in the Maori language by the word TARA, which denotes the MENTULA, manly mettle, the hair on the skin, the PUBES, things prickly and pointed, and the rays of the sun on the horizon. FILLAN is probably the Scottish form of "PERRAN," the Cornish saint who has preserved the meaning of RENN (Eg.), the Little One, in the place-name of "PERRAN THE LITTLE."

Sufficient has now been said of the roots in Africa beyond Egypt.

In conclusion, a word of explanation on the plan and object of this work, which cannot be fully unfolded in the first two volumes. It is a *sine quâ non* for the Egyptian origines to be thus far established as the foundation of all that has to follow, and, to some extent, correlation must and would commence in this comparative process, before the myths themselves had been related, and the fundamental nature of typology interpreted. For this reason, conclusions already attained by the writer had to be occasionally stated, glanced at, or implied, which must appear to the reader the sheerest, and sometimes most unwarrantable assumptions, until the evidence for such conclusions can be completely set forth.

Allusions to matters not yet in the reader's mind will of necessity cause some present perplexity. This was unavoidable. The writer was compelled to talk the language of typology, so to say, before the grammar had been presented to the reader. Also, there are things here of which an Egyptologist only can have any previous inkling. But nothing has been asserted without warrant. Nothing has been introduced wantonly. All that is new, and strange, and startling, has its place, or will find it, and be found in it. There is nothing mystical in mythology, but some doctrine, dogma, or religious rite will be traced to it in the sequel. The following volumes will be devoted to the typology of the whole subject : the science of typology ; the typology of the Genesis, Eden, the Tree, the Fall; typology of the Deluge and Ark ; typology of the Gods, the Great Mother; the Mother and Messiah son ; the Two Truths of Egypt ; the Biune Being, the triads and the trinity ; typology of time, of number, of the Word, or logos ; typology of the cross, and the crossing; typology of the mummy and the KA; typology of naming and of sounds; typology of the astronomical allegory ; the great pyramid and the great year. Each one of these types will supply further evidence of what is here termed the Egyptian origin, in corroboration of the present witnesses in words and myths. The first thought of the reader may be that the typology should have preceded these two volumes. But the writer had to show cause *why* the world should be troubled at all on the subject of typology, and offer some reasonable ground for hope that a bottom might at length be found in the hitherto unbridged abyss. It remains to be shown how the " Types " originated in phenomena, of necessity and for use ; how they became the symbols of expression in mythology and language, and how theology by its perversions and misinterpretations has established a reign of error through the whole domain of religion.

The last volume will be chiefly devoted to tracing the current theology and eschatology as the outcome, deposit, development, and final form of the ancient typology and mythology ; it will also contain a copious index to the contents of the whole work.

The writer hopes to be able to furnish a not altogether inadequate representation of the primitive system of thought and its expression in types and myths, so far as it has been possible for him to recover the broken moulds and piece together the scattered remains.

Any help that may be kindly offered will be thankfully accepted, and all errors in matters of fact which may be pointed out shall be frankly acknowledged in the next volume. A pioneering work of a nature so preliminary and primitive will be certain to contain mistakes, oversights, redundancy of details, and still graver errors. That which was probable in any case is inevitable in the present. But,

> If half my grapnels hold their ground,
>   An anchorage made firm and fast
> Will serve to show that we have found
>   The old sea-bottom of the past.